Second Conference on Machine Translation (WMT 2017)

Copenhagen, Denmark
7 – 8 September 2017

ISBN: 978-1-5108-4749-1

WMT 2017

**Second Conference on
Machine Translation**

Proceedings

September 7-8, 2017
Copenhagen, Denmark

Introduction

The Second Conference on Machine Translation (WMT 2017) took place on Thursday and Friday, September 7–8, 2017 in Copenhagen, Denmark, immediately preceding the Conference on Empirical Methods in Natural Language Processing (EMNLP 2017).

This is the second time WMT has been held as a conference. The first time WMT was held as a conference was at ACL 2016 in Berlin, Germany. Prior to being a conference, WMT was held 10 times as a workshop. WMT was held for the first time at HLT-NAACL 2006 in New York City, USA. In the following years the Workshop on Statistical Machine Translation was held at ACL 2007 in Prague, Czech Republic, ACL 2008, Columbus, Ohio, USA, EACL 2009 in Athens, Greece, ACL 2010 in Uppsala, Sweden, EMNLP 2011 in Edinburgh, Scotland, NAACL 2012 in Montreal, Canada, ACL 2013 in Sofia, Bulgaria, ACL 2014 in Baltimore, USA, and EMNLP 2015 in Lisbon, Portugal.

The focus of our conference was to use parallel corpora for machine translation. Recent experimentation has shown that the performance of MT systems varies greatly with the source language. In this conference we encouraged researchers to investigate ways to improve the performance of MT systems for diverse languages, including morphologically more complex languages, languages with partial free word order, and low-resource languages.

Prior to the conference, in addition to soliciting relevant papers for review and possible presentation, we conducted 8 shared tasks. This consisted of three translation tasks: Machine Translation of News, Biomedical Translation, and Multimodal Machine Translation, two evaluation tasks: Metrics and Quality Estimation, as well as the Automatic Post-Editing, Neural MT Training, and the Bandit Learning tasks. Two of these tasks were run at WMT for the first time. The Neural MT Training task provide comparable conditions and encouraging researchers to explore training methods that lead to improved and more robust translation quality and help speed up the training. The Bandit Learning Task encourages participants to train and improve MT systems by learning from weak or partial feedback instead of the commonly used gold-standard human-generated translations.

The results of all shared tasks were announced at the conference, and these proceedings also include overview papers for the shared tasks, summarizing the results, as well as providing information about the data used and any procedures that were followed in conducting or scoring the tasks. In addition, there are short papers from each participating team that describe their underlying system in greater detail

Like in previous years, we have received a far larger number of submissions than we could accept for presentation. This year we have received 40 full research paper submissions. In total, WMT 2017 featured 16 full paper oral presentations and 59 shared task poster presentations.

Holger Schwenk gave the invited on "Multilingual Representations and Applications in NLP".

We would like to thank the members of the Program Committee for their timely reviews. We also would like to thank the participants of the shared task and all volunteers who helped with the evaluations.

Ondřej Bojar, Christian Buck, Rajen Chatterjee, Christian Federmann, Yvette Graham Barry Haddow, Matthias Huck, Antonio Jimeno Yepes, Philipp Koehn, Julia Kreutzer, Varvara Logacheva Christof Monz, Matteo Negri, Aurélie Névéol, Mariana Neves, Matt Post, Stefan Riezler, Raphael Rubino, Artem Sokolov, Lucia Specia, Marco Turchi, and Karin Verspoor

Co-Organizers

Organizers:

Ondřej Bojar (Charles University in Prague)
Christian Buck (University of Edinburgh)
Rajen Chatterjee (FBK)
Christian Federmann (MSR)
Yvette Graham (DCU)
Barry Haddow (University of Edinburgh)
Matthias Huck (University of Edinburgh)
Antonio Jimeno Yepes (IBM Research Australia)
Philipp Koehn (University of Edinburgh / Johns Hopkins University)
Julia Kreutzer (Heidelberg University)
Varvara Logacheva (University of Sheffield)
Christof Monz (University of Amsterdam)
Matteo Negri (FBK)
Aurélie Névéol (LIMSI, CNRS)
Mariana Neves (Federal Institute for Risk Assessment / Hasso Plattner Institute)
Matt Post (Johns Hopkins University)
Stefan Riezler (Heidelberg University)
Raphael Rubino (Saarland University)
Artem Sokolov (Heidelberg University, Amazon Development Center, Berlin)
Lucia Specia (University of Sheffield)
Marco Turchi (FBK)
Karin Verspoor (University of Melbourne)

Invited Speaker:

Holger Schwenk (Facebook AI Research)

Program Committee:

Tim Anderson (Air Force Research Laboratory)
Eleftherios Avramidis (German Research Center for Artificial Intelligence (DFKI))
Daniel Beck (University of Melbourne)
Arianna Bisazza (University of Amsterdam)
Graeme Blackwood (IBM Research)
Frédéric Blain (University of Sheffield)
Ozan Caglayan (LIUM, Le Mans University)
Marine Carpuat (University of Maryland)
Francisco Casacuberta (Universitat Politècnica de València)
Daniel Cer (Google)
Mauro Cettolo (FBK)
Rajen Chatterjee (Fondazione Bruno Kessler)
Boxing Chen (NRC)
Colin Cherry (NRC)
David Chiang (University of Notre Dame)

Eunah Cho (Karlsruhe Institute of Technology)
Kyunghyun Cho (New York University)
Vishal Chowdhary (MSR)
Jonathan Clark (Microsoft)
Marta R. Costa-jussà (Universitat Politècnica de Catalunya)
Praveen Dakwale (University of Amsterdam)
Steve DeNeefe (SDL Language Weaver)
Michael Denkowski (Amazon.com, Inc.)
Markus Dreyer (Amazon.com)
Nadir Durrani (QCRI)
Desmond Elliott (University of Edinburgh)
Marzieh Fadaee (University of Amsterdam)
Marcello Federico (FBK)
Minwei Feng (IBM Watson Group)
Yang Feng (Institute of Computing Technology, Chinese Academy of Sciences)
Andrew Finch (NICT)
Orhan Firat (Google Research)
Marina Fomicheva (Universitat Pompeu Fabra)
José A. R. Fonollosa (Universitat Politècnica de Catalunya)
Mikel L. Forcada (Universitat d'Alacant)
George Foster (National Research Council)
Alexander Fraser (Ludwig-Maximilians-Universität München)
Markus Freitag (IBM Research)
Ekaterina Garmash (University of Amsterdam)
Ulrich Germann (University of Edinburgh)
Hamidreza Ghader (Informatics Institute, University of Amsterdam)
Jesús González-Rubio (Universitat Politècnica de València)
Cyril Goutte (National Research Council Canada)
Thanh-Le Ha (Karlsruhe Institute of Technology)
Nizar Habash (New York University Abu Dhabi)
Jan Hajic (Charles University)
Greg Hanneman (Carnegie Mellon University)
Christian Hardmeier (Uppsala universitet)
Eva Hasler (SDL)
Yifan He (Bosch Research and Technology Center)
Kenneth Heafield (University of Edinburgh)
Carmen Heger (Iconic)
John Henderson (MITRE)
Felix Hieber (Amazon Research)
Stéphane Huet (Université d'Avignon)
Young-Sook Hwang (SKPlanet)
Gonzalo Iglesias (SDL)
Doug Jones (MIT Lincoln Laboratory)
Marcin Junczys-Dowmunt (Adam Mickiewicz University, Poznań)
Roland Kuhn (National Research Council of Canada)
Shankar Kumar (Google)
Ákos Kádár (Tilburg University)

David Langlois (LORIA, Université de Lorraine)

William Lewis (Microsoft Research)

Qun Liu (Dublin City University)

Shujie Liu (Microsoft Research Asia, Beijing, China)

Saab Mansour (Apple)

Daniel Marcu (ISI/USC)

Arne Mauser (Google, Inc)

Mohammed Mediani (Karlsruhe Institute of Technology)

Abhijit Mishra (IBM Research India)

Maria Nadejde (University of Edinburgh)

Preslav Nakov (Qatar Computing Research Institute, HBKU)

Jan Niehues (Karlsruhe Institute of Technology)

Kemal Oflazer (Carnegie Mellon University - Qatar)

Tsuyoshi Okita (Kyushuu institute of technology university)

Daniel Ortiz-Martínez (Technical University of Valencia)

Martha Palmer (University of Colorado)

Siddharth Patwardhan (IBM Watson)

Pavel Pecina (Charles University)

Stephan Peitz (Apple)

Sergio Penkale (Lingo24)

Jan-Thorsten Peter (RWTH Aachen University)

Maja Popović (Humboldt University of Berlin)

Preethi Raghavan (IBM Research TJ Watson)

Stefan Riezler (Heidelberg University)

Baskaran Sankaran (IBM T.J. Watson Research Center)

Jean Senellart (SYSTRAN)

Rico Sennrich (University of Edinburgh)

Wade Shen (MIT)

Michel Simard (NRC)

Patrick Simianer (Heidelberg University)

Linfeng Song (University of Rochester)

Sara Stymne (Uppsala University)

Katsuhito Sudoh (Nara Institute of Science and Technology (NAIST))

Felipe Sánchez-Martínez (Universitat d'Alacant)

Aleš Tamchyna (Charles University in Prague, UFAL MFF)

Jörg Tiedemann (University of Helsinki)

Christoph Tillmann (IBM Research)

Ke M. Tran (University of Amsterdam)

Dan Tufiş (Research Institute for Artificial Intelligence, Romanian Academy)

Marco Turchi (Fondazione Bruno Kessler)

Ferhan Ture (Comcast Labs)

Masao Utiyama (NICT)

David Vilar (Amazon)

Stephan Vogel (Qatar Computing Research Institute)

Martin Volk (University of Zurich)

Taro Watanabe (Google)

Bonnie Webber (University of Edinburgh)

Marlies van der Wees (University of Amsterdam)
Marion Weller-Di Marco (LMU München, Universität Stuttgart)
Philip Williams (University of Edinburgh)
Hua Wu (Baidu)
Joern Wuebker (Lilt, Inc.)
François Yvon (LIMSI/CNRS)

Conference Program

Thursday, September 7, 2016

8:45–9:00   *Opening Remarks*

9:00–10:30   **Session 1: Shared Tasks Overview Presentations I**

9:00–9:40   *Shared Task: News Translation*

Findings of the 2017 Conference on Machine Translation (WMT17)
Ondřej Bojar, Rajen Chatterjee, Christian Federmann, Yvette Graham, Barry Haddow, Shujian Huang, Matthias Huck, Philipp Koehn, Qun Liu, Varvara Logacheva, Christof Monz, Matteo Negri, Matt Post, Raphael Rubino, Lucia Specia and Marco Turchi

9:40–10:10   *Shared Task: Multimodal Translation*

Findings of the Second Shared Task on Multimodal Machine Translation and Multilingual Image Description
Desmond Elliott, Stella Frank, Loïc Barrault, Fethi Bougares and Lucia Specia

10:10–10:30   *Shared Task: Biomedical Translation*

Findings of the WMT 2017 Biomedical Translation Shared Task
Antonio Jimeno Yepes, Aurelie Neveol, Mariana Neves, Karin Verspoor, Ondrej Bojar, Arthur Boyer, Cristian Grozea, Barry Haddow, Madeleine Kittner, Yvonne Lichtblau, Pavel Pecina, Roland Roller, Rudolf Rosa, Amy Siu, Philippe Thomas and Saskia Trescher

10:30-11:00   *Coffee Break*

11:00–12:30   Session 2: Shared Tasks Poster Session I

11:00–12:30   *Shared Task: News Translation*

CUNI submission in WMT17: Chimera goes neural
Roman Sudarikov, David Mareček, Tom Kocmi, Dusan Varis and Ondřej Bojar

LIMSI@WMT'17
Franck Burlot, Pooyan Safari, Matthieu Labeau, Alexandre Allauzen and François
Yvon

SYSTRAN Purely Neural MT Engines for WMT2017
Yongchao Deng, Jungi Kim, Guillaume Klein, Catherine KOBUS, Natalia Segal,
Christophe Servan, Bo Wang, Dakun Zhang, Josep Crego and Jean Senellart

FBK's Participation to the English-to-German News Translation Task of WMT 2017
Mattia Antonino Di Gangi, Nicola Bertoldi and Marcello Federico

The JHU Machine Translation Systems for WMT 2017
Shuoyang Ding, Huda Khayrallah, Philipp Koehn, Matt Post, Gaurav Kumar and
Kevin Duh

*The TALP-UPC Neural Machine Translation System for German/Finnish-English
Using the Inverse Direction Model in Rescoring*
Carlos Escolano, Marta R. Costa-jussà and José A. R. Fonollosa

LIUM Machine Translation Systems for WMT17 News Translation Task
Mercedes García-Martínez, Ozan Caglayan, Walid Aransa, Adrien Bardet, Fethi
Bougares and Loïc Barrault

*Extending hybrid word-character neural machine translation with multi-task learn-
ing of morphological analysis*
Stig-Arne Grönroos, Sami Virpioja and Mikko Kurimo

The AFRL-MITLL WMT17 Systems: Old, New, Borrowed, BLEU
Jeremy Gwinnup, Timothy Anderson, Grant Erdmann, Katherine Young, Michaeel
Kazi, Elizabeth Salesky, Brian Thompson and Jonathan Taylor

University of Rochester WMT 2017 NMT System Submission
Chester Holtz, Chuyang Ke and Daniel Gildea

Thursday, September 7, 2016 (continued)

17:15–17:30   *Target-side Word Segmentation Strategies for Neural Machine Translation*
Matthias Huck, Simon Riess and Alexander Fraser

Friday, September 8, 2017

9:00–10:30   **Session 5: Shared Tasks Overview Presentations II**

9:00–9:20   *Shared Task: Quality Estimation*

9:20–9:40   *Shared Task: Metrics*

Results of the WMT17 Metrics Shared Task
Ondřej Bojar, Yvette Graham and Amir Kamran

9:40–10:00   *Shared Task: Automatic Post-Editing*

10:00–10:15   *Shared Task: Bandit Learning*

A Shared Task on Bandit Learning for Machine Translation
Artem Sokolov, Julia Kreutzer, Kellen Sunderland, Pavel Danchenko, Witold Szymaniak, Hagen Fürstenau and Stefan Riezler

10:15–10:30   *Shared Task: Neural Training*

Results of the WMT17 Neural MT Training Task
Ondřej Bojar, Jindřich Helcl, Tom Kocmi, Jindřich Libovický and Tomáš Musil

10:30-11:00   *Coffee Break*

11:00–12:30   Session 6: Shared Tasks Poster Session II

11:00–12:30   *Shared Task: Quality Estimation*

Sentence-level quality estimation by predicting HTER as a multi-component metric
Eleftherios Avramidis

Predicting Translation Performance with Referential Translation Machines
Ergun Biçici

Bilexical Embeddings for Quality Estimation
Frédéric Blain, Carolina Scarton and Lucia Specia

Improving Machine Translation Quality Estimation with Neural Network Features
Zhiming Chen, Yiming Tan, Chenlin Zhang, Qingyu Xiang, Lilin Zhang, Maoxi Li
and Mingwen WANG

UHH Submission to the WMT17 Quality Estimation Shared Task
Melania Duma and Wolfgang Menzel

*Predictor-Estimator using Multilevel Task Learning with Stack Propagation for
Neural Quality Estimation*
Hyun Kim, Jong-Hyeok Lee and Seung-Hoon Na

Unbabel's Participation in the WMT17 Translation Quality Estimation Shared Task
André F. T. Martins, Fabio Kepler and Jose Monteiro

Feature-Enriched Character-Level Convolutions for Text Regression
Gustavo Paetzold and Lucia Specia

11:00–12:30   *Shared Task: Metrics*

UHH Submission to the WMT17 Metrics Shared Task
Melania Duma and Wolfgang Menzel

MEANT 2.0: Accurate semantic MT evaluation for any output language
Chi-kiu Lo

Blend: a Novel Combined MT Metric Based on Direct Assessment — CASICT-DCU submission to WMT17 Metrics Task
Qingsong Ma, Yvette Graham, Shugen Wang and Qun Liu

CUNI Experiments for WMT17 Metrics Task
David Mareček, Ondřej Bojar, Ondřej Hübsch, Rudolf Rosa and Dusan Varis

chrF++: words helping character n-grams
Maja Popović

bleu2vec: the Painfully Familiar Metric on Continuous Vector Space Steroids
Andre Tättar and Mark Fishel

11:00–12:30   *Shared Task: Automatic Post-Editing*

LIG-CRIStAL Submission for the WMT 2017 Automatic Post-Editing Task
Alexandre Berard, Laurent Besacier and Olivier Pietquin

Multi-source Neural Automatic Post-Editing: FBK's participation in the WMT 2017 APE shared task
Rajen Chatterjee, M. Amin Farajian, Matteo Negri, Marco Turchi, Ankit Srivastava and Santanu Pal

The AMU-UEdin Submission to the WMT 2017 Shared Task on Automatic Post-Editing
Marcin Junczys-Dowmunt and Marcin Junczys-Dowmunt

Ensembling Factored Neural Machine Translation Models for Automatic Post-Editing and Quality Estimation
Chris Hokamp

Neural Post-Editing Based on Quality Estimation
Yiming Tan, Zhiming Chen, Liu Huang, Lilin Zhang, Maoxi Li and Mingwen Wang

CUNI System for WMT17 Automatic Post-Editing Task
Dusan Varis and Ondřej Bojar

Sense-Aware Statistical Machine Translation using
Adaptive Context-Dependent Clustering

Xiao Pu
EPFL & Idiap Research Inst.
Martigny, Switzerland
xiao.pu@idiap.ch

Nikolaos Pappas
Idiap Research Institute
Martigny, Switzerland
nikolaos.pappas@idiap.ch

Andrei Popescu-Belis
Idiap Research Institute
Martigny, Switzerland
apbelis@idiap.ch

Abstract

Statistical machine translation (SMT) systems use local cues from n-gram translation and language models to select the translation of each source word. Such systems do not explicitly perform word sense disambiguation (WSD), although this would enable them to select translations depending on the hypothesized sense of each word. Previous attempts to constrain word translations based on the results of generic WSD systems have suffered from their limited accuracy. We demonstrate that WSD systems can be adapted to help SMT, thanks to three key achievements: (1) we consider a larger context for WSD than SMT can afford to consider; (2) we adapt the number of senses per word to the ones observed in the training data using clustering-based WSD with K-means; and (3) we initialize sense-clustering with definitions or examples extracted from WordNet. Our WSD system is competitive, and in combination with a factored SMT system improves noun and verb translation from English to Chinese, Dutch, French, German, and Spanish.

1 Introduction

Selecting the correct translation of polysemous words remains an important challenge for machine translation (MT). While some translation options may be interchangeable, substantially different senses of source words must generally be rendered by different words in the target language. In this case, an MT system should identify – implicitly or explicitly – the correct sense conveyed by each occurrence in order to select the appropriate translation.

> **Source:** And I do really like this *shot*, because it shows all the detritus that's sort of embedded in the sole of the sneakers.
>
> **Baseline SMT:** Und ich mag dieses *Bild* ...
>
> **Online NMT:** Und ich mag diesen *Schuss* wirklich, ...
>
> **Sense-aware MT:** Und ich mag diese *Aufnahme* wirklich, ...
>
> **Reference translation:** Ich mag diese *Aufnahme* wirklich, ...

Figure 1: Example of sense-aware translation that is closer to a reference translation than a baseline statistical MT system or an online neural one.

Current statistical or neural MT systems perform word sense disambiguation (WSD) implicitly, for instance through the n-gram frequency information stored in the translation and language models. However, the context taken into account by an MT system when performing implicit WSD is limited. For instance, in the case of phrase-based SMT, it is the order of the language model (often between 3 and 5) and the length of n-grams in the phrase table (seldom above 5). In attention-based neural MT systems, the context extends to the entire sentence, but is not specifically trained to be used for WSD.

For instance, Figure 1 shows an English sentence translated into German by a baseline statistical MT, an online neural MT, and the sense-aware MT system proposed in this paper. The word *shot* is respectively translated as *Schuss* (gun shot), *Bild* (drawing) and *Aufnahme* (picture) by the online NMT, the baseline system, and our sense-aware system. The latter selects a correct sense, which is identical to the reference translation, while the first two are incorrect (especially the online NMT).

Proceedings of the Conference on Machine Translation (WMT), Volume 1: Research Papers, pages 1–10
Copenhagen, Denmark, September 7–11, 2017. ©2017 Association for Computational Linguistics

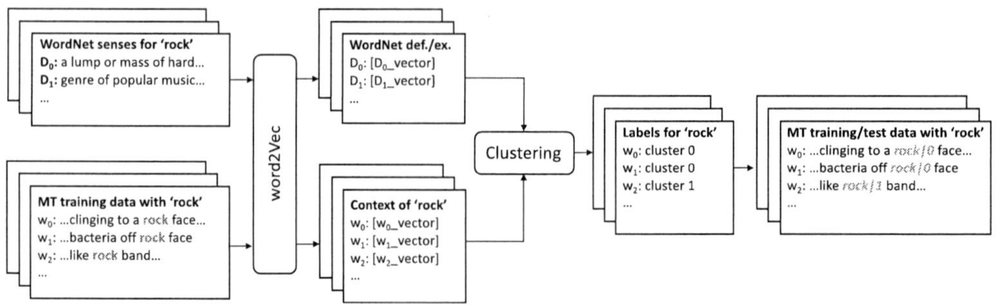

Figure 2: Adaptive WSD for MT: vectors from WordNet definitions (or examples) are clustered with context vectors of each occurrence (here of *'rock'*), resulting in sense labels used as factors for MT.

In this paper, we introduce a sense-aware statistical MT system that performs explicit WSD, and uses for this task a larger context than is accessible to state-of-the-art SMT. Our WSD system performs context-dependent clustering of word occurrences and is initialized with knowledge from WordNet, in the form of vector representations of definitions or examples for each sense. The labels of the resulting clusters are used as abstract source-side sense labels within a factored phrase-based SMT system. The stages of our method are presented in Figure 2, and will be explained in detail in Section 3.

Our results, presented in Section 5, show first that our WSD system is competitive on the SemEval 2010 WSD task, but especially that it helps SMT to increase its BLEU scores and to improve the translation of polysemous nouns and verbs, when translating from English into Chinese, German, French, Spanish or Dutch, in comparison to an SMT baseline that is not aware of word senses.

With respect to previous work that used WSD for MT, discussed in Section 2, we innovate on the following points:

- we design a sense clustering method with explicit knowledge (WordNet definitions or examples) to disambiguate polysemous nouns and verbs;

- we represent each token by its context vector, obtained from word2vec word vectors in a large window surrounding the token;

- we adapt the possible number of senses per word to the ones observed in the training data rather than constraining them by the full list of senses from WordNet;

- we use the abstract sense labels for each analyzed word as factors in an SMT system.

2   Related Work

Word sense disambiguation aims to identify the sense of a word appearing in a given context (Agirre and Edmonds, 2007). Resolving word sense ambiguities should be useful, in particular, for lexical choice in MT.

An initial investigation found that an SMT system which makes use of off-the-shelf WSD does not yield significantly better quality translations than a SMT system not using it (Carpuat and Wu, 2005). However, another study (Vickrey et al., 2005) reformulated the task of WSD for SMT as predicting possible target translations rather than senses of ambiguous source words, and showed that WSD improved such a simplified word translation task. Subsequent studies which adopted this formulation (Cabezas and Resnik, 2005; Chan et al., 2007; Carpuat and Wu, 2007), successfully integrated WSD to hierarchical or phrase-based SMT. These systems yielded slightly better translations compared to SMT baselines in most cases (0.15–0.30 BLEU).

Although the WSD reformulation above proved helpful for SMT, it did not determine whether actual source-side senses are helpful or not for end-to-end SMT. Xiong and Zhang (2014) attempted to answer this question by performing word sense induction for large scale data. In particular, they proposed a topic model that automatically learned sense clusters for words in the source language. In this way, on the one hand, they avoided using a pre-specified inventory of word senses as traditional WSD does, but on the other hand, they created the risk of discovering sense clusters which do not correspond to the common senses of words needed for MT. Hence, this study left open an important question, namely whether WSD based on semantic resources such as WordNet (Fellbaum, 1998) can be successfully integrated with SMT.

Neale et al. (2016) attempted such an integration, by using a WSD system based on a sense graph from WordNet (Agirre and Soroa, 2009). This system detects the senses of words in context using a random walk algorithm over the sense graph. The authors used it to specify the senses of the source words and integrate them as contextual features with a MaxEnt-based translation model for English-Portuguese MT. Similarly, Su et al. (2015) built a large weighted graph model of both source and target word dependencies and integrated them as features to a SMT model. However, apart from the sense graph, WordNet provides also textual information such as sense definitions and examples, which should be useful for disambiguating senses, but were not used in the above studies. Here, we aim to exploit this information to perform word sense induction from large scale monolingual data (in a first phase), thus combining the benefits of semantic ontologies and word sense induction for WSD.

Several other studies integrated additional information from a larger context using factored-based MT models (Koehn and Hoang, 2007). Birch et al. (2007) used supertags from a Combinatorial Categorial Grammar as factors in phrase-based translation model. Avramidis and Koehn (2008) added source-side syntactic information for each word for translating from a morphologically poorer language to a richer one (English-Greek). The levels of improvement achieved with factored models such as the ones above range from 0.15 to 0.50 BLEU points. Here, we also observe improvements in the upper part of this range, and they are consistent across several language pairs.

3 Adaptive Sense Clustering for SMT

In this section, we describe our adaptive WSD method and show how we integrate it with SMT, as represented in Figure 2 above. In a nutshell, we consider all source words that have more than one sense (synset) in WordNet, and extract from WordNet the definition of each sense and, if available, the example. We associate to them word embeddings built using word2vec. For each occurrence of these words in the training data, we also build vectors for their contexts (i.e. neighboring words) using the same model. All the vectors are passed to a clustering algorithm, resulting in the labeling of each occurrence with a cluster number that will be used as a factor in statistical MT.

Our method answers several limitations of previous supervised or unsupervised WSD methods. Supervised methods require data with manually sense-annotated labels and are therefore often limited to a small number of word types: for instance, only 50 nouns and 50 verbs were targeted in SemEval 2010[1] (Manandhar et al., 2010). On the contrary, our method does not require labeled texts for training, and applies to all word types appearing with multiple senses in WordNet.

Unsupervised methods often pre-define the number of possible senses for each ambiguous word before clustering the various occurrences according to the senses. If these numbers come from WordNet, the senses may be too fine-grained for the needs of translation, especially when a specific domain is targeted. In contrast, as we explain below, our WSD method initializes a context-dependent clustering algorithm with information from WordNet senses for each word (nouns and verbs), but then adapts the number of clusters to the observed training data for MT.

3.1 Representing Definitions, Examples and Contexts of Word Occurrences

For each noun or verb *type* W_t appearing in the training data, as identified by the Stanford POS tagger,[2] we extract the senses associated to it in WordNet[3] by using NLTK.[4] Specifically, we extract the set of definitions $D_t = \{d_{tj}|j = 1, \ldots, m_t\}$ and the set of examples of use $E_t = \{e_{tj}|j = 1, \ldots, n_t\}$, each of them containing multiple words. While most of the senses are accompanied by a definition, only a smaller subset also include an example of use, as it appears from the four last columns of Table 1. Less frequently, some senses contain examples without definitions.

Each definition d_{tj} and example e_{tj} is represented by a vector, which is the average of the word embeddings over all the words constituting them (except stopwords). Formally, these are $d_{tj} = (\sum_{w_l \in d_{tj}} \vec{w_l})/m_t$ and respectively $\vec{e_{tj}} = (\sum_{w_l \in e'_{tj}} \vec{w_l})/n_t$. While the entire definition d_{tj} is used to build the vector, we do not consider all words in the example e_{tj}, but limit the sum to

---

[1] www.cs.york.ac.uk/semeval2010_WSI
[2] http://nlp.stanford.edu/software/
[3] https://wordnet.princeton.edu/
[4] See www.nltk.org/howto/wordnet.html

e'_{tj} i.e. we consider only a window of size c centered around the noun or verb of type W_t (similarly to the window used for context representation below) to avoid noise from long examples.

All the word vectors $\vec{w}_l$ above are word2vec pre-trained embeddings from Google[5] (Mikolov et al., 2013). If d is the dimensionality of the word vector space, then all vectors $\vec{w}_l$, $\vec{d}_{tj}$, and $\vec{e}_{tj}$ are in $\mathcal{R}^d$. Each definition vector $\vec{d}_{tj}$ or example vector $\vec{e}_{tj}$ for a word type W_t will be considered as a center vector for each sense during the clustering procedure.

Similarly, each word *token* w_i in a source sentence is represented by the average vector $\vec{u}_i$ of the words in its context, which is defined as a window of c words centered in w_i. The value c of the context size is even, since we calculate the vector $\vec{u}_i$ for w_i by averaging vectors from $c/2$ words before w_i and from $c/2$ words after it. We stop nevertheless at the sentence boundaries, and filter out stop words before averaging.

We will now explain how to cluster according to their senses all vectors $\vec{u}_i$ for the occurrences w_i of a given word type W_t, using as initial centers either the definition or the example vectors.

3.2 Clustering Word Occurrences According to their Senses

We aim to group all occurrences w_i of a given word type W_t into clusters according to the similarity of their senses, which we will model as the similarity of their context vectors. The correctness of this hypothesis will be supported by the empirical results. We will modify the k-means algorithm in several ways to achieve an optimal clustering of word senses for MT.

The original k-means algorithm (MacQueen, 1967) aims to partition a set of items, which are here tokens $w_1, w_2, \ldots, w_n$ of a same word type W_t, represented through their embeddings $\vec{u}_1, \vec{u}_2, \ldots, \vec{u}_n$ where $\vec{u}_i \in \mathcal{R}^d$. The goal of k-means is to partition (or cluster) them into k sets $S = \{S_1, S_2, \ldots, S_k\}$ so as to minimize the within-cluster sum of squares, as follows:

$$S = \arg\min_S \sum_{i=1}^{k} \sum_{\vec{u} \in S_i} ||\vec{u} - \vec{\mu}_i||^2, \qquad (1)$$

where $\vec{\mu}_i$ is the centroid of each set S_i. At the first iteration, when there are no clusters yet, the

^{5}`code.google.com/archive/p/word2vec/`

algorithm selects k random points to be the centroids of the k clusters. Then, at each subsequent iteration t, k-means calculates for each candidate cluster a new point to be the centroid of the observations, defined as their average vector, as follows:

$$\vec{\mu}_i^{t+1} = \frac{1}{|S_i^t|} \sum_{\vec{u}_j \in S_i^t} \vec{u}_j \qquad (2)$$

We make the following modifications to the original k-means algorithm, to make it adaptive to the word senses observed in the training data.

1. We define the initial number of clusters k_t for each ambiguous word type W_t in the data as the number of its senses in Word-Net (but this number may be reduced by the final re-clustering described below at point 3). Specifically, we run two series of experiments (the results of which will be compared in Section 5.1.1): one in which each k_t is set to m_t, i.e. the number of senses that possess a definition in WordNet, and another one in which we consider only senses that are illustrated with an example, hence setting each k_t to n_t. These settings avoid fixing the number of clusters k_t arbitrarily for each ambiguous word type.

2. We initialize the centroids of the clusters to the vectors representing the senses from WordNet, either using their definition vectors $\vec{d}_{tj}$ in one series of experiments, or their example vectors $\vec{e}_{tj}$ in the other one. This second modification attempts to provide a reasonably accurate starting point for the clustering process.

3. After running the k-means algorithm, we reduce the number of clusters for each word type by merging the clusters which contain fewer than 10 tokens with the nearest larger cluster. This is done by calculating the cosine similarity between each token vector $\vec{u}_i$ and the centroids of the larger clusters and assigning the tokens to the closest large cluster. This re-clustering adapts the final number of clusters to the observed occurrences in the training data. Indeed, when there are few occurrences of a sense for a given ambiguous word type in the data, the SMT is likely not able to translate them properly due to the lack of training samples.

Finally, after clustering the training data, we use the centroids to assign each *new token from the test data* to a cluster, i.e. an abstract sense label, by selecting the closest centroid to it in terms of cosine distance in the embedding space.

3.3 Integration with Machine Translation

Our adaptive WSD system assigns a sense number for each ambiguous word token in the source-side of a parallel corpus. To pass this information to an SMT system, we use a factored phrase-based translation model (Koehn and Hoang, 2007). The factored model offers a principled way to supplement words with additional information – such as, traditionally, part-of-speech tags – without requiring any intervention in the translation tables. The features are combined in a log-linear way with those of a standard phrase-based decoder, and the goal remains to find the most probable target sentence for a given source sentence. To each source noun or verb token, we add a sense label obtained from our adaptive WSD system. To all the other words, we add a NULL label.[6] The translation system will thus take the source-side sense labels into consideration during the training and the decoding processes.

4 Datasets, Preparation and Settings

We evaluate our sense-aware SMT on the UN Corpus[7] (Rafalovitch and Dale, 2009) and on the Europarl Corpus[8] (Koehn, 2005). We select 0.5 million parallel sentences for each language pair from Europarl, as shown in Table 1. We also use the smaller WIT3 Corpus[9] (Cettolo et al., 2012), a collection of transcripts of TED talks, to evaluate the impact of costly model choices, namely the type of the resource (definition vs. examples), the length of the context window, and the k-means method (adaptive vs. original).

Before assigning sense labels, we first tokenize all the texts and identify the parts of speech (POS) using the Stanford POS tagger[10]. Then, we filter out the stopwords and the nouns which are proper names according to the Stanford Name Entity Recognizer[10]. Furthermore, we convert the

---

[6] In practice, these labels are simply appended to the tokens in the data following a vertical bar, e.g. 'rock|1' or 'great|NULL'.

[7] http://www.uncorpora.org/

[8] http://www.statmt.org/europarl/

[9] http://wit3.fbk.eu/

[10] http://nlp.stanford.edu/software/

plural forms of nouns to their singular form and the verb forms to infinitive using the stemmer and lemmatizer from NLTK[11], which is essential because WordNet has description entries only for singular nouns and infinitive form of verbs. The pre-processed text is used for assigning sense labels to each occurrence of a noun or verb which has more than one sense in WordNet.

For translation, we train and tune baseline and factored phrase-based models with Moses[12] (Koehn et al., 2007). We also carried out pilot experiments with neural machine translation (NMT). However, due to the large datasets NMT requires for training, its performance was below SMT on the datasets above, and sense labels did not improve it. We thus focus on SMT in what follows, and leave WSD for NMT for future studies.

We select the optimal model configuration based on the MT performance, measured with the traditional BLEU score (Papineni et al., 2002), on the WIT3 corpus for EN/ZH and EN/DE. Unless otherwise stated, we use the following settings in the k-means algorithm, starting from the implementation provided in Scikit-learn (Pedregosa et al., 2011):

- we use the definition of each sense for initializing the centroids in the adaptive k-means methods (and compare this later with using the examples);

- we set k_t equal to m_t, i.e. the number of senses of an ambiguous word type W_t;

- the window size for the context surrounding each occurrence is set to $c = 8$.

For the evaluation of intrinsic WSD performance, we use the V-metric, the F_1-metric, and their average, as used for instance at SemEval 2010 (Manandhar et al., 2010). To measure the impact of WSD on MT, besides BLEU, we also measure the actual impact on the nouns and verbs that appear in WordNet with several senses, by comparing how many of them are translated as in the reference translation, by our system vs. the baseline. For a certain set of tokens in the source data, we note as N_{improved} the number of tokens which are translated by our system as in the reference translation, but whose baseline translation differs from it. Conversely, we note as N_{degraded} the number of tokens which are translated by the

---

[11] http://www.nltk.org/

[12] http://www.statmt.org/moses/

		Training		Development		Testing		Definitions		Examples	
		# lines	# tokens	# lines	# tokens	# lines	# tokens	# nouns	# verbs	# nouns	# verbs
EN/ZH	WIT3	150,000	3M	10,000	0.3M	50,000	1M	6,052	2,435	2,049	1,932
	UN	500,000	13M	5,000	0.14M	50,000	1.5M	8,165	3,382	2,810	2,716
EN/DE	WIT3	140,000	2.8M	5,000	0.16M	50,000	1M	8,308	2,384	3,662	2,042
	Europarl	500,000	14M	5,000	0.14M	50,000	1.4M	6,373	3,323	2,608	2,668
EN/FR	Europarl	$\sim$	$\sim$	$\sim$	$\sim$	$\sim$	$\sim$	8,279	4,022	2,276	2,054
EN/ES	Europarl	$\sim$	$\sim$	$\sim$	$\sim$	$\sim$	$\sim$	8,716	4,048	2,478	2,359
EN/NL	Europarl	$\sim$	$\sim$	$\sim$	$\sim$	$\sim$	$\sim$	8,667	4,023	2,439	2,318

Table 1: Statistics of the corpora used for machine translation: '$\sim$' indicates a similar size, though not identical texts, because the English source texts for the different language pairs from Europarl are different. Hence, the number of words found in WordNet differ as well.

baseline system as in the reference, but differently by our system. We will use the normalized coefficient $\rho = (N_\text{improved} - N_\text{degraded})/T$, where T is the total number of tokens, as a metric focusing explicitly on the words submitted to WSD.[13]

5 Results

Using the data, settings, and metrics above, we investigate first the impact of two model choices on the performance: centroid initialization for k-means (definition or examples vs. random), and the length of the context window for each word. Then, we evaluate our adaptive clustering method on the WSD task, to estimate its intrinsic quality, and finally measure WSD+MT performance.

5.1 Optimal Values of the Parameters

5.1.1 Initialization of Adaptive k-means

We examine first the impact of the initialization of the sense clusters, on the WIT3 Corpus. In Table 2, we present the BLEU scores of our WSD+MT system in two conditions: when the k-means clusters are initialized with vectors from the definitions vs. from the examples provided in the WordNet synsets of ambiguous words. Moreover, we provide BLEU scores of baseline systems and oracle ones (i.e. using correct senses as factors), as well as the ρ score indicating the relative improvement of ambiguous words in our system wrt. the baseline. The use of definitions outperforms the use of examples, probably because there are more words with definitions than with examples in WordNet (twice as many, as shown in Table 1 in Section 4), but also because definitions may provide more helpful words to build the initial vectors, as they are more explicit than the examples.

All the values of ρ show clear improvements over the baseline, with up to 4% for DE/EN. As for the oracle scores, they outperform the baseline by a factor of 2–3 compared to our system.

Pair	Resource	BLEU			ρ (%)
		Baseline	Factored	Oracle	
EN/ZH	Definitions	15.23	**15.54**	16.24	+2.25
	Examples		15.41	15.85	+1.60
EN/DE	Definitions	19.72	**20.23**	20.99	+3.96
	Examples		19.98	20.45	+2.15

Table 2: Performance of our WSD+MT factored system for two language pairs from WIT3, with two initialization conditions for the k-means clusters, i.e. definitions or examples for each sense.

In addition, we compare the two initialization options above with random initializations of k-means clusters, in Table 3. To offer a fair comparison, we set the number of clusters, in the case of random initializations, respectively to the number of synsets with definitions or examples, for each word type. Clearly, our adaptive, informed initializations of clusters are beneficial to MT.

Resource	k-means initialization	
	Specific	Random
Definitions	**15.54**	15.34
Examples	**15.41**	15.27

Table 3: Performance of our WSD+MT factored system for EN-ZH from WIT3, comparing the two initialization conditions for the k-means clusters, i.e. definitions or examples for each sense, with random initializations.

5.1.2 Length of the Context Window

We investigate the effect of the size of the context window surrounding each ambiguous token, i.e. the number of words surrounding it that are considered for building its vector representation. Figure 3 displays the BLEU score of our WSD+MT

---

[13]The values of N_improved and N_degraded are obtained using automatic word alignment. They do not capture, of course, the absolute correctness of a candidate translation, but only its identity or not with one reference translation.

	System	V-score			F_1-score			Average			#clusters
		All	Nouns	Verbs	All	Nouns	Verbs	All	Nouns	Verbs	
Base.	MFS	0	0	0	64.85	57.00	72.70	32.42	29.50	25.40	1.00
	Random	4.40	4.60	4.20	32.35	30.60	34.10	18.45	17.60	19.30	4.00
	1ClusterPerIns	31.70	35.80	25.60	0.12	0.11	0.12	15.40	17.90	12.90	89.15
Top systems	Hermit (Jurgens and Stevens, 2010)	16.20	16.70	15.60	25.55	26.70	24.40	20.85	21.70	20.00	10.78
	UoY (Korkontzelos and Manandhar, 2010)	15.70	20.60	8.50	49.80	38.20	66.60	32.75	29.40	**37.50**	11.54
	KSU KDD (Elshamy et al., 2010)	15.70	18.00	12.40	36.90	24.60	54.70	26.30	21.30	33.50	17.50
	Duluth-WSI (Pedersen, 2010)	9.00	11.40	5.70	41.10	37.10	46.70	25.05	24.20	26.20	4.15
	Duluth-WSI-SVD-Gap (Pedersen, 2010)	0.00	0.00	0.10	63.30	57.00	72.40	31.65	28.50	36.20	1.02
	KCDC-PT (Kern et al., 2010)	1.90	1.00	3.10	61.80	56.40	69.70	31.85	28.70	36.40	1.50
	KCDC-GD (Kern et al., 2010)	6.90	5.90	8.50	59.20	51.60	70.00	33.05	28.70	39.20	2.78
	Duluth-Mix-Gap (Pedersen, 2010)	3.00	2.90	3.00	59.10	54.50	65.80	31.05	29.70	34.40	1.61
Ours	**Adaptive k-means + definition**	13.65	14.70	12.60	56.70	53.70	59.60	**35.20**	**34.20**	36.10	4.45
	Adaptive k-means + example	11.35	11.00	11.70	53.25	47.70	58.80	32.28	29.30	35.25	3.58

Table 4: WSD results from the SemEval 2010 shared task in terms of V-score, F_1 score and their average. Our adaptive k-means using definitions (last but one line) outperforms all the other systems on the average of V and F_1, when considering both nouns and verbs, or nouns only.

factored system when varying this size, on EN/ZH translation in the WIT3 Corpus, along with the (constant) score of the baseline. The performance of our system improves with the size of the window, reaching a peak around 8–10. This result highlights the importance of a longer context compared to the typical settings of SMT systems, which generally do not go beyond 6. It also suggests that MT systems which exploit effectively longer context, as we show here with a sense-aware factored MT system for ambiguous nouns and verbs, can significantly improve their lexical choice and their overall translation quality.

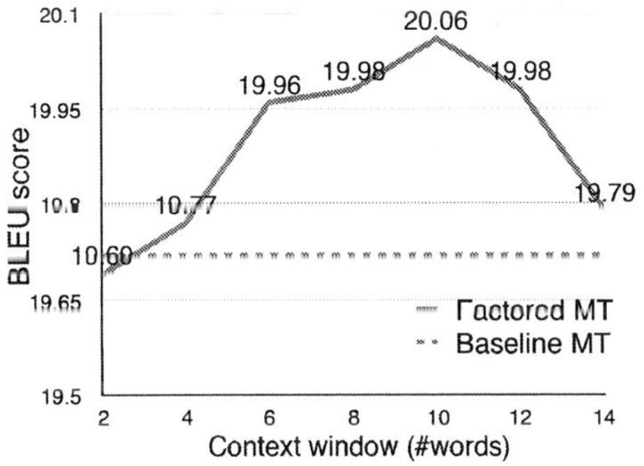

Figure 3: BLEU scores of our WSD+MT factored system on EN/ZH WIT3 data, along with the baseline score (constant), when the size of the context window around each ambiguous token (for building its context vector) varies from 2 to 14.

5.2 Word Sense Disambiguation Results

We evaluate in this section our WSD system on the dataset from the SemEval 2010 shared task (Man-andhar et al., 2010), to assess how competitive it is, while acknowledging that our system uses external knowledge not available to SemEval participants.

Table 4 shows the WSD results in terms of V-score and F_1-score, comparing our method (bottom two lines) with other WSD systems that participated in SemEval 2010 (top four systems for each metric). We add three baselines provided by the task organizers for comparison: (1) Most Frequent Sense (MFS), which groups all occurrences of a word into one cluster, (2) 1Cluster-PerInstance, which produces one cluster for each occurrence of a word, and (3) Random, which randomly assigns an occurrence to 1 out of 4 clusters (4 is the average number of senses from the ground-truth).

The V-score is biased towards systems generating a higher number of clusters than the number of gold standard senses. F_1-score measures the classification performance, i.e. how well a method assigns two occurrences of a word belonging to the same gold standard class. Hence, this metric favors systems that generate fewer clusters (for instance, if all instances were grouped into 1 cluster, the F_1-score would be high). As these two metrics are biased towards either small or large numbers of clusters, their average is a useful metric as well.

Table 4 shows that k-means initialized with definitions achieves high performance and ranks among the top systems for each metric individually, outperforming all other systems on the averaged metric (especially over nouns or all words). Moreover, the adaptive k-means method finds an

Language pair	Corpus	BLEU			ρ (%)
		Baseline	Factored	Oracle	
EN/ZH	UN	23.25	**23.69**	24.44	+2.26
EN/DE	Europarl	20.78	**21.32**	21.95	+1.57
EN/FR	Europarl	31.96	**32.20**	32.98	+1.21
EN/ES	Europarl	39.95	**40.37**	41.06	+1.04
EN/NL	Europarl	23.56	**23.84**	24.79	+1.38

Table 5: BLEU scores of our WSD+MT factored system, with both noun and verb senses, along with baseline MT and oracle WSD+MT, on five language pairs.

Language pair	Baseline	Factored (Nouns)				Factored (Verbs)			
		nouns		nouns + verbs	Oracle	verbs		nouns + verbs	Oracle
		BLEU	ρ (%)	ρ (%)		BLEU	ρ (%)	ρ (%)	
EN/ZH	23.25	**23.61**	+1.78	+1.93	24.05	**23.35**	+3.30	+3.14	24.17
EN/DE	20.78	**21.31**	+1.65	+1.48	21.45	**21.30**	+1.81	+1.79	21.87
EN/FR	31.96	**32.08**	+0.90	+0.82	32.36	**32.15**	+2.03	+2.13	32.98
EN/ES	39.95	**40.28**	+1.05	+0.96	40.59	**40.24**	+2.08	+1.15	41.06
EN/NL	23.56	**23.79**	+1.13	+0.87	24.05	**23.70**	+2.58	+2.71	24.46

Table 6: BLEU scores of our WSD+MT factored system, trained separately on disambiguated nouns vs. verbs, and tested separately or jointly, along with baseline MT and oracle WSD+MT, on five language pairs.

average number of senses of 4, which is close to the ground-truth value provided by SemEval (4.46). These results show that our method, despite its simplicity, is effective and provides competitive performance against prior art, partly thanks to additional knowledge not available to the shared task systems.

5.3 Machine Translation Results

Table 5 displays the performance of our factored MT systems trained with noun and verb senses on five language pairs by using the dataset mentioned in Table 1. Our system performs consistently better than the MT baseline on all pairs, with the largest improvements achieved on EN/ZH and EN/DE. To better understand the improvements over the baseline MT, we also provide the BLEU score of an oracle system which has access to the reference translation of the ambiguous words through the alignment provided by GIZA++. According to the results, our factored MT system bridges around 40% of the gap between the baseline MT system and the oracle system on EN/DE and 30% on EN/ZH.

As shown in Table 6, the translation quality of our factored MT outperforms the baseline when trained with either noun senses or verb senses separately. However, in some cases, our factored MT system trained with both noun and verb senses performs worse than with noun and verb senses separately. This may be due to the lack of sufficient training data to learn reliably using all the additional factors – as we observed when training on the smaller WIT3 Corpus.

Lastly, Table 7 shows the confusion matrix for our factored MT and the baseline MT systems when comparing the reference translation of nouns and verbs separately, using GIZA++ alignment. In particular, the confusion matrix displays the number of labeled tokens which are translated as in the reference or not ('Correct' vs. 'Incorrect'). As we can observe, the number of tokens that our factored MT system translates correctly while the baseline MT does not, is two times largers than the number of tokens that the baseline MT system finds correctly while our factored MT does not.

6 Conclusion

We presented a sense-aware statistical MT system which uses a larger context than standard ones, through an adaptive context-dependent k-means clustering algorithm for WSD. The algorithm utilizes semantic information from WordNet to identify the dominant clusters, which correspond to senses in the source side of a parallel corpus. The proposed adaptive k-means method is straightforward, yet it provides competitive WSD performance on data from the SemEval 2010 shared task. For MT, our experiments with five language pairs show that our sense-aware MT system consistently improves over the baseline. As future work, we plan to integrate sense information for ambiguous words to neural MT and investigate

		Factored (Nouns)				Factored (Verbs)			
		nouns		nouns + verbs		verbs		nouns + verbs	
		Correct	Incorrect	Correct	Incorrect	Correct	Incorrect	Correct	Incorrect
EN/ZH	Correct	138,876	4,402	138,264	5,075	37,132	1,166	36,647	1,527
Baseline	Incorrect	8,454	75,690	9,472	74,541	3,939	41,728	4,149	41,077
EN/DE	Correct	91,966	1,473	91,376	2,035	18,370	664	18,214	812
Baseline	Incorrect	4,268	71,037	4,525	69,931	1,892	47,105	2,029	46,795

Table 7: Detailed confusion matrix of our factored MT system and the baseline MT system with respect to the reference on the EN/DE pair from Europarl corpus and the EN/ZH from UN corpus.

other effective ways to enable access to longer context.

Acknowledgments

We are grateful for their support to the Swiss National Science Foundation (SNSF) under the Sinergia MODERN project (grant n. 147653, see www.idiap.ch/project/modern/) and to the European Union under the Horizon 2020 SUMMA project (grant n. 688139, see www.summa-project.eu). We thank the reviewers for their helpful suggestions.

References

Eneko Agirre and Philip Edmonds. 2007. *Word Sense Disambiguation: Algorithms and Applications*. Springer Science & Business Media.

Eneko Agirre and Aitor Soroa. 2009. Personalizing PageRank for word sense disambiguation. In *Proceedings of the 12th Conference of the European Chapter of the Association for Computational Linguistics*. Athens, Greece, pages 33–41.

Eleftherios Avramidis and Philipp Koehn. 2008. Enriching morphologically poor languages for statistical machine translation. In *Proceedings of the 46th Annual Meeting of the Association for Computational Linguistics*. Columbus, Ohio, pages 763–770.

Alexandra Birch, Miles Osborne, and Philipp Koehn. 2007. CCG supertags in factored statistical machine translation. In *Proceedings of the Second Workshop on Statistical Machine Translation*. Prague, Czech Republic, pages 9–16.

Clara Cabezas and Philip Resnik. 2005. Using WSD techniques for lexical selection in statistical machine translation. Technical report, DTIC Document.

Marine Carpuat and Dekai Wu. 2005. Word sense disambiguation vs. statistical machine translation. In *Proceedings of the 43rd Annual Meeting of Association for Computational Linguistics*. Michigan, USA, pages 387–394.

Marine Carpuat and Dekai Wu. 2007. Improving statistical machine translation using word sense disambiguation. In *Proceedings of the 2007 Joint Conference on Empirical Methods in Natural Language Processing and Computational Natural Language Learning*. Prague, Czech Republic, pages 61–72.

Mauro Cettolo, Christian Girardi, and Marcello Federico. 2012. WIT[3]: Web inventory of transcribed and translated talks. In *Proceedings of the 16th Conference of the European Association for Machine Translation (EAMT)*. Trento, Italy, pages 261–268.

Yee Seng Chan, Hwee Tou Ng, and David Chiang. 2007. Word sense disambiguation improves statistical machine translation. In *Proceedings of the 45th Annual Meeting of the Association of Computational Linguistics*. Prague, Czech Republic, pages 33–40.

Wesam Elshamy, Doina Caragea, and William H Hsu. 2010. KSU KDD: Word sense induction by clustering in topic space. In *Proceedings of the 5th international workshop on semantic evaluation (SemEval-2010)*. Association for Computational Linguistics, Los Angeles, California, pages 367–370.

Christiane Fellbaum, editor. 1998. *WordNet: An Electronic Lexical Database*. The MIT Press, Cambridge, MA, USA.

David Jurgens and Keith Stevens. 2010. Hermit: Flexible clustering for the Semeval-2 WSI task. In *Proceedings of the 5th international workshop on semantic evaluation (SemEval-2010))*. Association for Computational Linguistics, Los Angeles, California, pages 359–362.

Roman Kern, Markus Muhr, and Michael Granitzer. 2010. KCDC: Word sense induction by using grammatical dependencies and sentence phrase structure. In *Proceedings of the 5th international workshop on semantic evaluation (SemEval-2010)*. Association for Computational Linguistics, Los Angeles, California, pages 351–354.

Philipp Koehn. 2005. Europarl: A parallel corpus for statistical machine translation. In *Proceedings of MT summit*. Phuket, Thailand, pages 79–86.

Philipp Koehn and Hieu Hoang. 2007. Factored translation models. In *Proceedings of the 2007 Joint Conference on Empirical Methods in Natural Language Processing and Computational Natural Language Learning*. Prague, Czech Republic, pages 868–876.

Philipp Koehn, Hieu Hoang, Birch, et al. 2007. Moses: Open source toolkit for statistical machine translation. In *Proceedings of the 45th annual meeting of the Association for Computational Linguistics*. pages 177–180.

Ioannis Korkontzelos and Suresh Manandhar. 2010. Uoy: Graphs of ambiguous vertices for word sense induction and disambiguation. In *Proceedings of the 5th international workshop on semantic evaluation (SemEval-2010)*. Los Angeles, California, pages 355–358.

James MacQueen. 1967. Some methods for classification and analysis of multivariate observations. In *Proceedings of the 5th Berkeley symposium on mathematical statistics and probability*. Oakland, CA, USA, pages 281–297.

Suresh Manandhar, Ioannis P Klapaftis, Dmitriy Dligach, and Sameer S Pradhan. 2010. SemEval-2010 task 14: Word sense induction and disambiguation. In *Proceedings of the 5th international workshop on semantic evaluation (SemEval-2010)*. Association for Computational Linguistics, Los Angeles, California, pages 63–68.

Tomas Mikolov, Ilya Sutskever, Kai Chen, Greg S Corrado, and Jeff Dean. 2013. Distributed representations of words and phrases and their compositionality. In *Advances in Neural Information Processing Systems*. pages 3111–3119.

Steven Neale, Luıs Gomes, Eneko Agirre, Oier Lopez de Lacalle, and António Branco. 2016. Word sense-aware machine translation: Including senses as contextual features for improved translation models. In *Proceedings of the Tenth International Conference on Language Resources and Evaluation (LREC 2016)*. Portoroz, Slovenia, pages 2777–2783.

Kishore Papineni, Salim Roukos, Todd Ward, and Wei-Jing Zhu. 2002. BLEU: A method for automatic evaluation of machine translation. In *Proceedings of the 40th Annual Meeting of Association for Computational Linguistics*. Philadelphia, USA, pages 311–318.

Ted Pedersen. 2010. Duluth-WSI: SenseClusters applied to the sense induction task of SemEval-2. In *Proceedings of the 5th international workshop on semantic evaluation (SemEval-2010)*. Association for Computational Linguistics, Los Angeles, California, pages 363–366.

Fabian Pedregosa, Gaël Varoquaux, Alexandre Gramfort, Vincent Michel, Bertrand Thirion, Olivier Grisel, Mathieu Blondel, Peter Prettenhofer, Ron Weiss, Vincent Dubourg, Jake Vanderplas, Alexandre Passos, David Cournapeau, Matthieu Brucher, Matthieu Perrot, and Édouard Duchesnay. 2011. Scikit-learn: Machine learning in python. *Journal of Machine Learning Research* 12:2825–2830.

Alexandre Rafalovitch and Robert Dale. 2009. United Nations general assembly resolutions: A six-language parallel corpus. In *Proceedings of the MT Summit*. Ontario, Canada, pages 292–299.

Jinsong Su, Deyi Xiong, Shujian Huang, Xianpei Han, and Junfeng Yao. 2015. Graph-Based collective lexical selection for statistical machine translation. In *Proceedings of the Conference on Empirical Methods in Natural Language Processing*. Lisbon, Portugal, pages 1238–1247.

David Vickrey, Luke Biewald, Marc Teyssier, and Daphne Koller. 2005. Word-sense disambiguation for machine translation. In *Proceedings of the Conference on Human Language Technology and Empirical Methods in Natural Language Processing*. Vancouver, British Columbia, Canada, pages 771–778.

Deyi Xiong and Min Zhang. 2014. A sense-based translation model for statistical machine translation. In *Proceedings of the 52nd Annual Meeting of the Association for Computational Linguistics*. Baltimore MD, USA, pages 1459–1469.

Improving Word Sense Disambiguation in Neural Machine Translation with Sense Embeddings

Annette Rios[*] and **Laura Mascarell**[*] and **Rico Sennrich**[†*]
[*]Institute of Computational Linguistics, University of Zurich
[†]School of Informatics, University of Edinburgh

Abstract

Word sense disambiguation is necessary in translation because different word senses often have different translations. Neural machine translation models learn different senses of words as part of an end-to-end translation task, and their capability to perform word sense disambiguation has so far not been quantified. We exploit the fact that neural translation models can score arbitrary translations to design a novel cross-lingual word sense disambiguation task that is tailored towards evaluating neural machine translation models. We present a test set of 7,200 lexical ambiguities for German→English, and 6,700 for German→French, and report baseline results. With 70% of lexical ambiguities correctly disambiguated, we find that word sense disambiguation remains a challenging problem for neural machine translation, especially for rare word senses. To improve word sense disambiguation in neural machine translation, we experiment with two methods to integrate sense embeddings. In a first approach we pass sense embeddings as additional input to the neural machine translation system. For the second experiment, we extract lexical chains based on sense embeddings from the document and integrate this information into the NMT model. While a baseline NMT system disambiguates frequent word senses quite reliably, the annotation with both sense labels and lexical chains improves the neural models' performance on rare word senses.

1 Introduction

Semantically ambiguous words present a special challenge to machine translation systems: in order to produce a correct sentence in the target language, the system has to decide which meaning is accurate in the given context. Errors in lexical choice can lead to wrong or even incomprehensible translations. However, quantitatively assessing errors of this type is challenging, since automatic metrics such as BLEU (Papineni et al., 2002) do not provide a sufficiently detailed analysis.

Several ways of evaluating lexical choice for machine translation have been proposed in previous work. Cross-lingual lexical choice tasks have been created for the evaluation of word sense disambiguation (WSD) systems (Mihalcea et al., 2010; Lefever and Hoste, 2013), and have been applied to the evaluation of MT systems (Carpuat, 2013). Vickrey et al. (2005) evaluate lexical choice in a blank-filling task, where the translation of an ambiguous source word is blanked from the reference translation, and an MT system is tested as to whether it can predict it. In all these tasks, a word-level translation (or set of translations) is defined as the gold label. A major problem is that an MT system will be punished for producing a synonym, paraphrase, or inflected variant of the predefined gold label. We thus propose a more constrained task where an MT system has to select one out of a predefined set of translations.

Neural machine translation (NMT) (Sutskever et al., 2014; Bahdanau et al., 2015) has recently emerged as the new state of the art in machine translation, producing top-ranked systems in recent shared tasks (Luong and Manning, 2015; Sennrich et al., 2016a; Neubig, 2016). The strengths and weaknesses of NMT have been the subject of recent research, and previous studies involving human analysis have consistently found NMT to be

Proceedings of the Conference on Machine Translation (WMT), Volume 1: Research Papers, pages 11–19
Copenhagen, Denmark, September 7–11, 2017. ©2017 Association for Computational Linguistics

more fluent than phrase-based SMT (Neubig et al., 2015; Bojar et al., 2016; Bentivogli et al., 2016), but results in terms of adequacy are more mixed. Bentivogli et al. (2016) report improvements in lexical choice based on HTER matches on the lemma-level, while Bojar et al. (2016) found no clear improvement in a direct assessment of adequacy. Neubig et al. (2015) perform an error annotation in which the number of lexical choice errors even increases slightly by reranking a syntax-based statistical machine translation system with an NMT model.

We aim to allow for a large-scale, reproducible method of assessing the capability of an NMT model to perform lexical disambiguation. NMT systems can not only be used to generate translations of a source sentence, but also to assign a probability $P(T|S)$ for any given pair of a source sentence S and a target sentence T. We use this feature to create a test set with artificially introduced lexical disambiguation errors. Comparing the scores of an NMT model on these contrastive translations to the score of the reference allows us to assess how well the model can distinguish different senses in ambiguous words.

We have created two test sets for the language pairs German-English and German-French with about 6,500 and 6,700 sentence pairs respectively.[1] Based on the performance of state-of-the-art NMT systems on these test sets, we discuss the capability of NMT to perform lexical disambiguation.

Furthermore, we present two methods to improve word sense disambiguation in neural machine translation by allowing the model to learn sense-specific word embeddings. Both methods are based on an external word sense disambiguation. While the first method passes sense labels as additional input to an NMT system, the second is motivated by the hypothesis that document-level context is valuable for disambiguation. We model this context via lexical chains, i.e. sequences of semantically-similar words in a given text that express the topic of the segment they cover in a condensed form. Our method is inspired by Galley and McKeown (2003), who present an approach to build English lexical chains automatically using WordNet (Miller, 1995) and evaluate its performance on a sense disambiguation task. Instead

of WordNet, we use sense embeddings in order to determine the similarity between the words in a document and thus find and annotate the lexical chains. Experimental results show the potential of lexical chains at disambiguating word senses.

2 Contrastive Translations

The test set consists of sentence pairs that contain at least one ambiguous German word. In order to produce contrastive translation pairs, we create an automatically modified version of the reference translation where we replace the original translation of a given ambiguous word with the translation of one of its other meanings. We cluster different translations that overlap in meaning, i.e. that are (at least sometimes) used interchangeably. We do not produce any contrastive translations that belong to the same cluster as the reference translation.

As an example, we show the sense clusters that we consider for two ambiguous German words:

> *Schlange:*
> serpent, snake
> line, queue
>
> *Abzug:*
> withdrawal, departure   *rétraction, sortie*
> trigger   *gâchette*
> discount, subtraction   *déduction, soustraction*

Table 1 shows an example of source, reference, and contrastive sentences.

Our approach is inspired by Sennrich (2017), who use contrastive translation pairs to evaluate various error types, including morpho-syntactic agreement and polarity errors. Apart from focusing on another error type, namely word sense errors, our approach differs in that we pair a human reference translation not just with one contrastive example, but a set of contrastive examples, i.e. a set of incorrect translations of the semantically ambiguous source word. The model is considered correct if it scores the human reference translation higher than all of the contrastive translations. Note that this evaluation does not directly assess the translation output of a system, which might be different from the set of translations that are scored, or the search performance of a system. Instead, its focus is to identify specific model errors.

3 Lexical Choice Errors

In a first step, we compile a list of German nouns that have semantically distinct translations in English and French from the lexical translation tables

---

12

of existing German-English and German-French phrase-based MT systems, and we clean these lists manually. We then extract sentence pairs from parallel corpora for all ambiguous words in our lists. Since for most ambiguous words, one or more of their meanings are relatively rare, a large amount of parallel text is necessary to extract a sufficiently balanced number of examples.[2]

When creating the test set, our goal is to produce contrastive translations that cannot be easily identified as wrong based on grammatical or phonological features. We do not consider ambiguities across word classes (*Flucht* - 'flight, escape' vs. *flucht* - 'he/she curses'). Furthermore, we do not consider German words with different meanings distinguished by gender (*der Leiter* (m.) - 'leader' vs. *die Leiter* (f.) - 'ladder').

Contrastive translations are produced automatically based on a replacement of the target word with the specified contrastive variants. We ensure that contrastive translations match the original translation in number; in French, we also limit replacements to those that match the original translation in gender, and take into account elision for vowel-initial words.

We consider both plural and singular forms in German, but exclude word forms that are unambiguous. For instance, the German singular word *Schuld* can refer to *debt* or *guilt*, however, the plural form *Schulden* can only be translated as *debts*.

Furthermore, we exclude a small number of cases where the context in either source or target sentence clearly indicates the meaning: For instance, if the German word *Absatz* ('heel', 'sales', 'paragraph') is followed by a number, the transla-

tion is in all likelihood 'paragraph' and contrastive sentences with 'heel' or 'sales' will not present a challenge for the model.

Following our strategy of focusing on difficult cases, we oversample the less frequent word senses for the test set to reduce the performance of a simple most frequent sense baseline to that of random guessing. Specifically, we include 100 test instances per word sense, or the total amount of available sentence pairs if less than 100 were found in the parallel data.

For German-English, the test set contains 84 word senses, with on average 3.5 contrastive translations per reference; for German-French, it contains 71 word senses, with an average of 2.2 contrastive translations per reference. A full list of word senses can be found in the appendix.

We include the location of the sentence in the original corpus in our metadata to allow future experiments with document-level information.[3]

4 Sense Embeddings in Neural Machine Translation

In addition to the evaluation of a standard NMT model on the word sense disambiguation task detailed in the previous section, we present two experiments on German→English and German→French to improve lexical choice using methods from WSD. In a first approach, we compute sense embeddings and include the resulting sense labels into the NMT model as additional input features (Alexandrescu and Kirchhoff, 2006; Sennrich and Haddow, 2016). For our second experiment, instead of adding the labels directly to the input, we use them to build lexical chains of similar words in the given document. These lexical chains contain information about the topic and/or domain of the document, and we include them as additional features into our NMT model.

4.1 Sense Embeddings

Sense embeddings are vector representations of word senses in a vector space, but unlike word embeddings, where every word form receives a vector representation, with sense embeddings we obtain separate vector representations for each sense of a given word. To compute the sense embeddings we

---

[2]Sentence pairs have been extracted from the following corpora:

- WMT test and development sets 2006-2016 (de-en) and 2006-2013 (de-fr)
- Crédit Suisse News Corpus `https://pub.cl.uzh.ch/projects/b4c/de/`
- corpora from OPUS ((Tiedemann, 2012)):
  - Global Voices (`http://opus.lingfil.uu.se/GlobalVoices.php`)
  - Books (`http://opus.lingfil.uu.se/Books.php`)
  - EU Bookshop Corpus (`http://opus.lingfil.uu.se/EUbookshop.php`)
  - OpenSubtitles 2016 (German-French) (`http://opus.lingfil.uu.se/OpenSubtitles2016.php`)
- MultiUN (Ziemski et al., 2016)

[3]A snapshot of the corpora used to extract the examples can be found at `http://data.statmt.org/ContraWSD/`.

source:	*Also nahm ich meinen amerikanischen Reisepass und stellte mich in die **Schlange** für Extranjeros.*
reference:	*So I took my U.S. passport and got in the **line** for Extranjeros.*
contrastive:	*So I took my U.S. passport and got in the **snake** for Extranjeros.*
contrastive:	*So I took my U.S. passport and got in the **serpent** for Extranjeros.*
source:	*Er hat zwar schnell den Finger am **Abzug**, aber er ist eben neu.*
reference:	*Il a la **gâchette** facile mais c'est parce qu'il débute.*
contrastive:	*Il a la **soustraction** facile mais c'est parce qu'il débute.*
contrastive:	*Il a la **déduction** facile mais c'est parce qu'il débute.*
contrastive:	*Il a la **sortie** facile mais c'est parce qu'il débute.*
contrastive:	*Il a la **rétraction** facile mais c'est parce qu'il débute.*

Table 1: Contrastive Translations

use $SenseGram$[4] (Pelevina et al., 2016), which has been shown to perform as good as stat-of-the-art unsupervised WSD systems.

The method to learn the sense embeddings using $SenseGram$ consists of four steps that we briefly summarise here. First, the method learns word embeddings using the $word2vec$ toolkit (Mikolov et al., 2013).[5] It then uses these word embeddings to build a word similarity graph, where each word is linked to its 200 nearest neighbours. Next, it induces a sense inventory, where each sense is represented by a cluster of words (e.g. the sense of *table-furniture* is represented with the word cluster *desk*, *bench*, *dining table*, *surface*, and *board*). The sense inventory of each word is obtained through clustering the ego-networks of its related words. Finally, the method computes the sense embedding of each word sense by averaging the vectors of the words in the corresponding cluster.

Once the sense embeddings are learned, we label all content words in the data with their corresponding sense and include this information as additional features.

4.2 Lexical Chains

As described above, $SenseGram$ allows us to disambiguate a word based on the context in which it occurs. Based on the disambiguated words, we can detect the lexical chains, i.e. chains of semantically similar words within a given document. To compute the semantic similarity between two word senses, we calculate the cosine similarity between their sense embeddings.[6] The closer to 1.0 the resulting value is, the higher their semantic similarity. To distinguish between similar and non-similar senses, we set a threshold of 0.85 that we manually picked by looking at how different values affect the resulting lexical chains: a lower threshold builds lexical chains containing sense words that are not sufficiently related, whereas a higher threshold results in semantically strong, but possibly incomplete lexical chains that do not cover all words belonging to the chain.

We use the method proposed by Mascarell (2017) to detect lexical chains in a document. This method is inspired by Morris and Hirst (1991)'s approach, which manually finds lexical chains in a document using a thesaurus to obtain the similarity between words. As detailed in Section 4.1, we use sense embeddings instead of a dictionary to compute the semantic similarity.

Given a document as input, our method processes sentences and their content words sequentially. For each sentence, it computes the semantic similarity between the current content word c and each previous content word c' in the previous five sentences, based on the approach by Morris and Hirst (1991). If c and c' are semantically similar, our method proceeds as follows:

- If c and c' are not part of a chain, create a new chain with c and c'.

- If c' is in a chain ch_i, append c to ch_i.

---

[4]`https://github.com/tudarmstadt-lt/sensegram`

[5]Embeddings for our models were learned on the following corpora:

- SdeWaC (Faaß and Eckart, 2013) (∼768M words)
- Common Crawls (∼775M words)
- Europarl (∼47M words)
- News Commentary (∼6M words)

[6]Using sense embeddings instead of word embeddings for this task ensures that we can recognize similar words even if they are polysemic and not all of their senses are related. For instance, *mouse* and *rat* are related if *mouse* refers to the animal, but not if *mouse* refers to the computer device.

- If c and c' are in two different chains, merge both chains.

Since every linked word in the chain provides context for disambiguation, the method creates as many links as possible between similar words. Therefore, it also preserves one-transitive links: c_i links to c_{i+l} by transitivity if c_i links to c_{i+k} and c_{i+k} to c_{i+l}, where $i<k<l$ (Morris and Hirst, 1991).

As Morris and Hirst (1991) indicate, words linked by one-transitive links are semantically related, but words further apart in the chain might not be: In their paper, they point to the lexical chain {*cow, sheep, wool, scarf, boots, hat, snow*}. While consecutive words in the chain such as *wool* and *scarf* are semantically related, *cow* and *snow* are not.

To provide the NMT model with the detected lexical chains in the source, we represent this discourse knowledge in the input as a combination of features. Accordingly, each word in the lexical chain is annotated with its linked words as factors. For example, if the German word *Absatz* is linked in the lexical chain to *Wirtschaft* ('economy') and *Verkauf* ('sale'), it is represented as *Absatz|Wirtschaft|Verkauf*. The resulting vector representation of *Absatz* is the vector concatenation of each individual feature's embeddings.

Since all words in the input must have the same number of factors, each word that is not part of a lexical chain is annotated with itself as factors. Similarly, words linked to only one word are annotated with the corresponding linked word in the chain and the word itself.

5   Evaluation

We present an evaluation with two basic neural MT systems, trained with Nematus (Sennrich et al., 2017), using byte pair encoding (BPE) on both source and target side (Sennrich et al., 2016b). For both the German-English and the German-French experiments, we train a model on 2.1 million sentence pairs from Europarl (v7) and News Commentary (v11).[7] We use these corpora because they contain document boundaries, which is a requirement for the lexical chains experiments.

We present further results for models that use additional source-side features, a) the sense labels themselves and b) lexical chains. The feature is

given its own embedding space, and the model can thus learn sense-specific embeddings. If a word is segmented into multiple subword units by BPE, the additional input feature of the word is repeated for each unit. Vocabulary size for all models is 90,000.

We train the models for a week, using Adam (Kingma and Ba, 2015) to update the model parameters on minibatches of the size 80. Every 10,000 minibatches, we validate our model on a held out development set via BLEU and perplexity. The maximum length of the sentences is 50. The total size of the embedding layer is 500 for both the baseline and the system trained with additional input features, and the dimension of the hidden layer is 1024. For the experiments with additional input features, we divide the embedding size equally among the features. Conceivably, keeping the dimensionality of the word embedding constant and adding more parameters for additional features would result in better performance, but we wanted to rule out that any performance improvements are solely due to an increase in model size.

To assess a model's capability to distinguish different meanings of ambiguous words, we let it assign a score to the reference translation and to the artificially created contrastive translations. If the score of the reference translation is higher than the scores of all contrastive translations, this counts as a correct decision.

system	accuracy
de-en ($N = 7243$)	
NMT baseline	0.7095
NMT sense labels	0.7138
NMT lexical chains	0.7034
human	≈ 0.96
de-fr ($N = 6746$)	
NMT baseline	0.7023
NMT sense labels	0.6998
NMT lexical chains	0.7083
human	≈ 0.93

Table 2: Word sense disambiguation accuracy

German	*Sehen Sie die **Muster**?*
reference	*Do you see the **patterns**?*
contrastive	*Do you see the **examples**?*

Table 4: Ambiguous sentence pair

[7] http://opus.lingfil.uu.se/News-Commentary11.php

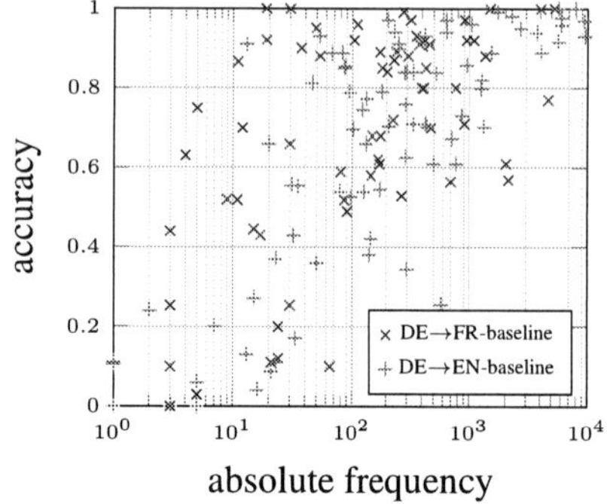
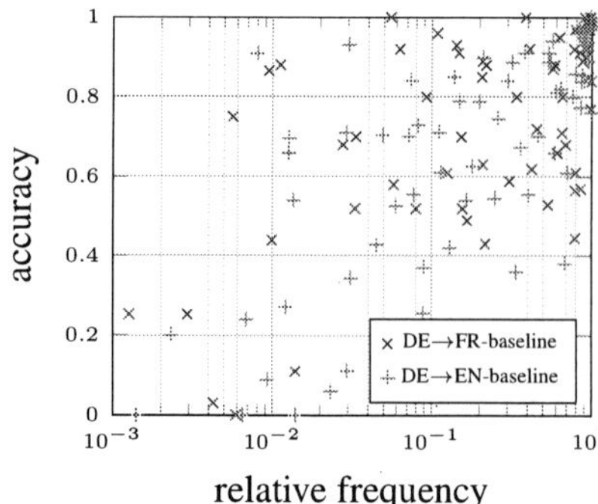

Figure 1: Word sense disambiguation accuracy by word sense frequency in training set (absolute, or relative to source word frequency).

| | | de-en | | | | de-fr | | |
| | | baseline | sense labels | lexical chains | | baseline | sense labels | lexical chains |
frequency	senses[*]	accuracy	accuracy	accuracy	senses[*]	accuracy	accuracy	accuracy
>10000	2	0.9840	0.9840	0.9840	2	0.9900	0.9900	0.9900
>5000	7	**0.9639**	0.9534	0.9459	1	1.0000	1.0000	0.9900
>2000	4	**0.9386**	0.9284	0.9284	3	0.7375	**0.7725**	0.7150
>1000	6	0.8598	**0.8632**	0.8427	3	0.9333	**0.9367**	0.9167
>500	8	**0.7410**	0.7308	0.7090	6	0.8260	0.8260	**0.8361**
>200	17	0.7800	0.7734	**0.7900**	16	0.8444	**0.8475**	0.8406
>100	9	0.6058	0.6095	**0.6156**	9	**0.7544**	0.7456	0.6933
>50	8	**0.7899**	0.7645	0.7630	6	0.5160	0.5200	**0.6420**
>20	9	0.4055	**0.4521**	0.3945	8	0.5276	0.5430	**0.5469**
0-20	14	0.3127	**0.3664**	0.3237	17	0.4924	0.4611	**0.5156**

Table 3: Accuracy of word sense prediction by frequency of word sense in training set (* number of senses in frequency range).

	baseline	sense labels	lexical chains
de-en	17.1	16.9	17.1
de-fr	14.6	14.6	14.7

Table 5: Average BLEU scores on newstest 2009-2013

As Table 2 shows, both the German→French and the German→English baseline model achieve an accuracy of 0.70 on the test set. We also report accuracy of a smaller-scale human evaluation, in which two human annotators (one per language pair) were asked to identify the correct translation for a random sample of the test set (N=100–150). The annotation was performed purely on sentence-level, without any document context, and shows that some ambiguities are even hard for a human to resolve without context. Consider the sentence pairs in Table 4 for such an example. We speculate that both humans and MT systems should be able to resolve more ambiguities with wider con-

text. Even with only sentence-level information, the gap between human and NMT performance is sizeable, between 23 and 26 percentage points.

An important indicator of how well a word sense is translated by NMT is its frequency in the training data. Figure 1 illustrates the relationship between the frequency of a word sense in the training data (both absolute and relative to the frequency of the source word) and the accuracy the model achieves on the test set.

There is a high correlation between word sense frequency and accuracy: for German→English, Spearman's ρ is 0.75 for the correlation between accuracy and absolute frequency, and 0.77 for the correlation between accuracy and relative frequency. For German→French, ρ is 0.58 for both. It is unsurprising that the most frequent word sense is preferred by the model, and that accuracy for it is high. We hence want to highlight performance on rarer word senses. Table 3 shows the word sense accuracy of the NMT models grouped by frequency classes and the number of senses in each class. All models achieve close to 100% accuracy on words that occur more than 10,000 times in the training data. For the rare senses however, the NMT models are much less reliable: for word senses seen 0-20 times in training, the baseline accuracy is between 31-49%.

The annotation of the source side with sense labels improves the accuracy on the test set by 0.43% for German→English, while the lexical chains does not improve the model on average. On the other hand for German→French, the lexical chains result in an improvement of 0.6%, but the annotation with sense labels does not lead to a better score on the test set on average. As shown in Table 3, there is little room for improvement for frequent word senses, and sense labels and lexical chains show the strongest improvements over the baseline for the less frequent word senses. Table 5 contains the average BLEU scores on the newstest 2009-2013 test sets.

6 Conclusions

This paper introduces a novel lexical decision task for the evaluation of NMT models, and presents test sets for German-English and German-French. This task allows for the automatic and quantitative analysis of the ability of NMT models to perform lexical disambiguation, a phenomenon that has previously been remarked to be challenging for NMT. First evaluations with NMT models show that lexical choice is resolved well for frequent word senses, but not for infrequent word senses. Additional experiments to add a) sense labels to content words and b) topic knowledge in the form of lexical chains to the NMT model shows that semantic information improves lexical choice especially for word senses that do not occur frequently in the training data. We find that the inclusion of sense labels improves lexical choice on our test set 0.43% for German→English. Furthermore, we gain a small increase of 0.6% in accuracy with lexical chains for German→French.

We consider the performance of the baseline NMT systems respectable, given that the test set was created to be challenging, and has a strong focus on difficult cases. Our experiments indicate that NMT models perform poorly for rare word senses, and we observe moderate improvements for these rare word senses by using methods from WSD to complement the disambiguation capability of the main NMT model. Still, the problem is far from solved, and there is a sizeable difference of 23-26 percentage points between NMT performance and human performance. We hope that the release of our test set will inspire and support future research on the problem of word sense disambiguation for machine translation. In our human experiments, we also found evidence that wider document context is necessary to solve this task.

Acknowledgments

We are grateful to the Swiss National Science Foundation (SNF) for support of the project CoN-Tra (grant number 105212_169888) and the Synergia MODERN project (grant number 147653).

References

Andrei Alexandrescu and Katrin Kirchhoff. 2006. Factored Neural Language Models. In *Proceedings of the Human Language Technology Conference of the NAACL*. New York, NY, USA, pages 1–4.

Dzmitry Bahdanau, Kyunghyun Cho, and Yoshua Bengio. 2015. Neural Machine Translation by Jointly Learning to Align and Translate. In *Proceedings of the International Conference on Learning Representations (ICLR 2015)* . San Diego, CA, USA.

Luisa Bentivogli, Arianna Bisazza, Mauro Cettolo, and Marcello Federico. 2016. Neural versus Phrase-Based Machine Translation Quality: a Case Study. In *Proceedings of the Conference on Empirical Methods in Natural Language Processing (EMNLP 2016)*. Austin, Texas, USA.

Ondřej Bojar, Rajen Chatterjee, Christian Federmann, Yvette Graham, Barry Haddow, Matthias Huck, Antonio Jimeno Yepes, Philipp Koehn, Varvara Logacheva, Christof Monz, Matteo Negri, Aurelie Neveol, Mariana Neves, Martin Popel, Matt Post, Raphael Rubino, Carolina Scarton, Lucia Specia, Marco Turchi, Karin Verspoor, and Marcos Zampieri. 2016. Findings of the 2016 Conference on Machine Translation (WMT16). In *Proceedings of the First Conference on Machine Translation, Volume 2: Shared Task Papers*. Berlin, Germany, pages 131–198.

Marine Carpuat. 2013. A Semantic Evaluation of Machine Translation Lexical Choice. In *Proceedings of the 7th Workshop on Syntax, Semantics and Structure in Statistical Translation*. Atlanta, Georgia, pages 1–10.

Gertrud Faaß and Kerstin Eckart. 2013. SdeWaC – A Corpus of Parsable Sentences from the Web. In *Language Processing and Knowledge in the Web*, Springer Berlin Heidelberg, volume 8105, pages 61–68.

Michel Galley and Kathleen McKeown. 2003. Improving Word Sense Disambiguation in Lexical Chaining. In *Proceedings of the 18th International Joint Conference on Artificial Intelligence (IJCAI-03)*. Acapulco, Mexico, pages 1486–1488.

Diederik P. Kingma and Jimmy Ba. 2015. Adam: a Method for Stochastic Optimization. In *Proceedings of the 3rd International Conference on Learning Representations ((ICLR2015))*. San Diego, CA, USA.

Els Lefever and Véronique Hoste. 2013. SemEval-2013 Task 10: Cross-lingual Word Sense Disambiguation. In *Second Joint Conference on Lexical and Computational Semantics (*SEM), Volume 2: Proceedings of the Seventh International Workshop on Semantic Evaluation (SemEval 2013)*. Atlanta, Georgia, USA, pages 158–166.

Minh-Thang Luong and Christopher D. Manning. 2015. Stanford Neural Machine Translation Systems for Spoken Language Domains. In *Proceedings of the International Workshop on Spoken Language Translation 2015*. Da Nang, Vietnam.

Laura Mascarell. 2017. Lexical Chains meet Word Embeddings in Document-level Statistical Machine Translation. In *Proceedings of the 3rd Workshop on Discourse in Machine Translation*. Copenhagen, Denmark.

Rada Mihalcea, Ravi Sinha, and Diana McCarthy. 2010. SemEval-2010 Task 2: Cross-lingual Lexical Substitution. In *Proceedings of the 5th International Workshop on Semantic Evaluation*. Los Angeles, California, pages 9–14.

Tomas Mikolov, Kai Chen, Greg Corrado, and Jeffrey Dean. 2013. Efficient Estimation of Word Representations in Vector Space. In *Proceedings of Workshop at the International Conference on Learning Representations (ICLR 2013)*. Scottsdale, AZ, USA.

George A Miller. 1995. WordNet: A Lexical Database for English. *Communications of the ACM* 38(11):39–41.

Jane Morris and Graeme Hirst. 1991. Lexical Cohesion Computed by Thesaural Relations as an Indicator of the Structure of Text. *Computational Linguistics* 17(1):21–48.

Graham Neubig. 2016. Lexicons and Minimum Risk Training for Neural Machine Translation: NAIST-CMU at WAT2016. In *Proceedings of 3rd Workshop on Asian Translation (WAT 2016)*. Osaka, Japan.

Graham Neubig, Makoto Morishita, and Satoshi Nakamura. 2015. Neural Reranking Improves Subjective Quality of Machine Translation: NAIST at WAT2015. In *Proceedings of the 2nd Workshop on Asian Translation (WAT2015)*. Kyoto, Japan, pages 35–41.

Kishore Papineni, Salim Roukos, Todd Ward, and Wei-Jing Zhu. 2002. BLEU: A Method for Automatic Evaluation of Machine Translation. In *Proceedings of the 40th Annual Meeting on Association for Computational Linguistics*. Philadelphia, Pennsylvania, pages 311–318.

Maria Pelevina, Nikolay Arefiev, Chris Biemann, and Alexander Panchenko. 2016. Making Sense of Word Embeddings. In *Proceedings of the 1st Workshop on Representation Learning for NLP*. Berlin, Germany, pages 174–183.

Rico Sennrich. 2017. How Grammatical is Character-level Neural Machine Translation? Assessing MT Quality with Contrastive Translation Pairs. In *Proceedings of the 15th Conference of the European Chapter of the Association for Computational Linguistics (EACL)*. Valencia, Spain.

Rico Sennrich, Orhan Firat, Kyunghyun Cho, Alexandra Birch, Barry Haddow, Julian Hitschler, Marcin Junczys-Dowmunt, Samuel Läubli, Antonio Valerio Miceli Barone, Jozef Mokry, and Maria Nadejde. 2017. Nematus: a Toolkit for Neural Machine Translation. In *Proceedings of the Demonstrations at the 15th Conference of the European Chapter of the Association for Computational Linguistics*. Valencia, Spain.

Rico Sennrich and Barry Haddow. 2016. Linguistic Input Features Improve Neural Machine Translation. In *Proceedings of the First Conference on Machine Translation*. Berlin, Germany, volume 1 Research Papers, pages 83–91.

Rico Sennrich, Barry Haddow, and Alexandra Birch. 2016a. Edinburgh Neural Machine Translation Systems for WMT 16. In *Proceedings of the First Conference on Machine Translation*. Berlin, Germany, volume 2 Shared Task Papers, pages 371–376.

Rico Sennrich, Barry Haddow, and Alexandra Birch. 2016b. Neural Machine Translation of Rare Words with Subword Units. In *Proceedings of the 54th Annual Meeting of the Association for Computational Linguistics (Volume 1: Long Papers)*. Berlin, Germany, pages 1715–1725.

Ilya Sutskever, Oriol Vinyals, and Quoc V. Le. 2014. Sequence to Sequence Learning with Neural Networks. In *Advances in Neural Information Processing Systems 27: Annual Conference on Neural Information Processing Systems 2014*. Montreal, Quebec, Canada, pages 3104–3112.

Jörg Tiedemann. 2012. Parallel Data, Tools and Interfaces in OPUS. In *Proceedings of the Eighth International Conference on Language Resources and Evaluation (LREC-2012)*. European Language Resources Association (ELRA), Istanbul, Turkey, pages 2214–2218.

David Vickrey, Luke Biewald, Marc Teyssier, and Daphne Koller. 2005. Word-Sense Disambiguation for Machine Translation. In *Proceedings of the conference on Human Language Technology and Empirical Methods in Natural Language Processing (HLT '05)*. Vancouver, British Columbia, Canada, pages 771–778.

Michał Ziemski, Marcin Junczys-Dowmunt, and Bruno Pouliquen. 2016. The United Nations Parallel Corpus v1.0. In *Proceedings of the Tenth International Conference on Language Resources and Evaluation LREC*. European Language Resources Association (ELRA), Portorož, Slovenia, pages 3530–3534.

Word Representations in Factored Neural Machine Translation

Franck Burlot[*]
LIMSI, CNRS, Université Paris Saclay

Mercedes García-Martínez[*]
LIUM, University of Le Mans

Loïc Barrault
LIUM, University of Le Mans

Fethi Bougares
LIUM, University of Le Mans

François Yvon
LIMSI, CNRS, Université Paris Saclay

Abstract

Translation into a morphologically rich language requires a large output vocabulary to model various morphological phenomena, which is a challenge for neural machine translation architectures. To address this issue, the present paper investigates the impact of having two output factors with a system able to generate separately two distinct representations of the target words. Within this framework, we investigate several word representations that correspond to different distributions of morpho-syntactic information across both factors. We report experiments for translation from English into two morphologically rich languages, Czech and Latvian, and show the importance of explicitly modeling target morphology.

1 Introduction

Open vocabularies remain a challenge for Neural Machine Translation (NMT) (Cho et al., 2014; Bahdanau et al., 2015), both for linguistic and computational reasons. From a linguistic standpoint, morphological variation and lexical productivity cause word forms unseen in training to occur in source texts, which may also require to generate novel target word forms. Using very large input/output vocabularies partially mitigates these issues, yet may cause serious instability (when computing embeddings of rare or unseen words) and complexity issues (when dealing with large softmax layers).

Several proposals have been put forward to address these problems, which are particularly harmful when one language is a morphologically rich language (MRL), exhibiting larger token/type ratio than is observed for English. One strategy is to improve NMT's internal procedures: for instance by using a structured output layer (Mnih and Hinton, 2008) or by altering the training or decoding criteria (Jean et al., 2015). An alternative approach is to work with representations designed to remove some variations via source-side or target-side normalization procedures; or more radically to consider character-based representations (Ling et al., 2015; Luong and Manning, 2016; Costa-jussà and Fonollosa, 2016), which are however much more costly to train, and make long distance dependencies even longer.

None has however been as successful as the recent proposal of Sennrich et al. (2016b) which seems to achieve a right balance between a limited vocabulary size and an ability to translate a fully open vocabulary. In a nutshell, this approach decomposes source and target tokens into smaller units of variable length (using what is now termed as a "Byte Pair Encoding" or BPE in short): this means that (a) all source tokens can be represented as a sequence of such units, which crucially are all seen in training; (b) all possible target words can also be generated; (c) the size of the output layer can be set to remain within tractable limits; (d) most frequent words are kept as BPE units, which preserves the locality of many dependencies.

In this work, we consider possible ways to extend this approach by also supplying target-side linguistic information in order to help the system generate correct target word forms. Our proposal relies on two distinct components (a) linguistically or data-driven normalization procedures manipulating various source and target word segmentations, as well as eg. multiple factors on the target side (see § 4), and (b) a neural architecture equipped with a dual output layer to predict the target in two simpler tasks generating the lexi-

---

[*]Both authors have contributed equally to this work.

Proceedings of the Conference on Machine Translation (WMT), Volume 1: Research Papers, pages 20–31
Copenhagen, Denmark, September 7–11, 2017. ©2017 Association for Computational Linguistics

cal unit and the morphological information (§ 3). These components are assessed separately and in conjunction using translation from English into two MRLs: Czech and Latvian. Our experiments show improvement over a strong (Denkowski and Neubig, 2017) BPE-to-BPE baseline, incorporating ensemble of models and backtranslated data (§ 5). Overall, they suggest that BPE representations, which loosely simulates concatenative morphological processes, is complementary to feature-based morphological representations.

2 Related Work

Translating from and into MRLs has recently attracted some attention from the research community, as these languages compound a number of difficulties for automatic translation, such as the need to analyze or generate word forms unseen in training, or to handle variation in word order.

To mitigate the unknown word problem, a first approach consists in translating into target *stems* (Minkov et al., 2007; Toutanova et al., 2008); the right form is then selected from the full paradigms in a second step using a classifier. Target words may also be represented as lemmas complemented with side information. Bojar (2007); Bojar and Kos (2010); Bojar et al. (2012) use such a representation for two statistical MT systems: the first one translates from English into Czech lemmas decorated with source-side information and the second one performs a monotone translation into fully inflected Czech.

Fraser et al. (2012) propose a target morphology normalization for German words represented as lemmas followed by a sequence of morphological tags and introduce a linguistically motivated selection of these when translating from English. The selection step consists in predicting the tags that have been removed during normalization, using a specific Conditional Random Field (CRF) model for each morphological attribute to predict. Finally, word forms are produced via look-up in a morphological dictionary. This approach is extended by Weller et al. (2013), who takes verbal subcategorization frames into account, thus enabling the CRFs to make better predictions. Note that Burlot et al. (2016) and El Kholy and Habash (2012b,a) propose related approaches respectively for translating into Czech and Arabic.

Factored word representations have also been considered in neural language models (Niehues et al., 2016; Alexandrescu and Kirchhoff, 2006; Wu et al., 2012), and more recently in a neural machine translation architecture as input features (Sennrich and Haddow, 2016) and in the output by separating the lemma and morphological factors (García-Martínez et al., 2016). One contribution of the current paper is the investigation of new variants of the latter architecture. There have been other attempts with dual training objectives in NMT. In (Chen et al., 2016), a *guided alignment training* using topic information of the sentence as a second objective helps the decoder to improve the translation. Multi-task and multilingual learning in NMT have also been considered in several papers (Luong et al., 2015; Dong et al., 2015; Firat et al., 2016), where training batches have to carefully balance tasks and language pairs. In contrast to these approaches, our factored NMT (FNMT) system produces several outputs *simultaneously*.

3 Model Architectures

The baseline NMT system used in this paper is an implementation of a standard NMT model with attention mechanism (Bahdanau et al., 2015). It consists of a sequence to sequence encoder-decoder of two recurrent neural networks (RNN), one used by the encoder and the other by the decoder. This architecture integrates a bidirectional RNN encoder (see bottom left part with green background of Figure 1). Each input sentence word x_i ($i \in 1 \dots N$ with N the source sequence length) is encoded into an annotation a_i by concatenating the hidden states of a forward and a backward RNN. Each annotation $a_1 \dots a_N$ thus represents the whole sentence with a focus on the word(s) being processed. The decoder is based on a conditional gated recurrent unit (GRU) (Firat and Cho, 2016) made of two GRUs interleaved with the attention mechanism. The attention mechanism computes a context vector C_j as a convex combination of annotation vectors, where the weights of each annotation are computed locally using a feed-forward network. The decoder RNN takes as input the embedding of the previous output word in the first GRU, the context vector C_j in the second GRU and its hidden state. The softmax output layer is connected to the network through a non-linear layer which takes as input the embedding of the previous output word as well as the context vector and the output of the decoder from the second GRU (both adapted with a linear transformation, respectively, L_C and L_R). Finally, the output probabilities for each word in the target vocabulary are computed with a softmax. The word with the highest probability is the translation output at each time step. The encoder and the decoder are trained jointly to maximize the conditional probability of the reference translation.

The Factored NMT system of García-Martínez et al. (2016) is an extension of the standard NMT architecture that allows the system *to generate several output symbols at the same time*, as presented in Figure 1.

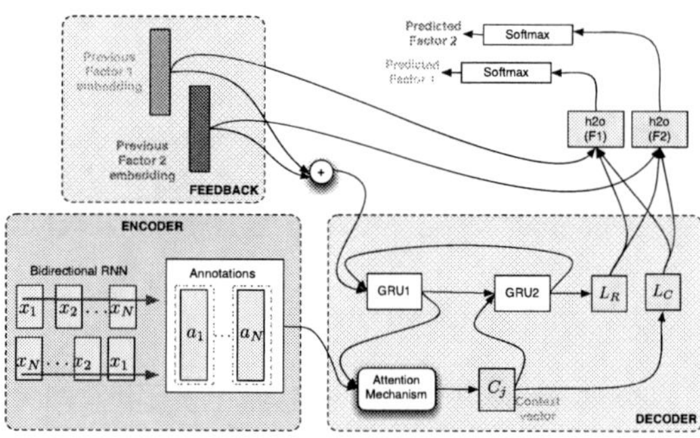

Figure 1: Factored NMT system.

The encoder and the attention mechanism of the Factored NMT are the same as the standard NMT model. However, the decoder has been modified to produce multiple outputs. The two outputs are constrained to have the same length. The decoder feedback is also modified to use information from the multiple output streams. The concatenation of the embeddings of the pair of generated symbols is used to feed the decoder's cGRU at each timestep.

Two types of FNMT models have been used for this work. Their architecture differ after the generation of the decoder state. The first model contains a single hidden-to-output (*h2o*) layer which is used by the two separate softmax. This layer uses the context vector, the decoder's hidden state and the concatenation of the embeddings of the previous generated tokens. The second model is one contribution of the current work. As shown in Figure 1), it contains two separated *h2o* layers. They are similar to the *h2o* layer in the first model except that instead of using the concatenation of the embeddings of the previously generated factors, each *h2o* layer receives only the embedding of the factor it is generating. The two separated *h2o* layers allow the system to have more weights specialized for each output.

4 Word Representations

This paper focuses on the question of word representations, which we understand not only in terms of word segmentation, but also as the quantity of morpho-syntactic information encoded in a word. We introduce three representations varying in the quantity of grammatical information they contain:

- **fully inflected words**: this is a baseline setup where all the lexical and grammatical information is encoded in a single factor.

- **normalized words**: only a well chosen subset of morphological features is kept in the first factor; the second factor corresponds to the Part of Speech (PoS).

- **lemmas**: the output splits the lexical content of the word (first factor: lemma) and its grammatical content (second factor: PoS).

These differences are illustrated in Table 1.

4.1 Normalizing Word Forms

Translating from English into a MRL is made difficult by linguistic divergences, as English lacks many of the morphological contrasts that exist in the MRL. Normalization is needed to reduce the morphological variability on the MRL side so as to limit the number of types in the target, and to mitigate sparsity issues. This strategy is used for instance by Burlot et al. (2016) who remove the case mark from Czech nouns, which is not predictable from their English counterpart(s).

Normalization is usually performed using handcrafted rules and requires expert knowledge for each language pair. In this paper, normalized words are obtained with an automatic data-driven method[1] introduced in (Burlot and Yvon, 2017b).

In a nutshell, this method performs a clustering of the MRL vocabulary by grouping together words that tend to share the same translation(s) in English. This translational similarity is based on the conditional entropy of lexical translation models estimated, for each MRL word form, using automatic word alignments. The clustering procedure merges two words whenever the resulting cluster does not increase the conditional entropy, which ensures a minimal loss of information during the whole process.

---

[1]The source code is available at github.com/franckbrl/bilingual_morph_normalizer

The actual normalization algorithm is delexicalized and operates at the level of PoS. Each word is represented as a lemma, a coarse PoS and a sequence of morphological tags (e.g. *kočka+Noun+Sing+Accusative*). Translational similarities are computed on such words and are combined to provide a PoS-level similarity between two tag sequences. Successive merge operations group into one cluster different such tag sequences. As a result of this procedure, we represent words as a lemma and a cluster identificator (ID) taking the form of a coarse PoS and an arbitrary integer, such as *kočka+Noun+7* in Table 1. In this example, the cluster ID *Noun+7* stands for a set of fine-grained PoS, such as {*Sing+Nominative, Sing+Accusative, ...* }.

This representation introduces a direct correspondence between the first and the second factor in our architecture, since the former (the cluster ID) constraints the set of possible values of the latter (the fine-grained PoS), which is notably used in our constrained decoding procedure (§ 5.4).

4.2 Word Representation Setup

The example of Table 1 shows that words are also varying along a second dimension: in addition to considering unsegmented lexical units (be it fully inflected words, normalized words or lemmas), we also investigate the impact of a segmentation of these units using BPE (Sennrich et al., 2016b).

In this scenario, BPE segmentation is performed on fully inflected words and lemmas. For its application to normalized words, the cluster ID was considered as a minimal unit that cannot be segmented (just like any other character), in order to avoid segmentations like *kočka+No- un+7*. For these setups, the PoS information (second factor) is replicated for all subparts of a word.

We finally use an alternative representation with normalized words to which BPE segmentation is applied and cluster IDs are systematically split from the lemma. Whenever the FNMT system predicts a lemma in the first factor, it is forced to predict a null PoS in the second factor. On the other hand, when a split cluster ID is predicted, the second factor should output an actual PoS. This specific treatment of the second factor is expected to give the system a better ability to map a word to a compatible PoS, thus avoiding, for instance, the prediction of a verbal PoS for the Czech noun *kočka* (cat).

These different word representations imply a progressive reduction of the target vocabulary. We computed the vocabulary size of Czech on the parallel data used to train the systems (§ 5.1) over unsegmented words. We thus have 2.1M fully inflected words, 1.9M normalized words, 1.5M normalized words with split clusters (lemmas and clusters), and 1.4M lemmas.

5 Experiments

We introduce here the experimental setup for all the reported systems translating from English into Czech and Latvian.

5.1 Data and Preprocessing

Our experimental setting follows the guidelines of the WMT'17[2] news translation task. The pre-processing of English data relies on in-house tools (Déchelotte et al., 2008). All the Czech data were tokenized and truecased the Moses toolkit (Koehn et al., 2007). PoS-tagging was performed with Morphodita (Straková et al., 2014). The pre-processing of Latvian was provided by Tilde.[3] Latvian PoS-tags were obtained with the LU MII Tagger (Paikens et al., 2013).

For English-to-Czech, the parallel data used consisted in nearly 20M sentences from a subset of WMT data relevant to the news domain: News-commentary, Europarl and specific categories of the Czeng corpus (news, paraweb, EU, fiction). Newstest-2015 was used for validation and the systems are tested on Newstest-2016 and 2017. The normalization of the Czech data was trained on the parallel data used to train the MT systems, except Czeng fiction and paraweb subcorpora, which amounts to over 10M sentences.

A part of these systems was also trained on synthetic parallel data (Sennrich et al., 2016a) (see § 6). The Czech monolingual corpus News-2016 was backtranslated to English using the single best system provided by the University of Edinburgh from WMT'16.[4] In order to prevent learning from being too biased towards the synthetic source of this set, we used initial bitext parallel data as well. We added five copies[5] of News-commentary and

---

[2]www.statmt.org/wmt17
[3]www.tilde.com
[4]http://data.statmt.org/rsennrich/wmt16_systems/
[5]Adding multiple copies of the same corpus into the training set can be seen as a coarse way to weight different corpora and favor in-domain bibtext.

	fully infl.	norm. words		lemmas	
	Single factor	factor 1	factor 2	factor 1	factor 2
plain	kočky	kočka+N+7	N+Pl+Nom	kočka	N+Pl+Nom
BPE	ko- čky	ko- čka+N+7	N+Pl+Nom N+Pl+Nom	ko- čka	N+Pl+Nom N+Pl+Nom
+ split cls		ko- čka- N+7	null null N+Pl+Nom		

Table 1: Multiple representations for the Czech word *kočky* (cats). *N* stands for noun, *Pl* for plural and *Nom* for nominative case.

the news subcorpus from Czeng, as well as 5M sentences from the Czeng EU corpus randomly selected after running modified Moore-Lewis filtering with XenC (Rousseau, 2013).

The English-to-Latvian systems used all the parallel data provided at WMT'17. The DCEP corpus was filtered with the Microsoft sentence aligner[6] and using modified Moore-Lewis. We kept the best 1M sentences, which led to a total of almost 2M parallel sentences. The systems were validated on 2k sentences held out from the LETA corpus and we report results on Newsdev-2017 and newstest-2017. The normalization of Latvian data was trained on the same parallel sentences used to train the MT systems.

Training was carried out for a part of these systems on synthetic parallel data. We used a back-translation of the monolingual corpora news-2015 and 2016 provided by the University of Edinburgh (Moses system). To these corpora were added 10 copies of the LETA corpus, as well as 2 copies of Europarl and Rapid.

Bilingual BPE models for each language pair and system setup were learned on the bitext parallel data. 90k merge operations were performed to obtain the final vocabularies. For (F)NMT models, the vocabulary size of the second factors is only 1.5k for Czech and 376 for Latvian. The number of parameters in (F)NMT systems increases around 2.5% for Czech and 7% in Latvian.

5.2 System Setup

Only sentences with a maximum length of 50 were kept in the training data, except for the setup where cluster IDs were split in normalized words. In this case, we set the maximum length to 100. For the training of all models, we used NMTPY, a Python toolkit based on Theano (Caglayan et al., 2017) and available as free software[7]. We used the standard NMT system on fully inflected words and the

FNMT architecture described in § 3 on all other word representations.

All systems (F)NMT systems have an embedding dimension of 512 and hidden states of dimension 1024 for both the encoder and the decoder. Dropout is enabled on source embeddings, context vector, as well as output layers. When training starts, all parameters are initialized with Xavier (Glorot and Bengio, 2010). In order to slightly speed up the training on the actual parallel data, the learning rate was set to 0.0004, patience to 30 with validation every 20k updates. On the synthetic data, we finally set the learning rate to 0.0001 and performed validation every 5k updates. These systems were tuned with Adam optimizer (Kingma and Ba, 2014) and have been training for approximately 1 month.

5.3 Reinflection

The factored systems predict at each time step a lexical unit and a PoS-tag, which requires a non-trivial additional step producing sentences in a fully inflected language. We refer to this process as reinflection.

Given a lexical unit and a PoS-tag, word forms are retrieved with a dictionary look-up. In the context of MRL, deterministic mappings from a lemma and a PoS to a form are very rare. Instead, the dictionary often contains several word forms corresponding to the same lexical unit and morphological analysis.

A first way to solve this ambiguity is to simply compute unigram frequencies of each word form, which was done over all the monolingual data available at WMT'17 for both Czech and Latvian. During a dictionary look-up, ambiguities can then be solved by taking the most frequent word form. The downside of this procedure is that it ignores important information given by the target monolingual context. For instance, the Czech preposition *s* (with) will have different forms according to the right-side context: *s tebou* (with you), but *se mnou* (with me). A solution is to let an inflected-word-based system select the correct word form from the dictionary. To this end, k-best hypotheses from the dictionary are generated. Given a sentence containing lemmas and PoS, we perform a beam search going through each word and keeping at each step the k-best reinflection hypotheses according to the unigram model mentioned above.

For Czech reinflection, we used the Morphodita generator (Straková et al., 2014). Since we had no such tool for Latvian, all monolingual data available at WMT'17 were automatically tagged using the LU MII Tagger (Paikens et al., 2013) and we gathered the result in a look-up table. As one could expect, we obtained a large table (nearly 2.5M forms) in which we observed a lot of noise.

5.4 Constrained Decoding

The factored system described in § 3 outputs a lexical unit and a PoS-tag at each time step. A peculiarity of this system is that the predictions of both factors are independent. There is only a weak dependency due to the fact that both share the same decoder state and context vector. As a consequence, the best hypothesis for the first factor can well be incompatible with the best hypothesis for the second factor, and the risks of such mismatches only get worse when top-n hypotheses are considered, as in beam search.

Our constrained decoding procedure aims at enforcing a strong consistency between factors. Each word in the target vocabulary is first associated with a specific set of PoS-tags. The decoding procedure is modified as follows: for each candidate target word, we only retain the compatible PoS tags, and select the top-n hypotheses to be kept in the beam from this filtered list. This constraint ensures that the beam search does not evaluate incompatible pairs of factors. (e.g. the PoS *Preposition* and the word *cat*).

With a dictionary, creating such a mapping is trivial for full lemmas, but less obvious in the case of BPE units. Since the latter can be generated from different words having different grammatical classes, the size of the set of possible PoS can grow quickly. For normalized words, things are much easier and do not even require a dictionary, as the mapping between cluster IDs and compatible PoS is learnt during the normalization process (see § 4.1). Thus constrained decoding was only performed for (a) unsegmented lemmas, and (b) unsegmented and segmented normalized words.

6 Automatic Evaluation

Results are reported using the following automatic metrics: BLEU (Papineni et al., 2002), BEER (Stanojević and Sima'an, 2014) which tunes a large number of features to maximize the human ranking correlation at sentence level and CharacTER (Wang et al., 2016), a character-level version of TER which has shown a high correlation with human rankings (Bojar et al., 2016). Each score on fully inflected word systems is averaged from two independent runs (for both single and ensembled models).

6.1 Experiments with Bitext

The results using the bitext provided at the WMT'17 the evaluation campaign are presented in Table 2 for English-to-Czech [8] and in Table 3 for English-to-Latvian.

We can observe that using the constrained decoding consistently improves the results, except when using split clusters. In this last case, the system is forced to predict a PoS in the second factor whenever it has generated a cluster ID in the first factor. Since there is a reduced quantity of such cluster IDs, the model has no difficulty to learn the constraints by itself and therefore to map a cluster ID exclusively to a specific subset of PoS. In the Latvian lemma setup, we observe that the improvement using constrained decoding is lower than for Czech (see Table 3), which is probably due to the quality of the noisy look-up table we have created for Latvian (see § 5.1). Note that we have no such dependency on the lexical resources at decoding time for the normalized word setups, where improvements are comparable across both language pairs.

The systems using BPE tokens significantly outperform word-level systems, which confirms the analysis of Sennrich et al. (2016b). The results show that BPE units are even more efficient when applied to normalized words, providing significant improvements over segmented inflected words of 1.79 and 1.85 BLEU points for Czech, and 0.78 and 1.06 for Latvian.

The lemma representation was tested with the two FNMT models presented in § 3, one model using a single hidden-to-output layer (*single h2o layer*) and the other model using two separated hidden-to-output layers (*separated h2o layers*).

---

[8] At decoding time, Czech systems performed better with a beam size of 2, which was used to provide these results.

	Newstest-2016			Newstest-2017		
	BLEU ↑	BEER ↑	CTER ↓	BLEU ↑	BEER ↑	CTER ↓
word-to-word						
fully inflected w.	15.74	47.29	74.79	12.76	44.81	78.90
factored norm						
sep. h2o layers	16.63	49.78	68.02	13.70	47.13	72.81
+ constrained dec.	17.71	50.38	66.94	14.88	47.81	71.44
factored lemmas						
single h2o layer	16.73	50.50	65.51	14.09	48.15	69.85
+ constrained dec.	17.42	50.94	64.95	14.93	48.76	69.26
sep. h2o layers	16.54	50.12	66.35	13.89	47.78	70.63
+ constrained dec.	17.56	50.73	65.48	14.66	48.26	69.96
BPE-to-BPE						
fully inflected w.	18.24	52.29	60.05	15.08	49.54	65.38
factored norm						
sep. h2o layers	18.59	53.01	59.95	15.89	50.49	66.75
+ constrained dec.	20.03	53.96	58.90	16.93	51.14	64.13
split clusters	19.74	53.90	59.95	16.31	50.73	64.49
+ constrained dec.	19.71	53.96	59.85	16.38	50.83	64.35
factored lemmas						
single h2o layer	17.30	51.82	61.19	14.19	48.98	66.28
sep. h2o layers	17.34	52.22	60.62	14.73	49.61	65.34

Table 2: Scores for English-to-Czech systems trained on official bitext data

We observe mixed results, here: the system with the *single h2o* layer has slightly better results for the word-to-word systems, but the BPE-to-BPE factored lemma system obtains better performance with the *separated h2o layers* architecture. For that reason, we decided to only use the *separated h2o layers* architecture for the next set of experiments involving synthetic data which is the aim of the next section.

6.1.1 Experiments with Selected Bitext and Synthetic Data

Table 4 and 5 show the results of using selected parts of bitext and synthetic parallel data (see section 5.1) for both language pairs. Each model trained with a selection of bitext and synthetic data was initialized with the parameters of its counterpart trained on bitext. The BPE vocabulary used was the same as in the model used for initialization, which led the systems to generate unknown words. In our experiments, we forced the decoder to avoid unknown token generation.

By using synthetic data, we are able to obtain a large improvement for all systems, which is in line with (Sennrich et al., 2016a). We notice that the contrasts present in the previous section between the various word representations are less clear now. The baseline system (first two rows) is the system which benefits the most from the additional data with +5.7 and +6.9 BLEU for Czech and Latvian. The performance of factored systems has also increased, but to a lesser extent,

leading to slightly worse results compared to the baseline system. This situation changes when the reinflected hypotheses are rescored. We are then able to surpass the baseline system with normalized words.

The two language pairs react differently to k-best hypotheses rescoring (+*k-best rescored* in the tables). For Czech, this has nearly no impact on translation quality according to the metrics, whereas it provides an important improvement in Latvian: +2.03 and +0.84 BLEU in the split cluster setup. Note that this specific setup gives the best score we could achieve on newsdev-2017, without n-best rescoring or model ensembling. We interpret this situation as a result of the difference in quality observed for the Czech and Latvian dictionaries used for reinflection. Indeed, since Morphodita contains exclusively useful Czech reinflection candidates, a simple unigram model is sufficient to select the right word forms, making the generation of 10-best reinflection hypotheses useless.[9] On the other hand, the hypotheses returned by the look-up table we have used to generate Latvian word forms were noisy and required a rescoring from an MT system based on fully inflected words.[10] We obtained the best results for

---

[9] Our experiments with 50-best and 100-best reinflections did not show any improvement.

[10] We assume that the word form generation at this step requires information from the monolingual context only, and could be modeled with a simple target language model, although this needs to be confirmed empirically.

	Newsdev-2017			Newstest-2017		
	BLEU ↑	BEER ↑	CTER ↓	BLEU ↑	BEER ↑	CTER ↓
words-to-words						
fully inflected w.	15.15	48.18	76.97	10.61	43.44	85.67
factored norm						
sep. h2o layers	14.91	50.56	69.49	10.42	45.94	78.83
+ constrained dec.	15.57	50.78	69.65	11.38	46.28	78.93
factored lemmas						
single h2o layer	13.96	49.53	68.36	9.68	45.24	77.07
+ constrained dec.	14.02	49.48	69.97	9.94	45.21	78.11
sep. h2o layers	13.92	49.93	68.45	9.71	45.10	77.51
+ constrained dec.	14.38	49.74	70.04	10.07	45.26	78.08
BPEs-to-BPEs						
fully inflected w.	16.22	51.63	64.44	11.29	47.02	71.95
factored norm						
sep. h2o layers	15.69	52.35	64.14	10.94	47.80	73.51
+ constrained dec.	16.81	52.72	64.02	12.16	48.25	72.93
split clusters	16.99	52.95	64.65	12.35	48.64	72.40
+ constrained dec.	17.00	52.96	64.61	12.35	48.65	72.32
factored lemmas						
single h2o layer	14.45	50.86	67.14	10.45	46.36	72.25
sep. h2o layers	14.39	50.72	66.05	10.69	46.44	72.96

Table 3: Scores for English-to-Latvian systems trained on official bitext.

	Newstest-2016			Newstest-2017		
	BLEU ↑	BEER ↑	CTER ↓	BLEU ↑	BEER ↑	CTER ↓
fully inflected w.	23.94	57.30	52.77	20.00	54.45	58.40
+ ensemble	24.34	57.51	52.48	20.16	54.62	58.22
factored norm						
sep. h2o layers	22.26	56.49	53.43	18.74	53.76	59.18
+ constrained dec.	23.02	56.76	53.29	19.34	54.03	58.67
split clusters	23.37	57.44	52.66	19.77	54.58	58.44
+ constrained dec.	23.39	57.43	52.71	19.76	54.59	58.51
+ k-best rescored	23.43	57.45	52.64	19.79	54.60	58.49
+ n-best rescored	24.19	57.88	52.19	20.56	54.99	57.96
+ ensemble	24.55	58.00	51.97	20.68	55.08	57.93
factored lemmas						
sep. h2o layers	22.30	56.63	53.46	19.34	54.16	58.76
+ k-best rescored	22.35	56.60	53.49	19.36	54.17	58.71
+ n-best rescored	23.39	57.25	52.73	19.83	54.57	58.35
+ ensemble	24.05	57.59	52.27	20.22	54.80	57.89

Table 4: Scores for English-to-Czech systems (BPE-to-BPE) trained on selected bitext and synthetic parallel data.

this Latvian setup by generating the 100-best re-inflection hypotheses, which provides less dependency on the quality of the dictionary and relies more on the knowledge learned by a word-form-aware system. Despite the fact that such a rescoring procedure is costly in terms of computational time, we observe that it can be a helpful solution when no resources of quality are available.

Czech n-best reinflection, as opposed to k-best, turned out to be efficient, bringing the lemma-based systems to the level of the baselines and even above for the normalized word setups. Whereas it does not improve with Latvian normalized words, we observe a positive impact on the lemma-based systems. We assume that rescoring

the n-best list is a way to rely on an inflected-word-based system to make important decisions related to translation, as opposed to the much simpler monolingual process of reinflection mentioned above. Latvian split-cluster models seem to have nothing to learn from such systems.

Factored norm performs best among all the presented models, showing consistent BLEU improvements over the baselines of 0.25 and 0.56 for Czech, and 0.57 and 0.89 for Latvian. We finally notice that ensembling two models slightly reduces those contrasts, and lemma-based systems are the ones that benefit the most from model ensembling. Conclusions are not easy to draw, since across the different setups, the level of indepen-

	Newsdev-2017			Newstest-2017		
	BLEU ↑	BEER ↑	CTER ↓	BLEU ↑	BEER ↑	CTER ↓
fully inflected w.	22.05	57.34	53.32	14.84	51.78	63.08
+ ensemble	22.41	57.78	52.67	15.12	52.11	62.64
factored norm						
sep. h2o layers	18.81	55.65	56.07	13.57	50.94	64.24
+ constrained dec.	20.05	56.14	56.13	14.44	51.26	63.60
split clusters	20.85	56.77	54.13	14.50	51.84	63.04
+ constrained dec.	20.86	56.80	54.02	14.57	51.87	62.96
+ k-best rescored	22.89	57.88	52.77	15.41	52.39	62.40
+ n-best rescored	22.62	57.43	53.66	15.73	52.77	61.78
+ ensemble	22.69	57.61	52.91	16.04	52.99	61.41
factored lemmas						
sep. h2o layers	18.93	56.01	54.36	13.98	51.26	63.9
+ k-best rescored	20.56	56.94	53.42	14.80	51.78	63.19
+ n-best rescored	21.59	57.62	52.83	15.31	52.34	62.64
+ ensemble	21.90	57.83	52.38	15.35	52.31	62.46

Table 5: Scores for English-to-Latvian systems (BPEs-to-BPEs) trained on selected bitext and synthetic parallel data.

dence of the two ensembled models is suspected to be quite different. [11]

It is important to note that automatic metrics may not do justice to the lexical and grammatical choices made by the factored systems. In an attempt to focus on the grammaticality of the FNMT systems, we conducted a qualitative analysis of the outputs.

7 Qualitative Evaluation

7.1 Attention in Factored Systems

In a factored NMT setup, the attention mechanism distributes weights across all positions in the input sentence in order to make two predictions, one for each factor, which is an important difference from single-objective NMT. An illustration of the impact of this difference is shown in Figure 2 for the ensembles of two English-to-Czech models introduced in § 6.

In this sentence, the system based on fully inflected words (translation on the top) erroneously predicts the verbal present tense in *nevyhýbá* (does not avoid). We can see that the target subword unit *nevy@@* is rather strongly linked to the source *didn't*, which allowed the system to correctly predict negative polarity. On the other hand, the ending of the verb *á* is not linked by attention to this same source word, from which the morphological feature of past should have been conveyed. We observe in (a) that the lemma-based system attention aligns the target position to both the source auxil-

iary *didn't* and the lexical verb's first subword unit *shir@@*, which enables the successful prediction of the right lemma and morphology, i.e. negation (N) and past (R). The normalized word based system in (b) shows an even more explicit modelization of this morphological phenomenon. While the lemma *nevyhýbat@@* is strongly related to the same English segment *shir@@*, it is only slightly linked to the English auxiliary. *didn't* is instead clearly associated to the cluster ID *V+20* that gathers negative past tense PoS-tags, enabling the right prediction in the second factor. In this last setup, the system has to deal, at each time step in the output sentence, with either a lexical phenomenon or a grammatical one.

Target-side grammatical phenomena being more explicitly modeled in factored NMT, it is generally easier for the attention mechanism to spot an English grammatical word (auxiliary, preposition, negative particle, etc.), which enables a better prediction in the second factor output. We assume that this peculiarity ensures a better source-to-target grammatical adequacy.

7.2 Measuring Morphological Consistency

We provide here an attempt to understand more systematically whether an *a priori* intuition of factored NMT systems is verified. The intuition is that dividing the task of translating a sentence into two easier joint tasks, namely the prediction of a lexical unit and of a set of morphological features, should encourage the system to produce a higher level of grammaticality.

To this end, we have used a part of the test suite

---

[11]Performing independently two system runs for ensembling would have given results easier to analyze, which we were not able to provide due to the cost of such practice.

target	system	nouns	adjectives			verbs				mean
		case	gender	number	case	number	person	tense	polarity	
Czech	**fully inflected w.**	.208	.295	.272	.310	.125	.070	.086	.061	.178
	factored norm.	**.165**	.308	**.236**	.273	**.105**	**.059**	**.067**	**.042**	**.157**
	factored lemmas	.206	**.278**	.240	**.269**	.125	.074	.090	.067	.169
Latvian	**fully inflected w.**	.263	.640	.623	.669	.140	.233	.142		.387
	factored norm.	.220	**.580**	**.577**	**.617**	.108	.170	.111		**.340**
	factored lemmas	**.213**	.608	.606	.643	**.099**	**.163**	**.092**		.346

Table 6: Morphological prediction consistency (Entropy).

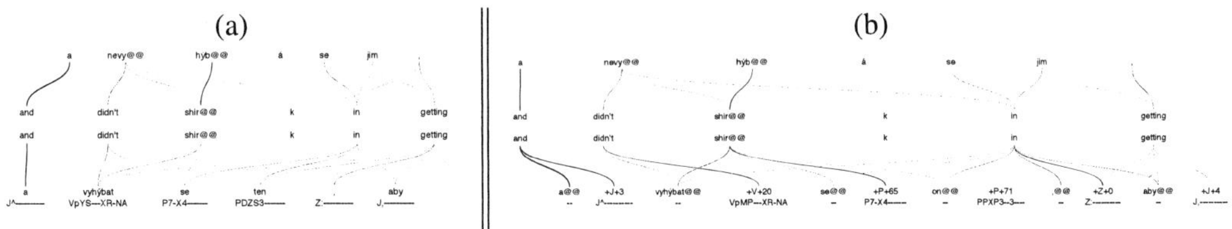

Figure 2: An example of attention weight distribution in FNMT (bottom) and fully inflected words (top) output systems aligned to the source sentence (middle) for English-to-Czech. (a) corresponds to the factored lemmas system and (b) factored norm system

provided by Burlot and Yvon (2017a), who propose an evaluation of the morphological competence of a machine translation system performed on an automatically produced test suite. For each source test sentence from a monolingual corpus (the *base*), several *variants* are generated, containing exactly one difference with the base, and focusing on a specific *target* lexeme of the base. We took the part of the test labeled as "C-set" that focuses on a word in the *base* sentence and produces *variants* containing synonyms and antonyms of this word. Thus the consistency of morphological choices is tested over lexical variation (eg. synonyms and antonyms all having the same tense) and the success is measured based on the average normalized entropy of morphological features in the set of target sentences. The systems used are the ensembles of two models introduced in § 6 (the inflected word system is our best system for each language pair).

The results of this procedure are shown in Table 6. Entropy demonstrates how confident a system is *wrt.* a specific morphological feature across synonyms and antonyms. While NMT systems on fully inflected words are well-known to produce fluent outputs, we always observe a lower entropy with the factored systems over all features, except for the lemma-based system on Czech verbs. This tends to show that the prediction of any morphological feature is more confident when it is explicitly modeled by a separate objective focused on morphology, disregarding lexical variations.

8 Conclusion

In this paper, we have presented various models integrating factored word representations for neural machine translation systems. Additionally to results with automatic metrics reporting significant improvements over a strong baseline, we provided a qualitative analysis focusing on the grammatical competence of FNTM systems that showed the benefits of explicitly modeling morpho-syntactic information.

Our experiments have shown that the cluster ID from the morphological normalization of target words brings useful information to the system by enabling a better correspondence of both factors' predictions. This specificity, as well as the improvements given by constrained decoding, brings us to future work focusing on the modelization of a stronger dependency of the second factor towards the first one in the FNMT architecture.

Acknowledgments

This work has been partly funded by the European Unions Horizon 2020 research and innovation programme under grant agreement No. 645452 (QT21) and the French National Research Agency (ANR) through the CHIST-ERA M2CR project, under the contract number ANR-15-CHR2-0006-01.

References

Andrei Alexandrescu and Katrin Kirchhoff. 2006. Factored neural language models. In *Proceedings of the Human Language Technology Conference of the NAACL, Companion Volume: Short Papers.* NAACL-Short '06, pages 1–4.

Dzmitry Bahdanau, Kyunghyun Cho, and Yoshua Bengio. 2015. Neural machine translation by jointly learning to align and translate. In *Proc. ICLR 2015.* San Diego, CA.

Ondřej Bojar. 2007. English-to-Czech factored machine translation. In *Proc. of the 2nd WMT.* Prague, Czech Republic, pages 232–239.

Ondřej Bojar, Yvette Graham, Amir Kamran, and Miloš Stanojević. 2016. Results of the WMT16 Metrics Shared Task. In *Proc. WMT.* Berlin, Germany, pages 199–231.

Ondřej Bojar, Bushra Jawaid, and Amir Kamran. 2012. Probes in a taxonomy of factored phrase-based models. In *Proceedings of the Seventh Workshop on Statistical Machine Translation.* Stroudsburg, PA, USA, WMT '12, pages 253–260.

Ondřej Bojar and Kamil Kos. 2010. Failures in English-Czech phrase-based MT. In *Proc. of the 5th WMT.* pages 60–66.

Franck Burlot, Elena Knyazeva, Thomas Lavergne, and François Yvon. 2016. Two-Step MT: Predicting Target Morphology. In *Proc. IWSLT.* Seattle, USA.

Franck Burlot and François Yvon. 2017a. Evaluating the morphological competence of machine translation systems. In *Proceedings of the Second Conference on Machine Translation (WMT'17).* Association for Computational Linguistics, Copenhagen, Denmark.

Franck Burlot and François Yvon. 2017b. Learning morphological normalization for translation from and into morphologically rich language. *The Prague Bulletin of Mathematical Linguistics (Proc. EAMT)* (108):49–60.

Ozan Caglayan, Mercedes García-Martínez, Adrien Bardet, Walid Aransa, Fethi Bougares, and Loïc Barrault. 2017. Nmtpy: A flexible toolkit for advanced neural machine translation systems. *arXiv preprint arXiv:1706.00457* .

Wenhu Chen, Evgeny Matusov, Shahram Khadivi, and Jan-Thorsten Peter. 2016. Guided alignment training for topic-aware neural machine translation. *CoRR abs/1607.01628.*

Kyunghyun Cho, Bart van Merrienboer, Dzmitry Bahdanau, and Yoshua Bengio. 2014. On the properties of neural machine translation: Encoder-decoder approaches. In *Proc. SSST@EMNLP.* Doha, Qatar, pages 103–111.

R. Marta Costa-jussà and R. José A. Fonollosa. 2016. Character-based neural machine translation. In *Proceedings of the 54th Annual Meeting of the Association for Computational Linguistics (Volume 2: Short Papers).* pages 357–361.

Daniel Déchelotte, Gilles Adda, Alexandre Allauzen, Olivier Galibert, Jean-Luc Gauvain, Hélène Maynard, and François Yvon. 2008. LIMSI's statistical translation systems for WMT'08. In *Proceedings of NAACL-HLT Statistical Machine Translation Workshop.* Columbus, Ohio.

Michael Denkowski and Graham Neubig. 2017. Stronger Baselines for Trustable Results in Neural Machine Translation. *arXiv preprint arXiv:1706.09733* .

Daxiang Dong, Hua Wu, Wei He, Dianhai Yu, and Haifeng Wang. 2015. Multi-task learning for multiple language translation. In *ACL.*

Ahmed El Kholy and Nizar Habash. 2012a. Rich morphology generation using statistical machine translation. In *Proc. INLG.* pages 90–94.

Ahmed El Kholy and Nizar Habash. 2012b. Translate, predict or generate: Modeling rich morphology in statistical machine translation. In *Proc. EAMT.* Trento, Italy, pages 27–34.

Orhan Firat and Kyunghyun Cho. 2016. Conditional gated recurrent unit with attention mechanism. `github.com/nyu-dl/dl4mt-tutorial/ blob/master/docs/cgru.pdf.`

Orhan Firat, Kyunghyun Cho, and Yoshua Bengio. 2016. Multi-way, multilingual neural machine translation with a shared attention mechanism. *arXiv preprint arXiv:1601.01073* .

Alexander Fraser, Marion Weller, Aoife Cahill, and Fabienne Cap. 2012. Modeling inflection and word-formation in SMT. In *Proc. EACL.* Avignon, France, pages 664–674.

Mercedes García-Martínez, Loïc Barrault, and Fethi Bougares. 2016. Factored neural machine translation architectures. In *Proceedings of the International Workshop on Spoken Language Translation.* Seattle, USA, IWSLT'16.

Xavier Glorot and Yoshua Bengio. 2010. Understanding the difficulty of training deep feedforward neural networks. In *Proceedings of the International Conference on Artificial Intelligence and Statistics (AISTATS'10). Society for Artificial Intelligence and Statistics.*

Sébastien Jean, Kyunghyun Cho, Roland Memisevic, and Yoshua Bengio. 2015. On using very large target vocabulary for neural machine translation. In *Proceedings of the 53rd Annual Meeting of the Association for Computational Linguistics and the 7th International Joint Conference on Natural Language Processing (Volume 1: Long Papers).* Beijing, China, pages 1–10.

Diederik Kingma and Jimmy Ba. 2014. Adam: A method for stochastic optimization. *arXiv preprint arXiv:1412.6980* .

Philipp Koehn, Hieu Hoang, Alexandra Birch, Chris Callison-Burch, Marcello Federico, Nicola Bertoldi, Brooke Cowan, Wade Shen, Christine Moran, Richard Zens, Chris Dyer, Ondřej Bojar, Alexandra Constantin, and Evan Herbst. 2007. Moses: Open source toolkit for statistical MT. In *Proc. ACL:Systems Demos*. Prague, Czech Republic, pages 177–180.

Wang Ling, Isabel Trancoso, Chris Dyer, and Alan W. Black. 2015. Character-based neural machine translation. *CoRR* abs/1511.04586. http://arxiv.org/abs/1511.04586.

Minh-Thang Luong, Quoc V. Le, Ilya Sutskever, Oriol Vinyals, and Lukasz Kaiser. 2015. Multitask sequence to sequence learning. *CoRR* abs/1511.06114.

Minh-Thang Luong and D. Christopher Manning. 2016. Achieving open vocabulary neural machine translation with hybrid word-character models. In *Proceedings of the 54th Annual Meeting of the Association for Computational Linguistics (Volume 1: Long Papers)*. pages 1054–1063.

Einat Minkov, Kristina Toutanova, and Hisami Suzuki. 2007. Generating complex morphology for machine translation. In *Proc. ACL*. Prague, Czech Republic, pages 128–135.

A. Mnih and G.E. Hinton. 2008. A scalable hierarchical distributed language model. In *Advances in Neural Information Processing Systems 21*. volume 21, pages 1081–1088.

Jan Niehues, Thanh-Le Ha, Eunah Cho, and Alex Waibel. 2016. Using factored word representation in neural network language models. In *Proceedings of the First Conference on Machine Translation*. Association for Computational Linguistics, Berlin, Germany, pages 74–82.

Peteris Paikens, Laura Rituma, and Lauma Pretkalnina. 2013. Morphological analysis with limited resources: Latvian example. In *Proc. NODALIDA*. pages 267–277.

Kishore Papineni, Salim Roukos, Todd Ward, and Wei-Jing Zhu. 2002. Bleu: a method for automatic evaluation of machine translation. In *Proceedings of the 40th Annual Meeting on Association for Computational Linguistics*. Stroudsburg, PA, USA, ACL '02, pages 311–318.

Anthony Rousseau. 2013. XenC: An open-source tool for data selection in natural language processing. *The Prague Bulletin of Mathematical Linguistics* 100:73–82.

Rico Sennrich and Barry Haddow. 2016. Linguistic input features improve neural machine translation. *CoRR* abs/1606.02892.

Rico Sennrich, Barry Haddow, and Alexandra Birch. 2016a. Improving neural machine translation models with monolingual data. In *Proc. ACL*.

Rico Sennrich, Barry Haddow, and Alexandra Birch. 2016b. Neural machine translation of rare words with subword units. In *Proceedings of the 54th Annual Meeting of the Association for Computational Linguistics (Volume 1: Long Papers)*. Association for Computational Linguistics, pages 1715–1725.

Miloš Stanojević and Khalil Sima'an. 2014. Fitting sentence level translation evaluation with many dense features. In *Proc. EMNLP*. Doha, Qatar, pages 202–206.

Jana Straková, Milan Straka, and Jan Hajič. 2014. Open-Source Tools for Morphology, Lemmatization, POS Tagging and Named Entity Recognition. In *Proc. ACL: System Demos*. Baltimore, MA, pages 13–18.

Kristina Toutanova, Hisami Suzuki, and Achim Ruopp. 2008. Applying morphology generation models to machine translation. In *Proc. ACL-08: HLT*. Columbus, OH, pages 514–522.

Weiyue Wang, Jan-Thorsten Peter, Hendrik Rosendahl, and Hermann Ney. 2016. CharacTer: Translation Edit Rate on Character Level. In *Proc. WMT*. Berlin, Germany, pages 505–510.

Marion Weller, Alexander M. Fraser, and Sabine Schulte im Walde. 2013. Using subcategorization knowledge to improve case prediction for translation to german. In *ACL (1)*. The Association for Computer Linguistics, pages 593–603.

Youzheng Wu, Hitoshi Yamamoto, Xugang Lu, Shigeki Matsuda, Chiori Hori, and Hideki Kashioka. 2012. Factored recurrent neural network language model in TED lecture transcription. In *IWSLT*.

Modeling Target-Side Inflection in Neural Machine Translation

Aleš Tamchyna[1,2] and **Marion Weller-Di Marco**[1,3] and **Alexander Fraser**[1]
[1]LMU Munich, [2]Memsource, [3]University of Stuttgart
`ales.tamchyna@memsource.com dimarco@ims.uni-stuttgart.de`
`fraser@cis.lmu.de`

Abstract

NMT systems have problems with large vocabulary sizes. Byte-pair encoding (BPE) is a popular approach to solving this problem, but while BPE allows the system to generate any target-side word, it does not enable effective generalization over the rich vocabulary in morphologically rich languages with strong inflectional phenomena. We introduce a simple approach to overcome this problem by training a system to produce the lemma of a word and its morphologically rich POS tag, which is then followed by a deterministic generation step. We apply this strategy for English–Czech and English–German translation scenarios, obtaining improvements in both settings. We furthermore show that the improvement is not due to only adding explicit morphological information.

1 Introduction

Neural machine translation (NMT) has recently become the new state of the art. Despite a large body of recent research, NMT still remains a relatively unexplored territory.

In this work, we focus on one of these less studied areas, namely target-side morphology. NMT systems typically produce outputs word-by-word and at each step, they evaluate the probability of all possible target words. When translating to morphologically rich languages, due to the large size of target-side vocabularies, NMT systems run into scalability issues and struggle with vocabulary coverage.

Byte-pair encoding (BPE, Sennrich et al. (2016b)) is currently perhaps the most successful approach to addressing these problems. How-

ever, while BPE allows the system to generate any target-side word (possibly as a concatenation of smaller segments), it does not enable effective generalization over the many different surface forms possible for a single lemma, which had been shown to be useful in phrase-based SMT (Bojar and Kos, 2010).

We see three main problems associated with rich target-side morphology in NMT: (i) NMT systems have no explicit connection between different surface forms of a single target-side lexeme (lemma), leading to data sparsity, (ii) there is no explicit information about morphological features of target-side words, and (iii) NMT systems cannot systematically generate unseen surface forms of known lemmas: while the combination of subword segments obtained with BPE splitting can technically generate new forms, this is not a linguistically informed way to generate new words, and is furthermore restricted to "simple" concatenative word formation processes.

We propose a simple two-step approach to achieve morphological generalization in NMT. In the first step, we use an encoder-decoder NMT system with attention and BPE (Bahdanau et al., 2014; Sennrich et al., 2016b) to generate a sequence of interleaving morphological tags and lemmas. In the second step, we use a morphological generator to produce the final inflected output. This decomposition addresses all three of the problems outlined above:

- the presence of lemmas allows the system to model different inflections jointly and better capture lexical correspondence with the source,

- morphological information is explicit and allows the system to easily learn target-side morpho-syntactic patterns including agreement,

32

Proceedings of the Conference on Machine Translation (WMT), Volume 1: Research Papers, pages 32–42
Copenhagen, Denmark, September 7–11, 2017. ©2017 Association for Computational Linguistics

- unseen surface forms can be generated simply by combining a known lemma and a known tag.

While simple, the approach is very effective and leads to significant improvements in translation quality in a medium-resource setting for English–Czech translation. Similarly, experiments in an English–German setting lead to improved translation results and also show that the proposed strategy can be applied to other language pairs.

2 Two-Step NMT

We work within the standard encoder-decoder framework with an attention mechanism as proposed by Bahdanau et al. (2014), using the Nematus implementation (Sennrich et al., 2017). To model target-side morphology, the system is trained on an intermediate representation consisting of interleaved lemmas and morphological tags providing the full set of relevant inflection features. Decoding is followed by a second step which is fully deterministic. We use the predicted pairs of (tag+features, lemma) as input to a morphological generator which outputs the final inflected surface forms. In the rare cases where the generator fails to output any surface form, we simply output the lemma.

Our approach is inspired by the successful results of Nadejde et al. (2017), where the authors interleave target-side words and CCG supertags and observe improvements by learning to also predict the target-side syntax. Our experiments in the English–Czech translation task will, however, show that the improvement we obtain is not a similar effect, but instead requires the improved generalization obtained through mapping inflected forms to their lemmas and the ability to generate correct surface forms.

In this paper, we first apply our tag lemma strategy to an English–Czech translation setting. We show that it is effective and also investigate potential effects of tag prediction interacting with morphological generalization. A second set of experiments concerns English–German translation: here, the focus is rather put on modeling linguistic phenomena, including German word formation. While Czech has a more complex morphology than German, German has the additional problem of compounds that make translation challenging; one system variant thus includes simple compound handling.

3 Modeling Czech Morphology

Czech is a Slavic language with a rich inflectional morphology. There are seven cases for nouns and adjectives, four genders and two grammatical numbers. Surface forms of verbs follow complex rules as well, as they encode number, person, tense and several other phenomena. Due to its fusional nature, there is a degree of syncretism in Czech – words with different morphological features may share the same surface form.

As such, Czech is a suitable example for evaluating our approach. We use the Czech positional tagset in our work (Hajič and Vidová-Hladká, 1998). Figure 1 illustrates the input and output to our network and the baseline. Figure 2 illustrates the tagset on an example. For Czech morphological analysis, tagging and generation, we use the MorphoDiTa toolkit (Straková et al., 2014), which achieves state-of-the-art results in lemmatization and tagging and its coverage in morphological generation is very high. Morphological generation is based on a lexicon of lemmas and their paradigms and it is fully deterministic.

4 Modeling German Morphology

To obtain the representation of interleaved lemmas and tag+feature sequences for German, we apply a slightly different pipeline than for the English–Czech setting. Instead of representing a word by a simple lemma and a morphological tag, we use a morphological analyzer covering also productive formation processes – the morphologically complex analyses of the lemma ("stem") allow us to easily handle compounds, which pose a considerable challenge when translating into German.

4.1 Linguistic Resources

The key linguistic knowledge sources to model German morphology are the constituency parser BitPar (Schmid, 2004) to obtain morphological analyses in the sentence context, and the morphological tool SMOR (Schmid et al., 2004) to analyze and generate inflected German surface forms.

SMOR is a a morphological analyzer for German inflection and word formation processes implemented in finite state technology. In particular, it also covers productive word formation processes such as compounding or derivation. SMOR functions in two directions: *surface form → stem+features* and *stem+features → surface form*. Thus, when preparing the target-side training data,

	input:	there are a million different kinds of pizza .
	baseline:	existují miliony druhů piz@ @ zy .
	morphgen:	VB-P—3P-AA— existovat NNIP1——A—- milión NNIP2——A—- druh NNFS2——A—- pizza Z:————- .

Figure 1: Examples of input and output training sequences for the baseline and the proposed system. BPE splits are denoted by "@ @".

Category	Value	Description
POS	A	adjective
sub-POS	A	adjective, general
gender	I	masculine inanimate
number	P	plural
case	7	instrumental
possgender	–	*(possessor's gender)*
possnumber	–	*(possessor's number)*
person	–	*(person, verbs)*
tense	–	*(tense, verbs)*
grade	2	comparative degree
negation	A	affirmative (not negated)
voice	–	*(voice, verbs)*
reserve1	–	*(unused)*
reserve2	–	*(unused)*
var	–	*(style, variant)*

Figure 2: Czech positional tagset. Feature values for the word *kulatějšími*, tag `AAIP7----2A----`.

each inflected surface form is analyzed, and then replaced by its stem and respective morphological features, as illustrated for the verb *trifft* below:

surface	*trifft*
stem	`treffen<+V><3><Sg><Pres><Ind>`

For the inflection process after translation, SMOR is used in the reverse direction to output an inflected form when given a stem+feature sequence.

4.2 German Inflectional Features

German has a rich nominal and verbal morphology, and even though it exhibits a relatively high degree of syncretism, it has a high lemma–to–inflected forms ratio. For example, adjectives can have up to 6 different inflected forms, such as *blau, blaue, blaues, blauer, blauen, blauem* ('blue').

Nominal Inflection   Unlike in English, where only the feature number is expressed for nouns, German nominal inflection is applied to determiners, adjectives and nouns. The following four features are relevant for nominal inflection:

case	*nominative, accusative, dative, genitive*
gender	*feminine, masculine, neuter*
number	*singular, plural*
str/wk	*strong, weak*

To efficiently handle syncretism, SMOR has the artificial value *NoGend*, that is used when a surface form is the same for all three values of gender; this is typical for plural forms. Similarly, the feature strong/weak[1] does not need to be specified if the surface forms are the same; we thus add the dummy-value `<NA>` to always have a sequence of four values. Words that are subject to nominal inflection are replaced by their SMOR analysis that is split into stem and the tag-feature sequence:

`STEM <+Tag><Gend><Case><Num><St/Wk>`

Verbal Morphology   German verbal morphology requires the modeling of these features:

person	*1,2,3*
number	*singular, plural*
tense	*present, past*
mood	*indicative, subjunctive*

These features refer to morphologically expressed properties in a single word; further instances of the feature tense, in particular future tense, are realized as compound tenses. Our modeling of verbal inflection, is restricted to the word-level, and the decision how to combine auxiliaries and full verbs is left to the translation model. Verb forms are represented as follows in the stemmed format:

finite	`STEM <+V><Pers><Num><Tense><Mood>`
participle	`STEM <+V><PPast>`
infinitive	`STEM <+V><Inf>`

4.3 Building the stemmed representation

Table 1 illustrates the process of deriving the fully specified stemmed representation by combining morphological analyses and rich parse tags; the column *infl* indicates whether a word is inflected. As a German surface form can have many possible analyses (cf. below), the parse tags are needed to

---

[1] Strong/weak inflection is determined by the setting of definite/indefinite articles in combination with the other feature: for example, the NP *das blaue Auto* ('the blue car') is inflected differently when occurring with an indefinite article (*ein blaues Auto*) in the function of subject or direct object.

English sentence	and what you 're seeing here is a cloud of densely packed , hydrogen-sulfide-rich water coming out of a volcanic axis on the sea floor

EN gloss	DE surface	parse-tags	infl.	fully specified stemmed representation
and	und	KON	0	`und[KON]`
here	hier	ADV	1	`hier[ADV]`
sees	sieht	VVFIN-Sg	1	`sehen||<+V><3><Sg><Pres><Ind>`
one	man	PIS-Nom.Sg	0	`man[PIS]`
a	eine	ART-Acc.Sg.Fem	1	`eine<Indef>||<+ART><Fem><Acc><Sg><St>`
cloud	Wolke	NN-Acc.Sg.Fem	1	`Wolke||<+NN><Fem><Acc><Sg><NA>`
of	von	APPR-Dat	0	`von[APPR-Dat]`
dense	dichtem	ADJA-Dat.Sg.Neut	1	`dicht<Pos>||<+ADJ><Neut><Dat><Sg><St>`
hydrogen-sulfide-rich	hydrogensulfid-reichem	ADJA-Dat.Sg.Neut	1	`Hydrogen<NN>Sulfid<NN>` `reich<Pos>||<+ADJ><Neut><Dat><Sg><St>`
water	Wasser	NN-Dat.Sg.Neut	1	`Wasser||<+NN><Neut><Dat><Sg><NA>`
,	,	$,	0	`,[$]`
that	das	PRELS-Nom.Sg.Neut	0	`das[PRELS]`
from	aus	APPR-Dat	0	`aus[APPR-Dat]`
a	einer	ART-Dat.Sg.Fem	1	`eine<Indef>||<+ART><Fem><Dat><Sg><St>`
volcanic	vulkanischen	ADJA-Dat.Sg.Fem	1	`vulkanisch||<+ADJ><Pos>` `<NoGend><Dat><Sg><Wk>`
longitudinal axis	Langsachse	NN-Dat.Sg.Fem	1	`längs<ADJ>Achse||<+NN><Fem><Dat><Sg><NA>`
on	an	APPR-Dat	0	`an[APPR-Dat]`
the	dem	ART-Dat.Sg.Masc	1	`die<Def>||<+ART><Masc><Dat><Sg><St>`
sea floor	Meeresboden	NN-Dat.Sg.Masc	1	`Meer<NN>Boden||<+NN><Masc><Dat><Sg><NA>`
oozes	tritt	VVFIN-Sg	1	`treten||<+V><3><Sg><Pres><Ind>`
.	.	$.	0	`.[$]`

Table 1: Example for the fully specified representation used in the NMT system. The double-pipe symbol || indicates the boundary between the word(stem) and the tag with the full set of inflectional features.

disambiguate the morphological analyses.

---

vulkanischen

```
vulkanisch<+ADJ><Pos><Neut><Gen><Sg>
vulkanisch<+ADJ><Pos><Masc><Acc><Sg>
vulkanisch<+ADJ><Pos><Masc><Gen><Sg>
vulkanisch<+ADJ><Pos><NoGend><Acc><Pl><Wk>
vulkanisch<+ADJ><Pos><NoGend><Dat><Pl>
vulkanisch<+ADJ><Pos><NoGend><Dat><Sg><Wk>
vulkanisch<+ADJ><Pos><NoGend><Gen><Pl><Wk>
vulkanisch<+ADJ><Pos><NoGend><Nom><Pl><Wk>
vulkanisch<+ADJ><Pos><Fem><Gen><Sg><Wk>
```

The stem and the tag-feature sequence (or the bare tag for non-inflected words) are separated, allowing the model to learn lexical relations between source- and target-side separately from target-side morpho-syntactic patterns. As the addition of tags effectively doubles the length of German sentences, we also add tags (obtained with tree-tagger, Schmid (1994)) on the source-side to balance the source/target side sentence lengths.

4.4 Reduction of Vocabulary Size

One of the main objectives of the two-step approach is to reduce the target-side vocabulary size. Table 2 shows the most frequent fragments on the end of words obtained through BPE splitting on the German surface data – while it is difficult to generalize without the actual context, most tend to be inflectional suffixes. While this type of splitting does make sense, it also seems that there is some redundancy, and a systematic generalization is impossible. Furthermore, a mere segmentation of surface forms does not cover non-concatenative phenomena such as "Umlautung": for example, the concatenation of *Haus-* (lemma: 'house') and *-er* (typical plural suffix) does not result in the correct plural form (*Häuser*) – thus, two "lemmas" are required to guarantee correct inflections of words that undergo Umlautung when working with surface forms. Table 3 shows the reduction of vocabulary in the stemmed representation: replacing inflected forms with their stems leads to

freq	part	freq	part	freq	part
2469	ten	1257	sten	1077	ern
2157	te	1214	es	1077	-
1738	en	1169	ter	1058	den
1607	er	1148	gen	1040	s
1474	ung	1 078	ischen	1015	ungen

Table 2: The most frequent fragments on word ends after BPE from the German surface data.

	vocabulary size	vocabulary size w/ BPE
DE surface data	121.892	22.712
DE morph	97.587	21.663
DE morph-split	68.533	21.892

Table 3: Overview of vocabulary size in the German TED data (BPE: Byte Pair Encoding).

a considerable reduction of the vocabulary size; compound splitting leads to a further reduction.

4.5 Simple Compound Handling

Another factor contributing to a high vocabulary size is the productivity of German compounds; in SMT, compound handling has been found to improve translation quality, e.g. Stymne et al. (2011) and Cap et al. (2014). In addition to inflectional morphology, SMOR also provides a derivational analysis, including splitting into compound parts: for example, the compound *Häuser|markt* ('house market') is analyzed as `Haus<NN>Markt<+NN><...>`. In particular, the modifier is represented by its base form `Haus`, covering the non-concatenative process of "Umlautung" (*Haus ↔ Häuser*).

In the stemmed representation, this may already present an indirect advantage, as compounds fragmented through BPE splitting can match other stemmed occurrences of that word. An obvious idea at this point is to go a step further and add compound splitting to the pre-processing of the German data. Using the SMOR annotation, compounds are split at mid-word adjective and noun borders. For example, the word *Meeres|boden* ('sea bottom') from table 1 is split into two subwords separated by the modifier's tag:

```
Meer §§<NN>§§ Boden <+NN><...>
```

This notation separates lexical parts from SMOR markup, thus allowing the model to learn compound patterns. After translation, the compound

corpus	sents	src tokens	tgt tokens
train	114k	2309k	1908k
test2012	1385	25150	20682
test2013	1327	28454	24107

Table 4: Sizes of English-Czech corpora.

stems are concatenated and then inflected.

On the English side, it is assumed that the equivalents of compounds are already separate words. For this system variant, however, the English side was slightly simplified by aggressive hyphen splitting, and replacing nouns and verbs by their lemma form, accompanied by a tag indicating the type of inflection. Our hope is that this representation will be more parallel to the compound-split representation in German.

5 Experimental Evaluation

In this section, we describe our experiments with English-Czech and English-German translation.

5.1 Czech

We use the IWSLT training and test sets in English-Czech experiments[2]. The training set consists of transcribed TED talks as collected in the WIT3 corpus (Cettolo et al., 2012). We use IWSLT test set 2012 as the held-out set and the 2013 test set for evaluation. Table 4 summarizes the basic data statistics.

We use the Nematus toolkit for training the NMT systems (Sennrich et al., 2017). We run BPE training on both sides of the training data with 49500 splits. We set the vocabulary size to 50000 word types. The embedding size is set to 500, the dimension of the hidden layer is 1024. We optimize the model using Adam (Kingma and Ba, 2014) and we use the default early stopping criterion in Nematus. We do not apply drop-out anywhere in the model. Following Nadejde et al. (2017), we set the maximum sequence length to 50 for the baseline and to 100 for systems which produce interleaved outputs.

Our *baseline* system is a standard Nematus setup with the parameters described above. We refer to our two-step setup as *morphgen* from now on. For comparison, we also evaluate a third setting where we train the system to output sequences of morphological tags interleaved with the surface

---

[2]`http://workshop2016.iwslt.org`

system	BLEU (dev)	BLEU (test)
baseline	12.60	12.89
morphgen	**14.05**	**14.57**
serialization	11.49	12.07

Table 5: English-Czech: BLEU scores of NMT system variants.

	baseline	morphgen	Δ
IWSLT	12.89	14.57	1.68
250k	14.87	17.51	2.64
500k	16.96	20.05	**3.09**
1M	18.07	20.95	2.88
2M	20.04	**22.31**	2.27

Table 6: English-Czech: BLEU scores of systems with larger parallel training data.

forms. We refer to this contrastive experiment as *serialization* – our aim is to tease apart the possible benefit of explicitly predicting target-side morphological tags from the improvements due to morphological generalization.

Note that BPE is applied in all system variants. However, due to a reduced vocabulary size in the *morphgen* setting, the splits are uncommon and morphological tags are never split (this is an effect of BPE, not a hard constraint).

Because NMT system results can vary significantly due to randomness in initialization and training, we run system training end-to-end for each variant three times. We then select the best run based on BLEU as measured on the development set (test2012) and then evaluate it on the final test set (test2013).

Importantly, the network was able to learn the correct structure for both *morphgen* and *serialization* systems. The outputs are well-formed sequences of interleaving tags and lemmas/forms.

Table 5 shows the obtained results. In our main experiment, our two-step system achieves a substantial improvement of roughly 1.7 BLEU points, showing that two-step in the neural context works for English to Czech translation for this data size.

In the serialization experiment, we see that, surprisingly, the *serialization* system does not outperform the baseline setup. This stands in contrast to the use of CCG supertags by Nadejde et al. (2017), which was effective in this framework. The result there showed that using CCG supertags which handle syntactic generalization helps produce a better sequence of surface forms. We attribute our result to the trade-off between providing the system with explicit morpho-syntactic information (which is weaker information than CCG supertags) and increasing the sequence length (which complicates training). It is possible that with larger training data, *serialization* might still outperform the baseline, but our main result has shown that morphological generalization on this data size is beneficial.

Scaling to Larger Data The observed improvements are certainly at least partially due to reduced data sparsity: because Czech is a morphologically rich language, there is a high number of distinct surface forms. We help the system generalize by essentially dividing the information that surface forms carry into two different "streams": one for morpho-syntax (tags) and the other for semantics (lemmas).

One possible concern with the proposed approach is the ability to scale to larger training data. Data sparsity could be such a major issue only when training data are small and once we scale up, the observed benefits might disappear as the system gets more robust statistical estimates for the individual surface forms.

We run a targeted experiment with larger sizes of parallel training data to determine whether the improvements hold. We always use the main training set described above but additionally, we add a random sample from the CzEng 1.0 parallel corpus (Bojar et al., 2012) to achieve training data sizes of 250 thousand up to 2 million parallel sentences (total).

Table 6 shows the results. We observe the highest difference in the 500k setting (over 3 BLEU points absolute) and while the improvement decreases slightly as we add more data, the difference is still around 2.3 BLEU points even in the largest evaluated setting, which is an encouraging result.

Note that due to the increased computational cost, scores for larger system variants are only based on a single training run.

Analysis and Discussion We now further analyze our two-step system, *morphgen*, in the IWSLT data setting. We first look at cases where the generator failed to produce the surface form. We found only a handful of cases; these mostly involved unknown proper names (Braper, Hvanda).

In just four cases, the tag proposed by the network was not compatible with the lemma (i.e., the network made an error).

In order to determine where the improvement comes from, we analyze the number of novel surface forms produced by the system. We find that indeed, unseen word forms *are* generated by the system but not nearly as many as we expected: only 125 novel tokens were found in the test set (114 word types). Out of these, 14 forms are confirmed by the reference sentences (note that the unconfirmed words may still be correct within the system output).

It seems that the system mostly benefits from the decomposition that we proposed – Czech lemmas are more easily mapped to source-side English words than the many inflected forms associated with each lemma. The interleaving tags then help explicitly train the morpho-syntactic structure of the sentences and allow the second step to deterministically generate the final translations. While morphological generalization does indeed occur, it is not the source of most of the observed improvement. When we use surface forms together with the annotations (in our serialization experiment), we see no improvement.

Finally, we report the results of a blind manual annotation contrasting outputs of *baseline* and *morphgen*. For each instance, the annotator had access to the reference translation and both outputs. The task was to rank which translation is better or to mark both as equal quality. The annotator analyzed 200 sentences. In 130 cases, the translations were judged as equal. Out of the remaining 70 sentences, the *morphgen* system was marked as better in 48 cases and the baseline won in 22 cases.

5.2 German

The initial English–German experiments are evaluated on IWSLT training and test data, which consists of transcribed TED talks. The system is optimized on the 2012 dev-set (1165 sentences), and tested on the 2013 test-set (1363 sentences) and the 2014 test-set (1305 sentences). The training data consists of 184.879 parallel sentences, after filtering out sentences shorter than 5 or longer than 50 words, as well as sentences that could not be parsed. Prior to training the NMT system, the (stemmed) source- and target-data undergo BPE splitting (29500 splits), in order to keep the vo-

TED'13	run-1	run-2	avg.
baseline	19.87	20.15	20.01
morph-gen	20.73	20.98	20.86
morph-gen-split	20.88	21.18	21.03

TED'14	run-1	run-2	avg.
baseline	19.02	18.68	18.85
morph-gen	20.01	19.93	19.97
morph-gen-split	20.07	20.76	20.42

Table 7: English–German: lowercased BLEU for two test sests (1363 and 1305 sentences).

	baseline	morph-gen	morph-gen-split
250k	18.75	20.55	20.51
500k	21.39	22.79	23.00

Table 8: English–German: lowercased BLEU for newstest'16 (2169 sentences) trained on 250k and 500k sentences news-mix data.

cabulary within the predefined limit.

The translation experiments are carried out with the Nematus toolkit (Sennrich et al., 2017), using the training parameters as displayed below, in combination with the default early stopping criterion in Nematus:

vocab	30k	dropout	yes
dim_word	500	dropout_emb	0.2
dim	1024	dropout_hid	0.2
lrate	0.0001	dropout_src	0.1
opt	adam	dropout_trg	0.1
maxlen	50(100)		

The sentence length is set to 50 for the baseline system, and extended to 100 for the morph-gen systems, because the addition of the morphological tags doubles the sentence length.

Table 7 shows the results for the English–German translation experiments, averaged over two training runs: on both test sets, the system generating inflected forms based on stems and features is better than the baseline.

Despite SMOR's complicated structure, the resulting stems are generally well-formed; for uninflectable stems (mostly made-up words such as `Parunelogramm<+NN><Neut><Gen><Sg>`), the markup is simply removed.

The addition of compound splitting leads to a minor further improvement. We consider this a promising result, indicating that segmentation using the rich information provided by SMOR can be helpful; we plan to explore this further in future work.

Generation of novel words A closer look at the translation output reveals that there are indeed new word forms generated by the *morph-gen* system. For the TED'13 set, for example, the *morph-gen* system output a total of 261 words that are not in the training data or the English input sentence. Of these, 112 are names or nonsense words produced by concatenating BPE segments[3]. The other 149 words are morphologically well-formed, though not necessarily semantically sound (e.g. *Schokoladenredakteur*: 'chocolate editor' as proposed translation for 'smart-ass editor') or appropriate in the translation context. Thus, we compared the novel words with the reference translations: 23 words (21 nouns, 2 adjectives) were found in the reference of the respective sentence. Of course, this under-estimates the number of useful new creations, as a valid translation does not necessarily need to match exactly with the reference. For the *morph-gen-split* system, only 27 matches with the reference were found in a set of 328 unseen forms.

Different Domain and Larger Corpus To assess the influence of domain and corpus size, we also evaluate the approach to model German morphology in a larger news corpus setting. To obtain a training corpus that is diverse, but still restricted in size, we combined randomly selected sentences (between 5-50 words) from the 4 parallel corpora provided for EN–DE translation at the WMT'17 shared task[4] (selected in equal parts from Europarl, CommonCrawl, News-Commentary and RapidCorpus), resulting in a set of 250k and 500k sentences The model is optimized on newstest'15 and evaluated on newstest'16; table 8 shows the results for the surface form baseline and the morphological generation systems with and without compound handling. As for the TED data set, the morphological generation systems outperforms the systems trained on surface data, but the improvement for the system trained on 500k sentences is slightly lower than for the system trained on 250k sentences. The systems with additional compound splitting obtained the same result as the basis morphological generation system (250k), or were slightly better (500k). With regard to the effectiveness of compound handling, it is difficult to draw a clear conclusion, but, looking also at the

results obtained in the TED setting, it seems that there is a tendency that compound handling leads to a slight improvement. As compounding is a productive word formation process that is challenging to cover even in large corpora, compound handling might be useful also when using larger data training corpora.

6   Related Work

Generation of unseen morphological variants has been tackled in various ways in the context of phrase-based models and other SMT approaches. Notably, two-step SMT was proposed to address this problem (Toutanova et al., 2008; Bojar and Kos, 2010; Fraser et al., 2012). In two-step SMT, a separate prediction model (such as a linear-chain CRF) is used to either directly predict the surface form (as in Toutanova et al. (2008)) or used to predict the grammatical features, following which morphological generation is performed (as in Bojar and Kos (2010); Fraser et al. (2012)). Our work differs from their work in that we do not use a separate prediction model, but instead rely on predicting the lemmas and surface-forms as a single sequence in a neural machine translation model.

Huck et al. (2017b) recently proposed an approach related to two-step MT where the unseen surface forms are added as synthetic phrases directly in the system phrase table and a context-aware discriminative model is applied to score the unseen variants. Unlike our work, the authors report diminishing improvements as training data grows larger. Our approach learns a more robust underlying model thanks to the reduced data sparsity. Unlike Huck et al. (2017b), our improvements are therefore not only due to the ability to generate words which were not seen in the training data.

Factored translation models (Koehn and Hoang, 2007) can deal with unseen word forms thanks to generation steps. One of the original goals of factored MT was in fact the scenario where the system produces lemmas and tags and then a generation step could be used to produce the inflected forms. Factored models failed to achieve this goal due to lemmas and tags being predicted independently, leading to many invalid combinations, and due to the involved combinatorial explosion.

García-Martínez et al. (2016) attempt to include target-side factors in neural MT. Unlike our simple technique, their approach requires modifications

---

[3]Into this category, we also count non-wellformed generations by SMOR caused by incorrect transitional elements in compounds, e.g. *Oszillationengenerator* vs. *Oszillationsgenerator*.

[4]http://www.statmt.org/wmt17/translation-task.html

to the network architecture. The authors work with English-French translation and they report mixed results.

Another successful attempt to learn novel inflections in SMT is back-translation (Bojar and Tamchyna, 2011). By using an MT system trained to translate *lemmas* in the opposite direction, it is possible to create synthetic parallel data which contain unseen word forms of known lemmas on the target side. There are two main downsides to this approach. The first is that the source language contains translation errors, which may affect translation quality. The second is that the substitution of different surface forms for the same target language lemma may result in incoherent translations, where the context no longer agrees with the chosen surface form. Sennrich et al. (2016a) propose to use back-translation in NMT to include language modeling data, but the "inverse" NMT system is not able to translate unseen target word forms (no lemmatization is done) and therefore this method does not learn novel inflections. Applying BPE splitting can technically lead to new inflected word forms, but this requires an appropriate segmentation into base form and inflectional suffixes which might not always be the case, in particular for infrequent words.

A very similar method to our two-step setting was independently proposed for use in a natural language generation (NLG) pipeline for morphologically rich languages (Dušek, 2017). However, in this scenario, the approach was not better than a baseline which operated on surface forms.

Finally, there has been further more recent work on alternatives to using BPE segmentation for NMT. Ataman et al. (2017) looked at segmentation for Turkish, which is an agglutinative language. Huck et al. (2017a) presents an approach for segmenting German with a focus on compound splitting and splitting suffixes off of stems using a stemmer, which may allow generalization in a similar way to our work. It would be interesting to compare with these approaches in future work.

7   Conclusion

In this work we showed that a simple setup, interspersing lemmas and rich morphological tags, followed by deterministic generation of the resulting surface form, results in impressive gains in NMT of English to Czech. Applying the technique to an English to German system also resulted in considerable improvements. For English–German, the addition of compound handling yielded promising results. Furthermore, among the novel word forms for German, most were compounds – as compounding is a very productive process, this is also a challenging problem when using larger corpora. Exploring strategies for better segmentation and compound handling is an interesting task that we plan to investigate further.

We believe that while simple, this technique effectively addresses the fundamental problems of rich target-side morphology: (i) sparse data and lack of connection between different forms of a single target lexeme, (ii) lack of explicit morphological information, and (iii) inability to generate unseen forms of known lexemes. Our results indicate that most of the improvement comes from the first two properties.

Perhaps a modified training criterion could be used to encourage the system to generalize more; in the standard setting, the system probably learns to strongly condition the lemma on the tag and avoids the risk of generating new pairs. In the situations where a novel form is required, the system may either bypass this by producing a synonymous word or paraphrase, or it might simply produce an ungrammatical form of the correct lemma. This phenomenon deserves more examination which we leave to future work.

We further analyzed the serialization scenario, showing that the effect here is not due to training the system to also predict morphological tags, which is in contrast with the result of Nadejde et al. (2017). It is likely that the two approaches are complementary, the rich information in CCG supertags could bring additional benefit to the morphological generalization that we perform. We plan to investigate this in future work.

Acknowledgments

This project has received funding from the European Union's Horizon 2020 research and innovation programme under grant agreement No 644402 (HimL). This project has received funding from the European Research Council (ERC) under the European Union's Horizon 2020 research and innovation programme (grant agreement No 640550).

References

Duygu Ataman, Matteo Negri, Marco Turchi, and Marcello Federico. 2017. Linguistically motivated vocabulary reduction for neural machine translation from Turkish to English. In *Proceedings of EAMT*.

Dzmitry Bahdanau, Kyunghyun Cho, and Yoshua Bengio. 2014. Neural machine translation by jointly learning to align and translate. *CoRR* abs/1409.0473. http://arxiv.org/abs/1409.0473.

Ondřej Bojar, Zdeněk Žabokrtský, Ondřej Dušek, Petra Galuščáková, Martin Majliš, David Mareček, Jiří Maršík, Michal Novák, Martin Popel, and Aleš Tamchyna. 2012. The Joy of Parallelism with CzEng 1.0. In *Proc. of LREC*. ELRA, pages 3921–3928.

Ondřej Bojar and Kamil Kos. 2010. 2010 failures in english-czech phrase-based mt. In *Proceedings of the Joint Fifth Workshop on Statistical Machine Translation and Metrics-MATR*. Association for Computational Linguistics, Stroudsburg, PA, USA, WMT '10, pages 60–66. http://dl.acm.org/citation.cfm?id=1868850.1868855.

Ondřej Bojar and Aleš Tamchyna. 2011. Improving Translation Model by Monolingual Data. In *Proceedings of the Sixth Workshop on Statistical Machine Translation*. Association for Computational Linguistics, Edinburgh, Scotland, pages 330–336. http://www.aclweb.org/anthology/W11-2138.

Fabienne Cap, Alexander Fraser, Marion Weller, and Aoife Cahill. 2014. How to Produce Unseen Teddy Bears: Improved Morphological Processing of Compounds in SMT. In *Proceedings of the 14th Conference of the European Chapter of the Association for Computational Linguistics (EACL)*. Göteborg, Sweden, pages 579–587.

Mauro Cettolo, Christian Girardi, and Marcello Federico. 2012. Wit^3: Web inventory of transcribed and translated talks. In *Proceedings of the 16th Conference of the European Association for Machine Translation (EAMT)*. Trento, Italy, pages 261 268.

Ondřej Dušek. 2017. *Novel methods in natural language generation for spoken dialogue systems*. Ph.D. thesis.

Alexander Fraser, Marion Weller, Aoife Cahill, and Fabienne Cap. 2012. Modeling Inflection and Word-Formation in SMT. In *Proceedings of the 13th Conference of the European Chapter of the Association for Computational Linguistics*. Association for Computational Linguistics, Avignon, France, pages 664–674. http://www.aclweb.org/anthology/E12-1068.

Mercedes García-Martínez, Loïc Barrault, and Fethi Bougares. 2016. Factored neural machine translation. *CoRR* abs/1609.04621. http://arxiv.org/abs/1609.04621.

Jan Hajič and Barbora Vidová-Hladká. 1998. Tagging inflective languages: Prediction of morphological categories for a rich, structured tagset. In *Proceedings of the COLING - ACL Conference*. pages 483–490.

Matthias Huck, Simon Riess, and Alexander Fraser. 2017a. Target-side word segmentation strategies for neural machine translation. In *Proceedings of the Second Conference on Machine Translation (WMT)*. Copenhagen, Denmark.

Matthias Huck, Aleš Tamchyna, Ondřej Bojar, and Alexander Fraser. 2017b. Producing unseen morphological variants in statistical machine translation. In *Proceedings of the 15th Conference of the European Chapter of the Association for Computational Linguistics (EACL)*.

Diederik P. Kingma and Jimmy Ba. 2014. Adam: A method for stochastic optimization. *CoRR* abs/1412.6980. http://arxiv.org/abs/1412.6980.

Philipp Koehn and Hieu Hoang. 2007. Factored translation models. In *Proceedings of the 2007 Joint Conference on Empirical Methods in Natural Language Processing and Computational Natural Language Learning (EMNLP-CoNLL)*. Association for Computational Linguistics, Prague, Czech Republic, pages 868–876. http://www.aclweb.org/anthology/D/D07/D07-1091.

Maria Nadejde, Siva Reddy, Rico Sennrich, Tomasz Dwojak, Marcin Junczys-Dowmunt, Philipp Koehn, and Alexandra Birch. 2017. Syntax-aware neural machine translation using CCG. *CoRR* abs/1702.01147. http://arxiv.org/abs/1702.01147.

Helmut Schmid. 1994. Probabilistic part-of-speech tagging using decision trees. In *Proceedings of the International Conference on New Methods in Language Processing*. Manchester, UK, pages 44–49.

Helmut Schmid. 2004. Efficient Parsing of Highly Ambiguous Context-Free Grammars with Bit Vectors. In *Proceedings of the International Conference on Computational Linguistics*. Geneva, Switzerland, pages 162–168.

Helmut Schmid, Arne Fitschen, and Ulrich Heid. 2004. SMOR: A German Computational Morphology Covering Derivation, Composition, and Inflection. In *Proceedings of the 4th International Conference on Language Resources and Evaluation (LREC)*. Lisbon, Portugal, pages 1263–1266.

R. Sennrich, O. Firat, K. Cho, A. Birch, B. Haddow, J. Hitschler, M. Junczys-Dowmunt, S. Läubli, A. Valerio Miceli Barone, J. Mokry, and M. Nădejde. 2017. Nematus: a Toolkit for Neural Machine Translation. *ArXiv e-prints* .

Rico Sennrich, Barry Haddow, and Alexandra Birch. 2016a. Improving neural machine translation models with monolingual data. In *Proceedings of the 54th Annual Meeting of the Association for Computational Linguistics, ACL 2016*. http://aclweb.org/anthology/P/P16/P16-1009.pdf.

Rico Sennrich, Barry Haddow, and Alexandra Birch. 2016b. Neural machine translation of rare words with subword units. In *Proceedings of the 54th Annual Meeting of the Association for Computational Linguistics, ACL 2016*. http://aclweb.org/anthology/P/P16/P16-1162.pdf.

Jana Straková, Milan Straka, and Jan Hajič. 2014. Open-Source Tools for Morphology, Lemmatization, POS Tagging and Named Entity Recognition. In *Proceedings of 52nd Annual Meeting of the Association for Computational Linguistics: System Demonstrations*. Association for Computational Linguistics, Baltimore, Maryland, pages 13–18. http://www.aclweb.org/anthology/P/P14/P14-5003.pdf.

Sara Stymne, Nicola Candedda, and Lars Ahrenberg. 2011. Generation of Compound Words in Statistical Machine Translation into Compounding Languages. *Computational Linguistics* 39(4):1067–1108.

Kristina Toutanova, Hisami Suzuki, and Achim Ruopp. 2008. Applying morphology generation models to machine translation. In *Proceedings of ACL-08: HLT*. Association for Computational Linguistics, Columbus, Ohio, pages 514–522. http://www.aclweb.org/anthology/P/P08/P08-1059.

Evaluating the morphological competence of Machine Translation Systems

Franck Burlot and **François Yvon**
LIMSI, CNRS, Université Paris-Saclay, France
`firstname.lastname@limsi.fr`

Abstract

While recent changes in Machine Translation state-of-the-art brought translation quality a step further, it is regularly acknowledged that the standard automatic metrics do not provide enough insights to fully measure the impact of neural models. This paper proposes a new type of evaluation focused specifically on the morphological competence of a system with respect to various grammatical phenomena. Our approach uses automatically generated pairs of source sentences, where each pair tests one morphological contrast. This methodology is used to compare several systems submitted at WMT'17 for English into Czech and Latvian.

1   Introduction

It is nowadays unanimously recognized that Machine Translation (MT) engines based on the neural encoder-decoder architecture with attention (Cho et al., 2014; Bahdanau et al., 2014) constitute the new state-of-the-art in statistical MT, at least for open-domain tasks (Sennrich et al., 2016a). The previous phrase-based (PBMT) architectures were complex (Koehn, 2010) and hard to diagnose, and Neural MT (NMT) systems, which dispense with any sort of symbolic representation of the learned knowledge, are probably worse in this respect. Furthermore, the steady progress of MT engines makes automatic metrics such as BLEU (Papineni et al., 2002) or METEOR (Banerjee and Lavie, 2005) less appropriate to evaluate and compare modern NMT systems. To better understand the strength and weaknesses of these new architectures, it is thus necessary to investigate new, more focused, evaluation procedures.

Error analysis protocols, as proposed eg. by Vilar et al. (2006); Popović and Ney (2011) for PBMT, are obvious candidates for such studies and have been used eg. in (Bentivogli et al., 2016). Recently, various new proposals have been put forward to better diagnose neural models, notably by Linzen et al. (2016); Sennrich (2017), who focus respectively on the syntactic competence of Neural Language Models (NLMs) or of NMT; and by Isabelle et al. (2017); Burchardt et al. (2017), who resuscitate an old tradition of designing test suites.

Inspired by these (and other) works (see § 4), we propose in this paper a new evaluation scheme aimed at specifically assessing the *morphological* competence of MT engines translating from English into a Morphologically Rich Language (MRL). Morphology poses two main types of problems in MT: (a) morphological variation in the source increases the occurrence of Out-of-Vocabulary (OOV) source tokens, the translation of which is difficult to coin; (b) morphological variation in the target forces the MT to generate forms that have not been seen in training. Morphological complexity is alo often associated to more flexible word orderings, which is mostly a problem when translating from a MRL (Bisazza and Federico, 2016). Reducing these issues is a legitimate and important goal for many language pairs.

Our method for measuring the morphological competence of MT systems (detailed in § 2) is mainly based on the analysis of minimal pairs, each representing a contrast that is expressed syntactically in English and morphologically in the MRL. By comparing the automatic translations of these pairs, it is then possible to approximately assess whether a given MT system has succeeded in generating the correct word form, carrying the proper morphological marks. In § 3, we illustrate the potential of our evaluation protocol in a large-scale comparison of multiple MT engines having participated to the WMT'17 News Transla-

Proceedings of the Conference on Machine Translation (WMT), Volume 1: Research Papers, pages 43–55
Copenhagen, Denmark, September 7–11, 2017. ©2017 Association for Computational Linguistics

tion tasks for the pairs English-Czech and English-Latvian.[1] We finally relate our protocol to conventional metrics (§ 4), and conclude in § 5 by discussing possible extensions of this methodology, for instance to other (sets of) language pairs.

2 Evaluation Protocol

2.1 Morphological competence and its assessment

In traditional linguistics, morphology is "the branch of the grammar that deals with the internal structure of words" (Matthews, 1974, p. 9); the "structure of words" being further subdivided into inflections, derivations (word formation) and compounds. Languages exhibit a large variety of formal processes to express morphological/lexical relatedness of a set of word forms: alternations in suffix/prefix are the most common processes in Indo-European languages, where other language families recourse to circumfixation, reduplication, transfixation, or tonal alternations. They also greatly differ in the phenomena that are expressed through morphological alternations versus grammatical constructions.

Our evaluation protocol is designed to assess the robustness of MT in the presence of morphological variation in the source and target, looking how source alternations (possibly implying to translate source OOVs) are reproduced in the target (possibly implying to generate target OOVs).

The general principle is as follows: for each source test sentence (the *base*), we generate one (or several) *variant(s)* containing exactly one difference with the base, focusing on a specific *target* lexeme of the base; the variant differs on a feature that is expressed morphologically in the target, such as the person, number or tense of a verb; or the number or case of a noun or an adjective. This configuration is illustrated in Table 1, where the first pair is an example of the *tense* contrast and the second pair an instance of the *polarity* contrast.

We consider that a system behaves correctly with respect to a given contrast if the translation of the base and the variant reproduce the targeted contrast: for the first example in Table 1, we expect to see in the translation of (1.a) and (1.b) different word forms accounting for the difference of verb tense: the translation of the variant should have a past form and any other case is considered as an error. Other modifications between the two

translations, such as the selection of different lemmas for both forms or any modification of the context, are considered irrelevant with respect to the specific morphological feature at study, and are therefore ignored. In the following sections, we detail and justify our strategy for generating contrastive pairs.

2.2 Sentence selection and morphological contrasts

We consider the set of contrasts listed in Table 2. We distinguish three subsets (denoted A, B, and C), which slightly differ in their generation and scoring procedures.

Our choice for selecting this particular set of tests was dictated by a mixture of linguistic and also more practical reasons. From a linguistic standpoint, we were looking to cover a large variety of morphological phenomena in the target language, in particular we wished to include test instances for all open domain word classes (noun, verbs, adjectives). Our first set of tests (set A) is akin to paradigm completion tasks, adopting here a rather loose sense of "paradigm" which also includes simple derivational phenomena such as the formation of comparative for adjectives and mostly checks whether the morphological feature inserted in the source sentence has been translated. Tests in the set B look at various agreement phenomena, while tests in set C are more focused on the consistency of morphological choices. These three categories of tests slightly differ in their generation and scoring procedures.

For each contrast in the A and B sets, sentence generation takes the following steps:[2]

1. collect a sufficiently large number of short sentences (length < 15) containing a source word of interest for at least one morphological variation;

2. generate a variant as prescribed by the contrast (see below);

3. compute an average language model (LM) score for the pair (base, variant);

4. remove the 33% worst pairs based on their LM score;

5. randomly select 500 pairs for inclusion into the final test.

[1] http://statmt.org/wmt17/.

[2] Examples of test pairs are given as supplementary material in the appendix.

base	(1.a) The thing that **horrifies** me is the forgetfulness.		
variant	(1.b) The thing that **horrified** me is the forgetfulness.		
base	(2.a) Traffic deaths **fall** as gas prices climb.		
variant	(2.b) Traffic deaths **do not fall** as gas prices climb.		

Table 1: Generating minimal contrastive pairs

name	contrast	target	description
A-1	number	noun	base contains a singular noun, variant contains the plural form
A-2	number	pronoun	base contains a singular pronoun, variant contains the plural form
A-3	gender	pronoun	base contains a masculine pronoun, variant contains the feminine form
A-4	tense:future	verb	base and variant only differ in the tense of the main verb - present in the base, future in the variant
A-5	tense:past	verb	base and variant only differ in the tense of the main verb - present in the base, past in the variant
A-6	comparative	adjective	base contains the bare adjective, variant the comparative form
A-7	polarity	verb	base and variant only differ in the polarity of the main verb - affirmative in the base, negative in the variant
B-1	complex NP	pronoun	base contains a pronoun, variant contains a complex NP of the form *adj noun*
B-2	coordinated noun	pronoun	base contains a pronoun, variant contains a coordinated NP of the form *noun and noun*
B-3	coordinated verbs	verbs	base contain a simple verb, variant contains a coordinated VP of the form *verb and verb*
B-4	prep-case	preposition	base and variant differ in one preposition which implies a different case in the target (eg. *during* vs. *before*, *with* vs. *without*)
C-1	hyponyms	adjective	base contains an adjective, (4) variants with hyponyms
C-2	hyponyms	noun	base contains a noun, (4) variants with hyponyms
C-3	hyponyms	verb	base contains a verb, (4) variants with hyponyms

Table 2: A set of morphological contrasts. See text for details.

For set A, the creation of the variant (step 2) consists in replacing a word according to the morphological phenomenon to evaluate (see examples Table 1). This word is selected in such a way that its modification does not require a modification of any other word in the sentence. For instance, a singular subject noun is not replaced by its plural form, since the verb agreeing with it would also need to be replaced accordingly. Indeed, more than one modification would go against our initial idea of generating minimal pairs reflecting exactly one single contrast.

For B-1 (complex NPs), we spot a personal pronoun that we changed into an NP consisting in an adjective and a noun. Both words are generated randomly with the only constraint that the noun should refer to a human subject and the adjective to a psychological state, yielding NPs such as "the happy linguist" or "the gloomy philosopher". In order to ensure that the context corresponds to a human subject, we selected pronouns that unambiguously refer to humans, such as "him", "her", "we" (avoiding "them"). For B-2 (coordinated NPs) the pronoun in the base sentence is transformed into a complex NP consisting of two coordinated nouns. Note that adjectives associated to these nouns, as well as adverbs, have been randomly inserted in order to produce some variation in the constructions. The B-3 contrasts are produced in a similar fashion, targeting verbs instead of nouns, with an additional random generation of a discourse marker that should not interfere with the translation, yielding variants like "he **said** and, as a matter of fact, **shouted**".[3] Those inser-

---

[3]The coordinated verbs are in bold, the discourse marker is underlined.

tions were performed in order to increase the distance between the two verbs, making agreement between them harder. Finally, the B-4 contrasts are produced in the same way as for the A-set and simply consist in modifying a preposition.

The C-set variants select a noun, an adjective or a verb and replace it with a random hyponym, producing an arbitrary number of sentences. Sentence selection slightly differs from the description above: during step 2, we generate as many variants as possible. Each variant is then scored with a language model and only the top four variants are kept, leading to buckets of five sentences. Those buckets are finally filtered in the same way as for the A and B sets, removing the 33% worst buckets based on their LM score (step 3).

All the sentences were selected from the English News-2008 corpus provided at WMT. The choice of the news domain was dictated by our intention to evaluate systems submitted at WMT'17[4] News Translation task. Sentences longer than 15 tokens were removed in order to ensure a better focus on a specific part of the sentence in the MT output. The modifications of English sentences were based on a morpho-syntactic analysis produced with the TreeTagger (Schmid, 1994) and using the Pymorphy morphological generator[5] to change the inflection of a word. Hyponyms (synonyms and/or antonyms) were generated with WordNet (Miller, 1995). The 5-gram language model used for sentence selection was learned with KenLM (Heafield, 2011) on all English monolingual data available at WMT'15.

2.3 Scoring Procedures

Regarding the scoring procedure, we again distinguish three cases (examples are in Table 3).

- set A: we compare the translations of base and variant and search for the word(s) in variant that are not in base. If one of these words contains the morphological feature associated with the source sentence modification, we report a success. Accuracy of each morphological feature is averaged over all the samples. In this set, we thus evaluate morphological information that should be conveyed from the source sentence, which leads to an assessment on the grammatical adequacy of the output towards the source.

- set B: we compare the translations of base and variant and check that (a) a pronoun in the former is replaced by a NP in the latter (b) the adjective and the noun in the NP share the same gender, number and case. A distinct accuracy rate per feature can then be reported; note that the situation is different in the complex and coordinated tests, as in the latter case some agreement properties may differ in the base and variant (eg. the NP gender agreement depends on the noun gender that may be different from the pronoun gender in base). For the test triggered by prepositions (B-4), we check whether the first noun on the right of a preposition carries the required case mark. Moreover, since we have prepositions associated to nouns in both base and variant, we performed this test on both sentences. This evaluation set checks for agreement and provides an insight about the morphological fluency of the produced translations.

- set C : in this set of tests, we wish to assess the consistency of morphological features with respect to lexical variation in a fixed context; accordingly, we measure the success based on the average normalized entropy of morphological features in the set of target sentences. Such scores can be computed either globally or on a per feature basis. The entropy is null when all variants have the same morphological features, the highest possible consistency; conversely, the normalized entropy is 1 when the five sentences contain different morphological features. For each set C-1, C-2 and C-3, we report average scores over 500 samples. In this setup, we measure the degree of certainty to which a system predicts morphological features across small lexical variations.

Our scoring procedure needs access to morphological information in the target. For A and B sets, the translated sentences are passed through a morphological analysis, where several PoS can be associated with a word. This makes the evaluation less dependent on the tagger's accuracy. Therefore, when checking whether a specific morphological feature appears in the output (eg. negation of a verb), we look for at least one PoS tag indicating negation, ignoring all the others.

For Czech, we used the Morphodita analyzer (Straková et al., 2014). We had no such resource

---

[4]www.statmt.org/wmt17/
[5]http://pymorphy.readthedocs.io/

Base&Variant(s)	Output	Result
A-set		
I am hungry	mám hlad	
I am not hungry	**nemám** hlad	negation found
B-set		
I see him	vidím ho	noun and adjective both
I see a crazy researcher	vidím **bláznivého výzkumníka**	have accusative form
C-set		
I agree with the president	souhlasím s **prezidentem**	all nouns bear
I agree with the director	souhlasím s **ředitelem**	the same
I agree with the minister	souhlasím s **ministrem**	intrumental case
I agree with the driver	souhlasím s **řidičem**	
I agree with the painter	souhlasím s **malířem**	(Entropy = 0.0)

Table 3: Examples of sentences that pass the tests.

for Latvian and therefore used the LU MII Tagger (Paikens et al., 2013) to parse all Latvian monolingual data available at WMT'17. We then extracted a dictionary consisting of words and associated PoS from the automatic parses. We finally performed a coarse cleaning of this dictionary by removing the PoS that were predicted less than 100 times for a specific word. To run the morphological analysis of Latvian, we parsed the translated sentences with the tagger, then augmented the tagger predictions with our dictionary, producing the desired ambiguous analysis of the Latvian outputs.

For the C-set, the translated sentence analyses are disambiguated: each word is mapped to a single PoS. This was required to compute the entropy. Indeed, we need to select only one morphological value for each base and variant sentence, given that the entropy is normalized according the total number of sentences in the bucket.

3 Experiments

We have run the presented morphological evaluation[6] on several systems among which some were submitted at WMT'17. The description of the latter can be found in the proceedings of the Second Conference on Machine Translation (2017a). We briefly summarize the types of systems included in the English-to-Czech study:

- Phrase-based systems: The **Moses baseline** was trained on WMT'17 data and was not submitted at WMT'17. **UFAL Chimera**[7] was submitted at WMT'16 and is described in (Tamchyna et al., 2016).

- Word based NMT: **NMT words** is a system trained on WMT'17 parallel data with a target vocabulary of 80k tokens. It was not submitted at WMT'17 and is used for contrast.

- BPE-based NMT: **LIMSI NMT** (Burlot et al., 2017) is based on NMTPY (Caglayan et al., 2017), **UEDIN NMT** (Sennrich et al., 2017a) on Nematus (Sennrich et al., 2017b) and **UFAL NMT** (Bojar et al., 2017b) on Neural Monkey (Helcl and Libovický, 2017).

- NMT modeling target morphology: **LIMSI FNMT** (Burlot et al., 2017) and **LIUM FNMT** (García-Martínez et al., 2017) use a factored output predicting words and PoS, and **UFAL NMT Chim.** (Bojar et al., 2017b) uses Chimera (Bojar et al., 2013). All these models also use BPE segmentation.

These systems are representative of different models across statistical MT history. Phrase-based systems are a former state of the art that word-based NMT struggled to improve. The new state of the art is an NMT setup with an open vocabulary provided by byte pair encoding (BPE) segmentation (Sennrich et al., 2016b). Finally, we have a set of systems that are optimized in order to improve target morphology. The automatic scores of the systems submitted at WMT'17[8] are in Table 4 where we report BLEU, BEER (Stanojević and Sima'an, 2014) and CharacTER (Wang et al., 2016).[9] We also computed a morphology accuracy for these systems. Using output-to-reference alignments produced by METEOR on lemmas, we

---

[6]The test suite and the scripts used for evaluation can be downloaded at `github.com/franckbrl/morpheval`.

[7]Chimera (Bojar et al., 2013) consists in a phrase-based factored system (Moses), a deep-syntactic transfer-based system (TectoMT) and a rule-based post-processing system.

[8]We were not able to provide such scores for the other systems, since we did not have access to their translations of WMT'17 official test sets.

[9]Outputs were taken from `matrix.statmt.org`. The scores are computed on tokenized and truecased outputs.

System	BLEU $\uparrow$	BEER $\uparrow$	CTER $\downarrow$	Acc.
LIMSI NMT	19.81	54.50	58.40	85.59
UFAL NMT	19.78	54.52	57.62	85.31
UEDIN NMT	23.06	56.52	56.04	86.98
LIMSI FNMT	20.45	54.98	58.09	85.42
LIUM FNTM	20.14	54.81	57.91	84.98
UFAL NMT Chim.	21.00	55.04	59.39	85.28

Table 4: Scores of the English-to-Czech WMT'17 submissions on the official test set.

checked whether aligned words shared the same form. Our assumption is that two different forms associated to the same lemma correspond to two different inflections of the same lexeme, which allows us to locate positions that likely correspond to morphological errors.

Table 5 lists the results for the A-set tests, which evaluate the morphological adequacy of the output wrt. the source sentence. The last column provides the mean of all scores for one system. We can note that all BPE-based NMT systems have a much higher performance than the phrase-based systems.[10] We explain the poor performance of the word-based NMT system by the use of a too small closed vocabulary: over the 18,500 sentences of the test suite, 12,016 unknown words were produced by this system. However, when it comes to predicting the morphology of closed class words, this systems performs much better: the accuracy computed for pronoun gender and number is similar to the ones of best BPE-based systems. As opposed to nouns and verbs (open classes), the set of pronouns in Czech is quite small; having observed all their inflections, the word-based system is in a better position to convey the target form.

Despite important differences in automatic metric scores between UEDIN NMT system and LIMSI FNMT, we see that the latter always outperforms the former, except for the feminine pronoun prediction. The overall morphological accuracies (Table 4) show that UEDIN NMT provides more similar word forms with the reference translation, but these global scores fail to show the higher adequacy performance of LIMSI FNMT highlighted in the A-set.

The results of the B-set evaluation for Czech are in Table 6 and are an estimate of the morphological fluency of the output. We observe here again

that morphological phenomena such as agreement are better modeled by sequence-to-sequence models using BPE segmentation than phrase-based or word-based NMT systems. The overall best performance of UEDIN and UFAL NMT has to be noted, since both outperform systems that explicitly model target morphology.

The results for the C-set for English-to-Czech are shown in Table 7. We now observe that factored systems are less sensitive to lexical variations and make more stable morphological predictions. The differences with the entropy values computed for the phrase-based systems are spectacular, especially for verbal morphology. We understand this poor performance for phrase-based systems as a consequence of the initial assumption those systems rely on: the concatenation of phrases to constitute an output sentence does not help to provide a single morphological prediction in slightly various contexts.

As an attempt to evaluate the error margin of our evaluation results, we have run a manual check of our evaluation measures. For this, we have taken all 500 sentence pairs reflecting past tense (A-set), as well as case (pronouns to nouns in B-set), and took translations from different systems randomly. We report on cases where the modification of the source created a "bad" (meaningless or ungrammatical) variant, as well as sample translations erroneously considered successful or unsuccessful. For past tense, we observe a low quantity of false positive (1.6%) and false negative (0.4%). The ratio of bad sources is quite low as well (3%), and is mostly related to cases where a word was given the wrong analysis in the first place, such as a noun labeled by the PoS-tagger as a verb, which was then turned into a past form. For pronouns to nouns, there are nearly no bad source sentences (0.2%): the transformation of pronouns into noun phrases is quite easy and safe. While false positive labels are lower (0.2%), there is a higher amount of false positive (4.4%), which was mainly due to our word-based NMT system that generates many unknown words and presents important differences between base and variant: several adjectives and nouns, not corresponding to the ones we generated in the source sentence, could then be considered during the evaluation.

For English-to-Latvian, we have represented the same types of systems as for Czech, with an additional hybrid system. The scores and mor-

---

[10]The prediction quality of future tense by PBMT systems is however comparable to that of NMT systems. We assume that this is due to the possibility to generate an analytic form of this tense (auxiliary + infinitive) that is easier to form well than its synthetic form (morphological phenomenon).

System	verbs			pronouns		others		mean
	past	future	neg.	fem.	plur.	noun nb.	compar.	
Moses baseline	61.0%	87.2%	73.8%	91.6%	78.0%	72.6%	70.9%	76.4%
UFAL PBMT	92.2%	**88.6%**	78.8%	75.6%	79.8%	86.0%	72.2%	81.9%
NMT words	74.6%	60.6%	91.6%	89.2%	71.6%	44.0%	47.8%	68.5%
UFAL NMT	91.0%	90.4%	95.0%	**92.4%**	**80.8%**	**96.6%**	70.6%	88.1%
LIMSI NMT	92.6%	86.2%	**96.0%**	91.4%	79.2%	94.6%	**76.2%**	88.0%
UEDIN NMT	92.4%	87.0%	94.2%	93.0%	78.0%	95.8%	73.8%	87.7%
LIMSI FNMT	94.2%	88.0%	95.4%	91.2%	80.0%	96.2%	75.0%	**88.6%**
LIUM FNTM	**93.4%**	84.0%	94.6%	91.6%	80.2%	96.2%	73.4%	87.6%
UFAL NMT Chim.	92.6%	86.6%	88.2%	85.4%	80.2%	89.2%	70.6%	84.7%

Table 5: Sentence pair evaluation for English-to-Czech (A-set).

System	coordinated verbs			coord.n	pronouns to nouns			prep.	mean
	number	person	tense	case	gender	number	case	case	
Moses baseline	53.2%	53.6%	47.6%	92.6%	68.0%	69.4%	69.4%	86.2%	67.5%
UFAL PBMT	67.4%	69.2%	59.2%	93.2%	92.4%	92.4%	91.8%	89.6%	81.9%
NMT words	60.0%	58.8%	51.8%	64.0%	22.8%	23.2%	22.6%	62.2%	45.7%
LIMSI NMT	76.6%	77.0%	69.2%	90.4%	90.8%	92.6%	92.2%	95.3%	85.5%
UFAL NMT	81.4%	80.0%	74.0%	**94.2%**	**94.4%**	**94.6%**	**94.8%**	**97.0%**	88.8%
UEDIN NMT	**83.6%**	**84.2%**	**77.6%**	92.8%	93.6%	94.4%	94.0%	95.8%	**89.5%**
LIMSI FNMT	77.6%	77.4%	70.6%	89.0%	91.4%	90.8%	91.6%	96.1%	85.6%
LIUM FNTM	80.8%	79.6%	71.8%	89.6%	90.6%	90.4%	90.8%	95.8%	86.2%
UFAL NMT Chim.	75.8%	74.6%	68.0%	92.6%	87.8%	87.8%	88.2%	92.9%	83.5%

Table 6: Sentence pair evaluation for English-to-Czech (B-set).

phological accuracies of the systems submitted at WMT'17 are in Table 8.

- Phrase-based systems: The **Moses baseline** was trained on WMT'17 data and **TILDE PBMT** was provided by TILDE[11] and is described in (Peter et al., 2017). These systems did not take part in the official WMT'17 evaluation campaign.

- Word-based NMT: **NMT words** is a system trained on WMT'17 parallel data with a 80K target vocabulary. It was not submitted at WMT'17 and is used here as a contrast.

- BPE-based NMT. **LIMSI NMT** (Burlot et al., 2017) is based on NMTPY and **UEDIN NMT** (Sennrich et al., 2017a) on Nematus.

- NMT modeling target morphology: **LIMSI FNMT** (Burlot et al., 2017) and **LIUM FNMT** (García-Martínez et al., 2017) use a factored output predicting words and PoS.

- Hybrid system: **TILDE hybrid** is an ensemble of NMT models using a PBMT to process rare and unknown words. It was submitted at WMT'17 (Pinnis et al., 2017).

The results for the A-set evaluation are in Table 9. Compared to the previous Czech evaluation, there is a less clear difference between phrase-based and NMT systems based on BPE. Indeed, TILDE hybrid has the best mean performance and is only 5 points above our Moses baseline. A possible reason for that situation is the lower amount of parallel data available for English-Latvian, compared to English-Czech. We notice that there is no significant difference between the two NMT systems and LIMSI FNMT. With this language pair, word-based NMT performs significantly worse than all other systems on all morphological features, which is confirmed by the fluency evaluation in Table 10. Here, the factored systems tend to have a better verbal fluency, whereas NMT systems perform better on nominal agreement: LIMSI FNMT has the best mean score, but is only 0.2 points above UEDIN NMT. The best system, TILDE hybrid, is now 21.1 points above the Moses baseline, which again seems to be the main reason for such high overall morphological accuracy in Table 8.

Table 11 confirms the higher performance of NMT and factored NMT systems, with a clear advantage for TILDE hybrid, which has the best accuracy in terms of fluency, like in the previous Table 10, which tends to show some correlation between both types of tests.

[11] http://www.tilde.com/mt

	nouns	adjectives			verbs				mean
System	case	gender	number	case	number	person	tense	negation	
Moses baseline	.381	.482	.420	.453	.415	.300	.354	.269	.384
UFAL PBMT	.272	.376	.331	.376	.198	.134	.150	.105	.243
NMT words	.419	.561	.537	.460	.513	.477	.491	.467	.491
UFAL NMT	.193	.325	.271	.317	.154	.084	.105	.075	.191
LIMSI NMT	.205	.303	.262	.301	.138	.068	.082	**.054**	.177
UEDIN NMT	.217	.302	.276	.300	.124	.065	.086	**.054**	.178
LIMSI FNMT	**.197**	.287	.255	.292	**.110**	**.062**	**.081**	.056	**.168**
LIUM FNTM	.206	**.278**	**.240**	**.269**	.125	.074	.090	.067	.169
UFAL NMT Chim.	.214	.353	.302	.359	.185	.114	.129	.097	.219

Table 7: Sentence group evaluation for English-to-Czech with Entropy (C-set).

System	BLEU ↑	BEER ↑	CTER ↓	Acc.
LIMSI NMT	15.91	52.91	61.56	85.36
UEDIN NMT	17.20	53.77	65.60	85.99
LIMSI FNMT	16.93	53.73	60.57	85.57
LIUM FNTM	16.13	52.81	61.90	84.05
TILDE hybrid	20.28	55.46	57.46	87.95

Table 8: Scores of the English-to-Latvian WMT'17 submissions on the official test set.

	verbs		pronouns		nouns	mean
System	past	future	fem.	plur.	number	
Moses baseline	67.0%	83.2%	68.6%	83.6%	63.6%	73.2%
TILDE PBMT	68.8%	70.4%	56.0%	71.8%	65.0%	66.4%
NMT words	56.8%	64.0%	38.6%	71.4%	59.2%	58.0%
UEDIN NMT	74.6%	83.6%	57.0%	88.6%	69.4%	74.6%
LIMSI NMT	68.8%	84.6%	64.2%	86.8%	73.0%	75.5%
LIMSI FNMT	69.6%	82.8%	62.0%	**89.0%**	70.6%	74.8%
LIUM FNMT	73.0%	81.2%	**76.8%**	86.6%	**73.2%**	**78.2%**
TILDE hybrid	**79.6%**	**92.0%**	49.4%	87.2%	71.2%	75.9%

Table 9: Sentence pair evaluation for English-to-Latvian (A-set).

When it comes to morphological correction of the output, our evaluation clearly shows the superiority of BPE-based NMT systems over phrase-based ones. On the other hand, while we observed that factored models obtain a higher performance in terms of adequacy, NMT models are still very close to them in terms of fluency. Finally, factored models, as well as TILDE hybrid, clearly showed more confidence in their predictions through slight lexical variations.

4 Related work: evaluating morphology

Automatic metrics Despite their well-known flaws, "general purpose" automatic metrics such as BLEU (Papineni et al., 2002), TER (Snover et al., 2006) or METEOR (Banerjee and Lavie, 2005) remain the preferred way to measure progress in Machine Translation. Evaluation campaigns aimed at comparing systems have long abandoned these measures and resort to human judgments, such as ranking (Callison-Burch et al., 2007) or direct assessment (Bojar et al., 2016). To compensate for the inability of eg. BLEU to detect improvements targeting specific difficulties of MT, several problem-specific measures have been introduced over the years such as the LR-Score (Birch and Osborne, 2010) to measure the correctness of reordering decisions, MEANT (Lo and Wu, 2011) to measure the transfer of entailment relationships, or CharacTER (Wang et al., 2016)

to better assess the success of translation into a MRL. Stanojević and Sima'an (2014)'s BEER is a nice example of a sophisticated metric, based on a trainable mixture of multiple metrics: for MRLs, the inclusion of character n-gram matches and of reordering scores proves critical to reach good correlation with human judgments. In comparison, the proposal of Wang et al. (2016) simply computes a TER-like score at the character level, thereby partially crediting a system for predicting the right lemma with the wrong morphology.

Error typologies Error analysis protocols, as proposed by Vilar et al. (2006); Popović and Ney (2011); Stymne (2011) for PBMT systems are obvious candidates for running diagnosis studies and have been used eg. by Bentivogli et al. (2016); Toral Ruiz and Sánchez-Cartagena (2017); Costa-jussà (2017); Klubička et al. (2017). These works differ in the language pairs and in the error typology considered. Bentivogli et al. (2016) only recognizes three main error types which are automatically recognized based on aligning the hypotheses and references – for instance a morphological error is detected when the word form is wrong, whereas the lemma is correct; this definition is also adopted in (Toral Ruiz and Sánchez-Cartagena, 2017), and decomposed at the level of morphological features in (Peter et al., 2016); (Klubička et al., 2017) use a more detailed ty-

	coordinated verbs			coord.n	pronouns to nouns			prep.	mean
System	number	person	tense	case	gender	number	case	case	
Moses baseline	50.2%	37.4%	50.6%	42.2%	21.4%	24.0%	14.8%	45.1%	35.7%
TILDE PBMT	49.6%	32.8%	50.2%	**47.6%**	24.0%	25.4%	19.0%	48.5%	37.1%
NMT words	43.0%	36.0%	43.6%	15.6%	7.8%	8.0%	7.8%	44.1%	25.7%
UEDIN NMT	70.6%	60.8%	72.0%	30.2%	46.4%	44.8%	43.4%	56.7%	53.1%
LIMSI NMT	69.2%	57.6%	70.4%	41.8%	40.0%	40.8%	35.8%	54.6%	51.3%
LIMSI FNMT	72.4%	63.4%	73.2%	34.8%	43.0%	42.2%	41.4%	55.5%	53.2%
LIUM FNMT	**78.0%**	**67.0%**	**78.6%**	37.2%	38.6%	38.0%	35.6%	56.1%	53.6%
TILDE hybrid	69.0%	61.8%	69.4%	35.4%	**54.6%**	**53.0%**	**53.2%**	**58.3%**	**56.8%**

Table 10: Sentence pair evaluation for English-to-Latvian (B-set).

	nouns	adjectives			verbs			mean
System	case	gender	number	case	number	person	tense	
Moses baseline	.467	.738	.717	.753	.271	.352	.285	.512
TILDE PBMT	.436	.755	.735	.768	.254	.337	.258	.506
NMT words	.385	.751	.732	.764	.329	.353	.337	.522
UEDIN NMT	.234	.598	.596	.628	.115	.190	.114	.354
LIMSI NMT	.255	.616	.610	.644	.139	.221	.134	.374
LIMSI FNMT	.233	**.587**	.582	.612	.117	.182	.113	.346
LIUM FNMT	.213	.608	.606	.643	.099	.163	.092	.346
TILDE hybrid	**.198**	**.587**	**.581**	**.608**	**.088**	**.123**	**.090**	**.325**

Table 11: Sentence group evaluation for English-to-Latvian with Entropy (C-set).

pology derived from the MQM proposal[12] and adapted to the English:Croatian pair – morphological errors mostly correspond to "word form" errors and are too subtle to be automatically detected. A common finding of these studies is that NMT generates better agreements than alternatives such as PBMT or Hierarchical MT.

Test suites The work of Isabelle et al. (2017); Burchardt et al. (2017) resuscitates an old tradition of using carefully designed test suites King and Falkedal (1990); Lehmann et al. (1996) to explore the ability of NMT to handle specific classes of difficulties. Test suites typically include a small set of handcrafted sentences for each targeted type of difficulty. For instance, Isabelle et al. (2017) focuses on translating from English into French and is based on a set of 108 short sentences illustrating situations of morphosyntactic, lexico-syntactic and syntactical divergences between these two languages. Assessing a system's ability to handle these difficulties requires a human judge to decide whether the automated translation has successfully "crossed" the bridge between languages.[13] A similar methodology is used in the work of Burchardt et al. (2017), who use a test suite of approximately 800 segments covering a wide array of translation difficulties for the pair English-German. Test suites enable to directly evaluate and compare specific abilities of MT Engines, including morphological competences: again, both studies found that NMT is markedly better than PBMT when it comes to phenomena such as word agreement. The downside is the requirement to have expert linguists prepare the data as well as evaluate the success of the MT system, which is a rather expensive price to pay to get a diagnostic evaluation.

Automatic test suites The work by Linzen et al. (2016) specifically looks at the prediction of the correct agreement features in increasingly complex contexts generated by augmenting the distance between the head and its dependent and the number of intervening distractors. A language model is deemed correct if it scores the correct agreement higher than any wrong one. One intriguing finding of this study is the very good performance of RNNs, provided that they receive the right kind of feedback in training. A similar approach is adapted for MT by Sennrich (2017), who looks at a wider range of phenomena. Contrastive pairs as automatically produced as follows: given a correct (source, target) pair $p = (\mathbf{f}, \mathbf{e})$, introduce one error in $\mathbf{e}$ yielding an alternative couple $p' = (\mathbf{f}, \mathbf{e}')$. A system is deemed to perform correctly wrt. this contrastive pair if it scores p higher than p'. This approach is fully automatic, looks at a wide range of contexts and phenomena and

---

[12] http://www.qt21.eu/mqm-definition

[13] Note that this is a *local* evaluation – a system can produce a bad overall translation, yet pass the test.

also enables to focus on specific errors types; a downside is the fact that the evaluation never considers whether **e** is the system's best choice given source **f**. Regarding specifically morphology, this study mostly considers (subject-verb, as well as modifier-head noun) agreement errors, but only compares error rates of variants of NMT systems.

A typology of evaluation protocols The variety of evaluation protocols found in the literature can be categorized along the following dimensions:

- *holistic* vs *analytic*: a holistic metric provides a global sentence- or document-level score, of which the morphological ability is only one part; an analytic metric focuses on specific difficulties;

- *coarse* vs *fine-grain*: a coarse (analytic) metric only provides global appreciation of morphological competence; while a fine-grain metric distinguishes various types of errors;

- *natural* vs *hand-crafted* vs *artificial*: for the sake of this study, this distinction relates to the design of the test sentences – were they invented for the purpose of the evaluation or found in a corpus, or even generated using automatic processing ?

- *automatic* vs *human-judgment*: is scoring fully automatic or is a human judge involved ?

- scores can be distance-based, such as a global comparison with a reference translation, or a Boolean value that denotes success or failure wrt. a local test, or based on a comparison of model scores;

Based on this analysis, the work reported here is analytic/fine-grain, uses artificial data, and computes automatic scores based on a local comparison with an expected value (mostly). This is the only one of that kind we are aware of.

5 Conclusion and Outlook

In this paper, we have presented a new protocol for evaluating the morphological competence of a Machine Translation system, with the aim to measure progresses in handling complex morphological phenomena in the source or the target language. We have presented preliminary experiments for two language pairs, which show that NMT systems with BPE outperform in many ways the phrase-based MT systems. Interestingly, they also reveal subtle differences among NMT systems and indicate specific areas where improvements are still needed. This work will be developed in three main directions:

- improve the generation and scoring algorithms: our procedure for generating sentences relies on automatic morphological analysis, which can be error prone, and on crude heuristics. While these two sources of noise likely have a small impact on the final results, which represent an average over a large number of sentences, we would like to better evaluate these effects, and, if needed, apply the necessary fixes;

- refine our analysis of automatic scores: the numbers reported in § 3 are averages over multiple sentences, and could be subjected to more analyses such as looking more precisely at OOVs, or taking frequency effects in considerations. This would allow to assess a system's ability to generate the right form for frequent vs rare vs unseen lemmas or morphological features. Frequency is also often correlated with regularity, and we also would like to assess morphological competence along those lines. Likewise, analyzing performance in agreement tests with respect to the distance between two coordinated nouns or verbs might also be revealing.

- increase the set of tests: we have focused on translating English into two MRLs having similar properties. Future work includes the generation of additional inflectional contrasts (introducing for instance mood or aspect, which are morphologically marked in many languages) as well as derivational contrasts (such as diminutives for nouns, or antonyms for adjectives). Again, this implies to improve our scoring and generation algorithms, and to adapt them to new languages.

Acknowledgements

The authors thank the participants to the WMT'17 News Translation task who kindly translated our test sets into Latvian and Czech. This work has been partly funded by the European Union's Horizon 2020 research and innovation programme under grant agreement No. 645452 (QT21).

References

Dzmitry Bahdanau, Kyunghyun Cho, and Yoshua Bengio. 2014. Neural machine translation by jointly learning to align and translate. *CoRR* abs/1409.0473.

Satanjeev Banerjee and Alon Lavie. 2005. METEOR: An automatic metric for MT evaluation with improved correlation with human judgments. In *Proceedings of the ACL Workshop on Intrinsic and Extrinsic Evaluation Measures for Machine Translation*. Ann Arbor, Michigan, pages 65–72.

Luisa Bentivogli, Arianna Bisazza, Mauro Cettolo, and Marcello Federico. 2016. Neural versus phrase-based machine translation quality: a case study. In *Proceedings of the 2016 Conference on Empirical Methods in Natural Language Processing*. Austin, Texas, pages 257–267.

Alexandra Birch and Miles Osborne. 2010. LRscore for evaluating lexical and reordering quality in MT. In *Proceedings of the Joint Fifth Workshop on Statistical Machine Translation and MetricsMATR*. Association for Computational Linguistics, WMT '10, pages 327–332.

Arianna Bisazza and Marcello Federico. 2016. A survey of word reordering in statistical machine translation: Computational and language phenomena. *Computational Linguistics* 42(2):163–205.

Ondřej Bojar, Christian Buck, Rajen Chatterjee, Christian Federmann, Yvette Graham, Barry Haddow, Matthias Huck, Antonio Jimeno Yepes, Philipp Koehn, Julia Kreutzer, Varvara Logacheva, Christof Monz, Matteo Negri, Aurélie Névéol, Mariana Neves, Matt Post, Stefan Riezler, Artem Sokolov, Lucia Specia, Marco Turchi, and Karin Verspoor. 2017a. Proceedings of the second conference on machine translation, WMT 2017. The Association for Computational Linguistics, Copenhagen, Denmark.

Ondřej Bojar, Rajen Chatterjee, Christian Federmann, Yvette Graham, Barry Haddow, Matthias Huck, Antonio Jimeno Yepes, Philipp Koehn, Varvara Logacheva, Christof Monz, Matteo Negri, Aurelie Neveol, Mariana Neves, Martin Popel, Matt Post, Raphael Rubino, Carolina Scarton, Lucia Specia, Marco Turchi, Karin Verspoor, and Marcos Zampieri. 2016. Findings of the 2016 conference on machine translation. In *Proceedings of the First Conference on Machine Translation*. Association for Computational Linguistics, Berlin, Germany, pages 131–198.

Ondřej Bojar, Tom Kocmi, David Mareček, Roman Sudarikov, and Dusan Varis. 2017b. CUNI submission in WMT17: Chimera goes neural. In *Proceedings of the Second Conference on Machine Translation (WMT'17)*. Copenhagen, Denmark.

Ondřej Bojar, Rudolf Rosa, and Tamchyna Aleš. 2013. Chimera – three heads for English-to-Czech translation. In *Proceedings of the Eight Workshop on Statistical Machine Translation*. Sofia, Bulgaria, pages 92–98.

Aljoscha Burchardt, Vivien Macketanz, Jon Dehdari, Georg Heigold, Jan-Thorsten Peter, and Philip Williams. 2017. A Linguistic Evaluation of Rule-Based, Phrase-Based, and Neural MT Engines. In *Proceedings of the European Conference on Machine Translation*. Prague, Czech Republic, EAMT'17, pages 159–170.

Franck Burlot, Pooyan Safari, Matthieu Labeau, Alexandre Allauzen, and François Yvon. 2017. LIMSI@WMT'17. In *Proceedings of the Second Conference on Machine Translation (WMT'17)*. Copenhagen, Denmark.

Ozan Caglayan, Mercedes García-Martínez, Adrien Bardet, Walid Aransa, Fethi Bougares, and Loïc Barrault. 2017. NMTPY: A Flexible Toolkit for Advanced Neural Machine Translation Systems. *arXiv preprint arXiv:1706.00457* .

Chris Callison-Burch, Cameron Fordyce, Philipp Koehn, Christof Monz, and Josh Schroeder. 2007. (meta-) evaluation of machine translation. In *Proceedings of the Second Workshop on Statistical Machine Translation*. Prague, Czech Republic, pages 136–158.

Kyunghyun Cho, Bart van Merrienboer, Dzmitry Bahdanau, and Yoshua Bengio. 2014. On the properties of neural machine translation: Encoder–decoder approaches. In *Proceedings of SSST-8, Eighth Workshop on Syntax, Semantics and Structure in Statistical Translation*. Doha, Qatar, pages 103–111.

Marta. R Costa-jussà. 2017. Why Catalan-Spanish neural machine translation ? analysis, comparison and combination with standard rule and phrase-based technologies. In *Proceedings of the Fourth Workshop on NLP for Similar Languages, Varieties and Dialects (VarDial)*. Association for Computational Linguistics, pages 55–62.

Mercedes García-Martínez, Ozan Caglayan, Walid Aransa, Adrien Bardet, Fethi Bougares, and Loïc Barrault. 2017. Lium machine translation systems for wmt17 news translation task. In *Proceedings of the Second Conference on Machine Translation*. Copenhagen, Denmark.

Kenneth Heafield. 2011. KenLM: Faster and Smaller Language Model Queries. In *Proceedings of the Sixth Workshop on Statistical Machine Translation*. Edinburgh, Scotland, pages 187–197.

Jindrich Helcl and Jindřich Libovický. 2017. Neural monkey: An open-source tool for sequence learning. *Prague Bulletin of Mathematical Linguistics* 107:1–11.

Pierre Isabelle, Colin Cherry, and George Foster. 2017. A challenge set approach to evaluating machine translation. *ArXiv e-prints* .

Margaret King and Kirsten Falkedal. 1990. Using test suites in evaluation of machine translation systems. In *COLNG 1990 Volume 2: Papers presented to the 13th International Conference on Computational Linguistics*.

Filip Klubička, Antonio Toral Ruiz, and Víctor M. Sánchez-Cartagena. 2017. Fine-grained human evaluation of neural versus phrase-based machine translation. In *Proceedings of the European Conference on Machine Translation*. Prague, Czech Republic, EAMT'17, pages 121—-132.

Philipp Koehn. 2010. *Statistical Machine Translation.* Cambridge University Press.

Sabine Lehmann, Stephan Oepen, Sylvie Regnier-prost, Klaus Netter, Veronika Lux, Judith Klein, Kirsten Falkedal, Frederik Fouvry, Dominique Estival, Eva Dauphin, Hervé Compagnion, Judith Baur, Lorna Balkan, and Doug Arnold. 1996. TSLNP – test suites for natural language processing. In *Proceedings of the 16th International Conference on Computational Linguistics (COLING 96)*. pages 711–716.

Tal Linzen, Emmanuel Dupoux, and Yoav Goldberg. 2016. Assessing the ability of LSTMs to learn syntax-sensitive dependencies. *Transactions of the Association for Computational Linguistics* 4:521–535.

Chi-kiu Lo and Dekai Wu. 2011. MEANT: an inexpensive, high-accuracy, semi-automatic metric for evaluating translation utility based on semantic roles. In *Proceedings of the 49th Annual Meeting of the Association for Computational Linguistics: Human Language Technologies*. Association for Computational Linguistics, pages 220–229.

Peter H. Matthews. 1974. *Morphology.* Cambridge University Press.

George A. Miller. 1995. Wordnet: A lexical database for english. *Communications of the ACM* 38(11):39–41.

Peteris Paikens, Laura Rituma, and Lauma Pretkalnina. 2013. Morphological analysis with limited resources: Latvian example. In *Proc. NODALIDA*. pages 267–277.

Kishore Papineni, Salim Roukos, Todd Ward, and Wei-Jing Zhu. 2002. BLEU: a method for automatic evaluation of machine translation. In *Proceedings of the 40th Annual Meeting on Association for Computational Linguistics*. Association for Computational Linguistics, Stroudsburg, PA, USA, pages 311–318.

Jan-Thorsten Peter, Tamer Alkhouli, Hermann Ney, Matthias Huck, Fabienne Braune, Alexander Fraser, Aleš Tamchyna, Ondřej Bojar, Barry Haddow,

Rico Sennrich, Frédéric Blain, Lucia Specia, Jan Niehues, Alex Waibel, Alexandre Allauzen, Lauriane Aufrant, Franck Burlot, Elena Knyazeva, Thomas Lavergne, François Yvon, Mārcis Pinnis, and Stella Frank. 2016. The QT21/HimL combined machine translation system. In *Proceedings of the First Conference on Machine Translation*. Association for Computational Linguistics, Berlin, Germany, pages 344–355.

Jan-Thorsten Peter, Hermann Ney, Ondřej Bojar, Ngoc-Quan Pham, Jan Niehues, Alex Waibel, Franck Burlot, François Yvon, Mārcis Pinnis, Valters Šics, Joost Bastings, Miguel Rios, Wilker Aziz, Philip Williams, Frédéric Blain, and Lucia Specia. 2017. The QT21 Combined Machine Translation System for English to Latvian. In *Proceedings of the Second Conference on Machine Translation (WMT'17)*. Copenhagen, Denmark.

Mārcis Pinnis, Rihards Krišlauks, Toms Miks, Daiga Deksne, and Valters Šics. 2017. Tilde's Machine Translation Systems for WMT 2017. In *Proceedings of the Second Conference on Machine Translation (WMT 2017), Volume 2: Shared Task Papers*. Copenhagen, Denmark.

Maja Popović and Hermann Ney. 2011. Towards automatic error analysis of machine translation output. *Computational Linguistics* 37(4):657–688.

Helmut Schmid. 1994. Probabilistic part-of-speech tagging using decision trees. In *Proceedings of International Conference on New Methods in Language Processing*. Manchester, UK.

Rico Sennrich. 2017. How grammatical is character-level neural machine translation? assessing mt quality with contrastive translation pairs. In *Proceedings of the 15th Conference of the European Chapter of the Association for Computational Linguistics: Volume 2, Short Papers*. Association for Computational Linguistics, pages 376–382.

Rico Sennrich, Alexandra Birch, Anna Currey, Ulrich Germann, Barry Haddow, Antonio Valerio Miceli Barone, and Philip Williams. 2017a. The University of Edinburgh's Neural MT Systems for WMT17. In *Proceedings of the Second Conference on Machine Translation, Volume 2: Shared Task Papers*. Copenhagen, Denmark.

Rico Sennrich, Orhan Firat, Kyunghyun Cho, Alexandra Birch, Barry Haddow, Julian Hitschler, Marcin Junczys-Dowmunt, Samuel Läubli, Antonio Valerio Miceli Barone, Jozef Mokry, and Maria Nadejde. 2017b. Nematus: a toolkit for neural machine translation. In *Proceedings of the Software Demonstrations of the 15th Conference of the European Chapter of the Association for Computational Linguistics*. Association for Computational Linguistics, Valencia, Spain, pages 65–68.

Rico Sennrich, Barry Haddow, and Alexandra Birch. 2016a. Edinburgh Neural Machine Translation Systems for WMT 16. In *Proceedings of the First Conference on Machine Translation*. Berlin, Germany, pages 371–376.

Rico Sennrich, Barry Haddow, and Alexandra Birch. 2016b. Neural machine translation of rare words with subword units. In *Proceedings of the 54th Annual Meeting of the Association for Computational Linguistics (Volume 1: Long Papers)*. Association for Computational Linguistics, pages 1715–1725.

Matthew Snover, Bonnie Dorr, Richard Schwartz, Linnea Micciulla, and John Makhoul. 2006. A study of translation edit rate with targeted human annotation. In *Proceedings of the seventh conference of the Association for Machine Translation in the America (AMTA)*. Boston, Massachusetts, USA, pages 223–231.

Miloš Stanojević and Khalil Sima'an. 2014. Fitting sentence level translation evaluation with many dense features. In *Proceedings of the 2014 Conference on Empirical Methods in Natural Language Processing*. Doha, Qatar, EMNLP, pages 202–206.

Jana Straková, Milan Straka, and Jan Hajič. 2014. Open-Source Tools for Morphology, Lemmatization, POS Tagging and Named Entity Recognition. In *Proc. ACL: System Demos*. Baltimore, MA, pages 13–18.

Sara Stymne. 2011. Blast: A tool for error analysis of machine translation output. In *Proceedings of the 49th Annual Meeting of the Association for Computational Linguistics: Human Language Technologies: Systems Demonstrations*. Association for Computational Linguistics, HLT '11, pages 56–61.

Aleš Tamchyna, Roman Sudarikov, Ondřej Bojar, and Alexander Fraser. 2016. Cuni-lmu submissions in wmt2016: Chimera constrained and beaten. In *Proceedings of the First Conference on Machine Translation*. Berlin, Germany, pages 385–390.

Antonio Toral Ruiz and M. Víctor Sánchez-Cartagena. 2017. A multifaceted evaluation of neural versus phrase based machine translation for 9 language directions. In *Proceedings of the 15th Conference of the European Chapter of the Association for Computational Linguistics: Volume 1, Long Papers*. Association for Computational Linguistics (ACL), Valencia, Spain, pages 1063–1073.

David Vilar, J. Xu, D.H. Luis Fernando, and Hermann Ney. 2006. Error analysis of statistical machine translation output. In *Proceedings of the Fifth International Conference on Language Resources and Evaluation*. Genoa, Italy, LREC'06.

Weiyue Wang, Jan-Thorsten Peter, Hendrik Rosendahl, and Hermann Ney. 2016. CharacTer: Translation Edit Rate on Character Level. In *Proceedings of the First Conference on Machine Translation*. Berlin, Germany, WMT, pages 505–510.

Target-side Word Segmentation Strategies
for Neural Machine Translation

Matthias Huck, Simon Riess, Alexander Fraser

Center for Information and Language Processing
LMU Munich
Munich, Germany

{mhuck,fraser}@cis.lmu.de,riess.simon@campus.lmu.de

Abstract

For efficiency considerations, state-of-the-art neural machine translation (NMT) requires the vocabulary to be restricted to a limited-size set of several thousand symbols. This is highly problematic when translating into inflected or compounding languages. A typical remedy is the use of subword units, where words are segmented into smaller components. Byte pair encoding, a purely corpus-based approach, has proved effective recently.

In this paper, we investigate word segmentation strategies that incorporate more linguistic knowledge. We demonstrate that linguistically informed target word segmentation is better suited for NMT, leading to improved translation quality on the order of magnitude of $+0.5$ BLEU and -0.9 TER for a medium-scale English→German translation task.

Our work is important in that it shows that linguistic knowledge can be used to improve NMT results over results based only on the language-agnostic byte pair encoding vocabulary reduction technique.

1 Introduction

Inflection and nominal composition are morphological processes which exist in many natural languages. Machine translation into an inflected language or into a compounding language must be capable of generating words from a large vocabulary of valid word surface forms, or ideally even be open-vocabulary. In NMT, though, dealing with a very large number of target symbols is expensive in practice.

While, for instance, a standard dictionary of German, a compounding language, may cover 140 000 vocabulary entries,[1] NMT on off-the-shelf GPU hardware is nowadays typically only tractable with target vocabularies below 100 000 symbols.

This issue is made worse by the fact that compound words are not a closed set. More frequently occurring compound words may be covered in a standard dictionary (e.g., "Finanztransaktionssteuer", English: "financial transaction tax"), but the compounding process allows for words to be freely joined to form new ones (e.g., "Finanztransaktionssteuerzahler", English: "financial transaction tax payer"), and compounding is highly productive in a language like German.

Furthermore, a dictionary lists canonical word forms, many of which can have many inflected variants, with morphological variation depending on case, number, gender, tense, aspect, mood, and so on. The German language has four cases, three grammatical genders, and two numbers. German exhibits a rich amount of morphological word variations also in the verbal system. A machine translation system should ideally be able to produce any permissible compound word, and all inflections for each canonical form of all words (including compound words).

Previous work has drawn on byte pair encoding to obtain a fixed-sized vocabulary of subword units. In this paper, we investigate word segmentation strategies for NMT which are linguistically more informed. Specifically, we explore and empirically compare:

- Compound splitting.
- Suffix splitting.
- Prefix splitting.
- Byte pair encoding (BPE).
- Cascaded applications of the above.

---

[1] Duden, 26th ed., 2013, cf. http://www.duden.de/ueber_duden/auflagengeschichte.

Proceedings of the Conference on Machine Translation (WMT), Volume 1: Research Papers, pages 56–67
Copenhagen, Denmark, September 7–11, 2017. ©2017 Association for Computational Linguistics

Our empirical evaluation focuses on target-language side segmentation, with English→German translation as the application task. Our proposed approaches improve machine translation quality by up to +0.5 BLEU and −0.9 TER, respectively, compared with using plain BPE.

Advantages of linguistically-informed target word segmentation in NMT are:

1. *Better vocabulary reduction* for practical tractability of NMT, as motivated above.

2. *Reduction of data sparsity.* Learning lexical choice is more difficult for rare words that appear in few training samples (e.g., rare compounds), or when a single form from a source language with little inflection (such as English) has many target-side translation options which are morphological variants. Splitting compounds and separating affixes from stems can ease lexical selection.

3. *Better open vocabulary translation.* With target-side word segmentation, the NMT system can generate sequences of word pieces at test time that have not been seen in this combination in training. It may produce new compounds, or valid morphological variants that were not present in the training corpus, e.g. by piecing together a stem with an inflectional suffix in a new, but linguistically admissible way. Using a linguistically informed segmentation should better allow the system to try to learn the linguistic processes of word formation.

2 Word Segmentation Strategies

2.1 Byte Pair Encoding

A technique in the manner of the Byte Pair Encoding (BPE) compression algorithm (Gage, 1994) can be adopted in order to segment words into smaller subword units, as suggested by Sennrich et al. (2016b). The BPE word segmenter conceptionally proceeds by first splitting all words in the whole corpus into individual characters. The most frequent adjacent pairs of symbols are then consecutively merged, until a specified limit of merge operations has been reached. Merge operations are not applied across word boundaries. The merge operations learned on a training corpus can be stored and applied to other data, such as test sets.

suffixes
-e, -em, -en, -end, -enheit, -enlich, -er, -erheit, -erlich, -ern, -es, -est, -heit, -ig, -igend, -igkeit, -igung, -ik, -isch, -keit, -lich, -lichkeit, -s, -se, -sen, -ses, -st, -ung

prefixes
ab-, an-, anti-, auf-, aus-, auseinander-, außer-, be-, bei-, binnen-, bitter-, blut-, brand-, dar-, des-, dis-, durch-, ein-, empor-, endo-, ent-, entgegen-, entlang-, entzwei-, epi-, er-, extra-, fehl-, fern-, fest-, fort-, frei-, für-, ge-, gegen-, gegenüber-, grund-, heim-, her-, hetero-, hin-, hinter-, hinterher-, hoch-, homo-, homöo-, hyper-, hypo-, inter-, intra-, iso-, kreuz-, los-, miss-, mit-, mono-, multi-, nach-, neben-, nieder-, non-, pan-, para-, peri-, poly-, post-, pro-, prä-, pseudo-, quasi-, schein-, semi-, stock-, sub-, super-, supra-, tief-, tod-, trans-, ultra-, um-, un-, unab-, unan-, unauf-, unaus-, unbe-, unbei-, undar-, undis-, undurch-, unein-, unent-, uner-, unfehl-, unfort-, unfrei-, unge-, unher-, unhin-, unhinter-, unhoch-, unmiss-, unmit-, unnach-, unter-, untief-, unum-, ununter-, unver-, unvor-, unweg-, unwider-, unzer-, unzu-, unüber-, ur-, ver-, voll-, vor-, voran-, voraus-, vorüber-, weg-, weiter-, wider-, wieder-, zer-, zu-, zurecht-, zurück-, zusammen-, zuwider-, über-

Table 1: German affixes which our suffix splitter and prefix splitter separate from the word stem.

An advantage of BPE word segmentation is that it allows for a reduction of the amount of distinct symbols to a desired order of magnitude. The technique is purely frequency-based. Frequent sequences of characters will be joined through the merge operations, resulting in common words not being segmented. Words containing rare combinations of characters will not be fully merged from the character splitting all the way back to their original form. They will remain split into two or more subword units in the BPE-segmented data. On the downside, the BPE algorithm has no notion of morphosyntax, narrowing down its capabilities at modeling inflection and compounding. BPE also has no guidelines for splitting words into syllables. This way no phonetic or semantic substructures are taken into account. Therefore BPE splits often appear arbitrary to the human reader, since it appears frequently that subword units ignore syllable boundaries entirely.

Nevertheless, NMT systems incorporating BPE word segmentation have achieved top translation quality in recent shared tasks (Sennrich et al., 2016a; Bojar et al., 2016). We designed our linguistically-informed segmentation techniques by looking at the shortcomings of BPE segmentations.

2.2 Compound Splitting

BPE word segmentation operates bottom-up from characters to larger units. Koehn and Knight (2003) have proposed a frequency-based word segmentation method that starts from the other end, top-down inspecting full words and looking into whether they are composed of parts which are proper words themselves. Any composed word is segmented into parts such that the geometric mean of word frequencies of its parts (counted in the original corpus) is maximized. This technique represents a suitable approach for compound splitting in natural language processing applications. It has been successfully applied in numerous statistical machine translation systems, mostly on the source language side, but sometimes also on the target side (Sennrich et al., 2015).

The difference in nature between BPE word segmentation and frequency-based compound splitting (bottom-up and top-down) leads to quite different results. While BPE tends to generate unintuitive splits, compound splitting nearly always comes up with reasonable word splits. On the other hand there are many possible intuitive word splits that compound splitting does not catch.

2.3 Suffix Splitting

Morphological variation in natural languages is often realized to a large extent through affixation. In the German language there are several suffixes that unambiguously mark a word as an adjective, noun, or verb. By splitting these telling suffixes, we can automatically include syntactic information. Even though this underlying relationship between suffix and morphological function is sometimes ambiguous—especially for verbs—reasonable guesses about the POS of a word with which we are not familiar are only possible by considering its suffix.

Information retrieval systems take advantage of this observation and reduce search queries to stemmed forms by means of simply removing common suffixes, prefixes, or both. The Porter stemming algorithm is a well-known affix stripping method (Porter, 1980). In such algorithms, some basic linguistic knowledge about the morphology of a particular language is taken into account in order to come up with a few handwritten rules which would detect common affixes and delete them. We can benefit from the same idea for the segmentation of word surface forms.

We have modified the Python implementation of the German Snowball stemming algorithm from NLTK[2] for our purposes. The Snowball stemmer removes German suffixes via some language-specific heuristics. In order to obtain a segmenter, we have altered the code to not drop suffixes, but to write them out separately from the stem. Our Snowball segmenter splits off the German suffixes that are shown in Table 1. Some of them are inflectional, others are used for nominalization or adjectivization. The suffix segmenter also splits sequential appearances of suffixes into multiple parts according to the Snowball algorithm's splitting steps, but always retaining a stem with a minimum length of at least three characters.

Table 2 shows some relationships between German suffixes and their English translations. Especially nominalizations and participles are particularly consistent, which makes translation rather unambiguous. Even though an exact translation from every German suffix to one specific English suffix cannot be established, this shows that a set of German suffixes translates into a set of English suffixes. Some suffixes indeed have an unambiguous translation like German *-los* to English *-less* or German *-end* to English *-ing*. These relationships might be due to the shared roots of the German and English language. Especially for other Germanic languages this promises transferability of our results.

It seems to be a reasonable assumption that other languages also have a certain set of possible suffixes which correspond to each type of word. For these relationships our approach may be able to automatically and cheaply add (weak) POS information, which might improve translation quality, but this will require further investigation in future work.

We would also like to study the relationship between stemming quality and resulting NMT translation quality. Weissweiler and Fraser (2017) have introduced a new stemmer of German and showed that it performs better than Snowball using comparison with gold standards. This may serve as an interesting starting point.

2.4 Prefix Splitting

Similarly to our Snowball suffix segmenter, we have written a small script to split off prefixes.

---

[2]`http://www.nltk.org/_modules/nltk/stem/snowball.html`

German suffixes unambiguously marking nouns

-ung, -heit, -nis, -keit, -sal, -schaft, -ling, -tum

English nominalizations with *-ness* are translated consistently by adding one of these suffixes

busyness – Geschäftigkeit
abstractness – Abstraktheit
kindness – Freundlichkeit
coziness – Behaglichkeit
giftedness – Begabung
sadness – Traurigkeit
tiredness – Müdigkeit
laziness – Faulheit

But a simple mapping between German and English noun suffixes does not exist

Abholzung – deforestation
Segmentierung – segmentation
Trockenheit – aridity
Obrigkeit – autority
Genauigkeit – precision
Bündnis – alliance
Gefängnis – prison
Verhältnis – relationship

German suffixes typical for adjectives

-ig, -lig, -isch, -sam, -bar, -haft, -los

Adjective derivation using these suffixes

achtsam – mindful
wendig – agile
begehbar – accessible
sichtbar – visible
nahrhaft – nutricious
essbar – edible
fettig – greasy
ethisch – ethical
moralisch – morally
laienhaft – unprofessional

-los with consistent English counterpart *-less*

taktlos – tactless
reglos – motionless
rastlos – restless
schamlos – shameless

German participles ending with *-end*

hängend – hanging
stehend – standing
schlafend – sleeping
lachend – laughing

Table 2: Examples illustrating the use of German suffixes.

The common German verb prefix *ver-* shows no obvious pattern in English translations

verstehen – to understand
sich verirren – to get lost
vergehen – to vanish
sich versprechen – to misspeak oneself
verfehlen – to miss
aus Versehen – unintentionally
verbieten – to prohibit
vergessen – to forget

Another common German verb prefix, *be-*, also shows no obvious pattern

behaupten – to claim
beschuldigen – to accuse
bewerben – to apply for
beladen – to load
betonen – to emphasize
bewahren – to preserve

The common German prefix *auf-* (English: *on, up*) has relatively consistent pattern in English translation

aufstellen – to put up
aufsetzen – to sit up
aufgehen – to give up
aufstehen – to stand up
aufblasen – to blow up
aufgeben – to give up
aufbauen – to set up
aufhören – to stop

German verb *setzen* (English: *to sit down*) with different prefixes

absetzen – to drop off
besetzen – to occupy
ersetzen – to replace
zersetzen – to decompose
umsetzen – to realize
widersetzen – to defy

Table 3: Examples illustrating the use of German prefixes.

Here, we specifically target verb and adjective prefixes and thus only segment lowercase words, excluding nouns which are written in uppercase in German text. We consider the prefixes as shown in Table 1. We sort them descending by length, checking for longer prefix matches first. Negational prefixes (beginning with *un-*, but not *unter-*) are additionally segmented after *un-*; e.g., *unab-* becomes *un- ab-*. In case the remaining part starts with either of the two verb infixes *-zu-* or *-ge-*, we also segment after that infix. We require the final stem to be at least three characters long.

While suffixes tend to contain morphological information, German prefixes change—sometimes radically—the semantics of the word stem. Some prefixes, especially those indicating local relationships, have a relatively clear and consistent translation. On the other hand, certain prefixes change the meaning more subtly and also more ambiguously. Therefore some prefixes lead to a simple translation while others change the meaning too radically.

Table 3 shows how the meaning of German verbs can change by adding different prefixes to a common stem. The example for *setzen – to sit down* illustrates that each of the combinations is semantically so different from the others that their translations have to be learned separately. This also means that splitting the prefix might not benefit the machine translation system, since generalization is hardly possible.

The examples given in Table 3 also suggest that a single verb prefix may affect the semantics of the word in ambiguous ways when applied to different verb stems. The very common German prefix *ver-*, for instance, which often indicates an incorrectly performed action (like *sich versprechen – to misspeak oneself* or *verfehlen – to miss*), still has a lot of different applications. This variety shows that prefixes clearly carry information, but still it is highly ambiguous and therefore might not benefit the translation process.

The German prefix *auf – up, on* has a relatively unambiguous translation, though, and hence splitting it might support the machine translation system. A possible improvement might be only splitting these unambiguously translatable prefixes (which in general are prepositions indicating the direction of the altered verb), but this remains to be investigated in future research.

2.5 Cascaded Application of Segmenters

Affix splitting and compound splitting can be applied in combination, by cascading the segmenters and preprocessing the data first with the suffix splitter, then optionally with the prefix splitter, and then with the compound splitter. In a cascaded application, the compound splitter is applied to word stems only, and the counts for computing the geometric means of word frequencies for compound splitting are collected after affix splitting.

When cascading the compound splitter with affix splitting, we introduce a minor modification. Our standalone compound splitter takes the filler letter "*s*" and "*es*" into account, which often appear in between word parts in German noun compounding. For better consistency of the compound splitting component with affix splitting, we additionally allow for more fillers, namely: suffixes, suffixes followed by "*s*", and "*zu*".

The methods for compound splitting, suffix splitting, and prefix splitting provide linguistically more sound approaches for word segmentation, but they do not arbitrarily reduce the amount of distinct symbols. For a further reduction of the number of target-side symbols, we may want to apply a final BPE segmentation step on top of the other segmenters. BPE will not re-merge words that have been segmented before. It can benefit from the prior segmentation provided to it and come up with a potentially better sequence of merge operations. Affixes will be learned as subwords but not joined with the stem. This improves the quality of resulting BPE splits. BPE no longer combines arbitrary second to last syllables with their suffixes, which makes learning the other—non affix—syllables easier.

We deliberately decided against joint/bilingual BPE, for multiple reasons. (1.) In cascaded segmentations, BPE operations are learned from training data after previous splitters in the pipeline have been applied. With joint BPE, the source would be affected, being preprocessed slightly differently in different setups. Instead, we opted for conducting BPE-50K separately over English. The source is hence equal in all setups, which we believe renders the evaluation more sound. (2.) When tying source+target in joint-BPE, vocabulary sizes cannot be controlled independently on each side. Joint-BPE with 59500 operations for instance yields 46K German types in the data, but an English corpus containing only 26K types.

BPE	*sie alle versch ## icken vorsätzlich irreführende Dokumente an Kleinunternehmen in ganz Europa .*
compound + BPE	*sie alle verschicken vorsätzlich #L irre @@ führende Dokumente an #U klein @@ unter @@ nehmen in ganz Europa .*
suffix + BPE	*sie all $$e verschick $$en vorsätz $$lich irreführ $$end $$e Dokument $$e an Kleinunternehm $$en in ganz Europa .*
suffix + compound + BPE	*sie all $$e verschick $$en vorsätz $$lich #L Irre @@ führ $$end $$e Dokument $$e an #U klein @@ Unternehm $$en in ganz Europa .*
suffix + prefix + compound + BPE	*sie all $$e ver$$ schick $$en vor$$ sätz $$lich #L Irre @@ führ $$end $$e Dokument $$e an #U klein @@ Unternehm $$en in ganz Europa .*
English	*they all mail deliberately deceptive documents to small businesses across Europe .*

Table 4: Different word segmentation strategies applied to a training sentence. ## is a BPE split-point, ver§§ is prefix *ver*, $$en is the suffix *en*, #U and #L are upper and lower case indicators for compounds, @@ indicates a compound merge-point, @s@ would indicate a compound merged with the letter *s* between the parts, etc.

(3.) Joint-BPE may boost transliteration capabilities. Generally, we would however recommend to extract BPE operations monolingually to better capture the properties of the individual language. We argue that well justified segmentation cannot be language-independent. (4.) We would not expect fundamentally different findings when switching to joint-BPE everywhere.

2.6 Reversibility

Target-side word segmentation needs to be reversible in postprocessing. We introduce special markers to enable reversibility of word splits. For suffixes, we attach a marker to the beginning of each suffix token; for prefixes to the end of each split prefix.

Fillers within segmented compounds receive attached markers on either side. When a compound is segmented into parts with no filler between them, we place a separate special marker token in the middle which is not attached to any of the parts. It indicates the segmentation and has two advantages over attaching it to any of the parts: (1.) The tokens of the parts are exactly the same as when they appear as words outside of a compound. The NMT system does not perceive them as different symbols. (2.) There is more flexibility at producing new compounds that have not been seen in the training corpus. The NMT system can decide to place any symbol into a token sequence that would form a compound, even the ones which were never part of a compound in training. The vocabulary is more open in that respect.

We adhere to the same rationale for split markers in BPE word segmentation. A special marker token is placed separately between subword units, with whitespace around it. In our experience, attaching the marker to BPE subword units does not improve translation quality over our practice.

The compound splitter alters the casing of compound parts to the variants that appears most frequently in the corpus. When merging compounds in postprocessing, we need to know whether to lowercase or to uppercase the compound. We let the translation system decide and introduce another special annotation in order to allow for this. When we segment compounds, we always place an indicator symbol before the initial part of the split compound token sequence, which can be either #L or #U. It specifies the original casing of the compound (lower or upper).

The effect of different segmentation strategies on the word splits in an example sentence is shown in Table 4.

Preprocessing	#types	#tokens
tokenized	303 K	39 M
compound	139 K	45 M
suffix	217 K	54 M
suffix + compound	98 K	60 M
suffix + prefix + compound	88 K	63 M
BPE	46 K	42 M
compound + BPE	46 K	46 M
suffix + BPE	45 K	56 M
suffix + compound + BPE	43 K	60 M
suffix + prefix + compound + BPE	43 K	64 M

Table 5: Target-side training corpus statistics.

System	test2007		test2008	
	BLEU	TER	BLEU	TER
top 50K voc. (source & target)	25.5	60.9	25.2	60.9
BPE	25.8	60.7	25.6	60.9
compound + BPE	25.9	60.3	25.5	60.6
suffix + BPE	**26.3**	60.0	**26.0**	**60.1**
suffix + compound + BPE	26.2	**59.8**	25.8	60.2
suffix + prefix + compound + BPE	26.1	**59.8**	25.9	60.6
suffix + prefix + compound, 50K	25.9	59.9	25.5	60.3
phrase-based (Huck et al., 2015)	22.6	–	22.1	–

Table 6: English→German experimental results on Europarl (case-sensitive BLEU and TER).

3 Machine Translation Experiments

3.1 Experimental Setup

We conduct an empirical evaluation using encoder-decoder NMT with attention and gated recurrent units as implemented in Nematus (Sennrich et al., 2017). We train and test on English–German Europarl data (Koehn, 2005). The data is tokenized and frequent-cased using scripts from the Moses toolkit (Koehn et al., 2007). Sentences with length >50 after tokenization are excluded from the training corpus, all other sentences (1.7 M) are considered in training under every word segmentation scheme. We set the amount of merge operations for BPE to 50K. Corpus statistics of the German data after different preprocessings are given in Table 5. On the English source side, we apply BPE separately, also with 50K merge operations.

For comparison, we build a setup denoted as *top 50K voc. (source & target)* where we train on the tokenized corpus without any segmentation, limiting the vocabulary to the 50K most frequent words on each side and replacing rare words by *"UNK"*. In a setup denoted as *suffix + prefix + compound, 50K*, we furthermore examine whether BPE can be

omitted in a cascaded application of target word segmenters. Here, we use the top 50K target symbols after suffix, prefix, and compound splitting, but still apply BPE to the English source.

It is important to note that the amount of distinct target symbols in the setups ranges between 43K-46K; 50K for top-50K-voc systems. There are no massive vocabulary size differences. We always apply 50K BPE operations. Minor divergences in the number of types naturally occur amongst the various cascaded segmentations. The linguistically-informed splitters segment more, resulting in more tokens. We chose BPE-50K because the vocabulary is reasonably large while training fits onto GPUs with 8 GB of RAM. Larger vocabularies come at the cost of either more RAM or adjustment of other parameters (e.g., batch size or sentence length limit). From hyperparameter search over reduced vocabulary sizes we would not expect important insights, so we do not do this.

In all setups the training samples are always the same. We removed long sentences after tokenization but before segmentation, which affects all setups equally. No sentences are discarded after that stage (Nematus' maxlen > longest sequence in data).

We configure dimensions of 500 for the embeddings and 1024 for the hidden layer. We train with the Adam optimizer (Kingma and Ba, 2015), a learning rate of 0.0001, batch size of 50, and dropout with probability 0.2 applied to the hidden layer.[3] We validate on the *test2006* set after every 10 000 updates and do early stopping when the validation cost has not decreased for ten epochs.

We evaluate case-sensitive with BLEU (Papineni et al., 2002) and TER (Snover et al., 2006), computed over postprocessed hypotheses against the raw references with `mteval-v13a` and `tercom.7.25`, respectively.

3.2 Experimental Results

The translation results are reported in Table 6. Cascading compound splitting and BPE slightly improves translation quality as measured in TER. Cascading suffix splitting with BPE or with compound splitting plus BPE considerably improves translation quality by up to +0.5 BLEU or −0.9 TER over pure BPE. Adding in prefix splitting is less effective. We conjecture that prefix

---

[3]In preliminary experiments, we found dropout for source, target, and embeddings did not yield additional gains.

System \ Words in output	BPE-merged		compound-merged		suffix-merged		prefix-merged	
	tokens	types	tokens	types	tokens	types	tokens	types
BPE	1 075	1 032	–	–	–	–	–	–
	(1.9 %)	(13.4 %)	–	–	–	–	–	–
compound + BPE	271	255	2 766	1 738	–	–	–	–
	(0.5 %)	(3.3 %)	(4.9 %)	(22.6 %)	–	–	–	–
suffix + BPE	443	427	–	–	19 152	4 915	–	–
	(0.8 %)	(5.6 %)	–	–	(33.7 %)	(64.0 %)	–	–
suffix + compound + BPE	111	106	2 568	1 597	19 028	5 022	–	–
	(0.2 %)	(1.4 %)	(4.5 %)	(20.4 %)	(33.7 %)	(64.1 %)	–	–
suffix + prefix + compound + BPE	100	95	2 566	1 577	19 063	4 990	4 601	1 667
	(0.2 %)	(1.2 %)	(4.5 %)	(20.2 %)	(33.5 %)	(64.0 %)	(8.1 %)	(21.4 %)

Table 7: Statistics over words in system outputs for *test2008*, after desegmentation.

System \ Words in output	overall		
	tokens	types	ratio
BPE	57 334	7 700	0.134
compound + BPE	56 827	7 692	0.135
suffix + BPE	56 849	7 674	0.135
suffix + compound + BPE	56 461	7 839	0.139
suffix + prefix + compound + BPE	56 875	7 797	0.137
reference	57 073	8 975	0.157

Table 8: Overall types and tokens, measured on *test2008* after desegmentation (hypotheses translations) or after tokenization (reference).

System	avg. sent. length
BPE	28.7
compound + BPE	28.4
suffix + BPE	28.4
suffix + compound + BPE	28.2
suffix + prefix + compound + BPE	28.4
reference	28.5

Table 9: Average sentence lengths on *test2008*.

System \ Words in output	unseen vocabulary	
	tokens	types
BPE	197	194
	(0.3 %)	(2.5 %)
compound + BPE	280	257
	(0.5 %)	(3.3 %)
suffix + BPE	139	138
	(0.2 %)	(1.8 %)
suffix + compound + BPE	262	238
	(0.5 %)	(3.0 %)
suffix + prefix + compound + BPE	265	234
	(0.5 %)	(3.0 %)

Table 10: Productivity at open vocabulary translation, measured on *test2008* system outputs (after desegmentation) against the vocabulary of the tokenized training data.

splitting does not help because German verb prefixes often radically modify the meaning. When prefixes are split off, the decoder's embeddings layer may therefore become less effective (as the stem may be confusable with a completely different word).

We also evaluated casing manually. Manual inspection of the first fifty #L / #U occurrences in one of the hyptheses reveals that none is misplaced, and casing is always correctly indicated.

3.3 Analysis

In order to better understand the impact of the different target-side segmentation strategies, we analyze and compare the output of our main setups. Particularly, we turn our attention on the words in the translation outputs for the *test2008* set. For the analysis, in order to achieve comparable vocabularies in the various outputs, we apply desegmentation to all of the plain hypotheses produced by the systems. However, we do not run the full postprocessing pipeline: detruecasing and detokenization are omitted.

First, we count the number of words in the desegmented translations that have been merged together from subword components in the plain system outputs. Table 7 shows the statistics. The table rows contain the absolute amounts and relative frequencies of words with subword unit parts in the desegmented hypotheses, for running words in the text (types) and in terms of the vocabulary in the *test2008* translation output. The frequencies are relative to all words in the respective output. Note that when cascaded word segmentation was applied, a single desegmented word may be composed of multiple subword units that originate from different word splitters. We find that compared to the pure BPE system, many more words

OOV types	A	B	C	D	E
A	0	1621 (21.1 %)	1583 (20.6 %)	1584 (20.6 %)	1626 (21.1 %)
B	1612 (21.0 %)	0	1589 (20.7 %)	1469 (19.1 %)	1434 (18.7 %)
C	1559 (20.3 %)	1574 (20.5 %)	0	1451 (18.9 %)	1456 (19.0 %)
D	1726 (22.0 %)	1620 (20.7 %)	1617 (20.6 %)	0	1435 (18.3 %)
E	1725 (22.1 %)	1542 (19.8 %)	1579 (20.3 %)	1392 (17.9 %)	0
R	3641 (40.6 %)	3676 (41.0 %)	3624 (40.4 %)	3604 (40.2 %)	3634 (40.5 %)

Table 11: Systems compared against each other in terms of types found in *test2008* hypothesis translations, after desegmentation. (OOV words of output of vertical system wrt. vocabulary present in output of horizontal system.) *A*: BPE. *B*: compound + BPE. *C*: suffix + BPE. *D*: suffix + compound + BPE. *E*: suffix + prefix + compound + BPE. *R*: reference translation.

OOV tokens	A	B	C	D	E
A	0	1804 (3.1 %)	1763 (3.1 %)	1801 (3.1 %)	1826 (3.2 %)
B	1814 (3.2 %)	0	1793 (3.2 %)	1663 (2.9 %)	1612 (2.8 %)
C	1741 (3.1 %)	1768 (3.1 %)	0	1647 (2.9 %)	1648 (2.9 %)
D	1942 (3.4 %)	1803 (3.2 %)	1801 (3.2 %)	0	1565 (2.8 %)
E	1958 (3.4 %)	1734 (3.0 %)	1794 (3.2 %)	1554 (2.7 %)	0
R	4506 (7.9 %)	4582 (8.0 %)	4484 (7.9 %)	4484 (7.9 %)	4520 (7.9 %)

Table 12: Systems compared against each other in terms of tokens found in *test2008* hypothesis translations, after desegmentation.

Output similarity	A	B	C	D	E
A	100	61.6	61.3	60.4	60.1
B	61.6	100	61.4	62.0	62.1
C	61.3	61.4	100	62.5	62.9
D	60.5	62.0	62.5	100	63.0
E	60.1	62.1	62.9	63.0	100

Table 13: System outputs (after desegmentation) evaluated against each other with BLEU. (Hypothesis translation of vertical system against output of horizontal system as the reference in `multi-bleu.perl`.)

are merged from subword unit parts in the other systems.

Table 8 presents the overall amount of types and tokens in the hypothesis translations and in the reference. The pure BPE system exhibits the lowest type/token ratio, whereas the type/token ratio in the reference is higher than in all the machine translation outputs.

Average sentence lengths are given in Table 9. The pure BPE system produces sentences that are slightly longer than the ones in the reference. All other setups tend to be below the average reference sentence length, the shortest sentences being produced by the *suffix + compound + BPE* system.

Next, we look into how often the open vocabulary capabilities of the systems lead to the generation of words which are not present in the tokenized training corpus. We denote these words as "unseen". Table 10 reveals that only small fractions of the words formed from subword unit parts (as counted before, Table 7) are unseen. The relative frequency of produced unseen words is smaller than—or equal to—half a percent in the running text. The setups trained with compound-split target data produce unseen words a bit more often. While at first glance it might seem disappointing that the systems' open vocabulary capabilities do not come into effect more heavily, this observation however emphasizes that we have succeeded at training neural models that adhere to word formation processes which lead to valid forms.

A straightforward follow-up question is how lexically dissimilar the various system outputs are. In Tables 11 and 12, we compare all hypotheses pairwise against each other, measuring the amount of words in one hypothesis that does not appear in the vocabulary present in a translation from another system. We basically calculate cross-hypothesis out-of-vocabulary (OOV) rates. Table 11 shows the results on type level, Table 12 on token level. We furthermore compare against the reference. The system outputs are lexically quite dissimilar, but much closer to each other than to the reference.

We can finally follow the very same rationale by evaluating the system outputs against each other with BLEU, calculating the BLEU score of one hypothesis against another hypothesis rather than against a reference translation. The result, presented in Table 13, reaffirms that the different systems have each learned to translate in different ways, based on the respective segmentation of the training data.

Our cascaded *suffix + compound + BPE* target word segmentation strategy was employed for LMU Munich's participation in the WMT17 shared tasks on machine translation of news and of biomedical texts. We refer the reader to the system description paper (Huck et al., 2017a), where we include some interesting translation examples from the news translation task. We note that our system was ranked first in the human evaluation of the news task, despite having a lower BLEU score than Edinburgh's submission. BLEU, which tries to automatically predict how humans will evaluate quality, may unfairly penalize approaches like ours, but more study is needed.

4   Related Work

The SMT literature has a wide diversity of approaches in dealing with translation to morphologically rich languages. One common theme is modeling the relationship between lemmas and surface forms using morphological knowledge, e.g., (Toutanova and Suzuki, 2007; Koehn and Hoang, 2007; Bojar and Kos, 2010; Fraser et al., 2012; Weller et al., 2013; Tamchyna et al., 2016; Huck et al., 2017b). This problem has been studied for NMT by Tamchyna et al. (2017), and it would be interesting to compare with their approach.

Our work is closer in spirit to previous work on integrating morphological segmentation into SMT. Some examples of early work here include work on Arabic (Lee et al., 2003) and Czech (Goldwater and McClosky, 2005). More recent work includes work on Arabic, such as (Habash, 2007), and work on Turkish (Oflazer and Durgar El-Kahlout, 2007; Yeniterzi and Oflazer, 2010). Unsupervised morphological splitting, using, e.g., Morfessor has also been tried, particularly for dealing with agglutinative languages (Virpioja et al., 2007). Our work is motivated by the same linguistic observations as theirs.

Other studies, e.g., (Popović et al., 2006; Stymne, 2008; Cap et al., 2014), model German compounds by splitting them into single simple words in the SMT training data, and then predicting where to merge simple words as a postprocessing step (after SMT decoding). This has similarities to our use of compound splitting and markers in NMT.

There is also starting to be interest in alternatives to BPE in NMT. The Google NMT system (Wu et al., 2016) used wordpiece splitting, which is similar to but different from BPE and would be interesting to evaluate in future work. Ataman et al. (2017) considered both supervised and unsupervised splitting of agglutinative morphemes in Turkish, which is closely related to our ideas. An important difference here is that Turkish is an agglutinative language, while German has fusional inflection and very productive compounding.

We are also excited about early work on character-based NMT such as (Lee et al., 2016), which may eventually replace segmentation models like those in our work (or also replace BPE when linguistically aware segmentation is not available). However, at the current stage of research character-based approaches require very long training times and extensive optimization of hyperparameters to make them work, and still do not seem to be able to produce state-of-the-art translation quality on a wide range of tasks. More research is needed in making character-based NMT robust and accessible to many research groups.

5   Conclusion

Linguistically motivated target-side word segmentation improves neural machine translation into an inflected and compounding language. The system can learn linguistic word formation processes from the segmented data. For German, we have shown that cascading of suffix splitting—or suffix splitting and compound splitting—with BPE yields the best results. In future work we will consider alternative sources of linguistic knowledge about morphological processes and also evaluate high performance unsupervised segmentation.

Acknowledgments

This project has received funding from the European Union's Horizon 2020 research and innovation programme under grant agreement № 644402 (HimL). This project has received funding from the European Research Council (ERC) under the European Union's Horizon 2020 research and innovation programme (grant agreement № 640550).

References

Duygu Ataman, Matteo Negri, Marco Turchi, and Marcello Federico. 2017. Linguistically motivated vocabulary reduction for neural machine translation from turkish to english. In *Proceedings of EAMT*.

Ondřej Bojar, Rajen Chatterjee, Christian Federmann, Yvette Graham, Barry Haddow, Matthias Huck, Antonio Jimeno Yepes, Philipp Koehn, Varvara Logacheva, Christof Monz, Matteo Negri, Aurelie Neveol, Mariana Neves, Martin Popel, Matt Post, Raphael Rubino, Carolina Scarton, Lucia Specia, Marco Turchi, Karin Verspoor, and Marcos Zampieri. 2016. Findings of the 2016 Conference on Machine Translation. In *Proceedings of the First Conference on Machine Translation*, pages 131–198, Berlin, Germany. Association for Computational Linguistics.

Ondřej Bojar and Kamil Kos. 2010. 2010 Failures in English-Czech Phrase-Based MT. In *Proceedings of the Joint Fifth Workshop on Statistical Machine Translation and MetricsMATR*, pages 60–66, Uppsala, Sweden. Association for Computational Linguistics.

Fabienne Cap, Alexander Fraser, Marion Weller, and Aoife Cahill. 2014. How to produce unseen teddy bears: Improved morphological processing of compounds in SMT. In *Proceedings of the 14th Conference of the European Chapter of the Association for Computational Linguistics (EACL)*, pages 579–587.

Alexander Fraser, Marion Weller, Aoife Cahill, and Fabienne Cap. 2012. Modeling inflection and word-formation in SMT. In *Proceedings of the 13th Conference of the European Chapter of the Association for Computational Linguistics (EACL)*, pages 664–674, Avignon, France.

Philip Gage. 1994. A New Algorithm for Data Compression. *C Users J.*, 12(2):23–38.

Sharon Goldwater and David McClosky. 2005. Improving statistical MT through morphological analysis. In *Proceedings of the Human Language Technology Conference and Conference on Empirical Methods in Natural Language Processing (HLT-EMNLP)*, Vancouver, Canada.

Nizar Habash. 2007. Syntactic preprocessing for statistical machine translation. In *MTSUMMIT*, Copenhagen, Denmark.

Matthias Huck, Alexandra Birch, and Barry Haddow. 2015. Mixed-Domain vs. Multi-Domain Statistical Machine Translation. In *Proc. of MT Summit XV, vol.1: MT Researchers' Track*, pages 240–255, Miami, FL, USA.

Matthias Huck, Fabienne Braune, and Alexander Fraser. 2017a. LMU Munich's Neural Machine Translation Systems for News Articles and Health Information Texts. In *Proceedings of the Second Conference on Machine Translation*, Copenhagen, Denmark. Association for Computational Linguistics.

Matthias Huck, Aleš Tamchyna, Ondřej Bojar, and Alexander Fraser. 2017b. Producing Unseen Morphological Variants in Statistical Machine Translation. In *Proceedings of the 15th Conference of the European Chapter of the Association for Computational Linguistics: Volume 2, Short Papers*, pages 369–375, Valencia, Spain. Association for Computational Linguistics.

Diederik P. Kingma and Jimmy Ba. 2015. Adam: A method for stochastic optimization. *CoRR*, abs/1412.6980.

Philipp Koehn. 2005. Europarl: A Parallel Corpus for Statistical Machine Translation. In *Proceedings of the MT Summit X*, Phuket, Thailand.

Philipp Koehn and Hieu Hoang. 2007. Factored translation models. In *Conference on Empirical Methods in Natural Language Processing and Conference on Computational Natural Language Learning (EMNLP-CONLL)*, Prague, Czech Republic.

Philipp Koehn, Hieu Hoang, Alexandra Birch, Chris Callison-Burch, Marcello Federico, Nicola Bertoldi, Brooke Cowan, Wade Shen, Christine Moran, Richard Zens, Chris Dyer, Ondrej Bojar, Alexandra Constantin, and Evan Herbst. 2007. Moses: Open Source Toolkit for Statistical Machine Translation. In *Proceedings of the 45th Annual Meeting of the Association for Computational Linguistics Companion Volume Proceedings of the Demo and Poster Sessions*, pages 177–180, Prague, Czech Republic. Association for Computational Linguistics.

Philipp Koehn and Kevin Knight. 2003. Empirical Methods for Compound Splitting. In *Proceedings of the 10th Conference of the European Chapter of the Association for Computational Linguistics*, pages 187–194, Budapest, Hungary. Association for Computational Linguistics.

Jason Lee, Kyunghyun Cho, and Thomas Hofmann. 2016. Fully character-level neural machine translation without explicit segmentation. *CoRR*, abs/1610.03017.

Young-Suk Lee, Kishore Papineni, Salim Roukos, Ossama Emam, and Hany Hassan. 2003. Language model based Arabic word segmentation. In *Proceedings of the 41st Annual Meeting of the Association for Computational Linguistics (ACL)*, Sapporo, Japan.

Kemal Oflazer and Ilknur Durgar El-Kahlout. 2007. Exploring Different Representational Units in English-to-Turkish Statistical Machine Translation. In *Proceedings of the Second Workshop on Statistical Machine Translation*, pages 25–32, Prague, Czech Republic. Association for Computational Linguistics.

Kishore Papineni, Salim Roukos, Todd Ward, and Wei-Jing Zhu. 2002. Bleu: a Method for Automatic Evaluation of Machine Translation. In *Proceedings of 40th Annual Meeting of the Association for Computational Linguistics*, pages 311–318, Philadelphia, Pennsylvania, USA. Association for Computational Linguistics.

Maja Popović, Daniel Stein, and Hermann Ney. 2006. Statistical machine translation of German compound words. In *FinTAL - 5th International Conference on Natural Language Processing, Springer Verlag, LNCS*, pages 616–624, Turku, Finland.

Martin Porter. 1980. An algorithm for suffix stripping. *Program: electronic library and information systems*, 14(3):130–137.

Rico Sennrich, Orhan Firat, Kyunghyun Cho, Alexandra Birch, Barry Haddow, Julian Hitschler, Marcin Junczys-Dowmunt, Samuel Läubli, Antonio Valerio Miceli Barone, Jozef Mokry, and Maria Nadejde. 2017. Nematus: a Toolkit for Neural Machine Translation. In *Proceedings of the Software Demonstrations of the 15th Conference of the European Chapter of the Association for Computational Linguistics*, pages 65–68, Valencia, Spain. Association for Computational Linguistics.

Rico Sennrich, Barry Haddow, and Alexandra Birch. 2016a. Edinburgh Neural Machine Translation Systems for WMT 16. In *Proceedings of the First Conference on Machine Translation*, pages 371–376, Berlin, Germany. Association for Computational Linguistics.

Rico Sennrich, Barry Haddow, and Alexandra Birch. 2016b. Neural Machine Translation of Rare Words with Subword Units. In *Proceedings of the 54th Annual Meeting of the Association for Computational Linguistics (Volume 1: Long Papers)*, pages 1715–1725, Berlin, Germany. Association for Computational Linguistics.

Rico Sennrich, Philip Williams, and Matthias Huck. 2015. A tree does not make a well-formed sentence: Improving syntactic string-to-tree statistical machine translation with more linguistic knowledge. *Computer Speech & Language*, 32(1):27–45.

Matthew Snover, Bonnie Dorr, Richard Schwartz, Linnea Micciulla, and John Makhoul. 2006. A Study of Translation Edit Rate with Targeted Human Annotation. In *Proceedings of the Conference of the Association for Machine Translation in the Americas (AMTA)*, pages 223–231, Cambridge, MA, USA.

Sara Stymne. 2008. German compounds in factored statistical machine translation. In *GoTAL 2008: Proceedings of the 6th International Conference on Natural Language Processing*, pages 464–475. Springer Verlag.

Aleš Tamchyna, Alexander Fraser, Ondřej Bojar, and Marcin Junczys-Dowmunt. 2016. Target-Side Context for Discriminative Models in Statistical Machine Translation. In *Proceedings of the 54th Annual Meeting of the Association for Computational Linguistics (Volume 1: Long Papers)*, pages 1704–1714, Berlin, Germany. Association for Computational Linguistics.

Aleš Tamchyna, Marion Weller-Di Marco, and Alexander Fraser. 2017. Target-Side Inflection in Neural Machine Translation. In *Proceedings of the Second Conference on Machine Translation*, Copenhagen, Denmark. Association for Computational Linguistics.

Kristina Toutanova and Hisami Suzuki. 2007. Generating case markers in machine translation. In *Proceedings of the North American Chapter of the Association for Computational Linguistics and Human Language Technologies Conference (NAACL-HLT)*, pages 49–56, Rochester, NY.

Sami Virpioja, Jaakko J. Väyrynen, Mathias Creutz, and Markus Sadeniemi. 2007. Morphology-aware statistical machine translation based on morphs induced in an unsupervised manner. In *PROC. OF MT SUMMIT XI*, pages 491–498.

Leonie Weissweiler and Alexander Fraser. 2017. Developing a stemmer for German based on a comparative analysis of publicly available stemmers. In *Proceedings of the German Society for Computational Linguistics and Language Technology (GSCL)*, Berlin, Germany.

Marion Weller, Alexander Fraser, and Sabine Schulte im Walde. 2013. Using subcategorization knowledge to improve case prediction for translation to German. In *Proceedings of the 51st Annual Conference of the Association for Computational Linguistics (ACL)*, pages 593–603, Sofia, Bulgaria.

Yonghui Wu, Mike Schuster, Zhifeng Chen, Quoc V. Le, Mohammad Norouzi, Wolfgang Macherey, Maxim Krikun, Yuan Cao, Qin Gao, Klaus Macherey, Jeff Klingner, Apurva Shah, Melvin Johnson, Xiaobing Liu, Lukasz Kaiser, Stephan Gouws, Yoshikiyo Kato, Taku Kudo, Hideto Kazawa, Keith Stevens, George Kurian, Nishant Patil, Wei Wang, Cliff Young, Jason Smith, Jason Riesa, Alex Rudnick, Oriol Vinyals, Greg Corrado, Macduff Hughes, and Jeffrey Dean. 2016. Google's neural machine translation system: Bridging the gap between human and machine translation. *CoRR*, abs/1609.08144.

Reyyan Yeniterzi and Kemal Oflazer. 2010. Syntax-to-morphology mapping in factored phrase-based statistical machine translation from English to Turkish. In *Proceedings of the 48th Annual Conference of the Association for Computational Linguistics (ACL)*, Uppsala, Sweden. Association for Computational Linguistics.

Predicting Target Language CCG Supertags Improves Neural Machine Translation

Maria Nădejde[1] and **Siva Reddy**[1] and **Rico Sennrich**[1] and **Tomasz Dwojak**[1,2]
Marcin Junczys-Dowmunt[2] and **Philipp Koehn**[3] and **Alexandra Birch**[1]
[1]School of Informatics, University of Edinburgh
[2]Adam Mickiewicz University
[3]Dep. of Computer Science, Johns Hopkins University
{m.nadejde,siva.reddy, rico.sennrich, a.birch}@ed.ac.uk
{t.dwojak,junczys}@amu.edu.pl,phi@jhu.edu

Abstract

Neural machine translation (NMT) models are able to partially learn syntactic information from sequential lexical information. Still, some complex syntactic phenomena such as prepositional phrase attachment are poorly modeled. This work aims to answer two questions: 1) Does explicitly modeling target language syntax help NMT? 2) Is tight integration of words and syntax better than multitask training? We introduce syntactic information in the form of CCG supertags in the decoder, by interleaving the target supertags with the word sequence. Our results on WMT data show that explicitly modeling target-syntax improves machine translation quality for German→English, a high-resource pair, and for Romanian→English, a low-resource pair and also several syntactic phenomena including prepositional phrase attachment. Furthermore, a tight coupling of words and syntax improves translation quality more than multitask training. By combining target-syntax with adding source-side dependency labels in the embedding layer, we obtain a total improvement of 0.9 BLEU for German→English and 1.2 BLEU for Romanian→English.

1 Introduction

Sequence-to-sequence neural machine translation (NMT) models (Sutskever et al., 2014; Cho et al., 2014b; Bahdanau et al., 2015) are state-of-the-art on a multitude of language-pairs (Sennrich et al., 2016a; Junczys-Dowmunt et al., 2016). Part of the appeal of neural models is that they can learn to implicitly model phenomena which underlie high quality output, and some syntax is indeed captured by these models. In a detailed analysis, Bentivogli et al. (2016) show that NMT significantly improves over phrase-based SMT, in particular with respect to morphology and word order, but that results can still be improved for longer sentences and complex syntactic phenomena such as prepositional phrase (PP) attachment. Another study by Shi et al. (2016) shows that the encoder layer of NMT partially learns syntactic information about the source language, however complex syntactic phenomena such as coordination or PP attachment are poorly modeled.

Recent work which incorporates additional source-side linguistic information in NMT models (Luong et al., 2016; Sennrich and Haddow, 2016) show that even though neural models have strong learning capabilities, explicit features can still improve translation quality. In this work, we examine the benefit of incorporating global syntactic information on the target-side. We also address the question of how best to incorporate this information. For language pairs where syntactic resources are available on both the source and target-side, we show that approaches to incorporate source syntax and target syntax are complementary.

We propose a method for tightly coupling words and syntax by interleaving the target syntactic representation with the word sequence. We compare this to loosely coupling words and syntax using a multitask solution, where the shared parts of the model are trained to produce either a target sequence of words or supertags in a similar fashion to Luong et al. (2016).

We use CCG syntactic categories (Steedman, 2000), also known as *supertags*, to represent syntax explicitly. Supertags provide global syntactic information locally at the lexical level. They encode subcategorization information, capturing short and long range dependencies and attach-

Proceedings of the Conference on Machine Translation (WMT), Volume 1: Research Papers, pages 68–79
Copenhagen, Denmark, September 7–11, 2017. ©2017 Association for Computational Linguistics

ments, and also tense and morphological aspects of the word in a given context. Consider the sentence in Figure 1. This sentence contains two PP attachments and could lead to several disambiguation possibilities (*"in"* can attach to *"Netanyahu"* or *"receives"*, and *"of"* can attach to *"capital"*, *"Netanyahu"* or *"receives"*). These alternatives may lead to different translations in other languages. However the supertag $((S[dcl]\backslash NP)/PP)/NP$ of *"receives"* indicates that the preposition *"in"* attaches to the verb, and the supertag $(NP\backslash NP)/NP$ of *"of"* indicates that it attaches to *"capital"*, thereby resolving the ambiguity.

Our research contributions are as follows:

- We propose a novel approach to integrating target syntax at word level in the decoder, by interleaving CCG supertags in the target word sequence.

- We show that the target language syntax improves translation quality for German→English and Romanian→English as measured by BLEU. Our results suggest that a tight coupling of target words and syntax (by interleaving) improves translation quality more than the decoupled signal from multitask training.

- We show that incorporating source-side linguistic information is complimentary to our method, further improving the translation quality.

- We present a fine-grained analysis of SNMT and show consistent gains for different linguistic phenomena and sentence lengths.

2 Related work

Syntax has helped in statistical machine translation (SMT) to capture dependencies between distant words that impact morphological agreement, subcategorisation and word order (Galley et al., 2004; Menezes and Quirk, 2007; Williams and Koehn, 2012; Nadejde et al., 2013; Sennrich, 2015; Nadejde et al., 2016a,b; Chiang, 2007). There has been some work in NMT on modeling source-side syntax implicitly or explicitly. Kalchbrenner and Blunsom (2013); Cho et al. (2014a) capture the hierarchical aspects of language implicitly by using convolutional neural networks, while Eriguchi et al. (2016) use the parse tree of the source sentence to guide the recurrence and attention model in tree-to-sequence NMT. Luong

et al. (2016) co-train a translation model and a source-side syntactic parser which share the encoder. Our multitask models extend their work to attention-based NMT models and to predicting target-side syntax as the secondary task. Sennrich and Haddow (2016) generalize the embedding layer of NMT to include explicit linguistic features such as dependency relations and part-of-speech tags and we use their framework to show source and target syntax provide complementary information.

Applying more tightly coupled linguistic factors on the target for NMT has been previously investigated. Niehues et al. (2016) proposed a factored RNN-based language model for re-scoring an n-best list produced by a phrase-based MT system. In recent work, Martínez et al. (2016) implemented a factored NMT decoder which generated both lemmas and morphological tags. The two factors were then post-processed to generate the word form. Unfortunately no real gain was reported for these experiments. Concurrently with our work, Aharoni and Goldberg (2017) proposed serializing the target constituency trees and Eriguchi et al. (2017) model target dependency relations by augmenting the NMT decoder with a RNN grammar (Dyer et al., 2016). In our work, we use CCG supertags which are a more compact representation of global syntax. Furthermore, we do not focus on model architectures, and instead we explore the more general problem of including target syntax in NMT: comparing tightly and loosely coupled syntactic information and showing source and target syntax are complementary.

Previous work on integrating CCG supertags in factored phrase-based models (Birch et al., 2007) made strong independence assumptions between the target word sequence and the CCG categories. In this work we take advantage of the expressive power of recurrent neural networks to learn representations that generate both words and CCG supertags, conditioned on the entire lexical and syntactic target history.

3 Modeling Syntax in NMT

CCG is a lexicalised formalism in which words are assigned with syntactic categories, i.e., supertags, that indicate context-sensitive morpho-syntactic properties of a word in a sentence. The combinators of CCG allow the supertags to capture global syntactic constraints locally. Though NMT

Source-side

BPE:	Obama	receives	Net+	an+	yahu	in	the	capital	of	USA
IOB:	O	O	B	I	E	O	O	O	O	O
CCG:	NP	((S[dcl]\NP)/PP)/NP	NP	NP	NP	PP/NP	NP/N	N	(NP\NP)/NP	NP

Target-side

NP Obama ((S[dcl]\NP)/PP)/NP receives NP Net+ an+ yahu PP/NP in NP/N the N capital (NP\NP)/NP of NP USA

Figure 1: Source and target representation of syntactic information in syntax-aware NMT.

captures long range dependencies using long-term memory, short-term memory is cheap and reliable. Supertags can help by allowing the model to rely more on local information (short-term) and not having to rely heavily on long-term memory.

Consider a decoder that has to generate the following sentences:

1. What$_{(S[wq]/(S[q]/NP))/N}$ city is$_{(S[q]/PP)/NP}$ the Taj Mahal in?

2. Where$_{S[wq]/(S[q]/NP)}$ is$_{(S[q]/NP)/NP}$ the Taj Mahal?

If the decoding starts with predicting "*What*", it is ungrammatical to omit the preposition "*in*", and if the decoding starts with predicting "*Where*", it is ungrammatical to predict the preposition. Here the decision to predict "*in*" depends on the first word, a long range dependency. However if we rely on CCG supertags, the supertags of both these sequences look very different. The supertag (S[q]/PP)/NP for the verb "*is*" in the first sentence indicates that a preposition is expected in future context. Furthermore it is likely to see this particular supertag of the verb in the context of (S[wq]/(S[q]/NP))/N but it is unlikely in the context of S[wq]/(S[q]/NP). Therefore a succession of local decisions based on CCG supertags will result in the correct prediction of the preposition in the first sentence, and omitting the preposition in the second sentence. Since the vocabulary of CCG supertags is much smaller than that of possible words, the NMT model will do a better job at generalizing over and predicting the correct CCG supertags sequence.

CCG supertags also help during encoding if they are given in the input, as we saw with the case of PP attachment in Figure 1. Translation of the correct verb form and agreement can be improved with CCG since supertags also encode tense, morphology and agreements. For example, in the sentence "*It is going to rain*", the supertag (S[ng]\NP[expl])/(S[to]\NP) of "*going*"

indicates the current word is a verb in continuous form looking for an infinitive construction on the right, and an expletive pronoun on the left.

We explore the effect of target-side syntax by using CCG supertags in the decoder and by combining these with source-side syntax in the encoder, as follows.

Baseline decoder The baseline decoder architecture is a conditional GRU with attention ($cGRU_{attn}$) as implemented in the Nematus toolkit (Sennrich et al., 2017). The decoder is a recursive function computing a hidden state s_j at each time step $j \in [1, T]$ of the target recurrence. This function takes as input the previous hidden state s_{j-1}, the embedding of the previous target word y_{j-1} and the output of the attention model c_j. The attention model computes a weighted sum over the hidden states $h_i = [\overrightarrow{h_i}; \overleftarrow{h_i}]$ of the bi-directional RNN encoder. The function g computes the intermediate representation t_j and passes this to a *softmax* layer which first applies a linear transformation (W_o) and then computes the probability distribution over the target vocabulary. The training objective for the entire architecture is minimizing the discrete cross-entropy, therefore the loss l is the negative log-probability of the reference sentence.

$$s'_j = GRU_1(y_{j-1}, s_{j-1}) \tag{1}$$

$$c_j = ATT([h_1; ...; h_{|x|}], s'_j) \tag{2}$$

$$s_j = cGRU_{attn}(y_{j-1}, s_{j-1}, c_j) \tag{3}$$

$$t_j = g(y_{j-1}, s_j, c_j) \tag{4}$$

$$p_y = \prod_{j=1}^{T} p(y_j | x, y_{1:j-1}) = \prod_{j=1}^{T} softmax(t_j W_o) \tag{5}$$

$$l = -log(p_y) \tag{6}$$

Target-side syntax When modeling the target-side syntactic information we consider different

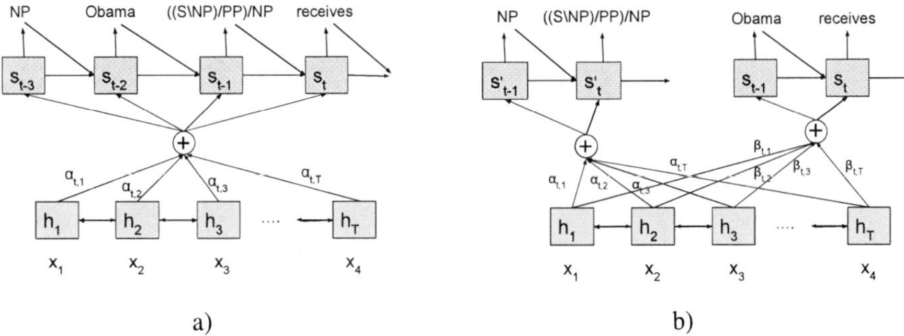

Figure 2: Integrating target syntax in the NMT decoder: a) interleaving and b) multitasking.

strategies of coupling the CCG supertags with the translated words in the decoder: interleaving and multitasking with shared encoder. In Figure 2 we represent graphically the differences between the two strategies and in the next paragraphs we formalize them.

- **Interleaving** In this paper we propose a tight integration in the decoder of the syntactic representation and the surface forms. Before each word of the target sequence we include its supertag as an extra token. The new target sequence y' will have the length $2T$, where T is the number of target words. With this representation, a single decoder learns to predict both the target supertags and the target words conditioned on previous syntactic and lexical context. We do not make changes to the baseline NMT decoder architecture, keeping equations (1) - (6) and the corresponding set of parameters unchanged. Instead, we augment the target vocabulary to include both words and CCG supertags. This results in a shared embedding space and the following probability of the target sequence y', where y'_j can be either a word or a tag:

$$y' = y_1^{tag}, y_1^{word}, \ldots, y_T^{tag}, y_T^{word} \qquad (7)$$

$$p_{y'} = \prod_j^{2T} p(y'_j | x, y'_{1:j-1}) \qquad (8)$$

At training time we pre-process the target sequence to add the syntactic annotation and then split only the words into *byte-pair-encoding* (BPE) (Sennrich et al., 2016b) sub-units. At

testing time we delete the predicted CCG supertags to obtain the final translation. Figure 1 gives an example of the target-side representation in the case of interleaving. The supertag *NP* corresponding to the word *Netanyahu* is included only once before the three BPE subunits *Net+ an+ yahu*.

- **Multitasking – shared encoder** A loose coupling of the syntactic representation and the surface forms can be achieved by co-training a translation model with a secondary prediction task, in our case CCG supertagging. In the multitask framework (Luong et al., 2016) the encoder part is shared while the decoder is different for each of the prediction tasks: translation and tagging. In contrast to Luong et al., we train a separate attention model for each task and perform multitask learning with target syntax. The two decoders take as input the same source context, represented by the encoder's hidden states $h_i = [\overrightarrow{h_i}; \overleftarrow{h_i}]$. However, each task has its own set of parameters associated with the five components of the decoder: GRU_1, ATT, $cGRU_{att}$, g, $softmax$. Furthermore, the two decoders may predict a different number of target symbols, resulting in target sequences of different lengths T_1 and T_2. This results in two probability distributions over separate target vocabularies for the words and the tags:

$$p_y^{word} = \prod_j^{T_1} p(y_j^{word} | x, y_{1:j-1}^{word}) \qquad (9)$$

$$p_y^{tag} = \prod_k^{T_2} p(y_k^{tag} | x, y_{1:k-1}^{tag}) \qquad (10)$$

The final loss is the sum of the losses for the two decoders:

$$l = -(log(p_y^{word}) + log(p_y^{tag})) \qquad (11)$$

We use EasySRL to label the English side of the parallel corpus with CCG supertags[1] instead of using a corpus with gold annotations as in Luong et al. (2016).

Source-side syntax – shared embedding While our focus is on target-side syntax, we also experiment with including source-side syntax to show that the two approaches are complementary.

Sennrich and Haddow propose a framework for including source-side syntax as extra features in the NMT encoder. They extend the model of Bahdanau et al. by learning a separate embedding for several source-side features such as the word itself or its part-of-speech. All feature embeddings are concatenated into one embedding vector which is used in all parts of the encoder model instead of the word embedding. When modeling the source-side syntactic information, we include the CCG supertags or dependency labels as extra features. The baseline features are the subword units obtained using BPE together with the annotation of the subword structure using IOB format by marking if a symbol in the text forms the beginning (B), inside (I), or end (E) of a word. A separate tag (O) is used if a symbol corresponds to the full word. The word level supertag is replicated for each BPE unit. Figure 1 gives an example of the source-side feature representation.

4 Experimental Setup and Evaluation

4.1 Data and methods

We train the neural MT systems on all the parallel data available at WMT16 (Bojar et al., 2016) for the German↔English and Romanian↔English language pairs. The English side of the training data is annotated with CCG lexical tags[2] using EasySRL (Lewis et al., 2015) and the available pre-trained model[3]. Some longer sentences cannot be processed by the parser and therefore we eliminate them from our training and test data. We report the sentence counts for the filtered data

	train	dev	test
DE-EN	4,468,314	2,986	2,994
RO-EN	605,885	1,984	1,984

Table 1: Number of sentences in the training, development and test sets.

sets in Table 1. Dependency labels are annotated with ParZU (Sennrich et al., 2013) for German and SyntaxNet (Andor et al., 2016) for Romanian.

All the neural MT systems are attentional encoder-decoder networks (Bahdanau et al., 2015) as implemented in the Nematus toolkit (Sennrich et al., 2017).[4] We use similar hyper-parameters to those reported by (Sennrich et al., 2016a; Sennrich and Haddow, 2016) with minor modifications: we used mini-batches of size 60 and Adam optimizer (Kingma and Ba, 2014). We select the best single models according to BLEU on the development set and use the four best single models for the ensembles.

To show that we report results over strong baselines, table 2 compares the scores obtained by our baseline system to the ones reported in Sennrich et al. (2016a). We normalize diacritics[5] for the English→Romanian test set. We did not remove or normalize Romanian diacritics for the other experiments reported in this paper. Our baseline systems are generally stronger than Sennrich et al. (2016a) due to training with a different optimizer for more iterations.

	This work	Sennrich et. al
DE→EN	31.0	28.5
EN→DE	27.8	26.8
RO→EN	28.0	27.8
EN→RO[1]	25.6	23.9

Table 2: Comparison of baseline systems in this work and in Sennrich et al. (2016a). Case-sensitive BLEU scores reported over newstest2016 with *mteval-13a.perl*. [1]Normalized diacritics.

During training we validate our models with BLEU (Papineni et al., 2002) on development sets: newstest2013 for German↔English and newsdev2016 for Romanian↔English. We evaluate the systems on newstest2016 test sets for both lan-

---

[1]We use the same data and annotations for the *interleaving* approach.

[2]The CCG tags include features such as the verb tense (e.g. [ng] for continuous form) or the sentence type (e.g. [pss] for passive).

[3]https://github.com/uwnlp/EasySRL

[4]https://github.com/rsennrich/nematus

[5]There are different encodings for letters with cedilla (ş,ţ) used interchangeably throughout the corpus. https://en.wikipedia.org/wiki/Romanian_alphabet#ISO_8859

guage pairs and use bootstrap resampling (Riezler and Maxwell, 2005) to test statistical significance. We compute BLEU with *multi-bleu.perl* over tokenized sentences both on the development sets, for early stopping, and on the test sets for evaluating our systems.

Words are segmented into sub-units that are learned jointly for source and target using BPE (Sennrich et al., 2016b), resulting in a vocabulary size of 85,000. The vocabulary size for CCG supertags was 500.

For the experiments with source-side features we use the BPE sub-units and the IOB tags as baseline features. We keep the total word embedding size fixed to 500 dimensions. We allocate 10 dimensions for dependency labels when using these as source-side features and when using source-side CCG supertags we allocate 135 dimensions.

The *interleaving* approach to integrating target syntax increases the length of the target sequence. Therefore, at training time, when adding the CCG supertags in the target sequence we increase the maximum length of sentences from 50 to 100. On average, the length of English sentences for newstest2013 in BPE representation is 22.7, while the average length when adding the CCG supertags is 44. Increasing the length of the target recurrence results in larger memory consumption and slower training.[6]. At test time, we obtain the final translation by post-processing the predicted target sequence to remove the CCG supertags.

4.2 Results

In this section, we first evaluate the syntax-aware NMT model (SNMT) with target-side CCG supertags as compared to the baseline NMT model described in the previous section (Bahdanau et al., 2015; Sennrich et al., 2016a). We show that our proposed method for tightly coupling target syntax via *interleaving*, improves translation for both German→English and Romanian→English while the *multitasking* framework does not. Next, we show that SNMT with target-side CCG supertags can be complemented with source-side dependencies, and that combining both types of syntax brings the most improvement. Finally, our experiments with source-side CCG supertags confirm that global syntax can improve translation either

as extra information in the encoder or in the decoder.

Target-side syntax We first evaluate the impact of target-side CCG supertags on overall translation quality. In Table 3 we report results for German→English, a high-resource language pair, and for Romanian→English, a low-resource language pair. We report BLEU scores for both the best single models and ensemble models. However, we will only refer to the results with ensemble models since these are generally better.

The SNMT system with target-side syntax improves BLEU scores by 0.9 for Romanian→English and by 0.6 for German→English. Although the training data for German→English is large, the CCG supertags still improve translation quality. These results suggest that the baseline NMT decoder benefits from modeling the global syntactic information locally via supertags.

Next, we evaluate whether there is a benefit to tight coupling between the target word sequence and syntax, as apposed to loose coupling. We compare our method of *interleaving* the CCG supertags with *multitasking*, which predicts target CCG supertags as a secondary task. The results in Table 3 show that the multitask approach does not improve BLEU scores for German→English, which exhibits long distance word reordering. For Romanian→English, which exhibits more local word reordering, multitasking improves BLEU by 0.6 relative to the baseline. In contrast, the *interleaving* approach improves translation quality for both language pairs and to a larger extent. Therefore, we conclude that a tight integration of the target syntax and word sequence is important. Conditioning the prediction of words on their corresponding CCG supertags is what sets SNMT apart from the multitasking approach.

Source-side and target-side syntax We now show that our method for integrating target-side syntax can be combined with the framework of Sennrich and Haddow (2016) for integrating source-side linguistic information, leading to further improvement in translation quality. We evaluate the syntax-aware NMT system, with CCG supertags as target-syntax and dependency labels as source-syntax. While the dependency labels do not encode global syntactic information, they disambiguate the grammatical function of words. Ini-

---

[6]Roughly 10h30 per 100,000 sentences (20,000 batches) for SNMT compared to 6h for NMT.

model	syntax	strategy	German→English		Romanian→English	
			single	ensemble	single	ensemble
NMT	-	-	31.0	32.1	28.1	28.4
SNMT	target – CCG	interleaving	32.0	**32.7***	29.2	**29.3****
Multitasking	target – CCG	shared encoder	31.4	32.0	28.4	29.0*
SNMT	source – dep	shared embedding	31.4	32.2	28.2	28.9
	+ target – CCG	+ interleaving	32.1	**33.0****	29.1	**29.6****

Table 3: Experiments with target-side syntax for German→English and Romanian→English. BLEU scores reported for baseline NMT, syntax-aware NMT (SNMT) and multitasking. The SNMT system is also combined with source dependencies. Statistical significance is indicated with * $p < 0.05$ and ** $p < 0.01$, when comparing against the NMT baseline.

tially, we had intended to use global syntax on the source-side as well for German→English, however the German CCG tree-bank is still under development.

From the results in Table 3 we first observe that for German→English the source-side dependency labels improve BLEU by only 0.1, while Romanian→English sees an improvement of 0.5. Source-syntax may help more for Romanian→English because the training data is smaller and the word order is more similar between the source and target languages than it is for German→English.

For both language pairs, target-syntax improves translation quality more than source-syntax. However, target-syntax is complemented by source-syntax when used together, leading to a final improvement of 0.9 BLEU points for German→English and 1.2 BLEU points for Romanian→English.

Finally, we show that CCG supertags are also an effective representation of global-syntax when used in the encoder. In Table 4 we present results for using CCG supertags as source-syntax in the embedding layer. Because we have CCG annotations only for English, we reverse the translation directions and report BLEU scores for English→German and English→Romanian. The BLEU scores reported are for the ensemble models over newstest2016.

For English→German BLEU increases by 0.7 points and for English→Romanian by 0.5 points. In contrast, Sennrich and Haddow (2016) obtain an improvement of only 0.2 for English→German using dependency labels which encode only the grammatical function of words. These results confirm that representing global syntax in the encoder provides complementary information that

model	syntax	EN→DE	EN→RO
NMT	-	28.3	25.6
SNMT	source – CCG	**29.0***	**26.1***

Table 4: Results for English→German and English→Romanian with source-side syntax. The SNMT system uses the CCG supertags of the source words in the embedding layer. *$p < 0.05$.

the baseline NMT model is not able to learn from the source word sequence alone.

4.3 Analyses by sentence type

In this section, we make a finer grained analysis of the impact of target-side syntax by looking at a breakdown of BLEU scores with respect to different linguistic constructions and sentence lengths[7].

We classify sentences into different linguistic constructions based on the CCG supertags that appear in them, e.g., the presence of category (NP\NP)/(S/NP) indicates a subordinate construction. Figure 3 a) shows the difference in BLEU points between the syntax-aware NMT system and the baseline NMT system for the following linguistic constructions: coordination *(conj)*, control and raising *(control)*, prepositional phrase attachment *(pp)*, questions and subordinate clauses *(subordinate)*. In the figure we use the symbol "*" to indicate that syntactic information is used on the target (eg. de-en*), or both on the source and target (eg. *de-en*). We report the number of sentences for each category in Table 5.

With target-syntax, we see consistent improvements across all linguistic constructions for Romanian→English and across all but *control and raising* for German→English. In particular, the in-

---

[7]Document-level BLEU is computed over each subset of sentences.

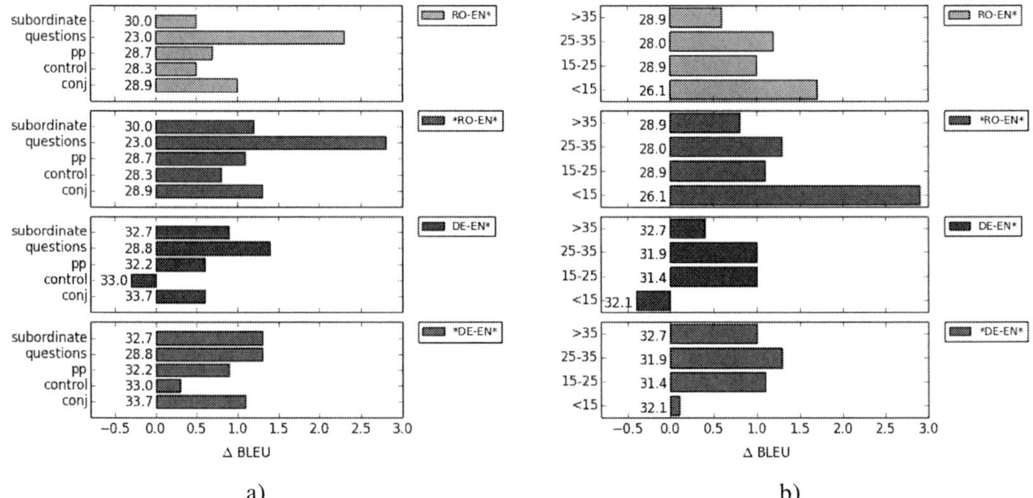

Figure 3: Difference in BLEU points between SNMT and NMT, relative to baseline NMT scores, with respect to a) linguistic constructs and b) sentence lengths. The numbers attached to the bars represent the BLEU score for the baseline NMT system. The symbol * indicates that syntactic information is used on the target (eg. de-en*), or both on the source and target (eg. *de-en*)

	sub.	qu.	pp	contr.	conj
RO↔EN	742	90	1,572	415	845
DE↔EN	936	114	2,321	546	1,129

Table 5: Sentence counts for different linguistic constructions.

crease in BLEU scores for the *prepositional phrase* and *subordinate* constructions suggests that target word order is improved.

For German→English, there is a small decrease in BLEU for the *control and raising* constructions when using target-syntax alone. However, source-syntax adds complementary information to target-syntax, resulting in a small improvement for this category as well. Moreover, combining source and target-syntax increases translation quality across all linguistic constructions as compared to NMT and SNMT with target syntax alone. For Romanian→English, combining source and target-syntax brings an additional improvement of 0.7 for *subordinate* constructs and 0.4 for *prepositional phrase attachment*. For German→English, on the same categories, there is an additional improvement of 0.4 and 0.3 respectively. Overall, BLEU scores improve by more than 1 BLEU point for most linguistic constructs and for

both language pairs.

Next, we compare the systems with respect to sentence length. Figure 3 b) shows the difference in BLEU points between the syntax-aware NMT system and the baseline NMT system with respect to the length of the source sentence measured in BPE sub-units. We report the number of sentences for each category in Table 6.

	<15	15-25	25-35	>35
RO↔EN	491	540	433	520
DE↔EN	918	934	582	560

Table 6: Sentence counts for different sentence lengths.

With target-syntax, we see consistent improvements across all sentence lengths for Romanian→English and across all but short sentences for German→English. For German→English there is a decrease in BLEU for sentences up to 15 words. Since the German→English training data is large, the baseline NMT system learns a good model for short sentences with local dependencies and without subordinate or coordinate clauses. Including extra CCG supertags increases the target sequence without adding information about complex lin-

DE - EN Question

Source	Oder wollen Sie herausfinden , **über** was andere reden ?
Ref.	Or do you want to find out what others are talking **about** ?
NMT	Or would you like to find out **about** what others are talking **about** ?
SNMT	Or do you want to find out what$_{NP/(S[dcl]/NP)}$ others are$_{(S[dcl]\backslash NP)/(S[ng]\backslash NP)}$ talking$_{(S[ng]\backslash NP)/PP}$ **about**$_{PP/NP}$?

DE - EN Subordinate

Source	...dass die Polizei jetzt sagt , ..., und dass Lamb in seinem Notruf **Prentiss zwar als seine Frau bezeichnete** ...
Ref.	...that police are now saying ..., and that while Lamb **referred to Prentiss as his wife** in the 911 call ...
NMT	...police are now saying ..., and that in his emergency call **Prentiss he called his wife** ...
SNMT	...police are now saying ..., and that lamb , in his emergency call , **described**$_{((S[dcl]\backslash NP)/PP)/NP}$ **Prentiss as his wife** ....

Figure 4: Comparison of baseline NMT and SNMT with target syntax for German→English.

guistic phenomena. However, when using both source and target syntax, the effect on short sentences disappears. For Romanian→English there is also a large improvement on short sentences when combining source and target syntax: 2.9 BLEU points compared to the NMT baseline and 1.2 BLEU points compared to SNMT with target-syntax alone.

With both source and target-syntax, translation quality increases across all sentence lengths as compared to NMT and SNMT with target-syntax alone. For German→English sentences that are more than 35 words, we see again the effect of increasing the target sequence by adding CCG supertags. Target-syntax helps, however BLEU improves by only 0.4, compared to 0.9 for sentences between 15 and 35 words. With both source and target syntax, BLEU improves by 0.8 for sentences with more than 35 words. For Romanian→English we see a similar result for sentences with more than 35 words: target-syntax improves BLEU by 0.6, while combining source and target syntax improves BLEU by 0.8. These results confirm as well that source-syntax adds complementary information to target-syntax and mitigates the problem of increasing the target sequence.

4.4 Discussion

Our experiments demonstrate that target-syntax improves translation for two translation directions: German→English and Romanian→English. Our proposed method predicts the target words together with their CCG supertags.

Although the focus of this paper is not improving CCG tagging, we can also measure that SNMT is accurate at predicting CCG supertags. We compare the CCG sequence predicted by the SNMT models with that predicted by EasySRL

and obtain the following accuracies: 93.2 for Romanian→English, 95.6 for German→English, 95.8 for German→English with both source and target syntax.[8]

We conclude by giving a couple of examples in Figure 4 for which the SNMT system with target syntax produced more grammatical translations than the baseline NMT system.

In the example **DE-EN Question** the baseline NMT system translates the preposition *"über"* twice as *"about"*. The SNMT system with target syntax predicts the correct CCG supertag for *"what"* which expects to be followed by a sentence and not a preposition: NP/(S[dcl]/NP). Therefore the SNMT correctly re-orders the preposition *"about"* at the end of the question.

In the example **DE-EN Subordinate** the baseline NMT system fails to correctly attach *"Prentiss"* as an object and *"his wife"* as a modifier to the verb *"called (bezeichnete)"* in the subordinate clause. In contrast the SNMT system predicts the correct sub-categorization frame of the verb *"described"* and correctly translates the entire predicate-argument structure.

5 Conclusions

This work introduces a method for modeling explicit target-syntax in a neural machine translation system, by interleaving target words with their corresponding CCG supertags. Earlier work on syntax-aware NMT mainly modeled syntax in the encoder, while our experiments suggest modeling syntax in the decoder is also useful. Our results show that a tight integration of syntax in the decoder improves translation quality for both

---

[8]The multitasking model predicts a different number of CCG supertags than the number of target words. For the sentences where these numbers match, the CCG supetagging accuracy is 73.2.

German→English and Romanian→English language pairs, more so than a loose coupling of target words and syntax as in multitask learning. Finally, by combining our method for integrating target-syntax with the framework of Sennrich and Haddow (2016) for source-syntax we obtain the most improvement over the baseline NMT system: 0.9 BLEU for German→English and 1.2 BLEU for Romanian→English. In particular, we see large improvements for longer sentences involving syntactic phenomena such as subordinate and coordinate clauses and prepositional phrase attachment. In future work, we plan to evaluate the impact of target-syntax when translating into a morphologically rich language, for example by using the Hindi CCGBank (Ambati et al., 2016).

Acknowledgements

We thank the anonymous reviewers for their comments and suggestions. This project has received funding from the European Union's Horizon 2020 research and innovation programme under grant agreements 644402 (HimL), 644333 (SUMMA) and 645452 (QT21).

References

Roee Aharoni and Yoav Goldberg. 2017. Towards string-to-tree neural machine translation. In *Proceedings of the 55th Annual Meeting of the Association for Computational Linguistics (Volume 2: Short Papers)*, Vancouver, Canada. Association for Computational Linguistics.

Bharat Ram Ambati, Tejaswini Deoskar, and Mark Steedman. 2016. Hindi CCGbank: CCG Treebank from the Hindi Dependency Treebank. In *Language Resources and Evaluation*.

Daniel Andor, Chris Alberti, David Weiss, Aliaksei Severyn, Alessandro Presta, Kuzman Ganchev, Slav Petrov, and Michael Collins. 2016. Globally normalized transition-based neural networks. In *Proceedings of the 54th Annual Meeting of the Association for Computational Linguistics (Volume 1: Long Papers)*, pages 2442–2452, Berlin, Germany. Association for Computational Linguistics.

Dzmitry Bahdanau, Kyunghyun Cho, and Yoshua Bengio. 2015. Neural machine translation by jointly learning to align and translate. In *Proceedings of the International Conference on Learning Representations (ICLR)*.

Luisa Bentivogli, Arianna Bisazza, Mauro Cettolo, and Marcello Federico. 2016. Neural versus phrase-based machine translation quality: a case study. In *Proceedings of the 2016 Conference on Empirical Methods in Natural Language Processing, EMNLP 2016, Austin, Texas, USA, November 1-4, 2016*, pages 257–267.

Alexandra Birch, Miles Osborne, and Philipp Koehn. 2007. Ccg supertags in factored statistical machine translation. In *Proceedings of the Second Workshop on Statistical Machine Translation*, StatMT '07, pages 9–16, Stroudsburg, PA, USA. Association for Computational Linguistics.

Ondřej Bojar, Rajen Chatterjee, Christian Federmann, Yvette Graham, Barry Haddow, Matthias Huck, Antonio Jimeno Yepes, Philipp Koehn, Varvara Logacheva, Christof Monz, Matteo Negri, Aurelie Neveol, Mariana Neves, Martin Popel, Matt Post, Raphael Rubino, Carolina Scarton, Lucia Specia, Marco Turchi, Karin Verspoor, and Marcos Zampieri. 2016. Findings of the 2016 conference on machine translation. In *Proceedings of the First Conference on Machine Translation*, pages 131–198, Berlin, Germany. Association for Computational Linguistics.

David Chiang. 2007. Hierarchical phrase-based translation. *Comput. Linguist.*, 33(2):201–228.

Kyunghyun Cho, Bart van Merrienboer, Dzmitry Bahdanau, and Yoshua Bengio. 2014a. On the properties of neural machine translation: Encoder–decoder approaches. In *Proceedings of SSST-8, Eighth Workshop on Syntax, Semantics and Structure in Statistical Translation*, pages 103–111, Doha, Qatar. Association for Computational Linguistics.

Kyunghyun Cho, Bart van Merriënboer, Çağlar Gülçehre, Dzmitry Bahdanau, Fethi Bougares, Holger Schwenk, and Yoshua Bengio. 2014b. Learning phrase representations using rnn encoder–decoder for statistical machine translation. In *Proceedings of the 2014 Conference on Empirical Methods in Natural Language Processing (EMNLP)*, pages 1724–1734, Doha, Qatar. Association for Computational Linguistics.

Chris Dyer, Adhiguna Kuncoro, Miguel Ballesteros, and Noah A. Smith. 2016. Recurrent neural network grammars. In *Proceedings of the 2016 Conference of the North American Chapter of the Association for Computational Linguistics: Human Language Technologies*, pages 199–209, San Diego, California. Association for Computational Linguistics.

Akiko Eriguchi, Kazuma Hashimoto, and Yoshimasa Tsuruoka. 2016. Tree-to-sequence attentional neural machine translation. In *Proceedings of the 54th Annual Meeting of the Association for Computational Linguistics (Volume 1: Long Papers)*, pages 823–833, Berlin, Germany. Association for Computational Linguistics.

Akiko Eriguchi, Yoshimasa Tsuruoka, and Kyunghyun Cho. 2017. Learning to parse and translate improves neural machine translation. In *Proceedings of the

55th Annual Meeting of the Association for Computational Linguistics (Volume 2: Short Papers), Vancouver, Canada. Association for Computational Linguistics.

Michel Galley, Mark Hopkins, Kevin Knight, and Daniel Marcu. 2004. What's in a translation rule? In *Proceedings of Human Language Technologies: Conference of the North American Chapter of the Association of Computational Linguistics*, HLT-NAACL '04.

Marcin Junczys-Dowmunt, Tomasz Dwojak, and Hieu Hoang. 2016. Is Neural Machine Translation Ready for Deployment? A Case Study on 30 Translation Directions. In *Proceedings of the IWSLT 2016*.

Nal Kalchbrenner and Phil Blunsom. 2013. Recurrent continuous translation models. In *Proceedings of the 2013 Conference on Empirical Methods in Natural Language Processing*, pages 1700–1709, Seattle, Washington, USA. Association for Computational Linguistics.

Diederik Kingma and Jimmy Ba. 2014. Adam: A method for stochastic optimization. *arXiv preprint arXiv:1412.6980*.

Mike Lewis, Luheng He, and Luke Zettlemoyer. 2015. Joint a* ccg parsing and semantic role labelling. In *Empirical Methods in Natural Language Processing*.

Minh-Thang Luong, Quoc V Le, Ilya Sutskever, Oriol Vinyals, and Lukasz Kaiser. 2016. Multi-task sequence to sequence learning. In *Proceedings of International Conference on Learning Representations (ICLR 2016)*.

Mercedes García Martínez, Loïc Barrault, and Fethi Bougares. 2016. Factored Neural Machine Translation Architectures. In *International Workshop on Spoken Language Translation (IWSLT'16)*.

Arul Menezes and Chris Quirk. 2007. Using dependency order templates to improve generality in translation. In *Proceedings of the Second Workshop on Statistical Machine Translation*, pages 1–8.

Maria Nadejde, Alexandra Birch, and Philipp Koehn. 2016a. Modeling selectional preferences of verbs and nouns in string-to-tree machine translation. In *Proceedings of the First Conference on Machine Translation*, pages 32–42, Berlin, Germany. Association for Computational Linguistics.

Maria Nadejde, Alexandra Birch, and Philipp Koehn. 2016b. A neural verb lexicon model with source-side syntactic context for string-to-tree machine translation. In *Proceedings of the International Workshop on Spoken Language Translation (IWSLT)*.

Maria Nadejde, Philip Williams, and Philipp Koehn. 2013. Edinburgh's Syntax-Based Machine Translation Systems. In *Proceedings of the Eighth Workshop on Statistical Machine Translation*, pages 170–176, Sofia, Bulgaria.

Jan Niehues, Thanh-Le Ha, Eunah Cho, and Alex Waibel. 2016. Using factored word representation in neural network language models. In *Proceedings of the First Conference on Machine Translation*, Berlin, Germany.

Kishore Papineni, Salim Roukos, Todd Ward, and Wei-Jing Zhu. 2002. Bleu: A method for automatic evaluation of machine translation. In *Proceedings of the 40th Annual Meeting on Association for Computational Linguistics*, ACL '02, pages 311–318, Stroudsburg, PA, USA. Association for Computational Linguistics.

Stefan Riezler and John T. Maxwell. 2005. On some pitfalls in automatic evaluation and significance testing for mt. In *Proceedings of the ACL Workshop on Intrinsic and Extrinsic Evaluation Measures for Machine Translation and/or Summarization*, pages 57–64, Ann Arbor, Michigan. Association for Computational Linguistics.

Rico Sennrich. 2015. Modelling and Optimizing on Syntactic N-Grams for Statistical Machine Translation. *Transactions of the Association for Computational Linguistics*, 3:169–182.

Rico Sennrich, Orhan Firat, Kyunghyun Cho, Alexandra Birch, Barry Haddow, Julian Hitschler, Marcin Junczys-Dowmunt, Samuel Läubli, Antonio Valerio Miceli Barone, Jozef Mokry, and Maria Nadejde. 2017. Nematus: a toolkit for neural machine translation. In *Proceedings of the Software Demonstrations of the 15th Conference of the European Chapter of the Association for Computational Linguistics*, pages 65–68, Valencia, Spain. Association for Computational Linguistics.

Rico Sennrich and Barry Haddow. 2016. Linguistic input features improve neural machine translation. In *Proceedings of the First Conference on Machine Translation*, pages 83–91, Berlin, Germany.

Rico Sennrich, Barry Haddow, and Alexandra Birch. 2016a. Edinburgh neural machine translation systems for wmt 16. In *Proceedings of the First Conference on Machine Translation*, pages 371–376, Berlin, Germany. Association for Computational Linguistics.

Rico Sennrich, Barry Haddow, and Alexandra Birch. 2016b. Neural machine translation of rare words with subword units. In *Proceedings of the 54th Annual Meeting of the Association for Computational Linguistics (Volume 1: Long Papers)*, Berlin, Germany. Association for Computational Linguistics.

Rico Sennrich, Martin Volk, and Gerold Schneider. 2013. Exploiting Synergies Between Open Resources for German Dependency Parsing, POS-tagging, and Morphological Analysis. In *Proceedings of the International Conference Recent Advances in Natural Language Processing 2013*, pages 601–609, Hissar, Bulgaria.

Xing Shi, Inkit Padhi, and Kevin Knight. 2016. Does string-based neural mt learn source syntax? In *Proceedings of the 2016 Conference on Empirical Methods in Natural Language Processing*, pages 1526–1534, Austin, Texas. Association for Computational Linguistics.

Mark Steedman. 2000. *The syntactic process*, volume 24. MIT Press.

Ilya Sutskever, Oriol Vinyals, and Quoc V. Le. 2014. Sequence to sequence learning with neural networks. In *Proceedings of the 27th International Conference on Neural Information Processing Systems*, NIPS'14, pages 3104–3112.

Philip Williams and Philipp Koehn. 2012. Ghkm rule extraction and scope-3 parsing in moses. In *Proceedings of the Seventh Workshop on Statistical Machine Translation*, pages 388–394.

Exploiting Linguistic Resources for Neural Machine Translation Using Multi-task Learning

Jan Niehues and **Eunah Cho**
Institute for Anthropomatics and Robotics
KIT - Karlsruhe Institute of Technology, Germany
`firstname.lastname@kit.edu`

Abstract

Linguistic resources such as part-of-speech (POS) tags have been extensively used in statistical machine translation (SMT) frameworks and have yielded better performances. However, usage of such linguistic annotations in neural machine translation (NMT) systems has been left under-explored.

In this work, we show that multi-task learning is a successful and a easy approach to introduce an additional knowledge into an end-to-end neural attentional model. By jointly training several natural language processing (NLP) tasks in one system, we are able to leverage common information and improve the performance of the individual task.

We analyze the impact of three design decisions in multi-task learning: the tasks used in training, the training schedule, and the degree of parameter sharing across the tasks, which is defined by the network architecture. The experiments are conducted for an German to English translation task. As additional linguistic resources, we exploit POS information and named-entities (NE). Experiments show that the translation quality can be improved by up to 1.5 BLEU points under the low-resource condition. The performance of the POS tagger is also improved using the multi-task learning scheme.

1 Introduction

Recently, there has been a dramatic change in the state-of-the-art techniques for machine translation (MT). In a traditional method, often the best per-formance is achieved by using a complicated combination of several statistical models, which are individually trained. For example, POS information was shown to be very helpful to model word reordering between languages, as shown in Niehues and Kolss (2009). While the recent development of end-to-end trained neural models (Bahdanau et al., 2014) showed significant gains over traditional approaches, they are often trained only on the parallel data in an end-to-end fashion. In most cases, therefore, they do not facilitate other knowledge sources.

When parallel data is sparse, exploiting other knowledge sources can be crucial for performance. Two techniques to integrate the additional resources are well studied. In one technique, we train a tool on the additional resources (e.g. POS tagger) and then annotate the parallel data using this tool. This technique has been applied extensively in SMT systems (e.g. Niehues and Kolss (2009)) as well as in some NMT systems (e.g. Sennrich and Haddow (2016)). The second technique would be to use the annotated data directly to train the model.

The goal of this work is to integrate the additional linguistic resources directly into neural models, in order to achieve better performance. To do so, we build a multi-task model and train several NLP tasks jointly.

We use an attention-based sequence-to-sequence model for all tasks. Experiments show that we are able to improve the performance on the German to English machine translation task measured in BLEU, BEER and CharacTER. Furthermore, we analyze three important decisions when designing multi-task models. First, we investigated the influence of secondary tasks. Also, we analyze the influence of training schedule, e.g. whether we need to adjust it in order to get the best performance on the target task. And finally,

Proceedings of the Conference on Machine Translation (WMT), Volume 1: Research Papers, pages 80–89
Copenhagen, Denmark, September 7–11, 2017. ©2017 Association for Computational Linguistics

we evaluated the amount of parameter sharing enforced by different model architectures.

The main contributions of this paper are (1) that we show multi-task learning is possible within attention-based sequence-to-sequence models, which are state-of-the-art in machine translation and (2) that we analyze the influence of three main design decisions.

2 Related Work

Motivated by the success of using features learned from linguistic resources in various NLP tasks, there have been several approaches including external information into neural network-based systems.

The POS-based information has been integrated for language models in Wu et al. (2012); Niehues et al. (2016). In the neural machine translation, using additional word factors like POS-tags has shown to be beneficial (Sennrich and Haddow, 2016).

The initial approach for multi-task learning for neural networks was presented in Collobert et al. (2011). The authors used convolutional and feed forward networks for several tasks such as semantic parsing and POS tagging. This idea was extended to sequence to sequence models in Luong et al. (2015).

A special case of multi-task learning for attention based models has been explored. In multilingual machine translation, for example, the tasks are still machine translation tasks but they need to consider different language pairs. In this case, a system with an individual encoder and decoder (Firat et al., 2016b) as well as a system with a shared encoder-decoder (Ha et al., 2016; Johnson et al., 2016) has been proposed.

2.1 Attention Models

Recently, state-of-the art performance in machine translation was significantly improved by using neural machine translation. In this approach, a recurrent neural network (RNN) based encoder decoder architecture is used to transform the source sentence into the target sentence.

In the encoder, an RNN is used to encode the source sentence into a fixed size of continuous space representation by inserting the source sentence word-by-word into the network. First, source words are encoded into a one-hot encoding. Then a linear transformation of this into a con-

tinuous space, referred to as word embeddings, is learned. An RNN model will learn the source sentence representation over these word embeddings. In a second step, the decoder is initialized by the representation of the source sentence and is then generating the target sequence one word after the other using the last generated word as input for the RNN. In order to get the output probability at each target position, a softmax layer that get the hidden state of the RNN as input is used (Sutskever et al., 2014).

The main drawback of this approach is that the whole source sentence has to be stored in a fixed-size context vector. To overcome this problem, Bahdanau et al. (2014) introduced the soft attention mechanism. Instead of only considering the last state of the encoder RNN, they use a weighted sum of all hidden states. Using these weights, the model is able to put attention on different parts of the source sentence depending on the current status of the decoder RNN. In addition, they extended the encoder RNN to a bi-directional one to be able to get information from the whole sentence at every position of the encoder RNN. A detailed description of the NMT framework can be found in Bahdanau et al. (2014).

3 Multi-task Learning

In a traditional NLP pipeline, a named entity recognition or machine translation system employ POS information by using the POS tags as additional features. For example, the system will learn that the probability of a word being a named entity is higher if the word is marked as a noun. First, a POS tagger is used to annotate the input data. Combining the statistical models used for POS tagging and named entity recognition might not be straightforward.

Recent advances in deep learning approaches, e.g. CNN or RNN-based models (Labeau and Löser K., 2015), made it straightforward to use very similar techniques throughout different NLP tasks. Therefore, there are new methods to combine the tasks. Instead of using the output of a model as input for another one, for example, we can build one model for all tasks. The model is then automatically able to learn to share as much information across the tasks as necessary.

For building a model that can learn three NLP tasks, we use the attention-based encoder-decoder model, which is a standard in state-of-the-art machine translation systems. The two non-MT tasks can also be modeled by converting them into a translation problem. Instead of translating the source words into the target language, we *translate* the words into labels, either POS-tags or NE-labels.

In this work, we study several crucial design aspects when applying attention-based encoder-decoder model for a multi-task learning scenario. First, we consider different architectures of the network in order to assess how much parameter sharing is useful between the tasks. In general, sharing more information across the tasks is preferred. However, if the tasks differ from each other greatly, it might be helpful to restrict the degree of sharing. In addition, the training schedule of each task has to be addressed. While all three tasks are handled as a form of translation, certain distinctions and special processes needed to be asserted. In Section 3.3 we address this issue.

3.1 Architecture

The general attentional encoder-decoder model consists of three main parts: the encoder E, the attention model A and the decoder D. Figure 1 gives an overview of this layout.

Our baseline considers the scenario where we have separate models for each task. Therefore, all three parts (encoder, attention model, and decoder) stand separately for each task. We will have nine components E_{MT}, E_{POS}, E_{NE}, A_{MT}, A_{POS}, A_{NE}, D_{MT}, D_{POS}, D_{NE} in total.

The one main design decision for a multi-task learning architecture is the degree of sharing across the tasks. Motivated by architectures proposed for multi-lingual machine translation (Dong et al., 2015; Firat et al., 2016a; Ha et al., 2016), we analyze the impact of different degrees of sharing in the output quality. When sharing more parameters between the tasks, the models are able to learn more from the training data of other tasks. If the tasks are very distant, on the other hand, it might be harmful to share the parameters.

Shared encoder *(shrd Enc)* One promising way is to share components that handle the same type of data. Since all our tasks share English as input here is the encoder.

In this architecture, we therefore use one encoder for all tasks. This is the minimal degree of sharing we consider in our experiments. A common encoder E_{ALL} is used for all tasks, but separate attention models A_{MT}, A_{POS}, A_{NE} and decoders D_{MT}, D_{POS}, D_{NE} are used.

Shared attention *(shrd Att)* The next component is the attention model which connects the encoder and decoder. While the output should be different for the addressed tasks, the type of input is the same. Therefore, it might be helpful to share more information between the models.

In a second architecture, we also share the attention model in addition to the encoder. So in this setup, we have one encoder E_{ALL}, one attention model A_{ALL} and three decoder D_{MT}, D_{POS}, D_{NE}.

Shared decoder *(shrd Dec)* Finally, we explore whether it is possible to share all information across the tasks and let the model learn how to represent the different tasks. Thus, in this scheme, we aim to share the decoder partially. The only thing that is not shared is the final softmax layer.

In this architecture, the decoder RNN has to model the generation of target words as well as that of labels. Therefore, we have only one encoder E_{ALL}, one attention model A_{ALL} and one decoder D_{ALL}. In the decoder, however, we have separated output layers for each task.

Figure 1 depicts which layers are shared depending on the architecture.

3.2 Training Schedule

In this section, we discuss the influence of the training schedule on the quality of the model.

Throughout our experiments we used a mini-batch size of 512 tokens. The weight updates were determined using the Adam algorithm.

The training has to be adapted to the multi-task scenario. The main decision is how to present the training examples to the training algorithm. We only consider one task in each mini-batch. Although the model structure is the same for all tasks, the models for the individual tasks have different weights. Therefore, parallelization on the GPU would be less efficient when using different tasks within one batch. In order to train our model on all tasks in parallel, we randomly shuffle the mini-batches from all tasks. This is our default training schedule. One issue in the multi-task scenario is that the data size might vary. In this case, the model will mainly concentrate on the task with the most data and not achieve the best performance on each task.

Figure 1: Overview on the different architectures used for multi-task learning

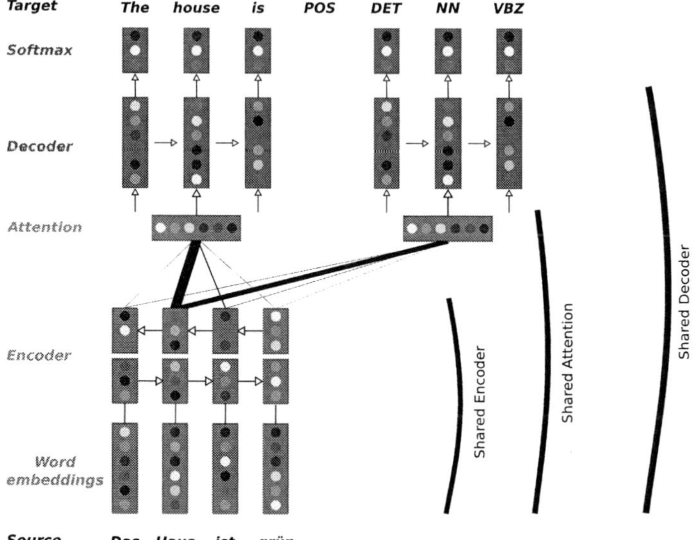

This challenge is strongly related with the problem of domain adaptation in machine translation, where a large out-of-domain data is available but only a small amount of in-domain data. For this scenario, first training on all data and then fine-tuning on the in-domain data was very successful (Lavergne et al., 2011; Cho et al., 2016). Therefore, we adapt this approach to the multi-task scenario. In this case, we first trained the model on all tasks and then continued training only on the main task. We will refer to this training schedule as adapted.

3.3 Target Length

While all tasks are modeled as a translation problem in this work, the nature of each task is largely different. One main difference between the translation task and the other two tasks is the length of the target sequence. While it is unknown in the translation task, it is known and fixed for the other two cases. During training this does not matter as the target sequence is given. For testing the system, however, this issue is crucial to address.

In our initial experiment, it was shown that the POS tagger was able to learn the correct target length in most of the cases. For some sentences, however, the estimated target length was not correct. Therefore, the prior knowledge of sequence length is used during decoding so that label sequences are generated with the correct target length. It is worth to mention that the desired length of the labels is not exactly the length of the input to the model itself. Our model uses inputs with subwords units generated by byte-pair encoding (Sennrich et al., 2016).

4 Experimental Setup

We conduct experiments using the multi-task approach on three different tasks: machine translation from German to English, German fine-grained POS tagging and German NE tagging. As briefly mentioned in Section 1, multi-task approach can be helpful when data is sparse. In order to simulate this, we deploy only German to English TED data for the translation task.

4.1 Data

For the translation task, we used 4M tokens of the WIT corpus (Cettolo et al., 2012) for German to English as training data. We used *dev2010* for validation and *tst2013* and *tst2014* for testing, provided by the IWSLT. We only used training examples shorter than 60 words per sentence.

The POS tagger was trained on 720K tokens the Tiger Corpus (Brants et al., 2004). This corpus contains German newspaper text. Consequently, it is out-of-domain data for the machine translation task. The development and the test data are also from this corpus. The POS tag set consists of 54 tags and the fine-grained POS tags with morphological annotations has 774 labels.

Finally, we trained the German named-entity

tagger on 450K tokens of the GermEval 2014 NER Shared Task data (Benikova et al., 2014). The corpus is extracted from Wikipedia and the training data consists of 24K sentences.

We preprocess the parallel data by tokenizing and true-casing. In addition, we trained a byte-pair encoding (Sennrich et al., 2016) with 40K subwords on the source and target side of the TED corpus jointly. We then applied the subwords to all German and English corpora.

4.2 System Architecture

For all our experiments, we use an attentional encoder-decoder model. The baseline systems use this architecture as well. The encoder uses word embeddings of size 256 and a bidirectional LSTM (Hochreiter and Schmidhuber, 1997; Schuster and Paliwal, 1997) with 256 hidden layers for each direction. For the attention, we use a multi-layer perceptron with 512 hidden units and tanh activation function. The decoder uses conditional GRU units with 512 hidden units. The models are all trained with Adam, where we restarted the algorithm twice and early stopping is applied using log-likelihood of the concatenated validation sets from the considered tasks. For the adapted schedule, Adam is started once again when training only on the target task. The model is implemented in lamtram (Neubig, 2015)[1].

4.3 Evaluation

The machine translation output is evaluated with BLEU (Papineni et al., 2002), BEER (Stanojevic and Sima'an, 2014) and CharacTER (Wang et al., 2016). For the POS tags, we report error rates on the small label set as well as on the large label set.

5 Results

In this section, we present the results from our experiments and analysis.

5.1 Initial experiments on the architecture

The results of the initial experiments on the machine translation tasks are shown in Table 1. The table displays the performance on the validation set and on both test sets. For all experiments, we first show the BLEU score, then the BEER score and finally the characTER.

First, we show the results of the baseline neural MT system trained on the parallel data (single task). As mentioned in the beginning, we simulated a low-resource condition in these experiments by only using the data from TED, which are roughly 185K sentences.

We evaluated models that are trained both on the translation and POS tagging task. Although the POS data is out-of-domain and significantly smaller than the parallel training data for the translation task (ca. 20% of the size), we see improvements for all three architectures consistently in three metrics. The BLEU scores is improved by more than 1 point and the characTER is reduced by more than 1.5 points. The BEER metric score is improved by more than a half point on both sets.

In a more detailed look at this task, we see that the model sharing the most (*shrd Dec*) performs better than the baseline, but worse than the other two. Therefore, we can conclude that it is helpful to separate the tasks when the components work on different types of data. Whether it is helpful to share the attention layer (*shrd Att*) or not (*shrd Enc*) is not clear from this experiment. Therefore, we concentrate on these two architectures in the following experiments.

5.2 Impact of design decisions

Following the initial experiment, we address the following three design questions:

- What kind of influence does the secondary task have?

- How do the different architectures perform?

- Do we need to adapt the training schedule?

In order to clarify the impact of the three hyperparameters (the architectures, the tasks and the training) we performed experiments based on possible combinations. We used two most promising architectures, *shrd Enc* and *shrd Att* as discussed in Section 5.1. We use three task combinations, *POS+MT*, *NE+MT* and *NE+POS+MT*. Two training strategies are applied with and without adaptation as described in Section 3.2. These 12 systems are evaluated on the two test sets using three different metrics. Consequently, in total we have 72 measurements for the 12 systems.

Since a first view on the results did not clearly reveal a best performing system, we conducted a more detailed analysis by averaging the results

---

[1] The extension to handle multi-task training can be downloaded *https://github.com/isl-mt/lamtram*

Task(s)	Arch.	Valid	Test	
		dev 2010	tst2013	tst2014
MT	-	29.91/62.16/51.06	30.85/62.27/51.16	26.12/58.73/55.17
POS + MT	shrd Enc	30.62/62.77/48.35	31.97/62.72/49.69	27.08/58.99/54.50
	shrd Att	30.51/62.27/49.09	31.76/62.68/49.59	26.86/58.84/53.88
	shrd Dec	30.36/62.34/49.28	31.26/62.31/50.35	26.52/58.48/54.00
Adapted NE + POS + MT	shrd Enc	30.70/62.96/48.60	32.30/63.25/49.22	27.78/59.74/53.49

Table 1: Results of multi-task learning architectures on the machine translation task (BLEU/BEER/characTER)

over several configurations. First, we analyze the influence of adapting the training schedule by fine-tuning on the MT task. Out of the 12 systems, six systems used an adapted training schedule.

As shown in the first line of Table 2 (*All*), when averaging over the six systems using the adapted training schedule and tested both test sets, we see improvements in all considered metrics compare to the systems using the default training schedule. The BLEU score improved by 0.4 BLEU points, BEER by 0.2 and characTER by 0.4. Furthermore, we compared each of the 36 measurements using the adapted schedule with the corresponding measurement using the default training schedule. Thus, the scores are calculated on same test set, based on the same metric. The model differs whether it is trained using the default or adapted training schedule. How often the system with an adapted schedule performs better is shown in the last column of Table 2. When directly comparing these systems, in 25 out of 36 cases the ones with the adapted schedule perform better.

We analyzed the influence of the architecture as well as tasks considered in training in the same way. The influence of both aspects, however, was not as clear as the one from the training schedule. In order to get a deeper understanding, we analyzed in which cases it is more helpful to adapt the training schedule. As a first step, we looked at the correlation between the training schedule and the two different architectures. The results are shown in the next lines of Table 2.

Compared to the systems using the *shrd Enc* layout, we observe even bigger improvements when applying the adapted schedule. The averaged BLEU score is improved by 0.7 BLEU points. Furthermore, the system with the adapted training schedule performs better, in almost all cases. For the *shrd Att* model, in contrast, we gain nearly no improvements from the adapted sched-

ule. We also observed that the system with the default schedule performs better in 10 out of 18 cases.

One reason for this can be that the default training schedule may not perform as well any more when only a few parameters are observed in every batch. In this case, continuing and concentrating on one task seems to be very important.

In addition, we evaluate the correlation between the tasks involved and the training schedule. The results are shown in the same table. The adapted training schedule has no effect when training on named entities and machine translation. The effect when training on POS tagging and MT is also relatively small. When training the three tasks together, however, the system with an adapted schedule performs always better than the system with the default one. The average BLEU is improved by 0.7. The BEER score and characTER are also improved by 0.5 and 1.2 points.

Inspired by the results, we build the adapted *shrd Enc* model trained on all three tasks, as shown in Table 1. This model improved the performance by 1.5 BLEU points over the baseline system. Also the BEER score is improved by 1 and the characTER score reduced by 1.8 to 2 points.

5.3 POS Tagging Performance

In addition to the results on the task of translation, we also evaluated the performance on the task of POS tagging. The results are shown in Table 3.

For the validation and test data, we show the error rate on the small tag sets as well as the error rate on the morpho-syntactic tag set. In the table, we always first show the results for the small test set.

The baseline system trained only on the Tiger corpus achieves an error rate of 5.49, for the POS tags in the validation set. For the morpho-syntactic tag of the validation set, it achieves 11.36. The

Systems	Default Schedule	Adapted Schedule	Adapted better
All	29.48/60.89/52.05	29.89/61.08/51.64	25/36
shrd Enc	29.34/60.85/52.31	30.00/61.25/51.50	17/18
shrd Att	29.62/61.93/51.78	29.78/60.93/51.79	8/18
POS + MT	29.41/60.81/51.92	29.78/61.00/51.90	8/12
NE + MT	29.60/61.00/51.76	29.79/60.96/51.77	5/12
NE + POS + MT	29.42/60.87/52.46	30.09/61.46/51.25	12/12

Table 2: Impact of the training schedule in the machine translation task (BLEU/BEER/characTER)

Task(s)	Model	Default schedule		Adaptation schedule	
		Valid	Test	Valid	Test
POS	-	5.49/11.36	10.13/17.27	-	-
POS + MT	shrd Enc	3.99/9.98	7.55/14.98	3.57/8.82	6.24/13.24
	shrd Att	3.86/9.55	6.98/14.17	3.16/8.23	5.52/12.25
	shrd Dec	3.57/9.28	7.40/14.62	3.53/8.94	5.81/12.56
NE + POS + MT	shrd Enc	3.42/9.00	5.86/12.87	3.00/8.00	5.06/11.62
	shrd Att	3.08/8.45	6.23/13.28	2.78/7.87	5.49/12.10

Table 3: Results of different multi-task architectures on the POS task

performance on the test data is 10.13 and 17.27 for both tag sets. In all systems we used one system the generate the both tag sets. The small tags were evaluated by removing the morhpo-syntactic information from the output

It is clear that all models outperform the baseline. It seems to be very helpful for the POS task to jointly train the model along with the translation task. The MT data is significantly larger than the POS data, which is beneficial for this task.

A more detailed look shows that model adaptation is beneficial for a good performance. In all cases the performance is improved by adapting the model to the POS task. Therefore, when the data of the main task is small compared to the overall training data, adapting on the main task is even more important.

Furthermore, we see improvements when using a third task in all cases. Facilitating this combination of tasks is also helpful for POS tagging.

As we observed in the MT task, the impact and differences brought from each architecture are not huge. The architectures considered in this work perform similar. Even the system sharing all components achieves a comparable performance on this task.

The best performing model, however, is the *shred Enc* model, trained on all three tasks and adapted to the task. This model achieved an error of 5.06 on the small tag set. Compared to the baseline performance of 10.13, we can see that the error rate is halved. On the fine-grained tag set, we see an improvement from 17.27 to 11.62, which is a more than 30% reduction in error rate.

5.4 Analysis and Examples

In order to show the influence of the other tasks, we show translation examples in Table 4. For the examples we use the multi-task system trained on all three tasks with the *shrd Enc* architecture.

A common problem of many neural MT systems is that they do not translate parts of the source sentence, or that parts of the source sentence are translated twice. The baseline system suffers from this, as shown in the first two examples. The translation of the multi-task system is improved compared to the baseline in several aspects. In the first example, the baseline system is not translating the German compound *Geburtsfehler* into *birth defect* correctly, but into *birth*. Although the multi-task system does not generate the translation that exactly matches the reference the translation is understandable. In the second example, the phrase *of 10* is not repeated. One explanation for this could be that the additional information from the POS data leads to a better encoding of the structure of the source sentence.

The influence of the named-entity training examples on the translation quality is clearer. In several cases, the model is able to handle named enti-

German	sie ist kein Geburtsfehler.
Reference	it's not a birth defect.
Baseline	she's not born.
Multi-task	it's not a birth error.
German	das bedeutet, dass 8 von 10 Entscheidungen...
Reference	that means that eight out of 10 of the decisions...
Baseline	that means that eight of 10 of 10 choices...
Multi-task	that means that eight of 10 decisions...
German	...["Benjamin Franklin" von Walter Isaacson]["John Adams" von David McCullough]...
Reference	...["Benjamin Franklin" by Walter Isaacson]["John Adams" by David McCullough]...
Baseline	...[Benjamin Franklin, from Walter Franklin"][The "John Adams"]...
Multi-task	...["Benjamin Franklin" from Walter Isaacson],["John Adams" from David McCullough...
German	darum habe ich infantile Zerebralparese, ...
Reference	as a result, I have cerebral palsy,
Baseline	that's why I have the infantile,
Multi-task	I have infantile cerebral palsy,
German	Prousts Freunde hätten das Land verlassen müssen, ..
Reference	you know, Proust's boyfriends would have to leave the country ...
Baseline	Prolled friends had to have left the country ...
Multi-task	Proulcss friends have to leave the country ...

Table 4: Translation examples

ties better. As shown in the third and fourth example, the NMT system is not able to copy a named entity from the source to the target, nor to translate rare words. In the third example, the baseline system is not able to generate the correct last name of the first author *Isaacson*, but is generating the last name from the book title. In the second part of the example, the baseline system completely deletes the author. In contrast, the multi-task system is able to generate the correct sequence. In the fourth example the multi-task example is able to translate *Zerebralparese (cerebral palsy)*, while the baseline system is not able to do it.

We would like to note that as shown in the last example, there are also several cases where the NMT system is not able to translate names or rare words correctly.

6 Conclusion

In this paper we proposed the use of multi-task learning for attention-based encoder-decoder models in order to exploit linguistic resourced for NMT. By training the models not only on the machine translation task, but also on other NLP tasks, we yielded clear improvements on the translation performance. Results show that multi-task learning improves the translation up to 1.5 BLEU

points and 2 characTER points. As a by product, we were also able to improved the performance of the POS tagging by 30% to 50% relatively. This is especially helpful since data annotation for many NLP tasks is very time-consuming and expensive. It suggests that multi-task learning is a promising approach to exploit any linguistic annotated data, which is especially important if we have a low-resource condition.

We addressed the influence of three design decisions: the involved tasks, the training schedule and the architecture of the model. The largest influence on the final performance was given by the training schedule . By adapting the system on the individual tasks, we were able to make most use of available additional resources. In this case, we showed that both additional resources, the data for POS tagging as well as the named entity-annotated corpus, were beneficial for the translation quality. It is worth mentioning that this was achieved using corpora from a different domain, i.e. spoken TED talks versus written style. Furthermore, these corpora were significantly smaller than the available parallel data. Finally, the amount of parameter sharing defined by the architecture of the model has less influence on the final performance. Although, the best performance on both tasks was achieved with a model sharing only the encoder between the tasks.

In this work, the performance of machine translation task was improved by adopting multi-task training with other source language NLP tasks. In future work, we will also investigate methods to include target-language NLP tasks into the joint framework.

Acknowledgments

The project leading to this application has received funding from the European Union's Horizon 2020 research and innovation programme under grant agreement n° 645452. This work was supported by the Carl-Zeiss-Stiftung.

References

D. Bahdanau, K. Cho, and Y. Bengio. 2014. Neural machine translation by jointly learning to align and translate. *CoRR* abs/1409.0473.

D. Benikova, C. Biemann, M. Kisselew, and S. Pado. 2014. Germeval 2014 named entity recognition shared task: Companion paper. In *Proceedings of the KONVENS GermEval workshop*. Hildesheim, Germany, pages 104–112.

S. Brants, S. Dipper, P. Eisenberg, S. Hansen-Schirra, E. König, W. Lezius, C. Rohrer, G. Smith, and H. Uszkoreit. 2004. Tiger: Linguistic interpretation of a german corpus. *Research on Language and Computation* 2(4):597–620. https://doi.org/10.1007/s11168-004-7431-3.

M. Cettolo, C. Girardi, and M. Federico. 2012. Wit: Web inventory of transcribed and translated talks. In *Proceedings of the 16th Conference of the European Association for Machine Translation (EAMT)*. Trento, Italy, pages 261–268.

E. Cho, J. Niehues, T-L Ha, M. Sperber, M. Mediani, and A. Waibel. 2016. Adaptation and combination of nmt systems: The kit translation systems for iwslt 2016. In *Proceedings of the 13th International Workshop on Spoken Language Translation (IWSLT 2016)*. Seattle, USA.

R. Collobert, J. Weston, L. Bottou, M. Karlen, K. Kavukcuoglu, and P. Kuksa. 2011. Natural language processing (almost) from scratch. *J. Mach. Learn. Res.* 12:2493–2537.

D. Dong, H. Wu, W. He, D. Yu, and H. Wang. 2015. Multi-task learning for multiple language translation. In *Proceedings of the 53st Annual Meeting of the Association for Computational Linguistics (ACL 2015)*. Beijing, China.

O. Firat, K. Cho, and Y. Bengio. 2016a. Multiway, multilingual neural machine translation with a shared attention mechanism. In *Proceedings of the 2012 Conference of the North American Chapter of the Association for Computational Linguistics: Human Language Technologies (NAACL-HLT 2016)*. San Diego, California, USA, pages 866–875.

O. Firat, B. Sankaran, Y. Al-Onaizan, F. T. Yarman-Vural, and K. Cho. 2016b. Zero-resource translation with multi-lingual neural machine translation. In *Proceedings of the Conference on Empirical Methods in Natural Language Processing (EMNLP 2016)*. Austin, USA, pages 268–277.

T-L Ha, J. Niehues, and A. Waibel. 2016. Toward multilingual neural machine translation with universal encoder and decoder. In *Proceedings of the 13th International Workshop on Spoken Language Translation (IWSLT 2016)*. Seattle, USA.

S. Hochreiter and J. Schmidhuber. 1997. Long short-term memory. *Neural Comput.* 9(8):1735–1780. https://doi.org/10.1162/neco.1997.9.8.1735.

M. Johnson, M. Schuster, Q. V. Le, M. Krikun, Y. Wu, Z. Chen, N. Thorat, F. B. Viegas, M. Wattenberg, G. Corrado, M. Hughes, and J. Dean. 2016. Google's multilingual neural machine translation system: Enabling zero-shot translation. *CoRR* abs/1611.04558.

M. Labeau and Allauzen Löser K. 2015. Non-lexical neural architecture for fine-grained pos tagging. In *Proceedings of the Conference on Empirical Methods in Natural Language Processing (EMNLP 2015)*. Lisbonne, Portugal, page 6.

T. Lavergne, H-S Le, A. Allauzen, and F. Yvon. 2011. Limsi's experiments in domain adaptation for iwslt11. In M-Y Hwang and S. St??ker, editors, *Proceedings of the Eights International Workshop on Spoken Language Translation (IWSLT 2011)*. San Francisco, CA, pages 62–67.

M-T Luong, Q. V. Le, I. Sutskever, O. Vinyals, and L. Kaiser. 2015. Multi-task sequence to sequence learning. *CoRR* abs/1511.06114.

G. Neubig. 2015. lamtram: A toolkit for language and translation modeling using neural networks.

J. Niehues, T-L Ha, E. Cho, and A. Waibel. 2016. Using factored word representation in neural network language models. In *Proceedings of the First Conference on Statistical Machine Translation (WMT 2016)*. Berlin, Germany.

J. Niehues and M. Kolss. 2009. A pos-based model for long-range reorderings in smt. In *Proceedings of the Fourth Workshop on Statistical Machine Translation (WMT 2009)*. Athens, Greece.

K. Papineni, S. Roukos, T. Ward, and W-J Zhu. 2002. Bleu: A method for automatic evaluation of machine translation. In *Proceedings of the 40th Annual Meeting of the Association for Computational Linguistics (ACL 2002)*. Philadelphia, Pennsylvania, pages 311–318. https://doi.org/10.3115/1073083.1073135.

M. Schuster and K. K. Paliwal. 1997. Bidirectional recurrent neural networks. *IEEE Transactions on Signal Processing* 45(11):2673–2681.

R. Sennrich and B. Haddow. 2016. Linguistic input features improve neural machine translation. In *Proceedings of the First Conference on Statistical Machine Translation (WMT 2016)*. Berline, Germany, pages 83–91.

R. Sennrich, B. Haddow, and A. Birch. 2016. Neural machine translation of rare words with subword units. In *Proceedings of the 54st Annual Meeting of the Association for Computational Linguistics (ACL 2016)*. Berlin, Germany.

M. Stanojevic and K. Sima'an. 2014. Fitting sentence level translation evaluation with many dense features. In *Proceedings of the 2014 Conference on Empirical Methods in Natural Language Processing (EMNLP)*. Doha, Qatar, pages 202–206.

I. Sutskever, O. Vinyals, and Q. V. Le. 2014. Sequence to sequence learning with neural networks. In *Advances in Neural Information Processing Systems 27: Annual Conference on Neural Information Processing Systems 2014*. Quebec, Canada, pages 3104–3112.

W. Wang, J-T Peter, H. Rosendahl, and H. Ney. 2016. Character: Translation edit rate on character level. In *Proceedings of the First Conference on Statistical Machine Translation (WMT 2016)*. Berlin, Germany, pages 505–510.

Y. Wu, X. Lu, H. Yamamoto, S. Matsuda, C. Hori, and H. Kashioka. 2012. Factored language model based on recurrent neural network. In *Proceedings of the 24rd International Conference on Computational Linguistics (COLING 2012)*. Bombay, India.

Tree as a Pivot: Syntactic Matching Methods in Pivot Translation

Akiva Miura[†], Graham Neubig[‡,†], Katsuhito Sudoh[†], Satoshi Nakamura[†]
[†] Nara Institute of Science and Technology, Japan
[‡] Carnegie Mellon University, USA
miura.akiba.lr9@is.naist.jp   gneubig@cs.cmu.edu
sudoh@is.naist.jp   s-nakamura@is.naist.jp

Abstract

Pivot translation is a useful method for translating between languages with little or no parallel data by utilizing parallel data in an intermediate language such as English. A popular approach for pivot translation used in phrase-based or tree-based translation models combines source-pivot and pivot-target translation models into a source-target model, as known as *triangulation*. However, this combination is based on the constituent words' surface forms and often produces incorrect source-target phrase pairs due to semantic ambiguity in the pivot language, and interlingual differences. This degrades translation accuracy. In this paper, we propose a approach for the triangulation using syntactic subtrees in the pivot language to distinguish pivot language words by their syntactic roles to avoid incorrect phrase combinations. Experimental results on the United Nations Parallel Corpus show the proposed method gains in all tested combinations of language, up to 2.3 BLEU points.[1]

1 Introduction

In statistical machine translation (SMT) (Brown et al., 1993), it is known that translation with models trained on larger parallel corpora can achieve greater accuracy (Dyer et al., 2008). Unfortunately, large bilingual corpora are not readily available for many language pairs, particularly those that do not include English. One effective solution to overcome the scarceness of bilingual data is to introduce a pivot language for which paral-

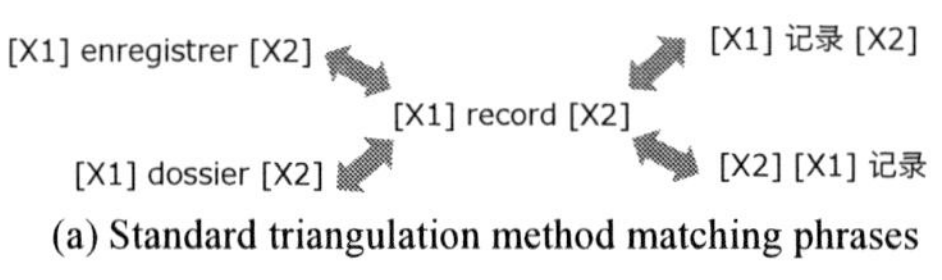

(a) Standard triangulation method matching phrases

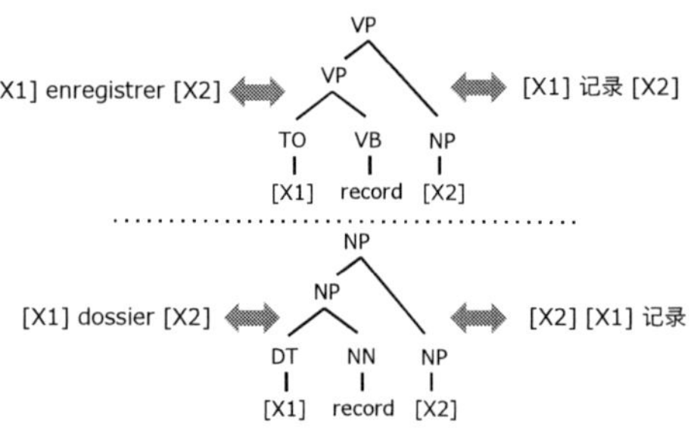

(b) Proposed triangulation method matching subtrees

Figure 1: Example of disambiguation by parse subtree matching (Fr-En-Zh), [X1] and [X2] are non-terminals for sub-phrases.

lel data with the source and target languages exists (de Gispert and Mariño, 2006).

Among various methods using pivot languages, one popular and effective method is the triangulation method (Utiyama and Isahara, 2007; Cohn and Lapata, 2007), which first combines source-pivot and pivot-target translation models (TMs) into a source-target model, then translates using this combined model. The procedure of triangulating two TMs into one has been examined for different frameworks of SMT and its effectiveness has been confirmed both in Phrase-Based SMT (PBMT) (Koehn et al., 2003; Utiyama and Isahara, 2007) and in Hierarchical Phrase-Based SMT (Hiero) (Chiang, 2007; Miura et al., 2015). However, word sense ambiguity and interlingual differences of word usage cause difficulty in accurately learning correspondences between source and target phrases, and thus the accuracy obtained by triangulated models lags behind that of models

---

[1]Code to replicate the experiments can be found at https://github.com/akivajp/wmt2017

Proceedings of the Conference on Machine Translation (WMT), Volume 1: Research Papers, pages 90–98
Copenhagen, Denmark, September 7–11, 2017. ©2017 Association for Computational Linguistics

trained on direct parallel corpora.

In the triangulation method, source-pivot and pivot-target phrase pairs are connected as a source-target phrase pair when a common pivot-side phrase exists. In Figure 1 (a), we show an example of standard triangulation on Hiero TMs that combines hierarchical rules of phrase pairs by matching pivot phrases with equivalent surface forms. This example also demonstrates problems of ambiguity: the English word "record" can correspond to several different parts-of-speech according to the context. More broadly, phrases including this word also have different possible grammatical structures, but it is impossible to uniquely identify this structure unless information about the surrounding context is given.

This varying syntactic structure will affect translation. For example, the French verb "enregistrer" corresponds to the English verb "record", but the French noun "dossier" also corresponds to "record" — as a noun. As a more extreme example, Chinese is a languages that does not have inflections according to the part-of-speech of the word. As a result, even in the contexts where "record" is used with different parts-of-speech, the Chinese word "记录" will be used, although the word order will change. These facts might result in an incorrect connection of "[X1] enregister [X2]" and "[X2] [X1] 记录" even though proper correspondence of "[X1] enregister [X2]" and "[X1] dossier [X2]" would be "[X1] 记录 [X2]" and "[X2] [X1] 记录". Hence a superficial phrase matching method based solely on the surface form of the pivot will often combine incorrect phrase pairs, causing translation errors if their translation scores are estimated to be higher than the proper correspondences.

Given this background, we hypothesize that disambiguation of these cases would be easier if the necessary syntactic information such as phrase structures are considered during pivoting. To incorporate this intuition into our models, we propose a method that considers syntactic information of the pivot phrase, as shown in Figure 1 (b). In this way, the model will distinguish translation rules extracted in contexts in which the English symbol string "[X1] record [X2]" behaves as a verbal phrase, from contexts in which the same string acts as nominal phrase.

Specifically, we propose a method based on Synchronous Context-Free Grammars (SCFGs)

(Aho and Ullman, 1969; Chiang, 2007), which are widely used in tree-based machine translation frameworks (§2). After describing the baseline triangulation method (§3), which uses only the surface forms for performing triangulation, we propose two methods for triangulation based on syntactic matching (§4). The first places a hard restriction on exact matching of parse trees (§4.1) included in translation rules, while the second places a softer restriction allowing partial matches (§4.2). To investigate the effect of our proposed method on pivot translation quality, we perform experiments of pivot translation on the United Nations Parallel Corpus (Ziemski et al., 2016), which shows that our method indeed provide significant gains in accuracy (of up to 2.3 BLEU points), in almost all combinations of 5 languages with English as a pivot language (§5). In addition, as an auxiliary result, we compare pivot translation using the proposed method with zero-shot neural machine translation, and find that triangulation of symbolic translation models still significantly outperforms neural MT in the zero-resource scenario.

2 Translation Framework

2.1 Synchronous Context-Free Grammars

In this section, first we cover SCFGs, which are widely used in machine translation, particularly hierarchical phrase-based translation (Hiero) (Chiang, 2007). In SCFGs, the elementary structures used in translation are synchronous rewrite rules with aligned pairs of source and target symbols on the right-hand side:

$$X \to \langle \overline{s}, \overline{t} \rangle \tag{1}$$

where X is the head symbol of the rewrite rule, and s and $\overline{t}$ are both strings of terminals and non-terminals on the source and target side respectively. Each string in the right side pair has the same number of indexed non-terminals, and identically indexed non-terminals correspond to each-other. For example, a synchronous rule could take the form of

$$X \to \langle X_0 \text{ of } X_1, X_1 \text{ 的 } X_0 \rangle . \tag{2}$$

Synchronous rules can be extracted based on parallel sentences and automatically obtained word alignments. Each extracted rule is scored with phrase translation probabilities in both directions $\phi(\overline{s}|\overline{t})$ and $\phi(\overline{t}|\overline{s})$, lexical translation probabilities in both directions $\phi_{lex}(\overline{s}|\overline{t})$ and $\phi_{lex}(\overline{t}|\overline{s})$, a word penalty counting the terminals in $\bar{t}$, and a constant phrase penalty of 1.

At translation time, the decoder searches for the target sentence that maximizes the derivation probability, which is defined as the sum of the scores of the rules used in the derivation, and the log of the language model (LM) probability over the target strings. When not considering an LM, it is possible to efficiently find the best translation for an input sentence using the CKY+ algorithm (Chappelier et al., 1998). When using an LM, the expanded search space is further reduced based on a limit on expanded edges, or total states per span, through a procedure such as cube pruning (Chiang, 2007).

2.2 Hierarchical Rules

In this section, we specifically cover the rules used in Hiero. Hierarchical rules are composed of initial head symbol S, and synchronous rules containing terminals and single kind of non-terminals X.[2] Hierarchical rules are extracted using the same phrase extraction procedure used in phrase-based translation (Koehn et al., 2003) based on word alignments, followed by a step that performs recursive extraction of hierarchical phrases (Chiang, 2007).

For example, hierarchical rules could take the form of:

$$X \rightarrow \langle \text{Officers, 主席团 成员} \rangle \tag{3}$$

$$X \rightarrow \langle \text{the Committee, 委员会} \rangle \tag{4}$$

$$X \rightarrow \langle X_0 \text{ of } X_1, X_1 \text{ 的 } X_0 \rangle . \tag{5}$$

From these rules, we can translate the input sentence by derivation:

$$
\begin{aligned}
S \quad &\rightarrow \quad \langle X_0,\ X_0 \rangle \\
&\Rightarrow \quad \langle X_1 \text{ of } X_2,\ X_2 \text{ 的 } X_1 \rangle \\
&\Rightarrow \quad \langle \text{Officers of } X_2,\ X_2 \text{ 主席团 成员} \rangle \\
&\Rightarrow \quad \langle \text{Officers of the Committee,} \\
&\qquad\qquad \text{委员会 的 主席团 成员} \rangle
\end{aligned}
$$

The advantage of Hiero is that it is able to achieve relatively high word re-ordering accuracy (compared to other symbolic SMT alternatives such as standard phrase-based MT) without language-dependent processing. On the other hand, since it does not use syntactic information and tries to extract all possible combinations of rules, it has the tendency to extract very large translation rule tables and also tends to be less syntactically faithful in its derivations.

2.3 Explicitly Syntactic Rules

An alternative to Hiero rules is the use of synchronous context-free grammar or synchronous tree-substitution grammar (Graehl and Knight, 2004) rules that explicitly take into account the syntax of the source side (tree-to-string rules), target side (string-to-tree rules), or both (tree-to-tree rules). Taking the example of tree-to-string (T2S) rules, these use parse trees on the source language side, and the head symbols of the synchronous rules are not limited to S or X, but instead use non-terminal symbols corresponding to the phrase structure tags of a given parse tree. For example, T2S rules could take the form of:

$$X_{\text{NP}} \rightarrow \langle \text{(NP (NNS Officers)), 主席团 成员} \rangle \tag{6}$$

$$X_{\text{NP}} \rightarrow \langle \text{(NP (DT the) (NNP Committee)), 委员会} \rangle \tag{7}$$

$$X_{\text{PP}} \rightarrow \langle \text{(PP (IN of) } X_{\text{NP},0}\text{), } X_0 \text{ 的} \rangle \tag{8}$$

$$X_{\text{NP}} \rightarrow \langle \text{(NP } X_{\text{NP},0}\ X_{\text{PP},1}\text{), } X_1\ X_0 \rangle \tag{9}$$

Here, parse subtrees of the source language rules are given in the form of S-expressions.

From these rules, we can translate from the parse tree of the input sentence by derivation:

$$
\begin{aligned}
X_{\text{ROOT}} \quad &\rightarrow \quad \langle X_{\text{NP},0},\ X_0 \rangle \\
&\Rightarrow \quad \langle \text{(NP } X_{\text{NP},1}\ X_{\text{PP},2}\text{), } X_2\ X_1 \rangle \\
&\Rightarrow \quad \langle \text{(NP (NP (NNS Officers) } X_{\text{PP},2}\text{)), } X_2 \text{ 主席团 成员} \rangle \\
&\overset{*}{\Rightarrow} \quad \left\langle
\begin{array}{l}
\text{(NP} \\
\quad \text{(NP (NNS Officers))} \\
\quad \text{(PP (IN of)} \\
\quad\quad \text{(NP (DT the)} \\
\quad\quad\quad \text{(NNP Committee))))}
\end{array}
,\ \text{委员会 的 主席团 成员}
\right\rangle
\end{aligned}
$$

In this way, it is possible in T2S translation to obtain a result conforming to the source language's grammar. This method also has the advantage the number of less-useful synchronous rules extracted by syntax-agnostic methods such as Hiero are reduced, making it possible to learn more compact rule tables and allowing for faster translation.

3 Standard Triangulation Method

In the triangulation method by Cohn and Lapata (2007), we first train source-pivot and pivot-target rule tables as T_{SP} and T_{PT} respectively. Then we search T_{SP} and T_{PT} for source-pivot and pivot-target rules having a common pivot phrase, and

---

[2]It is also standard to include a glue rule $S \rightarrow \langle X_0,\ X_0 \rangle$, $S \rightarrow \langle S_0\ X_1,\ S_0\ X_1 \rangle$, $S \rightarrow \langle S_0\ X_1,\ X_1\ S_0 \rangle$ to fall back on when standard rules cannot result in a proper derivation.

synthesize them into source-target rules to create rule table T_{ST}:

$$X \to \langle \bar{s}, \bar{t} \rangle \in T_{ST}$$
$$s.t. \ X \to \langle \bar{s}, \bar{p} \rangle \in T_{SP} \ \wedge \ X \to \langle \bar{p}, \bar{t} \rangle \in T_{PT}. \quad (10)$$

For all the combined source-target rules, phrase translation probability $\phi(\cdot)$ and lexical translation probability $\phi_{lex}(\cdot)$ are estimated according to the following equations:

$$\phi\left(\bar{t}|\bar{s}\right) = \sum_{\bar{p} \in T_{SP} \cap T_{PT}} \phi\left(\bar{t}|\bar{p}\right) \phi\left(\bar{p}|\bar{s}\right), \quad (11)$$

$$\phi\left(\bar{s}|\bar{t}\right) = \sum_{\bar{p} \in T_{SP} \cap T_{PT}} \phi\left(\bar{s}|\bar{p}\right) \phi\left(\bar{p}|\bar{t}\right), \quad (12)$$

$$\phi_{lex}\left(\bar{t}|\bar{s}\right) = \sum_{\bar{p} \in T_{SP} \cap T_{PT}} \phi_{lex}\left(\bar{t}|\bar{p}\right) \phi_{lex}\left(\bar{p}|\bar{s}\right), (13)$$

$$\phi_{lex}\left(\bar{s}|\bar{t}\right) = \sum_{\bar{p} \in T_{SP} \cap T_{PT}} \phi_{lex}\left(\bar{s}|\bar{p}\right) \phi_{lex}\left(\bar{p}|\bar{t}\right). (14)$$

The equations (11)-(14) are based on the memoryless channel model, which assumes:

$$\phi\left(\bar{t}|\bar{p}, \bar{s}\right) = \phi\left(\bar{t}|\bar{p}\right), \quad (15)$$

$$\phi\left(\bar{s}|\bar{p}, \bar{t}\right) = \phi\left(\bar{s}|\bar{p}\right) \quad (16)$$

For example, in equation (15), it is assumed that the translation probability of target phrase given pivot and source phrases is never affected by the source phrase. However, it is easy to come up with examples where this assumption does not hold. Specifically, if there are multiple interpretations of the pivot phrase as shown in the example of Figure 1, source and target phrases that do not correspond to each other semantically might be connected, and over-estimation by summing products of the translation probabilities is likely to cause failed translations.

4 Triangulation with Syntactic Matching

In the previous section, we explained about the standard triangulation method and mentioned that the pivot side ambiguity causes incorrect estimation of translation probability and the translation accuracy might decrease. To address this problem, it is desirable to be able to distinguish pivot-side phrases that have different syntactic roles or meanings, even if the symbol strings are exactly equivalent. In the following two sections, we describe two methods to distinguish pivot phrases that have syntactically different roles, one based on exact matching of parse trees, and one based on soft matching.

4.1 Exact Matching of Parse Subtrees

In the exact matching method, we first train pivot-source and pivot-target T2S TMs by parsing the pivot side of parallel corpora, and store them into rule tables as T_{PS} and T_{PT} respectively. Synchronous rules of T_{PS} and T_{PT} take the form of $X \to \langle \hat{p}, \bar{s} \rangle$ and $X \to \langle \hat{p}, \bar{t} \rangle$ respectively, where $\hat{p}$ is a symbol string that expresses pivot-side parse subtree (S-expression), $\bar{s}$ and $\bar{t}$ express source and target symbol strings. The procedure of synthesizing source-target synchronous rules essentially follows equations (11)-(14), except using T_{PS} instead of T_{SP} (direction of probability features is reversed) and pivot subtree $\hat{p}$ instead of pivot phrase $\bar{p}$. Here $\bar{s}$ and $\bar{t}$ do not have syntactic information, therefore the synthesized synchronous rules should be hierarchical rules explained in §2.2.

The matching condition of this method has harder constraints than matching of superficial symbols in standard triangulation, and has the potential to reduce incorrect connections of phrase pairs, resulting in a more reliable triangulated TM. On the other hand, the number of connected rules decreases as well in this restricted triangulation, and the coverage of the triangulated model might be reduced. Therefore it is important to create TMs that are both reliabile and have high coverage.

4.2 Partial Matching of Parse Subtrees

To prevent the problem of the reduction of coverage in the exact matching method, we also propose a partial matching method that keeps coverage just like standard triangulation by allowing connection of incompletely equivalent pivot subtrees. To estimate translation probabilities in partial matching, we first define *weighted triangulation* generalizing the equations (11)-(14) of standard triangulation with weight function $\psi(\ )$:

$$\phi\left(\bar{t}|\bar{s}\right) = \sum_{\hat{p_T}} \sum_{\hat{p_S}} \phi\left(\bar{t}|\hat{p_T}\right) \psi\left(\hat{p_T}|\hat{p_S}\right) \phi\left(\hat{p_S}|\bar{s}\right), \quad (17)$$

$$\phi\left(\bar{s}|\bar{t}\right) = \sum_{\hat{p_S}} \sum_{\hat{p_T}} \phi\left(\bar{s}|\hat{p_S}\right) \psi\left(\hat{p_S}|\hat{p_T}\right) \phi\left(\hat{p_T}|\bar{t}\right), \quad (18)$$

$$\phi_{lex}\left(\bar{t}|\bar{s}\right) = \sum_{\hat{p_T}} \sum_{\hat{p_S}} \phi_{lex}\left(\bar{t}|\hat{p_T}\right) \psi\left(\hat{p_T}|\hat{p_S}\right) \phi_{lex}\left(\hat{p_S}|\bar{s}\right), \quad (19)$$

$$\phi_{lex}\left(\bar{s}|\bar{t}\right) = \sum_{\hat{p_S}} \sum_{\hat{p_T}} \phi_{lex}\left(\bar{s}|\hat{p_S}\right) \psi\left(\hat{p_S}|\hat{p_T}\right) \phi_{lex}\left(\hat{p_T}|\bar{t}\right) \quad (20)$$

where $\hat{p_S} \in T_{SP}$ and $\hat{p_T} \in P_{PT}$ are pivot parse subtrees of source-pivot and pivot-target synchronous rules respectively. By adjusting $\psi(\cdot)$, we can control the magnitude of the penalty for the case of incompletely matched connections. If we define $\psi(\hat{p_T}|\hat{p_S}) = 1$ when $\hat{p_T}$ is equal to $\hat{p_S}$ and $\psi(\hat{p_T}|\hat{p_S}) = 0$ otherwise, equations (17)-(20) are equivalent with equations (11)-(14).

Better estimating $\psi(\cdot)$ is not trivial, and co-occurrence counts of $\hat{p_S}$ and $\hat{p_T}$ are not available. Therefore we introduce a heuristic estimation method as follows:

$$\psi(\hat{p_T}|\hat{p_S}) = \frac{w(\hat{p_S},\hat{p_T})}{\sum_{\hat{p}\in T_{PT}} w(\hat{p_S},\hat{p})} \cdot \max_{\hat{p}\in T_{PT}} w(\hat{p_S},\hat{p}) \quad (21)$$

$$\psi(\hat{p_S}|\hat{p_T}) = \frac{w(\hat{p_S},\hat{p_T})}{\sum_{\hat{p}\in T_{SP}} w(\hat{p},\hat{p_T})} \cdot \max_{\hat{p}\in T_{SP}} w(\hat{p},\hat{p_T}) \quad (22)$$

$$w(\hat{p_S},\hat{p_T}) = \begin{cases} 0 & (flat(\hat{p_S}) \neq flat(\hat{p_T})) \\ \exp\left(-d\left(\hat{p_S},\hat{p_T}\right)\right) & (otherwise) \end{cases} \quad (23)$$

$$d(\hat{p_S},\hat{p_T}) = TreeEditDistance(\hat{p_S},\hat{p_T}) \quad (24)$$

where $flat(\hat{p})$ returns the symbol string of $\hat{p}$ keeping non-terminals, and $TreeEditDistance(\hat{p_S},\hat{p_T})$ is minimum cost of a sequence of operations (contract an edge, uncontract an edge, modify the label of an edge) needed to transform $\hat{p_S}$ into $\hat{p_T}$ (Klein, 1998).

According to equations (21)-(24), we can assure that incomplete match of pivot subtrees leads $d(\cdot) \geq 1$ and penalizes such that $\psi(\cdot) \leq 1/e^d \leq 1/e$, while exact match of subtrees leads to a value of $\psi(\cdot)$ at least $e \approx 2.718$ times larger than when using partially matched subtrees.

5   Experiments

5.1   Experimental Set-Up

To investigate the effect of our proposed approach, we evaluate the translation accuracy through pivot translation experiments on the United Nations Parallel Corpus (UN6Way) (Ziemski et al., 2016). UN6Way is a line-aligned multilingual parallel corpus that includes data in English (En), Arabic (Ar), Spanish (Es), French (Fr), Russian (Ru) and Chinese (Zh), covering different families of languages. It contains more than 11M sentences for each language pair, and is therefore suitable for multilingual translation tasks such as pivot translation. In these experiments, we fixed English as the pivot language considering that it is the language most frequently used as a pivot language. This has the positive side-effect that accurate phrase structure parsers are available in the pivot language, which is good for our proposed method. We perform pivot translation on all the combinations of the other 5 languages, and compared the accuracy

of each method. For tokenization, we adopt SentencePiece,[3] an unsupervised text tokenizer and detokenizer, that is although designed mainly for neural MT, we confirmed that it also helps to reduce training time and even improves translation accuracy in our Hiero model as well. We first trained a single shared tokenization model by feeding a total of 10M sentences from the data of all the 6 languages, set the maximum shared vocabulary size to be 16k, and tokenized all available text with the trained model. We used English raw text without tokenization for phrase structure analysis and for training Hiero and T2S TMs on the pivot side. To generate parse trees, we used the Cky-lark PCFG-LA parser (Oda et al., 2015), and filtered out lines of length over 60 tokens from all the parallel data to ensure accuracy of parsing and alignment. About 7.6M lines remained. Since Hiero requires a large amount of computational resources for training and decoding, so we decided not to use all available training data but first 1M lines for training each TM. As a decoder, we use Travatar (Neubig, 2013), and train Hiero and T2S TMs with its rule extraction code. We train 5-gram LMs over the target side of the same parallel data used for training TMs using KenLM (Heafield, 2011). For testing and parameter tuning, we used the first 1,000 lines of the 4,000 lines test and dev sets respectively. For the evaluation of translation results, we first detokenize with the SentencePiece model and re-tokenized with the tokenizer of the Moses toolkit (Koehn et al., 2007) for Arabic, Spanish, French and Russian and re-tokenized Chinese text with Kytea tokenizer (Neubig et al., 2011), then evaluated using case-sensitive BLEU-4 (Papineni et al., 2002).

We evaluate 6 translation methods:

Direct:
Translating with a Hiero TM directly trained on the source-target parallel corpus without using pivot language (as an oracle).

Tri. Hiero:
Triangulating source-pivot and pivot-target Hiero TMs into a source-target Hiero TM using the traditional method (baseline, §3).

Tri. TreeExact
Triangulating pivot-source and pivot-target T2S TMs into a source-target Hiero TM using

---

[3] https://github.com/google/sentencepiece

Source	Target	BLEU Score [%]		
		Direct	Tri. Hiero (baseline)	Tri. TreeExact (proposed 1)	Tri. TreePartial (proposed 2)
Ar	Es	38.49	34.20	‡ 34.97	‡ **35.94**
	Fr	33.34	29.93	‡ 30.68	‡ **30.83**
	Ru	24.63	22.94	‡ 23.94	‡ **24.15**
	Zh	27.27	22.78	‡ **25.17**	‡ 25.07
Es	Ar	27.18	22.97	‡ 24.09	‡ **24.45**
	Fr	43.24	38.74	‡ 39.62	‡ **40.12**
	Ru	28.83	26.35	‡ 27.25	‡ **27.41**
	Zh	27.08	24.54	25.00	† **25.16**
Fr	Ar	25.10	21.65	21.40	† **22.13**
	Es	45.20	40.16	‡ 41.03	‡ **41.99**
	Ru	27.42	24.71	† 25.24	‡ **25.64**
	Zh	25.84	23.16	**23.56**	23.53
Ru	Ar	22.53	19.82	19.86	**20.35**
	Es	37.60	34.56	34.96	‡ **35.62**
	Fr	34.05	30.75	† 31.43	‡ **31.67**
	Zh	28.03	24.88	25.07	**25.12**
Zh	Ar	20.09	16.66	17.01	‡ **17.73**
	Es	30.66	27.84	27.99	**28.05**
	Fr	25.97	23.82	24.34	† **24.35**
	Ru	21.16	18.63	‡ 19.58	‡ **19.59**

Table 1: Comparison of each triangulation methods. Bold face indicates the highest BLEU score in pivot translation, and daggers indicate statistically significant gains over Tri. Hiero († : $p < 0.05$, ‡ : $p < 0.01$).

the proposed exact matching of pivot subtrees (proposed 1, §4.1).

Tri. TreePartial

Triangulating pivot-source and pivot-target T2S TMs into a source-target Hiero TM using the proposed partial matching of pivot subtrees (proposed 2, §4.2)

5.2 Experimental Results

The result of experiments using all combinations of pivot translation tasks for 5 languages via English is shown in Table 1. From the results, we can see that the proposed partial matching method of pivot subtrees in triangulation outperforms the standard triangulation method for all language pairs and achieves higher or almost equal scores than proposed exact matching method. The exact matching method also outperforms the standard triangulation method in the majority of the language pairs, but has a lesser improvement than partial matching method. In Table 2 we show the comparison of coverage of each proposed triangulated method. From this table, we can see that the

exact matching method reduces several percent in number of unique phrases while the partial matching method keeps the same coverage with surface-form matching. We can consider that it is one of the reasons of the difference in improvement stability between the partial and exact matching methods.

We show an example of a translated sentences for which pivot-side ambiguity is resolved in the the syntactic matching methods:

Source Sentence in French:
La Suisse encourage **tous les États parties** à soutenir le travail conceptuel que fait actuellement le Secrétariat .

Corresponding Sentence in English:
Switzerland encourages all parties to support the current conceptual work of the secretariat.

Reference in Spanish:
Suiza alienta a **todos los Estados partes** a que apoyen la actual labor *conceptual* de la Secretaría .

Source	Target	Number of source-side unique phrases/words	
		Tri. TreeExact	Tri. TreePartial
Ar	Es	2.580M / 5,072	2.646M / 5,077
	Fr	2.589M / 5,067	2.658M / 5,071
	Ru	2.347M / 5,085	2.406M / 5,088
	Zh	2.324M / 5,034	2.386M / 5,040
Es	Ar	1.942M / 5,182	2.013M / 5,188
	Fr	2.062M / 5,205	2.129M / 5,210
	Ru	1,978M / 5,191	2.037M / 5,197
	Zh	1,920M / 5,175	1.986M / 5,180
Fr	Ar	2.176M / 5,310	2.233M / 5,316
	Es	2.302M / 5,337	2.366M / 5,342
	Ru	2.203M / 5.311	2.266M / 5,318
	Zh	2.162M / 5.313	2.215M / 5,321
Ru	Ar	2.437M / 5,637	2.505M / 5,644
	Es	2.478M / 5.677	2.536M / 5,682
	Fr	2.479M / 5,661	2.531M / 5,665
	Zh	2.466M / 5,682	2.515M / 5,688
Zh	Ar	1.480M / 9,428	1.556M / 9,474
	Es	1.504M / 9,523	1.570M / 9,555
	Fr	1.499M / 9,490	1,568M / 9,520
	Ru	1.518M / 9,457	1.593M / 9,487

Table 2: Comparison of rule table coverage in proposed triangulation methods.

Direct:

Suiza alienta a todos los Estados partes a que apoyen el trabajo conceptual que se examinan en la Secretaría . (BLEU+1: 55.99)

Tri. Hiero:

Suiza *conceptuales* para apoyar la labor que en estos momentos la Secretaría alienta a todos los Estados Partes . (BLEU+1: 29.74)

Tri. TreeExact:

Suiza alienta a **todos los Estados Partes** a apoyar la labor conceptual que actualmente la Secretaría . (BLEU+1: 43.08)

Tri. TreePartial:

Suiza alienta a **todos los Estados Partes** a apoyar la labor conceptual que actualmente la Secretaría . (BLEU+1: 43.08)

The results of Tri.TreeExact and Tri.TreePartial are same in this example. We find that the derivation in Tri.Hiero uses rule $X \rightarrow \langle X_0$ _parties $X_1, X_1 X_0$ _Partes$\rangle$[4]

causing incorrect re-ordering of phrases followed by steps of incorrect word selection.[5] On the other hand, derivation in Tri.TreeExact and Tri.TreePartial uses rule $X \rightarrow \langle$ _tous _les X_0 _parties, _todos X_0 _Partes$\rangle$[6] synthesized from T2S rules with common pivot subtree (NP (DT all) (NP' X_{NNP} (NNS parties)). We can confirm that the derivation improves word-selection and word-reordering by using this rule.

5.3 Comparison with Neural MT:

Recent results (Firat et al., 2016; Johnson et al., 2016) have found that neural machine translation systems can gain the ability to perform translation with zero parallel resources by training on multiple sets of bilingual data. However, previous work has not examined the competitiveness of these methods with pivot-based symbolic SMT frameworks such as PBMT or Hiero. In this section, we compare a zero-shot NMT model (detailed parameters in Table 3) with our pivot-based Hiero models.

---

[4]The words emphasized with underline and wavy-underline in the example correspond to X_0 and X_1 respectively.

[5]For example, the word "conceptuales" with italic face in Tri.Hiero takes the wrong form and position.

[6]The words emphasized in bold face in the example correspond to the rule.

vocabulary size:	16k (shared)
source embedding size:	512
target embedding size:	512
output embedding size:	512
encoder hidden size:	512
decoder hidden size:	512
LSTM layers:	1
attention type:	MLP
attention hidden size:	512
optimizer type:	Adam
loss integration type:	mean
batch size:	2048
max iteration:	200k
dropout rate:	0.3
decoder type:	Luong+ 2015

Table 3: Main parameters of NMT training

Direct NMT is trained with the same data of Direct Hiero, Cascade NMT translates by bridging source-pivot and pivot-target NMT models, and Zero-Shot NMT is trained on single shared model with pvt $\leftrightarrow$ {src,target} parallel data according to Johnson et al. (2016). To train and evaluate NMT models, we adopt NMTKit.[7] From the results we see the tendency of NMT that directly trained model achieves high translation accuracy even for translation between languages of different families, on the other hand, the accuracy is drastically reduced in the situation when there is no source-target parallel corpora for training. Cascade is one immediate method connecting two TMs, and NMT cascade translation shows the medium performance in this experiment. In our setting, while bilingually trained NMT systems were competitive or outperformed Hiero based models, zero-shot translation is uniformly weaker. This may be because we used only 1 LSTM layer for encoder/decoder, or because the amount of parallel corpora or language pairs were not sufficient. Thus, we can posit that while zero-shot translation has demonstrated reasonable results in some settings, successful zero-shot translation systems are far from trivial to build, and pivot-based symbolic MT systems such as PBMT or Hiero may still be a competitive alternative.

---

[7]https://github.com/odashi/nmtkit

6 Conclusion

In this paper, we have proposed a method of pivot translation using triangulation with exact or partial matching method of pivot-side parse subtrees. In experiments, we found that these triangulated models are effective in particular when allowing partial matching. To estimate translation probabilities, we introduced heuristic that has no guarantee to be optimal. Therefore in the future, we plan to explore more refined estimation methods that utilize machine learning.

Acknowledgments

Part of this work was supported by JSPS KAKENHI Grant Numbers JP16H05873 and JP17H06101.

References

Alfred V. Aho and Jeffrey D. Ullman. 1969. Syntax directed translations and the pushdown assembler. *Journal of Computer and System Sciences* 3(1):37–56.

Peter F. Brown, Vincent J.Della Pietra, Stephen A. Della Pietra, and Robert L. Mercer. 1993. The Mathematics of Statistical Machine Translation: Parameter Estimation. *Computational Linguistics* 19:263–312.

Jean-Cédric Chappelier, Martin Rajman, et al. 1998. A Generalized CYK Algorithm for Parsing Stochastic CFG. In *Proc. TAPD*. Citeseer, volume 98, pages 133–137.

David Chiang. 2007. Hierarchical Phrase-Based Translation. *Computational Linguistics* 33(2):201–228.

Trevor Cohn and Mirella Lapata. 2007. Machine Translation by Triangulation: Making Effective Use of Multi-Parallel Corpora. In *Proc. ACL*. pages 728–735.

Adrià de Gispert and José B. Mariño. 2006. Catalan-English Statistical Machine Translation without Parallel Corpus: Bridging through Spanish. In *Proc. of LREC 5th Workshop on Strategies for developing machine translation for minority languages*. pages 65–68.

Chris Dyer, Aaron Cordova, Alex Mont, and Jimmy Lin. 2008. Fast, Easy, and Cheap: Construction of Statistical Machine Translation Models with MapReduce. In *Proc. WMT*. pages 199–207.

Orhan Firat, Baskaran Sankaran, Yaser Al-Onaizan, Fatos T. Yarman Vural, and Kyunghyun Cho. 2016. Zero-Resource Translation with Multi-Lingual Neural Machine Translation. In *Proc. EMNLP*. pages 268–277.

Source	Target	BLEU Score [%]				
		Direct Hiero	Direct NMT	Tri. TreePartial	Cascade NMT	Zero-Shot NMT
Ar	Es	38.49	38.25	35.94	31.62	8.18
	Fr	33.34	33.16	30.83	26.91	8.57
	Ru	24.63	27.00	24.15	21.67	5.79
	Zh	27.27	30.04	25.07	23.70	5.04
Es	Ar	27.18	26.02	24.45	21.21	5.22
	Fr	43.24	41.83	40.12	31.84	15.04
	Ru	28.83	30.65	27.41	23.60	7.57
	Zh	27.08	32.36	25.16	26.03	8.62
Fr	Ar	25.10	23.28	22.13	18.66	8.08
	Es	45.20	44.49	41.99	32.93	14.37
	Ru	27.42	28.29	25.64	20.87	8.77
	Zh	25.84	29.10	23.53	23.14	11.95
Ru	Ar	22.53	23.19	20.35	19.71	3.18
	Es	37.60	38.67	35.62	31.25	10.42
	Fr	34.05	33.26	31.67	27.34	9.76
	Zh	28.03	31.39	25.12	24.25	9.46
Zh	Ar	20.09	20.17	17.73	16.89	10.38
	Es	30.66	32.69	28.05	26.01	6.13
	Fr	25.97	27.68	24.35	23.35	7.12
	Ru	21.16	23.17	19.59	18.40	3.21

Table 4: Comparison of SMT and NMT in multilingual translation tasks.

Jonathan Graehl and Kevin Knight. 2004. Training Tree Transducers. In *Proc. NAACL.* pages 105–112.

Kenneth Heafield. 2011. KenLM: Faster and Smaller Language Model Queries. In *Proc, WMT.* pages 187–197.

Melvin Johnson, Mike Schuster, Quoc V. Le, Maxim Krikun, Yonghui Wu, Zhifeng Chen, Nikhil Thorat, Fernanda B. Viégas, Martin Wattenberg, Greg Corrado, Macduff Hughes, and Jeffrey Dean. 2016. Google's Multilingual Neural Machine Translation System: Enabling Zero-Shot Translation. *CoRR* abs/1611.04558. http://arxiv.org/abs/1611.04558.

Philip N. Klein. 1998. Computing the Edit-Distance Between Unrooted Ordered Trees. In *Proc. of European Symposium on Algorithms.* pages 91–102.

Philipp Koehn, Hieu Hoang, Alexandra Birch, Chris Callison-Burch, Marcello Federico, Nicola Bertoldi, Brooke Cowan, Wade Shen, Christine Moran, Richard Zens, Chris Dyer, Ondrej Bojar, Alexandra Constantin, and Evan Herbst. 2007. Moses: Open Source Toolkit for Statistical Machine Translation. In *Proc. ACL.* pages 177–180.

Phillip Koehn, Franz Josef Och, and Daniel Marcu. 2003. Statistical Phrase-Based Translation. In *Proc. NAACL.* pages 48–54.

Akiva Miura, Graham Neubig, Sakriani Sakti, Tomoki Toda, and Satoshi Nakamura. 2015. Improving Pivot Translation by Remembering the Pivot. In *Proc. ACL.* pages 573–577.

Graham Neubig. 2013. Travatar: A Forest-to-String Machine Translation Engine based on Tree Transducers. In *Proc. ACL Demo Track.* pages 91–96.

Graham Neubig, Yosuke Nakata, and Shinsuke Mori. 2011. Pointwise Prediction for Robust, Adaptable Japanese Morphological Analysis. In *Proc. ACL.* pages 529–533.

Yusuke Oda, Graham Neubig, Sakriani Sakti, Tomoki Toda, and Satoshi Nakamura. 2015. Ckylark: A More Robust PCFG-LA Parser. In *Proc. NAACL.* pages 41–45.

Kishore Papineni, Salim Roukos, Todd Ward, and Wei-Jing Zhu. 2002. BLEU: a Method for Automatic Evaluation of Machine Translation. In *Proc. ACL.* pages 311–318.

Masao Utiyama and Hitoshi Isahara. 2007. A Comparison of Pivot Methods for Phrase-Based Statistical Machine Translation. In *Proc. NAACL.* pages 484–491.

Michał Ziemski, Marcin Junczys-Dowmunt, and Bruno Pouliquen. 2016. The United Nations Parallel Corpus v1.0. In *Proc. LREC.* pages 3530–3534.

Deep Architectures for Neural Machine Translation

Antonio Valerio Miceli Barone[†]   Jindřich Helcl[*]   Rico Sennrich[†]
Barry Haddow[†]   Alexandra Birch[†]
[†]School of Informatics, University of Edinburgh
[*]Faculty of Mathematics and Physics, Charles University
{amiceli, bhaddow}@inf.ed.ac.uk
{rico.sennrich, a.birch}@ed.ac.uk
helcl@ufal.mff.cuni.cz

Abstract

It has been shown that increasing model depth improves the quality of neural machine translation. However, different architectural variants to increase model depth have been proposed, and so far, there has been no thorough comparative study.

In this work, we describe and evaluate several existing approaches to introduce depth in neural machine translation. Additionally, we explore novel architectural variants, including deep transition RNNs, and we vary how attention is used in the deep decoder. We introduce a novel "BiDeep" RNN architecture that combines deep transition RNNs and stacked RNNs.

Our evaluation is carried out on the English to German WMT news translation dataset, using a single-GPU machine for both training and inference. We find that several of our proposed architectures improve upon existing approaches in terms of speed and translation quality. We obtain best improvements with a BiDeep RNN of combined depth 8, obtaining an average improvement of 1.5 BLEU over a strong shallow baseline.

We release our code for ease of adoption.

1 Introduction

Neural machine translation (NMT) is a well-established approach that yields the best results on most language pairs (Bojar et al., 2016; Cettolo et al., 2016). Most systems are based on the sequence-to-sequence model with attention (Bahdanau et al., 2015) which employs single-layer recurrent neural networks both in the encoder and in the decoder.

Unlike feed-forward networks where depth is straightforwardly defined as the number of non-input layers, recurrent neural network architectures with multiple layers allow different connection schemes (Pascanu et al., 2014) that give rise to different, orthogonal, definitions of depth (Zhang et al., 2016) which can affect the model performance depending on a given task. This is further complicated in sequence-to-sequence models as they contain multiple sub-networks, recurrent or feed-forward, each of which can be deep in different ways, giving rise to a large number of possible configurations.

In this work we focus on *stacked* and *deep transition* recurrent architectures as defined by Pascanu et al. (2014). Different types of stacked architectures have been successfully used for NMT (Zhou et al., 2016; Wu et al., 2016). However, there is a lack of empirical comparisons of different deep architectures. Deep transition architectures have been successfully used for language modeling (Zilly et al., 2016), but not for NMT so far. We evaluate these architectures, both alone and in combination, varying the connection scheme between the different components and their depth over the different dimensions, measuring the performance of the different configurations on the WMT news translation task.[1]

Related work includes that of Britz et al. (2017), who have performed an exploration of NMT architectures in parallel to our work. Their experiments, which are largely orthogonal to ours, focus on embedding size, RNN cell type (GRU vs. LSTM), network depth (defined according to the architecture of Wu et al. (2016)), attention mechanism and beam size. Gehring et al. (2017) recently proposed a NMT architecture based on convolutions over fixed-sized windows

---

[1] http://www.statmt.org/wmt17/
translation-task.html

Proceedings of the Conference on Machine Translation (WMT), Volume 1: Research Papers, pages 99–107
Copenhagen, Denmark, September 7–11, 2017. ©2017 Association for Computational Linguistics

rather than RNNs, and they reported results for different model depths and attention mechanism configurations. A similar feedforward architecture which uses multiple pervasive attention mechanisms rather than convolutions was proposed by Vaswani et al. (2017), who also report results for different model depths.

2 NMT Architectures

All the architectures that we consider in this work are GRU (Cho et al., 2014a) sequence-to-sequence transducers (Sutskever et al., 2014; Cho et al., 2014b) with attention (Bahdanau et al., 2015). In this section we describe the baseline system and the variants that we evaluated.

2.1 Baseline Architecture

As our baseline, we use the NMT architecture implemented in Nematus, which is described in more depth by Sennrich et al. (2017b). We augment it with layer normalization (Ba et al., 2016), which we have found to both improve translation quality and make training considerably faster.

For our discussion, it is relevant that the baseline architecture already exhibits two types of depth:

- *recurrence transition depth* in the decoder RNN which consists of two GRU transitions per output word with an attention mechanism in between, as described in Firat and Cho (2016).

- *feed-forward depth* in the attention network that computes the alignment scores and in the output network that predicts the target words. Both these networks are multi-layer perceptrons with one tanh hidden layer.

2.2 Deep Transition Architectures

In a deep transition RNN (DT-RNN), at each time step the next state is computed by the sequential application of multiple transition layers, effectively using a feed-forward network embedded inside the recurrent cell. In our experiments, these layers are GRU transition blocks with independently trainable parameters, connected such that the "state" output of one of them is used as the "state" input of the next one. Note that each of these GRU transition is not individually recurrent, recurrence only occurs at the level of the whole multi-layer cell, as the "state" output of the last

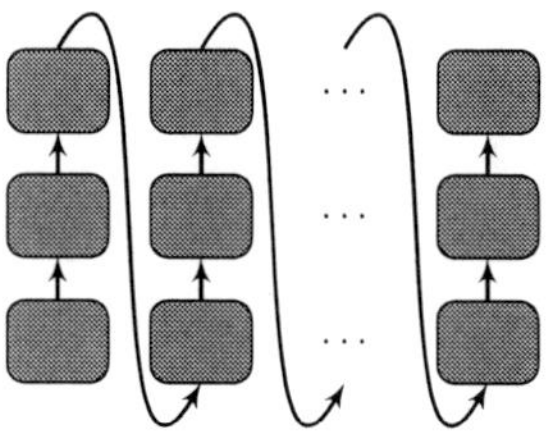

Figure 1: Deep transition decoder

GRU transition for the current time step is carried over as the "state" input of the first GRU transition for the next time step.

Applying this architecture to NMT is a novel contribution.

2.2.1 Deep Transition Encoder

As in a baseline shallow Nematus system, the encoder is a bidirectional recurrent neural network. Let L_s be the encoder recurrence depth, then for the i-th source word in the forward direction the forward source word state $\overrightarrow{h}_i \equiv \overrightarrow{h}_{i,L_s}$ is computed as:

$$\overrightarrow{h}_{i,1} = \mathrm{GRU}_1\left(x_i, \overrightarrow{h}_{i-1,L_s}\right)$$
$$\overrightarrow{h}_{i,k} = \mathrm{GRU}_k\left(0, \overrightarrow{h}_{i,k-1}\right) \text{ for } 1 < k \leq L_s$$

where the input to the first GRU transition is the word embedding x_i, while the other GRU transitions have no external inputs. Recurrence occurs as the previous word state $\overrightarrow{h}_{i-1,L_s}$ enters the computation in the first GRU transition for the current word.

The reverse source word states are computed similarly and concatenated to the forward ones to form the bidirectional source word states $C \equiv \left\{\left[\overrightarrow{h}_{i,L_s} \overleftarrow{h}_{i,L_s}\right]\right\}$.

2.2.2 Deep Transition Decoder

The deep transition decoder is obtained by extending the baseline decoder in a similar way. Recall that the baseline decoder of Nematus already has a transition depth of two, with the first GRU transition receiving as input the embedding of the previous target word and the second GRU transition receiving as input a context vector computed by the attention mechanism. We extend this decoder architecture to an arbitrary transition depth L_t as follows:

$$s_{j,1} = \text{GRU}_1\left(y_{j-1}, s_{j-1,L_t}\right)$$
$$s_{j,2} = \text{GRU}_2\left(\text{ATT}(C, s_{j,1}), s_{j,1}\right)$$
$$s_{j,k} = \text{GRU}_k\left(0, s_{j,k-1}\right) \text{ for } 2 < k \leq L_t$$

where y_{j-1} is the embedding of the previous target word and $\text{ATT}(C, s_{i,1})$ is the context vector computed by the attention mechanism. GRU transitions other than the first two do not have external inputs. The target word state vector $s_j \equiv s_{j,L_t}$ is then used by the feed-forward output network to predict the current target word. A diagram of this architecture is shown in Figure 1.

The output network can be also made deeper by adding more feed-forward hidden layers.

2.3 Stacked architectures

A stacked RNN is obtained by having multiple RNNs (GRUs in our experiments) run for the same number of time steps, connected such that at each step the bottom RNN takes "external" inputs from the outside, while each of the higher RNN takes as its "external" input the "state" output of the one below it. Residual connections between states at different depth (He et al., 2016) are also used to improve information flow. Note that unlike deep transition GRUs, here each GRU transition block constitutes a cell that is individually recurrent, as it has its own state that is carried over between time steps.

2.3.1 Stacked Encoder

In this work we consider two types of bidirectional stacked encoders: an architecture similar to Zhou et al. (2016) which we denote here as *alternating* encoder (Figure 2), and one similar to Wu et al. (2016) which we denote as *biunidirectional* encoder (Figure 3).

Our contribution is the empirical comparison of these architectures, both in isolation and in combination with the deep transition architecture.

We do not consider stacked unidirectional encoders (Sutskever et al., 2014) as bidirectional encoders have been shown to outperform them (e.g. Britz et al. (2017)).

Alternating Stacked Encoder The forward part of the encoder consists of a stack of GRU recurrent neural networks, the first one processing words in

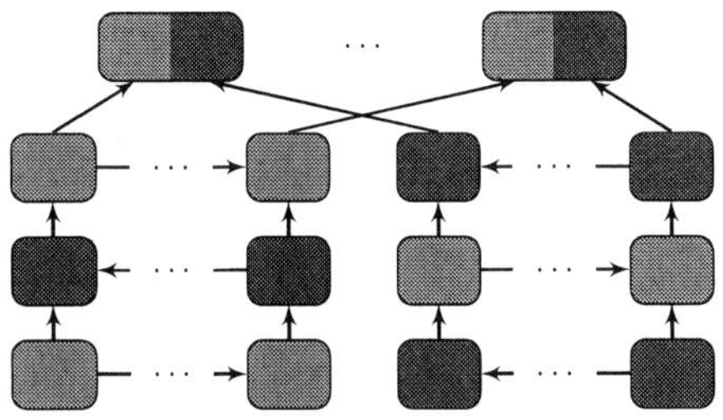

Figure 2: Alternating stacked encoder (Zhou et al., 2016).

the forward direction, the second one in the backward direction, and so on, in alternating directions. For an encoder stack depth D_s, and a source sentence length N, the forward source word state $\overrightarrow{w}_i \equiv \overrightarrow{w}_{i,D_s}$ is computed as:

$$\overrightarrow{w}_{i,1} = \overrightarrow{h}_{i,1} = \text{GRU}_1\left(x_i, \overrightarrow{h}_{i-1,1}\right)$$
$$\overrightarrow{h}_{i,2k} = \text{GRU}_{2k}\left(\overrightarrow{w}_{i,2k-1}, \overrightarrow{h}_{i+1,2k}\right)$$
$$\text{for } 1 < 2k \leq D_s$$
$$\overrightarrow{h}_{i,2k+1} = \text{GRU}_{2k+1}\left(\overrightarrow{w}_{i,2k}, \overrightarrow{h}_{i-1,2k+1}\right)$$
$$\text{for } 1 < 2k+1 \leq D_s$$
$$\overrightarrow{w}_{i,j} = \overrightarrow{h}_{i,j} + \overrightarrow{w}_{i,j-1}$$
$$\text{for } 1 < j \leq D_s$$

where we assume that $\overrightarrow{h}_{0,k}$ and $\overrightarrow{h}_{N+1,k}$ are zero vectors. Note the residual connections: at each level above the first one, the word state of the previous level $\overrightarrow{w}_{i,j-1}$ is added to the recurrent state of the GRU cell $\overrightarrow{h}_{i,j}$ to compute the the word state for the current level $\overrightarrow{w}_{i,j}$.

The backward part of the encoder has the same structure, except that the first level of the stack processes the words in the backward direction and the subsequent levels alternate directions.

The forward and backward word states are then concatenated to form bidirectional word states $C \equiv \{[\overrightarrow{w}_{i,D_s} \overleftarrow{w}_{i,D_s}]\}$. A diagram of this architecture is shown in Figure 2.

Biunidirectional Stacked Encoder In this encoder the forward and backward parts are shallow, as in the baseline architecture. Their word states are concatenated to form shallow bidirectional word states $w_i \equiv [\overrightarrow{w}_{i,1} \overleftarrow{w}_{i,1}]$ that are then used as inputs for subsequent stacked GRUs which operate only in the forward sentence direction, hence the name "biunidirectional". Since residual connections are also present, the higher depth

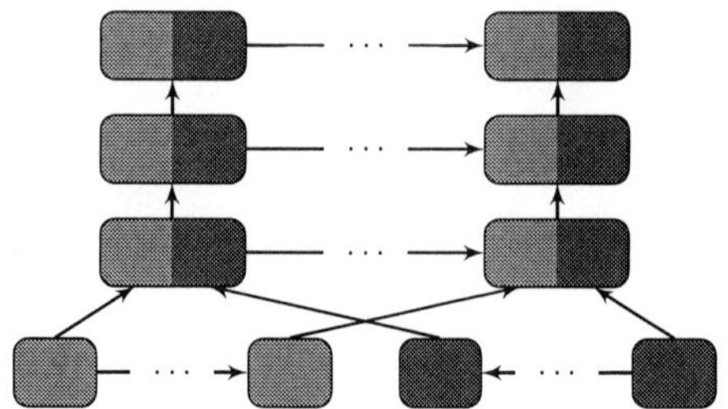

Figure 3: Biunidirectional stacked encoder (Wu et al., 2016).

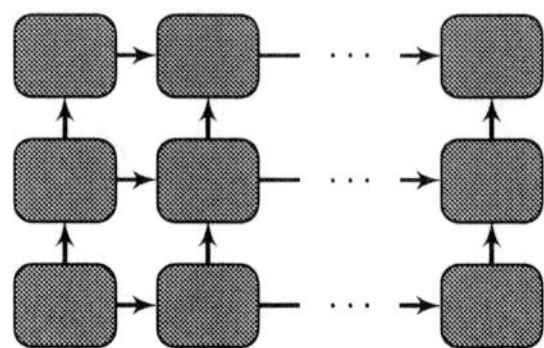

Figure 4: Stacked RNN decoder

GRUs have a state size twice that of the base ones. This architecture has shorter maximum information propagation paths than the alternating encoder, suggesting that it may be less expressive, but it has the advantage of enabling implementations with higher model parallelism. A diagram of this architecture is shown in Figure 3.

In principle, alternating and biunidirectional stacked encoders can be combined by having D_{sa} alternating layers followed by D_{sb} unidirectional layers.

2.3.2 Stacked Decoder

A stacked decoder can be obtained by stacking RNNs which operate in the forward sentence direction. A diagram of this architecture is shown in Figure 4.

Note that the base RNN is always a conditional GRU (cGRU, Firat and Cho, 2016) which has transition depth at least two due to the way that the context vectors generated by the attention mechanism are used in Nematus. This opens up the possibility of several architectural variants which we evaluated in this work:

Stacked GRU The higher RNNs are simple GRUs which receive as input the state from the previous level of the stack, with residual connec-

tions between the levels.

$$s_{j,1,1} = \mathrm{GRU}_{1,1}\left(y_{j-1}, s_{j-1,1,2}\right)$$
$$c_{j,1} = \mathrm{ATT}(C, s_{j,1,1})$$
$$s_{j,1,2} = \mathrm{GRU}_{1,2}\left(c_{j,1}, s_{j,1,1}\right)$$
$$r_{j,1} = s_{j,1,2}$$
$$s_{j,k,1} = \mathrm{GRU}_k\left(r_{j,k-1}, s_{j-1,k,1}\right)$$
$$r_{j,k} = s_{j,k,1} + r_{j,k-1}$$
$$\text{for } 1 < k \leq D_t$$

Note that the higher levels have transition depth one, unlike the base level which has two.

Stacked rGRU The higher RNNs are GRUs whose "external" input is the concatenation of the state below and the context vector from the base RNN. Formally, the states $s_{j,k,1}$ of the higher RNNs are computed as:

$$s_{j,k,1} = \mathrm{GRU}_k\left([r_{j,k-1}, c_{j,1}], s_{j-1,k,1}\right)$$
$$\text{for } 1 < k \leq D_t$$

This is similar to the deep decoder by Wu et al. (2016).

Stacked cGRU The higher RNNs are conditional GRUs, each with an independent attention mechanism. Each level has two GRU transitions per step j, with a new context vector $c_{j,k}$ computed in between:

$$s_{j,k,1} = \mathrm{GRU}_{k,1}\left(r_{j,k-1}, s_{j-1,k,1}\right)$$
$$c_{j,k} = \mathrm{ATT}(C, s_{j,k,1})$$
$$s_{j,k,2} = \mathrm{GRU}_{k,2}\left(c_{j,k}, s_{j,1,1}\right)$$
$$\text{for } 1 < k \leq D_t$$

Note that unlike the stacked GRU and rGRU, the higher levels have transition depth two.

Stacked crGRU The higher RNNs are conditional GRUs but they reuse the context vectors from the base RNN. Like the cGRU there are two GRU transition per step, but they reuse the context vector $c_{j,1}$ computed at the first level of the stack:

$$s_{j,k,1} = \mathrm{GRU}_{k,1}\left(r_{j,k-1}, s_{j-1,k,1}\right)$$
$$s_{j,k,2} = \mathrm{GRU}_{k,2}\left(c_{j,1}, s_{j,1,1}\right)$$
$$\text{for } 1 < k \leq D_t$$

2.4 BiDeep architectures

We introduce the *BiDeep RNN*, a novel architecture obtained by combining deep transitions with stacking.

A BiDeep encoder is obtained by replacing the D_s individually recurrent GRU cells of a stacked encoder with multi-layer deep transition cells each composed by L_s GRU transition blocks.

For instance, the BiDeep alternating encoder is defined as follows:

$$\overrightarrow{w}_{i,1} = \overrightarrow{h}_{i,1} = \text{DTGRU}_1\left(x_i, \overrightarrow{h}_{i-1,1}\right)$$

$$\overrightarrow{h}_{i,2k} = \text{DTGRU}_{2k}\left(\overrightarrow{w}_{i,2k-1}, \overrightarrow{h}_{i+1,2k}\right)$$
$$\text{for } 1 < 2k \leq D_s$$

$$\overrightarrow{h}_{i,2k+1} = \text{DTGRU}_{2k+1}\left(\overrightarrow{w}_{i,2k}, \overrightarrow{h}_{i-1,2k+1}\right)$$
$$\text{for } 1 < 2k+1 \leq D_s$$

$$\overrightarrow{w}_{i,j} = \overrightarrow{h}_{i,j} + \overrightarrow{w}_{i,j-1}$$
$$\text{for } 1 < j \leq D_s$$

where each multi-layer cell DTGRU_k is defined as:

$$v_{k,1} = \text{GRU}_{k,1}\left(\text{in}_k, \text{state}_k\right)$$
$$v_{k,t} = \text{GRU}_{k,t}\left(0, v_{k_t-1}\right) \text{ for } 1 < k \leq L_s$$
$$\text{DTGRU}_k\left(\text{in}_k, \text{state}_k\right) = v_{k,L_s}$$

It is also possible to have different transition depths at each stacking level.

BiDeep decoders are similarly defined, replacing the recurrent cells (GRU, rGRU, cGRU or cr-GRU) with deep transition multi-layer cells.

3 Experiments

All experiments were performed with Nematus (Sennrich et al., 2017b), following Sennrich et al. (2017a) in their choice of preprocessing and hyperparameters. For experiments with deep models, we increase the depth by a factor of 4 compared to the baseline for most experiments; in preliminary experiments, we observed diminishing returns for deeper models.

We trained on the parallel English–German training data of WMT-2017 news translation task, using newstest2013 as validation set. We used early-stopping on the validation cross-entropy and selected the best model based on validation BLEU.

We report cross-entropy (CE) on newstest2013, training speed (on a single Titan X (Pascal) GPU),

and the number of parameters. For translation quality, we report case-sensitive, detokenized BLEU, measured with mteval-v13a.pl, on newstest2014, newstest2015, and newstest2016.

We release the code under an open source license, including it in the official Nematus repository.[2] The configuration files needed to replicate our experiments are available in a separate repository.[3]

3.1 Layer Normalization

Our first experiment is concerned with layer normalization. We are interested to see how essential layer normalization is for our deep architectures, and compare the effect of layer normalization on a baseline system, and a system with an alternating encoder with stacked depth 4. Results are shown in Table 1. We find that layer normalization is similarly effective for both the shallow baseline model and the deep encoder, yielding an average improvement of 0.8–1 BLEU, and reducing training time substantially. Therefore we use it for all the subsequent experiments.

3.2 Deep Encoders

In Table 2 we report experimental results for different architectures of deep encoders, while the decoder is kept shallow.

We find that all the deep encoders perform substantially better than baseline (+0.5–+1.2 BLEU), with no consistent quality differences between each other. In terms of number of parameters and training speed, the deep transition encoder performs best, followed by the alternating stacked encoder and finally the biunidirectional encoder (note that we trained on a single GPU, the biunidirectional encoder may be comparatively faster on multiple GPUs due to its higher model parallelism).

3.3 Deep Decoders

Table 3 shows results for different decoder architectures, while the encoder is shallow. We find that the deep decoders all improve the cross-entropy, but the BLEU results are more varied: deep output[4] decreases BLEU scores (but note that the baseline

---

[2] `https://github.com/EdinburghNLP/nematus`

[3] `https://github.com/Avmb/deep-nmt-architectures`

[4] deep feed-forward output with shallow RNNs in both the encoder and decoder

encoder	CE	BLEU			parameters (M)	training speed (words/s)	early stop (10^4 minibatches)
		2014	2015	2016			
baseline	49.98	21.2	23.8	28.4	**98.0**	**3350**	44
+layer normalization	**47.53**	**21.9**	**24.7**	**29.3**	98.1	2900	**29**
alternating (depth 4)	49.25	21.8	24.6	28.9	**135.8**	**2150**	46
+layer normalization	**46.29**	**22.6**	**25.2**	**30.5**	135.9	1600	**29**

Table 1: Layer normalization results. English→German WMT17 data.

encoder	depth			CE	BLEU			parameters (M)	training speed (words/s)
	s. bidir.	s. forw.	trans.		2014	2015	2016		
shallow	1	-	1	47.53	21.9	24.7	29.3	98.1	2900
alternating	4	-	1	**46.29**	22.6	25.2	**30.5**	135.9	1600
biunidirectional	1	3	1	46.79	22.4	**25.4**	30.0	173.7	1500
deep transition	1	-	4	46.54	**22.9**	**25.4**	30.2	**117.0**	**1900**

Table 2: Deep encoder results. English→German WMT17 data. Parameters and speed are highlighted for the deep recurrent models.

has already some depth), stacked GRU performs similarly to the baseline (-0.1–+0.2 BLEU) and stacked rGRU possibly slightly better (+0.1–+0.2 BLEU).

Other deep RNN decoders achieve higher gains. The best results (+0.6 BLEU on average) are achieved by the stacked conditional GRU with independent multi-step attention (cGRU). This decoder, however, is the slowest one and has the most parameters.

The deep transition decoder performs well (+0.5 BLEU on average) in terms of quality and is the fastest and smallest of all the deep decoders that have shown quality improvements.

The stacked conditional GRU with reused attention (crGRU) achieves smaller improvements (+0.3 BLEU on average) and has speed and size intermediate between the deep transition and stacked cGRU decoders.

3.4 Deep Encoders and Decoders

Table 4 shows results for models where both the encoder and the decoder are deep, in addition to the results of the best deep encoder (the deep transition encoder) + shallow decoder reported here for ease of comparison.

Compared to deep transition encoder alone, we generally see improvements in cross-entropy, but not in BLEU. We evaluate architectures similar to Zhou et al. (2016) (alternating encoder + stacked GRU decoder) and (Wu et al., 2016) (biunidirectional encoder + stacked rGRU decoder), though they are not straight replications since we used GRU cells rather than LSTMs and the implementation details are different. We find that the former architecture performs better in terms of BLEU

scores, model size and training speed.

The other variants of alternating encoder + stacked or deep transition decoder perform similarly to alternating encoder + stacked rGRU decoder, but do not improve BLEU scores over the best deep encoder with shallow decoder. Applying the BiDeep architecture while keeping the total depth the same yields small improvements over the best deep encoder (+0.2 BLEU on average), while the improvement in cross-entropy is stronger. We conjecture that deep decoders may be better at handling subtle target-side linguistic phenomena that are not well captured by the 4-gram precision-based BLEU evaluation.

Finally, we evaluate a subset of architectures with a combined depth that is 8 times that of the baseline. Among the large models, the BiDeep model yields substantial improvements (average +0.6 BLEU over the best deep encoder, +1.5 BLEU over the shallow baseline), in addition to cross-entropy improvements. The stacked-only model, on the other hand, performs similarly to the smaller models, despite having even more parameters than the BiDeep model. This shows that it is useful to combine deep transitions with stacking, as they provide two orthogonal kinds of depth that are both beneficial for neural machine translation.

3.5 Error Analysis

One theoretical difference between a stacked RNN and a deep transition RNN is that the distance in the computation graph between timesteps is increased for deep transition RNNs. While this allows for arguably more expressive computations to be represented, in principle it could reduce the ability to remember information over long dis-

decoder	high RNN stacked	decoder RNN depth		output depth	CE	BLEU			params. (M)	training speed (words/s)
		trans.	type			2014	2015	2016		
shallow	-	1	1	1	47.53	21.9	24.7	29.3	98.1	2900
stacked	GRU	4	1	1	46.73	21.8	24.6	29.5	**117.0**	**2250**
stacked	rGRU	4	1	1	46.72	22.1	25.0	29.4	135.9	2150
stacked	cGRU	4	1	1	**44.76**	**22.8**	**25.5**	29.6	164.3	1300
stacked	crGRU	4	1	1	45.88	22.5	24.7	29.7	145.4	1750
deep transition	-	1	8	1	45.98	22.4	24.9	**30.0**	**117.0**	2200
deep output	-	1	1	4	47.21	21.5	24.2	28.7	98.9	2850

Table 3: Deep decoder results. English→German WMT17 data. Parameters and speed are highlighted for the deep recurrent models.

encoder	decoder	decoder high RNN type	encoder depth			decoder depth		CE	BLEU			params. (M)	training speed (words/s)
			bidir.	forw.	trans.	stacked	trans.		2014	2015	2016		
shallow	shallow	-	1	-	1	1	1	47.53	21.9	24.7	29.3	98.1	2900
deep tran.	shallow	-	1	-	4	1	1	46.54	22.9	25.4	30.2	117.0	1900
(Zhou et al., 2016) (ours)													
alternating	stacked	GRU	4	-	1	4	1	45.89	22.9	25.3	30.1	154.9	1480
(Wu et al., 2016) (ours)													
biunidir.	stacked	rGRU	1	3	1	4	1	46.15	22.4	24.7	29.6	211.5	1280
alternating	stacked	rGRU	4	-	1	4	1	46.00	23.0	**25.7**	30.5	173.7	1400
alternating	stacked	cGRU	4	-	1	4	1	44.32	22.9	**25.7**	29.8	202.1	970
deep tran.	deep tran.	-	1	-	4	1	8	45.52	22.7	**25.7**	30.1	**136.0**	**1570**
BiDeep altern.	BiDeep	rGRU	2	-	2	2	4/2	**43.52**	**23.1**	25.5	**30.6**	145.4	1480
BiDeep altern.	BiDeep	rGRU	4	-	2	4	4/2	**43.26**	**23.4**	**26.0**	**31.0**	**214.7**	**980**
alternating	stacked	rGRU	8	-	1	8	1	44.32	22.9	25.5	30.5	274.6	880

Table 4: Deep encoder–decoder results. English→German WMT17 data. Transition depth 4/2 means 4 in the base RNN of the stack and 2 in the higher RNNs. The last two models are large and their results are highlighted separately.

tances, since each layer may lose information during forward computation or backpropagation. This may not be a significant issue in the encoder, as the attention mechanism provides short paths from any source word state to the decoder, but the decoder contains no such shortcuts between its states, therefore it might be possible that this negatively affects its ability to model long-distance relationships in the target text, such as subject–verb agreement.

Here, we seek to answer this question by testing our models on Lingeval97 (Sennrich, 2017), a test set which provides contrastive translation pairs for different types of errors. For the example of subject-verb agreement, contrastive translations are created from a reference translation by changing the grammatical number of the verb, and we can measure how often the NMT model prefers the correct reference over the contrastive variant.

In Figure 5, we show accuracy as a function of the distance between subject and verb. We find that information is successfully passed over long distances by the deep recurrent transition network. Even for decisions that require information to be carried over 16 or more words, or at least 128 GRU transitions[5], the deep recurrent transition network

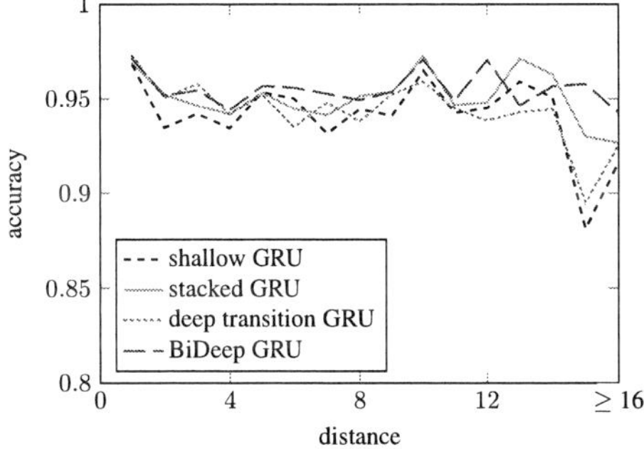

Figure 5: Subject-verb agreement accuracy as a function of distance between subject and verb.

achieves an accuracy of over 92.5% ($N = 560$), higher than the shallow decoder (91.6%), and similar to the stacked GRU (92.7%). The highest accuracy (94.3%) is achieved by the BiDeep network.

4 Conclusions

In this work we presented and evaluated multiple architectures to increase the model depth of neural machine translation systems.

We showed that *alternating stacked* encoders (Zhou et al., 2016) outperform *biunidirectional*

---

[5]some decisions may not require the information to be passed on the target side because the decisions may be possible based on source-side information.

stacked encoders (Wu et al., 2016), both in accuracy and (single-GPU) speed. We showed that *deep transition* architectures, which we first applied to NMT, perform comparably to the stacked ones in terms of accuracy (BLEU, cross-entropy and long-distance syntactic agreement), and better in terms of speed and number of parameters.

We found that depth improves BLEU scores especially in the encoder. Decoder depth, however, still improves cross-entropy if not strongly BLEU scores.

The best results are obtained by our BiDeep architecture which combines both stacked depth and transition depth in both the (alternating) encoder and the decoder, yielding better accuracy for the same number of parameters than systems with only one kind of depth.

We recommend to use combined architectures when maximum accuracy is the goal, or use deep transition architectures when speed or model size are a concern, as deep transition performs very positively in the quality/speed and quality/size trade-off.

While this paper only reports results for one translation direction, the effectiveness of the presented architectures across different data conditions and language pairs was confirmed in follow-up work. For the shared news translation task of this year's Conference on Machine Translation (WMT17), we built deep models for 12 translation directions, using a deep transition architecture or a stacked architecture (alternating encoder and rGRU decoder), and observe improvements for the majority of translation directions (Sennrich et al., 2017a).

Acknowledgments

The research presented in this publication was conducted in cooperation with Samsung Electronics Polska sp. z o.o. - Samsung R&D Institute Poland.

This project received funding from the European Union's Horizon 2020 research and innovation programme under grant agreements 645452 (QT21), 644402 (HimL) and 688139 (SUMMA).

References

Lei Jimmy Ba, Ryan Kiros, and Geoffrey E. Hinton. 2016. Layer Normalization. *CoRR* abs/1607.06450.

Dzmitry Bahdanau, Kyunghyun Cho, and Yoshua Bengio. 2015. Neural Machine Translation by Jointly Learning to Align and Translate. In *Proceedings of the International Conference on Learning Representations (ICLR)*.

Ondřej Bojar, Rajen Chatterjee, Christian Federmann, Yvette Graham, Barry Haddow, Matthias Huck, Antonio Jimeno Yepes, Philipp Koehn, Varvara Logacheva, Christof Monz, Matteo Negri, Aurelie Neveol, Mariana Neves, Martin Popel, Matt Post, Raphael Rubino, Carolina Scarton, Lucia Specia, Marco Turchi, Karin Verspoor, and Marcos Zampieri. 2016. Findings of the 2016 Conference on Machine Translation (WMT16). In *Proceedings of the First Conference on Machine Translation, Volume 2: Shared Task Papers*. Association for Computational Linguistics, Berlin, Germany, pages 131–198.

Denny Britz, Anna Goldie, Minh-Thang Luong, and Quoc V. Le. 2017. Massive Exploration of Neural Machine Translation Architectures. *CoRR* abs/1703.03906.

Mauro Cettolo, Jan Niehues, Sebastian Stüker, Luisa Bentivogli, and Marcello Federico. 2016. Report on the 13th IWSLT Evaluation Campaign. In *IWSLT 2016*. Seattle, USA.

Kyunghyun Cho, B van Merrienboer, Dzmitry Bahdanau, and Yoshua Bengio. 2014a. On the properties of neural machine translation: Encoder-decoder approaches. In *Eighth Workshop on Syntax, Semantics and Structure in Statistical Translation (SSST-8), 2014*.

Kyunghyun Cho, Bart van Merrienboer, Caglar Gulcehre, Dzmitry Bahdanau, Fethi Bougares, Holger Schwenk, and Yoshua Bengio. 2014b. Learning Phrase Representations using RNN Encoder–Decoder for Statistical Machine Translation. In *Proceedings of the 2014 Conference on Empirical Methods in Natural Language Processing (EMNLP)*. Doha, Qatar, pages 1724–1734.

Orhan Firat and Kyunghyun Cho. 2016. Conditional Gated Recurrent Unit with Attention Mechanism. https://github.com/nyu-dl/dl4mt-tutorial/blob/master/docs/cgru.pdf. Published online, version `adbaeea`.

Jonas Gehring, Michael Auli, David Grangier, Denis Yarats, and Yann N. Dauphin. 2017. Convolutional Sequence to Sequence Learning. *CoRR* abs/1705.03122.

Kaiming He, Xiangyu Zhang, Shaoqing Ren, and Jian Sun. 2016. Deep Residual Learning for Image Recognition. In *2016 IEEE Conference on Computer Vision and Pattern Recognition, CVPR 2016, Las Vegas, NV, USA, June 27-30, 2016*. pages 770–778.

Razvan Pascanu, Çağlar Gülçehre, Kyunghyun Cho, and Yoshua Bengio. 2014. How to Construct Deep Recurrent Neural Networks. In *International Conference on Learning Representations 2014 (Conference Track)*.

Rico Sennrich. 2017. How Grammatical is Character-level Neural Machine Translation? Assessing MT Quality with Contrastive Translation Pairs. In *Proceedings of the 15th Conference of the European Chapter of the Association for Computational Linguistics: Volume 2, Short Papers*. Association for Computational Linguistics, Valencia, Spain, pages 376–382.

Rico Sennrich, Alexandra Birch, Anna Currey, Ulrich Germann, Barry Haddow, Kenneth Heafield, Antonio Valerio Miceli Barone, and Philip Williams. 2017a. The University of Edinburgh's Neural MT Systems for WMT17. In *Proceedings of the Second Conference on Machine Translation, Volume 2: Shared Task Papers*. Copenhagen, Denmark.

Rico Sennrich, Orhan Firat, Kyunghyun Cho, Alexandra Birch, Barry Haddow, Julian Hitschler, Marcin Junczys-Dowmunt, Samuel Läubli, Antonio Valerio Miceli Barone, Jozef Mokry, and Maria Nadejde. 2017b. Nematus: a Toolkit for Neural Machine Translation. In *Proceedings of the Software Demonstrations of the 15th Conference of the European Chapter of the Association for Computational Linguistics*. Association for Computational Linguistics, Valencia, Spain, pages 65–68.

Ilya Sutskever, Oriol Vinyals, and Quoc V Le. 2014. Sequence to sequence learning with neural networks. In *Advances in neural information processing systems*. pages 3104–3112.

Ashish Vaswani, Noam Shazeer, Niki Parmar, Jakob Uszkoreit, Llion Jones, Aidan N Gomez, Lukasz Kaiser, and Illia Polosukhin. 2017. Attention Is All You Need. *arXiv preprint arXiv:1706.03762* .

Yonghui Wu, Mike Schuster, Zhifeng Chen, Quoc V. Le, Mohammad Norouzi, Wolfgang Macherey, Maxim Krikun, Yuan Cao, Qin Gao, Klaus Macherey, Jeff Klingner, Apurva Shah, Melvin Johnson, Xiaobing Liu, Lukasz Kaiser, Stephan Gouws, Yoshikiyo Kato, Taku Kudo, Hideto Kazawa, Keith Stevens, George Kurian, Nishant Patil, Wei Wang, Cliff Young, Jason Smith, Jason Riesa, Alex Rudnick, Oriol Vinyals, Greg Corrado, Macduff Hughes, and Jeffrey Dean. 2016. Google's Neural Machine Translation System: Bridging the Gap between Human and Machine Translation. *CoRR* abs/1609.08144.

Saizheng Zhang, Yuhuai Wu, Tong Che, Zhouhan Lin, Roland Memisevic, Ruslan R Salakhutdinov, and Yoshua Bengio. 2016. Architectural Complexity Measures of Recurrent Neural Networks. In *Advances in Neural Information Processing Systems 29*. pages 1822–1830.

Jie Zhou, Ying Cao, Xuguang Wang, Peng Li, and Wei Xu. 2016. Deep Recurrent Models with Fast-Forward Connections for Neural Machine Translation. *TACL* 4:371–383.

Julian Georg Zilly, Rupesh Kumar Srivastava, Jan Koutník, and Jürgen Schmidhuber. 2016. Recurrent highway networks. *arXiv preprint arXiv:1607.03474* .

Biasing Attention-Based Recurrent Neural Networks Using External Alignment Information

Tamer Alkhouli and Hermann Ney

Human Language Technology and Pattern Recognition Group
Computer Science Department
RWTH Aachen University
D-52056 Aachen, Germany
`<surname>@i6.informatik.rwth-aachen.de`

Abstract

This work explores extending attention-based neural models to include alignment information as input. We modify the attention component to have dependence on the current source position. The attention model is then used as a lexical model together with an additional alignment model to generate translation. The attention model is trained using external alignment information, and it is applied in decoding by performing beam search over the lexical and alignment hypotheses. The alignment model is used to score these alignment candidates. We demonstrate that the attention layer is capable of using the alignment information to improve over the baseline attention model that uses no such alignments. Our experiments are performed on two tasks: WMT 2016 English→Romanian and WMT 2017 German→English.

1 Introduction

Neural machine translation (NMT) has emerged recently as a successful end-to-end statistical machine translation approach. The best performing NMT systems use an attention mechanism that focuses the attention of the decoder on parts of the source sentence (Bahdanau et al., 2015). The attention component is computed as an intermediate part of the model, and is trained jointly with the rest of the model. The approach is appealing because (1) it is end-to-end, where the neural model is trained from scratch without assistance from other trained models, and (2) the attention component is trained jointly with the rest of the model, requiring no pre-computed alignments.

In this work, we raise the question whether the attention component is self-sufficient to attend to the source side, and if it can still benefit from explicit dependence on the alignment information. To this end, we modify the attention model to bias the attention layer towards the alignment information, and evaluate the model in a generative framework consisting of two steps: alignment prediction followed by lexical translation.

Two decades ago, (Vogel et al., 1996) applied hidden Markov models to machine translation. The idea was based on introducing word alignments as hidden variables, while using the first-order Markov assumption to simplify the dependencies of the alignment sequence. The approach decomposed the translation process using a lexical model and an alignment model. These models were simple tables enumerating all possible translation and alignment combinations. Nowadays, HMM is used with IBM models to generate word alignments, which are needed to train phrase-based systems.

Alkhouli et al. (2016) and Wang et al. (2017) apply the hidden Markov model decomposition using feedforward lexical and alignment neural network models. In this work, we are interested in using more expressive models. Namely, we leverage attention models as lexical models and use them with bidirectional recurrent alignment models. These recurrent models are able to encode unbounded source and target context in comparison to feedforward networks.

The attention-based translation model is conditioned on the full source sentence, but it has no explicit dependence on alignments as input. We propose to bias the attention mechanism using alignment information, while still allowing the model to compute attention weights dynamically. Conditioning the model on the alignment information as such makes it possible to combine with an alignment model in a generative story. We demonstrate

Proceedings of the Conference on Machine Translation (WMT), Volume 1: Research Papers, pages 108–117
Copenhagen, Denmark, September 7–11, 2017. ©2017 Association for Computational Linguistics

that the attention model can benefit from such external alignment information on two WMT tasks: the 2016 English→Romanian task and the 2017 German→English task.

2 Related Work

Alignment-based neural models have explicit dependence on the alignment information either at the input or at the output of the network. They have been extensively and successfully applied in the literature on top of conventional phrase-based systems (Sundermeyer et al., 2014a; Tamura et al., 2014; Devlin et al., 2014). In this work, we focus on using the models directly to perform standalone neural machine translation.

Alignment-based neural models were proposed in (Alkhouli et al., 2016) to perform neural machine translation. They mainly used feedforward alignment and lexical models in decoding. In this work, we investigate recurrent models instead. We use a modified attention model as a lexical model and apply it together with a recurrent alignment neural model.

Deriving neural models for translation based on the HMM framework can also be found in (Yang et al., 2013; Yu et al., 2017). Alignment-based neural models were also applied to perform summarization and morphological inflection (Yu et al., 2016). The work used a monotonous alignment model, where training was done by marginalizing over the alignment hidden variables, which is computationally expensive. In this work, we use non-monotonous alignment models. In addition, we train using pre-computed Viterbi alignments which speeds up neural training. In (Yu et al., 2017), alignment-based neural models were used to model alignment and translation from the target to the source side (inverse direction), and a language model was included in addition. They showed results on a small translation task. In this work, we present results on translation tasks containing tens of millions of words. We do not include a language model in any of our systems.

There is plenty of work on modifying attention models to capture more complex dependencies. (Cohn et al., 2016) introduces structural biases from word-based alignment concepts like fertility and Markov conditioning. These are internal modifications that leave the model self-contained. Our modifications introduce alignments as external information to the model. (Arthur et al., 2016) include lexical probabilities to bias attention. (Chen et al., 2016; Mi et al., 2016) add an extra term dependent on the alignments to the training objective function to guide neural training. This is only applied during training but not during decoding. Our work modifies the attention component directly, and we can choose whether to apply the alignment bias during decoding or not. We show that using alignment bias during search alongside an alignment model improves translation.

3 Alignment-Based Translation

Given a source sentence $f_1^J = f_1...f_j...f_J$, a target sentence $e_1^I = e_1...e_i...e_I$, and an alignment sequence $b_1^I = b_1...b_i...b_I$, where $j = b_i$ is the source position aligned to the target position i, we model translation using an alignment model and a lexical model:

$$p(e_1^I|f_1^J) = \sum_{b_1^I} p(e_1^I, b_1^I|f_1^J) \tag{1}$$

$$\approx \max_{b_1^I} \prod_{i=1}^{I} \underbrace{p(e_i|b_i, b_1^{i-1}, e_1^{i-1}, f_1^J)}_{\text{lexical model}} \cdot$$

$$\underbrace{p(b_i|b_1^{i-1}, e_1^{i-1}, f_1^J)}_{\text{alignment model}}$$

Both the lexical model and the alignment model have rich dependencies including the full source context f_1^J, the full alignment history b_1^{i-1}, and the full target history e_1^{i-1}. The lexical model has an extra dependence on the current source position b_i. First-order HMMs simplify the dependence on the alignment history and limit it to the predecessor alignment point b_{i-1}. This allows an efficient computation of the sum over the alignment sequence given in Eq. (1) using dynamic programming. In this work, we stick to the maximum approximation, and keep the full dependence on the alignment history b_1^{i-1}. We use recurrent neural networks to model the unbounded source, target and alignment context. Nevertheless, the models we describe can be simplified easily to drop the full dependence on the alignment history, in which case integrated training using the sum can be performed as suggested by Wang et al. (2017).

4 Attention-Based Translation Model

The standard attention-based translation model has three main components: The encoder, the decoder, and the attention component. The model

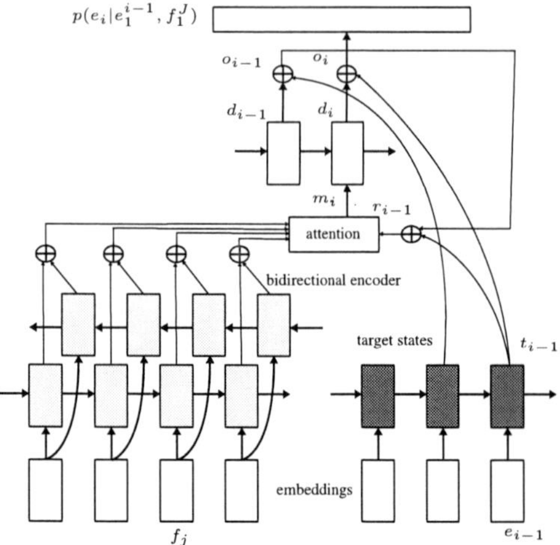

Figure 1: Attention model architecture.

architecture is illustrated in Fig. (1). We use long short-term memory (LSTM) recurrent layers throughout this work (Hochreiter and Schmidhuber, 1997; Gers et al., 2000, 2003). We include a bidirectional encoder where we sum the forward and backward source state representations:

$$\overrightarrow{h_j} = \mathrm{LSTM}(\overrightarrow{h}_{j-1}, F f_j)$$
$$\overleftarrow{h_j} = \mathrm{LSTM}(\overleftarrow{h}_{j+1}, F f_j)$$
$$h_j = Y \overleftarrow{h}_j + Z \overrightarrow{h}_j \tag{2}$$

where Y and Z are weight matrices, F is the source word embedding matrix, and $f_j \in \{0,1\}^{|V_f| \times 1}$ is the one-hot vector of the source word at position j. $|V_f|$ is the size of the source vocabulary. The parameterization of the recurrent layer is abstracted away using the LSTM notation for simplicity. We use an LSTM layer to represent the state of the target sequence:

$$t_{i-1} = \mathrm{LSTM}(t_{i-2}, E e_{i-1}) \tag{3}$$

where E is the target word embedding matrix, and $e_{i-1} \in \{0,1\}^{|V_e| \times 1}$ is the one-hot vector of the target word at position $i-1$. $|V_e|$ is the size of the target vocabulary. The attention weights are normalized using the softmax function according

to the following equations:

$$\alpha_{ij} = \frac{\exp(s_{ij})}{\sum_{j=1}^{J} \exp(s_{ij})}$$
$$s_{ij} = v^T \tanh(W h_j + M r_{i-1} + a)$$
$$r_{i-1} = R o_{i-1} + L t_{i-1} \tag{4}$$
$$o_{i-1} = A d_{i-1} + B t_{i-2}$$
$$d_{i-1} = \mathrm{LSTM}(d_{i-2}, m_{i-1}) \tag{5}$$
$$m_i = \sum_{j=1}^{J} \alpha_{ij} h_j$$

where α_{ij} denotes the normalized attention weights, s_{ij} denotes the unnormalized attention scores, r_{i-1} is the translation state computed using the decoder state at the previous step o_{i-1} and the target state t_{i-1} which in turn is computed using the target word e_{i-1}. The decoder state d_i is computed using an LSTM over the attended source positions m_i. v and a are vectors, and A, B, W, M, R, and L are weight matrices.

The final target word probability is computed as a softmax function of the decoder state $o_i \in \mathbb{R}^{|V_e| \times 1}$:

$$p(e_i = w | e_1^{i-1}, f_1^J) = \frac{\exp(o_{iw})}{\sum_{v=1}^{|V_e|} \exp(o_{iv})}$$

5 Alignment-Biased Attention

In order to use the attention model as an alignment-dependent lexical model, we introduce a dependence on the alignment information b_i. We modify the attention mechanism according to the following equation:

$$s_{ij} = v^T \tanh(W h_j + M r_{i-1} + a + \delta_{j,b_i} c) \tag{6}$$

where c is a vector, and δ_{j,b_i} is the Kronecker delta:

$$\delta_{j,b_i} = \begin{cases} 1, & \text{if } j = b_i \\ 0, & \text{otherwise.} \end{cases}$$

We also experiment with a bias term that includes the aligned source state h_{b_i}:

$$s_{ij} = v^T \tanh(W h_j + M r_{i-1} + a + \delta_{j,b_i} D h_{b_i}) \tag{7}$$

which we refer to as source alignment bias. D is an additional weight matrix. Note that the model will have full dependence on the alignment history due to Eq. (5) and Eq. (4) (cf. Fig. (1)). This dependency can be simplified by removing both the

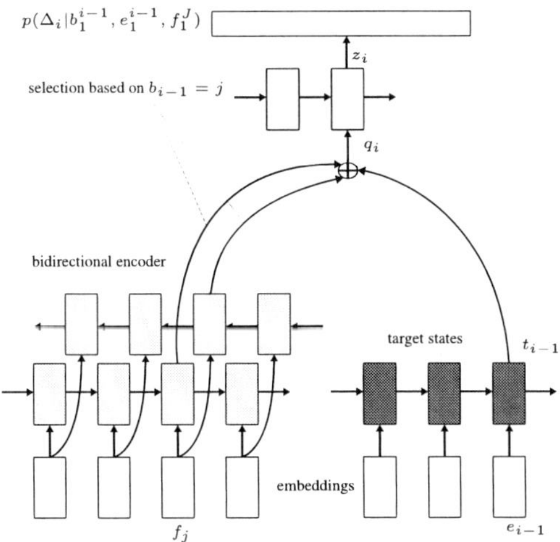

Figure 2: Bidirectional alignment model (BAM).

recurrency in Eq. (5), and the recurrent input o_{i-1} that feeds r_{i-1} in Eq. (4). In this work, however, we stick to the richer representation and keep the full dependence on the alignment history.

If the alignment information is pre-computed, e.g. through IBM/HMM training, using it as an alignment bias might risk that the original attention part will learn nothing and that it becomes completely dependent on the alignment information. To alleviate this problem, we include the alignment bias term during training for some batches and drop it for others. In our experiments, we randomly include the bias term for 50% of the training batches.

6 Recurrent Alignment Model

We use a recurrent alignment model to score alignments. The model architecture is shown in Fig. (2). Following (Alkhouli et al., 2016), the alignment model predicts the relative jump $\Delta_i = b_i - b_{i-1}$ from the previous source position b_{i-1} to the current source position b_i. This model has a bidirectional source encoder consisting of two recurrent layers (yellow), and a recurrent layer maintaining the target state (red). The most recent target state computed including word e_{i-1} is paired with the source states at position b_{i-1}, which is a hard alignment obtained externally and not computed by the model. We pair the source state h_j at position $j = b_{i-1}$ with the target state t_{i-1} at position $i-1$ to predict the jump Δ_i to the next source

position b_i according to the following equations:

$$q_i = U t_{i-1} + h_{b_{i-1}}$$
$$z_i = \text{LSTM}(z_{i-1}, q_i) \tag{8}$$

where U is a weight matrix, q_i is the paired source and target states, and z_i is the decoder state used to predict the jump from b_{i-1} to b_i. $h_{b_{i-1}}$ and t_{i-1} are defined in Eq. (2), and Eq. (3), respectively. Removing the recurrency in Eq. (8) results in a first-order model over the alignment sequence.

7 Training

In this work, we train the attention and the alignment model separately. We obtain the alignments using IBM/HMM training. While this breaks up the simplicity of end-to-end training of attention models, we want to note that this is not central to the proposed approach. Integrated training using the sum instead of the maximum approximation in Eq. (1) can be performed using the Baum-Welch algorithm similar to (Yu et al., 2017; Wang et al., 2017), but the models need to give up the recurrency over the alignment information. Alternatively, the maximum approximation can be used to find the Viterbi alignments without changing the models, where training proceeds by alternating between aligning the training data and model estimation. In this work, however, we focus on the modeling aspect and leave integrated training to future work.

8 Alignment-Based Decoding

Similar to (Alkhouli et al., 2016), we combine the lexical and alignment neural models in a beam based decoder. Since the models depend on the alignment information, we also have to hypothesize alignments during decoding. In training, we assume that each target position is aligned to exactly one source position. During decoding, we hypothesize all source positions for each target position. We assign the models separate weights and obtain the best translation as follows

$$e_1^{\hat{I}} = \arg\max_{I, e_1^I} \left\{ \frac{1}{I} \max_{b_1^I} \left\{ \sum_{i=1}^{I} \lambda \log p(e_i | b_1^i, e_1^{i-1}, f_1^J) \right.\right.$$
$$\left.\left. + (1-\lambda) \log p(\Delta_i | b_1^{i-1}, e_1^{i-1}, f_1^J) \right\} \right\} \tag{9}$$

where λ is the lexical model weight, which we tune on the development set using grid search.

| | WMT 2016 | | WMT 2017 | |
	English	Romanian	German	English
Sentences	604K		3.55M	
Running Words	15.5M	15.8M	85M	86M
Vocabulary	92.3K	128.3K	671K	587K
Neural Network Vocabulary	56.1K	80.9K	188K	131K

Table 1: Corpora and NN statistics.

9 Experiments

9.1 Setup

This section presents experiments on two WMT shared translation tasks: the 2016 English→Romanian task[1] and the 2017 German→English task.[2] The corpora statistics are shown in Tab. (1). We use the full bilingual data of the English→Romanian task. For the German→English task, we choose the common crawl, news commentary and European parliament bilingual data. The data is filtered by removing sentences longer than 100 words. We also remove sentences where five or more consecutive source words are unaligned according to IBM1/HMM/IBM4 training. This is to remove noisy sentence pairs that are frequent in the common crawl corpus. We do not use any kind of synthetic or back-translated data in this work.

We reduce the vocabulary size by replacing singletons with the unknown token for both English and Romanian corpora in the English→Romanian task. Since we have more data in the German→English task, we replace words occurring less than 6 times in the German corpus and less than 4 times in the English corpus by the unknown token. The reduced vocabularies are what we refer to as the neural network vocabulary in Tab. (1). To handle the large output vocabularies, all lexical models use a class-factored output layer, with 1000 singleton classes dedicated to the most frequent words, and 1000 classes shared among the rest of the words. The classes are trained using a separate tool to optimize the maximum likelihood training criterion with the bigram assumption. The alignment model uses a small output layer of 201 nodes, determined by a maximum jump length of 100 (forward and backward). We train using stochastic gradient descent and halve the learning rate when the development perplexity increases.

We train feedforward models to compare to (Alkhouli et al., 2016). The models have two hidden layers, the first has 1000 nodes and the second has 500 nodes. We use a 9-word source window, and a 5-gram target history. 100 nodes are used for word embeddings. The bidirectional alignment models have 4 LSTM layers as shown in Fig. (2). We use 200-node source and target word embeddings and 200 nodes in each LSTM layer.

The attention models also use 200-node LSTM layers, and 200-node source and target embeddings. The internal dimension of the attention component is also set to 200 nodes, i.e. $v, a, c \in \mathbb{R}^{200 \times 1}$.

Each model is trained on 4-12 CPU cores using the Intel MKL library, and takes about 2–4 days on average to converge.

We apply attention models with alignment bias and feedforward models in decoding using a decoder similar to that proposed in (Alkhouli et al., 2016). The decoder hypothesizes each source position for every target position being translated. Beam search is applied where the search nodes consist of both lexical and alignment hypotheses. When the attention model is applied without the alignment bias term, the decoder simplifies to hypothesizing lexical translations only. To speed up decoding of long sentences, we limit alignment hypotheses to the source positions $j \in \{i - 20, ..., i + 20\}$, where i is the current target position being translated. We use a beam size of 16 in all experiments. The alignments used during training are a result of IBM1/HMM/IBM4 training using GIZA++ (Och and Ney, 2003).

We use grid search to optimize the lexical model weights (cf. Eq. (9)). We find that the attention model receives a weight of 0.8, while the alignment model is assigned a weight of 0.2. We tune this on the development set of each task. We use 1000 sentence pairs of `newsdev2016` as the development set of the English→Romanian task, and `newstest2015` for tuning the German→English model weights.

[1] http://www.statmt.org/wmt16/
[2] http://www.statmt.org/wmt17/

These same datasets are used to halve the learning rate during model training.

All translation experiments are performed using an extension of the *Jane* toolkit (Vilar et al., 2010; Wuebker et al., 2012). The neural networks are trained using an extension of the *rwthlm* toolkit (Sundermeyer et al., 2014b). All results are measured in case-insensitive BLEU [%] (Papineni et al., 2002) using *mteval* from the *Moses* toolkit (Koehn et al., 2007). Case-insensitive TER [%] scores are computed with *TERCom* (Snover et al., 2006). Word classes are trained using an in-house tool (Botros et al., 2015) similar to *mkcls*.

9.2 Results

We compare our proposed system to three baseline systems on the WMT 2016 English→Romanian task and the WMT 2017 German→English task. The results are shown in Tab. (2). We set up a baseline system using a feedforward lexical model and a feedforward alignment model, to compare to the models used in (Alkhouli et al., 2016). This is shown in row 1. We first check the effect of using a recurrent alignment model (row 2) instead of the feedforward model. This brings an improvement of up to 1.6% BLEU. The attention baseline (row 3) performs much better in comparison, scoring up to 3.1% BLEU better than the feedforward system. This model has no alignment bias component. We note here that the German→English training data size is about 5.7 times more than that of the English→Romanian task, which can explain the small gap in performance between the systems in row 2 and row 3 on the German→English task, as the feeforward networks have large hidden layers of 1000 and 500 nodes, while the recurrent models use hidden layers of size 200.

We train an attention model by adding the alignment bias term in Eq. (6). We bias the attention model randomly during training for 50% of the training batches. During decoding, we include a bidirectional alignment model to score the alignment hypotheses (rows 4, 5). The combination of the alignment-biased attention model and the bidirectional alignment model (row 4) outperforms the standard attention model (row 3). This shows that the model learns to use the alignment information. We also compare to adding source alignment bias as given by Eq. (7) (row 5). We observe no difference to the case of constant alignment bias (row 4) on these tasks. Overall, we improve BLEU by

1.7% and 1.1% on the English→Romanian and the German→English task, respectively.

9.3 Alignment Model

In Tab. (3), we analyze the effect of the alignment model on the system. We observe that if the alignment model is dropped, the attention model is unable to score the alignments hypothesized during decoding on its own (row 4). If we drop the alignment model in decoding, we also have to exclude the alignment bias term when computing attention weights during decoding (row 3) (the bias term is still included in training). In this case, the translation degrades to the baseline performance.

9.4 Block out

In Tab. (3) we also investigate the effect of block out. On the English→Romanian task which has less training data in comparison to German→English, we observe that block out helps improve the system (row 2 vs. 5). This is because it avoids overfitting the alignment information, allowing the attention component to learn to attend on its own. This can be verified when comparing row 3 to row 6: When block out is used in training, and the attention model is used afterwards in decoding alone without an alignment model, it is able to perform close to the baseline attention performance if block out is used. Without using block out, the model fails to attend to the source side properly on its own.

9.5 Alignment Quality

We analyze the word alignment quality using 504 manually word-aligned German-English sentence pairs that were extracted from the Europarl corpus (Vilar et al., 2006). In Tab. (4), we compare the baseline attention system to the proposed alignment-based system. The alignments of the baseline attention system are generated by aligning each target word to the source position having the maximum attention weight. We observe that the baseline attention system has a high AER in comparison to the proposed system, which reduces AER from 44.9% to 29.7%. This corresponds to 1.1% BLEU improvement. It is worth noting that the high AER of the baseline system is likely because the model is not trained to align, and that the attention weights it produces are soft alignments. In comparison, our system uses an alignment model that explicitly learns to model alignments.

#	lexical model	alignment model	bias term	WMT En→Ro newstest2016 BLEU[%]	TER[%]	WMT De→En newstest2017 BLEU[%]	TER[%]
1	feedforward	feedforward	-	20.0	64.2	24.2	58.6
2	feedforward	bidirectional	-	21.6	62.7	25.5	57.6
3	attention	-	-	23.1	60.6	25.7	57.6
4	attention	bidirectional	$\delta_{j,bi}\, c$	24.8	58.1	26.8	55.6
5	attention	bidirectional	$\delta_{j,bi}\, D\, h_{b_i}$	24.8	58.1	26.8	55.5

Table 2: Translation results on the WMT 2016 English→Romanian task and the WMT 2017 German→English task.

#	lexical model	alignment model	decode w/ align bias	train w/ block out	WMT En→Ro newstest2016 BLEU[%]	TER[%]	WMT De→En newstest2017 BLEU[%]	TER[%]
1	attention baseline	-	-	-	23.1	60.6	25.7	57.6
2		bidirectional	yes		24.8	58.1	26.8	55.6
3		-	no	yes	23.1	60.6	25.7	59.4
4	+ alignment bias	-	yes		degenerate		degenerate	
5		bidirectional	yes	no	23.7	59.2	26.7	55.8
6		-	no		degenerate		degenerate	

Table 3: The effect of using the alignment model in decoding and block out in training . The alignment bias term used here is $\delta_{j,bi}\, c$. Rows 1 and 2 are the same as rows 3 and 4 in Tab. (2). Block out means including the alignment bias term for 50% of the training batches.

	newstest2017 BLEU[%]	Europarl AER[%]
attention baseline	25.7	44.9
proposed system	26.8	29.7

Table 4: A comparison between the WMT German→English proposed system and the baseline attention system in terms of the alignment error rate (AER). The attention baseline and the proposed system are the same ones shown in Tab. (2), rows 3 and 4, respectively.

To illustrate what happens when we include the source alignment bias term, we take a sample from the translation hypotheses of the German→English system in Tab. (2, row 5), and compare it to the output of the standard attention model Tab. (2, row 3). The sample is chosen from the development set `newstest2015`. The German sentence *"diese schreckliche Erfahrung wird uns immer verfolgen ."* has the reference translation " *this horrible experience will stay with us ."*

In Fig. (3), we illustrate the best translation hypothesis and the corresponding attention weights produced by the standard attention model. Fig. (4) shows the same thing for the attention model using source alignment bias. We observe that the latter is able to generate a good translation while being able to attend to the source sentence in a proper order. On the other hand, the standard attention model has a problem in the first half of the hypothesis, where it attends to the second half of the source sentence instead. It ends up confusing the object and the subject. A more acceptable, though inaccurate, translation of 'verfolgen' under such reordering would be 'followed by', but the system fails to generate this translation.

Fig. (5) shows the curve of tuning the lexical model weight. We observe that the weight is robust against small changes. The best results in terms of BLEU are achieved when $\lambda = 0.8$.

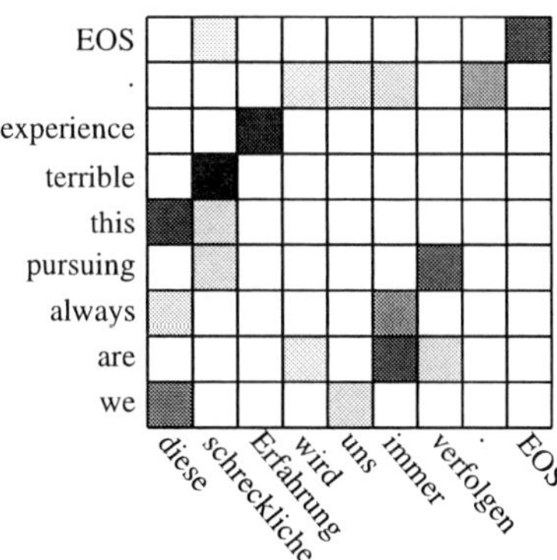

Figure 3: A translation example produced by the standard attention system in Tab. (2), row 3. EOS denotes the sentence end symbol. The shading degree corresponds to the attention weight.

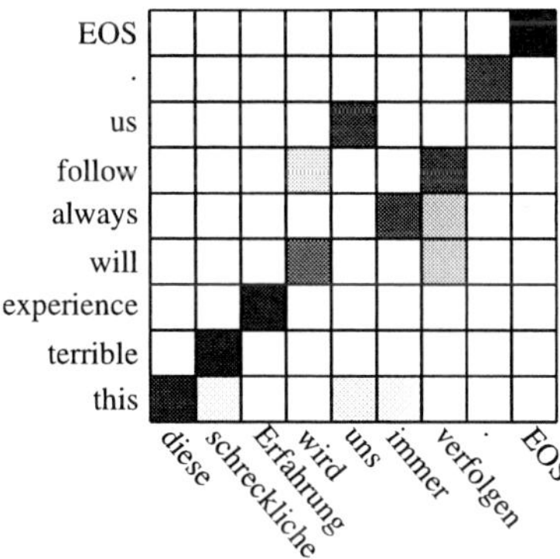

Figure 4: A translation example produced by our best system using source alignment bias, given in Tab. (2), row 5. EOS denotes the sentence end symbol. The shading degree corresponds to the attention weight.

10 Conclusion

We presented a modification of the attention model to bias it using external alignment information. We also presented a bidirectional recurrent neural network alignment model to be used alongside the proposed attention model. We used the two models in a generative scheme of alignment generation followed by lexical translation. We demonstrated improvements over the standard attention model on two WMT tasks. We provided evidence that enabling the alignment bias term for all training samples makes the attention mechanism overfit the alignments on non-large datasets. To remedy this, we proposed to apply the alignment bias on half of the training samples, which

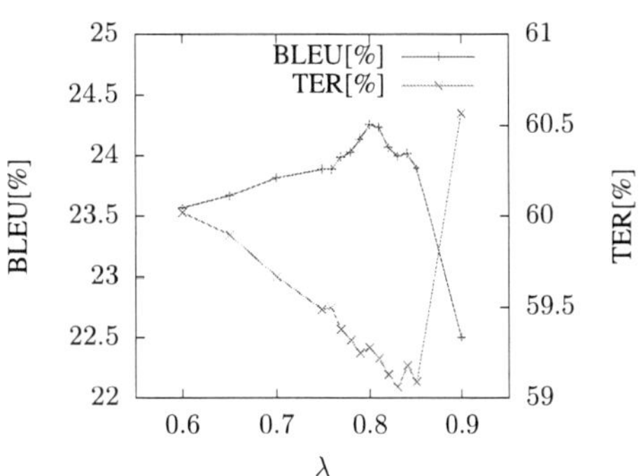

Figure 5: Grid search tuning of the lexical weight of the system in Tab. (2, row 4). The results are computed on the development set of the English→Romanian task.

yielded our best system.

While this work depends on pre-computed alignments to train the attention and alignment models, this is not central to our approach. In future work, we plan to perform integrated training by alternating between alignment generation and model estimation. Alignment generation can be performed using forced alignment where beam search is performed over the alignment positions, while fixing the lexical translations to the reference translation. This can eliminate the need for pre-computing alignments using ad hoc methods like IBM1/ HMM/IBM4 training.

Acknowledgements

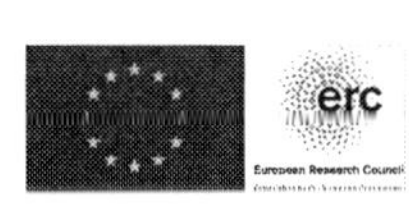

The work reported in this paper results from two projects, SEQCLAS and QT21. SEQCLAS has received funding from the European Research Council (ERC) under the European Union's Horizon 2020 research and innovation programme under grant agreement n° 694537. QT21 has received funding from the European Union's Horizon 2020 research and innovation programme under grant agreement n° 645452. The work reflects only the authors' views and neither the European Commission nor the European Research Council Executive Agency are responsible for any use that may be made of the information it contains.

Tamer Alkhouli was partly funded by the 2016 Google PhD Fellowship for North America, Europe and the Middle East.

The authors would like to thank Kazuki Irie for contributing to the attention layer implementation.

References

Tamer Alkhouli, Gabriel Bretschner, Jan-Thorsten Peter, Mohammed Hethnawi, Andreas Guta, and Hermann Ney. 2016. Alignment-based neural machine translation. In *Proceedings of the First Conference on Machine Translation*, pages 54–65, Berlin, Germany.

Philip Arthur, Graham Neubig, and Satoshi Nakamura. 2016. Incorporating discrete translation lexicons into neural machine translation. In *Proceedings of the 2016 Conference on Empirical Methods in Natural Language Processing*, pages 1557–1567, Austin, Texas.

Dzmitry Bahdanau, Kyunghyun Cho, and Yoshua Bengio. 2015. Neural machine translation by jointly learning to align and translate. In *International Conference on Learning Representations*, San Diego, Calefornia, USA.

Rami Botros, Kazuki Irie, Martin Sundermeyer, and Hermann Ney. 2015. On efficient training of word classes and their application to recurrent neural network language models. In *Interspeech*, pages 1443–1447, Dresden, Germany.

Wenhu Chen, Evgeny Matusov, Shahram Khadivi, and Jan-Thorsten Peter. 2016. Guided alignment training for topic-aware neural machine translation. In *Proceedings of the 2016 Conference of the Association for Machine Translation in the Americas (AMTA)*, pages 121–134, Austin, Texas.

Trevor Cohn, Cong Duy Vu Hoang, Ekaterina Vymolova, Kaisheng Yao, Chris Dyer, and Gholamreza Haffari. 2016. Incorporating structural alignment biases into an attentional neural translation model. In *Proceedings of the 2016 Conference of the North American Chapter of the Association for Computational Linguistics: Human Language Technologies*, pages 876–885, San Diego, California.

Jacob Devlin, Rabih Zbib, Zhongqiang Huang, Thomas Lamar, Richard Schwartz, and John Makhoul. 2014. Fast and Robust Neural Network Joint Models for Statistical Machine Translation. In *52nd Annual Meeting of the Association for Computational Linguistics*, pages 1370–1380, Baltimore, MD, USA.

Felix A. Gers, Jürgen Schmidhuber, and Fred Cummins. 2000. Learning to forget: Continual prediction with LSTM. *Neural computation*, 12(10):2451–2471.

Felix A. Gers, Nicol N. Schraudolph, and Jürgen Schmidhuber. 2003. Learning precise timing with lstm recurrent networks. *The Journal of Machine Learning Research*, 3:115–143.

Sepp Hochreiter and Jürgen Schmidhuber. 1997. Long short-term memory. *Neural computation*, 9(8):1735–1780.

Philipp Koehn, Hieu Hoang, Alexandra Birch, Chris Callison-Burch, Marcello Federico, Nicola Bertoldi, Brooke Cowan, Wade Shen, Christine Moran, Richard Zens, Chris Dyer, Ondřej Bojar, Alexandra Constantine, and Evan Herbst. 2007. Moses: Open Source Toolkit for Statistical Machine Translation. pages 177–180, Prague, Czech Republic.

Haitao Mi, Zhiguo Wang, and Abe Ittycheriah. 2016. Supervised attentions for neural machine translation. In *Proceedings of the 2016 Conference on Empirical Methods in Natural Language Processing*, pages 2283–2288, Austin, Texas.

Franz J. Och and Hermann Ney. 2003. A Systematic Comparison of Various Statistical Alignment Models. *Computational Linguistics*, 29(1):19–51.

Kishore Papineni, Salim Roukos, Todd Ward, and Wei-Jing Zhu. 2002. Bleu: a Method for Automatic Evaluation of Machine Translation. In *Proceedings of the 41st Annual Meeting of the Association for Computational Linguistics*, pages 311–318, Philadelphia, Pennsylvania, USA.

Matthew Snover, Bonnie Dorr, Richard Schwartz, Linnea Micciulla, and John Makhoul. 2006. A Study of Translation Edit Rate with Targeted Human Annotation. In *Proceedings of the 7th Conference of the Association for Machine Translation in the Americas*, pages 223–231, Cambridge, Massachusetts, USA.

Martin Sundermeyer, Tamer Alkhouli, Joern Wuebker, and Hermann Ney. 2014a. Translation Modeling with Bidirectional Recurrent Neural Networks. In *Conference on Empirical Methods on Natural Language Processing*, pages 14–25, Doha, Qatar.

Martin Sundermeyer, Ralf Schlüter, and Hermann Ney. 2014b. rwthlm - the RWTH Aachen university neural network language modeling toolkit. In *Interspeech*, pages 2093–2097, Singapore.

Akihiro Tamura, Taro Watanabe, and Eiichiro Sumita. 2014. Recurrent neural networks for word alignment model. In *52nd Annual Meeting of the Association for Computational Linguistics*, pages 1470–1480, Baltimore, MD, USA.

David Vilar, Maja Popović, and Hermann Ney. 2006. AER: Do we need to "improve" our alignments? In *Proceedings of International Workshop on Spoken Language Translation*, pages 205–212, Kyoto, Japan.

David Vilar, Daniel Stein, Matthias Huck, and Hermann Ney. 2010. Jane: Open source hierarchical translation, extended with reordering and lexicon models. In *ACL 2010 Joint Fifth Workshop on Statistical Machine Translation and Metrics MATR*, pages 262–270, Uppsala, Sweden.

Stephan Vogel, Hermann Ney, and Christoph Tillmann. 1996. HMM-Based Word Alignment in Statistical Translation. In *Proceedings of the 16th conference on Computational linguistics*, volume 2, pages 836–841, Copenhagen, Denmark.

Weiyue Wang, Tamer Alkhouli, Derui Zhu, and Hermann Ney. 2017. Hybrid neural network alignment and lexicon model in direct hmm for statistical machine translation. In *Proceedings of the 55th Annual Meeting of the Association for Computational Linguistics*, Vancouver, Canada.

Joern Wuebker, Matthias Huck, Stephan Peitz, Malte Nuhn, Markus Freitag, Jan-Thorsten Peter, Saab Mansour, and Hermann Ney. 2012. Jane 2: Open source phrase-based and hierarchical statistical machine translation. In *International Conference on Computational Linguistics*, pages 483–491, Mumbai, India.

Nan Yang, Shujie Liu, Mu Li, Ming Zhou, and Nenghai Yu. 2013. Word alignment modeling with context dependent deep neural network. In *51st Annual Meeting of the Association for Computational Linguistics*, pages 166–175, Sofia, Bulgaria.

Lei Yu, Phil Blunsom, Chris Dyer, Edward Grefenstette, and Tomás Kociský. 2017. The neural noisy channel. In *Proceedings of the International Conference on Learning Representations*, volume abs/1611.02554.

Lei Yu, Jan Buys, and Phil Blunsom. 2016. Online segment to segment neural transduction. In *Proceedings of the 2016 Conference on Empirical Methods in Natural Language Processing*, pages 1307–1316, Austin, Texas.

Effective Domain Mixing for Neural Machine Translation

Reid Pryzant[*]
Stanford University
rpryzant@stanford.edu

Denny Britz[*]
Google Brain
dennybritz@google.com

Quoc V. Le
Google Brain
qvl@google.com

Abstract

Neural Machine Translation (NMT) models are often trained on heterogeneous mixtures of domains, from news to parliamentary proceedings, each with unique distributions and language. In this work we show that training NMT systems on naively mixed data can degrade performance versus models fit to each constituent domain. We demonstrate that this problem *can* be circumvented, and propose three models that do so by jointly learning domain discrimination and translation. We demonstrate the efficacy of these techniques by merging pairs of domains in three languages: Chinese, French, and Japanese. After training on composite data, each approach outperforms its domain-specific counterparts, with a model based on a discriminator network doing so most reliably. We obtain consistent performance improvements and an average increase of 1.1 BLEU.

1 Introduction

Neural Machine Translation (NMT) (Kalchbrenner and Blunsom, 2013; Sutskever et al., 2014; Cho et al., 2014) is an end-to-end approach for automated translation. NMT has shown impressive results (Bahdanau et al., 2015; Luong et al., 2015a; Wu et al., 2016) often surpassing those of phrase-based systems while addressing shortcomings such as the need for hand-engineered features.

In many translation settings (e.g. web translation, assistant translators), input may come from more than one domain. Each domain has unique properties that could confound models not explicitly fitted to it. Thus, an important problem is to effectively mix a diversity of training data in a multi-domain setting.

Our problem space is as follows: how can we train a translation model on multi-domain data to improve test-time performance in each *constituent* domain? This setting differs from the majority of work in domain adaptation, which explores how models trained on some source domain can be effectively applied to *outside* target domains. This setting is important, because previous research has shown that both standard NMT and adaptation methods degrade performance on the original source domain(s) (Farajian et al., 2017; Haddow and Koehn, 2012). We seek to prove that this problem can be overcome, and hypothesize that leveraging the heterogeneity of composite data rather than dampening it will allow us to do so.

To this extent, we propose three new models for multi-domain machine translation. These models are based on discriminator networks, adversarial learning, and target-side domain tokens. We evaluate on pairs of linguistically disparate corpora in three translation tasks (EN-JA, EN-ZH, EN-FR), and observe that unlike naively training on mixed data (as per current best practices), the proposed techniques consistently improve translation quality in each individual setting. The most significant of these tasks is EN-JA, where we obtain state-of-the-art performance in the process of examining the ASPEC corpus (Nakazawa et al., 2016) of scientific papers and Sub-Crawl, a new corpus based on an anonymous manuscript (Anonymous, 2017). In summary,

---

[*]Equal Contribution.

Proceedings of the Conference on Machine Translation (WMT), Volume 1: Research Papers, pages 118–126
Copenhagen, Denmark, September 7–11, 2017. ©2017 Association for Computational Linguistics

our contributions are as follows:

- We show that mixing data from heterogeneous domains leads to suboptimal results compared to the single-domain setting, and that the more distant these domains are, the more their merger degrades downstream translation quality.

- We demonstrate that this problem can be circumvented and propose novel, general-purpose techniques that do so.

2 Neural Machine Translation

Neural machine translation (Sutskever et al., 2014) directly models the conditional log probability $\log p(\boldsymbol{y}|\boldsymbol{x})$ of producing some translation $\boldsymbol{y} = y_1, ..., y_m$ of a source sentence $\boldsymbol{x} = x_1, ..., x_n$. It models this probability through the *encoder-decoder* framework. In this approach, an *encoder* network encodes the source into a series of vector representations $\boldsymbol{H} = \boldsymbol{h}_1, ..., \boldsymbol{h}_n$. The *decoder* network uses this encoding to generate a translation one target token at a time. At each step, the decoder casts an attentional distribution over source encodings (Luong et al., 2015b; Bahdanau et al., 2014). This allows the model to focus on parts of the input before producing each translated token. In this way the decoder is decomposing the conditional log probability into

$$\log p(\boldsymbol{y}|\boldsymbol{x}) = \sum_{t=1}^{m} \log p(y_t|y_{<t}, \boldsymbol{H}) \qquad (1)$$

In practice, stacked networks with recurrent Long Short-Term Memory (LSTM) units are used for both the encoder and decoder. Such units can effectively distill structure from sequential data (Elman, 1990).

The cross-entropy training objective in NMT is formulated as,

$$\mathcal{L}_{gen} = \sum_{(\mathbf{x},\mathbf{y})\in\mathcal{D}} -\log p(\mathbf{y}|\mathbf{x}) \qquad (2)$$

Where $\mathcal{D}$ is a set of (source, target) sequence pairs $(\mathbf{x}, \mathbf{y})$.

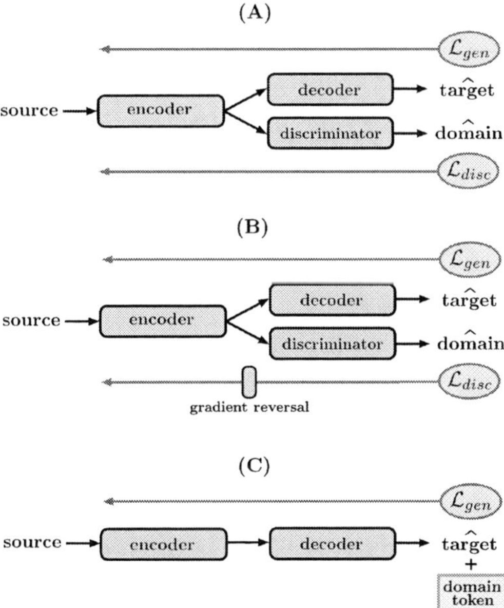

Figure 1: The novel mixing paradigms under consideration. Discriminative mixing (A), adversarial discriminative mixing (B), and target-side token mixing (C) are depicted.

3 Models

We now describe three models we are proposing that leverage the diversity of information in heterogeneous corpora. They are summarized in Figure 1. We assume dataset $\mathcal{D}$ consists of source sequences $\boldsymbol{X}$, target sequences $\boldsymbol{Y}$ and domain class labels $\boldsymbol{D}$ that are only known at training time.

3.1 Discriminative Mixing

In the Discriminative Mixing approach, we add a discriminator network on top of the source encoder that takes a single vector encoding of the source $\boldsymbol{c}$ as input. This network maximizes $P(d|\boldsymbol{H})$, the predicted probability of the correct domain class label d conditioned on the hidden states of the encoder $\boldsymbol{H}$. It does so by minimizing the negative cross-entropy loss $\mathcal{L}_{disc} = -\log p(d|\boldsymbol{H})$. In other words, the discriminator uses the encoded representation of the source sequence to predict the correct domain. Intuitively, this forces the encoder to encode domain-related information into the features it generates. We hypothesize that this information will be useful during the decoding process.

The encoder can employ an arbitrary mechanism to distill the source into a single-vector representation c. In this work, we use an attention mechanism over the encoder states H, followed by a fully connected layer. We set c to be the attention context, and calculate it according to Bahdanau et al. (2015):

$$c = \sum_j a_j h_j$$
$$a = \text{softmax}(\hat{a})$$
$$\hat{a}_i = v_a^T \tanh(W_a h_i)$$

The discriminator can be an arbitrary neural network. For this work, we fed c into a fully connected layer with a tanh nonlinearity, then passed the result through a softmax to obtain probabilities for each domain class label.

The discriminator is optimized jointly with the rest of the Sequence-to-Sequence network. If $\mathcal{L}_{gen}$ is the standard sequence generator loss described in Section 2, then the final loss we are optimizing is the sum of the generator and discriminator loss $\mathcal{L} = \mathcal{L}_{gen} + \mathcal{L}_{disc}$.

3.2 Adversarial Discriminative Mixing

We also experiment with an adversarial approach to domain mixing. This approach is similar to that of 3.1, except that when backpropagating from the discriminator network to the encoder, we reverse the gradients by multiplying them by -1. Though the discriminator is still using $\nabla \mathcal{L}_{disc}$ to update its parameters, with the inclusion of the reversal layer, we are implicitly directing the encoder to optimize with $-\nabla \mathcal{L}_{disc}$. This has the opposite effect of what we described above. The discriminator still learns to distinguish between domains, but the encoder is forced to compute domain-invariant representations that are not useful to the discriminator. We hope that such representations lead to better generalization across domains.

Note the connections between this technique and that of the Generative Adversarial Network (GAN) paradigm (Goodfellow et al., 2014). GANs optimize two networks with two objective functions (one being the negation of the other) and periodically freeze the parameters of each network during training. We are training a single network without freezing any of its components. Furthermore, we reverse

gradients in lieu of explicitly defining a second, negated loss function. Last, the adversarial parts of this model are trained jointly with translation in a multitask setting.

Note also that the representations computed by this model are likely to be applicable to unseen, outside domains. However, this setting is outside the scope of this paper and we leave its exploration to future work. For our setting, we hypothesize that the domain-agnostic encodings encouraged by the discriminator may yield improvements in mixed-domain settings as well.

3.3 Target Token Mixing

A simpler alternative to adding a discriminator network is to prepend a domain token to the target sequence. Such a technique can be readily incorporated into any existing NMT pipeline and does not require changes to the model. In particular, we add a single special vocabulary word such as "domain=subtitles", per domain and prepend this token to each target sequence therein.

The decoder must learn, similar to the more complex discriminator above, to predict the correct domain token based on the source representation at the first step of decoding. We hypothesize that this technique has a similar regularizing effect as adding a discriminator network. During inference, we remove the first predicted token corresponding to the domain.

The advantage of this approach verses the similar techniques discussed in related work (Section 5) is that in our proposed method, the model must learn to predict the domain based on the source sequence alone. It does not need to know the domain a-priori.

4 Experiments

4.1 Datasets

For the Japanese translation task we evaluate our domain mixing techniques on the standard ASPEC corpus (Nakazawa et al., 2016) consisting of 3M scientific document sentence pairs, and the SubCrawl corpus, consisting of 3.2M colloquial sentence pairs harvested from freely available subtitle repositories on the World Wide Web. We use standard train/dev/test splits (3M, 1.8k, and 1.8k examples, respectively) and preprocess the data using subword units[1] (Sennrich et al., 2015) to learn a shared English-Japanese vocabulary of size 32,000. To allow for fair comparisons, we use the same vocabulary and sentence segmentation for all experiments, including single-domain models.

To prove its generality, we also evaluate our techniques on a small set of about 200k/1k/1k training/dev/test examples of English Chinese (EN-ZH) and English-French (EN-FR) language pairs. For EN-ZH, we use a news commentary corpus from WMT'17[2] and a 2012 database dump of TED talk subtitles (Tiedemann, 2012). For EN-FR, we use professional translations of European Parliament Proceedings (Koehn, 2005) and a 2016 dump of the OpenSubtitles database (Lison and Tiedemann, 2016).

The premise of evaluating on mixed-domain data is that the domains undergoing mixing are in fact disparate. We need to quantifiably measure the disparity therein to obtain fair, valid, and explainable results. Thus, we measured the distances between the domains of each language pair with A-distance, an important part of the upper generalization bounds for domain adaptation (Ben-David et al., 2007). Due to the intractability of computing A-distances, we instead compute a proxy for A-distance, $\hat{d}_A$, which is given theoretical justification in Ben-David et al. (2007) and used to measure domain distance in Gani et al. (2015); Glorot et al. (2011). The proxy A-distance is obtained by measuring the generalization error ϵ of a linear bag-of-words SVM classifier trained to discriminate between the two domains, and setting $\hat{d}_A = 2(1-2\epsilon)$. Note that by nature of its formulation, $\hat{d}_A$ is only useful in comparative settings, and means little in isolation (Ben-David et al., 2007). However, it has a minimum value of 1, implying exact domain match, and a maximum of 2, implying that domains are polar opposites.

4.2 Experimental Protocol

All models are implemented using the Tensorflow framework and based on the Sequence-to-Sequence implementation of Britz et al.

(2017)[3]. We use a 4-layer bidirectional LSTM encoder with 512 units, and a 4-layer LSTM decoder. Recall from Section 3 that we use Bahdanau-style attention Bahdanau et al. (2015). Dropout of 0.2 (0.8 keep probability) is applied to the input of each cell. We optimize using Adam and a learning rate of 0.0001 (Kingma and Ba, 2014; Abadi et al., 2016). Each model is trained on 8 Nvidia K40m GPUs with a batch size of 128. The combined Japanese dataset took approximately a week to reach convergence.

During training, we save model checkpoints every hour and choose the best one using the BLEU score on the validation set. To calculate BLEU scores for the EN-JA task, we follow the instruction from WAT [4] and use the KyTea tokenizer (Neubig et al., 2011). For the EN-FR and EN-ZH tasks, we follow the WMT '16 guidlines and tokenize with the Moses `tokenizer.perl` script (Koehn et al., 2007).

4.3 Results

The results of our proxy-A distance experiment are given in Table 1. $\hat{d}_A$ is a purely comparative metric that has little meaning in isolation (Ben-David et al., 2007), so it is evident that the EN-JA and EN-ZH domains are more disparate, while the EN-FR domains are more similar.

Lanuage	Domain 1	Domain 2	$\hat{d}_A$
Japanese	ASPEC	SubCrawl	1.89
Chinese	News	TED	1.73
French	Europarl	OpenSubs	1.23

Table 1: Proxy A-distances ($\hat{d}_A$) for each domain pair.

To understand the interactions between these models and mixed-domain data, we train and test on ASPEC, SubCrawl, and their concatenation. We do the same for the French and Chinese baselines

In general, our results support the hypothesis that the naive concatenation of data from disparate domains can degrade in-domain translation quality (Table 2). In both the EN-JA and EN-FR settings, the domains undergoing mixing are disparate enough to *degrade*

---

[1]Using https://github.com/google/sentencepiece

[2]http://www.statmt.org/wmt17/translation-task.html

[3]https://github.com/google/seq2seq

[4]http://lotus.kuee.kyoto-u.ac.jp/WAT/evaluation/

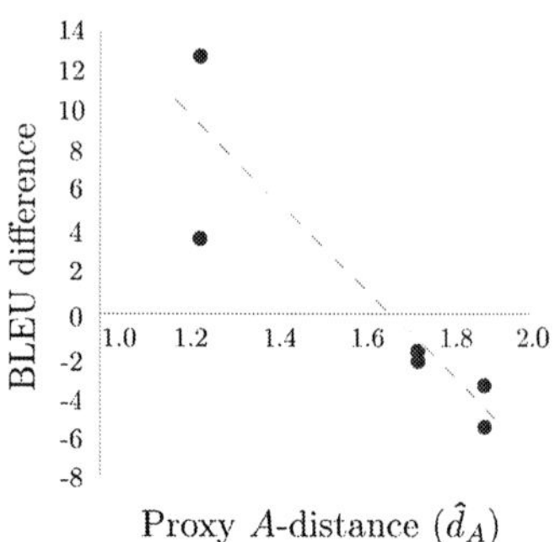
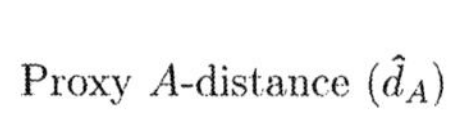
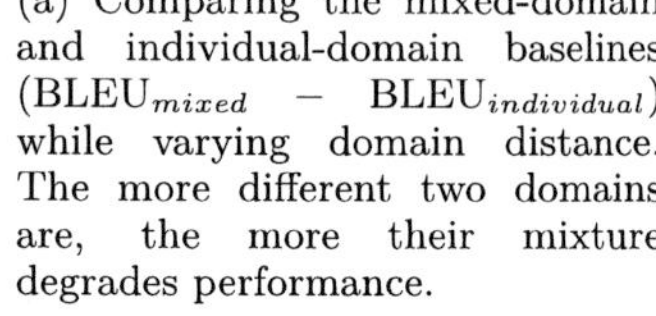

(a) Comparing the mixed-domain and individual-domain baselines ($BLEU_{mixed} - BLEU_{individual}$) while varying domain distance. The more different two domains are, the more their mixture degrades performance.

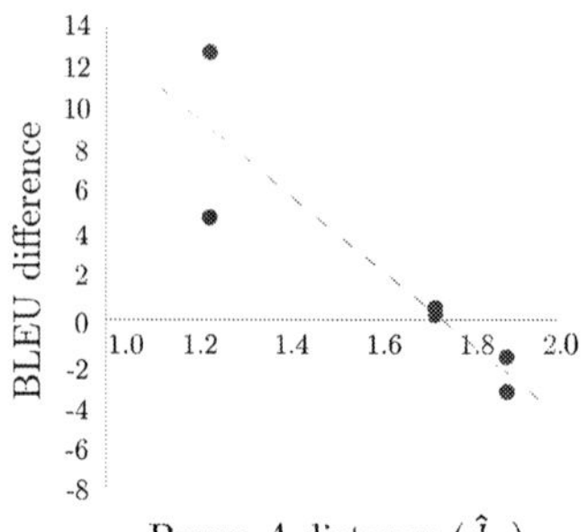

(b) Comparing the proposed discriminator and individual-domain baseline ($BLEU_{discriminator} - BLEU_{individual}$) while varying domain distance. Compared to Figure 2a, performance is less degraded when using the discriminator.

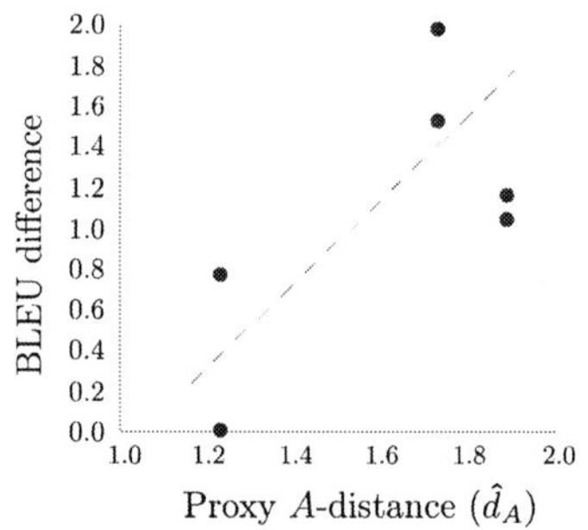

(c) Comparing the proposed discriminator approach and mixed-domain baseline ($BLEU_{discriminator} - BLEU_{mixed}$) while varying domain distance. The discriminator always improves over the baseline, and this is accentuated when the merged domains are more distant.

Figure 2: Comparative performance and domain distance. Trends corresponding to a least-squares fit are indicated with dashed lines.

performance when mixed, and the proposed techniques recover some of this performance drop. In the EN-ZH setting, we observe that even when similar domains are mixed performance can drop. Notably, in this setting, the proposed techniques successfully *improve* performance over single-domain training.

For a more detailed perspective on this result, Figure 2a depicts the mixed-domain/individual-domain performance differential as a function of domain distance. The two share a negative association, suggesting that the most distant two domains are, the more their merger degrades performance. This degradation is particularly strong in Japanese due the vast structural differences between formal and casual language. The vocabularies, conjugational patterns, and word attachments all follow different rules in this case (Hori, 1986).

We then trained and tested our proposed methods on the same mixed data (Table 2). Our results generally agree with the hypothesis that the diversity of information in heterogeneous data *can* be leveraged to improve in-domain translation. Overall, we find that all of the proposed methods outperform their respective baselines in most settings, but that the discriminator appears the most reliable. It bested its counterparts in 4 of 6 trials, and was

EN-JA Model	ASPEC	SubCrawl
ASPEC	38.87	3.85
SubCrawl	2.74	16.91
ASPEC + SubCrawl	33.85	14.34
Discriminator	35.01	**15.38**
Adv. Discriminator	29.87	13.31
Target Token	**35.05**	14.92

EN-FR Model	Europarl	OpenSubs
Europarl	34.51	13.36
OpenSubtitles	13.12	15.2
Europarl + OpenSubs	38.26	27.9
Discriminator	39.03	**27.91**
Adv. Discriminator	38.38	25.67
Target Token	**39.1**	25.32

EN-ZH Model	News	TED
News	12.75	3.12
TED	2.79	8.41
News + TED	11.36	6.67
Discriminator	**12.88**	**8.64**
Adv. Discriminator	12.15	8.16
Target Token	11.98	7.69

Table 2: BLEU scores for models trained on various domains and languages (both mixed and unmixed). Rows correspond to training domains and columns correspond to test domains. Note that our single-domain AS-PEC results are state-of-the-art, indicating the strength of these baselines.

the only approach that outperformed both individually fit and naively mixed baselines in every trial.

Figure 2c depicts the dynamics of the discriminator approach. More specifically, this figure shows the discriminator/naive-mixing performance differential as a function of domain distance. The two share a positive association, suggesting that the more distant two domains are, the more the discriminator helps performance. This may be because it is easier to classify distant domains, so the discriminator can fit the data better and its gradients encourage the upstream encoder to include more useful domain-related structure.

The adversarial discriminator architecture yielded improvements on the small datasets, but underperformed on EN-JA. It is possible that the grammatical differences inherent to casual and polite domains are such that semantic information was lost in the process of forcing their encoded distributions to match. Additionally, adversarial objective functions are notoriously difficult to optimize on, and this model was prone to falling into poor local optimum during training.

The simpler target token approach also yields improvement over the baselines, just barely surpassing that of the Discriminator for ASPEC. This approach has the practical benefit of requiring no architectural changes to an off-the-shelf NMT system.

Our EN-FR results are particularly interesting. Though the data seem like they should come from sufficiently distant domains (parliament proceedings and subtitles), the domains are actually quite close according to d_A (Table 1). Since these domains are so close, their merger is able to improve baseline performance. Thus, if the source and target domain are sufficiently close, then their merger does indeed help.

Next, we investigated the optimization dynamics of these models by examining their learning curves. Curves for the baselines and discriminative models trained on EN-JA data are depicted in Figure 3a. Single-domain training clearly outperforms mixed training, and it appears that adding a discriminative strategy provides additional gains. From Figure 3b we can see that the discriminator approach (not reversing gradients), learns to fit the domain distribution quickly, implying that the Japanese domains were in fact quite distant and easily classifiable.

5 Related Work

Our work builds on a recent literature on domain adaptation strategies in Neural Machine Translation. Prior work in this space has proposed two general categories of methods.

The first proposed method is to take models trained on the source domain and finetune on target-domain data. Luong and Manning (2015); Zoph et al. (2016) explores how to improve transfer learning for a low-resource language pair by finetuning only parts of the network. Chu et al. (2017) empirically evaluate domain adaptation methods and propose mixing source and target domain data during finetuning. Freitag and Al-Onaizan (2016) explored finetuning using only a small subset of target domain data. Note that we did not compare directly against these techniques because they are intended to transfer knowledge to a new domain and perform well on only the target domain. We are concerned with multi-domain settings, where performance on *all* constituent domains is important.

A second strain of "multi-domain" thought in NMT involves appending a domain indicator token to each source sequence (Kobus et al., 2016). Similarly, Johnson et al. (2016) use a token for cross-lingual translation instead of domain identification. This idea was further refined by Chu et al. (2017), who integrated source-tokenization into the domain finetuning paradigm. While it requires no changes to the NMT architecture, these approaches are inherently limited because they stipulate that domain information for unseen test examples be known. For example, if using a trained model to translate user-generated sentences, we do not know the domain a-priori, and this approach cannot be used.

Apart from the recent progress in domain adaptation for NMT, we draw on work that transfers knowledge between domains in semisupervised settings. Our strongest influence is adversarial domain adaptation (Ganin et al., 2015), where feature distributions in the source and target domains are matched

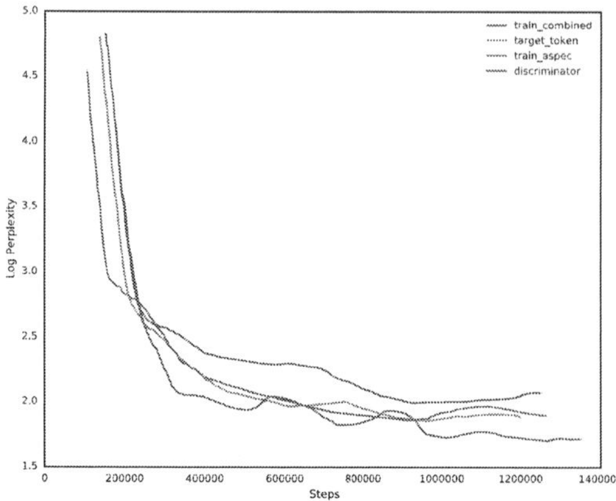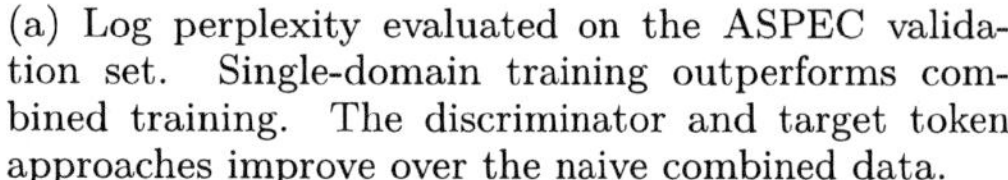

(a) Log perplexity evaluated on the ASPEC validation set. Single-domain training outperforms combined training. The discriminator and target token approaches improve over the naive combined data.

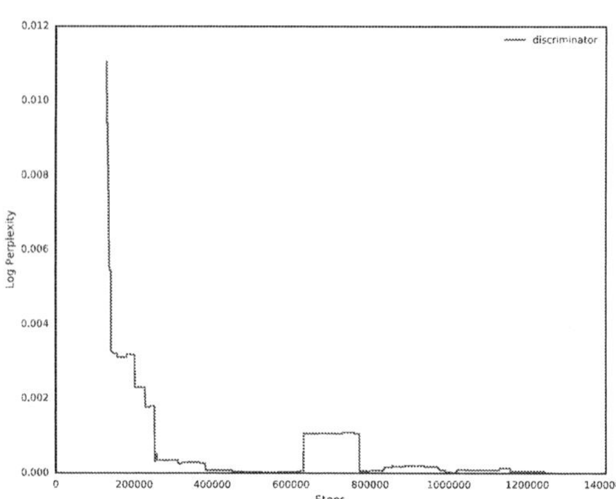

(b) Discriminator training loss over time on the EN-JA data. The discriminator learns to fit the data almost perfectly after a few hundred thousand iterations

Figure 3: Training curves for domain mixing and discriminator loss.

with a Domain-Adversarial Neural Network (DANN). Another approach to this problem is that of Long et al. (2015), which measures and minimizes the distance between domain distribution means before training, thereby negating any unique properties.

There is some overlap between past research in multi-domain statistical machine translation (SMT) and the ideas of this paper. (Farajian et al., 2017) compared the efficacy of phrase-based SMT and NMT on multiple-domain data, observing similar performance degradations as us in mixed-domain settings. However, that study did not seek to understand the issue and offered no explanation, analysis, or solution to the problem. Another line of work merged data by only selecting examples with a propensity for relevance in a multi-domain setting (Mandal et al., 2008; Axelrod et al., 2011). In a strategy that echos NMT fine-tuning, Pecina et al. (2012) used a variety of in-domain development sets to tune hyperparameters to a generalized setting. Similar to our domain discriminator network, Clark et al. (2012) crafted domain-specific features that are used by the decoder. However, some of these systems' features are downstream of binary indicators for domain identity. This approach, then, faces the same inherent limitations as source-tokenization: domain knowledge is required for inference. Furthermore, the domain features of this system are integral to the decoding process, while our discriminator network is an independent module that can be detached during inference.

6 Conclusion

We presented three novel models for applying Neural Machine Translation to multi-domain settings, and demonstrated their efficacy across six domains in three language pairs, and in the process achieved a new state-of-the-art in EN-JA translation. Unlike the naive combining of training data, these models improve their translational ability on each constituent domain. Furthermore, these models are the first of their kind to not require knowledge of each example's domain at inference time. All the proposed approaches outperform the naive combining of training data, so we advise practitioners to implement whichever most easily fits into their pre-existing pipelines, but an approach based on a discriminator network offered the most reliable results.

In future work we hope to explore the dynamics of adversarial discriminative training objectives, which force the model to learn domain-agnostic features, in the related problem of adaptation to unseen test-time domains.

References

Martín Abadi, Ashish Agarwal, Paul Barham, Eugene Brevdo, Zhifeng Chen, Craig Citro, Greg S Corrado, Andy Davis, Jeffrey Dean, Matthieu Devin, et al. 2016. Tensorflow: Large-scale machine learning on heterogeneous distributed systems. *arXiv preprint arXiv:1603.04467* .

Anonymous. 2017. Subcrawl: A colloquial parallel corpus for english-japanese translation. *Manuscript submitted for publication.* .

Amittai Axelrod, Xiaodong He, and Jianfeng Gao. 2011. Domain adaptation via pseudo in-domain data selection. In *Proceedings of the conference on empirical methods in natural language processing*. Association for Computational Linguistics, pages 355–362.

Dzmitry Bahdanau, Kyunghyun Cho, and Yoshua Bengio. 2014. Neural machine translation by jointly learning to align and translate. *arXiv preprint arXiv:1409.0473* .

Dzmitry Bahdanau, Kyunghyun Cho, and Yoshua Bengio. 2015. Neural machine translation by jointly learning to align and translate. In *ICLR*.

Shai Ben-David, John Blitzer, Koby Crammer, Fernando Pereira, et al. 2007. Analysis of representations for domain adaptation. *Advances in neural information processing systems* 19:137.

D. Britz, A. Goldie, T. Luong, and Q. Le. 2017. Massive Exploration of Neural Machine Translation Architectures. *ArXiv e-prints* .

Kyunghyun Cho, Bart van Merrienboer, Çaglar Gülçehre, Fethi Bougares, Holger Schwenk, and Yoshua Bengio. 2014. Learning phrase representations using RNN encoder-decoder for statistical machine translation. In *EMNLP*.

Chenhui Chu, Raj Dabre, and Sadao Kurohashi. 2017. An empirical comparison of simple domain adaptation methods for neural machine translation. *CoRR* abs/1701.03214. http://arxiv.org/abs/1701.03214.

Jonathan H Clark, Alon Lavie, and Chris Dyer. 2012. One system, many domains: Open-domain statistical machine translation via feature augmentation .

Jeffrey L Elman. 1990. Finding structure in time. *Cognitive science* 14(2):179–211.

M Amin Farajian, Marco Turchi, Matteo Negri, Nicola Bertoldi, and Marcello Federico. 2017. Neural vs. phrase-based machine translation in a multi-domain scenario. *EACL 2017* page 280.

Markus Freitag and Yaser Al-Onaizan. 2016. Fast domain adaptation for neural machine translation. *CoRR* abs/1612.06897. http://arxiv.org/abs/1612.06897.

Yaroslav Gani, Evgeniya Ustinova, Hana Ajakan, Pascal Germain, Hugo Larochelle, François Laviolette, Mario Marchand, and Victor Lempitsky. 2015. Domain-adversarial training of neural networks. arxiv preprint. *arXiv preprint arXiv:1505.07818* .

Y. Ganin, E. Ustinova, H. Ajakan, P. Germain, H. Larochelle, F. Laviolette, M. Marchand, and V. Lempitsky. 2015. Domain-Adversarial Training of Neural Networks. *ArXiv e-prints* .

Xavier Glorot, Antoine Bordes, and Yoshua Bengio. 2011. Domain adaptation for large-scale sentiment classification: A deep learning approach. In *Proceedings of the 28th international conference on machine learning (ICML-11)*. pages 513–520.

Ian Goodfellow, Jean Pouget-Abadie, Mehdi Mirza, Bing Xu, David Warde-Farley, Sherjil Ozair, Aaron Courville, and Yoshua Bengio. 2014. Generative adversarial nets. In *Advances in neural information processing systems*. pages 2672–2680.

Barry Haddow and Philipp Koehn. 2012. Analysing the effect of out-of-domain data on smt systems. In *Proceedings of the Seventh Workshop on Statistical Machine Translation*. Association for Computational Linguistics, pages 422–432.

Motoko Hori. 1986. A sociolinguistic analysis of the japanese honorifics. *Journal of pragmatics* 10(3):373–386.

Melvin Johnson, Mike Schuster, Quoc V. Le, Maxim Krikun, Yonghui Wu, Zhifeng Chen, Nikhil Thorat, Fernanda B. Viégas, Martin Wattenberg, Greg Corrado, Macduff Hughes, and Jeffrey Dean. 2016. Google's multilingual neural machine translation system: Enabling zero-shot translation. *CoRR* abs/1611.04558. http://arxiv.org/abs/1611.04558.

Nal Kalchbrenner and Phil Blunsom. 2013. Recurrent continuous translation models. In *EMNLP*.

Diederik Kingma and Jimmy Ba. 2014. Adam: A method for stochastic optimization. *arXiv preprint arXiv:1412.6980* .

Catherine Kobus, Josep Crego, and Jean Senellart. 2016. Domain control for neural machine translation. *arXiv preprint arXiv:1612.06140* .

Philipp Koehn. 2005. Europarl: A parallel corpus for statistical machine translation. In *MT summit*. volume 5, pages 79–86.

Philipp Koehn, Hieu Hoang, Alexandra Birch, Chris Callison-Burch, Marcello Federico, Nicola Bertoldi, Brooke Cowan, Wade Shen, Christine Moran, Richard Zens, et al. 2007. Moses: Open source toolkit for statistical machine translation. In *Proceedings of the 45th annual meeting of the ACL on interactive poster and demonstration sessions*. Association for Computational Linguistics, pages 177–180.

Pierre Lison and Jörg Tiedemann. 2016. Opensubtitles2016: Extracting large parallel corpora from movie and tv subtitles. In *Proceedings of the 10th International Conference on Language Resources and Evaluation*.

Mingsheng Long, Yue Cao, Jianmin Wang, and Michael I Jordan. 2015. Learning transferable features with deep adaptation networks. In *ICML*. pages 97–105.

Minh-Thang Luong and Christopher D Manning. 2015. Stanford neural machine translation systems for spoken language domains. In *Proceedings of the International Workshop on Spoken Language Translation*.

Minh-Thang Luong, Hieu Pham, and Christopher D. Manning. 2015a. Effective approaches to attention-based neural machine translation. In *EMNLP*.

Minh-Thang Luong, Hieu Pham, and Christopher D Manning. 2015b. Effective approaches to attention-based neural machine translation. *arXiv preprint arXiv:1508.04025* .

Arindam Mandal, Dimitra Vergyri, Wen Wang, Jing Zheng, Andreas Stolcke, Gokhan Tur, D Hakkani-Tur, and Necip Fazil Ayan. 2008. Efficient data selection for machine translation. In *Spoken Language Technology Workshop, 2008. SLT 2008. IEEE*. IEEE, pages 261–264.

Toshiaki Nakazawa, Manabu Yaguchi, Kiyotaka Uchimoto, Masao Utiyama, Eiichiro Sumita, Sadao Kurohashi, and Hitoshi Isahara. 2016. Aspec: Asian scientific paper excerpt corpus. In *Proceedings of the Ninth International Conference on Language Resources and Evaluation (LREC 2016)*. pages 2204–2208.

Graham Neubig, Yosuke Nakata, and Shinsuke Mori. 2011. Pointwise prediction for robust, adaptable japanese morphological analysis. In *Proceedings of the 49th Annual Meeting of the Association for Computational Linguistics: Human Language Technologies: short papers-Volume 2*. Association for Computational Linguistics, pages 529–533.

Pavel Pecina, Antonio Toral, and Josef Van Genabith. 2012. Simple and effective parameter tuning for domain adaptation of statistical machine translation. In *COLING*. pages 2209–2224.

Rico Sennrich, Barry Haddow, and Alexandra Birch. 2015. Neural machine translation of rare words with subword units. *arXiv preprint arXiv:1508.07909* .

Ilya Sutskever, Oriol Vinyals, and Quoc V. Le. 2014. Sequence to sequence learning with neural networks. In *NIPS*.

Jörg Tiedemann. 2012. Parallel data, tools and interfaces in opus. In *LREC*. volume 2012, pages 2214–2218.

Yonghui Wu, Mike Schuster, Zhifeng Chen, Quoc V. Le, Mohammad Norouzi, Wolfgang Macherey, Maxim Krikun, Yuan Cao, Qin Gao, Klaus Macherey, Jeff Klingner, Apurva Shah, Melvin Johnson, Xiaobing Liu, Lukasz Kaiser, Stephan Gouws, Yoshikiyo Kato, Taku Kudo, Hideto Kazawa, Keith Stevens, George Kurian, Nishant Patil, Wei Wang, Cliff Young, Jason Smith, Jason Riesa, Alex Rudnick, Oriol Vinyals, Greg Corrado, Macduff Hughes, and Jeffrey Dean. 2016. Google's neural machine translation system: Bridging the gap between human and machine translation. *CoRR* abs/1609.08144.

Barret Zoph, Deniz Yuret, Jonathan May, and Kevin Knight. 2016. Transfer learning for low-resource neural machine translation. *CoRR* abs/1604.02201. http://arxiv.org/abs/1604.02201.

Multi-Domain Neural Machine Translation through Unsupervised Adaptation

M. Amin Farajian[1,2], **Marco Turchi**[1], **Matteo Negri**[1], **Marcello Federico**[1]

[1]Fondazione Bruno Kessler, Trento, Italy

[2]University of Trento, Trento, Italy

{farajian,turchi,negri,federico}@fbk.eu

Abstract

We investigate the application of Neural Machine Translation (NMT) under the following three conditions posed by real-world application scenarios. First, we operate with an input stream of sentences coming from many different domains and with no predefined order. Second, the sentences are presented without domain information. Third, the input stream should be processed by a single generic NMT model. To tackle the weaknesses of current NMT technology in this unsupervised multi-domain setting, we explore an efficient instance-based adaptation method that, by exploiting the similarity between the training instances and each test sentence, dynamically sets the hyperparameters of the learning algorithm and updates the generic model on-the-fly. The results of our experiments with multi-domain data show that local adaptation outperforms not only the original generic NMT system, but also a strong phrase-based system and even single-domain NMT models specifically optimized on each domain and applicable only by violating two of our aforementioned assumptions.

1 Introduction

The progress towards a more pervasive integration of machine translation (MT) into industrial translation workflows has to confront two interconnected problems. On one side, MT technology should be able to guarantee a high level of flexibility to deliver good-quality output in a wide range of use scenarios (language combinations, genres, domains). On the other side, the infrastructures required to reach this objective should be scalable enough to enable the industrial deployment of MT at reasonable cost.

The first problem is a well known one in (statistical) MT: regardless of the paradigm adopted, performance is bounded by the similarity between training and test data. The scenario addressed in this paper, in which the input stream comes from a variety of different domains, is a typical example where models trained on generic parallel corpora suffer from data diversity. Indeed, processing sentences from diverse domains becomes more and more difficult when the distance from the training instances increases. The more the domains a system is exposed to, the higher the chance to experience drops in translation quality under unseen conditions. To cope with this issue, MT systems should be flexible enough to adapt to a variety of linguistic differences (*e.g.* lexical, structural) between different data points.

The second problem is more practical: in absence of flexible models, multi-domain translation scenarios call for infrastructures based on multiple specialised systems, each of which is tuned to maximise performance in a given domain. This solution, however, has two evident drawbacks: *i)* domain-specific models can only be invoked by input sentences presented along with domain information, so that each instance is processed by the right model, and *ii)* each time a new domain has to be covered, a new dedicated model has to be trained with domain-specific data. In real-world application scenarios, however, translation requests rarely come with domain information, the notion of domain is *per se* fuzzy, domain-specific data can be hard to acquire and, most importantly, architectures' costs and scalability are of utmost concern. When maintenance costs and architecture scalability come into play, a preferable solution would be to rely on one single model, capable to adapt on-the-fly to input streams of diverse data,

Proceedings of the Conference on Machine Translation (WMT), Volume 1: Research Papers, pages 127–137
Copenhagen, Denmark, September 7–11, 2017. ©2017 Association for Computational Linguistics

without any supervision.

Neural machine translation (Bahdanau et al., 2014), which has recently become the dominant approach in MT, is not immune to the aforementioned problems. Domain drifts are in fact hard to manage by NMT, due to its inherent characteristics. Different from the phrase-based paradigm, in which training data is explicitly memorised and used in the form of basic translation constituents (phrases), NMT generates a more implicit representation of the data, by compressing and distributing the information over its internal parameters. Moreover, given the amount of data and time required for training, high flexibility and fast adaptation capabilities of single generic models become key requirements to unleash NMT's potential in industry applications.

To pursue these objectives, we investigate the application of an unsupervised method to adapt on-the-fly a generic NMT model (M_g) and improve translation quality for an input stream of diverse, multi-domain sentences presented in random order. Our approach is based on a retrieval mechanism that, given an input sentence q, extracts from the pool of parallel data the top (*source*, *target*) pairs in terms of similarity between the *source* and q. The retrieved pairs are then used to fine-tune the model (M_q), which is then applied to translate q. Finally, the adapted model is reset to the original parameters (M_g), the next input sentence is read, and so on. In order to learn more efficiently from the retrieved set, we introduce a dynamic method that, based on the similarity between the test sentence and the retrieved pairs, decides about the hyperparameters to be used by the learning algorithm (*i.e.* learning rate and number of epochs).

In our experiments with multi-domain data, we observe significant improvements by our approach over the generic NMT system, a strong generic phrase-based MT system, and also specialised NMT models fine-tuned on each domain using domain-specific data. In particular, by dynamically setting the model hyperparameters, our solution is able to outperform the strong pool of domain-specific NMT systems by +2.8 BLEU scores, in overall.

2   Related Works

Domain adaptation has been extensively studied in machine translation. The existing works in this field mostly rely on the assumption of knowing the target domain in advance and having in-domain training data of reasonable size. This dataset is then used to train specific models that are interpolated with generic ones using standard log-linear methods (Koehn and Schroeder, 2007) or mixture models (Foster and Kuhn, 2007).

In line with the work presented in this paper, (Eck et al., 2004) and (Zhao et al., 2004) proposed to perform an instance selection step in which for each test document/sentence a small set of similar documents/sentences is retrieved from the pool of training data and used to build more specific language models. (Hildebrand et al., 2005) further extended this approach and proposed to build local translation models using the set of retrieved sentence pairs.

As in SMT, recent works in domain adaptation for neural MT share the assumption of knowing the target domain in advance and report significant improvements by adapting the generic system to the target domain as an offline step (Luong and Manning, 2015). More recently, (Li et al., 2016)[1] proposed an instance-based adaptation technique for NMT in which for each translation segment a set of similar sentence pairs is retrieved. This small training set is then used to update the model before translating the given test sentence. In order to reduce the cost of computing the similarity of the test segment and all the sentences in the pool, they suggest a three-step process in which, as the first step, all the sentence pairs containing at least one of the test words are retrieved. This large set is then filtered by measuring the similarity between the source sentences and the test using the Dice coefficient measure (Dice, 1945), and keeping the top 1000. The remaining sentences are then ranked based on their Levenshtein distance to the test sentence. To cope with the risk of training a model on sentence pairs with low similarity to the test sentence, the first best retrieved sentence pair is used only if its similarity is higher than a threshold (*i.e.* 0.4), otherwise they use the top-128 training pairs. Moreover, to keep under control the possibility of overfitting, they suggest to train the system for only one epoch over the retrieved set.

To further investigate the potential of the instance selection approach, we study if properly

---

[1]This work is a non-archival document that has not been peer reviewed for publication. For the sake of completeness we reported it in this paper and compared our results with our reimplementation of this method.

setting the hyperparameters in the learning algorithm can boost NMT performance. For this purpose, we take a different direction from (Li et al., 2016) by proposing a strategy to dynamically select the number of epochs and learning rate based on the similarity between the best retrieved sentence pair and the test segment. We empirically prove the effectiveness of this method in a multi-domain application scenario and show that only our adaptive approach is able to produce better translation quality than the PBMT system and the strong pool of specialised NMT systems.

3   Neural Machine Translation

We build our adaptive NMT approach on top of the state-of-the-art sequence-to-sequence model proposed by (Bahdanau et al., 2014). This model relies on a two-step process: first, a recurrent neural network encodes the source sentence word by word into a sequence of hidden states; then, another recurrent neural network decodes the source hidden sequence into the target string. Both the encoder and decoder networks are implemented with *gated recurrent units* (Cho et al., 2014). In particular, the decoder network operates like a language model: it predicts the next target word from the last target word, the last hidden state of the decoder, and a convex combination of the encoder hidden states. The weights of this convex combination are dynamically computed through a simple feed-forward network, called *attention model*. Intuitively, similarly to a word alignment model, the attention model informs the decoder about the encoder hidden states corresponding to the next target word. The decoder actually predicts a full distribution over the target language vocabulary. Thus, the generation of a translation requires sampling at each step the most probable target word from the distribution and then feeding it back to the decoder as input for the next step. The decoding phase is initialised with a conventional delimiter symbol and terminates when the same symbol is output. Better translations are actually produced by integrating the decoder generative process with a beam search, that considers multiple input and output word hypotheses at each step. Training of the presented NMT architecture involves estimating many parameters, such as word embedding matrices, GRU layers in both the encoder and decoder networks, and the attention model weights. Training is carried out via maximum-likelihood estimation over a large collection of parallel sentences. In particular, optimization is performed via stochastic gradient descent (SGD), by iterating over batches of training data randomly shuffled after each epoch (Goodfellow et al., 2016). More formally, starting from a random initialisation of the parameters, at each iteration a batch B is extracted and each parameter w is moved one step in the opposite direction of the mean gradient of the log-likelihood (L), evaluated on the entries of B:

$$\Delta w = -\eta \frac{1}{|B|} \sum_{(s,t) \in B} \frac{\partial L(s,t)}{\partial w} \qquad (1)$$

The size of the step Δw is moderated by a *learning rate* η which can either be fixed for all parameters and all iterations, or vary along one or both dimensions (Goodfellow et al., 2016). During training, the SGD procedure typically goes through several so-called epochs, *i.e.* the number of times the whole training data is processed.

The above presented training procedure is also used to adapt an already trained NMT model to a new task for which representative training data is available (Luong and Manning, 2015). In this paper, we investigate the application of the adaptation procedure under extreme conditions, that is when the training data is made of few samples.

4   Unsupervised Instance-based Adaptation

We consider the scenario in which translation requests from a variety of domains are presented in random order to a single generic system. We also assume that each input sentence is presented without information about the domain it comes from. In this setting, the system needs to perform an unsupervised adaptation step on-the-fly and produce the translation.

To this aim, we experiment with an approach in which, given a generic NMT model (M_g), the pool of parallel data (C_p), and a sentence to be translated (q), the following three steps are performed: (1) q is used as a query to retrieve from C_p a set of (*source, target*) pairs (C_q) in which the *source* is similar to q; (2) this set is used to locally adapt the hyperparameters (HP_q) of M_g; (3) the resulting locally-tuned model (M_q) is applied to translate q. If C_q is empty, the generic model is used to translate q. The pseudo code of this approach is shown in Algorithm 1.

Algorithm 1 RetrieveAdaptTranslate

```
1:  ▷ M_g: generic NMT model
2:  ▷ S: stream of sentences to be translated
3:  ▷ RT: text retrieval module
4:  ▷ C_q: retrieved parallel sentences
5:  ▷ q*: translated segment
6:  procedure RAT(M_g, RT, S)
7:      ▷ For each segment to be translated
8:      while pop q from S do
9:          ▷ Local copy of the generic model
10:         M_q:=M_g
11:         ▷ Instance selection
12:         C_q:=Retrieve(RT,q)
13:         if C_q ≠ ∅ then
14:             ▷ Model optimization
15:             HP_q:=SetHP(C_q, q)
16:             M_q:=Adapt(M_g, C_q, HP_q)
17:         ▷ Translate the segment with M_q
18:         q*:=Translate(M_q, q)
19:         ▷ Post the translated segment
20:         Post q*
```

Instance selection and parameter optimization are the two key steps of this algorithm. On one hand, since instance selection aims to retrieve the most relevant sentences from C_p, the similarity measure plays an important role as the quality of the material used for local tuning directly affects the next processing steps. In this paper, we use Lucene (McCandless et al., 2010), an open-source information retrieval library that is highly optimized for text search purposes. However, since the similarity measure used in Lucene is based on *tf-idf* counts (Baeza-Yates and Ribeiro-Neto, 2011), it does not consider the order of the words and n-grams in the query and in the retrieved sentences, which is an important aspect for MT model training. In order to take advantage also of this information, we first query Lucene to retrieve a large set of candidates and then re-score them using the sentence-level BLEU (Chen and Cherry, 2014), so that the sentences with higher BLEU score are ranked first. Finally, the top-n similar sentences are used to update the model. This approach is reasonably fast, since it takes advantage of Lucene in searching in a large set of data and then computes the BLEU scores on just few candidates.

The optimization phase, on the other hand, needs to effectively adapt the model parameters with a very small set of parallel data featuring different levels of similarity. In order to tune at best its parameters with respect to the input sentence q, the system has in fact to learn as much as possible from highly similar points in C_q, and keep under control the risk of overfitting in the case of instances with low similarity. The learning rate and number of times the system iterates over the retrieved sentence pairs hence become crucial aspects during optimization. Differently from (Li et al., 2016), who keeps these factors fixed, in this paper we propose a simple yet effective method that dynamically decides about the hyperparameters of the learning algorithm (*i.e.* HP_q) based on the relevance of the retrieved sentence pairs to the input segment. To this aim, we define two functions that for the retrieved samples with high similarity to the test segment increase the learning rate and number of epochs, so that the system can leverage more the information of the training set and vice versa. The idea is to overfit more the NMT system on sentences that are similar to the test sentence while avoiding drastic changes in case of tuning with low similarity sentence pairs. In Section 6, we investigate the effect of dynamically setting these parameters on the final performance of the system. As the results show, our dynamic method significantly improves the performance of the adaptive system, outperforming the strong PBMT system and the oracle NMT systems fine-tuned specifically to each domain.

5   Experimental Setup

5.1   Data

Our experiments are carried out on an English to French translation task, where the training data is a collection of publicly available corpora from different domains: European Central Bank (ECB), Gnome, JRC-Acquis (JRC), KDE4, OpenOffice (OOffice), PHP, Ubuntu, and translated UN documents (UN-TM).[2] Since the size of these corpora is relatively small for training robust MT systems, in particular NMT solutions, we added the News Commentary data from WMT'13[3](WMT_nc), as well as the CommonCrawl (CommonC.) and Europarl corpora as out-domain data, so to reach a total of ~5.8M sentence pairs.

From each specific domain a set of size 500 sentence pairs is randomly selected as development set, and 1,000 sentence pairs are used as held-

---

[2]All the corpora are available in http://opus.lingfil.uu.se
[3]http://www.statmt.org/wmt13/

	Segments	Tok/Typ	Avg. Len
ECB	142.4K	76.7	20.5
Gnome	236.1K	102.1	7.2
JRC	678.9K	146.3	15.4
KDE4	160.7K	25.3	6.4
OOffice	32.9K	40.8	11.2
PHP	36.7K	26.0	6.5
Ubuntu	7.5K	5.1	5.2
UN-TM	37.6K	69.6	21.9
WMT_nc	189.1K	65.3	24.6
CommonC.	2.6M	80.3	20.9
Europarl	1.7M	364.3	22.9

Table 1: Statistics of the English side of the training corpora.

	Segments	Tok/Typ	Avg. Sim
ECB	1,000	5.5	50.5
Gnome	982	3.8	70.2
JRC	757	5.1	54.7
KDE4	988	7.0	34.8
OOffice	976	5.8	30.3
PHP	352	4.1	55.7
Ubuntu	997	2.7	27.7
UN-TM	910	7.1	65.1
WMT	1,000	2.2	11.9

Table 2: Statistics of the English side of the test corpora.

out test corpus. Duplicated sentence pairs are removed from each corpus separately, resulting in a total of 3,527 dev and 6,962 test corpora for all the domains. To analyze the performance of the system on generic data, two subsets of size 500 and 1000 sentence pairs are randomly selected from the WMT'13 test data as dev and test corpora. The statistics of the training and test corpora are reported in Tables 1 and 2, respectively, showing that the considered domains are extremely diverse in terms of average sentence length and average word frequency. The *Avg.* *Sim* column in Table 2 reports the average similarity of the test sentences and the source side of the most relevant sentence pair retrieved from the pool of training data. The scores are computed using the sentence-level BLEU (Chen and Cherry, 2014). Since our adaptation approach updates the model by leveraging these retrieved sentences, their average similarity can be a reliable indicator for predicting the performance gain after adaptation. In other words, the system can learn more from the retrieved samples in the case of corpora with higher sentence similarity (*e.g.* Gnome) than the datasets with lower average BLEU score (*e.g.* WMT). In Section 6 we analyze these features and their impact on the system performance.

Finally, the analysis of the characteristics of Gnome, KDE4, OpenOffice, PHP, and Ubuntu, which are often referred to as IT domain corpora, evidences another important issue in developing domain-specific MT systems. As the statistics of Table 1 show, these corpora are extremely diverse in terms of average sentence length and word frequency, which are likely to correspond to different levels of difficulty for MT and, in turn, to large differences in final translation quality.

5.2 Neural MT System

All our experiments with NMT are conducted with an in-house developed and maintained branch of the Nematus toolkit[4] which is an implementation of the attentional encoder-decoder architecture (Bahdanau et al., 2014). Since handling large vocabularies is one of the main bottlenecks for the existing NMT systems, state-of-the-art approaches are trained on corpora in which the less frequent words are segmented into their sub-word units (Sennrich et al., 2016) by applying a modified version of the byte pair encoding (BPE) compression algorithm (Gage, 1994). This makes the NMT systems capable of dealing with new and rare words. As recommended in (Sennrich et al., 2016), in order to increase the consistency in segmenting the source and target text, we combined both sides of the training data, and set the number of merge rules to 89,500, resulting in vocabularies of size 78K and 86K tokens respectively for English and French. We use mini-batches of size 100, word embeddings of size 500, and GRU layers of size 1,024. The maximum sentence length is set to 50. The models are trained using Adagrad (Duchi et al., 2011) by reshuffling the training set at each epoch, and are evaluated every 10,000 mini-batches with BLEU (Papineni et al., 2002).

5.3 Terms of Comparison

We compare our adaptive NMT system with a generic NMT and a strong PBMT system trained on the *pool* of all the training data. For training the PBMT system we used the open source Moses

---

[4]https://github.com/rsennrich/nematus

toolkit (Koehn et al., 2007). The word alignment models were trained with FastAlign (Dyer et al., 2013). We trained the 5-gram language models with the KenLM toolkit (Heafield et al., 2013) on the target side of the pooled corpora. Feature weights were tuned with batch MIRA (Cherry and Foster, 2012) to maximize BLEU on the dev set. Details of the generic NMT system are described in Section 5.2. In Table 3, the results on the dev set are reported. Although trained on the same dataset, it is interesting to note that, the performance of the generic NMT system is by far lower than the PBMT system. A possible explanation is that the PBMT system can explicitly memorise and use translation options learned from the training data, while the NMT system generates a more implicit representation of the data. This might have a fundamental role in domain-specific and very repetitive datasets.

Similarly to (Luong and Manning, 2015), in order to improve the performance of the generic NMT system on the target domains, we separately adapted multiple instances of the generic NMT model to each specific domain (using only the corresponding training data). This is done by using the same configurations and training criteria used for the generic model, described in Section 5.2. We refer to these strong systems as *oracles*, because they exploit knowledge of the domain labels both at the training and test time. As we see in Table 3, this offline adaptation significantly improves the performance of the NMT system, resulting in translations with higher quality than the strong PBMT system. However, as mentioned earlier, this approach requires information of the target domain and assumes having sufficient amount of time and data to train domain-specific systems for each test domain.

The recently proposed approach by (Li et al., 2016) is the first attempt in this field that tries to cope with these limitations. In this paper we implement this method and compare it with our adaptive strategy (*i.e. Adaptive Baseline*), which differs in how the retrieved sentences are ranked (*i.e.* sentence-level BLEU) and in using only the top-1 retrieved pair for updating the model. As shown in Table 3, our method performs identically to the Li et al. (2016) system that uses a larger number of training samples in the case of low similarities. So, for efficiency reasons, in all our experiments we use our approach and we keep only the first best sentence pair for updating the model.

6 Unsupervised Neural MT Adaptation

In this section we discuss the dynamic setting of the hyperparameters of the learning algorithm and their impact on the performance of the system.

6.1 Model Adaptation: Learning Rate

Once the set of relevant sentence pairs is extracted, we need to update the generic model accordingly. As described in Section 3, the learning rate controls the contribution of the new information for updating the model parameters by determining the magnitude of the update steps. Deciding about the learning rate value is very important for the SGD algorithm in general, but becomes even more crucial in our scenario where we need to adjust the parameters by using only a small training set. In order to approximate the optimal value, we performed a set of experiments on our dev set in which the learning rate is gradually increased until the overall performance of the system starts to degrade (Figure 2).

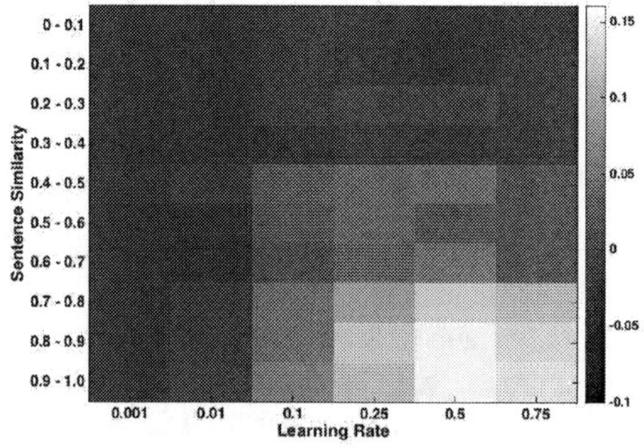

Figure 1: The effect of different learning rates on the adaptive system performance on the dev set. Darker cells show performance degradations or no gain over the *NMT generic*, while brighter cells represent larger gains over the generic system.

However, if the similarity between the retrieved sentence and the test sentence is low, by applying larger learning rates we run the risk of making drastic parameter changes in the wrong direction, which can result in lower quality translations and global performance degradations. The low results of the system when using learning rate of 0.75 empirically confirms this.

| | PBMT | NMT | | Li *et al.* | | Adaptive | |
		Generic	Oracle		Baseline	Dynamic Lrate	Dynamic Lrate-Epochs
Overall	54.6	45.7	55.9	53.2	53.2	53.6	57.5
ECB	56.1	46.3	56.3	50.9	51.1	51.0	53.7
Gnome	88.1	62.3	90.5	75.2	74.6	79.0	91.2
JRC	65.7	59.9	64.7	67.3	66.6	66.8	70.2
KDE4	50.1	45.7	54.3	50.5	50.4	50.4	53.1
OOffice	37.5	32.0	41.5	35.7	36.5	36.2	39.3
PHP	46.6	29.7	39.3	37.1	39.8	39.6	48.0
Ubuntu	50.1	47.9	47.7	49.1	49.5	51.5	53.1
UN-TM	72.8	54.4	78.4	70.0	70.3	70.3	77.6
WMT	26.7	30.5	26.8	29.0	29.7	30.6	30.3

Table 3: Comparison of the performance of generic PBMT and NMT, domain-specific oracles, and the adaptive NMT systems on the dev corpora in terms of BLEU.

To further analyze the effect of different learning rates on sentences with different levels of similarity, we measured the average performance gain of the adaptive system (over *NMT generic* in terms of sentence-level BLEU) in each similarity range when using different learning rates (Figure 1). The darker cells represent settings in which there is a drop in performance or no gain over the generic system, while brighter cells correspond to the configurations where the performance of the adaptive system is higher. We observe that updating the model with large learning rates on less relevant samples results in performance degradation (*i.e.* the darker cells in the top-right side of the figure). This suggests to apply more conservative learning rates to less relevant training samples, while increasing it to larger values for higher similarity levels. Based on this analysis, we developed a dynamic learning rate method that, for each similarity range in Figure 1, selects the learning rate that provides the largest gain over the generic NMT model (*i.e. Adaptive Dynamic-Lrate*). For instance, it uses the learning rate of 0.01 for the sentences in the similarity range of [0.0-0.1], and sets the learning rate to 0.5 for the samples with the similarity between 0.9 and 1.0. The results of this system are reported in Table 3. By comparing these results against the best performing system with fixed learning rate (*i.e. Adaptive Baseline*), we see that dynamically setting the learning rate improves the performance by +0.4 BLEU points[5] in overall (53.6 vs 53.2), which further reduces the gap between the generic and specialized NMTs.

---

[5]The difference is statistically significant with $p < 0.05$.

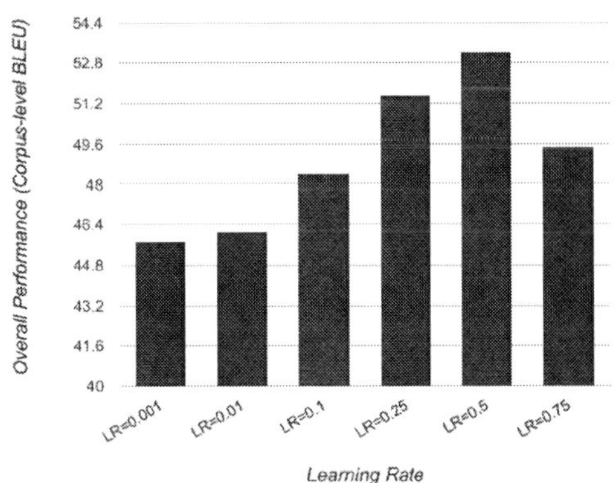

Figure 2: The effect of different learning rates on the adaptive system performance on dev data.

6.2 Model Adaptation: Number of Epochs

As described in Section 3, during training/adaptation the training samples are processed iteratively and the network parameters are updated accordingly. The number of epochs plays an important role in this process. Setting it to a large value may result in overfitting, which limits the generalization capability of the model, while performing only few epochs results in underfitting, where the system does not learn effectively from the samples. In order to analyze the effect of this factor on the final performance of the system, we run another set of experiments in which the maximum number of epochs is gradually increased until the overall results start to degrade (similar to what we did in the analysis of the learning rates in the previous section). In

	PBMT	NMT Generic	NMT Oracle	Adaptive Lrate-Epochs
Overall	54.5	44.9	55.6	**58.4**
ECB	58.6	46.5	58.0	**58.7**
Gnome	90.5	61.5	93.8	**94.9**
JRC	66.3	56.5	62.6	**69.7**
KDE4	50.6	46.4	55.7	**56.2**
OOffice	37.1	31.8	39.9	**40.3**
PHP	47.0	33.4	39.7	**50.5**
Ubuntu	45.8	45.3	46.9	**48.8**
UN-TM	69.7	52.1	75.7	**75.9**
WMT	26.0	**30.7**	26.6	**30.7**

Table 4: Comparison of the generic PBMT, NMT, and domain-specific NMT oracles against the adaptive system with dynamic learning rate and dynamic number of epochs. The reported BLEU scores are computed on the test corpora.

these experiments we used the dynamic learning rates described in Section 6.1. We observed that increasing the maximum number of epochs up to 9 helps to improve the overall performance of the system, while using larger number of updates leads in performance degradation due to the aforementioned overfitting issue.

Similarly to the experiments in Section 6.1, the relation between the number of epochs and the sentence similarity is first explored and, then, it is used to devise an approach that can automatically set the number of updates. This analysis suggests to set the number of epochs proportional to the level of similarity of the training instance.

The results of our adaptive system using dynamic learning rate and number of epochs (*i.e. Adaptive Dynamic Lrate-Epochs*) on the dev set are reported in Table 3. As the results show, dynamically deciding about the number of epochs improves the performance of the system by +3.9 BLEU scores, outperforming all our adaptive systems and the approach of (Li et al., 2016) by a large margin. More detailed analysis of the system shows that dynamically setting the number of epochs is in particular beneficial for the domains with high similarity, where it allows the system to leverage more the information of the training sample by performing more updates. In fact, the significant improvements over *Adaptive Dynamic Lrate* in the domains with high sentence similarities (*e.g.* +12.2 in case of Gnome and +7.4 in

case of UN-TM) and the smaller gains in the domains with low similarities (*e.g.* +1.7 in case of Ubuntu) empirically proves this. Our investigation into the correlation of the performance gain by the adaptive system and similarity of the retrieved sentence, shows that there is a correlation of 0.9 between these two factors, further supporting our domain-wise analysis.

The results of the experiments on the test set are reported in Table 4 and show that our adaptive system outperforms the generic NMT system and both the strong PBMT system and domain-specific oracles by a large margin (+14.5, +3.9 and +2.8). This confirms that local adaptation of the generic NMT models to small set of relevant training samples can effectively improve the final performance of the system, making it a reasonable solution for the multi-domain application scenarios where maintaining several domain-specific MT engines is not feasible.

Our further analysis on the outputs of the generic and the adaptive systems reveals that the adaptive system produces sentences that are more similar to the references in terms of length (*i.e.* 14.4 vs 15.1 words per sentence, compared to 15.3 of the reference). Moreover, by analyzing the errors of the systems using TER we note that the adaptive system effectively reduces the lexical errors by 14%. This shows that our adaptive approach helps the system to produce translations that are more similar to the reference both in terms of length and structure.

7 Further Analysis

In Table 5 we present four examples taken from the dev set, for which the performance of the *Generic*, *Baseline* and *Adaptive* [6] systems is compared. The first example (from ECB) shows a case that the retrieved source sentence is highly similar to the test sentence. Comparing the outputs produced by the three systems we see that the adaptation step in the *Baseline* helps the system to produce translations that are closer to the reference but it still translates "*such management*" literally to "*cetter gestion*" which is a less fluent translation than "*celle-ci*" in this context. This shows that in this case the system could not leverage all the information provided by the retrieved pair in just one

---

[6]To make it short, we refer to the adaptive system with dynamic learning rate and epochs (*Adaptive Dynamic Lrate-Epochs*) as *Adaptive*.

epoch. However, by performing more epochs the *Adaptive* system is able to effectively adapt to the retrieved pair and correctly translate the given test.

The second example (from KDE4) shows another case where the retrieved pair is highly similar to the test sentence on the surface level but is different in terms of semantics. The English word *"collapse"* is translated into *"réduire"* and *"Groupe"* in French, which are semantically different. However, given the retrieved pair, both the *Baseline* and *Adaptive* system learn to translate it to *"Groupe"* which is not a correct translation in the context of the test sentence.

The next example (from JRC) presents the issue of inconsistent translations. As we see, the retrieval method is able to retrieve a sentence pair whose its source side is identical to the test sentence but is translated differently. In this case both the *Baseline* and *Adaptive* system effectively learn the information given by the retrieved pair and learn to produce the exact translation as the retrieved target (*i.e. Ret.Trg*). However, since the translation provided by the retrieved pair is different than the reference, they are eventually penalized in terms of BLEU.

The last example (from WMT) shows a case of low-similar retrieved pair and the need for a more conservative adaptation. In this case the *Baseline* replaces the French term *"une aide"* with *"des services d'"*, learned aggressively from the retrieved pair, while the *Adaptive* system learns to only replace *"aide"* with *"services"*, leading in a higher quality translation. However, both the systems fail to learn the correct translation of *"and"* (*i.e. "et de"*) in this context, which is provided by the retrieved target (*i.e. Ret.Trg*).

These observations open to interesting research avenues that we plan to address in future work. These include: *i)* developing semantic-aware retrieval methods that, in addition to the surface form of the sentences, also consider their semantic similarities (KDE4 example). *ii)* handling inconsistent translations to avoid being biased towards an specific translation where other correct translations exist for the given sentence or phrase (JRC example) *iii)* developing adaptation methods that are able to leverage more efficiently the small amount of information provided by the low similar retrieved training samples (WMT example).

8 Conclusion

In this paper we investigated an instance-based adaptive Neural MT approach that effectively handles translation requests from multiple domains in an unsupervised manner, that is without knowing the domain labels. Given an input sentence, it updates a background generic model on-the-fly by means of a single training instance selected among all available training data. Differently from previous works, we enhance this approach by proposing a method to dynamically set the hyperparameters of the learning algorithm (*i.e.* learning rate and number of epochs) before updating the model. When tested in a multi-domain scenario, our approach was able to significantly outperform the generic NMT and PBMT systems and the single-domain NMT models specifically optimized on each domain.

Acknowledgments

This work has been partially supported by the EC-funded H2020 projects QT21 (grant no. 645452) and ModernMT (grant no. 645487).

References

R. Baeza-Yates and B. Ribeiro-Neto. 2011. *Modern Information Retrieval: The Concepts and Technology Behind Search*. Addison Wesley.

Dzmitry Bahdanau, Kyunghyun Cho, and Yoshua Bengio. 2014. Neural machine translation by jointly learning to align and translate. *arXiv preprint arXiv:1409.0473* .

Boxing Chen and Colin Cherry. 2014. A systematic comparison of smoothing techniques for sentence-level BLEU. In *Proceedings of the Ninth Workshop on Statistical Machine Translation, WMT@ACL 2014, June 26-27, 2014, Baltimore, Maryland, USA*. pages 362–367. http://aclweb.org/anthology/W/W14/W14-3346.pdf.

Colin Cherry and George Foster. 2012. Batch tuning strategies for statistical machine translation. In *Proceedings of the 2012 Conference of the North American Chapter of the Association for Computational Linguistics: Human Language Technologies*. Association for Computational Linguistics, Stroudsburg, PA, USA, NAACL HLT '12, pages 427–436. http://dl.acm.org/citation.cfm?id=2382029.2382089.

Kyunghyun Cho, Bart van Merrienboer, Çaglar Gülçehre, Fethi Bougares, Holger Schwenk, and

Src	a participating NCB may decide to abstain from such management or to pool such management with one or more other participating NCBs .
Ref	une BCN participante peut décider de ne pas participer à cette gestion ou d' assumer celle-ci en commun avec une ou plusieurs autres BCN participantes .
Ret.Src	a euro area NCB may decide to abstain from such management or to pool such management with one or more other euro area NCBs .
Ret.Trg	une BCN de la zone euro peut décider de ne pas participer à cette gestion ou d' assumer celle-ci en commun avec une ou plusieurs autres BCN de la zone euro .
Generic	une BCN participante peut décider de s' abstenir de cette gestion ou de créer une telle gestion avec une ou plusieurs autres BCN participantes .
Baseline	une BCN participante peut décider de ne pas participer à cette gestion ou d' assumer cette gestion avec une ou plusieurs autres BCN participantes .
Adaptive	une BCN participante peut décider de ne pas participer à cette gestion ou d' assumer celle-ci en commun avec une ou plusieurs autres BCN participantes .
Src	collapse all categories
Ref	réduire toutes les catégories
Ret.Src	collapse all folders
Ret.Trg	Groupe tous les dossiers
Generic	réduire toutes les catégories
Baseline	Groupe toutes les catégories
Adaptive	Groupe toutes les catégories
Src	this Decision is addressed to the Member States .
Ref	les États membres sont destinataires de la présente décision .
Ret.Src	this Decision is addressed to the Member States .
Ret.Trg	la présente décision est adressée aux États membres .
Generic	les États membres sont destinataires de la présente décision .
Baseline	la présente décision est adressée aux États membres .
Adaptive	la présente décision est adressée aux États membres .
Src	in addition , they limited the right of individuals and groups to provide assistance to voters wishing to register .
Ref	de plus , ils ont limité le droit de personnes et de groupes de fournir une assistance aux électeurs désirant s' inscrire .
Ret.Src	in addition , we provide assistance and advice to real estate investors and promoters .
Ret.Trg	enfin , nous proposons des services d' assistance et de conseil aux investisseurs et promoteurs immobiliers .
Generic	en outre , ils ont limité le droit des personnes et des groupes à fournir une aide aux électeurs souhaitant s' inscrire .
Baseline	en outre , ils ont limité le droit des personnes et des groupes à fournir des services d' assistance aux électeurs souhaitant s' inscrire .
Adaptive	en outre , ils ont limité le droit des personnes et des groupes à fournir une assistance aux électeurs souhaitant s' inscrire .

Table 5: Translation examples for comparing Generic, Baseline and the Adaptive NMT systems.

Yoshua Bengio. 2014. Learning phrase representations using RNN encoder-decoder for statistical machine translation. *CoRR* abs/1406.1078. http://arxiv.org/abs/1406.1078.

Lee Raymond Dice. 1945. Measures of the amount of ecologic association between species. *Ecology* 26(3):297–302. http://www.jstor.org/pss/1932409.

John Duchi, Elad Hazan, and Yoram Singer. 2011. Adaptive Subgradient Methods for Online Learning and Stochastic Optimization. *Journal of Machine Learning Research* .

Chris Dyer, Victor Chahuneau, and Noah A. Smith. 2013. A simple, fast, and effective reparameterization of ibm model 2. In *In Proc. NAACL*.

Matthias Eck, Stephan Vogel, and Alex Waibel. 2004. Language model adaptation for statistical machine translation based on information retrieval. In *In Proceedings of the 4th International Conference on language resources and evaluation (LREC-2004*. pages 327–330.

George Foster and Roland Kuhn. 2007. Mixture-model adaptation for SMT. In *Proceedings of the Second Workshop on Statistical Machine Translation*. Association for Computational Linguistics, Prague, Czech Republic, pages 128–135. http://www.aclweb.org/anthology/W/W07/W07-0217.

Philip Gage. 1994. A New Algorithm for Data Compression. *C Users J.* 12(2):23–38. http://dl.acm.org/citation.cfm?id=177910.177914.

Ian Goodfellow, Yoshua Bengio, and Aaron Courville. 2016. *Deep Learning*. MIT Press. http://www.deeplearningbook.org.

Kenneth Heafield, Ivan Pouzyrevsky, Jonathan H. Clark, and Philipp Koehn. 2013. Scalable modified kneser-ney language model estimation. In *Proceedings of the 51st Annual Meeting of the Association for Computational Linguistics (Volume 2: Short Papers)*. Association for Computational Linguistics, Sofia, Bulgaria, pages 690–696. http://www.aclweb.org/anthology/P13-2121.

Almut Silja Hildebrand, Mattias Eck, Stephan Vogel, and Alex Waibel. 2005. Adaptation of the translation model for statistical machine translation based on information retrieval. In *Proceedings of the 10th annual conference of the European association for machine translation*. Budapest, Hungary, page 133142.

Philipp Koehn, Hieu Hoang, Alexandra Birch, Chris Callison-Burch, Marcello Federico, Nicola Bertoldi, Brooke Cowan, Wade Shen, Christine Moran, Richard Zens, Chris Dyer, Ondřej Bojar, Alexandra Constantin, and Evan Herbst. 2007. Moses: Open source toolkit for statistical machine translation. In *Proceedings of the 45th Annual Meeting of the ACL on Interactive Poster and Demonstration Sessions*. Association for Computational Linguistics, Stroudsburg, PA, USA, ACL '07, pages 177–180. http://dl.acm.org/citation.cfm?id=1557769.1557821.

Philipp Koehn and Josh Schroeder. 2007. Experiments in domain adaptation for statistical machine translation. In *Proceedings of the Second Workshop on Statistical Machine Translation*. Association for Computational Linguistics, Prague, Czech Republic, pages 224–227. http://www.aclweb.org/anthology/W/W07/W07-0233.

Xiaoqing Li, Jiajun Zhang, and Chengqing Zong. 2016. One sentence one model for neural machine translation. *CoRR* abs/1609.06490. http://arxiv.org/abs/1609.06490.

Minh-Thang Luong and Christopher D Manning. 2015. Stanford Neural Machine Translation Systems for Spoken Language Domains. In *Proceedings of the International Workshop on Spoken Language Translation*.

M. McCandless, E. Hatcher, and O. Gospodnetić. 2010. *Lucene in Action*. Manning Pubs Co Series. Manning. https://books.google.it/books?id=XrJBPgAACAAJ.

Kishore Papineni, Salim Roukos, Todd Ward, and Wei-Jing Zhu. 2002. Bleu: a method for automatic evaluation of machine translation. In *Proceedings of 40th Annual Meeting of the Association for Computational Linguistics*. Association for Computational Linguistics, Philadelphia, Pennsylvania, USA, pages 311–318. https://doi.org/10.3115/1073083.1073135.

Rico Sennrich, Barry Haddow, and Alexandra Birch. 2016. Neural Machine Translation of Rare Words with Subword Units. In *Proceedings of the 54th Annual Meeting on Association for Computational Linguistics*. Association for Computational Linguistics.

Bing Zhao, Matthias Eck, and Stephan Vogel. 2004. Language model adaptation for statistical machine translation with structured query models. In *Proceedings of the 20th International Conference on Computational Linguistics*. Association for Computational Linguistics, Stroudsburg, PA, USA, COLING '04. https://doi.org/10.3115/1220355.1220414.

Adapting Neural Machine Translation
with Parallel Synthetic Data

Mara Chinea-Ríos and **Álvaro Peris** and **Francisco Casacuberta**
Pattern Recognition and Human Language Technology Research Center
Universitat Politècnica de València, València, Spain
`{machirio, lvapeab, fcn}@prhlt.upv.es`

Abstract

Recent works have shown that the usage of a synthetic parallel corpus can be effectively exploited by a neural machine translation system. In this paper, we propose a new method for adapting a general neural machine translation system to a specific task, by exploiting synthetic data.

The method consists in selecting, from a large monolingual pool of sentences in the source language, those instances that are more related to a given test set. Next, this selection is automatically translated and the general neural machine translation system is fine-tuned with these data.

For evaluating the adaptation method, we first conducted experiments in two controlled domains, with common and well-studied corpora. Then, we evaluated our proposal on a real e-commerce task, yielding consistent improvements in terms of translation quality.

1 Introduction

Neural machine translation (NMT) (Sutskever et al., 2014; Cho et al., 2014a; Bahdanau et al., 2015) has obtained state-of-the art performance in several domains and language pairs (Sennrich et al., 2016b; Wu et al., 2016). Given the nature of NMT paradigms, the limitation for obtaining bilingual corpora—or their availability—has been one of the major obstacles faced when building competitive NMT systems. Recently, the idea of using synthetic corpora in NMT has reported promising results with regard to the data scarcity in NMT. Many different works demonstrated that the combination of real parallel corpora with synthetic bilingual corpus enhances the NMT trans-

lation quality (Sennrich et al., 2016a; Zhang and Zong, 2016a; Cheng et al., 2016).

Following these good results, we aim to adapt general NMT models to real, specific tasks by using synthetic parallel data. The core idea is to select the most valuable instances from a large pool of monolingual source sentences, with respect to a given test set. Next, we automatically translate them. Therefore, we obtain a synthetic parallel corpus, related to our test set domain. Such synthetic corpus can be used to fine-tune a NMT system to the domain at hand.

The main contributions of this paper involve the necessary steps required to adapt a NMT system to a specific domain:

- We propose a novel method to create the most adequate synthetic corpus leverages a vector-space representation of sentences, relying on the word embeddings by Mikolov et al. (2013a) and Le and Mikolov (2014).

- We describe the pipeline of our adaptation process, relating the selection, translation and fine-tuning processes.

- We study our adaptation technique on two classical domains. Additionally, we validate our technique on a real e-commerce translation task.

- Results show important improvements over a baseline system.

This paper is structured as follows. NMT technology is briefly described in Section 2. Section 3 summarizes the related work. In Section 4, we present our selection method and we describe the adaptation pipeline. Section 5 presents the experimental set-up and corpora. Results are analyzed and discussed in Section 6. Finally, conclusions and future work are traced in Section 7.

138

Proceedings of the Conference on Machine Translation (WMT), Volume 1: Research Papers, pages 138–147
Copenhagen, Denmark, September 7–11, 2017. ©2017 Association for Computational Linguistics

2 Neural Machine Translation

Neural machine translation is an instantiation of sequence-to-sequence learning: given a sequence of words in the source language, we must produce the corresponding sequence of words in the target language. This is usually done by means of the encoder–decoder architecture: the encoder computes a representation of the input sequence, while the decoder takes it and generates, word by word, the sentence in the target language (Sutskever et al., 2014). In this work, we use a NMT system featuring long short-term memory (LSTM) units (Hochreiter and Schmidhuber, 1997)—in both the encoder and decoder—and equipped with an attention mechanism (Bahdanau et al., 2015).

The input to the system is a sequence of words in the source language. A word embedding matrix projects each word from the discrete to a continuous space. The sequence of word embeddings is then processed by a bidirectional (Schuster and Paliwal, 1997) LSTM network, which produces a sequence of annotations by concatenating the hidden states from the forward and backward layers.

At each decoding timestep, the attention mechanism computes a weighted mean of the sequence of annotations. The weights are given according to a soft alignment model that weights each annotation with the previous decoding state. This can be seen as a joint, dynamic representation of the input sentence.

The decoder is another LSTM network, conditioned to the representation computed by the attention model and the previously generated word. Finally, a deep output layer (Pascanu et al., 2014) computes a distribution over the target language vocabulary.

The model is jointly trained by stochastic gradient descent (SGD), aiming to maximize the log-likelihood over a bilingual parallel corpus. At decoding time, the model approximates the most likely target sentence with beam-search (Sutskever et al., 2014).

3 Related work

Since Kalchbrenner and Blunsom (2013), Sutskever et al. (2014) and Cho et al. (2014b) proposed the first NMT systems, this has been a boiling research topic. A singular effort has been spent into leverage the advantages that this technology brings in. One of them is the ability of NMT systems to rapidly adapt to a given domain, when they are already trained on a general domain. This is useful either for creating domain-dependent NMT systems or for low-resource tasks. Thus, Luong and Manning (2015) tackled the informal speech translation task by starting from a system trained on the WMT data and adapting it to the translation task at hand.

In phrase-based statistical machine translation (SMT), synthetic bilingual corpora have been mainly proposed as a mean to exploit the vast amount of monolingual data available. By applying a self-training scheme, the synthetic parallel data can be obtained by automatically translating a source-side monolingual corpus (Ueffing et al., 2007; Wu et al., 2008). Other works used target-side corpora to build the synthetic parallel corpus (Bertoldi and Federico, 2009; Lambert et al., 2011).

Inspired by these works in SMT, research referring the inclusion of monolingual data in NMT has a growing interest. Different works have tackled the inclusion of monolingual data, either in source (Zhang and Zong, 2016b) and target language (Gulcehre et al., 2015, 2017).

Moreover, Sennrich et al. (2016a) showed that parallel data is not strictly necessary for performing domain adaptation: the usage of synthetic data has positive effects on the NMT system. For obtaining the synthetic data they automatically translated a large monolingual corpus. This synthetic-based approach obtained better results than other methods aimed to exploit monolingual data (e.g. Gulcehre et al. (2015)). Domain adaptation in NMT systems is also integrated in commercial systems, such as SYSTRAN (Crego et al., 2016).

4 Adaptation using synthetic corpus

As described in the previous section, synthetic parallel data have been widely used to boost the translation quality of NMT. In this work, we further extend their application by adapting NMT models with synthetic parallel data. In certain language pairs or domains where parallel corpora are scarce or even non-existent, a model adjusted with synthetic data can improve the performance with respect to a more general model.

The core idea is that, once a model has been trained on a large, general corpus, we can adapt it to a new domain, by fine-tuning it exclusively using the synthetic data. For doing this, we create an

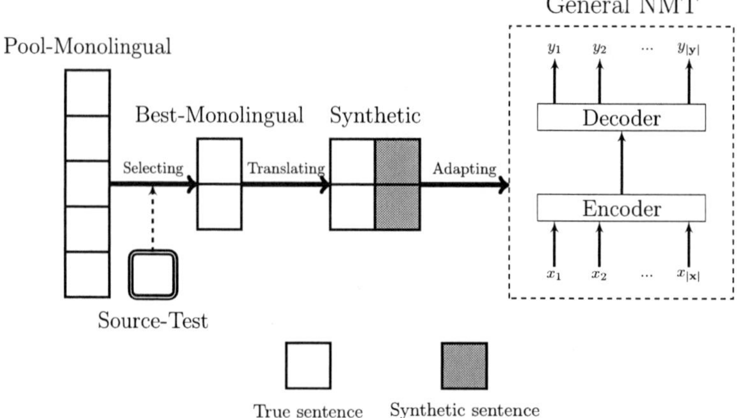

Figure 1: The process of building an adequate synthetic parallel corpus for a given test set.

ad-hoc, specific synthetic corpus in which appear the features from our target-domain data. This corpus is constructed by selecting from a large monolingual pool of sentences—in the source language—those instances that are related with our in-domain dataset. Next, we automatically translate these sentences into the target language. Finally, using this synthetic corpus, we fine-tune a NMT system trained on a more general domain. Figure 1 shows the pipeline of our adaptation process.

In this section, we describe our technique for creating adequate synthetic corpora, based on a vector-space representation of sentences, and the NMT adaptation process.

4.1 Continuous vector-space representation

The idea of representing words or sentence in a continuous vector-space employing neuronal networks was initially proposed by Hinton (1986) and Elman (1990). Continuous vector-space representations (CVR) of words or sentences have been widely leveraged in a variety of natural language applications and demonstrated solid results across a variety of tasks, such as speech recognition (Schwenk, 2007), part-of-speech tagging (Socher et al., 2011), sentiment classification and identification (Glorot et al., 2011) or machine translation (Cho et al., 2014a; Mikolov et al., 2013b).

In this paper, we use a sophisticated CVR of the sentences involved in our data selection method. Specifically, we follow the CVR approach presented by Le and Mikolov (2014). In this work, the authors adapted the continuous Skip-Gram model

(Mikolov et al., 2013a) to generate representative vectors of sentences and documents. Thus, with this technique, we obtain a particular vector that represents a complete sentence by means of the the Skip-Gram architecture.

4.2 Synthetic creation method

For creating an adequate synthetic corpus for adapting a NMT system, we select from a large pool of monolingual text the most related sentences for our task at hand. We present a novel selection technique, based on the CVR of the sentences.

The intuition is to select sentences whose vector-space representation is similar to the representation of our in-domain instances, assuming that similar sentences will have similar vectors (Le and Mikolov, 2014).

Having a continuous vector space representation of the test sentences allows us to compute a centroid. This can be seen as prototype of the sentences present in the test set.

Provided that similar sentences have similar vector-space representations (Mikolov et al., 2013b), we assume that vectors from the in-domain corpus will be clustered. On the other hand, vectors from the general pool of sentences are likely to be more disperse. The idea of our method is to create a hypersphere in the continuous space, with center in our test set centroid, containing all sentences from the test set. Hopefully, only a selection of the sentences from the general pool will be contained in this hypersphere. The hyper-sphere radius is established according to some similarity metric between the centroid of the test set, and the furthest of the test sentences.

As similarity metric we consider the cosine similarity, defined as:

$$cos(\mathbf{F}_1, \mathbf{F}_2) = \frac{\mathbf{F}_1 \cdot \mathbf{F}_2}{\|\mathbf{F}_1\| \cdot \|\mathbf{F}_2\|} \tag{1}$$

where $\mathbf{F}_1$ and $\mathbf{F}_2$ are two z-dimensional vectors.

The centroid is defined as an average of the representations of the sentences from our in-domain corpus $\mathcal{T}$ (made up of T sentences):

$$\mathbf{F}_\mathcal{T} = \frac{1}{|T|} \sum_t^{|T|} \mathbf{F}_{\mathbf{x}_t} \tag{2}$$

where $\mathbf{F}_{\mathbf{x}_t} \in \mathbb{R}^z$ is the z-dimensional representation of the sentence $\mathbf{x}_t$ and $\mathbf{F}_\mathcal{T} \in \mathbb{R}^z$ denotes the centroid of our test set.

Data: Pool $\mathcal{P}$; test data $\mathcal{T}$
Result: Source synthetic corpus $\mathcal{S}$
1   $\mathbf{F}_\mathcal{T} := centroid(\mathcal{T})$;
2   $\rho := \infty$;
3   $\mathcal{S} := \emptyset$;
4   **forall** $\mathbf{x}_t \in \mathcal{T}$ **do**
5   **if** $cos(\mathbf{F}_{\mathbf{x}_t}, \mathbf{F}_\mathcal{T}) \leq \rho$ **then**
6       $\rho := cos(\mathbf{F}_{\mathbf{x}_t}, \mathbf{F}_\mathcal{T})$
7   **end**
8   **end**
9   **forall** $\mathbf{x}_p \in \mathcal{P}$ **do**
10   **if** $cos(\mathbf{F}_{\mathbf{x}_p}, \mathbf{F}_\mathcal{T}) \geq \rho$ **then**
11       $\mathcal{S} \cup \{\mathbf{x}_p\}$;
12   **end**
13 **end**

Algorithm 1: Pseudo-code for selecting synthetic corpora.

Algorithm 1 shows the selection procedure. Here, $\mathbf{x}_t \in \mathcal{T}$, is a sentence from our source test data $\mathcal{T}$; and $\mathbf{F}_{\mathbf{x}_t}$ is the vector-space representation of $\mathbf{x}_t$. Analogously, $\mathcal{P}$ is the pool of candidate sentences, $\mathbf{x}_p \in \mathcal{P}$ is a source candidate sentence, $\mathbf{F}_{\mathbf{x}_p}$ is the vector-space representation of $\mathbf{x}_p$, and $|\mathcal{P}|$ is the number of sentences in $\mathcal{P}$. Then, our objective is to select data from $\mathcal{P}$ such that it is the most suitable for translating data belonging to the source test data $\mathcal{T}$.

Algorithm 1 introduces several functions:

- $centroid(\cdot)$: calculates the centroid (Eq. 2) for the test corpus $\mathcal{T}$.
- $cos(\cdot, \cdot)$: computes the cosine similarity (Eq. 1) between two different vectors.

ρ represents the radius of the hyper-sphere, which is computed in lines 4 to 8 (the first **forall** loop) in Algorithm 1.

4.3 Adapting with the selection

In our adaptation framework, we assume that we have a NMT model trained on a general domain. We also have a large monolingual pool of sentences (in the source language) and the source part of the test set.

As first step, we compute the distributed representation of the sentences in our large pool. Next, we select sentences from the monolingual pool, given the test set, according to Algorithm 1. This subset of sentences are expected to be related with our in-domain test data. We translate them by means of machine translation (see Section 5.3 for further details). Now we have a synthetic parallel corpus, relating our in-domain task. Finally, we fine-tune the general NMT model with these data.

5 Experiments

In this section, we describe the experimental framework employed to assess the performance of the NMT adaptation method described in Section 4. For this purpose, we studied its behavior in three corpora. Two of them refer to controlled tasks; while the last one belongs to a real e-commerce task.

5.1 Corpora

We performed the experiments on English→Spanish translation. Our out-of-domain training data was the Common Crawl (COMMON) corpus which was collected from web sources. We chose the 1 Billion Words corpus (Chelba et al., 2013) as the large pool of monolingual sentences. For validation, we chose the News-commentary test 2013 (dev13) dataset. For testing, we used corpus from three different domains: Xerox printer manuals (XRCE–Test) (Barrachina et al., 2009), Information Technology[1] (IT–Test) and Electronic Commerce (E-Com–Test). This last corpus was obtained from a real e-commerce website (*Cachitos de Plata*[2]). Statistics of all corpora are provided in Table 1.

---

[1] http://metashare.metanet4u.eu/
qtleapcorpus
[2] http://cachitosdeplata.com

Table 1: Corpora main figures, in terms of number of sentences ($|S|$), number of words ($|W|$), vocabulary size ($|V|$) and average sentence length ($\overline{|W|}$).

Corpus		$|S|$	$|W|$	$|V|$	$\overline{|W|}$
1 Billion Words	EN	30.3M	800M	800k	26.4
COMMON	EN	1.5M	30M	456k	20.0
	ES		31M	522k	20.0
dev2013	EN	2.7k	48.9k	7.5k	18.1
	ES		52.6k	9.1k	19.5
XRCE – Test	EN	1.1k	8.4k	1.6k	7.6
	ES		10.1k	1.7k	9.2
IT – Test	EN	857	15.6k	2.1k	18.2
	ES		17.4k	2.4k	20.3
E-Com – Test	EN	886	7.3k	874	8.2
	ES		8.6k	973	9.7

5.2 Evaluation

Translation quality was assessed according to the following well-known metrics:

- BLEU (BiLingual Evaluation Understudy) (Papineni et al., 2002), measures n-gram precision with respect to a reference set, with a penalty for sentences that are too short.

- TER (Translation Error Rate) (Snover et al., 2006), is an error metric that computes the minimum number of edits (including swaps) required to modify the system hypotheses so that they match the reference.

For all results, we computed their confidence intervals ($p = 0.05$) by means of bootstrap resampling (Koehn, 2004).

5.3 Machine translation systems

We used NMT-Keras (Peris, 2017) for building the NMT system, as described in Section 2. We applied joint byte pair encoding (BPE) (Sennrich et al., 2016b), learning $32,000$ merge operations, on the out-of-domain dataset. Following the findings from Britz et al. (2017), we used LSTM units. Due to practical reasons, we used single-layered LSTMs. The LSTM, word embedding and attention MLP sizes were 512 each. We applied layer normalization (Ba et al., 2016) and Gaussian noise ($\sigma = 0.01$) to the weights (Graves, 2011). We clipped the L_2 norm of the gradients to 1 (Pascanu et al., 2012). We used Adam (Kingma and Ba, 2014) with a learning rate of 0.0002 (Wu et al., 2016). The size of the beam was set to 6.

We trained further the NMT system using the selected synthetic data. For this training, we used vanilla SGD with an initial learning rate of 0.05. Such hyperparameters were set according the results observed in the development set. From this exploration, we also noticed that the application of more sophisticated SGD optimizers (e.g. Adam) is tricky, as they update the model on a more aggressive way. Therefore, if we apply excessively large updates, the knowledge from the general model is somehow lost.

We also tested our method with ensembles of NMT systems. Ensembles were made up of 4 models sampled at different points of the training process. Such points were evenly chosen (each $2,000$ updates) around the single model which obtained the highest performance on the development set.

Finally, we used Moses toolkit as phrase-based reference (Koehn et al., 2007). We used a 5-gram language model with modified Kneser-Ney smoothing (Kneser and Ney, 1995), built with the SRILM toolkit (Stolcke, 2002). The phrase table was generated employing symmetrised word alignments obtained with GIZA++ (Och and Ney, 2003). The log-lineal combination weights were optimized using MERT (Minimum Error Rate Training) (Och, 2003).

Table 2: Main figures of the selections obtained by Algorithm 1 for each test set ($\mathcal{T}$), employed for adapting the NMT system. $|S|$ denotes number of sentences; $|W|$, number of words; $|V|$, vocabulary size and $\overline{|W|}$, average sentence length.

$\mathcal{T}$		$|S|$	$|W|$	$|V|$	$\overline{|W|}$
XRCE – Test	EN	180k	2.2M	54k	9.4
	ES		1.7M	58k	12.2
IT – Test	EN	150k	2.5M	76k	16.7
	ES		3.0M	78k	20.0
E-Com – Test	EN	300k	3.2M	100k	10.6
	ES		4.1M	100k	13.6

5.4 Corpus creation

The process for building synthetic parallel corpora begins with the selection from the monolingual pool. The selection method presented in Section 4.2, requires to set the dimension of the vector-space representation. We set it to 200, according to preliminary research, and it was maintained for all the experiments reported in this paper.

Table 3: Selection examples from each domain.

	Selected sentence
XRCE	id rather send files electronically use current antivirus and a firewall images are stored on a one terabyte built in hard drive which includes a DVD burner
IT	the technology would also be available to ipod touch users although they would have to buy a microphone and headphones to make calls pc world reported if you want to find panorama archive material on delicious the easiest way to search is to use the single word on the right hand column my personal have is tweetdeck which although designed for photo uploading amongst other things
E-Com	it is perfect for your collection pasta is inexpensive easy and really romantic another shows the dust forming into clumps along magnetic lines like pearls on a necklace

Once we obtained the monolingual selections, we translated them. In order to speed up this process, we split the selection and translate it using Moses and NMT. Both systems were trained on the out-of-domain data. In the case of the NMT system, we applied the same BPE subword segmentation to all data. Therefore, the potential vocabulary differences across tasks were effectively leveraged by using subword units.

6 Results and analysis

In this section, we present and discuss the results obtained. We start by analyzing the selection obtained by Algorithm 1. Next, we present the translation results obtained in all tasks. Finally, in order to get some insights of the system behavior, we analyze several representative examples.

6.1 Analysis of the selection

Table 2 shows the features of the selection for each corpus. Note that the average length of the sentences belonging to each selection is tightly related to the sentence length from each test set (Table 1).

Therefore, the selections from XRCE and E-Com had shorter sentences, while the selection obtained from the IT corpus had longer ones. As shown in the following sections, this was a key factor that affected the machine translation systems performance.

Moreover, Table 3 shows some samples from each domain, selected by our selection technique. We can notice that such samples are related to the correspondent test set domain. Thus, sentences from XRCE and IT domains refer to a technological field. As illustrated in Table 2, sentences selected from the IT corpus were notoriously longer than those selected from XRCE. Sentences selected from the E-Com task are related to jewelry or economy. Given the E-Com domain—an electronic shop of silver jewelry—these sentences are also coherent.

6.2 Quantitative results

Table 4 shows the results on the XRCE and IT tasks. The general NMT model performed worse than Moses in out-of-domain tasks. The use of a 4-model ensemble was very helpful. Nevertheless, it still had a lower performance than Moses.

The TER values of the general NMT system in the XRCE task were unusually high. This is due to the corpus features: As shown in Table 1, the XRCE–Test set has an average sentence length of 9 words. The general NMT model generated sentences with an average of 13 words, because it was trained on general-domain data. The TER metric greatly penalizes this behavior, because it must delete the exceeding words. Therefore, TER results of the NMT system were surprisingly high. In the case of Moses, the average sentence length of the sentences generated by Moses was 9.5. Because the generation was bounded by the phrase and language models.

The addition of synthetic data significantly improved the NMT systems, in all cases. Taking the reference of a single NMT model, the gains ranged from 5 to 7 BLEU points. The performance of a single fine-tuned NMT model was also clearly better than fine-tuned ensembles.

Especially critical were the enhancements in terms of TER. In the XRCE task, the synthetic data improved TER by almost 40 and 20 points, for single model and ensembles, respectively. Due to the addition of synthetic data, the system learned to produce shorter translations (around 5 words shorter, in average), and therefore, greatly diminishing TER. In the IT task, the synthetic data also improved TER, but to a lower extent. This is because the IT task is closer to the out-of-domain corpus. Therefore, the adaptation benefits brought by the synthetic data were less crucial than in the XRCE task.

It is worth noting that the adaptation of the

Table 4:   Translation results for the XRCE and IT tasks. BLEU and TER results given in percentage. Σ denotes an ensemble of 4 neural models. $\overline{|W|}$ is the average number of words per sentence.

System	XRCE			IT		
	BLEU	TER	$\overline{|W|}$	BLEU	TER	$\overline{|W|}$
Moses	26.2 ± 0.8	59.0 ± 0.8	9.1	33.4 ± 0.6	45.6 ± 0.6	20.4
NMT	20.4 ± 1	94.5 ± 5.1	12.8	29.0 ± 0.8	53.5 ± 0.8	15.3
NMT$^{\Sigma}$	25.5 ± 0.8	76.8 ± 2.0	11.3	31.4 ± 0.8	51.2 ± 0.8	15.3
NMT + Synthetic	27.5 ± 0.8	56.7 ± 0.8	8.6	34.1 ± 0.7	45.7 ± 0.7	17.8
NMT$^{\Sigma}$ + Synthetic	27.3 ± 0.8	56.3 ± 0.8	8.4	33.8 ± 0.7	46.3 ± 0.7	18.1

NMT system was very fast. The system only required to be trained on $\sim 15,000$ samples in order to achieve the best results. Using a GPU, the fine-tuning of the NMT model can be done in minutes.

Table 5 shows the results on the real E-Com task. This was a very specific task. In these cases, the single NMT model also yielded worse performance in terms of BLEU than Moses, but when applying an ensemble, the results were significantly enhanced. In terms of BLEU, even beating Moses.

Table 5: E-Com – Test set results. BLEU and TER results given in percentage. Σ denotes an ensemble of 4 neural models. $\overline{|W|}$ is the average number of words per sentence.

System	E-Com		
	BLEU	TER	$\overline{|W|}$
Moses	21.1 ± 0.8	56.7 ± 0.7	9.4
NMT	16.9 ± 1.0	104.7 ± 6.3	14.1
NMT$^{\Sigma}$	23.0 ± 1.0	80.8 ± 2.9	12.0
NMT + Synthetic	25.5 ± 1.0	59.1 ± 1.0	8.7
NMT$^{\Sigma}$ + Synthetic	25.8 ± 1.0	61.1 ± 2.6	8.7

The NMT systems behaviored similarly to the XRCE task in terms of TER. The E-Com corpus had similar features than XRCE–Test (in this case, 9.7 words per sentence). Therefore, we observed the same phenomenon: as we introduced in-domain-related sentences, the system learned to produce shorter sentences, diminishing TER consequently.

The use of synthetic data again greatly improved the system. The results were coherent with the previous experiments: A single, fine-tuned model, significantly outperformed the general system (+9 BLEU points). A sole adapted system was even better than a general model ensemble. With respect to Moses, we also found major enhancements in terms of BLEU.

It is also noticeable the ensemble of systems trained with synthetic data did not improve the performance of a single fine-tuned system. This is probably due to the fact that the adaptation was performed from an already trained model and with few data. Therefore, the systems belonging to the ensemble were quite similar, all of them around the same local minimum. Therefore, potential enhancements from the ensembles were diluted.

Finally, we should remark than the E-Com task belongs to a real-world scenario. This corpus is not designed for experimental purposes. It contains elements that distort the experiment, and therefore yield to unpredictable results. In such open scenarios, a human evaluation should be the next step to take.

6.3   Qualitative results

Some translation examples from each corpus are shown in Table 6. In the first example, all the systems presented the similar error at the beginning of the translation (*especificación del*). This is because that was the most likely translation in our corpora, both the real and synthetic ones.

In the second example, Moses was not able to correctly identify the right meaning of the word (*windows*) in the sentence to translate. It should be left untranslated, as it is a proper noun. The NMT systems were able to detect it. Also, Moses, NMT and NMT+Synth systems presented the same lexical choice error at the word (*deberían*).

Finally, we show the translation examples for the e-commerce domain. Moses obtained the worst translation. The NMT$^{\Sigma}$ method was not able to obtain the word (*precioso*), as provided in the reference, but instead it a synonym (*hermoso*). Nevertheless, note that, although this may not be an actual mistake in translation terms, it will be penalized by BLEU and TER. The NMT+Synth ob-

Table 6: Translation examples for each domain with the MT systems built: Src (source sentence), Moses (moses system), NMT (NMT system), NMT$^\Sigma$ (NMT system with ensemble), NMT + Synth (NMT using synthetic corpus) and Ref (reference).

XRCE	Src	specifying the output file format 2-29
	Moses	*especificando el* formato de salida 2-29
	NMT	*especificar el* formato de archivo de salida 2-29 .
	NMT$^\Sigma$	*especificar el* formato de archivo de salida *de 29 a 29* .
	NMT+Synth	*especificar el* formato de archivo de salida 2-29
	Ref	especificación del formato de archivo de salida 2-29
IT	Src	almost all apps installed on windows 8 should work correctly in windows 8.1 .
	Moses	casi todas las aplicaciones instaladas en *las ventanas* 8 *debería* funcionar correctamente en *ventanas* 8.1 .
	NMT	casi todas las aplicaciones instaladas en windows 8 *deben* funcionar correctamente en windows 8.1 .
	NMT$^\Sigma$	casi todas las aplicaciones instaladas en windows 8 deberían funcionar correctamente en windows 8.1 .
	NMT+Synth	casi todas las aplicaciones instaladas en windows 8 *debería* funcionar correctamente en windows 8.1 .
	Ref	casi todas las aplicaciones instaladas en windows 8 deberían funcionar correctamente en windows 8.1 .
E-Com	Src	they are a lovely set of small and thin strips silver intertwined .
	Moses	son un *conjunto* de pequeñas y *encantadoras tiras finas plata interrelacionado* .
	NMT	son un precioso conjunto de *tiras de película pequeña y delgada* .
	NMT$^\Sigma$	son un *hermoso* conjunto de pequeñas y finas tiras de plata .
	NMT+Synth	son un precioso conjunto de pequeñas y finas tiras de plata .
	Ref	son un precioso conjunto de pequeñas y finas tiras de plata entrelazada .

tained the closer translation to the reference. Even though, the system was unable to obtain a translation for the word (*intertwined*).

7 Conclusions

In this work we presented an instance selection method and applied it to collect the most adequate sentences for translating a corpus from a specific domain. We selected domain-related instances from a large monolingual corpus, automatically translated them and fine-tuned a NMT system, originally trained on a more general domain. Results showed significant improvements in terms of BLEU and TER with respect to the original model. Moreover, we found that it is preferable to use a single fine-tuned model than an ensemble of general models. It is also worth mentioning that, once the selection was performed, the adaptation of NMT systems to new domains was very fast (few minutes).

As byproduct of the evaluation carried out in this work, we can also conclude two main points. First, to use a single automatic metric for evaluating machine translation is risky, as every automatic metric is likely to be distorted. In order to have more confidence about the performance of a machine translation system, it should be tested on more metrics. Second, when applying NMT systems to tasks with different features than the training data, we should control the length of the output sentences. This can be achieved either with some heuristics or adapting with an in-domain corpus.

We leave the study of this control as future work.

As additional future work, we intend to prove our methods in more domains and different language pairs in order to establish its robustness. Moreover, we want to observe the influence of the quality and nature of the synthetic data in our pipeline. Therefore, we aim to study the influence of different translation methods or technologies when translating the monolingual corpus. We should also study if adding source synthetic data instead of target synthetic data affects the system. Finally, given the good results obtained, we want to leverage the bondages of the synthetic data, using it in different applications.

Acknowledgments

The research leading to these results has received funding from the Generalitat Valenciana under grant PROMETEOII/2014/030 and the FPI (2014) grant by Universitat Politècnica de València. We also acknowledge NVIDIA for the donation of a GPU used in this work.

References

Jimmy Lei Ba, Jamie Ryan Kiros, and Geoffrey E Hinton. 2016. Layer normalization. *arXiv:1607.06450*.

Dzmitry Bahdanau, Kyunghyun Cho, and Yoshua Bengio. 2015. Neural machine translation by jointly learning to align and translate. *arXiv:1409.0473*.

Sergio Barrachina, Oliver Bender, Francisco Casacuberta, Jorge Civera, Elsa Cubel, Shahram Khadivi,

Antonio Lagarda, Hermann Ney, Jesús Tomás, Enrique Vidal, and Juan-Miguel Vilar. 2009. Statistical approaches to computer-assisted translation. *Computational Linguistics* 35:3–28.

Nicola Bertoldi and Marcello Federico. 2009. Domain adaptation for statistical machine translation with monolingual resources. In *Proceedings of the Workshop on Statistical Machine Translation*. pages 182–189.

Denny Britz, Anna Goldie, Thang Luong, and Quoc Le. 2017. Massive exploration of neural machine translation architectures. *arXiv:1703.03906*.

Ciprian Chelba, Tomas Mikolov, Mike Schuster, Qi Ge, Thorsten Brants, Phillipp Koehn, and Tony Robinson. 2013. One billion word benchmark for measuring progress in statistical language modeling. *arXiv:1312.3005*.

Yong Cheng, Wei Xu, Zhongjun He, Wei He, Hua Wu, Maosong Sun, and Yang Liu. 2016. Semi-supervised learning for neural machine translation. *arXiv:1606.04596*.

Kyunghyun Cho, Bart Van Merriënboer, Dzmitry Bahdanau, and Yoshua Bengio. 2014a. On the properties of neural machine translation: Encoder-decoder approaches. *arXiv:1409.1259*.

Kyunghyun Cho, Bart van Merriënboer, Dzmitry Bahdanau, and Yoshua Bengio. 2014b. On the properties of neural machine translation: Encoder-decoder approaches. In *Proceedings of the Workshop on Syntax, Semantic and Structure in Statistical Translation*. pages 103–111.

Josep Maria Crego, Jungi Kim, Guillaume Klein, Anabel Rebollo, Kathy Yang, Jean Senellart, Egor Akhanov, Patrice Brunelle, Aurelien Coquard, Yongchao Deng, Satoshi Enoue, Chiyo Geiss, Joshua Johanson, Ardas Khalsa, Raoum Khiari, Byeongil Ko, Catherine Kobus, Jean Lorieux, Leidiana Martins, Dang-Chuan Nguyen, Alexandra Priori, Thomas Riccardi, Natalia Segal, Christophe Servan, Cyril Tiquet, Bo Wang, Jin Yang, Dakun Zhang, Jing Zhou, and Peter Zoldan. 2016. SYSTRAN's pure neural machine translation systems. *arXiv:1610.05540*.

Jeffrey L Elman. 1990. Finding structure in time. *Cognitive science* 14(2):179–211.

Xavier Glorot, Antoine Bordes, and Yoshua Bengio. 2011. Domain adaptation for large-scale sentiment classification: A deep learning approach. In *Proceedings of the International Conference on Machine Learning*. pages 513–520.

Alex Graves. 2011. Practical variational inference for neural networks. In *Advances in Neural Information Processing Systems*. pages 2348–2356.

Caglar Gulcehre, Orhan Firat, Kelvin Xu, Kyunghyun Cho, Loic Barrault, Huei-Chi Lin, Fethi Bougares, Holger Schwenk, and Yoshua Bengio. 2015. On using monolingual corpora in neural machine translation. *arXiv:1503.03535*.

Caglar Gulcehre, Orhan Firat, Kelvin Xu, Kyunghyun Cho, and Yoshua Bengio. 2017. On integrating a language model into neural machine translation. *Computer Speech & Language* 45:137 – 148.

Geoffrey E Hinton. 1986. Learning distributed representations of concepts. In *Proceedings of the Annual Meeting of the Cognitive Science Society*. pages 12–24.

Sepp Hochreiter and Jürgen Schmidhuber. 1997. Long short-term memory. *Neural Computation* 9(8):1735–1780.

Nal Kalchbrenner and Phil Blunsom. 2013. Recurrent continuous translation models. In *Proceedings of the Conference on Empirical Methods in Natural Language Processing*. pages 1700–1709.

Diederik Kingma and Jimmy Ba. 2014. Adam: A method for stochastic optimization. *arXiv:1412.6980*.

Reinhard Kneser and Hermann Ney. 1995. Improved backing-off for m-gram language modeling. In *Proceedings of the International Conference on Acoustics, Speech and Signal Processing*. pages 181–184.

Philipp Koehn. 2004. Statistical significance tests for machine translation evaluation. In *Proceedings of the Conference on Empirical Methods in Natural Language Processing*. pages 388–395.

Philipp Koehn, Hieu Hoang, Alexandra Birch, Chris Callison-Burch, Marcello Federico, Nicola Bertoldi, Brooke Cowan, Wade Shen, Christine Moran, Richard Zens, Chris Dyer, Ondřej Bojar, Alexandra Constantin, and Evan Herbst. 2007. Moses: Open source toolkit for statistical machine translation. In *Proceedings of the Annual Meeting of the Association for Computational Linguistics*. pages 177–180.

Patrik Lambert, Holger Schwenk, Christophe Servan, and Sadaf Abdul-Rauf. 2011. Investigations on translation model adaptation using monolingual data. In *Proceedings of the Workshop on Statistical Machine Translation*. pages 284–293.

Quoc V Le and Tomas Mikolov. 2014. Distributed representations of sentences and documents. *arXiv:1405.4053*.

Minh-Thang Luong and Christopher D Manning. 2015. Stanford neural machine translation systems for spoken language domains. In *Proceedings of the International Workshop on Spoken Language Translation*. pages 76–79.

Tomas Mikolov, Kai Chen, Greg Corrado, and Jeffrey Dean. 2013a. Efficient estimation of word representations in vector space. *arXiv:1301.3781*.

Tomas Mikolov, Quoc V Le, and Ilya Sutskever. 2013b. Exploiting similarities among languages for machine translation. *arXiv:1309.4168*.

Franz Josef Och. 2003. Minimum error rate training in statistical machine translation. In *Proceedings of the Annual Meeting of the Association for Computational Linguistics*. pages 160–167.

Franz Josef Och and Hermann Ney. 2003. A systematic comparison of various statistical alignment models. *Computational Linguistics* 29(1):19–51.

Kishore Papineni, Salim Roukos, Todd Ward, and Wei-Jing Zhu. 2002. Bleu: a method for automatic evaluation of machine translation. In *Proceedings of the Annual Meeting of the Association for Computational Linguistics*. pages 311–318.

Razvan Pascanu, Caglar Gulcehre, Kyunghyun Cho, and Yoshua Bengio. 2014. How to construct deep recurrent neural networks. *arXiv:1312.6026*.

Razvan Pascanu, Tomas Mikolov, and Yoshua Bengio. 2012. On the difficulty of training recurrent neural networks. *arXiv:1211.5063*.

Álvaro Peris. 2017. NMT-Keras. `https://github.com/lvapeab/nmt-keras`. GitHub repository.

Mike Schuster and Kuldip K. Paliwal. 1997. Bidirectional recurrent neural networks. *IEEE Transactions on Signal Processing* 45(11):2673–2681.

Holger Schwenk. 2007. Continuous space language models. *Computer Speech & Language* 21(3):492–518.

Rico Sennrich, Barry Haddow, and Alexandra Birch. 2016a. Improving neural machine translation models with monolingual data. In *Proceedings of the Annual Meeting of the Association for Computational Linguistics*. pages 86–96.

Rico Sennrich, Barry Haddow, and Alexandra Birch. 2016b. Neural machine translation of rare words with subword units. In *Proceedings of the Annual Meeting of the Association for Computational Linguistics*. pages 1715–1725.

Matthew Snover, Bonnie Dorr, Richard Schwartz, Linnea Micciulla, and John Makhoul. 2006. A study of translation edit rate with targeted human annotation. In *Proceedings of the Association for Machine Translation in the Americas*. pages 223–231.

Richard Socher, Cliff C Lin, Chris Manning, and Andrew Y Ng. 2011. Parsing natural scenes and natural language with recursive neural networks. In *Proceedings of the International Conference on Machine Learning*. pages 129–136.

Andreas Stolcke. 2002. SRILM - an extensible language modeling toolkit. In *Proceedings of the International Conference on Spoken Language Processing*. pages 901–904.

Ilya Sutskever, Oriol Vinyals, and Quoc V. Le. 2014. Sequence to sequence learning with neural networks. In *Proceedings of the Advances in Neural Information Processing Systems*. volume 27, pages 3104–3112.

Nicola Ueffing, Gholamreza Haffari, Anoop Sarkar, et al. 2007. Transductive learning for statistical machine translation. In *Proceedings of the Annual Meeting of the Association for Computational Linguistics*. pages 25–35.

Hua Wu, Haifeng Wang, and Chengqing Zong. 2008. Domain adaptation for statistical machine translation with domain dictionary and monolingual corpora. In *Proceedings of the Annual Meeting of the Association for Computational Linguistics*. pages 993–1000.

Y. Wu, M. Schuster, Z. Chen, Q. V. Le, M. Norouzi, W. Macherey, M. Krikun, Y. Cao, Q. Gao, K. Macherey, J. Klingner, A. Shah, M. Johnson, X. Liu, Ł. Kaiser, S. Gouws, Y. Kato, T. Kudo, H. Kazawa, K. Stevens, G. Kurian, N. Patil, W. Wang, C. Young, J. Smith, J. Riesa, A. Rudnick, O. Vinyals, G. Corrado, M. Hughes, and J. Dean. 2016. Google's Neural Machine Translation System: Bridging the Gap between Human and Machine Translation. *arXiv:1609.08144*.

Jiajun Zhang and Chengqing Zong. 2016a. Bridging neural machine translation and bilingual dictionaries. *arXiv:1610.07272*.

Jiajun Zhang and Chengqing Zong. 2016b. Exploiting source-side monolingual data in neural machine translation. In *Proceedings of the Conference on Empirical Methods in Natural Language Processing*. pages 1535–1545.

Copied Monolingual Data Improves Low-Resource Neural Machine Translation

Anna Currey, Antonio Valerio Miceli Barone, and **Kenneth Heafield**
School of Informatics, University of Edinburgh
`a.currey@sms.ed.ac.uk`
`{amiceli, kheafiel}@inf.ed.ac.uk`

Abstract

We train a neural machine translation (NMT) system to both translate source-language text and copy target-language text, thereby exploiting monolingual corpora in the target language. Specifically, we create a bitext from the monolingual text in the target language so that each source sentence is identical to the target sentence. This copied data is then mixed with the parallel corpus and the NMT system is trained like normal, with no metadata to distinguish the two input languages.

Our proposed method proves to be an effective way of incorporating monolingual data into low-resource NMT. On Turkish↔English and Romanian↔English translation tasks, we see gains of up to 1.2 BLEU over a strong baseline with back-translation. Further analysis shows that the linguistic phenomena behind these gains are different from and largely orthogonal to back-translation, with our copied corpus method improving accuracy on named entities and other words that should remain identical between the source and target languages.

1 Introduction

Neural machine translation (NMT) systems require a large amount of training data to make generalizations, both on the source side (in order to interpret the text well enough to translate it) and on the target side (in order to produce fluent translations). This data typically comes in the form of parallel corpora, in which each sentence in the source language is matched to a translation in the target language. Recent work (Gulcehre et al., 2015; Sennrich et al., 2016b) has investigated incorporating monolingual training data (particularly on the target side) into NMT. This effectively converts machine translation into a semi-supervised problem that takes advantage of both labeled (parallel) and unlabeled (monolingual) data. Adding monolingual data to NMT is important because sufficient parallel data is unavailable for all but a few language pairs and domains.

In this paper, we introduce a straightforward method for adding target-side monolingual training data to an NMT system without changing its architecture or training algorithm. This method converts a monolingual corpus in the target language into a parallel corpus by copying it, so that each source sentence is identical to its corresponding target sentence. This copied corpus is then mixed with the original parallel data and used to train the NMT system, with no distinction made between the parallel and the copied data.

We focus on language pairs with small amounts of parallel data where monolingual data has the most impact. On the relatively low-resource language pairs of English↔Turkish and English↔Romanian, we find that our copying technique is effective both alone and combined with back-translation. This is the case even when no additional monolingual data is used (i.e. when the copied corpus and the back-translated corpus are identical on the target side). This implies that back-translation does not make full use of monolingual data in low-resource settings, which makes sense because it relies on low-resource (and therefore low-quality) translation in the reverse direction.

Proceedings of the Conference on Machine Translation (WMT), Volume 1: Research Papers, pages 148–156
Copenhagen, Denmark, September 7–11, 2017. ©2017 Association for Computational Linguistics

2 Related Work

Early work on incorporating monolingual data into NMT concentrated on target-side monolingual data. Jean et al. (2015) and Gulcehre et al. (2015) used a 5-gram language model and a recurrent neural network language model (RNNLM), respectively, to re-rank NMT outputs. Gulcehre et al. (2015) also integrated a pre-trained RNNLM into NMT by concatenating hidden states. Sennrich et al. (2016b) added monolingual target data directly to NMT using null source sentences and freezing encoder parameters while training with the monolingual data. Our method is similar, although instead of using a null source sentence, we use a copy of the target sentence and train the encoder parameters on the copied sentence.

Sennrich et al. (2016b) also created synthetic parallel data by translating target-language monolingual text into the source language. To perform this process, dubbed *back-translation*, they first trained an initial target→source machine translation system on the available parallel data. They then used this model to translate the monolingual corpus from the target language to the source language. The resulting back-translated data was combined with the original parallel data and used to train the final source→target NMT system. Since this back-translation method outperforms previous methods that only train the decoder (Gulcehre et al., 2015; Sennrich et al., 2016b), we use it as our baseline. In addition, our method stacks with back-translation in both the target→source and source→target systems; we can use source text to improve the back-translations and target text to improve the final outputs.

In the mirror image of back-translation, Zhang and Zong (2016) added source-side monolingual data to NMT by first translating the source data into the target language using an initial machine translation system and then using this translated data and the original parallel data to train their NMT system. Our method is orthogonal: it could improve the initial system or be used alongside the translated data in the final system. They also considered a multitask shared encoder setup where the monolingual source data is used in a sentence re-ordering task.

More recent approaches have used both source and target monolingual data while simultaneously training source→target and target→source NMT systems. Cheng et al. (2016) accom-

plished this by concatenating source→target and target→source NMT systems to create an autoencoder. Monolingual data was then introduced by adding an autoencoder objective. This can be interpreted as back-translation with joint training. He et al. (2016) similarly used a small amount of parallel data to pre-train source→target and target→source NMT systems; they then added monolingual data to the systems by translating a sentence from the monolingual corpus into the other language and then translating it back into the original language, using reinforcement learning with rewards based on the language model score of the translated sentence and the similarity of the reconstructed sentence to the original. Our approach also employs an autoencoder, but rather than concatenate two NMT systems, we have flattened them into one standard NMT system.

Our approach is related to multitask systems. Luong et al. (2016) proposed conjoined translation and autoencoder networks; we use a single shared encoder. Further work used the same encoder and decoder for multi-way translation (Johnson et al., 2016). We have repurposed the idea to inject monolingual text for low-resource NMT. Their work combined multiple translation directions (e.g. French→English, German→English, and English→German) into one system. Our work combines e.g. English→English and Turkish→English into one system for the purpose of improving Turkish→English quality. They used only parallel data; our goal is to inject monolingual data.

3 Neural Machine Translation

We evaluate our approach using sequence-to-sequence neural machine translation (Cho et al., 2014; Kalchbrenner and Blunsom, 2013; Sutskever et al., 2014) augmented with attention (Bahdanau et al., 2015). We briefly explain these models here.

Neural machine translation is an end-to-end approach to machine translation that learns to directly model $p(y \mid x)$ for a source-target sentence pair (x, y). The system consists of two recurrent neural networks (RNNs): the encoder and the decoder. In our experiments, the encoder is a bidirectional RNN with gated recurrent units (GRUs) that maps the source sentence into a vector representation. The decoder is an RNN language model conditioned on the source sentence. This is augmented with an attention mechanism, which assigns weights to each of the words in the source sentence when modeling target words. This model is trained to minimize word-level cross-entropy loss; at test time, translations are generated using beam search.

4 Copied Monolingual Data for NMT

We propose a method for incorporating target-side monolingual data into low-resource NMT that does not rely heavily on the amount or quality of the parallel data. We first convert the target-side monolingual corpus into a bitext by making each source sentence identical to its target sentence; i.e., the source side of the bitext is a copy of the target side. We refer to this bitext as the *copied corpus*. The copied corpus is then mixed with the bilingual parallel corpus and no distinction is made between the two corpora. Finally, we train our NMT system with a single encoder and decoder using this mixed data. We are able to use the same encoder for both the parallel and the copied source sentences because we use byte pair encoding (Sennrich et al., 2016c) to represent the source and target words in the same vocabulary.

This copying method can also be combined with the back-translation method of Sennrich et al. (2016b). This is done by shuffling the parallel, back-translated, and copied corpora together into a single dataset and training the NMT system like normal, again making no distinction between the three corpora during training. We experiment with using the same monolingual data as the basis for both the back-translated and copied corpora (so that the target sides of the back-translated and copied corpora are identical) and with using two separate monolingual datasets for these purposes. Note that in the former case, each sentence in the original monolingual corpus occurs twice in the training data.

5 Experiments

5.1 Experimental Setup

5.1.1 Training Details

We train attentional sequence-to-sequence models (Bahdanau et al., 2015) implemented in Nematus (Sennrich et al., 2017). We use hidden layers of size 1024 and word embeddings of size 512. The models are trained using Adam (Kingma and Ba, 2015) with a minibatch size of 80 and a maximum

Language pair	Parallel	Monolingual
EN↔TR	207 373	414 746
EN↔RO	608 320	608 320
EN↔DE	5 852 458	10 000 000

Table 1: Number of parallel and monolingual training sentences for each language pair.

sentence length of 50. We apply dropout (Gal and Ghahramani, 2016) in all of our EN↔TR and EN↔RO systems with a probability of 0.1 on word layers and 0.2 on all other layers. No dropout is used for EN↔DE. For all models, we use early stopping based on perplexity on the validation dataset. We decode using beam search on a single model with a beam size of 12, except for EN↔DE where we use a beam size of 5. For the experiments which use back-translated versions of the monolingual data, the target→source systems used to create the back-translations have the same setup as those used in the final source→target experiments.

5.1.2 Data and Preprocessing

We evaluate our models on three language pairs: English (EN) ↔ Turkish (TR), English ↔ Romanian (RO), and English ↔ German (DE). As shown in Table 1, these pairs each have vastly different amounts of parallel data. All of these languages have a substantial amount of monolingual data available.

The EN↔TR and EN↔DE data comes from the WMT17 news translation shared task,[1] while the EN↔RO data comes from the WMT16 shared task (Bojar et al., 2016). We use all of the available parallel data for each language pair, and the monolingual data comes from News Crawl 2015 (EN↔RO) or News Crawl 2016 (EN↔TR and EN↔DE). To create our monolingual datasets we randomly sample from the full monolingual sets.

For all language pairs, we tokenize and truecase the parallel and monolingual training data; we also apply byte pair encoding (BPE) to split words into subword units (Sennrich et al., 2016c). For each language pair, we learn a shared BPE model with 90,000 merge operations. Both the BPE model and the truecase model are learned on parallel data only (not on monolingual data). For RO→EN, we remove diacritics from the source training data, following the recommendation by Sennrich et al. (2016a).

---

[1] http://statmt.org/wmt17

BLEU	**EN→TR**		**TR→EN**		**EN→RO**	**RO→EN**	**EN→DE**		**DE→EN**	
	2016	**2017**	**2016**	**2017**	**2016**	**2016**	**2016**	**2017**	**2016**	**2017**
baseline	12.8	14.2	18.5	18.3	23.8	34.5	**33.3**	**26.6**	40.1	33.8
+ copied	**14.0**†	**15.2**†	**18.9**‡	**18.6**‡	**24.5**†	**35.7**†	**33.3**	26.3	**40.2**	**34.0**

Table 2: Translation performance in BLEU with and without copied monolingual data. Statistically significant differences are marked with † ($p < 0.01$) and ‡ ($p < 0.05$).

5.2 Translation Performance

We evaluate our models compared to a baseline containing parallel and back-translated data on the newstest2016 (all language pairs) and newstest2017 (EN↔TR and EN↔DE) test sets. For each model, we report case-sensitive detokenized BLEU (Papineni et al., 2002) calculated using `mteval-v13a.pl`.

The BLEU scores for each language pair and each system are shown in Table 2. The only difference between the baseline and the *+ copied* systems is the addition of the copied corpus during training. Note that the copied and the back-translated corpora are created using identical monolingual data, which means that in the *+ copied* system, each sentence from the monolingual corpus occurs twice in the training data (once as part of the copied corpus and once as part of the back-translated corpus).

For EN↔TR and EN↔DE, we use about twice as much monolingual as parallel data, so the ratio of parallel to back-translated to copied data is 1:2:2. For EN↔RO, we use a 1:1:1 ratio. In addition, for EN↔DE, we oversample the parallel corpus twice in order to balance the parallel and monolingual data.

For EN↔TR and EN↔RO, we observe statistically significant improvements (up to 1.2 BLEU) when adding the copied corpus. This indicates that our copied monolingual method can help improve NMT in cases where only a moderate amount of parallel data is available. For EN↔DE, we do not see improvements from adding the copied data; we conjecture that this occurs because this is a high-resource language pair. However, the EN↔DE systems trained with the copied corpus also do not perform any worse that those without.

5.3 Fluency

Adding copied target-side monolingual data results in a significant improvement in translation performance as measured by BLEU for EN↔TR and EN↔RO. Motivated by a desire to better understand the source of these improvements, we further experiment with the outputs for each system described in section 5.2. In particular, we want to examine whether these gains are simply due to the monolingual data improving the fluency of the NMT system.

In order to evaluate the fluency of each system, we train 5-gram language models for each language using KenLM (Heafield, 2011). The models are trained on the full monolingual News Crawl 2015 and 2016 datasets. This data is preprocessed as described in section 5.1, except that no subword segmentation is used.

We use these language models to measure perplexity on the outputs of the baseline systems (trained using parallel and back-translated data) and the *+ copied* systems (trained using parallel, back-translated, and copied data). The language models are also queried on the reference translations for comparison. For all language pairs except EN↔RO, we concatenate newstest2016 and newstest2017 into a single dataset to find the perplexity.

Table 3 displays the perplexities for each system output and the reference. Interestingly, the perplexities for the baseline and the *+ copied* systems are similar for all language pairs. In particular, improvements in BLEU (see Table 2) do not necessarily correlate to improvements in perplexity. This indicates that the gains from the *+ copied* system may not solely be due to fluency.

5.4 Pass-through Accuracy

Since the copied monolingual data adds an autoencoder element to the NMT training, it is possible that the systems trained with copied data learn how to better pass through named entities and other relevant words than the baselines. In order to test this hypothesis, we detect words that are identical in each sentence in the source and the reference for the tokenized test data (excluding words that contain only one character and ignoring case). We then count how many of these words occur in the corresponding sentence in the translation output from each system. We calculate the pass-through

Perplexity	EN→TR	TR→EN	EN→RO	RO→EN	EN→DE	DE→EN
reference	700.0	146.7	202.4	118.1	231.0	116.5
baseline	**921.1**	**341.6**	**328.2**	248.4	**490.6**	317.3
+ copied	921.6	344.2	344.8	**245.5**	493.3	**314.2**

Table 3: Language model perplexities for the outputs of each NMT system.

Accuracy	EN→TR	TR→EN	EN→RO	RO→EN	EN→DE	DE→EN
baseline	77.3%	85.0%	71.5%	85.3%	78.5%	**91.4%**
+ copied	**82.0%**	**89.1%**	**78.5%**	**91.5%**	**78.6%**	91.1%

Table 4: Pass-through accuracy for the outputs of each NMT system.

accuracy as the percent of such words that appear in the output; these results are shown in Table 4.

For all language pairs except for EN↔DE, there is a large improvement in pass-through accuracy when the copied data is added during training. This closely mirrors the BLEU results discussed in section 5.2. These results suggest that a key advantage of using copied data is that the model learns to pass appropriate words through to the target output more successfully. Table 5 shows some examples of translations with improved pass-through accuracy for the + *copied* systems.

5.5 Additional EN-TR Experiments

In this section, we describe a number of additional experiments on EN→TR in order to investigate the effects of different experimental setups and aspects of the data. Note that the BLEU scores in this section are not directly comparable with those in Table 2, since a different subset of the monolingual data is used for some of these experiments. All BLEU scores reported in this section are on newstest2016 unless otherwise noted.

5.5.1 Double Back-Translated Data

In section 5.2, we report significant gains from our + *copied* systems over baselines trained on parallel and back-translated data for EN↔TR and EN↔RO, even while using the same monolingual data as the basis for both the copied and the back-translated corpora. However, in our experiments, we use particularly high-quality in-domain monolingual data. As a result, it is possible that these improvements are due to using this monolingual data twice (in the form of the back-translated and copied corpora) rather than to using the copied monolingual corpus.

In order to evaluate this, we consider an additional configuration in which we train using two copies of the same back-translated corpus (instead of using one copy of each of the back-translated corpus and the copied corpus). The results for this experiment are in Table 6. For both test sets, the + *copied* system performs better than the system with double back-translated data by about 1 BLEU point. This indicates that our copied corpus improves NMT performance, and that this is not simply due to the higher weight given to the high-quality monolingual data.

5.5.2 Different Copied Data

In our initial experiments, we use the same monolingual corpus to create the back-translated and the copied data. Here, we consider a variation in which we use different monolingual data for these purposes. This is done by cutting the monolingual corpus in half and back-translating only half of it, leaving the rest for copied data. Note that this means that the original monolingual corpus is the same size (twice the size of the parallel data; see Table 1), but each monolingual sentence only occurs once in the training data, rather than twice as before.

The results for these experiments are shown in Table 7. The baseline is trained on back-translations of all of the monolingual data, and the + *same copied* system contains the full copied corpus. The + *different copied* system uses different data for copying and back-translation. Both copied systems outperform the baseline, although the + *same copied* system does slightly better.

5.5.3 Copied Data Without Back-translation

Our results in section 5.2 show that our copied corpus method stacks with back-translation to improve translation performance when there is not much parallel data available. In this section, we study whether the copied corpus can aid NMT when no back-translated data is used. If so, this would be advantageous, as the copied corpus method is much simpler to apply than back-

RO→EN	
source	... a afirmat Angel Ubide, analist șef în cadrul **Peterson** Institute for International Economics.
reference	... said Angel Ubide, senior fellow at the **Peterson** Institute for International Economics.
baseline	... "said Angel Ubide, chief analyst at the **Carson** Institute for International Economics.
+ copied	... "said Angel Ubide, chief analyst at **Peterson** Institute for International Economics.
source	Les **Dissonances** a aparut pe scena muzicala în 2004 ...
reference	Les **Dissonances** appeared on the music scene in 2004 ...
baseline	Les **Dissonville** appeared on the music scene in 2004 ...
+ copied	Les **Dissonances** appeared on the music scene in 2004 ...

TR→EN	
source	**Metcash**, Bay **Douglass**'ın yorumlarına bir yanıt vermeyi reddetti.
reference	**Metcash** has declined to respond publicly to Mr **Douglass**' comments.
baseline	**Metah** declined to give an answer to Mr. **Doug**'s comments.
+ copied	**Metcash** declined to respond to a response to Mr. **Douglass**'s comments.
source	PSV teknik direktörü Phillip **Cocu**, şöyle dedi: "Çok kötü bir sakatlanma."
reference	Phillip **Cocu**, the PSV coach, said: "It's a very bad injury."
baseline	PSV coach Phillip **Coker** said: "It was a very bad injury.
+ copied	PSV coach Phillip **Cocu** said: "It's a very bad injury."

Table 5: Comparison of translations generated by baseline and + *copied* systems.

BLEU	2016	2017
parallel + back-translated	12.4	14.2
parallel + double back-translated	13.1	14.1
parallel + back-translated + copied	**14.0**	**15.2**

Table 6: EN→TR translation performance when using the back-translated corpus twice vs. the back-translated and copied corpora.

	BLEU
baseline	12.4
+ same copied	**13.6**
+ different copied	13.3

Table 7: EN→TR translation performance when using the same or different data for copied and back-translated corpora.

	BLEU
parallel only	9.4
parallel + small copied	11.7
parallel + large copied	12.0
parallel + small back-translated	**12.0**
parallel + large back-translated	**12.4**

Table 8: EN→TR translation performance without back-translated data. We include systems trained with parallel and back-translated data (without copied data) for comparison.

	BLEU
baseline	12.4
+ copied	**13.6**
+ EN data	**13.6**

Table 9: EN→TR translation performance with EN monolingual data.

translation and does not require the training of an additional target→source machine translation system. We experiment with both a small copied corpus (about 200k sentences) and a large copied corpus (about 400k sentences).

The results for systems trained with only parallel and copied data are in Table 8. Both the small copied corpus and the large copied corpus yield large improvements (2.3-2.6 BLEU) over using parallel data only, and their performance is only slightly worse (0.3-0.4 BLEU) than the corresponding systems trained with only back-translated and parallel data.

5.5.4 Source Monolingual Data

Although we have concentrated thus far on incorporating target-side monolingual data into NMT, source-side monolingual data also has the poten-

tial to help translation performance. In particular, a source copied corpus can be used when training the target→source system for back-translation. Here, we test this strategy on EN→TR NMT with EN monolingual data. For this purpose, we randomly sample about 400k English sentences (twice the size of the parallel corpus) from the News Crawl 2015 monolingual corpus.

The results for this experiment are shown in Table 9. Although both copied systems improve over the baseline, adding the EN monolingual data does not result in further improvement over the target-only copied model, despite taking much longer to train.

BLEU	1:1	2:1	3:1
baseline	12.0	12.4	12.8
+ copied	**13.0**	**13.6**	**13.8**

Table 10: EN→TR translation performance with different amounts of monolingual data.

5.5.5 Amount of Monolingual Data

Finally, we study the effectiveness of the copied monolingual corpus when the amount of monolingual data is varied. We consider three different monolingual corpus sizes: the same size as the parallel data (200k sentences; *1:1*), twice the size of the parallel data (400k sentences; *2:1*), and three times the size of the parallel data (600k sentences; *3:1*). We compare these different sizes for the baseline (parallel and back-translated data) and the + *copied* systems (parallel, back-translated, and copied data, where the back-translated and copied data are identical on the target side). Each smaller monolingual corpus is a subset of the larger monolingual corpora. Note that we do not oversample the parallel data to balance the different data sources.

Table 10 displays the results when different amounts of monolingual data are used. Note that we vary the amount of back-translated data in the baseline and of back-translated and copied data in the + *copied* system. For both the baseline and + *copied*, adding more monolingual data consistently yields small improvements (0.2-0.6 BLEU). In addition, the + *copied* system performs about 1.0 BLEU better than the baseline regardless of the amount of monolingual data. This is surprising since we do not oversample the parallel data at all. For the *2:1* and *3:1* cases, the systems see far less parallel than synthetic data, but the overall translation performances still improve.

6 Discussion

Our proposed method of using a copied target-side monolingual corpus to augment training data for NMT proved to be beneficial for EN↔TR and EN↔RO translation, resulting in improvements of up to 1.2 BLEU over a strong baseline. We showed that our method stacks with the previously proposed back-translation method of Sennrich et al. (2016b) for these language pairs. For EN↔DE, however, there was no significant difference between systems trained with the copied corpus and those trained without it. There was much more parallel training data for EN↔DE than for EN↔RO (nearly 10 times as much) and EN↔TR (about 28 times as much), so it is possible that the gains that would have come from the copied corpus were already achieved with the parallel data. Overall, the copied monolingual corpus either helped or was indifferent, so training with this corpus is not risky. In addition, it does not require any more monolingual data besides what is used for back-translation.

We initially assumed that the copied monolingual corpus was helping to improve the fluency of the target outputs. However, further study of the outputs did not necessarily support this assumption, as noted in section 5.3. Our method did improve accuracy when copying proper nouns and other words that are identical in the source and target languages; this is at least part of the explanation for the increases in BLEU score when using the copied corpus.

Subsequent experiments revealed various factors that influenced the effectiveness of the copied monolingual corpus. An unexpected finding was that doubling and tripling the size of the monolingual corpus (whether used as copied or back-translated data) resulted in small improvements (0.2-0.6 BLEU). We had originally thought that using much more monolingual than parallel data would result in a worse performance, since the system would see true parallel data less often than copied or back-translated data, but this did not turn out to be the case. Not having to limit the amount of monolingual data based on the availability of parallel data is an advantage for language pairs with much more monolingual than parallel data.

7 Conclusion

In this paper, we introduced a method for improving neural machine translation using monolingual data, particularly for low-resource scenarios. Augmenting the training data with monolingual data in which the source side is a copy of the target side proved to be an effective way of improving EN↔TR and EN↔RO translation, while not damaging EN↔DE (high-resource) translation. This technique could be used in combination with back-translation or with parallel data only. In addition, using much more monolingual than parallel data did not hinder performance, which is beneficial for the common case where a large amount of monolingual data is available but the language pair has little parallel data.

In the future, we plan on studying the effects of the quality of the monolingual data, since our copied corpus technique might in principle pose the risk of adding noise to the NMT system. In particular, we would like to apply a data selection method when creating the monolingual corpus, as the similarity of the monolingual and parallel data has been shown to have an effect on NMT (Cheng et al., 2016). We also hope to find an effective way of adding source monolingual training data. Finally, it would be interesting to do a manual evaluation of our method to confirm the BLEU and perplexity findings reported in sections 5.2 and 5.3.

Acknowledgments

This work was conducted within the scope of the Horizon 2020 Innovation Action *Health in My Language*, which has received funding from the European Union's Horizon 2020 research and innovation programme under grant agreement No 644402. This work was partially funded by the Amazon Academic Research Awards program. We used Azure credits donated by Microsoft to The Alan Turing Institute. This work was supported by The Alan Turing Institute under the EPSRC grant EP/N510129/1.

References

Dzmitry Bahdanau, Kyunghyun Cho, and Yoshua Bengio. 2015. Neural machine translation by jointly learning to align and translate. In *3rd International Conference on Learning Representations*.

Ondřej Bojar, Rajen Chatterjee, Christian Federmann, Yvette Graham, Barry Haddow, Matthias Huck, Antonio Jimeno Yepes, Philipp Koehn, Varvara Logacheva, Christof Monz, Matteo Negri, Aurélie Névéol, Mariana Neves, Martin Popel, Matt Post, Raphael Rubino, Carolina Scarton, Lucia Specia, Marco Turchi, Karin Verspoor, and Marcos Zampieri. 2016. Findings of the 2016 Conference on Machine Translation. In *Proceedings of the First Conference on Machine Translation*, pages 131–198. Association for Computational Linguistics.

Yong Cheng, Wei Xu, Zhongjun He, Wei He, Hua Wu, Maosong Sun, and Yang Liu. 2016. Semi-supervised learning for neural machine translation. In *Proceedings of the 54th Annual Meeting of the ACL*, pages 1965–1974. Association for Computational Linguistics.

Kyunghyun Cho, Bart Van Merriënboer, Caglar Gulcehre, Dzmitry Bahdanau, Fethi Bougares, Holger Schwenk, and Yoshua Bengio. 2014. Learning phrase representations using RNN encoder-decoder

for statistical machine translation. In *Proceedings of the 2014 Conference on Empirical Methods in Natural Language Processing*, pages 1724–1734. Association for Computational Linguistics.

Yarin Gal and Zoubin Ghahramani. 2016. A theoretically grounded application of dropout in recurrent neural networks. In *Advances in Neural Information Processing Systems 29*.

Caglar Gulcehre, Orhan Firat, Kelvin Xu, Kyunghyun Cho, Loïc Barrault, Huei-Chi Lin, Fethi Bougares, Holger Schwenk, and Yoshua Bengio. 2015. On using monolingual corpora in neural machine translation. *arXiv preprint arXiv:1503.03535*.

Di He, Yingce Xia, Tao Qin, Liwei Wang, Nenghai Yu, Tieyan Liu, and Wei-Ying Ma. 2016. Dual learning for machine translation. In *Advances in Neural Information Processing Systems 29*.

Kenneth Heafield. 2011. KenLM: faster and smaller language model queries. In *Proceedings of the Sixth Workshop on Statistical Machine Translation*, pages 187–197. Association for Computational Linguistics.

Sébastien Jean, Orhan Firat, Kyunghyun Cho, Roland Memisevic, and Yoshua Bengio. 2015. Montreal neural machine translation systems for WMT15. In *Proceedings of the Tenth Workshop on Statistical Machine Translation*, pages 134–140. Association for Computational Linguistics.

Melvin Johnson, Mike Schuster, Quoc V Le, Maxim Krikun, Yonghui Wu, Zhifeng Chen, Nikhil Thorat, Fernanda Viégas, Martin Wattenberg, Greg Corrado, Macduff Hughes, and Jeffrey Dean. 2016. Google's multilingual neural machine translation system: Enabling zero-shot translation. *arXiv preprint arXiv:1611.04558*.

Nal Kalchbrenner and Phil Blunsom. 2013. Recurrent continuous translation models. In *Proceedings of the 2013 Conference on Empirical Methods in Natural Language Processing*, pages 1700–1709. Association for Computational Linguistics.

Diederik Kingma and Jimmy Ba. 2015. Adam: A method for stochastic optimization. In *3rd International Conference on Learning Representations*.

Minh Thang Luong, Quoc V Le, Ilya Sutskever, Oriol Vinyals, and Lukasz Kaiser. 2016. Multi-task sequence to sequence learning. In *4th International Conference on Learning Representations*.

Kishore Papineni, Salim Roukos, Todd Ward, and Wei-Jing Zhu. 2002. BLEU: a method for automatic evaluation of machine translation. In *Proceedings of the 40th Annual Meeting of the ACL*, pages 311–318. Association for Computational Linguistics.

Rico Sennrich, Orhan Firat, Kyunghyun Cho, Alexandra Birch, Barry Haddow, Julian Hitschler, Marcin

Junczys-Dowmunt, Samuel Läubli, Antonio Valerio Miceli Barone, Jozef Mokry, and Maria Nadejde. 2017. Nematus: a toolkit for neural machine translation. In *Proceedings of the EACL 2017 Software Demonstrations*, pages 65–68. Association for Computational Linguistics.

Rico Sennrich, Barry Haddow, and Alexandra Birch. 2016a. Edinburgh neural machine translation systems for WMT 16. In *Proceedings of the First Conference on Machine Translation*, pages 371–376. Association for Computational Linguistics.

Rico Sennrich, Barry Haddow, and Alexandra Birch. 2016b. Improving neural machine translation models with monolingual data. In *Proceedings of NAACL-HLT*, pages 86–96. Association for Computational Linguistics.

Rico Sennrich, Barry Haddow, and Alexandra Birch. 2016c. Neural machine translation of rare words with subword units. In *Proceedings of the 54th Annual Meeting of the ACL*, pages 1715–1725. Association for Computational Linguistics.

Ilya Sutskever, Oriol Vinyals, and Quoc V Le. 2014. Sequence to sequence learning with neural networks. In *Advances in Neural Information Processing Systems 27*.

Jiajun Zhang and Chengqing Zong. 2016. Exploiting source-side monolingual data in neural machine translation. In *Proceedings of the 2016 Conference on Empirical Methods in Natural Language Processing*, pages 1535–1545. Association for Computational Linguistics.

Guiding Neural Machine Translation Decoding with External Knowledge

Rajen Chatterjee[1,2], Matteo Negri[2], Marco Turchi[2],
Marcello Federico[2], Lucia Specia[3], and Frédéric Blain[3]

[1]University of Trento, Trento, Italy
[2]Fondazione Bruno Kessler, Trento, Italy
[3]University of Sheffield, Sheffield, UK
{chatterjee,negri,turchi,federico}@fbk.eu
{l.specia,f.blain}@sheffield.ac.uk

Abstract

Differently from the phrase-based paradigm, neural machine translation (NMT) operates on word and sentence representations in a continuous space. This makes the decoding process not only more difficult to interpret, but also harder to influence with external knowledge. For the latter problem, effective solutions like the XML-markup used by phrase-based models to inject fixed translation options as constraints at decoding time are not yet available. We propose a "guide" mechanism that enhances an existing NMT decoder with the ability to prioritize and adequately handle translation options presented in the form of XML annotations of source words. Positive results obtained in two different translation tasks indicate the effectiveness of our approach.

1 Introduction

The need to enforce fixed translations of certain source words is a well known problem in machine translation (MT). For instance, this is an issue in application scenarios in which the translation process has to comply with specific terminology and/or style guides. In such situations it is generally necessary to consider external resources to guide the decoder in order to ensure consistency or meet other specific requirements. Terminology lists, which provide the decoder with the expected translations of specific words or phrases, are a typical example of external knowledge used to guide the process to meet such constraints. Meeting predefined constraints, however, does not represent the only case in which an external guidance can support decoding. In ensemble MT architectures, for example, the output of a translation system specialised in handling specific phenomena (*e.g.* numbers or dates) can be used to guide another decoder without changing its underlying model.

Phrase-based statistical MT (PBSMT), which explicitly manipulates symbolic representations of the basic constituents (phrases) in the source and target languages, provides solutions to address these needs. For instance, the XML markup implemented in the Moses toolkit (Koehn et al., 2007) allows one to supply the expected translations to the decoder in the form of tags surrounding the corresponding source phrases.

To our knowledge, solutions to this problem are not yet available for neural machine translation (NMT), which has recently emerged as the dominant approach for MT. In particular, no work has been done to address the needs of the translation industry, in which language service providers usually receive translation requests that must be satisfied in short time, often taking into account external knowledge that defines specific customers' constraints. In this case, the time-consuming retraining routines of NMT are not viable, thus making methods to inject external knowledge without retraining of paramount importance.

To address this gap, we investigate problems arising from the fact that NMT operates on implicit word and sentence representations in a continuous space, which makes influencing the process with external knowledge more complex. In particular, we attempt to answer the following questions: *i)* How to enforce the presence of a given translation recommendation in the decoder's output? *ii)* How to place these word(s) in the right position? *iii)* How to guide the translation of out-of-vocabulary terms?

Our solution extends an existing NMT decoder (Sennrich et al., 2016a) by introducing the possibility to guide the translation process with constraints provided as XML annotations of the

Proceedings of the Conference on Machine Translation (WMT), Volume 1: Research Papers, pages 157–168
Copenhagen, Denmark, September 7–11, 2017. ©2017 Association for Computational Linguistics

source words with the corresponding translation options. The guidance mechanism supervises the process, generating the final output with the expected translations, in the right place, including cases of external words unknown to the model.

To test our approach, we experiment in two scenarios that pose different challenges to NMT. The first one is a translation task in which source sentences contain XML-annotated domain-specific terms. The presence of few annotated terms poses fewer constraints to the decoder in generating the output sentence. The second scenario is an automatic post-editing (APE) task, in which the NMT model is trained to translate "monolingually" from draft machine-translated sentences into human-quality post-edits. The external guidance is provided by word-level quality judgements (Blatz et al., 2004) indicating the "good" words in the machine-translated sentence that should be kept in the final APE output. In this case, the large number of "good" words already present in the original MT output poses more constraints to the decoding process. In both scenarios, our guidance mechanism achieves significant performance gains over the original NMT decoder.

2   Related Work

In PBSMT, the injection of external knowledge in the decoder is usually handled with the so-called XML markup, a technique used to guide the decoder by supplying the desired translation for some of the source phrases. The supplied translation choice can be injected in the output by using different strategies, all rather straightforward. Examples include manipulating the phrase table by either replacing entries that cover the specific source phrase, or adding the alternative phrase translations to it, so that they are in competition. This problem has only recently started to be explored in NMT and, in most of the cases, the proposed solutions integrate external knowledge at training stage. Time-consuming training routines, however, limit the suitability of this strategy for applications requiring real-time translations. In Gulcehre et al. (2015), monolingual data is used to train a neural language model that is integrated in the NMT decoder by concatenating their hidden states. In Arthur et al. (2016), the probability of the next target word in the NMT decoder is biased by using lexicon probabilities computed from a bilingual lexicon. When the external knowledge is

in the form of linguistic information, such as POS tags or lemmas, Sennrich and Haddow (2016) propose to compute separate embedding vectors for each linguistic information and then concatenate them, without altering the decoder. Other solutions exploit the strengths of PBSMT systems to improve NMT by pre-translating the source sentence. In Niehues et al. (2016), the NMT model is fed with a concatenation of the source and its PBSMT translation. Some of these solutions lead to improvements in performance, but they all require time-intensive training of the NMT models to use an enriched input representation or to optimize the parameters of the model. (Stahlberg et al., 2016) proposed an approach which can be used at decoding time. A hierarchical PBSMT system is used to generate the translation lattices, which are then re-scored by the NMT decoder. During decoding, the NMT posterior probabilities are adjusted using the posterior scores computed by the hierarchical model. However, by representing the additional information as a translation lattice, this approach does not allow the use of external knowledge in the form of bilingual terms or quality judgements as we do in §5 and §6. A different technique is post-processing the translated sentences. Jean et al. (2015) and Luong and Manning (2015) replace the unknown words either with the most likely aligned source word or with the translation determined by another word alignment model.

The closest approach to ours is the one by (Hokamp and Liu, 2017). They explore all the possible constraints (or translation options) at each time step making sure not to generate a constraint that have already been generated in the previous timestep. Their approach generates all the constraints in the final output, thus implicitly it assumes that only one translation options is provided as constraint for a given source word/phrase. However, in a more realistic scenario (*e.g.* in presence of a termbase or when the target language is more inflected than the source language), a source word can have multiple translation options from which the decoder should decide the best one on-the-fly depending on the source context. Our approach can handle both scenarios thus being more suitable in practice. In this paper we consider the possibility of having multiple translation options for a single word. For this reason, we can not compare the guided decoder against the approach proposed in (Hokamp and Liu, 2017). In addition to the application in MT to customize NMT output to meet customer-specific needs (Task 1), our approach can also be used to add quality judgements within NMT at decoding time (Task 2).

3   NMT decoding

In this section we first provide a general introduction to NMT as it is currently commonly implemented in systems like the one used in our experiments. Then, we discuss its limitations with respect to our problem: guiding decoding with external knowledge.

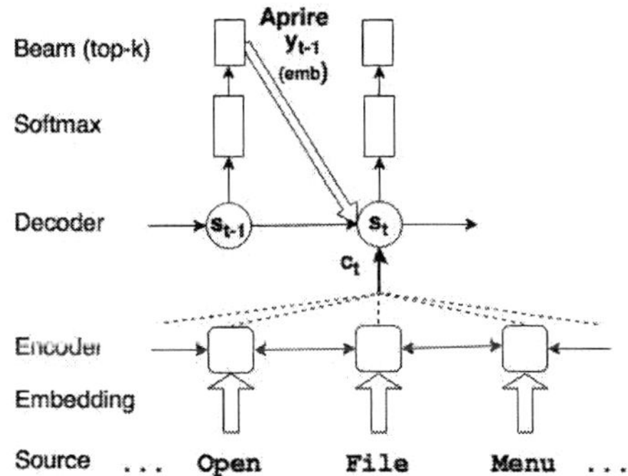

Figure 1: Overview of NMT decoding.

As shown in Figure 1, NMT starts by mapping all words of the source sentence into a continuous space, through an embedding layer. The word embeddings are processed by a bidirectional recurrent layer, implemented with gated recurrent units (GRUs) (Cho et al., 2014), which encodes each source word together with its left and right context in a sequence of hidden states. Once all the hidden states of the encoder are computed, the decoder starts generating the target string one word at the time. The decoder layer is implemented as a unidirectional GRU-based RNN.[1] The decoder hidden state at time t (s_t) is recursively updated via the previous hidden state (s_{t-1}), the embedding of the previously generated target word (y_{t-1}), and the input context (c_t). The context is generated as a convex combination of the encoder hidden states, whose weights ($\alpha_{t,j}$) are computed by a so-called attention model (Bahdanau et al., 2014). The attention model weights $\alpha_{t,j}$ are computed with a feed-forward neural network and can be interpreted as probability distributions over the

source positions ($j = 1, \ldots, m$).

Finally, the decoder linearly combines the embedding of y_{t-1}, s_t, and c_t and applies a *softmax* transformation to compute a language model over the target vocabulary which, through s_t, is actually conditioned on all the previous target words $y_0, \ldots, y_{t-1}$ (where y_0 is a conventional sentence delimiter symbol). This language model is used to sample the new target word y_t, which is fed back to the decoder layer to continue the process of generating target words until the sentence delimiter word is produced. When a beam search strategy is employed, the most probable K target words ($y_{t,i}$ $i = 1, \ldots, K$) are sampled instead, and used as alternative hypotheses for the next decoding step. The process does not diverge because only K best target words are again selected from the resulting K target language model distributions. Through simple bookkeeping, the best target word sequence is computed that maximises the product of all the corresponding language model scores.

In this NMT workflow, there is no easy way to integrate partial translations provided by an external resource, such as a bilingual dictionary. Differently from a PBSMT decoder that is aware of which source phrase is translated at each step, the NMT decoder does not have this information. The only indirect connection between the target word y_t generated at time t and the corresponding source positions (words) is represented by the attention model weights $\alpha_{t,j}$, which are used to create the context vector c_t from the encoder hidden states. Moreover, differently from decoding in PBSMT, the NMT architecture described above does not apply any coverage constraint on the source positions. Thus, there is no guarantee that the output generated by NMT covers (*i.e.* translates) each source word exactly once.

4   Guided NMT decoding

To overcome the aforementioned problems, we present a novel technique called "guided decoding" that forces the decoder to generate particular translations given as external knowledge. Translation hints are provided in the form of annotations of individual source words in the input text. Our decoder accepts input in an XML format similar to the one adopted in the Moses toolkit,[2] which contains the source sentence and its annotations

---

[1] The implementation in Nematus (Sennrich et al., 2016a) we are building on deploys two GRUs, but this variation does not play any important role here.

[2] goo.gl/ObB6QL

as shown below (for English-German):

<seg id="1702"> enter the <n transla-tion="Benutzer"> user</n> name and password </seg>

The annotations are placed in a *"n"* tag that has the attribute *"translation"* to hold the translation recommendation for the corresponding source word. The decoder parses the XML input and creates two parallel input streams: one that contains source words and another that contains the corresponding suggestions or the empty string. Then, the overall process is carried out similarly to the previously described NMT system but with a different interaction between the beam search and the network. In particular, after a new beam of K-top target words is generated, the "guide" mechanism checks the K hypotheses and their attention model weights to possibly influence the beam search with the external suggestions. This is done by: *i)* prioritizing the hypotheses that can generate the suggestions provided (§4.1); *ii)* performing look-ahead steps with the beam search to evaluate the current hypothesis (§4.2) and *iii)* applying different strategies to manage out-of-vocabulary (OOV) terms (§4.3).

4.1   Forcing the presence of a given term

In PBSMT, XML markups can be easily handled: when looking for translation options for each source phrase, the decoder checks both the external suggestions and the options in the phrase table. However, the NMT process is too complex to follow a similar approach. When generating a target word, NMT assumes a continuous representation of the whole source sentence through a context vector. In particular: *i)* all the source words can in principle contribute to generate a target word, and *ii)* different hypotheses may focus on different source words in the same decoding step. Thus, it is not guaranteed that the output at a given time step is solely dependent on a particular source word and, in turn, it is not clear how the external suggestions could be used. We tackle this issue by using the probability distribution of the source positions obtained from the attention model used to create the context vector. At each step of the beam search, for each of the K generated target words we look for the most probable source position provided by the attention model. If the corresponding source word has a suggestion, then we replace the target word by the given suggestion and update the

score of the hypotheses; otherwise, we keep the original target word.

4.2   Placing the term in the right position

The guiding mechanism in §4.1 allows the decoder to generate a given translation by replacing options inside the beam. However, the method does not consider cases in which one source word position is involved in the generation of multiple target words. This may happen when the decoder has its attention on a particular source word more than once (*e.g.* an article and a noun in the target referring to the same noun in the source). In these situations, it could happen that valid translation options are erroneously replaced and the external suggestion is reproduced multiple times in the output. For instance, in Figure 2, the source word *"application"* which the attention model refers to for both *"die"* and *"Anwendung"* would be translated as *"Anwendung Anwendung"*.

To address this problem and to make our approach more robust to possible attention model nuances, we relax the hard replacement of a translation option if it differs from the provided suggestion. In particular, if the conditions for a replacement occur, we also check if the beam search would nevertheless generate the suggestion from the current word, within a small number of steps. If this happens, we keep the current word in place since we know that the actual suggestion will be generated in the short future. If the suggestion is not reachable, then we force the replacement.

Algorithm 1 illustrates the modified beam search process that generates the K best hypotheses for the next target word. Starting from the beam at time $t-1$, a new state S_t is computed and returned. The state contains the best K target words (y_t), their corresponding decoder hidden states (s_t), cumulative language model scores (q_t), backtracking indexes to the parent entries in the previous state (b_t), and source indexes having the largest attention weight (α_t). In addition, the modified beam search algorithm maintains, for each of the K entries, the list of suggestions (L_t) that have been generated within that hypothesis so far. The algorithm accesses the global variable $\tilde{y}[j]$, which contains for each source position j either a provided target word suggestion or the empty word $\emptyset$. The algorithm proceeds by computing the normal beam search step (line 14) and initializing the lists of generated suggestions with the list of the

Algorithm 1 Guided Beam Search Step

```
 1:  ▷ K: size of beam
 2:  ▷ L_t: K lists of generated suggestions
 3:  ▷ N: look-ahead step to check reachability
 4:  ▷ S_t = [y_t, s_t, q_t, b_t, α_t]: state information
 5:  ▷ y_t: K target words
 6:  ▷ s_t: K decoder layer hidden states
 7:  ▷ q_t: K cumulative language model scores
 8:  ▷ b_t: K backtracking indexes
 9:  ▷ α_t: K highest-attention-indexes
10:  ▷ Global variable with suggestions:
11:  ▷   ỹ[j]: target word for source position j
12:  procedure GUIDEDBEAMSEARCH(K,L_{t-1},N,S_{t-1})
13:      ▷ Perform a step of beam search
14:      S_t := BeamSearchStep(S_{t-1})
15:      ▷ Copy generated suggestions from parent
16:      L_t := UpdateLists(b_t, L_{t-1})
17:      ▷ for each entry of the beam
18:      for k ∈ {1,...,K} do
19:          ▷ Check suggestion for source word α_{t,k}
20:          if ỹ[α_{t,k}] ≠ ∅ ∧ α_{t,k} ∉ L_{t,k} then
21:              ỹ := ỹ[α_{t,k}]
22:              if y_{t,k} ≠ ỹ then
23:                  ▷ if ỹ is not generated by N steps
24:                  if !Reachable(S_t, ỹ, k, N) then
25:                      ▷ Force suggestion in beam
26:                      y_{t,k} = ỹ;
27:                      ▷ Update suggestion list
28:                      Add(α_{t,k}, L_{t,k})
29:                  end if
30:              else
31:                  ▷ Suggestion is generated
32:                  Add(α_{t,k}, L_{t,k})
33:              end if
34:          end if
35:      end for
36:      return (L_t, S_t)
37:  end procedure
```

corresponding parents (line 16) that are accessible through the backtracking indexes. The main loop (line 18) checks, for each beam entry, the source position that received the highest weight by the corresponding attention model. If this source position ($\alpha_{t'k}$) corresponds to a non-empty suggestion and if the suggestion has not been generated by one of the predecessors of this entry, then the algorithm decides whether or not this suggestion ($\tilde{y}$) has to be forced in the beam. In particular, there are two cases for which action is taken. First, if the suggestion is different from the word in the beam (line 22) and the suggestion will not be generated by one of its next N successors, then the suggestion will replace the current word (line 26). The list of generated suggestions by this hypothesis is updated accordingly. Second, if the suggestion is equal to the word in the beam (line 30), then the suggestion has been generated directly by the beam search and the corresponding list is updated (line 32). The algorithm finally returns the

updated lists of generated suggestions and the updated beam search state.

This algorithm can generate both continuous and discontinuous target phrases:

Continuous phrases are those in which consecutive target words are pointed by the same source word. The phrase pair (*"application"*, *"die Anwendung"*) in Figure 2 falls in this category. With a look-ahead window set to 1 in the algorithm, the decoder will be able to generate bigram phrases (such as *"die Anwendung"*). With larger look-ahead windows, longer phrases can be generated.

Discontinuous phrases are those in which target words pointed by the same source word are intermingled with other words for which the attention points elsewhere. The phrase pair (*"quit"*, *"haben verlassen"*) in Figure 2 falls in this category. In these cases, the guided beam search should look at least two steps in the future. The time step value maps the distance (number of words) between the left and right sub-parts of the target phrase. In our example, the distance is 4 (*i.e.* 4 steps are needed to reach *"verlassen"* from *"haben"*) so, if we set the look-ahead window to 4, the decoder can generate the annotation *"verlassen"* after emitting *"haben"*.

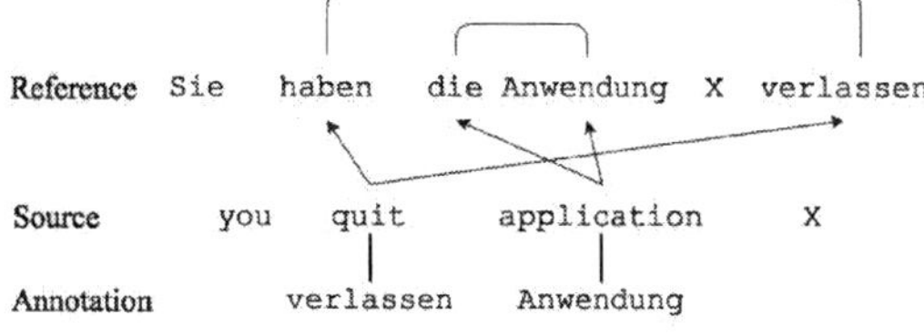

Figure 2: An example showing continuous (*"die Anwendung"*) and discontinuous (*"haben...verlassen"*) target phrases.

4.3 Guiding the translation of OOV terms

The last problem is dealing with suggestions that are OOV words. In NMT, it is common practice to replace OOV words by the unknown token (UNK) and use its corresponding embedding. The questions are: *i)* if an OOV suggestion is given by the external resource, should the modified beam search force it into the beam?, and *ii)* which target word embedding should be used in the next step? To answer these questions, we implemented a lookup table to store all the OOV suggestions along with their unique *id* before initializing the decoder. These *id*s are used for OOV suggestions by the beam search instead of the *id* associated by default to the UNK token. To get the embeddings for OOV suggestions, we tested different strategies, which are discussed in §5.2 and §6.2.

5 Task 1: Machine Translation

In our first experiment, we use guided decoding in a standard MT setting. Our goal is to improve MT performance by exploiting prior knowledge supplied as translation recommendations for domain-specific terms. The suggested terms (*i.e.* the constraints posed to the decoder) are usually few, thus leaving a large degree of freedom to the NMT decoder while generating the output.

5.1 Experimental setting

NMT models. We evaluate guided decoding in its ability to improve the performance of two different English to German NMT models, both obtained with the Nematus toolkit (Sennrich et al., 2016a). The first system operates at word level and it is trained by using part of the JRC-Acquis corpus (Steinberger et al., 2006), Europarl (Koehn, 2005) and OpenSubtitles2013 (Tiedemann, 2009), which results in at total of about 1.8M parallel sentence pairs. The size of the vocabulary, word embedding, and hidden units is respectively set to 40K, 600, and 600, and parameters are optimised with Adagrad (Duchi et al., 2011) using a learning rate of 0.01. The batch size is set to 100, and the model is trained for 300K updates ($\sim$17 epochs). At test stage, the word-level system is supplied with terminology lists containing term recommendations at the level of granularity of full words. The second system is trained on sub-word units by using the Byte-Pair Encoding (BPE) technique (Gage, 1994), which has been proposed by Sennrich et al. (2016b) as a successful way to reduce the OOV rate. The system used in our evaluation is the pre-trained model built for the best English-German submission (Sennrich et al., 2016a) at the News Translation task at WMT'16 (Bojar et al., 2016). At test stage, it is supplied with terminology lists containing term recommendations in BPE format. In all the experiments we use a default beam size of 12.

Test data. We experiment with two domain-specific English-German test sets containing 850 segments each: *i)* a subset of the EMEA corpus

(Tiedemann, 2009) for the medical domain and *ii)* an information technology corpus extracted from software manuals (Federico et al., 2014). Word-level term lists for both domains are obtained by processing the test data with the "Terminology as a Service" platform,[3] a cloud-based system that supports automatic bilingual term extraction from user uploaded documents. The BPE-level version of each word-level term list is obtained as follows. First, each entry is segmented with the BPE rules available along with the pre-trained Nematus model. Then, the segmented entries are aligned by running MGiza++ (Gao and Vogel, 2008) trained on the BPE-level WMT'16 training data. Finally, all the one-to-one aligned sub-units are extracted to form the sub-word level bilingual term dictionaries. The word and sub-word bilingual dictionaries are used to annotate the respective test sets. This results in the annotation of $\sim$5K words and $\sim$7.5K sub-words. The term rate (#Term/#Tokens) in the two test sets is respectively 18.9% (IT: 21.5% and Medical: 17.7%) and 20.1% (IT: 23.2% and Medical: 18.0%).

5.2 Results and discussion

Our results on the MT task are reported in Table 1, which shows system performance on the concatenation of the test sets from the two target domains. Performance is measured with BLEU (Papineni et al., 2002), and statistical significance is computed with bootstrap resampling (Koehn, 2004). The result of the word-level baseline system is computed after post-processing its output following the approach of Jean et al. (2015), which was customized to our scenario. This method (see §2) is driven by the attention model to replace the UNK tokens in the output with their corresponding recommendation supplied as external knowledge. This post-processing strategy is not used for the BPE-level baseline because it implicitly addresses the problem of OOVs.

We evaluate our guided decoder incrementally, by adding one at a time the mechanisms described in §4. In the discussion, we do not compare the performance of BPE-based and word-based models because the former were trained and optimized with larger training data for the news translation task at WMT'16. Results, instead, will be discussed in terms of the contribution yield by each mechanism on top of previous best results.

---

[3] `http://www.taas-project.eu`

The baseline decoder (`Baseline`) performs better than our basic guided decoder (`GDec_base`), which considers translation recommendations only in the case of known terms as described in §4.1. This indicates that the problem of constraining the NMT output using a bilingual dictionary can not be addressed by simply emitting the recommendations whenever the corresponding source term has the highest attention.

	words || BPE
`Baseline`	22.62 || 25.64
`GDec_base`	21.68 || 25.25
`GDec_base+oov`	23.04† || 25.66
`GDec_base+oov+reach`	**25.51†** || **28.42†**

Table 1: BLEU results of different decoders on the MT task ("†" indicates statistically significant differences wrt. `Baseline` with p<0.05).

`GDec_base+oov` extends `GDec_base` with the mechanism to handle OOV annotations as described in §4.3. In order to generate word embeddings for OOV terms, we tested several strategies: *i)* using the embedding of the unknown word, *ii)* using the embedding of the best target word in the beam, *iii)* using the embedding of the previous word (y_{t-1}), and *iv)* using the average of the embeddings of all the previous words ($y_{1,..,t-1}$). The best results are obtained when using the embedding of the unknown word which, on further investigation, resulted to be close to rare words in terms of cosine similarity. As of now, this proximity to rare words suggests that it can model OOVs better than the other strategies, but deeper investigations on this aspect are certainly an interesting topic for future analysis. The ability to handle OOVs yields statistically significant improvements (+0.4 BLEU) over the baseline for the word-based model. In contrast, since the BPE-based systems can implicitly mitigate the OOV problem (as discussed in §5.1), our strategy results in marginal improvements over the BPE baseline.

Finally, `GDec_base+oov+reach` combines OOV handling with the method to avoid repetitions and to manage the insertion positions described in §4.2. Since it uses a look-ahead (LA) hyper-parameter in order to validate the translation options, we experimented with different values ranging from 1 to 9. By varying the LA window, performance increases both for the word-level and the BPE-level models up to the highest scores achieved with LA=6. Increasing LA beyond 6 does not yield further gains. Using LA=1 performs slightly worse (-0.4 BLEU) than LA=6, indicating that this mechanism is already effective even at small values (*i.e.* on our data, a large number of problematic cases involve continuous phrases like the example in Figure 2). This full-fledged guided decoder achieves a statistically significant improvement of $\sim$3 BLEU points over both word-level and BPE-level baselines. A per-domain results' analysis shows similar gains over the `Baseline` for word-based (IT: +4.3, Medical: +2.6) and for BPE-based NMT (IT: +3.9, Medical: +2.0).

To better understand the behaviour of our decoder, we further analysed its output. First, the percentage of translation recommendations produced in the MT output ($\frac{\#TermsInTranslation}{\#AnnotatedTerms}$) was computed both for the `Baseline`, and for the `GDec_base+oov+reach` decoders. As expected, the `Baseline` achieves lower results (BPE-level: 70.81%, Word-level: 65.38%) compared to the full-fledged `GDec_base+oov+reach` (BPE-level: 94.08%, Word-level: 87.19%). Indeed, as a generic NMT system, it is not able to properly handle domain-specific terms (the BPE representation helps to reduce OOVs but does not guarantee correct realizations in the target language). Second, a preliminary error analysis was carried out by looking at the word alignments returned by the attention model. This revealed that the majority of the errors produced by our decoder can be found in sentences in which the annotated source words never receive the highest attention, thus making the corresponding recommendations unreachable.

Manual Analysis: We manually analyzed some samples to understand the effect of using GDec in the translation task. We observe that when fed with a list of translation options in the form of xml annotations, GDec is able to generate the correct terms. Moreover, these local improvements also help GDec to fix other parts of the translation. Examples illustrating these effects are provided in Table 2. Example 1 shows that the baseline system (Base) translates the word "browse" in the source sentence (Src) to "stöbern" (En: "rummage around") but the post-editors prefers to use in the reference "durchsuche" (En: "search") which is then generated by the GDec. Example 2 illustrates a case where post-editors prefer to preserve the terms in the source language rather than translating them. The baseline system translates "plastics labs" to "Kunststofflabore" (En: "Plastic laboratories"), however, it should be preserved *as-is* in the final output as done by GDec. Another interesting example highlighting the effect of choosing a correct term on the overall translation quality is provided in example 3. The term "zugewiesen" translation of the source word "assigned" helps GDec to correct other parts of the final translation, like generating "es gibt keine" (En: "There is no") which is otherwise missing in the baseline translation.

6 Task 2: Automatic Post-Editing

In our second experiment, we apply guided decoding in an automatic post-editing task. The goal of automatic post-editing (APE) is to correct errors in an MT-ed text. The problem is typically approached as a "monolingual translation" task, in which models are trained on parallel corpora containing (*MT_output*, *MT_post-edit*) pairs, with MT post-edits coming from humans (Simard et al., 2007; Chatterjee et al., 2015b, 2017). In their attempt to translate the entire input sentence, APE systems usually tend to over-correct the source words, *i.e.* to use all applicable correction options. This can happen even when the input is correct, often resulting in text deterioration (Bojar et al., 2015). To cope with this problem, neural-based APE decoders would benefit from external knowledge indicating words in the input which are correct and thus should not be modified during decoding. For that we propose to use word-level binary quality estimation labels (Blatz et al., 2004; de Souza et al., 2014) to annotate the "good" words that should be kept. Due to the relatively high quality of the MT outputs (62.11 BLEU), source sentences will usually contain many terms annotated as "good". This, compared to the MT task, poses more constraints on the decoder.

6.1 Experimental setting

NMT models. We use the pre-trained model built for the best English-German submission (Junczys-Dowmunt and Grundkiewicz, 2016) at the WMT'16 APE task. This available model was trained with Nematus over a data set of ~4M back-translated pairs, and then adapted to the task-specific data segmented using the BPE technique.

Test data. In this experiment, we use the English-German data released at the WMT'16 APE shared task (Bojar et al., 2016). To annotate the test set, instead of relying on automatic quality, predictions, we exploit oracle labels indicating "good" words (to be kept in the output) and "bad" words (to be replaced by the decoder). To this aim, we first aligned each MT output with the corresponding human post-edit using TER (Snover et al., 2006). Then, each MT word that was aligned with itself in the post-edit was annotated as "good". This resulted in a high number of "good" labels (on average, 79.4% of the sentence terms). It is worth noting that, by construction, the resulting quality labels are "gold" annotations that current word-level quality estimation systems can only approximate. These make them suitable for our testing purposes, as they allow us to avoid the noise introduced by sub-optimal predictors. The BPE-level version of the test set is obtained by projecting the word-level QE tags into the sub-words (all sub-words of a word receive the original word tag). If a sub-word was labelled as "good", then we annotate it with itself to indicate that the decoder must generate the sub-word in the output.

6.2 Results and discussion

Our results on the APE task are reported in Table 3. Performance is measured with the two WMT'16 APE task metrics, namely TER and BLEU (Bojar et al., 2016). The statistical significance for BLEU is computed using paired bootstrap resampling, while for TER we use stratified approximate randomization (Yeh, 2000).

Our first baseline (Base-MT), the same used at WMT, corresponds to the original MT output left untouched. Our second baseline (Base-APE) is a neural APE system that was trained on (*MT_output*, *MT_post-edit*) pairs but ignores the information from the QE annotations. Base-APE improves the Base-MT up to 3.14 BLEU points.

Similar to §5.2, the evaluation of our guided decoder is performed incrementally. GDec_base forces the "good" words in the automatic translation to appear in the output according to the mechanism described in §4.1. This basic guidance mechanism yields only marginal improvements over the Base-MT and is far behind the Base-APE. This can be explained by the large number of constraints (*i.e.* "good" words to be

	Src: <n translation="durchsuchen‖Durchsuchen"> browse </n> all products

Src: <n translation="durchsuchen‖Durchsuchen"> browse </n> all products
Base: stöbern alle Produkte
GDec: durchsuchen Sie alle Produkte
Ref: durchsuchen Sie alle Produkte

Src: <n translation="produkt‖Produkt"> Product </n> 4 - <n translation="plastics‖Plastics"> Plastics </n> <n translation="labs‖Labs"> Labs </n>
Base: Produkt 4 - Kunststofflabore
GDec: Produkt 4 - Plastics Labs
Ref: Produkt 4 - Plastics Labs

Src: There is no limit on the number of valve gates that can be <n translation="zugewiesen"> assigned </n> to a model .
Base: die Anzahl der Ventiltore , die einem Modell zugeordnet werden können , ist nicht begrenzt .
GDec: es gibt keine Grenze für die Anzahl der Ventiltore , die einem Modell zugewiesen werden können .
Ref: Es gibt keine Begrenzung für die Anzahl der Anschnitte , die zugewiesen werden können.

Table 2: Examples covering some cases where GDec improves over the baseline for the MT task

	BLEU ($\uparrow$)	TER ($\downarrow$)
Base-MT	62.11	24.76
Base-APE	65.25	23.67
GDec_base	62.68†	23.97†
GDec_base+OOV	62.69†	23.96†
GDec_base+OOV+reach	**67.03†**	**22.45†**

Table 3: Performance of different decoders on the APE task measured in terms of TER ($\downarrow$) and BLEU score ($\uparrow$) ("†" indicates statistically significant differences wrt. Base-APE with p<0.05).

kept), which drastically reduces the freedom of the decoder to generate surrounding words. This is confirmed by manual inspection: many original MT segments were missing function words that depended on the "good" words present in the sentence. These insertions are easily performed by the unconstrained Base-APE decoder but are unreachable by GDec_base, which is only able to keep the annotated words.

GDec_base+OOV integrates the mechanism to handle OOV annotations described in §4.3. Since the model is trained on the BPE segment corpus, the problem of OOV is already tackled by the model itself. Thus, we do not observe a significant contribution by this mechanism, which is in-line with our results on BPE in the MT task.

GDec_base+OOV+reach is our full-fledged system, which manages repetitions and insertion positions as illustrated in §4.2. Its ability to better model the surroundings of the annotated words allows this technique to achieve statistically significant improvements (+1.78 BLEU, -1.22 TER)

over the strong Base-APE decoder.

To better appreciate the ability of the APE decoder to leverage the QE labels and to avoid overcorrection, we compute the APE precision (Chatterjee et al., 2015a) as the ratio of the number of sentences an APE system improves (with respect to the MT output) over all the sentences it modifies. The GDec_base+OOV+reach decoder gains 9 precision points over Base-APE (72% vs. 63%) confirming that guided decoding supported by QE labels can improve also APE output quality.

Manual Analysis: Similar to the MT task we performed a manual analysis of the outputs generated by different APE systems. Examples capturing various aspects of the workings of GDec in this task are provided in Table 4. The labels Src, MT, Base, GDec, and Ref respectively represents the source sentence, machine translation output, baseline APE output, GDec full-fledge output, and the reference translation. Example 1 shows the capability of GDec to preserve the MT words in the final output that are correctly generated by the MT system. In this example the word "Gibt" (En: "Specifies") is preserved by GDec which is otherwise translated to "Legt" (En: "Sets") by the baseline system. Example 2 shows that guiding the neural decoder by marking the MT word "gewährleisten" (En: "ensure") as "Good" not only helps to preserve it in the final output but also help to improve other parts of the translation like "um ein ähnliches" (En: "a similar") which is otherwise untouched by the baseline APE system.

Src: Specifies the source for the glow .	
MT: <n translation="gibt|Gibt">Gibt</n> die Quelle</n> für</n> das Glü@@ hen aus .	
Base: Legt die Quelle für das Glühen fest .	
GDec: Gibt die Quelle für das Glühen aus .	
Ref: Gibt die Quelle für den Schein an .	
Src: Map Japanese indirect fonts across platforms to ensure a similar appearance .	
MT: ... zu einem ähnlichen Erscheinungsbild <n translation="gewährleisten"> gewährleisten </n> .	
Base: ... " auf einem ähnlichen Erscheinungsbild an .	
GDec: ... " auf , um ein ähnliches Erscheinungsbild zu gewährleisten .	
Ref: ... zu , um ein ähnliches Erscheinungsbild zu gewährleisten .	
Src: All values , even primitive values , are objects .	
MT: alle Werte , auch Grund@@ werte , <n translation="handelt">handelt</n> <n translation="es">es</n> <n translation="sich">sich</n> <n translation="um">um</n> <n translation="Objekte">Objekte</n> .	
Base: Alle Werte , auch Grundwerte , sind Objekte .	
GDec: Alle Werte , auch Grundwerte , handelt es sich um Objekte .	
Ref: Bei allen Werten , auch Grundwerten , handelt es sich um Objekte .	

Table 4: Examples covering some cases where GDec improves over the baseline for APE task.

Example 3 illustrates that GDec can be very useful to avoid the problem of over-correction. The MT segment in this example is almost a correct translation of the source sentence and should be left untouched but the baseline APE system modifies it deteriorating the overall translation quality. However, when the MT word is annotated to itself by the xml tags, GDec is able to preserve this word thereby avoiding over-correction and retaining the translation quality.

7 Conclusion

We presented a novel method for guiding the behaviour of an NMT decoder with external knowledge supplied in the form of translation recommendations (*e.g.* terminology lists). Our approach supervises the translation process, ensuring that the final output includes the expected translations, in the right place, including cases of added OOV words. Evaluation results on two tasks indicate the effectiveness of our proposed solution, which significantly improves over a standard NMT decoder.

Acknowledgments

This work has been partially supported by the EC-funded H2020 projects QT21 (grant agreement no. 645452) and ModernMT (grant agreement no. 645487).

References

Philip Arthur, Graham Neubig, and Satoshi Nakamura. 2016. Incorporating Discrete Translation Lexicons into Neural Machine Translation. In *Proceedings of the 2016 Conference on Empirical Methods in Natural Language Processing*. Association for Computational Linguistics, Austin, Texas.

Dzmitry Bahdanau, Kyunghyun Cho, and Yoshua Bengio. 2014. "neural machine translation by jointly learning to align and translate". *arXiv preprint arXiv:1409.0473* .

John Blatz, Erin Fitzgerald, George Foster, Simona Gandrabur, Cyril Goutte, Alex Kulesza, Alberto Sanchis, and Nicola Ueffing. 2004. Confidence Estimation for Machine Translation. In *Proceedings of the 20th International Conference on Computational Linguistics*.

Ondřej Bojar, Rajen Chatterjee, Christian Federmann, Yvette Graham, Barry Haddow, Matthias Huck, Antonio Jimeno Yepes, Philipp Koehn, Varvara Logacheva, Christof Monz, Matteo Negri, Aurelie Neveol, Mariana Neves, Martin Popel, Matt Post, Raphael Rubino, Carolina Scarton, Lucia Specia, Marco Turchi, Karin Verspoor, and Marcos Zampieri. 2016. Findings of the 2016 Conference on Machine Translation. In *Proceedings of the First Conference on Machine Translation*. Association for Computational Linguistics, Berlin, Germany.

Ondřej Bojar, Rajen Chatterjee, Christian Federmann, Barry Haddow, Matthias Huck, Chris Hokamp, Philipp Koehn, Varvara Logacheva, Christof Monz, Matteo Negri, Matt Post, Carolina Scarton, Lucia Specia, and Marco Turchi. 2015. Findings of the 2015 Workshop on Statistical Machine Translation.

In *Proceedings of the Tenth Workshop on Statistical Machine Translation*. Association for Computational Linguistics, Lisbon, Portugal.

Rajen Chatterjee, Gebremedhen Gebremelak, Matteo Negri, and Marco Turchi. 2017. Online Automatic Post-editing for MT in a Multi-Domain Translation Environment. In *Proceedings of the 15th Conference of the European Chapter of the Association for Computational Linguistics*. Valencia, Spain, pages 525–535.

Rajen Chatterjee, Marco Turchi, and Matteo Negri. 2015a. The FBK Participation in the WMT15 Automatic Post-editing Shared Task. In *Proceedings of the Tenth Workshop on Statistical Machine Translation*. Lisbon, Portugal.

Rajen Chatterjee, Marion Weller, Matteo Negri, and Marco Turchi. 2015b. Exploring the Planet of the APEs: a Comparative Study of State-of-the-art Methods for MT Automatic Post-Editing. In *Proceedings of the 53rd Annual Meeting of the Association for Computational Linguistics*. Beijing, China.

Kyunghyun Cho, Bart van Merrienboer, Dzmitry Bahdanau, and Yoshua Bengio. 2014. On the Properties of Neural Machine Translation: Encoder-Decoder Approaches. In *Proceedings of SSST@EMNLP 2014, Eighth Workshop on Syntax, Semantics and Structure in Statistical Translation*. Doha, Qatar.

José G. C. de Souza, Jesús González-Rubio, Christian Buck, Marco Turchi, and Matteo Negri. 2014. FBK-UPV-UEdin participation in the WMT14 Quality Estimation shared-task. In *Proceedings of the Ninth Workshop on Statistical Machine Translation*. Baltimore, MD, USA.

John C. Duchi, Elad Hazan, and Yoram Singer. 2011. Adaptive Subgradient Methods for Online Learning and Stochastic Optimization. *Journal of Machine Learning Research* .

Marcello Federico, Nicola Bertoldi, Mauro Cettolo, Matteo Negri, Marco Turchi, Marco Trombetti, Alessandro Cattelan, Antonio Farina, Domenico Lupinetti, Andrea Martines, Alberto Massidda, Holger Schwenk, Loïc Barrault, Frederic Blain, Philipp Koehn, Christian Buck, and Ulrich Germann. 2014. THE MATECAT TOOL. In *Proceedings of COLING 2014, the 25th International Conference on Computational Linguistics: System Demonstrations*. Dublin, Ireland.

Philip Gage. 1994. A New Algorithm for Data Compression. *C Users Journal* 12(2).

Qin Gao and Stephan Vogel. 2008. Parallel Implementations of Word Alignment Tool. In *Software Engineering, Testing, and Quality Assurance for Natural Language Processing*.

Caglar Gulcehre, Orhan Firat, Kelvin Xu, Kyunghyun Cho, Loïc Barrault, Huei-Chi Lin, Fethi Bougares, Holger Schwenk, and Yoshua Bengio. 2015. On Using Monolingual Corpora in Neural Machine Translation. *arXiv e-prints* .

Chris Hokamp and Qun Liu. 2017. Lexically Constrained Decoding for Sequence Generation Using Grid Beam Search. *CoRR* abs/1704.07138.

Sébastien Jean, Kyunghyun Cho, Roland Memisevic, and Yoshua Bengio. 2015. On Using Very Large Target Vocabulary for Neural Machine Translation. In *Proceedings of the 53rd Annual Meeting of the Association for Computational Linguistics and the 7th International Joint Conference on Natural Language Processing*. Beijing, China.

Marcin Junczys-Dowmunt and Roman Grundkiewicz. 2016. Log-linear Combinations of Monolingual and Bilingual Neural Machine Translation Models for Automatic Post-Editing. In *Proceedings of the First Conference on Machine Translation*. Berlin, Germany.

Philipp Koehn. 2004. Statistical Significance Tests for Machine Translation Evaluation. In *Proceedings of the 2004 Conference on Empirical Methods in Natural Language Processing*.

Philipp Koehn. 2005. Europarl: A Parallel Corpus for Statistical Machine Translation. In *Conference Proceedings: the tenth Machine Translation Summit*. AAMT, Phuket, Thailand.

Philipp Koehn, Hieu Hoang, Alexandra Birch, Chris Callison-Burch, Marcello Federico, Nicola Bertoldi, Brooke Cowan, Wade Shen, Christine Moran, Richard Zens, Chris Dyer, Ondřej Bojar, Alexandra Constantin, and Evan Herbst. 2007. Moses: Open Source Toolkit for Statistical Machine Translation. In *Proceedings of the 45th Annual Meeting of the ACL on Interactive Poster and Demonstration Sessions*.

Minh-Thang Luong and Christopher D Manning. 2015. Stanford Neural Machine Translation Systems for Spoken Language Domains. In *Proceedings of the International Workshop on Spoken Language Translation*.

Jan Niehues, Eunah Cho, Thanh-Le Ha, and Alex Waibel. 2016. Pre-Translation for Neural Machine Translation. In *International Conference on Computational Linguistics*.

Kishore Papineni, Salim Roukos, Todd Ward, and Wei-Jing Zhu. 2002. Bleu: a Method for Automatic Evaluation of Machine Translation. In *Proceedings of the 40th Annual Meeting of the Association for Computational Linguistics*.

Rico Sennrich and Barry Haddow. 2016. Linguistic Input Features Improve Neural Machine Translation. In *Proceedings of the First Conference on Machine Translation*. Berlin, Germany.

Rico Sennrich, Barry Haddow, and Alexandra Birch. 2016a. Edinburgh Neural Machine Translation Systems for WMT 16. In *Proceedings of the First Conference on Machine Translation*. Berlin, Germany.

Rico Sennrich, Barry Haddow, and Alexandra Birch. 2016b. Neural Machine Translation of Rare Words with Subword Units. In *Proceedings of the 54th Annual Meeting of the Association for Computational Linguistics*.

Michel Simard, Cyril Goutte, and Pierre Isabelle. 2007. Statistical Phrase-Based Post-Editing. In *Proceedings of the Annual Conference of the North American Chapter of the Association for Computational Linguistics (NAACL HLT)*. Rochester, New York, pages 508–515.

Matthew Snover, Bonnie Dorr, Richard Schwartz, Linnea Micciulla, and John Makhoul. 2006. A Study of Translation Edit Rate with Targeted Human Annotation. In *Proceedings of Association for Machine Translation in the Americas*. Cambridge, Massachusetts, USA, pages 223–231.

Felix Stahlberg, Eva Hasler, Aurelien Waite, and Bill Byrne. 2016. Syntactically Guided Neural Machine Translation. In *Proceedings of the 54th Annual Meeting of the Association for Computational Linguistics*. Berlin, Germany.

Ralf Steinberger, Bruno Pouliquen, Anna Widiger, Camelia Ignat, Tomaz Erjavec, Dan Tufis, and Dániel Varga. 2006. The JRC-Acquis: A Multilingual Aligned Parallel Corpus with 20+ Languages. In *Proceedings of the 5th International Conference on Language Resources and Evaluation (LREC'2006)*. Genoa, Italy.

Jörg Tiedemann. 2009. News from OPUS - A Collection of Multilingual Parallel Corpora with Tools and Interfaces. In *Recent Advances in Natural Language Processing*, John Benjamins, Amsterdam/Philadelphia, Borovets, Bulgaria.

Alexander Yeh. 2000. More Accurate Tests for the Statistical Significance of Result Differences. In *Proceedings of the 18th Conference on Computational Linguistics - Volume 2*.

Findings of the 2017 Conference on Machine Translation (WMT17)

Ondřej Bojar
Charles University

Rajen Chatterjee
FBK

Christian Federmann
Microsoft Research

Yvette Graham
Dublin City University

Barry Haddow
Univ. of Edinburgh

Shujian Huang
Nanjing University

Matthias Huck
LMU Munich

Philipp Koehn
JHU / Edinburgh

Qun Liu
Dublin City University

Varvara Logacheva
MIPT Moscow

Christof Monz
Univ. of Amsterdam

Matteo Negri
FBK

Matt Post
Johns Hopkins Univ.

Raphael Rubino
DFKI & Saarland Univ.

Lucia Specia
Univ. of Sheffield

Marco Turchi
FBK

Abstract

This paper presents the results of the WMT17 shared tasks, which included three machine translation (MT) tasks (news, biomedical, and multimodal), two evaluation tasks (metrics and run-time estimation of MT quality), an automatic post-editing task, a neural MT training task, and a bandit learning task.

1 Introduction

We present the results of the shared tasks of the Second Conference on Statistical Machine Translation (WMT) held at EMNLP 2017. This conference builds on eleven previous editions of WMT as workshops and conference (Koehn and Monz, 2006; Callison-Burch et al., 2007, 2008, 2009, 2010, 2011, 2012; Bojar et al., 2013, 2014, 2015, 2016a).

This year we conducted several official tasks. We report in this paper on three tasks:

- news translation (Section 2, Section 3)
- quality estimation (Section 4)
- automatic post-editing (Section 5)

The conference featured additional shared tasks that are described in separate papers in these proceedings:

- metrics (Bojar et al., 2017a)
- multimodal machine translation and multilingual image description (Elliott et al., 2017)
- biomedical translation (Jimeno Yepes et al., 2017)
- neural MT training (Bojar et al., 2017b)
- bandit learning (Sokolov et al., 2017)

In the news translation task (Section 2), participants were asked to translate a shared test set, optionally restricting themselves to the provided training data (constraint condition). We held 14 translation tasks this year, between English and each of Chinese, Czech, German, Finnish, Latvian, Russian, and Turkish. The Latvian and Chinese translation tasks were new this year. Latvian is a lesser resourced data condition on challenging language pair. Chinese allowed us to co-operate with an ongoing evaluation campaign on Asian languages organized alongside the Chinese Workshop on Machine Translation (CWMT).[1] System outputs for each task were evaluated both automatically and manually.

The human evaluation (Section 3) involves asking human judges to score sentences output by anonymized systems. We obtained large numbers of assessments from researchers who contributed evaluations proportional to the number of tasks they entered. In addition, we used Mechanical Turk to collect further evaluations. This year, the official manual evaluation metric is based on judgments of adequacy on a 100 point scale, a method we explored last year with convincing results in terms of the trade-off between annotation effort and reliable distinctions between systems.

The quality estimation task (Section 4) this year included three subtasks: sentence-level prediction of post-editing effort scores, word and phrase-level prediction of good/bad labels. Datasets

---

[1] http://nlp.nju.edu.cn/cwmt2017/evaluation.en.html

Proceedings of the Conference on Machine Translation (WMT), Volume 2: Shared Task Papers, pages 169–214
Copenhagen, Denmark, September 7–11, 2017. ©2017 Association for Computational Linguistics

were released with English→German IT translations and German→English Pharmaceutical translations for all subtasks.

The automatic post-editing task (Section 5) examined automatic methods for correcting errors produced by an unknown machine translation system. Participants were provided with training triples containing source, target and human post-edits, and were asked to return automatic post-edits for unseen (source, target) pairs. In this third round, the task focused on correcting English→German translations in the IT domain and German→English translations in the Pharmaceutical domain.

The primary objectives of WMT are to evaluate the state of the art in machine translation, to disseminate common test sets and public training data with published performance numbers, and to refine evaluation and estimation methodologies for machine translation. As before, all of the data, translations, and collected human judgments are publicly available.[2] We hope these datasets serve as a valuable resource for research into statistical machine translation, automatic evaluation, or prediction of translation quality. News translations are also available for interactive visualization and comparison of differences between systems at `http://wmt.ufal.cz/` using MT-CompareEval (Sudarikov et al., 2016).

2 News Translation Task

The recurring WMT task examines translation between English and other languages in the news domain. As in the previous years, we include German, Czech, Russian, Finnish, and Turkish. New languages this years are Latvian and Chinese.

We created a test set for each language pair by translating newspaper articles and provided training data.

2.1 Test data

The test data for this year's task was selected from online sources, as before. We took about 1500 English sentences and translated them into the other 5 languages, and then additional 1500 sentences from each of the other languages and translated them into English. This gave us test sets of about 3000 sentences for our English-X language pairs, which have been either originally written in English and translated into X, or vice versa. The composition of the test documents is shown in Table 1.

The stories were translated by professional translators, funded by the EU Horizon 2020 projects CRACKER and QT21 (German, Czech, Latvian), by Yandex[3], a Russian search engine company (Turkish, Russian), and by BAULT, a research community on building and using language technology funded by the University of Helsinki (Finnish). The Chinese–English task was sponsored by Nanjing University, Xiamen University, the Institutes of Computing Technology and of Automation, Chinese Academy of Science, Northeastern University (China) and Datum Data Co., Ltd. All of the translations were done directly, and not via an intermediate language.

For Latvian, the test set size was 2000 sentences, and an additional 2000 sentences were released as development set.

2.2 Training data

As in past years we provided parallel corpora to train translation models, monolingual corpora to train language models, and development sets to tune system parameters. Some training corpora were identical from last year (Europarl[4], Common Crawl, SETIMES2 , Russian-English parallel data provided by Yandex, Wikipedia Headlines provided by CMU) and some were updated (United Nations, CzEng v1.6 (Bojar et al., 2016b), News Commentary v12, monolingual news data). A new corpis is the EU Press Release parallel corpus for German, Finnish, and Latvian.

For Latvian and Chinese a number of new corpora were released. For Latvian this data was prepared by the University of Latvia and Tilde, the Chinese corpora were prepared by the Institutes of Computing Technology and of Automation, Chinese Academy of Science, Northeastern University (China) and Datum Data Co., Ltd.

Some statistics about the training materials are given in Figure 1.

2.3 Submitted systems

We received 103 submissions from 31 institutions. The participating institutions and their entry names are listed in Table 2; each system did not necessarily appear in all translation tasks. We also

---

[2] `http://statmt.org/wmt17/results.html`

[3] `http://www.yandex.com/`

[4] As of Fall 2011, the proceedings of the European Parliament are no longer translated into all official languages.

Europarl Parallel Corpus

	German ↔ English		Czech ↔ English		Finnish ↔ English		Latvian ↔ English	
Sentences	1,920,209		646,605		1,926,114		637,599	
Words	50,486,398	53,008,851	14,946,399	17,376,433	37,814,266	52,723,296	11,957,078	15,412,186
Distinct words	381,583	115,966	172,461	63,039	693,963	115,896	289,849	137,244

News Commentary Parallel Corpus

	German ↔ English		Czech ↔ English		Russian ↔ English		Chinese ↔ English	
Sentences	270,769		211,284		222,390		332,525	
Words	6,087,255	5,924,001	4,057,726	4,545,443	4,759,919	5,068,124	–	5,123,145
Distinct words	285,017	181,203	295,447	157,800	317,074	169,315	–	164,103

Common Crawl Parallel Corpus

	German ↔ English		Czech ↔ English		Russian ↔ English	
Sentences	2,399,123		161,838		878,386	
Words	54,575,405	58,870,638	3,529,783	3,927,378	21,018,793	21,535,122
Distinct words	1,640,835	823,480	210,170	128,212	764,203	432,062

EU Press Release Parallel Corpus

	German ↔ English		Finnish ↔ English		Latvian ↔ English	
Sentences	1,329,041		583,223		306,588	
Words	22,078,112	22,998,930	6,823,630	10,063,161	4,250,672	5,135,993
Distinct words	642,591	347,021	465,355	189,316	200,773	121,401

Latvian Parallel Corpora

	LETA News Latvian ↔ English		Online Books Latvian ↔ English		Corpus of Eu. Parliament Latvian ↔ English	
Sentences	15,671		9,577		3,542,280	
Words	340,394	438,666	63,233	82,665	30,177,230	37,158,634
Distinct words	62,734	41,252	19,191	9,104	604,110	416,932

Chinese Parallel Corpora

	casia2015	casict2011	casict2015	datum2011	datum2017	neu2017
Sentences	1,050,000	1,936,633	2,036,834	1,000,004	999,985	2,000,000
Words (en)	20,571,578	34,866,598	22,802,353	24,632,984	25,182,185	29,696,442
Distinct words (en)	470,452	627,630	435,010	316,277	312,164	624,420

Yandex 1M Parallel Corpus

	Russian ↔ English	
Sentences	1,000,000	
Words	24,121,459	26,107,293
Distinct	701,809	387,646

Wiki Headlines Parallel Corpus

	Russian ↔ English		Finnish ↔ English	
Sentences	514,859		153,728	
Words	1,191,474	1,230,644	269,429	354,362
Distinct	282,989	251,328	127,576	96,732

CzEng Parallel Corpus

	Czech ↔ English	
Sentences	62,493,539	
Words	611,094,888	688,534,994
Distinct	8,017,713	5,738,815

United Nations Parallel Corpus

	Russian ↔ English		Chinese ↔ English	
Sentences	23,239,280		15,886,041	
Words	482,966,738	524,719,646	–	372,612,596
Distinct	3,857,656	2,737,469	–	1,981,413

Figure 1: Statistics for the training sets used in the translation task. The number of words and the number of distinct words (case-insensitive) is based on the provided tokenizer.

Language	Sources (Number of Documents)
English	ABC News (1), BBC (9), Brisbane Times (1), CBS News (5), CNN (1), Daily Mail (10), Euronews (1), Fox News (2), Globe and Mail (1), Guardian (3), Independent (2), Los Angeles Times (1), Novinite (1), New York Times (8), Reuters (4), Russia Today (3), Scotsman (1), Sydney Morning Herald (4), Telegraph (1), The Local (1), UPI (4)
Chinese	Ifeng (82), People Daily (14), Sina (14), Xinhua (8)
Czech	aktuálně.cz (10), blesk.cz (4), blisty.cz (1), deník.cz (1), iDNES.cz (14), ihned.cz (4), lidovky.cz (8), Novinky.cz (5), Reflex (1), tyden.cz (4), ZDN (2)
German	Abendzeitung München (1), Abendzeitung Nürnberg (1), ARD (1), Augsburger Allgemeine (1), Bergedorfer Zeitung (1), Braunschweiger Zeitung (1), Der Standard (2), Deutsche Welle (1), Dülmener Zeitung (1), Euronews (1), Frankfurter Rundschau (2), Generalanzeiger Bonn (1), Göttinger Tageblatt (1), Handelsblatt (4), In Franken (4), In Südthüringen (1), Kieler Nachrichten (2), Kreisanzeiger (1), Kreiszeitung (3), Krone (1), Kölner Stadt Anzeiger (2), Merkur (1), Morgenpost (3), Neue Presse Coburg (1), Nordbayerischer Kurier (1), oe24 (1), Potzdamer Neueste Nachrichten (1), Passauer Neue Presse (1), Pforzheimer Zeitung (1), Rheinzeitung (1), Rundschau (1), Schwarzwälder Bote (2), Südkurier (1), Süddeutsche Zeitung (1), Usinger Anzeiger (1), Westfälischer Anzeiger (1), Westfälische Nachrichten (3), Westdeutsche Zeitung (4), Zeit (1), Waiblinger Kreiszeitung (4).
Finnish	Etelä-Saimaa (2), Etelä-Suomen Sanomat (1), Helsingin Sanomat (14), Ilkka (10), Iltalehti (16), Ilta-Sanomat (16), Kaleva (9), Kansan Uutiset (3), Karjalainen (10), Kouvolan Sanomat (2), Loimaan Lehti (1).
Latvian	Dienas Bizness (3), Delfi (11), Diena (13), grenet.lv (1), LSM (10), NRA (9), Talsu Vestis (1), TV Net (21)
Russian	aif (), dp.ru (2), eg-online.ru (2), gazeta.ru (5), gzt-sv.ru (1), Izvestiya (7), Kommersant (16), Lenta (17), lgng (5), MK RU (4), nov-pravda.ru (1), Novaya Gazeta (3), pnp.ru (4), rg.ru (1), rusplit.ru (1), Vedomosti (1), Versia (2), Vesti (3), VM News (1), zr.ru (3)
Turkish	Sabah (96), Sözcü (19)

Table 1: Composition of the test set. For more details see the XML test files. The `docid` tag gives the source and the date for each document in the test set, and the `origlang` tag indicates the original source language.

Europarl Language Model Data

	English	German	Czech	Finnish	Latvian
Sentences	2,218,201	2,176,537	668,595	2,120,739	667, 241
Words	59,848,044	53,534,167	14,946,399	39,511,068	12,092,389
Distinct words	123,059	394,781	172,461	711,868	160,312

News Language Model Data

	English	German	Czech	Russian	Finnish
Sentences	166,127,560	221,793,141	59,184,372	31,285,072	10,938,701
Words	3,816,723,867	3,938,344,482	974,167,234	572,672,132	137,162,922
Distinct words	5,895,731	17,824,672	4,011,712	2,929,646	,3557,784

Common Crawl Language Model Data

	English	German	Czech	Russian	Finnish	Romanian	Turkish
Sent.	3,074,921,453	2,872,785,485	333,498,145	1,168,529,851	157,264,161	288,806,234	511,196,951
Words	65,128,419,540	65,154,042,103	6,694,811,063	23,313,060,950	2,935,402,545	8,140,378,873	11,882,126,872
Dist.	342,760,462	339,983,035	50,162,437	101,436,673	47,083,545	37,846,546	88,463,295

Test Set

	Czech ↔ EN		German ↔ EN		Finnish ↔ EN		Latvian ↔ EN	
Sentences.	3,005		3,004		3,002		2,001	
Words	54,630	61,958	60,963	64,760	45,472	62,769	39,064	47,832
Distinct words	14,462	8,544	12,514	8,997	16,156	8,552	11,708	7,435

	Russian ↔ EN		Turkish ↔ EN		Chinese ↔ EN	
Sentences.	3,001		3,007		2,001	
Words	59,912	69,847	55,303	67,927	–	54,011
Distinct words	17,391	9,386	14,864	8,664	–	7,710

Figure 2: Statistics for the training and test sets used in the translation task. The number of words and the number of distinct words (case-insensitive) is based on the provided tokenizer.

ID	Institution
AALTO	Aalto University(Grönroos et al., 2017)
AFRL-MITLL	Air Force Research Lab / MIT Lincoln Lab (Gwinnup et al., 2017)
APERTIUM	Apertium / Helsinki University (Hurskainen and Tiedemann, 2017)
C-3MA	Tartu-Riga-Zürich (Rikters et al., 2017)
CASICT-DCU	Chinese Academy of Sciences / Dublin City University (Zhang et al., 2017)
CU-CHIMERA	Charles University (Sudarikov et al., 2017)
FBK	Fondazione Bruno Kessler (Di Gangi et al., 2017)
HUNTER	Hunter College, City University of New York (Xu et al., 2017)
HY	Helsinki University (Östling et al., 2017)
JAIST	Japan Advanced Institute of Science and Technology (Trieu et al., 2017)
JHU	Johns Hopkins University (Ding et al., 2017)
KIT	Karlsruhe Institute of Technology (Pham et al., 2017)
LIMSI	LIMSI (Burlot et al., 2017)
LIUM-CVC	University of Le Mans / Universitat Autonoma de Barcelona (García-Martínez et al., 2017)
LMU	LMU Munich (Huck et al., 2017)
NMT-AVE-MULTI-CS	
NRC	National Research Council, Canada
OREGON	Orgon State University
PJATK	Polish-Japanese Academy of Information (Wolk and Marasek, 2017)
PROMT	PROMT Rule-Based System
QT21	QT21 project system combination (Peter et al., 2017b)
ROCMT	University of Rochester (Holtz et al., 2017)
RWTH	RWTH Aachen (Peter et al., 2017a)
SOGOU	Sogou Inc. (Wang et al., 2017)
SYSTRAN	Systran (Deng et al., 2017)
TALP-UPC	TALP, Technical University of Catalonia (Escolano et al., 2017)
TILDE	Tilde (Pinnis et al., 2017)
UEDIN	University of Edinburgh (Sennrich et al., 2017)
USFD	University of Sheffield
UU	Uppsala University
XMU	Xiamen University (Tan et al., 2017b)

Table 2: Participants in the shared translation task. Not all teams participated in all language pairs. The translations from the commercial and online systems were not submitted by their respective companies but were obtained by us, and are therefore anonymized in a fashion consistent with previous years of the workshop.

included 39 online statistical MT systems (originating from 4 services), which we anonymized as ONLINE-A,B,F,G.

For presentation of the results, systems are treated as either *constrained* or *unconstrained*, depending on whether their models were trained only on the provided data. Since we do not know how they were built, these online and commercial systems are treated as unconstrained during the automatic and human evaluations.

3 Human Evaluation

A human evaluation campaign is run each year to assess translation quality and to determine the final ranking of systems taking part in the competition. This section describes how preparation of evaluation data, collection of human assessments, and computation of the official results of the shared task is carried out this year.

In previous years, we asked human annotators to rank the outputs of five systems. From these rankings, we produced pairwise translation comparisons, and applied the TrueSkill algorithm (Herbrich et al., 2007; Sakaguchi et al., 2014) to produce system rankings. We refer to this approach as the *relative ranking* (RR) approach, so named because the pairwise comparisons denote only relative ability between a pair of systems, and cannot be used to infer absolute quality. For example, RR can be used to discover which systems perform better than others, but RR does not provide any information about the absolute quality of system translations, i.e. it provides no information about how far a given system is from producing perfect output according to a human user.

Work on evaluation over the past few years has provided fresh insight into ways to collect *direct assessments* (DA) of machine translation quality (Graham et al., 2013, 2014, 2016), and last year's evaluation campaign included parallel assessment of a subset of News task language pairs evaluated with RR and DA. DA has some clear advantages over RR, namely the evaluation of absolute translation quality and the ability to carry out evaluations through quality controlled crowd-sourcing. As established last year (Bojar et al., 2016a), DA results (via crowd-sourcing) and RR results (produced by researchers) correlate strongly, with Pearson correlation ranging from 0.920 to 0.997 across several source languages into English and at 0.975 for English-to-Russian (the only pair evaluated out-of-English). This year, we thus employ DA only. Where possible, we collect DA judgments via the crowd-sourcing platform, Amazon's Mechanical Turk, and as in previous year's we ask participating teams to provide manual evaluation of system outputs via Appraise with a new implementation of DA. Researcher involvement is needed particularly for translations out-of-English.

Human assessors are asked to rate a given translation by how adequately it expresses the meaning of the corresponding reference translation (i.e. no bilingual speakers are needed) on an analogue scale, which corresponds to an underlying absolute 0–100 rating scale. Since DA involves evaluation of a single translation per screen, this allows the sentence length restriction usually applied during manual evaluation to be removed for both researchers and crowd-sourced workers.[5] Figure 3 shows one DA screen as completed by researchers on Appraise, while Figure 4 provides a screenshot of DA shown to crowd-sourced workers on Amazon's Mechanical Turk.

The annotation is organized into "HITs" (following the Mechanical Turk's term "human intelligence task"), each containing 100 such screens and requiring about half an hour to finish. Appraise users were allowed to pause their annotation at any time, Amazon interface did not allow any pauses. More details of composition of HITs are given in Section 3.3 and details on time spent in Section 3.6 below.

3.1 Evaluation Campaign Overview

In terms of the News translation task manual evaluation, a total of 151 individual researcher accounts were involved, and 754 turker accounts.[6] Researchers in the manual evaluation came from 29 different research groups and contributed judgments of 125,693 translations, while 237,200 translation assessment scores were submitted in total by the crowd.[7]

Under ordinary circumstances, each assessed translation would correspond to a single individual scored segment. However, since many systems

---

[5]The maximum sentence length with RR was 30 in WMT16.

[6]Numbers do not include the 954 workers on Mechanical Turk who did not pass quality control.

[7]Numbers include quality control items for workers who passed quality control but omit the additional 151,200 assessments collected on Mechanical Turk where a worker did not pass quality control.

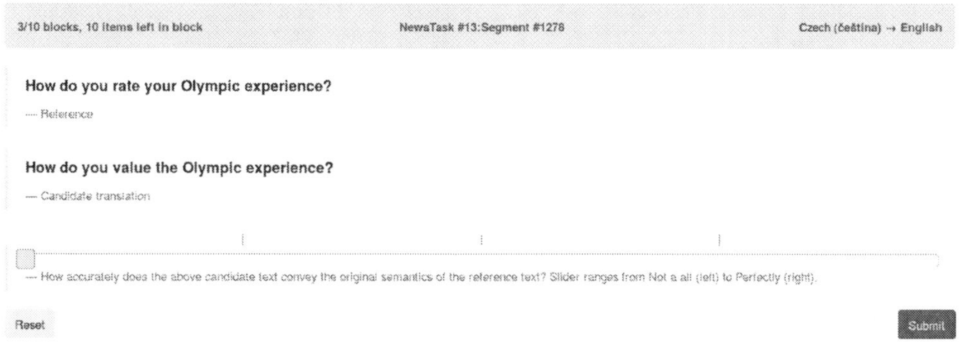

Figure 3: Screen shot of Direct Assessment in the Appraise interface used in the human evaluation campaign. The annotator is presented with a reference translation and a single system output randomly selected from competing systems (anonymized), and is asked to rate the translation on a sliding scale.

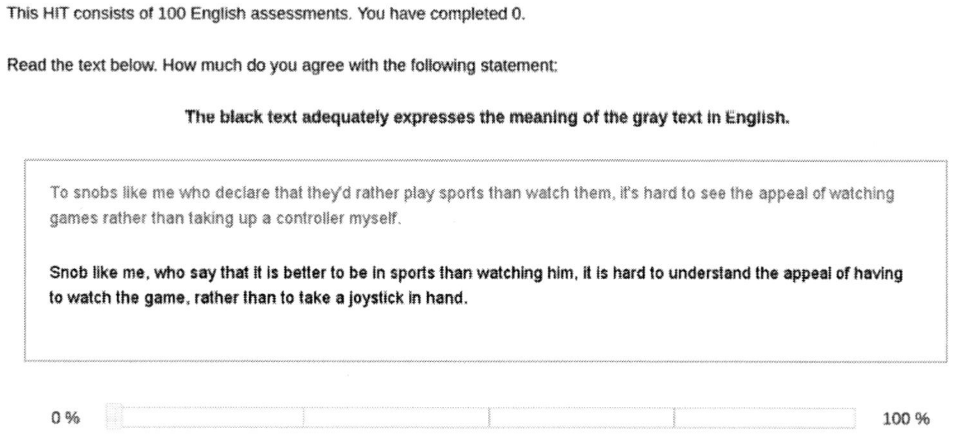

Figure 4: Screen shot of Direct Assessment as carried out by workers on Mechanical Turk.

can produce the same output for a particular input sentence, we are often able to take advantage of this and use a single assessment for multiple systems. This year we only combine human assessments in this way if the string of text belonging to multiple systems is exactly identical. For example, even small differences in punctuation disqualify the potential combination of similar system outputs into a single human assessment, and this is due to lack of evidence about what kinds of minor differences might impact human evaluation.

Table 3 shows the numbers of segments for which distinct MT systems participating in the News task produced identical outputs. English to Czech is the only language pair to include systems that do not belong to the news task, the additional NMT Training task systems, and we include a breakdown of duplicate translations by each task for that language pair in Table 3. The biggest saving in terms of exact duplicate translations for multiple systems was made in the News task for English to German.

3.2 Data Collection

The system ranking is produced from a large set of human assessments, each of which indicates the absolute quality of the output of a system. Annotations are collected in an evaluation campaign that enlists participants in the shared task to help. Each team is asked to contribute 8 hours anno-

Language Pair	# Systems	# Segs	# Total Segs	# Unique Segs	Overall Saving
Chinese→English	16	2,001	32,016	30,772	3.9 %
Czech→English	4	3,005	12,020	11,501	4.3 %
German→English	11	3,004	33,044	29,513	10.7 %
Finnish→English	6	3,002	18,012	17,766	1.4 %
Latvian→English	9	2,001	18,009	17,441	3.2 %
Russian→English	9	3,001	27,009	25,430	5.8 %
Turkish→English	10	3,007	30,070	28,672	4.6 %
English→Chinese	11	2,001	22,011	21,626	1.7 %
English→Czech	14	3,005	42,070	37,774	10.2 %
News	8	3,005	24,040	21,261	11.6 %
NMT Training	6	3,005	18,030	17,098	5.2 %
English→German	16	3,004	48,064	41,918	12.8 %
English→Finnish	12	3,002	36,024	34,688	3.7 %
English→Latvian	17	2,001	34,017	30,928	9.1 %
English→Russian	9	3,001	27,009	25,807	4.5 %
English→Turkish	8	3,007	24,056	23,540	2.1 %

Table 3: Total segments prior to sampling for manual evaluation and savings made by combining identical segments (Segs) produced by multiple MT systems in the News (all language pairs) and NMT Training task (English→Czech only).

tation time, which we estimated this year at 16 100-translation HITs per primary system submitted. We continue to use the open-source Appraise[8] (Federmann, 2012) tool for our data collection, in addition to Amazon Mechanical Turk.[9] Table 4 shows total numbers of human assessments collected in WMT17 contributing to final scores for systems.

When summarizing and comparing annotation times recorded on Appraise and Mechanical Turk, both encounter possible challenges in terms of idle times exaggerating summary statistics. We explore this issue in detail in Section 3.6, and for the summary that follows, assessment times for Appraise that appear to include very lengthy idle times are each replaced with a realistic average time per assessment, as described in Section 3.6. In total, our human annotators spent nearly 24 days and 22 hours working on Appraise, and 47 days and 23 hours annotating via crowdsourcing.[10] This gives an average annotation time of 4 hours per researcher using Appraise and 1 hour 32 minutes contribution by individual workers on Mechanical Turk.[11] Compared to last year's

RR evaluation, we see a reduction in average time commitment per researcher, which was 6.4 hours in WMT16.

In this year's evaluation, since it is the first time DA has been used with non-crowdsourced human evaluators, estimates of expected assessment completion times were used to guess the required time commitment by each participating team. Similar to the previous campaigns, several of the Appraise annotators passed the mark of required numbers of annotations (the maximum number being 5,240 translation assessments) with the most patient annotator contributing close to 22.5 hours of work. However, for one language pair, English to Latvian, insufficient annotations were contributed by researchers, which we suspect was caused by the difficulty in sourcing Latvian speakers.

Nonetheless, the effort that goes into the manual evaluation campaign each year is impressive, and we are grateful to all participating individuals and teams. We believe that human annotation provides the best decision basis for evaluation of machine translation output and it is great to see continued contributions on this large scale.

---

[8] https://github.com/cfedermann/Appraise

[9] https://www.mturk.com

[10] Numbers do not include the 2,106,918 seconds of annotation provided by workers who did not pass quality control.

[11] Times for Mechanical Turk workers do not include workers who failed to pass quality control checks. Some but not all of the HITs that do not pass quality control checks are rejected and therefore go unpaid. A portion of unusable data is accepted and paid due to the possibility that some diligent workers may simply lack the required literary skills to pass quality control.

Language Pair	Systems	Comps	Comps/Sys	Assessments	Assess/Sys
Chinese→English	16	–	–	38,736	2,421
Czech→English	4	–	–	21,992	5,498
German→English	11	–	–	36,189	3,290
Finnish→English	6	–	–	27,545	4,591
Latvian→English	9	–	–	30,321	3,369
Russian→English	9	–	–	24,837	2,760
Turkish→English	10	–	–	25,853	2,585
English→Chinese	11	–	–	16,253	1,478
English→Czech	15	–	–	32,564	2,171
English→German	16	–	–	10,229	639
English→Finnish	12	–	–	8,289	691
English→Latvian	17	–	–	6,882	405
English→Russian	9	–	–	25,798	2,866
English→Turkish	8	–	–	2,219	277
Total Researcher	153	–	–	107,902	705
Total Crowd	85	–	–	199,805	2,351
Total WMT17	**153**	–	–	**307,707**	**2,011**
WMT16	138	569,287	4,125.2	284,644	2,062
WMT15	131	542,732	4,143.0	271,366	2,071
WMT14	110	328,830	2,989.3	164,415	1,494
WMT13	148	942,840	6,370.5	471,420	3,185
WMT12	103	101,969	999.6	50,985	495
WMT11	133	63,045	474.0	31,522	237

Table 4: Amount of data (assessments after removal of quality control items and "de-collapsing" *multi-system outputs*) collected in the WMT17 manual evaluation campaign. The final six rows report summary information from previous years of the workshop. Note how many rankings we get for Czech language pairs; these include systems from the NMT Training shared task.

3.3 Crowd Quality Control

Translations are arranged in sets of 100-translation HITs as this allows a minimum number of pairs of quality control translations to be collected from each worker who participates, while at the same time allowing sufficient separation of assessment of quality control translation pairs so that human assessors are highly unlikely to simply remember the score they assigned to the initial assessed translation. Details of the three kinds of quality control translation pairs employed by DA are provided in Table 5: we repeat pairs (expecting a similar judgement), damage MT outputs (expecting significantly worse scores) and use references instead of MT outputs (expecting high scores). Bad reference pairs are created automatically by replacing a phrase within a given translation with a phrase of the same length randomly selected from n-grams extracted from the full test set of reference transla-

tions belonging to that language pair. This means that the replacement phrase in itself will comprise a fluent sequence of words (making it difficult to tell that the sentence is low quality without reading the entire sentence) while at the same time making its presence highly likely to sufficiently change the meaning of the MT output so that it causes a noticeable degradation. The length of the phrase to be replaced is determined by the number of words in the translation to be degraded, as follows:

Translation Length (N)	# Words Replaced in Translation
1	1
2–5	2
6–8	3
9–15	4
16–20	5
>20	$\lfloor N/4 \rfloor$

Repeat Pairs:	Original System output (10)	An exact repeat of it (10);
Bad Reference Pairs:	Original System output (10)	A degraded version of it (10);
Good Reference Pairs:	Original System output (10)	Its corresponding reference translation (10);

Table 5: Quality control translation pairs hidden within 100-translation HITs, numbers of items are provided in parentheses.

In total, 60 items in a 100-translation HIT serve in quality control checks but 40 of those are regular judgements of MT system outputs (we exclude assessments of bad references and ordinary reference translations when calculating final scores). The effort wasted for the sake of quality control is thus 20%.

3.4 Annotator Agreement

When an analogue (or 0–100 point, in practice) scale is employed, agreement cannot be measured using the conventional Kappa coefficient, ordinarily applied to evaluation of human assessment where judgments are discrete categories or preferences. Instead, we filter crowd-sourced human assessors by how consistently they rate translations of known distinct quality using bad reference pairs described previously. Quality filtering via bad reference pairs is especially important for the crowd-sourced portion of the manual evaluation. Due to the anonymous nature of crowd-sourcing, when collecting assessments of translations it is likely to encounter workers who attempt to game the service, as well as submission of inconsistent and even robotic HITs. We therefore employ DA's quality control mechanism, facilitated by the use of DA's analogue rating scale.

Assessments belonging to a given crowd-sourced worker who has not demonstrated that they can reliably score bad reference translations significantly lower than corresponding genuine system output translations are filtered out. The p-value produced in a paired significance test of bad reference pair score distributions is used as an estimate of human assessor reliability. Assessments of workers whose p-value does not fall below the conventional 0.05 threshold are omitted from the evaluation of systems, since they do not reliably score degraded translations lower than corresponding MT output translations.

Table 6 shows the number of unique workers who evaluated MT output on Mechanical Turk via DA, those who met our filtering requirement by showing a significantly lower score for bad reference items, and the proportion of those workers who simultaneously showed no significant dif-

ference between scores they attributed in repeat assessment of identical translations. The idea is that the repeated input should receive a very similar score. Assuming that annotators do not remember their previous assessment for the repeated sentence, the "Exact Rep." corresponds to intra-annotator agreement and it reaches very high scores of 97–100%.

We also see in Table 6 that the number of excluded Mechanical Turk workers can be high for many languages, between 42 and 58% for English HITs, 72% for Russian and 81% for Chinese. The variance in English annotations for different source languages are consistent with previous DA evaluations and we do not believe this is caused in any significant way by the source language. With respect to the choice of target language, however, in general DA evaluation for languages with fewer speakers on Mechanical Turk, such as Russian and Chinese, do tend to encounter higher rates of gaming. Since HITs are slower to complete, due to fewer workers with that language, HITs are live for a longer duration on the service and gamer-type workers have a greater opportunity to attempt payment for them.

This year, bad reference items were only collected for crowd-sourced assessments. For information on quality control statistics for non crowd-sourced workers see this year's human evaluation of the APE task, Section 5.5, where student volunteers were employed and although only 11 annotators were involved in total, 100% of those passed DA's quality control filter.

3.5 Producing the Human Ranking

All research and crowd data that passed quality control were combined to produce the overall shared task results. In order to iron out differences in scoring strategies of distinct human assessors, human assessment scores for translations were first standardized according to each individual human assessor's overall mean and standard deviation score, for both researchers and crowd. Average standardized scores for individual segments belonging to a given system are then computed, before the final overall DA score for that

	All	(A) Sig. Diff. Bad Ref.	(A) & No Sig. Diff. Exact Rep.
Czech→English	154	89 (58%)	87 (98%)
German→English	398	201 (51%)	194 (97%)
Finnish→English	264	106 (40%)	102 (96%)
Latvian→English	332	123 (37%)	122 (99%)
Russian→English	274	148 (54%)	144 (97%)
Turkish→English	344	107 (31%)	103 (96%)
Chinese→English	386	161 (42%)	158 (98%)
English→Russian	82	23 (28%)	23 (100%)
English→Chinese	43	8 (19%)	8 (100%)
Total	**1708**	**754 (44%)**	**733 (97%)**

Table 6: Number of unique Mechanical Turk workers, (A) those whose scores for bad reference pairs were significantly different and numbers of unique human assessors in (A) whose scores for exact repeat assessments also showed no significant difference.

system is computed as the average of its segment scores (Ave z in Table 7). Results are also reported for average scores for systems, computed in the same way but without any score standardization applied (Ave % in Table 7).

Table 7 includes final DA scores for all systems participating in WMT17 translation task. Clusters are identified by grouping systems together according to which systems significantly outperform all others in lower ranking clusters, according to Wilcoxon rank-sum test. Figure 5 shows the underlying head-to-head significance test results for all pairs of systems.

3.6 Crowd versus Researcher Results Comparison

Finally, although we have combined all data collected via crowd-sourcing and researchers to produce the overall results of the shared task, sufficient assessments were collected to produce system scores independently in both set-ups for three language pairs. Table 8 shows the Pearson correlation between DA scores for systems when evaluated by researchers with scores produced via crowd-sourcing, showing high levels of agreement reached overall for all language pairs as correlations range from 0.98 to 0.997.

In terms on annotation times, some differences in the way HIT durations are recorded within Appraise and Mechanical Turk make a comparison of annotation times for researchers and crowd-sourced workers not entirely straightforward. On the one hand, it is possible for a Mechanical Turk

(Mturk) worker, attempting to game the system, to leave the window idle in order to obscure a lack of effort, while on Appraise, researcher annotation times will naturally include idle times due to interruptions of some kind.

The degree to which annotation times can be exaggerated for Mturk workers is quite limited, however. Firstly, since we impose quality control checks throughout Mturk HITs, it won't be possible for many workers to meet the quality threshold without genuinely spending a minimum amount of time on assessments. Additionally, we impose a hard time limit of 90 minutes duration to each 100-translation HIT on Mturk (this corresponds to an average maximum completion time of 54 seconds per translation) which limits the amount of exaggeration of completion times that can take place. The situation on Appraise is quite different however, and idle times could potentially severely skew annotation time analysis.

Figure 6(a) shows annotation times recorded for our HITs on Mechanical Turk and Figure 6(b) shows equivalent times for Appraise, where both sets of completion times have been sorted from shortest to longest duration. Examining the y-axis of the Appraise plot in Figure 6(b) shows the maximum completion time for a single translation to be at a whopping 329,578 seconds (3.8 days), revealing the extent to which the inclusion of idle times for Appraise runs the risk of exaggerating annotation times for researchers, while on Mechanical Turk, Figure 6(a), the 90 minute HIT du-

Chinese→English

#	Ave %	Ave z	System
1	73.2	0.209	SogouKnowing-nmt
	73.8	0.208	uedin-nmt
	72.3	0.184	xmunmt
4	69.9	0.113	online-B
	70.4	0.109	online-A
	69.8	0.079	NRC
7	67.9	0.023	jhu-nmt
	66.9	−0.016	afrl-mitll-opennmt
	67.1	−0.026	CASICT-DCU_NMT
	65.4	−0.058	ROCMT
11	64.3	−0.107	Oregon-State-Uni-S
12	61.7	−0.209	PROMT-SMT
	61.2	−0.265	NMT-Ave-Multi-Cs
	60.0	−0.276	UU-HNMT
	59.6	−0.279	online-F
	59.3	−0.305	online-G

English→Chinese

#	Ave %	Ave z	system
1	73.2	0.208	SogouKnowing-nmt
	72.5	0.178	uedin-nmt
	72.0	0.165	xmunmt
4	69.8	0.065	online-B
	69.5	0.056	jhu-nmt
	68.5	0.035	CASICT-DCU_NMT
	68.2	0.010	online-A
8	64.8	−0.111	Oregon-State-Uni-S
9	59.2	−0.300	UU-HNMT
10	55.9	−0.438	online-G
11	53.1	−0.504	online-F

Czech→English

#	Ave %	Ave z	system
1	74.6	0.181	uedin-nmt
2	71.9	0.068	online-B
3	68.3	−0.068	online-A
4	62.7	−0.268	PJATK

English→Czech

#	Ave %	Ave z	system
1	62.0	0.308	uedin-nmt
2	59.7	0.240	online-B
3	55.9	0.111	limsi-factored-norm
	55.2	0.102	LIUM-FNMT
	55.2	0.090	LIUM-NMT
	54.1	0.050	CU-Chimera
	53.3	0.029	online-A
8	44.9	−0.236	TT-ufal-8GB
9	42.2	−0.315	TT-afrl-4GB
	41.9	−0.327	PJATK
	40.7	−0.373	TT-base-8GB
	40.5	−0.376	TT-afrl-8GB
13	36.5	−0.486	TT-ufal-4GB
	36.6	−0.493	TT-denisov-4GB

German→English

#	Ave %	Ave z	system
1	78.2	0.213	online-B
	76.6	0.169	online-A
	76.6	0.165	KIT
	76.6	0.162	uedin-nmt
	75.8	0.131	RWTH-nmt-ensemb
	74.5	0.098	SYSTRAN
7	72.9	0.029	LIUM-NMT
8	70.2	−0.058	TALP-UPC
	69.8	−0.072	online-G
	68.6	−0.103	C-3MA
11	64.1	−0.260	online-F

English→German

#	Ave %	Ave z	system
1	72.9	0.257	LMU-nmt-reranked
2	70.2	0.158	online-B
	69.8	0.139	uedin-nmt
	68.9	0.092	SYSTRAN
	66.9	0.035	LMU-nmt-single
	66.7	0.022	KIT
	66.4	0.015	xmu
	66.6	0.006	LIUM-NMT
	66.0	−0.003	RWTH-nmt-ensemb
10	60.1	−0.233	online-A
	60.3	−0.234	PROMT-Rule-based
	58.9	−0.270	C-3MA
	58.1	−0.301	fbk-nmt-comb
	55.2	−0.391	TALP-UPC
	54.9	−0.440	online-F
	53.2	−0.491	online-G

Finnish→English

#	Ave %	Ave z	system
1	73.8	0.407	online-B
2	67.5	0.220	online-G
3	62.6	0.041	online-A
4	58.8	−0.095	TALP-UPC
5	52.1	−0.316	Hunter-MT
6	44.6	−0.559	apertium

English→Finnish

#	Ave %	Ave z	system
1	59.6	0.378	online-B
	57.8	0.305	HY-HNMT
3	51.6	0.090	online-G
	51.3	0.060	jhu-nmt-latt-resc
	49.3	−0.004	AaltoHnmtMultitask
6	46.4	−0.102	AaltoHnmtFlatcat
	46.7	−0.109	online-A
	45.8	−0.115	HY-SMT
	43.5	−0.192	HY-AH
	43.4	−0.204	jhu-pbmt
11	40.8	−0.298	TALP-UPC
12	8.0	−1.428	apertium

Latvian→English

#	Ave %	Ave z	system
1	76.2	0.266	online-B
	76.2	0.245	tilde-nc-nmt-smt
3	71.4	0.087	uedin-nmt
	71.0	0.083	tilde-c-nmt-smt
5	67.3	−0.039	online-A
6	64.4	−0.137	jhu-pbmt
7	63.4	−0.187	C-3MA
	62.2	−0.199	Hunter-MT
9	56.3	−0.436	PJATK

English→Latvian

#	Ave %	Ave z	system
1	54.4	0.196	tilde-nc-nmt-smt
	51.6	0.121	online-B
	51.1	0.104	tilde-c-nmt-smt
	50.8	0.075	limsi-fact-norm
	50.0	0.058	usfd-cons-qt21
	47.1	−0.014	QT21-Comb
	47.3	−0.027	usfd-cons-kit
	45.7	−0.063	KIT
	45.2	−0.072	uedin-nmt
	44.9	−0.099	tilde-nc-smt
	43.2	−0.157	LIUM-FNMT
	43.0	−0.198	LIUM-NMT
	40.1	−0.253	HY-HNMT
	37.5	−0.341	online-A
	36.1	−0.368	jhu-pbmt
	33.3	−0.457	C-3MA
17	18.8	−0.947	PJATK

Russian→English

#	Ave %	Ave z	system
1	82.0	0.271	online-B
2	77.6	0.126	online-G
3	76.5	0.081	NRC
	76.1	0.057	online-A
	74.9	0.017	afrl-mitll-comb
	74.6	0.005	afrl-mitll-opennmt
	74.2	0.002	uedin-nmt
	74.7	−0.011	jhu-pbmt
9	65.9	−0.288	online-F

English→Russian

#	Ave %	Ave z	system
1	75.4	0.402	online-B
2	68.2	0.166	uedin-nmt
3	66.5	0.105	online-H
4	65.9	0.080	PROMT-Rule-based
	65.2	0.061	online-A
	65.2	0.054	online-G
7	62.6	−0.018	jhu-pbmt
8	57.3	−0.194	afrl-mitll-backtra
9	46.5	−0.568	online-F

Turkish→English

#	Ave %	Ave z	system
1	68.8	0.294	online-B
	68.5	0.282	online-A
3	61.1	0.050	uedin-nmt
4	58.6	−0.029	online-G
	58.0	−0.083	afrl-mitll-m2w
	57.0	−0.093	afrl-mitll-comb
	56.7	−0.097	LIUM-NMT
8	53.5	−0.183	PROMT-SMT
9	46.4	−0.436	jhu-pbmt
	45.5	−0.475	JAIST

English→Turkish

#	Ave %	Ave z	system
1	53.4	0.513	online-B
2	44.0	0.206	uedin-nmt
3	39.1	0.071	online-A
	35.5	−0.032	online-G
5	32.2	−0.129	LIUM-NMT
6	18.0	−0.554	jhu-nmt-latt-resc
	16.7	−0.597	jhu-pbmt
	15.7	−0.602	JAIST

Table 7: Official results of WMT17 News translation task. Systems ordered by standardized mean DA score, though systems within a cluster are considered tied. Lines between systems indicate clusters according to Wilcoxon rank-sum test at p-level $p \leq 0.05$. Systems with gray background indicate use of resources that fall outside the constraints provided for the shared task.

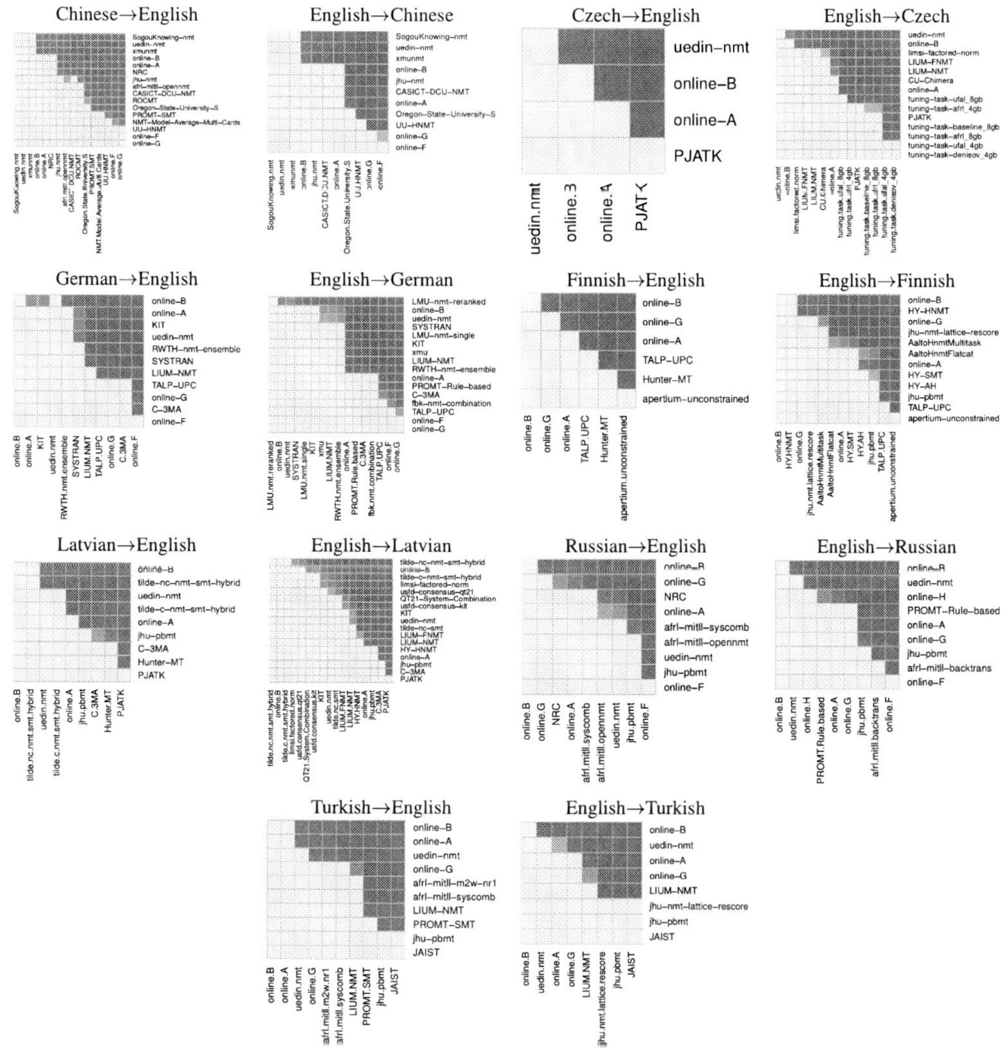

Figure 5: Wilcoxon rank-sum significance test results for pairs of systems competing in the News translation task, where a green cell denotes a significant win for the system in a given row over the system in a given column, at $p \leq 0.05$.

	r	# Researcher	# Crowd
Czech→English	0.997	2,915	2,445
Finnish→English	0.996	1,261	3,245
English→Russian	0.980	867	1,889

Table 8: Pearson correlation (r) between overall DA standardized mean adequacy scores collected via crowd-sourcing (Mturk) and from researchers participating in the shared task (Appraise), numbers of assessments per system (#) are also provided for each set-up.

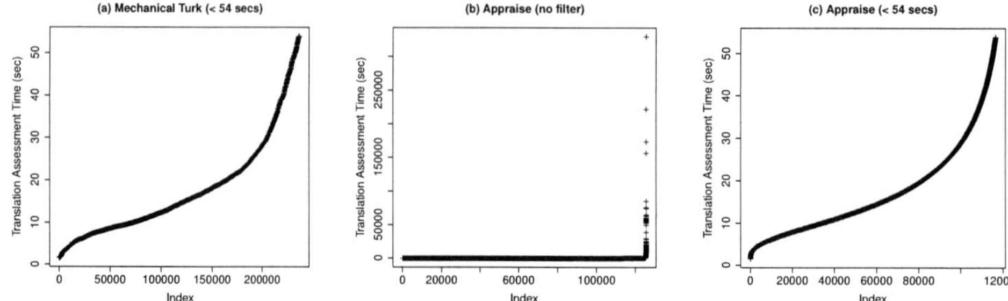

Figure 6: Comparison of Completion Times for (a) Mechanical Turk Assessments; (b) Appraise Assessments (unfiltered); (c) Appraise Assessments (with reasonable cut-off imposed)

ration constraint we impose means that the maximum annotation time per translation is just under 54 seconds.

Although it is possible that assessment times for Mechanical Turk HITs in Figure 6(a) still contain a degree of idle-time exaggeration themselves, the extent to which they could possibly obscure assessment times is vastly less than that of Appraise. Prior to analysis of assessment times, we therefore impose a reasonable limit on what could be considered a realistic maximum annotation time for assessment of a single translation with DA on Appraise. Just to remind ourselves, the assessment of a single translation on Appraise includes: (i) reading a reference translation; (ii) reading the MT output; (iii) considering how well the latter expresses the meaning of the former; (iv) assigning a score via the analogue rating scale; (v) pressing the submit button. We apply the same maximum cut-off applied within Mturk assessments of 54 seconds per translation assessment to Appraise annotation times analysis therefore, which is a reasonable maximum duration for a single translation assessment. Figure 6(c) shows a plot of sorted assessment times for Appraise assessments when this cut-off is applied.

Once overly lengthy idle times have been omitted, it is possible to compare the speed at which researchers and crowd-sourced workers complete DA assessments, in addition to comparing annotation times in this year's DA evaluation with WMT16's RR evaluation as both were completed by researchers. Table 9 shows average annotation times for each human annotator type, and annotation scheme. Annotation times for DA in terms of the average time taken to assess a single translation are straightforward to compute, since a single

	DA Crowd	DA Researcher	RR Researcher
WMT16	19.6	–	20.8
WMT17	17.5	17.1	–

Table 9: Average annotation time per translation (in seconds)

translation is assessed per screen. Each RR assessment is made up of a relative ranking of five MT output translations, however. Therefore to compute average annotation times for a single translation with RR we simply divide the average time to evaluate five translations by five.

Before comparing annotation times, it is important to note that we must take care comparing annotations times collected in two different year's evaluation campaigns, as for researchers, the annotators involved in the evaluation will have some overlap, this is less likely for crowd-sourced workers and in both cases the data involved comes from two different data sets. The evaluation produced by researchers in WMT16 and WMT17 does, however, provide the first data enabling a comparison of annotation speeds for researchers employing DA and RR. Annotation times analysis should only provide an approximate indication of speeds as opposed to tried and tested findings, however, which we hope to provide in the future.

Table 9 shows the reduction in average annotation time resulting from DA's simpler assessment set-up for researchers, from 20.8 seconds per assessment with RR to 17.1 seconds with DA, an approximate reduction of 18%.

Comparing annotation speeds for crowd-sourced workers evaluating with DA in both WMT16 and WMT17, we also see a slight speed up from 19.6 to 17.5 seconds. It is difficult to conclude from a comparison of crowd-sourced workers that this as a genuine speed up as it is likely due at least in part to variance in annotation styles of two different groups of workers drawn from a very large crowd. For example, average annotation times of crowd-sourced workers in the APE task this year was 13.6 seconds with DA where a distinct set of workers was also employed.

In terms of researchers versus crowd-sourced workers evaluating with DA, when we compare this year's results, researchers appear to be marginally quicker, on average approximately 0.4 seconds faster per translation assessment. Although again, this comparison includes average annotation times of crowd-sourced workers that can naturally vary from one group to the next.

Finally, we include a brief comparison in terms of projected time commitments required by participants in future evaluations when the methodology employed is DA rather than RR. In subsequent evaluations, since we have verified that DA results produced by quality controlled crowdsourcing correspond very closely to researcher results, it should be possible to collect all to-English evaluations via crowd-sourcing. This means that the switch to DA may result in only requiring participants to make a time commitment in terms of out-of-English language pairs. For some research groups this will cut the required manual evaluation time commitment in half.

Assuming a similar number of language pairs as in WMT17 (14 language pairs), an RR manual evaluation, which in previous years required manual evaluation of 100 HITs (each containing 15 translations), amounts to a commitment of assessment of 1,500 translations per submitted system. Considering researchers took on average 20.8 seconds per translation, a team wishing to participate in all language pairs would require a total time commitment of approximately (1,500 x 20.8 seconds x 14 = 436,800 seconds) 121.3 hours. In comparison for DA, even if we stick with the same number of translations per submission (1,500), when we take into account the fact that all of the to-English language pairs can be crowd-sourced as well as the quicker annotation time for DA, the time commitment for such a team would be reduced by approximately 60% to (1,500 x 17.1 seconds x 7 = 179,550 seconds) 49.9 hours.

4 Quality Estimation Task

This shared task builds on its previous five editions to further examine automatic methods for estimating the quality of machine translation output at run-time, without the use of reference translations. It includes the (sub)tasks of word-level, phrase-level and sentence-level estimation. In addition to advancing the state of the art at all prediction levels, our goals include:

- To test the effectiveness of larger (domain-specific and professionally annotated) datasets. We do so by significantly increasing the size of one of last year's training sets.

- To study the effect of language direction and domain. We do so by providing two datasets created in similar ways, but for different domains and language directions.

- To investigate the utility of detailed information logged during post-editing. We do so by providing a score for perceived post-editing effort, post-editing time, keystrokes, and actual edits.

- To measure progress over years at all prediction levels. We do so by using last year's test set for comparative experiments.

This year's shared task provides new training and test datasets for all tasks, and allows participants to explore any additional data and resources deemed relevant. All tasks make use of a large dataset produced from post-editions by professional translators. The data is domain-specific (IT and Pharmaceutical domains) and substantially larger than in previous years. An in-house, in-domain SMT system was used to produce translations for all tasks. System-internal information was made available under request. The data is publicly available but since it was provided by industry collaborators it is subject to specific terms and conditions. However, these have no practical implications on the use of this data for research purposes.

The three tasks are defined as follows: Task 1 at sentence level (Section 4.4), Task 2 at word level (Section 4.5), and Task 3 at phrase level (Section 4.6). Two datasets are used for all tasks (Section 4.3): English-German and German-English SMT translations labelled with task-specific labels. Participants were also provided with a baseline set of features for each task, and a software package to extract these and other quality estimation features and perform model learning (Section 4.1). Participants (Section 4.2) could submit up to two systems for each task. A discussion on the main goals and findings from this year's task is given in Section 4.7.

4.1 Baseline systems

Sentence-level baseline system: For Task 1, QUEST++[12] (2015) was used to extract 17 MT system-independent features from the source and translation (target) files and parallel corpora:

- Number of tokens in the source and target sentences.
- Average source token length.
- Average number of occurrences of the target word within the target sentence.
- Number of punctuation marks in source and target sentences.
- Language model (LM) probability of source and target sentences based on models built using the source or target sides of the parallel corpus used to train the SMT system.
- Average number of translations per source word in the sentence as given by the IBM model 1 extracted using the SMT parallel corpus, and thresholded such that $P(t|s) > 0.2$ or $P(t|s) > 0.01$.
- Percentage of unigrams, bigrams and trigrams in frequency quartiles 1 (lower frequency words) and 4 (higher frequency words) in the source language extracted from the source side of the SMT parallel corpus.
- Percentage of unigrams in the source sentence seen in the source side of the SMT parallel corps.

These features were used to train a Support Vector Regression (SVR) algorithm using a Radial Basis Function (RBF) kernel within the SCIKIT-LEARN toolkit.[13] The γ, ϵ and C parameters were optimised via grid search with 5-fold cross validation on the training set, resulting in γ=0.01, ϵ = 0.0825, $C = 20$. This baseline system has proved robust across a range of language pairs, MT systems, and text domains for predicting various

forms of post-editing effort (2012; 2013; 2014; 2015; 2016a).

Word-level baseline system: For Task 2, the baseline features were extracted with the MARMOT tool (Logacheva et al., 2016). These are 28 features that have been deemed the most informative in previous research on word-level QE. 22 of them were taken from the feature set described in (Luong et al., 2014), and had also been used as a baseline feature set at WMT16:

- Word count in the source and target sentences, and source and target token count ratio. Although these features are sentence-level (i.e. their values will be the same for all words in a sentence), the length of a sentence might influence the probability of a word being wrong.
- Target token, its left and right contexts of 1 word.
- Source word aligned to the target token, its left and right contexts of 1 word. The alignments were given by the SMT system that produced the automatic translations.
- Boolean dictionary features: target token is a stopword, a punctuation mark, a proper noun, or a number.
- Target language model features:
  - The order of the highest order ngram which starts and end with the target token.
  - The order of the highest order ngram which starts and ends with the source token.
  - The part-of-speech (POS) tags of the target and source tokens.
  - Backoff behaviour of the ngrams (t_{i-2}, t_{i-1}, t_i), (t_{i-1}, t_i, t_{i+1}), (t_i, t_{i+1}, t_{i+2}), where t_i is the target token (backoff behaviour is computed as described by (2011)).

In addition to that, 6 new features were included which contain combinations of other features, and which proved useful in (Kreutzer et al., 2015; Martins et al., 2016):

- Target word + left context.
- Target word + right context.
- Target word + aligned source word.
- POS of target word + POS of aligned source word.

---

[12] https://github.com/ghpaetzold/questplusplus

[13] http://scikit-learn.org/

- Target word + left context + source word.
- Target word + right context + source word.

The baseline system models the task as a sequence prediction problem using the Linear-Chain Conditional Random Fields (CRF) algorithm within the CRFSuite tool (Okazaki, 2007). The model was trained using passive-aggressive optimisation algorithm.

We note that this baseline is different from the one used last year. In Section 4.7 we present results comparing this against last year's baseline.

Phrase-level baseline system: The phrase-level system is identical to the one used in last year's shared task. The phrase-level features were also extracted with MARMOT, but they are different from the word-level features. They are based on the sentence-level features in QUEST++.[14] These are the so-called "black-box" features — features that do not use the internal information from the MT system. The baseline uses the following 72 features:

- Source phrase frequency features:
    - average frequency of ngrams (unigrams, bigrams, trigrams) in different quartiles of frequency (the low and high frequency ngrams) in the source side of the SMT parallel corpus.
    - percentage of distinct source ngrams (unigrams, bigrams, trigrams) seen in the source side of the SMT parallel corpus.

- Translation probability features:
    - average number of translations per source word in the phrase as given by the IBM model 1 extracted using the SMT parallel corpus (with different translation probability thresholds: 0.01, 0.05, 0.1, 0.2, 0.5).
    - average number of translations per source word in the phrase as given by the IBM model 1 extracted using the SMT parallel corpus (with different translation probability thresholds: 0.01, 0.05, 0.1, 0.2, 0.5) weighted by the frequency of each word in the source side of the parallel SMT corpus.

- Punctuation features:
    - difference between numbers of various punctuation marks (periods, commas, colons, semicolons, question and exclamation marks) in the source and the target phrases.
    - difference between numbers of various punctuation marks normalised by the length of the target phrase.
    - percentage of punctuation marks in the target or source phrases.

- Language model features:
    - log probability of the source or target phrases based on models built using the source or target sides of the parallel corpus used to train the SMT system.
    - perplexity of the source and the target phrases using the same models as above.

- Phrase statistics:
    - lengths of the source or target phrases.
    - ratio between the source and target phrase lengths.
    - average length of tokens in source or target phrases.
    - average occurrence of target word within the target phrase.

- Alignment features:
    - number of unaligned target words, using the word alignment provided by the SMT decoder.
    - number of target words aligned to more than one source word.
    - average number of alignments per word in the target phrase.

- Part-of-speech features:
    - percentage of content words in the source or target phrases.
    - percentage of words of a particular part of speech tag (verb, noun, pronoun) in the source or target phrases.
    - ratio of numbers of words of a particular part of speech (verb, noun, pronoun) between the source and target phrases.
    - percentage of numbers and alphanumeric tokens in the source or target phrases.

[14]http://www.quest.dcs.shef.ac.uk/quest_files/features_blackbox

– ratio between the percentage of numbers and alphanumeric tokens in the source and target phrases.

This feature set was designed for sentences. We expect that phrases, being sequences of words of varied length, are similar to sentences and can be treated analogously in QE. On the other hand, unlike sentences, phrases are related to their neighbouring phrases, and in this respect they are similar to words. Therefore, analogously to the baseline word-level system, we treat phrase-level QE as a sequence labelling task, and model it using Conditional Random Fields. The phrase-level baseline system is trained with CRFSuite toolkit using passive-aggressive optimisation algorithm.

4.2 Participants

Table 10 lists all participating teams submitting systems to any of the tasks. Each team was allowed up to two submissions for each task and language pair. In the descriptions below, participation in specific tasks is denoted by a task identifier (T1 = task1, T2 = task 2, T3 = task 3).

CDACM (T2, T3): The submissions from CDACM use a recurrent neural network language model (RNN-LM) architecture for word-level QE as described in (Patel and M, 2016), and explore the word-level predictions for phrase-level QE. CDACM's WMT16 submission was modified to add other RNN variants, such as LSTMs, deep LSTMs and GRUs. Another difference with respect to the WMT16 submission is the addition of the predicted history (only previous prediction) and characters of the word as additional features to the RNN model. This modified architecture predicts the label (OK/BAD) in a slot rather than predicting the word as in the case of standard RNN-LMs. The input to the system is a word sequence, similar to the standard RNN-LM. Bilingual models were also used and performed better than monolingual models. The code for these models is freely available.[15]

DCU (T2): DCU's submission is an ensemble of neural MT systems with different input factors, designed to jointly tackle both the automatic post-editing and word-level QE.

Word-level features which have proven effective for QE, such as part-of-speech tags and dependency labels are included as input factors to NMT systems. NMT systems using different input representations are ensembled together in a log-linear model which is tuned for the F_1-mult metric using MERT (Och, 2003). The output of the ensemble is a pseudo-reference that is then TER aligned with the original MT to obtain OK/BAD tags for each word in the MT hypothesis.

DFKI (T1): These submissions investigate alternative machine learning models for the prediction of the HTER score on the sentence-level task. Instead of directly predicting the HTER score, the systems use a single-layer perceptron with four outputs that jointly predict the number of each of the four distinct post-editing operations that are then used to calculate the HTER score. This also gives the possibility to correct invalid (e.g. negative) predicted values prior to the calculation of the HTER score. The two submissions use the baseline features and the English-German submission also uses features from (Avramidis, 2017a).

JXNU (T1): The JXNU submissions use features extracted from a neural network, including embedding features and cross-entropy features of the source sentences and their machine translations. The sentence embedding features are extracted through global average pooling from word embedding, which are trained using the WORD2VEC toolkit. The sentence cross-entropy features are calculated by a recurrent neural network language model. They experimented with different sentence embedding dimensions of the source sentences and translation outputs, as well as different sizes of the training corpus. The experimental results show that the neural network features lead to significant improvements over the baseline, and that combining the neural network features with baseline features leads to further improvement.

POSTECH (T1, T2, T3): POSTECH's submissions to the sentence/word/phrase-level QE tasks are based on predictor-estimator architecture (Kim et al., 2017; Kim and Lee, 2016), which is the two-stage end-to-end

---

[15]https://github.com/patelrajnath/rnn4nlp

ID	Participating team
CDACM	Centre for Development of Advanced Computing, India (Patel and M, 2016)
DCU	Dublin City University (Hokamp, 2017)
DFKI	German Research Centre for Artificial Intelligence, Germany (Avramidis, 2017b)
JXNU	Jiangxi Normal University, China (Chen et al., 2017)
POSTECH	Pohang University of Science and Technology, Republic of Korea (Kim et al., 2017)
RTM	Referential Translation Machines, Turkey (Biçici, 2017)
SHEF	University of Sheffield, UK (Blain et al., 2017; Paetzold and Specia, 2017)
UHH	University of Hamburg, Germany (Duma and Menzel, 2017)
Unbabel	Unbabel, Portugal (Martins et al., 2017b)

Table 10: Participants in the WMT17 quality estimation shared task.

neural QE model. The predictor-estimator architecture consists of two types of stacked neural network models: 1) a word prediction model based on bidirectional and bilingual recurrent neural network language model trained on additional large-scale parallel corpora and 2) a neural quality estimation model trained on quality-annotated noisy parallel corpora. To jointly learn the two-stage model, a stack propagation method was applied (Zhang and Weiss, 2016). In addition, a "multilevel model" was developed where a task-specific predictor-estimator model was trained using not only task-specific training examples but also all the other training examples of QE subtasks. All the submitted runs are ensembles that combine a set of neural models, trained under different settings of varying dimensionalities and shuffling of training examples.

RTM (T1, T2, T3): The RTM systems are improved versions over WMT16's RTM submissions which average prediction scores from different models using weights based on their training performance to improve the overall test performance. They also use new features representing substring distances, punctuation tokens, character n-grams, and alignment crossings.

SHEF (T1, T2, T3): The SHEF team participated in all the three sub tasks. For task 1, two types of systems were submitted: CNN and QUEST-EMB. The CNN submissions are based on convolutional neural networks. The system first transforms the source and target sentences into sequences of character embeddings, and then passes them through a series of deep parallel stacked convolution/max pooling layers. The baseline features are provided through a multi-layer perceptron,

and then concatenated with the character-level information. Finally, the concatenation is passed onto another multi-layer perceptron and the very last layer outputs HTER values. The two submissions differ in the the use of standard (CNN+BASE-Single) and multi-task learning (CNN+BASE-Multi) for training. The QUEST-EMB submission follows the word embeddings approach used by (Scarton et al., 2016) for document-level QE. Here in-domain word embeddings are used instead of embeddings obtained general purpose data (same as in task 2, below). Word embeddings were averaged to generate a single vector for each sentence. Source and target word embeddings were then concatenated with the baseline features and given to an SVM regressor for model building.

For the word-level task SHEF investigated a new approach based on predicting the strength of the lexical relationships between the source and target sentences (BMAPS). Following the work by (Madhyastha et al., 2014), a bilinear model is trained from three matrices corresponding to the training data, the development set and a "truth" matrix between them, which is built from the word alignments and the gold labels to indicate which lexical items form a pair, and whether or not their lexical relation is OK or BAD. The first two matrices are built from 300 dimension word vectors computed with pre-trained in-domain word embeddings. They train their model over 100 iterations with the l_2 norm as regulariser and using the *forward-backward splitting* algorithm (FOBOS) (Duchi and Singer, 2009) as optimisation method. They report results considering the word and its context versus the word in isolation, as well as variants with and without the gold labels at training time.

187

Finally, for the phrase-level task, SHEF made use of predictions generated by BMAPS for task 2 and the phrase labelling approaches in (Blain et al., 2016). These approaches use the number of BAD word-level predictions in a phrase: an optimistic version labels the phrase as OK if at least half of the words in it are predicted to be OK, and a super-pessimistic version labels the phrase as BAD if any word is in is predicted to be BAD.

UHH (T1): The UHH-STK submission is based on sequence and tree kernels applied on the source and target input data for predicting the HTER score. The kernels use a back-translation of the MT output into the source language as an additional input data representation. Further hand-crafted features were defined in the form of the scores of the kernel functions applied on the pair of source and back-translation sentences. The submitted runs outperformed the baseline systems for both language pairs.

Unbabel (T1, T2): For word level, the "stacked" system stacks a linear and a neural model similar to the ones submitted by Unbabel at WMT16. The "full-stacked-src-mt" system incorporates the output of an APE system, converted to OK/BAD tags, as an additional feature, similar to their work in (Martins et al., 2017a). The sentence-level submissions use and normalise the word-level predictions as percentage of words edited to generate an HTER score.

4.3 Datasets

One of the main differences between this year's and previous years' tasks is the considerably larger size of human-labelled datasets made available to participants for training. Whereas the last year we released a corpus of $12,000$ instances (plus $1,000$ and $2,000$ for development and test, respectively), this year this figure was doubled. In contrast to last year, we also provide datasets for two language pairs.

The structure used for the data have been the same since WMT15. Each data instance consists of (i) a source sentence, (ii) its automatic translation into the target language, (iii) the manually post-edited version of the automatic translation, (iv) a free reference translation of the source sentence. Post-edits are used to extract labels for the

different levels of granularity, which allows using the same datasets for all three QE tasks.

The first dataset contains texts in **IT domain** translated **from English into German**. This is a superset of the last year's data: $11,000$ sentences from the same source were added to the training set. Their translations were produced using the same statistical MT system and post-edited by professional translators who are native speakers of German. The dataset statistics are outlined in Table 11.

The second dataset belongs to **pharmaceutical domain** and provides translations **from German into English**. It contains $25,000$ instances for training. Analogously to the IT dataset, automatic translations were generated with a statistical MT system and post-edited by professional translators. The dataset statistics are shown in Table 12. The Table shows another feature of this dataset: it contains much fewer errors than the IT one.

	Sentences	Words	% of BAD words
Training	23,000	404,198	20.55
Development	1,000	19,487	19.55
Test	2,000	35,577	19.70

Table 11: Statistics of the English–German dataset.

	Sentences	Words	% of BAD words
Training	25,000	453,666	12.55
Development	1,000	18,152	11.71
Test	2,000	36,119	11.52

Table 12: Statistics of the German–English dataset.

4.4 Task 1: Predicting sentence-level quality

This task consists in scoring (and ranking) translation sentences according to the proportion of their words that need to be fixed. HTER (Snover et al., 2006b) is used as quality score, i.e. the minimum edit distance between the machine translation and its manually post-edited version.

Labels HTER labels were computed using the TERCOM tool[16] with default settings (tokenised, case insensitive, exact matching only), with scores capped to 1.

---

[16]http://www.cs.umd.edu/~snover/tercom/

Evaluation Evaluation was performed against the true HTER label and/or ranking, using the following metrics:

- Scoring: Pearson's r correlation score (primary metric, official score for ranking submissions), Mean Average Error (MAE) and Root Mean Squared Error (RMSE).

- Ranking: Spearman's ρ rank correlation and DeltaAvg.

Statistical significance on Pearson r was computed using the William's test.[17]

Results Tables 13 and 14 summarise the results for Task 1 on German–English and English–German datasets, respectively, ranking participating systems best to worst using Pearson's r correlation as primary key. Spearman's ρ correlation scores should be used to rank systems for the ranking variant.

The top three systems are the same for both datasets, and the ranking of systems according to their performance is similar for both datasets. They are all based on neural models that first model the problem of word-level prediction and then somehow generalise such predictions for sentence level QE, either by using them directly (Unbabel) or building a model from word to sentence-level prediction (POSTECH). We also note that the majority of the systems perform better than the baseline, although five submissions are not significantly different from it.

4.5 Task 2: Predicting word-level quality

This task evaluates the extent to which we can detect word-level errors in MT output. Often, the overall quality of a translated segment is significantly harmed by specific errors in a small proportion of the words. Various classes of errors can be found in translations, but for this task we consider all error types together, aiming at making a binary distinction between correct (OK) and incorrect (BAD) tokens.

Labels The binary labels for the datasets (OK and BAD) were derived automatically from the TERCOM tool with default settings and disabled shifts (option "-d 0"). We aligned automatically translated sentences with their post-edited version and labelled each word in the automatic translation

with an edit operation: insertion, deletion, substitution or no edit (correct word). We mark each edited word as BAD, and the remainingn as OK.

Evaluation Analogously to the last year's task, the primary evaluation metric is the multiplication of F_1-scores for the OK and BAD classes, denoted as F_1-mult. Unlike previously used F_1-BAD score this metric is not biased towards "pessimistic" labellings. We also report F_1-scores for individual classes for completeness. We test the significance of the results using randomisation tests (Yeh, 2000) with Bonferroni correction (Abdi, 2007).

Results The results for Task 2 are summarised in Tables 15 and 16, ordered by the F_1-mult metric.

The top two systems are the same as for the sentence-level task. This is perhaps not surprising since these are essentially word-level predictors: POSTECH and Unbabel. These along with DCU's submissions (which were specifically designed for the English–German word-level task), are all based on neural models.

4.5.1 Word-level predictions for sentence-level QE

Given that some submissions to the sentence-level task which were actually based on word-level predictions performed very well at sentence level, here we study the performance of *all* teams participating in the word-level task for sentence-level prediction. The percentage of words labelled as BAD in a sentence can essentially be seen as a sentence-level HTER score. Participants were also invited to submit an additional word-level system tuned to optimise sentence-level scores, but we are not aware of systems that did so.

In order to obtain sentence-level scores from word-level predictions we computed HTER for each sentence in the test set as the percentage of words classified as BAD. We then evaluated the submissions in terms of sentence-level metrics: Pearson correlation, MAE, RMSE. Table 17 shows the performance of the word-level systems on the sentence level task for the German–English dataset and their comparison with the participants of the Task 1. It can be clearly seen that word-level predictions are very close to sentence-level ones: systems of different levels are well distributed along the ranked list.

The submissions by POSTECH and Unbabel show that word-level and sentence-level systems

---

---

[17]`https://github.com/ygraham/mt-qe-eval`

Model	Pearson r	MAE	RMSE	Spearman ρ	DeltaAvg
• POSTECH/Combined-MultiLevel-Ensemble	0.728	0.091	0.133	0.691	10.64
POSTECH/SingleLevel-Ensemble	0.715	0.094	0.136	0.669	10.44
Unbabel/full-stacked-src-mt	0.626	0.121	0.179	0.613	9.74
RTM/RTM-MIX	0.600	0.109	0.157	0.570	8.94
RTM/RTM-TREE	0.585	0.119	0.158	0.573	9.18
Unbabel/stacked	0.580	0.106	0.170	0.574	7.72
SHEF/QUEST-EMB-SCALE	0.558	0.121	0.161	0.561	8.79
JXNU/Emb+RNNLM+QuEst+SVM	0.531	0.130	0.167	0.520	8.62
UHH/STK1	0.503	0.137	0.172	0.503	8.17
UHH/STK2	0.489	0.140	0.175	0.482	7.97
BASELINE	0.441	0.128	0.175	0.446	6.81
DFKI/SLP4	0.398	0.123	0.188	0.396	5.82
SHEF/CNN+BASE-Single	0.390	0.136	0.179	0.388	6.39
SHEF/CNN+BASE-Multi	0.350	0.162	0.202	0.387	6.41

Table 13: Official results of the WMT17 Quality Estimation Task 1 for the German–English dataset. The winning submission is indicated by a • and is statistically significantly different from all others. Submissions in the grey area are those which are not significantly different from the baseline.

Model	Pearson r	MAE	RMSE	Spearman ρ	DeltaAvg
• POSTECH/Combined-MultiLevel-Ensemble	0.695	0.102	0.137	0.725	12.32
POSTECH/SingleLevel-Ensemble	0.673	0.107	0.141	0.703	11.98
Unbabel/full-stacked-src-mt	0.641	0.128	0.169	0.652	11.36
Unbabel/stacked	0.589	0.129	0.176	0.610	10.28
JXNU/Emb+RNNLM+QuEst+SVM	0.522	0.126	0.163	0.545	9.54
UHH/STK2	0.509	0.130	0.166	0.534	9.41
UHH/STK1	0.508	0.129	0.165	0.533	9.49
SHEF/QUEST-EMB-SCALE	0.496	0.126	0.166	0.513	8.96
RTM-MIX	0.454	0.130	0.171	0.477	8.64
RTM-PLS-GBR	0.430	0.131	0.173	0.452	8.23
SHEF/CNN+BASE-Single	0.416	0.135	0.174	0.444	8.13
SHEF/CNN+BASE-Multi	0.402	0.135	0.178	0.452	8.16
BASELINE	0.397	0.136	0.175	0.425	7.45
DFKI/SLP4	0.113	0.153	0.204	0.136	2.5

Table 14: Official results of the WMT17 Quality Estimation Task 1 for the English–German dataset. The winning submission is indicated by a • and is statistically significantly different from all others. Submissions in the grey area are those which are not significantly different from the baseline.

Model	F_1-mult	F_1-BAD	F_1-OK
• POSTECH/Combined-MultiLevel-Ensemble	0.535	0.569	0.940
• Unbabel/full-stacked-src	0.529	0.562	0.941
POSTECH/SingleLevel-Ensemble	0.516	0.552	0.936
Unbabel/stacked	0.466	0.497	0.936
BASELINE	0.342	0.365	0.939
CDACM/RNN	0.333	0.370	0.900
RTM/s4-RTM-GLMd	0.329	0.350	0.939
SHEF/BMAPS-unigram	0.088	0.210	0.419
SHEF/BMAPS-nolabel-unigram	0.082	0.209	0.391

Table 15: Official results of the WMT17 Quality Estimation Task 2 for the German–English dataset. The winning submissions are indicated by a • and are statistically significantly different from all others. Submissions in the grey area are those which are not significantly different from the baseline.

Model	F_1-mult	F_1-BAD	F_1-OK
• POSTECH/Combined-MultiLevel-Ensemble	0.568	0.628	0.904
• Unbabel/full-stacked-src-mt	0.566	0.625	0.906
• DCU/SRC-APE-QE-TUNED	0.559	0.614	0.910
• DCU/AVG-ALL	0.556	0.611	0.910
POSTECH/SingleLevel-Ensemble	0.543	0.607	0.894
Unbabel/stacked	0.512	0.581	0.882
CDACM/RNN	0.370	0.457	0.809
BASELINE	0.361	0.407	0.886
RTM/s5-RTM-GLMd	0.285	0.322	0.884
RTM/s4-RTM-GLMd	0.261	0.293	0.889
SHEF/BMAPS-unigram	0.097	0.302	0.322
SHEF/BMAPS-nolabel-unigram	0.157	0.325	0.484

Table 16: Official results of the WMT17 Quality Estimation Task 2 for the English–German dataset. The winning submissions are indicated by a • and are statistically significantly different from all others. Submissions in the grey area are those which are not significantly different from the baseline.

trained on the same data using the same (or similar) methods yield very close results: the POSTECH sentence-level systems occupy the first two positions in the list, while their word-level systems follow. The corresponding word-level and sentence-level systems by Unbabel are even closer, their differences are not statistically significant. This is expected since Unbabel's submission to the sentence-level task was based on their predictions for the word-level task. Finally, the baselines for the two task do not show significant differences in their performance either, although they are based on very different features and models.

Overall, these results suggest that word-level QE models can indeed be successfully used to predict sentence-level quality of translation. Additionally, sentence-level metrics proved suitable for the evaluation of word-level QE models (the rankings of word-level submissions produced by F_1-mult and Pearson r metrics have correlation coefficient of 0.96). Results for the English–German task show the same trend.

4.6 Task 3: Predicting phrase-level quality

This level of granularity was first introduced in the shared task at WMT16. The goal is to predict MT quality at the level of phrases.

Labels The phrase-level QE task requires segmenting training and test sentences into phrases. We used the segmentation produced by the SMT system which generated automatic translations for the datasets. The phrase-level labels were produced from binary word-level labels: we labelled a phrase as OK if all words in it were correct (OK

words). Any phrase with one or more BAD words was labelled as BAD.

Evaluation In contrast to the last year's phrase-level shared task, where we used word-level metrics to evaluate phrase-level submissions, this time we resort to phrase-level F_1 scores. The reason for that is that the word-level metrics were unable to differentiate between various systems. Therefore, here our primary metric is the phrase-level version of F_1-mult, and we also report phrase-level F_1-BAD and F_1-OK. Statistical significance was computed using randomised test with Bonferroni correction as in task 2.

Results The results of the phrase-level task are represented in Tables 18 and 19. These results follow from those for the word-level task, with POSTECH showing significantly better results overall.

4.7 Discussion

In what follows, we discuss the main findings of this year's shared task based on the goals we had previously identified for it.

Larger training data To test the effectiveness of larger (domain-specific and professionally annotated) datasets, we increase the size of last year's training set for English–German. In order to check if the increased training data size helps improve the systems' performance we compare the baseline systems for all tasks trained on last year's versus this year's dataset, with parameters optimised on the same development sets.

Model	Pearson r	MAE	RMSE
• POSTECH/Combined-MultiLevel-Ensemble	0.728	0.091	0.133
POSTECH/SingleLevel-Ensemble	0.715	0.094	0.136
word POSTECH/Combined-MultiLevel-Ensemble	0.687	0.092	0.149
word POSTECH/SingleLevel-Ensemble	0.674	0.095	0.153
Unbabel/full-stacked-src-mt	0.626	0.121	0.179
word Unbabel/full-stacked-src-mt	0.625	0.147	0.242
RTM/RTM-MIX	0.600	0.109	0.157
RTM/RTM-TREE	0.585	0.119	0.158
Unbabel/stacked	0.580	0.106	0.170
word Unbabel/stacked	0.580	0.147	0.242
SHEF2/QUEST-EMB-SCALE	0.558	0.121	0.161
JXNU/Emb+RNNLM+QuEst+SVM	0.531	0.130	0.167
UHH/STK1	0.503	0.137	0.172
UHH/STK2	0.489	0.140	0.175
word BASELINE	0.455	0.118	0.197
word CDACM/RNN	0.450	0.132	0.198
BASELINE	0.441	0.128	0.175
word RTM/s4-RTM-GLMd	0.425	0.122	0.201
DFKI/SLP4	0.398	0.123	0.188
SHEF1/CNN+BASE-Single	0.390	0.136	0.179
SHEF1/CNN+BASE-Multi	0.350	0.162	0.202
word SHEF/BMAPS-nolabel-unigram	0.180	0.592	0.628
word SHEF/BMAPS-unigram	0.167	0.574	0.613

Table 17: Additional results of the WMT17 Quality Estimation Task 1 for the German–English dataset: using for the word-level predictions for sentence-level QE, evaluated for scoring. The winning submission is indicated by a • and is statistically significantly different from all others. Submissions in the grey area are those which are not significantly different from the baselines. The word-level systems are denoted with prefix **word**.

Model	F_1-**mult**	F_1-BAD	F_1-OK
• POSTECH/PredictorEstimator-Combined-MultiLevel-Ensemble	0.561	0.615	0.912
POSTECH/PredictorEstimator-SingleLevel-Ensemble	0.543	0.599	0.906
CDACM/RNN	0.381	0.444	0.858
BASELINE	0.360	0.397	0.907
RTM/s5-RTM-GLMd	0.284	0.312	0.908
RTM/s4-RTM-GLMd	0.278	0.306	0.908
SHEF/BMAPS-unigram-opti	0.141	0.299	0.473
SHEF/BMAPS-unigram-nolabel-opti	0.132	0.300	0.440

Table 18: Official results for the WMT17 Quality Estimation Task 3 for the German-English data. The winning submission is indicated by a • and is statistically significantly different from all others. The gray area indicates the submissions whose results are not statistically different from the baseline.

Model	F_1-**mult**	F_1-BAD	F_1-OK
• POSTECH/PredictorEstimator-Combined-MultiLevel-Ensemble	0.586	0.679	0.863
POSTECH/PredictorEstimator-SingleLevel-Ensemble	0.549	0.652	0.843
CDACM/RNN	0.391	0.535	0.731
BASELINE	0.327	0.402	0.814
SHEF/BMAPS-unigram-opti	0.226	0.409	0.553
SHEF/BMAPS-unigram-nolabel-opti	0.148	0.388	0.380

Table 19: Official results for the WMT17 Quality Estimation Task 3 for the English–German data. The winning submission is indicated by a • and is statistically significantly different from all others. The gray area indicates the submissions whose results are not statistically different from the baseline.

In Table 20 we show the performance of the baseline systems for all tasks trained on the WMT16 and WMT17 English–German datasets and tested on the WMT16 test set. The performance improves for all tasks when using the WMT17 training set, which is much larger. However, the gain for the word-level and phrase-level tasks is smaller than that for sentence level. For the word-level task, we also include experiments with the WMT16 baseline system, which was simpler than the WMT17 baseline system. We observe larger improvement from the new word-level features which we included in this year's baseline system than from the larger training set. This suggests that better features/models can lead to larger performance gains than more data, at least for the word-level task.

2016 word-level baseline			
Training set	F_1-mult	F_1-BAD	F_1-OK
2016 data	0.324	0.368	0.880
2017 data	0.335	0.378	0.886
2017 word-level baseline			
Training set	F_1-mult	F_1-BAD	F_1-OK
2016 data	0.341	0.384	0.887
2017 data	0.360	0.404	0.892
Phrase-level baseline			
Training set	F_1-mult	F_1-BAD	F_1-OK
2016 data	0.311	0.389	0.799
2017 data	0.328	0.403	0.812
Sentence-level baseline			
Training set	Pearson r	MAE	RMSE
2016 data	0.351	0.135	0.184
2017 data	0.397	0.136	0.175

Table 20: Comparison of baseline English–German systems trained on WMT16 and WMT17 datasets (tested on the WMT16 test set) for all tasks.

Progress over years Progress over years is a difficult factor to measure. We attempted to do so this year for the first time given the similarity between the tasks this and last year for the English–German data. We do so by requesting participants in this year's task to submit results using their WMT17 systems on the WMT16 test sets. We note however that this comparison is also affected by the increased size of the training set for this language pair in the current edition of the task. Therefore, the WMT17 systems may be better systems because of better techniques but also because of larger amounts of training data.

In Table 21 we compare the results from WMT16 and WMT17 systems on the WMT16 test set at sentence level, where WMT16 systems are highlighted in cyan background. Overall, it can be clearly seen that WMT17 systems perform better: last year's top system is only the 4th best compared to the WMT17 submissions, and half of WMT16 participants are below this year's baseline. It is important to note that the baseline performs much better than last year because of the additional training data – as shown in Table 20 – since the baseline system itself did not change.

Table 22 shows the results for word-level systems, which indicates a similar trend: systems also improved from last year's submissions, with last year's winner being outperformed by four other systems, and the majority of WMT16 participants performing closely to this year's baseline (which we note is a stronger model than last year's baseline as previously discussed).

Finally, the same trend is observed when comparing phrase-level systems submitted to WMT16 and WMT17 in Table 23. The only difference is that although the new data improved the performance of the phrase-level baseline system, this improvement did not change its position in the systems ranking.

Overall, the (Person r and F_1-mult) scores of the winning submissions this year is much higher than in last year's results, which we believe to be a combination of better techniques as well as better (larger) data.

The progress of state-of-the-art QE models can also be tracked by the performance of recurring participants: the results of systems by POSTECH (tasks 1, 2, 3) and CDACM (task 2) teams are better this year.

We note the increasing popularity of neural networks and their improving performance for QE: although some of the last year's winners (e.g. YSDA team which won the sentence-level task) did not use neural networks, all WMT17 winners and the majority of best-performing systems use neural networks for model building.

Languages and domains To study the effect of language direction and domain, we provided two datasets created in similar ways, but for different domains and language directions, as was previously mentioned. The QE performance on these datasets varies considerably, with German–English showing higher scores for the sentence-

Model	Pearson r	MAE	RMSE
• POSTECH/PredictorEstimator-Combined-MultiLevel-Ensemble	0.714	0.096	0.134
POSTECH/PredictorEstimator-SingleLevel-Ensemble	0.686	0.101	0.139
JXNU/Emb+RNNLM+QuEst+SVM	0.527	0.122	0.163
• YSDA/SNTX+BLEU+SVM	0.525	12.30	16.41
UHH/STK2	0.524	0.124	0.162
UHH/STK1	0.516	0.123	0.163
SHEF/QUEST-EMB-SCALE	0.499	0.124	0.167
POSTECH/SENT-RNN-QV2	0.460	13.58	18.60
SHEF-LIUM/SVM-NN-emb-QuEst	0.451	12.88	17.03
POSTECH/SENT-RNN-QV3	0.447	13.52	18.38
SHEF-LIUM/SVM-NN-both-emb	0.430	12.97	17.33
SHEF/CNN+BASE-Single	0.421	0.131	0.174
UGENT-LT3/SCATE-SVM2	0.412	19.57	24.11
BASELINE 2017	0.399	0.132	0.175
SHEF/CNN+BASE-Multi	0.397	0.135	0.184
UFAL/MULTIVEC	0.377	13.60	17.64
RTM/RTM-FS-SVR	0.376	13.46	17.81
UU/UU-SVM	0.370	13.43	18.15
UGENT-LT3/SCATE-SVM1	0.363	20.01	24.63
RTM/RTM-SVR	0.358	13.59	18.06
BASELINE 2016	0.351	13.53	18.39
SHEF/SimpleNets-SRC	0.320	13.92	18.23
SHEF/SimpleNets-TGT	0.283	14.35	18.22
RTM-PLS-GBR	0.163	0.150	0.192
RTM-TREE	0.155	0.148	0.190
DFKI/SLP4	0.132	0.154	0.206

Table 21: Comparison of official results of WMT17 and WMT16 sentence-level QE task on the English–German WMT16 test set. The winning submission is indicated by a • and is statistically significantly different from all others. WMT16 systems are highlighted with cyan.

level task, both in terms of the baseline systems the winning submissions, and English–German showing generally higher scores for the word and phrase-level tasks (except for the baseline system in the phrase-level task). Even though the performance scores may not be directly comparable, we can make some interesting observations. We believe that the main reasons for these differences are related to the general quality of the MT systems and – as a consequence – the distribution of quality labels in the QE datasets, and – to a lesser extent – the sizes of the QE training sets, which are slightly different (see Tables 11 and 12).

The quality of the translations in each dataset is very different. As shown in Tables 11 and 12, the German–English dataset contains much fewer errors. Indeed, when building the SMT systems that generated these translations, we observed very different BLEU scores: 35.9 for English–German (IT domain), and 53.4 for German–English (Pharma domain). This difference in quality is not due to training settings, since these were the same for both datasets, except that for English–German the SMT training set was much larger (7.2 vs 2.09 million sentences). Details on the SMT models and data used to build such models are given in (Specia et al., 2017a). In addition to the well-known fact that translating into English normally leads to better quality than translating from English, we hypothesise that this difference could be due to higher token repetition rate in the German–English dataset. The difference in quality was confirmed by the average HTER score obtaining from the post-editing of these test sets: 0.25 for English–German and 0.19 for German–English.[18] The fact that the German–English dataset contains fewer errors makes it harder for the word and phrase-level tasks to achieve high F_1-mult as

---

[18]We note that these BLEU and HTER scores were measured on a superset of this data, as described in (Specia et al., 2017a)

Model	F_1-**mult**	F_1-BAD	F_1-OK
• POSTECH/Combined-MultiLevel-Ensemble	0.581	0.637	0.913
• DCU/SRC-APE-QE-TUNED	0.575	0.627	0.917
• DCU/AVG-ALL	0.573	0.625	0.917
POSTECH/SingleLevel-Ensemble	0.561	0.619	0.906
• Unbabel/ensemble	0.495	0.560	0.885
Unbabel/linear	0.463	0.529	0.875
UGENT LT3/SCATE-RF	0.411	0.492	0.836
CDACM/RNN	0.391	0.469	0.833
UGENT-LT3/SCATE-ENS	0.381	0.464	0.821
POSTECH/WORD-RNN-QV3	0.380	0.447	0.850
POSTECH/WORD-RNN-QV2	0.376	0.454	0.828
UAlacant/SBI-Online-baseline	0.367	0.456	0.805
BASELINE 2017	0.360	0.404	0.892
CDACM/RNN	0.353	0.419	0.842
SHEF/SHEF-MIME-1	0.338	0.403	0.839
SHEF/SHEF-MIME-0.3	0.330	0.391	0.845
BASELINE 2016	0.324	0.368	0.880
RTM/s5-RTM-GLMd	0.308	0.349	0.882
RTM/s5-RTM-GLMd	0.305	0.353	0.865
UAlacant/SBI-Online	0.290	0.406	0.715
RTM/s4-RTM-GLMd	0.286	0.326	0.878
RTM/s4-RTM-GLMd	0.273	0.307	0.888
SHEF/BMAPS-unigram	0.158	0.316	0.501
SHEF/SHEF/BMAPS-nolabel-unigram	0.098	0.296	0.330

Table 22: Comparison of official results of WMT17 and WMT16 word-level QE task on the English–German WMT16 test set. Winning submissions are indicated by a • and are statistically significantly different from all others. WMT16 systems are highlighted with cyan.

Model	F_1-**mult**	F_1-BAD	F_1-OK
• POSTECH/Combined-MultiLevel-Ensemble	0.603	0.693	0.869
POSTECH/SingleLevel-Ensemble	0.562	0.662	0.849
CDACM/RNN	0.403	0.541	0.744
POSTECH/RNN-QV3	0.393	0.518	0.759
POSTECH/RNN-QV2	0.388	0.504	0.771
CDACM/RNN	0.378	0.500	0.756
USFD2/CONTEXT	0.364	0.467	0.780
USFD2/W&SLP4PT	0.363	0.475	0.764
RTM/s5-RTM-GLMd	0.342	0.420	0.814
RTM/s4-RTM-GLMd	0.336	0.411	0.817
RTM/s5-RTM-GLMd	0.331	0.413	0.802
BASELINE 2017	0.328	0.403	0.812
BASELINE 2016	0.311	0.389	0.799
RTM/s4-RTM-GLMd	0.306	0.376	0.815
UAlacant/SBI-Online-baseline	0.275	0.502	0.547
SHEF/BMAPS-unigram-opti	0.233	0.415	0.562
SHEF/BMAPS-unigram-nolabel-opti	0.149	0.398	0.373
UAlacant/SBI-Online	0.146	0.456	0.320

Table 23: Comparison of official results of WMT17 and WMT16 phrase-level QE task on the English–German WMT16 test set. The winning submission is indicated by a • and is statistically significantly different from all others. WMT16 systems are highlighted with cyan.

the models will have a strong bias towards predicting words or phrases as OK. In fact, if we take the word-level task, the difference between F_1-BAD and F_1-OK scores is much more noticeable for German–English (0.569 vs 0.940, respectively – Table 15) than for English–German (0.628 vs 0.904, respectively – Table 16), showing that the systems tend to overpredict OK labels for German–English. The same applies to the phrase-level task. For the sentence-level task, the skewed distribution towards good quality translations does not have the same effect, perhaps due to the prediction of an aggregated (HTER) score and the metric used for evaluation.

Additional evidence To investigate the utility of detailed information logged during post-editing, we offered to participants other sources of information: post-editing time, keystrokes, and actual edits. Surprisingly, no participating system requested these additional labels. The DFKI submission re-created some of this information by further annotating words with the actual edit operations, as obtained from the HTER alignments. Instead of predicting the HTER score, the systems attempted to predict the number of each of the four post-editing operations (add, replace, shift, delete) at the sentence level. However, this did not lead to positive results. In future editions of the task, we plan to make this detailed post-editing information available again and suggest clear ways of using it.

5 Automatic Post-editing Task

The WMT shared task on MT automatic post-editing (APE), this year at its third round at WMT, aims to evaluate systems for the automatic correction of errors in a machine translated text. As pointed out by (Chatterjee et al., 2015b), from the application point of view the task is motivated by its possible uses to:

- Improve MT output by exploiting information unavailable to the decoder, or by performing deeper text analysis that is too expensive at the decoding stage;

- Cope with systematic errors of an MT system whose decoding process is not accessible;

- Provide professional translators with improved MT output quality to reduce (human) post-editing effort;

- Adapt the output of a general-purpose MT system to the lexicon/style requested in a specific application domain.

The third round of the APE task proposed to participants the same general evaluation framework of the previous ones (Bojar et al., 2015, 2016a). It consists in a "black box" scenario in which the MT system that produced the translations is unknown to the participants and cannot be modified.

This year the task has been extended by including German-English as a new language direction in addition to English-German, which was the only language pair covered in the 2016 round. For both directions, participants operated with domain-specific data (`information technology` for EN-DE and `pharmacological` for DE-EN),[19] with post-edits collected from professional translators.[20] All data has been provided by the European Project QT21.[21]

As in 2016, TER and BLEU computed between automatic and human post-edits have been respectively used as primary and secondary evaluation metrics. In continuity with the previous round, a manual evaluation has also been carried out to gain further insights on final output quality. However, while in 2016 Appraise[22] (Federmann, 2012) was employed for manual evaluation, this year the German to English evaluation was carried out via direct human assessment (Graham et al., 2016) and quality controlled crowd-sourcing on Amazon's Mechanical Turk[23], while the English to German evaluation was completed, again via direct assessment, but translation students were employed as opposed to crowd-sourcing.

In terms of participants and submitted runs, this year's round replicated the success of the 2016 edition. On English-German we had 7 participants (one more than in 2016), with a total of 15 submitted runs. On German-English (a more challenging direction due to a much higher quality of the original MT output), we had 2 participants, with a total of 5 submitted runs.

Building on the recent success of neural ap-

---

[19] As opposed to the general news domain data used in the first round, which proved to be more difficult to handle due to scarce repetitiveness.

[20] As opposed to the less coherent crowdsourced material used in the first round.

[21] http://www.qt21.eu/

[22] https://github.com/cfedermann/Appraise

[23] https://www.mturk.com

proaches to APE, this year all the submissions relied on neural end-to-end solutions. The adoption of multi-source models (able to combine information from raw MT output and the original source text) and the extensive use of available synthetic data (to increase the size of the training set) are other traits common to several systems.

On both directions, all participants managed to beat the baseline, at least with their primary submission. Top results achieved impressive improvements up to -4.9 TER and +7.6 BLEU points on English-German and smaller, but statistically significant gains up to -0.25 TER and +0.3 BLEU on German-English. The manual evaluation of participants' primary submissions confirmed the jump in performance of this year's systems in the English-German task. Although all of them are still below human quality, the gap has been reduced with respect to the 2016 round, three systems are almost on par in the top tier (last year it was only one) and the improvements over the baseline are significantly better than the original MT output prior to post-editing for all participants (last year this was only true for the top submission).

5.1 Task description

Similar to previous years, participants were provided with training and development data consisting of (*source*, *target*, *human post-edit*) triplets, and were asked to return automatic post-edits for a test set of unseen (*source*, *target*) pairs.

5.1.1 Data

Previous rounds of the APE task suggested (Bojar et al., 2015) and confirmed (Bojar et al., 2016a) the dependence of system results on data repetitiveness. In the 2015 pilot task, dealing with "general-domain" news data and crowdsourced post-edits proved to be very difficult due to data sparsity issues that prevented participants to learn from the training set useful correction patterns reapplicable to the test set. In 2016, the switch to more repetitive (in other terms, less sparse) domain-specific data post-edited by professional translators resulted in a higher applicability of the learned correction patterns. The effect of this switch was made evident by final results: while none of the submitted runs was able to beat the baseline in the pilot round, more than half of the submissions significantly outperformed it in 2016. Based on these outcomes, and to give stability to

a relatively young task, also this year we opted for the adoption of domain-specific data post-edited by professionals for both language directions.

Training and development sets consist of (*source*, *target*, *human post-edit*) triplets in which:

- The source (SRC) is a tokenized sentence with length between 3 and 30 tokens;

- The target (TGT) is a tokenized translation of the source. Translations were obtained from statistical MT systems.[24] This information, however, was unknown to participants, for which the MT system was a black-box.

- The human post-edit (PE) is a manually-revised version of the target, done by professional translators.

Test data consists of (*source*, *target*) pairs having similar characteristics of those in the training set. Human post-edits of the test target instances were left apart to measure system performance.

English-German data were drawn from the `Information Technology` (IT) domain. Training and test sets respectively contain 11,000 and 2,000 triplets. The data released for the 2016 round of the task (15,000 instances) and the artificially generated post-editing triplets (4 million instances) used by last year's winning system (Junczys-Dowmunt and Grundkiewicz, 2016) were also provided as additional training material.

German-English data were drawn from the `Pharmacological` domain. Training and development sets respectively contain 25,000 and 1,000 triplets, while the test set consists of 2,000 instances.

Table 24 provides some basic statistics about the data (the same used for the sentence-level quality estimation task), which has been released by the European Project QT21 (Specia et al., 2017b).[25] In addition, Tables 25 and 26 provide a view of the data from a task difficulty standpoint. Table 25 shows the repetition rate (RR) values of the data sets released in the three rounds

---

[24]We used phrase-based MT systems trained with generic and in-domain parallel training data, leveraging pre-reordering techniques (Herrmann et al., 2013), and taking advantage of POS and word class-based language models.

[25]For both language directions, the source sentences and reference translations were provided by TAUS (https://www.taus.net/).

	Tokens			Types			Lemmas		
	SRC	TGT	PE	SRC	TGT	PE	SRC	TGT	PE
EN-DE									
Train (23,000)	384448	403306	411246	18220	27382	31652	10946	21959	25550
Dev (1,000)	17827	19355	19763	2931	3333	3506	1922	2686	2806
Test (2,000)	65120	69812	71483	8061	9765	10502	2626	3976	4282
DE-EN									
Train (25,000)	437833	453096	456163	29745	19866	19172	23532	15422	14131
Dev (1,000)	17578	18130	18313	4426	3583	3642	3589	2828	2836
Test (2,000)	35087	36082	36480	6987	5391	5488	5590	4255	4255

Table 24: Data statistics.

of the WMT APE task. RR measures the repetitiveness inside a text by looking at the rate of non-singleton n-gram types (n=1...4) and combining them using the geometric mean. Larger values indicate a higher text repetitiveness and, as discussed in (Bojar et al., 2016a), suggest a higher chance of learning from the training set correction patterns that are applicable also to the test set. In (Bojar et al., 2016a) we considered the large differences in repetitiveness between APE15 and APE16 data as a possible motivation for the significant baseline improvements achieved by participants in the second round of the task. As we will see in Section 5.4, similar explanations hold for this year's results, in which the higher repetitiveness of English-German data likely contributed to facilitate the task in comparison with the German-English direction.

Table 26 shows, for the same data sets, the Translation Error Rate (TER) (Snover et al., 2006a) and the BLEU score (Papineni et al., 2002) of the original target translations, computed against the human post-edits. In this case, numeric evidence of a higher quality of the original translations can indicate a smaller room for improvement for APE systems (having, at the same time, less to learn during training and less to correct at test stage). On one side, indeed, training on good (or near-perfect) automatic translations can drastically reduce the number of learned correction patterns. On the other side, testing on similarly good translations can drastically reduce the number of corrections required and the applicability of the learned patterns, thus making the task potentially more difficult. Together with the lower repetition rates observed, also the large differences in translation quality between the two APE17 language directions (62.49 BLEU for APE17_EN-DE

vs 79.54 for APE17_DE-EN) suggest a higher difficulty for the German-English task. Further indications in this direction are provided by Figures 7 and 8, which plot the TER distribution for the test items in the two data sets. As can be seen, the quality of English-German data is much more balanced compared to German-English, with about 50% of the test items distributed over the first five bins. In particular, what makes a big difference between the two test sets is the proportion of "perfect" test instances having TER=0 (i.e. items that should not be modified by the APE systems). While for English-German they represent 14.0% of the total, for German-English they are about 45.0% of the test data. This means that, for almost half of the German-English test set, any correction made by the APE systems will be unnecessary and penalized by automatic evaluation metrics. This difficult scenario calls for conservative and precise systems able to properly fix errors only in the remaining 50% of the data.

5.1.2 Evaluation metric

System performance was evaluated by computing the distance between *automatic* and *human* post-edits of the machine-translated sentences present in the test set (i.e. for each of the $2,000$ target test sentences). Similar to last year, this distance was measured in terms of TER and BLEU (case-sensitive).[26] Systems were ranked based on the average TER calculated on the test set by using the

---

[26]In the case of TER, the baseline is computed by averaging the distances between each machine-translated sentence and its human-revised version. The actual evaluation metric is the human-targeted TER (HTER). For the sake of clarity, since TER and HTER compute edit distance in the same way (the only difference is in the origin of the correct sentence used for comparison), henceforth we will use TER to refer to both metrics.

		APE15	APE16	APE17_EN-DE	APE17_DE-EN
	SRC	2.905	6.616	7.216	5.225
RR	TGT	3.312	8.845	9.531	6.841
	PE	3.085	8.245	8.946	6.293

Table 25: Repetition Rate (RR) of the WMT15 (English-Spanish, news domain, crowdsourced post-edits), WMT16 (English-German, IT domain, professional post-editors), WMT17_EN-DE (English-German, IT domain, professional post-editors) and WMT17_DE-EN (German-English, pharmacological domain, professional post-editors) APE task data.

	APE15	APE16	APE17_EN-DE	APE17_DE-EN
TER	23.84	24.76	24.48	15.55
BLEU	n/a	62.11	62.49	79.54

Table 26: Translation quality (TER/BLEU of TGT and proportion of TGTs with TER=0) of the WMT15, WMT16, WMT17_EN-DE and WMT17_DE-EN data.

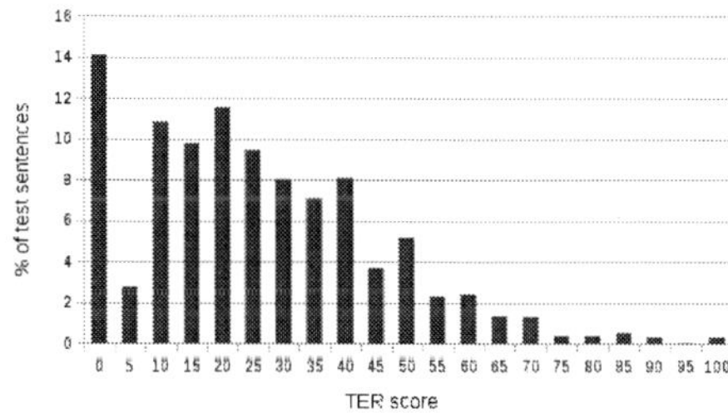

Figure 7: TER distribution over the **EN-DE** test set

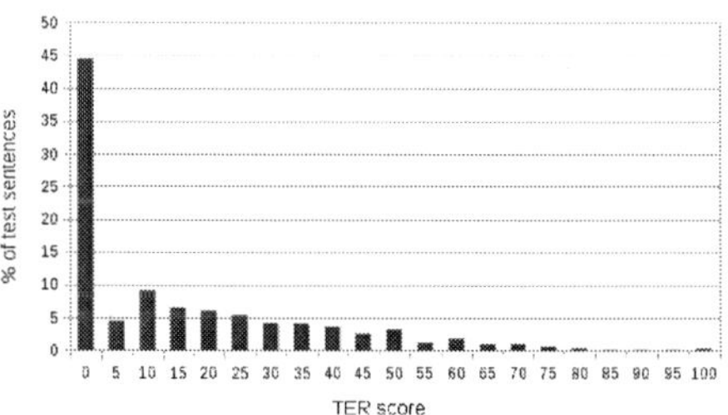

Figure 8: TER distribution over the **DE-EN** test set

TERcom[27] software: lower average TER scores correspond to higher ranks. BLEU was computed using the multi-bleu.perl package[28] available in MOSES.

5.1.3 Baselines

Also this year, the official baseline results are the TER and BLEU scores calculated by comparing the raw MT output with the human post-edits. In practice, the baseline APE system is a *"do-nothing"* system that leaves all the test targets unmodified. Baseline results, the same shown in Table 26, are also reported in Tables 28-29 for comparison with participants' submissions.

In continuity with the previous rounds, we used as additional term of comparison a re-implementation of the method firstly proposed by Simard et al. (2007). It relies on a phrase-based post-editing approach to the task, which represented the common backbone of APE systems before the spread of neural solutions. The system is based on Moses (Koehn et al., 2007); translation and reordering models were estimated following the Moses protocol with default setup using

MGIZA++ (Gao and Vogel, 2008) for word alignment. For language modeling we used the KenLM toolkit (Heafield, 2011) for standard n-gram modeling with an n-gram length of 5. Finally, the system was tuned on the development set, optimizing TER/BLEU with Minimum Error Rate Training (Och, 2003). The results of this additional term of comparison are also reported in Tables 28-29.

For each submitted run, the statistical significance of performance differences with respect to the baseline and our re-implementation of Simard et al. (2007) was calculated with the bootstrap test (Koehn, 2004).

5.2 Participants

Seven teams participated in the English-German task by submitting a total of fifteen runs. Two of them also participated in the German-English task with five submitted runs. Participants are listed in Table 27, and a short description of their systems is provided in the following.

Adam Mickiewicz University. AMU's (EN-DE) participation explores and combines multiple neural architectures available in the Marian toolkit.[29] They include single source (either

[27]http://www.cs.umd.edu/~snover/tercom/

[28]https://github.com/moses-smt/mosesdecoder/blob/master/scripts/generic/multi-bleu.perl

[29]https://github.com/marian-nmt/marian

ID	Participating team
EN-DE	
AMU	Adam Mickiewicz University, Poland (Junczys-Dowmunt and Grundkiewicz, 2017)
CUNI	Univerzita Karlova v Praze, Czech Republic (Variš and Bojar, 2017)
DCU	Dublin City University, Ireland (Hokamp, 2017)
FBK	Fondazione Bruno Kessler, Italy (Chatterjee et al., 2017)
JXNU	Jiangxi Normal University, Nanchang, China (Tan et al., 2017a)
LIG	University of Lille & University Grenoble, France (Berard et al., 2017)
USAAR	Saarland University, Germany
DE-EN	
FBK	Fondazione Bruno Kessler, Italy (Chatterjee et al., 2017)
LIG	University of Lille & University Grenoble, France (Berard et al., 2017)

Table 27: Participants in the WMT17 Automatic Post-editing task.

$src \rightarrow pe$ or $mt \rightarrow pe$) and multi-source models ($\{src, mt\} \rightarrow pe$), the latter being able to combine information from raw MT output and original source language input. Different attention mechanisms are explored, including soft attention (looking at information anywhere in the source sequence during decoding) and hard monotonic attention (looking at one encoder state at a time from left to right, thus being more conservative and faithful to the original input), which are combined in different ways in the case of multi-source models. The artificial data provided by Junczys-Dowmunt and Grundkiewicz (2016) are used to boost performance by increasing the size of the corpus used for training.

Univerzita Karlova v Praze. CUNI's (EN-DE) system is based on the character-to-character neural network architecture described in (Lee et al., 2016). This architecture was compared with the standard neural network architecture proposed by Bahdanau et al. (2014) which uses byte-pair encoding (Sennrich et al., 2015) for generating translation tokens. During the experiments, two setups have been compared for each architecture: *i)* a single encoder with SRC and MT sentences concatenated, and *ii)* a two-encoder system, where each SRC and MT sentence is fed to a separate encoder. The submitted system uses the two-encoder architecture with a character-level encoder and decoder. The initial state of the decoder is a weighted combination of the final states of the encoders. Attention is computed separately over each encoder. The model was trained using both the WMT17 training data and the artificial data provided by Junczys-Dowmunt and Grundkiewicz (2016). The WMT17 training dataset was sampled to match the

size of the artificial data. The submitted primary submission used beam-search for decoding while greedy decoding was used for the contrastive submission.

Dublin City University. DCU's (EN-DE) submission is an ensemble of neural MT systems with different input factors, designed to jointly tackle both the APE task and the Word-Level QE task. Word-Level features which have proven effective for QE, such as word-alignments, part-of-speech tags, and dependency labels, are included as input factors to neural machine translation systems, which are trained to output Post-Edited MT hypotheses. Concatenated *source + MT hypothesis* are also used as an input representation for some models. The system makes extensive use of the synthetic training data provided by Junczys-Dowmunt and Grundkiewicz (2016), as well as min-risk training for fine-tuning (Shen et al., 2016). The neural systems, which use different input representations but share the same output vocabulary, are then ensembled together in a log-linear model which is tuned for the TER metric using MERT.

Fondazione Bruno Kessler. FBK's (EN-DE & DE-EN) submission extends the existing NMT implementation in the Nematus toolkit (Sennrich et al., 2016) to train an ensemble of multi-source neural APE systems. Building on previous participations based on the phrase-based paradigm (Chatterjee et al., 2015a, 2016), and similar to (Libovický et al., 2016), such systems jointly learn from source and target information in order to increase robustness and precision of the automatic corrections. The n-best hypotheses produced by this ensemble are further re-ranked using features based on the edit distance between the original MT output and each APE hypothesis, as well as other statistical models (n-gram language model and operation sequence model). For English-German, generic models are trained using the ~4M synthetic data provided by Junczys-Dowmunt and Grundkiewicz (2016), and then fine-tuned with in-domain data. Similarly, for German-English, synthetic post-editing training data are created by round-trip translation of a sub-set of parallel data released in the medical task at WMT'14 (Bojar et al., 2014).

Jiangxi Normal University. JXNU's (EN-DE) system contains three neural automatic post-editing models: *npe_baseline*, *npe_minor* and *npe_single*. Based on Junczys-Dowmunt and Grundkiewicz (2016), the *npe_baseline* model is created and trained with the training set officially released by the evaluation campaign. The *npe_minor* model is obtained by fine-tuning *npe_baseline* with a triplets corpus including raw machine translation outputs needing four or less edit operations. The *npe_single* model is obtained by fine-tuning *npe_baseline* with a triplets corpus containing machine translations needing at most two edit operations. The output of these three systems is integrated into an n-best list of translations hypotheses, which are scored and ranked by means of a sentence-level QE approach (Specia et al., 2013) and a statistical language model (Stolcke, 2002). Since the raw machine translation outputs can be classified into five grades according to the above sentence-level QE score, the best output can be selected from the n-best list in accordance with the raw MT outputs' grading. The features used by these models can mitigate the over-correction problem emerged in previous rounds of the APE task (Bojar et al., 2016a).

University of Lille & University of Grenoble. LIG's (EN-DE & DE-EN) submission is a neural-based APE system that exploits the approach proposed by Libovický et al. (2016): instead of predicting words, it predicts edit operations (*keep*, *delete*, or *insert* a word). An advantage of this approach, is that it is very easy to learn to replicate the ("*do-nothing*") baseline, by just predicting *keep* operations. By contrast, it can be hard for a classic NMT model to learn the identity function, in particular because of the unknown word

problem, and because of the limited amounts of training data. LIG's submission proposes a number of improvements over this method: the simplest model ('*Contrastive-Forced*') uses a task-specific attention mechanism, which forces the decoder to look at the right word in the input (i.e., the word being post-edited). This simple approach gives very good results on the English-German task in limited data conditions. Finally, they also propose a chained architecture ('*Contrastive-Chained*'), which uses two different models (and two different training objectives): a translation model ($src \rightarrow mt$), and a post-editing model ($mt \rightarrow pe$). The attention vectors over src learned by the translation model are used by the post-editing model to give additional contextual information (when predicting a new edit operation, it can look at the mt word to post-edit, and at the src words that are aligned to this word.) This approach is a way to incorporate the source sentence into the proposed framework, and gives promising results on the English-German task, when adding more data ('*primary*' models).

Saarland University. USAAR's (EN-DE) submission combines a neural model and an operation sequence (OSM) phrase-based (Pal et al., 2016c) model. The neural system is trained on a bidirectional (forward-backward) RNN-based encoder-decoder[30] MT model (Bahdanau et al., 2014) trained for $mt \rightarrow pe$ translation. The network has been trained for 5 days using a hyper-parameter setting similar to (Pal et al., 2016b). Training data consists of WMT-2016, 2017 APE data (23K) and 4.5M artificial APE data (Junczys-Dowmunt and Grundkiewicz, 2016). The OSM phrase-based system (Pal et al., 2016c) consists of three basic components: corpus pre-processing, hybrid word alignment (Pal et al., 2016a) and a vanilla setting of a phrase-based MT system integrated with the hybrid word alignment. The model used 23K (*target, human post-edit*) data for training. Experiments on the WMT-2017 test set using both the neural and the OSM-based APE systems revealed that the neural system provides better performance for short sentences (less than 15 words) and the OSM-based APE model performs better for the longer ones. A manual inspection indicates that the neural system suffers from a "lack of coverage" while translating longer sentences. There-

---

[30]The system used is GroundHog – `https://github.com/lisa-groundhog/GroundHog`.

fore, the final submission was based on a mix of neural translations for short test sentences and OSM translations for the longer ones.

5.3 TER/BLEU results

Participants' TER and BLEU results are shown in Tables 28 (English-German) and 29 (German-English). The submitted runs are ranked based on the average TER (case-sensitive), which is the APE task primary evaluation metric. Overall, similar to last year, TER and BLEU rankings do not show major differences. The main ones can be found in the English-German task where: *i)* two mid-ranked primary submissions (USAAR and JXNU) are inversely ordered by the two metrics, and *ii)* the phrase-based APE (worse in terms of TER) would outperform the *"do-nothing"* strategy by around 0.48 BLEU points. In the German-English task, TER and BLEU rankings differ in the ordering of a primary submission and the *"do-nothing"* baseline, but the negligible score differences are not significant. As we will see in Section5.5, for English-German, the human evaluation based on direct assessment (DA) suggests a third different ranking that is slightly closer to the BLEU-based one (two primary submissions are ranked in the same position, while with TER this happens only in one case). On German-English, a slight preference is confirmed for the BLEU-based ranking as shown by the small difference (0.1) in average DA scores in favour of the *"do-nothing"* baseline over the second-ranked primary submission. However, due to the small differences in systems' architectures and results, it's not surprising that different metrics and evaluation criteria produce slightly different rankings. Also this year, it's hence difficult to draw definite conclusions about which automatic metric is more reliable.

English-German Compared to previous rounds of the APE task, the most noticeable aspect is that this year, for the first time, all participants managed to beat the MT baseline at least with their primary submission.[31] This steady improvement has been mainly driven by the massive migration to the neural approach, which in 2016 allowed the winning system to achieve impressive results (-3.24 TER, +5.54 BLEU with respect to the baseline). This year, the gains on English-German data

---

[31] In 2015, none of the submitted runs were able to consistently improve over the raw MT output. Last year, only half of the runs outperformed this baseline.

are even larger, with the winning system scoring -4.88 TER and +7.58 BLEU points better than the MT baseline. The technology advancement is evident if we look at our second term of comparison: the re-implementation of the phrase-based approach by Simard et al. (2007). Last year, on English-German, the results of this method were better than the baseline and in a middle position in the official participants' ranking. This year, on the same language direction, they are almost identical to those achieved in 2016, but also: *i)* worse than the baseline in terms of TER (+0.21), *ii)* slightly better in terms of BLEU (+0.48) and *iii)* competitive only against the contrastive submission of one participant. Considering the distance between the same phrase-based approach and the baseline as an indicator of the task difficulty across different rounds of the task, we hypothesize that the good results achieved by this year's participants are mainly due to improved techniques rather than "easier" test data. Indeed, for English-German where a comparison with last year is possible, the close repetition rate and BLEU scores reported in Tables 25 and 26 reveal a similar level of difficulty for the APE16 and APE_17 test data.

ID	Avg. TER	BLEU
FBK Primary	19.6	70.07
AMU Primary	19.77	69.5
AMU Contrastive	19.83	69.38
DCU Primary	20.11	69.19
DCU Contrastive	20.25	69.33
FBK Contrastive	20.3	69.11
FBK_USAAR Contr.	21.55	67.28
USAAR Primary	23.05	65.01
LIG Primary	23.22	65.12
JXNU Primary	23.31	65.66
LIG Contrastive-Forced	23.51	64.52
LIG Contrastive-Chained	23.66	64.46
CUNI Primary	24.03†	64.28
USAAR Contrastive	24.17	63.55
Baseline	24.48	62.49
(Simard et al., 2007)	24.69	62.97
CUNI Contrastive	25.94	61.65

Table 28: Results for the WMT17 APE **EN-DE** task – average TER (↓), BLEU score (↑). The † indicates a difference from the MT baseline that is not statistically significant.

German-English On German-English, the improvements of the top submission over the baseline are smaller (-0.26 TER, +0.28 BLEU) but still statistically significant. Such smaller gains, ob-

ID	Avg. TER	BLEU
FBK Primary	15.29	79.82
FBK Contrastive	15.31	79.64†
LIG Primary	15.53†	79.49†
Baseline	15.55	79.54
LIG Contrastive-Forced	15.62†	79.48†
LIG Contrastive-Chained	15.68	79.35
(Simard et al., 2007)	15.74	79.28†

Table 29: Results for the WMT17 APE **DE-EN** task – average TER (↓), BLEU score (↑). The † indicates differences from the MT baseline that are not statistically significant.

tained by systems based on the same approaches adopted for the English-German task, confirm our initial expectations about the different level of difficulty of the two language directions. The interaction between low repetition rates and high translation quality, which certainly played a role in reducing the gap between the primary submissions and the *"do-nothing"* MT baseline, is hence an interesting aspect for more thorough explorations in future rounds of the APE task. Also in this case, however, the lowest results achieved by the phrase-based APE baseline (with both metrics) confirm that the switch to neural methods represents a technology advancement in the right direction.

5.4 System/performance analysis

Although all participants built their systems under the same general neural paradigm, results' distribution in a 4.5 TER (and 6.5 BLEU) points interval suggests differences in systems' behaviour that it is worth to explore further. To this aim, and as a complement to global TER/BLEU scores, also this year we performed a more fine-grained analysis of the changes made by each system to the test instances.

5.4.1 Macro indicators: modified, improved and deteriorated sentences

Tables 30 and 31 show the number of modified, improved and deteriorated sentences, respectively for the English-German and the German-English tasks. It's worth noting that, as in the previous rounds and for both language directions, the number of sentences modified by each system is higher than the sum of the improved and the deteriorated ones. This difference is represented by modified sentences for which the corrections do not yield TER variations. This grey area, for which quality improvement/degradation can not be automati-

cally assessed, contributes to motivate the human evaluation discussed in Section 5.5

English-German. As expected, differently from last year where the amount of test sentences modified by the participants had a much larger variance due to the different approaches applied, this year the top English-German systems show a quite homogeneous behaviour. In 2016, out of 11 submitted runs, the number of sentences modified by the top 3 primary submissions (the best one being neural and the others being phrase-based) ranged between 421 and 1,613 (respectively 21.0% and 80.6% of the total). This year, out of 15 submitted runs (all neural-based), the top 3 primary submissions have a number of modified sentences that falls in a much smaller range between 1,583 and 1,607 (between 79.1% and 80.0% of the total). The same holds for systems' precision (i.e. the proportion of improved sentences out of the total amount of modified test items). The top 3 primary submissions, indeed, have a precision ranging in a two points interval from 63.6% to 65.6%, while last year the proportion for the top 3 primary runs was more spread in a 11 points interval from 57.9% to 68.8%. Overall, lower ranked systems show a tendency to either modify less sentences (all submissions with less than 1,000 modified sentences are in the bottom half of the ranking), or to do it with lower precision (all submissions with less than 60.0% precision are in the bottom half of the ranking), or a combination of the two, as in the case of the phrase-based approach (Simard et al., 2007), which is the second less aggressive method and by far the less precise one. In general, looking at system precision numbers, it's worth noting that the close results between the top submissions still leave large room for improvement. Indeed, in the case of the best systems, more than 30 points in precision represent a huge gap to be filled before considering APE a solved problem.

German-English. In this case, the higher difficulty of the task (due to lower repetition rate and higher translation quality, as discussed in Section 5.1.1) changes the global picture provided by our macro indicators. Although the two participating systems were developed under the neural paradigm, their different behaviour is evident from the amount of modified sentences: the two primary submissions respectively modified 270

Systems	Modified	Improved	Deteriorated
FBK Primary	1,607 (80.3%)	1,035 (64.4%)	334 (20.7%)
AMU Primary	1,583 (79.1%)	1,040 (65.6%)	322 (20.3%)
AMU Contrastive	1,583 (79.1%)	1,044 (65.9%)	326 (20.5%)
DCU Primary	1,592 (79.6%)	1,014 (63.6%)	361 (22.6%)
DCU Contrastive	1,558 (77.9%)	1,012 (64.9%)	329 (21.1%)
FBK Contrastive	1,597 (79.8%)	996 (62.3%)	344 (21.5%)
FBK_USAAR Contrastive	1,675 (83.7%)	920 (55.0%)	482 (28.7%)
USAAR Primary	744 (37.2%)	461 (61.9%)	160 (21.5%)
LIG Primary	1,168 (58.4%)	629 (53.8%)	306 (26.1%)
JXNU Primary	1,385 (69.2%)	678 (48.9%)	404 (29.1%)
LIG Contrastive-Forced	719 (35.9%)	412 (57.3%)	166 (23.1%)
LIG Contrastive-Chained	814 (40.7%)	422 (51.8%)	217 (26.6%)
CUNI Primary	1,513 (75.6%)	713 (47.1%)	515 (34.0%)
USAAR Contrastive	306 (15.3%)	179 (58.4%)	76 (24.8%)
(Simard et al., 2007)	571 (28.5%)	211 (36.9%))	244 (42.7%)
CUNI Contrastive	1577 (78.8%)	644 (40.8%)	663 (42.0%)

Table 30: Number of test sentences modified, improved and deteriorated by each run submitted to the **EN-DE** task.

Systems	Modified	Improved	Deteriorated
FBK Primary	270 (13.5%)	108 (40.0%)	78 (28.9%)
FBK Contrastive	364 (18.2)	135 (37.0%)	118 (32.4%)
LIG Primary	64 (3.2%)	27 (42.1%)	24 (37.5%)
LIG Contrastive-Forced	47 (2.3%)	13 (27.6%)	21 (44.7%)
LIG Contrastive-Chained	64 (3.2%)	27 (42.1%)	46 (71.9%)
(Simard et al., 2007)	139 (6.9%)	30 (21.6%)	69 (49.6%)

Table 31: Number of test sentences modified, improved and deteriorated by each run submitted to the **DE-EN** task.

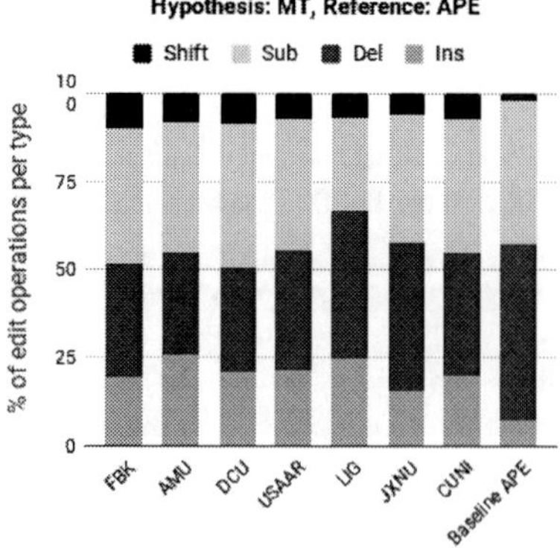

Figure 9: System behaviour (primary submissions) for **EN-DE** – TER(MT, APE)

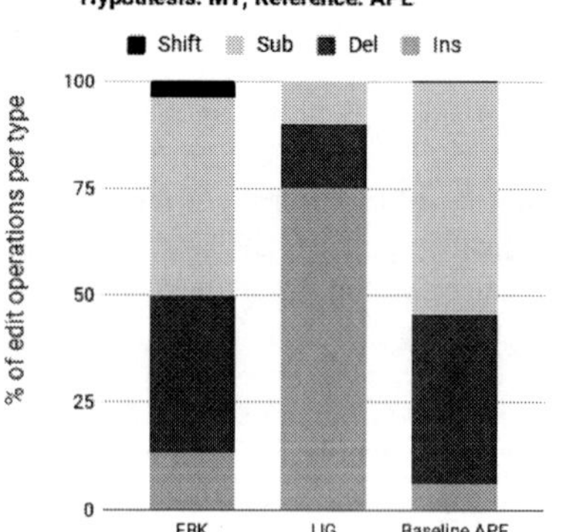

Figure 10: System behaviour (primary submissions) for **DE-EN** – TER(MT, APE)

(13.5%) and 64 (3.2%) test items. On one side, the small number of modified sentences compared to English-German indicates systems' ability to keep under control the number of unnecessary corrections. If we consider that almost half of the test items are "perfect" translations that should be kept unchanged (see Table 26), a rather conservative approach is indeed a desired behaviour. On the other side, however, precision scores are much lower compared to those observed in the English-German task. Even for an "easy" target language like English, coping with data featuring low repetition rates and high translation quality is hence a still open challenge.

5.4.2 Micro indicators: edit operations

Also this year we performed a more fine-grained analysis of systems' behaviour in order to discover possible differences in the way they correct the test set instances. To this aim, we looked at the distribution of the edit operations done by each system (insertions, deletions, substitutions and shifts) by computing the TER between the original MT output and the output of each system taken as reference (only for the primary submissions). The outcomes of this analysis are shown in Figures 9 (English-German) and 10 (German-English).

English-German. As expected, compared to last year, the plot in Figure 9 does not show large differences between similar neural-based submissions. All of them are characterized by a rather homogeneous distribution of the types of correction patterns applied, with a slight dominance of substitutions for the top submissions (between 37.0% and 40.0%) and a slight dominance of deletions for the others (between 34.5% and 42.1%). Another quite visible correlation is the one between shift operations and performance results, which tend to decrease for systems that perform less reordering (also last year, the winning neural system had a significantly larger amount of shifts compared to the others). Interestingly, also in this case the phrase-based baseline (the weakest APE system in terms of results) is a clear outlier. It performs the lowest number of shifts (2.2% vs 9.7% of the top submission), the lowest number of insertions (7.1% vs 19.5%) and the largest number of deletions (50.2% vs 32.1%). This indicates a scarce capability of the phrase-based approach to learn reordering rules and its tendency to replace them with more radical deletion operations.

German-English. As shown by Figure 10, the two primary submissions for this task have a quite different behaviour. In addition to the large differences in the number of modified, improved and deteriorated sentences (see Table 31), the distribution of the edit operations performed on test data indicates opposite strategies. Also in this case, the distribution is more homogeneous for the best performing system, with a dominance of substitutions and around 4.0% of shifts (though less than in the English-German task, where they were around 10.0%). The second system has a much

more unbalanced distribution, with lots of insertions and no shifts in the few sentence corrections it returned. The distribution for the phrase-based APE baseline is more similar to the best system but, as shown in Table 31, its corrections are by far the less reliable ones. Apart from these considerations, it is hard to draw clear conclusions since the different correction strategies of the three methods result in close final scores. Indeed, as shown in Table 29, only 0.24 TER and 0.33 BLEU points separate the two primary systems, while 0.45 TER and 0.54 BLEU points separate the best system from the phrase-based baseline. The small improvements of the primary submissions over the *"do-nothing"* MT baseline suggest that, independently from the different correction strategies applied, both primary submissions definitely suffered from the large amount of "perfect" translation in the test set (around 45.0%). However, while automatic evaluation metrics like TER and BLEU always penalize unnecessary corrections of good translations, there is a chance that some of these corrections are acceptable paraphrases rather than sentence deteriorations. One of the objectives of the human evaluation discussed in the next section is to check if this phenomenon has a visible impact on performance.

5.5 Human evaluation

To assess the quality of the output of the APE systems and produce a ranking based on human judgment, as well as analyze how humans perceive TER/BLEU performance differences between the submitted systems, a human evaluation of the quality of automatic post-edits was carried out using Direct Assessment (DA) (Graham et al., 2013, 2016). Since sufficient crowd-sourced workers are available for assessing English on Mechanical Turk, the DA evaluation for German to English was completed via quality-controlled crowdsourcing. For English to German, DA judgments were provided by 10 native German speakers from Saarland University, studying language technologies and translation. This subsection describes the human evaluation procedure and presents the results of the evaluation of participants' primary submissions.

5.5.1 Evaluation procedure

Direct Assessment, which is described in more detail in Section 3, elicits human assessments of translation adequacy on an analogue rating scale

Language Pair	EN-DE	DE-EN
# Systems	9	4
# Segs	2,000	2,000
# Total Segs	18,000	8,000
# Unique Segs	9,767	3,415
Overall Saving	46%	57%

Table 32: Total segments prior to sampling for manual evaluation and savings made by combining identical segments (Segs) produced by multiple APE systems.

	Systems	Assess	Assess/Sys
EN-DE	9	11,492	1,277
DE-EN	4	7,193	1,798

Table 33: Amount of data (assessments after "de-collapsing" *multi-system outputs*) collected in the WMT17 APE manual evaluation campaign and numbers of assessments per system.

(0–100), where human assessors are asked to rate how adequately the APE system output expresses the meaning of the human reference translation. DA scores for systems and segments have been shown to be highly repeatable in self-replication experiments (Graham et al., 2015). Thus, DA overcomes the previous challenges associated with lack of reliability of human assessment of MT.

Since we also have a human post-edit available for each MT output in the test set, to make DA outcomes more informative we also included the human post-edits as a hidden system in the evaluation, which will provide some insight into an achievable DA score for a potential system that achieved human-quality post-editing. Additionally, we included the original MT output without any post-editing as a hidden system to discover the baseline DA score for each language pair.

When running the APE manual evaluation, it was possible in many cases to take advantage of the fact that multiple systems can produce identical outputs, as was begun in evaluation of the News task in WMT15 (Bojar et al., 2015). Table 32 shows numbers of translations in total for all APE systems, as well as savings in terms of annotation effort that was gained by combining identical system outputs prior to running the evaluation, where, as expected, a substantial saving was made due to the fact that the systems quite often produced the same output. In terms of human effort involved in carrying out the manual evaluation, Table 33 shows numbers of judgments collected in total for each language pair and number of assessments contributing to the final DA score for APE systems on average.

When carrying out a manual evaluation of any kind, it is important to consider the consistency of annotators with the aim of estimating, where the evaluation to be repeated, how likely it would be that the same conclusions would be drawn.

When an analogue scale is employed for human assessment, consistency of human assessors cannot be evaluated in the usual way, such as the Kappa coefficient, commonly employed for evaluating the consistency of human assessors when discrete quality judgments or relative preference judgments are collected. Instead, for analogue scale data, we examine the consistency of individual human assessors according to their ability to discriminate between the quality of pairs of known worse quality translations, known as bad reference pairs, where original translations produced by the APE systems are degraded automatically. In addition, repeat assessments of the same translation are given to human assessors to see how reliably they assign similar scores to similar quality translations. Hiding bad reference and repeat translation pairs within hits allows a significance test to be carried out for each human judge investigating if their score distributions show a significant difference where there should be one, and another test to check that no significant difference shows up for repeated assessment of the same translation.

As such, proportions of human assessors and whether they discriminate between the quality of bad reference pairs and repeat translations are shown in Table 34. Notably, all of the student translators (for EN-DE) passed the DA's quality control mechanism by assigning significantly lower scores to degraded translations, while 54%, a usual number of crowd-sourced workers (for DE-EN), passed quality control.

Proportions of workers showing a non significant difference in repeat items at first appears lower than usual for DA, at 91% for EN-DE and 93% for DE-EN, as this proportion has been between 97 and 100% for DA in past evaluations. However, on closer inspection, the total number of assessors showing a significant difference for repeat items is as low as three assessors and proportions are therefore exaggerated due to the low number of workers involved in the evaluation overall.

	All	(A) Sig. Diff. Bad Ref.	(A) & No Sig. Diff. Exact Rep.
EN-DE	11	11 (100%)	10 (91%)
DE-EN	54	29 (54%)	27 (93%)

Table 34: Number of unique Mechanical Turk workers, (A) those whose scores for bad reference pairs were significantly different and numbers of unique human assessors in (A) whose scores for exact repeat assessments also showed no significant difference.

Prior to computing final DA scores for systems, in order to iron out differences in scoring strategies of distinct human assessors, human assessment scores for translations were first standardized according to each individual human assessor's overall mean and standard deviation score. Average standardized scores for individual segments belonging to a given system are then computed, before the final overall DA score for that system is computed as the average of its segment scores.

5.5.2 Human evaluation results

Table 35 includes DA results for English-German and Table 36 shows results for German-English APE systems. Clusters are identified by grouping systems together according to which systems significantly outperform all others in lower ranking clusters, according to Wilcoxon rank-sum test.

#	Ave %	Ave z	System
−	84.8	0.520	HUMAN POST_EDIT
1	78.2	0.261	AMU
	77.9	0.261	FBK
	76.8	0.221	DCU
4	73.8	0.115	JXNU
5	71.9	0.038	USAAR
	71.1	0.014	CUNI
	70.2	−0.020	LIG
−	68.6	−0.083	NO POST_EDIT

Table 35: **EN-DE** DA Human evaluation results showing average raw DA scores (Ave %) and average standardized scores (Ave z), lines between systems indicate clusters according to Wilcoxon rank-sum test at p-level $p \leq 0.05$.

Figures 11 and 12 show head to head significance test results for English-German and German-English systems participating in the APE task, as well as the two additional "systems" where either no post-editing or human post-editing was

#	Ave %	Ave z	System
−	81.9	0.199	HUMAN POST_EDIT
1	76.8	0.040	FBK
	75.3	−0.007	LIG
	75.4	−0.008	NO POST_EDIT

Table 36: **DE-EN** DA Human evaluation results showing average raw DA scores (Ave %) and average standardized scores (Ave z), lines between systems indicate clusters according to Wilcoxon rank-sum test at p-level $p \leq 0.05$.

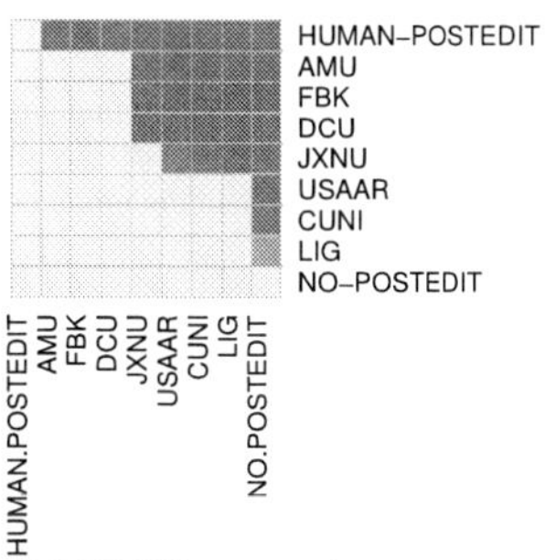

Figure 11: **EN-DE** Wilcoxon rank-sum significance test results for pairs of systems competing in the APE task, where a green cell denotes a significant win for the system in a given row over the system in a given column, at $p \leq 0.05$.

carried out, where a darker shade of green signifies a lower p-value and a conclusion made with more certainty.

English-German. For this language direction, the ranking produced by DA is slightly different from those based on TER/BLEU. This is not surprising if we consider the close performance results measured with automatic metrics. With primary submissions compressed in a relatively small TER/BLEU interval, different system orders are in fact likely to emerge also from manual evalua-

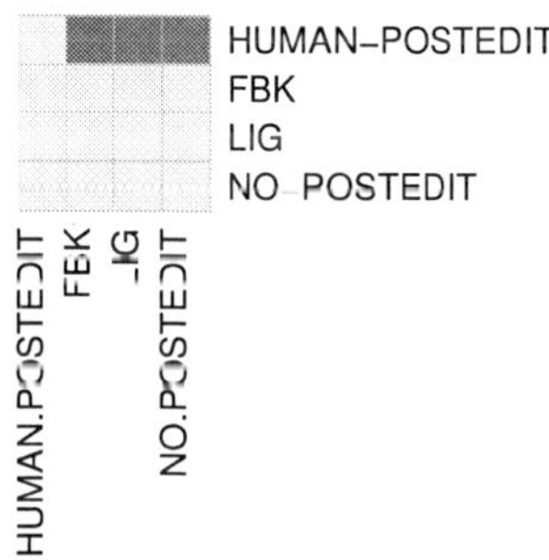

Figure 12: **DE-EN** Wilcoxon rank-sum significance test results for pairs of systems competing in the APE task, where a green cell denotes a significant win for the system in a given row over the system in a given column, at $p \leq 0.05$.

tion. Overall, as shown in Table 35, three systems emerge as significantly better than the others. This ranking is comparable to the one obtained with automatic metrics, although the top two systems (FBK and AMU) are switched, but this is in-line with the human evaluation that showed no significant difference between the two. This is also in-line with TER/BLEU rankings, for which the three systems are the only primary systems with TER<20.00 and BLEU>69.00. In agreement with the BLEU-based ranking, the JXNU submission ranks in fourth position in its own cluster. This represents the main difference with the TER-based ranking (in which it occupies the 6th place), which suggests a higher agreement between DA and BLEU. The remaining three systems, which feature rather close TER/BLEU scores, are positioned in the same lower cluster, though in a different order, again with small raw DA score differences.

Apart from these general considerations, which are difficult to project into conclusive indications about the reliability of our two automatic metrics, two major outcomes are evident. First, the technology advancement with respect to the 2016 round is also confirmed by DA scores, which indicate that all the systems are significantly better than the "*do-nothing*" baseline (NO POST_EDIT). Last year, in contrast, all participants but one were in the same cluster of the baseline. The downside is that, despite the significant progress made, APE systems are still far from human quality. Average DA scores indicate that the distance between the top primary submissions and human post-edits is in fact similar to the distance that separates them from the primary submissions in the bottom cluster.

German-English. Also DA scores confirm the higher difficulty of the German-English task. As expected, also in this case human quality is much higher, with a gap that is even larger compared to the distance observed in Figure 35. Moreover, while in terms of automatic metrics the improvement over the baseline for the top ranked system was statistically significant, the DA-based ranking places the two primary systems in the same cluster of the baseline.

5.6 Lessons learned and outlook

The third round of the APE task has marked a further step forward from the previous ones both in terms of participants (one more than in 2016) and, most importantly, in terms of the deployed technology. Concerning the latter aspect, the wide adoption of neural approaches has led, for the first time, to significant improvements over the baselines for all participants. On English-German data we observed the largest gains, which are up to -4.9 TER and +7.6 BLEU points for the top submission. On German-English, a more difficult task due to lower repetition rate and higher translation quality of the test data, the improvements of the top submission over the baseline are smaller (-0.26 TER, +0.28 BLEU) but still statistically significant. With respect to previous years, similar design and training choices (e.g. the use of multi-source solutions and additional synthetic training data), produced a more compact ranking of the participating systems but, at the same time, resulted in submissions that still feature different behaviour that deserve closer inspection in future.

Despite the technology improvement, some major challenges are still open. The main one is how to better handle the difficult case in which an automatic translation is already (or near-) perfect and APE systems should abstain from performing useless (or risky) corrections. Another limitation of current solutions is their inefficacy in generalizing the learned correction patterns, so that training data featuring low repetitiveness can be better exploited to learn useful correction patterns.

From the performance evaluation standpoint, the selection of the best metric is still debatable. TER (the official one in all the APE rounds so far) and BLEU produce slightly different rankings, which both differ from those produced by human evaluation with direct assessment. The comparison with DA indicates a small preference for the BLEU-based ranking, but drawing definite conclusions about the suitability of the two metrics is difficult due to the small performance differences observed. Most likely, future rounds of the task will hence keep the the evaluation setting unaltered, possibly focusing on the aforementioned challenges to increase the level of difficulty and further raise the interest on the APE problem.

Acknowledgments

This work was supported in parts by the QT21, QTLeap, EXPERT and CRACKER projects funded by the European Commission (7th Framework Programme and H2020). Further datasets were donated by University of Helsinki and Yandex. The APE task organizers would also like to thank Text&Form for producing the manual post-edits and the annotators involved in the manual evaluation.

References

Hervé Abdi. 2007. The bonferroni and šidák corrections for multiple comparisons. *Encyclopedia of measurement and statistics*, 3:103–107.

Eleftherios Avramidis. 2017a. Comparative quality estimation for machine translation: Observations on machine learning and features. *The Prague Bulletin of Mathematical Linguistics (PBML)*, 108:307–318.

Eleftherios Avramidis. 2017b. Sentence-level quality estimation by predicting HTER as a multi-component metric. In *Proceedings of the Second Conference on Machine Translation*, Copenhagen, Denmark. Association for Computational Linguistics.

Dzmitry Bahdanau, Kyunghyun Cho, and Yoshua Bengio. 2014. Neural machine translation by jointly learning to align and translate. *arXiv preprint arXiv:1409.0473*.

Alexandre Berard, Laurent Besacier, and Olivier Pietquin. 2017. LIG-CRIStAL Submission for the WMT 2017 Automatic Post-Editing Task. In *Proceedings of the Second Conference on Machine Translation*, Copenhagen, Denmark. Association for Computational Linguistics.

Ergun Biçici. 2017. Predicting Translation Performance with Referential Translation Machines. In *Proceedings of the Second Conference on Machine Translation*, Copenhagen, Denmark. Association for Computational Linguistics.

Frédéric Blain, Varvara Logacheva, and Lucia Specia. 2016. Phrase level segmentation and labelling of machine translation errors. *LREC16*.

Frédéric Blain, Carolina Scarton, and Lucia Specia. 2017. Bilexical Embeddings for Quality Estimation. In *Proceedings of the Second Conference on Machine Translation*, Copenhagen, Denmark. Association for Computational Linguistics.

Ondřej Bojar, Christian Buck, Christian Federmann, Barry Haddow, Philipp Koehn, Johannes Leveling, Christof Monz, Pavel Pecina, Matt Post, Herve Saint-Amand, Radu Soricut, Lucia Specia, and Aleš Tamchyna. 2014. Findings of the 2014 workshop on statistical machine translation. In *Proceedings of the Ninth Workshop on Statistical Machine Translation*, pages 12–58, Baltimore, Maryland, USA. Association for Computational Linguistics.

Ondřej Bojar, Yvette Graham, and Amir Kamran. 2017a. Results of the WMT17 Metrics Shared Task. In *Proceedings of the Second Conference on Machine Translation*, Copenhagen, Denmark. Association for Computational Linguistics.

Ondřej Bojar, Jindřich Helcl, Tom Kocmi, Jindřich Libovický, and Tomáš Musil. 2017b. Results of the WMT17 Neural MT Training Task. In *Proceedings of the Second Conference on Machine Translation*, Copenhagen, Denmark. Association for Computational Linguistics.

Ondřej Bojar, Christian Buck, Chris Callison-Burch, Christian Federmann, Barry Haddow, Philipp Koehn, Christof Monz, Matt Post, Radu Soricut, and Lucia Specia. 2013. Findings of the 2013 Workshop on Statistical Machine Translation. In *Proceedings of the Eighth Workshop on Statistical Machine Translation*, pages 1–44, Sofia, Bulgaria. Association for Computational Linguistics.

Ondřej Bojar, Rajen Chatterjee, Christian Federmann, Yvette Graham, Barry Haddow, Matthias Huck, Antonio Jimeno Yepes, Philipp Koehn, Varvara Logacheva, Christof Monz, Matteo Negri, Aurelie Neveol, Mariana Neves, Martin Popel, Matt Post, Raphael Rubino, Carolina Scarton, Lucia Specia, Marco Turchi, Karin Verspoor, and Marcos Zampieri. 2016a. Findings of the 2016 conference on machine translation. In *Proceedings of the First Conference on Machine Translation*, pages 131–198, Berlin, Germany. Association for Computational Linguistics.

Ondřej Bojar, Rajen Chatterjee, Christian Federmann, Barry Haddow, Matthias Huck, Chris Hokamp, Philipp Koehn, Varvara Logacheva, Christof Monz, Matteo Negri, Matt Post, Carolina Scarton, Lucia Specia, and Marco Turchi. 2015. Findings of the 2015 Workshop on Statistical Machine Translation. In *Proceedings of the Tenth Workshop on Statistical Machine Translation*, pages 1–46, Lisbon, Portugal. Association for Computational Linguistics.

Ondřej Bojar, Ondřej Dušek, Tom Kocmi, Jindřich Libovický, Michal Novák, Martin Popel, Roman Sudarikov, and Dušan Variš. 2016b. CzEng 1.6: Enlarged Czech-English Parallel Corpus with Processing Tools Dockered. In *Text, Speech and Dialogue: 19th International Conference, TSD 2016, Brno, Czech Republic, September 12-16, 2016, Proceedings*. Springer Verlag. In press.

Franck Burlot, Pooyan Safari, Matthieu Labeau, Alexandre Allauzen, and François Yvon. 2017. LIMSI@WMT'17. In *Proceedings of the Second Conference on Machine Translation*, Copenhagen, Denmark. Association for Computational Linguistics.

Chris Callison-Burch, Cameron Shaw Fordyce, Philipp Koehn, Christof Monz, and Josh Schroeder. 2007. (Meta-) evaluation of machine translation. In *Proceedings of the Second Workshop on Statistical Machine Translation*, pages 136–158, Prague, Czech

Republic. Association for Computational Linguistics.

Chris Callison-Burch, Cameron Shaw Fordyce, Philipp Koehn, Christof Monz, and Josh Schroeder. 2008. Further meta-evaluation of machine translation. In *Proceedings of the Third Workshop on Statistical Machine Translation*, pages 70–106, Columbus, Ohio. Association for Computational Linguistics.

Chris Callison-Burch, Philipp Koehn, Christof Monz, Kay Peterson, Mark Przybocki, and Omar Zaidan. 2010. Findings of the 2010 joint workshop on statistical machine translation and metrics for machine translation. In *Proceedings of the Joint Fifth Workshop on Statistical Machine Translation and MetricsMATR*, pages 17–53, Uppsala, Sweden. Association for Computational Linguistics.

Chris Callison-Burch, Philipp Koehn, Christof Monz, Matt Post, Radu Soricut, and Lucia Specia. 2012. Findings of the 2012 workshop on statistical machine translation. In *Proceedings of the Seventh Workshop on Statistical Machine Translation*, pages 10–48, Montreal, Canada. Association for Computational Linguistics.

Chris Callison-Burch, Philipp Koehn, Christof Monz, and Josh Schroeder. 2009. Findings of the 2009 Workshop on Statistical Machine Translation. In *Proceedings of the Fourth Workshop on Statistical Machine Translation*, pages 1–28, Athens, Greece. Association for Computational Linguistics.

Chris Callison-Burch, Philipp Koehn, Christof Monz, and Omar Zaidan. 2011. Findings of the 2011 workshop on statistical machine translation. In *Proceedings of the Sixth Workshop on Statistical Machine Translation*, pages 22–64, Edinburgh, Scotland. Association for Computational Linguistics.

Rajen Chatterjee, M. Amin Farajian, Matteo Negri, Marco Turchi, Ankit Srivastava, and Santanu Pal. 2017. Multi-source Neural Automatic Post-Editing: FBK's participation in the WMT 2017 APE shared task. In *Proceedings of the Second Conference on Machine Translation*, Copenhagen, Denmark. Association for Computational Linguistics.

Rajen Chatterjee, José G. C. de Souza, Matteo Negri, and Marco Turchi. 2016. The FBK Participation in the WMT 2016 Automatic Post-editing Shared Task. In *Proceedings of the 11th Workshop on Statistical Machine Translation (WMT)*.

Rajen Chatterjee, Turchi Turchi, and Matteo Negri. 2015a. The FBK Participation in the WMT15 Automatic Post-editing Shared Task. In *Proceedings of the 10th Workshop on Statistical Machine Translation (WMT)*.

Rajen Chatterjee, Marion Weller, Matteo Negri, and Marco Turchi. 2015b. Exploring the Planet of the APEs: a Comparative Study of State-of-the-art

Methods for MT Automatic Post-Editing. In *Proceedings of the 53rd Annual Meeting of the Association for Computational Linguistics)*, Beijing, China.

Zhiming Chen, Yiming Tan, Chenlin Zhang, Qingyu Xiang, Lilin Zhang, Maoxi Li, and Mingwen WANG. 2017. Improving Machine Translation Quality Estimation with Neural Network Features. In *Proceedings of the Second Conference on Machine Translation*, Copenhagen, Denmark. Association for Computational Linguistics.

Yongchao Deng, Jungi Kim, Guillaume Klein, Catherine KOBUS, Natalia Segal, Christophe Servan, Bo Wang, Dakun Zhang, Josep Crego, and Jean Senellart. 2017. SYSTRAN Purely Neural MT Engines for WMT2017. In *Proceedings of the Second Conference on Machine Translation*, Copenhagen, Denmark. Association for Computational Linguistics.

Mattia Antonino Di Gangi, Nicola Bertoldi, and Marcello Federico. 2017. FBK's Participation to the English-to-German News Translation Task of WMT 2017. In *Proceedings of the Second Conference on Machine Translation*, Copenhagen, Denmark. Association for Computational Linguistics.

Shuoyang Ding, Huda Khayrallah, Philipp Koehn, Matt Post, Gaurav Kumar, and Kevin Duh. 2017. The JHU Machine Translation Systems for WMT 2017. In *Proceedings of the Second Conference on Machine Translation*, Copenhagen, Denmark. Association for Computational Linguistics.

John Duchi and Yoram Singer. 2009. Efficient online and batch learning using forward backward splitting. *Journal of Machine Learning Research*, 10:2899–2934.

Melania Duma and Wolfgang Menzel. 2017. UHH Submission to the WMT17 Quality Estimation Shared Task. In *Proceedings of the Second Conference on Machine Translation*, Copenhagen, Denmark. Association for Computational Linguistics.

Desmond Elliott, Stella Frank, Loïc Barrault, Fethi Bougares, and Lucia Specia. 2017. Findings of the Second Shared Task on Multimodal Machine Translation and Multilingual Image Description. In *Proceedings of the Second Conference on Machine Translation*, Copenhagen, Denmark. Association for Computational Linguistics.

Carlos Escolano, Marta R. Costa-jussà, and José A. R. Fonollosa. 2017. The TALP-UPC Neural Machine Translation System for German/Finnish-English Using the Inverse Direction Model in Rescoring. In *Proceedings of the Second Conference on Machine Translation*, Copenhagen, Denmark. Association for Computational Linguistics.

Christian Federmann. 2012. Appraise: an open-source toolkit for manual evaluation of mt output. *The Prague Bulletin of Mathematical Linguistics*, 98:25–35.

Qin Gao and Stephan Vogel. 2008. Parallel Implementations of Word Alignment Tool. In *Proceedings of the ACL 2008 Software Engineering, Testing, and Quality Assurance Workshop*, pages 49–57, Columbus, Ohio.

Mercedes García-Martínez, Ozan Caglayan, Walid Aransa, Adrien Bardet, Fethi Bougares, and Loïc Barrault. 2017. LIUM Machine Translation Systems for WMT17 News Translation Task. In *Proceedings of the Second Conference on Machine Translation*, Copenhagen, Denmark. Association for Computational Linguistics.

Yvette Graham, Timothy Baldwin, Alistair Moffat, and Justin Zobel. 2013. Continuous measurement scales in human evaluation of machine translation. In *Proceedings of the 7th Linguistic Annotation Workshop and Interoperability with Discourse*, pages 33–41, Sofia, Bulgaria. Association for Computational Linguistics.

Yvette Graham, Timothy Baldwin, Alistair Moffat, and Justin Zobel. 2014. Is machine translation getting better over time? In *Proceedings of the 14th Conference of the European Chapter of the Association for Computational Linguistics*, pages 443–451, Gothenburg, Sweden. Association for Computational Linguistics.

Yvette Graham, Timothy Baldwin, Alistair Moffat, and Justin Zobel. 2016. Can machine translation systems be evaluated by the crowd alone. *Natural Language Engineering*, pages 1–28.

Yvette Graham, Nitika Mathur, and Timothy Baldwin. 2015. Accurate evaluation of segment-level machine translation metrics. In *Proceedings of the 2015 Conference of the North American Chapter of the Association for Computational Linguistics Human Language Technologies*, Denver, Colorado.

Stig-Arne Grönroos, Sami Virpioja, and Mikko Kurimo. 2017. Extending hybrid word-character neural machine translation with multi-task learning of morphological analysis. In *Proceedings of the Second Conference on Machine Translation*, Copenhagen, Denmark. Association for Computational Linguistics.

Jeremy Gwinnup, Timothy Anderson, Grant Erdmann, Katherine Young, Michaeel Kazi, Elizabeth Salesky, Brian Thompson, and Jonathan Taylor. 2017. The AFRL-MITLL WMT17 Systems: Old, New, Borrowed, BLEU. In *Proceedings of the Second Conference on Machine Translation*, Copenhagen, Denmark. Association for Computational Linguistics.

Kenneth Heafield. 2011. KenLM: Faster and Smaller Language Model Queries. In *Proceedings of the EMNLP 2011 Sixth Workshop on Statistical Machine Translation*, pages 187–197, Edinburgh, Scotland, United Kingdom.

Ralf Herbrich, Tom Minka, and Thore Graepel. 2007. Trueskill^{TM}: a bayesian skill rating system. In *Advances in neural information processing systems*, pages 569–576.

Teresa Herrmann, Jan Niehues, and Alex Waibel. 2013. Combining Word Reordering Methods on different Linguistic Abstraction Levels for Statistical Machine Translation. In *Proceedings of the Seventh Workshop on Syntax, Semantics and Structure in Statistical Translation*, Altanta, Georgia, USA.

Chris Hokamp. 2017. Ensembling Factored Neural Machine Translation Models for Automatic Post-Editing and Quality Estimation. In *Proceedings of the Second Conference on Machine Translation*, Copenhagen, Denmark. Association for Computational Linguistics.

Chester Holtz, Chuyang Ke, and Daniel Gildea. 2017. University of Rochester WMT 2017 NMT System Submission. In *Proceedings of the Second Conference on Machine Translation*, Copenhagen, Denmark. Association for Computational Linguistics.

Matthias Huck, Fabienne Braune, and Alexander Fraser. 2017. LMU Munich's Neural Machine Translation Systems for News Articles and Health Information Texts. In *Proceedings of the Second Conference on Machine Translation*, Copenhagen, Denmark. Association for Computational Linguistics.

Arvi Hurskainen and Jörg Tiedemann. 2017. Rulebased Machine translation from English to Finnish. In *Proceedings of the Second Conference on Machine Translation*, Copenhagen, Denmark. Association for Computational Linguistics.

Antonio Jimeno Yepes, Aurelie Neveol, Mariana Neves, Karin Verspoor, Ondrej Bojar, Arthur Boyer, Cristian Grozea, Barry Haddow, Madeleine Kittner, Yvonne Lichtblau, Pavel Pecina, Roland Roller, Rudolf Rosa, Amy Siu, Philippe Thomas, and Saskia Trescher. 2017. Findings of the WMT 2017 Biomedical Translation Shared Task. In *Proceedings of the Second Conference on Machine Translation*, Copenhagen, Denmark. Association for Computational Linguistics.

Marcin Junczys-Dowmunt and Roman Grundkiewicz. 2016. Log-linear combinations of monolingual and bilingual neural machine translation models for automatic post-editing. In *Proceedings of the First Conference on Machine Translation*, pages 751–758, Berlin, Germany. Association for Computational Linguistics.

Marcin Junczys-Dowmunt and Roman Grundkiewicz. 2017. An Exploration of Neural Sequence-to-Sequence Architecturesfor Automatic Post-Editing. In *Proceedings of the Second Conference on Machine Translation*, Copenhagen, Denmark.

Hyun Kim and Jong-Hyeok Lee. 2016. Recurrent neural network based translation quality estimation. In *Proceedings of the First Conference on Machine Translation*, pages 787–792, Berlin, Germany. Association for Computational Linguistics.

Hyun Kim, Jong-Hyeok Lee, and Seung-Hoon Na. 2017. Predictor-Estimator using Multilevel Task Learning with Stack Propagation for Neural Quality Estimation. In *Proceedings of the Second Conference on Machine Translation*, Copenhagen, Denmark. Association for Computational Linguistics.

Philipp Koehn. 2004. Statistical Significance Tests for Machine Translation Evaluation. In *Proceedings of EMNLP 2004*, pages 388–395, Barcelona, Spain.

Philipp Koehn, Hieu Hoang, Alexandra Birch, Chris Callison-Burch, Marcello Federico, Nicola Bertoldi, Brooke Cowan, Wade Shen, Christine Moran, Richard Zens, Chris Dyer, Ondrej Bojar, Alexandra Constantin, and Evan Herbst. 2007. Moses: Open Source Toolkit for Statistical Machine Translation. In *Proceedings of the 45th Annual Meeting of the Association for Computational Linguistics Companion Volume Proceedings of the Demo and Poster Sessions*, pages 177–180, Prague, Czech Republic.

Philipp Koehn and Christof Monz. 2006. Manual and automatic evaluation of machine translation between european languages. In *Proceedings on the Workshop on Statistical Machine Translation*, pages 102–121, New York City. Association for Computational Linguistics.

Julia Kreutzer, Shigehiko Schamoni, and Stefan Riezler. 2015. Quality estimation from scratch (quetch): Deep learning for word-level translation quality estimation. In *Proceedings of the Tenth Workshop on Statistical Machine Translation*, pages 316–322, Lisbon, Portugal. Association for Computational Linguistics.

Jason Lee, Kyunghyun Cho, and Thomas Hofmann. 2016. Fully character-level neural machine translation without explicit segmentation. *arXiv preprint arXiv:1610.03017*.

Jindřich Libovický, Jindřich Helcl, Marek Tlustý, Ondřej Bojar, and Pavel Pecina. 2016. CUNI at Post-editing and Multimodal Translation Tasks. In *Proceedings of the 11th Workshop on Statistical Machine Translation (WMT)*, Berlin, Germany.

Varvara Logacheva, Chris Hokamp, and Lucia Specia. 2016. MARMOT: A Toolkit for Translation Quality Estimation at the Word Level. In *Proceedings of the 10th edition of the Language Resources and Evaluation Conference*, Portorož, Slovenia.

Ngoc Quang Luong, Laurent Besacier, and Benjamin Lecouteux. 2014. Lig system for word level qe task at wmt14. In *Proceedings of the Ninth Workshop on Statistical Machine Translation*, pages 335–341, Baltimore, Maryland, USA. Association for Computational Linguistics.

Pranava Swaroop Madhyastha, Xavier Carreras, and Ariadna Quattoni. 2014. Learning task-specific bilexical embeddings. In *Proceedings of COLING 2014, the 25th International Conference on Computational Linguistics: Technical Papers*, pages 161–171, Dublin, Ireland.

André Martins, Marcin Junczys-Dowmunt, Fabio Kepler, Ramn Astudillo, Chris Hokamp, and Roman Grundkiewicz. 2017a. Pushing the limits of translation quality estimation. *Transactions of the Association for Computational Linguistics*, 5:205–218.

André F. T. Martins, Ramón Astudillo, Chris Hokamp, and Fabio Kepler. 2016. Unbabel's participation in the wmt16 word-level translation quality estimation shared task. In *Proceedings of the First Conference on Machine Translation*, pages 806–811, Berlin, Germany. Association for Computational Linguistics.

André F. T. Martins, Fabio Kepler, and Jose Monteiro. 2017b. Unbabel's Participation in the WMT17 Translation Quality Estimation Shared Task. In *Proceedings of the Second Conference on Machine Translation*, Copenhagen, Denmark. Association for Computational Linguistics.

Franz Josef Och. 2003. Minimum Error Rate Training in Statistical Machine Translation. In *Proceedings of the 41st Annual Meeting of the Association for Computational Linguistics*, ACL '03, pages 160–167, Sapporo, Japan.

Naoaki Okazaki. 2007. CRFsuite: a fast implementation of Conditional Random Fields.

Robert Östling, Yves Scherrer, Jörg Tiedemann, Gongbo Tang, and Tommi Nieminen. 2017. The Helsinki Neural Machine Translation System. In *Proceedings of the Second Conference on Machine Translation*, Copenhagen, Denmark. Association for Computational Linguistics.

Gustavo Paetzold and Lucia Specia. 2017. Feature-Enriched Character-Level Convolutions for Text Regression. In *Proceedings of the Second Conference on Machine Translation*, Copenhagen, Denmark. Association for Computational Linguistics.

Santanu Pal, Sudip Kumar Naskar, and Josef van Genabith. 2016a. Multi-engine and multi-alignment based automatic post-editing and its impact on translation productivity. In *Proceedings of COLING 2016, the 26th International Conference on Computational Linguistics: Technical Papers*, pages 2559–2570, Osaka, Japan. The COLING 2016 Organizing Committee.

Santanu Pal, Sudip Kumar Naskar, Mihaela Vela, and Josef van Genabith. 2016b. A Neural Network based Approach to Automatic Post-Editing. In *Proceedings of the 54th Annual Meeting of the Association for Computational Linguistics (Volume 2: Short Papers)*, pages 281–286, Berlin, Germany.

Santanu Pal, Marcos Zampieri, and Josef van Genabith. 2016c. Usaar: An operation sequential model for automatic statistical post-editing. In *Proceedings of the First Conference on Machine Translation*, pages 759–763, Berlin, Germany.

Kishore Papineni, Salim Roukos, Todd Ward, and Wei-Jing Zhu. 2002. BLEU: A Method for Automatic Evaluation of Machine Translation. In *Proceedings of the 40th Annual Meeting on Association for Computational Linguistics*, ACL '02, pages 311–318, Philadelphia, Pennsylvania.

Raj Nath Patel and Sasikumar M. 2016. Translation quality estimation using recurrent neural network. In *Proceedings of the First Conference on Machine Translation*, pages 819–824, Berlin, Germany. Association for Computational Linguistics.

Jan-Thorsten Peter, Andreas Guta, Tamer Alkhouli, Parnia Bahar, Jan Rosendahl, Nick Rossenbach, Miguel Graça, and Hermann Ney. 2017a. The RWTH Aachen University English-German and German-English Machine Translation System for WMT 2017. In *Proceedings of the Second Conference on Machine Translation*, Copenhagen, Denmark. Association for Computational Linguistics.

Jan-Thorsten Peter, Hermann Ney, Ondřej Bojar, Ngoc-Quan Pham, Jan Niehues, Alex Waibel, Franck Burlot, François Yvon, Mārcis Pinnis, Valters Sics, Joost Bastings, Miguel Rios, Wilker Aziz, Philip Williams, Frédéric Blain, and Lucia Specia. 2017b. The QT21 Combined Machine Translation System for English to Latvian. In *Proceedings of the Second Conference on Machine Translation*, Copenhagen, Denmark. Association for Computational Linguistics.

Ngoc-Quan Pham, Jan Niehues, Thanh-Le Ha, Eunah Cho, Matthias Sperber, and Alexander Waibel. 2017. The Karlsruhe Institute of Technology Systems for the News Translation Task in WMT 2017. In *Proceedings of the Second Conference on Machine Translation*, Copenhagen, Denmark. Association for Computational Linguistics.

Mārcis Pinnis, Rihards Krišlauks, Toms Miks, Daiga Deksne, and Valters Sics. 2017. Tilde's Machine Translation Systems for WMT 2017. In *Proceedings of the Second Conference on Machine Translation*, Copenhagen, Denmark. Association for Computational Linguistics.

Sylvain Raybaud, David Langlois, and Kamel Smali. 2011. this sentence is wrong. detecting errors in machine-translated sentences. *Machine Translation*, 25(1):1–34.

Matīss Rikters, Chantal Amrhein, Maksym Del, and Mark Fishel. 2017. C-3MA: Tartu-Riga-Zurich Translation Systems for WMT17. In *Proceedings of the Second Conference on Machine Translation*, Copenhagen, Denmark. Association for Computational Linguistics.

Keisuke Sakaguchi, Matt Post, and Benjamin Van Durme. 2014. Efficient elicitation of annotations for human evaluation of machine translation. In *Proceedings of the Workshop on Statistical Machine Translation*, Baltimore, Maryland. Association for Computational Linguistics.

Carolina Scarton, Daniel Beck, Kashif Shah, Karin Sim Smith, and Lucia Specia. 2016. Word embeddings and discourse information for quality estimation. In *Proceedings of the First Conference on Machine Translation*, pages 831–837, Berlin, Germany. Association for Computational Linguistics.

Rico Sennrich, Alexandra Birch, Anna Currey, Ulrich Germann, Barry Haddow, Kenneth Heafield, Antonio Valerio Miceli Barone, and Philip Williams. 2017. The University of Edinburgh's Neural MT Systems for WMT17. In *Proceedings of the Second Conference on Machine Translation*, Copenhagen, Denmark. Association for Computational Linguistics.

Rico Sennrich, Barry Haddow, and Alexandra Birch. 2015. Neural machine translation of rare words with subword units. *arXiv preprint arXiv:1508.07909*.

Rico Sennrich, Barry Haddow, and Alexandra Birch. 2016. Edinburgh neural machine translation systems for wmt 16. In *Proceedings of the First Conference on Machine Translation*, pages 371–376, Berlin, Germany. Association for Computational Linguistics.

Shiqi Shen, Yong Cheng, Zhongjun He, Wei He, Hua Wu, Maosong Sun, and Yang Liu. 2016. Minimum risk training for neural machine translation. In *Proceedings of the 54th Annual Meeting of the Association for Computational Linguistics (Volume 1: Long Papers)*, pages 1683–1692, Berlin, Germany.

Michel Simard, Cyril Goutte, and Pierre Isabelle. 2007. Statistical phrase-based post-editing. In *Human Language Technologies 2007: The Conference of the North American Chapter of the Association for Computational Linguistics; Proceedings of the Main Conference*, pages 508–515, Rochester, New York. Association for Computational Linguistics.

Matthew Snover, Bonnie Dorr, Richard Schwartz, Linnea Micciulla, and John Makhoul. 2006a. A study of translation edit rate with targeted human annotation. In *Proceedings of association for machine translation in the Americas*, pages 223–231.

Matthew Snover, Bonnie J. Dorr, Richard Schwartz, Linnea Micciulla, and John Makhoul. 2006b. A study of translation edit rate with targeted human annotation. In *5th Conference of the Association for Machine Translation in the Americas (AMTA)*, Boston, Massachusetts.

Artem Sokolov, Julia Kreutzer, Kellen Sunderland, Pavel Danchenko, Witold Szymaniak, Hagen Fürstenau, and Stefan Riezler. 2017. A Shared Task on Bandit Learning for Machine Translation. In *Proceedings of the Second Conference on Machine Translation*, Copenhagen, Denmark. Association for Computational Linguistics.

Lucia Specia, Frédéric Blain, Kim Harris, Aljoscha Burchardt, Viviven Macketanz, Inguna Skadiņa, Marco Turchi, and Matteo Negri. 2017a. Translation quality and productivity: A study on rich morphology languages. In *Proceedings of the 16th Machine Translation Summit*, Nagoya, Japan.

Lucia Specia, Kim Harris, Aljoscha Burchardt, Marco Turchi, Matteo Negri, and Inguna Skadina. 2017b. Translation Quality and Productivity: A Study on Rich Morphology Languages. In *Proceedings of the 16th Machine Translation Summit*, Nagoya, Japan.

Lucia Specia, Gustavo Paetzold, and Carolina Scarton. 2015. Multi-level Translation Quality Prediction with QuEst++. In *53rd Annual Meeting of the Association for Computational Linguistics and Seventh International Joint Conference on Natural Language Processing of the Asian Federation of Natural Language Processing: System Demonstrations*, pages 115–120, Beijing, China.

Lucia Specia, Kashif Shah, Jose G.C. de Souza, and Trevor Cohn. 2013. Quest - a translation quality estimation framework. In *Proceedings of the 51st Annual Meeting of the Association for Computational Linguistics: System Demonstrations*, pages 79–84, Sofia, Bulgaria.

A. Stolcke. 2002. Srilm - an extensible language modeling toolkit. In *ICSLP*, pages 901–904, Denver, CO.

Roman Sudarikov, David Mareček, Tom Kocmi, Dušan Variš, and Ondřej Bojar. 2017. CUNI Submission in WMT17: Chimera Goes Neural. In *Proceedings of the Second Conference on Machine Translation*, Copenhagen, Denmark. Association for Computational Linguistics.

Roman Sudarikov, Martin Popel, Ondřej Bojar, Aljoscha Burchardt, and Ondřej Klejch. 2016. Using MT-ComparEval. In *Translation Evaluation: From Fragmented Tools and Data Sets to an Integrated Ecosystem*, pages 76–82.

Yiming Tan, Zhiming Chen, Liu Huang, Lilin Zhang, Maoxi Li, and Mingwen Wang. 2017a. Neural Post-Editing Based on Quality Estimation. In *Proceedings of the Second Conference on Machine Translation*, Copenhagen, Denmark. Association for Computational Linguistics.

Zhixing Tan, Boli Wang, Jinming Hu, Yidong Chen, and xiaodong shi. 2017b. XMU Neural Machine Translation Systems for WMT 17. In *Proceedings of the Second Conference on Machine Translation*, Copenhagen, Denmark. Association for Computational Linguistics.

Long Trieu, Trung-Tin Pham, and Le-Minh Nguyen. 2017. The JAIST Machine Translation Systems for WMT 17. In *Proceedings of the Second Conference on Machine Translation*, Copenhagen, Denmark. Association for Computational Linguistics.

Dušan Variš and Ondřej Bojar. 2017. CUNI System for WMT17 Automatic Post-Editing Task. In *Proceedings of the Second Conference on Machine Translation*, Copenhagen, Denmark. Association for Computational Linguistics.

Yuguang Wang, Shanbo Cheng, Liyang Jiang, Jiajun Yang, Wei Chen, Muze Li, Lin Shi, Yanfeng Wang, and Hongtao Yang. 2017. Sogou Neural Machine Translation Systems for WMT17. In *Proceedings of the Second Conference on Machine Translation*, Copenhagen, Denmark. Association for Computational Linguistics.

Krzysztof Wolk and Krzysztof Marasek. 2017. PJIIT's systems for WMT 2017 Conference. In *Proceedings of the Second Conference on Machine Translation*, Copenhagen, Denmark. Association for Computational Linguistics.

Jia Xu, Yi Zong Kuang, Shondell Baijoo, Jacob Hyun Lee, Uman Shahzad, Mir Ahmed, Meredith Lancaster, and Chris Carlan. 2017. Hunter MT: A Course for Young Researchers in WMT17. In *Proceedings of the Second Conference on Machine Translation*, Copenhagen, Denmark. Association for Computational Linguistics.

Alexander Yeh. 2000. More Accurate Tests for the Statistical Significance of Result Differences. In *Coling-2000: the 18th Conference on Computational Linguistics*, pages 947–953, Saarbrücken, Germany.

Jinchao Zhang, Peerachet Porkaew, Jiawei Hu, Qiuye Zhao, and Qun Liu. 2017. CASICT-DCU Neural Machine Translation Systems for WMT17. In *Proceedings of the Second Conference on Machine Translation*, Copenhagen, Denmark. Association for Computational Linguistics.

Yuan Zhang and David Weiss. 2016. Stack-propagation: Improved representation learning for syntax. In *Proceedings of the 54th Annual Meeting of the Association for Computational Linguistics (Volume 1: Long Papers)*, pages 1557–1566, Berlin, Germany. Association for Computational Linguistics.

Findings of the Second Shared Task on Multimodal Machine Translation and Multilingual Image Description

Desmond Elliott
School of Informatics
University of Edinburgh
d.elliott@ed.ac.uk

Stella Frank
Centre for Language Evolution
University of Edinburgh
stella.frank@ed.ac.uk

Loïc Barrault and **Fethi Bougares**
LIUM
University of Le Mans
first.last@univ-lemans.fr

Lucia Specia
Department of Computer Science
University of Sheffield
l.specia@sheffield.ac.uk

Abstract

We present the results from the second shared task on multimodal machine translation and multilingual image description. Nine teams submitted 19 systems to two tasks. The multimodal translation task, in which the source sentence is supplemented by an image, was extended with a new language (French) and two new test sets. The multilingual image description task was changed such that at test time, only the image is given. Compared to last year, multimodal systems improved, but text-only systems remain competitive.

1 Introduction

The Shared Task on Multimodal Translation and Multilingual Image Description tackles the problem of generating descriptions of images for languages other than English. The vast majority of image description research has focused on English-language description due to the abundance of crowdsourced resources (Bernardi et al., 2016). However, there has been a significant amount of recent work on creating multilingual image description datasets in German (Elliott et al., 2016; Hitschler et al., 2016; Rajendran et al., 2016), Turkish (Unal et al., 2016), Chinese (Li et al., 2016), Japanese (Miyazaki and Shimizu, 2016; Yoshikawa et al., 2017), and Dutch (van Miltenburg et al., 2017). Progress on this problem will be useful for native-language image search, multilingual e-commerce, and audio-described video for visually impaired viewers.

The first empirical results for multimodal translation showed the potential for visual context to improve translation quality (Elliott et al., 2015; Hitschler et al., 2016). This was quickly followed by a wider range of work in the first shared task at WMT 2016 (Specia et al., 2016). The current shared task consists of two subtasks:

- Task 1: **Multimodal translation** takes an image with a source language description that is then translated into a target language. The training data consists of parallel sentences with images.

- Task 2: **Multilingual image description** takes an image and generates a description in the target language without additional source language information at test time. The training data, however, consists of images with independent descriptions in both source and target languages.

The translation task has been extended to include a new language, French. This extension means the Multi30K dataset (Elliott et al., 2016) is now triple aligned, with English descriptions translated into both German and French.

The description generation task has substantially changed since last year. The main difference is that source language descriptions are no longer observed for test images. This mirrors the real-world scenario in which a target-language speaker wants a description of image that does not already have source language descriptions associated with it. The two subtasks are now more distinct because multilingual image description requires the use of the image (no text-only system is possible because the input contains no text).

Another change for this year is the introduction of two new evaluation datasets: an extension of the

Proceedings of the Conference on Machine Translation (WMT), Volume 2: Shared Task Papers, pages 215–233
Copenhagen, Denmark, September 7–11, 2017. ©2017 Association for Computational Linguistics

existing Multi30K dataset, and a "teaser" evaluation dataset with images carefully chosen to contain ambiguities in the source language.

This year we encouraged participants to submit systems using unconstrained data for both tasks. Training on additional out-of-domain data is under-explored for these tasks. We believe this setting will be critical for future real-world improvements, given that the current training datasets are small and expensive to construct.

2 Tasks & Datasets

2.1 Tasks

The Multimodal Translation task (Task 1) follows the format of the 2016 Shared Task (Specia et al., 2016). The Multilingual Image Description Task (Task 2) is new this year but it is related to the Crosslingual Image Description task from 2016. The main difference between the Crosslingual Image Description task and the Multilingual Image Description task is the presence of source language descriptions. In last year's Crosslingual Image Description task, the aim was to produce a single target language description, given five source language descriptions and the image. In this year's Multilingual Image Description task, participants received only an unseen image at test time, without source language descriptions.

2.2 Datasets

The Multi30K dataset (Elliott et al., 2016) is the primary dataset for the shared task. It contains 31K images originally described in English (Young et al., 2014) with two types of multilingual data: a collection of professionally translated German sentences, and a collection of independently crowd-sourced German descriptions.

This year the Multi30K dataset has been extended with new evaluation data for the Translation and Image Description tasks, and an additional language for the Translation task. In addition, we released a new evaluation dataset featuring ambiguities that we expected would benefit from visual context. Table 1 presents an overview of the new evaluation datasets. Figure 1 shows an example of an image with an aligned English-German-French description.

In addition to releasing the parallel text, we also distributed two types of ResNet-50 visual features (He et al., 2016) for all of the images, namely the 'res4_relu' convolutional features (which preserve

En: A group of people are eating noddles.
De: Eine Gruppe von Leuten isst Nudeln.
Fr: Un groupe de gens mangent des nouilles.

Figure 1: Example of an image with a source description in English, together with German and French translations.

the spatial location of a feature in the original image) and averaged pooled features.

Multi30K French Translations

We extended the translation data in Multi30K dataset with crowdsourced French translations. The crowdsourced translations were collected from 12 workers using an internal platform. We estimate the translation work had a monetary value of €9,700. The translators had access to the source segment, the image and an automatic translation created with a standard phrase-based system (Koehn et al., 2007) trained on WMT'15 parallel text. The automatic translations were presented to the crowdworkers to further simplify the crowdsourcing task. We note that this did not end up being a post-editing task, that is, the translators did not simply copy and paste the suggested translations. To demonstrate this, we calculated text-similarity metric scores between the phrase-based system outputs and the human translations on the training corpus, resulting in 0.41 edit distance (measured using the TER metric), meaning that more than 40% of the words between these two versions do not match.

Multi30K 2017 test data

We collected new evaluation data for the Multi30K dataset. We sampled new images from five of the six Flickr groups used to create the original Flickr30K dataset using MMFeat (Kiela, 2016)[1]. We sampled additional images from two thematically related groups (Everything Outdoor and

---

[1] Strangers!, Wild Child, Dogs in Action, Action Photography, and Outdoor Activities.

	Training set		Development set	
	Images	Sentences	Images	Sentences
Translation	29,000	29,000	1,014	1,014
Description	29,000	145,000	1,014	5,070

	2017 test		COCO	
	Images	Sentences	Images	Sentences
Translation	1,000	1,000	461	461
Description	1,071	5,355	—	

Table 1: Overview of the Multi30K training, development, 2017 test, and Ambiguous COCO datasets.

Group	Task 1	Task 2
Strangers!	150	154
Wild Child	83	83
Dogs in Action	78	92
Action Photography	238	259
Flickr Social Club	241	263
Everything Outdoor	206	214
Outdoor Activities	4	6

Table 2: Distribution of images in the Multi30K 2017 test data by Flickr group.

Flickr Social Club) because Outdoor Activities only returned 10 new CC-licensed images and Flickr-Social no longer exists. Table 2 shows the distribution of images across the groups and tasks. We initially downloaded 2,000 images per Flickr group, which were then manually filtered by three of the authors. The filtering was done to remove (near) duplicate images, clearly watermarked images, and images with dubious content. This process resulted in a total of 2,071 images.

We crowdsourced five English descriptions of each image from Crowdflower[2] using the same process as Elliott et al. (2016). One of the authors selected 1,000 images from the collection to form the dataset for the Multimodal Translation task based on a manual inspection of the English descriptions. Professional German translations were collected for those 1,000 English-described images. The remaining 1,071 images were used for the Multilingual Image Description task. We collected five ad-

ditional independent German descriptions of those images from Crowdflower.

Ambiguous COCO

As a secondary evaluation dataset for the Multimodal Translation task, we collected and translated a set of image descriptions that potentially contain ambiguous verbs. We based our selection on the VerSe dataset (Gella et al., 2016), which annotates a subset of the COCO (Lin et al., 2014) and TUHOI (Le et al., 2014) images with OntoNotes senses for 90 verbs which are ambiguous, e.g. *play*. Their goals were to test the feasibility of annotating images with the word sense of a given verb (rather than verbs themselves) and to provide a gold-labelled dataset for evaluating automatic visual sense disambiguation methods.

Altogether, the VerSe dataset contains 3,518 images, but we limited ourselves to its COCO section, since for our purposes we also need the image descriptions, which are not available in TUHOI. The COCO portion covers 82 verbs; we further discarded verbs that are unambiguous in the dataset, i.e. although some verbs have multiple senses in OntoNotes, they all occur with one sense in VerSe (e.g. *gather* is used in all instances to describe the 'people gathering' sense), resulting in 57 ambiguous verbs (2,699 images). The actual descriptions of the images were not distributed with the VerSe dataset. However, given that the ambiguous verbs were selected based on the image descriptions, we assumed that in all cases at least one of the original COCO description (out of the five per image) should contain the ambiguous verb. In cases where more than one description contained the verb, we randomly selected one such description to be part of the dataset of descriptions containing ambiguous

En: A man on a motorcycle is <u>passing</u> another vehicle.
De: Ein Mann auf einem Motorrad <u>fährt</u> an einem anderen Fahrzeug vorbei.
Fr: Un homme sur une moto <u>dépasse</u> un autre véhicule.

En: A red train is <u>passing</u> over the water on a bridge
De: Ein roter Zug <u>fährt</u> auf einer Brücke über das Wasser
Fr: Un train rouge <u>traverse</u> l'eau sur un pont.

Figure 2: Two senses of the English verb "to pass" in their visual contexts, with the original English and the translations into German and French. The verb and its translations are underlined.

verbs. This resulted in 2,699 descriptions.

As a consequence of the original goals of the VerSe dataset, each sense of each ambiguous verb was used multiple times in the dataset, which resulted in many descriptions with the same sense, for example, 85 images (and descriptions) were available for the verb *show*, but they referred to a small set of senses of the verb.

The number of images (and therefore descriptions) per ambiguous verb varied from 6 (*stir*) to 100 (*pull, serve*). Since our intention was to have a small but varied dataset, we selected a subset of a subset of descriptions per ambiguous verb, aiming at keeping 1-3 instances per sense per verb. This resulted in 461 descriptions for 56 verbs in total, ranging from 3 (e.g. *shake, carry*) to 26 (*reach*) (the verb *lay/lie* was excluded as it had only one sense). We note that the descriptions include the use of the verbs in phrasal verbs. Two examples of the English verb "to pass" are shown in Figure 2. In the German translations, the source language verb did not require disambiguation (both German translations use the verb "fährt"), whereas in the French translations, the verb was disambiguated into "dépasse" and "traverse", respectively.

3 Participants

This year we attracted submissions from nine different groups. Table 3 presents an overview of the groups and their submission identifiers.

AFRL-OHIOSTATE (Task 1) The AFRL-OHIOSTATE system submission is an atypical Machine Translation (MT) system in that the image is the catalyst for the MT results, and not the textual content. This system architecture assumes an image caption engine can be trained in a target language to give meaningful output in the form of a set of the most probable n target language candidate captions. A learned mapping function of the encoded source language caption to the corresponding encoded target language captions is then employed. Finally, a distance function is applied to retrieve the "nearest" candidate caption to be the translation of the source caption.

CMU (Task 2) The CMU submission uses a multi-task learning technique, extending the baseline so that it generates both a German caption and an English caption. First, a German caption is generated using the baseline method. After the LSTM for the baseline model finishes producing a German caption, it has some final hidden state. Decoding is simply resumed starting from that final state with an independent decoder, separate vocabulary, and this time without any direct access to the image. The goal is to encourage the model to keep information about the image in the hidden state throughout the decoding process, hopefully improving the model output. Although the model is trained to produce both German and English captions, at evaluation time the English component of the model is ignored and only German captions are

ID	Participating team
AFRL-OHIOSTATE	Air Force Research Laboratory & Ohio State University (Duselis et al., 2017)
CMU	Carnegie Melon University (Jaffe, 2017)
CUNI	Univerzita Karlova v Praze (Helcl and Libovický, 2017)
DCU-ADAPT	Dublin City University (Calixto et al., 2017a)
LIUMCVC	Laboratoire d'Informatique de l'Université du Maine & Universitat Autonoma de Barcelona Computer Vision Center (Caglayan et al., 2017a)
NICT	National Institute of Information and Communications Technology & Nara Institute of Science and Technology (Zhang et al., 2017)
OREGONSTATE	Oregon State University (Ma et al., 2017)
SHEF	University of Sheffield (Madhyastha et al., 2017)
UvA-TiCC	Universiteit van Amsterdam & Tilburg University (Elliott and Kádár, 2017)

Table 3: Participants in the WMT17 multimodal machine translation shared task.

generated.

CUNI (Tasks 1 and 2) For Task 1, the submissions employ the standard neural MT (NMT) scheme enriched with another attentive encoder for the input image. It uses a hierarchical attention combination in the decoder (Libovický and Helcl, 2017). The best system was trained with additional data obtained from selecting similar sentences from parallel corpora and by back-translation of similar sentences found in the SDEWAC corpus (Faaß and Eckart, 2013).

The submission to Task 2 is a combination of two neural models. The first model generates an English caption from the image. The second model is a text-only NMT model that translates the English caption to German.

DCU-ADAPT (Task 1) This submission evaluates ensembles of up to four different multimodal NMT models. All models use global image features obtained with the pre-trained CNN VGG19, and are either incorporated in the encoder or the decoder. These models are described in detail in (Calixto et al., 2017b). They are model IMG_W, in which image features are used as words in the source-language encoder; model IMG_E, where image features are used to initialise the hidden states of the forward and backward encoder RNNs; and model IMG_D, where the image features are used as additional signals to initialise the decoder hidden state. Each image has one corresponding feature vector, obtained from the activations of the FC7 layer of the VGG19 network, and consist of a 4096D real-valued vector that encode information about the entire image.

LIUMCVC (Task 1) LIUMCVC experiment with two approaches: a multimodal attentive NMT with separate attention (Caglayan et al., 2016) over source text and convolutional image features, and an NMT where global visual features (2048-dimensional pool5 features from ResNet-50) are multiplicatively interacted with word embeddings. More specifically, each target word embedding is multiplied with global visual features in an element-wise fashion in order to visually contextualize word representations. With 128-dimensional embeddings and 256-dimensional recurrent layers, the resulting models have around 5M parameters.

NICT (Task 1) These are constrained submissions for both language pairs. First, a hierarchical phrase-based (HPB) translation system s built using Moses (Koehn et al., 2007) with standard features. Then, an attentional encoder-decoder network (Bahdanau et al., 2015) is trained and used as an additional feature to rerank the n best output of the HPB system. A unimodal NMT model is also trained to integrate visual information. Instead of integrating visual features into the NMT model directly, image retrieval methods are employed to obtain target language descriptions of images that are similar to the image described by the source sentence, and this target description information is integrated into the NMT model. A multimodal

NMT model is also used to rerank the HPB output. All feature weights (including the standard features, the NMT feature and the multimodal NMT feature) were tuned by MERT (Och, 2003). On the development set, the NMT feature improved the HPB system significantly. However, the multimodal NMT feature did not further improve the HPB system that had integrated the NMT feature.

OREGONSTATE (Task 1) The OREGON-STATE system uses a very simple but effective model which feeds the image information to both encoder and decoder. On the encoder side, the image representation was used as an initialization information to generate the source words' representations. This step strengthens the relatedness between image's and source words' representations. Additionally, the decoder uses alignment to source words by a global attention mechanism. In this way, the decoder benefits from both image and source language information and generates more accurate target side sentence.

UvA-TiCC (Task 1) The submitted systems are Imagination models (Elliott and Kádár, 2017), which are trained to perform two tasks in a multitask learning framework: a) produce the target sentence, and b) predict the visual feature vector of the corresponding image. The constrained models are trained over only the 29,000 training examples in the Multi30K dataset with a source-side vocabulary of 10,214 types and a target-side vocabulary of 16,022 types. The unconstrained models are trained over a concatenation of the Multi30K, News Commentary (Tiedemann, 2012) parallel texts, and MS COCO (Chen et al., 2015) dataset with a joint source-target vocabulary of 17,597 word pieces (Schuster and Nakajima, 2012). In both constrained and unconstrained submissions, the models were trained to predict the 2048D GoogleLeNetV3 feature vector (Szegedy et al., 2015) of an image associated with a source language sentence. The output of an ensemble of the three best randomly initialized models - as measured by BLEU on the Multi30K development set - was used for both the constrained and unconstrained submissions.

SHEF (Task 1) The SHEF systems utilize the predicted posterior probability distribution over the image object classes as image features. To do so, they make use of the pre-trained ResNet-152 (He et al., 2016), a deep CNN based image network that is trained over the 1,000 object categories on the Imagenet dataset (Deng et al., 2009) to obtain the posterior distribution. The model follows a standard encoder-decoder NMT approach using *softdot* attention as described in (Luong et al., 2015). It explores image information in three ways: a) to initialize the encoder; b) to initialize the decoder; c) to condition each source word with the image class posteriors. In all these three ways, non-linear affine transformations over the posteriors are used as image features.

Baseline — Task 1 The baseline system for the multimodal translation task is a text-only neural machine translation system built with the Nematus toolkit (Sennrich et al., 2017). Most settings and hyperparameters were kept as default, with a few exceptions: batch size of 40 (instead of 80 due to memory constraints) and ADAM as optimizer. In order to handle rare and OOV words, we used the Byte Pair Encoding Compression Algorithm to segment words (Sennrich et al., 2016b). The merge operations for word segmentation were learned using training data in both source and target languages. These were then applied to all training, validation and test sets in both source and target languages. In post-processing, the original words were restored by concatenating the subwords.

Baseline — Task 2 The baseline for the multilingual image description task is an attention-based image description system trained over only the German image descriptions (Caglayan et al., 2017b). The visual representation are extracted from the so-called *res4f_relu* layer from a ResNet-50 (He et al., 2016) convolutional neural network trained on the ImageNet dataset (Russakovsky et al., 2015). Those feature maps provide spatial information on which the model focuses through the attention mechanism.

4 Text-similarity Metric Results

The submissions were evaluated against either professional or crowd-sourced references. All submissions and references were pre-processed to lowercase, normalise punctuation, and tokenise the sentences using the Moses scripts.[3] The evaluation was performed using `MultEval` (Clark et al., 2011) with the primary metric of Meteor 1.5 (Denkowski and Lavie, 2014). We also report the results using BLEU (Papineni et al., 2002) and

---

[3]`https://github.com/moses-smt/`
`mosesdecoder/blob/master/scripts/`

TER (Snover et al., 2006) metrics. The winning submissions are indicated by •. These are the top-scoring submissions and those that are not significantly different (based on Meteor scores) according the approximate randomisation test (with p-value ≤ 0.05) provided by `MultEval`. Submissions marked with * are not significantly different from the Baseline according to the same test.

4.1 Task 1: English $\rightarrow$ German

4.1.1 Multi30K 2017 test data

Table 4 shows the results on the Multi30K 2017 test data with a German target language. It interesting to note that the metrics do not fully agree on the ranking of systems, although the four best (statistically indistinguishable) systems win by all metrics. All-but-one submission outperformed the text-only NMT baseline. This year, the best performing systems include both multimodal (LIUMCVC_MNMT_C and UvA-TiCC_IMAGINATION_U) and text-only (NICT_NMTrerank_C and LIUMCVC_MNMT_C) submissions. (Strictly speaking, the UvA-TiCC_IMAGINATION_U system is incomparable because it is an unconstrained system, but all unconstrained systems perform in the same range as the constrained systems.)

4.1.2 Ambiguous COCO

Table 5 shows the results for the out-of-domain ambiguous COCO dataset with a German target language. Once again the evaluation metrics do not fully agree on the ranking of the submissions.

It is interesting to note that the metric scores are lower for the out-of-domain Ambiguous COCO data compared to the in-domain Multi30K 2017 test data. However, we cannot make definitive claims about the difficulty of the dataset because the Ambiguous COCO dataset contains fewer sentences than the Multi30K 2017 test data (461 compared to 1,000).

The systems are mostly in the same order as on the Multi30K 2017 test data, with the same four systems performing best. However, two systems (DCU-ADAPT_MultiMT_C and OREGON-STATE_1NeuralTranslation_C) are ranked higher on this test set than on the in-domain Flickr dataset, indicating that they are relatively more robust and possibly better at resolving the ambiguities found in the Ambiguous COCO dataset.

4.2 Task 1: English $\rightarrow$ French

4.2.1 Multi30K Test 2017

Table 6 shows the results for the Multi30K 2017 test data with French as target language. A reduced number of submissions were received for this new language pair, with no unconstrained systems. In contrast to the English$\rightarrow$German results, the evaluation metrics are in better agreement about the ranking of the submissions.

Translating from English$\rightarrow$French is an easier task than English$\rightarrow$German systems, as reflected in the higher metric scores. This also includes the baseline systems where English$\rightarrow$French results in 63.1 Meteor compared to 41.9 for English$\rightarrow$German.

Eight out of the ten submissions outperformed the English$\rightarrow$French baseline system. Two of the best submissions for English$\rightarrow$German remain the best for English$\rightarrow$French (LIUMCVC_MNMT_C and NICT_NMTrerank_C), the text-only system (LIUMCVC_NMT_C) decreased in performance, and no UvA-TiCC_IMAGINATION_U system was submitted for French.

An interesting observation is the difference of the Meteor scores between text-only NMT system (LIUMCVC_NMT_C) and Moses hierarchical phrase-based system with reranking (NICT_NMTrerank_C). While the two systems are very close for the English$\rightarrow$German direction, the hierarchical system is better than the text-only NMT systems in the English$\rightarrow$French direction. This pattern holds for both the Multi30K 2017 test data and Ambiguous COCO test data.

4.2.2 Ambiguous COCO

Table 7 shows the results for the out-of-domain Ambiguous COCO dataset with the French target language. Once again, in contrast to the English$\rightarrow$German results, the evaluation metrics are in better agreement about the ranking of the submissions. The performance of all the models is once again in mostly agreement with the Multi30K 2017 test data, albeit lower. Both DCU-ADAPT_MultiMT_C and OREGON-STATE_2NeuralTranslation_C again perform relatively better on this dataset.

4.3 Task 2: English $\rightarrow$ German

The description generation task, in which systems must generate target-language (German) captions for a test image, has substantially changed since

	BLEU ↑	Meteor ↑	TER ↓
•LIUMCVC_MNMT_C	33.4	54.0	48.5
•NICT_NMTrerank_C	31.9	53.9	48.1
•LIUMCVC_NMT_C	33.2	53.8	48.2
•UvA-TiCC_IMAGINATION_U	33.3	53.5	47.5
UvA-TiCC_IMAGINATION_C	30.2	51.2	50.8
CUNI_NeuralMonkeyTextualMT_U	31.1	51.0	50.7
OREGONSTATE_2NeuralTranslation_C	31.0	50.6	50.7
DCU-ADAPT_MultiMT_C	29.8	50.5	52.3
CUNI_NeuralMonkeyMultimodalMT_U	29.5	50.2	52.5
CUNI_NeuralMonkeyTextualMT_C	28.5	49.2	54.3
OREGONSTATE_1NeuralTranslation_C	29.7	48.9	51.6
CUNI_NeuralMonkeyMultimodalMT_C	25.8	47.1	56.3
SHEF_ShefClassInitDec_C	25.0	44.5	53.8
SHEF_ShefClassProj_C	24.2	43.4	55.9
Baseline (text-only NMT)	19.3	41.9	72.2
AFRL-OHIOSTATE-MULTIMODAL_U	6.5	20.2	87.4

Table 4: Official results for the WMT17 Multimodal Machine Translation task on the English-German Multi30K 2017 test data. Systems with grey background indicate use of resources that fall outside the constraints provided for the shared task.

	BLEU ↑	Meteor ↑	TER ↓
•LIUMCVC_NMT_C	28.7	48.9	52.5
•LIUMCVC_MNMT_C	28.5	48.8	53.4
•NICT_1_NMTrerank_C	28.1	48.5	52.9
•UvA-TiCC_IMAGINATION_U	28.0	48.1	52.4
DCU-ADAPT_MultiMT_C	26.4	46.8	54.5
OREGONSTATE_1NeuralTranslation_C	27.4	46.5	52.3
CUNI_NeuralMonkeyTextualMT_U	26.6	46.0	54.8
UvA-TiCC_IMAGINATION_C	26.4	45.8	55.4
OREGONSTATE_2NeuralTranslation_C	26.1	45.7	55.9
CUNI_NeuralMonkeyMultimodalMT_U	25.7	45.6	55.7
CUNI_NeuralMonkeyTextualMT_C	23.2	43.8	59.8
CUNI_NeuralMonkeyMultimodalMT_C	22.4	42.7	60.1
SHEF_ShefClassInitDec_C	21.4	40.7	56.5
SHEF_ShefClassProj_C	21.0	40.0	57.8
Baseline (text-only NMT)	18.7	37.6	66.1

Table 5: Results for the Multimodal Translation task on the English-German Ambiguous COCO dataset. Systems with grey background indicate use of resources that fall outside the constraints provided for the shared task.

	BLEU ↑	Meteor ↑	TER ↓
•LIUMCVC_MNMT_C	55.9	72.1	28.4
•NICT_NMTrerank_C	55.3	72.0	28.4
DCU-ADAPT_MultiMT_C	54.1	70.1	30.0
LIUMCVC_NMT_C	53.3	70.1	31.7
OREGONSTATE_2NeuralTranslation_C	51.9	68.3	32.7
OREGONSTATE_1NeuralTranslation_C	51.0	67.2	33.6
CUNI_NeuralMonkeyMultimodalMT_C	49.9	67.2	34.3
CUNI_NeuralMonkeyTextualMT_C	50.3	67.0	33.6
Baseline (text-only NMT)	44.3	63.1	39.6
*SHEF_ShefClassInitDec_C	45.0	62.8	38.4
SHEF_ShefClassProj_C	43.6	61.5	40.5

Table 6: Results for the Multimodal Translation task on the English-French Multi30K Test 2017 data.

	BLEU ↑	Meteor ↑	TER ↓
•LIUMCVC_MNMT_C	45.9	65.9	34.2
•NICT_NMTrerank_C	45.1	65.6	34.7
•DCU ADAPT_MultiMT_C	44.5	64.1	35.2
OREGONSTATE_2NeuralTranslation_C	44.1	63.8	36.7
LIUMCVC_NMT_C	43.6	63.4	37.4
CUNI_NeuralMonkeyTexutalMT_C	43.0	62.5	38.2
CUNI_NeuralMonkeyMultimodalMT_C	42.9	62.5	38.2
OREGONSTATE_1NeuralTranslation_C	41.2	61.6	37.8
SHEF_ShefClassInitDec_C	37.2	57.3	42.4
*SHEF_ShefClassProj_C	36.8	57.0	44.5
Baseline (text-only NMT)	35.1	55.8	45.8

Table 7: Results for the Multimodal Translation task on the English-French Ambiguous COCO dataset.

	BLEU ↑	Meteor ↑	TER ↓
Baseline (target monolingual)	9.1	23.4	91.4
CUNI_NeuralMonkeyCaptionAndMT_C	4.2	22.1	133.6
CUNI_NeuralMonkeyCaptionAndMT_U	6.5	20.6	91.7
CMU_NeuralEncoderDecoder_C	9.1	19.8	63.3
CUNI_NeuralMonkeyBilingual_C	2.3	17.6	112.6

Table 8: Results for the Multilingual Image Description task on the English-German Multi30K 2017 test data.

last year. The main difference is that source language descriptions are no longer observed for images at test time. The training data remains the same and contains images with both source and target language descriptions. The aim is thus to leverage multilingual training data to improve a monolingual task.

Table 8 shows the results for the Multilingual image description task. This task attracted fewer submissions than last year, which may be because it was no longer possible to re-use a model designed for Multimodal Translation. The evaluation metrics do not agree on the ranking of the submissions, with major differences in the ranking using either BLEU or TER instead of Meteor.

The main result is that none of the submissions outperform the monolingual German baseline according to Meteor. All of the submissions are statistically significantly different compared to the baseline. However, the CMU_NeuralEncoderDecoder_C submission marginally outperformed the baseline according to TER and equalled its BLEU score.

5 Human Judgement Results

This year, we conducted a human evaluation in addition to the text-similarity metrics to assess the translation quality of the submissions. This evaluation was undertaken for the Task 1 German and French outputs for the Multi30K 2017 test data.

This section describes how we collected the human assessments and computed the results. We would like to gratefully thank all assessors.

5.1 Methodology

The system outputs were manually evaluated by bilingual Direct Assessment (DA) (Graham et al., 2015) using the Appraise platform (Federmann, 2012). The annotators (mostly researchers) were asked to evaluate the semantic relatedness between the source sentence in English and the target sentence in German or French. The image was shown along with the source sentence and the candidate translation and evaluators were told to rely on the image when necessary to obtain a better understanding of the source sentence (e.g. in cases where the text was ambiguous). Note that the reference sentence is not displayed during the evaluation, in order to avoid influencing the assessor. Figure 3 shows an example of the direct assessment interface used in the evaluation. The score of each translation candidate ranges from 0 (meaning that the meaning of the source is not preserved in the target language sentence) to 100 (meaning the meaning of the source is "perfectly" preserved). The human assessment scores are standardized according to each individual assessor's overall mean and standard deviation score. The overall score of a given system (z) corresponds to the mean standardized score of its translations.

5.2 Results

The French outputs were evaluated by seven assessors, who conducted a total of 2,521 DAs, resulting in a minimum of 319 and a maximum of 368 direct assessments per system submission, respectively. The German outputs were evaluated by 25 assessors, who conducted a total of 3,485 DAs, resulting in a minimum of 291 and a maximum of 357 direct assessments per system submission, respectively. This is somewhat less than the recommended number of 500, so the results should be considered preliminary.

Tables 9 and 10 show the results of the human evaluation for the English to German and the English to French Multimodal Translation task (Multi30K 2017 test data). The systems are ordered by standardized mean DA scores and clustered ac-

Figure 3: Example of the human direct assessment evaluation interface.

cording to the Wilcoxon signed-rank test at p-level $p \leq 0.05$. Systems within a cluster are considered tied. The Wilcoxon signed-rank scores can be found in Tables 11 and 12 in Appendix A.

When comparing automatic and human evaluations, we can observe that they globally agree with each other, as shown in Figures 4 and 5, with German showing better agreement than French. We point out two interesting disagreements: First, in the English→French language pair, CUNI_NeuralMonkeyMultimodalMT_C and DCU-ADAPT_MultiMT_C are significantly better than LIUMCVC_MNMT_C, despite the fact that the latter system achieves much higher metric scores. Secondly, across both languages, the text-only LIUM-CVC_NMT_C system performs well on metrics but does relatively poorly on human judgements, especially as compared to the multimodal version of the same system.

6 Discussion

Visual Features: do they help? Three teams provided text-only counterparts to their multimodal systems for Task 1 (CUNI, LIUMCVC, and ORE-GONSTATE), which enables us to evaluate the contribution of visual features. For many systems, visual features did not seem to help reliably, at least as measured by metric evaluations: in German, the CUNI and OREGONSTATE text-only systems outperformed the counterparts, while in French, there were small improvements for the CUNI multimodal system. However, the LIUMCVC multimodal system outperformed their text-only system

across both languages.

The human evaluation results are perhaps more promising: nearly all the highest ranked systems (with the exception of NICT) are multimodal. An intruiging result was the text-only LIUM-CVC_NMT_C, which ranked highly on metrics but poorly in the human evaluation. The LIUMCVC systems were indistinguishable from each other in terms of Meteor scores but the standardized mean direct assessment score showed a significant difference in performance (see Tables 11 and 12): further analysis of the reasons for humans disliking the text-only translations will be necessary.

The multimodal Task 1 submissions can be broadly categorised into three groups based on how they use the images: approaches useing double-attention mechanisms, initialising the hidden state of the encoder and/or decoder networks with the global image feature vector, and alternative uses of image features. The double-attention models calculate context vectors over the source language hidden states and location-preserving feature vectors over the image; these vectors are used as inputs to the translation decoder (CUNI_NeuralMonkeyMultimodalMT). Encoder and/or decoder initialisation involves initialising the recurrent neural network with an affine transformation of a global image feature vector (DCU-ADAPT_MultiMT, OREGON-STATE_1NeuralTranslation) or initialising the encoder and decoder with the 1000 dimension softmax probability vector over the object classes in ImageNet object recognition challenge

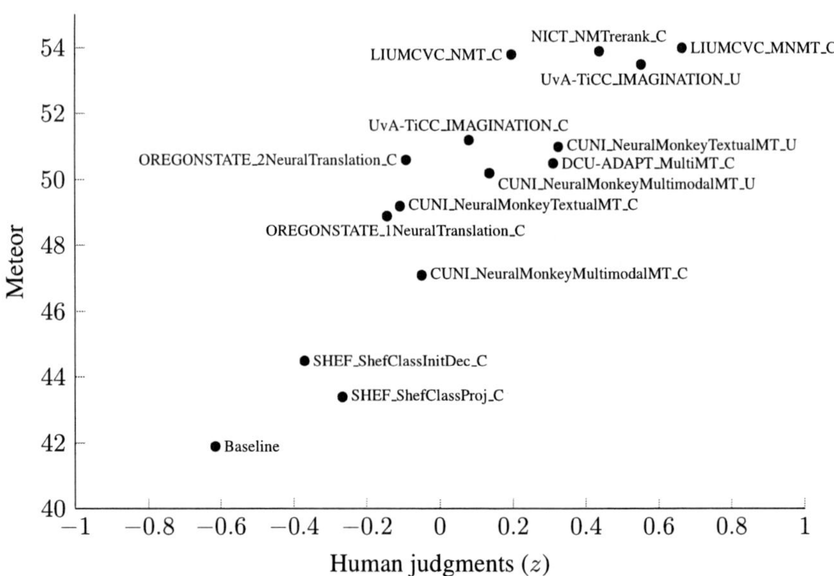

Figure 4: System performance on the English→German Multi30K 2017 test data as measured by human evaluation against Meteor scores. The AFRL-OHIOSTATE-MULTIMODAL_U system has been ommitted for readability.

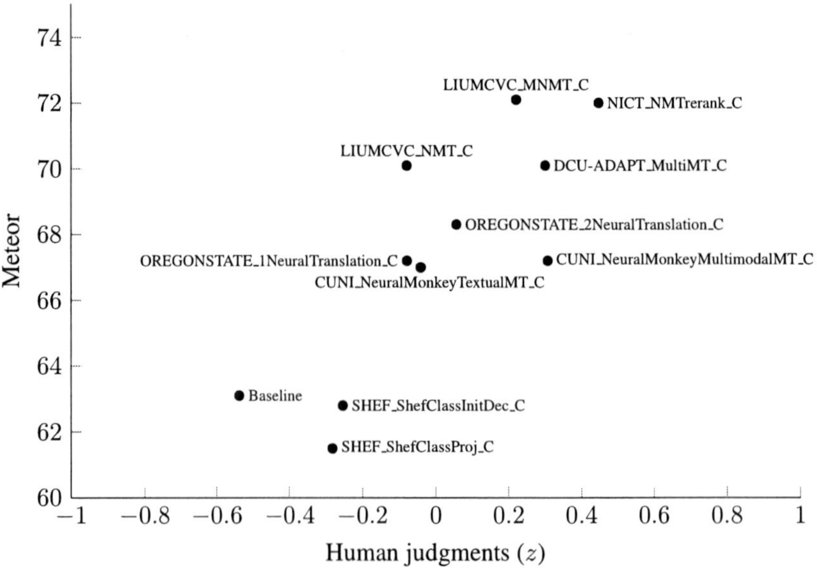

Figure 5: System performance on the English→French Multi30K 2017 test data as measured by human evaluation against Meteor scores.

English→German

#	Raw	z	System
1	77.8	0.665	LIUMCVC_MNMT_C
2	74.1	0.552	UvA-TiCC_IMAGINATION_U
3	70.3	0.437	NICT_NMTrerank_C
	68.1	0.325	CUNI_NeuralMonkeyTextualMT_U
	68.1	0.311	DCU-ADAPT_MultiMT_C
	65.1	0.196	LIUMCVC_NMT_C
	60.6	0.136	CUNI_NeuralMonkeyMultimodalMT_U
	59.7	0.08	UvA-TiCC_IMAGINATION_C
	55.9	-0.049	CUNI_NeuralMonkeyMultimodalMT_C
	54.4	-0.091	OREGONSTATE_2NeuralTranslation_C
	54.2	-0.108	CUNI_NeuralMonkeyTextualMT_C
	53.3	-0.144	OREGONSTATE_1NeuralTranslation_C
	49.4	-0.266	SHEF_ShefClassProj_C
	46.6	-0.37	SHEF_ShefClassInitDec_C
15	39.0	-0.615	Baseline (text-only NMT)
	36.6	-0.674	AFRL-OHIOSTATE_MULTIMODAL_U

Table 9: Results of the human evaluation of the WMT17 English-German Multimodal Translation task (Multi30K 2017 test data). Systems are ordered by standardized mean DA scores (z) and clustered according to Wilcoxon signed-rank test at p-level $p \leq 0.05$. Systems within a cluster are considered tied, although systems within a cluster may be statistically significantly different from each other (see Table 11). Systems using unconstrained data are identified with a gray background.

(SHEF_ShefClassInitDec). The alternative uses of the image features include element-wise multiplication of the target language embeddings with an affine transformation of a global image feature vector (LIUMCVC_MNMT), summing the source language word embeddings with affine-transformed 1000 dimension softmax probability vector (SHEF_ShefClassProj), using the visual features in a retrieval framework (AFRL-OHIOSTATE_MULTIMODAL), and learning visually-grounded encoder representations by learning to predict the global image feature vector from the source language hidden states (UvA-TiCC_IMAGINATION).

Overall, the metric and human judgement results in Sections 4 and 5 indicate that there is still a wide scope for exploration of the best way to integrate visual and textual information. In particular, the alternative approaches proposed in the LIUM-CVC_MNMT and UvA-TiCC_IMAGINATION submissions led to strong performance in both the metric and human judgement results, surpassing the more common approaches using initialisation and double attention.

Finally, the text-only NICT system ranks highly across both languages. This system uses hierarchical phrase-based MT with a reranking step based on a neural text-only system, since their multimodal system never outperformed the text-only variant in development (Zhang et al., 2017). This is in line with last year's results and the strong Moses baseline (Specia et al., 2016), and suggests a continuing role for phrase-based MT for small homogeneous datasets.

Unconstrained systems The Multi30k dataset is relatively small, so unconstrained systems use more data to complement the image description translations. Three groups submitted systems using external resources: UvA-TiCC, CUNI, and AFRL-OHIOSTATE. The unconstrained UvA-TiCC and CUNI submissions always outperformed their respective constrained variants by 2–3 Meteor points and achieved higher standardized mean DA scores. These results suggest that external parallel text corpora (UvA-TiCC and CUNI) and external monolingual image description datasets (UvA-TiCC) can usefully improve the quality of multimodal translation models.

However, tuning to the target domain remains important, even for relatively simple image captions.

227

			English→French
#	Raw	z	System
1	79.4	0.446	NICT_NMTrerank_C
	74.2	0.307	CUNI_NeuralMonkeyMultimodalMT_C
	74.1	0.3	DCU-ADAPT_MultiMT_C
4	71.2	0.22	LIUMCVC_MNMT_C
	65.4	0.056	OREGONSTATE_2NeuralTranslation_C
	61.9	-0.041	CUNI_NeuralMonkeyTextualMT_C
	60.8	-0.078	OREGONSTATE_1NeuralTranslation_C
	60.5	-0.079	LIUMCVC_NMT_C
9	54.7	-0.254	SHEF_ShefClassInitDec_C
	54.0	-0.282	SHEF_ShefClassProj_C
11	44.1	-0.539	Baseline (text-only NMT)

Table 10: Results of the human evaluation of the WMT17 English-French Multimodal Translation task (Multi30K 2017 test data). Systems are ordered by standardized mean DA score (z) and clustered according to Wilcoxon signed-rank test at p-level $p \leq 0.05$. Systems within a cluster are considered tied, although systems within a cluster may be statistically significantly different from each other (see Table 12).

We ran the best-performing English→German WMT'16 news translation system (Sennrich et al., 2016a) on the English→German Multi30K 2017 test data to gauge the performance of a state-of-the-art text-only translation system trained on only out-of-domain resources[4]. It ranked 10th in terms of Meteor (49.9) and 11th in terms of BLEU (29.0), placing it firmly in the middle of the pack, and below nearly all the text-only submissions trained on the in-domain Multi30K dataset.

The effect of OOV words The Multi30k translation training and test data are very similar, with a low OOV rate in the Flickr test set (1.7%). In the 2017 test set, 16% of English test sentences include a OOV word. Human evaluation gave the impression that these often led to errors propagated throughout the whole sentence. Unconstrained systems may perform better by having larger vocabularies, as well as more robust statistics. When we evaluate the English→German systems over only the 161 OOV-containing test sentences, the highest ranked submission by all metrics is the unconstrained UvA-TiCC_IMAGINATION submission, with +2.5 Metor and +2.2 BLEU over the second best system (LIUMCVC_NMT; 45.6 vs 43.1 Meteor and 24.0 vs 21.8 BLEU).

The difference over non-OOV-containing sentences is not nearly as stark, with constrained systems all performing best (both LIUMCVC systems, MNMT and NMT, with 56.6 and 56.3 Meteor, respectively) but unconstrained systems following close behind (UvA-TiCC with 55.4 Meteor, CUNI with 53.4 Meteor).

Ambiguous COCO dataset We introduced a new evaluation dataset this year with the aim of testing systems' ability to use visual features to identify word senses.

However, it is unclear whether visual features improve performance on this test set. The text-only NICT_NMTrerank system performs competitively, ranking in the top three submissions for both languages. We find mixed results for submissions with text-only and multimodal counterparts (CUNI, LIUMCVC, OREGONSTATE): LIUMCVC's multimodal system improves over the text-only system for French but not German, while the visual features help for German but not French in the CUNI and OREGONSTATE systems.

We plan to perform a further analysis on the extent of translation ambiguity in this dataset. We will also continue to work on other methods for constructing datasets in which textual ambiguity can be disambiguated by visual information.

Multilingual Image Description It proved difficult for Task 2 systems to use the English data to improve over the monolingual German baseline.

---

[4] `http://data.statmt.org/rsennrich/wmt16_systems/en-de/`

In future iterations of the task, we will consider a lopsided data setting, in which there is much more English data than target language data. This setting is more realistic and will push the use of multilingual data. We also hope to conduct human evaluation to better assess performance because automatic metrics are problematic for this task (Elliott and Keller, 2014; Kilickaya et al., 2017).

7 Conclusions

We presented the results of the second shared task on multimodal translation and multilingual image description. The shared task attracted submissions from nine groups, who submitted a total of 19 systems across the tasks. The Multimodal Translation task attracted the majority of the submissions. Human judgements for the translation task were collected for the first time this year and ranked systems broadly in line with the automatic metrics.

The main findings of the shared task are:

(i) There is still scope for novel approaches to integrating visual and linguistic features in multilingual multimodal models, as demonstrated by the winning systems.

(ii) External resources have an important role to play in improving the performance of multimodal translation models beyond what can be learned from limited training data.

(iii) The differences between text-only and multimodal systems are being obfuscated by the well-known shortcomings of text-similarity metrics. Multimodal systems often seem to be prefered by humans but not rewarded by metrics. Future research on this topic, encompassing both multimodal translation and multilingual image description, should be evaluated using human judgements.

In future editions of the task, we will encourage participants to submit the output of single decoder systems to better understand the empirical differences between approaches. We are also considering a Multilingual Multimodal Translation challenge, where the systems can observe two language inputs alongside the image to encourage the development of multi-source multimodal models.

Acknowledgements

This work was supported by the CHIST-ERA M2CR project (French National Research Agency No. ANR-15-CHR2-0006-01 – Loïc Barrault and Fethi Bougares), and by the MultiMT project (EU H2020 ERC Starting Grant No. 678017 – Lucia Specia). Desmond Elliott acknowledges the support of NWO Vici Grant No. 277-89-002 awarded to K. Sima'an, and an Amazon Academic Research Award. We thank Josiah Wang for his help in selecting the Ambiguous COCO dataset.

References

Dzmitry Bahdanau, Kyunghyun Cho, and Yoshua Bengio. 2015. Neural machine translation by jointly learning to align and translate. In *Proceedings of the International Conference on Learning Representations*.

Raffaella Bernardi, Ruket Cakici, Desmond Elliott, Aykut Erdem, Erkut Erdem, Nazli Ikizler-Cinbis, Frank Keller, Adrian Muscat, and Barbara Plank. 2016. Automatic description generation from images: A survey of models, datasets, and evaluation measures. *J. Artif. Intell. Res.*, 55:409–442.

Ozan Caglayan, Loïc Barrault, and Fethi Bougares. 2016. Multimodal attention for neural machine translation. *CoRR*, abs/1609.03976.

Ozan Caglayan, Walid Aransa, Adrien Bardet, Mercedes García-Martínez, Fethi Bougares, Loïc Barrault, Marc Masana, Luis Herranz, and Joost van de Weijer. 2017a. LIUM-CVC Submissions for WMT17 Multimodal Translation Task. In *Proceedings of the Second Conference on Machine Translation, Volume 2: Shared Task Papers*, pages 432–439.

Ozan Caglayan, Mercedes García-Martínez, Adrien Bardet, Walid. Aransa, Fethi. Bougares, and Loïc Barrault. 2017b. NMTPY: A Flexible Toolkit for Advanced Neural Machine Translation Systems. *CoRR*, 1706.00457.

Iacer Calixto, Koel Dutta Chowdhury, and Qun Liu. 2017a. DCU System Report on the WMT 2017 Multi-modal Machine Translation Task. In *Proceedings of the Second Conference on Machine Translation, Volume 2: Shared Task Papers*, pages 440–444.

Iacer Calixto, Qun Liu, and Nick Campbell. 2017b. Incorporating Global Visual Features into Attention Based Neural Machine Translation. In *Proceedings of the 2017 Conference on Empirical Methods in Natural Language Processing*.

Xinlei Chen, Hao Fang, Tsung-Yi Lin, Ramakrishna Vedantam, Saurabh Gupta, Piotr Dollár, and C. Lawrence Zitnick. 2015. Microsoft COCO captions: Data collection and evaluation server. *CoRR*, abs/1504.00325.

Jonathan H Clark, Chris Dyer, Alon Lavie, and Noah A Smith. 2011. Better hypothesis testing for statistical machine translation: Controlling for optimizer instability. In *49th Annual Meeting of the Association for Computational Linguistics: Human Language Technologies*, pages 176–181.

Jia Deng, Wei Dong, Richard Socher, Li-Jia Li, Kai Li, and Li Fei-Fei. 2009. ImageNet: A Large-Scale Hierarchical Image Database. In *IEEE Conference on Computer Vision and Pattern Recognition*.

Michael Denkowski and Alon Lavie. 2014. Meteor universal: Language specific translation evaluation for any target language. In *EACL 2014 Workshop on Statistical Machine Translation*.

John Duselis, Michael Hutt, Jeremy Gwinnup, James Davis, and Joshua Sandvick. 2017. The AFRL-OSU WMT17 Multimodal Translation System: An Image Processing Approach. In *Proceedings of the Second Conference on Machine Translation, Volume 2: Shared Task Papers*, pages 445–449.

Desmond Elliott and Ákos Kádár. 2017. Imagination improves Multimodal Translation. *CoRR*, abs/1705.04350.

Desmond Elliott and Frank Keller. 2014. Comparing automatic evaluation measures for image description. In *Proceedings of the 52nd Annual Meeting of the Association for Computational Linguistics: Short Papers*, pages 452–457.

Desmond Elliott, Stella Frank, and Eva Hasler. 2015. Multi-language image description with neural sequence models. *CoRR*, abs/1510.04709.

Desmond Elliott, Stella Frank, Khalil Simaan, and Lucia Specia. 2016. Multi30k: Multilingual english-german image descriptions. In *5th Workshop on Vision and Language*, pages 70–74.

Gertrud Faaß and Kerstin Eckart. 2013. SdeWaC–a corpus of parsable sentences from the web. In *Language processing and knowledge in the Web*, pages 61–68. Springer.

Christian Federmann. 2012. Appraise: An open-source toolkit for manual evaluation of machine translation output. *The Prague Bulletin of Mathematical Linguistics*, 98:25–35, September.

Spandana Gella, Mirella Lapata, and Frank Keller. 2016. Unsupervised visual sense disambiguation for verbs using multimodal embeddings. In *2016 Conference of the North American Chapter of the Association for Computational Linguistics: Human Language Technologies*, pages 182–192, San Diego, California.

Yvette Graham, Timothy Baldwin, Alistair Moffat, and Justin Zobel. 2015. Can machine translation systems be evaluated by the crowd alone. *Natural Language Engineering*, 23(1):3–30.

Kaiming He, Xiangyu Zhang, Shaoqing Ren, and Jian Sun. 2016. Deep residual learning for image recognition. In *IEEE Conference on Computer Vision and Pattern Recognition*, pages 770–778.

Jindřich Helcl and Jindřich Libovický. 2017. CUNI System for the WMT17 Multimodal Translation Task. In *Proceedings of the Second Conference on Machine Translation, Volume 2: Shared Task Papers*, pages 450–457.

Julian Hitschler, Shigehiko Schamoni, and Stefan Riezler. 2016. Multimodal Pivots for Image Caption Translation. In *54th Annual Meeting of the Association for Computational Linguistics*, pages 2399–2409.

Alan Jaffe. 2017. Generating Image Descriptions using Multilingual Data. In *Proceedings of the Second Conference on Machine Translation, Volume 2: Shared Task Papers*, pages 458–464.

Douwe Kiela. 2016. MMFeat: A toolkit for extracting multi-modal features. In *Proceedings of ACL-2016 System Demonstrations*, pages 55–60.

Mert Kilickaya, Aykut Erdem, Nazli Ikizler-Cinbis, and Erkut Erdem. 2017. Re-evaluating automatic metrics for image captioning. In *Proceedings of EACL 2017*, pages 199–209.

Philipp Koehn, Hieu Hoang, Alexandra Birch, Chris Callison-Burch, Marcello Federico, Nicola Bertoldi, Brooke Cowan, Wade Shen, Christine Moran, Richard Zens, et al. 2007. Moses: Open source toolkit for statistical machine translation. In *45th Annual meeting of Association for Computational Linguistics*, pages 177–180.

D.T. Le, R. Bernardi, and J.R.R. Uijlings. 2014. TUHOI: Trento Universal Human Object Interaction Dataset. In *Vision and Language Workshop at the 26th International Conference on Computational Linguistics*.

Xirong Li, Weiyu Lan, Jianfeng Dong, and Hailong Liu. 2016. Adding chinese captions to images. In *Proceedings of the 2016 ACM on International Conference on Multimedia Retrieval*, pages 271–275.

Jindřich Libovický and Jindřich Helcl. 2017. Attention strategies for multi-source sequence-to-sequence learning. *CoRR*, abs/1704.06567.

Tsung-Yi Lin, Michael Maire, Serge J. Belongie, Lubomir D. Bourdev, Ross B. Girshick, James Hays, Pietro Perona, Deva Ramanan, Piotr Dollár, and C. Lawrence Zitnick. 2014. Microsoft COCO: common objects in context. *CoRR*, abs/1405.0312.

Minh-Thang Luong, Hieu Pham, and Christopher D Manning. 2015. Effective approaches to attention-based neural machine translation. In *Proceedings of the 2015 Conference on Empirical Methods in Natural Language Processing*, pages 1412–1421.

Mingbo Ma, Dapeng Li, Kai Zhao, and Liang Huang. 2017. OSU Multimodal Machine Translation System Report. In *Proceedings of the Second Conference on Machine Translation, Volume 2: Shared Task Papers*, pages 465–469.

Pranava Swaroop Madhyastha, Josiah Wang, and Lucia Specia. 2017. Sheffield MultiMT: Using Object Posterior Predictions for Multimodal Machine Translation. In *Proceedings of the Second Conference on Machine Translation, Volume 2: Shared Task Papers*, pages 470–476.

Takashi Miyazaki and Nobuyuki Shimizu. 2016. Cross-lingual image caption generation. In *Proceedings of the 54th Annual Meeting of the Association for Computational Linguistics*, pages 1780–1790.

Franz Josef Och. 2003. Minimum error rate training in statistical machine translation. In *41st Annual Meeting on Association for Computational Linguistics*, pages 160–167, Sapporo, Japan.

Kishore Papineni, Salim Roukos, Todd Ward, and Wei-Jing Zhu. 2002. Bleu: A method for automatic evaluation of machine translation. In *40th Annual Meeting on Association for Computational Linguistics*, pages 311–318.

Janarthanan Rajendran, Mitesh M Khapra, Sarath Chandar, and Balaraman Ravindran. 2016. Bridge correlational neural networks for multilingual multimodal representation learning. In *Proceedings of the 2016 Conference of the North American Chapter of the Association for Computational Linguistics: Human Language Technologies*, pages 171–181.

Olga Russakovsky, Jia Deng, Hao Su, Jonathan Krause, Sanjeev Satheesh, Sean Ma, Zhiheng Huang, Andrej Karpathy, Aditya Khosla, Michael Bernstein, Alexander C. Berg, and Li Fei-Fei. 2015. ImageNet Large Scale Visual Recognition Challenge. *International Journal of Computer Vision (IJCV)*, 115(3):211–252.

Mike Schuster and Kaisuke Nakajima. 2012. Japanese and korean voice search. In *2012 IEEE International Conference on Acoustics, Speech and Signal Processing (ICASSP)*, pages 5149–5152.

Rico Sennrich, Barry Haddow, and Alexandra Birch. 2016a. Edinburgh neural machine translation systems for WMT 16. In *Proceedings of the First Conference on Machine Translation*.

Rico Sennrich, Barry Haddow, and Alexandra Birch. 2016b. Neural machine translation of rare words with subword units. In *54th Annual Meeting of the Association for Computational Linguistics*, pages 1715–1725, Berlin, Germany.

Rico Sennrich, Orhan Firat, Kyunghyun Cho, Alexandra Birch, Barry Haddow, Julian Hitschler, Marcin Junczys-Dowmunt, Samuel Läubli, Antonio Valerio Miceli Barone, Jozef Mokry, et al. 2017. Nematus: a toolkit for neural machine translation. In *Software Demonstrations of the 15th Conference of the European Chapter of the Association for Computational Linguistics*, pages 65–68.

Matthew Snover, Bonnie Dorr, Richard Schwartz, Linnea Micciulla, and John Makhoul. 2006. A study of translation edit rate with targeted human annotation. In *Proceedings of Association for Machine Translation in the Americas*.

Lucia Specia, Stella Frank, Khalil Sima'an, and Desmond Elliott. 2016. A shared task on multimodal machine translation and crosslingual image description. In *First Conference on Machine Translation*, pages 543–553.

Christian Szegedy, Vincent Vanhoucke, Sergey Ioffe, Jonathon Shlens, and Zbigniew Wojna. 2015. Rethinking the inception architecture for computer vision. *CoRR*, abs/1512.00567.

Jörg Tiedemann. 2012. Parallel data, tools and interfaces in opus. In *Eight International Conference on Language Resources and Evaluation (LREC'12)*.

Mesut Erhan Unal, Begum Citamak, Semih Yagcioglu, Aykut Erdem, Erkut Erdem, Nazli Ikizler Cinbis, and Ruket Cakici. 2016. Tasviret: Görüntülerden otomatik türkçe açıklama oluşturma İçin bir denektaçı veri kümesi (TasvirEt: A benchmark dataset for automatic Turkish description generation from images). In *IEEE Sinyal İşleme ve İletişim Uygulamaları Kurultayı (SIU 2016)*.

Emiel van Miltenburg, Desmond Elliott, and Piek Vossen. 2017. Cross-linguistic differences and similarities in image descriptions. In *Proceedings of the 10th International Conference on Natural Language Generation*.

Yuya Yoshikawa, Yutaro Shigeto, and Akikazu Takeuchi. 2017. Stair captions: Constructing a large-scale japanese image caption dataset. *CoRR*, abs/1705.00823.

Peter Young, Alice Lai, Micah Hodosh, and Julia Hockenmaier. 2014. From image descriptions to visual denotations: New similarity metrics for semantic inference over event descriptions. *Transactions of the Association for Computational Linguistics*, 2:67–78.

Jingyi Zhang, Masao Utiyama, Eiichro Sumita, Graham Neubig, and Satoshi Nakamura. 2017. NICT-NAIST System for WMT17 Multimodal Translation Task. In *Proceedings of the Second Conference on Machine Translation, Volume 2: Shared Task Papers*, pages 477–482, Copenhagen, Denmark.

A Significance tests

Tables 11 and 12 show the Wilcoxon signed-rank test used to create the clustering of the systems.

English→German

	LIUMCVC_MNMT_C	UvA-TiCC_IMAGINATION_U	NICT_NMTrerank_C	CUNI_NeuralMonkeyTextualMT_U	DCU-ADAPT_MultiMT_C	LIUMCVC_NMT_C	CUNI_NeuralMonkeyMultimodalMT_U	UvA-TiCC_IMAGINATION_C	CUNI_NeuralMonkeyMultimodalMT_C	OREGONSTATE_2NMT_C	CUNI_NeuralMonkeyTextualMT_C	OREGONSTATE_1NMT_C	SHEF_ShefClassProj_C	SHEF_ShefClassInitDec_C	BASELINE	AFRL-OHIOSTATE_MULTIMODAL_C
LIUMCVC_MNMT_C		2.8e-2	3.1e-4	4.8e-5	1.1e-6	4.5e-8	6.6e-10	6.2e-13	7.9e-18	1.0e-18	2.9e-17	3.2e-18	5.2e-26	1.2e-30	5.5e-41	3.1e-43
UvA-TiCC_IMAGINATION_U			4.9e-2	1.8e-2	1.2e-3	6.8e-5	3.5e-6	2.0e-8	3.2e-12	2.1e-13	4.7e-12	5.6e-13	3.2e-19	9.1e-24	3.9e-33	1.2e-34
NICT_NMTrerank_C				-	-	1.3e-2	1.6e-3	8.1e-5	9.6e-8	1.0e-8	4.6e-8	9.8e-9	1.3e-13	2.2e-17	2.2e-26	4.0e-28
CUNI_NMT_U					-	4.3e-2	1.3e-2	6.8e-4	2.4e-6	4.9e-7	1.3e-6	3.1e-7	1.6e-11	6.8e-15	3.8e-23	4.7e-25
DCU-ADAPT_MultiMT_C						-	4.0e-2	4.9e-3	3.0e-5	3.3e-6	1.3e-5	2.2e-6	1.4e-10	5.3e-14	9.8e-23	2.4e-24
LIUMCVC_NMT_C							-	-	5.7e-3	1.4e-3	2.2e-3	7.5e-4	2.2e-06	8.5e-09	2.0e-15	4.0e-17
CUNI_MNMT_U								-	1.7e-2	5.7e-3	5.6e-3	2.8e-3	4.5e-06	2.7e-08	1.2e-15	9.7e-18
UvA-TiCC_IMAGINATION_C									-	2.8e-2	3.3e-2	1.3e-2	6.2e-05	3.3e-07	3.5e-14	5.0e-16
CUNI_NMMT_C										-	-	-	6.5e-03	1.5e-04	1.5e-10	1.7e-12
OREGONSTATE_2NMT_C											-	-	1.9e-02	1.1e-03	2.0e-09	3.6e-11
CUNI_NMT_C												-	4.7e-02	3.3e-03	8.3e-08	2.1e-09
OREGONSTATE_1NMT_C													-	1.2e-02	9.1e-07	2.6e-08
SHEF_ShefClassProj_C														-	4.7e-05	1.3e-06
SHEF_ShefClassInitDec_C															2.0e-03	1.2e-04
BASELINE AFRL-OHIOSTATE_MULTIMODAL_C																-

Table 11: English → German Wilcoxon signed-rank test at p-level p ≤ 0.05. '-' means that the value is higher than 0.05.

	NICT_NMTrerank_C	CUNI_NeuralMonkeyMultimodalMT_C	DCU-ADAPT_MultiMT_C	LIUMCVC_MNMT_C	OREGONSTATE_2NeuralTranslation_C	CUNI_NeuralMonkeyTextualMT_C	OREGONSTATE_1NeuralTranslation_C	LIUMCVC_NMT_C	SHEF_ShefClassInitDec_C	SHEF_ShefClassProj_C	BASELINE
					English→French						
NICT_NMTrerank_C		-	-	1.0e-03	2.5e-05	5.5e-08	1.5e-09	1.8e-07	2.2e-16	6.8e-15	5.8e-26
CUNI_NeuralMonkeyMultimodalMT_C			-	8.8e-03	2.9e-04	5.2e-07	5.0e-08	2.9e-06	2.4e-14	1.1e-13	2.3e-24
DCU-ADAPT_MultiMT_C				2.2e-02	1.3e-03	6.7e-06	7.9e-07	2.3e-05	2.2e-12	1.3e-11	3.9e-21
LIUMCVC_MNMT_C					-	1.7e-02	2.7e-03	1.2e-02	5.3e-07	2.0e-06	5.9e-14
OREGONSTATE_2NeuralTranslation_C						-	-	-	1.7e-04	1.8e-04	7.3e-11
CUNI_NeuralMonkeyTextualMT_C							-	-	7.7e-03	7.7e-03	5.0e-08
OREGONSTATE_1NeuralTranslation_C								-	2.4e-02	1.8e-02	2.3e-07
LIUMCVC_NMT_C									1.8e-02	1.6e-02	5.6e-07
SHEF_ShefClassInitDec_C										-	3.2e-04
SHEF_ShefClassProj_C											1.8e-03
BASELINE											

Table 12: English → French Wilcoxon signed-rank test at p-level p $\leq$ 0.05. '-' means that the value is higher than 0.05.

Findings of the WMT 2017 Biomedical Translation Shared Task

Antonio Jimeno Yepes
IBM Research Australia

Aurélie Névéol
LIMSI, CNRS, Uni. Paris Saclay, France

Mariana Neves
HPI Uni. Potsdam, BfR, Germany

Karin Verspoor
Uni. Melbourne, Australia

Ondřej Bojar
Charles Uni., Czech Rep.

Arthur Boyer
LIMSI, CNRS,
Uni. Paris Saclay, France

Cristian Grozea
Fraunhofer Institute, Germany

Barry Haddow
Uni. Edinburgh, UK

Madeleine Kittner
Humboldt Uni., Germany

Yvonne Lichtblau
Humboldt Uni., Germany

Pavel Pecina
Charles Uni., Czech Rep.

Roland Roller
DFKI, Germany

Rudolf Rosa
Charles Uni., Czech Rep.

Amy Siu
MPI für Informatik, Germany

Philippe Thomas
DFKI, Germany

Saskia Trescher
Humboldt Uni., Germany

Abstract

Automatic translation of documents is an important task in many domains, including the biological and clinical domains. The second edition of the Biomedical Translation task in the Conference of Machine Translation focused on the automatic translation of biomedical-related documents between English and various European languages. This year, we addressed ten languages: Czech, German, English, French, Hungarian, Polish, Portuguese, Spanish, Romanian and Swedish. Test sets included both scientific publications (from the Scielo and EDP Sciences databases) and health-related news (from the Cochrane and UK National Health Service web sites). Seven teams participated in the task, submitting a total of 82 runs. Herein we describe the test sets, participating systems and results of both the automatic and manual evaluation of the translations.

1 Introduction

Automatic translation of texts allows readers to gain access to information present in documents written in a language in which the reader is not fluent. We identify two main use cases of machine translation (MT) in the biomedical domain: (a) making health information available to health professionals and the general public in their own language; and (b) assisting health professionals and researchers in writing reports of their research in English. In addition, it creates an opportunity for natural language processing (NLP) tools to be applied to domain-specific texts in languages for which few domain-relevant tools are available; i.e., the texts can be translated into a language for which there are more resources.

The second edition of the Biomedical Translation Task in the Conference for Machine Translation (WMT)[1] builds on the first edition (Bojar et al., 2016) by offering seven additional language pairs and new test sets. This year, we expanded to a total of ten languages in the biomedical task, namely, Czech (cs), German (de), English (en), French (fr), Hungarian (hu), Polish (pl), Portuguese (pt), Spanish (es), Romanian (ro) and Swedish (sv). Test sets included scientific publications from the Scielo and EDP Sciences databases and health-related news from Cochrane and the UK National Health Service (NHS).

Participants were challenged to build systems to enable translation from English to all other lan-

---

[1] http://www.statmt.org/wmt17/
biomedical-translation-task.html

Proceedings of the Conference on Machine Translation (WMT), Volume 2: Shared Task Papers, pages 234–247
Copenhagen, Denmark, September 7–11, 2017. ©2017 Association for Computational Linguistics

guages, as well as from French, Spanish and Portuguese to English. We provided both training and development data but the teams were allowed to use additional in-domain or out-of-domain training data. After release of the test sets, the participants had 10 days to submit results (automatic translations) for any of the test sets and languages. We allowed up to three runs per team for each language pair and test sets.

We evaluated the submission both automatically and manually. In this work, we report details on the challenge, test sets, participating teams, the results they obtained and the quality of the automatic translations.

2 Training and test sets

We released test sets from four sources, namely, Scielo, EDP, Cochrane and NHS, as presented in Table 1. For training and development data, we referred participants to various biomedical corpora: (a) Biomedical Translation Corpora Repository[2], which includes titles from MEDLINE® and the Scielo corpus (Neves et al., 2016); (b) UFAL Medical Corpus,[3] which includes EMEA and PatTR Medical, among others; (c) development data from the Khresmoi project.[4] We provide details of the test sets below.

Scielo. Similar to last year, this dataset consisted of titles and abstracts from scientific publications retrieved from the Scielo database[5] and addressed the following language pairs: es/en, en/es, pt/en and en/pt. There were not enough articles indexed in 2017 with French titles or abstracts, so we relied on another source for en/fr and fr/en language pairs (namely, EDP as described below). Similar to last year, we crawled the Scielo site for publications containing both titles and abstracts in both English/Spanish or English/Portuguese language pairs. We considered only articles published in 2017 until that point (April/2017). We tokenized the documents using Apache OpenNLP[6] (with specific models for each language). The test set dataset was automatically created by aligning

the GMA tool.[7] We manually checked the alignment of a sample and confirmed that around 88% of the sentences were correctly aligned.

EDP. Title and abstracts of scientific publications were collected from the open access publisher EDP Sciences[8] on March 15, 2017. The corpus comprises a selection of titles and abstracts of articles published in five journals in the fields of *Health* and *Life & Environmental Sciences*. The articles were originally written in French but the journals also publish the titles and abstracts in English, using a translation provided by the authors. The dataset was pre-processed for sentence segmentation using the Stanford CoreNLP toolkit[9] and aligned using YASA.[10] Manual evaluation conducted on a sample set suggests that 94% of the sentences are correctly aligned, with about 20% of the sentence pairs exhibiting additional content in one of the languages.

Cochrane and NHS. The test data was produced during the course of the KConnect[11] and HimL[12] projects. The test data contains health-related documents from Cochrane and NHS that were manually translated by experts from English to eight languages: cs, de, fr, hu, pl, ro, es and sv.

3 Participating teams and systems

We received submissions from seven teams, as summarized in Table 2. The teams came from a total of five countries (Germany, Japan, Poland, UK and USA) and from three continents. They include both research institutions and a company. An overview of the teams and their systems is provided below.

Hunter (Hunter College, City University of New York). The system from the Hunter College is based on Moses EMS, SRI-LM, GIZA++ (Xu et al., 2017). For the translation model, they generate word alignments using GIZA++ and mGIZA. For the language model, they relied on an interpolation of models that includes 6-grams with Kneser-Ney smoothing. Different corpora were used for the various languages

---

[2]https://github.com/
biomedical-translation-corpora/wmt-task
[3]https://ufal.mff.cuni.cz/ufal_
medical_corpus
[4]https://lindat.mff.cuni.cz/
repository/xmlui/handle/11234/1-2122
[5]http://www.scielo.org
[6]https://opennlp.apache.org/

[7]http://nlp.cs.nyu.edu/GMA/
[8]http://www.edpsciences.org
[9]https://stanfordnlp.github.io/
CoreNLP/
[10]http://rali.iro.umontreal.ca/rali/?q-
en/yasa
[11]http://k-connect.org
[12]http://www.himl.eu/

Test sets	en/cs	en/de	fr/en	en/hu	pt/en	es/en	en/fr	en/pl	en/pt	en/es	en/ro	en/sv
Scielo					189/1897	158/1180			188/1806	158/1082		
EDP			85/699				84/750					
Cochrane	25/467	25/467	25/467	25/467		25/467	25/467	25/467		25/467	25/467	25/467
NHS	25/1044	25/1044	25/1044	25/1044		25/1044	25/1044	25/1044		25/1044	25/1044	25/1044

Table 1: Overview of the test sets. We present the number of documents and sentences in each test set.

Team ID	Institution
Hunter	Hunter College, City University of New York
kyoto	Kyoto University
Lilt	Lilt Inc.
LMU	Ludwig Maximilian University of Munich
PJIIT	Polish-Japanese Academy of Information Technology
uedin-nmt	University of Edinburgh
UHH	University of Hamburg

Table 2: Overview of the participating teams.

to which they submitted runs. The system was tuned using the WMT16 test sets (in the case of French and English) and on the HimL test sets for Cochrane and NHS. For training data, the team relied on a variety of corpora, depending on the language pair, which included MEDLINE, Europarl, Scielo, News Commentary, UFAL, EMEA, Cordis, among others.

kyoto (Kyoto University). The system from the team from Kyoto University is based on two previous papers (Cromieres et al., 2016; Cromieres, 2016). The participants describe it as a classic neural machine translation (NMT) system, however, we do not have further information regarding the datasets that have been used to train and tune the system for the WMT challenge.

Lilt (Lilt Inc.). The system from the Lilt Inc.[13] uses an in-house implementation of a sequence-to-sequence model with Bahdanau-style attention. The final submissions are ensembles between models fine-tuned on different parts of the available data.

LMU (Ludwig Maximilian University of Munich). LMU Munich has participated with an en2de NMT system (Huck and Fraser, 2017). A distinctive feature of their system is a linguistically informed, cascaded target word segmentation approach. Fine-tuning for the domain of health texts was done using in-domain sections of the UFAL Medical Corpus v.1.0 as a training corpus. The learning rate was set to 0.00001, initialized with a pre-trained model, and optimized using only the in-domain medical data. The HimL tun-

ing sets were used for validation, and they tested separately on the Cochrane and NHS24 parts of the HimL devtest set.

PJIIT (Polish-Japanese Academy of Information Technology). PJIIT developed a translation model training, created adaptations of training settings for each language pair, and implemented byte pair encoding (BPE) (subword units) in their systems (Wolk and Marasek, 2017). Only the official parallel text corpora and monolingual models for the challenge evaluation campaign were used to train language models, and to develop, tune, and test their system. PJIIT explored the use of domain adaptation techniques, symmetrized word alignment models, the unsupervised transliteration models and the KenLM language modeling tool.

uedin-nmt (University of Edinburgh). The systems from the University of Edinburgh used a NMT trained with Nematus, an attentional encoder-decoder (Sennrich et al., 2017). Their setup follows the one from last year. This team again built BPE-based models with parallel and back-translated monolingual training data. New approaches this year included the use of deep architectures, layer normalization, and more compact models due to weight-tying and improvements in BPE segmentations.

UHH (University of Hamburg). All SMT models were developed using the Moses phrase-based MT toolkit and the Experiment Management System (Duma and Menzel, 2017). The preprocessing of the data consisted of tokenization, cleaning (6-80), lowercasing and normalizing punctuation. The tuning and the test sets were derived from WMT 2016 and WMT 2017. The SRILM toolkit

[13]https://lilt.com/

and Kneser-Ney discounting were used to estimate 5-gram language models (LM). For word alignment, GIZA++ with the default grow-diag-final-and alignment symmetrization method was used. Tuning of the SMT systems was performed with MERT. Commoncrawl and Wikipedia were used as general domain data for all language pairs except for EN/PT, where no Commoncrawl data was provided by WMT. As for the in-domain corpora, EMEA was used for all language pairs and Muchmore, ECDC, Pattr and Pubmed (all from UFAL Medical Corpus2) for the language pairs where data was available. The system made use of the training data provided by the previous Biomedical Task from 2016. The corpora corresponding to the general domain were concatenated into a single data source and the same procedure was applied for the in-domain corpora. This team investigated performing data selection for MT via Paragraph Vector and a Feed Forward Neural Network Classifier. Continuous distributed vector representations of the sentences were used as features for the classifier.

4 Evaluation

In this section, we present an overview of the submissions to the Biomedical Task and results in terms of both automatic and manual evaluation.

4.1 Submissions

An overview of the submissions is shown is Table 3. The participating teams submitted a total of 82 runs. No submissions were received for Swedish (en/sv) and Hungarian (en/hu).

4.2 Baselines

We provided baseline results only for the EDP and Scielo test sets, however, not for the other languages included in the Cochrane and NHS test sets.

Baseline. For the Scielo and EDP test sets, we compared the participants' results to our baseline system, which used the same approach as applied in last year's challenge (Bojar et al., 2016) for the evaluation of the Scielo dataset (Neves et al., 2016). The statistical machine translation (SMT) system used for the baseline was Moses (Koehn et al., 2007) with default settings. For es2en, en2es, fr2en, en2fr, pt2en and en2pt, the baseline system was trained as described in (Neves et al., 2016).

LIMSI baseline. For additional comparison, we also provided the results of an en2fr Moses-based system prepared by Ive et al. for their participation in the WMT16 biomedical track, which reflects the state of the art for this language pair (Ive et al., 2016a). The system uses in-domain parallel data provided for the biomedical task in 2016, as well as additional in-domain data[14] and out-of-domain data. However, we did not perform SOUL re-scoring.

4.3 Automatic evaluation

In this section, we provide the results for the automatic evaluation and rank the various systems based on those results. For the automatic evaluation, we computed BLEU scores at the sentence level using the multi-bleu and tokenization scripts as provided by Moses (`tokenizer` and `truecase`). For all test sets and language pairs, we compare the automatic translations to the reference one, as provided by each test set.

Results for the Scielo test sets are presented in Table 4. All three runs from the UHH team, for all four language pairs, obtained a much higher BLEU score than our baseline. However, this is not surprising given the simplicity of the methods used in the baseline system.

The BLEU scores for the EDP test set are presented in Table 5. While all system runs score above the baseline, only the Kyoto system outperforms the stronger baseline for en2fr. We rank the various submissions as follows:

- fr2en: Hunter (runs 1,2) < baseline < UHH (runs 1,2) < UHH (run 3) < kyoto (run 1).

- en2fr: baseline < Hunter (runs 1,2) < UHH (runs 1,2,3) < LIMSI baseline < kyoto (run 1) < kyoto (run 2).

The BLEU scores for the Cochrane test sets are presented in Table 6. The scores range from as low as 12.45 (for Polish) to as high as 48.99 (for Spanish). All scores were particularly high for Spanish (close to 50), but rather low for Polish and Czech (all below 30). While the BLEU value did not vary much for French (all around 30), these went from a range of 14 to 41 for Romanian. We rank the various submissions for each language as below:

---

[14]Cochrane translation corpus available at `http://www.translatecochrane.fr/corpus/` (Ive et al., 2016b)

Teams	en/cs	en/de	fr/en	pt/en	es/en	en/fr	en/pl	en/pt	en/es	en/ro
Hunter		CN	E2			C2NE2	CN			CN
kyoto			E			E2				
lilt		C2N2								
LMU		CN								
PJIIT	CN	CN					C3N3			CN
uedin-nmt	CN	CN					C2N2			C2N2
UHH		C3N3	E3	S3	S3	C3N3E3		S3	C3N3S3	

Table 3: Overview of submissions for each language pair and test set: [E]DP, [S]cielo, [C]ochrane and [N]HS. The number next to the letter indicates the number of runs that the team submitted for the corresponding test set.

Runs	pt/en	es/en	en/pt	en/es
baseline	36.35	31.50	30.52	27.31
UHH run1	43.84	37.14	39.14	36.08
UHH run2	43.93	37.47	39.38	35.93
UHH run3	43.88*	37.49*	39.21*	36.23*

Table 4: Results for the Scielo test sets. * indicates the primary run as identified by the participants.

Runs	fr/en	en/fr
baseline	17.47	12.32
LIMSI baseline	-	24.05
Hunter run1	15.10*	17.50*
Hunter run2	15.18	17.21
kyoto run1	25.21*	25.52
kyoto run2	-	27.04*
UHH run1	22.64	22.43
UHH run2	22.37	22.25
UHH run3	23.41*	22.79*

Table 5: Results for the EDP test sets. * indicates the primary run as declared by the participants.

- cs: PJIIT (run 1) < uedin-nmt (run 1).

- de: UHH (runs 1,2,3) < Hunter (run 1) < PIIJT (run 1) < lilt (run 1,2) < LMU < uedin-nmt (run 1).

- fr: Hunter (runs 1,2) < UHH (runs 1,2,3).

- pl: PIIJT (run 2) < Hunter (run 1) < PIIJT (runs 1,3) < uedin-nmt (run 2) < uedin-nmt (run 1).

- ro: Hunter (run 1) < PIIJT (run 1) < uedin-nmt (run 2) < uedin-nmt (run 1).

Finally, the BLEU scores for the NHS dataset are presented in Table 7. The scores range from as low as 10.56 (for Romanian, the lowest score across all test sets and languages) to as high as 41.22 (for Spanish). All scores were particularly high for Spanish (around 40), but rather low for Polish, Czech and Romanian (all below 30). We rank the various submissions for each language as shown below:

- cs: PJIIT (run 1) < uedin-nmt (run 1).

- de: UHH (runs 1,2,3) < Hunter (run 1) < PI-IJT (run 1) < lilt (run 1,2) < LMU < uedin-nmt (run 1).

- fr: Hunter (run 1) < UHH (runs 1,2) < UHH (run 3).

- pl: PIIJT (run 2) < Hunter (run 1), PIIJT (runs 1,3) < uedin-nmt (run 2) < uedin-nmt (run 1).

- ro: Hunter (run 1) < PIIJT (run 1) < uedin-nmt (run 2) < uedin-nmt (run 1).

The BLEU values were generally lower for NHS than the ones obtained for the same teams for the Cochrane test sets. However, the rankings of systems and runs are nearly the same for the Cochrane and NHS test sets. The only exceptions were in French, where run 3 from UHH was higher than the others from the team, and for Polish, where the scores for Hunter and PIIJT (runs 1,3) were nearly the same.

4.4 Manual evaluation

We required teams to identify a primary run for each language pair, in the case that they submitted more than one run. These are the runs for which we performed manual evaluation. The following runs were considered to be primary: Hunter (run1), kyoto (run2 for en/fr, run1 for fr/en), lilt (run1), LMU (run1), PJIIT (run3 for pl, otherwise, run1), uedin-nmt (run1), UHH (run3).

We computed pairwise combinations of translations either between two automated systems, or one automated system and the reference translation. We compared all systems (primary) to the reference translation, as well as to each other system. We ran manual validation for all target languages and test sets. The human validators were

Cochrane	cs	de	fr	pl	es	ro
Hunter run1	-	24.72*	30.75*	17.16*	-	14.74*
Hunter run2	-	-	30.76	-	-	-
lilt run1	-	34.91*	-	-	-	-
lilt run2	-	33.97	-	-	-	-
LMU	-	36.44*	-	-	-	-
PJIIT run1	19.96*	25.13*	-	18.86	-	24.91*
PJIIT run2	-	-	-	12.45	-	-
PJIIT run3	-	-	-	18.88*	-	-
uedin-nmt run1	28.54*	37.11*	-	29.04*	-	41.18*
uedin-nmt run2	-	-	-	27.69	-	38.89
UHH run1	-	22.03	32.46	-	48.99	-
UHH run2	-	22.37	32.59	-	48.45	-
UHH run3	-	22.63*	33.16*	-	48.70*	-

Table 6: Results for the Cochrane test sets. * indicates the primary run as informed by the participants.

NHS	cs	de	fr	pl	es	ro
Hunter	-	20.45*	22.99*	14.09*	-	10.56*
lilt run1	-	27.57*	-	-	-	-
lilt run2	-	26.79	-	-	-	-
LMU	-	29.46*	-	-	-	-
PJIIT run1	15.93*	21.88*	-	14.32	-	18.10*
PJIIT run2	-	-	-	10.75	-	-
PJIIT run3	-	-	-	14.34*	-	-
uedin-nmt run1	22.79*	33.06*	-	23.15*	-	29.32*
uedin-nmt run2	-	-	-	19.87	-	27.32
UHH run1	-	18.71	31.79	-	40.97	-
UHH run2	-	19.80	31.89	-	41.20	-
UHH run3	-	19.66*	33.36*	-	41.22*	-

Table 7: Results for the NHS test sets. * indicates the primary run as informed by the participants.

native speakers of the languages and were either members of the participating teams or colleagues from the research community.

The validation task was carried out using the Appraise tool[15] (Federmann, 2010). For each pairwise comparison, we validated a total of 100 randomly-chosen sentence pairs. The validation consisted of reading the two sentences (A and B), i.e., translations from two systems or from the reference, and choosing one of the options below:

- A<B: when the quality of translation B was higher than A.

- A=B: when both translation had similar quality.

- A>B: when the quality of translation A was higher than B.

- Flag error: when the translations did not seem to be derived from the same input sentence. This is usually derived from error in the corpus alignment (for the Scielo and EDP datasets).

The manual validation for the Scielo test sets is presented in Table 8, for the comparison of the only participating team (UHH) to the reference translation. For en2es, the automatic translation scored lower than the reference one in 53 out of 100 pairs, but could still beat the reference translation in 23 pairs. For en2pt, the automatic translation was better only on 13 sentences pairs, while they could achieve similar quality to the reference translation on 31 cases. In the case of translations from Spanish or Portuguese to English, the reference scored better than the UHH around the same proportion, while the latter could only beat the reference in very few cases.

We present the results for the manual evaluation of the EDP test sets in Table 9. Based on the number of times that a translation was validated as being better than another, we ranked the systems for each language as listed below:

- en2fr: Hunter < UHH < kyoto = reference

- fr2en: Hunter < UHH < kyoto < reference

Results for manual validation of the Cochrane test sets are presented in Table 10. We rank the various system as shown below:

Test set	Languages	Runs (A vs. B)	Total	A>B	A=B	A<B
Scielo	en2es	UHH vs. reference	100	23	24	53
	en2pt	UHH vs. reference	100	13	31	46
	es2en	UHH vs. reference	100	7	11	59
	pt2en	UHH vs. reference	100	10	20	50

Table 8: Results for the manual validation for the Scielo test sets. Values are absolute numbers (not percentages). They might not sum up to 100 due to the skipped sentences.

Test set	Languages	Runs (A vs. B)	Total	A>B	A=B	A<B
EDP	en2fr	UHH vs. reference	100	3	4	87
		UHH vs. Hunter	100	42	46	7
		UHH vs. kyoto	100	10	21	64
		Hunter vs. reference	100	0	2	93
		kyoto vs. reference	100	28	30	35
		Hunter vs. kyoto	100	3	10	82
	fr2en	UHH vs. reference	100	5	9	72
		UHH vs. Hunter	100	79	5	10
		UHH vs. kyoto	100	26	7	62
		Hunter vs. reference	100	2	4	79
		kyoto vs. reference	100	25	9	48
		Hunter vs. kyoto	100	3	9	81

Table 9: Results for the manual validation for the EDP test sets. Values are absolute numbers (not percentages). They might not sum up to 100 due to the skipped sentences.

- cs: PIIJT < uedin-nmt < reference

- de: UHH < Hunter = PJIIT < Lilt < LMU < uedin-nmt = reference

- fr: UHH < Hunter < reference

- pl: Hunter = PIIJT < uedin < reference

- es: UHH < reference

- ro: Hunter < PIIJT < uedin < reference

Results for manual validation of the NHS test sets are presented in Table 11. We rank the various system as shown below:

- cs: PIIJT < uedin-nmt < reference

- de: Hunter = UHH < PIIJT < Lilt < LMU = uedin-nmt < reference

- fr: UHH < Hunter < reference

- pl: Hunter < PIIJT < uedin < reference

- es: UHH < reference

- ro: Hunter < PIIJT < uedin < reference

For the Polish language in the NHS test set, the evaluator skipped too many sentences (68 out of 100) to enable a comparison between Hunter and PIIJT. However, we ranked the PIIJT system higher than Hunter given that the former scored 21

times better that the latter (in contrast to 7). However, there is inadequate data to support assigning a clear difference between the two systems. Indeed, both systems have similar quality for this language in the Cochrane test set.

5 Discussion

In this section we present, for each target language, some insights from the automatic validation, the quality of the translations, as well as future work that we plan to implement in the next edition of the challenges.

5.1 Performance of the systems

The results obtained by the teams show interesting point of discussion regarding the impact of methods and amount of training data. Considering all the results in Tables 4-7, the highest BLEU score (48.99) of all runs across all test sets was obtained by the UHH system for en2es (Cochrane test set). The same team also scored high (above 40) for the NHS en2es test set and for the Scielo pt2en test set. The only other team that obtained BLEU scores in the same range (above 40) was uedin-nmt for the Cochrane en2ro test set.

No automatic system was able to outperform or match the reference translations on manual evaluation; hence the automated systems all still have room for improvement. Interestingly, it can be noted that the best performing system on the EDP

Test set	Languages	Runs (A vs. B)	Total	A>B	A=B	A<B
Cochrane	cs	PIIJT vs. reference	100	4	1	95
		PIIJT vs. uedin-nmt	100	19	6	75
		uedin-nmt vs. reference	100	8	38	54
	de	Hunter vs. reference	100	5	12	83
		Hunter vs. Lilt	100	12	20	68
		Hunter vs. LMU	100	6	20	73
		Hunter vs. PJIIT	100	26	41	33
		Hunter vs. uedin-nmt	100	3	12	85
		Hunter vs. UHH	100	42	30	28
		Lilt vs. reference	100	19	22	59
		LMU vs. reference	100	17	32	51
		PJIIT vs. reference	100	2	8	90
		uedin-nmt vs. reference	100	31	29	40
		UHH vs. reference	100	93	6	1
		Lilt vs. LMU	100	23	24	50
		Lilt vs. PJIIT	100	66	19	15
		Lilt vs. uedin-nmt	100	14	22	63
		Lilt vs. UHH	100	81	8	11
		LMU vs. PJIIT	100	82	9	7
		LMU vs. uedin-nmt	100	19	50	31
		LMU vs. UHH	100	82	10	3
		PJIIT vs. uedin-nmt	100	14	22	64
		PJIIT vs. UHH	100	34	44	22
		uedin-nmt vs. UHH	100	87	5	8
	fr	UHH vs. reference	100	8	8	83
		UHH vs. Hunter	100	8	51	40
		Hunter vs. reference	100	11	10	79
	pl	Hunter vs. PJIIT	100	43	7	48
		Hunter vs. reference	100	4	8	88
		Hunter vs. uedin-nmt	100	16	0	84
		PJIIT vs. reference	100	3	11	86
		PJIIT vs. uedin-nmt	100	16	4	80
		uedin-nmt vs. reference	100	15	34	51
	es	UHH vs. reference	100	4	29	67
	ru	Hunter vs. PJIIT	100	6	20	74
		Hunter vs. reference	100	1	3	96
		Hunter vs. uedin-nmt	100	5	8	87
		PJIIT vs. reference	100	3	6	91
		PJIIT vs. uedin-nmt	100	20	21	59
		uedin-nmt vs. reference	100	4	32	64

Table 10: Results for the manual validation for the Cochrane test sets. Values are absolute numbers (not percentages). They might not sum up to 100 due to the skipped sentences.

Test set	Languages	Runs (A vs. B)	Total	A>B	A=B	A<B
NHS	cs	PIJT vs. reference	100	4	20	76
		PIJT vs. uedin-nmt	100	28	23	49
		uedin-nmt vs. reference	100	7	41	52
	de	Hunter vs. reference	100	0	9	91
		Hunter vs. Lilt	100	28	29	43
		Hunter vs. LMU	100	17	12	68
		Hunter vs. PJIIT	100	32	28	40
		Hunter vs. uedin-nmt	100	12	18	70
		Hunter vs. UHH	100	34	36	30
		Lilt vs. reference	100	2	35	63
		LMU vs. reference	100	4	30	62
		PJIIT vs. reference	100	1	24	74
		uedin-nmt vs. reference	100	5	45	46
		UHH vs. reference	100	2	18	79
		Lilt vs. LMU	100	19	44	33
		Lilt vs. PJIIT	100	46	24	30
		Lilt vs. uedin-nmt	100	11	23	66
		Lilt vs. UHH	100	47	28	25
		LMU vs. PJIIT	100	56	22	18
		LMU vs. uedin-nmt	100	37	27	33
		LMU vs. UHH	100	59	19	18
		PJIIT vs. uedin-nmt	100	8	24	68
		PJIIT vs. UHH	100	51	21	28
		uedin vs. UHH	100	63	29	8
	fr	UHH vs. reference	100	0	2	98
		UHH vs. Hunter	100	6	27	67
		Hunter vs. reference	100	11	23	65
	pl	Hunter vs. PJIIT	100	7	4	21
		Hunter vs. reference	100	14	2	84
		Hunter vs. uedin-nmt	100	8	11	48
		PJIIT vs. reference	100	9	8	83
		PJIIT vs. uedin-nmt	100	8	16	62
		uedin-nmt vs. reference	100	11	14	75
	es	UHH vs. reference	100	1	32	67
	ro	Hunter vs. PJIIT	100	10	38	52
		Hunter vs. reference	100	1	7	92
		Hunter vs. uedin-nmt	100	4	27	62
		PJIIT vs. reference	100	3	16	81
		PJIIT vs. uedin-nmt	100	24	34	41
		uedin-nmt vs. reference	100	6	26	68

Table 11: Results for the manual validation for the NHS test sets. Values are absolute numbers (not percentages). They might not sum up to 100 due to the skipped sentences.

en2fr dataset (Kyoto) compared very favorably to the reference and was found to be equal to or better than the reference in 62% (58/93) of the manually evaluated sentences. In general, the kyoto and uedin-nmt systems seemed to consistently outperform other competitors.

Regarding comparison of results to the ones obtained in the last year's edition of the challenge, we can only draw conclusions for the Scielo test set. The only participating team (UHH) obtained much higher BLEU scores for en2pt (39 vs. 19), pt2en (43 vs. 21) and es2en (37 vs. 30). However, results for en2es were just a little higher than last year's ones (36 vs. 33).

As the performance of the methods improves on the biomedical domain, it will make sense to introduce additional domain-oriented evaluation measures that provide a document-level assessment focused on the clinical validity of the translations, rather than the grammatical correctness and fluency.

5.2 Best-performing methods

For languages which received submissions from several systems, such as en2de over Cochrane and NHS data, the systems based on neural networks (e.g., uedin-nmt and LMU) performed substantially better than those based on SMT (e.g., UHH and Hunter). In many runs, the difference in BLEU score was greater than 10 points. The superiority of NMT systems was also observed in the EDP test set, as implemented in the Kyoto system. However, we also note that a state-of-the-art statistical system relying on rich in-domain and out-of-domain data still performs well (as seen in the strong results of the LIMSI system).

Finally, some teams submitted more than one run but we only observed significant differences in BLEU scores in a few cases, namely, kyoto (EDP en2fr test set), PJIIT (Cochrane/NHS pl test set), uedin (Cochrane/NHS pl and ro test sets). In the case of the PJIIT systems, the best performing one is an extended version of the base SMT system that includes domain adaptation, among other additional features. In the case of the uedin-nmt system, the best performing run relied on advanced techniques, such as +right-to-left re-ranking.

5.3 Differences across languages

Even if some teams relied on equal or similar methods for the different languages, the same system might perform better for certain languages then for others. This is probably due to amount (or quality) of training data available for each language and also due to different linguistic properties of the language pair in question.

For instance, the UHH team developed a SMT system which was trained on a variety of domain and out-of-the-domain data. This system achieved good performance for English, Portuguese and Spanish (around 30-48), but their results for German were much poorer (around 18-22). Indeed, the system obtained the lowest rank position for German for the Cochrane and NHS test sets. The participants report that this is probably due to the amount of training data available for this language (personal communication), even though other teams could obtain much higher BLEU scores for those same test sets, e.g., up to 37 points in the case of the uedin-nmt system.

Such differences across languages was also observed for other systems (higher than 10-20 points in the BLEU score). For instance, scores for the uedin-nmt system ranged from 22 (for Czech) to 41 (for Romanian). Interestingly, the scores for the Hunter system ranged from 10 (for Romanian, in contrast to higher scores from uedin-nmt system) to 30 (for French). The Hunter team seems to have used the same approach across all languages and all of these were trained on a variety of corpora. On the other hand, the uedin-nmt team seems to have used slightly different network architectures for each language (Sennrich et al., 2017).

5.4 Differences across datasets

Given that the methods and corpora seem to be largely the same for a particular language, differences in BLEU scores across the test sets are probably related to the the characteristics of these. Few teams submitted runs for more than one test set and only one team (UHH) submitted runs for all test set (for one particular language).

For Spanish, the UHH team obtained considerable differences in BLEU score for Scielo (around 36), NHS (around 41) and Cochrane (around 48). However, their system paper does not give much insight on the reason for such differences (Duma and Menzel, 2017). We can hypothesize that lower scores in the Scielo datasets are due to the fact that the reference translation is not a perfect translation of the source document and sentence alignment was performed automatically.

For French, the Hunter team obtained lower

scores in the EDP test set (around 17) and higher ones in the NHS (almost 23) and Cochrane test sets (around 30). Similarly, the UHH team obtained lower scores for the EDP (around 22) and higher ones for Cochrane and NHS (around 31-32). The reason for these differences is probably the same as for the Scielo test set: this is an automatically acquired test set, whose documents were automatically aligned. While the quality of the automatic alignment is high (estimated at 88% accuracy for Scielo and 94% for EDP), we can also note that the translations in these test sets are created by the authors of the articles who are neither professional translators nor native speakers of the all the languages involved.

On the other hand, differences also occurred between the Cochrane and NHS test sets, although these were manually translated by professionals. Such differences were small for most systems (24 vs. 20 for Hunter, 22 vs. 19 for UHH, 25 vs. 21 for PIIJT), for German in the Cochrane and NHS test sets, respectively. However, some cases show larger differences, such as the uedin-nmt system for Romanian (41 vs. 29 for Cochrane and NHS, respectively). We observed that that the average sentence length is higher for Cochrane (with some very long sentences included) while there are many short sentence fragments in the NHS test set. However, both can be problematic for MT as this can scramble long sentences, and trip up over sentence fragments since most of the training data consists of full sentences.

5.5 Differences between manual and automatic evaluations

We checked for differences between the manual and automatic evaluations, i.e., whether a team performed better than another in the manual evaluation but the other way round in the automatic evaluation. We observed small differences for Polish (Cochrane and NHS test sets) between the Hunter and PIIJT teams, but these are probably not significant and both systems have probably similar performance. We observed the same for the UHH and Hunter systems for German (NHS test set). However, we found a more interesting contradiction between Hunter and UHH systems for French in both Cohrane and NHS test sets. UHH obtained higher BLEU scores than Hunter (32-33 vs. 30 and 31-33 vs. 23, for Cochrane and NHS, respectively). However, in the manual evaluation,

our expert chose Hunter as being better than UHH in many more sentences (40 vs. 8 and 67 vs. 6, respectively).

5.6 Quality of the automatic translations

We provide an overview of the quality of the translations and the common errors that we identified during the manual validation.

Czech: The outputs of the weaker system, PIIJT, were rather unsurprising, featuring a wide range of well-known issues of phrase-based SMT, including inflection errors that violate both long-distance and short-distance morphological agreement, errors in missing or surplus negation, untranslated and uninflected rare words, wrong disambiguation of word meanings, etc. On the other hand, the quality of the neural uedint-nmt system is remarkably better, with no negation errors spotted, agreement errors generally limited to long-distance dependencies, only rare disambiguation errors (often domain-specific, e.g. "drug", "study", "review"), and a much bolder attempt at handling unknown or rare words. On one hand, we spotted cases where it would have been better to leave the word untranslated, or to only perform modest transliterations, as in "haemoglobin", which is similar enough to the "hemoglobin" used in Czech to be understandable as it is, but got translated to "hemoroidy" ("hemorrhoids") instead; on the other hand, both correct and incorrect translations of rare words were nearly always correctly inflected. Occasionally, we also noticed a missing or surplus word – especially with auxiliaries, such as reflexive pronouns or forms of the verb "be".

English: Overall, the assessor found the quality of translations into English improved from 2016. Some of the problems observed in the prior year persisted, including inappropriate capitalization of terms (terms were capitalized although they were neither proper nouns nor acronyms) for some translations. Other issues such as incorrect word order as well as untranslated and missing words were observed. Especially in fr2en translations, incorrect word order occurred when the noun-before-adjective grammar in French was erroneously preserved in English; for instance, "douleur oro-faciale" was translated as "pain oro-facial". Sometimes, however, untranslated words could still be deciphered because the French words were similar to the English equivalents, such as "biomatériaux" vs. "biomaterials", and "tolérance immunologique" vs. "immunological tolerance". As for missing words, translations were severely impacted when entire phrases were omitted, for instance when two consequences of a procedure were reduced to only one.

French: The quality of translations varied from poor to good. The issues that we encountered were similar to last year and included grammatical errors such as incorrect subject/verb or adjective/noun agreement, untranslated passages, incorrect lexical choice due to a lack of word sense disambiguation. One recurring mistake was the translation of the term "female" as "femelle", which is appropriate for animals instead of "femme", which is appropriate for humans. This year, the best systems showed an ability to successfully translate some acronyms. However, complex hyphenated terms remained challenging (for example, "38-year-old", "mid-60s", "immunoglobulin-like").

German: Overall, the quality of translations to German ranges from very good to poor. Comparing between the different systems, the translation with the better syntax, grammar and use of technical terms was preferred. When both translations were equally bad their performance was assigned equal. Poor translations are mostly characterized by incorrect syntax and grammar. Syntactic errors are usually due to missing predicates, the usage of two or more predicates in one sentence, and strange word order, especially in long sentences. This often led to confusion or even not understanding the meaning of a sentence. Usual grammar errors included incorrect conjugation of verbs as "wir suchte" instead of "wir suchten" (we searched). In well performing systems syntax and grammar are often correct. Their difference to the reference is often due to not using the most appropriate word. This does not influence the meaning of the sentence. Only as a native speaker one would rather use a different word. All systems seem to have problems with certain technical terms. Usually this occurs when the German translation is very different from the English term. For instance, "to restart a person's heart" is often word-by-word translated into "Neustart des Herzen" while in German this procedure is called "Reanimation des Herzens". The pairwise evaluation of the two best performing teams (LMU and uedin-nmt) indicates, that they often provide similar sentences in terms of grammar and token order.

Portuguese: Only one team (UHH) submitted translation for Portuguese (Scielo dataset). In comparison to submissions from the previous challenge (Bojar et al., 2016), we found the quality of the translations considerably better. As expected, longer sentences usually contained more mistakes and were harder to understand than shorter sentences, usually due to the wrong placement of the commas and conjunctions (e.g., and). For instance, the translation "diâmetro tubular, altura do epitélio seminífero e integridade" was derived from the English version of the reference clause "diâmetro dos túbulos seminíferos, altura e integridade do epitélio seminífero". However, the same can be also stated for some reference sentences, which could have a higher quality.

Regarding more common mistakes, we observed missing articles, such as "Extratos vegetais" versus "Os extratos das espécies vegetais". However, we observed fewer instances of untranslated English words in comparison to last year, which seems to indicate a better coverage of the biomedical terminology. In some sentences, such cases were observed for terms which were skipped by the translation system, such as "método de manometria de alta resolução" for "high-resolution manometry method for esophageal manometry". The same mistake was observed for acronyms, e.g., DPS (death of pastures syndrome) instead of SMP (síndrome da morte das pastagens). However, we also found correct translations for acronyms, e.g., SII (síndrome do intenstino irritavel) instead of IBS (irritable bowel syndrome). Finally, we observed other minor mistakes: (a) nominal concordance, e.g., "O fortalecimento muscular progressiva"; (b) wrong word ordering, e.g., "plantadas áreas florestais" instead of "áreas florestais plantadas"; (c) wrong verb tense, e.g., "coeficiente de correlação linear de Pearson spearmans determinado" instead of "determinou"; (d) wrong verb conjugation, e.g, "a umidade relativa, temperatura, velocidade do vento e intensidade de luz foi...", instead of "foram"; and (c) no contraction when necessary, e.g., "em as" instead of "nas".

Spanish: Compared to last year's challenge translations, the quality of the translations into Spanish is significantly better. Despite some small variations, many of the produced translations are valid translations of the original text. There are still cases in which there are mistakes such as with verb tenses "a menudo oír voces", which should be "a menudo oyen voces". There are translations with similar meaning but not entirely the same meaning such as "hace aparecer" vs. the reference translation "ocurren". In some cases, there are some incorrect phrases such as "teléfono NHS informar sobre" vs. the reference translation "llame por teléfono el sistema informativo de NHS en". Translation systems seem to have better alignment between masculine/feminine and singular/plural articles as compared to last year. In addition, the number of missing words is lower in the Spanish submissions.

Romanian: The quality varied from good translations to clearly underperforming ones. When both translations were good, the one that was grammatically correct was preferred. When one used an awkward language or did not use domain-specific terms such as "traumatism cranian" or "presiune intracraniana", the other one was preferred. We noticed that these translations can be very dangerous, especially when the form is good (and thus the appearance of quality is high). For instance, in one case, "vasopressor" was translated as "vasodilatatoare", which is the precise antonym. A frequent mistake was the translation of "trials" as "procese", which would have been correct for "law suits" but not for clinical trials. Somewhat confusing was translating "norepinephrine" as "noradrenaline", as they look different but are two names of the same substance. For the bad and very bad translations, errors abounded up to the point that both were equally useless and therefore marked as equal (in the sense of equally bad); this happened quite often. In general, we preferred translations that did not mislead and were still possible to understand despite their many flaws. Among the frequent translation errors, we identified the following: untranslated words, grammatical errors (case, gender), random characters and even Cyrillic (for no apparent reason) and context which were frequently not considered (e.g. "shots" translated to "gloante" and "impuscaturi", those words having to do with weapons not with syringes). Other strange errors included unrelated words from other fields, especially "subcontractantul copolimerului" or "transductoare AFC".

6 Conclusions

We presented the results of the second edition of the Biomedical task in the Conference for Machine Translation. The shared task addressed a total of ten languages and received submission from seven teams. In comparison to last year, we observed an increase on the performance of the systems in terms of higher BLEU scores as well as an improvement in the quality of the translations, as observed during manual validation. The methods used by the systems included statistical and neural machine translation techniques, but also incorporated many advanced features to boost the performance, such as domain adaptation.

Despite the comprehensive evaluation that we show here, there is still room for improvement in our methodology. All by professionals were rather small (up to 1000 sentences), which means that some of the our conclusions might not hold on a larger benchmark. Further, we did not perform statistical tests when ranking the various systems and runs in both manual and automatic evaluations. Furthermore, each combination of two translations or one translation and reference was evaluated by a single expert, given the high number of submissions and the difficulty of finding available experts. On the other hand, most results obtained through manual validation were consistent with the automatic validation, suggesting that automatic scoring is sufficiently meaningful.

Acknowledgments

We would like to thank the support of participants and colleagues in the manual validation of the translations. We thank Julia Ive and Franck Burlot for their assistance with the LIMSI translation system. The Cochrane and NHS test sets were provided by the EU H2020 projects HimL (contract no. 644402) and KConnect (contract no. 644753).

References

Ondřej Bojar, Rajen Chatterjee, Christian Federmann, Yvette Graham, Barry Haddow, Matthias Huck, Antonio Jimeno Yepes, Philipp Koehn, Varvara Logacheva, Christof Monz, Matteo Negri, Aurelie Neveol, Mariana Neves, Martin Popel, Matt Post, Raphael Rubino, Carolina Scarton, Lucia Specia, Marco Turchi, Karin Verspoor, and Marcos Zampieri. 2016. Findings of the 2016 Conference on Machine Translation. In *Proceedings of the First*

Conference on Machine Translation (WMT16) at the Conference of the Association of Computational Linguistics, pages 131–198.

Fabien Cromieres. 2016. Kyoto-NMT: a Neural Machine Translation implementation in Chainer. In *Proceedings of COLING 2016, the 26th International Conference on Computational Linguistics: System Demonstrations*. The COLING 2016 Organizing Committee, Osaka, Japan, pages 307–311.

Fabien Cromieres, Chenhui Chu, Toshiaki Nakazawa, and Sadao Kurohashi. 2016. Kyoto University Participation to WAT 2016. In *Proceedings of the 3rd Workshop on Asian Translation (WAT2016)*. The COLING 2016 Organizing Committee, Osaka, Japan, pages 166–174.

Mirela-Stefania Duma and Wolfgang Menzel. 2017. Automatic Threshold Detection for Data Selection in Machine Translation. In *Proceedings of the Second Conference on Machine Translation (WMT17) at the Conference on Empirical Methods in Natural Language Processing*.

Christian Federmann. 2010. Appraise: An open-source toolkit for manual phrase-based evaluation of translations. In *In LREC*.

Matthias Huck and Alexander Fraser. 2017. Lmu Munich's Neural Machine Translation Systems for News Articles and Health Information Texts. In *Proceedings of the Second Conference on Machine Translation (WMT17) at the Conference on Empirical Methods in Natural Language Processing*.

Julia Ive, Aurélien Max, and François Yvon. 2016a. Limsi's contribution to the wmt'16 biomedical translation task. In *Proceedings of the First Conference on Machine Translation*. Association for Computational Linguistics, Berlin, Germany, pages 469–476. http://www.aclweb.org/anthology/W/W16/W16-2337.

Julia Ive, Aurélien Max, François Yvon, and Philippe Ravaud. 2016b. Diagnosing high-quality statistical machine translation using traces of post-edition operations. In *Proceedings of the LREC 2016 Workshop: Translation evaluation From fragmented tools and data sets to an integrated ecosystem*. European Language Resources Association (ELRA), Portorož, Slovenia, pages 55–62. http://www.cracking-the-language-barrier.eu/wp-content/uploads/LREC-2016-MT-Eval-Workshop-Proceedings.pdf.

Philipp Koehn, Hieu Hoang, Alexandra Birch, Chris Callison-Burch, Marcello Federico, Nicola Bertoldi, Brooke Cowan, Wade Shen, Christine Moran, Richard Zens, Chris Dyer, Ondřej Bojar, Alexandra Constantin, and Evan Herbst. 2007. Moses: Open source toolkit for statistical machine translation. In *Proceedings of the 45th Annual Meeting of the ACL on Interactive Poster and Demonstration Sessions*. Association for Computational Linguistics,

Stroudsburg, PA, USA, ACL '07, pages 177–180. http://dl.acm.org/citation.cfm?id=1557769.1557821.

Mariana Neves, Antonio Jimeno Yepes, and Aurélie Névéol. 2016. The Scielo Corpus: a Parallel Corpus of Scientific Publications for Biomedicine. In Nicoletta Calzolari (Conference Chair), Khalid Choukri, Thierry Declerck, Sara Goggi, Marko Grobelnik, Bente Maegaard, Joseph Mariani, Helene Mazo, Asuncion Moreno, Jan Odijk, and Stelios Piperidis, editors, *Proceedings of the Tenth International Conference on Language Resources and Evaluation (LREC 2016)*. European Language Resources Association (ELRA), Paris, France.

Rico Sennrich, Alexandra Birch, Anna Currey, Ulrich Germann, Barry Haddow, Kenneth Heafield, Antonio Valerio Miceli Barone, and Philip Williams. 2017. The University of Edinburgh's Neural MT Systems for WMT17. In *Proceedings of the Second Conference on Machine Translation (WMT17) at the Conference on Empirical Methods in Natural Language Processing*.

Krzysztof Wolk and Krzysztof Marasek. 2017. PJIIT's systems for WMT 2017 Conference. In *Proceedings of the Second Conference on Machine Translation (WMT17) at the Conference on Empirical Methods in Natural Language Processing*.

Jia Xu, Yi Zong Kuang, Shondell Baijoo, Jacob Lee, Mir Ahmed, Uman Shahzad, Meredith Lancaster, and Chris Carlan. 2017. Supervised Study for Young Machine Translators: Hunter Machine Translation Systems for WMT17. In *Proceedings of the Second Conference on Machine Translation (WMT17) at the Conference on Empirical Methods in Natural Language Processing*.

CUNI Submission in WMT17: Chimera Goes Neural

Roman Sudarikov   **David Mareček**
Tom Kocmi   **Dušan Variš**   **Ondřej Bojar**

Charles University, Faculty of Mathematics and Physics
Institute of Formal and Applied Linguistics
Malostranské náměstí 25, 118 00 Prague, Czech Republic
`surname@ufal.mff.cuni.cz`

Abstract

This paper describes the neural and phrase-based machine translation systems submitted by CUNI to English-Czech News Translation Task of WMT17. We experiment with synthetic data for training and try several system combination techniques, both neural and phrase-based. Our primary submission CU-CHIMERA ends up being phrase-based backbone which incorporates neural and deep-syntactic candidate translations.

1 Introduction

The paper describes CUNI submissions for English-to-Czech WMT 2017 News Translation Task. We experimented with several neural machine translation (NMT) systems and we further developed our phrase-based statistical machine translation system Chimera, which was our primary system last year (Tamchyna et al., 2016).

This year, we planned our setup in a way that would allow us to experiment with neural system combination. To this end, we reserved the provided English-Czech parallel data for the training of the system combination and trained our "individual forward systems" on *almost only synthetic data*.

The structure of the paper is the following. In Section 2, we provide an overview of the relatively complex setup. Section 3 details how the training data for all the systems were prepared, including the description of MT systems used for back-translation. Section 4 is devoted to our individual forward translation systems, each of which could actually serve as a submission to the translation task. We do not stop there and train system combinations in Section 5. In Section 6, we present the systems we actually submitted to WMT17 and we conclude by Section 8.

2 Setup Overview

Our setup this year is motivated by the ability to use all the parallel data for system combination training. The overall sequence of system training is the following:

1. Use available monolingual data and last year's systems to prepare a synthetic parallel corpus using "back translation" (Section 3).

2. Train "individual forward systems" on this synthetic corpus (Section 4).

3. Apply individual forward systems to the source side of the genuine parallel data.

4. Train a (neural) system combination on this dataset (Section 5).

5. Apply individual forward systems to the test set and apply the trained combination system to their output (Section 5).

Each of the steps is fully described in the respective section of this paper. By "back-translated" data we mean that for English-to-Czech translation task, we created a synthetic English-Czech parallel corpus by "back-translating" Czech monolingual data into English. To distinguish back-translation Czech-to-English systems and the English-to-Czech systems to be submitted, we will call Czech-to-English systems "back-translation systems" and English-to-Czech systems "forward(-translation) systems".

3 Data Preparation

The section describes the data used for training of both Czech-to-English back-translation systems as well as English-to-Czech forward systems.

Proceedings of the Conference on Machine Translation (WMT), Volume 2: Shared Task Papers, pages 248–256
Copenhagen, Denmark, September 7–11, 2017. ©2017 Association for Computational Linguistics

Corpus	Sentences	Tokens Cs	Tokens En
Synthetic corpora			
NematusNews	59 190 187	985 887k	1 196 366k
MosesNews	59 146 101	985 017k	1 173 839k
XenC extracted corpora			
XenCNews	20 415 268	289 472k	334 322k
XenCMonoNews	12 498 680	95 687k	103 193k
Development corpora			
Dev	2 656	46k	55k
Eval	2 999	57k	67k

Table 1: Datasets

3.1 Back-Translated Data

To create back-translated data, we used the CzEng 1.6 Czech-English parallel corpus (Bojar et al., 2016) and the Czech News Crawl articles released for WMT2017[1] (called "mononews" for short).

We used two different back-translation systems: Moses (Koehn et al., 2007) trained by ourselves, and Marian[2] (known as AmuNMT before it included NMT training; Junczys-Dowmunt et al., 2016) using the pretrained Nematus (Sennrich et al., 2017) models[3] from WMT16 News Task.[4]

We used only the non-ensembled left-to-right run (i.e. no right-to-left rescoring as done by Sennrich et al., 2016a) with beam size of 5,[5] taking just the single-best output.

The Moses-based system used only a single phrase table translating from word form to word forms and twelve 10-gram language models built on individual years of English mononews.

We took all Czech mononews corpora available this year, concatenated and translated them using both systems described above and thus created two back-translated corpora on which we planned to train our forward systems.

The "Synthetic corpora" section of Table 1 shows the numbers of sentences and tokens of the resulting corpora. Despite having started with the same Czech monolingual corpus, the number of sentences differs slightly due to minor technical issues encountered by Moses.

In the following, the synthetic corpora created by the two MT systems will be referred to as NematusNews and MosesNews, respectively.

---

[1] http://www.statmt.org/wmt17/translation-task.html
[2] https://github.com/marian-nmt/marian
[3] http://data.statmt.org/rsennrich/wmt16_systems
[4] We decided to use Marian instead of Nematus since it was faster at the time we performed the translation.
[5] We chose beam size of 5, since our primary goal was to produce a 5-best list.

3.2 Domain-Selected Genuine Parallel Data

For the training of forward translation systems, we used primarily the synthetic corpora described in Section 3.1 above but also some additional sources described in this section.

The first source to mention is CzEng 1.6. We did not use the whole corpus as we did in our WMT16 submission (Tamchyna et al., 2016). Instead, we used the XenC toolkit (Rousseau, 2013) to extract domain-specific data from the whole corpus (referred to as "out-of-domain", in the following). We used two modes of XenC. Both of these modes estimate two language models from in-domain and out-of-domain corpora, using SRILM toolkit (Stolcke, 2002). The first mode is a filtering process based on a simple perplexity computation utilizing only one side of the corpora so that monolingual corpora are sufficient and the second mode is based on the bilingual cross-entropy difference as described by Axelrod et al. (2011).

We took two different corpora as our in-domain data:

- News section of CzEng 1.6 – which had 197 053 parallel English-Czech sentences. The extraction was performed both monolingually (perplexity) and bilingually (bilingual cross-entropy difference).

- Concatenated mononews corpora – which had 59 190 187 Czech sentences. The extraction was performed only monolingually.

The two different in-domain corpora were used because we wanted to estimate which of them would lead to better extracted corpus – a small parallel in-domain corpus or a larger monolingual corpus.

Based on these two representatives of in-domain texts, we extracted sentences from CzEng 1.6. We took top 20% of sentence pairs extracted monolingually (see XenCMonoNews in the section "XenC extracted corpora" in Table 1) and top 20% of sentence pairs extracted monolingually and bilingually (see XenCNews) in the same table. For XenCNews corpus monolingual and bilingual sentence extractions were made separately and then the results were unioned, i.e. concatenated and duplicates removed.

For the development and evaluation purposes, we used WMT2015 and WMT2016 test sets, respectively, see the "Development corpora" section in Table 1.

Finally, what we are combining, are the outputs of several forward translation systems: Nematus, Neural Monkey and TectoMT. During the development, we used the outputs of these systems on the test sets of WMT 2015 and 2016. For the test run, we translated the source of WMT news test set 2017.

All the corpora were tokenized using MorphoDita (Straková et al., 2014), i.e. even for synthetic corpora and combined systems, we de-BPE'd and detokenized the MT outputs and retokenized them.

4 Individual Forward Systems

This section describes our English-to-Czech systems. Each of them could be submitted to WMT17 but we combine them into just one system, see Section 5 below.

4.1 Baseline Nematus

We used Marian (formerly known as AmuNMT) (Junczys-Dowmunt et al., 2016) with pretrained English-to-Czech Nematus models[6] from WMT16 News Task as our baseline/benchmark and we also later included it in the final combined submission.

We used only the non-ensembled left-to-right run (i.e. no right-to-left rescoring as done by Sennrich et al., 2016a) with beam size of 12 (default value).

4.2 Neural Monkey

We use Neural Monkey[7] (Helcl and Libovický, 2017), an open-source neural machine translation and general sequence-to-sequence learning toolkit built using the TensorFlow machine learning library.

Neural Monkey is flexible in model configuration but for forward translation, we restrict our experiments to the standard encoder-decoder architecture with attention as preposed by Bahdanau et al. (2015). (Attempts to combine MT systems with Neural Monkey are described in Section 5.2 below.) We use the following model parameters which fit into 8GB GPU memory of NVIDIA GeForce GTX 1080. The encoder uses embeddings of size 600 and the hidden state of size 600.

Dropout is turned off[8] and maximum input sentence length is set to 50 tokens. The decoder uses attention mechanism and conditional GRU cells (Firat and Cho, 2016), with the hidden state of 600. Output embedding has the size of 600, dropout is turned off as well and the maximum output length is again 50 tokens. We use batch size of 60.

To reduce vocabulary size, we use byte pair encoding (Sennrich et al., 2016b) which breaks the all words into subword units defined in the vocabulary. The vocabulary is initialized with all letters and larger units are added on the basis of corpus statistics. Frequent words make it to the vocabulary, less frequent words are (deterministically) broken into smaller units from the vocabulary.

We set the vocabulary size to 30,000 subword units. The vocabulary is constructed jointly for the source and target side of the corpus and it is then shared between encoder and decoder.

During the inference, we use either greedy decoding or beam search with beam size of 50.[9]

4.3 Chimera 2016

The last individual forward system was based on CUNI's last year submission (Tamchyna et al., 2016). We experimented with several setups, see the list in Table 2.

Chimera itself is a hybrid system combination and we used the technique both here as an individual system as well as below in Section 5.3 for our final system combination.

The main components of the individual Chimera system are:

- **Synthetic phrase table** extracted from the main training data, ie. either or both of NematusNews and MosesNews as listed in Table 1.

- **In-domain phrase table** extracted from either or both of XenCNews and XenC-MonoNews.

- **Operation Sequence Model** (Durrani et al., 2013) trained on the NematusNews corpus.

---

[6] http://data.statmt.org/rsennrich/wmt16_systems

[7] http://ufal.mff.cuni.cz/neuralmonkey

[8] While dropout is useful for small datasets, Sennrich et al. (2016a) observed no gain from dropout with 8M training sentence pairs. Our training data is more than 7× larger.

[9] In contrast to what Tu et al. (2017, Table 1) observe for other implementations of the Bahdanau et al. (2015) model, Neural Monkey does not exhibit degradation of the quality of the top candidate with increasing beam size. We have thus no reason to keep beam size as small as usual.

	Phrase Tables	Additional	BLEU	Avg. BLEU
1.	XenCNews + TectoMT	-	20.88	-
2.	XenCMonoNews + TectoMT	-	20.08	-
3.	NematusNews	OSM	20.60	-
4.	MosesNews + TectoMT	-	20.79	-
5.	Mix(NematusNews, XenCNews) + TectoMT	-	21.60	-
6.	Mix(NematusNews, XenCMonoNews) + TectoMT	OSM	21.70	21.6
7.	Mix(NematusNews, XenCMonoNews) + TectoMT	-	21.87	21.7
8.	Mix(MosesNews, XenCNews) + TectoMT	-	21.30	-
9.	Mix(MosesNews, XenCMonoNews) + TectoMT	-	20.96	-
10.	Mix(MosesNews, NematusNews) + TectoMT	-	21.67	-
11.	Mix(MosesNews, NematusNews, XenCMonoNews) + TectoMT	-	21.52	-
12.	Mix(Moses, Nematus, XenCMonoNews, XenCNews) + TectoMT	-	21.81	-
	CHIMERA-TECTOMT-DEPFIX (secondary submission)			
	Mix(NematusNews, XenCMonoNews) + TectoMT	-	21.65	21.8

Table 2: Chimera-style combinations of various individual forward systems on WMT 2016 News.

- **TectoMT phrase table** (Žabokrtský et al., 2008) – a phrase table extracted from the outputs of TectoMT, a transfer-based deep-syntactic system, applied to the source side of the development and test sets.

The common components for all the tested systems are language models, which were taken from CUNI's last year submission. For some experiments we have used up to 4 phrase tables separately as Moses alternative decoding paths, trusting MERT (Och, 2003) to estimate weights. Alternatively (or when the number of the phrase tables would be even higher), we used the standard Moses phrase table mixing technique with uniform weights. Phrase tables mixed into one before MERT are listed as "Mix($table1, table2, ...$)" in the following.

MERT was done using the WMT2015 test set, and our internal evaluation was performed on WMT2016 test set, but with a different tokenization so the scores reported here are not directly comparable to the results at `http://matrix.statmt.org/`.

We report the results in Table 2, listing the used phrase tables and optionally OSM. The column "Average BLEU" was calculated based on 5 separate MERT runs.

It seems that training only on (in-domain) synthetic data is a viable option, lines 3 and 4 in Table 2 perform reasonably good and mixing the two sources of the synthetic data into one phrase table (line 10) instead of using the two of them simultaneously lead to an improvement of almost 1 BLEU point. At the same time, genuine parallel (and again in-domain) training data is equally good as each of the synthetic corpus, even if much smaller, see lines 1 and 2 trained on up to 20M sentence pairs instead of 59M synthetic sentences. Selecting the genuine parallel sentences both bilingually and monolingually (XenC-News) works usually better than selecting them only monolingually (XenCMonoNews), but there is a significant difference in corpus size so the numbers are not directly comparable.

The best-performing setup used the synthetic corpus created by Nematus (NematusNews), the (surprisingly) monolingually selected genuine parallel data (XenCMonoNews) and TectoMT (line 7 in Table 2). We used this setup as our main phrase-based translation system and also submitted is as a contrastive system under the name CHIMERA-TECTOMT-DEPFIX. Difference between line 7 and submitted system is in the TectoMT phrase table – line 7 system had TectoMT phrase-table without WMT 2017 test set, because internal evaluation was performed prior to the release of this test set.

5 Forward System Combination

This sections describes our experiments with system combination. We tried two neural and one Chimera-style approach.

As described in Section 3, the genuine parallel training data from CzEng was not directly used for the training of the forward systems (except for Chimera) so we could use this data to train our neural combination systems. We again opted to use only domain-specific part of CzEng, so we trained the systems on XenCNews as listed in Table 1.

5.1 Concatenative Neural System Combination

We experiment with system combination made by simple concatenation of individual system outputs together, inspired by Niehues et al. (2016).

To train the neural combination system, we create a synthetic parallel corpus with the following three sentences on the source side:

- Nematus English-to-Czech translation

- Neural Monkey English-to-Czech translation

- English source sentence

The sentence triples are concatenated with spaces between them, forming a single input string of tokens. The target side remains the same, i.e. a single Czech target sentence. As shown by Niehues et al. (2016), the attention mechanism is capable of synchronously following the source and one candidate translation, so we hoped it could follow two candidate translations as well (with the obvious complication due to much longer input sequences).

The translation system trained on such data might benefit from distinguishing the words based on the translation system they come from. We therefore add labels in form of prefixes to each the token to identify the originating the system (n- for Nematus output, m- for Neural Monkey, and s- for the English source).

We perform three experiments:

1. without labels,

2. with labels inserted before BPE splitting, which means that only the first part of individual tokens has the prefix,

3. with labels inserted after BPE splitting.

For training, we use Nematus NMT system (Sennrich et al., 2017), using shared vocabulary of size 50,000, RNN size 1024, embedding size 500, and batch size 80. The maximum sentence length is tripled to 150, instead of standard value of 50.

The results are in Table 3. It is obvious that the additional labels do not help. The best results were achieved without using labels and more labels worsen the final BLEU score. However, the concatenative system combination did not bring any improvement over the individual systems, it is worse than the best single system Nematus by

System	BLEU
Nematus	24.4
Neural Monkey	22.9
combination without labels	21.4
combination labelled before BPE	21.2
combination labelled after BPE	20.4

Table 3: Concatenative combination BLEU scores on WMT2016 News and comparison with the single systems.

3 BLEU points. This was partially caused by too short training time (about one week, 420,000 iterations, batch size 80).

We inspected the attention scores and confirmed that the decoder used all three sentences, however it prefers the Nematus translation and the English source sentence. It pays less attention to the Neural Monkey translation, which is understandable since the translation quality is lower.

5.2 Neural Monkey System Combination

Neural Monkey supports multiple encoders and a hierarchical attention model (Libovický et al., 2016). Due to time constraints, we did not finish these experiments for WMT17 but the work is still in progress.

The idea is to use a separate encoder for each input sentence and to combine their outputs before passing them to the target sentence decoder. The final encoder states are simply concatenated (and optionally resized by a linear layer) and the hidden states are all passed to the decoder for attention computation without distinguishing which encoder generated them. Libovický and Helcl (2017) suggest also other strategies for combining attention from multiple source encoders and we plan to further investigate them in the near future.

Since we are trying to combine outputs generated by Nematus and Neural Monkey, both trained on subword units, we decided to try a character-to-character architecture as introduced in Lee et al. (2016) for system combination, expecting better results due to differences in the used architectures. In the future, we also plan comparing this approach to the subword-level multi-encoder system combination.

We trained a baseline model using GeForce GTX 1080 with 8GB memory. We used a shared vocabulary of size 500 for all encoders and decoder. We used RNN size 256 and embedding

	Tables	BLEU	Avg. BLEU
1.	**Moses + Mix(TectoMT, Nematus, Neural Monkey 50) ***	24.11	24.1
2.	Moses + Mix(TectoMT, Nematus, Neural Monkey 1)	24.17	24.3
3.	Moses + Mix(TectoMT, Nematus, Neural Monkey)	23.86	23.9
4.	Moses + TectoMT + Mix(Nematus, Neural Monkey)	23.82	23.9
5.	Moses + Neural Monkey + Mix(TectoMT, Nematus)	23.75	23.7
6.	Moses + Nematus + Mix(TectoMT, Neural Monkey)	23.87	23.9
7.	Moses + Nematus + Neural Monkey + TectoMT	23.82	23.7
8.	Moses + Nematus + Neural Monkey	23.82	23.7
9.	Moses + TectoMT + Nematus	23.57	-
10.	**Moses + TectoMT + Neural Monkey 50**	23.57	-
11.	Moses + TectoMT + Neural Monkey 1	23.36	-
12.	Moses + TectoMT + Neural Monkey	22.96	22.9
13.	Moses + Neural Monkey	22.43	22.4
14.	**Moses + TectoMT**	21.65	21.8

Table 4: Chimera system combination evaluation on WMT 2016 News. Submitted systems in **bold**, with the primary marked with *.

300 for each encoder, highway depth of 2 and set of convolutional filters scaled down to fit the smaller memory and taking multiple encoders into account. The decoder RNN size was 512 and used embedding size 500. We trained the model for 10 days and obtained the BLEU score of 14.69 on the newstest2016 EN-CS development set. This is much lower than the individual combined systems.

The system performed poorly overall and we have to investigate whether the main reason for the failure is the character-to-character approach, the multi-encoder architecture, their combination, or simply some bugs in implementation. Further experiments are planned for the future to be able to draw better conclusions.

5.3 Chimera System Combination

Given the poor performance of our neural system combinations, we decided to try the same Chimera-style combination with all available systems, i.e. Nematus, Neural Monkey and Chimera 2016 described in Section 4.

We took the best phrase tables combination from Section 4.3: (1) A combination of mixed NematusNews and XenCMonoNews phrase table (called simply "Moses" in Table 4 because it is the phrase-based basis of the system), (2) phrase table generated from TectoMT output and (3) tried to add phrase tables extracted from Nematus and Neural Monkey translations of WMT2015–2017 test sets.

For Neural Monkey, we had several setups to extract phrase tables from:

- Neural Monkey – the output of the system described in Section 4.2 using greedy decoding,

- Neural Monkey 1 – decoding with beam search of 50 and taking only the first candidate translation to the phrase table,

- Neural Monkey 50 – decoding with beam search of 50 and taking all 50 candidate translations to the phrase table,

All combinations we have experimented with are shown in Table 4. The last column "Average BLEU" was calculated the same way as it was done in Section 4.3. Also the same 5 MERT runs were used for MultEval evaluation (Clark et al., 2011).

Basically, Table 4 confirms the well-know saying "more data helps". Using translations from different systems as additional phrase tables gave on average a 2.5 BLEU score boost, if we compare rows 1 or 2 and row 14.

We also see that using more than three phrase tables might lead to a lower BLEU score: Consider the system in the row 7 with four separate phrase tables (Avg. BLEU 23.7) and the system in the row 3 where three of the tables were first merged into one (Avg. BLEU 23.9). Moreover, Multeval comparison showed no significant difference between systems from rows 7 and 8, despite the effect of adding TectoMT table is generally

Systems	Depfix	News2017
Moses+TectoTM+Neural Monkey 50+Nematus *	+	20.5
Moses+TectoTM+Neural Monkey 1+Nematus	+	20.4
Moses+TectoTM+Neural Monkey 50	+	19.9
Neural Monkey 1	-	19.3
Moses+TectoTM	+	18.3

Table 5: Submitted systems comparison. Asterisk (*) denotes our primary submission, CU-Chimera.

#	Ave %	Ave z	BLEU	TER	CharacTER	BEER	System
1	62.0	0.308	22.8	0.667	0.588	0.540	uedin-nmt
2	59.7	0.240	20.1	0.703	0.612	0.519	online-B
3	55.9	0.111	20.2	0.696	0.607	0.524	limsi-factored-norm
	55.2	0.102	20.0	0.699	-	-	LIUM-FNMT
	55.2	0.090	20.2	0.701	0.605	0.522	LIUM-NMT
	54.1	0.050	20.5	0.696	0.624	0.523	CU-Chimera
	53.3	0.029	16.6	0.743	0.637	0.503	online-A
8	41.9	-0.327	16.2	0.757	0.697	0.485	PJATK

Table 6: Official results for English-to-Czech primary systems and some automatic metrics as evaluated by `http://matrix.statmt.org/`. For *TER metrics, lower is better.

positive. When TectoMT is added as the fourth table, MERT can probably no longer optimize the system to benefit from it.

We selected the system combination with Neural Monkey 50 as our primary submission (Avg. BLEU 24.1), because we believed, that it would be beneficial to have more translation variants. Unfortunately, we found only later that MultEval indicates a significant difference between systems from rows 1 and 2, supporting the single-best output of Neural Monkey (Avg. BLEU 24.3).

6 Results and Discussion

Our submitted systems are shown in Table 5. Depfix (Rosa et al., 2012) was applied only for the final submission. Scores in the last column are BLEU-cased evaluation results taken from `https://matrix.statmt.org`.

It is interesting to notice that Neural Monkey trained only on synthetic dataset preformed better than Moses trained on synthetic dataset with additional in-domain data.

One point of further investigation is to find out whether the combination of Moses and Neural Monkey is better because Moses provided some useful phrases or because it merely re-ranked Neural Monkey results of beam search output.

The next point is to experiment with mixing phrase tables techniques, examining e.g. non-uniform weights.

Table 6 displays the official results of English-to-Czech translation. We see that our CU-Chimera was second in terms of BLEU (20.5) and shared the second position with limsi-factored-norm in terms of TER (0.696) but considerably lost in manual evaluation, sharing the third rank with four other systems. For us, this confirms that BLEU overvalues short sequences that our phrase-based backbone of CU-Chimera was good at.

To summarize our results, we were able to considerably improve over our setup from the last year by adding the outputs of NMT to our strong combined system. Unfortunately, we failed in implementing *neural* system combination, mainly due to technical difficulties, and our final system thus suffers from the well-known limitations of PBMT.

7 Related Work

The idea of combining phrase-based and neural systems is not novel. Our concatenative approach follows Niehues et al. (2016) who saw PBMT as a pre-processing step and added the output of PBMT to the input of NMT system, obtaining improvements over a good-performing NMT ensemble of more than 1 BLEU for two different test sets for English-German translation.

Cho et al. (2016) use a weaker approach to system combination, mixing n-best lists of several variations of NMT systems (including those that already included PBMT output)

The multi-encoder approach we describe in Section 5.2 was very recently successfully applied by Zhou et al. (2017). The main difference in the application is that we tried to use character-level encoders instead of standard sub-word units, which was clearly overly ambitious given our limited computing and time resources.

8 Conclusion

In the paper, we presented our experiments with both phrase-based and neural approaches to machine translation.

Our results document that synthetic datasets can be nearly as good as genuine in-domain parallel data.

We experimented with three different approaches to MT system combination: two neural ones and one phrase-based. Due to time and resource limitations, we were not successful with the neural approaches, although there are good reasons (and new evidence) that they were very promising.

CU-Chimera, our primary submission to the WMT17 News Translation Task ends up being a phrase-based backbone which includes neural and deep-syntactic candidate translations.

Acknowledgments

This work has been in part supported by the European Union's Horizon 2020 research and innovation programme under grant agreements No 644402 (HimL) and 645452 (QT21), by the LINDAT/CLARIN project of the Ministry of Education, Youth and Sports of the Czech Republic (projects LM2015071 and OP VVV VI CZ.02.1.01/0.0/0.0/16_013/0001781), by the Charles University Research Programme "Progres" Q18+Q48, by the Charles University SVV project number 260 453 and by the grant GAUK 8502/2016.

References

Amittai Axelrod, Xiaodong He, and Jianfeng Gao. 2011. Domain Adaptation via Pseudo In-Domain Data Selection. In *Proceedings of the 2011 Conference on Empirical Methods in Natural Language Processing*.

Dzmitry Bahdanau, Kyunghyun Cho, and Yoshua Bengio. 2015. Neural Machine Translation by Jointly Learning to Align and Translate. In *Proceedings of the Third International Conference on Learning Representations (ICLR 2015)*. http://arxiv.org/abs/1409.0473.

Ondřej Bojar, Ondřej Dušek, Tom Kocmi, Jindřich Libovický, Michal Novák, Martin Popel, Roman Sudarikov, and Dušan Variš. 2016. Czeng 1.6: enlarged Czech-English parallel corpus with processing tools dockered. In *International Conference on Text, Speech, and Dialogue*. Springer, pages 231–238.

Eunah Cho, Jan Niehues, Thanh-Le Ha, Matthias Sperber, Mohammed Mediani, and Alex Waibel. 2016. Adaptation and Combination of NMT Systems: The KIT Translation Systems for IWSLT 2016. In *Proceedings of the 13th International Workshop on Spoken Language Translation (IWSLT 2016)-To be appeared*.

Jonathan H Clark, Chris Dyer, Alon Lavie, and Noah A Smith. 2011. Better hypothesis testing for statistical machine translation: Controlling for optimizer instability. In *Proceedings of the 49th Annual Meeting of the Association for Computational Linguistics: Human Language Technologies: short papers-Volume 2*. Association for Computational Linguistics, pages 176–181.

Nadir Durrani, Alexander M Fraser, Helmut Schmid, Hieu Hoang, and Philipp Koehn. 2013. Can markov models over minimal translation units help phrase-based smt? In *ACL (2)*. pages 399–405.

Orhan Firat and Kyunghyun Cho. 2016. Conditional Gated Recurrent Unit with Attention Mechanism. https://github.com/nyu-dl/dl4mt-tutorial/blob/master/docs/cgru.pdf. Published online, version `adbaeea`.

Jindřich Helcl and Jindřich Libovický. 2017. Neural Monkey: An Open-source Tool for Sequence Learning. *The Prague Bulletin of Mathematical Linguistics* 107:5–17. https://doi.org/10.1515/pralin-2017-0001.

Marcin Junczys-Dowmunt, Tomasz Dwojak, and Hieu Hoang. 2016. Is Neural Machine Translation Ready for Deployment? A Case Study on 30 Translation Directions. In *Proceedings of the 9th International Workshop on Spoken Language Translation (IWSLT)*. Seattle, WA.

Philipp Koehn, Hieu Hoang, Alexandra Birch, Chris Callison-Burch, Marcello Federico, Nicola Bertoldi, Brooke Cowan, Wade Shen, Christine Moran, Richard Zens, et al. 2007. Moses: Open source toolkit for statistical machine translation. In *Proceedings of the 45th annual meeting of the ACL on interactive poster and demonstration sessions*. Association for Computational Linguistics, pages 177–180.

Jason Lee, Kyunghyun Cho, and Thomas Hofmann. 2016. Fully Character-Level Neural Machine Translation without Explicit Segmentation. *CoRR* abs/1610.03017. http://arxiv.org/abs/1610.03017.

Jindřich Libovický and Jindřich Helcl. 2017. Attention Strategies for Multi-Source Sequence-to-Sequence Learning pages 196–202. http://aclweb.org/anthology/P17-2031.

Jindřich Libovický, Jindřich Helcl, Marek Tlustý, Ondřej Bojar, and Pavel Pecina. 2016. CUNI System for WMT16 Automatic Post-Editing and Multimodal Translation Tasks pages 646–654. http://www.aclweb.org/anthology/W16-2361.

Jan Niehues, Eunah Cho, Thanh-Le Ha, and Alex Waibel. 2016. Pre-Translation for Neural Machine Translation pages 1828–1836. http://aclweb.org/anthology/C/C16/C16-1172.pdf.

Franz Josef Och. 2003. Minimum error rate training in statistical machine translation. In *Proceedings of the 41st Annual Meeting on Association for Computational Linguistics-Volume 1*. Association for Computational Linguistics, pages 160–167.

Rudolf Rosa, David Mareček, and Ondřej Dušek. 2012. DEPFIX: A system for automatic correction of Czech MT outputs. In *Proceedings of the Seventh Workshop on Statistical Machine Translation*. Association for Computational Linguistics, pages 362–368.

Anthony Rousseau. 2013. Xenc: An open-source tool for data selection in natural language processing. *The Prague Bulletin of Mathematical Linguistics* 100:73–82.

Rico Sennrich, Orhan Firat, Kyunghyun Cho, Alexandra Birch, Barry Haddow, Julian Hitschler, Marcin Junczys-Dowmunt, Samuel Läubli, Antonio Valerio Miceli Barone, Jozef Mokry, and Maria Nadejde. 2017. Nematus: a Toolkit for Neural Machine Translation. In *Proceedings of the Software Demonstrations of the 15th Conference of the European Chapter of the Association for Computational Linguistics*. Association for Computational Linguistics, Valencia, Spain, pages 65–68. http://aclweb.org/anthology/E17-3017.

Rico Sennrich, Barry Haddow, and Alexandra Birch. 2016a. Edinburgh Neural Machine Translation Systems for WMT 16. In *Proceedings of the First Conference on Machine Translation*. Association for Computational Linguistics, Berlin, Germany, pages 646–654. http://www.anthology.aclweb.org/W/W16/W16-2361.pdf.

Rico Sennrich, Barry Haddow, and Alexandra Birch. 2016b. Neural Machine Translation of Rare Words with Subword Units. In *Proceedings of the 54th Annual Meeting of the Association for Computational Linguistics (Volume 1: Long Papers)*. Association for Computational Linguistics, Berlin, Germany, pages 1715–1725. http://www.aclweb.org/anthology/P16-1162.

Andreas Stolcke. 2002. SRILM – An Extensible Language Modeling Toolkit. In *Proc. Intl. Conf. on Spoken Language Processing*. volume 2, pages 901–904.

Jana Straková, Milan Straka, and Jan Hajič. 2014. Open-Source Tools for Morphology, Lemmatization, POS Tagging and Named Entity Recognition. In *ACL (System Demonstrations)*. pages 13–18.

Aleš Tamchyna, Roman Sudarikov, Ondřej Bojar, and Alexander Fraser. 2016. CUNI-LMU submissions in WMT2016: Chimera constrained and beaten. In *Proceedings of the First Conference on Machine Translation, Berlin, Germany. Association for Computational Linguistics*.

Zhaopeng Tu, Yang Liu, Lifeng Shang, and Xiaohua LiuAAAI 2017nd Hang Li. 2017. Neural Machine Translation with Reconstruction. In Satinder P. Singh and Shaul Markovitch, editors, *Proceedings of the Thirty-First AAAI Conference on Artificial Intelligence, February 4-9, 2017, San Francisco, California, USA.*. AAAI Press, pages 3097–3103.

Zdeněk Žabokrtský, Jan Ptáček, and Petr Pajas. 2008. TectoMT: Highly modular MT system with tectogrammatics used as transfer layer. In *Proceedings of the Third Workshop on Statistical Machine Translation*. Association for Computational Linguistics, pages 167–170.

Long Zhou, Wenpeng Hu, Jiajun Zhang, and Chengqing Zong. 2017. Neural System Combination for Machine Translation. In *Proceedings of the 55th Annual Meeting of the Association for Computational Linguistics (Volume 2: Short Papers)* . Association for Computational Linguistics, pages 378–384. https://doi.org/10.18653/v1/P17-2060.

LIMSI@WMT'17

Franck Burlot and **Pooyan Safari** and **Matthieu Labeau**
Alexandre Allauzen and **François Yvon**
LIMSI, CNRS, Université Paris Saclay, 91 403 Orsay, France
`firstname.lastname@limsi.fr`

Abstract

This paper describes LIMSI's submissions
to the news shared task at WMT'17 for
English into Czech and Latvian, as well
as related experiments. This year's novelties consist in the use of a neural machine
translation system with a factored output
predicting simultaneously a lemma decorated with morphological information and
a fine-grained part-of-speech. Such a type
of system drew our attention to the specific step of reinflection, where lemmas
and parts-of-speech are transformed into
fully inflected words. Finally, we ran experiments showing an efficient strategy for
parameter initialization, as well as data filtering procedures.

1 Introduction

The contribution of LIMSI laboratory to the WMT
2017 News shared task consisted in the submission of different systems for English-to-Czech, as
well as with this year's "guest" language pair:
English-to-Latvian.

Our main focus was on translation into morphologically rich languages (MRL), a challenging
question in current state-of-the-art neural machine
translation (NMT) architectures. Indeed, the variety of target word forms in these languages requires the use of an open vocabulary. To tackle this
issue, we have experimented with a factored neural machine translation system predicting simultaneously at each timestep a normalized word and a
fine-grained part-of-speech (section 3). A normalized word (section 5.2) is a specific representation
where we removed part of the morphological content of the word, keeping only the features that are
relevant to the source language.

Such a factored architecture required a non-
trivial step consisting in reinflecting the MT predictions, i.e. transforming normalized words and
parts-of-speech into fully inflected words. To this
end, we have experimented with a character-based
language model that is used to select ambiguous word forms returned by a look-up table (section 5.5).

Further experiments show the use of an autoencoder to initialize the NMT system's encoder
(section 4.1), which enables a faster convergence
of the parameter and therefore a lower training
time.

Finally, we report experiments performed with
different data filtering procedures (section 4.2) and
their impact on translation quality.

2 Data and Preprocessing

The pre-processing of English data relies on in-
house tools (Déchelotte et al., 2008). All the
Czech data were tokenized and truecased using the
Moses toolkit (Koehn et al., 2007). PoS-tagging
was performed with Morphodita (Straková et al.,
2014). The pre-processing of Latvian was provided by TILDE.[1] Latvian PoS-tags were obtained
with the LU MII Tagger (Paikens et al., 2013). All
the data used to train our systems were provided at
WMT'17.[2]

For English-to-Czech, the parallel data used
consisted in nearly 20M sentences from a subset
of WMT data relevant to the news domain: News-
commentary, Europarl and specific categories of
the Czeng corpus (news, paraweb, EU, fiction).
Newstest-2015 was used for validation and the
systems are tested on Newstest-2016 and 2017.

All systems were also trained on synthetic parallel data (Sennrich et al., 2016a). The Czech

---

[1] `www.tilde.com`
[2] `www.statmt.org/wmt17`

Proceedings of the Conference on Machine Translation (WMT), Volume 2: Shared Task Papers, pages 257–264
Copenhagen, Denmark, September 7–11, 2017. ©2017 Association for Computational Linguistics

monolingual corpus News-2016 was backtranslated to English using the single best system provided by the University of Edinburgh from WMT'16.[3] We then added five copies of News-commentary and the news subcorpus from Czeng, as well as 5M sentences from the Czeng EU corpus randomly selected after running modified Moore-Lewis filtering with XenC (Rousseau, 2013). This resulted in about 14M parallel sentences.

The English-to-Latvian systems used all the parallel data provided at WMT'17. The DCEP corpus was filtered with the Microsoft sentence aligner[4] and using modified Moore-Lewis. We kept the best 1M sentences, which led to a total of almost 2M parallel sentences. The systems were validated on 2k sentences held out from the LETA corpus and we report results on newsdev-2017 and newstest-2017.

Training was carried on with synthetic parallel data. We used a backtranslation of the monolingual corpora News-2015 and 2016 provided by the University of Edinburgh (Moses system). To these corpora were added 10 copies of the LETA corpus, as well as 2 copies of Europarl and Rapid.

Bilingual Byte Pair Encoding (BPE) models (Sennrich et al., 2016b) for each language pair and system setup were learned on the bibtext (ie. not synthetic) parallel data used for the MT system. 90k merge operations where performed to obtain the final vocabularies.

3 System Setup

Results are reported for two NMT systems: Nematus (Sennrich et al., 2017) and NMTPY (Caglayan et al., 2017).

3.1 NMTPY

Once the data was preprocessed, only sentences of a maximum length of 50 were kept in the training data, except for the setup where cluster IDs were split in normalized words (see § 5). In this case, we set the maximum length to 100.

All NMTPY systems have an embedding dimension of 512 and hidden states of dimension 1024 for both encoder and decoder, which are implemented as GRU units. Dropout is enabled on

source embeddings, encoder states, as well as output layer. When training starts, all parameters are initialized with Xavier (Glorot and Bengio, 2010). In order to slightly speed up training on bitext parallel data, the learning rate was set to 0.0004, patience to 30 with validation every 20k updates. On synthetic data, we finally set the learning rate to 0.0001 and performed validation every 5k updates. These systems were tuned with Adam optimizer (Kingma and Ba, 2014) and have been training for approximately 1 month.

3.2 Nematus

The setup for Nematus is very similar to the one presented in the previous section. Training was performed on sentences with the same maximum length, the same embedding and hidden unit size. The difference lies in the fact that dropout for Nematus systems was enabled on all layers. The optimizer used was Adadelta (Zeiler, 2012) and all systems had their learning rate set to 0.0001.

4 Experiments

4.1 Parameter initialization

In order to speed up the convergence of the training procedure we tried to initialize the encoder parameters with an a priori-trained model, instead of using random initialization. For the English-to-Czech translation system, this initial model was trained to translate from English into English. In order to do so, the same English corpus was fed into the neural model on both source and target side. After few updates according to the BLEU score on the validation set (which was higher than 99) it was possible to stop the training of this model and use the encoder parameters for the initialization of the main NMT system.

4.2 Data Filtering

The English-Czech training data provided at WMT'17 was very large and some corpora contained a lot of noise. For instance, we noticed several duplicate sentences in the Czeng EU parallel corpus and entire paragraphs in it were in languages other than English-Czech. Therefore, we decided to experiment with a system not containing the Czeng EU corpus. However, this lead to a degradation in terms of BLEI (see Table 1).

In another attempt, instead of removing the EU corpus, a filtering process was performed to discard the duplicate sentences on both sides. As

---

[3]http://data.statmt.org/rsennrich/wmt16_systems/

[4]http://research.microsoft.com/apps/catalog/

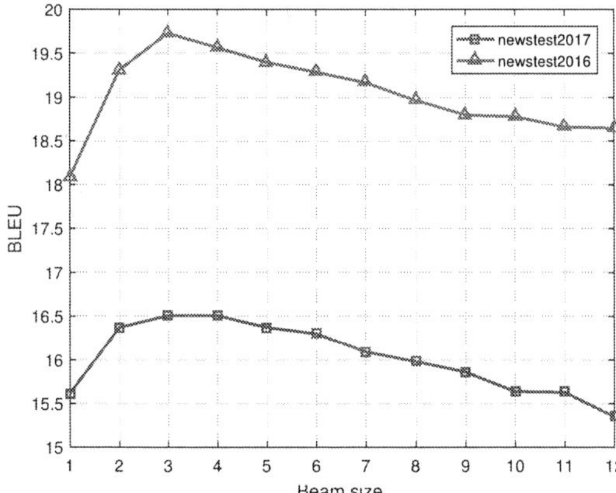

Figure 1: Comparison of different beam-size in terms of BLEU. The evaluation is performed on Newstest-2016 and Newstest-2017 English-Czech filtered data.

shown in Table 1, filtering the data results in an improvement in terms of BLEU for Newstest-2017, which is also consistent with the results we obtained on Newstest-2016 and validation set.

The filtering process was later followed by a sentence alignment check using the Microsoft sentence aligner. However, no further improvement was achieved with this method. The filtered-only data has shown the best performance on both Newstest-2016 and Newstest-2017 corpora.

Table 1: Comparison of BLEU scores of different filtering processes for English-to-Czech with Nematus systems. All the systems are evaluated with the beam search of size 2. The term "**basic**" is referred to the data without any filtering or alignment. The term **discard EU** is adopted to refer to the training without Czeng EU corpus.

data filtering	Newstest-2016	Newstest-2017
basic	18.66	15.67
discard EU	18.09	16.07
filt	**19.31**	**16.37**
filt+align	18.72	15.91

It is worthwhile to note that the model which had the best BLEU score performance on the validation data (Newstest-2015) resulted in the BLEU scores of 18.43 and 15.81 on Newstest-2016 and Newstest-2017, respectively.

Figure 1 shows the accuracy wrt. different sizes of beam during decoding. The model was trained using the English-Czech filtered data as reported in the **filt** row of the Table 1. We observed a sim-

ilar trend on both Newstest-2016 and Newstest-2017, where the best performance was obtained with a beam of size 3 for both test sets.

5 Submitted systems

5.1 Factored NMT

Additionally to standard NMTPY systems (baselines), our best submissions in terms of BLEU at WMT'17 consisted in factored NMT systems.

The architecture of such systems was introduced in (García-Martínez et al., 2016). The specific setup we have used for the following factored systems consisted in an architecture that enables training towards a dual objective: at each timestep in the output sentence, a word and a PoS-tag are produced. Each one of these objectives produces a cost, that is summed in order to compute the gradients to be backpropagated.

The encoder and attention mechanism remain the same as in the baseline architecture. While in the baseline a decoder state takes as input the embedding of the prediction made at the previous step, a factored NMT decoder unit takes as input a concatenation of the two previous predictions for each factor. In this situation, the factored NMT systems deal with two sets of embeddings on target side.

Another difference lies in the hidden-to-output layer. In our setup, we have used an architecture with two different such layers: the first one takes as input the representation of the previous prediction of the first factor (word) and the second one takes the previous second factor prediction (PoS). Each layer is then passed through a last feed-forward layer leading to distinct softmax layers.

While various word representations (Burlot et al., 2017) can be used in the first factor, our system predict at each timestep on the target side a normalized word and a PoS-tag.

	fully infl.	norm. words
plain	kočky	kočka+Noun+7
subword	ko- čky	ko- čka- Noun+7

Table 2: Different representations of the Czech word *kočky* (cats).

5.2 Normalization of Target Morphology

Both Czech and Latvian are morphologically rich languages, as opposed to the English source. Such

	Newstest-2016			Newstest-2017		
	BLEU ↑	BEER ↑	CTER ↓	BLEU ↑	BEER ↑	CTER ↓
baseline	24.24	57.41	52.81	19.89	54.51	58.29
factored	23.77	57.50	52.53	19.95	54.71	58.30
+ nk-best	**24.59**	**57.95**	**52.08**	**20.54**	**54.99**	**58.06**

Table 3: Scores for English-to-Czech systems

	Newsdev-2017			Newstest-2017		
	BLEU ↑	BEER ↑	CTER ↓	BLEU ↑	BEER ↑	CTER ↓
baseline	22.48	57.69	52.83	14.86	52.00	62.57
+ n-best	23.11	58.13	52.21	15.22	52.37	62.08
factored	21.33	57.11	53.56	15.10	52.19	62.52
+ nk-best	**24.19**	**58.72**	**51.89**	**16.30**	**53.18**	**61.11**

Table 4: Scores for English-to-Latvian systems

differences between the source and target languages leads to difficulties. Indeed, an English adjective, that is invariable, may be translated into multiple different word forms corresponding to the same lemma. Such a variety of forms on the target side leads to serious sparsity issues and makes the estimate of reliable translation probabilities hard.

To address this issue, both Czech and Latvian vocabularies have been normalized. The normalization of a MRL consists in selecting the morphosyntactic information that should remain encoded in a word. This selection is motivated by the fact that a target word contains more specificities than its source-side counterpart(s), leading to a lack of symmetry between both languages. For instance, when translating from English into Czech, target nouns mark grammatical case, which is removed in (Burlot et al., 2016) in order to make Czech nouns look more like their English translation(s).

Such a normalization is usually performed using hand-crafted rules and requires expert knowledge for each language pair. In this paper, normalized words are obtained with an automatic and data-driven method[5] introduced in (Burlot and Yvon, 2017a).

In a nutshell, it performs a clustering of the morphologically rich language by grouping together words that tend to share the same translation(s) in English. In order to measure this translation similarity and using word alignments, the conditional entropy of the translation probability distribution over the English vocabulary is computed for each word form. The model merges two words whenever the resulting aggregate cluster does not lead to an increase of conditional entropy, which guaranties a minimal loss of information during the clustering procedure.

The normalization model is delexicalized and operates at the level of PoS. Each word is represented as a lemma, a coarse PoS and a sequence of morphological tags (e.g. *kočka+Noun+Sing+Accusative*), therefore a merge consists in grouping into one cluster two different tag sequences. As a result of this procedure, we obtain words represented as a lemma and a cluster identificator (ID), i.e. a coarse PoS and an arbitrary integer, like *kočka+Noun+7* in Table 2. In this example, the cluster ID *Noun+7* stands for a set of fine-grained PoS, like { *Sing+Nominative, Sing+Accusative, ...* }.

In our setup, the cluster ID was systematically split from the lemma. BPE segmentation was thus learned and applied to lemmas. Whenever the factored NMT system predicts a lemma in the first factor, it is forced to predict a null PoS in the second factor. On the other hand, when a split cluster ID is predicted, the second factor should output an actual PoS. This specific treatment of the second factor is expected to give the system a better ability to map a word to a PoS that is relevant to it, thus avoiding, for instance, the prediction of a verbal PoS for the Czech noun *kočka* (cat).

The normalization of the Czech data was trained on the bibtext parallel data used to train the MT systems (see § 2), except Czeng fiction and paraweb subcorpora, which lead to over 10M sentences. As for the normalization of Latvian data it was trained on the same bitext parallel sentences used to train the MT systems.

5.3 Reinflection

The factored systems predict at each time step a normalized word and a PoS-tag, which requires a non-trivial additional step producing sentences in

---

[5]The source code is available at `github.com/franckbrl/bilingual_morph_normalizer`

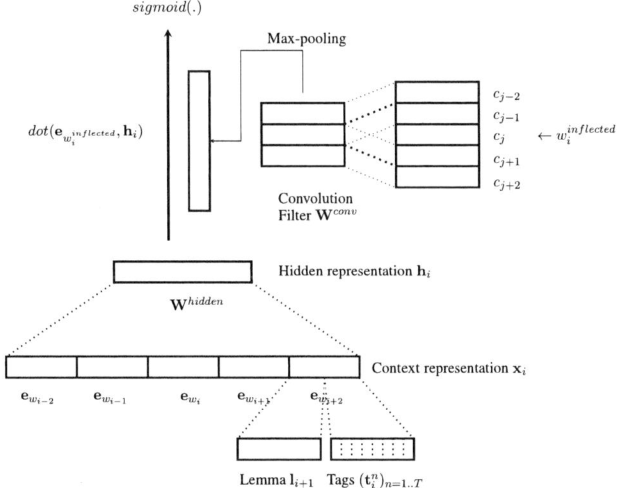

Figure 2: Architecture of the neural reinflection model

a fully inflected language. We refer to this last step as reinflection.

Given a lexical unit and a PoS-tag, word forms are retrieved with a dictionary lookup. In the context of MRL, deterministic mappings from a lemma and a PoS to a form are very rare. Instead, the dictionary often proposes several word forms corresponding to the same lexical unit and morphological analysis.

A first way to address this ambiguity is to simply compute unigram frequencies of each word form, which was done over all the monolingual data available at WMT'17 for both Czech and Latvian. During a dictionary lookup, ambiguities can then be solved by taking the most frequent word form. The downside of this procedure is that it ignores important information given by the target monolingual context. For instance, the Czech preposition *s* (with) will have different forms according to the right-side context: *s tebou* (with you), but *se mnou* (with me). A solution is to let a word-based system select the right word form from the dictionary. To this end, k-best hypothesis from the dictionary are generated. Given a sentence containing lemmas and PoS, we perform a beam search going through each word and keeping at each step the k-best reinflection hypothesis according to the unigram model mentioned above.

For Czech word form generation, we used the Morphodita generator (Straková et al., 2014). Since we had no such tool for Latvian, all monolingual data available at WMT'17 were automat-

ically tagged using the LU MII Tagger (Paikens et al., 2013) and we gathered the result in a dictionary. As one could expect, we obtained a large quantity of word forms (nearly 2.5M), among which a lot of noise was noticed.

5.4 Experimental Results

The systems we have submitted at WMT'17 are more specifically the following:

- English-to-Czech baseline: Ensemble of 5 best models.

- English-to-Czech factored: Ensemble of 2 best models with nk-best rescoring using the single best baseline.

- English-to-Latvian baseline: Ensemble of 3 best models with n-best rescoring using the single best Nematus system.

- English-to-Latvian factored: Ensemble of 3 best models with nk-best rescoring using the single best Nematus system.

The results are reported for these systems in tables 3 and 4, using BLEU, as well as BEER (Stanojević and Sima'an, 2014) and CharacTER (Wang et al., 2016), which have shown a high correlation with human rankings for MRL (Bojar et al., 2016).

As mentioned in Section 5.3, k-best hypothesis from factored systems are rescored using a fully inflected word-based system. For Czech, we set

	Newstest-2016			Newstest-2017		
	BLEU ↑	BEER ↑	CTER ↓	BLEU ↑	BEER ↑	CTER ↓
unigrams	24.24	57.41	52.81	19.89	54.51	58.29
+ n-best	24.47	57.91	52.16	20.53	54.99	58.05
neural	21.10	56.35	53.35	17.60	53.47	59.34
+ n-best	21.52	56.36	53.52	18.12	53.64	59.21

Table 5: Scores for different English-to-Czech reinflection methods.

	Newsdev-2017			Newstest-2017		
	BLEU ↑	BEER ↑	CTER ↓	BLEU ↑	BEER ↑	CTER ↓
unigrams	22.48	57.69	52.83	14.86	52.00	62.57
+ n-best	22.06	57.58	52.92	15.34	52.52	61.98
neural	17.48	55.38	54.82	12.39	50.75	63.85
+ n-best	17.96	55.69	54.43	12.64	50.89	63.62

Table 6: Scores for different English-to-Latvian reinflection methods.

k to 10. For Latvian, the $k = 100$ best hypothesis were taken from the dictionary, in order to mitigate the poor quality of this dictionary by relying more on the rescoring system. Additionally to the k-best hypothesis from the dictionary, we also took the n-best hypothesis from the factored NMT system ($n = 30$), which lead to the rescoring of nk-best hypothesis by an inflected word based system.

The improvement given by the nk-best setups show the advantage of using a word based model to select the right word forms instead of relying on simple unigram frequencies.

5.5 Reinflection Experiments

To address the disadvantages of the reinflection methods presented in section 5.3, we investigated a neural reinflection model. The general architecture is presented in figure 2. The model first takes as input a n-gram centered on the position to reinflect. To each position corresponds a lexical unit and T PoS-tags, which are represented by embeddings l_i and $(t_i^n)_{n=1..T}$. These are concatenated into a context representation x_i and transformed into a hidden representation $h_i = W^{hidden} x_i + b$.

The second input is a candidate inflected form $w_i^{inflected}$. We represent it as the sequence of its characters, and use a convolutional layer (Santos and Zadrozny, 2014) to build its vectorial representation $e_{w_i^{inflected}}$. The product of these two representations goes through a *sigmoid* activation function. We train the model in a supervised way, by feeding positive and negative examples of inflected forms, with labels 1 and 0. At test time, the model is given all possible inflected forms obtained in the dictionary, and we choose the one obtaining the best score.

However, our first results show accuracies under the performances of the unigram model presented in section 5.3, for both Czech and Latvian (see Tables 5 and 6). In future work, we plan to use such a model with a beam search.

6 Morphology prediction quality

In this section, we attempt to evaluate the improvement of our factored NMT systems over the baselines. To this end, we ran the evaluation introduced in (Burlot and Yvon, 2017b) over all our WMT submissions.

The evaluation of the morphological competence of a machine translation system is performed on an automatically produced test suite. For each source test sentence from a monolingual corpus (the *base*), one (or several) *variant(s)* are generated, containing exactly one difference with the base, focusing on a specific *target* lexeme of the base. These variants differ on a feature that is expressed morphologically in the target, such as the person, number or tense of a verb; or the number or case of a noun or an adjective. This artificial test set is then translated with a machine translation system. The machine translation system is deemed correct if the translations of the base and variant differ in the same way as their respective source. Another setup focuses on a word in the *base* sentence and produces *variants* containing antonyms and synonyms of this word. The expected translation is then synonyms and antonyms bearing the same morphological features as the initial word.

There are three types of contrasts implying different sorts of evaluation:

- A: We check whether the morphological feature inserted in the source sentence has been translated (eg. plural number of a noun). Ac-

	verbs			pronouns		others		mean
System	past	future	neg.	fem.	plur.	noun nb.	compar.	
NMT baseline	92.6%	86.2%	96.0%	91.4%	79.2%	94.6%	76.2%	88.0%
Factored NMT	94.2%	88.0%	95.4%	91.2%	80.0%	96.2%	75.0%	88.6%

Table 7: Sentence pair evaluation for English-to-Czech (A-set).

	coordinated verbs			coord.n	pronouns to nouns			prep.	mean
System	number	person	tense	case	gender	number	case	case	
NMT baseline	76.6%	77.0%	69.2%	90.4%	90.8%	92.6%	92.2%	95.3%	85.5%
Factored NMT	77.6%	77.4%	70.6%	89.0%	91.4%	90.8%	91.6%	96.1%	85.6%

Table 8: Sentence pair evaluation for English-to-Czech (B-set).

	nouns	adjectives			verbs				mean
System	case	gender	number	case	number	person	tense	negation	
NMT baseline	.205	.303	.262	.301	.138	.068	.082	.054	.177
Factored NMT	.197	.287	.255	.292	.110	.062	.081	.056	.168

Table 9: Sentence group evaluation for English-to-Czech with Entropy (C-set).

	verbs		pronouns		nouns	mean
System	past	future	fem.	plur.	number	
NMT baseline	68.8%	84.6%	64.2%	86.8%	73.0%	75.5%
Factored NMT	69.6%	82.8%	62.0%	89.0%	70.6%	74.8%

Table 10: Sentence pair evaluation for English-to-Latvian (A-set).

	coordinated verbs			coord.n	pronouns to nouns			prep.	mean
System	number	person	tense	case	gender	number	case	case	
NMT baseline	69.2%	57.6%	70.4%	41.8%	40.0%	40.8%	35.8%	54.6%	51.3%
Factored NMT	72.4%	63.4%	73.2%	34.8%	43.0%	42.2%	41.4%	55.5%	53.2%

Table 11: Sentence pair evaluation for English-to-Latvian (B-set).

	nouns	adjectives			verbs			mean
System	case	gender	number	case	number	person	tense	
NMT baseline	.255	.616	.610	.644	.139	.221	.134	.374
Factored NMT	.233	.587	.582	.612	.117	.182	.113	.346

Table 12: Sentence group evaluation for English-to-Latvian with Entropy (C-set).

curacy for all morphological features is averaged over all sentences. (Tables 7 and 10)

- B: We focus on various agreement phenomena by checking whether a given morphological feature is present in both words that need to agree (eg. case of two nouns). Accuracy is computed here as well. (Tables 8 and 11)

- C: We test the consistency of morphological choices over lexical variation (eg. synonyms and antonyms all having the same tense) and measure the success based on the average normalized entropy of morphological features in the set of target sentences. (Tables 9 and 12)

The A-set focuses on the morphological adequacy of the output towards the source sentence, which does not seem to have improved with factored NMT systems. The main improvement is related to the morphological fluency of the output (B and C-sets), although the contrasts are more visible for Latvian than for Czech.

7 Conclusions

This paper described LIMSI's submissions to the News shared task at WMT2017, consisting in English-to-Czech and English-to-Latvian systems that address the issues of translating into a morphologically rich language. Further experiments reported the benefits obtained with an efficient parameter initialization procedure, as well as data filtering.

Acknowledgments

This work has been partly funded by the European Union's Horizon 2020 research and innovation programme under grant agreement No. 645452 (QT21).

References

Ondřej Bojar, Yvette Graham, Amir Kamran, and Miloš Stanojević. 2016. Results of the wmt16 metrics shared task. In *Proc. WMT*. Berlin, Germany, pages 199–231.

Franck Burlot, Mercedes García-Martínez, Loïc Barrault, Fethi Bougares, and François Yvon. 2017. Word Representations in Factored Neural Machine Translation. In *Proceedings of the Second Conference on Machine Translation (WMT'17)*. Association for Computational Linguistics, Copenhagen, Denmark.

Franck Burlot, Elena Knyazeva, Thomas Lavergne, and François Yvon. 2016. Two-step mt: Predicting target morphology. In *Proc. IWSLT*. Seattle, USA.

Franck Burlot and François Yvon. 2017a. Learning morphological normalization for translation from and into morphologically rich language. *The Prague Bulletin of Mathematical Linguistics (Proc. EAMT)* (108):49–60.

Franck Burlot and François Yvon. 2017b. Evaluating the morphological competence of machine translation systems. In *Proceedings of the Second Conference on Machine Translation (WMT'17)*. Association for Computational Linguistics, Copenhagen, Denmark.

Ozan Caglayan, Mercedes García-Martínez, Adrien Bardet, Walid Aransa, Fethi Bougares, and Loïc Barrault. 2017. Nmtpy: A flexible toolkit for advanced neural machine translation systems. *arXiv preprint arXiv:1706.00457* .

Daniel Déchelotte, Gilles Adda, Alexandre Allauzen, Olivier Galibert, Jean-Luc Gauvain, Hélène Maynard, and François Yvon. 2008. LIMSI's statistical translation systems for WMT'08. In *Proceedings of NAACL-HLT Statistical Machine Translation Workshop*. Columbus, Ohio.

Mercedes García-Martínez, Loïc Barrault, and Fethi Bougares. 2016. Factored neural machine translation architectures. In *Proceedings of the International Workshop on Spoken Language Translation*. Seattle, USA, IWSLT'16.

Xavier Glorot and Yoshua Bengio. 2010. Understanding the difficulty of training deep feedforward neural networks. In *Proceedings of the International Conference on Artificial Intelligence and Statistics (AISTATS'10). Society for Artificial Intelligence and Statistics*.

Diederik Kingma and Jimmy Ba. 2014. Adam: A method for stochastic optimization. *arXiv preprint arXiv:1412.6980* .

Philipp Koehn, Hieu Hoang, Alexandra Birch, Chris Callison-Burch, Marcello Federico, Nicola Bertoldi, Brooke Cowan, Wade Shen, Christine Moran,

Richard Zens, Chris Dyer, Ondřej Bojar, Alexandra Constantin, and Evan Herbst. 2007. Moses: Open source toolkit for statistical MT. In *Proc. ACL:Systems Demos*. Prague, Czech Republic, pages 177–180.

Peteris Paikens, Laura Rituma, and Lauma Pretkalnina. 2013. Morphological analysis with limited resources: Latvian example. In *Proc. NODALIDA*. pages 267–277.

Anthony Rousseau. 2013. XenC: An open-source tool for data selection in natural language processing. *The Prague Bulletin of Mathematical Linguistics* (100):73–82.

Cicero D. Santos and Bianca Zadrozny. 2014. Learning character-level representations for part-of-speech tagging. In Tony Jebara and Eric P. Xing, editors, *Proceedings of the 31st International Conference on Machine Learning (ICML-14)*. JMLR Workshop and Conference Proceedings, pages 1818–1826.

Rico Sennrich, Orhan Firat, Kyunghyun Cho, Alexandra Birch, Barry Haddow, Julian Hitschler, Marcin Junczys-Dowmunt, Samuel Läubli, Antonio Valerio Miceli Barone, Jozef Mokry, and Maria Nadejde. 2017. Nematus: a toolkit for neural machine translation. In *Proceedings of the Software Demonstrations of the 15th Conference of the European Chapter of the Association for Computational Linguistics*. Association for Computational Linguistics, Valencia, Spain, pages 65–68.

Rico Sennrich, Barry Haddow, and Alexandra Birch. 2016a. Improving neural machine translation models with monolingual data. In *Proc. ACL*.

Rico Sennrich, Barry Haddow, and Alexandra Birch. 2016b. Neural machine translation of rare words with subword units. In *Proceedings of the 54th Annual Meeting of the Association for Computational Linguistics (Volume 1: Long Papers)*. Association for Computational Linguistics, pages 1715–1725.

Miloš Stanojević and Khalil Sima'an. 2014. Fitting sentence level translation evaluation with many dense features. In *Proc. EMNLP*. Doha, Qatar, pages 202–206.

Jana Straková, Milan Straka, and Jan Hajič. 2014. Open-Source Tools for Morphology, Lemmatization, POS Tagging and Named Entity Recognition. In *Proc. ACL: System Demos*. Baltimore, MA, pages 13–18.

Weiyue Wang, Jan-Thorsten Peter, Hendrik Rosendahl, and Hermann Ney. 2016. CharacTer: Translation Edit Rate on Character Level. In *Proc. WMT*. Berlin, Germany, pages 505–510.

Matthew D. Zeiler. 2012. Adadelta: An adaptive learning rate method. *CoRR* abs/1212.5701.

SYSTRAN Purely Neural MT Engines for WMT2017

Yongchao Deng, Jungi Kim, Guillaume Klein, Catherine Kobus, Natalia Segal,
Christophe Servan, Bo Wang, Dakun Zhang, Josep Crego, Jean Senellart

firstname.lastname@systrangroup.com
SYSTRAN / 5 rue Feydeau, 75002 Paris, France

Abstract

This paper describes SYSTRAN's systems submitted to the WMT 2017 shared news translation task for English-German, in both translation directions. Our systems are built using OpenNMT[1], an open-source neural machine translation system, implementing sequence-to-sequence models with LSTM encoder/decoders and attention. We experimented using monolingual data automatically back-translated. Our resulting models are further hyper-specialised with an adaptation technique that finely tunes models according to the evaluation test sentences.

1 Introduction

We participated in the WMT 2017 shared news translation task on two different translation directions: English→German and German→English.

The paper is structured as follows: Section 2 overviews our neural MT engine. Section 3 describes the set of experiments carried out to build the English→German and German→English neural translation models. Experiments and results are detailed in Section 3. Finally, conclusions are drawn in Section 4.

2 Neural MT System

Neural machine translation (NMT) is a new methodology for machine translation that has led to remarkable improvements, particularly in terms of human evaluation, compared to rule-based and statistical machine translation (SMT) systems (Crego et al., 2016; Wu et al., 2016). NMT has now become a widely-applied technique for machine translation, as well as an effective approach

for other related NLP tasks such as dialogue, parsing, and summarisation.

Our NMT system (Klein et al., 2017) follows the architecture presented in (Bahdanau et al., 2014). It is implemented as an encoder-decoder network with multiple layers of a RNN with Long Short-Term Memory (LSTM) hidden units (Zaremba et al., 2014). Figure 1 illustrates an schematic view of the MT network.

Source words are first mapped to word vectors and then fed into a bidirectional recurrent neural network (RNN) that reads an input sequence $s = (s_1, ..., s_J)$. Upon seeing the <eos> symbol, the final time step initialises a target RNN. The decoder is a RNN that predicts a target sequence $t = (t_1, ..., t_I)$, being J and I respectively the source and target sentence lengths. Translation is finished when the decoder predicts the <eos> symbol.

The left-hand side of the figure illustrates the bidirectional encoder, which actually consists of two independent LSTM encoders: one encoding the normal sequence (solid lines) that calculates a forward sequence of hidden states $(\overrightarrow{h_1}, ..., \overrightarrow{h_J})$, the second encoder reads the input sequence in reversed order (dotted lines) and calculates the backward sequence $(\overleftarrow{h_1}, ..., \overleftarrow{h_J})$. The final encoder outputs $(\overline{h_1}, ..., \overline{h_J})$ consist of the sum of both encoders final outputs. The right-hand side of the figure illustrates the RNN decoder. Each word l_i is predicted based on a recurrent hidden state h_i and a context vector c_i that aims at capturing relevant source-side information.

Figure 2 illustrates the attention layer. It implements the "general" attentional architecture from (Luong et al., 2015). The idea of a global attentional model is to consider all the hidden states of the encoder when deriving the context vector c_t. Hence, global alignment weights a_t are derived by

---

[1] http://opennmt.net

Proceedings of the Conference on Machine Translation (WMT), Volume 2: Shared Task Papers, pages 265–270
Copenhagen, Denmark, September 7–11, 2017. ©2017 Association for Computational Linguistics

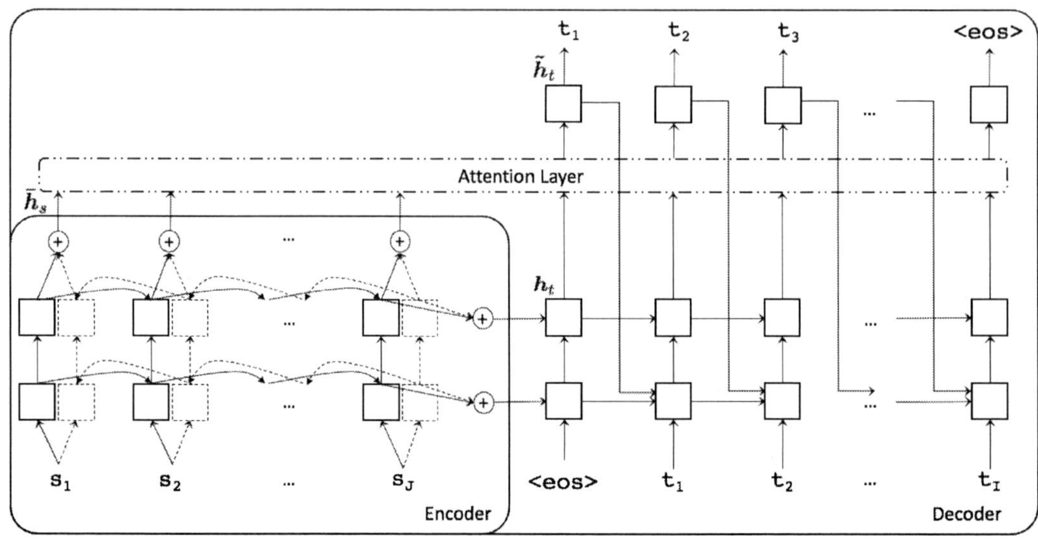

Figure 1: Schematic view of our MT network.

comparing the current target hidden state h_t with each source hidden state $\overline{h}_s$:

$$a_t(s) = \frac{exp(score(h_t, \overline{h}_s))}{\sum_{s'} exp(score(h_t, \overline{h}_{s'}))}$$

with the content-based score function:

$$score(h_t, \overline{h}_s) = h_t^T W_a \overline{h}_s$$

Given the alignment vector as weights, the context vector c_t is computed as the weighted average over all the source hidden states.

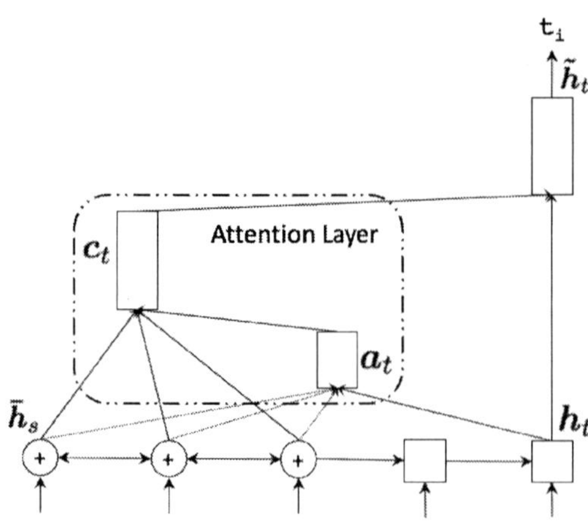

Figure 2: Attention layer of the MT network.

Note that for the sake of simplicity figure 1 illustrates a two-layers LSTM encoder/decoder while any arbitrary number of LSTM layers can be stacked. More details about our system can be found in (Crego et al., 2016).

3   Experiments

In this section we detail the corpora and training experiments used to build our English↔German neural translation models.

3.1   Corpora

We used the parallel corpora made available for the shared task: *Europarl v7*, *Common Crawl corpus*, *News Commentary v12* and *Rapid corpus of EU press releases*. Both English and German texts were preprocessed with standard tokenisation tools. German words were further preprocessed to split compounds, following a similar algorithm as the built-in for Moses. Additional monolingual data was also used for both German and English available for the shared task: *News Crawl: articles from 2016*. Basic statistics of the tokenised data are available in Table 1.

We used a byte pair encoding technique[2] (BPE) to segment word forms and achieve open-vocabulary translation with a fixed vocabulary of $30,000$ source and target tokens. BPE was originally devised as a compression algorithm, adapted to word segmentation (Sennrich et al., 2016b). It recursively replaces frequent consecutive bytes with a symbol that does not occur elsewhere. Each

---

[2]https://github.com/rsennrich/subword-nmt

	#sents	#words	vocab.	L_{mean}
Parallel				
En	4.6M	103.7M	627k	22.6
De	4.6M	104.5M	836k	22.8
Monolingual				
En	20,6M	463,6M	1.18M	22.5
De	34,7M	620,8M	3.36M	17.8

Table 1: *English-German parallel and monolingual corpus statistics. L_{mean} indicates mean sentence lengths. M stand for millions, k for thousands.*

such replacement is called a merge, and the number of merges is a tuneable parameter. Encodings were computed over the union of both German and English training corpora after preprocessing, aiming at improving consistency between source and target segmentations.

Finally, case information was considered by the network as an additional feature. It allowed us to work with a lowercased vocabulary and treat recasing as a separate problem (Crego et al., 2016).

3.2 Training Details

All experiments employ the NMT system detailed in Section 2. The encoder and the decoder consist of a four-layer stacked LSTM with $1,000$ cells each. We use a bidirectional RNN encoder. Size of word embedding is 500 cells. We use stochastic gradient descent, a minibatch size of 64 sentences and 0.3 for dropout probability. Maximum sentence length is set to 80 tokens. All experiments are performed on NVidia GeForce GTX 1080 on a single GPU per optimisation work. Newstest2008 (2008) is employed as validation test set and newstest from 2009 to 2016 (2009-16) as internal test sets.

3.2.1 Training on parallel data

Table 2 outlines training work. All parallel data (**P**) is used on each training epoch. Row LR indicates the learning rate value used for each epoch. Note that learning rate was initially set to 1.0 during several epochs until no or little perplexity (PPL) reduction is measured on the validation set. Afterwards, additional epochs are performed with learning rate decayed by 0.7 at each epoch. BLEU score (averaged over the eight internal test sets) after each training epoch is also shown. Note that all BLEU scores shown in this paper are computed

using `multi-bleu.perl`[3]. Training time per epoch is also shown in row Time measured in number of hours.

As expected, a perplexity reduction is observed for the initial epochs, until epochs 9 (German→English) and 8 (English→German) where little or no improvement is observed. The decay mode is then started allowing to further boost accuracy (between 1.5 and 2.0 BLEU points) after 5 additional epochs.

3.2.2 Training on parallel and synthetic data

Following (Sennrich et al., 2016a), we selected a subset of the available target-side in-domain monolingual corpora, translate it into the source side (back-translate) of the respective language pair, and then use this synthetic parallel data for training. The best performing models for each translation direction (epoch 13 on Table 2 of both translation directions) were used to back-translate monolingual data. (Sennrich et al., 2016a) motivate the use of monolingual data with domain adaptation, reducing overfitting, and better modelling of fluency.

Synthetic corpus was then divided into i different splits containing each 4.5 million sentence pairs (except for the last split that contains less sentences). Table 3 shows continuation of the training work using at each epoch the union of the entire parallel data together with a split of the monolingual back-translated data (**P+M**$_i$). Hence, balancing the amount of reference and synthetic data, summing up to around 9 million sentence pairs per epoch. Note that training work described in Table 3 is built as continuation of the model at epoch 13 on Table 2. Table 3 shows also BLEU scores over newstest2017 for the best performing network.

As for the experiments detailed in Table 2, once all splits of the synthetic corpus were used to train our models with learning rate always set to 1.0 (5 epochs for German→English and 8 epochs for English→German), we began a decay mode. In this case, we decided to reduce the amount of training examples from 9 to 5 millions due to time restrictions. To select the training data we employed the algorithm detailed in (Moore and Lewis, 2010). It aims at identifying sentences in a generic corpus that are closer to domain-

---

[3] `https://github.com/moses-smt/ mosesdecoder/blob/master/scripts/ generic/multi-bleu.perl`

Epoch	1	2	3	4	5	6	7	8	9	10	11	12	13
German→English													
Data	P	P	P	P	P	P	P	P	P	P	P	P	P
Time (hours)	24	24	24	24	24	24	24	24	24	24	24	24	24
LR	1.0	1.0	1.0	1.0	1.0	1.0	1.0	1.0	1.0	0.7^1	0.7^2	0.7^3	0.7^4
PPL (2008)	20.90	17.01	15.38	14.67	14.18	13.75	13.57	13.29	13.00	12.47	12.05	11.49	11.40
BLEU (2009-16)	20.07	22.06	23.02	24.17	24.59	24.40	24.99	25.11	25.42	25.65	26.14	26.48	26.87
English→German													
Data	P	P	P	P	P	P	P	P	P	P	P	P	P
Time (hours)	24	24	24	24	24	24	24	24	24	24	24	24	24
LR	1.0	1.0	1.0	1.0	1.0	1.0	1.0	1.0	0.7^1	0.7^2	0.7^3	0.7^4	0.7^5
PPL (2008)	20.85	16.52	14.84	13.89	13.62	13.13	12.59	12.66	11.72	11.20	10.94	10.75	10.55
BLEU (2009-16)	15.63	17.41	18.85	19.61	19.92	20.38	20.34	20.55	21.13	21.63	21.70	22.22	22.50

Table 2: *Training on parallel data.*

Epoch	1	2	3	4	5	6	7	8	9	10	11	12	13
German→English													
Data	$P+M_1$	$P+M_2$	$P+M_3$	$P+M_4$	$P+M_5$	P'+M'	P'+M'	P'+M'	P'+M'	P'+M'			
Time (hours)	45	45	45	45	32	25	25	25	25	25			
LR	1.0	1.0	1.0	1.0	1.0	0.7^1	0.7^2	0.7^3	0.7^4	0.7^5			
PPL (2008)	13.33	13.23	13.26	1347	12.63	12.25	11.87	11.60	11.40	11.33			
BLEU (2009-16)	26.85	27.37	27.37	27.01	27.77	27.91	28.34	28.54	28.75	28.73			
BLEU (2017)										32.35			
English→German													
Data	$P+M_1$	$P+M_2$	$P+M_3$	$P+M_4$	$P+M_5$	$P+M_6$	$P+M_7$	$P+M_8$	P'+M'	P'+M'	P'+M'	P'+M'	P'+M'
Time (hours)	46	46	46	46	46	46	46	40	25	25	25	25	25
LR	1.0	1.0	1.0	1.0	1.0	1.0	1.0	1.0	0.7^1	0.7^2	0.7^3	0.7^4	0.7^5
PPL (2008)	12.87	12.91	12.38	12.23	12.19	12.00	12.26	11.65	11.51	11.19	10.80	10.70	10.58
BLEU (2009-16)	21.81	22.26	22.52	22.65	22.59	22.75	22.79	22.93	23.35	23.56	23.79	23.96	24.07
BLEU (2017)													26.41

Table 3: *Training on parallel and synthetic data.*

specific data. Figure 3 outlines the algorithm. In our experiments, parallel and monolingual back-translated corpus are considered as the generic corpora (**P+M**) while all available newstest test sets, from 2009 to 2017, are considered as the domain-specific data (**T**). Hence, we aim at selecting from **P+M** the closest 5 million sentences to the newstest2009-17 data (2.5 from the **P** and 2.5 from the **M** subsets).

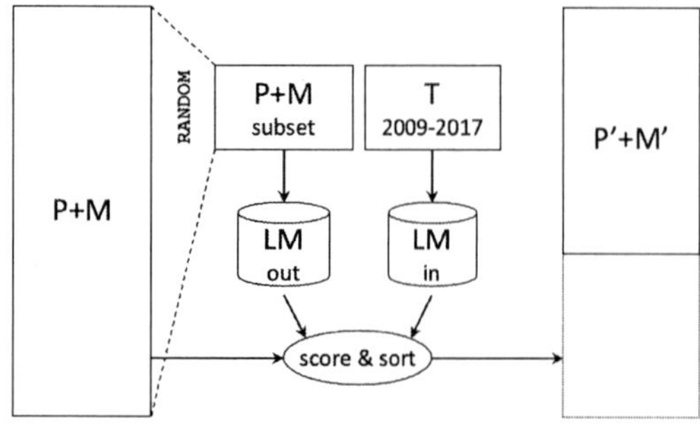

Figure 3: Data selection process.

Obviously, we base our selection procedure on

the source-side text of each translation direction as references for newstest2017 are not available.

Sentences s of the generic corpus are scored in terms of cross-entropy computed from two language models: a 3-gram LM trained on the domain-specific data $H_{in}(s)$ and a 3-gram LM trained on a random sample taken from itself $H_{out}(s)$. Finally, sentences of the generic corpus are sorted regarding the computation of the difference between domain-specific and generic scores $H_{in}(s) - H_{out}(s)$ (score & sort).

3.2.3 Hyper-specialisation on news test sets

Similar to domain adaptation, we explore a post-process approach, which hyper-specialises a neural network to a specific domain by running additional training epochs over newly available in-domain data (Servan et al., 2016). In our context, we utilise all newstest sets (**T**) (around $25,000$ sentences), as in-domain data and run a single learning iteration in order to fine tune the resulting network. Translations are not available for newstest2017, instead we use the single best hypotheses produced by the best performing system in Table 3. In a similar task, (Crego and Senellart, 2016) report translation accuracy gains by employing a neural system trained over a synthetic corpus built from source reference sentences and target translation hypotheses. The authors claim that text simplification is achieved when translating with an automatic engine compared to reference (human) translations, leading to higher accuracy results.

Table 4 details the hyper-specialisation training work. Note that the entire hyper-specialisation process was performed on approximately 6 minutes. We used a learning rate set to 0.7. Further experiments need to be conducted for a better understanding of the learning rate role in hyper-specialisation work.

Epoch	1	1
German→English		
Data	T	T-2017
Time (seconds)	365	305
LR	0.7^1	0.7^1
BLEU (2017)	$32,87$	$32,66$
English→German		
Data	T	T-2017
Time (seconds)	372	308
LR	0.7^1	0.7^1
BLEU (2017)	$26,98$	$26,80$

Table 4: *Hyper-specialisation on news test sets.*

Accuracy gains are obtained despite using automatic (noisy) translation hypotheses to hyper-specialise: $+0.52$ (German→English) and $+0.57$ (English→German). In order to measure the impact of using newstest2017 as training data (sefl-training) we repeated the hyper-specialisation experiment using as training data newstest sets from 2009 to 2016. This is, excluding newstest2017 (**T-2017**). Slightly lower accuracy results were obtained by this second configuration (last column in Table 4) but still outperforming the systems without hyper-specialisation: $+0.31$ (German→English) and $+0.39$ (English→German).

4 Conclusions

We described SYSTRAN's submissions to the WMT 2017 shared news translation task for English-German. Our systems are built using OpenNMT. We experimented using monolingual data automatically back-translated. Our resulting models were successfully hyper-specialised with an adaptation technique that finely tunes models

according to the evaluation test sentences. Note that all our submitted systems are single networks. No ensemble experiments were carried out, what typically results in higher accuracy results.

Acknowledgements

We would like to thank the anonymous reviewers for their careful reading of the paper and their many insightful comments and suggestions.

References

Dzmitry Bahdanau, Kyunghyun Cho, and Yoshua Bengio. 2014. Neural machine translation by jointly learning to align and translate. *CoRR* abs/1409.0473. Demoed at NIPS 2014: http://lisa.iro.umontreal.ca/mt-demo/. http://arxiv.org/abs/1409.0473.

Josep Crego, Jungi Kim, Guillaume Klein, Anabel Rebollo, Kathy Yang, Jean Senellart, Egor Akhanov, Patrice Brunelle, Aurelien Coquard, Yongchao Deng, Satoshi Enoue, Chiyo Geiss, Joshua Johanson, Ardas Khalsa, Raoum Khiari, Byeongil Ko, Catherine Kobus, Jean Lorieux, Leidiana Martins, Dang-Chuan Nguyen, Alexandra Priori, Thomas Riccardi, Natalia Segal, Christophe Servan, Cyril Tiquet, Bo Wang, Jin Yang, Dakun Zhang, Jing Zhou, and Peter Zoldan. 2016. Systran's pure neural machine translation systems. *CoRR* abs/1610.05540. http://arxiv.org/abs/1610.05540.

Josep Maria Crego and Jean Senellart. 2016. Neural machine translation from simplified translations. *CoRR* abs/1612.06139. http://arxiv.org/abs/1612.06139.

Guillaume Klein, Yoon Kim, Yuntian Deng, Jean Senellart, and Alexander M. Rush. 2017. Opennmt: Open-source toolkit for neural machine translation. In *Accepted to ACL 2017 Conference Demo Papers*. Association for Computational Linguistics, Vancouver, Canada.

Thang Luong, Hieu Pham, and Christopher D. Manning. 2015. Effective approaches to attention-based neural machine translation. In *Proceedings of the 2015 Conference on Empirical Methods in Natural Language Processing*. Association for Computational Linguistics, Lisbon, Portugal, pages 1412–1421. http://aclweb.org/anthology/D15-1166.

Robert C. Moore and William Lewis. 2010. Intelligent selection of language model training data. In *Proceedings of the ACL 2010 Conference Short Papers*. Association for Computational Linguistics, Uppsala, Sweden, pages 220–224. http://www.aclweb.org/anthology/P10-2041.

Rico Sennrich, Barry Haddow, and Alexandra Birch. 2016a. Improving neural machine translation models with monolingual data. *Proceedings of the 54th Annual Meeting of the Associa-tion for Computational Linguistics* pages 86–96. http://www.aclweb.org/anthology/P16-1009.

Rico Sennrich, Barry Haddow, and Alexandra Birch. 2016b. Neural machine translation of rare words with subword units. In *Proceedings of the 54th Annual Meeting of the Association for Computational Linguistics (Volume 1: Long Papers)*. Association for Computational Linguistics, Berlin, Germany, pages 1715–1725. http://www.aclweb.org/anthology/P16-1162.

Christophe Servan, Josep Maria Crego, and Jean Senellart. 2016. Domain specialization: a post-training domain adaptation for neural machine translation. *CoRR* abs/1612.06141. http://arxiv.org/abs/1612.06141.

Yonghui Wu, Mike Schuster, Zhifeng Chen, Quoc V. Le, Mohammad Norouzi, Wolfgang Macherey, Maxim Krikun, Yuan Cao, Qin Gao, Klaus Macherey, Jeff Klingner, Apurva Shah, Melvin Johnson, Xiaobing Liu, ÅĄukasz Kaiser, Stephan Gouws, Yoshikiyo Kato, Taku Kudo, Hideto Kazawa, Keith Stevens, George Kurian, Nishant Patil, Wei Wang, Cliff Young, Jason Smith, Jason Riesa, Alex Rudnick, Oriol Vinyals, Greg Corrado, Macduff Hughes, and Jeffrey Dean. 2016. Google's neural machine translation system: Bridging the gap between human and machine translation. Technical report, Google. https://arxiv.org/abs/1609.08144.

Wojciech Zaremba, Ilya Sutskever, and Oriol Vinyals. 2014. Recurrent neural network regularization. *CoRR* abs/1409.2329. http://arxiv.org/abs/1409.2329.

FBK's Participation to the English-to-German News Translation Task of WMT 2017

Mattia A. Di Gangi[1,2] and **Nicola Bertoldi**[2] and **Marcello Federico**[2]

[1]ICT International Doctoral School - University of Trento, Italy

[2]Fondazione Bruno Kessler - Trento, Italy

{digangi,bertoldi,federico}@fbk.eu

Abstract

In this paper we report on FBK's participation to the English-to-German news translation task of the Second Conference on Machine Translation (WMT'17). The submitted system is based on Neural Machine Translation using byte-pair encoding segmentation on both source and target languages for open-vocabulary translations. Back-translations of news monolingual data are used for improving the translations fluency on the in-domain data. With respect to last year's evaluation, our baseline outperforms the 2016 best system's baseline on the test sets 2015 and 2016. However, in our set-up back-translations produced a smaller improvement than expected. The final submission is given by the combination of 7 systems, including a system trained only on true parallel data and two right-to-left systems, which improves over our single best system by 1.5 BLEU points.

1 Introduction

FBK's participation to the news translations shared task in WMT 17 focused this year on the English-German language direction. Our purpose was to explore the state of the art and build a competitive neural machine translation [3] system in order to gain a practical knowledge of the available tools. With respect to our participation in the IWSLT 2016 evaluation campaign, we switched from the Nematus-Theano framework to the OpenNMT-Torch framework [16]. The reasons were twofold: higher baseline performance and significantly faster training.

In our primary submission we used back-translations [22], BPE-encoding [23] and system combination [11]. In this paper, we report about the tools used for the submitted system and the choices we have taken in terms of hyper-parameters and used data.

The presentation is structured as follows: in Section 2 we briefly introduce the theoretical background for NMT. In Section 3 we describe our baseline system. In Sections 4 and 5 we describe the details of the back-translations and system combination, which have been used for our final submission. Evaluation results are discussed in Section 6, while Section 7 is devoted to discussion and conclusions.

2 Neural Machine Translation

Neural machine translation [25] represents the state of the art for machine translation since the outstanding results obtained on IWSLT2015 [17] IWSLT2016 [1, 7] and WMT16 [24, 5] where the neural models greatly outperformed phrase-based systems. NMT is based on the encoder-decoder-attention architecture [3] which jointly learns the translation and the alignment model with a sequence-to-sequence learning model. Given a sequence of words $f_1, f_2, \ldots, f_m$ in the source language, they are used to index an embedding look-up table and retrieve the vectors $\mathbf{x_1}, \mathbf{x_2}, \ldots, \mathbf{x_m}$ representing the words. The embeddings are processed by a bi-directional RNN

$$\overrightarrow{\mathbf{h}}_j = g(\mathbf{x}_j, \overrightarrow{\mathbf{h}}_{j-1}), \quad j = 1, ..m$$

$$\overleftarrow{\mathbf{h}}_j = g(\mathbf{x}_j, \overleftarrow{\mathbf{h}}_{j+1}), \quad j = m, .., 1$$

$$\mathbf{h}_j = merge(\overrightarrow{\mathbf{h}}_j, \overleftarrow{\mathbf{h}}_j)$$

where $merge$ is a function for merging the output of the RNNs, like the vector concatenation or the point-wise sum, and g is the LSTM [13] or the GRU [8] function. The sequence of vectors produced by the bidirectional RNN is the encoded

Proceedings of the Conference on Machine Translation (WMT), Volume 2: Shared Task Papers, pages 271–275
Copenhagen, Denmark, September 7–11, 2017. ©2017 Association for Computational Linguistics

representation of the source sentence.

The decoder takes as input the encoder outputs (or states) and produces a sequence of target words $e_1, e_2, \ldots, e_l$. The decoder works by progressively predicting the probability of the next target word e_i given the previously generated target words and the source context vector c_i. At each step, the decoder computes a word embeddings $\mathbf{y}_{i-1}$ of the previous target word, applies one or more recurrent layers, an attention model function and a softmax layer. The recurrent layers produce an hidden state $\mathbf{s}_i$

$$\mathbf{s}_i = g(\mathbf{y}_{i-1}, \mathbf{s}_{i-1})$$

where, g can be computed with one or more LSTM or GRU layers. The output of the RNN is then used by the attention model to weight the source vectors according to their similarity with it.

$$\alpha_{ij} = \frac{\exp(score(\mathbf{s}_i, \mathbf{h}_j))}{\sum_{k=1}^{m} \exp(score(\mathbf{s}_i, \mathbf{h}_k))}$$

The weights are used to compute a weighted average of the encoder outputs, which represents the source context

$$\mathbf{c}_i = \sum_{j=1}^{m} \alpha_{ij}\mathbf{h}_j$$

The source context vector is then combined with the output of the last RNN layer in a new vector $\mathbf{z}_i$ that is passed as input to the softmax layer to compute the probability for each word in the vocabulary to be the next word, such that:

$$p(e \mid e_{i-1}, c_i) \propto \exp(\mathbf{e}^\top \mathbf{z}_i)$$

where $\mathbf{e}^\top$ represents the transpose of the one-hot vector representation of word e. Let Θ be the set of all the network parameters, then the objective of the training is to find parameter values maximizing the likelihood of the training set S, i.e.:

$$\sum_{(\mathbf{f},\mathbf{e}) \in S} \sum_{i=1}^{|e|} \log p(e_i | e_{<i}, \mathbf{c}_i; \Theta)$$

3 Baseline

Our baseline is a neural machine translation system trained on the four parallel corpora released for the task. Our preprocessing pipeline involved normalizing the punctuation, de-escaping the special characters, tokenization and truecasing for

Table 1: Number of training sentences.

	original	cleaned
commoncrawl	2,399,123	2,228,833
europarl-v7	1,920,209	1,719,859
news-comm-v12	270,769	255,944
rapid2016	1,329,041	1,277,997

both English and German. We also filtered out sentence pairs with source or target length greater than 50 or length ratio in one direction more than 1:9. In Table 1 we report the number of sentences before and after the cleaning step. The last step of the preprocessing is the BPE segmentation [23]. We trained $45,000$ BPE merge rules over the joint parallel data, which resulted in a vocabulary sizes of $43,853$ words for English and $47,465$ for German.

The NMT architecture consists of 2 LSTM layers both in the encoder and in the decoder. We used LSTM RNNs instead of the GRU RNNs, as they performed better in our preliminary experiments. Our result is hence coherent with what reported in [6]. The word embeddings size and the number of hidden units for each LSTM layer are fixed to 500. The encoder is a bidirectional LSTM [21] with 500 hidden units equally divided among the two directions. The optimizer of choice is SGD [20] with exponential decay. In preliminary experiments, using different and smaller datasets, this optimizer outperformed Adagrad [10] and Adam [15]. Figure 1 shows the validation scores after each epoch on the validation sets with the different optimizers. In [7] Adagrad led to better results on the IWSLT En-Fr validation set, thus we argue that the choice of the optimizer depends on the dataset and the NMT implementation. The latter is not considered in studies comparing different optimizers [2]

We set the initial learning rate to 1.0 and the exponential decay to 0.9. The decay starts from epoch 9. The results of the baseline are reported in the first row of Table 3, where they are compared with our submissions. The model was trained on a single GPU for 21 epochs with a minibatch size of 120. Each epoch required about 9 hours.

4 Monolingual Data

In order to leverage monolingual data we followed the state-of-the-art practice of using back-

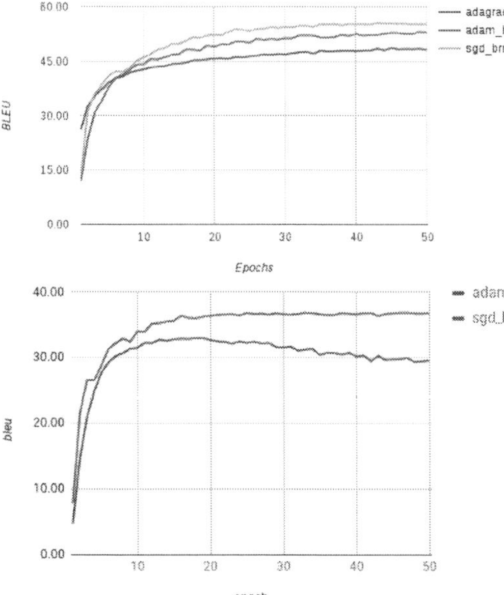

Figure 1: Comparison between different optimizers in terms of BLEU. In the top Figure SGD with exponential decay is the best performing against Adam and Adagrad in a private dataset. In the bottom Figure the trend is confirmed on IWSLT EN-FR data.

translated data. A German-to-English MT system was used to translate the news monolingual sentences. As we did not plan to participate in the opposite direction, we decided to use a phrase-based MT to performing back-translations.

The system of choice was MMT [4], an opensource PBMT system for industrial use, which has been trained using all available parallel data. The language model was trained on sentences randomly sampled from the English monolingual newscrawl data for a total of 1B words. The log-linear model weights were tuned on 1000 sentences sampled from newstest2013 and newstest2014 After tuning, the system obtained a BLEU score of 25.04 on newstest2015 de-en. With ModernMT we were able to translate $250,000$ sentences per day on a single CPU. We translated in total about $30M$ newscrawl sentences from 2013 to 2016. In a first experiment we trained a model until convergence on this huge synthetic parallel data and then fine-tuned on the true parallel data. In this setting, the system trained on the synthetic data converged before finishing the first epoch, and the following

Table 2: Results of the single systems used for combination

System	newstest2015	newstest2016
Sys1	23.95	28.53
Sys2	25.41	29.68
Sys3	**25.69**	**30.21**
Sys4	25.26	28.69

fine-tuning reached only 23 Bleu scores on newstest2015, thus we decided not to use this data for the final submission. Our best single system continued the training of the baseline on a new dataset consisting of both the parallel sentences and $5M$ back-translated parallel sentences randomly sampled from the $30M$ set.

As we describe in the following section, we used monolingual data also for the system combination.

5 System Combination

Our primary submission has been produced by merging the outputs of different systems with Jane's system combination tool [11].

For a system combination of m systems we build m confusion networks that are then merged to form a single confusion network. For each of the small networks, only one of the systems is chosen as the primary system, which is the system that decides the word order. The sentences from every secondary systems are then aligned to the primary. We perform word alignment using METEOR [9], a tool that uses four criteria for aligning words: 1) exact match; 2) stem, which matches two words if their stems computed with the Snowball Stemmer [19] are the same; 3) synonym, which uses the WordNet [18] synsets database; 4) paraphrase, which matches phrases if they are in an internal paraphrase table. When no criterion is matched, there is a match with the empty string.

The confusion networks are initialized with the primary system sentences, then the words from the secondary hypothesis are added to the network according to the alignment. The final confusion network is obtained by the union of the m networks. The output sentence is produced from the confusion network by majority voting. Each hypothesis receives a system weight, and the weights are optimized using a development set. In our case the development set is newstest2015 and the validation set is newstest2016

The systems involved in the combination are from

System	2015	2016	2017
Baseline (sys4)	25.26	28.69	24.20
+ Synthetic (sys3)	25.69	30.21	24.80
System Combination	**28.10***	**32.84**	**26.30**

Table 3: Our results on newstest 2015-17.
*The system has been tuned on newstest2015.

4 different NMT systems that used different training data:

1. A NMT system trained on parallel + synthetic[1] for 12 epochs

2. An NMT trained on parallel + synthetic right to left for 11 epochs[2]

3. The tuning of the baseline for 7 epochs more on parallel + synthetic data

4. The baseline system

For each system, with the exception of the baseline, we used the weights of last two epochs. This gave us an improvement on the validation set of 0.5 Bleu points. We improved the system combination by adding a 5-grams language model with modified Kneser-Ney smoothing [14] without pruning, trained on $\sim$ 500M tokens with KenLM [12]. This improved the result by another +0.6 BLEU on the validation.

In Table 2 we present the results of the single systems on newstest 2015 and 16. As expected, the systems are quite different also in terms of performance, especially for newstest2016, thus we expected significant improvements.

Surprisingly, we found that our system trained from scratch on back-translated data performed worse than the baseline, while the right-to-left system trained on the same data is slightly better on newstest2015 and 1 Bleu point better on newstest2016. The best system is the one that was trained in two phases, during the first phase only on true parallel data, and continued after 21 epochs on true plus synthetic parallel sentences.

6 Results

In Table 3 we report the results in terms of Bleu scores, for the test sets from 2015 to 2017. On newstest2015 the baseline was already in par with last year's best single system [24], and the improvement obtained by back-translations is only of +0.4 Bleu scores. The improvement given by back-translations is more significant on newstest2016, for which our system was quite weak if compared with last year's best single system, and it improved by +1.6 Bleu. The improvement is small also for newstest2017, where it amounts to +0.6.

In the last row of the table the results of the system combination are reported. For newstest2015 we get an improvement of +2.4, but the weights are optimized according to this dataset. A similar improvement is obtained on newstest2016, where we gain +2.6 Bleu scores. The improvement is considerable but the best single system does not have state-of-the-art results on this dataset. On newstest2017 the improvement over our best single system is of +1.5 Bleu scores, thus it produced a final score of 26.30 for which it has been ranked 8th out of 21 systems.

From Tables 2 and 3 we can see that the back-translations gained a small improvement to our systems, specially when there has not been a previous training over only true parallel data (sys1 in Table 2). This is surely related to the number of back-translated sentences, which was maybe too high with respect to the number of parallel sentences. Another issue can be due to the quality of the back-translations that were done with a PBMT system, hence underperforming with respect to a state-of-the-art NMT system.

7 Conclusions

In this paper we have reported on our submission to the English-German news translation task of WMT17. We developed several NMT systems with the OpenNMT open-source tool that were trained over real and synthetic parallel data. We used BPE segmentation for open-vocabulary translation and back-translations to create additional synthetic translations. The best single system, trained on true parallel data and afterwards on true and synthetic parallel sentence pairs, obtained state-of-the-art results on newstest2015 but not on newstest2016 and newstest2017. Additional data created via back-translations did not pay off as hoped. The outputs of 4 different systems, including a right-to-left system, were combined using system combination, producing an improvement

---

[1] With synthetic we refer to 5M back-translated sentences randomly sampled from newscrawl.

[2] In a right-to-left system the target sentences are in reverse order.

of +1.5 BLEU on this year's test set.

Acknowledgments

This work has been partially supported by the EC-funded projects ModernMT (H2020 grant agreement no. 645487) and QT21 (H2020 grant agreement no. 645452).

References

[1] The University of Edinburgh's systems submission to the MT task at IWSLT, author=Junczys-Dowmunt, Marcin and Birch, Alexandra, booktitle=Proceedings of the ninth International Workshop on Spoken Language Translation (IWSLT), Seattle, WA, year=2016.

[2] P. Bahar, T. Alkhouli, J.-T. Peter, C. J.-S. Brix, and H. Ney. Empirical investigation of optimization algorithms in neural machine translation. *The Prague Bulletin of Mathematical Linguistics*, 108(1):13–25, 2017.

[3] D. Bahdanau, K. Cho, and Y. Bengio. Neural machine translation by jointly learning to align and translate. *arXiv preprint arXiv:1409.0473*, 2014.

[4] N. Bertoldi, R. Cattoni, M. Cettolo, M. A. Farajian, M. Federico, D. Caroselli, L. Mastrostefano, A. Rossi, M. Trombetti, U. Germann, and D. Madl. MMT: New open source MT for the translation industry. In *Proceedings of The 20th Annual Conference of the European Association for Machine Translation (EAMT)*, 2017.

[5] J. Bradbury and R. Socher. Metamind neural machine translation system for WMT 2016. In *Proceedings of the First Conference on Machine Translation, Berlin, Germany. Association for Computational Linguistics*, 2016.

[6] D. Britz, A. Goldie, T. Luong, and Q. Le. Massive exploration of neural machine translation architectures. *arXiv preprint arXiv:1703.03906*, 2017.

[7] R. Chatterjee, M. Farajian, C. Conforti, S. Jalalvand, V. Balaraman, M. Di Gangi, D. Ataman, M. Turchi, M. Negri, and M. Federico. FBK's neural machine translation systems for IWSLT 2016. In *Proceedings of 13th International Workshop on Spoken Language Translation (IWSLT 2016)*, 2016.

[8] K. Cho, B. Van Merrienboer, D. Bahdanau, and Y. Bengio. On the properties of neural machine translation: Encoder-decoder approaches. *arXiv preprint arXiv:1409.1259*, 2014.

[9] M. Denkowski and A. Lavie. Meteor 1.3: Automatic metric for reliable optimization and evaluation of machine translation systems. In *Proceedings of the Sixth Workshop on Statistical Machine Translation*, pages 85–91. Association for Computational Linguistics, 2011.

[10] J. Duchi, E. Hazan, and Y. Singer. Adaptive subgradient methods for online learning and stochastic optimization. *Journal of Machine Learning Research*, 12(Jul):2121–2159, 2011.

[11] M. Freitag, M. Huck, and H. Ney. Jane: Open source machine translation system combination. In *EACL*, pages 29–32, 2014.

[12] K. Heafield, I. Pouzyrevsky, J. H. Clark, and P. Koehn. Scalable modified Kneser-Ney language model estimation. In *Proceedings of the 51st Annual Meeting of the Association for Computational Linguistics*, pages 690–696, Sofia, Bulgaria, August 2013.

[13] S. Hochreiter and J. Schmidhuber. Long short-term memory. *Neural computation*, 9(8):1735–1780, 1997.

[14] F. James. Modified kneser-ney smoothing of n-gram models. *Research Institute for Advanced Computer Science, Tech. Rep. 00.07*, 2000.

[15] D. Kingma and J. Ba. Adam: A method for stochastic optimization. *arXiv preprint arXiv:1412.6980*, 2014.

[16] G. Klein, Y. Kim, Y. Deng, J. Senellart, and A. M. Rush. OpenNMT: Open-Source Toolkit for Neural Machine Translation. *ArXiv e-prints*.

[17] M.-T. Luong and C. D. Manning. Stanford neural machine translation systems for spoken language domains. In *Proceedings of the International Workshop on Spoken Language Translation*, 2015.

[18] G. A. Miller and C. Fellbaum. Wordnet then and now. *Language Resources and Evaluation*, 41(2):209–214, 2007.

[19] M. F. Porter. Snowball: A language for stemming algorithms, 2001.

[20] H. Robbins and S. Monro. A stochastic approximation method. *The annals of mathematical statistics*, pages 400–407, 1951.

[21] M. Schuster and K. K. Paliwal. Bidirectional recurrent neural networks. *IEEE Transactions on Signal Processing*, 45(11):2673–2681, 1997.

[22] R. Sennrich, B. Haddow, and A. Birch. Improving neural machine translation models with monolingual data. *arXiv preprint arXiv:1511.06709*, 2015.

[23] R. Sennrich, B. Haddow, and A. Birch. Neural machine translation of rare words with subword units. *arXiv preprint arXiv:1508.07909*, 2015.

[24] R. Sennrich, B. Haddow, and A. Birch. Edinburgh neural machine translation systems for WMT 16. *arXiv preprint arXiv:1606.02891*, 2016.

[25] I. Sutskever, O. Vinyals, and Q. V. Le. Sequence to sequence learning with neural networks. In *Advances in neural information processing systems*, pages 3104–3112, 2014.

The JHU Machine Translation Systems for WMT 2017

Shuoyang Ding[†] **Huda Khayrallah**[†] **Philipp Koehn**[†]
Matt Post[‡] **Gaurav Kumar**[†] **and Kevin Duh**[‡]
[†]Center for Language and Speech Processing
[‡]Human Language Technology Center of Excellence
Johns Hopkins University
{dings, huda, phi}@jhu.edu,
{post, gkumar, kevinduh}@cs.jhu.edu

Abstract

This paper describes the Johns Hopkins University submissions to the shared translation task of EMNLP 2017 Second Conference on Machine Translation (WMT 2017). We set up phrase-based, syntax-based and/or neural machine translation systems for all 14 language pairs of this year's evaluation campaign. We also performed neural rescoring of phrase-based systems for English-Turkish and English-Finnish.

1 Introduction

The JHU 2017 WMT submission consists of phrase-based systems, syntax-based systems and neural machine translation systems. In this paper we discuss features that we integrated into our system submissions. We also discuss lattice rescoring as a form of system combination of phrase-based and neural machine translation systems.

The JHU phrase-based translation systems for our participation in the WMT 2017 shared translation task are based on the open source Moses toolkit (Koehn et al., 2007) and strong baselines of our submission last year (Ding et al., 2016). The JHU neural machine translation systems were built with the Nematus (Sennrich et al., 2016c) and Marian (Junczys-Dowmunt et al., 2016) toolkits. Our lattice rescoring experiments are also based on a combination of these three toolkits.

2 Phrase-Based Model Baselines

Although the focus of research in machine translation has firmly moved onto neural machine translation, we still built traditional phrase-based statistical machine translation systems for all language pairs. These submissions also serve as a baseline of where neural machine translation systems stand with respect to the prior state of the art.

Our systems are very simmilar to the JHU systems from last year (Ding et al., 2016).

2.1 Configuration

We trained our systems with the following settings: a maximum sentence length of 80, grow-diag-final-and symmetrization of GIZA++ alignments, an interpolated Kneser-Ney smoothed 5-gram language model with KenLM (Heafield, 2011) used at runtime, hierarchical lexicalized reordering (Galley and Manning, 2008), a lexically-driven 5-gram operation sequence model (OSM) (Durrani et al., 2013) with 4 count-based supportive features, sparse domain indicator, phrase length, and count bin features (Blunsom and Osborne, 2008; Chiang et al., 2009), a distortion limit of 6, maximum phrase-length of 5, 100-best translation options, compact phrase table (Junczys-Dowmunt, 2012) minimum Bayes risk decoding (Kumar and Byrne, 2004), cube pruning (Huang and Chiang, 2007), with a stack-size of 1000 during tuning and 5000 during test and the no-reordering-over-punctuation heuristic (Koehn and Haddow, 2009). We optimize feature function weights with k-best MIRA (Cherry and Foster, 2012).

We used POS and morphological tags as additional factors in phrase translation models (Koehn and Hoang, 2007) for the German-English language pairs. We also trained target sequence models on the in-domain subset of the parallel corpus using Kneser-Ney smoothed 7-gram models. We used syntactic preordering (Collins et al., 2005) and compound splitting (Koehn and Knight, 2003) for the German-to-English systems. We did no language-specific processing for other languages.

We included Och cluster language model, with 4 additional language models trained on 50, 200,

Proceedings of the Conference on Machine Translation (WMT), Volume 2: Shared Task Papers, pages 276–282
Copenhagen, Denmark, September 7–11, 2017. ©2017 Association for Computational Linguistics

Language Pair	Sentences
German–English	21,243
Czech–English	21,730
Finnish–English	2,870
Latvian–English	984
Russian-English	11,824
Turkish–English	1,001
Chinese–English	1,000

Table 1: Tuning set sizes for phrase and syntax-based system

500, and 2000 clusters (Och, 1999) using `mkcls`. In addition, we included a large language model based on the CommonCrawl monolingual data (Buck et al., 2014).

The systems were tuned on a very large tuning set consisting of the test sets from 2008-2015, with a total of up to 21,730 sentences (see Table 1). We used `newstest2016` as development test set. Significantly less tuning data was available for Finnish, Latvian, and Turkish.

2.2 Results

Table 2 shows results for all language pairs, except for Chinese–English, for which we did not built phrase-based systems. Our phrase-based systems were clearly outperformed by NMT systems for all language pairs, by a difference of 3.2 to 8.3 BLEU points. The difference is most dramatic for languages with rich morphology (Turkish, Finnish).

3 Syntax-based Model Baselines

We built syntax-based model baselines for both directions of Chinese-English language pairs because our previous experiments indicate that syntax-based machine translation systems generally outperform phrase-based machine translation systems by a large margin. Our system setup was largely based on our syntax-based system setup for last year's evaluation (Ding et al., 2016).

3.1 Configuration

Our syntax-based systems were trained with all the CWMT and UN parallel data provided for the evaluation campaign. We also used the monolingual data from news crawl 2007-2016, the English Gigaword, and the English side of Europarl corpus. The CWMT 2008 multi-reference dataset were used for tuning (see statistics in Table 1).

For English data, we used the scripts from Moses (Koehn et al., 2007) to tokenize our data, while for Chinese data we carried out word segmentation with Stanford word segmenter (Chang et al., 2008). We also normalized all the Chinese punctuations to their English counterparts to avoid disagreement across sentences. We parsed the tokenized data with Berkeley Parser (Petrov and Klein, 2007) using the pre-trained grammar provided with the toolkit, followed by right binarization of the parse. Finally, truecasing was performed on all the English texts. Due to the lack of casing system, we did not perform truecasing for any Chinese texts.

We performed word alignment with fast-align (Dyer et al., 2013) due to the huge scale of this year's training data and grow-diag-final-and heuristic for alignment symmetrization. We used the GHKM rule extractor implemented in Moses to extract SCFG rules from the parallel corpus. We set the maximum number of nodes (except target words) in the rules (`MaxNodes`) to 30, maximum rule depth (`MaxRuleDepth`) to 7, and the number of non-part-of-speech, non-leaf constituent labels (`MaxRuleSize`) to 7. We also used count bin features for the rule scoring as our phrase-based systems (Blunsom and Osborne, 2008)(Chiang et al., 2009). We used the same language model and tuning settings as the phrase-based systems.

While BLEU score was used both for tuning and our development experiments, it is ambiguous when applied for Chinese outputs because Chinese does not have explicit word boundaries. For discriminative training and development tests, we evaluate the Chinese output against the automatically-segmented Chinese reference with `multi-bleu.perl` scripts in Moses (Koehn et al., 2007).

3.2 Results

Our development results on `newsdev2017` are shown in Table 3. Similar to the phrase-based system, the syntax-based system is also outperformed by NMT systems for both translation directions.

4 Neural Machine Translation[1]

We built and submitted neural machine translation systems for both Chinese-English and English-Chinese language pairs. These systems are trained

---

[1] All the scripts and configurations that were used to train our neural machine translation systems can be retrieved at `https://github.com/shuoyangd/nmt4clsp`

Language Pair	JHU 2016	Baseline	Och LM	Och+CC LM	Och+CC LM	Best NMT
			newstest2016		newstest2017	
English-Turkish	9.22	9.22	9.11	9.30	9.8	18.1 +8.3
Turkish-English	12.94	13.03	12.92	12.83	12.6	20.1 +7.5
English-Finnish	13.76	14.12	14.04	13.99	14.5	20.7 +6.2
Finnish-English	19.08	19.72	19.36	19.16	20.5	-
English-Latvian	-	18.66	18.71	18.85	14.4	20.1 +5.7
Latvian-English	-	25.82	26.03	26.12	16.8	20.0 +3.2
English-Russian	23.99	21.45		23.16	25.3	29.8 +4.5
Russian-English	27.88	24.47		27.22	31.5	34.7 +3.2
English-Czech	23.56			23.05	19.1	22.8 +3.7
Czech-English	30.37	29.84	29.98	29.80	26.5	30.9 +4.4
English-German	28.35	28.95		28.39	21.6	28.3 +6.7
German-English	34.50		34.20	33.87	29.7	35.1 +5.4

Table 2: Phrase-Based Systems (cased BLEU scores)

with all the CWMT and UN parallel data provided for the evaluation campaign and `newsdev2017` as the development set. For the back-translation experiments, we also included some monolingual data from new crawl 2016, which is back-translated with our basic neural machine translation system.

4.1 Preprocessing

We started by following the same preprocessing procedures for our syntax-based model baselines except that we didn't do parsing for our training data for neural machine translation systems. After these procedures, we then applied Byte Pair Encoding (BPE) (Sennrich et al., 2016c) to reduce the vocabulary size in the training data. We set the number of BPE merging operations as 49500. The resulting vocabulary size for Chinese and English training data are 64126 and 35335, respectively.

4.2 Training

We trained our basic neural machine translation systems (labeled `base` in Table 3) with Nematus (Sennrich et al., 2017). We used batch size 80, vocabulary size of 50k, word dimension 500 and hidden dimension 1024. We performed dropout with dropout rate 0.2 for the input bi-directional encoding and the hidden layer, and 0.1 for the source and target word embedding. To avoid gradient explosion, gradient clipping constant 1.0 was used. We chose AdaDelta (Zeiler, 2012) as the optimization algorithm for training and used decay rate $\rho = 0.95$, $\varepsilon = 10^{-6}$.

We performed early stopping according to the validation error on the development set. The validation were carried out every 5000 batch updates. The early stopping was triggered if the validation error does not decrease for more than 10 validation runs, i.e. more than 50k batch updates.

4.3 Decoding and Postprocessing

To enable faster decoding for validation, test and back-translation experiments (in Section 4.4), we used the decoder from Marian (Junczys-Dowmunt et al., 2016) toolkit. For all the steps where decoding is involved, we set the beam size of RNN search to 12.

The postprocessing we performed for the final submission starts with merging BPE subwords and detokenization. We then performed de-trucasing for English output, while for Chinese output we re-normalized all the punctuations to their Chinese counterparts. Note that for fair comparison, we used the same evaluation methods for English-Chinese experiments as we did for the English-Chinese syntax-based system, which means we do not detokenzize our Chinese output for our development results.

4.4 Enhancements: Back-translation, Right-to-left models, Ensembles

To investigate the effectiveness of incorporating monolingual information with back-translation (Sennrich et al., 2016b), we continued training on top of the `base` system to build another system (labeled `back-trans` below) that has some exposure to the monolingual data. Due to the time and hardware constraints, we only took a random sample of

Language Pairs	Syntax	base single	base ensemble	back-trans single	back-trans ensemble
Chinese-English	16.22	17.81	**18.46**	17.52	18.16
English-Chinese	14.43	17.22	17.95	17.76	**18.60**

Table 3: Chinese-English and English-Chinese System Development Results on `newsdev2017` (cased BLEU scores). Bold scores indicate best and submitted systems.

2 million sentences from news crawl 2016 monolingual corpus and 1.5 million sentences from preprocessed CWMT Chinese monolingual corpus from our syntax-based system run and back-translated them with our trained `base` system. These back-translated pseudo-parallel data were then mixed with an equal amount of random samples from real parallel training data and used as the data for continued training. All the hyperparameters used for the continued training are exactly the same as those in the initial training stage.

Following the effort of (Liu et al., 2016) and (Sennrich et al., 2016a), we also trained right-to-left (`r2l`) models with a random sample of 4 million sentence pairs for both translation directions of Chinese-English language pairs, in the hope that they could lead to better reordering on the target side. But they were not included in the final submission because they turned out to hurt the performance on development set. We conjecture that our `r2l` model is too weak compared to both `base` and `back-trans` models to yield good reordering hypotheses.

We performed model averaging over the 4-best models for both `base` and `back-trans` systems as our combined system. The 4-best models are selected among the model dumps performed every 10k batch updates in training, and we select the models that has the highest BLEU scores on the development set. The model averaging was performed with the `average.py` script in Marian (Junczys-Dowmunt et al., 2016).

4.5 Results

Results of our neural machine translation systems on `newsdev2017` are also shown in Table 3. Both of our neural machine translation systems outperform their syntax-based counterparts by 2-4 BLEU points.

The results also indicate that the 4-best averaging ensemble uniformly performs better than single systems. However, the back-translation experiments for Chinese-English system do not improve performance. We hypothesize that the amount of our back-translated data is not sufficient to improve the model. Experiments with full-scale back-translated monolingual data are left for future work.

5 Rescoring

We use neural machine translation (NMT) systems to rescore the output of the phrase-based machine translation (PBMT) systems. We use two methods to do this, 500-best list rescoring, and lattice rescoring. Rescoring was performed on English-Turkish, and English-Finnish translation tasks. We combined the baseline PBMT models from Table 2, with basic NMT systems.

5.1 NMT Systems

We build basic NMT systems for this task. We preprocess the data by tokenizing, truecasing, and applying Byte Pair Encoding (Sennrich et al., 2015) with 49990 merge operations. We trained the NMT systems with Nematus (Sennrich et al., 2017) on the released training corpora. We used the following settings: batch size of 80, vocabulary size of 50000, word dimension 500, and hidden dimension 1000. We performed dropout with a rate of 0.2 for the input bi directional encoding and the hidden layer, and 0.1 for the source and target word embedding. We used Adam as the optimizer (Kingma and Ba, 2014).

We performed early stopping according to the validation error on the development set. Validation was carried out every 20000 batch updates. The early stopping was triggered if the validation error does not decrease for more than 10 validation runs, if early stopping is not triggered, we run for a maximum of 50 epochs.

We create ensembles by averaging the 3 best validation models with the `average.py` script in Marian (Junczys-Dowmunt et al., 2016).

Language Pair	PBMT	NMT	NMT-Ens	N-best	Lattice	N-best	Lattice
			newstest2016			newstest2017	
English-Turkish	9.2	8.1	8.5	9.4	**9.9**	9.4	**10.4**
English-Finnish	14.1	12.6	13.6	14.6	**15.5**	14.3	**16.0**

Table 4: Comparison of PBMT, NMT, NMT-Ensembles, and neural rescoring of PBMT output in the form of N-best lists or lattices (cased BLEU scores)

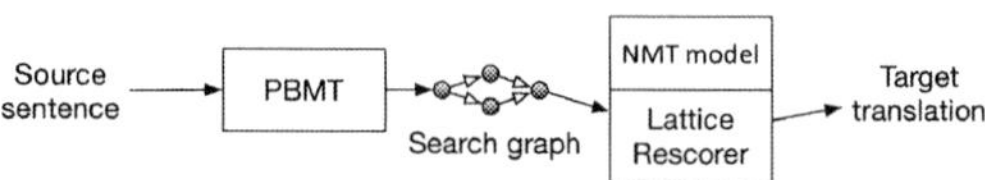

Figure 1: The neural lattice rescorer pipeline.

5.2 500-best Rescoring

We rescore 500-best candiate lists by first generating 500-best lists from Moses (Koehn et al., 2007) using the -N-best-list flag. We then use the Nematus (Sennrich et al., 2017) N-best list rescoring to rescore the list using our NMT model.

5.3 Lattice Rescoring

We also rescore PBMT lattices. We generate search graphs from the PBMT system by passing the -output-search-graph parameter to Moses. The search graphs are then converted to the OpenFST format (Allauzen et al., 2007) and operations to remove epsilon arcs, determinize, minimize and topsort are applied. Since the search graphs may be prohibitively large in size, we prune them to a threshold; we tune this threshold.[2]

The core difficulty in lattice rescoring with NMT is that its RNN architecture does not permit efficient recombination of hypotheses on the lattice. Therefore, we apply a stack decoding algorithm (similar to the one used in PBMT) which groups hypotheses by the number of target words (the paper describing this work is under review). Figure 5.3 describes this pipeline.

5.4 Results

We use newstest2016 as a developement set, and report the official results from newstest2017.

Tables 5 and 6 show the development set results for pruning thresholds of .1, .25, and .5 and stack sizes of 1, 10, 100, 1000. We chose not to use a stack size of 1000 in our final systems because the improvement in devset BLEU over a stack size of

	.1	.25	.5
1	9.60	9.51	9.11
10	9.82	9.86	9.28
100	9.86	9.90	9.43
1000	9.88	**9.92**	-

Table 5: Grid search on the pruning (.1, .25, .5) and stack parameters (1, 10, 100, 1000) for English-Turkish newstest2016 (cased BLEU)

	.1	.25	.5
1	14.85	15.06	14.96
10	14.92	15.30	15.32
100	14.92	15.33	15.49
1000	14.94	15.29	**15.53**

Table 6: Grid search on the pruning (.1, .25, .5) and stack parameters (1, 10, 100, 1000) for English-Finnish newstest2016 (cased BLEU)

100 is not large. For our final English-Turkish system, we use a pruning threshold of .25 and a stack size of 100; for our final English-Finnish system we use a pruning threshold of .5 and a stack size of 100.

Table 4 shows development results for the baseline PBMT, NMT systems, as well as the NMT ensembles, 500-best rescoring, and lattice rescoring. We also report test results for the 500-best rescoring, and lattice rescoring. On newstest2016, lattice rescoring outperforms 500-best rescoring by .5-1.1 BLEU, and on newstest2017, lattice rescoring outperforms 500-best rescoring by 1-1.7 BLEU. 500-best rescoring also outperforms PBMT, NMT system, and the NMT ensembles. While these results are not competitive with the best systems on newstest2017 in the evaluation campaign, it is interesting to note that lattice rescoring gave good performance among the models we compared. For future work it is worth re-running the lattice rescoring experiment using stronger baseline PBMT and NMT models.

---

[2] Pruning removes arcs that do not appear on a lattice path whose score is within than $t \otimes w$, where w is the weight of the FSTs shortest path, and t is the pruning threshold.

6 Conclusion

We submitted phrase-based systems for all 14 language pairs, syntax-based systems for 2 pairs, neural systems for 2 pairs, and two types of rescored systems for 2 pairs. While many of these systems underperformed neural systems, they provide a strong baseline to compare the new neural systems to the previous state-of-the-art phrase-based systems. The gap between our neural systems and the top performing ones can be partially explained by a lack of large-scale back-translated data, which we plan to include in future work.

References

Cyril Allauzen, Michael Riley, Johan Schalkwyk, Wojciech Skut, and Mehryar Mohri. 2007. OpenFst: A General and Efficient Weighted Finite-State Transducer Library. In *Proceedings of the Ninth International Conference on Implementation and Application of Automata, (CIAA 2007)*. Springer, volume 4783 of *Lecture Notes in Computer Science*, pages 11–23. http://www.openfst.org.

Phil Blunsom and Miles Osborne. 2008. Probabilistic Inference for Machine Translation. In *Proceedings of the 2008 Conference on Empirical Methods in Natural Language Processing*. Association for Computational Linguistics, Honolulu, Hawaii, pages 215–223.

Christian Buck, Kenneth Heafield, and Bas Van Ooyen. 2014. N-gram Counts and Language Models from the Common Crawl. *LREC* 2:4.

Pi-Chuan Chang, Michel Galley, and Christopher D Manning. 2008. Optimizing Chinese Word Segmentation for Machine Translation Performance. In *Proceedings of the third workshop on statistical machine translation*. Association for Computational Linguistics, pages 224–232.

Colin Cherry and George Foster. 2012. Batch Tuning Strategies for Statistical Machine Translation. In *Proceedings of the 2012 Conference of the North American Chapter of the Association for Computational Linguistics: Human Language Technologies*. Association for Computational Linguistics, Montréal, Canada, pages 427–436.

David Chiang, Kevin Knight, and Wei Wang. 2009. 11,001 New Features for Statistical Machine Translation. In *Proceedings of Human Language Technologies: The 2009 Annual Conference of the North American Chapter of the Association for Computational Linguistics*. Association for Computational Linguistics, Boulder, Colorado, pages 218–226.

Michael Collins, Philipp Koehn, and Ivona Kucerova. 2005. Clause Restructuring for Statistical Machine Translation. In *Proceedings of the 43rd Annual Meeting of the Association for Computational Linguistics (ACL'05)*. Association for Computational Linguistics, Ann Arbor, Michigan, pages 531–540.

Shuoyang Ding, Kevin Duh, Huda Khayrallah, Philipp Koehn, and Matt Post. 2016. The JHU Machine Translation Systems for WMT 2016. In *Proceedings of the First Conference on Machine Translation*. Association for Computational Linguistics, Berlin, Germany, pages 272–280.

Nadir Durrani, Alexander Fraser, Helmut Schmid, Hieu Hoang, and Philipp Koehn. 2013. Can Markov Models Over Minimal Translation Units Help Phrase-Based SMT? In *Proceedings of the 51st Annual Meeting of the Association for Computational Linguistics*. Association for Computational Linguistics, Sofia, Bulgaria.

Chris Dyer, Victor Chahuneau, and Noah A Smith. 2013. A Simple, Fast, and Effective Reparameterization of IBM Model 2. Association for Computational Linguistics.

Michel Galley and Christopher D. Manning. 2008. A Simple and Effective Hierarchical Phrase Reordering Model. In *Proceedings of the 2008 Conference on Empirical Methods in Natural Language Processing*. Honolulu, Hawaii, pages 848–856.

Kenneth Heafield. 2011. KenLM: Faster and Smaller Language Model Queries. In *Proceedings of the Sixth Workshop on Statistical Machine Translation*. Edinburgh, Scotland, United Kingdom, pages 187–197.

Liang Huang and David Chiang. 2007. Forest Rescoring: Faster Decoding with Integrated Language Models. In *Proceedings of the 45th Annual Meeting of the Association of Computational Linguistics*. Association for Computational Linguistics, Prague, Czech Republic, pages 144–151.

M. Junczys-Dowmunt. 2012. A phrase table without phrases: Rank encoding for better phrase table compression. In Mauro Cettolo, Marcello Federico, Lucia Specia, and Andy Way, editors, *Proceedings of th 16th International Conference of the European Association for Machine Translation (EAMT)*. pages 245–252.

Marcin Junczys-Dowmunt, Tomasz Dwojak, and Hieu Hoang. 2016. Is Neural Machine Translation Ready for Deployment? A Case Study on 30 Translation Directions. In *Proceedings of the 9th International Workshop on Spoken Language Translation (IWSLT)*. Seattle, WA.

Diederik P. Kingma and Jimmy Ba. 2014. Adam: A Method for Stochastic Optimization. *CoRR* abs/1412.6980.

Philipp Koehn and Barry Haddow. 2009. Edinburgh's Submission to all Tracks of the WMT 2009 Shared Task with Reordering and Speed Improvements to Moses. In *Proceedings of the Fourth Workshop on Statistical Machine Translation*. Association for Computational Linguistics, Athens, Greece, pages 160–164.

Philipp Koehn and Hieu Hoang. 2007. Factored Translation Models. In *Proceedings of the 2007 Joint Conference on Empirical Methods in Natural Language Processing and Computational Natural Language Learning (EMNLP-CoNLL)*. Association for Computational Linguistics, Prague, Czech Republic, pages 868–876.

Philipp Koehn, Hieu Hoang, Alexandra Birch, Chris Callison-Burch, Marcello Federico, Nicola Bertoldi, Brooke Cowan, Wade Shen, Christine Moran, Richard Zens, Chris Dyer, Ondrej Bojar, Alexandra Constantin, and Evan Herbst. 2007. Moses: open source toolkit for statistical machine translation. In *ACL*. Association for Computational Linguistics.

Philipp Koehn and Kevin Knight. 2003. "empirical methods for compound splitting". In *Proceedings of Meeting of the European Chapter of the Association of Computational Linguistics (EACL)*.

Shankar Kumar and William J. Byrne. 2004. Minimum Bayes-Risk Decoding for Statistical Machine Translation. In *HLT-NAACL*. pages 169–176.

Lemao Liu, Masao Utiyama, Andrew Finch, and Eiichiro Sumita. 2016. Agreement on target-bidirectional neural machine translation. In *Proceedings of NAACL-HLT*. pages 411–416.

Franz Josef Och. 1999. An Efficient Method for Determining Bilingual Word Classes. In *Proceedings of the 9th Conference of the European Chapter of the Association for Computational Linguistics (EACL)*. pages 71–76.

Slav Petrov and Dan Klein. 2007. Improved Inference for Unlexicalized Parsing. In *HLT-NAACL*. volume 7, pages 404–411.

Rico Sennrich, Orhan Firat, Kyunghyun Cho, Alexandra Birch, Barry Haddow, Julian Hitschler, Marcin Junczys-Dowmunt, Samuel Läubli, Antonio Valerio Miceli Barone, Jozef Mokry, and Maria Nadejde. 2017. Nematus: a Toolkit for Neural Machine Translation. In *Proceedings of the Software Demonstrations of the 15th Conference of the European Chapter of the Association for Computational Linguistics*. Association for Computational Linguistics, Valencia, Spain, pages 65–68.

Rico Sennrich, Barry Haddow, and Alexandra Birch. 2015. Neural Machine Translation of Rare Words with Subword Units. *CoRR* abs/1508.07909.

Rico Sennrich, Barry Haddow, and Alexandra Birch. 2016a. Edinburgh Neural Machine Translation Systems for WMT 16. In *Proceedings of the First Conference on Machine Translation, WMT 2016, colocated with ACL 2016, August 11-12, Berlin, Germany*. pages 371–376.

Rico Sennrich, Barry Haddow, and Alexandra Birch. 2016b. Improving Neural Machine Translation Models with Monolingual Data. In *Proceedings of the 54th Annual Meeting of the Association for Computational Linguistics, ACL 2016, August 7-12, 2016, Berlin, Germany, Volume 1: Long Papers*.

Rico Sennrich, Barry Haddow, and Alexandra Birch. 2016c. Neural Machine Translation of Rare Words with Subword Units. In *Proceedings of the 54th Annual Meeting of the Association for Computational Linguistics, ACL 2016, August 7-12, 2016, Berlin, Germany, Volume 1: Long Papers*.

Matthew D Zeiler. 2012. ADADELTA: an adaptive learning rate method. *arXiv preprint arXiv:1212.5701*.

The TALP-UPC Neural Machine Translation System for German/Finnish-English Using the Inverse Direction Model in Rescoring

Carlos Escolano, Marta R. Costa-jussà and **José A. R. Fonollosa**
TALP Research Center, Universitat Politècnica de Catalunya, Barcelona
carlos.escolano@tsc.upc.edu, {marta.ruiz,jose.fonollosa}@upc.edu

Abstract

In this paper, we describe the TALP-UPC participation in the News Task for German-English and Finish-English. Our primary submission implements a fully character to character neural machine translation architecture with an additional rescoring of a n-best list of hypothesis using a forced back-translation to the source sentence. This model gives consistent improvements on different pairs of languages for the language direction with the lowest performance while keeping the quality in the direction with the highest performance.

Additional experiments are reported for multilingual character to character neural machine translation, phrase-based translation and the additional Turkish-English language pair.

1 Introduction

Neural Machine Translation (MT) has been proven to reach state-of-the-art results in the last couple of years. The baseline encoder-decoder architecture has been improved by an attention-based mechanism citebahdanau:2015, subword units (Sennrich et al., 2016b), character-based encoders (Costa-jussà and Fonollosa, 2016) or even with generative adversarial nets (Yang et al., 2017), among many others.

Despite its successful beginnings, the neural MT approach still has many challenges to solve and improvements to incorporate into the system. However, since the system is computationally expensive and training models may last for several weeks, it is not feasible to conduct multiple experiments for a mid-sized laboratory. For the same reason, it is also relevant to report negative results on NMT.

In this system description, we describe our participation on German-English and Finnish-English for the News Task. Our system is a fully character-to-character neural MT (Lee et al., 2016) system with additional rescoring from the inverse direction model. In parallel to our final system, we also experimented with multilingual character to character system using German, Finnish and Turkish on the source side and English on the target side. Unfortunately, these last experiments did not work. All our systems are contrasted with a standard phrase-based system built with Moses (Koehn et al., 2007).

2 Char-to-char Neural MT

Our system uses the architecture from (Lee et al., 2016) where a character-level neural MT model maps the source character sequence to the target character sequence. The main difference in the encoder architecture respect to the standard neural MT model from (Bahdanau et al., 2015) is the use of a segmentation-free fully character-level network that extends initial character-based approaches like (Kim et al., 2015; Costa-jussà and Fonollosa, 2016). In the encoder, the network architecture includes character embeddings, convolution layers, max pooling and highway layers. The resulting character-based representation is then used as input to a bidirectional recurrent neural network. The main difference in the decoder architecture is that the single-layer feedforward network computes the attention score of next target character (instead of word) to be generated with every source segment representation. And afterwards, a two-layer character-level decoder takes the source context vector from the attention mechanism and predicts each target character.

Proceedings of the Conference on Machine Translation (WMT), Volume 2: Shared Task Papers, pages 283–287
Copenhagen, Denmark, September 7–11, 2017. ©2017 Association for Computational Linguistics

3 Rescoring with inverse model

The motivation behind this technique is the idea that a good translation of a sentence has to be able to produce the original sentence with high probability when it is back-translated to the original source. We expect to be able to produce the source sentence from the translation with high probability only if the information of the source sentence is preserved.

In this approach, the first direct NMT decoder uses the standard beam search algorithm to generate an n-best list of translation hypothesis with its corresponding score

The list of translation outputs and the source sentence are then fed to the inverse *forced decoder* to calculate the probability of generating the original source sentence using each of them as input.

At this point, for each translation candidate we have two probabilities: the one obtained at the first translation step and the one obtained from the inverse *forced decoding*. A simple linear combination of scores is then used to rerank and select the best translation. Specifically, for this decision task, we used the rescoring tools provided by *Moses* that allow us to create a weighted model (using a validation set). For each sentence its final score is calculated as $w1 \cdot s1 + w2 \cdot s2$, where $w1$ and $s1$ are the weight and score (logarithm of the probability) of the translation model, while $w2$ and $p2$ are the weight and score (logarithm of the probability) provided by the forced decoder in the inverse direction. The hypothesis with the highest score is then returned as the final translation.

4 System description

In this section we detail experimental corpora, architecture and parameters that we used to build our WMT 2017 submissions. We report additional details from contrastives systems that we used internally to compare our submissions.

As mentioned earlier, our submissions use a char-to-char neural MT architecture for German-English and Finnish-English. Additional contrastive submissions that we did not present in the WMT evaluation include: a standard phrase-based MT system built with Moses (Koehn et al., 2007) and a multilingual char-to-char neural MT system from the same paper (Lee et al., 2016), where we train different source languages to the same target language. The main difference with the multilingual architecture is that the number of convo-

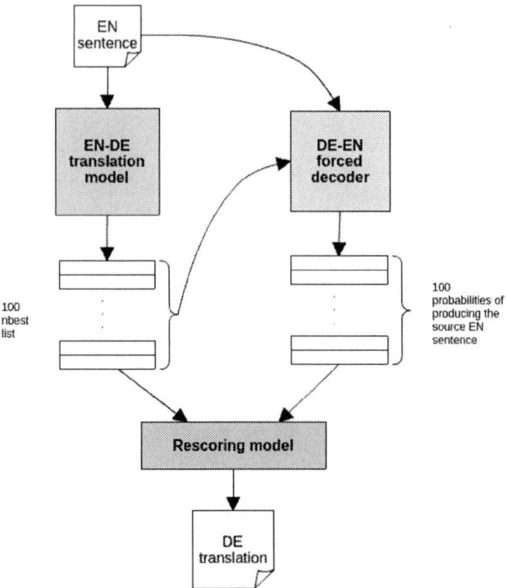

Figure 1: Overview of the architecture. In the image applied to a english-german translation

lutional filters varies. We built contrastive submissions on the phrase-based system for German-English, Finnish-English and we also built it for a language pair that we did not present in the evaluation which was Turkish-English. Multilingual char-to-char was only built for German,Finnish and Turkish to English.

4.1 Data and Preprocess

For the three language pairs that we experimented with, we used all data parallel data available in the evaluation[1]. For German-English, we used: *europarl v.7, news commentary v.12, common crawl* and *rapid corpus of EU press releases*. We also used automatically back-translated in-domain monolingual data (Sennrich et al., 2016a). For Finnish-English, we used *europarl v.8, wiki headlines* and *rapid corpus of EU press releases*. For Turkish-English, we used *setimes2*. All our systems falled into the constrained category. Also note that only for German-English we took advantage of the monolingual corpus provided.

Preprocessing consisted in cleaning empty sentences, limiting sentences up to 50 words, tokenization and truecasing for each language using tools from Moses (Koehn et al., 2007). Table 1 shows details about the corpus statistics after preprocessing. For German and Finnish pairs

---

[1] http://www.statmt.org/wmt17/translation-task.html

LP	L	Set	S	W	V
DeEn	De	Train	9659106	203634165	1721113
		Dev	2999	62362	12674
		Test	2169	44085	9895
		Eval	3004	60965	12763
	En	Train	9659106	210205446	954387
		Dev	2999	64503	9506
		Test	2169	46830	7871
		Eval	3004	64706	9434
FiEn	Fi	Train	2468673	37755811	863898
		Dev	3000	47779	16236
		Test	2870	43069	15748
		Eval	3002	45456	16239
	En	Train	2468673	52262051	240625
		Dev	3000	63519	9059
		Test	2870	60149	8961
		Eval	3002	62412	8956
TuEn	Tu	Train	200290	4248508	158276
		Dev	1001	16954	6463
		Test	3000	54128	15898
		Eval	3007	55293	15264
	En	Train	299290	4713025	73906
		Dev	1001	22136	4318
		Test	3000	66394	9503
		Eval	3007	67839	9181

Table 1: Corpus Statistics. Number of sentences (S),words (W), vocabulary (V). M stands for millions and K stands for thousands.

the evaluation set is news2016 challenge test and the test set is the news2015 test. For Turkish news2016 developement and test set were employed.

Table 2 shows the total vocabulary size in characters (characters) for each language. We also show the limited vocabulary size that we used to train (vocabulary) and the coverage of this limited vocabulary (coverage).

4.2 Parameters and Training Details

- **Moses**. We used the following parameters: grow-diag-final word alignment symmetrization, lexicalized reordering, relative frequencies (conditional and posterior probabilities) with phrase discounting, lexical weights, phrase bonus, accepting phrases up to length 10, 5-gram language model with kneser-ney smoothing, word bonus and MERT optimisation (Koehn et al., 2007).

- **Char-to-char neural MT**. For the embedding of the source sentence, we use set of convolutional layers which number kernels are (200-200-250-250-300-300-300-300) and their lengths are (1-2-3-4-5-6-7-8) respectively. Additionally 4 highway layers are employed. And a bidirectional LSTM layer of 512 units for encoding. The maximum souce sentence's length is 450 during training and 500 for decoding both during training and sampling.

- **Multilingual char-to-char neural MT**. As proposed in the original work (Lee et al., 2016), we implement this model with slightly more convolutional filters than the char-to-char model, namely (200-250- 300-300-400-400-400-400). Also the maximum sentence lenght used for training is 400 for this model. The other parameters of the network are set to the same values than in the bilingual models.

4.3 Results

Table 3 shows results for the systems that we trained in this evaluation: phrase-based, char-to-char neural MT with and without inverse model rescoring and multilingual char-to-char neural MT. We submitted the best systems from Table 3 for German-English and Finnish-English, which is the char-to-char neural MT with rescoring of the inverse model. We computed statistical signficance based on (Clark et al., 2011). Our proposed method obtains a better BLEU score with $> 95\%$ statistical significance.

4.3.1 German ⟷ English

This language pair was trained for 1.000.000 of updates (batches). We generated a 100 n-best list and did rescoring using force decoding over the inverse direction.

4.3.2 Finnish ⟷ English

This model trained for 900.000 updates (batches) for both language pairs. Rescoring is applied to the 100 n-best list using the force decoded probabilities obtained from the inverse model.

4.3.3 Turkish ⟷ English

This model trained for 200.000 updates. For this model rescoring did not produce significative improvement in the results as seen in 3. Also analyzinfg the results obtained we came to the conclusion that the corpus employed of approximately 200.000 sentences was not big enough to train the char2char model specially when compared with the resuts obtained using the phrase based model.

4.3.4 Multilingual

This model trained for 1.200.000 updates using all parallel data provided for the competition in German-English, Finnish-English, Turkish-English. As we can see in 3 the results obtained by the bilingual models outperform the ones obtained by this model. It is also worth to mention the case performance in Turkish where 0 BLEU

Language	Pair	Characters	Vocabulary	Coverage(%)
German(DE)	DE-EN/EN-DE	2379	300	99
English(EN)	DE-EN/EN-DE	2540	300	99
Finnish(FI)	FI-EN/EN-FI	439	300	99
English(EN)	FI-EN/EN-FI	438	300	99
Turkish(TU)	TU-EN/EN-TU	140	140	100
English(EN)	TU-EN/EN-TU	160	160	100

Table 2: Characters, vocabulary size and coverage for each language.

System	DeEn		EnDe		FiEn		EnFi		TuEn		EnTu	
	test	eval	test	eval	test	eval	test	eval	test	eval	test	eval
Phrase	23.59	22.71	18.25	17.93	9.71	11.35	13.67	**15.62**	**11.10**	**9.77**	**7.25**	**8.33**
Char2Char	**28.63**	**32.07**	21.08	26.61	**14.75**	15.75	11.54	11.21	5.87	6.77	6.23	4.73
+Rescoring	**28.63**	**32.07**	**21.37**	**26.98**	**14.75**	15.75	**11.98**	**11.63**	5.87	6.77	6.23	4.73
Multilingual	24.91	29.81	-	-	12.66	13.06	-	-	0	0	-	-

Table 3: BLEU results. In bold, best results.

score was obtained. This may be also explained by the limited corpus used for this language pair compared to the ones employed for German and Finnish.

System	Examples
Truth	CHIO : " goldene Sportpyramide " fr Bernhard Langer der Grund war durchaus berzeugend .
Char2Char	CHIO : " Golden Sport **Pyradid** " fr Bernhard Langer . er **hatte** grndlich berzeugt
+Rescoring	CHIO : " Golden Sport Pyramid " fr Bernhard Langer . er war grndlich berzeugt .

Table 4: Examples of German translation with and without rescoring.

System	Examples
Truth	Louis Galicia sanoi , ett Frank ypyi alkuun hostelleissa, mutta ett skettin " hnen asiansa sujuivat vihdoinkin hyvin ".
	hn oli hyvntahtoinen ja hnell oli suuri sydn .
	kyll , tilaisuudessa kteltiin
Char2Char	Louis Galicia sanoi , ett Frank ji aluksi houkutteluihin, mutta hiljattain : " asiat sujuivat lopultakin hyvin ".hn oli ystvllinen henki.kyll annettiin ktti.hn oli
	ystvllinen henki.
	kyll annettiin ktti .
+Rescoring	Louis Galicia sanoi , ett Frank ji aluksi houkutteluihin, mutta hiljattain : " asiat sujuivat vihdoin hyvin ".
	hn oli ystvllinen ja suuri sydmen henki.
	kyll annettiin kdellisyytt .

Table 5: Examples of Finnish translation with and without rescoring.

Table 4 shows several translation output examples. The first example shows how the rescoring technique can help when a word has been incorrectly spelled. In the second example, we see the correction of a badly translated word.

Table 5 shows some examples of Finnish translations. The examples show how even if the rescoring is not able to generate the correct translation it is able to produce a more similar word than the model without rescoring.

5 Conclusions

In this paper, we have described the TALP-UPC participation in the News Task. Our system implements a char-to-char neural MT with rescoring of the inverse direction model. This model gives consistent improvements on different pairs of languages for the language direction with lowest performance while keeping invariant the language direction with highest performance.

Acknowledgements

This study has been funded by the Spanish *Ministerio de Economía y Competitividad* and the European Regional Development Fund, through the postdoctoral senior grant *Ramón y Cajal* and the contract TEC2015-69266-P (MINECO/FEDER, EU).

References

Dzmitry Bahdanau, Kyunghyun Cho, and Yoshua Bengio. 2015. Neural machine translation by jointly learning to align and translate. volume abs/1409.0473. http://arxiv.org/abs/1409.0473.

Jonathan H. Clark, Chris Dyer, Alon Lavie, and Noah A. Smith. 2011. Better hypothesis testing for statistical machine translation: Controlling for optimizer instability. In *Proceedings of the 49th Annual Meeting of the Association for Computational Linguistics: Human Language Technologies: Short Papers - Volume 2*. Association for Computational Linguistics, Stroudsburg, PA, USA, HLT '11, pages 176–181. http://dl.acm.org/citation.cfm?id=2002736.2002774.

Marta R. Costa-jussà and José A. R. Fonollosa. 2016. Character-based neural machine translation. In *Proceedings of the 54th Annual Meeting of the Association for Computational Linguistics (Volume 2: Short Papers)*. Association for Computational Linguistics, Berlin, Germany, pages 357–361. http://anthology.aclweb.org/P16-2058.

Yoon Kim, Yacine Jernite, David Sontag, and Alexander M. Rush. 2015. Character-aware neural language models. *CoRR* abs/1508.06615. http://arxiv.org/abs/1508.06615.

Philipp Koehn, Hieu Hoang, Alexandra Birch, Chris Callison-Burch, Marcello Federico, Nicola Bertoldi, Brooke Cowan, Wade Shen, Christine Moran, Richard Zens, Chris Dyer, Ondřej Bojar, Alexandra Constantin, and Evan Herbst. 2007. Moses: Open source toolkit for statistical machine translation. In *Proceedings of the 45th Annual Meeting of the ACL on Interactive Poster and Demonstration Sessions*. Association for Computational Linguistics, Stroudsburg, PA, USA, ACL '07, pages 177–180. http://dl.acm.org/citation.cfm?id=1557769.1557821.

Jason Lee, Kyunghyun Cho, and Thomas Hofmann. 2016. Fully character-level neural machine translation without explicit segmentation. *CoRR* abs/1610.03017. http://arxiv.org/abs/1610.03017.

Rico Sennrich, Barry Haddow, and Alexandra Birch. 2016a. Edinburgh neural machine translation systems for wmt 16. *arXiv preprint arXiv:1606.02891*.

Rico Sennrich, Barry Haddow, and Alexandra Birch. 2016b. Neural machine translation of rare words with subword units. In *Proceedings of the 54th Annual Meeting of the Association for Computational Linguistics (Volume 1: Long Papers)*. Association for Computational Linguistics, Berlin, Germany, pages 1715–1725. http://www.aclweb.org/anthology/P16-1162.

Zhen Yang, Wei Chen, Feng Wang, and Bo Xu. 2017. Improving neural machine translation with conditional sequence generative adversarial nets. *CoRR* abs/1703.04887. http://arxiv.org/abs/1703.04887.

LIUM Machine Translation Systems for WMT17 News Translation Task

Mercedes García-Martínez, Ozan Caglayan[†], Walid Aransa
Adrien Bardet, Fethi Bougares, Loïc Barrault
LIUM, University of Le Mans
[†]`ozancag@gmail.com`
`FirstName.LastName@univ-lemans.fr`

Abstract

This paper describes LIUM submissions to WMT17 News Translation Task for English↔German, English↔Turkish, English→Czech and English→Latvian language pairs. We train BPE-based attentive Neural Machine Translation systems with and without factored outputs using the open source *nmtpy* framework. Competitive scores were obtained by ensembling various systems and exploiting the availability of target monolingual corpora for back-translation. The impact of back-translation quantity and quality is also analyzed for English→Turkish where our post-deadline submission surpassed the best entry by +1.6 BLEU.

1 Introduction

This paper describes LIUM Neural Machine Translation (NMT) submissions to WMT17 News Translation Task for English↔German, English↔Turkish, English→Czech and English→Latvian language pairs. We experimented with and without back-translation data for English↔German and English↔Turkish which are respectively described in Sections 3 and 4. For the latter pair, we also present an analysis about the impact of back-translation quality and quantity as well as two architectural ablations regarding the initialization and the output of recurrent decoder (Section 3).

Experiments for English→Czech and English→Latvian are performed using Factored NMT (FNMT) (García-Martínez et al., 2016) systems. FNMT is an extension of NMT which aims at simultaneously predicting the canonical form of a word and its morphological information needed to generate the final surface form. The details and results are presented in section 5. All submitted systems[1] are trained using the open source `nmtpy`[2] framework (Caglayan et al., 2017).

2 Baseline NMT

Our baseline NMT is an attentive encoder-decoder (Bahdanau et al., 2014) implementation. A bi-directional Gated Recurrent Unit (GRU) (Chung et al., 2014) encoder is used to compute source sentence annotation vectors. We equipped the encoder with layer normalization (Ba et al., 2016), a technique which adaptively normalizes the incoming activations of each hidden unit with a learnable gain and bias, after empirically observing that it improves both convergence speed and translation performance.

A conditional GRU (CGRU) (Firat and Cho, 2016; Sennrich et al., 2017) decoder with attention mechanism is used to generate a probability distribution over target tokens for each decoding step t. The hidden state of the CGRU is initialized using a non-linear transformation of the average encoder state produced by the encoder. Following Inan et al. (2016); Press and Wolf (2017), the feedback embeddings (input to the decoder) and the output embeddings are **tied** to enforce learning a single target representation and decrease the number of total parameters by target vocabulary size × embedding size.

We used Adam (Kingma and Ba, 2014) as the optimizer with a learning rate of $4e-4$. Weights are initialized with Xavier scheme (Glorot and Bengio, 2010) and the total gradient norm is clipped to 5 (Pascanu et al., 2013). When stated, three dropouts (Srivastava et al., 2014) are applied after source embeddings, encoder hidden

---

[1]Backtranslations and other data can be found at `http://github.com/lium-lst/wmt17-newstask`
[2]`http://github.com/lium-lst/nmtpy`

Proceedings of the Conference on Machine Translation (WMT), Volume 2: Shared Task Papers, pages 288–295
Copenhagen, Denmark, September 7–11, 2017. ©2017 Association for Computational Linguistics

states and pre-softmax activations respectively. The training is early stopped if validation set BLEU (Papineni et al., 2002) does not improve for a given number of consecutive validations. A beam size of **12** is used for beam-search decoding. Other hyper-parameters including layer dimensions and dropout probabilities are detailed for each language pair in relevant sections.

3 English↔Turkish

3.1 Training

We use SETIMES2 which consists of 207K parallel sentences for training, newsdev2016 for early-stopping, and newstest2016 for model selection (internal test). All sentences are normalized and tokenized using *normalize-punctuation* and *tokenizer* [3] from Moses (Koehn et al., 2007). Training sentences that have less than 3 and more than 50 words are filtered out and a joint Byte Pair Encoding (BPE) model (Sennrich et al., 2016b) with 16K merge operations is learned on train+newsdev2016. The resulting training set has 200K sentences and 5.5M tokens (Table 1) where $\sim$63% and $\sim$50% of English and Turkish vocabularies is composed of a common set of tokens.

Language	# BPE Tokens
English	10041 = 6285 Common + 3756 En
Turkish	12433 = 6285 Common + 6148 Tr
Combined	16189

Table 1: Sub-word statistics for English, Turkish and Combined vocabularies.

All models use **200**-dimensional embeddings and GRU layers with **500** hidden units. The dropout probability P_{drop} is used for all 3 dropouts and set to 0.2 and 0.3 for EN→TR and TR→EN respectively. The validation BLEU is computed after each $\sim$1/4 epoch and the training stops if no improvement is achieved after 20 consecutive validations.

Data Augmentation Due to the low-resource characteristic of EN↔TR, additional training data has been constructed using back-translations (BT) (Sennrich et al., 2016a) where target-side monolingual data is translated to source language to form a Source→Target synthetic corpus. newscrawl2016 (1.7M sentences) and

newscrawl2014 (3.1M sentences) are used as monolingual data for Turkish and English respectively. Although we kept the amount of synthetic data around $\sim$150K sentences for submitted systems to preserve *original-to-synthetic* ratio, we present an analysis about the impact of synthetic data quantity/quality as a follow-up study in Section 3.3. All back-translations are produced using the NMT systems described in this study.

3-way Tying (3WT) In addition to tying feedback and output embeddings (Section 2), we experiment with 3-way tying (3WT) (Press and Wolf, 2017) only for **EN→TR** where we use the **same** embeddings for source, feedback and output embeddings. A *combined* vocabulary of $\sim$16K tokens (Table 1) is then used to form a bilingual representation space.

Init-0 Decoder The attention mechanism (Bahdanau et al., 2014) introduces a time-dependent context vector (weighted sum of encoder states) as an auxiliary input to the decoder allowing implicit encoder-to-decoder connection through which the error back-propagates towards source embeddings. Although this makes it unnecessary to initialize the decoder, the first hidden state of the decoder is generally derived from the last (Bahdanau et al., 2014) or average encoder state (Sennrich et al., 2017) in common practice. To understand the impact of this, we train additional **Init-0** EN→TR systems where the decoder is initialized with an all-zero vector instead of average encoder state.

3.2 Submitted Systems

Each system is trained twice with different seeds and the one with better newstest2016 BLEU is kept when reporting single systems. Ensembles by default use the best early-stop checkpoints of both seeds unless otherwise stated. Results for *both* directions are presented in Table 2.

TR→EN baseline (E1) achieves 14.2 BLEU on newstest2017. The (E2) system trained with additional 150K BT data surpasses the baseline by $\sim$2 BLEU on newstest2017. The EN→TR system used for BT is a single (T5) system which is itself a BT-enhanced NMT. A contrastive system (E3) with less dropout ($P_{drop} = 0.2$) is used for our final submission which is an ensemble of 4 systems (2 runs of E2 + 2 runs of E3). In overall, an improvement of $\sim$3.7 BLEU over the baseline sys-

---

[3]The tokenizer is slightly modified to fix handling of apostrophe splitting in Turkish.

tem is achieved by making use of a small quantity of BT data and ensembling.

EN→TR baseline (T1) achieves 11.1 BLEU on newstest2017 (Table 2). (T2) which is augmented with 150K synthetic data, improves over (T1) by 2.5 BLEU. It can be seen that once 3-way tying (3WT) is enabled, a consistent improvement of up to 0.6 BLEU is obtained on newstest2017. We conjecture that 3WT is beneficiary (especially in a low-resource regime) when the intersection of vocabularies is a large set since the embedding of a common token will now receive as many updates as its occurrence count in both sides of the corpus. On the other hand, the initialization method of the decoder does not seem to incur a significant change in BLEU. Finally, using an ensemble of 4 3WT-150K-BT systems with different decoder initializations (2xT5 + 2xT6), an overall improvement of 4.9 BLEU is obtained over (T1). As a side note, 3WT reduces the number of parameters by ∼10% (12M→10.8M).

System	3WT	nt2016	nt2017
TR→EN ($P_{drop} = 0.3$)			
(E1) Baseline (200K)	×	14.2	14.2
(E2) E1 + 150K-BT	×	16.6	16.1
(E3) E1 + 150K-BT ($P_{drop} = 0.2$)	×	16.4	16.3
Ensemble (2xE2 + 2xE3)	×	18.1	**17.9**
EN→TR ($P_{drop} = 0.2$)			
(T1) Baseline (200K)	×	10.9	11.1
(T2) T1 + 150K-BT	×	12.7	13.6
(T3) T1 + 150K-BT + Init0	×	12.8	13.5
(T4) Baseline (200K)	✓	11.5	11.6
(T5) T4 + 150K-BT	✓	13.4	14.2
(T6) T4 + 150K-BT + Init0	✓	13.3	14.0
Ensemble (2xT5 + 2xT6)	✓	14.7	**16.0**

Table 2: EN↔TR: Underlined and **bold** scores represent contrastive and primary submissions respectively.

3.3 Follow-up Work

We dissect the output layer of CGRU NMT (Sennrich et al., 2017) which is conditioned (Equation 1) on the hidden state h_t of the decoder, the feedback embedding y_{t-1} and the weighted context vector c_t. We experiment with a *simple output* (Equation 2) which depends only on h_t similar to Sutskever et al. (2014). The target probability distribution is computed (Equation 3) using softmax on top of this output transformed with W_o.

$$o_t = \tanh(\mathbf{W_h}h_t + y_{t-1} + \mathbf{W_c}c_t) \quad (1)$$

$$o_t = \tanh(\mathbf{W_h}h_t) \quad (2)$$

$$P(y_t) = \mathrm{softmax}(\mathbf{W_o}o_t) \quad (3)$$

System	# Sents	nt2016 Single	nt2016 Ens	nt2017 Single	nt2017 Ens
(B0) Only SETIMES2	200K	11.5	12.8	11.6	13.0
(B1) Only 1.0M-BT-E1	1.0M	13.6	14.5	14.8	16.3
(B2) B0 + 150K-BT-E1	350K	13.2	14.2	14.3	15.4
(B3) BT-E2		13.4	14.1	14.2	14.9
(B4) B0 + 690K-BT-E1	890K	14.8	15.4	15.9	17.1
(B5) BT-E2		14.7	15.6	16.1	16.9
(B6) B0 + 1.0M-BT-E1	1.2M	**14.9**	**15.6**	**16.2**	**17.5**
(B7) BT-E2		14.9	15.5	16.0	17.0
(B8) B0 + 1.7M-BT-E1	1.9M	14.7	15.4	16.4	17.1
(B9) BT-E2		14.8	15.7	16.1	16.7

Table 3: Impact of back-translation quantity and quality for EN→TR: all systems are 3WT, (B0) is the same as (T4) from Table 2.

As a second follow-up experiment, we analyse the impact of BT data quantity and quality on final performance. Four training sets are constructed by taking the original 200K training set and gradually growing it with BT data of size 150K, 690K, 1.0M and 1.7M (all-BT) sentences respectively. The source side of the monolingual Turkish data used to create the synthetic corpus are translated to English using two different TR→EN systems namely (E1) and (E2) where the latter is better than former on newstest2016 by 2.4 BLEU (Table 2).

The results are presented in Table 3 and 4. First, (B1) trained with *only* synthetic data turns out to be superior than the baseline (B0) by 3.2 BLEU. The ensemble of (B1) even surpasses our primary submission. Although this may indicate the impact of training set size for NMT where a large corpus with synthetic source sentences leads to better performance than a human-translated but small corpus, a detailed analysis would be necessary to reveal other possible reasons.

Second, it is evident that increasing the amount of BT data is beneficial regardless of *original-to-synthetic* ratio: the system (B6) achieves +4.6 BLEU compared to (B0) on newstest2017 (11.6→16.2). The single (B6) is even slightly better than our ensemble submission (Table 4). The +2.4 BLEU gap between back-translators E1 and E2 does not seem to affect final performance where both groups achieve more or less the same scores.

Finally, the *Simple Output* seems to perform slightly better than the original output formulation. In fact, our final *post-deadline* submission which surpasses the winning UEDIN system[4] by 1.6 BLEU (Table 4) is an ensemble of four (B6) systems two of them being *SimpleOut*. Conditioning the target distribution over the weighted context vector c_t creates an auxiliary gradient flow from the cross-entropy loss to the encoder by skipping the decoder. We conjecture that conditioning only over the decoder's hidden state h_t forces the network (especially the decoder) to better learn the target distribution. Same gradient flow also happens for feedback embeddings in the original formulation (Equation 1).

System	Single	Ens
LIUM	-	16.0
UEDIN	-	**16.5**
(B1) Only BT	14.8	16.3
(B6) SETIMES2 + BT	16.2	17.5
(B6) + *SimpleOut*	16.6	17.6
Ensemble (2xB6 + 2xB6-*SimpleOut*)	-	**18.1**

Table 4: Summary of follow-up results for EN→TR newstest2017: UEDIN is the best WMT17 matrix entry before deadline while LIUM is our primary submission (Table 2).

4 English↔German

We train two types of model: first is trained with only parallel data provided by WMT17 (5.6M sentences), the second uses the concatenation (9.3M sentences) of the provided parallel data and UEDIN WMT16 back-translation corpus [5]. Prior to training, all sentences are normalized, tokenized and truecased using *normalize-punctuation*, *tokenizer* and *truecaser* from Moses (Koehn et al., 2007). Training sentences with less than 2 and more than 100 units are filtered out. A joint Byte Pair Encoding (BPE) model (Sennrich et al., 2016b) with 50K merge operations is learned on the *training data*. This results in a vocabulary of 50K and 53K tokens for English and German respectively.

The training is stopped if no improvement is observed during 30 consecutive validations on *new-*

stest2015. Final systems are selected based on *newstest2016* BLEU.

4.1 Submitted Systems

EN→DE The baseline which is an NMT with **256**-dimensional embeddings and **512**-units GRU layers, obtained 23.26 BLEU on newstest2017 (Table 5). The addition of BT data improved this baseline by 1.7 BLEU (23.26→24.94). Our primary submission which achieved 26.60 BLEU is an ensemble of 4 systems: 2 best checkpoints of an NMT and 2 best checkpoints of an NMT with 0-initialized decoder (See section 3.1).

DE→EN Our primary DE→EN system (Table 5) is an ensemble without back-translation (No-BT) of two NMT systems with different dimensions: 256-512 and 384-640 for embeddings and GRU hidden units respectively. Our post-deadline submission which is an ensemble with back-translation (BT) improved over our primary system by +4.5 BLEU and obtained 33.9 BLEU on newstest2017. This ensemble consists of 6 different systems (by varying the seed and the embedding and the GRU hidden unit size) trained with WMT17 and back-translation data.

System	# Params	nt2016	nt2017
EN→DE Baseline	35.0M	29.11	23.26
+ synthetic		31.08	24.94
primary ensemble		33.89	**26.60**
DE→EN Baseline	52.9M	33.13	29.42
primary ensemble (No-BT)		33.63	*30.10*
+ synthetic		37.36	32.20
post-deadline ensemble (BT)		**39.07**	**33.90**

Table 5: BLEU scores computed with *mteval-v13a.pl* for EN↔DE systems on newstest2016 and newstest2017.

5 English→{Czech,Latvian}

The language pairs English→Czech and English→Latvian are translated using a Factored NMT (FNMT) system where two symbols are generated at the same time. The FNMT systems are compared to a baseline NMT system similar to the one described in Section 2.

5.1 Factored NMT systems

The FNMT system (García-Martínez et al., 2016) is an extension of NMT where the lemma and the Part of Speech (PoS) tags of a word (i.e. factors)

[4]http://matrix.statmt.org
[5]http://data.statmt.org/rsennrich/wmt16_backtranslations

are produced at the output instead of its surface form. The two output symbols are then combined to generate the word using external linguistic resources. The low frequency words in the training set can benefit from sharing the same lemma with other high frequency words, and also from sharing the factors with other words having the same factors. The lemma and its factors can sometimes generate new surface words which are unseen in the training data. The vocabulary of the target language contains only lemmas and PoS tags but the total number of surface words that can be generated (i.e. virtual vocabulary) is larger because of the external linguistic resources that are used. This allows the system to correctly generate words which are considered unknown words in word-based NMT systems.

We experimented with two types of FNMT systems which have a second output in contrast to baseline NMT. The first one contains a single hidden to output layer (*h2o*) which is then used by two separate softmaxes while the second one contains two separate *h2o* layers each specialized for a particular output. The lemma and factor sequences generated by these two outputs are constrained to have the same length.

The results reported in Tables 6 and 7 are computed with *multi-bleu.perl* which makes them consistently lower than official evaluation matrix scores[6].

5.2 Training

All models use **512**-dimensional embeddings and GRU layers with **1024** hidden units. The validation BLEU is computed after each 20K updates and the training stops if no improvement is achieved after 30 consecutive validations. The rest of the hyperparameters are the same as Section 2.

The NMT systems are trained using all the provided bitext processed by a joint BPE model with 90K merge operations. The sentences longer than 50 tokens are filtered out after BPE segmentation. For FNMT systems, BPE is applied on the lemma sequence and the corresponding factors are repeated when a split occurs.

We also trained systems with synthetic data which are initialized with a previously trained model on the provided bitext only. For these systems, the learning rate is set to 0.0001 and the validations are performed every 5K updates in order

to avoid overfitting on synthetic data and forgetting the previously learned weights. Two models with different seeds are trained for NMT and FNMT systems for ensembling purposes.

5.3 N-best Reranking

We experimented with different types of N-best reranking of hypotheses generated with beam search (beam size = 12) using our best FNMT. For each hypothesis, we generate the surface form with the factors-to-word procedure, which can be ambiguous. Since a single {lemma, factors} pair may lead to multiple possible words, k possible words are considered for each pair (with k being 10 for Czech and 100 for Latvian). Finally, the hypotheses are rescored with our best word-based NMT model to select the 1-best hypothesis.

For English→Latvian, we have also performed N-best reranking with two Recurrent Neural Network Language Models (RNNLM), a simple RNNLM (Mikolov et al., 2010) and GRU-based RNNLM included in *nmtpy*. The RNNLMs are trained on WMT17 Latvian monolingual corpus and the target side of the available bitext (175.2M words in total). For the FNMT system, the log probability obtained by our best word-based NMT model is also used in addition to the RNNLM scores. The reranking is done using the *nbest* tool provided by the CSLM toolkit[7] (Schwenk, 2010). (The score weights were optimized with CONDOR (Vanden Berghen and Bersini, 2005) to maximize the BLEU score on newsdev2017 set.)

5.4 English→Czech

The English→Czech systems are trained using approximately 20M sentences from the relevant news domain parallel data provided by WMT17. Early stopping is performed using newstest2015 and newstest2016 is used as internal test set. All datasets are tokenized and truecased using the Moses toolkit (Koehn et al., 2007). PoS tagging is performed with Morphodita toolkit (Straková et al., 2014) as well as the reinflection to go from factored representation to word. Synthetic data is generated from news-2016 monolingual corpus provided by Sennrich et al. (2016a). In order to focus more on the provided bitext, five copies of news-commentary and the *czeng* news dataset are added to the backtranslated data. Also, 5M sen-

---

[6]http://matrix.statmt.org

[7]http://github.com/hschwenk/cslm-toolkit

tences from the *czeng* EU corpus applying modified Moore-Lewis filtering with XenC (Rousseau, 2013). We end up with about 14M sentences and 322M words for English and 292M for Czech.

System	newstest2016	newstest2017
NMT		
(CS1) Baseline	18.30	14.90
(CS2) CS1 + synthetic	24.18	20.26
(CE1) Ensemble(CS2)	24.52	**20.44**
FNMT		
(CS3) single h2o layer	17.30	14.19
(CS4) sep. h2o layers	17.34	14.73
(CS5) CS4 + synthetic	22.30	19.34
(CS6) CS5 n-best reranking	23.39	19.83
(CE2) Ensemble(CS5) n-best reranking	24.05	**20.22**

Table 6: EN→CS. **Bold** scores represent primary submissions. Ensemble(CSn) correspond to the ensemble of 2 systems CSn trained with different seeds.

System	newsdev2017	newstest2017
NMT		
(LS1) Baseline	15.25	10.36
(LS2) LS1 + synthetic	21.88	<u>15.26</u>
(LS3) LS2 RNNLM reranking	21.98	**15.59**
(LE1) Ensemble(LS2)	22.34	15.46
(LE2) Ensemble(LS2) RNNLM reranking	22.46	16.04
FNMT		
(LS4) single h2o layer	14.45	10.45
(LS5) sep. h2o layers	14.39	10.69
(LS6) LS5 + synthetic	18.93	<u>13.98</u>
(LS7) LS6 n-best reranking	21.24	<u>15.28</u>
(LS8) LS6 RNNLM reranking	21.79	**15.51**
(LE3) Ensemble(LS6) n-best reranking	21.90	15.35
(LE4) Ensemble(LS6) RNNLM reranking	21.87	15.53

Table 7: EN→LV. <u>Underlined</u> and **bold** scores represent contrastive and primary submissions. Ensemble(Sn) correspond to the ensemble of 2 systems Sn trained with different seeds.

5.5 English→Latvian

The English→Latvian systems are trained using all the parallel data available for the WMT17 evaluation campaign. Data selection was applied to the DCEP corpus resulting in 2M parallel sentences.The validation set consists of 2K sentences extracted from the LETA corpus and newsdev2017 is used as internal test set.

Monolingual corpora news-2015 and 2016 were backtranslated with a Moses system Koehn et al. (2007). Similarly to Czech, we added ten copies of the LETA corpus and two copies of Europarl and *rapid* to perform corpus weighting. The final corpus contains 7M sentences and 172M words for English and 143M for Latvian.

All the Latvian preprocessing was provided by TILDE.[8] Latvian PoS-tagging is done with the LU MII Tagger (Paikens et al., 2013). Since there is no tool for Latvian to convert factors to words, all the available WMT17 monolingual data has been automatically tagged and kept in a dictionary. This dictionary maps the lemmas and factors to their corresponding word. After preprocessing, we filter out training sentences with a maximum length of 50 or with a source/target length ratio higher than 3.

5.6 Analysis

We observe that including the synthetic parallel data in addition to the provided bitext results in a big improvement in NMT and FNMT for both

language pairs (see systems CS2 and CS5 in Table 6 and LS2 and LS6 in Table 7). Applying the ensemble of several models also gives improvement for all systems (CS1-CS2 and LS1-LS4). N-best reranking of FNMT systems (systems CS6 and LS7) shows bigger improvement when translating into Latvian than into Czech. This is due to the quality of the dictionary used for reinflection in each language. The Morphodita tool for Czech includes only good candidates, besides a similar tool is not available for Latvian. The reranking with RNNLM gives an improvement for the NMT and FNMT systems when translating Latvian (LS3 and LS8). As a follow-up work after submission, we ensembled two models applying reranking for Latvian and got improvements (LE2-LE4). Finally, the submitted translations for NMT and FNMT systems obtain very similar automatic scores. However, FNMT systems explicitly model some grammatical information leading to different lexical choices, which might not be captured by the BLEU score. Human evaluation shows for EN-LV task that NMT system obtained 43% of standardized mean direct assessment score and FNMT system obtained 43.2% showing a small improvement in FNMT system. Both systems obtained 55.2% in EN-CS task. Other analysis has been done (Burlot and Yvon, 2017) about morphology strength showing good results in EN-LV task. FNMT system helps when the corpus is not huge, this is the case of EN-LV task but EN-CS dataset is huge. Therefore, NMT system has already the information to learn the morphology.

---

[8]`www.tilde.com`

6 Conclusion and Discussion

In this paper, we presented LIUM machine translation systems for WMT17 news translation task which are among the top submissions according the official evaluation matrix. All systems are trained using additional synthetic data which significantly improved final translation quality.

For English→Turkish, we obtained (post-deadline) state-of-the-art results with a small model (~11M params) by tying all the embeddings in the network and simplifying the output of the recurrent decoder. One other interesting observation is that the model trained using *only* synthetic data surpassed the one trained on genuine translation corpus. This may indicate that for low-resource pairs, the amount of training data is much more important than the correctness of source-side sentences.

For English→Czech and English→Latvian pairs, the best factored NMT systems performed equally well compared to NMT systems. However, it is important to note that automatic metrics may not be suited to assess better lexical and grammatical choices made by the factored systems.

Acknowledgments

This work was supported by the French National Research Agency (ANR) through the CHIST-ERA M2CR project, under the contract number ANR-15-CHR2-0006-01[9] and also partially supported by the MAGMAT project.

References

Jimmy Lei Ba, Jamie Ryan Kiros, and Geoffrey E Hinton. 2016. Layer normalization. *arXiv preprint arXiv:1607.06450* http://arxiv.org/abs/1607.06450.

Dzmitry Bahdanau, Kyunghyun Cho, and Yoshua Bengio. 2014. Neural machine translation by jointly learning to align and translate. *CoRR* abs/1409.0473. http://arxiv.org/abs/1409.0473.

Franck Burlot and François Yvon. 2017. Evaluating the morphological competence of machine translation systems. In *Proceedings of the Second Conference on Machine Translation (WMT'17)*. Association for Computational Linguistics, Copenhagen, Denmark.

Ozan Caglayan, Mercedes García-Martínez, Adrien Bardet, Walid Aransa, Fethi Bougares, and

Loïc Barrault. 2017. Nmtpy: A flexible toolkit for advanced neural machine translation systems. *arXiv preprint arXiv:1706.00457* http://arxiv.org/abs/1706.00457.

Junyoung Chung, Çaglar Gülçehre, KyungHyun Cho, and Yoshua Bengio. 2014. Empirical evaluation of gated recurrent neural networks on sequence modeling. *CoRR* abs/1412.3555. http://arxiv.org/abs/1412.3555.

Orhan Firat and Kyunghyun Cho. 2016. Conditional gated recurrent unit with attention mechanism. http://github.com/nyu-dl/dl4mt-tutorial/blob/master/docs/cgru.pdf.

Mercedes García-Martínez, Loïc Barrault, and Fethi Bougares. 2016. Factored neural machine translation architectures. In *Proceedings of the International Workshop on Spoken Language Translation*. Seattle, USA, IWSLT'16.

Xavier Glorot and Yoshua Bengio. 2010. Understanding the difficulty of training deep feedforward neural networks. In *Proceedings of the Thirteenth International Conference on Artificial Intelligence and Statistics*. PMLR, volume 9 of *Proceedings of Machine Learning Research*, pages 249–256. http://proceedings.mlr.press/v9/glorot10a.html.

Hakan Inan, Khashayar Khosravi, and Richard Socher. 2016. Tying word vectors and word classifiers: A loss framework for language modeling. *arXiv preprint arXiv:1611.01462* http://arxiv.org/abs/1611.01462.

Diederik Kingma and Jimmy Ba. 2014. Adam: A method for stochastic optimization. *arXiv preprint arXiv:1412.6980* http://arxiv.org/abs/1412.6980.

Philipp Koehn, Hieu Hoang, Alexandra Birch, Chris Callison-Burch, Marcello Federico, Nicola Bertoldi, Brooke Cowan, Wade Shen, Christine Moran, Richard Zens, Chris Dyer, Ondřej Bojar, Alexandra Constantin, and Evan Herbst. 2007. Moses: Open source toolkit for statistical machine translation. In *Proceedings of the 45th Annual Meeting of the ACL on Interactive Poster and Demonstration Sessions*. Association for Computational Linguistics, Stroudsburg, PA, USA, ACL '07, pages 177–180. http://dl.acm.org/citation.cfm?id=1557769.1557821.

Tomas Mikolov, Martin Karafiát, Lukás Burget, Jan Cernocký, and Sanjeev Khudanpur. 2010. Recurrent neural network based language model. In *INTERSPEECH 2010, 11th Annual Conference of the International Speech Communication Association, Makuhari, Chiba, Japan, September 26-30, 2010*. pages 1045–1048. http://www.isca-speech.org/archive/interspeech_2010/i10_1045.html.

Pēteris Paikens, Laura Rituma, and Lauma Pretkalniņa. 2013. Morphological analysis with limited resources: Latvian example. In *Proceedings of the

---

[9]http://m2cr.univ-lemans.fr

19th Nordic Conference of Computational Linguistics (NODALIDA 2013). Linköping University Electronic Press, Sweden, Oslo, Norway, pages 267–277. http://www.aclweb.org/anthology/W13-5624.

Kishore Papineni, Salim Roukos, Todd Ward, and Wei-Jing Zhu. 2002. Bleu: A method for automatic evaluation of machine translation. In *Proceedings of the 40th Annual Meeting on Association for Computational Linguistics*. Association for Computational Linguistics, Stroudsburg, PA, USA, ACL '02, pages 311–318. https://doi.org/10.3115/1073083.1073135.

Razvan Pascanu, Tomas Mikolov, and Yoshua Bengio. 2013. On the difficulty of training recurrent neural networks. In *Proceedings of the 30th International Conference on International Conference on Machine Learning - Volume 28*. JMLR.org, ICML'13, pages III–1310–III–1318. http://dl.acm.org/citation.cfm?id=3042817.3043083.

Ofir Press and Lior Wolf. 2017. Using the output embedding to improve language models. In *Proceedings of the 15th Conference of the European Chapter of the Association for Computational Linguistics: Volume 2, Short Papers*. Association for Computational Linguistics, Valencia, Spain, pages 157–163. http://www.aclweb.org/anthology/E17-2025.

Anthony Rousseau. 2013. XenC: An open-source tool for data selection in natural language processing. *The Prague Bulletin of Mathematical Linguistics* (100):73–82. http://ufal.mff.cuni.cz/pbml/100/art-rousseau.pdf.

Holger Schwenk. 2010. Continuous-space language models for statistical machine translation. *The Prague Bulletin of Mathematical Linguistics* (93):137–146. http://ufal.mff.cuni.cz/pbml/93/art-schwenk.pdf.

Rico Sennrich, Orhan Firat, Kyunghyun Cho, Alexandra Birch, Barry Haddow, Julian Hitschler, Marcin Junczys-Dowmunt, Samuel Läubli, Antonio Valerio Miceli Barone, Jozef Mokry, and Maria Nadejde. 2017. Nematus: a toolkit for neural machine translation. In *Proceedings of the Software Demonstrations of the 15th Conference of the European Chapter of the Association for Computational Linguistics*. Association for Computational Linguistics, Valencia, Spain, pages 65–68. http://aclweb.org/anthology/E17-3017.

Rico Sennrich, Barry Haddow, and Alexandra Birch. 2016a. Improving neural machine translation models with monolingual data. In *Proceedings of the 54th Annual Meeting of the Association for Computational Linguistics (Volume 1: Long Papers)*. Association for Computational Linguistics, Berlin, Germany, pages 86–96. http://www.aclweb.org/anthology/P16-1009.

Rico Sennrich, Barry Haddow, and Alexandra Birch. 2016b. Neural machine translation of rare words with subword units. In *Proceedings of the 54th Annual Meeting of the Association for Computational Linguistics (Volume 1: Long Papers)*. Association for Computational Linguistics, Berlin, Germany, pages 1715–1725. http://www.aclweb.org/anthology/P16-1162.

Nitish Srivastava, Geoffrey Hinton, Alex Krizhevsky, Ilya Sutskever, and Ruslan Salakhutdinov. 2014. Dropout: A simple way to prevent neural networks from overfitting. *J. Mach. Learn. Res.* 15(1):1929–1958. http://dl.acm.org/citation.cfm?id=2627435.2670313.

Jana Straková, Milan Straka, and Jan Hajič. 2014. Open-source tools for morphology, lemmatization, pos tagging and named entity recognition. In *Proceedings of 52nd Annual Meeting of the Association for Computational Linguistics: System Demonstrations*. Association for Computational Linguistics, Baltimore, Maryland, pages 13–18. http://www.aclweb.org/anthology/P14-5003.

Ilya Sutskever, Oriol Vinyals, and Quoc V. Le. 2014. Sequence to sequence learning with neural networks. In *Proceedings of the 27th International Conference on Neural Information Processing Systems*. MIT Press, Cambridge, MA, USA, NIPS'14, pages 3104–3112. http://dl.acm.org/citation.cfm?id=2969033.2969173.

Frank Vanden Berghen and Hugues Bersini. 2005. Condor, a new parallel, constrained extension of powell's uobyqa algorithm: Experimental results and comparison with the dfo algorithm. *J. Comput. Appl. Math.* 181(1):157–175. https://doi.org/10.1016/j.cam.2004.11.029.

Extending hybrid word-character neural machine translation with multi-task learning of morphological analysis

Stig-Arne Grönroos and **Sami Virpioja** and **Mikko Kurimo**

`stig-arne.gronroos@aalto.fi`

Department of Signal Processing and Acoustics, Aalto University, Finland

Abstract

This article describes the Aalto University entry to the English-to-Finnish news translation shared task in WMT 2017. Our system is an open vocabulary neural machine translation (NMT) system, adapted to the needs of a morphologically complex target language. The main contributions of this paper are 1) implicitly incorporating morphological information to NMT through multi-task learning, 2) adding an attention mechanism to the character-level decoder, combined with character segmentation of names, and 3) a new overattending penalty to beam search.

1 Introduction

The rich inflection, derivation and compounding in synthetic languages can result in very large vocabularies. In statistical machine translation (SMT) large vocabularies cause sparsity issues. While continuous space representations make neural machine translation (NMT) more robust towards such sparsity, it suffers from a different set of problems related to large vocabularies. A large vocabulary bloats memory and computation requirements, while still leaving the problem of out-of-vocabulary words unsolved.

Subword vocabularies have been proposed as a solution. While the benefits of using subwords in SMT have been at best moderate (Virpioja et al., 2007; Fishel and Kirik, 2010; Grönroos et al., 2015), subword decoding has become popular in NMT (Sennrich et al., 2015). A subword vocabulary of a moderate size ensures full coverage of an open vocabulary. The downside is an increase in the length of the input and output sequences. Long sequences cause a large increase in computation time, especially for architectures using the attention mechanism.

An alternative approach is the hybrid word-character decoder presented by Luong and Manning (2016). In the hybrid decoder, a word level decoder outputs frequent words as they are, while replacing infrequent words with a special <UNK> symbol. A second character-level decoder then expands these <UNK> symbols into surface forms.

In addition to providing moderate length of input and output sequences together with an open vocabulary, the hybrid word-character decoder makes it simple to use labels based on the level of words, provided for example by morphological analyzers and parsers. In SMT, such tools are typically used via factored translation models (Koehn and Hoang, 2007). Factored translation has also been successfully applied in NMT. For example, Sennrich and Haddow (2016) augment the source words with four additional factors: PoS, lemma, dependency label and subwords. García-Martínez et al. (2016) use a decomposed generation process, in which they first output lemma, PoS, tense, person, gender, and number, from which the surface form is generated using a rule-based morphological analyzer.

Neural machine translation provides another way to utilize external annotations, multi-task learning (MTL). MTL is a well established machine learning approach that aims at improving the generalization performance of a task using other related tasks (Caruana, 1998). For example, Luong et al. (2016) use autoencoding, parsing, and caption generation as auxiliary tasks to improve English-to-German translation. Eriguchi et al. (2017) combine NMT with a Recurrent Neural Network Grammar. The system learns to parse the target language as an auxiliary task when translating into English.

We propose an MTL approach inspired by fac-

Proceedings of the Conference on Machine Translation (WMT), Volume 2: Shared Task Papers, pages 296–302
Copenhagen, Denmark, September 7–11, 2017. ©2017 Association for Computational Linguistics

tored translation. The output of a morphological analyzer for the target sentence is used as an auxiliary prediction target, while sharing network parameters to a larger extent than in the approach of Luong et al. (2016).

This approach has two advantages over factored models. When training a system using factored output, embedded gold standard labels are given as input to the decoder. During translation gold standard labels are not available, and predicted labels are instead fed back in. The confidence of the predictions is not accounted for when feeding back the labels. This might worsen the problems caused by exposure bias, i.e., the mismatch between training and inference (Ranzato et al., 2016). If factored input is used, the external labeling tools need to be included also in the translation pipeline. In MTL such tools are only necessary during training.

In terms of computational cost, a factored model needs to predict the auxiliary labels also during translation, slowing down inference and complicating the beam search. A factored model might also need to use a larger beam to avoid hypotheses with the same surface form but different labels from crowding out more diverse hypotheses. In MTL, the auxiliary tasks are only performed during training, and no changes need to be made to the inference.

The main contributions of this paper are combining word-level labels from morphological analysis with a hybrid word-character decoder, and adding an attention mechanism to the character-level decoder. We also propose a new overattending penalty to the beam search.

2 Neural machine translation

Neural machine translation (NMT) is a framework for machine translation that uses a single neural network trained end-to-end. The recently proposed encoder-decoder network with attention mechanism (Bahdanau et al., 2014) has become accepted as the current standard in NMT.

The first part of the network, the encoder, reads a source sentence x and encodes it as a sequence of hidden states $s = (s_1, s_2, \ldots, s_N)$. The encoder is often implemented as a bidirectional recurrent network with long short-term memory units (bi-LSTM), in which case each hidden state is the concatenation of a state from the forward and backward encoders.

The last part of the network, the decoder, is implemented as a conditional recurrent language model which models the probability of the target sentence y as

$$
\begin{aligned}
\log p(\boldsymbol{y} \mid \boldsymbol{x}) &= \sum_t \log p(y_t \mid \boldsymbol{y}_{<t}, \boldsymbol{x}) \\
&= \sum_t \log p(y_t \mid h_t, c_t).
\end{aligned}
\tag{1}
$$

The encoder and decoder are linked by the attention mechanism. At each timestep, the attention mechanism computes a context vector c_t as a weighted average of the encoder hidden states s. The weights $a_{t,i}$ are determined by a layer that takes as input the current decoder hidden state h_t and each of the vectors s_i in turn.

$$
a_{t,i}(h, s) = \frac{\exp(\text{align}(\boldsymbol{h}_t, \boldsymbol{s}_i))}{\sum_j \exp(\text{align}(\boldsymbol{h}_t, \boldsymbol{s}_j))}
$$
$$
\text{align}(\boldsymbol{h}_t, \boldsymbol{s}_i) = \boldsymbol{v}_a^\top \tanh(W_a[\boldsymbol{h}_t; \boldsymbol{s}_i])
\tag{2}
$$

In effect, at each timestep the attention mechanism scans the entire source to decide which parts are relevant to focus on when generating the next output symbol.

Luong and Manning (2016) extend the word-level encoder-decoder model by adding character-level processing of rare words. On the encoder side, word embeddings for rare source words are produced by a character-level encoder, instead of using a universal <UNK> embedding. The hybrid model ensures an open vocabulary, while keeping the attended sequence shorter than using characters or subwords.

On the decoder side, the word-level decoder outputs <UNK> for rare words, while storing the decoder hidden state at that timestep. A separate character-level decoder expands these tokens into the surface form. The character-level encoder and decoder can be trained jointly with the word-level components, by backpropagating end-to-end.

In separate path initialization of the character-level decoder, the word-level LSTM output h is not used to seed the character-level decoder, but instead a counterpart vector $\breve{h}$ is calculated as

$$
\breve{h}_t = \tanh(\breve{W}[c_t; h_t])
$$

3 System description

Our system is based on the open-source Helsinki Neural Machine Translation (HNMT) software[1].

---

[1] Available from
`https://github.com/robertostling/hnmt`.

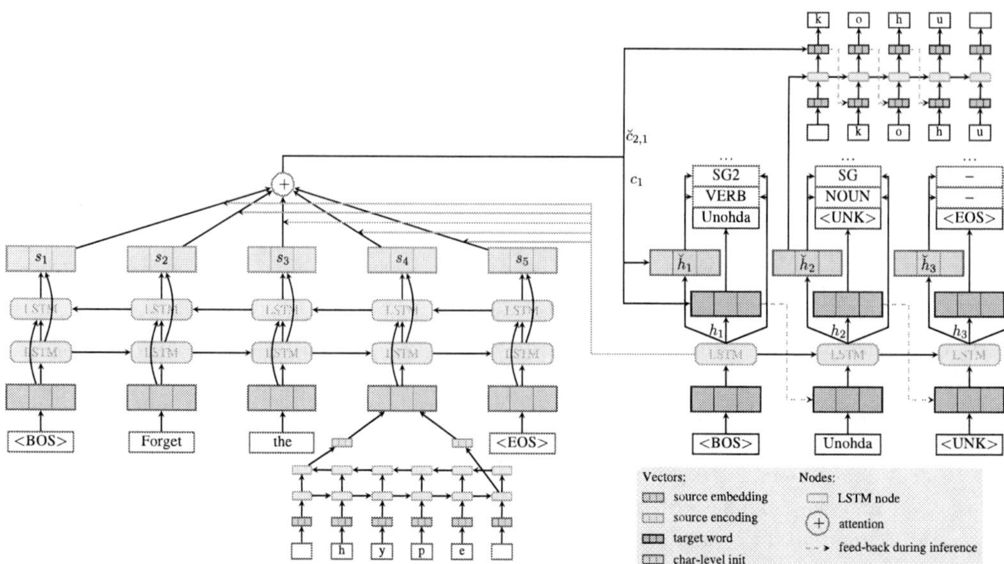

Figure 1: Our neural network architecture. In the example, "Forget the hype" is translated into "Unohda kohu". On the left side, the hybrid word-character encoder, using bi-LSTM for both levels. On the lower right side, the word-level attentional LSTM decoder, which predicts both word tokens and auxiliary labels. Above it, the predicted <UNK> is expanded by the attentional character-level decoder. For clarity, attention is only drawn for the first timestep of each decoder.

We extend[2] HNMT with a hybrid word-character decoder, multi-task learning, and improved beam search. An overview of the neural network architecture can be seen in Figure 1.

Hybrid encoder-decoder. HNMT implements a hybrid word-character encoder. Instead of the two-level unidirectional LSTM character-level encoders of Luong and Manning (2016), bi-LSTM encoders are used. The embedding for rare words is the concatenation of the last states of the forward and backward character-level encoders.

We extend HNMT with a hybrid word-character decoder, using separate path initialization of the character-level decoder. We also add an attention mechanism to the character-level decoder, yielding the character-level context vector $\check{c}_{t,t_c}$. The attended sequence is the same as for the word-level decoder: the word-level encoding s of the source sentence. To make it possible for the attentional character-level decoder to copy or transcribe on a subword-level, we perform character segmentation preprocessing on capitalized input words (after truecasing). The segmentation is described in Section 4.

Multi-task learning. The main task is transla-

tion into the target language surface form, while the auxiliary tasks consist of predicting the output of the FinnPos morphological analyzer for the target sentence. The auxiliary tasks provide additional supervision signals that can help the model learn grammar and morphology. The tasks share parameters more closely than the one-to-many multi-task learning setting defined by Luong et al. (2016). In addition to sharing the encoder, all parts of the word level decoder except the final feed-forward prediction layers are shared. A potential downside compared to using a separate decoder is that the label sequence must be of the same length and synchronous with the surface sequence. This tightly shared MTL matches perfectly with the hybrid word-character decoder, as the labeling is on the level of words. The work-around of repeating labels to match the length of a subword sequence was not explored in this work.

In MTL, the supervision from the labels is softer than when using a factored model. Uncertain labels could be ignored, by limiting the task to sentences with high-confidence labels. We did not use this opportunity, as FinnPos labels every input sentence, and does not provide confidence estimates. As all our data $\mathcal{D}$ is labeled, we control the influence of the auxiliary task using a multiplica-

---

[2]Our fork available from
https://github.com/Waino/hnmt .

tive weight on part of the cost function, instead of the minibatch mixing ratio used by Luong et al. (2016).

We train the whole model jointly to maximize

$$E_{(\boldsymbol{x},\boldsymbol{y},\boldsymbol{a})\in\mathcal{D}}[\log p(\boldsymbol{y},\boldsymbol{a}\mid \boldsymbol{x})]$$

where $\boldsymbol{a}$ are the labels: the cluster id of the lemma, the rounded log-frequency of the lemma, the PoS, and 5 morphological tags: number, case, person, mood, and tense. Each label is independently predicted from the concatenation of h and $\breve{h}$.

Beam search scoring function. We use beam search during decoding to find the optimal translation sequence $\boldsymbol{y}$. Instead of directly maximizing the probability, we maximize a score function $s(\boldsymbol{y},\boldsymbol{x})$, designed to alleviate two known issues in NMT: overtranslation and undertranslation.

Undertranslation is reduced by adding length normalization (lp) and a coverage penalty (cp), following Wu et al. (2016).

Unlike undertranslation, overtranslation is to some extent inherently reduced by the monotonically increasing generation log-probabilities. However, the inherent cost is not enough, leading us to add a penalty for overattending a source token (oap). The penalty is applied if the most attended source word has sum attention over 1.0. We use the maximum function instead of sum, in order not to increase the strength of the penalty for long input sentences. The overattending penalty is monotonically increasing, which enables us to include it when pruning active hypotheses.

The overattending penalty is not suitable if the decoder uses smaller units than the output of the encoder. Repeated attention is required if the decoder must output several subwords for each source token.

The scoring function is

$$s(\boldsymbol{y},\boldsymbol{x}) = -\log\big(p(\boldsymbol{y}\mid\boldsymbol{x})\big) + \mathrm{lp}(\boldsymbol{y})$$
$$+ \mathrm{cp}(\boldsymbol{y},\boldsymbol{x}) + \mathrm{oap}(\boldsymbol{y},\boldsymbol{x}), \qquad (3)$$

where

$$\mathrm{lp}(\boldsymbol{y}) = \frac{(|\boldsymbol{y}|+\lambda)^{\alpha}}{(1+\lambda)^{\alpha}} \qquad (4)$$

$$\mathrm{cp}(\boldsymbol{y},\boldsymbol{x}) = \beta \sum_{i=1}^{|\boldsymbol{x}|}\log\Big(\min(\sum_{j=1}^{|\boldsymbol{y}|} a_{ij}, 1.0)\Big) \qquad (5)$$

$$\mathrm{oap}(\boldsymbol{y},\boldsymbol{x}) = -\gamma\max\Big(\max_{i=1}^{|\boldsymbol{x}|}\big(\sum_{j=1}^{|\boldsymbol{y}|} a_{ij} - 1.0\big), 0.0\Big) \qquad (6)$$

The parameters α, β, γ, and λ control the strengths of the penalties.

Pruning in beam search. We use three types of pruning in the beam search.

First, at each step, for each hypothesis to be extended, we prune the list of candidates for the next symbol based on local probability, to only keep $beam\_width + 1$ candidates. This pruning improves speed without affecting the output.

Second, after at least one hypothesis has been completed, we keep track of the current best normalized score. This allows pruning active hypotheses by comparing their partially normalized score against the best normalized score, with adjustable pruning margin. The partially normalized score is calculated as the sum of the monotonically increasing parts of the scoring function

$$-\log\big(p(\boldsymbol{y}\mid\boldsymbol{x})\big) + \mathrm{oap}(\boldsymbol{y},\boldsymbol{x})$$

This pruning may affect the output by removing a hypothesis with a poor early score that could have improved later. To gain a speed-up, it is necessary to prune active hypotheses: limiting pruning to completed hypotheses cannot reduce the number of hypotheses in early stages, and thus cannot result in early clearing of the beam.

Completed hypotheses are moved from the beam to a separate heap. This clears out room in the beam for active hypotheses, but also means that the pruning of active hypotheses becomes essential for early stopping of the beam search.

The third type of pruning is applied to the heap of completed hypotheses based on normalized score, to only keep n best hypotheses. This pruning conserves memory and does not affect the ordering of the results.

4 Data

Our system participates in the constrained condition of the WMT shared task. As training data, we used the Europarl-v8, Rapid and Wikititles corpora, extended with backtranslated monolingual data, resulting in 6 091 184 parallel sentence pairs after cleaning. The backtranslated sentences were from the news.2014.fi corpus, translated with a PB-SMT model, trained with WMT16 constrained settings. Based on initial experiments we decided to use the full backtranslated set, for a ratio of ca 60% backtranslated to 40% parallel data, instead of sub-sampling to balance the ratio.

Configuration	newstest2016AB			newstest2017			
	chrF-1	chrF-2	BLEU	chrF-1	chrF-2	BLEU	TER
Hybrid decoder with MTL, ensemble of 4	56.79	**55.60**	21.46	57.30	**55.96**	20.28	**.673**
+ repetition removal	**57.07**	55.59	**21.55**	**57.57**	55.92	**20.31**	–
FlatCat subword decoder, ensemble of 4	55.77	55.41	20.01	54.10	53.98	17.15	.750
Hybrid decoder with MTL, single model	54.69	53.43	18.60	55.17	53.87	17.84	–

Table 1: Results of automatic evaluation. BLEU and chrF scores are percentages. TER from `http://matrix.statmt.org/matrix/systems_list/1871?metric_id=2` .

Configuration	newstest2016AB		
	chrF-1	chrF-2	BLEU
Hybrid decoder with MTL	56.79	55.60	21.46
No morphological tags	55.97	55.20	19.83
No log frequency	55.49	54.26	19.47
No clustered lemma	55.23	53.65	19.37
No PoS-tags	55.05	53.73	19.29
No multi-task learning	54.91	53.48	19.43
No character attention & name segmentation	52.12	50.80	17.16
No length penalty	56.68	55.52	21.35
No overattending penalty	56.68	55.53	21.33
No coverage penalty	56.43	54.93	20.97
No penalties	55.90	54.21	20.45

Table 2: Results of ablation experiments. All runs are ensembles of 4, to reduce variability.

Data preprocessing consists of filtering too long sentences, normalizing misencoded data, normalizing punctuation, deduplication, tokenization, statistical truecasing, filtering of untranslated sentences, and character segmentation of names on the source side.

Segmenting names into characters, when combined with attention on the character level, allows copying or transliteration on a character-to-character basis. It is applied using a rough heuristic: we segment any token longer than one character beginning with an upper case letter or digit. All segmented characters are marked using reserved symbols. The first and last characters of the sequence have distinct symbols separating them from word-internal characters.

The filtering of untranslated sentences was also performed using a rough heuristic, by filtering any sentences containing certain common English contractions and clitics that do not occur in Finnish. The target side training data, especially Europarl, contains hundreds of sentences with English phrases. A typical reason is discussions on the wording of English-language documents being drafted. The filtering was an attempt to alleviate a failure mode in which the system would instead of translating attempt (and fail) to output the English source.

A parallel corpus augmented with gold-standard labels for MTL is not available. We tag the target side of the parallel corpus using the statistical tagger FinnPos (Silfverberg et al., 2016). The resulting labels are noisy, but nonetheless provide supervision for the morphological analysis task.

We postprocess the output of FinnPos. The morpheme tag sequence is split, and tags are grouped by type. FinnPos lemmas are noisy, containing many remaining affixes and other mislemmatizations. We collapse numbers into a single number symbol, remove special characters, and cluster the remaining lemmas into 10 000 clusters with word2vec (Mikolov et al., 2013).

5 Training details

We use the following parameters for the network: weight of auxiliary task between 0.001 and 0.75, 64 dimensional character embeddings, 256 dimensional word embeddings, 128 dimensional aux embeddings, 2*256 dimensional encoder state, 1024 dimensional word decoder state, 1024 dimensional character decoder state, 256 dimensional attention, everything except 25k most frequent source words embedded by character level encoder, 50k most frequent target words output by word level decoder, 10k overlap between word level and character level vocabularies during training.

For training, we use Adam with initial learning rate 0.001 and gradient norm clipped to 5.0.

The systems have been tuned towards characterF-1.0 (Popovic, 2015, 2016). We optimize the beam search parameters, using a grid search. The optimal parameters were α 0.012,

β 0.3, γ 0.2, λ 3, pruning margin 1.4, and weight 0.8 for the character-level cost.

We use an ensemble procedure, in which the combined prediction is computed as the mean after the softmax layer of the predictions of 4 models. The primary system uses systems from 4 runs with different weights for the auxiliary task. The systems trained for comparison—a subword system based on Morfessor FlatCat and the systems in ablation experiments—were ensembled using 4 save points from a single run.

To include an example of subword NMT, we also submit our FlatCat system. As preprocessing, the target side has been segmented using Morfessor FlatCat (Grönroos et al., 2014), which was tuned to produce a subword lexicon of approximately 60k symbols. Segmenting names into characters is applied in addition to the FlatCat segmentation. The FlatCat segmented system uses WMT 2016 data only, i.e., omits the Rapid corpus.

The FlatCat subword system uses the standard HNMT decoder. It uses neither the hybrid word-character decoder nor MTL. We did however use the improved beam search with penalties.

6 Results

We evaluate the systems using characterF with β set to 1.0 and 2.0, and cased BLEU using the `mteval-v13a.pl` script. We also include Translation Error Rate (TER) results for the submitted systems. Our primary system has the best TER score of all participants.

As the development test set we use both reference translations of the newstest 2016 set. Table 1 shows the submitted ensemble systems, and the best single model for our primary system. As our system has a tendency to repeat certain words, we also evaluate the primary system after a postprocessing step in which consecutive repetitions are removed.

We perform ablation experiments for all new components in our system, by removing each of them separately (non-cumulative effect). Results are shown in Table 2.

All added components were beneficial. The largest improvement, +4.3 BLEU, comes from the attention mechanism in the character decoder, combined with segmenting names into characters.

Multi-task learning improves BLEU by +2.03. Not all auxiliary labels are equally important. PoS tags (+2.17 BLEU) and clustered lemmas (+2.09

BLEU) perform above average, and removing either of them yields worse BLEU than not using MTL at all. The results of both characterF measures differ in this, ranking not using MTL as worse than all the partial MTL variants.

The overattending penalty to the beam search gives a much more modest gain of +0.13 BLEU. The coverage penalty is the most important of the beam search penalties. In total, the beam search heuristics yield an improvement of +1.01 BLEU.

In the human evaluation, our primary system was ranked in the second of five clusters (tied 3rd to 5th place).

7 Discussion

All our added components improved the translation quality.

The largest improvement comes from the modifications intended to enable character-to-character copying: segmenting names into characters and character-level attention. However, the simple heuristic used for selecting words to segment can make translation more difficult in some cases, e.g. the names of institutions are typically capitalized, but translated on a term level. Replacing the heuristic with named-entity recognition or other more advanced methods is left for future work.

A common type of error made by our system is overtranslation through repetition. A possible explanation for the effect is the way that the levels of the hybrid word-character decoder are connected. There is no connection from the character level back to the word level. The surface forms generated by the character-level decoder are conditionally independent given the word-level hidden states, which can be similar to the states at adjacent time steps. The word-level decoder must decide on the number of words in an expression, which is a difficult task if the proportion of <UNK> tokens becomes large. The overattending penalty is only partially successful at reducing the repetition, and increasing the penalty weight deteriorates overall performance before eliminating the problem.

8 Conclusion

Our results show that translation into a morphologically complex language can be improved using word-level labels from morphological analysis combined with a hybrid word-character decoder. Adding an attention mechanism to the character decoder yields a large quality improvement.

Acknowledgements

This research has been supported by the Academy of Finland under the Finnish Centre of Excellence Program 2012–2017 (grant n°251170). Computer resources within the Aalto University School of Science "Science-IT" project were used. We wish to thank Jörg Tiedemann for the useful discussions and for sharing his backtranslations.

References

Dzmitry Bahdanau, Kyunghyun Cho, and Yoshua Bengio. 2014. Neural machine translation by jointly learning to align and translate. In *ICLR15*.

Rich Caruana. 1998. Multitask learning. In *Learning to learn*, Springer, pages 95–133.

Akiko Eriguchi, Yoshimasa Tsuruoka, and Kyunghyun Cho. 2017. Learning to parse and translate improves neural machine translation. *arXiv preprint arXiv:1702.03525* .

Mark Fishel and Harri Kirik. 2010. Linguistically motivated unsupervised segmentation for machine translation. In *Language Resources and Evaluation (LREC)*. Valletta, Malta.

Mercedes García-Martínez, Loïc Barrault, and Fethi Bougares. 2016. Factored neural machine translation. *arXiv preprint arXiv:1609.04621* .

Stig-Arne Grönroos, Sami Virpioja, and Mikko Kurimo. 2015. Tuning phrase-based segmented translation for a morphologically complex target language. In *WMT15*. Association for Computational Linguistics, Lisbon, Portugal, pages 105–111.

Stig-Arne Grönroos, Sami Virpioja, Peter Smit, and Mikko Kurimo. 2014. Morfessor FlatCat: An HMM-based method for unsupervised and semi-supervised learning of morphology. In *COLING14*. Association for Computational Linguistics, pages 1177–1185.

Philipp Koehn and Hieu Hoang. 2007. Factored translation models. In *EMNLP-CoNLL*. pages 868–876.

Minh-Thang Luong, Quoc V Le, Ilya Sutskever, Oriol Vinyals, and Lukasz Kaiser. 2016. Multi-task sequence to sequence learning. In *ICLR*.

Minh-Thang Luong and Christopher D. Manning. 2016. Achieving open vocabulary neural machine translation with hybrid word-character models. In *ACL16*.

Tomas Mikolov, Ilya Sutskever, Kai Chen, Greg S Corrado, and Jeff Dean. 2013. Distributed representations of words and phrases and their compositionality. In *Advances in neural information processing systems (NIPS)*. Lake Tahoe, NV, USA, pages 3111–3119.

Maja Popovic. 2015. chrF: character n-gram F-score for automatic MT evaluation. In *WMT15*. pages 392–395.

Maja Popovic. 2016. chrF deconstructed: β parameters and n-gram weights. In *WMT16*.

Marc'Aurelio Ranzato, Sumit Chopra, Michael Auli, and Wojciech Zaremba. 2016. Sequence level training with recurrent neural networks. In *International Conference on Learning Representations (ICLR)*.

Rico Sennrich and Barry Haddow. 2016. Linguistic input features improve neural machine translation. In *WMT16*. Association for Computational Linguistics, pages 83–91.

Rico Sennrich, Barry Haddow, and Alexandra Birch. 2015. Neural machine translation of rare words with subword units. In *ACL16*.

Miikka Silfverberg, Teemu Ruokolainen, Krister Lindén, and Mikko Kurimo. 2016. FinnPos: an open-source morphological tagging and lemmatization toolkit for Finnish. *Language Resources and Evaluation (LREC)* 50(4):863–878.

Sami Virpioja, Jaakko J Väyrynen, Mathias Creutz, and Markus Sadeniemi. 2007. Morphology-aware statistical machine translation based on morphs induced in an unsupervised manner. *Machine Translation Summit XI* 2007:491–498.

Yonghui Wu, Mike Schuster, Zhifeng Chen, Quoc V Le, Mohammad Norouzi, Wolfgang Macherey, Maxim Krikun, Yuan Cao, Qin Gao, Klaus Macherey, et al. 2016. Google's neural machine translation system: Bridging the gap between human and machine translation. *arXiv preprint arXiv:1609.08144* .

The AFRL-MITLL WMT17 Systems: Old, New, Borrowed, BLEU

Jeremy Gwinnup, Timothy Anderson,
Grant Erdmann, Katherine Young
Air Force Research Laboratory
{jeremy.gwinnup.1,timothy.anderson.20,
grant.erdmann,katherine.young.1.ctr}
@us.af.mil

Michaeel Kazi, Elizabeth Salesky,
Brian Thompson, Jonathan Taylor
MIT Lincoln Laboratory
{michaeel.kazi,elizabeth.salesky,
brian.thompson,jonathan.taylor}
@ll.mit.edu

Abstract

This paper describes the AFRL-MITLL machine translation systems and the improvements that were developed during the WMT17 evaluation campaign. This year, we explore the continuing proliferation of Neural Machine Translation toolkits, revisit our previous data-selection efforts for use in training systems with these new toolkits and expand our participation to the Russian–English, Turkish–English and Chinese–English translation pairs.

1 Introduction

As part of the 2017 Conference on Machine Translation (WMT, 2017) news-translation shared task, the MITLL and AFRL human language technology teams participated in the Russian–English, English–Russian, Turkish–English and Chinese–English tasks.

Our machine translation systems this year are a departure from our previous Moses (Koehn et al., 2007) based systems from WMT16 (Gwinnup et al., 2016). We employ systems built with the Nematus (Sennrich et al., 2017) toolkit as in our IWSLT2016 (Kazi et al., 2016) systems, the Nematus-compatible Marian training toolkit and AmuNMT decoder (Junczys-Dowmunt et al., 2016) and the OpenNMT (Klein et al., 2017) toolkit.

For the Russian–English and Turkish–English language pairs, we submitted an entry comprising the best systems combined using the Jane system combination method (Freitag et al., 2014) and the best-scoring single system for that language pair.

For the Chinese–English and English-Russian language pairs, we only submitted our single-best system.

2 Data and Preparation

2.1 Data Used

We utilized all available data sources provided for the language pairs we participated in, including the Commoncrawl (Smith et al., 2013), Yandex[1], UN v1.0 (Ziemski et al., 2016), SETimes (Tyers and Alperen, 2010) corpora.

2.2 Data Preparation

The Russian/English files were cleaned to remove blank lines, replace carriage returns with line feed characters, remove wrong-language text, and correct mixed alphabet spellings, following techniques outlined in (Young et al., 2016) and (Schwartz et al., 2014).

The number of non-parallel blank lines in the Russian/English news commentary files indicated some sentence alignment errors, so these files were re-processed using the NLTK Punkt (Kiss and Strunk, 2006) sentence segmenter and the Champollion sentence aligner (Ma, 2006) before cleaning. Altogether, 9537 of the original 236,314 newscommentary lines were removed during the clean-up process.

The Chinese files were word-segmented with Jieba[2] and the Stanford Chinese segmenter (Chang et al., 2008). The Chinese–English parallel data was cleaned to replace carriage returns and to remove wrong-language text. Lines with URLs in *http* were also removed, because of a difference in the Chinese and English tokenization. Altogether, the clean-up process removed 310,121 of the 21,248,495 lines in the combined file.

Portions of this work are sponsored by the Air Force Research Laboratory under Air Force contracts FA-8721-05-C-0002 and FA-8650-09-D-6939-029.

[1]https://translate.yandex.ru/corpus?lang=en
[2]https://github.com/fxsjy/jieba

Proceedings of the Conference on Machine Translation (WMT), Volume 2: Shared Task Papers, pages 303–309
Copenhagen, Denmark, September 7–11, 2017. ©2017 Association for Computational Linguistics

2.3 Subselection

We use our corpus subselection algorithm, defined in (Gwinnup et al., 2016). We use a vocabulary of up to 4-grams for subselection, after using byte-pair encoding (see Section 3) to produce sub-word units. We believe that selecting from subwords is especially beneficial in morphologically-complex languages like Turkish and Russian.

For Russian we conducted monolingual selection from provided Common Crawl, to match test sets from 2012-2016 (15K lines total). This corpus was broken into 571 chunks of one million lines each, and five thousand lines were selected from each (2.9M lines total). 3-gram and 4-gram sub-word subselection vocabulary was used.

For Turkish we conducted monolingual selection from Common Crawl, to match SE Times and dev/test 2016 corpora (212K lines total). This corpus was broken into 502 chunks of one million lines each, and 25 thousand lines were selected from each (12.5M lines total). 4-gram subword subselection vocabulary was used.

After this subselection process completed for various languages we then sampled the first 3000 (e.g. top-scoring) English sentences from each selected chunk. For Russian and Turkish, we utilized the entire subselected chunk. Final line-counts for these selected data sets are listed in Table 1.

Language	Final Lines
English	8,921,942
Russian	2,856,141
Turkish	5,011,001

Table 1: Final count of subselected lines per language used in training AFRL's backtranslation systems.

3 MT System Descriptions

This year we participated in the Russian–English, English–Russian, Turkish–English and Chinese–English translation pairs using a variety of toolkits and techniques. Of particular note, we employed byte-pair encoding (Sennrich et al., 2016b) (BPE) of the source and target training data to address the out-of-vocabulary(OOV) problem.

3.1 Russian–English

The Russian–English language pair has been our largest focus since our participation in WMT14.

We spent significant effort building a variety of systems described as described below.

3.1.1 AFRL Nematus/Marian Systems

Our Nematus/Marian systems follow the general approach of the WMT16 Edinburgh NMT systems (Sennrich et al., 2016a) with the following differences: We use the data selection algorithm described in Section 2.3 yielding approximately 5 million additional lines of backtranslated data.

In order to produce this backtranslated data we performed the following steps: 1) We first used Edinburgh's backtranslated data from WMT16 to produce a Nematus-based Russian–English system. 2) Once trained, we used the Amun decoder to translate the 2.8 million lines of subselected monolingual Commoncrawl Russian data into English. 3) The resulting data was then used to train an English–Russian Marian system that then used the Amun decoder to translate the 8.9 million lines of subselected English data to Russian. 4) Following this decoding, a final Russian–English system was trained using Marian with this backtranslated data. Three separate Marian training runs were performed with this final data set. Additionally, a Nematus system was trained for rescoring purposes where the English target data was reversed in word order. The combination of these final inputs was optimized with Drem (Erdmann and Gwinnup, 2015) to determine feature weights.

3.1.2 AFRL OpenNMT Systems

We trained four OpenNMT systems. Two systems employed the backtranslated data used in last year's University of Edinburgh NMT systems (Sennrich et al., 2017). The other two systems employed the subselected data as described in Section 2.3. All systems used 1000 hidden units and 600 unit word embeddings.

The two WMT16-based systems were each fine-tuned with `newstest2012-2015` data. One system was also incrementally trained with the same newstest data. The subselected systems had cased BLEU scores of 30.04 and 30.67 on `newstest2017` while the WMT16-based systems had BLEU scores of 32.16 and 32.78. They were all single systems.

Since OpenNMT currently does not support ensemble decoding, we decided to try doing system combination on the last four epochs of training. Taking the best system from the subselected data then gave a BLEU score of 33.95 while the best

WMT16-based systems increased to 33.23. Combining the four ensembles of each of those systems resulted in a score of 34.45 BLEU. This last ensemble system combination was done after the submission deadline.

3.1.3 MITLL Phrase-Based System

While similar to last year's phrase-based system (Gwinnup et al., 2016), this year's system differs in a few key ways: 1) We use Moses truecased training data, to make our tokenization scheme uniform; 2) We rescore using systems built from data made available by Edinburgh's WMT16 System (Sennrich et al., 2016a); 3) We updated our language models with the new monolingual data sources, and finally 4) We add an additional 4 million lines from the UN v1.0 corpus (Ziemski et al., 2016) into the parallel training data.

For the last item, we used Moore-Lewis (Moore and Lewis, 2010) filtering on the English side of the training data. The in-domain language model was trained on `news.2015.shuffled.en` using a single layer LSTM language model developed in-house. The out-of-domain language model (trained on UNv1.0) used the same vocabulary. We compared word vs character-level language model results, and noted that character-level language modeling did a good job of data cleanup (giving bad scores to personnel records and poorly formatted data). We swept data selection sizes of two, four, and eight million, and found the middle size consistently the best. Our phrase-based system results can be summarized in Table 2.

System	Cased BLEU
Baseline	24.95
Rescore	27.32
Rescore + UN ML-words	27.80
Rescore + UN ML-chars	27.86
Rescore + UN ML-both	28.05
Resc. + UN ML-both + new LMs	28.41

Table 2: MITLL phrase-based system scores on `newstest2016` measured in cased BLEU.

3.1.4 MITLL OpenNMT Systems

We trained an OpenNMT system with the same in-domain data as our phrase-based system, using the default 9 epochs at learning rate 1.0, and reducing the learning rate by 0.7 each epoch thereafter. This yielded a system with 29.07 BLEU on `newstest2016`. Creating an n-best list from the epoch 13 model and rescoring that n-best list with the models from epoch 11 and 12, combined with equal weight, yielded 29.55 BLEU.

3.1.5 AFRL Phrase-Based Systems

In order to provide diversity for system combination, we trained a Moses system with the provided parallel data and the subselected, backtranslated data as outlined in Section 3.1.1. We trained a 5-gram, BPE'd language model from the data used to train the BigLM used in our WMT15 (Gwinnup et al., 2015) systems.

3.2 English–Russian

Due to the surprising effectiveness of the Marian English–Russian translation system used to produce backtranslated data, we decided to enter this system in the English–Russian translation task. This system was used in Step 2 of the Russian–English training process detailed in Section 3.1.1. Results of decoding `newstest2017` are listed as entry 3 in Table 7.

3.3 Turkish–English

We apply the techniques employed in building our Russian–English systems to build Turkish–English translation systems.

3.3.1 AFRL Nematus/Marian Systems

For the Turkish–English task, the only provided parallel data was the SETimes corpus (Tyers and Alperen, 2010) of approximately 220,000 parallel lines. This presented a challenge for our goal of training a neural-based system similar to our Russian English system (Section 3.1.4). We adopted a multiple step approach as before, but first starting with a Turkish–English Moses (Koehn et al., 2007) system built on the SETimes corpus with BPE applied. An order-5 KenLM (Heafield, 2011) language model was built on a BPE'd version of the BigLM employed in our WMT15 system(Gwinnup et al., 2015). Hierarchical lexicalized reordering (Galley and Manning, 2008) and an order-5 Operation Sequence Model (Durrani et al., 2011) were also employed in this system. Drem (Erdmann and Gwinnup, 2015) was used to optimize system feature weights using the Expected Corpus Bleu (ECB) metric.

In the interest of speed, Moses2 (Hoang et al., 2016) was used to decode the subselected Turkish corpus. An English–Turkish Marian system was then trained (with default parameters) with the provided parallel data and the backtranslated data from the previous step. This system was then used to decode the English subselected corpus. Finally, our non-combination submission system was trained using both the parallel provided data and the data generated from the previous back-translation step. This final Marian system was trained with a source vocabulary of 70k, target vocabulary of 50k, a 2048-unit RNN hidden layer and a 512-unit word embedding layer. A Nematus system was trained with reversed target sentences to provide right-to-left(r2l) rescoring. Two Marian left-to-right (l2r) and one Nematus r2l training instances were run. Each of the 3 final models are an average of the 8 best-scoring model checkpoints for each distinct training run. These resulting l2r averaged models were used to ensemble decode the test set, with the averaged r2l model rescoring the resulting n-best lists. Finally, the one-best was output and submitted as System 5 in Table 7.

3.3.2 MITLL OpenNMT Systems

In the final week of the evaluation, to produce a diverse system, we attempted backtranslation, iteratively. We began with a Moses system trained on the SETimes corpus. We then took 800K sentences from `news.2016.shuffled` for either language. In training a Turkish to English MT system, we backtranslated the English news data into Turkish using the current best English–Turkish MT system. We then repeated the process in the other direction. In the interest of time, we used a small network with 256 sized word embeddings, 512 sized rnn, and learning rate decay starting at epoch 6. Each pass took one day. Perplexities converged after 3 iterations. See Table 3 below.

Iter	Forward ppl.	Backward ppl.
1	26.92	31.72
2	22.65	27.74
3	16.75	27.88

Table 3: MITLL OpenNMT Turkish–English system perplexities on `newsdev2016`.

3.3.3 AFRL Moses Phrase-Based Systems

For contrast, a phrase-based system was built in the same manner as described in Step 1 of Section 3.3.1, but using the provided and backtranslated data used in the final step. This system contributed

to the system combination listed as entry 4 of Table 7.

3.4 Chinese–English

3.4.1 MITLL Nematus and OpenNMT Systems

As in our other systems, we used Moore-Lewis filtering (on characters only here due to time constraints) to sort the data. In this case, we used the entire parallel training corpora provided (25M lines), and filtered it, since we had no prior knowledge of which corpora were useful. For our Nematus system, we took the top 20 million lines, using the subselection method as a form of data "cleanup". Since this system took a month to train, for our OpenNMT system we instead extracted the top 5M sentences, and this system trained in one week. The Nematus system trained to a BLEU score of 16.39 on `newstest2016`, ensembled to 18.59, and the single-best OpenNMT system trained to 18.30. (OpenNMT did not have ensemble decoding implemented at the time of the evaluation.) We also rescored the Nematus ensembled n-best list with our OpenNMT system. We used an n-best list size of 12, and achieved a score of 20.06 (+.06) on `newstest2017`.

3.4.2 AFRL OpenNMT Systems

Similarly to the Chinese–English systems in the previous section, we down-sampled the available parallel data using the algorithms described in (Gwinnup et al., 2016) resulting in a 5 million line parallel training set. OpenNMT systems were trained in the same manner described in Section 3.1.2. The outputs of the 8 best-scoring epochs were ensembled using system combination again in the same manner as the Russian–English systems. This resulting system is listed as entry 6 in Table 7.

3.4.3 AFRL Marian Systems

Again for contrast, we experimented using 5 million lines of down-selected data from the parallel UN corpus as in Section 3.4.2. We character-segmented all Chinese characters on the source side of the data, then applied a BPE model to any remaining non-Chinese words. This BPE model is the same as the one learned from and applied to the target side of the parallel training data. Interestingly, this approach limited the source vocabulary to only 22,000 terms. The target vocabulary is a more typical 40K due to the application of BPE.

Marian was used to train models with 1024, 2048, and 3072 hidden units in the RNN layer. We saw a performance gain when increasing the number of units from 1024 to 2048, but not from 2048 to 3072 (at least for this experiment). These scores are shown in the Table 4.

RNN width	cased BLEU
1024	17.75
2048	18.81
3072	18.84

Table 4: Chinese–English Marian systems with different RNN hiddenunit widths decoding `newstest2017` measured in cased BLEU.

3.5 System Combination

Jane System Combination (Freitag et al., 2014) was used to combine a variety of systems for our Russian–English and Turkish–English combination submissions. We show the individual system combination inputs and final scores for Russian–English in Table 5 and Turkish–English in Table 6. It is important to note that our single-best Russian–English submission did not contribute to the system-combination entry as this system was a late addition at the end of the evaluation period.

For each system combination, five experiment replicates were run to account for variance in the combination process. The resulting best replicate was submitted. Results are shown in Table 7.

4 Conclusion

We present a series of improvements to our Russian–English systems and apply these lessons learned to creating Turkish–English and Chinese–English systems.

While researchers in recent years have been searching for principled methods to combine the strengths of statistical and neural MT, we find that carefully devised system combination and ensembling provides provides aggregate improvement. Thus, "borrowing" the Jane system combination technique allows one to combine old and new for better BLEU.

Opinions, interpretations, conclusions and recommendations are those of the authors and are not necessarily endorsed by the United States Government. Cleared for public release on 22 June 2017. Originator reference number RH-17-117218. Case number 88ABW-2017-3080.

References

Pi-Chuan Chang, Michel Galley, and Christopher D. Manning. 2008. Optimizing Chinese word segmentation for machine translation performance. In *Proceedings of the Third Workshop on Statistical Machine Translation*. Association for Computational Linguistics, Columbus, Ohio, pages 224–232.

Nadir Durrani, Helmut Schmid, and Alexander Fraser. 2011. A joint sequence translation model with integrated reordering. In *Proc. of the 49th Annual Meeting of the Association for Computational Linguistics (ACL '11)*. Portland, Oregon, pages 1045–1054.

Grant Erdmann and Jeremy Gwinnup. 2015. Drem: The AFRL submission to the WMT15 tuning task. In *Proc. of the Tenth Workshop on Statistical Machine Translation*. Lisbon, Portugal, pages 422–427.

Markus Freitag, Matthias Huck, and Hermann Ney. 2014. Jane: Open source machine translation system combination. In *Conference of the European Chapter of the Association for Computational Linguistics*. Gothenburg, Sweden, pages 29–32.

Michel Galley and Christopher D. Manning. 2008. A simple and effective hierarchical phrase reordering model. In *Proc. of the Conference on Empirical Methods in Natural Language Processing*. EMNLP '08, pages 848–856.

Jeremy Gwinnup, Tim Anderson, Grant Erdmann, Katherine Young, Michaeel Kazi, Elizabeth Salesky, and Brian Thompson. 2016. *Proceedings of the First Conference on Machine Translation: Volume 2, Shared Task Papers*, Association for Computational Linguistics, chapter The AFRL-MITLL WMT16 News-Translation Task Systems, pages 296–302. https://doi.org/10.18653/v1/W16-2313.

Jeremy Gwinnup, Tim Anderson, Grant Erdmann, Katherine Young, Christina May, Michaeel Kazi, Elizabeth Salesky, and Brian Thompson. 2015. The AFRL-MITLL WMT15 system: There's more than one way to decode it! In *Proc. of the Tenth Workshop on Statistical Machine Translation*. Lisbon, Portugal, pages 112–119.

Kenneth Heafield. 2011. KenLM: faster and smaller language model queries. In *Proceedings of the EMNLP 2011 Sixth Workshop on Statistical Machine Translation*. Edinburgh, Scotland, United Kingdom, pages 187–197.

Hieu Hoang, Nikolay Bogoychev, Lane Schwartz, and Marcin Junczys-Dowmunt. 2016. Fast, scalable phrase-based smt decoding. In *Proceedings of the 12th Biennial Conference of the Association for Machine Translation in the Americas (AMTA2016)*.

Marcin Junczys-Dowmunt, Tomasz Dwojak, and Hieu Hoang. 2016. Is neural machine translation ready for deployment? a case study on 30 translation directions. In *Proc. of the 13th International Workshop on Spoken Language Translation (IWSLT'16)*. Seattle, Washington.

#	Description	cased BLEU
1	3x Marian Train ens, 8-best avg per, 1024 unit hidden + 1x Nematus r2l rescore, 8-best avg	31.44
2	2x Marian Train ens., 8-best avg per, 2048 unit hidden + 1x Nematus r2l rescore, 8-best avg	31.86
3	3x Marian Train ens., 8-best avg per, 2048 unit hidden + 1x Nematus r2l rescore, 8-best avg	32.25
4	Moses w/ BPE data, BPE'd BigLM from WMT15	30.53
5	OpenNMT with subsel, backtrans data, single decode	30.04
6	OpenNMT with backtrans data, finetune, inc. train	32.16
7	OpenNMT with backtrans data, finetune only	32.78
8	OpenNMT with UN data + Nematus rescore	33.24
9	OpenNMT with backtrans data, ensemble-syscomb 4-best	33.23
10	OpenNMT with subsel, backtrans data, ensemble syscomb 4-best	31.91
comb	Submitted System Combination	34.71

Table 5: Russian–English System Combination Inputs decoding `newstest2017` measured in cased BLEU.

#	Description	cased BLEU
1	2x Marian Train ens, 8-best avg per, 2048 unit hidden + 1x Nematus r2l rescore, 8-best avg	17.12
2	2x Marian Train ens, 8-best avg per, 2048 unit hidden + 1x Nematus r2l rescore, 8-best avg - alt. model	17.54
3	OpenNMT, iterative backtrans	15.98
4	Moses w/BPE data, BPE'd BigLM from WMT15	13.60
comb	Submitted System Combination	18.05

Table 6: Turkish–English System Combination Inputs decoding `newstest2017` measured in cased BLEU.

#	Lang	System	Cased BLEU
1	ru-en	System Combo	34.7
2	ru-en	OpenNMT-best	34.0
3	en-ru	Marian Backtrans	25.4
4	tr-en	System Combo	18.1
5	tr-en	Marian/Nematus	17.5
6	zh-en	Single-Best	21.3

Table 7: Submission system scores on `newstest2017` measured in cased BLEU.

Michaeel Kazi, , Elizabeth Salesky, Brian Thompson, Jonathan Taylor, Jeremy Gwinnup, Tim Anderson, Grant Erdmann, Eric Hansen, Brian Ore, Katherine Young, and Michael Hutt. 2016. The MITLL-AFRL IWSLT-2016 systems. In *Proc. of the 13th International Workshop on Spoken Language Translation (IWSLT'16)*. Seattle, Washington.

Tibor Kiss and Jan Strunk. 2006. Unsupervised multilingual sentence boundary detection. *Computational Linguistics, Volume 32, Number 4, December 2006* .

Guillaume Klein, Yoon Kim, Yuntian Deng, Jean Senellart, and Alexander M. Rush. 2017. Opennmt: Open-source toolkit for neural machine translation. *CoRR* abs/1701.02810. http://arxiv.org/abs/1701.02810.

Philipp Koehn, Hieu Hoang, Alexandra Birch, Chris Callison-Burch, Marcello Federico, Nicola Bertoldi, Brooke Cowan, Wade Shen, Christine Moran, Richard Zens, Chris Dyer, Ondřej Bojar, Alexandra Constantin, and Evan Herbst. 2007. Moses: Open source toolkit for statistical machine translation. In *Proc. of the 45th Annual Meeting of the ACL on Interactive Poster and Demonstration Sessions*. ACL '07, pages 177–180.

X. Ma. 2006. Champollion: A robust parallel text sentence aligner. In *Proceedings of the Fifth International Conference on Language Resources and Eval-*

uation (LREC'06). European Language Resources Association (ELRA).

Robert C. Moore and William Lewis. 2010. Intelligent selection of language model training data. In *Proceedings of the ACL 2010 Conference Short Papers*. Association for Computational Linguistics, Stroudsburg, PA, USA, pages 220–224.

Kishore Papineni, Salim Roukos, Todd Ward, and Wei-Jing Zhu. 2002. BLEU: A method for automatic evaluation of machine translation. In *Proc. of the 40th Annual Meeting of the Association for Computational Linguistics (ACL '02)*. Philadelphia, Pennsylvania, pages 311–318.

Lane Schwartz, Timothy Anderson, Jeremy Gwinnup, and Katherine Young. 2014. Machine translation and monolingual postediting: The AFRL WMT-14 system. In *Proceedings of the Ninth Workshop on Statistical Machine Translation (WMT'14)*. Baltimore, Maryland, USA, pages 186–194.

Rico Sennrich, Orhan Firat, Kyunghyun Cho, Alexandra Birch, Barry Haddow, Julian Hitschler, Marcin Junczys-Dwmunt, Samuel Läubli, Antonio Valerio Miceli Barone, Jozef Mokry, and Maria Nadejde. 2017. Nematus: a Toolkit for Neural Machine Translation. In *Proceedings of the Demonstrations at the 15th Conference of the European Chapter of the Association for Computational Linguistics*. Valencia, Spain.

Rico Sennrich, Barry Haddow, and Alexandra Birch. 2016a. Edinburgh neural machine translation systems for wmt 16. In *Proceedings of the First Conference on Machine Translation*. Association for Computational Linguistics, Berlin, Germany, pages 371–376.

Rico Sennrich, Barry Haddow, and Alexandra Birch. 2016b. Neural machine translation of rare words with subword units. In *Proceedings of the 54th Annual Meeting of the Association for Computational Linguistics (Volume 1: Long Papers)*. Association for Computational Linguistics, pages 1715–1725. https://doi.org/10.18653/v1/P16-1162.

Jason R. Smith, Herve Saint-Amand, Magdalena Plamada, Philipp Koehn, Chris Callison-Burch, and Adam Lopez. 2013. Dirt cheap web-scale parallel text from the common crawl. In *Proceedings of the 51st Annual Meeting of the Association for Computational Linguistics (ACL '13)*. Sofia, Bulgaria, pages 1374–1383.

Francis M. Tyers and Murat Sedar Alperen. 2010. South-east european times: A parallel corpus of balkan languages. In *Proceedings of the MultiLR Workshop at the Language Resources and Evaluation Conference, LREC2010*.

WMT. 2017. Findings of the 2017 Conference on Statistical Machine Translation. In *Proc. of the Second Conference on Statistical Machine Translation (WMT '17)*. Copenhagen, Denmark.

Katherine Young, Jeremy Gwinnup, and Lane Schwartz. 2016. A taxonomy of weeds: A field guide for corpus curators to winnowing the parallel text harvest. In *Proceedings of the 12th Biennial Conference of the Association for Machine Translation in the Americas (AMTA2016)*.

Michał Ziemski, Marcin Junczys-Dowmunt, and Bruno Pouliquen. 2016. The united nations parallel corpus v1.0. In *Proceedings of the Tenth International Conference on Language Resources and Evaluation (LREC 2016)*.

University of Rochester WMT 2017 NMT System Submission

Chester Holtz, Chuyang Ke, and **Daniel Gildea**
University of Rochester
`choltz2@u.rochester.edu`

Abstract

We describe the neural machine translation system submitted by the University of Rochester to the Chinese-English language pair for the WMT 2017 news translation task. We applied unsupervised word and subword segmentation techniques and deep learning in order to address (i) the word segmentation problem caused by the lack of delimiters between words and phrases in Chinese and (ii) the morphological and syntactic differences between Chinese and English. We integrated promising recent developments in NMT, including back-translations, language model reranking, subword splitting and minimum risk tuning.

1 Introduction

This paper presents the machine translation (MT) systems submitted by University of Rochester to the WMT 2017 news translation task. We participated in the Chinese-to-English and Latvian-to-English news translation tasks, but will focus on describing the system submitted for the Chinese-to-English task.

Chinese-to-English is a particularly challenging language pair for corpus-based MT systems due to the task of finding an optimal word segmentation for Chinese sentences as well as other linguistic differences between Chinese and English sentences. For example the fact that there may exist multiple possible meanings for characters depending on their context and that individual characters can be joined together to build compound words exacerbate the aforementioned segmentation problem. Additionally, translation performance is also affected by the frequent dropping of subjects and infrequent use of function words in Chinese sentences.

We used both word-level and morphological feature-based representations of Chinese to deal with data sparsity and reduce the size of the Chinese vocabulary. We experimented with both sub-phrase-based and character-based systems. Both RNN-based and 5-gram language models were trained with data extracted from the English news corpora provided and are used to rerank hypotheses proposed by the decoder.

The paper is organized as follows: in Section 2 we introduce our system and preprocessing methods for the Chinese language. Our main learning framework training settings are explained in Section 3. Our NMT, SMT, and submission results are presented in Section 4. The paper ends with some concluding remarks.

2 System Description

In this section we briefly introduce our preprocessing methods and the general encoder-decoder framework with attention (Sutskever et al., 2014; Cho et al., 2014; Bahdanau et al., 2014) used in our system. We closely followed the neural machine translation model proposed by Chorowski et al. (2015).

A neural machine translation model (Kalchbrenner and Blunsom, 2013; Cho et al., 2014; Sutskever et al., 2014) aims at building an end-to-end neural network framework, which takes as input a source sentence $X = (\mathbf{x}_1, ..., \mathbf{x}_{T_X})$ with length of T_X, and outputs its translation $Y = (\mathbf{y}_1, ..., \mathbf{y}_{T_Y})$ with length of T_Y, where $\mathbf{x}_t$ and $\mathbf{y}_t$ are the source and target language tokens, respectively. The framework is constructed as a composite of an encoder network and a decoder network.

Proceedings of the Conference on Machine Translation (WMT), Volume 2: Shared Task Papers, pages 310–314
Copenhagen, Denmark, September 7–11, 2017. ©2017 Association for Computational Linguistics

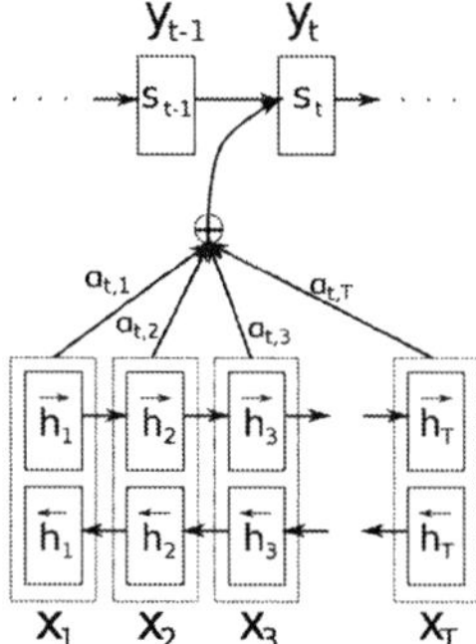

Figure 1: Illustration of the encoder-decoder framework from Bahdanau et al. (2014).

2.1 Morphological Analyzer

Word segmentation is considered an important first step for Chinese natural language processing tasks since individual Chinese words can be composed of multiple characters with no space appearing between words.

We employed the Jieba morphological analyzer (Junyi, 2013) to segment the source Chinese sentences into words. Jieba decomposes Chinese sentences into sequences of words by constructing a graph for all possible word combinations and finds the most probable sequence based on statistics derived from training data. For unknown words, an HMM-based model is used with the Viterbi algorithm.

2.2 Rare-Morpheme (BPE) Algorithm

If we simply apply the Chinese morphological analyzer to segment Chinese sentences into individual words and feed the words into our encoder, overfitting will occur; some words are so rare, that they only appear altogether with others. Thus, we enforced a thresholded on frequent words and applied the byte-pair-encoding (BPE) algorithm proposed by Gage (1994) and applied by Sennrich et al. (2016b) to NMT to further reduce the sparsity of our language data and to reduce the number of rare and out-of-vocabulary tokens.

2.3 Encoder

The encoder reads a sequence of source language tokens $X = (\mathbf{x}_1, \ldots, \mathbf{x}_{T_X})$, and outputs a sequence of hidden states $H = (h_1, \ldots, h_{T_X})$. A bidirectional recurrent neural network (BiRNN) (Bahdanau et al., 2014) consisting of a forward recurrent neural network (RNN) and a backward

RNN, is used to give additional positional representational power to the encoder. The lower part of Figure 1 illustrates the BiRNN structure.

The forward network reads the input sentence in a forward direction

$$\overrightarrow{h_t} = \overrightarrow{\phi_x}(i_x(\mathbf{x}_t), \overrightarrow{h_{t-1}}) \tag{1}$$

where for each input token $\mathbf{x}_t$, $i_x(\cdot) : X \to \mathbb{R}^n$ is a continuous embedding, that maps the t-th input token to a vector $i_x(\mathbf{x}_t)$ in a high dimensional space $\mathbb{R}^n$. A forward recurrent activation function $\overrightarrow{\phi_x}$ updates each forward hidden state $\overrightarrow{h_t}$, using the embedded token $i_x(\mathbf{x}_t)$ and the information of the previous hidden state $\overrightarrow{h_{t-1}}$.

Similarly, the reverse network reads the sentence in a reverse direction (right to left)

$$\overleftarrow{h_t} = \overleftarrow{\phi_x}(i_x(\mathbf{x}_t), \overleftarrow{h_{t+1}}) \tag{2}$$

and generates a sequence of backward hidden states.

The encoder utilizes information from both the forward RNN and the backward RNN to generate the hidden states $H = (h_1, \ldots, h_{T_X})$. For every input token $\mathbf{x}_t$, we concatenate its corresponding forward hidden state vector and the backward hidden state vector, such that $h_t = \begin{bmatrix} \overrightarrow{h_t} \\ \overleftarrow{h_t} \end{bmatrix}$.

2.4 Decoder

The upper part of Figure 1 illustrates the decoder. The decoder computes the conditional distribution over all possible translations based on the context information provided by the encoder (Bahdanau et al., 2014). More specifically, the decoder RNN tries to find a sequence of tokens in the target language that maximizes the following probability.

$$\log p(Y|X) - \sum_{t=1}^{T_Y} \log p(\mathbf{y}_t|\mathbf{y}_1, \ldots, \mathbf{y}_{t-1}, X) \tag{3}$$

Each hidden state s_t in the decoder is updated by

$$s_t = \phi_y(i_y(\mathbf{y}_{t-1}), s_{t-1}, c_t), \tag{4}$$

where i_y is the continuous embedding of a token in the target language. c_t is a context vector related to the t-th output token, such that

$$c_t = \sum_{l=1}^{T_X} h_l \cdot a_{tl} \tag{5}$$

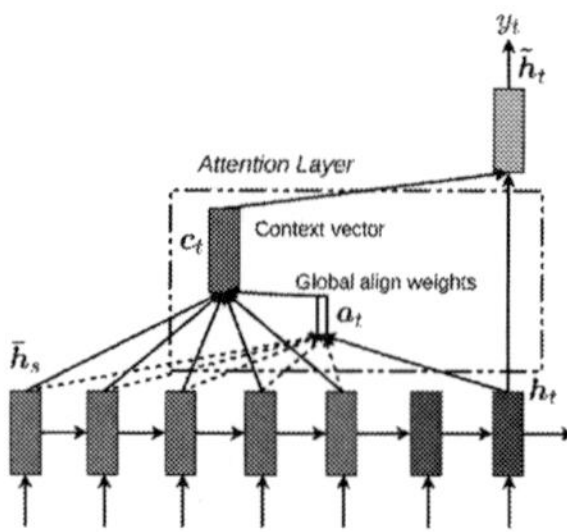

Figure 2: Illustration of Attention Mechanism from Luong et al. (2015).

and

$$a_{tl} = \frac{\exp(e_{tl})}{\sum_{k=1}^{T_x} \exp(e_{tk})} \quad (6)$$

Here, a_{tl} indicates the importance of the hidden state annotation h_l regarding to the previous hidden state s_{t-1} in the decoder RNN. e_{tk} measures how "matching" the input at position k and the output at position t are (Bahdanau et al., 2014; Chorowski et al., 2015); it is defined by a soft alignment model f_{align}, such that

$$e_{tk} = f_{\text{align}}(s_{t-1}, h_k). \quad (7)$$

Finally, each conditional probability in Equation 3 is generated by

$$p(\mathbf{y}_t|\mathbf{y}_1, \ldots, \mathbf{y}_{t-1}, X) = g(\mathbf{y}_{t-1}, s_t, c_t) \quad (8)$$

for some nonlinear function g.

2.5 Attention Mechanism

The soft-alignment mechanism f_{align} weighs each vector in the context set $C = (c_1, \ldots, c_{T_Y})$ according to its relevance given what has been translated (Bahdanau et al., 2014; Cho et al., 2014; Sutskever et al., 2014). It is commonly implemented as a feedforward neural network with a single hidden layer. This procedure can be understood as computing the alignment probability between the t-th target symbol and k-th source symbol.

The hidden state annotation $\mathbf{h}_t$, together with the previous target symbol $\mathbf{y}_{t-1}$ and the context vector c_t, is fed into a feedforward neural network to result in the conditional distribution and the whole network, consisting of the encoder, decoder and soft-alignment mechanism, is then tuned end-to-end to minimize the negative log-likelihood using stochastic gradient descent. In our system, the source sentence X is a sequence of sub-phrase and sub-word tokens extracted by the morphological analyzer and BPE algorithms, and the target sentence Y is represented as a sequence of sub-words.

2.6 Minimum Risk Tuning

We applied minimum risk training (Shen et al., 2016) to tune the model parameters post convergence of the cross-entropy loss by minimizing the expected risk for sentence-level BLEU scores where the risk is defined to be

$$R(\boldsymbol{\theta}) = \sum_{s=1}^{S} \mathbb{E}_{\mathbf{y}|\mathbf{x}^{(s)};\theta}[\Delta(\mathbf{y}, \mathbf{y}^{(s)})] \quad (9)$$

$$= \sum_{s=1}^{S} \sum_{\mathbf{y} \in Y(\mathbf{x}^{(s)})} P(\mathbf{y}|\mathbf{x}^{(s)};\boldsymbol{\theta})\Delta(\mathbf{y}, \mathbf{y}^{(s)}) \quad (10)$$

for candidate translations $Y(\mathbf{x}^{(s)})$ for $\mathbf{x}^{(s)}$. Details regarding methods to solve this problem can be found in Shen et al. (2016).

3 Experimental Settings

In this section, we describe the details of the experimental settings for our system.

3.1 Corpora and Preprocessing

Our model was trained on all available training parallel corpora for the ZH-EN language pair. The training data consists of approximately $2,000,000$ sentence pairs. We removed sentence pairs from our data when the source or target side is more than 50 tokens long. A set of $50,000,000$ sentences was sampled from the News Crawl 2007-15 data and was used to train our target side (English) language model. Additionally, we backtranslated a subset of these sentences and used the resulting source-target sentences to augment our training data.

Our training and development data were lowercased and preprocessed using the Moses tokenizer script (Koehn et al., 2007), Jieba, and BPE. We set the upper bound on the target vocabulary to $30,000$ sub-words and two additional tokens reserved for $\langle EOS \rangle$ and $\langle UNK \rangle$. For the source vocabulary, we constrained the size of BPE symbol vocabulary to $30,000$ tokens.

3.2 Synthetic Training Data

Sennrich et al. (2016a) introduced the augmentation of a parallel corpus by leveraging target-side monolingual data and empirically showed

that treating back-translations as additional training data reduced overfitting and increased fluency
of the translation model. We sampled monolingual
sentences from the same news data used to construct our language models. Due to computation
and time constraints, we were only able to augment our training data by an additional 190,000
sentence pairs. We hypothesize that increasing the
number of back-translated sentences in our training set will further improve our system's performance.

3.3 Neural Baseline

Our NMT baseline is an encoder-decoder model
with attention and dropout implemented with Nematus (Sennrich et al., 2017) and AmuNMT
(Junczys-Dowmunt et al., 2016). This baseline system without pre-tokenization or language model scoring achieves 17.32 uncased
BLEU on news-test2017 and 19.78 after source-
segmentation with the BPE algorithm.

We used beam search with a beam width of
8 to approximately find the most likely translations given a source sentence before introducing
features proposed by our language models and
reranking with the default Moses (Koehn et al.,
2007) implementation of K-best MIRA (Cherry
and Foster, 2012). Both language models were
trained on the English news data. Our unigram-
pruned 5-gram language model was trained with
KenLM (Heafield, 2011), and our RNN-based language model was trained with RNNLM (Mikolov
et al., 2011) with a hidden layer size of 300.

3.4 Statistical Baseline

For our SMT baseline, we trained a standard
phrase-based system on input segmented with
Jieba: Berkeley Aligner (IBM Model 1 and HMM,
both for 5 iterations); phrase table with up to 5
tokens per phrase, 40-best translation options per
source phrase, and Good-Turing smoothing; 4-
gram language model and pruning of singleton n-
grams; and the default K-best MIRA reordering.

This baseline system achieves an uncased
BLEU score of 7.46 on news-test2017.

4 Experimental Results

We compared the performance of our system to
several state-of-the-art algorithms. Our systems
(Character-level BiRNN, Morphological Subword
BiRNN) are marked in a bold font. It can be

System	Score
Moses Baseline (word)	7.5
Neural Baseline (word)	17.3
Neural Baseline (subword)	19.8
BiRNN (character)	12.5
BiRNN (word + subword)	21.6

Table 1: Test Results. Uncased BLEU scores of
the trained models computed over all sentences on
the development and test sets.

seen that our system outperformed the baselines,
whether using words or subwords as the input tokens. The experiments also showed that the rare-
morpheme algorithm significantly reduced some
potential overfitting, compared to the character-
level BiRNN.

4.1 Error Analysis

Error analysis on the validation set shows that the
two main sources of errors produced by the baseline are missing and incorrect words. These issues are addressed in our model by applying morphological segmentation in combination with BPE
and adding new backtranslated data to the training set. Our model's translation error rate (0.716)
is strictly lower than that of our baseline's output
(0.743). We attribute this reduction in error rate
to our system being able to more robustly model
multi-character words in Chinese.

5 Conclusion

We describe the University of Rochester neural
machine translation system for WMT'17 Chinese-
English news translation task, which employs
recent developments in the machine translation
field. Our results show that applying word and
morpheme-aware tokenization, minimum risk tuning, and language model reranking to an existing
MT framework help to improve the overall translation quality of the model.

Machine translation is a dynamic area, and there
are many opportunities for further exploration.

- **Other objectives**: Modify the encoder-
  decoder trainer and add secondary tasks for
  multi-task training (e.g. source sentence tagging) for explicit use of linguistic features.

- **Sentence reordering**: Reorder the training
  data in various ways to encourage the model
  to learn a more robust translation model.

- **Source-side monolingual data**: Leverage source-side monolingual data to improve translation performance.

Acknowledgments

The authors would like to thank the developers of Nematus (Sennrich et al., 2017) and Amunmt (Junczys-Dowmunt et al., 2016) as well as Theano (Al-Rfou et al., 2016). We acknowledge the support of the University of Rochester and the Center for Integrated Research Computing at the University of Rochester for computing support. Finally, we are grateful to the University of Edinburgh for centralizing the Chinese-English parallel corpora.

References

Rami Al-Rfou, Guillaume Alain, Amjad Almahairi, Christof Angermueller, Dzmitry Bahdanau, Nicolas Ballas, et al. 2016. Theano: A Python framework for fast computation of mathematical expressions. *arXiv:1409.1259*.

Dzmitry Bahdanau, Kyunghyun Cho, and Yoshua Bengio. 2014. Neural machine translation by jointly learning to align and translate. *arXiv:1409.0473*.

Colin Cherry and George Foster. 2012. Batch tuning strategies for statistical machine translation. In *Proceedings of the 2012 Conference the North American Association for Computational Linguistics: Human Language Technologies (HLT-NAACL 2012)*.

Kyunghyun Cho, Bart Van Merriënboer, Dzmitry Bahdanau, and Yoshua Bengio. 2014. On the properties of neural machine translation: Encoder-decoder approaches. *arXiv:1409.1259*.

Jan Chorowski, Dzmitry Bahdanau, Dmitriy Serdyuk, Kyunghyun Cho, and Yoshua Bengio. 2015. Attention-based models for speech recognition. In *Advances in Neural Information Processing Systems (NIPS 2015)*, pages 577–585.

Philip Gage. 1994. A new algorithm for data compression. *The C Users Journal*, 12(2):23–38.

Kenneth Heafield. 2011. Kenlm: Faster and smaller language model queries. In *Proceedings of the 2011 Workshop on Statistical Machine Translation (WMT11)*, pages 187–197.

Marcin Junczys-Dowmunt, Tomasz Dwojak, and Hieu Hoang. 2016. Is neural machine translation ready for deployment? a case study on 30 translation directions. In *Proceedings of the 9th International Workshop on Spoken Language Translation (IWSLT 2016)*.

Sun Junyi. 2013. Jieba. `http://github.com/fxsjy/jieba`.

Nal Kalchbrenner and Phil Blunsom. 2013. Recurrent continuous translation models. In *Proceedings of the 2013 Conference on Empirical Methods in Natural Language Processing (EMNLP 2013)*, pages 1700–1709.

Philipp Koehn, Hieu Hoang, Alexandra Birch, Chris Callison-Burch, Marcello Federico, Nicola Bertoldi, Brooke Cowan, Wade Shen, Christine Moran, Richard Zens, Chris Dyer, Ondrej Bojar, Alexandra Constantin, and Evan Herbst. 2007. Moses: Open source toolkit for statistical machine translation. *Association for Computational Linguistics (ACL)*.

Minh-Thang Luong, Hieu Pham, and Christopher Manning. 2015. Effective approaches to attention-based neural machine translation. In *Proceedings of the 2015 Conference on Empirical Methods in Natural Language Processing (EMNLP 2013)*.

Tomas Mikolov, Stefan Kombrink, Anoop Deoras, Lukas Burget, and Jan "Honza" Cernock. 2011. Rnnlm - recurrent neural network language modeling toolkit. In *Proceedings of Interspeech*.

Rico Sennrich, Orhan Firat, Kyunghyun Cho, Alexandra Birch, Barry Haddow, Julian Hitschler, Marcin Junczys-Dowmunt, Samuel Läubli, Antonio Valerio Miceli Barone, Jozef Mokry, and Maria Nadejde. 2017. Nematus: a toolkit for neural machine translation. In *Proceedings of the 15th Conference of the Association for Computational Linguistics (ACL 2017)*, pages 65–68.

Rico Sennrich, Barry Haddow, and Alexandra Birch. 2016a. Improving neural machine translation models with monolingual data. In *Proceedings of the 54th Annual Meeting of the Association for Computational Linguistics (ACL 2016)*.

Rico Sennrich, Barry Haddow, and Alexandra Birch. 2016b. Neural machine translation of rare words with subword units. In *Proceedings of the 54th Annual Meeting of the Association for Computational Linguistics (ACL 2016)*.

Shiqi Shen, Yong Cheng, Zhongjun He, Wei He, Hua Wu, Maosong Sun, and Yang Liu. 2016. Minimum risk training for neural machine translation. In *Proceedings of the 54th Annual Meeting of the Association for Computational Linguistics (ACL 2016)*.

Ilya Sutskever, Oriol Vinyals, and Quoc V Le. 2014. Sequence to sequence learning with neural networks. In *Advances in Neural Information Processing Systems (NIPS 2014)*, pages 3104–3112.

LMU Munich's Neural Machine Translation Systems
for News Articles and Health Information Texts

Matthias Huck, Fabienne Braune, Alexander Fraser

Center for Information and Language Processing
LMU Munich
Munich, Germany

{mhuck,braune,fraser}@cis.lmu.de

Abstract

This paper describes the LMU Munich English→German machine translation systems. We participated with neural translation engines in the WMT17 shared task on machine translation of news, as well as in the biomedical translation task. LMU Munich's systems deliver competitive machine translation quality on both news articles and health information texts.

1 Introduction

The Center for Information and Language Processing at LMU Munich has a strong track record at building statistical machine translation (SMT) systems for various language pairs, e.g. for translation between English and German, Czech, Romanian, Russian, or French. LMU has frequently participated in WMT machine translation shared tasks in recent years (Bojar et al., 2016, 2015, 2014, 2013), competing (and also collaborating) internationally in an open evaluation campaign with other leading research labs from both academia and industry.

Research on various different types of machine translation models has previously been conducted at LMU. Core SMT paradigms for LMU's past shared task participations include phrase-based models (Cap et al., 2015, 2014b; Weller et al., 2013, Sajjad et al., 2013), hierarchical phrase-based models (Huck et al., 2016; Peter et al., 2016), operation sequence models (Durrani et al., 2013), and hybrids of statistical approaches with rule-based and deep syntactic components (Tamchyna et al., 2016b).

At this year's *EMNLP 2017 Second Conference on Machine Translation (WMT17)*,[1] LMU participated in two shared tasks: the shared task

on *machine translation of news* and the *biomedical translation task*. We submitted the output of our English→German machine translation systems. The system for the news task was trained under "constrained" conditions, employing only permissible resources as defined by the shared task organizers. The system for the biomedical task builds upon our news task system, but was domain-adapted towards the medical domain via the usage of additional parallel training data from the in-domain sections of the UFAL Medical Corpus v.1.0.

We have trained *neural machine translation* (NMT) models this year. Neural network models for machine translation (Sutskever et al., 2014; Bahdanau et al., 2014) are now largely successful for many language pairs and domains. This has for instance become apparent with the University of Edinburgh's excellent results in the WMT16 news translation shared task with neural systems (Sennrich et al., 2016a), which outperformed most other submitted systems, including Edinburgh's own traditional SMT engines (Williams et al., 2016). LMU's English→German neural machine translation systems confirm this trend. We have achieved competitive performance—in terms of translation quality as measured with BLEU (Papineni et al., 2002)—in both shared tasks that we participated in.[2]

A unique characteristic of the LMU English→German NMT systems is a linguistically informed, cascaded word segmentation technique that we developed and applied to the German target language side of the training data. Amongst other aspects, SMT research at LMU is

---

[1] http://www.statmt.org/wmt17/

[2] Our LMU Munich primary system is ranked second in BLEU on the submission website, http://matrix.statmt.org/matrix/systems_list/1869, being outpaced by Edinburgh's WMT17 NMT setup only. In the human evaluation the LMU Munich primary system is ranked first (Bojar et al., 2017).

Proceedings of the Conference on Machine Translation (WMT), Volume 2: Shared Task Papers, pages 315–322
Copenhagen, Denmark, September 7–11, 2017. ©2017 Association for Computational Linguistics

focusing on investigating linguistically informed methods that improve machine translation into target languages which exhibit a more complex morphosyntax than English (Huck et al., 2017b; Tamchyna et al., 2016a; Ramm and Fraser, 2016; Weller-Di Marco et al., 2016; Braune et al., 2015; Cap et al., 2014a; Fraser et al., 2012). We are taking advantage of our group's longstanding experience regarding handling of complex morphosyntax in SMT, now enriching NMT with novel techniques that specifically tackle target-side morphosyntax.

In the following section of this paper (Section 2), we sketch our linguistically motivated target word segmentation technique. Then we describe how we trained and configured our neural machine translation systems (Section 3). Before concluding the paper, we present empirical results on the two translation tasks, which involve machine translation of news articles and of health information texts (Section 4).

2 Target-side Word Segmentation

Compounding and morphological variation are ubiquitous in the German language and have traditionally been challenging for machine translation into German. We believe that specifically targeting complex morphosyntactic phenomena in the output language is not only essential in traditional phrase-based machine translation, but keeps being valuable in NMT. Most previous work in NMT has focused on linguistically agnostic subword splitting, typically with the primary rationale of limiting the vocabulary size, which is required in NMT for efficiency considerations.

LMU is utilizing a more linguistically-informed target word segmentation approach. By doing so, we hope to achieve three major goals: better vocabulary reduction; reduction of data sparsity; and better open vocabulary translation.

We cascade three different word splitting methods on the German target side.

1. First we apply a suffix splitter that separates common German morphological suffixes from the word stems. We modified the German Snowball stemming algorithm from NLTK[3] for that purpose. Rather than stripping suffixes, our modified code splits them

off. It otherwise behaves just like the Snowball stemming algorithm.

2. Next we apply the empirical compound splitter as described by Koehn and Knight (2003) and as implemented in the Perl script which is part of the Moses toolkit (Koehn et al., 2007). We choose a fairly aggressive configuration of the compound splitter[4] in order to reduce the vocabulary size more than with its parameters as typically chosen for previous phrase-based translation setups in which German compound splitting was used.

3. Since the vocabulary size is still a bit large after suffix splitting and compound splitting, we adopt segmentation using the Byte Pair Encoding (BPE) technique (Gage, 1994; Sennrich et al., 2016c) on top of the other two word splitters. This last step is performed only for efficiency reasons in NMT. Without BPE, the vocabulary size is still almost 100K. We preferred something around 50K, which is more tractable in practice. Suffix splitting and compound splitting alone are not suitable for arbitrary reduction of the vocabulary size. However, we believe that they are more adequate word segmentation techniques than BPE is. So we prefer to split with those linguistically motivated methods, as far as practicable.

Special marker symbols allow us to revert the segmentation in postprocessing. We also introduce a case marker that is placed before any compound-split word in order to restore upper and lower casing, respectively, since the compound splitting approach modifies the casing of compound parts to the version of each part that (stand-alone) appears most frequently in the corpus.

We were running a comprehensive series of experiments with different target word segmentation strategies on Europarl data beforehand, and we found our cascaded word segmentation to perform clearly better than using BPE only. We furthermore tried prefix splitting, but the results looked less encouraging. Our Europarl results also suggested that the suffix splitting contributes more to improvements in translation quality than the compound splitting does. Huck et al. (2017a) provides further details. For our WMT17 shared task systems, we eventually decided to apply both suffix

[3]http://www.nltk.org/_modules/nltk/stem/snowball.html

[4]-min-size 4 -min-count 2 -max-count 999999999

splitting and compound splitting, but to omit prefix splitting.

The English source side is simply BPE-segmented.

3 Neural Translation System Setup

We utilize the Nematus implementation (Sennrich et al., 2017) to build encoder-decoder NMT systems with attention and gated recurrent units. We configure dimensions of 500 for the embeddings and 1024 for the hidden layer. We train with the Adam optimizer (Kingma and Ba, 2015), a learning rate of 0.0001, batch size of 50, and dropout with probability 0.2 applied to the hidden layer, but not to source, target, and embeddings. We validate every 10 000 updates and do early stopping when the validation cost has not decreased over ten consecutive control points.

Our initial baseline NMT system is trained using only data from the Europarl corpus (Koehn, 2005) and no other resources, with the Europarl `test2006` set used for validation. We tokenize and frequent-case the data with the standard scripts from the Moses toolkit (Koehn et al., 2007). For our Europarl-trained baseline, sentences of length >50 after tokenization are excluded from the training corpus, all other sentences (1.7 M) are kept in training.

The German compound split model and BPE merge operations are extracted from the Europarl data. In our cascaded word segmentation pipeline, the compound split model is extracted from the training data only after suffix splitting has been applied. Similarly, the BPE operations are extracted after suffix splitting and compound splitting have been applied to the German side of the training corpus. We set the amount of merge operations for BPE to 50K. On the English source side, we apply BPE separately, also with 50K merge operations.

3.1 News Translation Task

For the shared task on machine translation of news (Bojar et al., 2017), we successively improved our initial baseline by incrementally applying the following steps:

1. Adding the News Commentary (NC) and Common Crawl (CC) parallel training data as provided for WMT17 by the organizers of the news translation shared task. We initialize the optimization on the larger corpus with the Europarl-trained baseline model.

2. Adding synthetic training data. The use of automatically translated monolingual data as a supplementary training resource has proved to be effective in SMT for phrase-based, hierarchical, and neural systems (Ueffing et al., 2007; Lambert et al., 2011; Huck et al., 2011; Huck and Ney, 2012; Sennrich et al., 2016b). Sennrich et al. have publicly shared their backtranslations of monolingual WMT News Crawl corpora, which they created for their WMT16 participation (Sennrich et al., 2016a). We exploit the full amount of backtranslations of German data into English.[5] We concatenate the synthetic data and the human-generated parallel training data (Europarl + NC + CC). The optimization is initialized with the pre-trained model from the preceding step.

3. Fine-tuning towards the domain of news articles. We employ the `newstest` development sets from the years 2008 to 2014 as a training corpus. We reduce the learning rate to 0.000001, initialize with the pre-trained model from the preceding step, and optimize on only the small `Devsets2008-14` corpus.

4. Right-to-left reranking. We rerank an n-best list from the system in the preceding step with a right-to-left (r2l) model, where the order of the target sequence is reversed. Liu et al. (2016) have proposed right-to-left reranking for NMT. Earlier work by Freitag et al. (2013) had already established that reverse word order models can be beneficial in phrase-based and hierarchical phrase-based translation. Freitag et al. (2013) utilized reverse word order models by means of a system combination framework (Freitag et al., 2014), though.

Validation is done on `newstest2015` for each of the extended setups. The preprocessing pipeline is not altered when more training data is appended. Particularly, we keep applying the compound split model and BPE operations that have been extracted from only the Europarl corpus, and keep sticking to the vocabulary from Europarl. We force the system to suppress UNK tokens in inference at test time.

---

[5]`http://data.statmt.org/rsennrich/`
`wmt16_backtranslations/en-de/`

system \ newstest	2015 BLEU	2016 BLEU	2017 BLEU
baseline, Europarl-trained	19.4	22.8	18.3
+ NC & CC corpora	26.0	30.2	24.5
+ synthetic data	27.8	32.3	26.1
+ fine-tuning on Devsets2008-14	28.2	32.3	26.6
+ r2l reranking	**28.6**	**33.4**	**27.1**

Table 1: English→German translation results on newstest sets (case-sensitive BLEU). Extensions are applied incrementally.

system \ devtest	Cochrane BLEU	NHS24 BLEU
fine-tuning on Devsets2008-14	29.1	26.3
fine-tuning on Medical	35.0	29.5
+ r2l reranking	**35.8**	**30.3**

Table 2: English→German translation results on HimL biomedical sets (case-sensitive BLEU).

3.2 Biomedical Translation Task

For the biomedical translation task (Yepes et al., 2017), we started off with the pre-trained NMT model after step 2 of our news task system engineering and applied the following steps:

1. Fine-tuning towards the domain of health information texts. We employ the in-domain sections of the UFAL Medical Corpus v.1.0 as a training corpus.[6] We set the learning rate to 0.00001, initialize with the pre-trained model, and optimize on only the in-domain medical data.

2. Right-to-left reranking. An ensemble of domain-adapted r2l models worked best.

The HimL (Haddow et al., 2017) tuning sets are used for validation, and we tested separately on the Cochrane and NHS24 parts of the HimL devtest set.[7]

4 Empirical Results

We evaluate case-sensitive with BLEU (Papineni et al., 2002), computed over postprocessed hypotheses against the raw references with `mteval-v13a`. The results are reported in Table 1 for the news translation task and in Table 2 for the biomedical translation task.

In the news translation task, the Europarl-trained baseline does not get close to state-of-the-art performance on `newstest` sets. However,

this seems to be mostly due to a domain mismatch (Huck et al., 2015). Once we add in the News Commentary and Common Crawl parallel data, we are able to massively improve the translation quality, by around six to seven BLEU points. Synthetic data gives us a boost of about another two BLEU points. After fine-tuning on Devsets2008-14 towards news articles, we observe a further gain of 0.4 BLEU on `newstest2015` but no gain on `newstest2016`. Reranking with a right-to-left model is effective on all test sets again, with improvements in the range of 0.4 to 1.1 BLEU.

Two LMU submissions have been judged by humans in the manual evaluation for the WMT17 news translation task (Bojar et al., 2017): the output of our final setup with r2l reranking (as a primary submission; "*LMU-nmt-reranked*"), and the single system output without reranking (as a contrastive submission; "*LMU-nmt-single*"). Our primary submission is placed first amongst all evaluated systems. We conjecture that our linguistically-informed target word segmentation approach has contributed to a positive assessment by human evaluators. Interestingly, the contrastive submission was rated significantly worse, affirming the utility of r2l reranking.

A few example translations from our primary submission for the news task are shown in Table 3.

For the translation of health information texts, it is again crucial to adapt the NMT system to the domain. When applying the engine fine-tuned on out-of-domain news data (`Devsets2008-14`) to Cochrane and NHS24 devtest sets, we see quite a gap as compared to fine-tuning on the in-domain sections of the UFAL Medical Corpus. Right-to-left reranking improves the results by 0.8 BLEU for the biomedical task.

5 Conclusion

LMU Munich has participated with English→German neural machine translation systems in the WMT17 shared tasks on machine translation of news and of biomedical texts. A distinctive feature of LMU's NMT systems is a linguistically informed, cascaded target word segmentation approach. The LMU systems are very competitive in terms of translation quality, achieving top ranks amongst the participants in both tasks. Of all English→German systems manually evaluated in the news task, LMU's primary submission has received the highest human judgment scores.

---

[6]`https://ufal.mff.cuni.cz/ufal_medical_corpus`

[7]`http://www.himl.eu/test-sets`

source (preproc.)	the Kurdish community in Germany is expecting tens of thousands of people to arrive at short notice in search of protection , fleeing from Turkey to Germany .
LMU-nmt (plain)	die kurdisch \$\$e Gemeind \$\$e in #U deutsch @ @ Land rechnet damit , dass zehntaus \$\$end \$\$e Mensch \$\$en #L kurz @ @ Frist \$\$ig auf der Such \$\$e nach dem Schutz eintreff \$\$en , der aus der Türkei nach #U deutsch @ @ Land gefloh \$\$en ist .
LMU-nmt (postproc.)	Die kurdische Gemeinde in Deutschland rechnet damit, dass zehntausende Menschen kurzfristig auf der Suche nach dem Schutz eintreffen, der aus der Türkei nach Deutschland geflohen ist.
reference	Die Kurdische Gemeinde Deutschland rechnet kurzfristig mit zehntausenden Schutzsuchenden, die aus der Türkei nach Deutschland flüchten.
source (preproc.)	the situation only worsened over the past year when the world ' biggest producer , China , dumped steel into the global market en masse as a result of weakening domestic demand .
LMU-nmt (plain)	die Lag \$\$e verschlechtert \$\$e sich nur im vergang \$\$en \$\$en Jahr , als der #L Welt @ @ größt \$\$e Produzent , China , infolg \$\$e der schwä ## chelnd \$\$en #U binn @en@ nach @ @ Frag \$\$e #L Mass @en@ Haft Stahl in den global \$\$en Markt geworf \$\$en hat .
LMU-nmt (postproc.)	Die Lage verschlechterte sich nur im vergangenen Jahr, als der weltgrößte Produzent, China, infolge der schwächelnden Binnennachfrage massenhaft Stahl in den globalen Markt geworfen hat.
reference	Im vergangenen Jahr verschärfte sich die Lage weiter, als das weltgrößte Erzeugerland China angesichts der schwächelnden heimischen Nachfrage massenhaft Stahl auf den Weltmarkt warf.
source (preproc.)	analysts fear that separatist groups that had been more or less vanquished in recent years , like the Oro ## mo Liberation Front or the Og ## aden National Liberation Front , may try to exploit the turbulence and rearm .
LMU-nmt (plain)	Analyst \$\$en befürcht \$\$en , dass separatist \$\$isch \$\$e Grupp \$\$en , die in den letzt \$\$en Jahr \$\$en mehr oder wenig \$\$er bezwung \$\$en word \$\$en war \$\$en , wie die Oro ## mo @-@ #U Befreiung @s@ Front oder der O ## gad \$\$en National \$\$e #U Befreiung @s@ Front , versuch \$\$en könnt \$\$en , die Turbulenz \$\$en und die Aufrüst \$\$ung auszunutz \$\$en .
LMU-nmt (postproc.)	Analysten befürchten, dass separatistische Gruppen, die in den letzten Jahren mehr oder weniger bezwungen worden waren, wie die Oromo-Befreiungsfront oder der Ogaden Nationale Befreiungsfront, versuchen könnten, die Turbulenzen und die Aufrüstung auszunutzen.
reference	Analytiker befürchten, dass Separatisten wie die Oromo-Befreiungsfront oder die Nationale Befreiungsfront des Ogaden, die in den letzten Jahren mehr oder weniger bezwungen wurden, die Turbulenzen ausnützen und sich wieder bewaffnen könnten.
source (preproc.)	these cele ## bri ## ties are not relatives of famous people , or reality stars , or kids these days who know how to make a good S ## n ## ap ## chat video (although Jen ## ner is all of these things) .
LMU-nmt (plain)	dies \$\$e Pro ## minent \$\$en sind kein \$\$e Verwandt \$\$en berühmt \$\$er Mensch \$\$en oder Re ## ality @-@ Star \$\$s oder Kind \$\$er dies \$\$er Tag \$\$e , die wiss \$\$en , wie man ein gut \$\$es Sna ## p ## ch ## at @-@ Video mach \$\$en kann (obwohl J ## enn \$\$er all dies \$\$e Ding \$\$e ist) .
LMU-nmt (postproc.)	Diese Prominenten sind keine Verwandten berühmter Menschen oder Reality-Stars oder Kinder dieser Tage, die wissen, wie man ein gutes Snapchat-Video machen kann (obwohl Jenner all diese Dinge ist).
reference	Diese Berühmtheiten sind nicht mit berühmten Personen verwandt oder Reality Stars oder Jugendliche von heute, die wissen, wie man ein gutes Snapchat Video dreht (auch wenn davon alles auf Jenner zutrifft).
source (preproc.)	the specialists from the 3 ## 4th police inspectorate were able to prove that the thieves , who had travelled to Germany to commit the crimes , had committed four crimes .
LMU-nmt (plain)	die Spezialist \$\$en der 34. #U Polizei @ @ Inspektion konnt \$\$en beweis \$\$en , dass die Dieb \$\$e , die nach #U deutsch @ @ Land gereist war \$\$en , um die Verbrech \$\$en zu begeh \$\$en , vier Straftat \$\$en begang \$\$en hatt \$\$en .
LMU-nmt (postproc.)	Die Spezialisten der 34. Polizeiinspektion konnten beweisen, dass die Diebe, die nach Deutschland gereist waren, um die Verbrechen zu begehen, vier Straftaten begangen hatten.
reference	Die Spezialisten des Kriminalkommissariats 34 können den Dieben, die eigens zur Begehung von Straftaten nach Deutschland eingereist waren, vier Taten nachweisen.

Table 3: Example translations, produced with LMU Munich's primary machine translation system for the news task. The table shows the preprocessed English source, the plain system output, the postprocessed system output, and the German reference translation for every 479th sentence from the `newstest2017` evaluation set (excluding the very first of them, sentence 479, since it is too short to be interesting). ## is a BPE split-point, \$\$en is the suffix *en*, #U and #L are upper and lower case indicators for the first word of compounds, @ @ indicates a compound merge-point, @s@ indicates a compound merged with the letter *s* between the parts, etc.

Acknowledgments

This project has received funding from the European Union's Horizon 2020 research and innovation programme under grant agreement № 644402 (HimL). This project has received funding from the European Research Council (ERC) under the European Union's Horizon 2020 research and innovation programme (grant agreement № 640550).

References

Dzmitry Bahdanau, Kyunghyun Cho, and Yoshua Bengio. 2014. Neural Machine Translation by Jointly Learning to Align and Translate. *arXiv e-prints*, abs/1409.0473. Presented at ICLR 2015.

Ondřej Bojar, Christian Buck, Chris Callison-Burch, Christian Federmann, Barry Haddow, Philipp Koehn, Christof Monz, Matt Post, Radu Soricut, and Lucia Specia. 2013. Findings of the 2013 Workshop on Statistical Machine Translation. In *Proceedings of the Eighth Workshop on Statistical Machine Translation*, pages 1–44, Sofia, Bulgaria. Association for Computational Linguistics.

Ondřej Bojar, Christian Buck, Christian Federmann, Barry Haddow, Philipp Koehn, Johannes Leveling, Christof Monz, Pavel Pecina, Matt Post, Herve Saint-Amand, Radu Soricut, Lucia Specia, and Aleš Tamchyna. 2014. Findings of the 2014 Workshop on Statistical Machine Translation. In *Proceedings of the Ninth Workshop on Statistical Machine Translation*, pages 12–58, Baltimore, MD, USA. Association for Computational Linguistics.

Ondřej Bojar, Rajen Chatterjee, Christian Federmann, Yvette Graham, Barry Haddow, Matthias Huck, Antonio Jimeno Yepes, Philipp Koehn, Varvara Logacheva, Christof Monz, Matteo Negri, Aurelie Neveol, Mariana Neves, Martin Popel, Matt Post, Raphael Rubino, Carolina Scarton, Lucia Specia, Marco Turchi, Karin Verspoor, and Marcos Zampieri. 2016. Findings of the 2016 Conference on Machine Translation. In *Proceedings of the First Conference on Machine Translation*, pages 131–198, Berlin, Germany. Association for Computational Linguistics.

Ondřej Bojar, Rajen Chatterjee, Christian Federmann, Barry Haddow, Matthias Huck, Chris Hokamp, Philipp Koehn, Varvara Logacheva, Christof Monz, Matteo Negri, Matt Post, Carolina Scarton, Lucia Specia, and Marco Turchi. 2015. Findings of the 2015 Workshop on Statistical Machine Translation. In *Proceedings of the Tenth Workshop on Statistical Machine Translation*, pages 1–46, Lisbon, Portugal. Association for Computational Linguistics.

Ondřej Bojar et al. 2017. Findings of the 2017 Conference on Machine Translation. In *Proceedings of the Second Conference on Machine Translation*, Copenhagen, Denmark. Association for Computational Linguistics.

Fabienne Braune, Nina Seemann, and Alexander Fraser. 2015. Rule Selection with Soft Syntactic Features for String-to-Tree Statistical Machine Translation. In *Proceedings of the 2015 Conference on Empirical Methods in Natural Language Processing*, pages 1095–1101, Lisbon, Portugal. Association for Computational Linguistics.

Fabienne Cap, Alexander Fraser, Marion Weller, and Aoife Cahill. 2014a. How to Produce Unseen Teddy Bears: Improved Morphological Processing of Compounds in SMT. In *Proceedings of the 14th Conference of the European Chapter of the Association for Computational Linguistics*, pages 579–587, Gothenburg, Sweden. Association for Computational Linguistics.

Fabienne Cap, Marion Weller, Anita Ramm, and Alexander Fraser. 2014b. CimS – The CIS and IMS joint submission to WMT 2014 translating from English into German. In *Proceedings of the Ninth Workshop on Statistical Machine Translation*, pages 71–78, Baltimore, MD, USA. Association for Computational Linguistics.

Fabienne Cap, Marion Weller, Anita Ramm, and Alexander Fraser. 2015. CimS - The CIS and IMS Joint Submission to WMT 2015 addressing morphological and syntactic differences in English to German SMT. In *Proceedings of the Tenth Workshop on Statistical Machine Translation*, pages 84–91, Lisbon, Portugal. Association for Computational Linguistics.

Nadir Durrani, Alexander Fraser, Helmut Schmid, Hassan Sajjad, and Richárd Farkas. 2013. Munich-Edinburgh-Stuttgart Submissions of OSM Systems at WMT13. In *Proceedings of the Eighth Workshop on Statistical Machine Translation*, pages 122–127, Sofia, Bulgaria. Association for Computational Linguistics.

Alexander Fraser, Marion Weller, Aoife Cahill, and Fabienne Cap. 2012. Modeling Inflection and Word-Formation in SMT. In *Proceedings of the 13th Conference of the European Chapter of the Association for Computational Linguistics*, pages 664–674, Avignon, France. Association for Computational Linguistics.

Markus Freitag, Minwei Feng, Matthias Huck, Stephan Peitz, and Hermann Ney. 2013. Reverse Word Order Models. In *Proceedings of the XIV Machine Translation Summit*, pages 159–166, Nice, France.

Markus Freitag, Matthias Huck, and Hermann Ney. 2014. Jane: Open Source Machine Translation System Combination. In *Proceedings of the Demonstrations at the 14th Conference of the European Chapter of the Association for Computational Linguistics*, pages 29–32, Gothenburg, Sweden. Association for Computational Linguistics.

Philip Gage. 1994. A New Algorithm for Data Compression. *C Users J.*, 12(2):23–38.

Barry Haddow, Alexandra Birch, Ondřej Bojar, Fabienne Braune, Colin Davenport, Alex Fraser, Matthias Huck, Michal Kašpar, Květoslava Kovaříková, Josef Plch, Anita Ramm, Juliane Ried, James Sheary, Aleš Tamchyna, Dušan Variš, Marion Weller, and Phil Williams. 2017. HimL: Health in my Language. In *Proceedings of the EAMT 2017 User Studies and Project/Product Descriptions*, page 33, Prague, Czech Republic.

Matthias Huck, Alexandra Birch, and Barry Haddow. 2015. Mixed-Domain vs. Multi-Domain Statistical Machine Translation. In *Proceedings of MT Summit XV, vol.1: MT Researchers' Track*, pages 240–255, Miami, FL, USA.

Matthias Huck, Alexander Fraser, and Barry Haddow. 2016. The Edinburgh/LMU Hierarchical Machine Translation System for WMT 2016. In *Proceedings of the First Conference on Machine Translation*, pages 311–318, Berlin, Germany. Association for Computational Linguistics.

Matthias Huck and Hermann Ney. 2012. Pivot Lightly-Supervised Training for Statistical Machine Translation. In *Proceedings of the Tenth Conference of the Association for Machine Translation in the Americas (AMTA 2012)*, San Diego, CA, USA.

Matthias Huck, Simon Riess, and Alexander Fraser. 2017a. Target-side Word Segmentation Strategies for Neural Machine Translation. In *Proceedings of the Second Conference on Machine Translation*, Copenhagen, Denmark. Association for Computational Linguistics.

Matthias Huck, Aleš Tamchyna, Ondřej Bojar, and Alexander Fraser. 2017b. Producing Unseen Morphological Variants in Statistical Machine Translation. In *Proceedings of the 15th Conference of the European Chapter of the Association for Computational Linguistics: Volume 2, Short Papers*, pages 369–375, Valencia, Spain. Association for Computational Linguistics.

Matthias Huck, David Vilar, Daniel Stein, and Hermann Ney. 2011. Lightly-Supervised Training for Hierarchical Phrase-Based Machine Translation. In *Proceedings of the First workshop on Unsupervised Learning in NLP*, pages 91–96, Edinburgh, Scotland. Association for Computational Linguistics.

Diederik P. Kingma and Jimmy Ba. 2015. Adam: A method for stochastic optimization. *CoRR*, abs/1412.6980.

Philipp Koehn. 2005. Europarl: A Parallel Corpus for Statistical Machine Translation. In *Proceedings of the MT Summit X*, Phuket, Thailand.

Philipp Koehn, Hieu Hoang, Alexandra Birch, Chris Callison-Burch, Marcello Federico, Nicola Bertoldi, Brooke Cowan, Wade Shen, Christine Moran,

Richard Zens, Chris Dyer, Ondrej Bojar, Alexandra Constantin, and Evan Herbst. 2007. Moses: Open Source Toolkit for Statistical Machine Translation. In *Proceedings of the 45th Annual Meeting of the Association for Computational Linguistics Companion Volume Proceedings of the Demo and Poster Sessions*, pages 177–180, Prague, Czech Republic. Association for Computational Linguistics.

Philipp Koehn and Kevin Knight. 2003. Empirical Methods for Compound Splitting. In *Proceedings of the 10th Conference of the European Chapter of the Association for Computational Linguistics*, pages 187–194, Budapest, Hungary. Association for Computational Linguistics.

Patrik Lambert, Holger Schwenk, Christophe Servan, and Sadaf Abdul-Rauf. 2011. Investigations on Translation Model Adaptation Using Monolingual Data. In *Proceedings of the Sixth Workshop on Statistical Machine Translation*, pages 284–293, Edinburgh, Scotland. Association for Computational Linguistics.

Lemao Liu, Masao Utiyama, Andrew Finch, and Eiichiro Sumita. 2016. Agreement on Target-bidirectional Neural Machine Translation. In *Proceedings of the 2016 Conference of the North American Chapter of the Association for Computational Linguistics: Human Language Technologies*, pages 411–416, San Diego, CA, USA. Association for Computational Linguistics.

Kishore Papineni, Salim Roukos, Todd Ward, and Wei-Jing Zhu. 2002. Bleu: a Method for Automatic Evaluation of Machine Translation. In *Proceedings of 40th Annual Meeting of the Association for Computational Linguistics*, pages 311–318, Philadelphia, PA, USA. Association for Computational Linguistics.

Jan-Thorsten Peter, Tamer Alkhouli, Hermann Ney, Matthias Huck, Fabienne Braune, Alexander Fraser, Aleš Tamchyna, Ondřej Bojar, Barry Haddow, Rico Sennrich, Frédéric Blain, Lucia Specia, Jan Niehues, Alex Waibel, Alexandre Allauzen, Lauriane Aufrant, Franck Burlot, elena knyazeva, Thomas Lavergne, François Yvon, Mārcis Pinnis, and Stella Frank. 2016. The QT21/HimL Combined Machine Translation System. In *Proceedings of the First Conference on Machine Translation*, pages 344–355, Berlin, Germany. Association for Computational Linguistics.

Anita Ramm and Alexander Fraser. 2016. Modeling verbal inflection for English to German SMT. In *Proceedings of the First Conference on Machine Translation*, pages 21–31, Berlin, Germany. Association for Computational Linguistics.

Hassan Sajjad, Svetlana Smekalova, Nadir Durrani, Alexander Fraser, and Helmut Schmid. 2013. QCRI-MES Submission at WMT13: Using Transliteration Mining to Improve Statistical Machine Translation. In *Proceedings of the Eighth Workshop* on *Statistical Machine Translation*, pages 219–224, Sofia, Bulgaria. Association for Computational Linguistics.

Rico Sennrich, Orhan Firat, Kyunghyun Cho, Alexandra Birch, Barry Haddow, Julian Hitschler, Marcin Junczys-Dowmunt, Samuel Läubli, Antonio Valerio Miceli Barone, Jozef Mokry, and Maria Nadejde. 2017. Nematus: a Toolkit for Neural Machine Translation. In *Proceedings of the Software Demonstrations of the 15th Conference of the European Chapter of the Association for Computational Linguistics*, pages 65–68, Valencia, Spain. Association for Computational Linguistics.

Rico Sennrich, Barry Haddow, and Alexandra Birch. 2016a. Edinburgh Neural Machine Translation Systems for WMT 16. In *Proceedings of the First Conference on Machine Translation*, pages 371–376, Berlin, Germany. Association for Computational Linguistics.

Rico Sennrich, Barry Haddow, and Alexandra Birch. 2016b. Improving Neural Machine Translation Models with Monolingual Data. In *Proceedings of the 54th Annual Meeting of the Association for Computational Linguistics (Volume 1: Long Papers)*, pages 86–96, Berlin, Germany. Association for Computational Linguistics.

Rico Sennrich, Barry Haddow, and Alexandra Birch. 2016c. Neural Machine Translation of Rare Words with Subword Units. In *Proceedings of the 54th Annual Meeting of the Association for Computational Linguistics (Volume 1: Long Papers)*, pages 1715–1725, Berlin, Germany. Association for Computational Linguistics.

Ilya Sutskever, Oriol Vinyals, and Quoc V Le. 2014. Sequence to Sequence Learning with Neural Networks. In Z. Ghahramani, M. Welling, C. Cortes, N. D. Lawrence, and K. Q. Weinberger, editors, *Advances in Neural Information Processing Systems 27*, pages 3104–3112. Curran Associates, Inc.

Aleš Tamchyna, Alexander Fraser, Ondřej Bojar, and Marcin Junczys-Dowmunt. 2016a. Target-Side Context for Discriminative Models in Statistical Machine Translation. In *Proceedings of the 54th Annual Meeting of the Association for Computational Linguistics (Volume 1: Long Papers)*, pages 1704–1714, Berlin, Germany. Association for Computational Linguistics.

Aleš Tamchyna, Roman Sudarikov, Ondřej Bojar, and Alexander Fraser. 2016b. CUNI-LMU Submissions in WMT2016: Chimera Constrained and Beaten. In *Proceedings of the First Conference on Machine Translation*, pages 385–390, Berlin, Germany. Association for Computational Linguistics.

Nicola Ueffing, Gholamreza Haffari, and Anoop Sarkar. 2007. Semi-supervised model adaptation for statistical machine translation. *Machine Translation*, 21(2):77–94.

Marion Weller, Max Kisselew, Svetlana Smekalova, Alexander Fraser, Helmut Schmid, Nadir Durrani, Hassan Sajjad, and Richárd Farkas. 2013. Munich-Edinburgh-Stuttgart Submissions at WMT13: Morphological and Syntactic Processing for SMT. In *Proceedings of the Eighth Workshop on Statistical Machine Translation*, pages 232–239, Sofia, Bulgaria. Association for Computational Linguistics.

Marion Weller-Di Marco, Alexander Fraser, and Sabine Schulte im Walde. 2016. Modeling Complement Types in Phrase-Based SMT. In *Proceedings of the First Conference on Machine Translation*, pages 43–53, Berlin, Germany. Association for Computational Linguistics.

Philip Williams, Rico Sennrich, Maria Nadejde, Matthias Huck, Barry Haddow, and Ondřej Bojar. 2016. Edinburgh's Statistical Machine Translation Systems for WMT16. In *Proceedings of the First Conference on Machine Translation*, pages 399–410, Berlin, Germany. Association for Computational Linguistics.

Antonio Jimeno Yepes, Aurélie Névéol, Mariana Neves, Karin Verspoor, Ondřej Bojar, Arthur Boyer, Cristian Grozea, Barry Haddow, Madeleine Kittner, Yvonne Lichtblau, Pavel Pecina, Roland Roller, Amy Siu, Philippe Thomas, and Saskia Trescher. 2017. Findings of the WMT 2017 Biomedical Translation Shared Task. In *Proceedings of the Second Conference on Machine Translation*, Copenhagen, Denmark. Association for Computational Linguistics.

Rule-based Machine Translation from English to Finnish

Arvi Hurskainen
University of Helsinki
arvi.hurskainen@helsinki.fi

Jörg Tiedemann
University of Helsinki
jörg.tiedemann@helsinki.fi

Abstract

The paper describes a rule-based machine translation system adapted to English to Finnish translation. Although the translation system participates in the shared task of news translation in WMT 2017, the paper describes the strengths and weaknesses of the approach in general.

1 Credits

We are grateful to Pasi Tapanainen from Connexor OY for allowing us to use the en-fdg analyser of English as well as the Constraint Grammar (CG-3)[1] environment for a number of translation phases.

2 Introduction

The translation system described here is in stark contrast to the majority of systems participating in this conference. There are a number of reasons why we are interested in developing rule-based translation systems. One is the observation that, if we use statistical or neural translation systems, we will exclude 99.8 percent of languages out of development. Digitalization is supposed to break barriers between language groups, but in fact it currently increases them. The current hype on neural methods still accelerates the break between the small group of dominant languages and the less-resourced ones. If we want to avoid the break, we do not see any other way out than to put efforts in developing such systems that are affordable for less-resourced languages. At the same time, efforts for finding ways to overcome the problems of statistical systems are needed (Tiedemann et al 2016).

The approach described here deals with the English to Finnish translation system. However, the basic components of the system were developed with the language pair Swahili and English, for which Hurskainen developed rule-based translation systems to both directions (Hurskainen 1992, 1996, 2004, 2006, 2007, 2012).

A number of approaches for constructing rule-based systems have been studied. These include OpenLogos (Scott and Barreiro 2009; Barreiro et al 2011), Apertium (Forcada 2006), Grammatical Framework (Ranta 2011), and Nooj (Silbertztein 2015). Common to these approaches is the use of grammatical knowledge and lexicon of languages in translation. Although the approach that we have used has much in common with those, we did not implement any of them directly. The main reason is that we find it useful to have full control of all phases of the translation process, so that corrections can be made instantly at the correct point of the process. For the same reason we did not adapt such resources as Omorfi (Pirinen 2015). Instead we developed our own system for generating Finnish word forms.

The system described here deliberately avoids any statistical elements in translation process. The basic assumption is that running text can always be decomposed into structured units, and that these units can be described on more or less general level. The translation is not performed on the basis of surface word forms, but rather as a controlled sequence of operations, where the text in source language is processed into surface form of the target language. The basic components in the system are the lexicon and grammar of both languages.

On the abstract level, the language can be described by means of tags, each of which represents various degrees of abstractness. For example, POS tags are the most abstract ones, each representing a large set of members, whereas word lemmas are least abstract, and morphological tags are somewhere in between. The combination of the tags constitutes the knowledge, on the basis of which the text is converted into the surface form of the target language.

There are two guiding principles in this translation system. First, each word form should be given all linguistically correct interpretations. Second, all such operations that are conditional of context, such as selection, deletion, replacement, and adding, should be done in the environment, where context-sensitive rules can be written for controlling the process. For this rea-

---

[1] CG-3 is also termed as FDG-3, because within this environment it is possible to write also functional dependency rules.

Proceedings of the Conference on Machine Translation (WMT), Volume 2: Shared Task Papers, pages 323–329
Copenhagen, Denmark, September 7–11, 2017. ©2017 Association for Computational Linguistics

son, Constraint Grammar (Karlsson 1990, 1995; Karlsson et al 1995; Tapanainen 1996; Bick and Didriksen 2015) is in important role in the system.

Below is a description of various phases of the translation process.

3   Analysis of source text

The source text is first morphologically analysed, disambiguated and provided with syntactic description. In analysing the English text, we used the en-fdg parser (Järvinen and Tapanainen 1997). The parser has a fairly covering vocabulary, and it performs surface-syntax parsing as well as dependency parsing. However, it makes mistakes, and wrong assignments especially in POS categories are detrimental to translation results. Since we had no access to the source code of the parser, we had to devise our own mechanism to correct the mistakes.

The example sentence in (1) is used throughout in this paper.

(1)
```
1 He he subj:>2 @SUBJ %NH PRON PERS NOM SG3
2 will will v-ch:>3 @+FAUXV %AUX V AUXMOD
3 be be v-ch:>4 @-FAUXV %AUX V INF
4 hanging hang main:>0 @-FMAINV %VA ING
5 out out phr:>4 @ADVL %EH ADV
6 on on loc:>4 @ADVL %EH PREP
7 stages stage pcomp:>6 @<P %NH N NOM PL
8 for for subj:>11 @ADVL %EH PREP
9 years year pcomp:>8 @<P %NH N NOM PL
10 to to pm:>11 @INFMARK> %AUX INFMARK>
11 come come mod:>7 @-FMAINV %VA V INF
```

The en-fdg parser performs two types of syntactic mapping, and we had to choose one of them. Because the rule system, which we were going to use in the translation system, makes use of relative distances, we decided to use the surface-syntax option. The precise distances that the dependency parsing produces would probably not have much helped in translation. The modified form is in (2).

(2)
```
"<*he>" "he" %SUBJ CAPINIT PRON PERS NOM SG3
"<will>" "will" %+FAUXV V AUXMOD
"<be>" "be" %-FAUXV V INF
"<hanging>" "hang" %-FMAINV ING
"<out>" "out" %ADVL ADV
"<on>" "on" %ADVL PREP
"<stages>" "stage" %<P N PL NOM
"<for>" "for" %ADVL PREP
"<years>" "year" %<P N PL NOM
"<to>" "to" %INFMARK> INFMARK>
"<come>" "come" %-FMAINV V INF
```

4   Isolation of multiword expressions

Multiword expressions (MWE) are becoming an increasingly important component in machine translation. There is no covering list of MWEs of English, because the concept is very fluid. Many clusters of words can be successfully treated in more than one way. The general rule is that if translation through the normal rule system does not succeed, consider treating the cluster as a MWE. Treating a structure, which also could be handled with normal rules, as a MWE, often helps in disambiguation, because the MWE is given the lexical representation in target language for all members of the structure. In general, it is more safe to use MWE treatment is cases where both options are possible,

For this reason, MWEs are isolated prior to inserting the glosses (i.e. lexical words) of the target language. These MWEs are given the appropriate lexical interpretation (3).

(3)
```
"<*he>" "he" %SUBJ CAPINIT PRON PERS NOM SG3
"<will>" "will" %+FAUXV V AUXMOD
"<be>" "be" %-FAUXV V INF
"<hanging_out>" "hang_out" { hengailla V67 ,
roikkua V52-A } %-FMAINV ING
"<on>" "on" %ADVL PREP
"<stages>" "stage" %<P N PL NOM
"<for_years_to_come>" "for_year_to_come" {
tulevina vuosina , tuleviksi vuosiksi } ADV
```

We have used the CG-3 rule formalism (Tapanainen 1996) for implementing the MWEs, because it has a sophisticated system for controlling the rule application on the basis of context. It also removes all grammatical information on words, which are not relevant in further processing.

In English to Finnish MT, it is sensible to identify four types of MWEs, (a) those which have no inflection, (b) those where the first element (noun) carries the information on inflection, (c) those where the last element (noun) carries the information on inflection, and (d) those where the verb carries the needed information. In handling MWEs, it is also possible, and often needed, to add such new information that helps in achieving grammatically correct translation.

The rules for isolating MWEs are ordered so that the longer one wins. Problematic are such cases, where there are two contiguous MWE candidates with one or more shared members. This much discussed problem can be solved by adding context-based restrictions to rules for controlling rule application.

Although the different types of error-free CG rules are tedious to write manually, they can be produced with scripts from lexical lists.

5 Adding lexical glosses

The next step is to enrich each analysed word with the lexical representation of the target language. This is done so, that the POS category of the analysed word is found first, and then the lexical information is added from the lexicon of that POS category. In total, 13 POS categories are used in the system. Especially when translating from English, the identification of the correct POS category is important, because English is extremely ambiguous in this respect.

For making semantic disambiguation easier, the lexical glosses are ordered so that the most likely interpretation is the first one. There is no safe method for deciding which gloss should be considered as default, and often only thorough testing will help or statistical evidence can be used. Jörg Tiedemann has kindly helped in providing frequency lists produced using automatic word alignment (Östling and Tiedemann, 2016) on parallel corpora (mainly Europarl, Wikipedia headlines but also from OPUS[2]). Bilingual word lists are extracted from the aligned corpora and ranked by Dice scores and raw frequencies. Such words are discarded that include non-alphabetic characters and co-occurrence thresholds are used to further reduce the noise in the data. Separate lists are extracted for English multi-word-units that are aligned to single Finnish words and also for frequently aligned multi-word units on both sides. There is also a lemmatised version of the data. Lexical glosses are added in (4).

(4)
```
"<*he>" "he" { *hän Np9 FRONT , hänen , NO-
GLOSS , itse N8 FRONT } %SUBJ CAPINIT PRON
PERS NOM SG3
"<will>" "will" { NOGLOSS , aikoa V52-D ,
tulla V67 } %+FAUXV V AUXMOD
"<bo>" "bo" { olla V67b BE , eivät ole , ei
ole , NOGLOSS , joka Np13 , jotka Np14 } %-
FAUXV V INF
"<hanging_out>" "hang_out" { henkailla V67 ,
roikkua V52-A } %-FMAINV ING
"<on>" "on" { NOGLOSS M-ADE , NOGLOSS M-ILL ,
NOGLOSS M-PAR , NOGLOSS M-ELA , NOGLOSS M-ALL
, NOGLOSS M-ESS , NOGLOSS M-INE } %ADVL PREP
"<stages>" "stage" { vaihe N48 , lava N9 ,
näyttämö N2 FRONT } %<P N PL NOM
"<for_years_to_come>" "for_year_to_come" {
tulevina vuosina , tuleviksi vuosiksi } ADV
```

___
[2] Data available from http://opus.lingfil.uu.se and http://www.statmt.org/wmt16/translation-task.html

Because Finnish is a highly inflecting language, the lexicon needs precise instruction on inflection. Nouns and adjectives need a unique code for inflection in each case, in gradation, and in front/back concordance. Verbs have a large number of inflected forms, and also they follow gradation and front/back concordance rules. Not all of this need to be included into the transfer lexicon, but some anyway. For example, for transitive verbs it is useful to mark whether their preferred object case is partitive or accusative. Many of them use both, however, but in specific contexts. In addition to object argument, many verbs have also other arguments that require a certain case in inflection. Also such information should be added to the lexicon.

Compound words are common in Finnish, and their handling can be done in two places. The safest way is to handle them as MWEs. However, because compounding in Finnish is very productive, also more general methods should be provided. Compounds in Finnish are such that only the last member, the head, of the compound inflects. Therefore, it is possible to mark compound word candidates, which, if required contextual criteria are fulfilled, will be selected as first parts of the compound and later joined together with the second member. Even more than one member of compound words can thus be combined. This works with such English compounds that are composed of consecutive words without of-genitive structure.

For such words, for which there is no lexical gloss in the system, there is a default that the form in source language is copied as a gloss. It is given an inflection code according to the form of its last part.

Adding the lexical information is implemented using the Beta rewriting language.

6 Semantic disambiguation

Perhaps the most challenging phase in the current translation system is the semantic disambiguation. Much of the complexity comes directly from the source language English, the analysis of which does not offer many clues for performing semantic disambiguation. For example, English verbs do not mark whether they are transitive or intransitive, and the same verb functions in both roles. This creates a recurrent semantic disambiguation problem. The solution must be found on the basis of presence or absence of the object in the sentence. Also, the presence or absence of the agent in passive sentences helps in disambiguation. The distinction between transitive and intransitive verbs is one of the few cases, where rather global rules can be written on semantic disambiguation. Most of the rules are on a low level, applying to relatively few cases.

An example of complicated rules is to identify whether the word *with* starts a relative clause or whether it is in some other role. The identification alone does not suffice. One should also know whether it should be translated with singular or plural form.

The rules on punctuation are different in English and Finnish. These differences can be handled as part of semantic disambiguation.

Such words that can occur as proper nouns and ordinary words are a problem in translation. A partial solution is that such words that have a capital initial letter and are not sentence-initial are likely to occur in both roles and are marked as proper name candidates. Then, on the basis of the strict list and environment, the candidates are selected as proper names. However, this method does not work, if the word is sentence-initial, because in this position all words start with a capital letter.

If the language analyser would add the so-called supersenses to the analysis, the rule writing would become easier. Such comprehensive supersense categories have been established for English (Schneider and Noah 2015; Hollenstein et al 2016). The current system makes use of such sense categories as TIME, PLACE, ANIMACITY, HUMANNESS, TRANSITIVITY etc.. However, these categories are not part of the analyser, but they are implemented in the transfer rule system. The further development of the system might reveal, that more clustering should be made.

When semantic disambiguation rules are applied, the rest of readings are handled so that the first interpretation is selected and the rest are removed. Except for a few specific cases, the system does not leave ambiguity to the readings (5).

(5)
```
"<*he>" "he" { *hän Np9 FRONT } %SUBJ CAPINIT
PRON PERS NOM SG3
"<will>" "will" { NOGLOSS } %+FAUXV V AUXMOD
"<be>" "be" { NOGLOSS } %-FAUXV V INF
"<hanging_out>" "hang_out" { hengailla V67 }
%-FMAINV ING
"<on>" "on" { NOGLOSS } M-ADE %ADVL PREP
"<stages>" "stage" { näyttämö N2 FRONT } %<P
N PL NOM
"<for_years_to_come>" "for_year_to_come" {
tulevina vuosina } ADV
```

7 Controlling singular and plural

One could expect that singular matches with singular and plural with plural in two languages. This is not the case, however. A typical case is that whereas English uses plural forms in nouns that have a number as a modifier, Finnish uses singular. Also adjective and pronoun modifiers in such structures are in singular.

The en-fdg parser does not mark the number in adjectives and some verb forms, which is why such tags must be controlled in great detail.

8 Adding inflection tags

Because Finnish is a highly inflecting language, and English is not, there is little such information inherited from the analysis of the source language that can be used in constructing the correct Finnish word forms. Therefore, such instructions must be added, mostly on the basis of the information added in lexical mapping.

Adding inflection tags takes place in two phases. First, the primary constituents of the sentence are tagged. Such constituents include the verb, the subject, the object, the indirect object, and various modifiers of the verb.

In the second phase, adjective, pronoun, and number modifiers are given inflection tags on the basis of the inflection tag given to the noun head in the first phase of tagging.

Because rule writing for such a complex network is prone to multiple simultaneous mappings, the rules are hierarchically ordered and reapplication is prevented. The rules are ordered according to approximate security, the most secure ones first and the least secure ones last. By the secure rule we mean the likelihood that the rule works correctly in all contexts. There is no strict dichotomy between secure rules and other rules. Rather there is a continuum. Added inflection tags, some redundant, are displayed in (6).

(6)
```
"<*he>" "he" { *hän Np9 FRONT } %SUBJ CAPINIT
PRON PERS NOM SG3
"<will>" "will" { NOGLOSS } %+FAUXV V AUXMOD
SG PRES
"<be>" "be" { NOGLOSS } %-FAUXV V INF SG PRES
"<hanging_out>" "hang_out" { hengailla V67 }
%-FMAINV ING SG PRES
"<on>" "on" { NOGLOSS } M-ADE %ADVL PREP
"<stages>" "stage" { näyttämö N2 FRONT } %<P
N PL NOM ADE
"<for_years_to_come>" "for_year_to_come" {
tulevina vuosina } ADV
```

9 Marking stem boundary

There are 107 different inflection classes for Finnish nominals and verbs. The list of Kotimaisten Kielten Tutkimuskeskus (Research Centre of National Languages) has fewer categories, but they are insufficient for describing all word types. The number of inflection categories could certainly be reduced by applying a finite state machine for controlling part of variation.

There was no linguistic theory behind selecting the stem boundary marking. The solution was purely practical. The boundary mark was put to the point, which made it possible to produce all inflected forms of the word type.

10 Converting inflection tags to surface forms

Each inflection tag is converted to near-surface form using Beta-rules. The system first checks the inflection code, marks it as checked, and then looks for the other codes of that inflection class. If the path leads successfully to a surface form suffix, it is added after the suffix tag.

The process is not simple, however, because the reading may have two or three inflecting words, and each must be given the correct inflection. The danger of mixing the suffixes is avoided by joining the found suffix immediately to the word. A second, and possibly third, round is then run for finding the correct suffixes for the rest of words in that reading.

The suffixes are joined to the whole lexical word and not directly to the stem. This is done, because sometimes the correct front form can be decided only when the final part of the lexical word is present. Note that the inflection suffixes are not necessarily final. By default, suffixes are given the back vowel treatment (7). If the word requires front vowel treatment, conversion rules modify the suffix accordingly (8).

```
(7)
"<*he>" "he" { *h:än :Np9 FRONT } %SUBJ
CAPINIT PRON PERS NOM SG3
"<will>" "will" { NOGLOSS } %+FAUXV V AUXMOD
PRES SG
"<be>" "be" { NOGLOSS } %-FAUXV V INF PRES SG
"<hanging_out>" "hang_out" { hengail:la+ee
:V67 } %-FMAINV ING PRES SG
"<on>" "on" { NOGLOSS } M-ADE %ADVL PREP
"<stages>" "stage" { näyttämö:+illa :N2 FRONT
} %<P N PL ADE
"<for_years_to_come>"    "for_year_to_come"    {
tulevina vuosina } ADV
```

11 Front/back concordance

The decision on whether the ending of the word gets a front or back vowel treatment is done on the basis of the vowel structure of the word. In addition to this, the end part of the lexical word may affect the precise surface form of the word. For example, the rule may require that the back vowels of the suffix must be converted to corresponding front vowels. This conversion is not always one-to-one process, because a back vowel may have two corresponding front forms. This can be decided on the basis of the last vowel of the lexical word. Therefore the full lexical word must be present when conversion rules are applied. Front vowel conversion is displayed in (8).

```
(8)
"<*he>" "he" { *h:än } %SUBJ CAPINIT PRON
PERS NOM SG3
"<will>" "will" { NOGLOSS } %+FAUXV V AUXMOD
PRES SG
"<be>" "be" { NOGLOSS } %-FAUXV V INF PRES SG
"<hanging_out>" "hang_out" { hengail+ee } %-
FMAINV ING PRES SG
"<on>" "on" { NOGLOSS } M-ADE %ADVL PREP
"<stages>" "stage" { näyttämö:+illa } %<P N
PL ADE
"<for_years_to_come>"    "for_year_to_come"    {
tulevina vuosina } ADV
```

12 Controlling word order

POS tags are the most important keys in controlling the word order in target language. In the current language pair, the most important features that require word reordering are the prepositions and the of-genitive. Finnish most often uses postpositions, and it does not have equivalent for of-genitive. Also, passive structures with agent are missing in Finnish, which causes complex changes in word order.

We have written the reordering rules with Perl. In order to simplify rule-writing, we have moved the POS tag to the beginning of the reading of each word and changed the whole input into sentence-per-line format. Using this format, it is fairly easy to write new reordering rules. For each word type applies the same description, and only the POS tag changes. In case additional information is needed, it is available in the description of the word.

13 Discussion

The current translation system tries to make maximal use of the lexicon and grammar of source and target languages. A sentence in source language is converted through subsequent phases into target language. No purely statistical choices are used. In order to reduce unnecessary rule writing, defaults are used where feasible.

Such rules that need contextual control for their application are implemented using the CG3 environment. Such cases are, apart from the parsing component of English, the correction module for the output of the parser, the isolation and treatment of MWEs, the semantic disambiguation, the control of singular and plural forms, and the modules for adding primary and secondary tags for facilitating inflection. The rest of rules are implemented using rewriting rules in Beta or Perl, whichever is feasible in each case.

The periodic development with this language pair was started in 2015, using IT and medical domains as test environments. The work with news texts started in March 2017, and the work with this domain is just in the beginning. Especially the vocabulary of the domain is very defective, and also the isolation of MWEs needs much work.

Our own estimation of the feasibility of the rule-based approach to the current task is that the more grammatical the sentences are, the better the result. The ordinary news reporting can be translated satisfactorily, but sport news and other types of less grammatical texts are a big problem.

References

Barreiro Anabela, Bernard Scott, Walter Kasper and Bernd Kiefer, 2011. OpenLogos Rule-Based Machine Translation: Philosophy, Model, Resources and Customization. *Machine Translation*, volume 25 number 2, Pages 107-126, Springer, Heidelberg, 2011. ISSN 0922-6567, doi:10.1007/s10590-011-9091-z

Bick Eckhard and Tino Didriksen, 2015. CG-3 - Beyond Classical Constraint Grammar. In: Beáta Megyesi: *Proceedings of NODALIDA 2015*, May 11-13, 2015, Vilnius, Lithuania. pp. 31-39. Linköping: LiU Electronic Press. ISBN 978-91-7519-098-3.

Forcada Mikel L., 2006. Open-source machine translation: an opportunity for minor languages in B. Williams (ed.): *Proceedings of the Workshop "Strategies for developing machine translation for minority languages* (5th SALTMIL workshop on Minority Languages)" (organised in conjunction with LREC 2006 (22-28.05.2006)). Genoa, Italy, pp. 1-6.

Hollenstein Nora; Nathan Schneider and Bonnie Webber, 2016. Inconsistency Detection in Semantic Annotation. In *Proceedings of LREC-2016*. Pp. 3986-3990.

Hurskainen A., 1992. A Two-Level Computer Formalism for the Analysis of Bantu Morphology. An Application to Swahili. *Nordic Journal of African Studies*, 1(1), 87-122.

Hurskainen A., 1996. Disambiguation of morphological analysis in Bantu languages. In *Proceedings of the 16th conference on Computational Linguistics*. Copenhagen:ACL. Vol.1, pp.568-573.

Hurskainen A., 2004. Optimizing disambiguation in Swahili. In *Proceedings of the 20th International Conference on Computational Linguistics (COLING '04)*, Geneva, Switzerland, 23-27 August 2004, pp. 254–260. Genoa: [International Conference on Computational Linguistics].

Hurskainen A., 2006. Constraint Grammar in Unconventional Use: Handling complex Swahili idioms and proverbs. In: Suominen, Mickael et.al. (ed.) *A Man of Measure: Festschrift in Honour of Fred Karlsson on his 60th Birthday*. Special Supplement to SKY Jounal of Linguistics, Vol. 19 (ISSN 1796-279X), pp. 397-406. Turku: The Linguistic Association of Finland.

Hurskainen A., 2007. A rule-based environment for Swahili development. *MultiLingual*, 18(8), 53-58. ISSN 1523-0309.

Hurskainen A., 2012. Quality Swahili machine translation. *MultiLingual*, 23(7), 39-42. ISSN 1523-0309.

Järvinen Timo and Tapanainen Pasi, 1997. A Dependency Parser for English. *Technical Reports*, No. TR-1. Department of General Linguistics, University of Helsinki.

Karlsson Fred, 1990. Constraint grammar as a framework for parsing running text. In: Karlgren Hans (ed.), *Proceedings of 13th International Conference on Computational Linguistics*, volume 3, pp. 168-173, Helsinki, Finland.

Karlsson Fred, 1995. Designing a parser for unrestricted text. In: Karlsson F. et al (Eds), *Constraint Grammar: A Language-Independent System for Parsing Unrestricted Text*, 1-40. Berlin: Mouton de Gryuter.

Karlsson Fred; Atro Voutilainen, Juha Heikkilä and Arto Anttila, 1995. *Constraint Grammar. A Language-Independent System for Parsing Unrestricted Text*. Mouton the Gruyter.

Pirinen Tommi A., 2015. Omorfi —free and open source morphological lexical database for Finnish. In *Proceedings of the 20th Nordic Conference of Computational Linguistics NODALIDA 2015*, pages 313–315.

Ranta Aarne, *2011*. Grammatical Framework. Programming with Multilingual Grammars. *CSLI Publications, Center for the Study of Language and Information.* pp. 8–9. ISBN 978-1-57586-627-7.

Scott B. and Barreiro A. 2009. OpenLogos MT and the SAL representation language. In *Proceedings of the First International Workshop on Free/Open-Source Rule-Based Machine Translation* / Edited by Juan Antonio Pérez-Ortiz, Felipe Sánchez-Martínez, Francis M. Tyers. Alicante, Spain: Universidad de Alicante. Departamento de Lenguajes y Sistemas Informáticos. 2–3 November 2009, pp. 19–26.

Schneider Nathan and Noah A. Smith, 2015. A Corpus and Model Integrating Multiword Expressions and Supersenses. In *Proceedings of NAACL-HLT-2015.* Pp. 1537-1547

Silberztein M., 2015. *La formalisation des langues : l'approche de NooJ.* ISTE: London (426 p.).

Tapanainen Pasi, 1996. *The Constraint Grammar Parser CG-2.* University of Helsinki Publications No. 27.

Tapanainen Pasi, 1999. *Parsing in Two Frameworks: Finite-state and functional dependency grammar.* Ph.D. Dissertation, Department of General Linguistics, University of Helsinki.

Tiedemann Jörg, Fabienne Cap, Jenna Kanerva, Filip Ginter, Sara Stymne, Robert Östling and Marion Weller-Di Marco, 2016. *Phrase-Based SMT for Finnish with More Data, Better Models and Alternative Alignment and Translation Tools.* WMT 2016: 391-398.

Östling Robert and Jörg Tiedemann: Efficient Word Alignment with Markov Chain Monte Carlo. *The Prague Bulletin of Mathematical Linguistics (PBML)*, Number 106, pp. 125–146.

NRC Machine Translation System for WMT 2017

Chi-kiu Lo   **Boxing Chen**   **Colin Cherry**   **George Foster**[*]
Samuel Larkin   **Darlene Stewart**   **Roland Kuhn**

National Research Council Canada   Google Research
1200 Montreal Road, Ottawa, ON K1A 0R6, Canada   Montreal, Canada
`FirstName.LastName@nrc-cnrc.gc.ca`   `fosterg@google.com`

Abstract

We describe the machine translation systems developed at the National Research Council of Canada (NRC) for the Russian-English and Chinese-English news translation tasks of the Second Conference on Machine Translation (WMT 2017). We conducted several experiments to explore the best baseline settings for neural machine translation (NMT). In the Russian-English task, to our surprise, our best-performing system is one that rescores phrase-based statistical machine translation outputs using NMT rescoring features. On the other hand, in the Chinese-English task, which has far more parallel training data, NMT is able to outperform SMT significantly. The NRC MT systems is the best constrained system in Russian-English (out of nine participants) and the fourth best constrained system in Chinese-English (out of twenty participants) in WMT 2017 human evaluation.

1 Introduction

We present NRC's submission to the Russian-English and Chinese-English news translation task of WMT 2017. In contrast to last year, when we participated in the Russian-English task only, with our well-developed phrase-based statistical machine translation system (Lo et al., 2016; Larkin et al., 2010; Foster et al., 2009), this year we built large-scale state-of-the-art neural machine translation (NMT) systems for these two language pairs to facilitate further understanding and discussion of NMT.

Russian-English and Chinese-English are both challenging language pairs for machine transla-

tion. Russian is a highly inflectional and free word order language. The skewed Russian to English word type ratio introduces a data sparsity problem that cannot be solved by discarding word inflections, since they play an important role in disambiguating the meaning of sentences. Chinese does not have clear word boundaries. The number of Chinese word types created by automatic word segmentation software is high, while naive character segmentation would result in a skewed Chinese to English sentence length ratio. These characteristics make it difficult for machine translation systems to learn the correct association between words in Chinese and English.

Since this was the first time we deployed NMT models in an evaluation, we first tried to replicate the results of previous work (Sennrich et al., 2016a). Our NMT systems are based on Nematus (Sennrich et al., 2017). We used automatic back-translation (Sennrich et al., 2016b) of a sub-selected monolingual News corpus as additional training data, and all the training data is segmented into subword units using BPE (Sennrich et al., 2016c). We also experimented with pervasive dropout as implemented in Nematus.

For Russian-English, our WMT16 PBMT system scored higher than all the NMT systems we built this year. We therefore experimented with using the NMT systems as features for rescoring the 1000-best output from our WMT16 PBMT system. This strategy yielded almost 2 BLEU point improvement over the PBMT baseline. For Chinese-English, we exploited different domain adaptation techniques to boost the system performance on in-domain news translation. We also integrated various regularization methods to avoid the systems overfitting to the small development set.

The NRC Russian-English and Chinese-English news translation systems achieve competitive per-

---

[*]Work performed while at NRC.

330

Proceedings of the Conference on Machine Translation (WMT), Volume 2: Shared Task Papers, pages 330–337
Copenhagen, Denmark, September 7–11, 2017. ©2017 Association for Computational Linguistics

formance (third place in both language pairs) in the preliminary automatic evaluation of WMT 2017. In this paper, we discuss the lessons learned in building large-scale state-of-the-art NMT systems.

2 Russian-English news translation

We used all the Russian-English parallel corpora available for the constrained news translation task. They include the CommonCrawl corpus, the NewsCommentary v12 corpus, the Yandex corpus and the Wikipedia headlines corpus. In total, 2.6 million parallel Russian-English sentences are used to train the baseline system. We use the news translation test set of WMT 15 as development set and that of WMT 16 as test set. The Russian and English texts in the training/development/test corpora were kept in their original true case and tokenized, then the Russian and English texts were combined to train a BPE model with vocabulary size of 30k.

2.1 NMT baseline system

Our NMT baseline system is developed using Nematus (Sennrich et al., 2017). The dimension of word embeddings is set to 512 and that of the hidden layers is set to 1024. We train the models with rmsprop (Tieleman and Hinton, 2012), reshuffling the training corpus between epochs. We use mini-batches of size 100 and validate the model every 8000 minibatches against BLEU on the WMT 15 news translation test set. We perform early stopping on the baseline system. We use AmuNMT C++ decoder (Junczys-Dowmunt et al., 2016a) with a beam size of 4.

2.2 Synthetic training data

In statistical machine translation, large monolingual corpora in the output language have traditionally been used for training language models to make the system output more fluent. However, it is difficult to integrate language models in current NMT architectures. Instead of ignoring such large monolingual corpora, Sennrich et al. (2016b) exploited large corpora in the output language by translating a subset of them into the input language and then using the resulting synthetic sentence pairs as additional training data. We translated monolingual English text into Russian using an English to Russian NMT system mirroring

the one described in Section 2.1,[1] and then employed the machine-translated Russian and perfect English sentence pairs as additional data to train the Russian-English MT system.

To select sentences for back-translation, we used a semi-supervised convolutional neural network classifier (Chen and Huang, 2016). We sampled two million sentences from the English monolingual News Crawl 2015 & 2016 corpora according to their classifier scores, which reflect their similarity to the the English half of our development set.

2.3 Pervasive dropout

Pervasive dropout prevents the NMT system from overfitting. We apply the variant of Gal and Ghahramani (2016) pervasive dropout that is implemented in Nematus to all layers in the network. This variant has the characteristic that the random dropout is applied at the token level, instead of at the word-type level. We set the dropout probability for the source words, target words and embedding layers to 0.15. For the hidden layers, we set the dropout probability to 0.3.

2.4 Minimum risk training

Minimum risk training (MRT) (Shen et al., 2016) allows model optimization to arbitrary loss functions, which do not need to be differentiable, thus enabling direct model tuning against automatic MT evaluation metrics. It uses the MT evaluation metric as the loss function and minimizes the expected loss on the training data at sentence-level. We experimented with further model optimization using MRT on the whole training corpus against sentence BLEU at the final stage.

2.5 Greedy model averaging

A common practice for avoiding overfitting to the training data is ensembling the last few models saved as checkpoints. Recently, Junczys-Dowmunt et al. (2016b) showed that one can see nearly the same benefits by performing a component-wise average of all parameters across checkpoints. We extended this technique by using a greedy strategy to average a wider range of models. Instead of considering only the last few saved models, we considered 30 saved models having the best BLEU performance on the validation set one-by-one. For each checkpoint, in descending

---

[1] This scores 21.05 BLEU on the WMT 15 test set.

order of BLEU score, we add the checkpoint to our running average to create a model candidate. We then use the candidate to decode our development set. If this results in improved BLEU, we accept the candidate, and it becomes our new running average. We find that this process generally selects between 5 and 8 checkpoints to include in the average.

2.6 Portage - NRC WMT16 PBMT system

The core of the NRC WMT16 MT system (Lo et al., 2016) is *Portage* (Larkin et al., 2010). Portage is a conventional log-linear phrase-based SMT system.

The system was trained on all the Russian-English parallel training corpora and WMT 12 and WMT 13 Russian-English news translation test set and tuned on the WMT 14 test set. Both the Russian and English text in the parallel and monolingual corpora in the training/development/test corpora were tokenized and lowercased.

The system employed Russian lemmatization extensively in building word alignments for translation models, a hierarchical distortion model, a sparse feature model and neural network joint models or NNJMs (Devlin et al., 2014). The system also made extensive use of monolingual English corpora in building language models. Last but not least, it had comprehensive Russian OOV handling, which included a fallback Russian lemma-based phrase table and a Russian transliteration model.

2.7 Rescoring and truecasing

We rescored 1000-best lists output from the phrase-based decoder using a rescoring model (Och et al., 2004; Foster et al., 2009) consisting of 13 features: 3 NMT models, 2 language models, 5 NNJMs and 3 n-best features. The rescoring model was tuned using n-best MIRA (Cherry and Foster, 2012).

The three NMT systems used as rescoring features were: 1) baseline further trained with synthetic data, 2) dropout baseline further trained with synthetic data and with dropout turned off, and 3) the previous model optimized to the development set using minimum risk training.

The five NNJM rescoring features include two Russian-word NNJMs and three Russian-lemma ones. Following Devlin et al. (2014), we take advantage of the rescoring framework to have our NNJMs view each candidate translation from

	dev		test
	single		
System	best	ave.	
a: baseline	23.6	24.8	23.8
b: (a)+synthetic	25.6	26.3	25.3
c: dropout baseline	26.3	26.3	25.6
d: (c)+synthetic	27.7	27.8	26.6
e: (d)+mrt	27.8	27.8	26.1
f: WMT16 Portage	28.2	–	28.6
g: (f) rescored by (d)	29.9	–	29.6
h: (f) final rescoring	–	–	30.4

Table 1: Selected results from our Russian-English development experiments. The ave. column shows the result of greedy model averaging, where applicable.

perspectives not available during decoding. The Russian-lemma NNJMs are rescored using normal, target-to-source, and right-to-left perspectives. The Russian-word NNJMs are rescored using normal and right-to-left perspectives. The choice of which perspectives to include was made based on empirical devtest (WMT 16) performance.

The two language models were: a left-to-right 6-gram LM and a right-to-left 6-gram LM. Both were trained on the WMT 16 monolingual English training corpus,

The final output was truecased and detokenized in the same way as described in Lo et al. (2016).

2.8 Results

Table 1 shows the results of selected models from our development experiments. It can be seen that synthetic training data generated by back-translation of large output language monolingual corpora consistently improves the baseline by 1.4 to 2 BLEU. However, this result is rather disappointing by comparison with the exciting improvement reported in Sennrich et al. (2016a), i.e. 3-4 BLEU.

Another disappointing result is that model averaging does not work well with the dropout models. We can see model averaging yields around 1 BLEU gain on non-dropout systems. However, the improvement achieved by model averaging drops to 0-0.1 BLEU on dropout systems. In other experiments not shown here, we also saw no improvement from ensembling the checkpoints of our dropout systems.

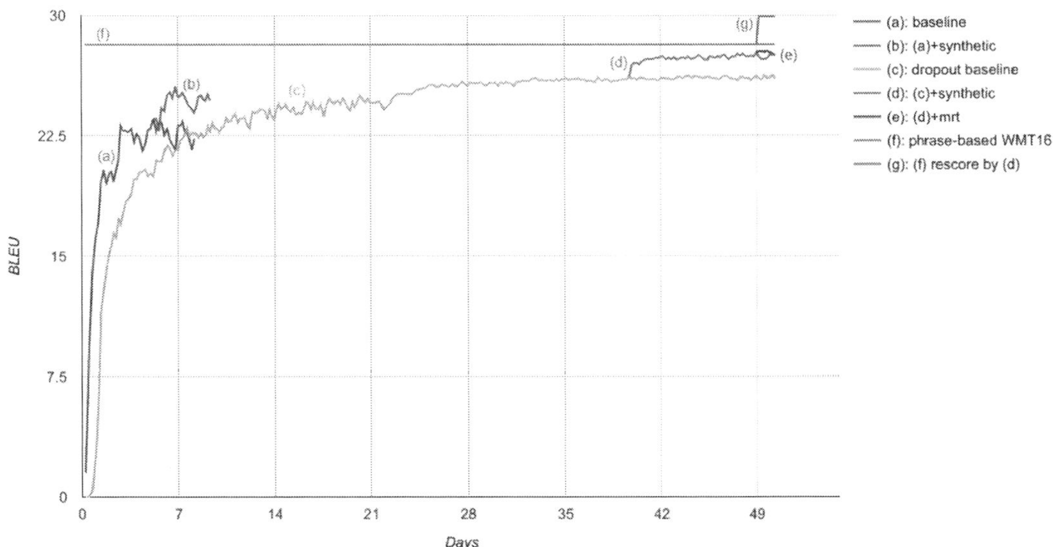

Figure 1: Russian-English learning curve on development set in cased BLEU of selected models: a) NMT baseline, b) NMT baseline further trained with synthetic data, c) NMT dropout baseline, d) NMT dropout baseline further trained with synthetic data while dropout is turned off, e) NMT dropout baseline with synthetic data optimized to sentence-level BLEU on the training data using MRT, f) our WMT16 PBMT submission and g) the PBMT rescored by one of the rescoring features.

The most interesting observation in our experiments is that the dropout baseline continues to improve over the course of many weeks. Figure 1 shows the learning curve of the selected models for all 7 weeks of development. Line (c) of this figure shows that the dropout baseline continues training and improving until the end of the evaluation campaign, achieving a development BLEU score that is 2.7 BLEU points beyond our best single NMT system that does not use dropout. This system can be further improved by adding synthetic data, as in line (d), however, we found that we needed to switch dropout off after adding the synthetic data.

Although in figure 1 we see that none of the NMT systems manage to beat our WMT16 PBMT submission, the more interesting result is that there is more than 1.8 BLEU gain on the development set and 1.1 BLEU gain on the test set by rescoring the PBMT 1000-best list using just one of our NMT systems and no other features, as in line (g). The final rescoring with weighted collections of NMT systems, language model features, NNJM features and n-best features shows 1.8 BLEU improvement over the WMT 16 submission on the test set.

3 Chinese-English news translation

We used all the Chinese-English parallel corpora available for the constrained news translation task. They include the UN corpus, the NewsCommentary v12 corpus and the CWMT corpus. In total, 25 million parallel Chinese-English sentences were used to train the baseline system. We used half of the WMT 17 news translation development set as our development set and the other half as internal test set. The English texts in the training/development/test corpora were tokenized and lowercased while the Chinese texts in the training/development/test corpora were segmented using the ICTCLAS segmenter (Zhang et al., 2003). Then the Chinese and English text were combined to train a BPE model with vocabulary size of 90k.

3.1 NMT baseline system

Our Chinese-English NMT baseline system is similar to the Russian-English baseline as described in section 2.1: Nematus-based, word embeddings with 512 dimensions, hidden layers with 1024 dimensions, etc.

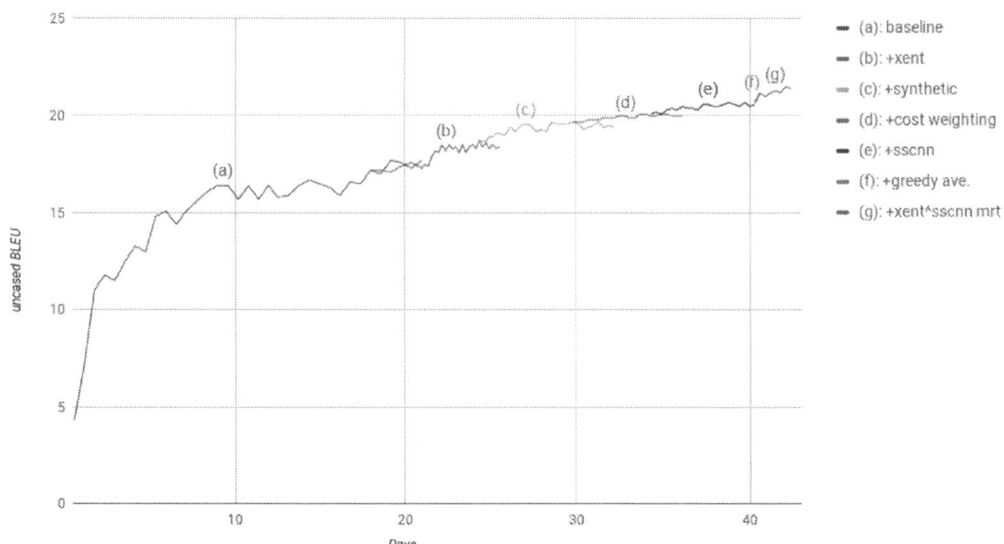

Figure 2: Chinese-English learning curves on the internal test set in uncased BLEU for selected models: a) NMT baseline, b) further trained with in-domain data selected by bilingual LM cross-entropy difference (xent), c) further trained with synthetic data, d) further trained with cost weighting, e) further trained with in-domain data selected by semi-supervised convolutional neural network classifier (sscnn), f) greedy model averaging and g) optimized against sentence-level BLEU on the intersection of the subsets of data selected by xent and sscnn using MRT.

3.2 Data selection and domain adaptation

Since the majority of the 25 million sentence pairs in the training corpus are general domain, we experimented with different data selection and domain adaptation techniques to further train the NMT system with data that are similar to the development set so as to perform better in the news domain.

Axelrod et al. (2011) introduced the bilingual language model cross-entropy difference as a similarity function for identifying sentence pairs from general-domain training corpora that are close to the target domain. We built four language models using the input and output sides of the training corpora and the development set respectively to select 3 million sentence pairs from the training corpora that are close to the news domain.

However, the development set, which consists of only 1k sentence pairs, is too tiny to be a suitable corpus for building the in-domain language models that will enable the bilingual LM cross-entropy difference data selection method to work effectively. Therefore, we also experimented with the semi-supervised convolutional neural network method in Chen and Huang (2016) to select 1 million sentence pairs from the training corpora that are close to the news domain.

Finally, we experimented with a cost weighting domain adaptation technique (Chen et al., 2017). This technique trains a domain classifier concurrently with the NMT system, and uses the classifier probabilities to weight training instances according to their similarity to the development set.

3.3 Synthetic training data

We generated synthetic Chinese and perfect English sentence pairs in a process similar to that described in section 2.2. We first used a semi-supervised convolutional neural network classifier (Chen and Huang, 2016) to sample 20 million sentences from the English monolingual News Crawl 2015 & 2016 corpora according to the development set. We then translated the selected sentences using a English-Chinese NMT baseline trained out-of-the-box using only the parallel corpora.

3.4 Greedy model averaging

Greedy model averaging is performed as described in section 2.5.

System	test
baseline	17.2
+biLM cross-entropy (xent) DS	18.7
+synthetic	19.7
+cost weighting DA	20.1
+sscnn DS	20.7
+greedy model averaging	21.2
+xent∩sscnn mrt	21.4
ensemble	24.2
rescoring	25.6

Table 2: Selected results in uncased BLEU from our Chinese-English development experiments.

3.5 Minimum risk training

In contrast to the way in which we carried out MRT for the Russian-English system in section 2.4, we optimized the Chinese-English system using MRT against sentence BLEU only on the intersection of the subsets of corpora selected by the LM cross-entropy and the semi-supervised CNN in section 3.2. The size of the intersection of the two subsets of corpora is 300k sentence pairs.

3.6 Ensembling, rescoring and truecasing

Applying different combinations of the techniques described in section 3.1 to 3.5, we built 14 different NMT systems. Their uncased BLEU on the test set ranged from 19.8 to 21.4. We ensembled all the systems together using Simplex-tuned weights.

We rescored 500-best lists output from the ensembled NMT system using a rescoring model (Och et al., 2004; Foster et al., 2009) consisting of 82 features: IBM models, RNN language models (Mikolov et al., 2010), n-gram language models trained on different data subsets, neural network joint models (NNJMs) (Devlin et al., 2014) and word, n-gram, word alignment posteriors (Foster et al., 2009), etc. The rescoring model was tuned using n-best MIRA (Cherry and Foster, 2012).

The final output was truecased and detokenized using heuristic methods.

3.7 Results

Figure 2 shows that all the components we described in section 3.2 to 3.5 help improve the NMT system. The uncased BLEU on the test set in table 2 shows that all the data selection and domain adaptation methods improve the NMT systems by 0.4 to 1.5 BLEU. Similar to the results we ob-

served in our Russian-English NMT systems, synthetic training data generated by back-translation of large output language monolingual corpora improved the NMT system score by 1 BLEU.

The most important observation in our experiments is that ensembling of NMT systems developed by different techniques achieves around 3 BLEU improvement and rescoring the n-best output from NMT systems also shows 1.4 BLEU gain on the test set.

4 Conclusion

We have presented the NRC submissions to the WMT 2017 Russian-English and Chinese-English news translation task. The Russian-English submitted system is our WMT 16 PBMT system rescored by three NMT models and other rescoring features. Our Chinese-English submitted system is an ensemble of fourteen NMT models rescored by a large set of additional features. Our system achieved the highest score for the Russian-English (among nine participants) and the fourth highest score for Chinese-English (among twenty participants) constrained news translation tasks in WMT 2017 human evaluation.

Our experiences in WMT 2017 illustrate the sharp divide between large- and medium-scale data scenarios when working with neural MT. For Russian-English, we found ourselves relying on techniques that are usually intended for low-resource scenarios, such as pervasive dropout and rescoring a phrase-based system. This is surprising, as 2.5 million sentence pairs would have been considered a large-data scenario in the not-too-distant past. Meanwhile, for Chinese-English, we were able to achieve strong individual neural systems, which were further strengthened by ensembling across various data selection and data weighting techniques. Our results also highlight the necessity to speed up convergence in the presence of dropout, so that it does not take weeks to train a single model.

References

Amittai Axelrod, Xiaodong He, and Jianfeng Gao. 2011. Domain Adaptation via Pseudo In-Domain Data Selection. In *Proceedings of the 2011 Conference on Empirical Methods in Natural Language Processing*. Association for Computational Linguistics, Edinburgh, Scotland, UK., pages 355–362. http://www.aclweb.org/anthology/D11-1033.

Boxing Chen, Colin Cherry, George Foster, and Samuel Larkin. 2017. Cost Weighting for Neural Machine Translation Domain Adaptation . In *1st Workshop of Neural Machine Translation*.

Boxing Chen and Fei Huang. 2016. Semi-supervised Convolutional Networks for Translation Adaptation with Tiny Amount of In-domain Data. In *Proceedings of the 20th SIGNLL Conference on Computational Natural Language Learning, CoNLL 2016, Berlin, Germany, August 11-12, 2016*. pages 314–323. http://aclweb.org/anthology/K/K16/K16-1031.pdf.

Colin Cherry and George Foster. 2012. Batch Tuning Strategies for Statistical Machine Translation. In *Proc. 2012 Conf. of the N. American Chapter of the Association for Computational Linguistics: Human Language Technologies*. Montréal, Canada, pages 427–436. http://www.aclweb.org/anthology/N12-1047.

Jacob Devlin, Rabih Zbib, Zhongqiang Huang, Thomas Lamar, Richard Schwartz, and John Makhoul. 2014. Fast and Robust Neural Network Joint Models for Statistical Machine Translation. In *Proceedings of the Annual Meeting of the Association for Computational Linguistics*. Baltimore, Maryland, pages 1370–1380. http://www.aclweb.org/anthology/P14-1129.

George Foster, Boxing Chen, Eric Joanis, Howard Johnson, Roland Kuhn, and Samuel Larkin. 2009. PORTAGE in the NIST 2009 MT Evaluation. *Technical report, NRC-CNRC.* .

Yarin Gal and Zoubin Ghahramani. 2016. A Theoretically Grounded Application of Dropout in Recurrent Neural Networks. In *Advances in Neural Information Processing Systems 29 (NIPS)*.

Marcin Junczys-Dowmunt, Tomasz Dwojak, and Hieu Hoang. 2016a. Is Neural Machine Translation Ready for Deployment? A Case Study on 30 Translation Directions. In *Proceedings of the 9th International Workshop on Spoken Language Translation (IWSLT)*. Seattle, WA.

Marcin Junczys-Dowmunt, Tomasz Dwojak, and Rico Sennrich. 2016b. The AMU-UEDIN Submission to the WMT16 News Translation Task: Attention-based NMT Models as Feature Functions in Phrase-based SMT. In *Proceedings of the First Conference on Machine Translation*. Association for Computational Linguistics, Berlin, Germany, pages 319–325. http://www.aclweb.org/anthology/W16-2316.

Samuel Larkin, Boxing Chen, George Foster, Uli Germann, Eric Joanis, J. Howard Johnson, and Roland Kuhn. 2010. Lessons from NRC's Portage System at WMT 2010. In *5th Workshop on Statistical Machine Translation*.

Chi-kiu Lo, Colin Cherry, George Foster, Darlene Stewart, Rabib Islam, Anna Kazantseva, and Roland Kuhn. 2016. NRC Russian-English Machine Translation System for WMT 2016. In *Proceedings of the First Conference on Machine Translation*. Association for Computational Linguistics, Berlin, Germany, pages 326–332. http://www.aclweb.org/anthology/W16-2317.

Tomas Mikolov, Martin Karafit, Luks Burget, Jan Cernock, and Sanjeev Khudanpur. 2010. Recurrent neural network based language model. In *INTERSPEECH*. ISCA, pages 1045–1048.

Franz Josef Och, Daniel Gildea, Sanjeev Khudanpur, Anoop Sarkar, Kenji Yamada, Alexander M Fraser, Shankar Kumar, Libin Shen, David Smith, Katherine Eng, Viren Jain, Zhen Jin, and Radev Dragomir. 2004. A Smorgasbord of Features for Statistical Machine Translation. In *Proceedings of the Human Language Technology Conference of the North American Chapter of the Association for Computational Linguistics: HLT-NAACL 2004*. pages 161–168.

Rico Sennrich, Orhan Firat, Kyunghyun Cho, Alexandra Birch, Barry Haddow, Julian Hitschler, Marcin Junczys-Dowmunt, Samuel Läubli, Antonio Valerio Miceli Barone, Jozef Mokry, and Maria Nadejde. 2017. Nematus: a Toolkit for Neural Machine Translation. In *Proceedings of the Software Demonstrations of the 15th Conference of the European Chapter of the Association for Computational Linguistics*. Association for Computational Linguistics, Valencia, Spain, pages 65–68. http://aclweb.org/anthology/E17-3017.

Rico Sennrich, Barry Haddow, and Alexandra Birch. 2016a. Edinburgh Neural Machine Translation Systems for WMT 16. In *Proceedings of the First Conference on Machine Translation*. Association for Computational Linguistics, Berlin, Germany, pages 371–376. http://www.aclweb.org/anthology/W16-2323.

Rico Sennrich, Barry Haddow, and Alexandra Birch. 2016b. Improving Neural Machine Translation Models with Monolingual Data. In *Proceedings of the 54th Annual Meeting of the Association for Computational Linguistics (Volume 1: Long Papers)*. Association for Computational Linguistics, Berlin, Germany, pages 86–96. http://www.aclweb.org/anthology/P16-1009.

Rico Sennrich, Barry Haddow, and Alexandra Birch. 2016c. Neural Machine Translation of Rare Words with Subword Units. In *Proceedings of the 54th Annual Meeting of the Association for Computational Linguistics (Volume 1: Long Papers)*. Association for Computational Linguistics, Berlin, Germany, pages 1715–1725. http://www.aclweb.org/anthology/P16-1162.

Shiqi Shen, Yong Cheng, Zhongjun He, Wei He, Hua Wu, Maosong Sun, and Yang Liu. 2016. Minimum Risk Training for Neural Machine Translation. In *Proceedings of the 54th Annual Meeting of the Association for Computational Linguistics (Volume 1: Long Papers)*. Association for Computational Linguistics, Berlin, Germany, pages 1683–1692. http://www.aclweb.org/anthology/P16-1159.

Tijmen Tieleman and Geoffrey Hinton. 2012. Lecture 6.5-rmsprop: Divide the gradient by a running average of its recent magnitude. In *COURSERA: Neural networks for machine learning*.

Hua-Ping Zhang, Hong-Kui Yu, De-Yi Xiong, and Qun Liu. 2003. HHMM-based Chinese Lexical Analyzer ICTCLAS. In *Proceedings of the Second SIGHAN Workshop on Chinese Language Processing*. Association for Computational Linguistics, Sapporo, Japan, pages 184–187.

The Helsinki Neural Machine Translation System[*]

Robert Östling
Department of Linguistics
Stockholm University

Yves Scherrer and **Jörg Tiedemann**
Department of Modern Languages
University of Helsinki

Gongbo Tang
Department of Linguistics and Philology
Uppsala University

Tommi Nieminen
Department of Modern Languages
University of Helsinki

Abstract

We introduce the Helsinki Neural Machine Translation system (HNMT) and how it is applied in the news translation task at WMT 2017, where it ranked first in both the human and automatic evaluations for English–Finnish. We discuss the success of English–Finnish translations and the overall advantage of NMT over a strong SMT baseline. We also discuss our submissions for English–Latvian, English–Chinese and Chinese–English.

1 Introduction

The Helsinki Neural Machine Translation system (HNMT) is a full-featured system for neural machine translation, with a particular focus on morphologically rich languages. We participated in the WMT 2017 shared task on news translation, obtaining the highest BLEU score for English–Finnish translation, while also performing well on English–Latvian and acceptably on English–Chinese and Chinese–English.

In addition to our participation in the shared task, this paper also details some of the other methods we have implemented and evaluated with HNMT, many of which yielded negative results and were subsequently not used in our submissions for the shared task.

1.1 HNMT

HNMT is based on the attentional encoder–decoder model due to Bahdanau et al. (2014). This is a rather minimalistic framework for NMT, and many extensions have been proposed. Of particular interest are those that allow proper and efficient

handling of morphologically rich languages, such as Finnish. We combine two such approaches: the hybrid character/word model of Luong and Manning (2016), which is used for the source language encoder, and the byte-pair encoding (BPE) technique of Sennrich et al. (2016c), which is used for the target language decoder and has been successfully used for Finnish previously (Sánchez-Cartagena and Toral, 2016). As BPE can be added as a simple pre- and post-processing step, it does not affect the structure of the translation model. This means that our system can be used with character, word and BPE level generation on the target side. The structure of the network, thus, consists of three Long Short-Term Memory (LSTM) (Hochreiter and Schmidhuber, 1997) layers:

1. A character-level encoder that transforms out-of-vocabulary source tokens into the same vector space as the source word embeddings.

2. A token-level bidirectional encoder that transforms a sequence of source word embeddings (or outputs from network (1) in case of OOV items) into an encoded sequence of the same length.

3. A character-, token- or BPE-level decoder that works as language model conditioned (via an attention mechanism) on the encoded source sequence from (2).

HNMT is implemented using Theano (Theano Development Team, 2016), which supports efficient training with a GPU. For optimization we use minibatch stochastic gradient descent with Adam (Kingma and Ba, 2015) for learning rate adaptation.

---

[*]The software is available from `https://github.com/robertostling/hnmt` under the GNU General Public License version 3.

Proceedings of the Conference on Machine Translation (WMT), Volume 2: Shared Task Papers, pages 338–347
Copenhagen, Denmark, September 7–11, 2017. ©2017 Association for Computational Linguistics

2 Tricks from the NMT arsenal

We have implemented and evaluated a number of proposed extensions to the basic attentional encoder–decoder model. Basic experiments were carried out on English–Finnish data, unless specified otherwise.

2.1 Layer normalization

Layer normalization (Ba et al., 2016) has been proposed as a technique for speeding up training of recurrent network models. We have implemented it into HNMT as the modified LSTM described by equations (20)–(22) in Ba et al. (2016). However, as preliminary experiments did not indicate any consistent effect of using layer normalization we did not include it in our evaluation.

2.2 Variational dropout

Gal and Ghahramani (2016) proposed a method for regularization of recurrent neural networks. This has also been implemented in HNMT, but preliminary experiments on Finnish did not indicate any improvement over the baseline system. While Sennrich et al. (2016a) reported large improvements for the Romanian news translation task at WMT 2016, the amount of training data is lower than what is available for Finnish, which should explain some of the difference. They also apply dropout on the word level, whereas the HNMT application currently only drops recurrent states.

2.3 Context gates

Context gates (Tu et al., 2017) introduce an explicit model for selecting to which extent the target sentence generation should focus on the source sentence or the target context, giving the network a chance to tune the balance between adequacy and fluency. While we obtained better cross-entropy on the development set, particularly early during training, the BLEU and chrF3 evaluations on development data made us decide against the slower context gates in the final run.

2.4 Coverage decoder

Wu et al. (2016) present an empirically determined method for using the attention vectors produced during decoding in the search algorithm, to bias the decoder towards translations with reasonable length and good coverage of the source sentence.[1] We performed a grid search of the parameter space for the length, coverage and overtranslation penalties, but did not find any that resulted in higher BLEU scores on the development set than the decoder without penalties.

2.5 Forward-Backward reranking

It is trivial to train a translation model to generate translations either from the beginning or the end of the target sentence. HNMT supports selecting translation direction, and combined with its n-best list and reranking features it is simple to generate candidate translations in both directions and to combine them based on their scores. This led to some minor improvements in our English–Finnish translations.

2.6 Ensembling

HNMT supports two general modes of ensembling, as well as their combination:

- Proper ensembling where $p(w) = \frac{1}{M} \sum_{m=1}^{M} p_m(w)$ is used to predict target symbol w, given predictions $p_m(w)$ for each model m in the ensemble.

- Parameter averaging where the model's parameter vector θ is computed as $\frac{1}{N} \sum_{m=1}^{M} \theta_m$ for each model m. This only works if the different θ_m are relatively similar, typically because they were saved at different points during the same training process.

The overhead for proper ensembling is linear in the number of ensembled systems, both for training (assuming one is building an ensemble of separately trained models) and inference, while parameter averaging is essentially free. HNMT allows proper ensembling of groups of models where the parameters are averaged within each group. This flexible structure allows a number of setups, which are explored further in Section 3.2.

3 English–Finnish

In our experiments, we used all English–Finnish parallel data sets provided by WMT except the Wiki headlines, which is a small and rather noisy data set that did not contribute anything in our experiments from last year. We also added substantial amounts of backtranslated data that has

---

[1]The HNMT implementation of this was contributed by Stig-Arne Grönroos.

been shown to help especially in neural machine translation (Sennrich et al., 2016b) but also in statistical MT (Tiedemann et al., 2016). Table 1 lists some basic statistics of the backtranslated data sets we created out of WMT's monolingual Finnish news data from 2014 and from 2016. We applied our best constrained phrase-based SMT model for Finnish to English from last year (Tiedemann et al., 2016) that uses a factored model with multiple translation paths, morphological tags and pseudo-tokens for case-markers that correspond to English prepositions (Tiedemann et al., 2015). The system scored 20.5% lowercased BLEU on the newstest 2016 data, which was the second-best system for the task in 2016.

	sentences	Finnish	English
news2014	1,378,833	17,117,137	23,818,547
news2016	4,144,406	55,637,304	76,161,439

Table 1: Backtranslated Finnish news data.

3.1 Preprocessing and postprocessing

We trained our models on tokenized and truecased data, except for the character-level models which were trained on raw untokenized data. For the former, we applied Moses tools for Unicode/punctuation normalisation, tokenization and truecasing using a model trained on the parallel training data.

We tested three different types of word segmentation: basic word-based segmentation, supervised morphological segmentation using OMorFi (Pirinen, 2015) and byte-pair encoding (BPE) (Sennrich et al., 2016c). For the latter, we opted for a fine-grained segmentation that results in a small vocabulary of 20,000 tokens when trained on the parallel data, expecting BPE to handle various cases of compound splitting and morphological segmentation. We always used the same BPE-based segmentation and did not try to optimize the BPE parameters in any way.

During development, we observed that the English development files contained a lot of verb form contractions (of the type *wouldn't*), but that such contracted forms appear rarely in the training data. Therefore, we also added a preprocessing routine to transform the contracted forms to their uncontracted equivalents.

Finally, we found that our tokenizer/detokenizer pipeline for Finnish did not handle the hyphen/dash distinction correctly. In Finnish, the '-'

sign can be used with spaces on both sides, without spaces, with a space only on the left, and with a space only on the right, as in the following examples:

(1)   a.   Draamaa Riossa - suomalaisnostaja pyörtyi...
      'Drama in Rio - Finnish lifter fainted...'
   b.   Kempinski-hotelli
      'Kempinski[-]hotel'
   c.   kissa ja hiiri -leikkiä
      'cat and mouse [-]game'
   d.   öljy- ja kaasutoiminnot
      'oil[-] and gas functions'

The tokenizer always introduces spaces on both sides, which means that the detokenizer is then unable to retrieve the original configuration. In order to remedy this problem, we applied a postprocessing step to the translated data. After detokenizing the output, for every hyphen sign, the four tokenization variants were generated and scored by the hybrid-to-character system; we then chose the tokenization variant with the highest score.

3.2 NMT Models

In preliminary experiments, we focused on different segmentation strategies for the source and target sides as well as on different proportions of backtranslations and parallel data. The models were evaluated on *newsdev2015* using lowercased BLEU and chrF3.[2] Table 2 shows some results.

In these experiments, we found BPE to be useful on the target side, but not so much on the source side. Character-level decoders are favoured by character-level evaluation scores such as chrF3, whereas BLEU favours decoders using larger units such as BPE. The best results were obtained with a combination of backtranslated and parallel data; using all backtranslations was slightly better than restricting the amount of backtranslations to match the size of the parallel data. The model based on supervised morphological segmentation followed by BPE encoding (OMorFi) yielded promising chrF3 results, but lagged behind in terms of BLEU. Further investigation is needed on the benefits and shortcomings of combining these segmentation approaches.

---

[2]The HNMT-internal BLEU computation is based on https://github.com/vikasnar/Bleu and on the NLTK tokenizer. The reported results are thus not directly comparable with official WMT results.

Encoder	Decoder	BLEU				chrF3			
		None	Only	Balanced	All	None	Only	Balanced	All
BPE	BPE	11.9	**14.4**	**15.7**	15.5	43.7	47.2	48.3	48.5
BPE	Char	9.2	13.0	13.7	14.0	41.0	**47.8**	**48.4**	48.6
Hybrid	BPE	**12.2**	13.8	15.4	15.3	43.4	47.0	48.1	49.0
Hybrid	Char	11.6	13.1	14.1	14.2	**46.3**	47.2	48.2	49.0
Hybrid	OMorFi	—	—	—	14.3	—	—	—	**49.2**

Table 2: Development results with different segmentation strategies for the source language encoder and the target language decoder and different proportions of backtranslated and parallel data (None = 2.5M sentences of parallel data + 0 sentences of backtranslated data; Only = 0 + 5.5M; Balanced = 2.5M + 2.5M; All = 2.5M + 5.5M).

BLEU	chrF3	M	SP/M	AVG
12.8	48.8	1	1	N/A
13.6	49.7	1	4	+
13.8	49.8	1	4	−
14.1	50.0	3	1	N/A
14.4	50.2	3	4	+
14.6	50.4	3	4	−

Table 3: Development results with different ensembling setups. Each configuration consists of M models, with SP/M savepoints per model, where the savepoints may be averaged (+AVG) or included as equal members in the ensemble (-AVG).

The model based on a hybrid encoder and a BPE decoder did not yield the best results in this preliminary evaluation, but showed the most robust performance across different evaluation types, training configurations and evaluation data (in particular, it outperformed other models on the *newstest2015* set). Therefore, four of our five submissions use that configuration. For comparison, we also submitted a system based on a character-level decoder.

We also investigated the effect of different ensembling combinations, and the result can be found in Table 3. In general, proper ensembling is better than savepoint averaging, but savepoint averaging is better than nothing. Further experiments revealed that the difference between an *ensemble of averaged savepoints from independent models* setup (second row from the bottom) and an *ensemble of several savepoints each from independent models* (bottom row) is not consistent, so we use the former (faster) variant for our official submissions.

The submitted character-decoder system uses 256 dimensions for word embeddings, 64 for character embeddings, 512 encoder state dimensions, 1024 decoder state dimensions, and 256 attention dimensions. We train four independent models for 72h each, and the savepoint with the best heldout chrF3 score is used (in practice we do not observe any significant overfitting, so this amounts to using nearly 72h of training for all models). Training data are the unprocessed versions of all parallel and backtranslated data. For decoding, we used proper ensembling of the four models, and averaging of the four last savepoints of each model (states were saved after each 5000 training batches).

The submitted BPE-decoder systems use the same model size as the character-decoder system. Again, we train four independent models for 72h each, using the preprocessed and BPE-encoded data, with hyphen retokenization applied as a postprocessing step. We provide two contrastive systems: one without input normalization, which shows a decrease of 0.3 BLEU, and one without hyphen retokenization, which shows a decrease of 0.9 BLEU (see Table 4).

We also propose an extended system that is based on the four models above and four additional backwards models (i.e., trained right-to-left). At test time, we generate a 10-best list of forward translations and a similar one of backward translations. We choose the best translation that occurred in both lists, or if the lists are disjoint, the translation with the highest likelihood according to the model (forward or backward) that generated it. This reranking only provided +0.1 BLEU; 48% of translations were chosen from the forward model, 22% from the backward model, and 30% occurred in both lists. This system has been ranked first in the automatic and manual evaluations.

3.3 SMT Baselines

Besides the neural MT models, we also trained various phrase-based SMT models to contrast our results with another popular paradigm. In particular, we were interested to see the effect of BPE segmentation and backtranslation on statis-

Decoder	IN	HR	Direction	BLEU
Char	+	N/A	fw	19.1
BPE	+	+	fw	20.6
BPE	−	+	fw	20.3
BPE	+	−	fw	19.7
BPE	+	+	fw+bw	**20.7**

Table 4: Submitted HNMT systems with official results. They vary with respect to decoder type, input normalization (IN), hyphen retokenization (HR), direction (forward or backward). The best result was submitted for manual evaluation, where it ranked #1 (tied with one unconstrained system).

tical MT. Both techniques are popular in neural MT but their impact on statistical MT has not been evaluated properly before. Therefore, we started a systematic comparison of different setups including various types of segmentations and data collections. All systems are based on Moses (Koehn et al., 2007) and we use standard configurations for training non-factored phrase-based SMT models using KenLM for language modeling (Heafield, 2011) and BLEU-based MERT for tuning. The only difference to the standard pipeline is the use of efmaral (Östling and Tiedemann, 2016), an efficient implementation of fertility-based IBM word alignment models with a Bayesian extension and Gibbs sampling.[3] Table 5 summarizes the results of our SMT experiments during development.

The first observation is that BPE (and also supervised morphological segmentation) is not very helpful. This is somewhat surprising as we expect a similar problem as with neural MT in the sense that the productive and rich morphology in Finnish causes problems due to data sparseness. We can see that some models benefit from BPE (see *back* and *opus*) especially if tuning is done on the word level and not on BPE-segmented output. However, we have to admit that we did not attempt to optimize the segmentation level and it can well be that the small BPE vocabulary in our setup is not working well for SMT.

Another observation is that the operation-sequence model does not lead to significant (or any) improvements. This is in contrast to related work and may be due to data sparseness again due to the morphological richness of Finnish.

The biggest surprise is the positive effect of backtranslated data. The models trained on those

<hr>

[3]Software available from https://github.com/robertostling/efmaral.

| *newsdev15* | segmentation | | | LM | |
data	src	trg	tuning	news	+CC
WMT	word	word	word	**12.51**	**13.74**
WMT	word	BPE	word	12.16	−
WMT	word	morf	word	11.58	−
WMT	BPE	BPE	BPE	11.91	−
WMT	BPE	BPE	word	12.24	12.95
back	word	word	word	12.69	**13.69**
back	BPE	BPE	BPE	12.73	−
back	BPE	BPE	word	**12.92**	13.50
WMT+back	word	word	word	−	**14.62**
WMT+back	BPE	BPE	BPE	12.94	−
WMT+back	BPE	BPE	word	13.40	14.44
+osm	word	word	word	−	14.04
+osm	BPE	BPE	word	12.85	14.58
opus	word	word	word	14.05	15.54
opus	BPE	BPE	word	14.45	15.63
+osm	word	word	word	−	**15.82**
+osm	BPE	BPE	word	−	15.57
newstest17					
WMT+back	BPE	BPE	word	−	**16.2**
opus+osm	BPE	BPE	word	−	**17.3**

Table 5: Phrase-based SMT tested on newsdev 2015 and newstest 2017 (lowercased BLEU). Different types of segmentation in source language text (src), target language text (trg) and during minimum-error rate training (tuning): word-based, byte-pair encoding (BPE) and OMorFi-based (morf). Different data sets for training: Europarl and Rapid2016 (WMT), backtranslated Finnish news (back) and all available data sets including parallel corpora from OPUS (opus). Additional component: operation-sequence model (osm).

data sets only are in fact better than the ones trained on the official training data provided by WMT. This demonstrates the strong domain mismatch between training and test data and the use of in-domain data, even very noisy ones, seems to lead to visible benefits. In combination, we can see substantial improvements over the individual models, which demonstrates the use of backtranslation even for SMT.

Another common outcome in SMT is the strong impact of language models. We can confirm this once again. Adding a second language model trained on common-crawl data (CC) has a strong influence on translation quality as we can see by the BLEU scores in Table 5.

In the manual evaluation, our best SMT system shared 6th rank with four other systems (interestingly a mix of phrase-based, rule-based and neural systems), of which two were constrained like ours.

3.4 NMT with Pre-translated Data

We were also interested in the combination of
SMT and NMT using the pre-translation approach
proposed by Niehues et al. (2016). In their model,
SMT-based translations of the source text are simply concatenated to the input to make it possible for an NMT system to draw information from
other MT models. Niehues et al. show that the
attention model is capable of learning the connections between the pre-translated part and the original source language input to jointly influence the
generated target language translations. The approach is straightforward and interesting because
it may improve the faithfulness (or adequacy) of
the translation engine, which can be a problem in
neural encoder–decoder models.

One challenge is that training data has to be
translated completely to make it possible to learn
the final NMT model. One of the problems discussed by Niehues et al. is the issue of overfitting
to the SMT-based translation if the SMT model is
trained on the same data set as will be used for
learning the NMT model. They propose to weaken
the phrase table by removing longer segments and,
hence, reducing the capacity of the SMT model to
create very generic translation options.

In our setup, we use a different strategy: Instead
of using the same data sets for training and translating, we use the backtranslated news data to train
a model that can be used to translate the parallel
WMT data (Europarl and Rapid2016). With this,
we get the same domain-mismatch as during test
time with a realistically weak model that avoids
over-trusting its capacity when training the NMT
model in pre-translated data. Furthermore, we use
a WMT-model trained on Europarl and Rapid2016
to translate the backtranslated news data from English back to Finnish again. The latter may be a
problem because of the significant noise added due
to the double backtranslation but we do not want
to discard the important news data completely.

Another difference in our setup is that we use
BPE-segmented SMT models to obtain segmented
output that we can use directly to be concatenated
with the original (BPE-segmented) source. We
mark the pre-translated part with a special suffix and then train a standard attention-based NMT
model. We use similar parameters as for our standard NMT experiments: 256-dimensional word
embeddings, encoder states and attentions, 512-
dimensional decoder states, and a vocabulary of

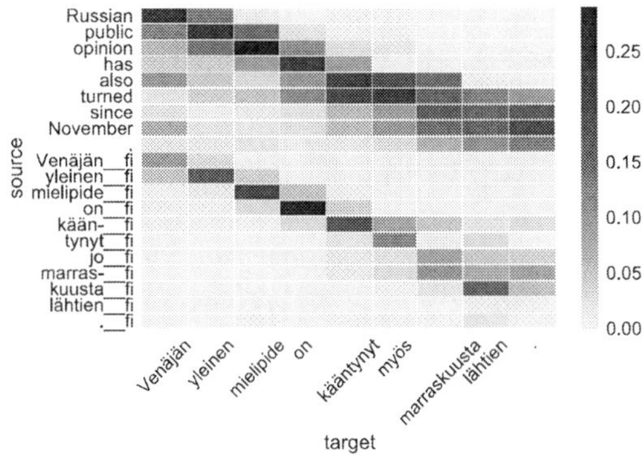

Figure 1: Attention with pre-translated data.

50,000 in source and target language. It turns out
that, indeed, the model learns to look at both the
source language and the pre-translated text, as we
can see in the attention plot in Figure 1.

Unfortunately, the training process is very slow
due to the extended input sequence and, hence,
converges very slowly. No useful model could be
submitted before the official deadline. Our final
system tested after the official submission is an ensemble of four independently trained models with
savepoint averaging over the last four savepoints
and reaches a lowercased BLEU score of 17.34%
on newsdev 2015 and 20.92% on newstest 2017 in
our internal evaluations (but only 19.8% BLEU in
the official on-line system). Even tough this looks
quite encouraging compared to the SMT scores,
it is still below the plain NMT models, which is,
of course, a bit disappointing. However, the results are not directly comparable and there is some
variation that needs to be accounted for. More detailed analyses are required to study the possible
contributions by the pre-translations. Further investigations of attention plots may reveal whether
the model still overfits to the SMT output, which
could be a good reason why it underperforms in
the end. The additional complexity and the increased length of the input sequences are certainly
other reasons for the negative outcome. It also
seems that the strong performance of the NMT
model also with respect to adequacy make it difficult to improve it further with a weaker SMT
model.

3.5 Manual Evaluation

The outputs of the best SMT and NMT systems
were partially reviewed and compared by a profes-

343

sional translator. The impression of the reviewer was that the perceived quality of NMT far exceeds that of SMT, mainly due to the superior fluency of NMT. The BLEU scores of the systems also indicate a significant quality difference in favor of NMT. However, single-reference BLEU scores are known to be unreliable indicators of quality for morphologically complex languages (Bojar et al., 2010), and they are also known to favor SMT over other MT methods (Callison-Burch et al., 2006). Due to this, it is possible that the BLEU scores, impressive as they are, do not reflect the real qualitative impact of NMT for English–Finnish MT.

To explore whether single-reference evaluation underestimates NMT quality, a sample of 68 sentences was extracted from the test set. Both SMT and NMT translations of the sample were postedited with minimal changes to the same quality level as the reference translation. The minimally edited MT was then used as a TER reference to obtain a more reliable estimate of the MT quality. The sample was chosen from sentences where SMT has a sentence-level TER that is at least 10 points lower than the corresponding NMT TER, since such differences can indicate evaluation errors. The sample was also restricted to sentences with an SMT TER lower than 40 to reduce postediting workload and filter out low-quality MT.

When postedited MT was used as a reference, total TER/BLEU for the sample changed from 24.7/50.2 to 12.5/76.0 for SMT and from 48.4/25.0 to 18.3/70.5 for NMT. While the score improved for both SMT and NMT, the improvement is clearly much larger for NMT. The test was then repeated for another sample of 68 sentences from the test set, this time selected from the sentences where NMT had lower sentence-level TER. The purpose of this sample was to see if evaluation errors affect single-reference scores for SMT to the same extent as for NMT. With the second sample, total TER/BLEU changed from 58.9/22.1 to 42.5/39.3 for SMT and from 28.2/48.5 to 12.1/77.01 for NMT, so the result was even more favorable for NMT. While the sample size was small, these results strongly suggest that single-reference BLEU scores indeed underestimate NMT quality.

4 English–Latvian

Training models for English–Latvian was a rather spontaneous decision and we did not spend a lot of time optimizing our settings. Backtranslations were produced with simplistic Latvian–English models. We used a quickly trained character-level NMT model to translate Latvian news data from 2016 and a standard phrase-based SMT model to translate parts of 2014-2016 news data. The statistics of the backtranslations are given in Table 6.

SMT	Sentences	Latvian	English
news2014	330,152	6,469,914	7,611,259
news2015	330,644	6,484,318	7,624,202
news2016	313,180	6,161,332	7,239,953
NMT	Sentences	Latvian	English
news2016	2,059,647	33,447,392	45,262,908

Table 6: Backtranslated Latvian news data using SMT and NMT.

4.1 NMT Models

We submitted one NMT system that follows the basic BPE-decoder system for English–Finnish in terms of model size and training settings. It is trained on the preprocessed versions of the parallel data and the NMT-based backtranslations. This system yielded a case-sensitive BLEU score of 16.8. We again applied hyphen retokenization as a postprocessing step, although it was less useful here than for Finnish (+0.1 BLEU). Again, we trained four independent models and used savepoint-averaging. For time reasons and given the low impact of forward-backward reranking observed for Finnish, we refrained from submitting such a system for English–Latvian.

4.2 SMT Baselines

The SMT models we trained use the provided data sets for training translation models and language models (including a second language model based on common crawl data) with the same tools as for our English–Finnish systems. We applied BPE to all data sets again with a rather fine-grained segmentation into 20,000 types on training data. Table 7 summarizes the results of our models on the *newstest* data from 2017.

We can see that the backtranslated data sets do not work very well in the Latvian case. A small improvement can be observed when combined with the provided training data but the quality of the backtranslations is too poor to have a strong impact on translation quality.

newstest 2017	BLEU
SMT WMT	13.29
SMT back	11.94
SMT WMT+back	13.74
SMT official score (WMT+back)	14.7
NMT official score (WMT+back)	17.3

Table 7: Statistical MT for English–Latvian tested on newstest 2017 (lowercased BLEU). The *official* score in the on-line evaluation system (lowercased) is surprisingly different from our own evaluations. The manual evaluation for English–Latvian produced no statistically significant ranking.

5 English–Chinese and Chinese–English

For English/Chinese, we performed experiments with the HNMT system only. We trained both English–Chinese and Chinese–English models, using all of the available parallel training data from the WMT/CWMT news translation task. After cleaning, 24,954,952 sentence pairs remained. Using the standard Moses tools, we tokenized and truecased the English data. Two methods were used for Chinese word segmentation, as detailed below.

All the models are trained by a hybrid character–word level encoder and a character-level decoder. The final submissions are generated by ensembles with parameters averaging. The official BLEU scores of these two tasks are shown in Table 8. The manual evaluation ranked our system in a shared last place (shared with four other systems) for Chinese–English, while it was ranked #9 (better than two unconstrained online systems) for English–Chinese.

5.1 Translating Chinese into English

Chinese is a language without word boundaries, so word segmentation is necessary before using our hybrid encoder with Chinese source sentences. There are different segmentation methods at different granularities, and they will lead to different translations. In the work of Su et al. (2017), they proposed a lattice-based recurrent encoder which applied three segmentations at different granularities (from the CTB, PKU and MSRA corpora). In our model, we just tried two segmentations: One is a fine-grained method implemented in Zpar (Zhang and Clark, 2011), the other is a coarse-granularity method by THULAC (Sun et al., 2016). The model with THULAC segmen-

newstest 2017	BLEU
English–Chinese	23.9
Chinese–English	15.9

Table 8: HNMT official results on English–Chinese language pair news translation task.

tation achieved a slightly lower BLEU score compared to the model with Zpar segmentation. Thus, we did not train more models on THULAC segmentation data after 6-day training. Unlike our results with English–Finnish translation, our experiments with BPE using a 30,000 size vocabulary did not yield any improvements.

The final submission uses Zpar for segmentation, a hybrid encoder with 60,000 item vocabulary, and a character-level decoder. We use dimensionalities of 256 for both word and character embedding, encoder LSTM and attention. The decoder uses an LSTM of size 512. We use a single model with parameters averaged from savepoints at 6, 9, 10, 12 and 14 days to generate the final submission. This is a rather unusual setup and different from the Finnish and Latvian submissions, but it shows parameter averaging works even when days have passed between savepoints. The beam size in the decoding is set to 10.

5.2 Translating English into Chinese

In addition to translating English into Chinese orthography (using Chinese characters, Hanzi), we also explored translating into romanized Chinese (using the Pinyin system), and then disambiguating the Pinyin to Hanzi with a 3-gram language model. This reduces the vocabulary to the circa 1300 syllables in Standard Mandarin. However, the final disambiguation step introduces new errors that were not outweighed by the easier task of predicting Pinyin output, and we did not pursue this method.

For our official submission, we used a hybrid encoder with 50,000 vocabulary size, and a character-level decoder. Again, we used a single model with parameters averaged from savepoints at 6, 7.5 and 11.5 days.

6 Conclusions

This paper introduces the Helsinki Neural Machine Translation system (HNMT) and its succesful application to the news translation task in WMT 2017. The models we trained handle well the translation into morphologically complex languages such as Finnish and our submission scored best among the participants in the English–Finnish task. The evaluations show that the neural models are superior to the strong SMT baselines that exploit the same tricks such as backtranslated data and automatic word segmentation. Manual inspections suggest that the advantage of NMT is even underestimated by single-reference BLEU scores. We also applied our models to English–Latvian and English–Chinese (in both directions) with a more moderate success. This is not very surprising for Latvian, for which we only invested about a week to set up the experiments and to train the models. For Chinese, manual evaluation will be important to judge the outcome of our systems fairly.

Acknowledgments

We wish to thank the anonymous reviewers, one of whom provided exceptionally thorough comments. The Finnish IT Center for Science (CSC) provided computational resources. We would also like to acknowledge the support by NVIDIA and their GPU grant. Gongbo Tang is supported by China Scholarship Council (No. 201607110016).

References

Jimmy Lei Ba, Jamie Ryan Kiros, and Geoffrey E. Hinton. 2016. Layer normalization. *ArXiv e-prints* .

Dzmitry Bahdanau, Kyunghyun Cho, and Yoshua Bengio. 2014. Neural machine translation by jointly learning to align and translate. *CoRR* abs/1409.0473.

Ondřej Bojar, Kamil Kos, and David Mareček. 2010. Tackling sparse data issue in machine translation evaluation. In *Proceedings of the ACL 2010 Conference Short Papers*. Association for Computational Linguistics, Uppsala, Sweden, pages 86–91. http://www.aclweb.org/anthology/P10-2016.

Chris Callison-Burch, Miles Osborne, and Philipp Koehn. 2006. Re-evaluating the role of bleu in machine translation research. In *In EACL*. pages 249–256.

Yarin Gal and Zoubin Ghahramani. 2016. A theoretically grounded application of dropout in recurrent neural networks. In D. D. Lee, M. Sugiyama, U. V. Luxburg, I. Guyon, and R. Garnett, editors, *Advances in Neural Information Processing Systems 29*, Curran Associates, Inc., pages 1019–1027. http://papers.nips.cc/paper/6241-a-theoretically-grounded-application-of-dropout-in-recurrent-neural-networks.pdf.

Kenneth Heafield. 2011. KenLM: Faster and Smaller Language Model Queries. In *Proceedings of the Sixth Workshop on Statistical Machine Translation*. Association for Computational Linguistics, Edinburgh, UK, pages 187–197.

Sepp Hochreiter and Jürgen Schmidhuber. 1997. Long short-term memory. *Neural Computation* 9(8):1735–1780. https://doi.org/10.1162/neco.1997.9.8.1735.

Diederik P. Kingma and Jimmy Ba. 2015. Adam: A method for stochastic optimization. In *The International Conference on Learning Representations*.

Philipp Koehn, Hieu Hoang, Alexandra Birch, Chris Callison-Burch, Marcello Federico, Nicola Bertoldi, Brooke Cowan, Wade Shen, Christine Moran, Richard Zens, Chris Dyer, Ondrej Bojar, Alexandra Constantin, and Evan Herbst. 2007. Moses: Open Source Toolkit for Statistical Machine Translation. In *ACL'07: Proceedings of the 45th Annual Meeting of the Association for Computational Linguistics, Demonstration Session*. Association for Computational Linguistics, pages 177–180.

Minh-Thang Luong and Christopher D. Manning. 2016. Achieving open vocabulary neural machine translation with hybrid word-character models. In *Proceedings of the 54th Annual Meeting of the Association for Computational Linguistics (Volume 1: Long Papers)*. Association for Computational Linguistics, Berlin, Germany, pages 1054–1063.

Jan Niehues, Eunah Cho, Thanh-Le Ha, and Alex Waibel. 2016. Pre-translation for neural machine translation. In *Proceedings of COLING 2016, the 26th International Conference on Computational Linguistics: Technical Papers*. The COLING 2016 Organizing Committee, Osaka, Japan, pages 1828–1836. http://aclweb.org/anthology/C16-1172.

Robert Östling and Jörg Tiedemann. 2016. Efficient word alignment with Markov Chain Monte Carlo. *Prague Bulletin of Mathematical Linguistics* 106:125–146. http://ufal.mff.cuni.cz/pbml/106/art-ostling-tiedemann.pdf.

Tommi A Pirinen. 2015. Development and use of computational morphology of finnish in the open source and open science era: Notes on experiences with omorfi development. *SKY Journal of Linguistics* 28:381–393.

Victor M Sánchez-Cartagena and Antonio Toral. 2016. Abu-MaTran at WMT 2016 translation task: Deep learning, morphological segmentation and tuning on character sequences. In *Proceedings of the First Conference on Machine Translation, Berlin, Germany. Association for Computational Linguistics*.

Rico Sennrich, Barry Haddow, and Alexandra Birch. 2016a. Edinburgh neural machine translation systems for wmt 16. In *Proceedings of the First Conference on Machine Translation*. Association for Computational Linguistics, Berlin, Germany, pages 371–376. http://www.aclweb.org/anthology/W16-2323.

Rico Sennrich, Barry Haddow, and Alexandra Birch. 2016b. Improving neural machine translation models with monolingual data. In *Proceedings of the 54th Annual Meeting of the Association for Computational Linguistics (Volume 1: Long Papers)*. Association for Computational Linguistics, Berlin, Germany, pages 86–96. http://www.aclweb.org/anthology/P16-1009.

Rico Sennrich, Barry Haddow, and Alexandra Birch. 2016c. Neural machine translation of rare words with subword units. In *Proceedings of the 54th Annual Meeting of the Association for Computational Linguistics (Volume 1: Long Papers)*. Association for Computational Linguistics, Berlin, Germany, pages 1715–1725. http://www.aclweb.org/anthology/P16-1162.

Jinsong Su, Zhixing Tan, Deyi Xiong, Rongrong Ji, Xiaodong Shi, and Yang Liu. 2017. Lattice-based recurrent neural network encoders for neural machine translation. In *Proceedings of the Thirty-First AAAI Conference on Artificial Intelligence (AAAI-17)*. pages 3302–3308.

Maosong Sun, Xinxiong Chen, Kaixu Zhang, Zhipeng Guo, and Zhiyuan Liu. 2016. Thulac: An efficient lexical analyzer for chinese .

Theano Development Team. 2016. Theano: A Python framework for fast computation of mathematical expressions. *arXiv e-prints* abs/1605.02688. http://arxiv.org/abs/1605.02688.

Jörg Tiedemann, Fabienne Cap, Jenna Kanerva, Filip Ginter, Sara Stymne, Robert Östling, and Marion Weller-Di Marco. 2016. Phrase-based SMT for finnish with more data, better models and alternative alignment and translation tools. In *Proceedings of the First Conference on Machine Translation*. Association for Computational Linguistics, Berlin, Germany, pages 391–398. http://www.aclweb.org/anthology/W16-2326.

Jörg Tiedemann, Filip Ginter, and Jenna Kanerva. 2015. Morphological segmentation and opus for finnish-english machine translation. In *WMT'15: Proceedings of the Tenth Workshop on Statistical Machine Translation*. pages 177–183.

Zhaopeng Tu, Yang Liu, Zhengdong Lu, Xiaohua Liu, and Hang Li. 2017. Context gates for neural machine translation. *Transactions of the Association for Computational Linguistics* 5:87–99. https://www.transacl.org/ojs/index.php/tacl/article/view/948.

Yonghui Wu et al. 2016. Google's neural machine translation system: Bridging the gap between human and machine translation. *CoRR* abs/1609.08144. http://arxiv.org/abs/1609.08144.

Yue Zhang and Stephen Clark. 2011. Syntactic processing using the generalized perceptron and beam search. *Computational Linguistics* 37:105–151.

The QT21 Combined Machine Translation System for English to Latvian

Jan-Thorsten Peter[1], Hermann Ney[1], Ondřej Bojar[2],
Ngoc-Quan Pham[3], Jan Niehues [3], Alex Waibel[3],
Franck Burlot[4], François Yvon[4], Mārcis Pinnis[5], Valters Šics[5],
Joost Bastings[6], Miguel Rios[6], Wilker Aziz[6],
Philip Williams[7], Frédéric Blain[8], Lucia Specia[8]

[1]RWTH Aachen University, Aachen, Germany
[2]Charles University, Prague, Czech Republic
[3]Karlsruhe Institute of Technology, Karlsruhe, Germany
[4]LIMSI, CNRS, Université Paris Saclay, 91 403 Orsay, France
[5]Tilde, Riga, Latvia
[6]University of Amsterdam, Amsterdam, Netherlands
[7]University of Edinburgh, Edinburgh, UK
[8]University of Sheffield, Sheffield, UK

Abstract

This paper describes the joint submission of the QT21 projects for the English→Latvian translation task of the *EMNLP 2017 Second Conference on Machine Translation* (WMT 2017). The submission is a system combination which combines seven different statistical machine translation systems provided by the different groups.

The systems are combined using either RWTH's system combination approach, or USFD's consensus-based system-selection approach. The final submission shows an improvement of 0.5 BLEU compared to the best single system on newstest2017.

1 Introduction

Quality Translation 21 (QT21) is a European machine translation research project with the aim of substantially improving statistical and machine learning based translation models for challenging languages and low-resource scenarios.

Members of the QT21 project have jointly built a combined statistical machine translation system, in order to achieve high-quality machine translation from English into Latvian.

Core components of the QT21 combined system for the WMT 2017 shared task for machine translation of news [1] are seven individual

English→Latvian translation engines which have been set up by different project partners.

The outputs of all these individual engines are combined using the system combination approach as implemented in Jane, RWTH's open source statistical machine translation toolkit (Freitag et al., 2014a). The Jane system combination is a mature implementation which previously has been successfully employed in other collaborative projects and for different language pairs (Peter et al., 2016; Freitag et al., 2013, 2014b,c).

As an alternative way of combining our systems, all outputs have been merged as the form of a n-best list and a consensus-based system-selection applied to obtain as best translation hypothesis the candidate that is most similar to the most likely translations amongst those systems.

2 Preprocessing

The training data was pre-processed using a custom language-specific tokeniser and the Moses truecaser (*truecase.perl*). For tokenisation, we used the Tilde's regular expression-based tokeniser for Latvian and English that takes into account language-specific characteristics (e.g., abbreviations, contractions, date, time, and numerical expressions, etc.) and non-translatable entities (e.g., phone numbers, e-mail addresses, XML tags, URLs, file paths, various identifiers and codes, etc.). Only the first word in each sentence was truecased.

The data (backtranslation included) is further cleaned using a simple language identifier from Shuyo (2010). We simply removed sentence pairs whose targets cannot be identified by the

---

[1]`http://www.statmt.org/wmt17/`
`translation-task.html`

Proceedings of the Conference on Machine Translation (WMT), Volume 2: Shared Task Papers, pages 348–357
Copenhagen, Denmark, September 7–11, 2017. ©2017 Association for Computational Linguistics

tool. The number of sentences being removed is approximately 50000.

3 Translation Systems

Each group contributed one or more systems. In this section the systems are presented in alphabetic order.

3.1 CUNI

The CUNI component of the system was built using Neural Monkey[2] (Helcl and Libovický, 2017), a flexible sequence-to-sequence toolkit implementing primarily the Bahdanau et al. (2015) model but useful also in multi-modal translation and multi-task training.

We used essentially the baseline setup of the system as released for the WMT17 NMT Training Task[3] (Bojar et al., 2017) for an 8GB GPU card. This involves BPE (Sennrich et al., 2016) with 30k merges, maximum sentence length for both source and target limited to 50 (BPE) tokens, no dropout and embeddings (both source and target) of 600, vocabulary shared between encoder and decoder, attention and conditional GRU (Firat and Cho, 2016). We experimented with the RNN size of the encoder and decoder and increased them to 800 instead of 600, at the expense of reducing batch size to 10. The batch size of 30 with this enlarged model would still fit into our GPU card but this run was prematurely interrupted due to a hardware failure and we noticed that it converges slower in terms of sentence pairs (not in terms of wallclock time), so we opted for a more efficient use of the training data by taking the smaller batch.

We trained on 5245514 sentence pairs mixing the genuine parallel data and synthetic data, as described in Section 2. Neural Monkey does not shuffle the corpus, so we shuffled it beforehand and kept the order identical for all training epochs.

The training ran for 15 days on NVIDIA GeForce GTX 1080 and processed 4.7 epochs but the best model (according to BLEU scores on the development set, "devset-b") was actually reached after 11M sentence pairs (early epoch 3), after 7 days.

Neither ensembling nor beam-search was used for the run, because they were not yet available

in Neural Monkey. Instead, the translations were generated using greedy search.

3.2 KIT

The neural machine translation models from KIT are built with the OpenNMT framework (Klein et al., 2017), which is a multi-layer LSTM encoder decoder network. We trained the models with 2.1 million parallel sentence pairs concatenated with 2.8 million pairs from backtranslation provided by University of Edinburgh. The networks have 1024 hidden units for each of 2 LSTM layers for both encoder and decoder. Furthermore, we experiment a number of features with the baseline:

First, we found out that using a context gate to mask activities between the decoder hidden state and the source context vector before producing the distribution at each time step (Tu et al., 2016a) is simple yet beneficial for performance. Second, we strengthen the attentional network with a coverage vector accumulating the previous attentional information, similar to the work of Mi et al. (2016) and Tu et al. (2016b).

Using the two techniques helps improve the BLEU score on the newsdev2017 set by 1.1 (tokenized) BLEU. By using ensembling 3 networks with different configs and rescoring using a model trained with reversed target sentences, we managed to reach 26.96 BLEU score for the development set, which yields 2.8 point of improvement compared to the baseline model. Details about the effect of each technique is described in Pham et al. (2017)

3.3 LIMSI

LIMSI's intput to this system combination consists of two NMT systems, both trained with the NMTPY framework (Caglayan et al., 2017) on bitext, then on synthetic parallel data. All of them were rescored with a Nematus system (Sennrich et al., 2017b). More details about these systems can be found in (Burlot et al., 2017b,a).

The first system, named baseline, is a BPE-to-BPE system. Bilingual sub-word units (Sennrich et al., 2016) were trained on the bitext parallel data with 90k merge operations. All the parameters of the neural network were initialized with Xavier. The system was optimized with Adam, dropout was enabled on source embeddings, encoder states, as well as output layer. The whole training process took approximately 1.5 months.

---

[2]http://ufal.mff.cuni.cz/neuralmonkey
[3]http://www.statmt.org/wmt17/nmt-training-task/

Individual Systems	newsdev2017/1				newsdev2017/2				newstest2017			
	BLEU	TER	CTER	BEER	BLEU	TER	CTER	BEER	BLEU	TER	CTER	BEER
Tilde smt	21.3	59.6	57.8	56.5	20.8	61.4	58.5	56.0	15.3	70.6	67.2	51.6
CUNI neuralmonkey	18.9	63.2	62.6	54.8	19.8	63.9	62.1	54.6	13.6	73.2	69.3	50.2
UvA	16.6	70.0	71.9	52.2	16.4	68.8	71.3	51.9	12.0	78.1	76.4	47.9
KIT	26.8	53.4	49.6	60.2	26.8	54.5	49.5	60.0	18.3	66.5	60.5	54.4
UEDIN NMT	25.7	55.1	51.6	59.5	25.6	56.4	50.4	59.4	17.8	67.9	66.7	53.5
UEDIN rescored by KIT	25.9	54.8	52.0	59.6	26.3	55.8	51.3	59.6	17.9	67.7	64.5	53.8
LIMSI factored	24.3	57.3	53.2	58.6	24.8	57.4	52.1	58.5	17.1	69.0	61.5	53.3
System Combination	27.4	53.1	50.9	60.2	27.9	53.9	51.0	59.9	18.8	66.0	67.8	54.3

Table 1: Results of the individual systems for the English→Latvian task. BLEU [%] and TER [%] scores are case-sensitive.

The results shown in Table 1 correspond to an ensemble of our three best models, which produced n-best hypothesis. Finally, these hypothesis were rescored using a Nematus system trained on the same data as the baseline and with similar hyperparameters.

The second system is an experiment with factored NMT, which is part of the NMTPY framework (García-Martínez et al., 2016). The hyperparameters mentioned above for the baseline also hold for this system. The specific setup we have used consisted in an architecture that enables training towards a dual objective: at each time-step in the output sentence, a normalized word and a PoS-tag are produced. To obtain the first factor vocabulary, all target words have been normalized (Burlot and Yvon, 2017a), i.e. all grammatical information that is redundant *wrt.* English has been removed from the words. In a nutshell, the normalization system performs a clustering of the morphologically rich language by grouping together words that tend to share the same translation(s) in English. As a result, words are represented by a lemma and a cluster identificator containing the morphological features that have been merged. In our setup, the cluster identificator was systematically split from the lemma. BPE segmentation was thus learnt and applied to lemmas.

Given a lexical unit and a PoS-tag, word forms are retrieved with a dictionary lookup. In the context of morphologically rich languages, deterministic mappings from a lemma and a PoS to a form are very rare. Instead, the dictionary often proposes several word forms corresponding to the same lexical unit and morphological analysis. To address this issue, we let a word-based system select the right word form from the dictionary. To this end, k-best hypothesis from the dictionary were generated, as well as the n-best hypothesis from the factored NMT system, leading to nk-best rescoring.

Our factored NMT system is an ensemble of two best models and rescoring is performed with our single best Nematus model.

3.4 Tilde

The Tilde system is a Moses phrase-based SMT system that was trained on the Tilde MT platform (Vasiļjevs et al., 2012). The system was trained using all available parallel data - 1.74 million unique sentence pairs after filtering, and 3 million unique sentence pairs that were acquired by re-translating a random selection of in-domain monolingual sentences with a neural machine translation system (Pinnis et al., 2017). The system has a 5-gram language model that was trained using KenLM (Heafield, 2011) on all available monolingual data (27.83 million unique sentences).

3.5 UEDIN

The University of Edinburgh's system is an attentional encoder-decoder (Bahdanau et al., 2015), trained using the Nematus toolkit (Sennrich et al., 2017c).

As training data, we used all parallel and synthetic data, which was tokenized, truecased, and filtered as described in Section 2. After filtering, the data was segmented into subword units using byte-pair-encoding (BPE), for which we used 90,000 operations, jointly learned over both sides of the parallel corpora.

We used word embeddings of size 512 and hidden layers of size 1024, with the size of the source and target network vocabularies fixed to the size of the respective BPE vocabularies. In order to reduce the size of the models, the target-side embedding weights were tied with the transpose of the output weight matrix (Press and Wolf, 2017). We used a deep transition architecture inspired by the one proposed by Zilly et al. (2016) for language modelling. In experiments conducted during feature development, we found that this gave consistent improvements across multiple language pairs. We also applied layer normalisation (Ba et al., 2016) to all recurrent and feed-forward layers, except for layers that are followed by a softmax. In preliminary experiments, we found that using layer normalisation led to faster convergence and resulted in slightly better performance.

We trained the models with adam (Kingma and Ba, 2015), using a learning rate of 0.0001 and mini-batch size of 80. Training was automatically stopped when the validation cross-entropy failed to reach a new minimum for 10 consecutive savepoints (saving every 10000 updates).

For our final system, we trained eight independent models: four left-to-right and four right-to-left. We used results on newsdev2017 to select one checkpoint from each model. An ensemble of the four left-to-right models was used to generate a 50-best list, which was rescored using the right-to-left models.

For a more detailed description of the system, see Sennrich et al. (2017a).

3.6 UvA: syntactically aware NMT with GCNs

We focus on exploiting structural information on the source side, i.e. in the encoder. We hypothesize that an encoder that incorporates syntax will lead to more informative representations of words, and that these representations, when used as context vectors by the decoder, will lead to an improvement in translation quality. Our model (Bastings et al., 2017) is an attentive encoder-decoder (Bahdanau et al., 2015) where in the encoder side we exploit the power of GCNs (Kipf and Welling, 2016) to induce syntactically-aware representations (Marcheggiani and Titov, 2017). GCNs operate by convolving nodes in a neighbourhood defined by a graph. In our case, a node corresponds to a position in the source sentence which is initially represented by a BiRNN hidden state. We then define a syntactic neighbourhood by following edges in an automatically produced dependency parse. Instead of relying on linear order only (as the BiRNN does), the GCN allows the encoder to 'teleport' over parts of the source

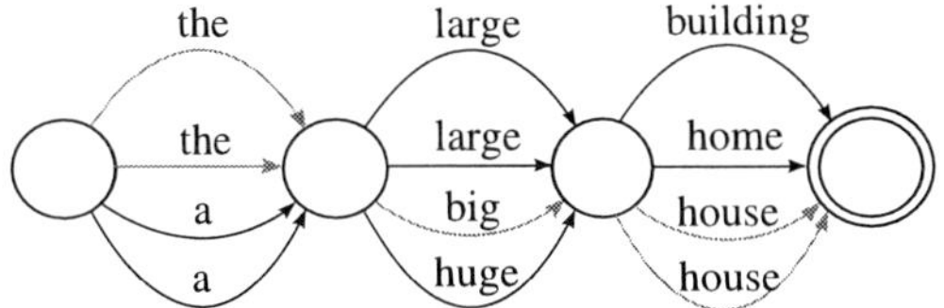

Figure 1: System A: *the large building*; System B: *the large home*; System C: *a big house*; System D: *a huge house*; Reference: *the big house*.

sentence connecting words that are potentially far apart. The model might not only benefit from this teleporting capability however; also the nature of the relations between words (i.e. dependency relation types and directionality) may be useful, and the GCN exploits this information.

4 System Combination

We conducted experiments with two methods for system combination that only require the translated hypotheses. This allows us choose the contributing systems without any restrictions.

4.1 Confusion Network

System combination produces consensus translations from multiple hypotheses which are obtained from different translation approaches, i.e., the systems described in the previous section. A system combination implementation developed at RWTH Aachen University (Freitag et al., 2014a) is used to combine the outputs of the different engines. The consensus translations outperform the individual hypotheses in terms of translation quality.

The first step in system combination is the generation of confusion networks (CN) from I input translation hypotheses. We need pairwise alignments between the input hypotheses, which are obtained from METEOR (Banerjee and Lavie, 2005). The hypotheses are then reordered to match a selected skeleton hypothesis in terms of word ordering. We generate I different CNs, each having one of the input systems as the skeleton hypothesis, and the final lattice is the union of all I generated CNs. In Figure 1 an example of a confusion network with $I = 4$ input translations is depicted. Decoding of a confusion network finds the best path in the network. Each arc is assigned a score of a linear model combination of M different models, which includes word penalty, 3-gram language model trained on the input hypotheses, a binary primary system feature that marks the primary hy-

Systems	newsdev2017/1				newsdev2017/2				newstest2017			
	BLEU	TER	CTER	BEER	BLEU	TER	CTER	BEER	BLEU	TER	CTER	BEER
KIT 20best Bleu	25.8	54.5	51.3	59.3	26.0	55.4	51.0	58.8	17.8	66.9	61.6	53.8
KIT 20best ChrF	25.4	55.0	50.5	59.6	25.7	56.0	50.4	59.2	17.6	68.0	60.9	53.9
KIT 20best Beer	26.0	54.1	50.2	60.0	26.3	55.0	50.6	59.6	18.0	66.7	60.8	54.2
LIMSI Factored 12best Bleu	19.7	60.4	55.7	55.4	19.9	61.0	54.8	55.3	14.2	71.7	63.9	50.8
LIMSI factored 12best ChrF	19.7	60.3	55.4	55.6	19.8	61.1	54.5	55.4	14.2	71.7	63.7	50.9
LIMSI factored 12best Beer	19.8	60.3	55.5	55.6	19.8	61.0	54.7	55.4	14.2	71.7	63.8	50.9
LIMSI factored 100best Bleu	21.5	59.1	55.5	55.9	21.3	59.8	54.8	55.7	15.3	70.7	63.6	51.2
LIMSI factored 100best ChrF	21.9	58.6	54.3	57.1	21.7	59.4	53.6	56.9	15.4	70.5	62.9	52.0
LIMSI factored 100best Beer	21.7	58.7	54.3	57.1	21.6	59.4	53.7	56.9	15.5	70.4	62.9	52.1
Consensus-based System-selection Bleu	19.8	72.5	60.1	51.8	20.5	72.9	59.7	51.6	17.4	69.7	61.9	53.3
Consensus-based System-selection ChrF	26.5	54.1	49.3	60.4	26.8	54.6	48.9	60.2	18.3	67.1	59.9	54.5
Consensus-based System-selection Beer	27.1	53.0	49.6	60.5	27.3	53.8	49.1	60.3	18.6	66.2	60.0	54.6
System Combination	27.4	53.1	50.9	60.2	27.9	53.9	51.0	59.9	18.8	66.0	67.8	54.3
System Combination + Cons-based Beer	27.4	52.7	50.0	60.5	27.7	53.6	51.7	60.2	18.7	66.1	62.0	54.4

Table 2: USFD rescoring and combination experiments English→Latvian task. BLEU [%] and TER [%] scores are case-sensitive.

pothesis, and a binary voting feature for each system. The binary voting feature for a system is 1 if and only if the decoded word is from that system, and 0 otherwise. The different model weights for system combination are trained with MERT (Och, 2003) and optimized towards $8 \cdot \text{BLEU} - \text{TER}$.

4.2 Consensus-based System Selection

As a secondary solution for system combination, we used USFD's consensus-based n-nbest list selection approach (Blain et al., 2017) for system combination by combining each system's output in the form of a n-best list. Inspired by DeNero et al. (2009)'s work on consensus-based Minimum Bayes Risk (MBR) decoding which compares different types of similarity metrics (BLEU, WER, etc.) under a SMT setup, USFD designed a re-ranking approach to empirically evaluate the effect of consensus on the varying n-best list in NMT.

Given a n-best list, each translation hypothesis is scored against the other MT candidates of the search space towards an automatic metric. In our experiment we considered three automatic metrics amongst the most widely used and which have been shown to be well correlated with human judgments (Bojar et al., 2016): BLEU, BEER (Stanojevic and Simaan, 2014) or CHRF (Popovic, 2015). The entire list of MT candidates is then entirely re-ranked according to the averaged score of each candidate. Different from most re-ranking approaches which make use of additional information usually treated as new model components and combined with the existing ones, we here focus only on the MT candidates. The difference between the consensus-based n-best list selection and an oracle translation is the absence of reference translation: each translation hypothesis is scored against all the other hypotheses used as references while in an oracle translation each translation hypothesis is scored against a single reference. This results in obtaining as best translation hypothesis the candidate that is most similar to the most likely translations.

5 Experimental Evaluation

Since only one development set was provided we split the given development set into two parts: newsdev2017/1 and newsdev2017/2. The first part was used as development set while the second part was our internal test set. The single systems and the system combintaion are optimized for the newsdev2017/1 set.

The single system scores in Table 2 show that the KIT system is the strongest single system closely followed by the UEDIN NMT system. The rescoreing of the UEDIN NMT nbest lists by KIT showed only a small improvement on newstest2017. The system combination of all these systems showed an improvement of 1.1 BLEU on newsdev2017/2 and 0.5 BLEU on official test set, newstest2017.

Table 3 shows a comparison between all systems by scoring the translation output against each other in TER and BLEU. We see that the outputs of the two best performing systems KIT and UEDIN are very close.

6 Morphology Evaluation

In order to get some insight regarding the quality of the morphological correctness of the outputs produced by the systems involved in the combina-

	CUNI	KIT	LIMSI	Tilde	UEDIN	UEDIN r.	UvA	USFD	Average
CUNI	-	38.1	32.4	23.9	37.8	38.2	22.3	40.2	33.3
KIT	43.8	-	49.3	29.9	60.1	62.6	28.3	77.0	49.3
LIMSI	49.8	33.2	-	26.1	48.6	49.4	27.5	56.7	41.4
Tilde	57.0	47.4	52.7	-	30.1	30.2	19.4	31.6	27.3
UEDIN	45.1	25.6	35.1	48.9	-	91.1	28.5	76.2	53.2
UEDIN rescored by KIT	44.5	23.8	34.3	48.4	5.4	-	28.7	78.4	54.1
UvA	62.9	56.6	57.5	65.8	57.1	56.7	-	30.3	26.4
USFD	42.0	13.9	28.1	45.9	15.8	14.2	54.7	-	55.8
Average	49.3	34.9	41.5	52.3	33.3	32.5	58.8	30.7	

Table 3: Comparison of system outputs against each other, generated by computing BLEU and TER on the system translations for newstest2017. One system in a pair is used as the reference, the other as candidate translation; we report the average over both directions. The USFD system is similar to the "Consensus-based System-selection Beer" in Table 2. The upper-right half lists BLEU [%] scores, the lower-left half TER [%] scores.

	verbs		pronouns		nouns	mean
System	past	future	fem.	plur.	number	
Tilde smt	68.8%	70.4%	56.0%	71.8%	65.0%	66.4%
UvA	75.2%	84.2%	46.4%	80.8%	66.8%	70.7%
UEDIN NMT	74.6%	83.6%	57.0%	88.6%	69.4%	74.6%
LIMSI NMT	68.8%	84.6%	64.2%	86.8%	73.0%	75.5%
LIMSI factored	69.6%	82.8%	62.0%	89.0%	70.6%	74.8%
KIT	74.2%	89.0%	56.6%	89.8%	71.6%	76.2%

Table 4: Sentence pair evaluation (A-set).

	coordinated verbs			coord.n	pronouns to nouns			prep.	mean
System	number	person	tense	case	gender	number	case	case	
Tilde smt	49.6%	32.8%	50.2%	47.6%	24.0%	25.4%	19.0%	48.5%	37.1%
UvA	61.8%	52.4%	63.2%	31.6%	36.8%	38.8%	36.6%	50.9%	46.5%
UEDIN NMT	70.6%	60.8%	72.0%	30.2%	46.4%	44.8%	43.4%	56.7%	53.1%
LIMSI NMT	69.2%	57.6%	70.4%	41.8%	40.0%	40.8%	35.8%	54.6%	51.3%
LIMSI factored	72.4%	63.4%	73.2%	34.8%	43.0%	42.2%	41.4%	55.5%	53.2%
KIT	73.4%	64.8%	74.0%	37.4%	51.4%	49.8%	48.8%	55.0%	56.8%

Table 5: Sentence pair evaluation (B-set).

	nouns	adjectives			verbs			mean
System	case	gender	number	case	number	person	tense	
Tilde smt	.436	.755	.735	.768	.254	.337	.258	.506
UvA	.295	.629	.613	.643	.157	.187	.160	.383
UEDIN	.234	.598	.596	.628	.115	.190	.114	.354
LIMSI NMT	.255	.616	.610	.644	.139	.221	.134	.374
LIMSI factored	.233	.587	.582	.612	.117	.182	.113	.346
KIT	.244	.599	.594	.633	.102	.186	.108	.352

Table 6: Sentence group evaluation with Entropy (C-set).

tion, we ran the evaluation method introduced in (Burlot and Yvon, 2017b). The evaluation of the morphological competence of a machine translation system is performed on an automatically produced test suite. For each source test sentence from a monolingual corpus (the *base*), one (or several) *variant(s)* are generated, containing exactly one difference with the base, focusing on a specific *target* lexeme of the base. These variants differ on a feature that is expressed morphologically in the target, such as the person, number or tense of a verb; or the number or case of a noun or an adjective. This artificial test set is then translated with a machine translation system. The machine translation system is deemed correct if the translations of the base and variant differ in the same way as their respective source. Another setup focuses on a word in the *base* sentence and produces *variants* containing antonyms and synonyms of this word. The expected translation is then synonyms and antonyms bearing the same morphological features as the initial word.

There are three types of contrasts implying different sorts of evaluation:

- A: We check whether the morphological feature inserted in the source sentence has been translated (eg. plural number of a noun). Accuracy for all morphological features is averaged over all sentences.

- B: We focus on various agreement phenomena by checking whether a given morphological feature is present in both words that need to agree (eg. case of two nouns). Accuracy is computed here as well.

- C: We test the consistency of morphological choices over lexical variation (eg. synonyms and antonyms all having the same tense) and measure the success based on the average normalized entropy of morphological features in the set of target sentences.

The results for the A-set are shown in Table 4 and reflect the adequacy of an output towards the source, or the quantity of morphological information that has been well conveyed from the source. Certain morphological features indicate rather low contrasts between statistical and neural systems (verb tense and pronoun gender), which shows the relevance of SMT systems in the combination.

Sets B and C are more forcused on target monolingual phenomena, such as agreement, and assess the level of fluency of a system output. Here, the observed contrasts between statistical and neural systems are far more obvious: all B-set SMT scores are below 50%, whereas NMT scores are always above. Here again, the superior performance of KIT is noticed, at least for sets A and B. As for the C-set, LIMSI factored, KIT and UEDIN show a comparable high confidence in their morphology predictions across lexical variety.

6.1 Consensus-based re-ranking

We report in Table 2 the results of the consensus-based approach for either system re-ranking or system combination.

First, we applied our approach on both KIT and LIMSI-factored outputs. While we never outperform original systems' performances, we observe that increasing the n-best size does help with a significant difference between LIMSI's system 12- or 100-best. One would note that in both cases, consensus-based n-best list re-ranking with BEER seems to be performing the best amongst all metrics.

Then, we applied our approach at system-level by combining the outputs of all systems described in Section 3. Once again, we observe better performance with BEER compared to the other two metrics, reaching similar results as the system combination based on confusion network. The only noticeable exception being the CTER score on newstest2017 which is significantly lower compared to the other system combination, most likely the benefit of using character-based metrics.

Finally, we combined both consensus-based selection confusion-based combination and although we observe similar performance to each system individually but a worse CTER.

7 Conclusion

Our combined effort shows again that the combination of different SMT systems results in a better overall system. The final result improved by 0.5 BLEU points. Consensus-based re-ranking showed a performance close to the confusion network approach.

Acknowledgments

This project has received funding from the European Union's Horizon 2020 research and innovation programme under grant agreements № 645452 (*QT21*).

References

Lei Jimmy Ba, Ryan Kiros, and Geoffrey E. Hinton. 2016. Layer Normalization. *CoRR* abs/1607.06450.

Dzmitry Bahdanau, Kyunghyun Cho, and Yoshua Bengio. 2015. Neural Machine Translation by Jointly Learning to Align and Translate. In *Proceedings of the International Conference on Learning Representations (ICLR)*. http://arxiv.org/abs/1409.0473.

Satanjeev Banerjee and Alon Lavie. 2005. METEOR: An Automatic Metric for MT Evaluation with Improved Correlation with Human Judgments. In *43rd Annual Meeting of the Assoc. for Computational Linguistics: Proc. Workshop on Intrinsic and Extrinsic Evaluation Measures for MT and/or Summarization*. Ann Arbor, MI, USA, pages 65–72.

Joost Bastings, Ivan Titov, Wilker Aziz, Diego Marcheggiani, and Khalil Sima'an. 2017. Graph convolutional encoders for syntax-aware neural machine translation. *arXiv preprint arXiv:1704.04675* Under review at EMNLP17.

Frédéric Blain, Pranava Swaroop Madhyastha, and Lucia Specia. 2017. Exploring hypotheses spaces in neural machine translation. In Asia-Pacific Association for Machine Translation (AAMT), editor, *Machine Translation Summit XVI*. Nagoya, Japan.

Ondrej Bojar, Yvette Graham, Amir Kamran, and Miloš Stanojevic. 2016. Results of the wmt16 metrics shared task. In *Proceedings of the First Conference on Machine Translation, Berlin, Germany. Association for Computational Linguistics*.

Ondřej Bojar, Jindřich Helcl, Tom Kocmi, Jindřich Libovický, and Tomáš Musil. 2017. Results of the WMT17 Neural MT Training Task. In *Proceedings of the Second Conference on Machine Translation (WMT17) Copenhagen, Denmark*

Franck Burlot, Mercedes García-Martínez, Loïc Barrault, Fethi Bougares, and François Yvon. 2017a. Word Representations in Factored Neural Machine Translation. In *Proceedings of the Second Conference on Machine Translation (WMT'17)*. Association for Computational Linguistics, Copenhagen, Denmark.

Franck Burlot, Pooyan Safari, Matthieu Labeau, Alexandre Allauzen, and François Yvon. 2017b. LIMSI@WMT'17. In *Proceedings of the Second Conference on Machine Translation (WMT'17)*. Association for Computational Linguistics, Copenhagen, Denmark.

Franck Burlot and François Yvon. 2017a. Learning morphological normalization for translation from and into morphologically rich language. *The Prague Bulletin of Mathematical Linguistics (Proc. EAMT)* (108):49–60.

Franck Burlot and Franois Yvon. 2017b. Evaluating the morphological competence of machine translation systems. In *Proceedings of the Second Conference on Machine Translation (WMT'17)*. Association for Computational Linguistics, Copenhagen, Denmark.

Ozan Caglayan, Mercedes García-Martínez, Adrien Bardet, Walid Aransa, Fethi Bougares, and Loïc Barrault. 2017. Nmtpy: A flexible toolkit for advanced neural machine translation systems. *arXiv preprint arXiv:1706.00457* http://arxiv.org/abs/1706.00457.

John DeNero, David Chiang, and Kevin Knight. 2009. Fast consensus decoding over translation forests. In *Proceedings of the Joint Conference of the 47th Annual Meeting of the ACL and the 4th International Joint Conference on Natural Language Processing of the AFNLP: Volume 2-Volume 2*. Association for Computational Linguistics, pages 567–575.

Orhan Firat and Kyunghyun Cho. 2016. Conditional gated recurrent unit with attention mechanism. https://github.com/nyu-dl/dl4mt-tutorial/blob/master/docs/cgru.pdf. Published online, version adbaeea.

Markus Freitag, Matthias Huck, and Hermann Ney. 2014a. Jane: Open Source Machine Translation System Combination. In *Proc. of the Conf. of the European Chapter of the Assoc. for Computational Linguistics (EACL)*. Gothenberg, Sweden, pages 29–32.

Markus Freitag, Stephan Peitz, Joern Wuebker, Hermann Ney, Nadir Durrani, Matthias Huck, Philipp Koehn, Thanh-Le Ha, Jan Niehues, Mohammed Mediani, Teresa Herrmann, Alex Waibel, Nicola Bertoldi, Mauro Cettolo, and Marcello Federico. 2013. EU-BRIDGE MT: Text Translation of Talks in the EU-BRIDGE Project. In *Proc. of the Int. Workshop on Spoken Language Translation (IWSLT)*. Heidelberg, Germany, pages 128–135.

Markus Freitag, Stephan Peitz, Joern Wuebker, Hermann Ney, Matthias Huck, Rico Sennrich, Nadir Durrani, Maria Nadejde, Philip Williams, Philipp Koehn, Teresa Herrmann, Eunah Cho, and Alex Waibel. 2014b. EU-BRIDGE MT: Combined Machine Translation. In *Proc. of the Workshop on Statistical Machine Translation (WMT)*. Baltimore, MD, USA, pages 105–113

Markus Freitag, Joern Wuebker, Stephan Peitz, Hermann Ney, Matthias Huck, Alexandra Birch, Nadir Durrani, Philipp Koehn, Mohammed Mediani, Isabel Slawik, Jan Niehues, Eunah Cho, Alex Waibel, Nicola Bertoldi, Mauro Cettolo, and Marcello Federico. 2014c. Combined Spoken Language Translation. In *Proc. of the Int. Workshop on Spoken Language Translation (IWSLT)*. Lake Tahoe, CA, USA, pages 57–64.

Mercedes García-Martínez, Loïc Barrault, and Fethi Bougares. 2016. Factored neural machine translation architectures. In *Proceedings of the International Workshop on Spoken Language Translation*. Seattle, USA, IWSLT'16.

Kenneth Heafield. 2011. KenLM : Faster and Smaller Language Model Queries. In *Proceedings of the Sixth Workshop on Statistical Machine Translation*. Association for Computational Linguistics, 2009, pages 187–197.

Jindřich Helcl and Jindřich Libovický. 2017. Neural Monkey: An open-source tool for sequence learning. *The Prague Bulletin of Mathematical Linguistics* (107):5–17. https://doi.org/10.1515/pralin-2017-0001.

Diederik P. Kingma and Jimmy Ba. 2015. Adam: A Method for Stochastic Optimization. In *The International Conference on Learning Representations*. San Diego, California, USA.

Thomas N. Kipf and Max Welling. 2016. Semi-supervised classification with graph convolutional networks. *CoRR* abs/1609.02907. http://arxiv.org/abs/1609.02907.

G. Klein, Y. Kim, Y. Deng, J. Senellart, and A. M. Rush. 2017. OpenNMT: Open-Source Toolkit for Neural Machine Translation. *ArXiv e-prints* .

Diego Marcheggiani and Ivan Titov. 2017. Encoding Sentences with Graph Convolutional Networks for Semantic Role Labeling. *ArXiv e-prints* https://arxiv.org/abs/1703.04826.

Haitao Mi, Baskaran Sankaran, Zhiguo Wang, and Abe Ittycheriah. 2016. Coverage embedding models for neural machine translation. *arXiv preprint arXiv:1605.03148* .

Franz Josef Och. 2003. Minimum Error Rate Training in Statistical Machine Translation. In *Proc. of the 41th Annual Meeting of the Association for Computational Linguistics (ACL)*. Sapporo, Japan, pages 160–167.

Jan-Thorsten Peter, Tamer Alkhouli, Hermann Ney, Matthias Huck, Fabienne Braune, Alexander Fraser, Ale Tamchyna, Ondrej Bojar, Barry Haddow, Rico Sennrich, Frdric Blain, Lucia Specia, Jan Niehues, Alex Waibel, Alexandre Allauzen, Lauriane Aufrant, Franck Burlot, Elena Knyazeva, Thomas Lavergne, Franois Yvon, Stella Frank, and Mārcis Pinnis. 2016. The qt21/himl combined machine translation system. In *ACL 2016 First Conference on Machine Translation*. Berlin, Germany, page 344355.

Ngoc-Quan Pham, Jan Niehues, Thanh-Le Ha, Eunah Cho, Matthias Sperber, and Alexander H Waibel. 2017. Kit system description for wmt 2017. In *WMT*.

Mārcis Pinnis, Rihards Krišlauks, Toms Miks, Daiga Deksne, and Valters Šics. 2017. Tilde's Machine Translation Systems for WMT 2017. In *Proceedings of the Second Conference on Machine Translation (WMT 2017), Volume 2: Shared Task Papers*.

Maja Popovic. 2015. chrf: character n-gram f-score for automatic mt evaluation. In *Proceedings of the 10th Workshop on Statistical Machine Translation (WMT-15)*. pages 392–395.

Ofir Press and Lior Wolf. 2017. Using the Output Embedding to Improve Language Models. In *Proceedings of the 15th Conference of the European Chapter of the Association for Computational Linguistics (EACL)*. Valencia, Spain.

Rico Sennrich, Alexandra Birch, Anna Currey, Ulrich Germann, Barry Haddow, Kenneth Heafield, Antonio Valerio Miceli Barone, and Philip Williams. 2017a. The University of Edinburgh's neural MT systems for WMT17. In *Proceedings of the Second Conference on Machine Translation, Volume 2: Shared Task Papers*. Association for Computational Linguistics, Copenhagen, Denmark.

Rico Sennrich, Orhan Firat, Kyunghyun Cho, Alexandra Birch, Barry Haddow, Julian Hitschler, Marcin Junczys-Dowmunt, Samuel Läubli, Antonio Valerio Miceli Barone, Jozef Mokry, and Maria Nadejde. 2017b. Nematus: a toolkit for neural machine translation. In *Proceedings of the Software Demonstrations of the 15th Conference of the European Chapter of the Association for Computational Linguistics*. Association for Computational Linguistics, Valencia, Spain, pages 65–68. http://aclweb.org/anthology/E17-3017.

Rico Sennrich, Orhan Firat, Kyunghyun Cho, Alexandra Birch, Barry Haddow, Julian Hitschler, Marcin Junczys-Dowmunt, Samuel Läubli, Antonio Valerio Miceli Barone, Jozef Mokry, and Maria Nadejde. 2017c. Nematus: a Toolkit for Neural Machine Translation. In *Proceedings of the Demonstrations at the 15th Conference of the European Chapter of the Association for Computational Linguistics*. Valencia, Spain.

Rico Sennrich, Barry Haddow, and Alexandra Birch. 2016. Neural Machine Translation of Rare Words with Subword Units. In *Proceedings of the 54th Annual Meeting of the Association for Computational Linguistics (ACL 2016)*. Berlin, Germany.

Nakatani Shuyo. 2010. Language detection library for java.

Miloš Stanojevic and Khalil Simaan. 2014. Beer: Better evaluation as ranking. In *Proceedings of the Ninth Workshop on Statistical Machine Translation*. pages 414–419.

Zhaopeng Tu, Yang Liu, Zhengdong Lu, Xiaohua Liu, and Hang Li. 2016a. Context gates for neural machine translation. *arXiv preprint arXiv:1608.06043* .

Zhaopeng Tu, Zhengdong Lu, Yang Liu, Xiaohua Liu, and Hang Li. 2016b. Modeling coverage for neural machine translation. *arXiv preprint arXiv:1601.04811* .

Andrejs Vasiļjevs, Raivis Skadiņš, and Jörg Tiedemann. 2012. Letsmt!: a cloud-based platform for do-it-yourself machine translation. In *Proceedings of the ACL 2012 System Demonstrations*. Association for Computational Linguistics, pages 43–48.

Julian Georg Zilly, Rupesh Kumar Srivastava, Jan Koutník, and Jürgen Schmidhuber. 2016. Recurrent highway networks. *arXiv preprint arXiv:1607.03474* .

The RWTH Aachen University English-German and German-English Machine Translation System for WMT 2017

Jan-Thorsten Peter, Andreas Guta, Tamer Alkhouli, Parnia Bahar,
Jan Rosendahl, Nick Rossenbach, Miguel Graça and Hermann Ney
Human Language Technology and Pattern Recognition Group
Computer Science Department
RWTH Aachen University
D-52056 Aachen, Germany
`<surname>@i6.informatik.rwth-aachen.de`

Abstract

This paper describes the statistical machine translation system developed at RWTH Aachen University for the English→German and German→English translation tasks of the *EMNLP 2017 Second Conference on Machine Translation* (WMT 2017). We use ensembles of attention-based neural machine translation system for both directions. We use the provided parallel and synthetic data to train the models. In addition, we also create a phrasal system using joint translation and reordering models in decoding and neural models in rescoring.

1 Introduction

We describe the statistical machine translation (SMT) systems developed by RWTH Aachen University for the German→English and English→German language pairs of the WMT 2017 evaluation campaign. After testing multiple systems and system combinations we submitted an ensemble of multiple NMT networks since it outperformed every tested system combination.

This paper is organized as follows. In Section 2 we describe our data preprocessing. Section 3 depicts the generation of synthetic data. Our translation software and baseline setups are explained in Section 4, including the attention-based recurrent neural network ensemble in Subsection 4.1 and phrasal joint translation and reordering (JTR) system in Subsection 4.2. Our experiments for each track are summarized in Section 5.

2 Preprocessing

We compared two different preprocessings for German→English for the attention-based recurrent neural network (NMT) system. The first preprocessing is similar to the preprocessing used in our WMT 2015 submission (Peter et al., 2015), which was optimized for phrase-based translation (PBT).

Secondly, we utilize a simplified version which uses tokenization, frequent casing, and simple categories only. Note, that the changes in preprocessing have a huge negative impact on the PBT system, while slightly improving the NMT system (Table 1). We therefore use the simplified version for all pure NMT experiments and use the old preprocessing for all other systems.

The phrasal JTR system uses the preprocessing technique that is optimized for PBT, as it relies on phrases as translation candidates. The preprocessing is similar to the one used in the WMT 2015 submission, but without any pre-ordering of source words. The English→German NMT system utilizes only the simplified preprocessing.

3 Synthetic Source Sentences

To increase the amount of usable parallel training data for the phrase-based and the neural machine translation systems, we translate a subset of the monolingual training data back to English in a similar way as described by (Bertoldi and Federico, 2009) and (Sennrich et al., 2016b).

We create a baseline German→English NMT system as described in 4.1 which is trained with all parallel data to translate 6.9M English sentences into German. For the other direction we use this newly created synthetic data and the parallel corpus to train a baseline English→German system, which in turn is used to translate additional 4.4M sentences from English to German.

Further, we append the synthetic data created by (Sennrich et al., 2016a). This results in additional 4.2M sentences for the German→English system and 3.6M for the opposite direction.

Proceedings of the Conference on Machine Translation (WMT), Volume 2: Shared Task Papers, pages 358–365
Copenhagen, Denmark, September 7–11, 2017. ©2017 Association for Computational Linguistics

Systems	PP	newstest2015				newstest2016				newstest2017			
		BLEU	TER	CTER	BEER	BLEU	TER	CTER	BEER	BLEU	TER	CTER	BEER
PBT	WMT15	27.9	52.7	53.9	60.5	33.6	47.8	49.1	63.5	28.9	52.2	54.3	60.8
PBT	simple	26.6	54.3	55.3	59.1	31.4	49.4	50.8	62.1	27.1	53.7	56.1	59.4
NMT	WMT15	27.3	53.0	52.7	59.7	32.1	48.4	48.4	62.8	27.7	53.0	53.0	59.9
NMT	simple	27.7	52.3	52.4	59.8	32.1	47.9	47.8	62.7	27.9	52.3	52.5	60.2

Table 1: Compares the performance of the preprocessing (PP) optimized for phrase-based systems (WMT15) or a very simple setup (simple), as described in Section 2 on a PBT and a Neural Machine Translation (NMT) system.

Individual Systems	newstest2015				newstest2016				newstest2017			
	BLEU	TER	CTER	BEER	BLEU	TER	CTER	BEER	BLEU	TER	CTER	BEER
Baseline	27.7	52.3	52.4	59.8	32.1	47.9	47.8	62.7	27.9	52.3	52.5	60.2
+ fertility	28.2	51.8	51.9	60.2	32.9	47.1	47.3	63.2	28.6	51.5	51.7	60.6
+ synthetic data	29.9	50.1	49.3	61.4	36.7	44.0	44.0	65.2	30.6	49.7	49.6	61.8
+ 2-layers decoder	30.7	49.7	48.3	61.8	37.5	43.6	43.4	65.5	31.8	49.1	49.1	62.3
+ filtered	30.8	49.7	48.5	61.8	37.9	43.1	42.8	65.8	31.7	49.1	48.9	62.2
+ anneling scheme	31.1	49.8	48.4	61.9	37.9	43.6	43.1	65.7	32.2	48.9	48.6	62.4
Base system	31.3	49.5	48.2	62.0	37.9	43.6	43.1	65.7	32.1	49.1	48.7	62.4
+ connected all LSTM cells	30.7	49.8	49.0	61.5	37.4	43.9	43.5	65.4	31.7	49.3	48.9	62.2
+ fertility	31.1	49.8	48.4	61.9	37.9	43.6	43.1	65.7	32.2	48.9	48.6	62.4
+ alignment feedback	31.3	49.8	48.3	61.9	37.7	43.6	43.2	65.6	32.2	49.1	48.4	62.4
Ensemble	32.0	48.9	47.5	62.3	38.8	42.7	42.5	66.2	33.1	48.3	47.7	63.0

Table 2: Results of the individual systems for the German→English task. The base system contains synthetic data, 2-decoder layers, filtered rapid data, and was trained with annealing learning rate instead of merging. Details are explained in Section 4.1.

4 SMT Systems

For the WMT 2017 evaluation campaign, we have employed two different translation system architectures for the German→English direction:

- phrasal joint translation and reordering
- attention-based neural network ensemble

The word alignments required by some models are obtained with GIZA++ (Och and Ney, 2003). We use mteval from the Moses toolkit (Koehn et al., 2007) and TERCom to evaluate our systems on the BLEU (Papineni et al., 2002) and TER (Snover et al., 2006) measures. Additional we use BEER (Stanojević and Sima'an, 2014) and CTER (Wang et al., 2016). All reported scores are case-sensitive and normalized.

4.1 Attention-Based Recurrent Neural Network

The best performing system provided by the RWTH is an attention-based recurrent neural network (NMT) similar to (Bahdanau et al., 2015). We use an implementation based on Blocks (van Merriënboer et al., 2015) and Theano (Bergstra et al., 2010; Bastien et al., 2012).

The encoder and decoder word embeddings are of size 620. The encoder consists of a bidirectional layer with 1000 LSTMs with peephole connections (Hochreiter and Schmidhuber, 1997a) to encode the source side. Additionally we ran experiments with two layers using 1000 LSTM nodes each where we optionally connect all internal states of the first LSTM layer to the second. The data is converted into subword units using byte pair encoding with 20000 operations (Sennrich et al., 2016c).

During training a batch size of 50 is used. The applied gradient algorithm is Adam (Kingma and Ba, 2014) with a learning rate of 0.001 and the four best models are averaged as described in the beginning of (Junczys-Dowmunt et al., 2016). Later experiments are done using Adam followed by an annealing scheme for learning rate reduction for SGD, as described in (Bahar et al., 2017).

The network is trained with 30% dropout for up to 500K iterations and evaluated every 10000 iterations on newstest2015. Decoding is done using a beam search with a beam size of 12.

If the neural network creates a special number token, the corresponding source number with the highest attention weight is copied to the target side. The synthetic training data is created and used as described in Section 3.

In addition, we tested methods to provide the alignment computation with supplementary information comparable with (Tu et al., 2016; Cohn et al., 2016). We model the word fertility and feedback the information of the last alignment points using a conventional layer with a window size of 5.

The final system was an ensemble of multiple systems each trained with slightly different settings as shown in Table 2 and 4.

4.2 Phrasal Joint Translation and Reordering System

The phrasal Joint Translation and Reordering (JTR) decoder is based on the implementation of the *source cardinality synchronous search* (SCSS) procedure described in (Zens and Ney, 2008). The system combines the flexibility of word-level models with the search accuracy of phrase candidates. It incorporates the JTR model (Guta et al., 2015), a language model (LM), a word class language model (wcLM) (Wuebker et al., 2013), phrasal translation probabilities, conditional JTR probabilities on phrase level and additional lexical models for smoothing purposes. The phrases are annotated with word alignments to allow for the application of word-level models.

A more detailed description of the translation candidate generation and the search procedure is given in (Peter et al., 2016). The phrase extraction and the estimation of the translation models are performed on all bilingual data excluding the rapid2016 corpus, the newstest2008-2013 and newssyscom2009 corpora and the first part of the synthetic data (Section 3). The non-synthetic data was filtered to contain only sentences with 4 unaligned words at most. In total, this results in 3.57M parallel and 6.94M synthetic sentences.

4.2.1 JTR Model

A JTR sequence $(\tilde{f}, \tilde{e})_1^{\tilde{I}}$ is an interpretation of a bilingual sentence pair (f_1^J, e_1^I) and its word alignment b_1^I. The joint probability $p(f_1^J, e_1^I, b_1^I)$ can be modeled as:

$$p(f_1^J, e_1^I, b_1^I) = p((\tilde{f}, \tilde{e})_1^{\tilde{I}})$$

$$= \prod_{i=1}^{\tilde{I}} p((\tilde{f}, \tilde{e})_i | (\tilde{f}, \tilde{e})_{i-n+1}^{i-1}).$$

The Viterbi alignments for both translation directions are obtained using GIZA++ (Och and Ney, 2003), merged and then used to convert the bilingual sentence pairs into JTR sequences. A 7-gram JTR joint model (Guta et al., 2015), which is responsible for estimating the translation and reordering probabilities, is trained on those. It is estimated with interpolated modified Kneser-Ney smoothing (Chen and Goodman, 1998) using the KenLM toolkit (Heafield et al., 2013).

4.2.2 Language Models

The phrase-based translation system uses two language models (LM) that are estimated with the KenLM toolkit (Heafield et al., 2013) and integrated into the decoder as separate models in the log-linear combination: A 5-gram LM and a 7-gram word-class language model (wcLM). Both use interpolated modified Kneser-Ney smoothing. For the word-class LM, we train 200 word classes on the target side of the bilingual training data using an in-house tool (Botros et al., 2015) similar to `mkcls` (Och, 2000). We have not tuned the number of word classes, but simply used 200, as it has proved to work well in previous systems. With these class definitions, we apply the technique described in (Wuebker et al., 2013) to estimate the wcLM on the same data as the conventional LM.

Both models are trained on all monolingual corpora, except the commoncrawl corpus, and the target side of the bilingual data (Section 4.2), which sums up to 365.44M sentences and 7230.15M running words, respectively.

4.2.3 Log-Linear Features in Decoding

In addition to the JTR model and the language models, JTR conditional models for both directions (Peter et al., 2016) are included into the log-linear framework. They are computed offline on the phrase level. Moreover, the system incorporates phrase translation models estimated as relative frequencies for both directions.

Because the JTR models are trained on Viterbi aligned word-pairs, they are limited to the context provided by the aligned word pairs and sensitive to the quality of the word alignments. To overcome this issue, we incorporate IBM 1 lexical models for both directions. The models are trained on all available bilingual data and the synthetic data, see Section 3.

The heuristic features used by the decoder are an enhanced low frequency penalty (Chen et al.,

360

2011), a penalty for unaligned source words and a symmetric word-level distortion penalty. Thus, different phrasal segmentations have the same reordering costs if they are equal in their word alignments. An additional word bonus helps to control the length of the hypothesized translation by counteracting the language model, which prefers translations to be rather short.

The decoder also incorporates a gap distance penalty (Durrani et al., 2011). All parameter weights are optimized using MERT (Och, 2003) towards the BLEU metric.

An attention-based recurrent neural model is applied as an additional feature in rescoring 1000-best lists, see Section 4.2.4.

4.2.4 Attention-based Recurrent Neural Network in Re-Ranking

An attention-based recurrent neural network similar to those in Subsection 4.1 is used within the log-linear framework for rescoring 1000-best lists generated by the phrasal JTR decoder. The model is trained on 6.96M sentences of the synthetic data.

The network uses the 30K most frequent words as source and target vocabulary, respectively. The decoder and encoder word embeddings are of size 500, the encoder uses a bidirectional LSTM layer with 1K units (Hochreiter and Schmidhuber, 1997b) to encode the source side. An LSTM layer with 1K units is used by the decoder.

Training is performed for up to 300K iterations with a batch size of 50 and Adam (Kingma and Ba, 2014) is used as the optimization algorithm. The parameters of the best four networks on newstest2015 with regards to BLEU score are averaged to produce the final model used in reranking.

4.2.5 Alignment-based Recurrent Neural Network in Re-Ranking

Besides the attention-based model, we apply recurrent alignment-based neural networks in 1000-best rescoring. These networks are similar to the ones used in rescoring in (Alkhouli et al., 2016).

We use a bidirectional alignment model that has a bidirectional encoder (2 LSTM layers), a unidirectional target encoder (1 LSTM layer), and an additional decoder LSTM layer. The model pairs each target state computed at target position $i - 1$ with its aligned bidirectional source state. The alignment information is obtain using GIZA++ in training, and from the 1000-best lists

during rescoring. The paired states are fed into the decoder layer. The model predicts the discrete jump from the previous to the current source position. The model is described in (Alkhouli and Ney, 2017).

We also use a bidirectional lexical model to score word translation. It uses an architecture similar to that of the alignment model, with the exception that pairing is done using the source states aligned to the target position i instead of $i - 1$. We also add weighted residual connections connecting the target states and the decoder states in the lexical model. We train two variants of this model, one including the target state, and one dropping it completely.

All models use four 200-node LSTM layers with the exception of the lexical model that includes the target state, which uses 350 nodes per layer. We use a class-factored output layer of 2000 classes, where 1000 classes are dedicated to the most frequent words, while the remaining 1000 classes are shared. This enables handling large vocabularies. The target vocabulary is reduced to 269K words, while the source vocabulary is reduced to 317K words

4.3 System Combination

System combination is applied to produce consensus translations from multiple hypotheses obtained from different translation approaches. The consensus translations typically outperform the individual hypotheses in terms of translation quality. A system combination implementation developed at RWTH Aachen University (Freitag et al., 2014) is used to combine the outputs of the different engines.

The first step in system combination is the generation of confusion networks (CN) from I input translation hypotheses. We need pairwise alignments between the input hypotheses. The alignments are obtained by METEOR (Banerjee and Lavie, 2005). The hypotheses are then reordered to match a selected skeleton hypothesis regarding the order of words. We generate I different CNs, each having one of the input systems as the skeleton hypothesis. The final lattice is the union of all I-many generated CNs.

The decoding of a confusion network consists of finding the shortest path in the network. Each arc is assigned a score of a linear model combination of M different models, which includes a

Individual Systems	newstest2015				newstest2016				newstest2017			
	BLEU	TER	CTER	BEER	BLEU	TER	CTER	BEER	BLEU	TER	CTER	BEER
Phrasal JTR + LM	29.7	52.5	50.5	61.3	33.9	48.0	46.5	64.2	29.4	53.1	51.6	61.2
+ wcLM	30.3	51.9	50.4	61.5	34.2	47.3	46.3	64.4	30.0	52.2	51.2	61.4
+ attention NMT	31.3	51.1	49.3	61.9	35.3	46.5	45.3	64.6	31.0	51.3	50.4	61.7
+ attention NMT	31.0	51.2	49.5	61.8	35.0	46.7	45.3	64.7	30.6	51.7	50.5	61.7
+ alignment NMT (x3)	30.9	51.0	49.6	61.8	35.3	46.5	45.6	64.8	30.7	51.6	50.7	61.7
+ attention NMT	31.3	50.9	49.3	61.9	35.3	46.4	45.3	64.8	30.9	51.2	50.2	61.8
NMT ensemble	32.0	48.9	47.5	62.3	38.8	42.7	42.5	66.2	33.1	48.3	47.7	63.0
System Combination	31.9	49.4	48.0	62.1	38.0	43.5	43.1	65.8	32.7	48.6	48.1	62.7

Table 3: Results of the individual systems for the German→English task. The system combination contains the system in line 3, 6, and 7.

word penalty, a 3-gram LM trained on the input hypotheses, a binary primary system feature that marks the primary hypothesis and a binary voting feature for each system. The binary voting feature for the system outputs 1 if the decoded word origins from that system and 0 otherwise.

The model weights for the system combination are trained with MERT.

5   Experimental Evaluation

We have mainly focused on building a strong German→English system and run most experiments on this task. We used newstest2015 as the development set.

After switching the preprocessing as described in Section 2, we have added the word fertility, which improves the baseline system by about 0.8 BLEU on newstest2016 as shown in Table 2. Adding the synthetic data as described in Section 3 gives a gain of 3.8 BLEU on newstest2016. Changing the number of layers in the decoder from one to two improves the performance by additional 0.8 BLEU. Filtering the rapid data corpus by scoring all bilingual sentences with an NMT system trained on all parallel data and removing the sentences with the worst scores improves the system on newstest2016 by 0.4 BLEU, but yield only in a small improvement on newstest2015. Surprisingly, it even decreases the performance on newstest2017, as observed at a later point in time. Switching from merging the 4 best networks in a training run to continuing the training with an annealing scheme for learning rate reduction for SGD, as described in (Bahar et al., 2017), has barely changed the performance on newstest2016. Nevertheless, we have decided to keep on using it, since it slightly helped on newstest2015.

We have used this, without the word fertility, as a base setup to train multiple systems with slightly different settings for an ensemble. In the first setting we use all LSTM states of the first decoder layer as input for the second decoder layer. This actually hurts the performance. Adding the word fertility or the alignment feedback as additional information does not have a large impact. Note, that the word fertility helpes when it is added to the baseline system - we are not sure why the effect disappears. Combining systems in one ensemble improves the system again by 1.1 BLEU on newstest2016.

We also combined the NMT system with the strongest phrasal JTR system and a few other combinations as well, but none of them has been able to improve over the NMT ensemble (Table 3). We therefore used the NMT system as our final submission. In the table, we can see that using three alignment-based models is comparable to using a single attention-based model. Note, however, that these models have relatively small LSTM layers of 200 and 350 nodes per layer. Meanwhile, the attention model uses 1000-node LSTM layers. When added on top of the alignment-based mix, the attention model only improves the mix slightly.

For the English→German system we have simply used the three best working NMT systems from the German→English setup and combined them in an ensemble. The word fertility and alignment feedback extensions also did not improve the performance, but the ensemble increased the overall performance by 1 BLEU on newstest2016. Due to computation time limitations, we did not succeed in building a phrasal JTR system on time.

6   Conclusion

The RWTH Aachen University has participated with a neural machine translation ensemble for the

Individual Systems	newstest2015				newstest2016				newstest2017			
	BLEU	TER	CTER	BEER	BLEU	TER	CTER	BEER	BLEU	TER	CTER	BEER
NMT	26.7	54.7	50.9	60.0	31.8	48.4	46.6	63.6	25.4	56.2	52.8	59.5
+ fertility	26.8	54.8	50.5	60.1	31.5	48.6	46.7	63.4	25.3	56.2	52.9	59.5
+ alignment feedback	26.3	55.5	51.5	59.7	31.3	48.8	47.0	63.3	25.1	56.7	53.1	59.3
Ensemble	27.4	54.1	50.2	60.4	32.8	47.4	45.7	64.1	26.0	55.5	51.9	59.9

Table 4: Results of the individual systems for the English→German task.

German→English and English→German WMT 2017 evaluation campaign. All networks are trained using all given parallel data, back-translated synthetic data, two LSTM layers in the decoder. The rapid corpus has been filtered to remove the most unlikely sentences. Adam followed by annealing scheme of learning rate reduction is used for optimization. Four networks are combined for the German→English ensemble and three for the English→German ensemble. In addition, we have submitted a phrasal JTR system, which has come close to the performance of a single neural machine translation network for newstest2017. Using system combination has not improved the performance of the best neural ensemble.

Acknowledgements

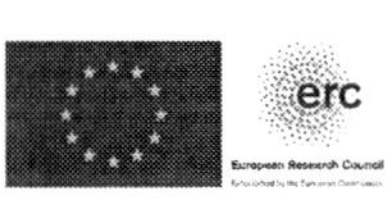
The work reported in this paper results from two projects, SEQCLAS and QT21. SEQCLAS has received funding from the European Research Council (ERC) under the European Union's Horizon 2020 research and innovation programme under grant agreement n° 694537. QT21 has received funding from the European Union's Horizon 2020 research and innovation programme under grant agreement n° 645452. The work reflects only the authors' views and neither the European Commission nor the European Research Council Executive Agency are responsible for any use that may be made of the information it contains. Tamer Alkhouli was partly funded by the 2016 Google PhD Fellowship for North America, Europe and the Middle East.

References

Tamer Alkhouli, Gabriel Bretschner, Jan-Thorsten Peter, Mohammed Hethnawi, Andreas Guta, and Hermann Ney. 2016. Alignment-based neural machine translation. In *Proceedings of the First Conference on Machine Translation*. Association for Computational Linguistics, Berlin, Germany, pages 54–65. http://www.aclweb.org/anthology/W16-2206.

Tamer Alkhouli and Hermann Ney. 2017. Biasing attention-based recurrent neural networks using external alignment information. In *Proceedings of the Second Conference on Machine Translation*. Association for Computational Linguistics, Copenhagen, Denmark.

Parnia Bahar, Tamer Alkhouli, Jan-Thorsten Peter, Christopher Brix, and Hermann Ney. 2017. Empirical investigation of optimization algorithms in neural machine translation. In *Conference of the European Association for Machine Translation*. Prague, Czech Republic, pages 13–26.

Dzmitry Bahdanau, Kyunghyun Cho, and Yoshua Bengio. 2015. Neural Machine Translation by Jointly Learning to Align and Translate. In *Proceedings of the International Conference on Learning Representations (ICLR)*. San Diego.

Satanjeev Banerjee and Alon Lavie. 2005. METEOR: An Automatic Metric for MT Evaluation with Improved Correlation with Human Judgments. In *43rd Annual Meeting of the Assoc. for Computational Linguistics: Proc. Workshop on Intrinsic and Extrinsic Evaluation Measures for MT and/or Summarization*. Ann Arbor, MI, pages 65–72.

Frédéric Bastien, Pascal Lamblin, Razvan Pascanu, James Bergstra, Ian J. Goodfellow, Arnaud Bergeron, Nicolas Bouchard, and Yoshua Bengio. 2012. Theano: new features and speed improvements. Deep Learning and Unsupervised Feature Learning NIPS 2012 Workshop.

James Bergstra, Olivier Breuleux, Frédéric Bastien, Pascal Lamblin, Razvan Pascanu, Guillaume Desjardins, Joseph Turian, David Warde-Farley, and Yoshua Bengio. 2010. Theano: a CPU and GPU math expression compiler. In *Proceedings of the Python for Scientific Computing Conference (SciPy)*. Oral Presentation.

Nicola Bertoldi and Marcello Federico. 2009. Domain adaptation for statistical machine translation with monolingual resources. In *Proceedings of the Fourth Workshop on Statistical Machine Translation*. Association for Computational Linguistics, Stroudsburg, PA, USA, StatMT '09, pages 182–189. http://dl.acm.org/citation.cfm?id=1626431.1626468.

Rami Botros, Kazuki Irie, Martin Sundermeyer, and Hermann Ney. 2015. On efficient training of word classes and their application to recurrent neural network language models. In *Interspeech*. Dresden, Germany, pages 1443–1447.

Boxing Chen, Roland Kuhn, George Foster, and Howard Johnson. 2011. Unpacking and Transforming Feature Functions: New Ways to Smooth Phrase Tables. In *MT Summit XIII*. Xiamen, China, pages 269–275.

Stanley F. Chen and Joshuo Goodman. 1998. An Empirical Study of Smoothing Techniques for Language Modeling. Technical Report TR-10-98, Computer Science Group, Harvard University, Cambridge, MA.

Trevor Cohn, Cong Duy Vu Hoang, Ekaterina Vymolova, Kaisheng Yao, Chris Dyer, and Gholamreza Haffari. 2016. Incorporating structural alignment biases into an attentional neural translation model. *CoRR* abs/1601.01085. http://arxiv.org/abs/1601.01085.

Nadir Durrani, Helmut Schmid, and Alexander Fraser. 2011. A joint sequence translation model with integrated reordering. In *Proceedings of the 49th Annual Meeting of the Association for Computational Linguistics: Human Language Technologies*. Portland, Oregon, USA, pages 1045–1054. http://www.aclweb.org/anthology/P11-1105.

Markus Freitag, Matthias Huck, and Hermann Ney. 2014. Jane: Open Source Machine Translation System Combination. In *Proc. of the Conf. of the European Chapter of the Assoc. for Computational Linguistics (EACL)*. Gothenberg, Sweden, pages 29–32.

Andreas Guta, Tamer Alkhouli, Jan-Thorsten Peter, Joern Wuebker, and Hermann Ney. 2015. A Comparison between Count and Neural Network Models Based on Joint Translation and Reordering Sequences. In *Proceedings of the 2015 Conference on Empirical Methods in Natural Language Processing*. Association for Computational Linguistics, Lisbon, Portugal.

Kenneth Heafield, Ivan Pouzyrevsky, Jonathan H. Clark, and Philipp Koehn. 2013. Scalable modified Kneser-Ney language model estimation. In *Proceedings of the 51st Annual Meeting of the Association for Computational Linguistics*. Sofia, Bulgaria, pages 690–696.

Sepp Hochreiter and Jürgen Schmidhuber. 1997a. Long short-term memory. *Neural Comput.* 9(8):1735–1780. https://doi.org/10.1162/neco.1997.9.8.1735.

Sepp Hochreiter and Jürgen Schmidhuber. 1997b. Long short-term memory. *Neural computation* 9(8):1735–1780.

Marcin Junczys-Dowmunt, Tomasz Dwojak, and Rico Sennrich. 2016. The AMU-UEDIN submission to the WMT16 news translation task: Attention-based NMT models as feature functions in phrase-based SMT. In *Proceedings of the First Conference on Machine Translation, WMT 2016, colocated with ACL 2016, August 11-12, Berlin, Germany*. pages 319–325. http://aclweb.org/anthology/W/W16/W16-2316.pdf.

Diederik P. Kingma and Jimmy Ba. 2014. Adam: A method for stochastic optimization. *CoRR* abs/1412.6980.

Philipp Koehn, Hieu Hoang, Alexandra Birch, Chris Callison-Burch, Marcello Federico, Nicola Bertoldi, Brooke Cowan, Wade Shen, Christine Moran, Richard Zens, Chris Dyer, Ondřej Bojar, Alexandra Constantine, and Evan Herbst. 2007. Moses: Open Source Toolkit for Statistical Machine Translation. Prague, Czech Republic, pages 177–180.

Franz J. Och. 2000. mkcls: Training of word classes for language modeling.

Franz Josef Och. 2003. Minimum Error Rate Training in Statistical Machine Translation. In *Proc. of the 41th Annual Meeting of the Association for Computational Linguistics (ACL)*. Sapporo, Japan, pages 160–167.

Franz Josef Och and Hermann Ney. 2003. A Systematic Comparison of Various Statistical Alignment Models. *Computational Linguistics* 29(1):19–51.

Kishore Papineni, Salim Roukos, Todd Ward, and Wei-Jing Zhu. 2002. Bleu: a Method for Automatic Evaluation of Machine Translation. In *Proceedings of the 41st Annual Meeting of the Association for Computational Linguistics*. Philadelphia, Pennsylvania, USA, pages 311–318.

Jan-Thorsten Peter, Andreas Guta, Nick Rossenbach, Miguel Graa, and Hermann Ney. 2016. The rwth aachen machine translation system for iwslt 2016. In *International Workshop on Spoken Language Translation*. Seattle, USA.

Jan-Thorsten Peter, Farzad Toutounchi, Joern Wuebker, and Hermann Ney. 2015. The rwth aachen german-english machine translation system for wmt 2015. In *EMNLP 2015 Tenth Workshop on Statistical Machine Translation*. Lisbon, Portugal, page 158163.

Rico Sennrich, Barry Haddow, and Alexandra Birch. 2016a. Edinburgh neural machine translation systems for wmt 16. In *Proceedings of the First Conference on Machine Translation*. Berlin, Germany, volume 2: Shared Task Papers, pages 368–373.

Rico Sennrich, Barry Haddow, and Alexandra Birch. 2016b. Improving neural machine translation models with monolingual data .

Rico Sennrich, Barry Haddow, and Alexandra Birch. 2016c. Neural machine translation of rare words with subword units pages 1715–1725.

Matthew Snover, Bonnie Dorr, Richard Schwartz, Linnea Micciulla, and John Makhoul. 2006. A Study of Translation Edit Rate with Targeted Human Annotation. In *Proceedings of the 7th Conference of the Association for Machine Translation in the Americas*. Cambridge, Massachusetts, USA, pages 223–231.

Miloš Stanojević and Khalil Sima'an. 2014. Fitting sentence level translation evaluation with many dense features. In *Proceedings of the 2014 Conference on Empirical Methods in Natural Language Processing (EMNLP)*. Association for Computational Linguistics, Doha, Qatar, pages 202–206. http://www.aclweb.org/anthology/D14-1025.

Zhaopeng Tu, Zhengdong Lu, Yang Liu, Xiaohua Liu, and Hang Li. 2016. Coverage-based neural machine translation. *CoRR* abs/1601.04811. http://arxiv.org/abs/1601.04811.

Bart van Merriënboer, Dzmitry Bahdanau, Vincent Dumoulin, Dmitriy Serdyuk, David Warde-Farley, Jan Chorowski, and Yoshua Bengio. 2015. Blocks and fuel: Frameworks for deep learning. *CoRR* abs/1506.00619. http://arxiv.org/abs/1506.00619.

Weiyue Wang, Jan-Thorsten Peter, Hendrik Rosendahl, and Hermann Ney. 2016. Character: Translation edit rate on character level. In *ACL 2016 First Conference on Machine Translation*. Berlin, Germany, pages 505–510.

Joern Wuebker, Stephan Peitz, Felix Rietig, and Hermann Ney. 2013. Improving statistical machine translation with word class models. In *Conference on Empirical Methods in Natural Language Processing*. Seattle, WA, USA, pages 1377–1381.

Richard Zens and Hermann Ney. 2008. Improvements in Dynamic Programming Beam Search for Phrase-based Statistical Machine Translation. In *International Workshop on Spoken Language Translation*. Honolulu, Hawaii, pages 195–205.

The Karlsruhe Institute of Technology Systems for the News Translation Task in WMT 2017

Ngoc-Quan Pham, Jan Niehues, Thanh-Le Ha,
Eunah Cho, Matthias Sperber, Alexander Waibel
Karlsruhe Institute of Technology, Karlsruhe, Germany
`firstname.lastname@kit.edu`

Abstract

We present our experiments in the scope of the news translation task in WMT 2017, in three directions: German→English, English→German and English→Latvian. The core of our systems is the encoder-decoder based neural machine translation models , enhanced with various modeling features, additional source side augmentation and output rescoring. We also experiment various methods in data selection and adaptation.

1 Introduction

We participate in the WMT 17 shared task on news translation with three directions: English-German, German-English and English-Latvian. The core of our submissions is the neural attentional encoder-decoder model, which we enhanced with different features such as context gates for more efficient attention and the coverage vector for maintaining attentional information during translation. Several techniques to integrated additional information into the source text have be investigated: Pre-translation with statistical systems, mono-lingual data and phrase-table entries. Finally, we combined different models using n-best lists reranking.

2 Data

This section describes the preprocessing steps for the parallel and monolingual corpora for the language pairs involved in the systems as well as the data selection methods investigated.

2.1 German↔English

As parallel data for our German↔English systems, we used Europarl v7 (EPPS), News Commentary v12 (NC), Rapid corpus of EU press releases, Common Crawl corpus, and simulated data. Except for the common crawl corpus, no special preprocessing was applied, but only tokenization and true-casing. For the common crawl corpus, we applied noise filtering using SVM as shown in Mediani et al. (2011). Around 900K sentence pairs are filtered out using this technique.

Synthetic data is motivated by Sennrich et al. (2015a). In order to exploit the monolingual data, we used the back-translation technique. We randomly select sentences from the data as much as our parallel data, and translate them with an inverse NMT system from the target to the source language. We use this synthetic data as an additional parallel training data. Summing all corpora, the preprocessed and noise-filtered parallel data reaches 8.3M sentences for each language.

For German monolingual data, we use News Crawl data. For English, we use News Crawl and News Discussions corpus. Same as for parallel data, only tokenization and true-casing are applied.

Once the data is preprocessed, we applied byte-pair encoding (BPE) (Sennrich et al., 2015b) on the corpus. In this work, we deploy two different operation sizes, 40K and 80K.

2.1.1 Monolingual data selection

We experimented with using domain adaptation techniques to select monolingual data for back-translation. In particular, we concatenated all news-test data sets up until 2013 to form our in-domain corpus, and used news-shuffle as background data. We used the method by Axelrod et al. (2015), a class-based extension of the widely used cross-entropy difference based data selection method by Moore and Lewis (2010). For word clustering, we used Clustercat (Dehdari et al., 2016) with 20 classes. We selected an amount of data equal to the available bilingual training data. Backtranslation was done as in (Sennrich et al.,

Proceedings of the Conference on Machine Translation (WMT), Volume 2: Shared Task Papers, pages 366–373
Copenhagen, Denmark, September 7–11, 2017. ©2017 Association for Computational Linguistics

2015a). We attempted this approach for both systems with English and German as target language. However, we did not observe any improvements over selecting monolingual data at random, and did not employ this method for our final system.

2.1.2 Parallel data selection

From previous MT evaluation campaigns (Cho et al., 2016), we notice that NMT systems work well when we do fine tuning on in-domain data after training our models on out-of-domain data. Since a clear in-domain corpus is not available in this task, we conducted parallel data selection experiments to build an in-domain corpus.

We followed the approach described in (Peris et al., 2016) to extract an in-domain data set from News Commentary corpus. More specifically, an LSTM-based neural network was utilized to classify every sentence in the general corpus whether we should include it into the in-domain corpus or not. The network is trained using a "golden" corpus as the in-domain one. We took the WMT development sets from 2008 to 2013, c.a. 16K sentence pairs, to be the golden corpus for this training. The outcome is the merge of the development sets and the selected sentences from News Commentary, resulting in c.a. 100K sentence-pair in-domain corpus.

2.2 English→Latvian

The parallel corpus English-Latvian contains 2.9 million sentences which are proprocessed by TILDE[1] with language specific tokenizers. The Latvian text is only true-cased on the first letter of the sentence. We also further clean the data by using the language detection library Shuyo (2010) and remove the lines that the target sentences cannot be recognized as Latvian by the tool, resulting in about 25K sentences removed. Aside from the main data provided by the organizer, we exploit the synthetically translated monolingual data (only the news2016 part), which is provided by University of Edinburgh with a Moses phrase-based system. The training data used for the final system consists of 5 million sentences in total. For validation, we use the the first $2,000$ sentences of the Leta corpus (the rest included in the training data) and use the newsdev2017 set ($2,003$ sentences) for testing. We train a BPE (Sennrich et al., 2015b) model on the training data (including the back-

translated part) with 40K operations, which is potentially helpful for a morphologically rich target language.

3 NMT Frameworks

Our systems consist of multiple neural encoder-decoder models trained using two different toolkits.

3.1 Nematus

We initially used the `nematus`[2] toolkit, in which we used the hyperparameters following previous works (Sennrich et al., 2017): minibatch size of 80, maximum sentence length of 50, word embedding size of 650, a one layer GRU with size 1,024 in the encoder and a conditional GRU decoder with hidden layer size 1,024. The gradients are scaled with norm of 1.0 and the gradient update method being used is Adam (Kingma and Ba, 2014) with learning rate 0.0001. Models are trained until the BLEU score on the validation set stops increasing. Checkpoints are saved every 20K iterations.

3.2 OpenNMT

We also employed the Torch-based (Collobert et al., 2011) toolkit OpenNMT (Klein et al., 2017) [3]. All models trained with this toolkit have two LSTM layers of 1,024 units each, and we also use the input-feeding method as described in (Luong et al., 2015). For optimization, the gradients are scaled at 5, and we experimentally use Adam with a high learning rate of 0.001 and then reduce it to 0.0005 when the perplexity of the model does not decrease anymore. Checkpoints are saved every epoch (all of the sentences are seen). We also enhanced the toolkits with different features, namely the Context Gate for attentional model (Tu et al., 2016a) and using coverage information during learning to translate (Tu et al., 2016b; Sankaran et al., 2016).

3.2.1 Context gates for machine translation

In conditional language models such as neural machine translation, the decoder makes prediction based on two sources of input: the decoder input at the current time step and the context vector queried by the attentional model. As analysed by (Tu et al., 2016a), it could be beneficial for the

---

[1] www.tilde.com

[2] https://github.com/rsennrich/nematus

[3] Our implementation for the WMT project can be found at https://github.com/isl-mt/OpenNMT

translation model to be able to control the influence of each prediction source. Concretely, inadequate translation can happen due to the bias over the current decoder input. We followed the authors to integrate a soft gating mechanism to alleviate this problem. Specifically, in our neural translation model, given the target hidden state h_t and the source context vector c_t, an attentional hidden state is formed by concatenation (Luong et al., 2015).

Alternatively, we use h_t and c_t to learn a soft context mask that prevents the activation of both states. The mentioned states are then masked with learned gates, and concatenated before being fed into the final linear regression layer.

Note that the authors (Tu et al., 2016a) built their model on top of the conditional GRU based network from Bahdanau et al. (2014), while ours are essentially an multi-layer LSTM decoder with an additional attention layer. Such difference leads to the minor change in terms of implementation, which may not replicate the same improvement as the original work.

3.2.2 Coverage mechanism for attention model

Various works have pointed out that the attention neural machine translation model can be benefit by constraining the attentional process to adequately cover the source words (Sankaran et al., 2016; Tu et al., 2016b; Mi et al., 2016; Luong et al., 2015). Different proposals share similar ideas which is to incorporate alignment information from the previous time steps into the attentional neural network. Our experiment inherits the neural fertility model from (Tu et al., 2016b) which uses an explicit vector to keep track of the alignment information. At every time step, the network makes an attentional decision with the help of the coverage vector, which is in turn updated using the alignment vector and the source context with a simple Gated Recurrent Unit (GRU).

4 Integration of Additional Resources

In this section, we show several techniques we applied in order to integrate additional resources into the translation. First, we integrate monolingual information using a multi-lingual NMT approach. In addition, we extracted information from PBMT systems.

4.1 Monolingual Data

When the encoder of an NMT system of a well-chosen architecture considers words across different languages, the model is expected to learn a good representation of the source words in a joint embedding space, in which words carrying similar meaning would have a close distance from each other. In turn, the shared information across source languages could help improve the choice of words in the target side. For example, the word *Flussufer* in German and the word *bank* in English should be projected in the joint embedding space in close proximity. This information might help to choose the French word *rive* over *banque*.

To make an attention NMT for single language pair translation to support a multilingual NMT that shared the common semantic space, (Ha et al., 2016b) suggested language-specific coding. Basically, language codes are appended to every word in source and target sentences and indicate the original language of the word. This information will be then passed to the training process of the NMT system. For example, an English-German sentence pair *excuse me* and *entschuldigen Sie* become *_en_excuse _en_me* and *_de_entschuldigen _de_Sie*. By doing so, they can train a single multilingual system that translates from several source languages to one or several target languages. When we have n English-German sentence pairs and m French-German sentence pairs, for example, we can train a single NMT system with a parallel corpus of $n + m$ sentence pairs. Then we can use the trained model to either translate from English or from French to German.

The aforementioned multilingual NMT can be used wisely as a novel way to utilize the monolingual data, which is not a trivial task in NMT systems. Particularly, if we want to translate from English to German, we can use a corpus in German as an additional German-German data similar to the way we utilize the French-German parallel corpus. Thus, the encoder is shared between the source and the target languages (English and German), and the attention is also shared across languages to help the decoder selects better German words in the target side. The system implemented this idea is referred as a *mix-source* system.

For this evaluation, we apply the idea of that multilingual NMT approach in the English-German direction in order to make use of the German monolingual corpus and gain additional improvements.

4.2 Pre-translation

One of the main problems of current NMT system is its limited vocabulary (Luong et al., 2014), generating difficulties when translating rare words. While the overall performance of NMT is significantly better on many tasks compared to SMT (Bojar et al., 2016), the translation of words seen only a few times is often not correct. In contrast, PBMT is able to memorize a translation it has observed only once in the training data. Therefore, we tried to combine the advantages of NMT and PBMT using pre-translation as described in (Niehues et al., 2016).

In the first step, we translate the source sentence f using the PBMT system generating a translation e^{SMT}. Then we use the NMT system to find the most probable translation e^* given the source sentence f and the PBMT translation e^{SMT}. Thus, we create a mixed input for the NMT system consisting of both sentences by concatenating them. This scheme, however, may lead to errors when the source and target languages have a same word in surface, but with different meanings, e.g. *die* in English is a verb, while it is an article in German. In order to prevent such errors, we use a separate vocabulary for each language. Using the BPE of the input (Sennrich et al., 2015b), we are able to encode any input words as well as any translation of the PBMT system. Thereby, the NMT is able to learn to copy translations of the PBMT system to the target side. The pre-translation method is applied on the German $\rightarrow$ English direction.

4.3 Integration of Selected Phrase Pairs

One main drawback of the aforementioned approach is that all training data as well as the test data has to be translated using a phrase-based MT system. Therefore, this is a time-consuming approach.

In a second approach to integrate information for rare words from the phrase-based MT system, we relied only on the phrase table. Using this technique, we annotate rare words with their possible translation according to the phrase table. In the first step, we need to identify the words for which we want to provide a possible translation. Then we need to select a translation from the phrase table and, finally, we need a method to provide the translation of the word optional to the NMT system.

In our approach, we consider all words that were split into several words by the byte pair encoding as rare words. For these words, we search their possible translations in the phrase table. We took the phrase pair with the longest source phrase that covers the word. If there are several translation options for this source phrase, we select the one where the log-sum of all fours probabilities in the phrase table is the highest.

We integrate this information into the source sentence, by appending the source phrase and the translation from the phrase table. We also annotate the beginning and end of the phrase with a special character. When we have the source sentence *Obama empfän@ @ gt Netanyahu* and a phrase pair *empfän@ @ gt ‖‖‖ receives* in the phrase table, we will generate the following input for the NMT system: *Obama # empfän@ @ gt ## receives # Netanyahu*

5 System Combination

Combination of different neural networks often leads to better performance, as shown in various applications of neural networks and previous NMT submissions in evaluation campaigns (Bojar et al., 2016). A successful technique is to ensemble different checkpoints of a model or models with different random initialization. While this is a very helpful technique, it has a potential drawback that it can only be performed easily for models using the same input and output representations.

In order to further extend the variety of models, we combine the output of several ensemble models by an n-best list combination. A first approach is to generate an n-best list from all or several of the models. Afterwards, we combine the n-best lists into a single one by creating the union of the n-best lists. Since every model only generated a subset of the joint list, we rescored the joint list by each model. Finally, we used a combination of all the scores to select the best entry for every source sentence. In previous work (Cho et al., 2017), it was shown that it is often sufficient to use the n-best list of the best model and rescore this n-best list with the different models. In our experiments, we used $n = 50$ for the n-best list size.

For systems to be combined, we use the NMT system generated by different frameworks (described in Section 3), as well as the pre-translation and multi-lingual systems (described in Section 4). We also combine systems using different BPE sizes. In addition, we use a system that generates the target sentence in the reversed order (Sennrich et al., 2015a; Liu et al., 2016; Huck et al., 2016).

After joining the n-best lists and rescoring it using the different systems, we have k scores for every entry in the n-best lists. In our experiments, we use two different techniques to combine the scores. The first method is to use the sum of all scores. Especially, if the performance of the different models is similar, we do not need to weigh the different models. Similar to the ensemble methods we can reach a good performance by using equal weights. In a second approach, we use the List-Net algorithms (Cao et al., 2007; Niehues et al., 2015) to find the optimal weights for the individual models.

5.1 ListNet-based Rescoring

In order to find the optimal weights for the different models, we use the ListNet algorithm (Cao et al., 2007; Niehues et al., 2015). This technique defines a probability distribution on the permutations of the list based on the scores of the individual models and another one based on a reference metric. In this set of experiments, we use the BLEU+1 score introduced by (Liang et al., 2006). Then we measure the cross entropy between both distributions as the loss function for our training. We trained the weights for the different models on the validation set also used during training the NMT systems.

Using this loss function, we can compute the gradient and use stochastic gradient descent. We use batch updates with ten samples and tune the learning rate on the development data.

The range of the scores of the different toolkits may greatly differ. Therefore, we rescaled all scores observed on the development data to the range of $[-1, 1]$ prior to rescoring.

6 Results

In this section, we describe the systems used to generate the final hypothesis for official test set. We participated in German→English, English →German, and English→Latvian translation tasks.

6.1 German→English

All German to English translation system are trained on the parallel data as well as back-translated data (Sennrich et al., 2015a) randomly selected from the monolingual news data. We use newstest2013 as validation data. Using this data, we train our initial system with the Nematus toolkit and a byte pair encoding size of 40K operations (*Nematus 40K*). The translation for all *Nematus* based systems are generated with ensembled system of different checkpoints. Although we also attempted to select the data for backtranslation as described in Section 2.1, initial experiments did not show improvements on the translation quality. Therefore, we use the randomly selected data for the remaining experiments.

In addition, we build a system with a reverse target order (R2L) (Liu et al., 2016) and the pre-translation. The pre-translation was generated by the PBMT system used in WMT 2016 (Ha et al., 2016a). Both performed slightly better than the baseline system.

When increasing the size of BPE operation to 80K, we observe the improvements on the translation quality, by 1.4 BLEU points.

In addition to Nematus, we also used the Open-NMT framework to build a network. For this language pair, we used the context gate, but not the coverage model. In contrast to the Nematus based systems, we did not ensemble different checkpoints. When using OpenNMT this technique did not yield an improvement in translation performance. When OpenNMT is trained using 40K BPE units (single system), we reach a BLEU score of 38.39. The default architecture of Open-NMT - utilizing two hidden layers - is deemed to be one reason for its outstanding performance.

In addition, we build a system using rare words annotated with their translations. In contrast to the baseline OpenNMT system, this configuration utilizes only half the hidden size. For comparison, a baseline system using this hidden size achieved a BLEU score of 36.91 on newstest2016. Although we did not improve the performance over the baseline, it was beneficial to use the system in the combination.

Finally, we generated an n-best list using the best performing system OpenNMT 40K. Then we used all the other models to rescore this n-best lists. The scores are combined linearly. The weights were optimized using the ListNet algorithm on newtest 2015. This resulted to the best performance of 39.10. The combination of all models improve the translation performance by another 0.7 BLEU points.

System	News2015	News2016
Nematus 40K	29.64	35.96
R2L		36.67
PreMT		36.86
Nematus 80K		37.38
OpenNMT 40K	31.48	38.39
RareWords	29.73	36.50
ListNet	32.33	**39.10**

Table 1: Experiments for German→English

System	Baseline	Adapted
Forward Normal	30.20	31.27
Forward Context Gate	30.44	31.36
Forward Ensembled	30.68	32.22
R2L	30.54	31.56
Mix-source	30.11	31.11
Pre-translation	30.67	-
Rescoring	-	**33.17**

Table 2: Experiments for English→German

6.2 English→German

Table 2 shows the results of the English→German translation task. The scores are reported in BLEU scores and evaluated on test2016. We used Open-NMT framework on the preprocessed data (parallel, sampled, back-translated as in Section 2.1). For all experiments, we used BPE operation at 40K.

The systems differ in the training method and the architectures. In the first series of experiments *Forward*, training sentences are seen in their natural direction (left-to-right in this case). For this type of experiments, we trained with two architectures: normal and with context gates. The *Context Gate* system got a small improvement over the normal one. The two architectures share the same vocabularies and ensembling them helped us to get more improvements. In the second series of experiments *R2L* the target sentences were reversed in order (right-to-left). And the third type is the mix-source systems described in Section 4.1 and in (Ha et al., 2016b). In addition, we also used a pre-translation system. The systems have different vocabularies and they were eventually combined using our ListNet-based rescoring (Section 5.1).

For each type of experiments, we conducted fine tuning on the small in-domain corpus mentioned in Section 2.1.2, and the best adapted model based on its BLEU score on test2015 was picked for the ensembling and/or rescoring. In all systems except for pre-translation, we observed considerable improvements, around 1 BLEU point, when applying fine tuning (c.f. *Adapted* column).

Finally, we rescored and combined four adapted systems (*Forward Ensembled*, *R2L*, *Mix-source* and *Pre-translation*) to get our submission system to the campaign. It achieved 33.17 BLEU points on test2016, 0.9 BLEU points better than the *Forward Ensembled* system and 1.6 BLEU points better than our best single system (*R2L*).

6.3 English→Latvian

The result of the English→Latvian translation task is illustrated in table 3. Our baseline models are trained with both frameworks using the concatenation of the actual parallel and back-translated data. We use dropout of 0.2 for both frameworks. For Nematus, the convergence was seen after about $540K$ iterations (about 9 epochs), with the best validation and test BLEU score achieved of 19.92 and 22.95 respectively. With OpenNMT, we obtained 20.62 and 24.11 BLEU points for the validation and test set, after training for 8 epochs (4 with high learning rate of 0.001, 2 with 0.0005 and last 2 with 0.00025.

Regarding the two enhancement features mentioned above, the simple Context Gate improved the scores by 0.2 and 0.6 on the two sets respectively, while integrating the coverage mechanism in the attention model yields a further 1.1 and 0.5 BLEU scores. The decoder recurrent network has always received previous context information through input-feeding. Surprisingly, the coverage vector still manages to improve the model performance. We assume that the gain comes from a stronger attention network, which has more parameters than the cosine similarity between the hidden state and the context, and the fact that the coverage vector can maintain a longer past attentional information compared to input-feeding.

It is notable that even though the improvement has been observed, it is not consistent throughout the sets. One possible explanation is the difference between the development (from Leta) and the test set (from news) in terms of domain and difficulty.

Regarding the consistency between BLEU score and perplexity, the model with higher BLEU score does not necessarily have lower perplexity (across different settings, for example baseline vs. coverage) even though we choose the model with the best perplexity for reporting BLEU scores.

This is the case even when these models share the same vocabulary. We can see that perplexity is a good measure to choose models within a single run, even though it is not informative to compare models with different network topologies.

By ensembling the three models, we managed improving the translation performance by 1.3 BLEU points. Our final submission is done by using another model trained with reversed target sentences to rescore the n-best list ($n = 20$) generated by the ensembled system, which improves about 0.4 BLEU.

System	LetaDev	News2016
Nematus 40K	19.92	22.95
OpenNMT 40K	20.62	24.11
+ Context Gate	20.88	24.71
+ Coverage Mode	21.91	**25.20**
Ensemble (3 models)	-	**26.54**
+ Reranking R2L	-	**26.96**

Table 3: Experiments for English→Latvian

7 Conclusion

In conclusion, we described our experiments in the news translation task in WMT 2016, in which we attempted to try out several techniques across different language pairs. The model-wise modifications such as context gate and coverage provided slight improvement, while we find out that NMT models can benefit greatly from adaptation and pre-translation. As observed in previous works, the most consistent gain mostly comes from system ensembling/combination and reranking.

Acknowledgments

The project leading to this application has received funding from the European Union's Horizon 2020 research and innovation programme under grant agreement n° 645452. The research by Thanh-Le Ha was supported by Ministry of Science, Research and the Arts Baden-Württemberg. The work by Jan Niehues was supported by the Carl-Zeiss-Stiftung.

References

Amittai Axelrod, Yogarshi Vyas, Marianna Martindale, and Marine Carpuat. 2015. Class-Based N-gram Language Difference Models for Data Selection. In *IWSLT (International Workshop on Spoken Language Translation)*. pages 180–187.

Dzmitry Bahdanau, Kyunghyun Cho, and Yoshua Bengio. 2014. Neural machine translation by jointly learning to align and translate. *arXiv preprint arXiv:1409.0473* .

Ondrej Bojar, Rajen Chatterjee, Christian Federmann, Yvette Graham, Barry Haddow, Matthias Huck, Antonio Jimeno Yepes, Philipp Koehn, Varvara Logacheva, Christof Monz, et al. 2016. Findings of the 2016 conference on machine translation (wmt16). In *Proceedings of the First Conference on Machine Translation (WMT)*. volume 2, pages 131–198.

Zhe Cao, Tao Qin, Tie yan Liu, Ming-Feng Tsai, and Hang Li. 2007. Learning to Rank: From Pairwise Approach to Listwise Approach. In *Proceedings of the 24th International Conference on Machine Learning*. Corvallis, OR, USA, pages 129–136.

Eunah Cho, Jan Niehues, Thanh-Le Ha, Matthias Sperber, Mohammed Mediani, and Alex Waibel. 2016. Adaptation and combination of nmt systems: The kit translation systems for iwslt 2016. In *Proceedings of the 13th International Workshop on Spoken Language Translation (IWSLT 2016)*.

Eunah Cho, Jan Niehues, Thanh-Le Ha, and Alexandre Waibel. 2017. Analyzing neural mt search and model performance. In *Proceedings of The First Workshop on Neural Machine Translation. Association ofr Computational Linguistics*.

Ronan Collobert, Koray Kavukcuoglu, and Clément Farabet. 2011. Torch7: A matlab-like environment for machine learning. In *BigLearn, NIPS Workshop*. EPFL-CONF-192376.

Jon Dehdari, Liling Tan, and Josef van Genabith. 2016. BIRA: Improved predictive exchange word clustering. In *Proceedings of the 2016 Conference of the North American Chapter of the Association for Computational Linguistics: Human Language Technologies (NAACL)*. Association for Computational Linguistics, San Diego, CA, USA, pages 1169–1174. http://www.aclweb.org/anthology/N16-1139.pdf.

Thanh-Le Ha, Eunah Cho, Jan Niehues, Mohammed Mediani, Matthias Sperber, Alexandre Allauzen, and Alexandre Waibel. 2016a. The karlsruhe institute of technology systems for the news translation task in wmt 2016. In *Proceedings of the First Conference on Machine Translation, Berlin, Germany. Association for Computational Linguistics*.

Thanh-Le Ha, Jan Niehues, and Alexander Waibel. 2016b. Toward multilingual neural machine translation with universal encoder and decoder. *arXiv preprint arXiv:1611.04798* .

Matthias Huck, Alexander Fraser, and Barry Haddow. 2016. The edinburgh/lmu hierarchical machine translation system for wmt 2016. In *Proc. of* the ACL 2016 First Conf. on Machine Translation (WMT16), Berlin, Germany, August.

Diederik Kingma and Jimmy Ba. 2014. Adam: A method for stochastic optimization. *arXiv preprint arXiv:1412.6980* .

G. Klein, Y. Kim, Y. Deng, J. Senellart, and A. M. Rush. 2017. OpenNMT: Open-Source Toolkit for Neural Machine Translation. *ArXiv e-prints* .

P. Liang, A. Bouchard-Côté, D. Klein, and B. Taskar. 2006. An End-to-end Discriminative Approach to Machine Translation. In *Proceedings of the 44th Annual Meeting of the Association for Computational Linguistics (ACL 2006)*. Sydney, Australia, pages 761–768.

Lemao Liu, Masao Utiyama, Andrew Finch, and Eiichiro Sumita. 2016. Agreement on target-bidirectional neural machine translation. In *Proceedings of NAACL-HLT*. pages 411–416.

Minh-Thang Luong, Hieu Pham, and Christopher D Manning. 2015. Effective approaches to attention-based neural machine translation. *arXiv preprint arXiv:1508.04025* .

Minh-Thang Luong, Ilya Sutskever, Quoc V Le, Oriol Vinyals, and Wojciech Zaremba. 2014. Addressing the rare word problem in neural machine translation.

Mohammed Mediani, Eunah Cho, Jan Niehues, Teresa Herrmann, and Alex Waibel. 2011. The KIT English-French Translation systems for IWSLT 2011. In *Proceedings of the 8th International Workshop on Spoken Language Translation*. San Francisco, CA, USA.

Haitao Mi, Baskaran Sankaran, Zhiguo Wang, and Abe Ittycheriah. 2016. Coverage embedding models for neural machine translation. *arXiv preprint arXiv:1605.03148* .

Robert C Moore and William Lewis. 2010. Intelligent Selection of Language Model Training Data. In *Proceedings of ACL*.

Jan Niehues, Eunah Cho, Thanh-Le Ha, and Alex Waibel. 2016. Pre-translation for neural machine translation. In *the 26th International Conference on Computational Linguistics (Coling 2016)*.

Jan Niehues, Quoc Khanh Do, Alexandre Allauzen, and Alex Waibel. 2015. Listnet-based MT Rescoring. *EMNLP 2015* page 248.

Álvaro Peris, Mara Chinea-Rios, and Francisco Casacuberta. 2016. Neural networks classifier for data selection in statistical machine translation. *arXiv preprint arXiv:1612.05555* .

Baskaran Sankaran, Haitao Mi, Yaser Al-Onaizan, and Abe Ittycheriah. 2016. Temporal attention model for neural machine translation. *arXiv preprint arXiv:1608.02927* .

Rico Sennrich, Orhan Firat, Kyunghyun Cho, Alexandra Birch, Barry Haddow, Julian Hitschler, Marcin Junczys-Dowmunt, Samuel Läubli, Antonio Valerio Miceli Barone, Jozef Mokry, and Maria Nadejde. 2017. Nematus: a toolkit for neural machine translation. In *Proceedings of the Software Demonstrations of the 15th Conference of the European Chapter of the Association for Computational Linguistics*. Association for Computational Linguistics, Valencia, Spain, pages 65–68. http://aclweb.org/anthology/E17-3017.

Rico Sennrich, Barry Haddow, and Alexandra Birch. 2015a. Improving neural machine translation models with monolingual data.

Rico Sennrich, Barry Haddow, and Alexandra Birch. 2015b. Neural machine translation of rare words with subword units. In *Proceedings of the 54th Annual Meeting of the Association for Computational Linguistics*. Berlin, Germany.

Nakatani Shuyo. 2010. Language detection library for java.

Zhaopeng Tu, Yang Liu, Zhengdong Lu, Xiaohua Liu, and Hang Li. 2016a. Context gates for neural machine translation. *arXiv preprint arXiv:1608.06043* .

Zhaopeng Tu, Zhengdong Lu, Yang Liu, Xiaohua Liu, and Hang Li. 2016b. Modeling coverage for neural machine translation. *arXiv preprint arXiv:1601.04811* .

Tilde's Machine Translation Systems for WMT 2017

Mārcis Pinnis and **Rihards Krišlauks** and **Toms Miks**
and **Daiga Deksne** and **Valters Šics**
Tilde, Vienibas gatve 75A, Riga, Latvia
{marcis.pinnis,rihards.krislauks,toms.miks}@tilde.lv
{daiga.deksne,valters.sics}@tilde.lv

Abstract

The paper describes Tilde's English-Latvian and Latvian-English machine translation systems for the WMT 2017 shared task in news translation. Both constrained and unconstrained systems are described. Our constrained systems were ranked as the best performing systems according to the automatic evaluation results. The paper gives details to how we pre-processed training data, the NMT system architecture that we used for training the NMT models, the SMT systems and their usage in NMT-SMT hybrid system configurations.

1 Introduction

The year 2016 marked the first time when neural machine translation (NMT) systems achieved significantly better results than statistical machine translation (SMT) systems for most of the translation directions in the news translation shared task of the WMT conference. This was achieved due to a number of architectural and data pre-processing novelties that the winning systems incorporated, for instance, the use of an attention mechanism in the decoder of the NMT system (Bahdanau et al., 2014), back-translation of additional in-domain monolingual data for domain adaptation of the NMT system after training of a broad domain model or during re-training of the whole NMT model, use of sub-word units to address the problem of out-of-vocabulary word translation, and others (Sennrich et al., 2016).

Since then, a number of further advances have been made in machine translation and related fields. A lot of effort has been invested in the search for the best hyper-parameter configurations and neural network architectures for NMT sys-

tem training (Britz et al., 2017). In particular, the use of long short-term memory (LSTM) cells and deep architectures has shown to allow increasing translation quality. Parallel to that, a number of novelties in neural network architectures have been introduced for other sequence processing tasks, some of which, like the multiplicative LSTM (MLSTM) units (Krause et al., 2016), promise advantages even over deep recurrent network architectures. For data pre-processing, we have shown that the language agnostic word splitting method using byte pair encoding (BPE) inconsistently splits words for morphologically rich languages and that the method can be improved by linguistically motivating word splitting (Pinnis et al., 2017b).

For the WMT 2017 shared task in news translation, we build upon the NMT toolkit Nematus (Sennrich et al., 2016) that achieved the best results in the WMT 2016 shared task. We also incorporate in our systems the latest advancements in the field, for instance, MLSTM recurrent layers, morphology-driven word splitting, better handling of unknown and rare words with robust NMT models, and hybrid methods. The improvements over the baseline NMT model have allowed us to develop the best scoring systems for the English-Latvian and Latvian-English translation directions.

The paper is further structured as follows: Section 2 provides an overview of our WMT 2017 systems, Section 3 describes the data and the different data processing workflows used for preparing the data for training, Section 4 describes SMT systems that were used in NMT-SMT hybrid system configurations, Section 5 describes the NMT architecture used for training of our NMT systems, Section 6 describes the hybrid NMT-SMT system architecture, Section 7 describes our evaluation results, and Section 8 concludes the paper.

Proceedings of the Conference on Machine Translation (WMT), Volume 2: Shared Task Papers, pages 374–381
Copenhagen, Denmark, September 7–11, 2017. ©2017 Association for Computational Linguistics

2 System Overview

For the WMT 2017 shared task, we developed both constrained and unconstrained MT systems. In total, we submitted five systems:

- Constrained English-Latvian and Latvian-English NMT-SMT hybrid systems.

- Unconstrained English-Latvian and Latvian-English NMT-SMT hybrid systems trained on significantly larger corpora.

- An unconstrained English-Latvian SMT system that achieves higher automatic evaluation results than the NMT-SMT hybrid systems.

3 Data

For training of MT systems, we used the WMT 2017 training data, however, for the unconstrained systems we also used resources from the Tilde Data Library.[1] All data were filtered using our data filtering methods (see Section 3.1), pre-processed with standard and custom pre-processing tools (see Section 3.2), and supplemented with synthetic data (see Section 3.3). For tuning and for decision-making during the development, we used the *newsdev2017* data set that was provided by the WMT 2017 organisers.

3.1 Data Filtering

Our previous research in NMT system development has shown that NMT systems are more sensitive to the noise present in the training data (Pinnis et al., 2017a) than SMT systems, therefore, we performed parallel data filtering to reduce potential non-parallelities and the negative effect of noise on the NMT systems. The filtering consisted of the following steps:

1. Long sentence filtering (longer than 1500 symbols or 80 tokens).

2. Sentence length difference filter (sentence pairs with a length ratio smaller than 0.3 were filtered out).

3. Incorrect language filtering using a language detection tool (Shuyo, 2010).

---

[1]Tilde Data Library is a parallel and monolingual data repository of the Tilde MT platform (http://www.tilde.com/mt/).

4. Low content overlap filter using the cross-lingual alignment tool *MPAligner* (Pinnis, 2013).

5. Bad encoding filter that filtered out sentences containing foreign and corrupt symbols.

6. Digit mismatch filter that showed to be an effective method for dealing with sentence segmentation issues in a number of corpora (including the Digital Corpus of European Parliament).

Training data statistics for both constrained and unconstrained systems are shown in Table 1.

3.2 Data Pre-processing

After filtering, all training data were pre-processed using the following steps:

1. *Normalisation of punctuation.* Only one standard of quotation marks and apostrophes were used, hyphenated tokens were split and the hyphens were replaced with a special symbol.

2. *Identification of non-translatable entities.* E-mail addresses, URLs, file addresses and XML tags were identified and replaced with place-holders.

3. *Tokenisation.* For tokenisation, we used the Tilde's regular expression-based tokeniser.

4. *Truecasing.* The Moses *truecase.perl* was used to truecase the first word of each sentence.

5. *Morphology-driven word splitting* (Pinnis et al., 2017b). Tokens were split using a morphological analyser and further processed with byte pair encoding (BPE) (Sennrich et al., 2015) to ensure an open vocabulary. For both languages, we used morphological analysers that were developed by Deksne (2013) using finite state transducer technology.

6. *Factorisation.* Following the work of Sennrich and Haddow (2016), who showed that linguistic input features allow increasing NMT system translation quality, we developed our NMT systems using factored models. Therefore, the source data were further factored using a language-specific tag-

Scenario	Lang. pair	Before filtering (Total / Unique)		After filtering (Unique)	
		Parallel	Monolingual	Parallel	Monolingual
Constrained	en-lv	4.51M / 1.92M	38.13M / 28.81M	1.61M	27.75M
	lv-en	4.51M / 1.92M	369.85M / 335.55M	1.61M	330.23M
Unconstrained	en-lv	39.28M / 15.78M	128.28M / 87.60M	12.69M	81.68M
	lv-en	39.28M / 15.78M	416.36M / 360.01M	12.69M	351.99M

Table 1: Training data statistics (sentence counts) for SMT and NMT systems before and after filtering

ger or parser. For Latvian, we used an averaged perceptron-based morpho-syntactic tagger (Nikiforovs, 2014) that was trained on the data from Pinnis and Goba (2011). For English, we used the lexicalized probabilistic parser (Klein et al., 2002) from the *Stanford CoreNLP* toolkit (Manning et al., 2014).

3.3 Synthetic Data

Similarly to the method by Pinnis et al. (2017b) that allows training NMT models that are more robust to unknown and rarely occurring words, we supplemented the parallel training data with synthetic parallel training sentences. To create the synthetic corpus, we performed word alignment on the parallel corpus using *fast-align* (Dyer et al., 2013). Then, we randomly replaced one to three unambiguously (one-to-one) aligned content words with unknown word *<UNK>* placeholders. Finally, we copied factor information from the original factored source sentence to the synthetic sentence.

Using the filtered and the synthetic training data, we trained initial target-to-source NMT models (see Section 5 for details on the NMT architecture). Then, we shuffled the available in-domain monolingual data (news articles or news commentary in the target language) and for each system back-translated a part of the monolingual data from the target language into the source language in order to create additional synthetic source-to-target parallel corpora. The data were selected such that the amount would approximately correspond to the original training data. Experiments with different back-translated data proportions showed that the best results could be achieved with a proportion of 1-to-1.

The back-translated parallel corpora were also supplemented with sentence pairs where content words with unambiguous alignments were randomly replaced with unknown word placeholders. Finally, the additional synthetic data were

Lang. pair	Synth. *<UNK>* sent.	Re-transl. sent.	Total
(C) en-lv	1.48M	3.09M	6.19M
(C) lv-en	1.48M	3.09M	6.19M
(U) en-lv	11.66M	21.69M	46.04M
(U) lv-en	11.66M	21.36M	45.71M

Table 2: Synthetic data and final NMT model training data statistics

added to the existing training data. The statistics of the synthetic corpora and the final training data for NMT system training are given in Table 2. It can be seen that the synthetic data creation process increased the size of the training data four times.

4 SMT Systems

SMT systems were trained using Moses (Koehn et al., 2007) in the Tilde MT platform (Vasiļjevs et al., 2012). All systems were trained using the filtered training data (see Table 1). Word alignment was performed using fast-align (Dyer et al., 2013). All SMT systems feature 7-gram translation models and the *wbe-msd-bidirectional-fe-allff*[2] reordering models. The systems have two language models that were trained using KenLM (Heafield, 2011) - an in-domain language model trained on the news article and news commentary corpora and an out-of-domain language model trained on the remaining monolingual data. The systems were tuned using MERT on the *news-dev2017* data set.

5 NMT System Architecture

The NMT system architecture is based on the implementation available with the Nematus toolkit that was used by Sennrich et al. (2016) to produce

---

[2]More about the different types of reordering models in Moses can be found online at http://www.statmt.org/moses/?n=FactoredTraining.BuildReorderingModel

Factor	English	Latvian
Word part	350	360
Position	5	5
Lemma	125	125
Part-of-speech tag	10	-
Syntactic function	10	-
Morpho-syntactic tag	-	10

Table 3: Dimensionality of each factor in the encoder's embedding layer

the top-scoring results for multiple language pairs in the WMT 2016 shared task in news translation. It is an encoder-decoder model with attention. The main distinction of our model is the use of multiplicative long short-term memory cells (Krause et al., 2016) instead of gated recurrent units (GRU) in the encoder and in the first cell of the decoder. We also use linguistic input features as described by Sennrich and Haddow (2016). I.e., each factor of a word part has its own embedding vector and in order to obtain one embedding vector for the whole word part, the individual embedding vectors are concatenated.

In more detail, the encoder's embedding layer has a total of 500 dimensions, which are split among the different input factors as specified in Table 5. It accommodates a vocabulary of 25 thousand sub-word units. The embedding layer is followed by a bidirectional MLSTM layer with 1024 dimensions for gates and cell states.

The decoder has a similar architecture to the implementation in the Nematus toolkit (Sennrich et al., 2017) which improves on the original attention-based NMT model (Bahdanau et al., 2014) by conditioning the attention weights on the previously decoded word in addition to the hidden state at the previous time-step. This is achieved by first computing an intermediate state

$$\hat{s}_t = \mathrm{GRU}(s_{t-1}, e_{y_{t-1}}),$$

then using it to compute the attention context

$$c_t = \mathrm{attention}(\hat{s}_t, h),$$

where s_{t-1} and $e_{y_{t-1}}$ are the decoder's hidden state and the embedding of the decoded word at the previous time-step respectively, and h is the annotation matrix produced by the encoder. The hidden state is then calculated as

$$s_t = \mathrm{GRU}(\hat{s}_t, c_t).$$

We modify this scheme by using an MLSTM cell to calculate the intermediate state

$$(\hat{s}_t, z_t) = \mathrm{MLSTM}(s_{t-1}, z_{t-1}, e_{y_{t-1}}),$$

where $\hat{s}_t$ and z_t are the MLSTM cell's output and hidden states respectively.

Similarly to the encoder, all of the gates and intermediate states of the decoder have a dimensionality of 1024. The decoder's embeddings have a dimensionality of 500.

For training, we also used dropout with the rate of 0.2 for hidden layers, and 0.1 for input and output embedding layers. For optimisation, we used Adadelta (Zeiler, 2012) with a learning rate of 0.0001, and we also used gradient clipping with a threshold of 1.

After training, 5 to 7 models that achieved the highest mixed metric evaluation results on the tuning data (i.e., the *newsdev2017* data set) were selected for ensemble decoding with a beam size of 12.

6 Hybrid System Architecture

After developing the initial NMT models, a preliminary manual analysis of the translations of the English-Latvian constrained system showed that only 34-44% of named entities within the tuning set were translated correctly. At the same time, the SMT system was able to handle approximately 70% of named entities correctly. Taking into account that our previous research in hybrid machine translation system development has shown that SMT systems in hybrid NMT-SMT system scenarios can handle rare and unknown word translation in hybrid scenarios better than the NMT models (Pinnis, 2016) alone, we decided to chain the NMT and SMT systems into a hybrid NMT-SMT system set up. In the hybrid set up, a sentence is at first translated with the NMT system, after which rare and unknown words that are left untranslated by the NMT system are translated with the SMT system.

The hybrid translation method performs translation in six steps as follows (see Table 4 for an example of a sentence processed through all of the hybrid translation steps):

1. First, rare and unknown words are identified in the source sentence and replaced by unknown word place-holders. Words are considered rare if they consist of at least one sub-word unit (or a sub-word unit bigram), which

Translation step	Example sentence
Source text	Šodien skatieties **Ikaunieces-Admidiņas** startu Rio spēlēs.
Pre-processed text	šodien skat@@ ieties **I@@ kaun@@ iec@@ es** – **Ad@@ mi@@ di@@ ņas** start@@ u Rio spēlē@@ s .
Text with identified rare words	šodien skat@@ ieties βIDβ – βIDβ start@@ u Rio spēlē@@ s .
NMT translation	watch the βIDβ – βIDβ start at the Rio Games today .
Moses XML with untranslated rare words	`<nmt translation="watch the">`šodien skatieties `</nmt>`Ikaunieces `<nmt translation="-">`-`</nmt>`**Admidiņas** `<nmt translation="start at the Rio Games today">`šodien startu Rio spēlēs`</nmt><nmt translation=".">`.`</nmt>`
Moses XML with identified untranslated person names	`<nmt translation="watch the">`šodien skatieties `</nmt><ne translation="Ikauniece" prob="1.0">`Ikaunieces`</ne>` `<nmt translation="-">`-`</nmt><ne translation="Admidina‖Admidins" prob="0.95‖0.05">`**Admidiņas**`</ne>` `<nmt translation="start at the Rio Games today">`šodien startu Rio spēlēs`</nmt><nmt translation=".">`.`</nmt>`
SMT translation	watch the **Ikauniece – Admidina** start at the Rio Games today .
Post-processed translation	Watch the **Ikauniece-Admidina** start at the Rio Games today.
NMT only transl. (for comparison)	Today, look at the start of the **Isolence-Admidias** in the Rio Games.

Table 4: Example of the NMT-SMT hybrid translation process

	Lang. pair	BPE count	BPE 2-gram
(C)	en-lv	25	1
	lv-en	35	0
(U)	en-lv	100	1
	lv-en	125	1

Table 5: Rare word detection thresholds

occurrence count in the training data is below a certain threshold. The thresholds for our submitted systems were empirically identified by analysing the hybrid method's performance on the tuning data. The thresholds are given in Table 5.

2. Then, the pre-processed sentence is translated with the NMT system. Our NMT models have been trained to leave the unknown word place-holders untranslated, i.e., to pass them through to the target side (Pinnis et al., 2017b). The capability of the NMT system to pass the place-holders through unchanged is vital for the further steps to work.

3. After translation, the NMT model's produced attention matrix is used to perform word alignment. Here, we also identify which source words correspond to each place-holder on the target side.

4. Then, a Moses XML document is prepared for the sentence such that the Moses SMT system will have to translate only the words that were replaced by the place-holders but leave the remaining part as it was translated by the NMT system.

5. Then, for the Latvian-English unconstrained system, we use a person name and surname dictionary to look-up translations of untranslated person names. The translations from the dictionary are merged in the Moses XML document so that the SMT system would be constrained to the translations found in the dictionary.

6. Finally, the Moses XML document is translated with the SMT system.

In the hybrid set-up, the same pre-processing and post-processing steps are used as for the individual NMT and SMT systems.

7 Results

We evaluated all MT systems using multiple automatic evaluation metrics including BLEU (Papineni et al., 2002), BEER 2.0 (Stanojevic and Sima'an, 2014), CharacTER (Wang et al., 2016),

Scenario	Lang. pair	System	BLEU (CS)	BEER 2.0	CharacTER	TER (CS)
(C)	en-lv	SMT	12.98 (12.36-13.60)	0.5086	0.6642	0.7582
		NMT	†19.49 (18.71-20.28)	0.5478	0.5877	0.6741
		Hybrid	†19.52 (18.70-20.34)	0.5482	0.5853	0.6729
	lv-en	SMT	15.47 (14.88-16.06)	0.5219	0.6606	0.7272
		NMT	†20.01 (19.31-20.64)	0.5494	0.6088	0.6725
		Hybrid	†20.06 (19.45-20.71)	0.5496	0.6081	0.6721
(U)	en-lv	SMT	20.43 (19.57-21.28)	0.5491	0.6126	0.6954
		NMT	20.04 (19.22-20.78)	0.5563	0.5832	0.6634
		Hybrid	20.08 (19.30-20.85)	0.5567	0.5827	0.6630
	lv-en	SMT	19.05 (18.42-19.67)	0.5515	0.6233	0.6928
		NMT	†22.02 (21.38-22.63)	0.5677	0.5838	0.6450
		Hybrid	†22.06 (21.41-22.74)	0.5683	0.5833	0.6442

Table 6: Automatic evaluation results of Tilde's systems (CS stands for case sensitive evaluation; the results are significant compared to the SMT system with $p = 0.01$†; the BLEU scores are given with a 95% confidence interval that was calculated using bootstrap resampling (Koehn, 2004))

and TER (Snover et al., 2006). The automatic evaluation results (see Table 6) on the *new-stest2017* data set show that for English-Latvian the constrained NMT system and for Latvian-English both the constrained and unconstrained NMT systems achieve significantly better results than the SMT systems. The difference between the quality of the unconstrained English-Latvian SMT and NMT systems is not statistically significant.

Since the automatic metrics have shown not to be sufficient to evaluate MT systems of the two different paradigms (Pinnis et al., 2017a), we also performed (blind) human comparative evaluation of the SMT and NMT system translations. Five professional translators were given the source sentence and translations of two MT systems and asked to select, which system (NMT, SMT, or neither) produces a better translation. The evaluation was performed on the tuning data set. In total, 200-250 sentences were evaluated in each evaluation task. The results in Figure 1 show that the NMT system translations are preferred more than the translations of the SMT systems. According to the methodology by Skadiņš et al. (2010), the results are weakly sufficient for all scenarios (except the Latvian-English unconstrained scenario for which the results are strongly sufficient) to conclude that the NMT systems produce better translations than the SMT systems.

The results also show that there is an insignificant quality increase for the hybrid systems over the NMT systems. The increase is minimal as only sentences that contain words with rare word parts

are translated differently. However, the hybrid scenario (and the components used in the hybrid scenario) allows us to integrate the NMT systems in our existing SMT infrastructure for formatting-rich document translation, which is a vital requirement for us to provide NMT services for customers.

Compared to other submitted systems, it is evident (see Table 7) that our constrained NMT-SMT hybrid systems significantly outperform other submitted systems.

8 Conclusions

In the paper, we have described English-Latvian and Latvian-English MT systems that were developed by Tilde for the WMT 2017 shared task in news translation. In total, we submitted five systems: four NMT-SMT hybrid systems (two constrained and two unconstrained systems) and one unconstrained English-Latvian SMT system that achieves similar translation quality as the NMT system according to automatic evaluation.

We have documented the methodology used to prepare the data for training of the systems, the SMT and NMT system training set-ups, the workflow for chaining the NMT and SMT systems into a hybrid NMT-SMT system, as well as our evaluation efforts.

The automatic and manual evaluation results show that three out of four NMT systems significantly outperform the SMT systems. Although the hybrid systems did not produce a significant improvement, the minimal improvement is con-

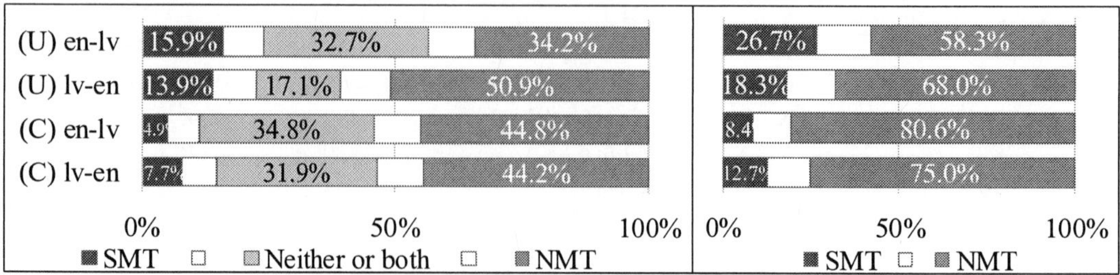

Figure 1: Results of the human comparative evaluation of Tilde's SMT and NMT systems

Lang. pair	System	BLEU (CS)	BEER 2.0	CharacTER	TER (CS)
en-lv	Tilde (hybrid)	†19.52 (18.74-20.31)	0.5482	0.5853	0.6729
	QT21 combination	18.03 (17.32-18.73)	0.5403	0.6455	0.7034
	KIT primary	17.72 (17.01-18.39)	0.5428	0.6051	0.6992
lv-en	Tilde (hybrid)	†20.83 (20.13-21.49)	0.5496	0.6081	0.6641
	UEDIN NMT	20.02 (19.39-20.63)	0.5462	0.6308	0.6719
	JHU SMT	17.67 (17.11-18.30)	0.5281	0.6485	0.7068

Table 7: Automatic evaluation results of the top three English-Latvian and Latvian-English constrained systems submitted for the WMT 2017 shared task on news translation (CS stands for case sensitive evaluation; the results are significant compared to other systems with $p = 0.01$†; the BLEU scores are given with a 95% confidence interval that was calculated using bootstrap resampling (Koehn, 2004))

sistent across all language pairs. The results also showed that in terms of automatic evaluation our submitted NMT-SMT hybrid systems significantly outperform the systems submitted by other participants of the shared task.

Acknowledgments

The research has been supported by the European Regional Development Fund within the research project "Neural Network Modelling for Inflected Natural Languages" No. 1.1.1.1/16/A/215.

References

Dzmitry Bahdanau, Kyunghyun Cho, and Yoshua Bengio. 2014. Neural machine translation by jointly learning to align and translate. *arXiv preprint arXiv:1409.0473* .

Denny Britz, Anna Goldie, Thang Luong, and Quoc Le. 2017. Massive exploration of neural machine translation architectures. *arXiv preprint arXiv:1703.03906* .

Daiga Deksne. 2013. Finite State Morphology Tool for Latvian. In *Proceedings of the 11th International Conference on Finite State Methods and Natural Language Processing*. pages 49–53.

Chris Dyer, Victor Chahuneau, and Noah A Smith. 2013. A Simple, Fast, and Effective Reparameterization of IBM Model 2. In *Proceedings of NAACL HLT 2013*. Atlanta, USA, June, pages 644–648.

Kenneth Heafield. 2011. KenLM : Faster and Smaller Language Model Queries. In *Proceedings of the Sixth Workshop on Statistical Machine Translation*. Association for Computational Linguistics, 2009, pages 187–197.

Dan Klein, Christopher D Manning, et al. 2002. Fast exact inference with a factored model for natural language parsing. *Advances in Neural Information Processing Systems (NIPS 2002)* pages 3–10.

Philipp Koehn. 2004. Statistical Significance Tests for Machine Translation Evaluation. In *Proceedings of the 2004 Conference on Empirical Methods in Natural Language Processing*. pages 388–395.

Philipp Koehn, Hieu Hoang, Alexandra Birch, Chris Callison-Burch, Marcello Federico, Nicola Bertoldi, Brooke Cowan, Wade Shen, Christine Moran, Richard Zens, Chris Dyer, Ondřej Bojar, Alexandra Constantin, and Evan Herbst. 2007. Moses: Open Source Toolkit for Statistical Machine Translation. In *Proceedings of the 45th Annual Meeting of the ACL on Interactive Poster and Demonstration Sessions*. Association for Computational Linguistics, Stroudsburg, PA, USA, ACL '07, pages 177–180.

Ben Krause, Liang Lu, Iain Murray, and Steve Renals. 2016. Multiplicative lstm for sequence modelling. *arXiv preprint arXiv:1609.07959* .

Christopher D Manning, Mihai Surdeanu, John Bauer, Jenny Rose Finkel, Steven Bethard, and David Mc-Closky. 2014. The stanford corenlp natural language processing toolkit. In *Proceedings of the ACL 2014 System Demonstrations*. pages 55–60.

Peteris Nikiforovs. 2014. Latvian NLP: Perceptron Tagger. https://github.com/pdonald/latvian.

Kishore Papineni, Salim Roukos, Todd Ward, and Wei-Jing Zhu. 2002. BLEU: a Method for Automatic Evaluation of Machine Translation. In *Proceedings of the 40th annual meeting on association for computational linguistics*. Association for Computational Linguistics, pages 311–318.

Mārcis Pinnis. 2013. Context Independent Term Mapper for European Languages. In *Proceedings of Recent Advances in Natural Language Processing (RANLP 2013)*. Hissar, Bulgaria, pages 562–570.

Mārcis Pinnis and Kārlis Goba. 2011. Maximum Entropy Model for Disambiguation of Rich Morphological Tags. In Cerstin Mahlow and Michael Piotrowski, editors, *Proceedings of the 2nd International Workshop on Systems and Frameworks for Computational Morphology*. Springer Berlin Heidelberg, Zurich, Switzerland, pages 14–22.

Mārcis Pinnis, Rihards Krišlauks, Daiga Deksne, and Toms Miks. 2017a. Evaluation of Neural Machine Translation for Highly Inflected and Small Languages. In *Proceedings of the 18th International Conference on Intelligent Text Processing and Computational Linguistics (CICLING 2017)*. Budapest, Hungary.

Mārcis Pinnis, Rihards Krišlauks, Daiga Deksne, and Toms Miks. 2017b. Neural Machine Translation for Morphologically Rich Languages with Improved Sub-word Units and Synthetic Data. In *Proceedings of the 20th International Conference of Text, Speech and Dialogue (TSD2017)*. Prague, Czechia.

Mrcis Pinnis. 2016. Towards Hybrid Neural Machine Translation for English-Latvian. In *Human Language Technologies The Baltic Perspective - Proceedings of the Seventh International Conference Baltic HLT 2016*. IOS Press, Riga, Latvia, pages 84–91.

Rico Sennrich, Orhan Firat, Kyunghyun Cho, Alexandra Birch, Barry Haddow, Julian Hitschler, Marcin Junczys-Dowmunt, Samuel Läubli, Antonio Valerio Miceli Barone, Jozef Mokry, et al. 2017. Nematus: a toolkit for neural machine translation. *arXiv preprint arXiv:1703.04357*.

Rico Sennrich and Barry Haddow. 2016. Linguistic Input Features Improve Neural Machine Translation. In *Proceedings of the First Conference on Machine Translation (WMT 2016) - Volume 1: Research Papers*. pages 83–91.

Rico Sennrich, Barry Haddow, and Alexandra Birch. 2015. Neural Machine Translation of Rare Words with Subword Units. In *Proceedings of the 54th Annual Meeting of the Association for Computational Linguistics (ACL 2015)*. Association for Computational Linguistics, Berlin, Germany.

Rico Sennrich, Barry Haddow, and Alexandra Birch. 2016. Edinburgh Neural Machine Translation Systems for WMT 16. In *Proceedings of the First Conference on Machine Translation (WMT 2016), Volume 2: Shared Task Papers*.

Nakatani Shuyo. 2010. Language detection library for java. http://code.google.com/p/language-detection/.

Raivis Skadiņš, Kārlis Goba, and Valters Šics. 2010. Improving SMT for Baltic Languages with Factored Models. In *Human Language Technologies: The Baltic Perspective: Proceedings of the Fourth International Conference, Baltic HLT 2010*. IOS Press, volume 219, pages 125–132.

Matthew Snover, Bonnie Dorr, Richard Schwartz, Linnea Micciulla, and John Makhoul. 2006. A Study of Translation Edit Rate with Targeted Human Annotation. In *Proceedings of the 7th biennial conference of the Association for Machine Translation in the Americas*. Cambridge, MA, USA, August, pages 223–231.

Miloš Stanojevic and Khalil Sima'an. 2014. B EER : BEtter Evaluation as Ranking. In *Proceedings of the Ninth Workshop on Statistical Machine Translation*. pages 414–419.

Andrejs Vasiļjevs, Raivis Skadiņš, and Jörg Tiedemann. 2012. LetsMT!: A Cloud-Based Platform for Do-It-Yourself Machine Translation. In Min Zhang, editor, *Proceedings of the ACL 2012 System Demonstrations*. Association for Computational Linguistics, Jeju Island, Korea, July, pages 43–48.

Weiyue Wang, Jan-thorsten Peter, Hendrik Rosendahl, and Hermann Ney. 2016. CharacTER : Translation Edit Rate on Character Level. In *Proceedings of the First Conference on Machine Translation (WMT 2016), Volume 2: Shared Task Papers*. Berlin, Germany, volume 2, pages 505–510.

Matthew D Zeiler. 2012. Adadelta: an adaptive learning rate method. *arXiv preprint arXiv:1212.5701*.

C-3MA: Tartu-Riga-Zurich Translation Systems for WMT17

Matīss Rikters
Faculty of Computing
University of Latvia
Riga, Latvia
matiss@lielakeda.lv

Chantal Amrhein
University of Zurich
Institute of Computational Linguistics
Zurich, Switzerland
chantal.amrhein@uzh.ch

Maksym Del and **Mark Fishel**
Institute of Computer Science
University of Tartu
Tartu, Estonia
{maksym.del, fishel}@ut.ee

Abstract

This paper describes the neural machine translation systems of the University of Latvia, University of Zurich and University of Tartu. We participated in the WMT 2017 shared task on news translation by building systems for two language pairs: English↔German and English↔Latvian. Our systems are based on an attentional encoder-decoder, using BPE subword segmentation. We experimented with back-translating the monolingual news corpora and filtering out the best translations as additional training data, enforcing named entity translation from a dictionary of parallel named entities, penalizing over- and under-translated sentences, and combining output from multiple NMT systems with SMT. The described methods give 0.7 - 1.8 BLEU point improvements over our baseline systems.

1 Introduction

We describe the neural machine translation (NMT) systems developed by the joint team of the University of Latvia, University of Zurich and University of Tartu (C-3MA). Our systems are based on an attentional encoder-decoder (Bahdanau et al., 2015), using BPE subword segmentation for open-vocabulary translation with a fixed vocabulary (Sennrich et al., 2016a). This paper is organized as follows: In Section 2 we describe our translation software and baseline setups. Section 3 describes our contributions for improving the baseline translations. Results of our experiments are summarized in Section 4. Finally, we conclude in Section 5.

2 Baseline Systems

Our baseline systems were trained with two NMT and one statistical machine translation (SMT) framework. For English↔German we only trained NMT systems, for which we used Nematus (NT) (Sennrich et al., 2017). For English↔Latvian, apart from NT systems, we additionally trained NMT systems with Neural Monkey (NM) (Helcl and Libovický, 2017) and SMT systems with LetsMT! (LMT) (Vasiļjevs et al., 2012).

In all of our NMT experiments we used a shared subword unit vocabulary (Sennrich et al., 2016b) of 35000 tokens. We clipped the gradient norm to 1.0 (Pascanu et al., 2013) and used a dropout of 0.2. Our models were trained with Adadelta (Zeiler, 2012) and after 7 days of training we performed early stopping.

For training the NT models we used a maximum sentence length of 50, word embeddings of size 512, and hidden layers of size 1000. For decoding with NT we used beam search with a beam size of 12.

For training the NM models we used a maximum sentence length of 70, word embeddings and hidden layers of size 600. For decoding with NM a greedy decoder was used. Unfortunately, at the time when we performed our experiments the beam search decoder for NM was still under development and we could not reliably use it.

3 Experimental Settings

3.1 Filtered Synthetic Training Data

Increasing the training data with synthetic back-translated corpora has proven to be useful in previous work (Sennrich et al., 2016a). The method

Proceedings of the Conference on Machine Translation (WMT), Volume 2: Shared Task Papers, pages 382–388
Copenhagen, Denmark, September 7–11, 2017. ©2017 Association for Computational Linguistics

Source	šodien , 21 : 16
Hypothesis	Sheodiennial
Perplexity	70455722055883
Source	lai izdzīvotu , nepieciešams aizpildīt ap 65 % , bet valsts apmaksā 10 % .
Hypothesis	it is necessary to fill around 65th and the state is paid to the population .
Perplexity	86070783032565
Source	potenciāli zaudētie mūža gadi ir gadi , kurus cilvēks būtu nodzīvojis līdz kādam noteiktam vecumam ,ja nebūtu miris nelaimes gadījumā , kādas slimības vai cita iemesla dēļ (līdz 64 gadu vecumam) .
Hypothesis	potential annualised annuity is a year that would have survived to a particular old age if it is not dead in an accident or for another reason to be in the age of 64 years old .
Perplexity	73076722556165
Source	tiekoties ar cilvēkiem Latvijā , " veiksmes stāsts " neesot jūtams .
Hypothesis	" we are talking about the people of Europe , " he said .
Perplexity	3.0285224517174
Source	liela daļa Latvijas iedzīvotāju ir piederīgi tā saucamajai " krievu pasaulei " , vai vismaz Krievija viņus saredz kā tai piederīgus - tie ir ne tikai Krievijas pilsoņi , bet arī krievvalodīgie , un tie kuriem ir pievilcīga Krievija un tās vērtības .
Hypothesis	a part of the Latvian population is a small and Russian world , or at least Russia sees them as being belonging to them - it is not only Russia ' civil , but also Russian and well known to live in the Russian civil society .
Perplexity	3.0276750775676

Table 1: Example sentences translated from Latvian into English that were filtered out from the back-translated news data.

consists of training the initial NMT systems on clean parallel data, then using them to translate monolingual data in the opposite direction and generate a supplementary parallel corpus with synthetic input and human-created output sentences. Nevertheless, more is not always better, as reported by Pinnis et al. (2017), where they stated that using some amount of back-translated data gives an improvement, but using double the amount gives lower results, while still better than not using any at all.

We used each of our NMT systems to back-translate 4.5 million sentences of the monolingual news corpora in each translation direction. First we removed any translations that contained at least one <unk> symbol. We trained a language model (LM) using CharRNN[1] with 4 million sentences from the monolingual news corpora of the target languages, resulting in three character-level RNN language models - English, German and Latvian. We used these language models to get perplexity scores for all remaining translations. The translations were then ordered by perplexity and the best (lowest) scoring 50% were used together with the sources as sources and references respectively for the additional filtered synthetic in-domain corpus. We chose scoring sentences with an LM instead of relying on neural network weights because 1) it is fast, reliable and ready to use without having to modify both NMT frameworks, and 2) it is an unbiased approach to score sentences when compared to having the system score its output by itself.

To verify that the perplexity score resembles human judgments, we took a small subset of the development sets and asked manual evaluators to rate each translation from 1 to 5. We sorted the translations by manual evaluation scores and automatically obtained perplexities, and calculated the overlap between the better halves of each. Results from this manual evaluation in Table 2 show that the LM perplexity score is good enough to separate the worst from the best translations, even though the correlation with human judgments is low.

---

[1] Multi-layer Recurrent Neural Networks (LSTM, GRU, RNN) for character - level language models in Torch https://github.com/karpathy/char-rnn

Some extreme examples of sentences translated from Latvian into English are listed in Table 1. The first one is just gibberish, the second is English, but makes little sense, the third one demonstrates unusual constructions like *annualised annuity*. The last two examples have a good perplexity score because they seem like good English, but when looking at the source, it is clear that in the fourth example there are some parts that are not translated.

As a result, the filtering approach brought an improvement of 1.1 - 4.9 BLEU (Papineni et al., 2002) on development sets and 1.5 - 2.8 BLEU on test sets when compared to using the full back-translated news corpora.

En→De	De→En	En→Lv	Lv→En
55%	56%	58%	56%

Table 2: Human judgment matches with LM perplexity for filtering on 200 random sentences from the *newsdev2017* dataset.

3.2 Named Entity Forcing

For our experiments with English↔German we enforced the translation of named entities (NE) using a dictionary which we built on the training data distributed for WMT 2017.

First, we performed named entity recognition (NER) using spaCy[2] for German and NLTK[3] for English. The reason for using different tools is that the spaCy output for English differed largely from the German one. NLTK performed much more similarly to the German spaCy output and, thus, it was easier to find NE translation pairs. We only considered NEs of type "person", "organisation" and "geographic location" for our dictionary.

Then we did word alignment using GIZA++ (Och and Ney, 2003) with the default *grow-diag-final-and* alignment symmetrization method. We created an entry in our translation dictionary for every pair of aligned (multi-word) NEs. Per entry we only kept the three most frequent translation options. Since there was still a lot of noise in the resulting dictionary, we decided to filter it automatically by removing entries that:

- did not contain alphabetical characters
  e.g. filtering out "⅔" aligned to "June"

- started with a dash
  e.g. filtering out "-Munich" aligned to "Hamburg"

- were longer than 70 characters or five tokens
  e.g. filtering out "Parliament's Committee on Economic and Monetary Affairs and Industrial Policy " aligned to "EU"

- differed from each other in length by more than 15 characters or two tokens
  e.g. filtering out "Georg" aligned to "Georg von Holtzbrinck"

When translating we made use of the alignment information given by the attention mechanism when translating with our NMT systems. We identified all NEs in the source text using the same tools as for the training data. For every source NE expression we searched for the most likely aligned translations by our systems via the attention matrix. We only considered source-translation pairs for which the attention to each other was highest in both directions.

Finally, for every such NE expression we checked whether there was a translation in our NE dictionary. If yes, we swapped the translation generated by our systems with the one in the dictionary. If not, we copied the NE expression from the source sentence to the target sentence. Since the attention is only given on the subword level, we needed to merge the subword units together before comparing the translations in the NE dictionary with the ones our systems produced. To avoid swapping too many correct translations, we defined some language-specific rules which, for example, took care of different cases in German.

We initially tested our approach on the *newstest2016* data (using our baseline system for the translation). For a qualitative perspective we looked at all of the NEs that were recognized in this text. We evaluated how many of them were changed by our algorithm and how many of these changes were positive, how many were negative and how many changed a wrong NE to another wrong NE. The results of this evaluation can be seen in Table 3. For *newstest2017* this approach gave a BLEU score improvement of 0.14 - 0.16.

3.3 Coverage Penalties

Under-translation and over-translation problems are results of lacking coverage in modern NMT systems (Tu et al., 2016). Attempts to address

---

[2]Industrial-Strength Natural Language Processing in Python - https://spacy.io/

[3]Natural Language Toolkit - http://www.nltk.org/

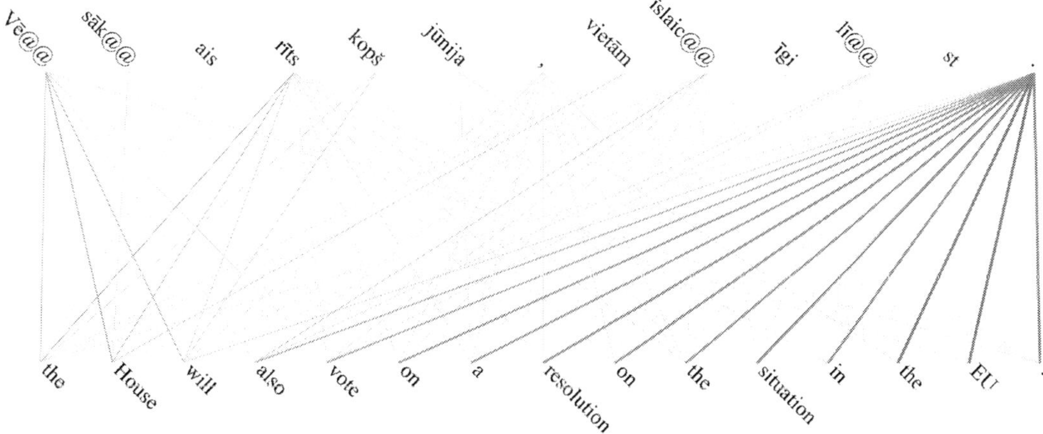

Figure 1: Attention alignment visualization of a translation, in which the strongest alignments are connected with the final token. Reference translation: *the coldest morning since June , brief local showers .,* hypothesis translation: *the House will also vote on a resolution on the situation in the EU .*

System	En→De		De→En	
Values	abs	rel (%)	abs	rel (%)
# recogn. NEs	4546	-	4201	-
# changed NEs	178	3.92	192	4.57
neg → pos	116	65.17	160	83.33
pos → neg	53	29.78	22	11.46
neg → neg	9	5.06	10	5.21

Table 3: Performance of NE enforcing on *newstest2016* data. The table shows how many NEs were recognized, how many of those were changed by our algorithm and how many of the changes were positive, negative or neutral.

these issues include both changes at training time and decoding time. Coverage penalty (Wu et al., 2016) is an example of a decoding time modification aimed at the under-translation problem. We designed coverage penalty variations that affect the over-translation issue as well.

More specifically, the coverage penalty is a part of the scoring function *s(Y,X)* that we use to rank candidate translations in beam search:

$$s(Y, X) = log(P(Y|X)) + cp(X; Y)$$

Coverage penalty from (Wu et al., 2016) is defined as follows:

$$cp(X; Y) = \beta * \sum_{i=1}^{|X|} log(min(\sum_{j=1}^{|Y|} p_{i,j}, 1.0)) \quad (1)$$

where $|Y|$ is the index of the last target word generated on the current beam search step, $|X|$ is the number of source words, and $p_{i,j}$ is the attention probability of the j-th target word y_j on the i-th source word x_i.

This expression penalizes the hypothesis if the sum of target word attentions on source words is below 1 (it is assumed that each target word is influenced by an attention probability mass equals to one; considering per word *fertility* might be a better choice), so it aims at reducing the under-translation problem. We extended equation 1 to penalize the hypothesis if the sum of target word attentions on source words not only below, but also above 1; we call it the coverage deviation penalty:

$$cdp(X; Y) = \beta * \sum_{i=1}^{|X|} log(abs(1 - \sum_{j=1}^{|Y|} p_{i,j})) \quad (2)$$

We also designed a perplexity penalty that implements the assumption that each target word should not be aligned with all source words by a little amount, but with some concrete parts of the source sentence. It penalizes the hypotheses where the target words have a high entropy of the attention distribution and called it the dispersion penalty:

$$dp(X; Y) = \beta * - \sum_{i=1}^{|X|} p_{i,|Y|} * log(p_{i,|Y|}) \quad (3)$$

Table 4 shows BLEU results. The dispersion

penalty with optimal weight improves BLEU considerably, with the change being statistically significant. We also tried combining different types of penalties, but got not improvements.

	BLEU change					
β	0.2	0.4	1	3	5	7
cp	**+0.3**	-1.0	-3.0	-	-	-
cdp	+0.0	+0.0	+0.1	-0.2	-	-
dp	+0.0	+0.0	+0.2	+0.5	**+0.7**	**+0.6**

Table 4: En→Lv BLEU score improvements with respect to different penalty types and values of β. Best score improvements are in bold

3.4 Hybrid System Combination

For translating between English↔Latvian we used all 3 systems in each direction and obtained the attention alignments from the NMT systems. For each direction we chose one main NMT system to provide the final translation for each sentence and, judging by the attention alignment distribution, tried to automatically identify unsuccessful translations. Two main types of unsuccessful translations that we noticed were when the majority of alignments are connected to only one token (example in Figure 1) or when all tokens strongly align one-to-one, hinting that the source may not have been translated at all (example in Figure 2). In the case of an unsuccessful translation, the hybrid setup checks the attention alignment distribution from the second NMT system and outputs either the sentence of that or performs a final back-off to the SMT output. This approach gave a BLEU score improvement of 0.1 - 0.3.

3.5 Post-processing

In post-processing of translation output we aimed to fix the most common mistakes that NMT systems tend to make. We used the output attention alignments from the NMT systems to replace any <unk> tokens with the source tokens that align to them with the highest weight. Any consecutive repeating n-grams were replaced with a single n-gram. The same was applied to repeating n-grams that have a preposition between them, i.e., *victim of the victim*. This approach gave a BLEU score improvement of 0.1 - 0.2.

System	En→De		De→En	
Dataset	Dev	Test	Dev	Test
Baseline NT	27.4	21.0	31.9	27.2
+filt. synth.	30.7	22.5	36.8	28.8
+NE forcing	30.9	**22.7**	36.9	**29.0**

Table 5: Experiment results for translating between English↔German. Submitted systems are in bold.

4 Results

The results of our English↔German systems are summarized in Table 5 and the results of our English↔Latvian systems - in Table 6. As mentioned in the subsections of Section 3 - each implemented modification gives a little improvement in the automated evaluation. Some modifications gave either no improvement for one or both language pairs or lead to lower automated evaluation results. These were either used for only the language pair that did show improvements on the development data or not used at all in the final setup.

System	En→Lv		Lv→En	
Dataset	Dev	Test	Dev	Test
Baseline NM	11.9	11.9	14.6	12.8
Baseline NT	12.2	10.8	13.2	11.6
Baseline LMT	19.8	12.9	24.3	13.4
+filt. synth. NM	16.7	13.5	15.7	14.3
+filt. synth. NT	16.9	13.6	15.0	13.8
NM+NT+LMT	-	**13.6**	-	**14.3**

Table 6: Experiment results for translating between English↔Latvian on development (*news-dev2017*) and test (*newstest2017*). Submitted systems are in bold.

4.1 Shared Task Results

Table 7 shows how our systems were ranked in the WMT17 shared news translation task against other submitted primary systems in the constraint track. Since the human evaluation was performed by showing evaluators only the reference translation and not the source, the human evaluation rankings are the same as BLEU, which also considers only the reference translation. One exception is the ranking for En→Lv, where an insufficient amount of evaluations were performed to cover all submitted systems, resulting in a tie for the 1st place across all but one submitted systems.

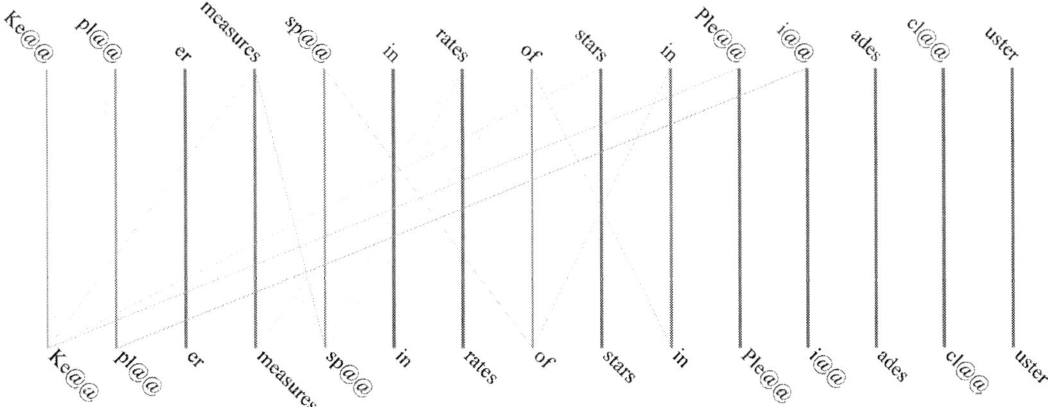

Figure 2: Attention alignment visualization of a translation, in which the all alignments are strong and mainly connected to only one-to-one. Reference translation: *Keplers izmēra zvaigžņu griešanās ātrumu Plejādes zvaigznājā .*, hypothesis translation: *Kepler measures spin rates of stars in Pleiades cluster*

System	BLEU	Rank	
		Human	
		Cluster	Ave %
De→En	6 of 7	6-7 of 7	7 of 7
En→De	10 of 11	9-11 of 11	9 of 11
En→Lv	11 of 12	1-11 of 12	11 of 12
Lv→En	5 of 6	4-5 of 6	4 of 6

Table 7: Automatic (BLEU) and human ranking of our submitted systems (C-3MA) at the WMT17 shared news translation task, only considering primary constrained systems. Human rankings are shown by clusters according to Wilcoxon signed-rank test at p-level p≤0.05, and standardized mean DA score (Ave %).

5 Conclusions

In this paper we described our submissions to the WMT17 News Translation shared task. Even though none of our systems were on the top of the list by automated evaluation, each of the implemented methods did give measurable improvements over our baseline systems. To complement the paper, we release open-source software[4] and configuration examples that we used for our systems.

---

[4]Scripts for Tartu Neural MT systems for WMT 17 - https://github.com/M4t1ss/C-3MA

Acknowledgments

The authors would like to thank Tilde for providing access to the LetsMT! SMT platform and the Institute of Electronics and Computer Science for providing GPU computing resources.

References

Dzmitry Bahdanau, Kyunghyun Cho, and Yoshua Bengio. 2015. Neural Machine Translation by Jointly Learning to Align and Translate. *Proceedings of the International Conference on Learning Representations (ICLR)* .

Jindřich Helcl and Jindřich Libovický. 2017. Neural monkey: An open-source tool for sequence learning. *The Prague Bulletin of Mathematical Linguistics* 107(1):5–17.

Franz Josef Och and Hermann Ney. 2003. A systematic comparison of various statistical alignment models. *Computational linguistics* 29(1):19–51.

Kishore Papineni, Salim Roukos, Todd Ward, and Wei-Jing Zhu. 2002. Bleu: a method for automatic evaluation of machine translation. In *Proceedings of the 40th annual meeting on association for computational linguistics*. Association for Computational Linguistics, pages 311–318.

Razvan Pascanu, Tomas Mikolov, and Yoshua Bengio. 2013. On the difficulty of training recurrent neural networks. *ICML (3)* 28:1310–1318.

Marcis Pinnis, Rihards Krislauks, Daiga Deksne, and Toms Miks. 2017. Neural machine translation for morphologically rich languages with improved subword units and synthetic data. In *International Conference on Text, Speech, and Dialogue*. Springer, pages 20–27.

Rico Sennrich, Orhan Firat, Kyunghyun Cho, Alexandra Birch, Barry Haddow, Julian Hitschler, Marcin Junczys-Dowmunt, Samuel Läubli, Antonio Valerio Miceli Barone, Jozef Mokry, et al. 2017. Nematus: a toolkit for neural machine translation. *EACL 2017* page 65.

Rico Sennrich, Barry Haddow, and Alexandra Birch. 2016a. Neural machine translation of rare words with subword units. In *Proceedings of the 54th Annual Meeting of the Association for Computational Linguistics (Volume 1: Long Papers)*. Association for Computational Linguistics, Berlin, Germany, pages 1715–1725. http://www.aclweb.org/anthology/P16-1162.

Rico Sennrich, Barry Haddow, and Alexandra Birch. 2016b. Neural Machine Translation of Rare Words with Subword Units. In *In Proceedings of the 54th Annual Meeting of the Association for Computational Linguistics (ACL 2016)*. Association for Computational Linguistics, Berlin, Germany, pages 1715–1725. http://www.research.ed.ac.uk/portal/files/25478429/subword_1.pdf http://arxiv.org/abs/1508.07909.

Zhaopeng Tu, Zhengdong Lu, Yang Liu, Xiaohua Liu, and Hang Li. 2016. Coverage-based neural machine translation. *CoRR* abs/1601.04811. http://arxiv.org/abs/1601.04811.

Andrejs Vasiļjevs, Raivis Skadiņš, and Jörg Tiedemann. 2012. LetsMT!: A Cloud-Based Platform for Do-It-Yourself Machine Translation. In Min Zhang, editor, *Proceedings of the ACL 2012 System Demonstrations*. Association for Computational Linguistics, Jeju Island, Korea, July, pages 43–48. http://www.aclweb.org/anthology/P12-3008.

Yonghui Wu, Mike Schuster, Zhifeng Chen, Quoc V. Le, Mohammad Norouzi, Wolfgang Macherey, Maxim Krikun, Yuan Cao, Qin Gao, Klaus Macherey, Jeff Klingner, Apurva Shah, Melvin Johnson, Xiaobing Liu, Lukasz Kaiser, Stephan Gouws, Yoshikiyo Kato, Taku Kudo, Hideto Kazawa, Keith Stevens, George Kurian, Nishant Patil, Wei Wang, Cliff Young, Jason Smith, Jason Riesa, Alex Rudnick, Oriol Vinyals, Greg Corrado, Macduff Hughes, and Jeffrey Dean. 2016. Google's neural machine translation system: Bridging the gap between human and machine translation. *CoRR* abs/1609.08144. http://arxiv.org/abs/1609.08144.

Matthew D Zeiler. 2012. Adadelta: an adaptive learning rate method. *arXiv preprint arXiv:1212.5701* .

The University of Edinburgh's Neural MT Systems for WMT17

Rico Sennrich, Alexandra Birch, Anna Currey, Ulrich Germann,
Barry Haddow, Kenneth Heafield, Antonio Valerio Miceli Barone and **Philip Williams**
University of Edinburgh, Scotland

Abstract

This paper describes the University of Edinburgh's submissions to the WMT17 shared news translation and biomedical translation tasks. We participated in 12 translation directions for news, translating between English and Czech, German, Latvian, Russian, Turkish and Chinese. For the biomedical task we submitted systems for English to Czech, German, Polish and Romanian. Our systems are neural machine translation systems trained with Nematus, an attentional encoder-decoder. We follow our setup from last year and build BPE-based models with parallel and back-translated monolingual training data. Novelties this year include the use of deep architectures, layer normalization, and more compact models due to weight tying and improvements in BPE segmentations. We perform extensive ablative experiments, reporting on the effectivenes of layer normalization, deep architectures, and different ensembling techniques.

1 Introduction

We participated in the WMT17 shared news translation task for 12 translation directions, translating between English and Czech, German, Latvian, Russian, Turkish and Chinese, and in the WMT17 shared biomedical translation task for English to Czech, German, Polish and Romanian.[1] We submitted neural machine translation systems trained with Nematus (Sennrich et al., 2017). Our setup is based on techniques described in last year's system description (Sennrich et al., 2016a), including the use of subword models (Sennrich et al.,

2016c), back-translated monolingual data, (Sennrich et al., 2016b), and re-ranking with right-to-left models.

This year, we experimented with deep network architectures, new ways to include monolingual data, and different ensembling variants. Other novelties include obtaining more compact models via better BPE segmentation and by weight tying (Press and Wolf, 2017), and speeding up model training with layer normalization (Ba et al., 2016) and adam (Kingma and Ba, 2015).

We perform extensive ablative experiments across language pairs to evaluate the effectiveness of each of these approaches. When comparing this year's baseline models to our best results, we show consistent increases in scores of 2.2–5 BLEU for our 12 news task language pairs. Among the constrained submissions to the news task, our submissions are ranked tied first for 11 out of the 12 translation directions in which we participated. For the biomedical task, we obtained the highest BLEU for all our submitted systems.

For the 6 language pairs for which we participated both in WMT16 and WMT17, we also show the scores of last year's systems. We observe solid improvements with increases of 1.5–3 BLEU for single models. Some of these improvements are due to differences in training data, preprocessing and hyperparameters, but most of the increase is due to layer normalization and deeper models. It is worth mentioning that our deeper models were trained on single GPUs, showing that the benefits of deeper models can be harnessed with limited hardware resources.

2 Novelties

Here we describe the main differences to last year's systems.

---

[1] We provide trained models and training commands at `http://data.statmt.org/wmt17_systems/`

Proceedings of the Conference on Machine Translation (WMT), Volume 2: Shared Task Papers, pages 389–399
Copenhagen, Denmark, September 7–11, 2017. ©2017 Association for Computational Linguistics

2.1 Subword Segmentation

Like last year, we use joint byte-pair encoding (BPE) for subword segmentation (Sennrich et al., 2016c) (except for ZH↔EN, where we train two separate BPE models). Joint BPE introduces undesirable edge cases in that it may produce subword units that have only been observed in one side of the parallel training corpus, and may thus be out-of-vocabulary at test time. To prevent this, we have modified our BPE script to only produce subword units at test time that have been observed in the source side of the training corpus.[2] Out-of-vocabulary subword units are recursively segmented into smaller units until this condition is met.

We use the same technique to disallow rare subword units (words occurring less than 50 times in the training corpus), both at test time and in the training corpus, both on the source-side and the target-side. This reduces the number of vocabulary symbols reserved for spurious, low-frequency subword units, and allows for more compact models. For example, for EN↔DE, using 90000 joint BPE operations, this filtering reduces the network vocabulary size for English from 80581 to 51092, with only a minor increase in sequence length (+0.2%). In preliminary experiments, this did not significantly affect BLEU, but slightly reduced the number of spurious OOVs produced – on EN→DE, unigram precision for OOVs increased from 0.34 to 0.36 on newstest2015 ($N = 1168$).

2.2 Layer Normalisation and Adam

This year, we use layer normalisation (Ba et al., 2016) for all systems. We apply layer normalisation to all recurrent and feed-forward layers, except for layers that are followed by a softmax. As SGD optimization algorithm, we use adam (Kingma and Ba, 2015) instead of adadelta (Zeiler, 2012), which we used last year.

In preliminary experiments, we found that both adam and layer normalisation lead to faster convergence, and result in better performance.

2.3 Deep Architectures

Miceli Barone et al. (2017) describe different deep recurrent architectures for neural machine translation. We use some of these architectures for our shared task submissions. We mainly use a *deep transition* architecture, but some runs use a

stacked architecture. Implementations of both of these architectures are available in Nematus.

For completeness, we here reproduce the description of the relevant deep architectures from (Miceli Barone et al., 2017). Note that some results reported by Miceli Barone et al. (2017) were obtained after the shared task submission, which explains why we did not choose the best-performing architecture, BiDeep.

2.3.1 Deep Transition Architecture

As in a baseline shallow Nematus system, the encoder is a bidirectional recurrent neural network. However, instead of being a simple GRU transition (Cho et al., 2014), the recurrence transition is itself composed of multiple GRU transitions with independently trainable parameters, all of which are executed sequentially for each input word.

Let L_s be the encoder recurrence depth, then for the i-th source word in the forward direction the forward source word state $\overrightarrow{h}_i \equiv \overrightarrow{h}_{i,L_s}$ is computed as

$$\overrightarrow{h}_{i,1} = \mathrm{GRU}_1\left(x_i, \overrightarrow{h}_{i-1,L_s}\right)$$
$$\overrightarrow{h}_{i,k} = \mathrm{GRU}_k\left(0, \overrightarrow{h}_{i,k-1}\right) \text{ for } 1 < k \leq L_s$$

where the input to the first GRU transition is the word embedding x_i, while the other GRU transitions have no external inputs. Note that each GRU transition is not internally recurrent, recurrence only occurs at the level of the whole multi-layer transition cell, as the previous word state $\overrightarrow{h}_{i-1,L_s}$ enters the computation in the first GRU transition. The reverse source word states are computed similarly and concatenated to the forward ones to form the bidirectional source word states $C \equiv \left\{\left[\overrightarrow{h}_{i,L_s} \overleftarrow{h}_{i,L_s}\right]\right\}$.

The deep transition decoder is obtained by extending the baseline decoder in a similar way. Note that the baseline decoder of Nematus has already a transition depth of two, with the first GRU transition receiving as input the embedding of the previous target word and the second GRU transition receiving as input a context vector computed by the attention mechanism. We extend this decoder architecture to an arbitrary transition depth L_t as follows

$$s_{j,1} = \mathrm{GRU}_1\left(y_{j-1}, s_{j-1,L_t}\right)$$
$$s_{j,2} = \mathrm{GRU}_2\left(\mathrm{ATT}(C, s_{j,1}), s_{j,1}\right)$$
$$s_{j,k} = \mathrm{GRU}_k\left(0, s_{j,k-1}\right) \text{ for } 2 < k \leq L_t$$

---

[2] `https://github.com/rsennrich/subword-nmt`

where y_{j-1} is the embedding of the previous target word and $\text{ATT}(C, s_{i,1})$ is the context vector computed by the attention mechanism. GRU transitions other than the first two do not have external inputs. The target word state vector $s_j \equiv s_{j,L_t}$ is then used by the feed-forward output network to predict the current target word.

In our experiments we use an encoder recurrence depth $L_s = 4$ and a decoder recurrence depth $L_t = 8$.

2.3.2 Stacked architecture

For our stacked architecture we use a variation of the one proposed by Zhou et al. (2016) with residual connections between the stack layers.

The forward encoder consists of a stack of GRU recurrent neural networks, the first one processing words in the forward direction, the second one in the backward direction, and so on, in alternating directions. For an encoder stack depth D_s, and a source sentence length N, the forward source word state $\overrightarrow{w}_i \equiv \overrightarrow{w}_{i,D_s}$ is computed as

$$\overrightarrow{w}_{i,1} = \overrightarrow{h}_{i,1} = \text{GRU}_1\left(x_i, \overrightarrow{h}_{i-1,1}\right)$$

$$\overrightarrow{h}_{i,2k} = \text{GRU}_{2k}\left(\overrightarrow{w}_{i,2k-1}, \overrightarrow{h}_{i+1,2k}\right)$$

$$\text{for } 1 < 2k \leq D_s$$

$$\overrightarrow{h}_{i,2k+1} = \text{GRU}_{2k+1}\left(\overrightarrow{w}_{i,2k}, \overrightarrow{h}_{i-1,2k+1}\right)$$

$$\text{for } 1 < 2k+1 \leq D_s$$

$$\overrightarrow{w}_{i,j} = \overrightarrow{h}_{i,j} + \overrightarrow{w}_{i,j-1}$$

$$\text{for } 1 < j \leq D_s$$

where we assume that source word indexes i start at 0 and $\overrightarrow{h}_{0,h}$ and $\overrightarrow{h}_{N+1,h}$ are zero vectors. Contrary to the deep transition encoder, each GRU transition here is a recurrent cell by itself. Note the residual connections: at each level above the first one, the word state of the previous level $\overrightarrow{w}_{i,j-1}$ is added to the recurrent state of the GRU cell $\overrightarrow{h}_{i,j}$ to compute the the word state for the current level $\overrightarrow{w}_{i,j}$. The backward encoder has the same structure, except that the first layer of the stack processes the words in the backward direction and the subsequent layers alternate directions. The forward and backward word states are then concatenated to form bidirectional word states $C \equiv \{[\overrightarrow{w}_{i,D_s}\overleftarrow{w}_{i,D_s}]\}$.

The stacked decoder has a similar structure, without any direction alternation. While the base GRU in the decoder is a conditional GRU with two

Table 1: BLEU scores for EN↔TR when adding copied monolingual data.

	TR→EN		EN→TR	
system	2016	2017	2016	2017
baseline	20.0	19.7	13.2	14.7
+copied	20.2	19.7	13.8	15.6

transitions, we use simple GRUs on higher layers. The "external" input to the higher layers is the concatenation of the state below and the context vector from the base RNN (Wu et al., 2016).

Where we have used the stacked architecture, we set both encoder and decoder depths to 4.

2.4 Monolingual Data

Like last year, we use back-translated monolingual data to augment our training data sets. We use two different training regimes to incorporate this monolingual data. In the *mixed* approach, we mix the synthetic and parallel data from the beginning of training, whilst in the *fine-tuned* approach we train a system using only the parallel data, then when this has converged we continue training using the parallel/synthetic mix. In both cases, the mixing proportions are set to 1:1, over-sampling from the smaller corpus where necessary. We find that the *mixed* approach is faster overall to train, although the fine-tuned approach has the advantage that the intermediate model could be adapted to a different domain using appropriate in-domain data.

For EN↔TR, we also experiment with a novel approach for incorporating target-side monolingual data. This consists of copying a monolingual corpus to convert it into a bitext where the source and target sides are identical. This copied bitext is then mixed with the parallel and back-translated data in order to train the NMT system; no distinction is made between the copied, back-translated, and parallel data during training. The mixing proportions of parallel, copied, and back-translated data we use in the EN↔TR experiments are 1:2:2, and we use the same monolingual data for both the copied and the back-translated corpora. More details can be found in Currey et al. (2017).

Table 1 shows the results of using the copied monolingual data while training. All systems are trained using parallel and back-translated data. Adding the copied monolingual data either yields modest improvements or does no damage, so we adopt this strategy for all EN↔TR experiments.

391

In preliminary experiments, we applied the same approach for EN↔LV (in a 1:1:1 ratio). Compared to our baseline EN↔LV systems, the addition of copied monolingual led to a slight decrease in translation quality (around 0.5 BLEU) on the devset and a slight improvement (0.1 BLEU) on the newstest2017 set.

2.5 Memory Efficiency

We reduce the memory footprint of our models by reducing the vocabulary sizes (Section 2.1), and by tying the weights of the target-side embedding and the transpose of the output weight matrix, which have the same dimensionality in our architecture (Press and Wolf, 2017). Using these techniques, we were able to train deep models on single GPUs (equipped with 8–12GB memory) without requiring model parallelism.

3 System Overview

3.1 Data and Preprocessing

All our systems are constrained and use data from the website of the shared task.[3]

For preprocessing, we use the Moses tokenizer with hyphen splitting ("-a" option), and perform truecasing with Moses scripts (Koehn et al., 2007). For subword segmentation, we use 90000 joint BPE operations, filtered according to section 2.1. The preprocessing pipeline was different for Russian and Chinese (because of non-Latin scripts). For EN→LV, we used the data that was prepared for the QT21 system combination (Peter et al., 2017). The variations are described in the language-specific sections below.

3.2 Baseline Systems

We train all systems with Nematus (Sennrich et al., 2017), which implements an attentional encoder-decoder with small modifications to the model in Bahdanau et al. (2015). We use word embedding sizes of 500 or 512, and hidden layer size 1024. We adapt the size of the network vocabulary to the size of the BPE vocabulary of the respective language.

We use adam (Kingma and Ba, 2015) as optimizer with a learning rate of 0.0001, and a batch sizes of 60 or 80 (depending on GPU memory). We filter out sentences with a length greater than 50 subwords. We tie the weights of the target-side

embedding and the transpose of the output weight matrix (Press and Wolf, 2017). We stop training when the validation cross-entropy fails to reach a new minimum for 10 consecutive save-points (saving every 10000 updates) and select the final model as the one having the best BLEU on validation.

For ensembling, we contrast two strategies:

- **checkpoint ensembles**, i.e. using the last N checkpoints of a single training run, which is a cheap way of obtaining an ensemble, and which we used in last year's submission.

- **independent ensembles**, i.e. training N models independently, potentially with different hyperparameters, which is more expensive, but likely to yield more diversity.

4 Experiments

4.1 Chinese ↔ English

For this language pair, we use all the available parallel data, except for 2000 sentence pairs from news-commentary which we hold back for validation. The English side is preprocessed using the same pipeline as for other language pairs, training a single BPE model with 59500 merge operations. For the Chinese side, we segment it using the Jieba[4] segmenter, except for Books 1–10 and data2011 which were already segmented. We then learn a BPE model on the segmented Chinese, also using 59500 merge operations.

For training the ZH→EN system we augment the parallel data with back-translation of the WMT news2016 monolingual corpus, translated using a shallow Nematus system built from the parallel data only. Since there was no monolingual news release for Chinese, we use LDC Chinese Gigaword (4th edition) to create synthetic data for EN→ZH, again using a shallow Nematus system for back-translation. In total we have approximately 24M parallel sentences, plus 20M sentences of synthetic data for ZH→EN and 8.5M for EN→ZH.

For ZH→EN we run 3 separate training runs in each direction (i.e. target left-right and target right-left). One run in each direction uses the stacked model architecture, and the fine-tuned training regime, whereas the other two use the deep transition architecture with a mixed training

---

regime. Initially we used a 2000 sentence portion of news-commentary for validation, but during the fine-tuning phase of the fine-tuned runs we switch to the development set released for the task (newsdev2017). For the mixed runs, we found that training converged and started to overfit the news-commentary validation set, so we restart with newsdev2017 as validation and ran to convergence. The final system is an ensemble of the best validation BLEU model from each of the three target left-right runs, rescored with the three target right-left runs, and reranked.

For EN→ZH we use the same training setup, with three runs for each target direction, and the same mix of models and training regimes. We use news-commentary as the validation set, except during the fine-tuning phase, where we use newsdev2017. The final system is an ensemble of four target left-right systems (the best validation BLEU model from each of the three runs, plus the same from the first run before fine-tuning), rescored with a similar ensemble of target right-left models and reranked. The final output is post-processed by removing all spaces (except when there was an ascii letter on either side) and then converting ascii full-stops and commas to their appropriate CJK unicode equivalents.

4.2 Czech ↔ English

To create the parallel corpus, we take the whole of CzEng 1.6pre (Bojar et al., 2016), plus the latest WMT releases of Europarl, News-commentary and CommonCrawl. We clean the corpus by running langid[5] over both sides and rejecting any parallel sentences whose English sides are not labelled as English, or whose Czech sides are not labelled as Czech, Slovak or Slovenian, by langid.[6] The rest of the preprocessing pipeline is the same as the general case (Section 3.1).

The parallel training data is augmented with synthetic parallel data created from the WMT news2016 monolingual corpus, back-translated using Edinburgh's WMT16 systems.[7] This provides about 20M synthetic parallel sentences for CS→EN and nearly 6M for EN→CS.

For CS→EN we use the stacked model architecture for all systems, training 4 target left-right

systems and 4 target right-left. The first of the left-right systems use the fine-tuned training regime, whereas the rest are all trained using the mixed regime. The final system is an ensemble of the left-right systems, with 12-best lists rescored with the right-left systems and reranked.

The same number of left-right and right-left models are used for EN→CS, with 2 of the left-right models using the fine-tuned training regime and the rest the mixed training regime. One of these fine-tuned models uses the stacked architecture whilst all the other EN→CS models use the deep transition architecture. Once again, the final system is an ensemble of the left-right models, rescored and reranked with the right-left systems.

4.3 German ↔ English

For the German-to-English and English-to-German system we use the pre-processed training data sets for the shared news translation task provided by the task organizers,[8] and supplement them with synthetic training data (Sennrich et al., 2016b) created by back-translating ca. 10 million sentences each from the 2016 monolingual news crawl data sets available through the web site for the shared task. For back-translation, we use Edinburgh's WMT16 systems.

Eight independent deep models are trained for each translation direction: four producing the translation left-to-right; four producing it right-to-left. The left-to-right models are ensembled to produce an n-best list of 50 translation hypotheses (beam size 50), which are then re-ranked by an ensemble of the four right-to-left models.

4.4 Latvian ↔ English

For EN→LV, we use the parallel data that was prepared for the QT21 system combination (Peter et al., 2017). The main differences from the standard preprocessing pipeline described in Section 3.1 are the use of a custom tokenizer with Latvian-specific handling of abbreviations, dates, numeric expressions, etc. and data filtering to remove noisy sentence pairs. For LV→EN, we apply the standard preprocessing pipeline after filtering the parallel corpus to remove the noisy sentence pairs identified during EN→LV preparation. In both cases, we reserve the first 2000 sentences of the (unfiltered) LETA news corpus for use as

---

[5] `https://github.com/saffsd/langid.py`

[6] Since langid does not use an estimate of prior language probability, this is a crude way of improving recall.

[7] The binary models are available at `http://data.statmt.org/rsennrich/wmt16_systems/`

[8] `http://data.statmt.org/wmt17/translation-task/preprocessed/de-en/`

a validation set during system development (with newsdev2017 used as a test set).

To produce LV→EN and EN→LV synthetic data we back-translate the WMT monolingual English and Latvian news 2016 corpora, respectively. We use phrase-based systems for back-translation, since these produced better translations (according to BLEU) than our preliminary parallel-only neural systems. The EN→LV synthetic data was subsequently filtered using the same method as for the original parallel data.

For the final system, we train eight independent models: four left-to-right and four right-to-left, from which we chose one model checkpoint from each based on the score on newsdev2017. The 50-best output from a left-to-right ensemble was rescored using the right-to-left models. When scoring translation candidates, we normalise the log probabilities by translation length, adjusted according to the method described in Wu et al. (2016). We optimise the length penalty (i.e., the alpha value in Wu et al. (2016)) on newsdev2017, setting it to 0.6 for EN→LV and 0.7 for LV→EN.

Our EN→LV models are also used in the QT21 system combination. For a description of the combined system and results, see Peter et al. (2017).

4.5 Russian ↔ English

We use the following resources from the WMT parallel data: News Commentary v12, Common Crawl, Yandex Corpus and UN Parallel Corpus V1.0. We do not use Wiki Headlines. To increase the consistency between English and Russian segmentation despite the differing alphabets, we transliterate the Russian vocabulary into Latin characters with ISO-9 to learn the joint BPE encoding, then transliterate the BPE merge operations back into Cyrillic. We apply the concatenation of the Cyrillic and Latin merge operations to the English and Russian side.

In order to incorporate in-domain parallel training data, we also use Edinburgh's WMT16 systems to backtranslate monolingual data. We translate the Russian (7.1M sentence) and English (20.4M sentences) News Crawl articles from 2016, which is combined with human-translated parallel data in a 1:1 mix. We used the deep transition architecture for our experiments.

For the final system, we train eight independent models: four left-to-right and four right-to-left, from which we choose one model checkpoint from

each based on the score on newsdev2017. The 50-best output from a left-to-right ensemble was rescored using the right-to-left models. There was a preprocessing error in the RU→EN backtranslation data and this is the reason that the submission result is worse than the corrected results published in this paper.

4.6 Turkish ↔ English

We use all of the available parallel training data to train our TR↔EN systems. This consists of about 200k parallel sentences after preprocessing. The preprocessing is as described in section 3.1, with the exception of the subword segmentation. For both directions, we do not include the modifications to subword segmentation described in section 2.1; i.e. we do not disallow rare subword units in the training corpus. This is done because of the relatively small amount of training data for this language pair.

In addition to the parallel training data, target-side monolingual data is incorporated into our systems. For both languages, we randomly select about 400k sentences from the WMT News Crawl 2016 corpus for this purpose. The same monolingual data is used as both back-translated and copied data (see section 2.4), and we use a mixed training regime for all experiments. We create the back-translated corpus using a shallow NMT system trained on the parallel training data.

We use the stacked model architecture for all systems. We train eight models for each translation direction: four left-to-right and four right-to-left. We ensemble the left-to-right models and take the 50 best translation hypotheses; these are reranked using an ensemble of the right-to-left models.

4.7 Biomedical Task Systems

4.7.1 Overview

The systems for EN→PL and EN→RO are created specifically for the WMT17 biomedical task using a similar model to the systems created for the news task. We use all the parallel data provided in the UFAL Corpus released for this task, first removing any parallel sentences where either side contains no ascii letters, then running the preprocessing pipeline as described in Section 3.1. For Romanian, we apply normalisation of "t-comma" and "s-comma" characters.

For EN→CS and EN→DE, our systems are

based on earlier work, so are created using different data sets. For EN→CS, our starting point is the Edinburgh WMT16 system, whereas for EN→DE we use all available data from OPUS[9] (gathered in May 2015) plus a small (10,000 sentence) corpus of translated Cochrane abstracts.

4.7.2 Synthetic Data

As in the news task, we seek to improve performance of the generic system by using in-domain training data, synthesising new data when there is insufficient naturally-occurring parallel data. We first tried fine-tuning with the EMEA corpus (drug information leaflets), but this did not give good results, probably because it is relatively small and not sufficiently close to the domain of interest.

Turning to back-translation as a source of parallel data for fine-tuning, we find that there is no good source of in-domain target language data. So, since the development and test sets are drawn from the websites of NHS 24 and Cochrane, we apply the following procedure in order to generate in-domain synthetic data:

1. Crawl the NHS 24 websites (`www.nhsinform`, `www.nhs24.com`, `www.scot.nhs.uk`) and the Cochrane websites (`www.cochrane.org` and `www.cochranelibrary.com`) to create English corpora of about 64k and 174k segments, respectively.

2. Machine translate each of these crawled corpora into the 4 target languages (Czech, German, Polish and Romanian). For all except for Polish, we used Edinburgh WMT16 system. For Polish we use a shallow Nematus system trained on OPUS.

3. Apply Moore Lewis selection (Moore and Lewis, 2010), using the translated Cochrane and NHS 24 crawls as in-domain data, to select from the monolingual CommonCrawl corpus (Buck et al., 2014) in each of the 4 languages. We restrict to sentences between 10 and 80 tokens long in CommonCrawl. We select corpora of between 4M and 10M sentences in each of 2 domains, by 4 languages.

4. Back-translate the selected corpora to English, again using either the Edinburgh WMT16 system for the language pair in question, or a Nematus system trained from OPUS.

An additional complication for Romanian is that the CommonCrawl corpus is particularly inconsistent in its use of diacritics (this is a problem we have observed to a lesser extent in other Romanian corpora). To fix this, we train a "diacritiser" for Romanian, which is actually an NMT system mapping Romanian text with diacritics stripped, to correct Romanian text. As training data for the diacritiser we use the Europarl, DGT and SETIMES2 corpora from OPUS. The diacritiser is applied to the CommonCrawl text selected above.

For the Romanian system we combine the corpora selected by both Cochrane and NHS 24, and train a single adapted system, for Polish we just use the corpus selected by the NHS 24 data, and for German and Czech we used the separate selected corpora to create adapted systems for each of Cochrane and NHS 24. We show the effect of this domain adaptation in Section 5.

4.7.3 System Details

For all language pairs, we use the HimL tuning sets for validation, and the HimL test sets as devtest sets.[10]

EN→CS We use shallow Nematus models, fine-tuned from Edinburgh's WMT16 system. There are separate fine-tuning runs for NHS 24 and Cochrane, each using 4M sentences randomly selected from CzEng, the synthetic corpus described above, and the EMEA corpus. The final system is an ensemble of the final 4 checkpoints.

EN→DE This is similar to EN→CS, except that the generic training corpus consists of about 44M sentence pairs from OPUS. For fine-tuning we use the synthetic corpus, EMEA, and 10M sentences randomly selected from the generic corpus. For Cochrane, we add 10k parallel sentences of abstracts from the Cochrane website.

EN→PL We use the UFAL corpus (39M sentence pairs) as the generic corpus, and the synthetic data and EMEA as the in-domain data (19M sentence pairs). The final system is an ensemble of four target left-right systems, reranked with two target left-right systems. One of each of the left-right and right-left systems uses the fine-tuned training regime and the stacked model architecture, whereas the others use the mixed regime and deep transition architecture. In the reranking, we apply a heuristic to remove hypotheses consisting

[9]`http://opus.lingfil.uu.se/`

[10]`http://www.himl.eu/test-sets`

Table 2: BLEU scores for translating news *into* English (WMT 2016 and 2017 test sets – WMT 2017 dev set is used where there was no 2016 test)

system	CS→EN		DE→EN		LV→EN		RU→EN		TR→EN		ZH→EN	
	2016	2017	2016	2017	2017d	2017	2016	2017	2016	2017	2017d	2017
WMT-16 single system	30.1	25.9	36.2	31.1	—	—	26.9	29.6	—	—	—	—
baseline	31.7	27.5	38.0	32.0	23.5	16.4	27.8	31.3	20.2	19.7	19.9	21.7
+layer normalization	32.6	28.2	38.6	32.1	24.4	17.0	28.8	32.3	19.5	18.8	20.8	22.5
+deep model	33.2	28.9	39.6	33.5	24.4	16.6	29.0	32.7	20.6	20.6	22.1	22.9
+checkpoint ensemble	33.8	29.4	39.7	33.8	25.7	17.7	29.5	33.3	20.6	21.0	22.5	23.6
+independent ensemble	34.6	30.3	40.7	34.4	27.5	18.5	29.8	33.6	22.1	21.6	23.4	25.1
+right-to-left reranking	35.6	31.1	41.0	35.1	28.0	19.0	30.5	34.6	22.9	22.3	24.0	25.7
WMT-17 submission[a]	—	30.9	—	35.1	—	19.0	—	30.8	—	20.1	—	25.7

[a] In some cases training did not converge until after the submission deadline. The contrastive/ablative results shown were obtained with the converged systems; this line reports the BLEU score for the system output submitted by the submission deadline.

Table 3: BLEU scores for translating news *out of* English (WMT 2016 and 2017 test sets – WMT 2017 dev set is used where there was no 2016 test)

system	EN→CS		EN→DE		EN→LV		EN→RU		EN→TR		EN→ZH	
	2016	2017	2016	2017	2017d	2017	2016	2017	2016	2017	2017d	2017
WMT16 single system	23.7	19.7	31.6	24.9	—	—	24.3	26.7	—	—	30.5	31.3
baseline	23.5	20.5	32.2	26.1	20.8	14.6	25.2	28.0	13.8	15.6	30.5	31.3
+layer normalization	23.3	20.5	32.5	26.1	21.6	14.9	25.8	28.7	14.0	15.7	31.6	32.3
+deep model	24.1	21.1	33.9	26.6	22.3	15.1	26.5	29.9	14.4	16.2	32.6	33.4
+checkpoint ensemble	24.7	22.0	33.9	27.5	23.4	16.1	27.3	31.0	15.0	16.7	32.8	33.5
+independent ensemble	26.4	22.8	35.1	28.3	24.7	16.7	28.2	31.6	15.5	17.6	35.4	35.8
+right-to-left reranking	26.7	22.8	36.2	28.3	25.0	16.9	–	–	16.1	18.1	35.7	36.3
WMT-17 submission[a]	–	22.8	–	28.3	–	16.9	–	29.8	–	16.5	–	36.3

[a] In some cases training did not converge until after the submission deadline. The contrastive/ablative results shown were obtained with the converged systems; this line reports the BLEU score for the system output submitted by the submission deadline.

of many repeated quotes, as well as a length normalisation trick (Wu et al., 2016). For the latter, we optimise alpha on the HimL test sets, setting it to 0.6 for NHS24 and 1.2 for Cochrane.

EN→RO The generic data for this system is the UFAL corpus (about 62M sentence pairs) with our in-domain set consisting of the synthetic data created as above and EMEA (about 11M sentence pairs). The final system is an ensemble of three deep target left-right systems, reranked with three target right-left systems. The first of the left-right runs used the stacked architecture, and the fine-tuned training regime, whereas the others used the deep transition architecture and mixed training. We again use the length normalisation trick, with alpha set to 0.7 for NHS 24.

5 Results

The main results for the news translation task are shown in Tables 2 and 3. We report case-sensitive, detokenized BLEU, using the NIST BLEU scorer.[11] For Chinese output, we split to characters using the script supplied for WMT17 before running BLEU.

For reporting single system scores, we arbitrarily choose the first system that we trained, out of the systems using the mixed training regime. In some cases we obtained improvements after the submission deadline, either due to longer training or preprocessing changes. In these cases the contrastive/ablative results show the best-performing systems, but we include the BLEU of the submitted system for completeness.

For the biomedical systems, we show results on the HimL test sets ("devtest") as well as the final released test sets in Table 4. The "+right-to-left reranking" system also introduces the tuned length normalisation.

For the language pairs for which we participated both in WMT16 and WMT17, we also show the scores of last year's systems. We observe solid improvements over these, with improvements of 1.5–3 BLEU for single models. Some of these improvements are visible in our baseline systems, which indicates that they are due to differences in training data, preprocessing and hyperparameters.

We have highlighted the performance improve-

---

[11] https://github.com/moses-smt/mosesdecoder/blob/master/scripts/generic/mteval-v13a.pl

Table 4: Contrastive experiments for biomedical task. Submitted system marked in bold.

| | EN→PL | | | | EN→RO | | | |
| | devtest | | test | | devtest | | test | |
system	Coch	NHS24	Coch	NHS24	Coch	NHS24	Coch	NHS24
baseline	19.8	24.3	26.2	18.2	35.4	29.5	36.8	23.0
+layer normalization	20.3	24.8	25.5	20.2	34.4	29.9	35.6	24.7
+deep model	20.6	24.5	25.9	20.2	36.7	30.0	37.8	27.3
+checkpoint ensemble	21.3	26.3	28.4	21.3	37.3	29.9	39.1	27.0
+independent ensemble	22.2	27.8	28.1	21.6	39.1	32.8	40.5	28.3
+right-to-left reranking	22.1	28.2	28.6	22.5	39.5	34.9	40.8	29.0
WMT17 submission[a]	–	–	**29.0**	**23.2**	–	–	**41.2**	**29.3**

[a] For the submitted systems we show the BLEU scores provided by the organisers, which used a different tokenisation to the other scores in the table. The outputs are all obtained using the +right-to-left reranking system

ments of two architecture variants, layer normalization and deep models, which lead to improvements in BLEU across most language pairs. We also show contrastive results for ensembling, comparing checkpoint ensembles to more expensive independent ensembles. We find that checkpoint ensembles generally yield performance improvements over a single model, but that independent ensembles are consistently more effective. Right-to-left reranking yielded an average improvement of 1 BLEU in our 2016 experiments; this year, improvements are smaller, and between 0 and 1 BLEU. We attribute this to the stronger performance of single models.

To show the effect of our domain adaptation for the biomedical task, we display results in Table 5 with and without the synthetic data. In this table, the "generic" system uses just the provided parallel data, with the stacked architecture. After training to convergence on this data, we then fine-tune the best model (selected by BLEU) using a 50-50 mixture of in-domain data (synthetic plus EMEA) and the generic parallel data. We report BLEU using the NIST scorer, for the best single model and an ensemble of the last four checkpoints, comparing the generic and the fine-tuned systems. Note that the system shown here is a different run to the single system shown in Table 4.

We can see that the adaptation has a positive effect on BLEU on all of the EN→PL test sets, however in EN→RO the effect is more mixed. We note that there are improvements on the corresponding single best models, but there seems to be a problem with the checkpoint ensemble for NHS 24. Looking more closely at the output we can see that when the BLEU score drops, the output is around 10% longer, due to the increased proportion of "nonsense" sentences. The checkpoint ensemble is perhaps being more affected by volatility

in training, as it selects models based on iteration count, rather than heldout performance.

An independent analysis of our EN→CS and EN→LV news systems' performance with regard to morphology can be found in Burlot and Yvon (2017).

6 Conclusions

This paper describes the University of Edinburgh's submissions to the WMT17 shared news translation and biomedical translation tasks. We perform extensive ablation experiments to report the effectiveness of different architecture choices and ensembling techniques. We report strong baselines that use both parallel and (back-translated) monolingual data, and already outperform our last year's submissions to WMT 2016. On top of these, we find that layer normalization and deep models lead to improvements across most language pairs. We also report performance gains from ensembling and re-ranking with right-to-left models, and find that gains have decreased slightly compared to last year's systems, despite using the more expensive strategy of ensembling independently trained models.

Among constrained submissions to the news task, our submissions are ranked tied 1st for 11 out of 12 translation directions in which we participated. EN→{CS, RU, LV, TR, ZH}, and {CS, DE, LV, RU, TR, ZH}→EN. In the biomedical task, we obtained the highest BLEU across all submissions, for all language/domain combinations that we submitted.

Acknowledgments

This project has received funding from the European Union's Horizon 2020 research and innovation programme under grant

Table 5: Effect of domain adaptation for biomedical task. We show the "generic" system (trained on parallel data only) and a "fine-tuned" system (the best generic system, fine-tuned on a mix of synthetic in-domain data, EMEA data and sampled parallel data). We show scores for both the single best system, and an ensemble of the last four checkpoints.

| | EN→PL | | | | EN→RO | | | |
| | devtest | | test | | devtest | | test | |
system	Coch	NHS24	Coch	NHS24	Coch	NHS24	Coch	NHS24
generic (single)	18.4	23.4	22.8	16.6	35.6	30.9	37.6	26.5
generic (ensemble 4)	19.9	24.3	23.6	19.9	37.5	33.3	39.2	27.9
fine-tuned (single)	20.7	26.5	27.2	19.5	36.7	30.1	38.6	27.0
fine-tuned (ensemble 4)	20.8	26.7	27.4	20.9	37.9	32.0	39.9	26.0

agreements 645452 (QT21), 644333 (TraMOOC), 644402 (HimL), 645487 (ModernMT), and 688139 (SUMMA). GPU time was supported by Microsoft's donation of Azure credits to The Alan Turing Institute. This work was supported by The Alan Turing Institute under the EPSRC grant EP/N510129/1.

References

Ba, Lei Jimmy, Ryan Kiros, and Geoffrey E. Hinton. 2016. "Layer Normalization." *CoRR*, abs/1607.06450.

Bahdanau, Dzmitry, Kyunghyun Cho, and Yoshua Bengio. 2015. "Neural Machine Translation by Jointly Learning to Align and Translate." *Proceedings of the International Conference on Learning Representations (ICLR)*.

Bojar, Ondřej, Ondřej Dušek, Tom Kocmi, Jindřich Libovický, Michal Novák, Martin Popel, Roman Sudarikov, and Dušan Variš. 2016. "CzEng 1.6: Enlarged Czech-English Parallel Corpus with Processing Tools Dockered." *Text, Speech and Dialogue: 19th International Conference, TSD 2016, Brno, Czech Republic, September 12-16, 2016, Proceedings*. In press.

Buck, Christian, Kenneth Heafield, and Bas van Ooyen. 2014. "N-gram Counts and Language Models from the Common Crawl." *Proceedings of the Language Resources and Evaluation Conference*. Reykjavik, Iceland.

Burlot, Franck and François Yvon. 2017. "Evaluating the morphological competence of Machine Translation Systems." *Proceedings of the Second Conference on Machine Translation (WMT'17)*. Copenhagen, Denmark.

Cho, Kyunghyun, Bart van Merrienboer, Caglar Gulcehre, Dzmitry Bahdanau, Fethi Bougares, Holger Schwenk, and Yoshua Bengio. 2014. "Learning Phrase Representations using RNN Encoder–Decoder for Statistical Machine Translation." *Proceedings of the 2014 Conference on Empirical Methods in Natural Language Processing (EMNLP)*, 1724–1734. Doha, Qatar.

Currey, Anna, Antonio Valerio Miceli Barone, and Kenneth Heafield. 2017. "Copied Monolingual Data Improves Low-Resource Neural Machine Translation." *Proceedings of the Second Conference on Machine Translation, Volume 1: Research Papers*. Copenhagen, Denmark.

Kingma, Diederik P. and Jimmy Ba. 2015. "Adam: A Method for Stochastic Optimization." *The International Conference on Learning Representations*. San Diego, California, USA.

Koehn, Philipp, Hieu Hoang, Alexandra Birch, Chris Callison-Burch, Marcello Federico, Nicola Bertoldi, Brooke Cowan, Wade Shen, Christine Moran, Richard Zens, Chris Dyer, Ondřej Bojar, Alexandra Constantin, and Evan Herbst. 2007. "Moses: Open Source Toolkit for Statistical Machine Translation." *Proceedings of the ACL-2007 Demo and Poster Sessions*, 177–180. Prague, Czech Republic.

Miceli Barone, Antonio Valerio, Jindřich Helcl, Rico Sennrich, Barry Haddow, and Alexandra Birch. 2017. "Deep Architectures for Neural Machine Translation." *Proceedings of the Second Conference on Machine Translation, Volume 1: Research Papers*. Copenhagen, Denmark.

Moore, Robert C. and William Lewis. 2010. "Intelligent Selection of Language Model Training Data." *Proceedings of the ACL 2010 Conference Short Papers*.

Peter, Jan-Thorsten, Hermann Ney, Ondřej Bojar, Ngoc-Quan Pham, Jan Niehues, Alex Waibel, Franck Burlot, François Yvon, Mārcis Pinnis, Valter Šics, Milos Stanojevic, Philip Williams, Frédéric Blain, and Lucia Specia. 2017. "The QT21 Combined Machine Translation System for English to Latvian." *Proceedings of the Second Conference on Machine Translation, Volume 2: Shared Task Papers*. Copenhagen, Denmark.

Press, Ofir and Lior Wolf. 2017. "Using the Output Embedding to Improve Language Models." *Proceedings of the 15th Conference of the European*

Chapter of the Association for Computational Linguistics (EACL). Valencia, Spain.

Sennrich, Rico, Orhan Firat, Kyunghyun Cho, Alexandra Birch, Barry Haddow, Julian Hitschler, Marcin Junczys-Dowmunt, Samuel Läubli, Antonio Valerio Miceli Barone, Jozef Mokry, and Maria Nadejde. 2017. "Nematus: a Toolkit for Neural Machine Translation." *Proceedings of the Demonstrations at the 15th Conference of the European Chapter of the Association for Computational Linguistics*. Valencia, Spain.

Sennrich, Rico, Barry Haddow, and Alexandra Birch. 2016a. "Edinburgh Neural Machine Translation Systems for WMT 16." *Proceedings of the First Conference on Machine Translation, Volume 2: Shared Task Papers*, 368–373. Berlin, Germany.

Sennrich, Rico, Barry Haddow, and Alexandra Birch. 2016b. "Improving Neural Machine Translation Models with Monolingual Data." *Proceedings of the 54th Annual Meeting of the Association for Computational Linguistics (Volume 1: Long Papers)*, 86–96. Berlin, Germany.

Sennrich, Rico, Barry Haddow, and Alexandra Birch. 2016c. "Neural Machine Translation of Rare Words with Subword Units." *Proceedings of the 54th Annual Meeting of the Association for Computational Linguistics (Volume 1: Long Papers)*, 1715–1725. Berlin, Germany.

Wu, Yonghui, Mike Schuster, Zhifeng Chen, Quoc V. Le, Mohammad Norouzi, Wolfgang Macherey, Maxim Krikun, Yuan Cao, Qin Gao, Klaus Macherey, Jeff Klingner, Apurva Shah, Melvin Johnson, Xiaobing Liu, Lukasz Kaiser, Stephan Gouws, Yoshikiyo Kato, Taku Kudo, Hideto Kazawa, Keith Stevens, George Kurian, Nishant Patil, Wei Wang, Cliff Young, Jason Smith, Jason Riesa, Alex Rudnick, Oriol Vinyals, Greg Corrado, Macduff Hughes, and Jeffrey Dean. 2016. "Google's Neural Machine Translation System: Bridging the Gap between Human and Machine Translation." *CoRR*, abs/1609.08144.

Zeiler, Matthew D. 2012. "ADADELTA: An Adaptive Learning Rate Method." *CoRR*, abs/1212.5701.

Zhou, Jie, Ying Cao, Xuguang Wang, Peng Li, and Wei Xu. 2016. "Deep Recurrent Models with Fast-Forward Connections for Neural Machine Translation." *Transactions of the Association for Computational Linguistics*, 4:371–383.

XMU Neural Machine Translation Systems for WMT 17

Zhixing Tan, Boli Wang, Jinming Hu, Yidong Chen and **Xiaodong Shi**

School of Information Science and Engineering, Xiamen University, Fujian, China

`{playinf, boliwang, todtom}@stu.xmu.edu.cn`
`{ydchen, mandel}@xmu.edu.cn`

Abstract

This paper describes the Neural Machine Translation systems of Xiamen University for the translation tasks of WMT 17. Our systems are based on the Encoder-Decoder framework with attention. We participated in three directions of shared news translation tasks: English→German and Chinese↔English. We experimented with deep architectures, different segmentation models, synthetic training data and target-bidirectional translation models. Experiments show that all methods can give substantial improvements.

1 Introduction

Neural Machine Translation (NMT) (Cho et al., 2014; Sutskever et al., 2014; Bahdanau et al., 2015) has achieved great success in recent years and obtained state-of-the-art results on various language pairs (Zhou et al., 2016; Sennrich et al., 2016a; Wu et al., 2016). This paper describes the NMT systems of Xiamen University (XMU) for the WMT 17. We participated in three directions of shared news translation tasks: English→German and Chinese↔English. We use two different NMTs for shared news translation tasks:

- MINiNMT: A deep NMT system (Zhou et al., 2016; Wu et al., 2016; Wang et al., 2017) with a simple architecture. The decoder is a stacked Long Short-Term Memory (LSTM) (Hochreiter and Schmidhuber, 1997) with 8 layers. The encoder has two variants. For English-German translation, we use an interleaved bidirectional encoder with 2 columns. Each column consists of 4 LSTMs. For Chinese-English translation, we use a stacked bidirectional encoder with 8 layers.

- DL4MT: Our reimplementation of dl4mt-tutorial[1] with minor changes. We also use a modified version of AmuNMT C++ decoder[2] for decoding. This system is used in the English-Chinese translation task.

We use both Byte Pair Encoding (BPE) (Sennrich et al., 2016c) and mixed word/character segmentation (Wu et al., 2016) to achieve open-vocabulary translation. Back-translation method (Sennrich et al., 2016b) is applied to make use of monolingual data. We also use target-bidiretional translation models to alleviate the label bias problem (Lafferty et al., 2001).

The remainder of this paper is organized as follows: Section 2 describes the architecture of MIN-INMT. Section 3 describes all experimental features used in WMT 17 shared translation tasks. Section 4 shows the results of our experiments. Section 5 shows the results of shared translation task. Finally, we conclude in section 6.

2 Model Description

Deep architectures have recently shown promising results on various language pairs (Zhou et al., 2016; Wu et al., 2016; Wang et al., 2017). We also experimented with a deep architecture as depicted in Figure 1. We use LSTM as the main recurrent unit and residual connections (He et al., 2016) to help training.

Given a source sentence $x = \{x_1, \ldots, x_S\}$ and a target sentence $y = \{y_1, \ldots, y_T\}$, the encoder maps the source sentence x into a sequence of annotation vectors $\{\mathbf{x}_i\}$. The decoder produces

---

[1] `https://github.com/nyu-dl/`
`dl4mt-tutorial`
[2] `https://github.com/emjotde/amunmt`

400

Proceedings of the Conference on Machine Translation (WMT), Volume 2: Shared Task Papers, pages 400–404
Copenhagen, Denmark, September 7–11, 2017. ©2017 Association for Computational Linguistics

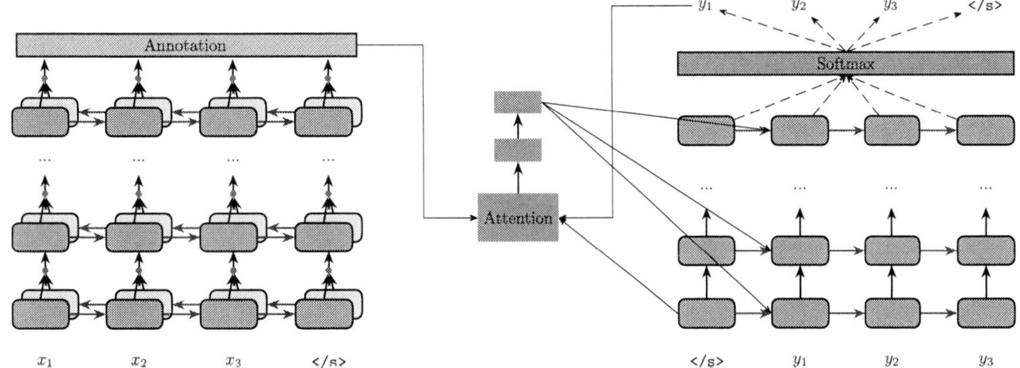

Figure 1: The architecture of our deep NMT system, which is inspired by Deep-Att (Zhou et al., 2016) and GNMT (Wu et al., 2016). Both the encoder and decoder adopt LSTM as its main recurrent unit. We also use residual connections (He et al., 2016) to help training, but here we omit it for clarity. We use black lines to denote input connections while use blue lines to denote recurrent connections.

translation y_t given the source annotation vectors $\{\mathbf{x}_i\}$ and target history $\boldsymbol{y}_{<t}$.

2.1 Encoder

2.1.1 Interleaved Bidirectional Encoder

The interleaved bidirectional encoder was introduced by (Zhou et al., 2016), which is also used in (Wang et al., 2017). Like (Zhou et al., 2016), our interleaved bidirectional encoder consists of two columns. In interleaved bidirectional encoder, the LSTMs in adjacent layers run in opposite directions:

$$\overrightarrow{\mathbf{x}}_t^i = \mathrm{LSTM}_i^f(\overrightarrow{\mathbf{x}}_t^{i-1}, \overrightarrow{\mathbf{s}}_{t+(-1)^i}^i) \qquad (1)$$

$$\overleftarrow{\mathbf{x}}_t^i = \mathrm{LSTM}_i^b(\overleftarrow{\mathbf{x}}_t^{i-1}, \overleftarrow{\mathbf{s}}_{t+(-1)^{i+1}}^i) \qquad (2)$$

Here $\mathbf{x}_t^0 \in \mathbb{R}^e$ is the word embedding of word x_t, $\mathbf{x}_t^i \in \mathbb{R}^h$ is the output of LSTM unit and $\mathbf{s}_t^i = (\mathbf{c}_t^i, \mathbf{m}_t^i)$ denotes the memory and hidden state of LSTM. We set both e and h to 512 in all our experiments. The annotation vectors $\mathbf{x}_i \in \mathbb{R}^{2h}$ are obtained by concatenating the final output $\overrightarrow{\mathbf{x}}^{L_{\mathrm{enc}}}$ and $\overleftarrow{\mathbf{x}}^{L_{\mathrm{enc}}}$ of two encoder columns. In our experiments, we set $L_{\mathrm{enc}} = 4$.

2.1.2 Stacked Bidirectional Encoder

To better exploit source representation, we adopt a stacked bidirectional encoder. As shown in Figure 1, all layers in the encoder are bidirectional. The

calculation is described as follows:

$$\overrightarrow{\mathbf{x}}^i = \mathrm{LSTM}_i^f(\mathbf{x}_t^{i-1}, \overrightarrow{\mathbf{s}}_{t-1}^i) \qquad (3)$$

$$\overleftarrow{\mathbf{x}}^i = \mathrm{LSTM}_i^b(\mathbf{x}_t^{i-1}, \overleftarrow{\mathbf{s}}_{t+1}^i) \qquad (4)$$

$$\mathbf{x}^i = [\overrightarrow{\mathbf{x}}^{iT}; \overleftarrow{\mathbf{x}}^{iT}]^T \qquad (5)$$

To reduce parameters, we reduce the dimension of hidden units from h to $h/2$ so that $\mathbf{x}^i \in \mathbb{R}^h$. The annotation vectors are taken from the output $\mathbf{x}^{L_{\mathrm{enc}}}$ of top LSTM layer. In our experiments, L_{enc} is set to 8.

2.2 Decoder

The decoder network is similar to GNMT (Wu et al., 2016). At each time-step t, let $\mathbf{y}_{t-1}^0 \in \mathbb{R}^e$ denotes the word embedding of y_{t-1} and $\mathbf{y}_{t-1}^1 \in \mathbb{R}^h$ denotes the output of bottom LSTM from previous time-step. The attention network calculates the context vector $\mathbf{a}_t$ as the weighted sum of source annotation vectors:

$$\mathbf{a}_t = \sum_{i=1}^{S} \alpha_{t,i} \cdot \mathbf{x}_i \qquad (6)$$

Different from GNMT (Wu et al., 2016), we use the concatenation of $\mathbf{y}_{t-1}^0$ and $\mathbf{y}_{t-1}^1$ as the query vector for attention network, as described follows:

$$\mathbf{h}_t = [\mathbf{y}_{t-1}^0{}^T; \mathbf{y}_{t-1}^1{}^T]^T \qquad (7)$$

$$e_{t,i} = \mathbf{v}_a^T \tanh(\mathbf{W}_a \mathbf{h}_t + \mathbf{U}_a \mathbf{x}_i) \qquad (8)$$

$$\alpha_{t,i} = \frac{\exp(e_{t,i})}{\sum_{j=1}^{S} \exp(e_{t,j})} \qquad (9)$$

This approach is also used in (Wang et al., 2017). The context vector $\mathbf{a}_t$ is then fed to all decoder LSTMs.

The probability of the next word y_t is simply modeled using a softmax layer on the output of top LSTM:

$$p(y_t|\boldsymbol{x}, \boldsymbol{y}_{<t}) = \text{softmax}(y_t, \mathbf{y}_t^{L_{\text{dec}}}) \qquad (10)$$

We set L_{dec} to 8 in all our experiments.

3 Experimental Features

3.1 Segmentation Approaches

To enable open-vocabulary, we use two approaches: BPE and mixed word/character segmentation.

In most of our experiments, we use BPE[3] (Sennrich et al., 2016c) with 50K operations. In our preliminary experiments, we found that BPE works better than UNK replacement techniques.

For English-Chinese translation task, we apply mixed word/character model (Wu et al., 2016) to Chinese sentences. We keep the most frequent 50K words and split other words into characters. Unlike (Wu et al., 2016), we do not add any prefixes or suffixes to the segmented Chinese characters. In post-processing step, we simply remove all the spaces.

3.2 Synthetic Training Data

We apply back-translation (Sennrich et al., 2016b) method to use monolingual data. For English-German and Chinese-English translation, we sample monolingual data from the NewsCrawl2016 corpora. For English-Chinese translation, we sample monolingual data from the XinhuaNet2011 corpus.

3.3 Target-bidirectional Translation

For Chinese-English translation, we also use a target-bidirectional model (Liu et al., 2016; Sennrich et al., 2016a) to rescore the hypotheses.

To train a target-bidirectional model, we reverse the target side of bilingual pairs from left-to-right (L2R) to right-to-left (R2L). We first output 50 candidates from the ensemble of 4 L2R models. Then we rescore candidates by interpolating L2R score and R2L score with uniform weights.

3.4 Training

For all our models, we adopt Adam (Kingma and Ba, 2015) ($\beta_1 = 0.9$, $\beta_2 = 0.999$ and $\epsilon = 1 \times 10^{-8}$) as the optimizer. The learning rate is set to 5×10^{-4}. We gradually halve the learning rate during the training process. As a common way to train RNNs, we clip the norm of gradient to a pre-defined value 5.0. The batch size is 128. We use dropout (Srivastava et al., 2014) to avoid overfitting with a keep probability of 0.8.

4 Results

4.1 Results on English-German Translation

System	Test (BLEU)
Baseline	25.7
+Synthetic	26.1
+Ensemble	**26.7**

Table 1: English-German translation results on newstest2017.

Table 1 show the results of English-German Translation. The baseline system is trained on preprocessed parallel data[4]. For synthetic data, we randomly sample 10M German sentences from NewsCrawl2016 and translate them back to English using an German-English model. However, we found random sampling do not work well. As a result, for Chinese-English translation, we select monolingual data according to development set. We first train one baseline model and continue to train 4 models on synthetic data with different shuffles. Next we ensemble 4 models and get the final results. We found this approach do not lead to substantial improvements.

4.2 Results on Chinese-English Translation

System	Test (BLEU)
Baseline	23.1
+Synthetic	23.7
+Ensemble	25.3
+R2L reranking	**26.0**

Table 2: Chinese-English translation results on newstest2017.

We use all training data (CWMT Corpus, UN Parallel Corpus and News Commentary) to train a

---

[3] https://github.com/rsennrich/subword-nmt

[4] http://data.statmt.org/wmt17/translation-task/preprocessed/de-en/

baseline system. The Chinese sentences are segmented using Stanford Segmenter[5]. For English sentences, we use the moses tokenizer[6]. We filter bad sentences according to the alignment score obtained by `fast-align` toolkit[7] and remove duplications in the training data. The preprocessed training data consists of 19M bilingual pairs. As noted earlier, the monolingual data is selected using newsdev2017. We first train 4 L2R models and one R2L model on training data, then we fine-tune our model on a mixture of 2.5M synthetic bilingual pairs and 2.5M bilingual pairs sampled from CWMT corpus. As shown in Table 2, we obtained +1.6 BLEU score when ensembling 4 models. When rescoring with one R2L model, we further gain +0.7 BLEU score.

4.3 Results on English-Chinese Translation

System	Test (BLEU)
Baseline	30.4
+Synthetic	34.3
+Ensemble	**35.8**

Table 3: English-Chinese translation results on newstest2017.

Table 3 show the results of English-Chinese Translation. We use our reimplementation of DL4MT to train English-Chinese models on CWMT and UN parallel corpus. The preprocessing steps, including word segmentation, tokenization, and sentence filtering, are almost the same as Section 4.2, except that we limited the vocabulary size to 50K and split all target side OOVs into characters. For synthetic parallel data, we use SRILM[8] to train a 5-gram KN language model on XinhuaNet2011 and select 2.5M sentences from XinhuaNet2011 according to their perplexities. We obtained +3.9 BLEU score when tuning the single best model on a mixture of 2.5M synthetic bilingual pairs and 2.5M bilingual pairs selected from CWMT parallel data randomly. We further gain +1.5 BLEU score when ensembling 4 models.

[5]https://nlp.stanford.edu/software/segmenter.shtml

[6]http://statmt.org/moses/

[7]https://github.com/clab/fast_align

[8]http://www.speech.sri.com/projects/srilm/

5 Shared Task Results

Table 4 shows the ranking of our submitted systems at the WMT17 shared news translation task. Our submissions are ranked (tied) first for 2 out of 3 translation directions in which we participated: EN↔ZH.

Direction	BLEU Rank	Human Rank
EN→DE	4	2-9 of 16
ZH→EN	2	1-3 of 16
EN→ZH	2	1-3 of 11

Table 4: Automatic (BLEU) and human ranking of our submitted systems at WMT17 shared news translation task.

6 Conclusion

We describe XMU's neural machine translation systems for the WMT 17 shared news translation tasks. All our models perform quite well on all tasks we participated. Experiments also show the effectiveness of all features we used.

Acknowledgments

This work was supported by the Natural Science Foundation of China (Grant No. 61573294, 61303082, 61672440), the Ph.D. Programs Foundation of Ministry of Education of China (Grant No. 20130121110040), the Foundation of the State Language Commission of China (Grant No. WT135-10) and the Natural Science Foundation of Fujian Province (Grant No. 2016J05161).

References

Dzmitry Bahdanau, KyungHyun Cho, and Yoshua Bengio. 2015. Neural machine translation by jointly learning to align and translate. In *Proceedings of ICLR*.

Kyunghyun Cho, Bart van Merrienboer, Caglar Gulcehre, Dzmitry Bahdanau, Fethi Bougares, Holger Schwenk, and Yoshua Bengio. 2014. Learning phrase representations using rnn encoder–decoder for statistical machine translation. In *Proceedings of the 2014 Conference on Empirical Methods in Natural Language Processing (EMNLP)*.

Kaiming He, Xiangyu Zhang, Shaoqing Ren, and Jian Sun. 2016. Deep residual learning for image recognition. In *Proceedings of the IEEE Conference on Computer Vision and Pattern Recognition*, pages 770–778.

Sepp Hochreiter and Jurgen Schmidhuber. 1997. Long short-term memory. *Neural Computation*, pages 1735–1780.

Diederik Kingma and Jimmy Ba. 2015. Adam: A method for stochastic optimization. In *Proceedings of ICLR*.

John Lafferty, Andrew McCallum, Fernando Pereira, et al. 2001. Conditional random fields: Probabilistic models for segmenting and labeling sequence data. In *Proceedings of the eighteenth international conference on machine learning, ICML*, volume 1, pages 282–289.

Lemao Liu, Masao Utiyama, Andrew Finch, and Eiichiro Sumita. 2016. Agreement on target-bidirectional neural machine translation. In *Proceedings of NAACL-HLT*, pages 411–416.

Rico Sennrich, Barry Haddow, and Alexandra Birch. 2016a. Edinburgh neural machine translation systems for wmt 16. *arXiv preprint arXiv:1606.02891*.

Rico Sennrich, Barry Haddow, and Alexandra Birch. 2016b. Improving neural machine translation models with monolingual data. In *Proceddings of ACL*.

Rico Sennrich, Barry Haddow, and Alexandra Birch. 2016c. Neural machine translation of rare words with subword units. In *Proceedings of ACL*.

Nitish Srivastava, Geoffrey Hinton, Alex Krizhevsky, Ilya Sutskever, and Ruslan Salakhutdinov. 2014. Dropout: A simple way to prevent neural networks from overfitting. *The Journal of Machine Learning Research*, 15(1):1929–1958.

Ilya Sutskever, Oriol Vinyals, and Quoc V Le. 2014. Sequence to sequence learning with neural networks. In *Advances in neural information processing systems*, pages 3104–3112.

Mingxuan Wang, Zhengdong Lu, Jie Zhou, and Qun Liu. 2017. Deep Neural Machine Translation with Linear Associative Unit. *arXiv preprint arXiv:1705.00861*.

Yonghui Wu, Mike Schuster, Zhifeng Chen, Quoc V Le, Mohammad Norouzi, Wolfgang Macherey, Maxim Krikun, Yuan Cao, Qin Gao, Klaus Macherey, et al. 2016. Google's neural machine translation system: Bridging the gap between human and machine translation. *arXiv preprint arXiv:1609.08144*.

Jie Zhou, Ying Cao, Xuguang Wang, Peng Li, and Wei Xu. 2016. Deep recurrent models with fast-forward connections for neural machine translation. *Transactions of the Association for Computational Linguistics*, 4:371–383.

The JAIST Machine Translation Systems for WMT 17

Hai-Long Trieu and **Trung-Tin Pham** and **Le-Minh Nguyen**
School of Information Science
Japan Advanced Institute of Science and Technology
{trieulh, tinpt, nguyenml}@jaist.ac.jp

Abstract

We describe the JAIST phrase-based machine translation systems that participated in the news translation shared task of the WMT17. In this work, we participated in the Turkish-English translation, in which only a small amount of bilingual training data is available, so that it is an example of the low-resource setting in machine translation. In order to solve the problem, we focus on two strategies: building a bilingual corpus from comparable data and exploiting existing parallel data based on phrase pivot translation. In order to utilize the strategies to enhance machine translation on the low-resource setting most effectively, we introduce a system combining the extracted corpus, the pivot translation, and the direct training data. Experimental results showed that our combined systems significantly improved the baseline models, which were trained on the small bilingual data.

1 Introduction

We participated in the WMT 17 news translation shared task for the Turkish-English language pair. The amount of bilingual training data for this language pair is small, which means that this machine translation task poses the problem of a low-resource setting. The problem causes a bottleneck for current data-driven machine translation methods including phrase-based and neural-based machine translation because there are few large bilingual corpora for most language pairs in the world (Irvine, 2013; Wang et al., 2016).

In our systems, we focus on two strategies to enhance machine translation for the low-resource setting: building a bilingual corpus from compa-

rable data, and exploiting existing parallel corpora based on the phrase pivot translation (Wu and Wang, 2007; Cohn and Lapata, 2007; Utiyama and Isahara, 2007). First, we built a bilingual corpus for Turkish-English based on parallel titles of Wikipedia articles. The parallel titles were extracted from Wikipedia articles' titles and interlanguage link records. Bilingual articles were collected based on the title pairs. Then, bilingual sentences were extracted from the article pairs using the Microsoft sentence aligner (Moore, 2002). Second, we exploited the phrase pivot translation method using six pivot languages to bridge the translation between Turkish and English. Finally, the two resources of the extracted corpus and the pivot translation were utilized with the direct bilingual training data in a combined system. Our combined systems achieved a significant improvement compared with the baseline model, which was trained on the direct bilingual data. The code and datasets used in our systems can be found at the repository.[1]

2 Methods

We describe approaches used in our systems. The Turkish-English bilingual data in this shared task embodies only 207k parallel sentences, which is an instance of machine translation task in low-resource setting. Our goal is to enhance the phrase-based machine translation on the low-resource setting by using two approaches: building a Turkish-English bilingual corpus from comparable data, and exploiting existing parallel corpora based on the phrase pivot translation method. The two approaches were then combined to enhance machine translation on the low-resource setting most effectively.

---

[1] https://github.com/nguyenlab/WMT17-JAIST

Proceedings of the Conference on Machine Translation (WMT), Volume 2: Shared Task Papers, pages 405–409
Copenhagen, Denmark, September 7–11, 2017. ©2017 Association for Computational Linguistics

2.1 Building A Turkish-English Bilingual Corpus from Comparable Data

We built a bilingual corpus for Turkish-English from comparable data to improve machine translation on the low-resource setting. We used Wikipedia, a free accessible resource containing articles in the same domain and topics in different languages, to build the corpus. In order to build a bilingual corpus from Wikipedia, we based on parallel titles of Wikipedia articles. Then, pairs of articles were crawled based on the parallel titles. Finally, sentences in the article pairs were aligned to extract parallel sentences. We describe these steps in more detail in this section.

Extracting Parallel Titles The content of Wikipedia can be obtained from their database dumps.[2] In order to extract parallel titles of Wikipedia articles, we used two resources for each language from the Wikipedia database dumps: the articles' titles and IDs in a particular language (ending with *-page.sql.gz*) and the interlanguage link records (file ends with *-langlinks.sql.gz*).

Collecting Parallel Articles After parallel titles of Wikipedia articles were extracted, we collected the article pairs using the parallel titles. We implemented a Java crawler for collecting the articles. The collected data was then preprocessed including sentence split and word tokenization using the Moses scripts.[3]

Sentence Alignment For each article pair, bilingual sentences were aligned using the Microsoft bilingual sentence aligner (Moore, 2002), one of the most powerful sentence alignment algorithms as shown in (Singh and Husain, 2005). After the sentence alignment step, we obtained a Turkish-English bilingual corpus with 48k parallel sentences, which is presented in Table 1.

	Turkish	English
Input articles	188,235	192,512
Input sentences	2,030,931	3,023,324
Bilingual articles	184,154	184,154
Aligned articles	22,100	22,100
Aligned sentences	48,554	48,554

Table 1: Building a bilingual corpus of Turkish-English from Wikipedia.

From the results, for 184k input bilingual articles, a small ratio of 22k articles were aligned. One of the main reasons is the characteristic of Wikipedia bilingual articles, in which each article in a language of a bilingual article pair is created separately by different authors with different styles of writing, background knowledge, etc. This leads to various challenges for aligning parallel sentences such as: the small portion of overlap in the article pair's content, the unbalance of sentence length, the unbalance of numbers of sentences in the articles. Further investigations on the Wikipedia data as well as different aligners and methods are needed to improve the performance on this task.

2.2 Phrase Pivot Translation

In order to enhance machine translation for the low-resource setting, we exploited existing bilingual corpora using the phrase pivot translation method (Cohn and Lapata, 2007; Utiyama and Isahara, 2007; Wu and Wang, 2007). In the phrase pivot translation method, source-pivot and pivot-target bilingual corpora are used to train phrase tables. Then, the source and target phrases are connected via common pivot phrases.

Given a source phrase s and a target phrase t of the source-pivot phrase table T_{SP} and the pivot-target phrase table T_{PT}, the phrase translation probability is estimated via common pivot phrases p based on the following feature function.

$$\phi(t|s) = \sum_{p \in (T_{SP}) \cap (T_{PT})} \phi(p|s)\phi(t|p) \quad (1)$$

Previous research showed the effectiveness of this method when source-target bilingual corpora are unavailable or in a limited amount.

In our systems, we used bilingual data sets of the SETIMES2 corpus (Tiedemann, 2009)[4], the same resource of the Turkish-English training data in this shared task, for training phrase pivot translation. We used six pivot languages to bridge the translation between Turkish and English: Bulgarian, Bosnian, Greek, Macedonian, Romanian, and Albanian. The bilingual corpora for the pivot translation are presented in Table 2.

For phrase pivot translation, we implemented the triangulation method of (Wu and Wang, 2007) using Java. One of the issues of the triangulation

---

No.	Pivot	tr-pvt	pvt-en	tr-en	en-tr
1	bg	206k	213k	393k	490k
2	bs	133k	138k	321k	374k
3	el	206k	226k	390k	472k
4	mk	202k	207k	387k	469k
5	ro	205k	212k	382k	457k
6	sq	206k	227k	379k	446k

Table 2: Bilingual corpora for Turkish-English pivot translation (the number of parallel sentences) and the number of pivoted phrase pairs in Turkish-English (**tr-en**) and English-Turkish (**en-tr**); **Pivot** languages: **bg** (Bulgarian), **bs** (Bosnian), **el** (Greek), **mk** (Macedonian), **ro** (Romanian), **sq** (Albanian); **tr-pvt (pvt-en)**: the bilingual corpus of Turkish and the pivot language (pivot-English)

method is that the number of pivoted phrase pairs is exploded (El Kholy et al., 2013). Therefore, we filtered the pivoted phrase tables by using a *n-best* technique in which for a set of *n* best target phrases was extracted for each source phrase (*n was set to 10 in our experiments*).

2.3 Combining Additional Resources

We exploited two resources to enhance machine translation for the low-resource setting: a bilingual corpus extracted from Wikipedia, and bilingual corpora of Turkish and English paired with the six pivot languages. Our goal now is to utilize the resource most effectively. We introduce a system incorporating the following components. First, we trained a phrase table based on the Wikipedia bilingual corpus, called *align* component. Second, using the phrase pivot translation, we obtained pivoted phrase table, called the *pivot* components. Additionally, we trained a phrase table using the Turkish-English training data, called *baseline* component. The components were combined to generate a phrase table for decoding. We adapted the linear interpolation (Sennrich, 2012) for combining phrase tables. Equation 2 describes the combination of the components.

$$p(t|s) = \lambda_d p_d(t|s) + \lambda_a p_a(t|s)$$
$$+ \lambda_{p_1} p_1(t|s) + \lambda_{p_2} p_2(t|s) + \lambda_{p_3} p_3(t|s)$$
$$+ \lambda_{p_4} p_4(t|s) + \lambda_{p_5} p_5(t|s) + \lambda_{p_6} p_6(t|s)$$
$$(2)$$

Where $p_d(t|s)$, $p_a(t|s)$ stand for the translation probability of the *baseline* and the *align* components, respectively. $p_i(t|s), i = 1..6$ stand for the translation probability of the six pivoted phrase tables.

The interpolation parameters λ_d, λ_a, and $\lambda_{p_i}(i = 1..6)$ in which $\lambda_d + \lambda_a + \lambda_{p_i} = 1$ were tuned based on the interpolation method (Sennrich, 2012) using the development set (*news-dev2016*) provided by the shared task.

3 Experiments

We describe the data sets, settings, and results of our systems in this section. We discuss the experimental results on three settings: building a bilingual corpus, using phrase pivot translation, and using the system combining the two components.

3.1 Training Data

We used the training, development, and test sets provided by the WMT 17 shared task. The Turkish-English training data contain 207k parallel sentences. For the development set, we used the *dev2016*. We evaluated our systems on the *tst2016*, and submitted the translation output for the *tst2017* test set.

For monolingual datasets to train language models, we used the monolingual datasets provided by the shared task: 40M sentences of Turkish and 40M sentences of English.

3.2 Baseline Systems

We conducted baseline experiments for phrase-based machine translation using the Moses toolkit (Koehn et al., 2007). The word alignment was trained using GIZA++ (Och and Ney, 2003) with the configuration *grow-diag-final-and*. 5-gram language models of Turkish and English were trained using KenLM (Heafield, 2011). For tuning, we used the batch MIRA (Cherry and Foster, 2012). The system's outputs were evaluated using the NIST-BLEU on the online system.[5]

3.3 Experimental Results

The results of the JAIST systems are presented in Table 3 and Table 4. We discuss the results for the three different settings.

3.3.1 Building A Bilingual Corpus

Although the aligned Wikipedia corpus contains a small number of parallel sentences (48k) compared with the direct training data (207k), the phrase-based models trained on the Wikipedia

---

[5]http://matrix.statmt.org/

Model	newsdev2016	newstest2016	newstest2017
baseline	12.28	12.3	12.0
align	7.67	8.1	7.9
pivot (bs)	7.47	11.0	7.6
baseline-align	13.35	12.9 (+0.6)	12.7 (+0.7)
baseline-pivot(bs)	12.39	13.1 (+0.8)	12.4 (+0.4)
baseline-pivot(bs)-align	13.02	13.0 (+0.7)	12.7 (+0.4)
baseline-pivot(6)-align	14.04	**13.7 (+1.4)**	**13.1 (+1.1)**

Table 3: Experimental results on the Turkish-English (BLEU); **baseline (align)**: the system trained on the baseline (the aligned Wikipedia) bilingual corpus; **pivot (bs), pivot (6)**: the phrase pivot translation system using one pivot language (bs: Bosnian) or using all of the 6 pivot languages; **baseline-pivot(6)-align**: the combined system of the baseline, align, and 6 pivot components.

Model	newsdev2016	newstest2016	newstest2017
baseline	8.66	9.3	9.9
align	5.96	6.3	6.6
pivot (bs)	6.01	8.2	6.3
baseline-align	8.87	9.3	10.0 (+0.1)
baseline-pivot	9.01	9.6 (+0.3)	9.7
baseline-pivot(bs)-align	8.98	9.6 (+0.3)	9.9
baseline-pivot(6)-align	10.11	**9.7 (+0.4)**	**10.4 (+0.5)**

Table 4: Experimental results on the English-Turkish translation (BLEU).

corpus showed a quite promising result: 7.9 BLEU point on the Turkish-English and 6.6 BLEU point on the English-Turkish. When the baseline model was combined with the align model, we achieved a significant improvement: +0.6 and +0.7 BLEU points on the Turkish-English of the *newstest2016* and *newstest2017*, respectively. The results showed the effectiveness of the extracted corpus to enhance machine translation on the low-resource setting. Nevertheless, the task becomes more challenging on the English-Turkish. Although the Wikipedia corpus showed the contribution on the Turkish-English translation, there was no improvement on the English-Turkish translation when we achieved only +0.1 BLEU point on the *newstest2017*.

3.3.2 Phrase Pivot Translation

For the phrase pivot translation models, using one pivot language (bs: Bosnian) showed the competitive performance on the newstest2016 of the Turkish-English: 11.0 BLEU point vs. 12.3 BLEU point (baseline), or 8.2 BLEU point vs. 9.3 BLEU point (baseline) on the English-Turkish.

When the pivot model (using one pivot language of Bosnian) was combine with the baseline model, we achieved the improvement on both translation directions: +0.8 BLEU point on the Turkish-English, and +0.3 BLEU point on the English-Turkish of the *newstest2016*. For the newstest2017, we achived the improvement only on

the Turkish-English (+0.4 BLEU point).

The results confirmed the contribution of the phrase pivot translation. Nevertheless, there was no improvement on some cases. Therefore, we seek to the combination of all components: the baseline, align, and pivot components (from one pivot language to six pivot languages).

3.3.3 Combined Systems

We would like to exploit the components most effectively to improve machine translation on the low-resource setting. The baseline, align, and pivot components were combined in a model. When using one pivot language (Bosnian), we achieved the improvement in most cases: +0.7 and +0.4 BLEU points on the *newstest2016* and *newstest2017* of the Turkish-English. For the English-Turkish, we achieved the improvement of +0.3 BLEU point on the *newstest2016*; however, there was no improvement on the *newstest2017*, in which the pivot model did not showed the contribution.

Interestingly, using six pivot languages showed the significant improvement in all settings. For the Turkish-English, we achieved +1.4 and +1.1 BLEU points on the *newstest2016* and *newstest2017*, respectively. For the English-Turkish, the combined system showed +0.4 BLEU point (newstest2016) and +0.5 BLEU point (newstest2017).

We submitted our systems using the settings

that combine the baseline, align, and six pivot languages in the phrase pivot translation.

4 Conclusion

We describe our phrase-based machine translation systems for Turkish-English participated in the WMT 17 news translation shared task. In this work, our goal is to enhance machine translation for the low-resource setting for Turkish-English, in which a only small training bilingual data is available. Two approaches were exploited in our systems: building a bilingual corpus from Wikipedia, and utilizing existing bilingual corpora using the phrase pivot translation method. In order to exploit the extracted data most effectively, we introduce a combined system of the aligned corpus, the pivot data, and the direct training data. We achieved a significant improvement on the *newstest2016* and *newstest2017*. The results showed the effectiveness of the extracted corpus and the pivot translation in improving machine translation on the low-resource setting. We released the Wikipedia corpus, which can be used to improve machine translation on Turkish-English in future work.

Acknowledgement

This work was supported by JSPS KAKENHI Grant number JP15K16048 and the VNU project "Exploiting Very Large Monolingual Corpora for Statistical Machine Translation" (code QG.12.49).

References

Colin Cherry and George Foster. 2012. Batch tuning strategies for statistical machine translation. In *Proceedings of HLT/NAACL*. Association for Computational Linguistics, pages 427–436.

Trevor Cohn and Mirella Lapata. 2007. Machine translation by triangulation: making effective use of multi-parallel corpora. In *Proceedings of ACL*. Association for Computational Linguistics, pages 728–735.

Ahmed El Kholy, Nizar Habash, Gregor Leusch, Evgeny Matusov, and Hassan Sawaf. 2013. Language independent connectivity strength features for phrase pivot statistical machine translation. In *Proceedings of ACL*. Association for Computational Linguistics, pages 412–418.

Kenneth Heafield. 2011. Kenlm: Faster and smaller language model queries. In *Proceedings of the Sixth Workshop on Statistical Machine Translation*. Association for Computational Linguistics, pages 187–197.

Ann Irvine. 2013. Statistical machine translation in low resource settings. In *Proceedings of HLT/NAACL*. Association for Computational Linguistics, pages 54–61.

Philipp Koehn, Hieu Hoang, Alexandra Birch, Chris Callison-Burch, Marcello Federico, Nicola Bertoldi, Brooke Cowan, Wade Shen, Christine Moran, Richard Zens, et al. 2007. Moses: Open source toolkit for statistical machine translation. In *Proceedings of ACL*. Association for Computational Linguistics, pages 177–180.

Robert C Moore. 2002. *Fast and accurate sentence alignment of bilingual corpora*. Springer.

Franz Josef Och and Hermann Ney. 2003. A systematic comparison of various statistical alignment models. *Computational Linguistics* 29(1):19–51.

Rico Sennrich. 2012. Perplexity minimization for translation model domain adaptation in statistical machine translation. In *Proceedings of EAMT*. pages 539–549.

Anil Kumar Singh and Samar Husain. 2005. Comparison, selection and use of sentence alignment algorithms for new language pairs. In *Proceedings of the ACL Workshop on Building and using Parallel texts*. Association for Computational Linguistics, pages 99–106.

Jörg Tiedemann. 2009. News from OPUS - A collection of multilingual parallel corpora with tools and interfaces. In N. Nicolov, K. Bontcheva, G. Angelova, and R. Mitkov, editors, *Recent Advances in Natural Language Processing*, John Benjamins, Amsterdam/Philadelphia, Borovets, Bulgaria, volume V, pages 237–248.

Masao Utiyama and Hitoshi Isahara. 2007. A comparison of pivot methods for phrase-based statistical machine translation. In *Proceedings of HLT/NAACL*. Association for Computational Linguistics, pages 484–491.

Pidong Wang, Preslav Nakov, and Hwee Tou Ng. 2016. Source language adaptation approaches for resource-poor machine translation. *Computational Linguistics* .

Hua Wu and Haifeng Wang. 2007. Pivot language approach for phrase-based statistical machine translation. In *Proceedings of ACL*. Association for Computational Linguistics, pages 856–863.

Sogou Neural Machine Translation Systems for WMT17

Yuguang Wang[*], **Xiang Li**[*†], **Shanbo Cheng**[*], **Liyang Jiang**[*], **Jiajun Yang**[*]
Wei Chen[*], **Lin Shi**[*], **Yanfeng Wang**[*], **Hongtao Yang**[*]
[*]Voice Interaction Technology Center, Sogou Inc., Beijing, China
[†]Key Laboratory of Intelligent Information Processing,
Institute of Computing Technology, Chinese Academy of Sciences
{wangyuguang, chengshanbo, chenweibj8871}@sogou-inc.com, lixiang@ict.ac.cn

Abstract

We describe the *Sogou* neural machine translation systems for the WMT 2017 Chinese↔English news translation tasks. Our systems are based on a multi-layer encoder-decoder architecture with attention mechanism. The best translation is obtained with ensemble and reranking techniques. We also propose an approach to improve the named entity translation problem. Our Chinese→English system achieved the highest cased BLEU among all 20 submitted systems, and our English→Chinese system ranked the third out of 16 submitted systems.[1]

1 Introduction

End-to-end neural machine translation (NMT) has recently been introduced as a promising paradigm with the potential to address many shortcomings of traditional statistical machine translation (SMT) systems, and has obtained state-of-the-art performance for several language pairs (Cho et al., 2014; Sutskever et al., 2014; Bahdanau et al., 2015; Sennrich et al., 2016a; Wu et al., 2016; Zhou et al., 2016). In this paper, we describe the *Sogou* NMT systems submissions for the WMT 2017 Chinese→English and English→Chinese translation tasks.

Overview of the systems can be described as follows: we implement a multi-layer attention-based encoder-decoder integrated with recent promising techniques in NMT, including that we use subword units based on byte pair encoding (BPE) rather than words as modelling units (Sennrich et al., 2016b) and layer normalization (Ba et al., 2016) to isolated layers. And we improve the performance using ensemble based four systems of the same network

trained with different random seeds of parameter initialization.

In addition, we improve the performance further by reranking the *n*-best translation lists with some effective features, including the target-bidirectional models, target-to-source models, and *n*-gram language models. And we use another NMT model to translate the recognized person names for the Chinese→English task, in order to improve the performance of unknown named entity translation.

Our Chinese→English system achieved the highest cased BLEU among all 20 submitted systems, and our English→Chinese system ranked the third out of 16 submitted systems.

2 Neural Machine Translation

Our NMT model follows the common attentional encoder-decoder networks (Bahdanau et al., 2015). We implement a deep multi-layer Long Short Term Memory (LSTM) recurrent neural network for both the encoder and decoder. In our setup, the encoder has one bi-directional LSTM layer followed by two uni-directional LSTM layers. The decoder has three uni-directional LSTM layers. Similar to the conditional GRU used in DL4MT (Firat and Cho, 2016), we use conditional LSTM (cLSTM) for the top layer of decoder instead of standard LSTM. The encoder takes the model's input sequence as input and encodes it into a fixed-size context vector. We only use the bottom layer output of the decoder to obtain attentional context vector, which is used to predict next target word at the top layer of decoder combining with the previous hidden state and the previously generated words.

We utilize layer normalization (Ba et al., 2016) to isolated LSTM layers, a method that adaptively learns to scale and shift the incoming activations of a neuron on a layer-by-layer basis at each time step. Layer normalization can stabilize the dynamics of hidden layers in the network and accelerate the convergence speed of deep neural networks.

---

[1] Automatic rankings are from http://matrix.statmt.org.

410

Proceedings of the Conference on Machine Translation (WMT), Volume 2: Shared Task Papers, pages 410–415
Copenhagen, Denmark, September 7–11, 2017. ©2017 Association for Computational Linguistics

All the weight parameters are initialized uniformly in [-0.02, 0.02], except for the square matrix weight parameters are initialized by orthogonal initialization (Henaff et al., 2016). We use dropout for the models as suggested by (Zaremba et al., 2015). We clip the gradient norm to 1.0 (Pascanu et al., 2013). Our main NMT decoder with a beam size of 10 is used in all experiments. We validate the model every 10,000 mini-batches via BLEU on the newsdev2017 data. We use a mini-batch size of 128, a hidden layer size 1024, a word embedding layer size of 512, filter out sentence pairs whose length exceeds 40 words, and reshuffle the training data between epochs as we proceed.

We use Adam (Kingma and Ma, 2014) to train the model with a learning rate 0.0001. We use the multi-GPUs training framework via asynchronous SGD (Dean et al., 2012) and data parallelism (copies of the full model on each GPU). We train the model on a host server with eight NVIDIA Tesla M40 GPUs. We train four systems of the same network with different random seeds of parameters initialization, perform early stop for each system, and use a widely used, simple ensemble method (prediction averaging) based on the best model of each system in order to improve the performance.

3 Experiment Techniques

This section describes several techniques integrated in our NMT system.

3.1 Reranking

In order to get better translation result, we explore different NMT variant models and n-gram language models as features in the reranking framework.

Target right-to-left NMT Model: The quality of the prefixes of translation hypotheses is much higher than that of the suffixes (Liu et al., 2016). In order to alleviate this unbalanced output problem, a variant right-to-left (R2L) NMT mode is trained on the training data, but the target data is inversed. We inverse the n-best lists generated by the main NMT model and calculate the likelihood which represents the conditional probabilities of reversed translations given the source sentences.

Target-to-source NMT Model: Moreover, the translation may be inadequate and repeat or miss out some words (Tu et al., 2016). In order to cope with the inadequateness, we use the target-to-source (T2S) reconstruction model trained with the swapped source and target training data. Because we participated in both the Chinese→English and English→Chinese tasks, the T2S model of Chinese→English is just the main NMT model of English→Chinese, and vice-versa.

N-gram language models: There exists a large amount of monolingual data for both Chinese and English. We train n-gram language models on each corpus and select the top k-best n-gram language models as reranking features based on perplexity (PPL) calculated on the newsdev2017 data. It is noted that we use character-level language models for English→Chinese task and word-level language models for Chinese→English. For English, the language model is trained on the "News Crawl: articles from 2016" provided by WMT 2016 has the lowest PPL, which is even much lower than the language model trained on English side of the training data.

We first generate an n-best lists with an ensemble model for a source sentence. Then we calculate the likelihood score with T2S and R2L models. We also use n-gram language models to compute PPL for the translation candidates. We treat each model score as an individual feature. We use k-batched MIRA (Cherry et al. 2012) to tune the weights for all the features. In order to get more diverse n-best lists, we also try to increase the beam size to further improve reranking.

3.2 NMT with Tagging Model

Translating rare words is hard for a conventional NMT model with a fixed relatively small vocabulary so that a single *unk* symbol is used to represent the large number of out-of-vocabulary (OOV) words.

Our proposed tagging model is similar to the placeholder mechanism (Crego et al., 2016), which aims at alleviating the rare words problem. When using tagging model to translate a sentence, we first use the pre-defined tags to replace the OOV words in the source sentence, then translate the source sentence with tags using the NMT model, and recover the tags in translation based on the attention weights and a bilingual translation dictionary finally.

The most significant difference between our tagging model and placeholder mechanism (Crego et al., 2016) is that we don't force beam search to generate tags, but only try to find exactly the same tag in the source side (if exists) when a tag is generated in the translation, and choose the one with the highest alignment probability based on attention weights. Given this information, we can find the source side to which a target tag is aligned, and obtain the translation of source tag via a bilingual dictionary.

Zhang et al., (2016) incorporated bilingual translation dictionary by using the dictionary to generate training data, where the bilingual dictionary is an external resource. While our work is of higher efficiency and the bilingual dictionary is trained from our training data alone.

In this paper, we use our CRF-based named entity recognize (NER) tagger to obtain the tags (placeholders). We also build the bilingual translation dictionary from scratch based on the training data.

Bilingual Translation Dictionary: The bilingual dictionary is generated by the following steps:

- Data preparation. We label both source-side and target-side words in the training data with our NER tagger and combine multi-words labelled with named-entities tags to a single word with specific marks so that we can recover the word to the original form.

- Word alignment. The word alignment is generated by using GIZA++ (Och and Ney, 2003) given the above data.

- Translation pairs extraction. The translation pairs are extracted according to the word alignment. We only extract those pairs whose both source and target side words are person name tags (labeled by our NER tagger), and represent the tag as a *$TERM* symbol in this paper.

The bilingual translation dictionary can not only be used as a lookup dictionary for tagging model, but also as the training data for the neural person name translation model in Sec. 3.3.

3.3 Named Entity Translation

Due to most of rare words in news data are person named entities, we propose an approach to translate the person named entities with an external character-based encoder-decoder model trained on the extracted parallel person names from the training data for the Chinese→English task individually, in order to improve the performance of rare words translation.

For the person named entity translation model, the size of the Chinese vocabulary is 3000 characters, the size of the English vocabulary is 30 characters, the size of hidden layers is 512, the size of embedding is 256, the size of mini-batch is 128, the sentence pairs whose length exceeds 30 characters are filtered out, and the training data is re-shuffled between epochs as we proceed. We validate the model every 1000 mini-batches via BLEU on the sample validation data (100 Chinese-English person names pairs). We only train the model on a single GPU and perform early stop.

Because many person names can be translated by the model, we only focus on the remaining person names aligned to the *unk* symbols in the target side according to the attention weights. Given an input sentence, we first recognize the person named entities with our NER tagger, then generate BPE segmentation for the plain sentence, and mark each subword unit which is part of a person named entity with a single name-aware symbol finally. During decoding, the text with BPE marker is first translated by our NMT model. We mark the source tokens to which each target *unk* symbol is most aligned with the method of Luong et al. (2015). If the marked source token is also a part of person named, the original person name is recovered via the BPE marker. Then we replace the recovered person names with a single *$TERM* symbol. Finally, we translate the text with *$TERM* symbols and BPE marker again, and replace the target *$TERM* symbols with the translation of original person names generated by our neural person named entity translation model.

Chinese Person Name	Translation
史婧琳 (Shǐ jìng lín)	Shi Jinglin
安东・瓦伊诺 (Ān dōng・wǎ yī nuò)	Anton Vaino
法土拉・葛兰 (Fǎ tǔ lā・gě lán)	Fethullah Gulen

Table 1: Examples of neural person named entity translation.

Our proposed method is similar to Li et al. (2016), but we only use the extracted parallel person names from training data instead of Wikipedia data. Although our method brings no significant improvement on BLEU, we find that it is useful for human evaluation especially when the source data contains person names. The translation of person names in Table 1 seems like the transliteration of Chinese person names.

In addition, we also replace all the number named entities greater than 5000 of source sentences with a single number-aware symbol. Then

the number-aware symbols of translation are recovered to their original number named entities
based the attention weights. Finally, the recovered
number named entities are translated with human
rules. By this mean, nearly most of number named
entities can be translated correctly.

4 Experiments Settings and Results

4.1 Data Processing

The training data for the two translation tasks consists of 12 million sentences pairs, including all the
CWMT 2017 training data and 3 million sentences
selected from the UN corpus by calculating the
PPL with an English language model trained on the
News Crawl: articles from 2016. We used the official newsdev2017 as validation set for both Chi-
nese→English and English→Chinese systems.

We first segmented the Chinese sentences with
our Chinese word segmentation tool and tokenized
English sentences with the scripts provided in Moses[2] (Koehn et al., 2007). Then we used BPE segmentation to process both source and target data.
300K subword symbols are used for the source side
and 150K subword symbols are used for target side.
For both Chinese→English and English→Chinese
systems, the size of the source vocabulary and target vocabulary is 300K and 150K respectively. We
created about 250K translation pairs for the bilingual dictionary described in Sec. 3.2.

4.2 Chinese→English Systems

Table 2 shows the Chinese→English translation results on validation set. We reported cased BLEU
scores calculated with Moses' *multi-bleu.pl*[3] script.
The baseline model is a conventional single-layer
encoder-decoder model where we used a bi-LSTM
layer for encoder and a cLSTM layer for decoder.
Other settings are the same as our deep NMT
model.

Our deep encoder-decoder model improves the
baseline by 0.8 BLEU. In order to get more diverse
models and better ensemble results, we trained four
deep models independently with different random
initializations. Then we selected the best model
based on validation set from four systems for

model ensemble. The ensemble result gives an additional improvement of 1.1 BLEU over the best
single deep NMT system.

To evaluate the influence of person named entity
translation on the performance of our NMT systems, we made an experiment on the newsdev2017
data. As a result, a little improvement by 0.1 BLEU
is achieved. One reason for such little improvement
is that the performance is calculated on word level,
the translation of person name is regarded wrong
even when there is only one letter difference. On
the other hand, the amount of training data with
$TERM symbols is insufficient, so that the model
is incapable to learn as good as the plain data.

System	BLEU
baseline	19.4
+deep model	20.2
+ensemble (4 deep models)	21.3
+named entity translation	21.4
+reranking (1 R2L, 4 T2S)	21.7
+reranking (beam size 100)	22.4
+reranking (10 language models)	**22.9**

Table 2: Chinese→English BLEU results on
development set. Submitted system is the last
system.

Additionally, to recover the case information, a
SMT-based recaser is trained on the English corpus
with Moses toolkit[4]. And we also use a few simple
uppercase rules, for example capitalizing the word
at the beginning of a sentence.

According to the experiments in (Liu et al.,
2016), a left-right/right-left reranking may also
help increase diversity. Hereafter, we used one T2L
model and four T2S models for reranking, resulting
in a 0.3 BLEU improvement. Due to the limitation
of beam search for NMT, we observed that most of
n-best lists are very similar. By increasing the beam
size from 10 to 100, we achieved another 0.7 BLEU
improvement. We also evaluated the influence of *n*-
gram language models for reranking. We trained
several 5-gram language models and selected top
ten best language models based on their PPL on
validation set. We achieved another improvement
by 0.5 BLEU. The last best system is our final submitted system.

---

[2] https://github.com/moses-smt/mosesdecoder/blob/mas-
ter/scripts/tokenizer/tokenizer.perl
[3] https://github.com/moses-smt/mosesdecoder/blob/mas-
ter/scripts/generic/multi-bleu.perl

[4] https://github.com/moses-smt/mosesdecoder/blob/mas-
ter/scripts/recaser/train-recaser.perl

4.3 English→Chinese Systems

Table 3 shows the English→Chinese translation results on validation set. All results are evaluated by character-level BLEU. Similar to the Chinese→English systems, a shallow model and four deep models are trained independently. The deep model brings a 0.4 BLEU improvement over the shallow model baseline. The ensemble system improves by 1.1 BLEU over single best deep model. The NE replacement improves by 0.1 BLEU. We also trained one R2L model and four T2S models for reranking. These variant models improve the system by 0.8 BLEU. We observed a 0.2 BLEU improvement by increasing the beam size from 10 to 100. Finally, we trained five Chinese language models for reranking, including three word-level 5-gram language models and two character-level 5-gram language models, for re-scoring the n-best lists, resulting in a 0.5 BLEU improvement. The last system is our final submitted English→Chinese system.

For English→Chinese translation task, if a target *unk* symbol cannot be recovered by named entity tagging and translation model, we directly replace the target *unk* symbol with its aligned English word according to the attention weights.

System	BLEU
baseline	31.6
+deep model	32.0
+ensemble (4 deep model)	33.1
+name entity translation	33.2
+reranking (1 R2L, 4 T2S)	34.0
+reranking (beam size 100)	34.2
+reranking (5 language models)	**34.7**

Table 3: English→Chinese translation BLEU results on development set. Submitted system is the last system.

5 Conclusion

We present the *Sogou* NMT systems for WMT 2017 Chinese↔English news translation tasks. For both translation directions, our final systems are improved by 3.1~3.5 BLEU over baseline systems by using the following techniques: 1) a deep NMT model; 2) ensemble of diverse deep NMT models; 3) reranking n-best lists with NMT variant models and n-gram language models; 4) named entity tagging and translation model. Our submitted Chinese→English system achieved the highest cased BLEU among all 20 submitted systems, and our English→Chinese system ranked third out of 16 submitted system.

References

Cho, Kyunghyun, Van Merrienboer, Bart, Gulcehre, Caglar, Bahdanau, Dzmitry, Bougares, Fethi, Schwenk, Holger, and Bengio, Yoshua. 2014. Learning Phrase Representations using RNN Encoder-Decoder for Statistical Machine Translation. In Proceedings of EMNLP, 2014.

Colin Cherry and Gorge Foster. Batch Tuning Strategies for Statistical Machine Translation, In Proceedings of NAACL, 2012.

Diederik Kingma and Jimmy Ba. Adam: A method for stochastic optimization. arXiv URL: https://arxiv.org/abs/1412.6980.

Dzmitry Bahdanau, Kyunghyun Cho, and Yoshua Bengio. Neural Machine Translation by Jointly Learning to Align and Translate. In Proceedings of ICLR, 2015.

Koehn, P., Och, F. J., and Marcu, D. Statistical phrase-based translation. In Proceedings of NAACL, 2003.

Ilya Sutskever, Oriol Vinyals, and Quoc V. Le. Sequence to sequence learning with neural networks. In Proceedings of NIPS, 2014.

Lei Jimmy Ba, Ryan Kiros, and Geoffrey E. Hinton. 2016. Layer normalization. CoRR 2016, arXiv URL: http://arxiv.org/abs/1607.06450.

Lemao Liu, Masao Utiyama, Andrew Finch, and Eiichiro Sumita. 2016. Agreement on Target-bidirectional Neural Machine Translation. In Proceedings of NAACL, 2016.

Jeffrey Dean, Greg S. Corrado, Rajat Monga, Kai Chen, Matthieu Devin, Quoc V. Le, Mark Z. Mao, MarcAurelio Ranzato, Andrew Senior, Paul Tucker, Ke Yang, Andrew Y. Ng. 2012. Large scale distributed deep networks. In Proceedings of NIPS, 2012.

Jiajun Zhang and Chengqing Zong. Bridging neural machine translation and bilingual dictionaries. URL: https://arxiv.org/abs/1610.07272.

Josep Crego, Jungi Kim, Guillaume Klein, Anabel Rebollo, Kathy Yang, Jean Senellart, Egor Akha-nov, Patrice Brunelle, Aurelien Coquard, Yongchao Deng, et al. 2016. Systran's pure neural machine translation systems. arXiv URL: https://arxiv.org/abs/1610.05540.

Mikael Henaff, Arthur Szlam, and Yann LeCun. Orthogonal RNNs and long-memory tasks. In Proceedings of ICML, 2016.

Orhan Firat and Kyunghyun Cho. Conditional gated recurrent unit with attention mechanism.

"github.com/nyu-dl/dl4mt-tutorial/blob/master/docs/cgru.pdf".

Razvan Pascanu, Tomas Mikolov, and Yoshua Bengio. On the difficulty of training recurrent neural networks. In Proceedings of ICML, 2013.

Rico Sennrich, Barry Haddow, and Alexandra Birch. 2016a. Edinburgh Neural Machine Translation Systems for WMT 16. In Proceedings of the First Conference on Machine Translation, Berlin, Germany. Association for Computational Linguistics.

Rico Sennrich, Barry Haddow, and Alexandra Birch. 2016b. Neural machine translation of rare words with subword units. In Proceedings of ACL, 2016.

Thang Luong, Ilya Sutskever, Quoc Le, Oriol Vinyals, and Wojciech Zaremba. Addressing the rare word problem in neural machine translation. In Proceedings of ACL, 2015.

Wojciech Zaremba, Ilya Sutskever, and Oriol Vinyals. 2015. Recurrent neural network regularization. In Proceedings of ICLR, 2015.

Xiaoqing Li, Jiajun Zhang and Chengqing Zong. 2016. Neural Name Translation Improves Neural Machine Translation. arXiv URL: https://arxiv.org/abs/1607.01856.

Yonghui Wu, Mike Schuster, Zhifeng Chen, Quoc V. Le, Mohammad Norouzi, Wolfgang Macherey, Maxim Krikun, Yuan Cao, Qin Gao, Klaus Macherey, Jeff Klingner, Apurva Shah, Melvin Johnson, Xiaobing Liu, Łukasz Kaiser, Stephan Gouws, Yoshikiyo Kato, Taku Kudo, Hideto Kazawa, Keith Stevens, George Kurian, Nishant Patil, Wei Wang, Cliff Young, Jason Smith, Jason Riesa, Alex Rudnick, Oriol Vinyals, Greg Corrado, Macduff Hughes, and Jeffrey Dean. 2016. Google's neural machine translation system: Bridging the gap between human and machine translation. arXiv URL: https://arxiv.org/abs/1609.08144.

Zhaopeng Tu, Yang Liu, Lifeng Shang, Xiaohua Liu, and Hang Li. 2016a. Neural machine translation with reconstruction. arXiv URL: https://arxiv.org/abs/1611.01874.

Zhou, Jie, Cao, Ying, Wang, Xuguang, Li, Peng, and Xu, Wei. 2016. Deep Recurrent Models with Fast-Forward Connections for Neural Machine Translation. arXiv URL: https://arxiv.org/abs/1606.04199.

Philipp Koehn, Hieu Hoang, Alexandra Birch, Chris Callison-Burch, Marcello Federico, Nicola Bertoldi, Brooke Cowan, Wade Shen, Christine Moran, Richard Zens, Chris Dyer, Ond'rej Bojar, Alexandra Constantin, and Evan Herbst. 2007. Moses: Open Source Toolkit for Statistical Machine Translation. In Proceedings of the ACL-2007 Demo and Poster Sessions, pages 177–180.

PJIIT's systems for WMT 2017 Conference

Krzysztof Wołk

Multimedia Department

Polish-Japanese Academy of Information
Technology, Koszykowa 86,
kwolk@pja.edu.pl

Krzysztof Marasek

Multimedia Department

Polish-Japanese Academy of Information
Technology, Koszykowa 86,
kmarasek@pja.edu.pl

Abstract

In this paper, we attempt to improve Statistical Machine Translation (SMT) systems between Czech, Latvian and English in WNT'17 News translation task. We also participated in the Biomedical task and produces translation engines from English into Polish, Czech, German, Spanish, French, Hungarian, Romanian and Swedish. To accomplish this, we performed translation model training, created adaptations of training settings for each language pair, and implemented BPE (subword units) for our SMT systems. Innovative tools and data adaptation techniques were employed. Only the official parallel text corpora and monolingual models for the WMT 2017 evaluation campaign were used to train language models, and to develop, tune, and test the system. We explored the use of domain adaptation techniques, symmetrized word alignment models, the unsupervised transliteration models and the KenLM language modeling tool. To evaluate the effects of different preparations on translation results, we conducted experiments and used the BLEU, NIST and TER metrics. Our results indicate that our approach produced a positive impact on SMT quality.

1 Introduction

Statistical Machine Translation (SMT) must deal with a number of problems to achieve high quality. These problems include the need to align parallel texts in language pairs and cleaning harvested parallel corpora to remove errors. This is especially true for real-world corpora developed from text harvested from the vast data available on the Internet. Out-Of-Vocabulary (OOV) words must also be handled, as they are inevitable in real-world texts (Wolk and Marasek, 2014a). The lack of enough parallel corpora for some less popular languages is another significant challenge for SMT. Since the approach is statistical in nature, a significant amount of quality language pair data is needed to improve translation accuracy. In addition, very general translation systems that work in a general text domain have accuracy problems in specific domains. SMT systems are more accurate on corpora from a domain that is not too wide. This exacerbates the data problem, calling for the enhancement of parallel corpora for particular text domains (Wolk and Marasek, 2014b). This paper describes SMT research that addresses these problems, particularly domain adaptation within the limits of permissible data for the WMT 2017 campaign. To accomplish this, we performed model training, created adaptations of training settings and data for each language pair. Innovative tools and data adaptation techniques were employed. We explored the use of domain adaptation techniques, symmetrized word alignment models, the unsupervised transliteration models, and the KenLM language modeling tool (Heafield, 2011). To evaluate the effects of different preparations on translation results, we conducted experiments and evaluated the results using standard SMT metrics (Koehn et al., 2007). The languages translated during this research were: Czech, Latvian and English in WNT'17 News translation task. We also participated in the Biomedical task and produces translation engines from English into Polish, Czech, German, Spanish, French, Hungarian, Romanian and Swedish. This paper is structured as follows: Section 2 explains the data preparation. Section 3 presents experimental

Proceedings of the Conference on Machine Translation (WMT), Volume 2: Shared Task Papers, pages 416–421
Copenhagen, Denmark, September 7–11, 2017. ©2017 Association for Computational Linguistics

setup and the results. Lastly in Section 4 we summarize the work.

2 Data preparation

This section describes our techniques for data preparation for our SMT systems. We give particular emphasis to preparation of the language data and models and our in-domain data adaptation approach.

2.1 Data pre-processing

The texts were encoded in UTF-8 format, separated into sentences, and provided in pairs of languages. Pre-processing, both automatic and manual, of this training data was required. There were a variety of errors found in this data, including spelling errors, unusual nesting of text, text duplication, and parallel text issues. For example in Polish-English corpora approximately 3% of the text in the training set contained spelling errors, and approximately 2% of the text had insertion errors. A tool described in (Wolk and Marasek, 2014b) was used to correct these errors automatically. Previous studies have found that such cleaning increases the BLEU score for SMT by a factor of 1.5–2 (Wolk and Marasek, 2014a). SyMGiza++, a tool that supports the creation of symmetric word alignment models, was used to extract parallel phrases from the data. This tool enables alignment models that support many-to-one and one-to-many alignments in both directions between two language pairs. SyMGiza++ is also designed to leverage the power of multiple processors through advanced threading management, making it very fast. Its alignment process uses four different models during training to progressively refine alignment results. This approach has yielded impressive results in Junczys-Dowmunt and Szał (2012). Out-Of-Vocabulary (OOV) words pose another significant challenge to SMT systems. If not addressed, unknown words appear, untranslated, in the output, lowering the translation quality. To address OOV words, we used implemented in the Moses toolkit Unsupervised Transliteration Model (UTM). UTM is an unsupervised, language-independent approach for learning OOV words (Moses statistical machine translation, 2015). We used the post-decoding transliteration option with this tool. UTM uses a transliteration phrase translation table to evaluate and score multiple possible transliterations (Durrani et al., 2014).

The KenLM tool was applied to the language model to train and binarize it. This library enables highly efficient queries to language models, saving both memory and computation time. The lexical values of phrases are used to condition the reordering probabilities of phrases. We used KenLM with lexical reordering set to hier-msdbidirectional-fe. This setting uses a hierarchical model that considers three orientation types based on both source and target phrases: monotone (M), swap (S), and discontinuous (D). Probabilities of possible phrase orders are examined by the bidirectional reordering model (Costa Jussa and Fonollosa, 2010; Moses statistical machine translation, 2013).

2.2 Domain adaptation

The news data sets have a rather a wide domain, but rather not as wide-ranging in topic as the variety of WMT permissible texts. The same goes to the biomedical task. Since SMT systems work best in a defined domain, this presents another considerable challenge. If not addressed, this would lead to lower translation accuracy. The quality of domain adaptation depends heavily on training data used to optimize the language and translation models in an SMT system. Selection and extraction of domain-specific training data from a large, general corpus addresses this issue (Axelrod, He and Gao, 2011). This process uses a parallel, general domain corpus and a general domain monolingual corpus in the target language. The result is a pseudo indomain sub-corpus. As described by Wang et al. in (2014), there are generally three processing stages in data selection for domain adaptation. First, sentence pairs from the parallel, general domain corpus are scored for relevance to the target domain. Second, resampling is performed to select the best scoring sentence pairs to retain in the pseudo in-domain sub-corpus. Those two steps can also be applied to the general domain monolingual corpus to select sentences for use in a language model. After collecting a substantial amount of sentence pairs (for the translation model) or sentences (for the language model), those models are trained on the sub-corpus that represents the target domain (Wang et al., 2014). Similarity measurement is required to select sentences for the pseudo in-domain sub-corpus. There are three state-of-the-art approaches for similarity measurement.

For Cosine tf-idf every document D_i is represented as a vector (w_{i1}, w_{i2},…,w_{in}) and n is the size of the vocabulary. So W_{ij} is calculated as follows:

$$W_{ij} = tf_{ij} \times log\,(idf_j)$$

In which $tf_{ij}i$ is the term frequency (TF) of the j-th word in the vocabulary in the document D_i and idf_j is the inverse document frequency (IDF) of the j-th word calculated. The likeness between the two texts is later explained as the cosine of the angle between two vectors. This formula is applied in accordance to Lü et al. (2007) and Hildebrand et al. (2005). This approach supposes that M is the size of query set and N is the number of sentences put together from general corpus according to each and every query. Thus, the size of the cosine tf-idf based quasi in-domain sub corpus is defined as:

$$Size_{Cos-IR} = M \times N$$

Perplexity is focused on the cross-entropy (Koehn 2004) that is the average of the negative logarithm of the word probabilities. Consider

$$H(p,q) = -\sum_{i=1}^{n} p(w_i)\log q(w_i)$$
$$= -\frac{1}{N}\sum_{i=1}^{n}\log q(w_i)$$

where p symbolizes the empirical distribution of the sample of the test. If w_i appeared n times in the test sample of N size, then $q(w_i)$ is the probability of the w_i event approximated from the training set.

For that, perplexity (pp) can be performed simply at the base point that is presented in the system, and is often applied as a cosmetic alternative of perplexity for the data selection as:

$$pp = b^{H(p,q)}$$

where b is the based of measured cross-entropy, $H(p,q)$ is the cross-entropy as given in (Koehn 2004) (often used as substitute of the perplexity in data selection Axelrod et al. 2011; Moore and Lewis 2010).

Let $H_I(p,q)$ and $H_O(p,q)$ be the cross-entropy of w_i string in accordance with the language model, which is subsequently, trained by general-domain dataset and in-domain dataset. While looking at the target (tgt) dimensions and the sources (src) of training data, there are three perplexity-based variants. The first one is known as basic cross-entropy defined as:

$$H_{I-src}(p,q)$$

The second is Moore-Lewis cross-entropy difference (Moore and Lewis 2010):

$$H_{I-src}(p,q) - H_{G-src}(p,q),$$

that attempts to choose the sentences that are more identical to I one and other but different to others in G. Both the standards mentioned above, consider only the sentences in the source language. Moreover, Axelrod et al. (2011) proposed a metric that adds cross-entropy differences over both sides:

$$[H_{I-src}(p,q) - H_{G-src}(p,q)]$$
$$+ \left[H_{I-tgt}(p,q)\right.$$
$$\left. - H_{G-tgt}(p,q)\right]$$

For instance, candidates with lower scores (Daumé III and Jagarlamudi 2011; Papineni et al. 2002; Mansour and Ney 2012) have higher relevancy to target specific domain. The size of the perplexity-based quasi in-domain subset must be equal to one another. In practice, we work with SRILM toolkit to train 5-gram LMs with interpolated modified Kneser-Ney discounting (Stolcke 2002; Chen and Goodman 1996).

In the realm of information theory and computer science, the Levenshtein distance is regarded as a string metric for the measurement of dissimilarity between two sequences. In casual terms, the Levenshtein distance between points or words is the minimum possible number of unique edits like the insertions or deletions in the data that is required to replace one word with another one.

Levenshtein distance also refers to the edit distance, only wider in its approach as it incorporates a wider area of subjects the distance metrics. It has a close association with pairwise string arrangement as well.

Mathematically, the Levenshtein distance between two strings a,b (of length $|a|$ and $|b|$ respectively) is given by $lev_{a,b}(|a|,|b|)$ where

$$lev_{a,b}(i,j)$$
$$= \begin{cases} \max(i,j) & if\ \min(i,j) = 0 \\ \min \begin{cases} lev_{a,b}(i-1,j)+1 \\ lev_{a,b}(i,j-1)+1 \\ lev_{a,b}(i-1,j-1)+1_{(a_i \neq b_j)} \end{cases} & otherwise. \end{cases}$$

where $1_{(a_i \neq b_j)}$ is the indicator function equal to 0 when $a_i = b_j$ and equal to 1 otherwise, and $lev_{a,b}(i,j)$ is the distance between the first i characters of a and the first j characters of b.

It is to be noted that the first component that is in the least correspondence of the deletion (from a to b), the second of the insertion and the third to match or mismatch, varying on whether the respective symbols are the matching.

In their study (Wang et al., 2014), Wang et al. found that a combination of these approaches provided the best performance in domain adaptation for Chinese-English corpora (Wang et al., 2014) In accordance with Wang et al. (2014)'s approach, we use a combination of the criteria at both the corpora and language models. The three similarity metrics are used to select different pseudo in-domain sub-corpora. The sub-corpora are then joined during resampling based on a combination of the three metrics. Similarly, the three metrics are combined for domain adaptation during translation. We empirically found acceptance rates that allowed us only to harvest 20% of most domain-similar data (Wang et al., 2014)

2.2 Sub-word units

Neural machine translation (NMT) models typically operate with a fixed vocabulary, but translation is an open-vocabulary problem. In SMT vocabularies that are disproportional are similar problem. Authors (Sutskever, Vinyals and Le, 2014) introduced a simple and effective approach, making the MT models capable of handling such problems by encoding rare and unknown words as sequences of subword units. This is based on the intuition that various word classes are translatable via smaller units than words, for instance names (via character copying or transliteration), compounds (via compositional translation), and cognates and loanwords (via phonological and morphological transformations). We applied this technique to our SMT engines for Slavic languages and obtained improved results of about 1.2 points in BLEU score.

3   Experimental setup

Various versions of our SMT systems were evaluated via experimentation. In preparation for experiments, we processed the corpora. This involved tokenization, cleaning, factorization,

conversion to lowercase, splitting, and final cleaning after splitting. Language models were developed and tuned using only the constrained training data. The Experiment Management System (Koehn et al., 2007) from the open source Moses SMT toolkit was used to conduct the experiments. Training of a 6-gram language model was accomplished in our resulting systems using the KenLM Modeling Toolkit instead of 5-gram SRILM (Stolcke, 2002) with an interpolated version of Kneser-Key discounting (interpolate – unk –kndiscount) that was used in our baseline systems. Word and phrase alignment was performed using SyMGIZA++ (Junczys-Dowmunt and Szał, 2012) instead of GIZA++. KenLM was also used, as described earlier, to binarize the language models. The OOV's were handled by using Unsupervised Transliteration Model (Durrani, 2014). The results are shown in Table 1. "BASE" in the tables represents the baseline SMT system. "EXT" indicates results for the baseline system, using the baseline settings but extended with additional permissible data (limited to permissible data) with data adaptation. "BEST" indicates the results when the new SMT settings were applied and using all permissible data after data adaptation. Three well-known metrics were used for scoring the results: Bilingual Evaluation Understudy (BLEU), the US National Institute of Standards and Technology (NIST) metric and Translation Error Rate (TER). The results show that the systems performed well on all data sets in comparison to the baseline SMT systems. Application of the new settings and use of all permissible data improved performance even more.

Task	Language and Direction	System	BLEU
News	CS->EN	BASE	21.18
News	CS->EN	EXT	22.67
News	CS->EN	BEST	23.9
News	EN->CS	BASE	14.04
News	EN->CS	EXT	15.44
News	EN->CS	BEST	16.6
News	LV->EN	BASE	10.09
News	LV->EN	EXT	12.17

News	LV->EN	BEST	12.9
News	EN->LV	BASE	8.78
News	EN->LV	EXT	9.78
News	EN->LV	BEST	10.4
Biomedical	EN->PL	BASE	12.45
Biomedical	EN->PL	EXT	18.62
Biomedical	EN->PL	BEST	18.86
Biomedical	EN->PL	BEST + BPE	18.88
Biomedical	EN->CS	BASE	14.56
Biomedical	EN->CS	EXT	18.12
Biomedical	EN->CS	BEST	19.96
Biomedical	EN->DE	BASE	21.43
Biomedical	EN->DE	EXT	24.64
Biomedical	EN->DE	BEST	25.13
Biomedical	EN->RO	BASE	19.43
Biomedical	EN->RO	EXT	23.18
Biomedical	EN->RO	BEST	24.91

Table 1: News and Biomedical Task Translation Results

4 Summary

We have improved our SMT systems for the WMT 2017 evaluation campaign using only permissible data. We cleaned, prepared, and tokenized the training data. Symmetric word alignment models were used to align the corpora. UTM was used to handle OOV words. A language model was created, binarized, and tuned. We performed domain adaptation of language data using a combination of similarity metrics. The results show a positive impact of our approach on SMT quality across the choose language pair. We also successfully used BPE inside SMT for morphologically rich language (Polish). This brings promise of improvement for other slavic languages as well.

References

Amittai Axelrod, Xiaodong He, Jianfeng Gao. 2011. *Domain adaptation via pseudo in-domain data selection*. Proceedings of the Conference on Empirical Methods in Natural Language Processing. Association for Computational Linguistics, p. 355-362.

Marta R. Costa-Jussa and Jose R. Fonollosa. 2010. Using linear interpolation and weighted reordering hypotheses in the Moses system, Barcelona, Spain

Hal Daumé III, Jagadesh Jagarlamudi. 2011. *Domain adaptation for machine translation by mining unseen words.* In: Proceedings of the 49th Annual Meeting of the Association for Computational Linguistics: Human Language Technologies (ACL-HLT '11). Association for Computational Linguistics, Stroudsburg, PA, USA, pp 407–412

Stanley Chen, Joshua Goodman. 1996. *An empirical study of smoothing techniques for language modeling.* In: Proceedings of the 34th Annual Meeting on Association for Computational Linguistics (ACL '96). Association for Computational Linguistics, Stroudsburg, PA, USA, pp 310–318. doi: 10.3115/981863.981904

Nadir Durrani, et al. 2014. *Integrating an Unsupervised Transliteration Model into Statistical Machine Translation*. EACL 2014. p. 148-153.

Kenneth Heafield. 2011. *KenLM: Faster and smaller language model queries*. Proceedings of the Sixth Workshop on Statistical Machine Translation. Association for Computational Linguistics, 2011. p. 187-197.

Almut Silja Hildebrand et al. 2005. *Adaptation of the translation model for statistical machine translation based on information retrieval.* In: Proceedings of EAMT 10th Annual Conference, 30-31 May 2005, Budapest, Hungary. Association for Computational Linguistics, Stroudsburg, PA, pp 133–142

Marcin Junczys-Dowmunt, Arkadiusz SZAŁ. 2012. *Symgiza++: symmetrized word alignment models for statistical machine translation.* Security and Intelligent Information Systems. Springer: Berlin Heidelberg. p. 379-390.

Philipp Koehn. 2004. *Pharaoh: a beam search decoder for phrase-based statistical machine translation models.* In: Proceedings of the

Antenna Measurement Techniques Association (AMTA '04). Springer, Berlin, Germany, pp 115–124

Philipp Koehn et al. 2007. Moses: Open Source Toolkit for Statistical Machine Translation, In: Proceedings of the ACL 2007 Demo and Poster Sessions, Prague, pp. 177–180

Yajuan Lü , Jin Huang, Qun Liu. 2007. *Improving statistical machine translation performance by training data selection and optimization.* In: Proceedings of the Joint Conference on Empirical Methods in Natural Language Processing and Computational Natural Language Learning (EMNLP-CoNLL '07). Association for Computational Linguistics, Stroudsburg, PA, USA, pp 343–350

Saab Mansour, Hermann Ney. 2012. *A simple and effective weighted phrase extraction for machine translation adaptation.* In: Proceedings of the 9th International Workshop on Spoken Language Translation (IWSLT '12). Springer-Verlag, Berlin, Heidelberg, pp 193–200

Robert Moore, William Lewis. 2010. *Intelligent selection of language model training data.* In: Proceedings of the 48th Annual Meeting of the Association for Computational Linguistics (ACL '10). Association for Computational Linguistics, Stroudsburg, PA, USA, pp 220–224

Moses statistical machine translation, "OOVs." Last revised February 13, 2015. Retrieved September 27, 2015 from: http://www.statmt.org/moses/?n=Advanced.OO Vs #ntoc2

Moses statistical machine translation, "Build reordering model." Last revised July 28, 2013.

Retrieved October 10, 2015 from: http://www.statmt.org/moses/?n=FactoredTrainin g. Build ReorderingModel

Kishore Papineni et al. 2002. *BLEU: a method for automatic evaluation of machine translation.* In: Proceedings of the Workshop on Automatic Summarization (ACL '02). Association for Computational Linguistics, Stroudsburg, PA, USA, pp 311–318. doi: 10.3115/1073083.1073135

Andreas Stolcke. 2002. SRILM - An Extensible Laguage Modeling Toolkit., INTERSPEECH, 2002.

Ilya Sutskever, Oriol Vinyals, & Quoc Le. 2014. *Sequence to sequence learning with neural networks.* In Advances in neural information processing systems (pp. 3104-3112).

Longyue Wang, Derek F. Wong, Lidia S. Chao, Yi Lu, and Junwen Xing. 2014. A Systematic Coparison of Data Selection Criteria for SMT Domain Adaptation., The Scientific World Journal, vol. 2014, doi:10.1155/2014/745485

Krzysztof Wołk, Krzysztof Marasek. 2014a. Polish - English Speech Statistical Machine Translation Systems for the IWSLT 2014, In: Proceedings of International Workshop on Spoken Language Translation, Lake Tahoe, California, USA, pp. 143- 148.

Krzysztof Wołk, Krzysztof Marasek. 2014b. A Sentence Meaning Based Alignment Method for Parallel Text Corpora Preparation. In: New Perspectives in Information Systems and Technologies, Volume 1. Springer International Publishing, 2014, p. 229- 237.

Hunter MT: A Course for Young Researchers in WMT17

Jia Xu and Yi Zong Kuang and Shondell Baijoo and Hyun Lee
and Uman Shahzad and Mir Ahmed and Meredith Lancaster and Chris Carlan
Hunter College, City University of New York
Jia.Xu@hunter.cuny.edu, {YiZong.Kuang38, shondell.baijoo41, hyun.lee16,
Uman.Shahzad34, Mir.Ahmed57, Meredith.Lancaster88, Chris.Carlan70}@myhunter.cuny.edu

Abstract

This paper documents an undergraduate course at Hunter College, in which one instructor, six undergraduates, and one high school student built 17 machine translation systems in six months from scratch. The team successfully participated in the second Conference on Machine Translation (WMT17) evaluation on the news task in Finnish-English and Latvian-English and on the bio-medical task in French-English, English-French, English-German, English-Romanian, and English-Polish.

1 Introduction

Machine learning has advanced the state-of-the-art of artificial intelligence at a rapid speed. There has been an increasing amount of related courses introduced. However, hands-on experience is of vital importance to novices (Lopez et al., 2013).

Through conventional education it may take many years for beginners to find a research direction in the field of machine translation. Introductory courses in this field can be either too theoretical or too detailed, leaving students lost in coding. Therefore, our goals were to make the material both detailed and comprehensive and also bring novelty and excitement into this course. We propose teaching methods that are centered around the machine translation competition. With this idea in mind we were able to achieve our goals because of three key factors. First, we were able to focus on the pragmatical aspects of the teaching material; second, the study was comprehensive, since we covered all the components of a machine translation system; and third, student motivation was enhanced, because the results were directly available in the MT community through the WMT evaluation. These key factors helped us to attain our goals optimally and efficiently.

We will discuss the teaching methods to introduce undergraduates to topics of advanced machine translation technology. We will describe the outcome, the machine translation systems in 17 languages, in particular the ones that were successfully submitted in the WMT17, as well as the research revised in this course. In conclusion, we will evaluate our course with feedback of students.

2 Backgrounds

At Hunter college, we experimentally designed an applied machine translation course to provide an opportunity for novice students to learn by competing against the best senior teams around the world in one of the most significant machine translation competitions, the WMT17. The students' levels ranged from high school to college senior, and none of them had any prior knowledge of machine learning or machine translation.

Hunter college offered supportive facilities for the course. Two students took an introductory C++ programming class (Software Analysis and Design I) (Hunter, 2016). Some students took an one-week "Linux introductory class" (Hunter, 2016) at the beginning of the semester. The open machine translation resources served as the basis of this course. "statmt.org" (SMT, 2017) provides excellent readings and software for the beginning student. "SMT Tutorial" (Knight, 1999) by Kevin Knight et. al. is an essential reading on machine translation, and the book "Statistical Machine Translation" (Koehn, 2010) by Philipp Koehn was recommended because it gives a more in-depth explanation.

We view machine translation as a high-dimensional, multiclass classification task. The reference book used was "Pattern Classification"

Proceedings of the Conference on Machine Translation (WMT), Volume 2: Shared Task Papers, pages 422–427
Copenhagen, Denmark, September 7–11, 2017. ©2017 Association for Computational Linguistics

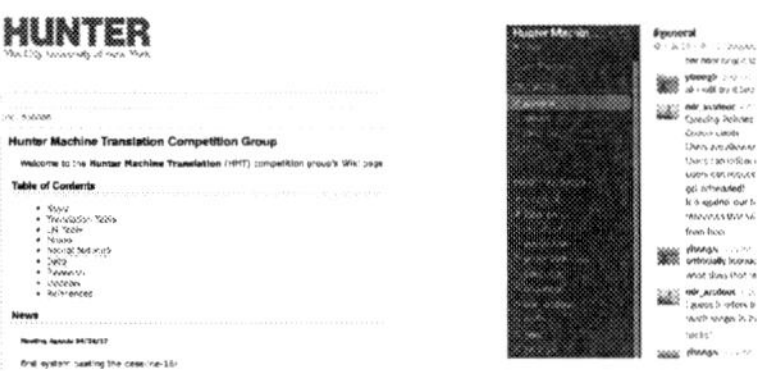

(a) Hunter MT Wiki page   (b) Chat room in Slack

Figure 1: Infrastructure for team coordination.

by Duda and Hart (Duda and Hart, 1973). With the insight in previous competitions, the instructor introduced basic methods on the blackboard in an interactive way, covering the following topics: Bayes Decision Rule, Maximum Likelihood, Word Alignment Models and Training, Search, Language Modeling, Cross-Validation, Domain Adaptation, Design Bagging, Neural Network, and Neural Machine Translation.

Team meetings took place weekly to discuss problems and solutions. Students set up a Wiki homepage called "Hunter MT" to share their work and post questions internally. A Slack Platform provided a coherent working atmosphere for students connecting with each other in real time. In our Slack board students had posted 13.9K messages and uploaded 131 files during this six-month course. Figure 1 contains screenshots of these homepages of the team.

The software development and machine translation systems were hosted in the High Performance Computing Center (HPCC) at the College of Staten Island (CSI) CUNY, located in New York City. Each student had their own account to conduct their experiments in their respective language pairs. Students shared their experiences within the team to avoid repeating experiments. Jobs were submitted and scheduled via queuing system. At HPCC, we used an infiniband cluster named Penzias and fat node server named Arrow. Penzias, which is a cluster, uses the Sandy Bridge chip and NVIDIA K20m GPU.

3 Core MT engine

We built phrase-based machine translation systems using the open software toolkit Moses (Koehn et al., 2007). We used an EMS script to run the translation pipeline, which includes preprocessing, word alignment training, tuning, testing, and error logs for debugging.

3.1 Pre- and Post-processing

For all language directions, we used the Moses default tokenization and true-casing tool. The pre-processing involved tokenization, truecasing, and cleaning. The experimental results showed that using truecasing produces a better result than not using it for most language directions.

3.2 Word alignment

Word alignments were generated based on GIZA++ (Och and Ney, 2000) and mGIZA (Gao and Vogel, 2008) for all language directions with the grow-diag-final option. We ran five iterations of Model 1 (Brown et al., 1993), five iterations of HMM (Vogel et al., 1996), and four iterations of IBM model-4 (Brown et al., 1993). Training sets included in-domain training data and selected out-of-domain training data that we will outline in detail for individual language pairs in Section 4 and Section 5.

We put a limit of 100 words maximum on the sentence length. For bio-medical tasks, the maximum sentence length was set to 80. The main reason for this was to shorten the time of the training process. Because there is more training data to handle in the bio-medical tasks than in the news tasks, considering both in-domain and out-of-domain corpora, we decided to place a heuristic threshold to shrink the training time to an acceptable one (a couple of days, depending on languages and processors in the HPCC).

3.3 Language model

The language models used were 7-gram SRILM (Stolcke, 2002) with Kneser-Ney smoothing (Kneser and Ney, 1991) and linear interpolation. Having the highest possible n-gram is generally good pratice, but due to limited time and the exponential rate of time needed to train the language model, we decided to use 7-gram to train the language model.

The English language model is shared among all foreign-language-to-English translation systems. It is a mixture language model with domain adaptation following (Xu et al., 2007). The language models trained on individual corpora is linearly interpolated on its n-gram probabilities. Their weights are optimized with respect to the perplexity on the development set

423

of German-English newstest2016. The individual training corpora are Europarl v7, a fraction of common crawl (due to limited computational resource), news commentary 2007-2016, DCEP, LETA, FAREWELL, RAPID, and news discussion. In addition to those, we also used NYT and XIN from GigaWord (WMT, 2017). Other language models were trained with all available corpora same as in English.

3.4 Tuning

The tuning set is the development set of WMT16 for most language pairs. We used MIRA (Hasler et al., 2011) to tune single systems to find out the optimal feature weights in the log-linear combination. We used 100-best in the tuning, and we also heuristically tuned the Moses parameters, such as maximum phrase length, stack size in search, nbest size, maximum sentence length, and search pruning options. The remaining parameters followed the default values in the EMS (Koehn et al., 2007). To rank the system, we used the BLEU (Papineni et al., 2002) score.

Below we describe our machine translation systems for language directions we submitted in the WMT17 evaluation.

4 Data Sets and Settings for News Task

The translation systems for different language pairs are built with the same methods as in Section 3. However, they are trained on different parallel training set. Table 1 shows the corpus used in the GIZA++ (Och and Ney, 2000) training for machine translation systems for each language direction. For each WMT17 evaluation task we participated in, we computed the number of sentences, the number of running words for the training set, the development set and the test set, respectively as shown in Table 2. We also computed the OOV rate of the running word and the OOV rate of the vocabulary (Voc.) for the source and target test set in each system.

4.1 Finnish-English

The parallel training set included corpora of Europarl version 7, Rapid 2016, and Titles. The translation result was evaluated on the WMT17 news test set of 2016.

4.2 Latvian-English

The parallel training set included corpora of Europarl version 7, Rapid 2016, LETA, FAREWELL, and DCEP. The translation result was evaluated on the WMT News Test set 2016.

5 Data Sets and Settings for Bio-medical Task

Below I will describe our submission systems in the bio-medical task (Yepes et al., 2017).

5.1 English-German

We used the WMT17 provided corpora for training and tuning, including Europarl v7, News Commentary v12, Rapid Corpus of EU press releases, and parts of the Common Crawl corpus. We added the previous years' test sets in the training.

Ultimately, we found that for German, increasing the maximum sentence length and phrase length increased the BLEU score by a few points. We also found that setting the language model order to 7 helped the BLEU score by one point. While these optimized parameters slowed down the training of the system as expected.

5.2 English-Polish

Both in-domain and selected out-of-domain corpora were used. The list of in-domain corpora used in this experiment came from the following sources: CESTA, ECDC, EMEA (open subtitle and news crawl), Medical Web Crawl, Medical Web Text from CzEng 1.6, MuchMore, PatTR Medical, and Subtitles. For out-of-domain corpora, the sources were the following: Cordis, EU-bookshop, EUROPARL, JRC-Acquis, MultiUN, News Commentary, OpenSubtitles, PatTR, and Rapid. The combined corpora totaled 39,442,076 lines, with a total of 302 million words. To preprocess the corpora, we used default Moses tokenizing tools. The resulting cleaned corpora totaled 39,321,672 lines.

5.3 English-Romanian

Because the Romanian language uses the alphabet system, for the Romanian system, we used a setting similar to that used for the Polish system. The corpora consisted of in-domain sources, such as ECDC, EMEA, and Subtitles. It also included out-of-domain sources, such as: EURO-BookShop, EUROPARL, JRC-Acquis, and Open Subtitles. The resulting corpora totaled 62 million lines and 416 million words. After preprocessing, to deal with the unique symbols in the language and to conform to a standard format of the text,

ID	Languages	Domain	BLEU[%]	Corpora	Test set
1	English-German	News	26.28	Europarl,Global,NC,Rapid	News Test 2016
2	German-English	News	33.61		News Test 2016
3	English-Czech	News	13.59	Europarl,CommonCrawl,News'12	News Test 2016
4	Czech-English	News	15.48		News Test 2016
5	English-Russian	News	15.88	CommonCrawl,NC,Wiki	News Test 2016
6	Russian-English	News	26.23		News Test 2016
7	Turkish-English	News	12.48	SETIMES2	News Test 2016
8	English-Turkish	News	10.93		News Test 2016
9	Finnish-English	News	18.53	Europarl,Rapid,Titles	News Test 2016
10	English-Finnish	News	12.82		News Test 2016
11	Latvian-English	News	24.61	Europarl,Rapid,LETA,FAREWELL,DCEP	News Dev 2017
12	English-Latvian	News	18.43		News Dev 2017
13	English-French	Bio	25.16	Europarl,Medline,NC,Scielo	Health Test 2016
14	French-English	Bio	24.46		Health Test 2016
15	English-German	Bio	29.56	Europarl,NC,UFAL,ECDC, Subtitles,EMEA,PatTR,Medical	Himl Test
16	English-Polish	Bio	18.70	Europarl,ECDC,EMEA,EUBS Subtitles,Cordis,JRC,Rapid	Himl Test
17	English-Romanian	Bio	17.36	Europarl,ECDC,EMEA, Subtitles,EUbookshop,JRC	Himl Test

Table 1: Translation systems in different language pairs in BLEU-c [%].

such as true-casing, the corpora was reduced to 61 million lines, which is a significant reduction compared to English-Polish. Using SRILM, we built a 5-gram language model.

6 System Outputs

Table 1 shows our system outputs for different language directions in the news and in the biomedical domain. All translation systems were only generated in this course. Each student was responsible for the translation systems of the language direction that interested them. The results are produced based on the training and test corpora listed in the last two columns, respectively.

Machine translation systems are built by students with the guidance and assistance of the course instructor, Jia Xu. Each student worked on different language directions: Yi Zong Kuang (15,16,17), Shondell Baijoo (1,2,11,12), Hyun Lee (13,14), Uman Shahzad (6,7,9,10), Mir Ahmed (3,4), Meredith Lancaster (5,6), and Chris Carlan (11,12). Yi Zong Kuang and Shondell Baijoo contributed to the Human evaluation in the News Track. Yi Zong Kuang, Shondell Baijoo, Hyun Lee worked on system descriptions together with the course instructor. Mixture language models and some translation systems are conducted by the instructor as example experiments.

7 Research Components

We applied two methods to improve over baseline systems. These are course exercises without being included in the final submission.

7.1 Design bagging

We applied the bagging (Breiman, 1996) and its improved version design bagging (Papakonstantinou et al., 2014) to train the systems. As shown in Algorithm 1 and Algorithm 2, the parallel training set is sampled into $m = 30$ blocks (subsets or bootstraps), each block contains b parallel sentences which is 50% of the whole parallel training data. $x \in R[0, N-1]$ means to uniform randomly assign an integer value to x in the range from 0 to $N-1$, where N is the size of the training data. Either bagging, see Algorithm 1 or design bagging, see Algorithm 2 is used to construct the blocks. Then each of the 30 blocks was used to train a machine translation system, with the same setting as described in Section 3. We translated the test set with each of these systems and then combined all 30 translation results with a system combination tool (Heafield and Lavie, 2010) whose weights were tuned on the development set.

7.2 Phrase-based language model

We also applied a phrase-based language model. The likelihood of a sentence is based on decomposed phrases instead of single words, given histories. This is achieved by treating phrase segmentation as a hidden variable and developing a complete phrase-based n-gram LM that was tailored for machine translation use. The details of this algorithm are described in (Xu and Chen, 2015).

Algorithm 1 Bagging	**Algorithm 2** Design Bagging
1: **Input:** block size b, number of blocks m, number of elements N.	1: **Input:** block size b, number of blocks m, number of elements N.
2: Initialize m empty blocks.	2: Initialize m empty blocks.
3: **for** $k = 0$ **to** $m - 1$ **do**	3: **for** $i = 1$ **to** $b \times m$ **do**
4: **for** $i = 0$ **to** $N - 1$ **do**	4: select current smallest block (if not unique, choose randomly)
5: $a[i] = i$	5: $S_1 \longleftarrow$ the set of elements not in this block
6: **end for**	6: $S_2 \longleftarrow$ set of elements that among the elements in S_1 appears the minimum of times in other blocks
7: **for** $i = 0$ **to** $2Nlog_2N - 1$ **do**	7: Choose randomly an element from S_2 and put it into the current block
8: $x \in R[0, N - 1]$	8: **end for**
9: $y \in R[0, N - 1]$	9: **Output:** m blocks each with b distinct elements.
10: Swap $a[x]$ and $a[y]$	
11: **end for**	
12: **for** $i = 0$ **to** $b - 1$ **do**	
13: $b[k][i] = a[i]$	
14: **end for**	
15: **end for**	
16: **Output:** m blocks each with b distinct elements.	

	Training Set		Dev Set		Test Set		OOV	
Languages	Sentences	Words	Sentences	Words	Sentences	Words	Words	Voc.
Latvian	4507745	56447016	2003	41245	974	21417	12.2%	5.8%
English	4507745	67601629	2003	49206	974	25496	8.0%	2.6%
Finnish	2633183	45235670	4500	72692	3002	46572	19.9 %	8.7 %
English	2633183	62847985	4500	98000	3000	64813	8.9 %	2.3 %
English	2794276	67279904	1000	21932	5023	140505	6.2 %	0.7 %
French	2794276	75320850	1000	27383	5023	192732	6.9 %	0.6 %
English	2061633	55855699	2495	45762	1931	34833	14.0 %	4.9 %
German	2061633	53356277	2495	43150	1931	35283	19.4 %	6.7 %
English	39321672	381409086	3922	69626	1931	34833	3.9 %	0.9%
Polish	39321672	307458011	7844	137396	1931	33527	3.5 %	1.3 %
English	61943814	536905597	3922	69626	1931	34833	4.0 %	0.9 %
Romanian	61943814	508776149	7844	137400	1931	37939	5.1 %	1.4 %

Table 2: Corpus statistics for various language directions

8 Teaching Outcome

As an outcome of the training, we performed an anonymous questionnaire on SurveyMonkey (surveymonkey, 2017) to evaluate the course and receive feedback. The overall rating of this course is satisfactory, with some comments for example: "The hands-on experience was by far the best." and "Being able to see the work was very important." In response to the question: What is the most valuable thing you learned? Students said "Understanding how research is done." At the same time, we also received such suggestions as "The tutorials and mini lectures were helpful and should be more frequent." and "more on Neural Network Machine Translation".

9 Summary

We described the teaching experience of a supervised study course of six undergraduates and a high school student. One course instructor guided young and fresh machine translation learners.

The teaching feedback is encouraging, and the products generated during this course were a cool surprise: 17 machine translation baseline systems and a successful participation of the WMT17.

Acknowledgments

We appreciate the strong support of the Department of Computer Science of Hunter College, the Office of the Dean of Arts and Science, as well as the Provost's Office at Hunter College. In particular, we thank Professor William Sakas for his arrangement and effort to make this course happen and to help outreaching course participants. We also thank Professor Susan Eppstein for her insightful advice on the course management. We are thankful to the High Performance Computing Center at the City University of New York for providing rich computational resources and IT services. Students got hardware and software support from CUNY HPC staff as well as basic training about usage of HPC systems. The Computer Science Department of CUNY Graduate Center offered location to host our seminars and supported the continuation of our team. Above all, we would like to thank Lampros Flokas, Pablo Gonzalez, Liam Geron, and Hussein Ghaly for the insight they brought from the reading group, as well as the effort they put into the CUNY machine translation systems built by the graduate study group.

References

Leo Breiman. 1996. Bagging predictors. *Machine Learning* 24(2):123–140.

Peter F. Brown, Stephen A. Della Pietra, Vincent J. Della Pietra, and R. L. Mercer. 1993. The mathematics of statistical machine translation: Parameter estimation. *Computational Linguistics* 19(2):263–311.

Richhard O. Duda and Peter E. Hart. 1973. *Pattern Classification and Scene Analysis*. John Wiley, New York, NY.

Qin Gao and Stephan Vogel. 2008. Parallel implementations of word alignment tool. In *Software Engineering, Testing, and Quality Assurance for Natural Language Processing*. Association for Computational Linguistics, pages 49–57.

Eva Hasler, Barry Haddow, and Philipp Koehn. 2011. Margin infused relaxed algorithm for moses. In *The Prague Bulletin of Mathematical Linguistics*. pages 69–78.

Kenneth Heafield and Alon Lavie. 2010. Voting on n-grams for machine translation system combination. AMTA.

Hunter. 2016. The website of CSci 135 course software analysis and design I at Hunter college. http://catalog.hunter.cuny.edu.

Hunter. 2016. The website of Hunter beginners' linux class. http://www.hunter.cuny.edu/csci/pressroom/news/beginners-linux-class.

Reinhard Kneser and Hermann Ney. 1991. Forming word classes by statistical clustering for statistical language modelling. In *1. Quantitative Linguistics Conf.*. Trier, Germany, pages 221–226.

Kevin Knight. 1999. A statistical MT tutorial workbook. Http://www.isi.edu/natural-language/mt/wkbk.rtf.

Philipp Koehn. 2010. *Statistical machine translation*. Cambridge University Press.

Philipp Koehn, Hieu Hoang, Alexandra Birch, Chris Callison-Burch, Marcello Federico, Nicola Bertoldi, Brooke Cowan, Wade Shen, Christine Moran, Richard Zens, et al. 2007. Moses: Open source toolkit for statistical machine translation. In *ACL on Interactive Poster and Demonstration Sessions*. Association for Computational Linguistics, pages 177–180.

Adam Lopez, Matt Post, Chris Callison-Burch, Jonathan Weese, Juri Ganitkevitch, Narges Ahmidi, Olivia Buzek, Leah Hanson, Beenish Jamil, Matthias Lee, et al. 2013. Learning to translate with products of novices: a suite of open-ended challenge problems for teaching mt. *Transactions of the Association for Computational Linguistics* 1:165–178.

Franz Josef Och and Hermann Ney. 2000. GIZA++: Training of statistical translation models.

Periklis A Papakonstantinou, Jia Xu, and Zhu Cao. 2014. Bagging by design (on the suboptimality of bagging). In *AAAI*. pages 2041–2047.

Kishore A. Papineni, Salim Roukos, Todd Ward, and Wei-Jing Zhu. 2002. BLEU: a method for automatic evaluation of machine translation. In *ACL*. Philadelphia, pages 311–318.

SMT. 2017. The homepage of statistical machine translation. Http://www.statmt.org.

Andreas Stolcke. 2002. SRILM - an extensible language modeling toolkit. In *Proceedings of IWSLT*. Denver, Colorado, pages 901–904.

surveymonkey. 2017. Free online survey software & questionnaire tool. Https://www.surveymonkey.com.

Stephan Vogel, Hermann Ney, and Christoph Tillmann. 1996. HMM-based word alignment in statistical translation. In *COLING96*. Copenhagen, Denmark, pages 836–841.

WMT. 2017. Conference on machine translation. Http://www.statmt.org/wmt17/.

Jia Xu and Geliang Chen. 2015. Phrase based language model for statistical machine translation. *arXiv preprint arXiv:1501.04324* .

Jia Xu, Yonggang Deng, Yuqing Gao, and Hermann Ney. 2007. Domain dependent statistical machine translation. In *In Proceedings of the MT Summit XI*. pages 515–520.

Antonio Jimeno Yepes, Aurélie Névéol, Mariana Neves, Karin Verspoor, Ondřej Bojar, Arthur Boyer, Cristian Grozea, Barry Haddow, Madeleine Kittner, Yvonne Lichtblau, Pavel Pecina, Roland Roller, Amy Siu, Philippe Thomas, and Saskia Trescher. 2017. Findings of the WMT 2017 Biomedical Translation Shared Task. In *Proceedings of the Second Conference on Machine Translation (WMT17) at EMNLP*. Copenhagen, Denmark.

CASICT-DCU Neural Machine Translation Systems for WMT17

Jinchao Zhang[1] Peerachet Porkaew[1] Jiawei Hu[1] Qiuye Zhao[1] Qun Liu[2,1]
[1]Key Laboratory of Intelligent Information Processing,
Institute of Computing Technology, Chinese Academy of Sciences
[2]ADAPT Centre, School of Computing, Dublin City University
{zhangjinchao,dingchunfa,hujiawei,zhaoqiuye,liuqun}@ict.ac.cn

Abstract

We participated in the WMT 2016 shared news translation task on English ↔ Chinese language pair. Our systems are based on the encoder-decoder neural machine translation model with the attention mechanism. We employ the Gated Recurrent Unit (GRU) with the linear associative connection to build deep encoder and address the unknown words with the dictionary replace approach. The dictionaries are extracted from the parallel training data with unsupervised word alignment method. In the decoding procedure, the translation probabilities of the target word from different models are averagely combined as the ensemble strategy. In this paper, we introduce our systems from data preprocessing to post-editing in details.

1 Introduction

We build the Neural Machine Translation systems CASICT-DCU for WMT17 English ↔ Chinese news translation task. Our systems are based on the encoder-decoder model with the attention mechanism, which is also known as the RNNSearch model (Bahdanau et al., 2015). To construct the deep RNN network, we employ the Gated Recurrent Unit (Cho et al., 2014b) with the linear associative connection (Wang et al., 2017) to ensure the fluent gradient propagation. Adadelta (Zeiler, 2012) algorithm is used to optimize the parameters and stochastic gradient descent algorithm with small learning rate is used in the fine-tuning stage. We extract dictionaries from parallel training data with the unsupervised method to address the unknown words in target translation according to the word alignment vector. During the decoding, the ensemble strategy is used to combine the translation probabilities of the target word from different models.

2 System Description

The neural machine translation model (Kalchbrenner and Blunsom, 2013; Cho et al., 2014b; Sutskever et al., 2014) aims to capture the translation knowledge through training a neural network in the end-to-end style. Our systems are built on the RNNSearch neural machine translation model. Formally, given a source sentence $\mathbf{x} = \mathbf{x}_1, ..., \mathbf{x}_m$ and a target sentence $\mathbf{y} = \mathbf{y}_1, ..., \mathbf{y}_n$, NMT models the translation probability as

$$P(\mathbf{y}|\mathbf{x}) = \prod_{t=1}^{n} P(\mathbf{y}_t|\mathbf{y}_{<t}, \mathbf{x}), \qquad (1)$$

where $\mathbf{y}_{<t} = \mathbf{y}_1, ..., \mathbf{y}_{t-1}$. The generation probability of $\mathbf{y}_t$ is

$$P(\mathbf{y}_t|\mathbf{y}_{<t}, \mathbf{x}) = g(\mathbf{y}_{t-1}, \mathbf{c}_t, \mathbf{s}_t), \qquad (2)$$

where $g(\cdot)$ is a softmax regression function, $\mathbf{y}_{t-1}$ is the newly translated target word and $\mathbf{s}_t$ is the hidden states of decoder which represents the translation status. The attention $\mathbf{c}_t$ denotes the related source words for generating $\mathbf{y}_t$ and is computed as the weighted-sum of source representation $\mathbf{h}$ upon an alignment vector α_t shown in Eq.(3) where the $align(\cdot)$ function is a feedforward network with $softmax$ normalization.

$$\mathbf{c}_t = \sum_{j=1}^{m} \alpha_{t,j} \mathbf{h}_j$$
$$\alpha_{t,j} = align(\mathbf{s}_t, \mathbf{h}_j) \qquad (3)$$

The hidden states $\mathbf{s}_t$ are updated as

$$\mathbf{s}_t = f(\mathbf{s}_{t-1}, \mathbf{y}_{t-1}, \mathbf{c}_t), \qquad (4)$$

Proceedings of the Conference on Machine Translation (WMT), Volume 2: Shared Task Papers, pages 428–431
Copenhagen, Denmark, September 7–11, 2017. ©2017 Association for Computational Linguistics

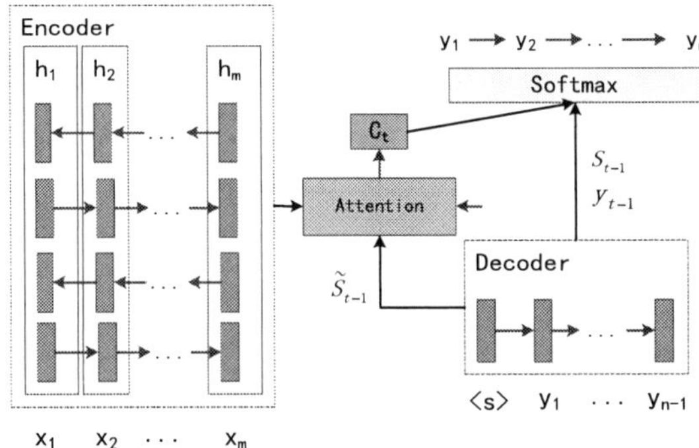

Figure 1: The general architecture of our systems.

where $f(\cdot)$ is a recurrent function.

We adopt a varietal attention mechanism[1] in our system which is implemented as

$$
\begin{aligned}
\widetilde{\mathbf{s}}_t &= f_1(\mathbf{s}_{t-1}, \mathbf{y}_{t-1}), \\
\alpha_{t,j} &= align(\widetilde{\mathbf{s}}_t, \mathbf{h}_j), \\
\mathbf{s}_t &= f_2(\widetilde{\mathbf{s}}_t, \mathbf{c}_t),
\end{aligned}
\tag{5}
$$

where $f_1(\cdot)$ and $f_2(\cdot)$ are recurrent functions.

To construct deep network, we use the linear associative unit (LAU) to ensure fluent gradient propagation. The LAU is computed as

$$
\begin{aligned}
r_t &= \sigma(W_{xr}x_t + W_{hr}h_{t-1}), \\
z_t &= \sigma(W_{xz}x_t + W_{hz}h_{t-1}), \\
g_t &= \sigma(W_{sg}x_t + W_{hg}h_{t-1}), \\
\widetilde{h}_t &= tanh((1 - r_t) \odot W_{xh}x_t + W_{hh}(r_t \odot h_{t-1})), \\
h_t &= ((1 - z_t) \odot h_{t-1} + z_t \odot \widetilde{h}_t) \odot (1 - g_t) + g_t \\
&\quad \odot (W_x x_t)
\end{aligned}
\tag{6}
$$

where W_* is the weight matrices, x_t is the input at time t and h_{t-1} is the hidden states at time $t-1$. The LAU allows the input linearly forward propagates in a certain scale to acquire fluent gradient back propagation. It works like residual connections (He et al., 2016) and fast-forward connections (Zhou et al., 2016) and makes build deep network possible. Our encoder is a 4 layers LAU network where forward LAU and backward LAU are alternately stacked. The general architecture of our systems is shown in Figure 1.

3 Pipeline Description

We introduce the pipeline of building the translation systems from data preprocessing to post edit-

ing in this section.

3.1 Data Preprocessing

For English ↔ Chinese news translation task, WMT 2017 provides tree parts of data: News Commentary v12, UN Parallel Corpus V1.0 and CWMT Corpus. We used all corpora to train our translation systems. For English sentences, the Moses tokenization script[2] is employed to execute the tokenization processing. For Chinese sentences, we used our in-house word segmentor called "PBCLAS" to do the word segmentation. The word segmentation criterion follows the Chinese People's Daily format. We filter the duplicated sentences and the sentences that are too long (more than 120 words) or too short (less than 5 words). The training corpus is case-sensitive.

3.2 Vocabulary

Our systems are based on the words rather than sub-words (Sennrich et al., 2016; Wu et al., 2016). For our system is serially trained on the single GPU with restricted memory space, the source vocabulary size is set to 100,000 and the target vocabulary size is set to 50,000. The words that out of the vocabulary are represented by the "UNK" symbol.

3.3 Training Details

The sentence length for training systems is up to 120. The word embedding dimension is set to 512 and the hidden layer size is 512. Square matrices are initialized in a random orthogonal way. Nonsquare matrices are initialized by sampling each element from the Gaussian distribution with mean 0 and variance 0.01^2. All biases are initialized to 0. Parameters are updated by Mini-batch Gradient Descent and the learning rate is controlled by the AdaDelta algorithm with the decay constant $\rho = 0.95$ and the denominator constant $\epsilon = 1e-6$. The batch size is 80. We use stochastic gradient descent with small learning rates as 0.0001 to fine-tune the models. Dropout strategy (Srivastava et al., 2014) is applied to the output layer with the dropout rate 0.5 to avoid over-fitting. The gradients of the cost function which have $L2$ norm larger than a predefined threshold 1.0 is normalized to the threshold to avoid gradients explosion (Pascanu et al., 2013). We exploit length normal-

---

[1]https://github.com/nyu-dl/dl4mt-tutorial/tree/master/session2

[2]https://github.com/moses-smt/mosesdecoder/tree/master/scripts/tokenizer/tokenizer.perl

ization (Cho et al., 2014a) on candidate translations and the beam size for decoding is 12.

3.4 UNK Replace

As the vocabulary sizes are restricted, target sentences may contain "UNK" symbols, which leads to sense ambiguity. We attempt to extract a dictionary to replace the "UNK" symbol in target sentence. We use the "fast_align" [3] word alignment tool to generate the word alignment and extract the dictionary through keeping the highest translation probability. We extract English $\rightarrow$ Chinese and Chinese $\rightarrow$ English dictionaries in this way.

At the decoding stage of NMT, we regard the source word that possesses highest alignment probability as the one that generates the target word. Once a "UNK" symbol is generated, we locate the corresponding source word and translate it with the dictionary. If the source word is not in the dictionary, it will be presented in the target sentence.

3.5 Model Ensemble

To add the diversity of systems, we train several models and combine them with the ensemble strategy. These models are initialized with different weight parameters. Each model produces the probability distribution on the target vocabulary at each step of decoding procedure. These probability distributions are averagely combined as the ultimate distribution for beam searching. For our UNK replace strategy, the word alignment vectors that produced by models are also averagely combined to determine the corresponding source word.

4 Experimental Results

4.1 English to Chinese

We ensemble 5 models for English to Chinese translation. The performance of the system on the validation set is presented in Table 1. We figure that the ensemble strategy brings +0.86 BLEU points improvement and the UNK replace approach provide further +1.57 BLEU points.

4.2 Chinese to English

We ensemble 6 models for Chinese to English translation. Table 2 presents the performance of system on the validation set. Same as the English

---

[3]https://github.com/clab/fast_align

Model	BLEU
Single Model	25.22
Ensemble 6	$26.08^{+0.86}$
+UNK Replace	$27.65^{+1.57}$

Table 1: The model performances on the validation set in English to Chinese direction.

to Chinese translation, the ensemble and UNK replace approaches can enhance the system performance over a single model. The ensemble strategy improves the system by +0.74 BLEU points and the UNK replace approach achieves further +0.51 BLEU point gain. Table 3 shows the performance of our systems on the test set.

Model	BLEU-cased
Single Model	18.13
Ensemble 5	$18.87^{+0.74}$
+ UNK Replace	$19.38^{+0.51}$

Table 2: The model performances on the validation set in Chinese to English direction.

Direction	BLEU	BLEU-cased
English $\rightarrow$ Chinese	30.5	30.5
Chinese $\rightarrow$ English	23.4	22.3

Table 3: The performance of our systems on the test set.

5 Conclusion

We present CASICT-DCU neural machine translation systems for the WMT17 shared news translation task on English $\leftrightarrow$ Chinese language pair. The Gated Recurrent Unit (GRU) with the linear associative connection are employed to build the deep encoder. We extract dictionaries from the parallel training data with unsupervised word alignment approach. We locate the source word that generates the "UNK" symbol in target sentence according to the word alignment vector and translate it with the dictionary. In the decoding procedure, the translation probabilities of the target word from different models are averagely combined as the ensemble strategy to further improve the performance.

Acknowledgments

Qun Liu's work is partially supported by Science Foundation Ireland in the ADAPT Centre for Digital Content Technology (www.adaptcentre.ie) at Dublin City University funded under the SFI Research Centres Programme (Grant 13/RC/2106) co-funded under the European Regional Development Fund.

References

Dzmitry Bahdanau, Kyunghyun Cho, and Yoshua Bengio. 2015. Neural machine translation by jointly learning to align and translate. In *Proceedings of ICLR2015*.

Kyunghyun Cho, Bart Van Merrienboer, Dzmitry Bahdanau, and Yoshua Bengio. 2014a. On the properties of neural machine translation: Encoderdecoder approaches. In *Eighth Workshop on Syntax,Semantics and Structure in Statistical Translation*.

Kyunghyun Cho, Bart van Merrienboer, Caglar Gulcehre, Dzmitry Bahdanau, Fethi Bougares, Holger Schwenk, and Yoshua Bengio. 2014b. Learning phrase representations using rnn encoder–decoder for statistical machine translation. In *Proceedings of EMNLP 2014*. Doha, Qatar, pages 1724–1734.

Kaiming He, Xiangyu Zhang, Shaoqing Ren, and Jian Sun. 2016. Deep residual learning for image recognition. In *Proceedings of the IEEE Conference on Computer Vision and Pattern Recognition*. pages 770–778.

Nal Kalchbrenner and Phil Blunsom. 2013. Recurrent continuous translation models. In *Proceedings of EMNLP2013*. Seattle, Washington, USA, pages 1700–1709.

Razvan Pascanu, Tomas Mikolov, and Yoshua Bengio 2013. On the difficulty of training recurrent neural networks. *ICML (3)* 28:1310 1318.

Rico Sennrich, Barry Haddow, and Alexandra Birch. 2016. Neural machine translation of rare words with subword units. In *Proceedings of ACL2016*. pages 1715–1725.

Nitish Srivastava, Geoffrey E Hinton, Alex Krizhevsky, Ilya Sutskever, and Ruslan Salakhutdinov. 2014. Dropout: a simple way to prevent neural networks from overfitting. *Journal of Machine Learning Research* 15(1):1929–1958.

Ilya Sutskever, Oriol Vinyals, and Quoc V. Le. 2014. Sequence to sequence learning with neural networks. *CoRR* abs/1409.3215.

Mingxuan Wang, Zhengdong Lu, Jie Zhou, and Qun Liu. 2017. Deep neural machine translation with linear associative unit. *CoRR* abs/1705.00861.

Yonghui Wu, Mike Schuster, Zhifeng Chen, Quoc V Le, Mohammad Norouzi, Wolfgang Macherey, Maxim Krikun, Yuan Cao, Qin Gao, Klaus Macherey, et al. 2016. Google's neural machine translation system: Bridging the gap between human and machine translation. *arXiv preprint arXiv:1609.08144* .

Matthew D Zeiler. 2012. Adadelta: an adaptive learning rate method. *arXiv preprint arXiv:1212.5701* .

Jie Zhou, Ying Cao, Xuguang Wang, Peng Li, and Wei Xu. 2016. Deep recurrent models with fast-forward connections for neural machine translation. In *Proceedings of EMNLP2016*.

LIUM-CVC Submissions for WMT17 Multimodal Translation Task

Ozan Caglayan[†], Walid Aransa, Adrien Bardet, Mercedes García-Martínez,
Fethi Bougares, Loïc Barrault
LIUM, University of Le Mans
[†]ozancag@gmail.com
FirstName.LastName@univ-lemans.fr

Marc Masana, Luis Herranz and Joost van de Weijer
CVC, Universitat Autonoma de Barcelona
{joost,mmasana,lherranz}@cvc.uab.es

Abstract

This paper describes the monomodal and multimodal Neural Machine Translation systems developed by LIUM and CVC for WMT17 Shared Task on Multimodal Translation. We mainly explored two multimodal architectures where either global visual features or convolutional feature maps are integrated in order to benefit from visual context. Our final systems ranked first for both En→De and En→Fr language pairs according to the automatic evaluation metrics METEOR and BLEU.

1 Introduction

With the recent advances in deep learning, purely neural approaches to machine translation, such as Neural Machine Translation (NMT), (Sutskever et al., 2014; Bahdanau et al., 2014) have received a lot of attention because of their competitive performance (Toral and Sánchez-Cartagena, 2017). Another reason for the popularity of NMT is its flexible nature allowing researchers to fuse auxiliary information sources in order to design sophisticated networks like multi-task, multi-way and multi-lingual systems to name a few (Luong et al., 2015; Johnson et al., 2016; Firat et al., 2017).

Multimodal Machine Translation (MMT) aims to achieve better translation performance by visually grounding the textual representations. Recently, a new shared task on Multimodal Machine Translation and Crosslingual Image Captioning (CIC) was proposed along with WMT16 (Specia et al., 2016). In this paper, we present MMT systems jointly designed by LIUM and CVC for the second edition of this task within WMT17.

Last year we proposed a multimodal attention mechanism where two different attention distributions were estimated over textual and image representations using *shared* transformations (Caglayan et al., 2016a). More specifically, convolutional feature maps extracted from a ResNet-50 CNN (He et al., 2016) pre-trained on the ImageNet classification task (Russakovsky et al., 2015) were used to represent visual information. Although our submission ranked first among multimodal systems for CIC task, it was not able to improve over purely textual NMT baselines in neither tasks (Specia et al., 2016). The winning submission for MMT (Caglayan et al., 2016a) was a phrase-based MT system rescored using a language model enriched with FC_7 global visual features extracted from a pre-trained VGG-19 CNN (Simonyan and Zisserman, 2014).

State-of-the-art results were obtained after WMT16 by using a *separate* attention mechanism for different modalities in the context of CIC (Caglayan et al., 2016b) and MMT (Calixto et al., 2017a). Besides experimenting with multimodal attention, Calixto et al. (2017a) and Libovický and Helcl (2017) also proposed a gating extension inspired from Xu et al. (2015) which is believed to allow the decoder to learn *when to attend* to a particular modality although Libovický and Helcl (2017) report no improvement over baseline NMT.

There have also been attempts to benefit from different types of visual information instead of relying on features extracted from a CNN pre-trained on ImageNet. One such study from Huang et al. (2016) extended the sequence of source embeddings consumed by the RNN with several regional features extracted from a region-proposal

432

Proceedings of the Conference on Machine Translation (WMT), Volume 2: Shared Task Papers, pages 432–439
Copenhagen, Denmark, September 7–11, 2017. ©2017 Association for Computational Linguistics

network (Ren et al., 2015). The architecture thus predicts a single attention distribution over a sequence of mixed-modality representations leading to significant improvement over their NMT baseline.

More recently, a radically different multi-task architecture called *Imagination* (Elliott and Kádár, 2017) is proposed to learn visually grounded representations by sharing an encoder between two tasks: a classical encoder-decoder NMT and a visual feature reconstruction using as input the source sentence representation.

This year, we experiment[1] with both convolutional and global visual vectors provided by the organizers to better exploit multimodality (Section 3). Data preprocessing for both English→{German,French} and training hyperparameters are detailed respectively in Section 2 and Section 4. The results based on automatic evaluation metrics are reported in Section 5. The paper ends with a discussion in Section 6.

2 Data

We use the Multi30k (Elliott et al., 2016) dataset provided by the organizers which contains 29000, 1014 and 1000 English→{German,French} image-caption pairs respectively for training, validation and Test2016 (the official evaluation set of WMT16 campaign) set. Following task rules we normalized punctuations, applied tokenization and lowercasing. A Byte Pair Encoding (BPE) model (Sennrich et al., 2016) with 10K merge operations is learned for each language pair resulting in 5234→7052 tokens for English→German and 5945→6547 tokens for English→French respectively.

We report results on Flickr Test2017 set containing 1000 image caption pairs and the additional ambiguous MSCOCO test set (Elliott et al., 2017) of 461 image-caption pairs.

Image Features We experimented with several types of visual representation using deep features extracted from convolutional neural networks (CNN) trained on large visual datasets. Following the current state-of-the-art in visual representation, we used a network with the ResNet-50 architecture (He et al., 2016) trained on the ImageNet dataset (Russakovsky et al., 2015) to extract two types of features: the 2048-dimensional features from the *pool5* layer and the 14x14x1024 features from the *res4f_relu* layer. Note that the former is a global feature while the latter is a feature map with roughly localized spatial information.

3 Architecture

Our baseline NMT is an attentive encoder-decoder (Bahdanau et al., 2014) variant with a Conditional GRU (CGRU) (Firat and Cho, 2016) decoder.

Let us denote source and target sequences X and Y with respective lengths M and N as follows where x_i and y_j are embeddings of dimension E:

$$X = (x_1, \ldots, x_M)$$
$$Y = (y_1, \ldots, y_N)$$

Encoder Two GRU (Chung et al., 2014) encoders with R hidden units each, process the source sequence X in forward and backward directions. Their hidden states are concatenated to form a set of *source annotations* **S** where each element s_i is a vector of dimension $C = 2 \times R$:

$$\mathbf{S} = \begin{bmatrix} \mathrm{GRU}_{\mathrm{Forw}}(\overrightarrow{X}) \\ \mathrm{GRU}_{\mathrm{Back}}(\overleftarrow{X}) \end{bmatrix} \in \mathbb{R}^{M \times C}$$

Both encoders are equipped with layer normalization (Ba et al., 2016) where each hidden unit adaptively normalizes its incoming activations with a learnable gain and bias.

Decoder A decoder block namely CGRU (two stacked GRUs where the hidden state of the first GRU is used for attention computation) is used to estimate a probability distribution over target tokens at each decoding step t.

The hidden state h_0 of the CGRU is initialized using a non-linear transformation of the average source annotation:

$$h_0 = \tanh \left(\mathbf{W_{init}} \cdot \frac{1}{M} \sum_i^M s_i \right), s_i \in \mathbf{S} \quad (1)$$

Attention At each decoding timestep t, an unnormalized attention score g_i is computed for each source annotation s_i using the first GRU's hidden state h_t and s_i itself:
($\mathbf{W_a} \in \mathbb{R}^C$, $\mathbf{W_s} \in \mathbb{R}^{C \times C}$ and $\mathbf{W_h} \in \mathbb{R}^{C \times R}$)

$$g_i = \mathbf{W_a^T} \tanh \left(\mathbf{W_s} s_i + b_s + \mathbf{W_h} h_t \right) + b_a \quad (2)$$

[1]A detailed tutorial for reproducing the results of this paper is provided at `https://github.com/lium-lst/wmt17-mmt`.

The context vector c_t is a weighted sum of s_i and its respective attention probability α_i obtained using a softmax operation over all the unnormalized scores:

$$\alpha_i = \text{softmax}\left([g_1, g_2, \ldots, g_M]\right)_i$$

$$c_t = \sum_i^M \alpha_i s_i$$

The final hidden state $\widetilde{h}_t$ is computed by the second GRU using the context vector c_t and the hidden state of the first GRU h_t.

Output The probability distribution over the target tokens is conditioned on the previous token embedding y_{t-1}, the hidden state of the decoder $\widetilde{h}_t$ and the context vector c_t, the latter two transformed with $\mathbf{W_{dec}}$ and $\mathbf{W_{ctx}}$ respectively:

$$o_t = \tanh(y_{t-1} + \mathbf{W_{dec}}\widetilde{h}_t + \mathbf{W_{ctx}}c_t)$$

$$P(y_t|y_{t-1}, \widetilde{h}_t, c_t) = \text{softmax}(\mathbf{W_o}o_t)$$

3.1 Multimodal NMT

3.1.1 Convolutional Features

The **fusion-conv** architecture extends the CGRU decoder to a multimodal decoder (Caglayan et al., 2016b) where convolutional feature maps of 14x14x1024 are regarded as 196 spatial annotations s'_j of 1024-dimension each. For each spatial annotation, an unnormalized attention score g'_j is computed (Equation 2) except that the weights and biases are specific to the visual modality and thus *not shared* with the textual attention:

$$g'_j = {\mathbf{W'_a}}^{\text{T}} \tanh\left(\mathbf{W_s}'s'_j + b'_s + \mathbf{W_h}'h_t\right) + b'_a$$

The visual context vector v_t is computed as a weighted sum of the spatial annotations s'_j and their respective attention probabilities β_j:

$$\beta_j = \text{softmax}\left([g'_1, g'_2, \ldots, g'_{196}]\right)_j$$

$$v_t = \sum_j^{196} \beta_j s'_j$$

The output of the network is now conditioned on a *multimodal* context vector which is the concatenation of the original context vector c_t and the newly computed visual context vector v_t.

3.1.2 Global pool5 Features

In this section, we present 5 architectures guided with global 2048-dimensional visual representation V in different ways. In contrast to the baseline NMT, the decoder's hidden state h_0 is initialized with an all-zero vector unless otherwise specified.

dec-init initializes the decoder with V by replacing Equation 1 with the following:

$$h_0 = \tanh\left(\mathbf{W_{img}} \cdot V\right)$$

(Calixto et al., 2017b) previously explored a similar configuration (IMG$_\text{D}$) where the decoder is initialized with the sum of global visual features extracted from FC7 layer of a pre-trained VGG-19 CNN and the last source annotation.

encdec-init initializes the bi-directional encoder and the decoder with V where e_0 represents the initial state of encoder (Note that in the baseline NMT, e_0 is an all-zero vector) :

$$e_0 = h_0 = \tanh\left(\mathbf{W_{img}} \cdot V\right)$$

ctx-mul modulates each source annotation s_i with V using element-wise multiplication:

$$s_i = s_i \odot \tanh\left(\mathbf{W_{img}} \cdot V\right)$$

trg-mul modulates each target embedding y_j with V using element-wise multiplication:

$$y_j = y_j \odot \tanh\left(\mathbf{W_{img}} \cdot V\right)$$

dec-init-ctx-trg-mul combines the latter two architectures with *dec-init* and uses separate transformation layers for each of them:

$$h_0 = \tanh\left(\mathbf{W_{img}} \cdot V\right)$$
$$s_i = s_i \odot \tanh\left(\mathbf{W'_{img}} \cdot V\right)$$
$$y_j = y_j \odot \tanh\left(\mathbf{W''_{img}} \cdot V\right)$$

4 Training

We use ADAM (Kingma and Ba, 2014) with a learning rate of $4e{-}4$ and a batch size of 32. All weights are initialized using Xavier method (Glorot and Bengio, 2010) and the total gradient norm is clipped to 5 (Pascanu et al., 2013). Dropout (Srivastava et al., 2014) is enabled after source embeddings X, source annotations $\mathbf{S}$ and pre-softmax activations o_t with dropout probabilities of $(0.3, 0.5, 0.5)$ respectively. $((0.2, 0.4, 0.4)$ for

En→De Flickr	# Params	Test2016 ($\mu \pm \sigma$/Ensemble)		Test2017 ($\mu \pm \sigma$/Ensemble)	
		BLEU	METEOR	BLEU	METEOR
Caglayan et al. (2016a)	62.0M	29.2	48.5		
Huang et al. (2016)	-	36.5	54.1		
Calixto et al. (2017a)	213M	36.5	55.0		
Calixto et al. (2017b)	-	37.3	55.1		
Elliott and Kádár (2017)	-	36.8	55.8		
Baseline NMT	4.6M	38.1 ± 0.8 / 40.7	57.3 ± 0.5 / 59.2	30.8 ± 1.0 / 33.2	51.6 ± 0.5 / 53.8
(D1) fusion-conv	6.0M	37.0 ± 0.8 / 39.9	57.0 ± 0.3 / 59.1	29.8 ± 0.9 / 32.7	51.2 ± 0.3 / 53.4
(D2) dec-init-ctx-trg-mul	6.3M	38.0 ± 0.9 / 40.2	57.3 ± 0.3 / 59.3	30.9 ± 1.0 / 33.2	51.4 ± 0.3 / 53.7
(D3) dec-init	5.0M	38.8 ± 0.5 / 41.2	57.5 ± 0.2 / 59.4	31.2 ± 0.7 / 33.4	51.3 ± 0.3 / 53.2
(D4) encdec-init	5.0M	38.2 ± 0.7 / 40.6	57.6 ± 0.3 / 59.5	31.4 ± 0.4 / 33.5	<u>51.9</u> ± 0.4 / 53.7
(D5) ctx-mul	4.6M	38.4 ± 0.3 / 40.4	<u>57.8</u> ± 0.5 / 59.6	31.1 ± 0.7 / 33.5	<u>51.9</u> ± 0.2 / 53.8
(D6) trg-mul	4.7M	37.8 ± 0.9 / 41.0	<u>57.7</u> ± 0.5 / **60.4**	30.7 ± 1.0 / 33.4	<u>52.2</u> ± 0.4 / **54.0**

Table 1: Flickr En→De results: underlined METEOR scores are from systems significantly different (p-value ≤ 0.05) than the baseline using the approximate randomization test of *multeval* for 5 runs. **(D6)** is the official submission of LIUM-CVC.

En→Fr.) An L_2 regularization term with a factor of $1e-5$ is also applied to avoid overfitting unless otherwise stated. Finally, we set E=128 and R=256 (Section 3) respectively for embedding and GRU dimensions.

All models are implemented and trained with the *nmtpy* framework[2] (Caglayan et al., 2017) using Theano v0.9 (Theano Development Team, 2016). Each experiment is repeated with 5 different seeds to mitigate the variance of BLEU (Papineni et al., 2002) and METEOR (Lavie and Agarwal, 2007) and to benefit from ensembling. The training is early stopped if validation set METEOR does not improve for 10 validations performed per 1000 updates. A beam-search with a beam size of 12 is used for translation decoding.

5 Results

All results are computed using *multeval* (Clark et al., 2011) with tokenized sentences.

5.1 En→De

Table 1 summarizes BLEU and METEOR scores obtained by our systems. It should be noted that since we trained each system with 5 different seeds, we report results obtained by ensembling 5 runs as well as the mean/deviation over these 5 runs. The final system to be submitted is selected based on ensemble Test2016 METEOR.

First of all, multimodal systems which use global *pool5* features *generally* obtain compara-

ble scores which are better than the baseline NMT in contrast to **fusion-conv** which fails to improve over it. Our submitted system (D6) achieves an ensembling score of 60.4 METEOR which is 1.2 better than NMT. Although the improvements are smaller, (D6) is still the best system on Test2017 in terms of ensembling/mean METEOR scores. One interesting point to be stressed at this level is that in terms of mean BLEU, (D6) performs worse than baseline on both test sets. Similarly, (D3) which has the best BLEU on Test2016, is the worst system on Test2017 according to METEOR. This is clearly a discrepancy between these metrics where an improvement in one does not necessarily yield an improvement in the other.

En→De	MSCOCO ($\mu \pm \sigma$/Ensemble)	
	BLEU	METEOR
Baseline NMT	26.4 ± 0.2 / 28.7	46.8 ± 0.7 / 48.9
(D1) fusion-conv	25.1 ± 0.7 / 28.0	46.0 ± 0.6 / 48.0
(D2) dec-init-ctx-trg-mul	26.3 ± 0.9 / 28.8	46.5 ± 0.4 / 48.5
(D3) dec-init	26.8 ± 0.5 / 28.8	46.5 ± 0.6 / 48.4
(D4) encdec-init	27.1 ± 0.9 / 29.4	47.2 ± 0.6 / **49.2**
(D5) ctx-mul	27.0 ± 0.7 / 29.3	47.1 ± 0.7 / 48.7
(D6) **trg-mul**	26.4 ± 0.9 / 28.5	<u>47.4</u> ± 0.3 / 48.8

Table 2: MSCOCO En→De results: the best Flickr system **trg-mul** (Table 1) has been used for this submission as well.

For the MSCOCO set no held-out set for model selection was available. Therefore, we submitted the system (D6) with best METEOR on Flickr Test2016.

---

[2] https://github.com/lium-lst/nmtpy

En→Fr	Test2016 ($\mu \pm \sigma$ / Ensemble)		Test2017 ($\mu \pm \sigma$ / Ensemble)	
	BLEU	METEOR	BLEU	METEOR
Baseline NMT	52.5 ± 0.3 / 54.3	69.6 ± 0.1 / 71.3	50.4 ± 0.9 / 53.0	67.5 ± 0.7 / 69.8
(F1) NMT + nol2reg	52.6 ± 0.8 / 55.3	69.6 ± 0.6 / 71.7	50.0 ± 0.9 / 52.5	67.6 ± 0.7 / 70.0
(F2) fusion-conv	53.5 ± 0.8 / 56.5	70.4 ± 0.6 / 72.8	51.6 ± 0.9 / 55.5	68.6 ± 0.7 / 71.7
(F3) dec-init	54.5 ± 0.8 / 56.7	71.2 ± 0.4 / 73.0	52.7 ± 0.9 / 55.5	69.4 ± 0.7 / 71.9
(F4) ctx-mul	54.6 ± 0.8 / 56.7	71.4 ± 0.6 / 73.0	52.6 ± 0.9 / 55.7	69.5 ± 0.7 / 71.9
(F5) trg-mul	54.7 ± 0.8 / 56.7	71.3 ± 0.6 / 73.0	52.7 ± 0.9 / 55.5	69.5 ± 0.7 / 71.7
ens-nmt-7	54.6	71.6	53.3	70.1
ens-mmt-6	**57.4**	**73.6**	**55.9**	**72.2**

Table 3: Flickr En→Fr results: Scores are averages over 5 runs and given with their standard deviation (σ) and the score obtained by ensembling the 5 runs. *ens-nmt-7* and *ens-mmt-6* are the submitted ensembles which correspond to the combination of 7 monomodal and 6 multimodal (global pool5) systems, respectively.

After scoring all the available systems (Table 2) we observe that (D4) is the best system according to ensemble metrics. This can be explained by the *out-of-domain/ambiguous* nature of MSCOCO where best generalization performance on Flickr is not necessarily transferred to this set.

Overall, (D4), (D5) and (D6) are the top systems according to METEOR on Flickr and MSCOCO test sets.

5.2 En→Fr

Table 5.1 shows the results of our systems on the official test set of last year (Test2016) and this year (test2017). F1 is a variant of the baseline NMT without L_2 regularization. F2 is a multimodal system using convolutional feature maps as visual features while F3 to F5 are multimodal systems using *pool5* global visual features. We note that all multimodal systems perform better than monomodal ones.

Compared to the MMT 2016 results, we can see that the fusion-conv (F2) system with separate attention over both modalities achieve better performance than monomodal systems. The results are further improved by systems F3 to F5 which use *pool5* global visual features. We conjecture that the way of integrating the global visual features into these systems does not seem to affect the final results since they all perform equally well on both test sets.

The submitted systems are presented in the last two lines of Table 5.1. Since we did not have all 5 runs with different seeds ready by the submission deadline, heterogeneous ensembles of different architectures and different seeds were considered. *ens-nmt-7* (contrastive monomodal submission) and *ens-mmt-6* (primary multimodal submission) correspond to ensembles of 7 monomodal and 6 multimodal (pool5) systems respectively. *ens-mmt-6* benefits from the heterogeneity of the included systems resulting in a slight improvement of BLEU and METEOR.

En→Fr	MSCOCO ($\mu \pm \sigma$ / ensemble)	
	BLEU	METEOR
Baseline NMT	41.2 ± 1.2 / 43.3	61.3 ± 0.9 / 63.3
(F1) NMT + nol2reg	40.6 ± 1.2 / 43.5	61.1 ± 0.9 / 63.7
(F2) fusion-conv	43.2 ± 1.2 / 45.9	63.1 ± 0.9 / 65.6
(F3) dec-init	43.3 ± 1.2 / 46.2	63.4 ± 0.9 / 66.0
(F4) ctx-mul	43.3 ± 1.2 / 45.6	63.4 ± 0.9 / 65.4
(F5) trg-mul	43.5 ± 1.2 / 45.5	63.2 ± 0.9 / 65.1
ens-nmt-7	43.6	63.4
ens-mmt-6	45.9	65.9

Table 4: MSCOCO En→Fr results: **ens-mmt-6**, the best performing ensemble on Test2016 corpus (see Table 5.1) has been used for this submission as well.

Results on the ambiguous dataset extracted from MSCOCO are presented in Table 4. We can observe a slightly different behaviour compared to the results in Table 5.1. The systems using the convolutional features are performing equally well compared to those using *pool5* features. One should note that no specific tuning was performed for this additional task since no specific validation data was provided.

6 Conclusion

We have presented the LIUM-CVC systems for English to German and English to French Multimodal Machine Translation evaluation campaign. Our systems were ranked first for both tasks in terms of automatic metrics. Using the *pool5* global visual features resulted in a better performance compared to multimodal attention architecture which makes use of convolutional features. This might be explained by the fact that the attention mechanism over spatial feature vectors cannot capture useful information from the extracted features maps. Another explanation for this is that source sentences contain most necessary information to produce the translation and the visual content is only useful to disambiguate a few specific cases. We also believe that reducing the number of parameters aggressively to around 5M allowed us to avoid overfitting leading to better scores in overall.

Acknowledgments

This work was supported by the French National Research Agency (ANR) through the CHIST-ERA M2CR project[3], under the contract number ANR-15-CHR2-0006-01 and by MINECO through APCIN 2015 under the contract number PCIN-2015-251.

References

Jimmy Lei Ba, Jamie Ryan Kiros, and Geoffrey E Hinton. 2016. Layer normalization. *arXiv preprint arXiv:1607.06450* http://arxiv.org/abs/1607.06450.

Dzmitry Bahdanau, Kyunghyun Cho, and Yoshua Bengio. 2014. Neural machine translation by jointly learning to align and translate. *CoRR* abs/1409.0473. http://arxiv.org/abs/1409.0473.

Ozan Caglayan, Walid Aransa, Yaxing Wang, Marc Masana, Mercedes García-Martínez, Fethi Bougares, Loïc Barrault, and Joost van de Weijer. 2016a. Does multimodality help human and machine for translation and image captioning? In *Proceedings of the First Conference on Machine Translation*. Association for Computational Linguistics, Berlin, Germany, pages 627–633. http://www.aclweb.org/anthology/W/W16/W16-2358.pdf.

Ozan Caglayan, Loïc Barrault, and Fethi Bougares. 2016b. Multimodal attention for neural machine translation. *CoRR* abs/1609.03976. http://arxiv.org/abs/1609.03976.

Ozan Caglayan, Mercedes García-Martínez, Adrien Bardet, Walid Aransa, Fethi Bougares, and Loïc Barrault. 2017. Nmtpy: A flexible toolkit for advanced neural machine translation systems. *arXiv preprint arXiv:1706.00457* http://arxiv.org/abs/1706.00457.

Iacer Calixto, Qun Liu, and Nick Campbell. 2017a. Doubly-attentive decoder for multimodal neural machine translation. *arXiv preprint arXiv:1702.01287* http://arxiv.org/abs/1702.01287.

Iacer Calixto, Qun Liu, and Nick Campbell. 2017b. Incorporating global visual features into attention-based neural machine translation. *arXiv preprint arXiv:1701.06521* http://arxiv.org/abs/1701.06521.

Junyoung Chung, Çaglar Gülçehre, KyungHyun Cho, and Yoshua Bengio. 2014. Empirical evaluation of gated recurrent neural networks on sequence modeling. *CoRR* abs/1412.3555. http://arxiv.org/abs/1412.3555.

Jonathan H. Clark, Chris Dyer, Alon Lavie, and Noah A. Smith. 2011. Better hypothesis testing for statistical machine translation: Controlling for optimizer instability. In *Proceedings of the 49th Annual Meeting of the Association for Computational Linguistics: Human Language Technologies: Short Papers - Volume 2*. Association for Computational Linguistics, Stroudsburg, PA, USA, HLT '11, pages 176–181. http://dl.acm.org/citation.cfm?id=2002736.2002774.

Desmond Elliott, Stella Frank, Loïc Barrault, Fethi Bougares, and Lucia Specia. 2017. Findings of the Second Shared Task on Multimodal Machine Translation and Multilingual Image Description. In *Proceedings of the Second Conference on Machine Translation*. Copenhagen, Denmark.

Desmond Elliott, Stella Frank, Khalil Sima'an, and Lucia Specia. 2016. Multi30k: Multilingual english-german image descriptions. In *Proceedings of the 5th Workshop on Vision and Language*. Association for Computational Linguistics, Berlin, Germany, pages 70–74. http://anthology.aclweb.org/W16-3210.

Desmond Elliott and Ákos Kádár. 2017. Imagination improves multimodal translation. *CoRR* abs/1705.04350. http://arxiv.org/abs/1705.04350.

Orhan Firat and Kyunghyun Cho. 2016. Conditional gated recurrent unit with attention mechanism. http://github.com/nyu-dl/dl4mt-tutorial/blob/master/docs/cgru.pdf.

Orhan Firat, Kyunghyun Cho, Baskaran Sankaran, Fatos T. Yarman Vural, and Yoshua Bengio. 2017. Multi-way, multilingual neural machine translation. *Comput. Speech Lang.* 45(C):236–252. https://doi.org/10.1016/j.csl.2016.10.006.

---

[3] http://m2cr.univ-lemans.fr

Xavier Glorot and Yoshua Bengio. 2010. Understanding the difficulty of training deep feedforward neural networks. In *Proceedings of the Thirteenth International Conference on Artificial Intelligence and Statistics*. PMLR, volume 9 of *Proceedings of Machine Learning Research*, pages 249–256. http://proceedings.mlr.press/v9/glorot10a.html.

K. He, X. Zhang, S. Ren, and J. Sun. 2016. Deep residual learning for image recognition. In *2016 IEEE Conference on Computer Vision and Pattern Recognition (CVPR)*. pages 770–778. https://doi.org/10.1109/CVPR.2016.90.

Po-Yao Huang, Frederick Liu, Sz-Rung Shiang, Jean Oh, and Chris Dyer. 2016. Attention-based multimodal neural machine translation. In *Proceedings of the First Conference on Machine Translation*. Association for Computational Linguistics, Berlin, Germany, pages 639–645. http://www.aclweb.org/anthology/W16-2360.

Melvin Johnson, Mike Schuster, Quoc V. Le, Maxim Krikun, Yonghui Wu, Zhifeng Chen, Nikhil Thorat, Fernanda Vigas, Martin Wattenberg, Greg Corrado, Macduff Hughes, and Jeffrey Dean. 2016. Google's multilingual neural machine translation system: Enabling zero-shot translation. Technical report, Google. https://arxiv.org/abs/1611.04558.

Diederik Kingma and Jimmy Ba. 2014. Adam: A method for stochastic optimization. *arXiv preprint arXiv:1412.6980* http://arxiv.org/abs/1412.6980.

Alon Lavie and Abhaya Agarwal. 2007. Meteor: An automatic metric for mt evaluation with high levels of correlation with human judgments. In *Proceedings of the Second Workshop on Statistical Machine Translation*. Association for Computational Linguistics, Stroudsburg, PA, USA, StatMT '07, pages 228–231. http://dl.acm.org/citation.cfm?id=1626355.1626389.

Jindrich Libovický and Jindrich Helcl. 2017. Attention strategies for multi-source sequence-to-sequence learning. *CoRR* abs/1704.06567. http://arxiv.org/abs/1704.06567.

Minh-Thang Luong, Quoc V Le, Ilya Sutskever, Oriol Vinyals, and Lukasz Kaiser. 2015. Multi-task sequence to sequence learning. *arXiv preprint arXiv:1511.06114* http://arxiv.org/abs/1511.06114.

Kishore Papineni, Salim Roukos, Todd Ward, and Wei-Jing Zhu. 2002. Bleu: A method for automatic evaluation of machine translation. In *Proceedings of the 40th Annual Meeting on Association for Computational Linguistics*. Association for Computational Linguistics, Stroudsburg, PA, USA, ACL '02, pages 311–318. https://doi.org/10.3115/1073083.1073135.

Razvan Pascanu, Tomas Mikolov, and Yoshua Bengio. 2013. On the difficulty of training recurrent neural networks. In *Proceedings of the 30th International Conference on International Conference on Machine Learning - Volume 28*. JMLR.org, ICML'13, pages III–1310–III–1318. http://dl.acm.org/citation.cfm?id=3042817.3043083.

Shaoqing Ren, Kaiming He, Ross Girshick, and Jian Sun. 2015. Faster r-cnn: Towards real-time object detection with region proposal networks. In *Proceedings of the 28th International Conference on Neural Information Processing Systems*. MIT Press, Cambridge, MA, USA, NIPS'15, pages 91–99. http://dl.acm.org/citation.cfm?id=2969239.2969250.

Olga Russakovsky, Jia Deng, Hao Su, Jonathan Krause, Sanjeev Satheesh, Sean Ma, Zhiheng Huang, Andrej Karpathy, Aditya Khosla, Michael Bernstein, Alexander C. Berg, and Li Fei-Fei. 2015. ImageNet Large Scale Visual Recognition Challenge. *International Journal of Computer Vision (IJCV)* 115(3):211–252. https://doi.org/10.1007/s11263-015-0816-y.

Rico Sennrich, Barry Haddow, and Alexandra Birch. 2016. Neural machine translation of rare words with subword units. In *Proceedings of the 54th Annual Meeting of the Association for Computational Linguistics (Volume 1: Long Papers)*. Association for Computational Linguistics, Berlin, Germany, pages 1715–1725. http://www.aclweb.org/anthology/P16-1162.

Karen Simonyan and Andrew Zisserman. 2014. Very deep convolutional networks for large-scale image recognition. *arXiv preprint arXiv:1409.1556* http://arxiv.org/abs/1409.1556.

Lucia Specia, Stella Frank, Khalil Sima'an, and Desmond Elliott. 2016. A shared task on multimodal machine translation and crosslingual image description. In *Proceedings of the First Conference on Machine Translation*. Association for Computational Linguistics, Berlin, Germany, pages 543–553. http://www.aclweb.org/anthology/W/W16/W16-2346.

Nitish Srivastava, Geoffrey Hinton, Alex Krizhevsky, Ilya Sutskever, and Ruslan Salakhutdinov. 2014. Dropout: A simple way to prevent neural networks from overfitting. *J. Mach. Learn. Res.* 15(1):1929–1958. http://dl.acm.org/citation.cfm?id=2627435.2670313.

Ilya Sutskever, Oriol Vinyals, and Quoc V. Le. 2014. Sequence to sequence learning with neural networks. In *Proceedings of the 27th International Conference on Neural Information Processing Systems*. MIT Press, Cambridge, MA, USA, NIPS'14, pages 3104–3112. http://dl.acm.org/citation.cfm?id=2969033.2969173.

Theano Development Team. 2016. Theano: A Python framework for fast computation of mathematical expressions. *arXiv e-prints* abs/1605.02688. http://arxiv.org/abs/1605.02688.

Antonio Toral and Víctor M. Sánchez-Cartagena. 2017.
A multifaceted evaluation of neural versus phrase-
based machine translation for 9 language directions.
In *Proceedings of the 15th Conference of the European Chapter of the Association for Computational
Linguistics: Volume 1, Long Papers*. Association for
Computational Linguistics, Valencia, Spain, pages
1063–1073. http://www.aclweb.org/anthology/E17-
1100.

Kelvin Xu, Jimmy Ba, Ryan Kiros, Kyunghyun
Cho, Aaron Courville, Ruslan Salakhudinov, Rich
Zemel, and Yoshua Bengio. 2015.   Show,
attend and tell: Neural image caption generation with visual attention.   In *Proceedings of the 32nd International Conference on
Machine Learning (ICML-15)*. JMLR Workshop
and Conference Proceedings, pages 2048–2057.
http://jmlr.org/proceedings/papers/v37/xuc15.pdf.

DCU System Report on the WMT 2017
Multi-modal Machine Translation Task

Iacer Calixto and **Koel Dutta Chowdhury** and **Qun Liu**
{iacer.calixto,koel.chowdhury,qun.liu}@adaptcentre.ie

Abstract

We report experiments with multi-modal neural machine translation models that incorporate global visual features in different parts of the encoder and decoder, and use the VGG19 network to extract features for all images. In our experiments, we explore both different strategies to include global image features and also how ensembling different models at inference time impact translations. Our submissions ranked 3rd best for translating from English into French, always improving considerably over an neural machine translation baseline across all language pair evaluated, e.g. an increase of 7.0–9.2 METEOR points.

1 Introduction

In this paper we report on our application of three different multi-modal neural machine translation (NMT) systems to translate image descriptions. We use encoder–decoder attentive multi-modal NMT models where each training example consists of one source variable-length sequence, one image, and one target variable-length sequence, and a model is trained to translate sequences in the source language into corresponding sequences in the target language while taking the image into consideration. We use the three models introduced in Calixto et al. (2017b), which integrate *global image features* extracted using a pre-trained convolutional neural network into NMT *(i)* as words in the source sentence, *(ii)* to initialise the encoder hidden state, and *(iii)* as additional data to initialise the decoder hidden state.

We are inspired by the recent success of multi-modal NMT models applied to the translation of image descriptions (Huang et al., 2016; Calixto

et al., 2017a). Huang et al. (2016) incorporate global visual features into NMT with some success, and Calixto et al. (2017a) propose to use local visual features instead, achieving better results. We follow Calixto et al. (2017b) and investigate whether we can achieve better results while still using *global visual features*, which are considerably smaller and simpler to integrate when compared to local features.

We expect that, by integrating visual information when translating image descriptions, we are able to exploit valuable information from both modalities when generating the target description, effectively grounding machine translation (Glenberg and Robertson, 2000).

2 Model Description

The models used in our experiments can be viewed as expansions of the attentive NMT framework introduced by Bahdanau et al. (2015) with the addition of a visual component that incorporates visual features from images. A bi-directional recurrent neural network (RNN) with gated recurrent unit (GRU) (Cho et al., 2014) is used as the encoder. The final annotation vector for a given source position i is the concatenation of forward and backward RNN hidden states, $h_i = [\overrightarrow{h_i}; \overleftarrow{h_i}]$.

We use the publicly available pre-trained convolution neural network VGG19[1] of Simonyan and Zisserman (2014) to extract global image feature vectors for all images. These features are the 4096D activations of the penultimate fully-connected layer FC7, henceforth referred to as q.

We now describe the three multi-modal NMT models used in our experiments. For a detailed explanation about these models, see Calixto et al. (2017b).

---

[1] http://www.robots.ox.ac.uk/˜vgg/research/very_deep/

Proceedings of the Conference on Machine Translation (WMT), Volume 2: Shared Task Papers, pages 440–444
Copenhagen, Denmark, September 7–11, 2017. ©2017 Association for Computational Linguistics

2.1 IMG$_{2W}$: Image as source words

In model IMG$_{2W}$, the image features are used as the first and last words of the source sentence, and the source-language attention model learns when to attend to the image representations. Specifically, given the global image feature vector $q \in \mathbb{R}^{4096}$:

$$d = W_I^2 \cdot (W_I^1 \cdot q + b_I^1) + b_I^2, \qquad (1)$$

where $W_I^1 \in \mathbb{R}^{4096 \times 4096}$ and $W_I^2 \in \mathbb{R}^{4096 \times d_x}$ are image transformation matrices, $b_I^1 \in \mathbb{R}^{4096}$ and $b_I^2 \in \mathbb{R}^{d_x}$ are bias vectors, and d_x is the source words vector space dimensionality, all trained with the model.

We directly use d as the first and last words of the source sentence. In other words, given the word embeddings for a source sentence $X = (x_1, x_2, \cdots, x_N)$, we concatenate the transformed image vector d to it, i.e. $X = (d, x_1, x_2, \cdots, x_N, d)$, and apply the forward and backward encoder RNN. By including images into the encoder in model IMG$_{2W}$, our intuition is that *(i)* by including the image as the *first word*, we propagate image features into the source sentence vector representations when applying the forward RNN to produce vectors $\overrightarrow{h_i}$, and *(ii)* by including the image as the *last word*, we propagate image features into the source sentence vector representations when applying the backward RNN to produce vectors $\overleftarrow{h_i}$.

2.2 IMG$_E$: Image for encoder initialisation

In the original attention-based NMT model of Bahdanau et al. (2015), the hidden state of the encoder is initialised with the zero vector $\overrightarrow{0}$. Instead, we propose to use two new single-layer feed-forward neural networks to compute the initial states of the forward and the backward RNN, respectively.

Similarly to what we do for model IMG$_{2W}$ described in Section 2.1, given a global image feature vector $q \in \mathbb{R}^{4096}$, we compute a vector d using Equation (1), only this time the parameters W_I^2 and b_I^2 project the image features into the same dimensionality as the hidden states of the source language encoder.

The feed-forward networks used to initialise the encoder hidden state are computed as in (2):

$$\overleftarrow{h}_{\text{init}} = \tanh\left(W_f d + b_f\right),$$
$$\overrightarrow{h}_{\text{init}} = \tanh\left(W_b d + b_b\right), \qquad (2)$$

where W_f and W_b are multi-modal projection matrices that project the image features d into the encoder forward and backward hidden states dimensionality, respectively, and b_f and b_b are bias vectors. $\overrightarrow{h}_{\text{init}}$ and $\overleftarrow{h}_{\text{init}}$ are directly used as the forward and backward RNN initial hidden states, respectively.

2.3 IMG$_D$: Image for decoder initialisation

To incorporate an image into the decoder, we introduce a new single-layer feed-forward neural network. Originally, the decoder initial hidden state is computed using a summary of the encoder hidden states. This is often the concatenation of the last hidden states of the encoder forward RNN and backward RNN, respectively $\overrightarrow{h}_N$ and $\overleftarrow{h}_1$, or the mean of the source-language annotation vectors h_i.

We propose to include the image features as additional input to initialise the decoder's hidden state, as described in (3):

$$s_0 = \tanh\left(W_{di}[\overleftarrow{h}_1; \overrightarrow{h}_N] + W_m d + b_{di}\right), \quad (3)$$

where s_0 is the decoder initial hidden state, W_m is a multi-modal projection matrix that projects the image features d into the decoder hidden state dimensionality and W_{di} and b_{di} are learned model parameters.

Once again we compute d by applying Equation (1) onto a global image feature vector $q \in \mathbb{R}^{4096}$, only this time the parameters W_I^2 and b_I^2 project the image features into the same dimensionality as the decoder hidden states.

3 Experiments

We report results for Task 1, specifically when translating from English into German (en–de) and French (en–fr). We conducted experiments on the constrained version of the shared task, which means that the only training data we used is the data released by the shared task organisers, i.e. the *translated Multi30k* (M30k$_T$) data set (Elliott et al., 2016) with the additional French image descriptions, included for the 2017 run of the shared task.

Our encoder is a bi-directional RNN with GRU, one 1024D single-layer forward RNN and one 1024D single-layer backward RNN. Throughout, we parameterise our models using 620D source and target word embeddings, and both are trained jointly with our model. All non-recurrent matrices are initialised by sampling from a Gaussian distribution ($\mu = 0, \sigma = 0.01$), recurrent matrices are random orthogonal and bias vectors are all initialised to $\vec{0}$. We apply dropout (Srivastava et al., 2014) with a probability of 0.3 in source and target word embeddings, in the image features, in the encoder and decoder RNNs inputs and recurrent connections, and before the readout operation in the decoder RNN. We follow Gal and Ghahramani (2016) and apply dropout to the encoder bidirectional RNN and decoder RNN using the same mask in all time steps.

The translated Multi30k training and validation sets contain 29k and 1014 images respectively, each accompanied by a sentence triple, the original English sentence and its gold-standard translations into German and into French.

We use the scripts in the Moses SMT Toolkit (Koehn et al., 2007) to normalise, lowercase and tokenize English, German and French descriptions and we also convert space-separated tokens into subwords (Sennrich et al., 2016). The subword models are trained jointly for English–German descriptions and separately for English–French descriptions using the English-German and English-French WMT 2015 data (Bojar et al., 2015). English–German models have a final vocabulary of 74K English and 81K German subword tokens, and English–French models 82K English and 82K French subword tokens. If sentences in English, German or French are longer than 80 tokens, they are discarded.

Finally, we use the 29K entries in the M30k$_T$ training set for training our models, and the $1,014$ entries in the M30k$_T$ development set for model selection, early stopping the training procedure in case the model stops improving BLEU scores on this development set. We evaluate our English–German models on three held-out test sets, the Multi30k 2016/2017 and the MSCOCO 2017 test sets, and our English–French models on the Multi30k 2017 and the MSCOCO 2017 test sets.

We evaluate translation quality quantitatively in terms of BLEU4 (Papineni et al., 2002), METEOR (Denkowski and Lavie, 2014), and TER (Snover et al., 2006).

Multi30k 2017				
Lang.	Model	BLEU4 ↑	METEOR↑	TER↓
en–de	NMT baseline	19.3	41.9	72.2
en–de	Ensemble	**29.8** (↑ 10.3)	**50.5** (↑ 8.6)	**52.3** (↓ 19.9)
en–fr	NMT baseline	44.3	63.1	39.6
en–fr	Ensemble	**54.1** (↑ 9.8)	**70.1** (↑ 7.0)	**30.0** (↓ 9.6)

Table 1: Results for the M30k$_T$ 2017 English–German and English–French test sets. All models are trained on the original M30k$_T$ training data. Our ensemble uses four multi-modal models, all independently trained: two models IMG$_D$, one model IMG$_E$, and one model IMG$_{2W}$.

MSCOCO 2017				
Lang.	Model	BLEU4 ↑	METEOR↑	TER↓
en–de	NMT baseline	18.7	37.6	66.1
en–de	Ensemble	**26.4** (↑ 7.7)	**46.8** (↑ 9.2)	**54.5** (↓ 11.6)
en–fr	NMT baseline	35.1	55.8	45.8
en–fr	Ensemble	**44.5** (↑ 9.4)	**64.1** (↑ 8.3)	**35.2** (↓ 10.6)

Table 2: Results for the MSCOCO 2017 English–German and English–French test sets. All models are trained on the original M30k$_T$ training data. Ensemble uses four multi-modal models, all trained independently: two models IMG$_D$, one model IMG$_E$, and one model IMG$_{2W}$.

3.1 Results

In Table 1, we show results when translating the Multi30k 2017 test sets. Models are trained on the original M30k$_T$ training data only. The NMT baseline is the attention-based NMT model of Bahdanau et al. (2015) and its results are the ones reported by the shared task organisers. When compared to other submissions of the multi-modal MT task under the constrained data regime, our models ranked sixth best when translating the English–German Multi30k 2017, and fourth best when translating the English–German MSCOCO 2017 test sets. When translating both the Multi30k 2017 and the MSCOCO 2017 English–French test sets, our models are ranked third best, scoring only 1–2 points (BLEU, METEOR) less than the best system.

In Table 2, we show results when translating the MSCOCO 2017 English–German and English–French test sets. Again, all models are trained on the original M30k$_T$ training data only. When compared to other submissions of the multi-modal MT task under the constrained data regime, our submission ranked fourth best for the English–German and third best for the English–French lan-

Multi30k 2016 (English→German)

	Ensemble?	BLEU4 ↑	METEOR↑	TER↓
$\text{NMT}_{\text{SRC+IMG}}$[1]	×	<u>39.0</u>	<u>56.8</u>	<u>40.6</u>
IMG_{D}	×	37.3	55.1	42.8
$\text{IMG}_{\text{D}} + \text{IMG}_{\text{E}}$	✓	40.1 (↑ 1.1)	58.5 (↑ 1.7)	40.7 (↑ 0.1)
$\text{IMG}_{\text{D}} + \text{IMG}_{\text{E}} + \text{IMG}_{\text{2W}}$	✓	41.0 (↑ 2.0)	58.9 (↑ 2.1)	39.7 (↓ 0.9)
$\text{IMG}_{\text{D}} + \text{IMG}_{\text{E}} + \text{IMG}_{\text{2W}} + \text{IMG}_{\text{D}}$	✓	**41.3** (↑ 2.3)	**59.2** (↑ 2.4)	**39.5** (↓ 1.1)

[1] This model is pre-trained on the English–German WMT 2015 (Bojar et al., 2015), consisting of ~4.3M sentence pairs.

Table 3: Results for the best model of Calixto et al. (2017a), which is pre-trained on the English–German WMT 2015 (Bojar et al., 2015), and different combinations of multi-modal models, all trained on the original M30k$_\text{T}$ training data only, evaluated on the M30k$_\text{T}$ 2016 test set.

guage pair, scoring only 1 to 1.5 points less than the best system. These are promising results, specially taking into consideration that we are using global image features, which are smaller and simpler than local features (used in Calixto et al. (2017a)).

Ensemble decoding We now report on how can ensemble decoding be used to improve multi-modal MT. In Table 3, we show results when translating the Multi30k 2016's test set. We ensembled different models by starting with one of Calixto et al. (2017b)'s best performing multi-modal models on this data set, IMG_{D}, and by adding new models to the ensemble one by one, until we reach a maximum of four independent models, all of which are trained separately and on the original M30k$_\text{T}$ training data only. We also report results for the best model of Calixto et al. (2017a), which is pre-trained on the English–German WMT 2015 (Bojar et al., 2015) and uses local visual features extracted with the ResNet-50 network (He et al., 2015).

We first note that adding more models to the ensemble seems to always improve translations by a large margin (∼ 3 BLEU/METEOR points). Adding model IMG_{2W} to the ensemble already consisting of models IMG_{E} and IMG_{D} still improves translations, according to all metrics evaluated. This is an interesting result, since compared to these other two multi-modal models, model IMG_{2W} performs the worst according to BLEU, METEOR and chrF3 (see Calixto et al. (2017b)). Our best results are obtained with an ensemble of four different multi-modal models.

By using an ensemble of four different multi-modal NMT models trained on the translated

Multi30k training data, we were able to obtain translations comparable to or even better than those obtained with the strong multi-modal NMT model of Calixto et al. (2017a), which is pre-trained on large amounts of WMT data and uses local image features.

4 Conclusions and Future work

In this work, we evaluated multi-modal NMT models which integrate *global image features* into both the encoder and the decoder. We experimented with ensembling different multi-modal NMT models introduced in Calixto et al. (2017b), and results show that these models can generate translations that compare favourably to multi-modal models that use local image features. We observe consistent improvements over a text-only NMT baseline trained on the same data, and these are typically very large (e.g., 7.0–9.2 METEOR points across language pairs and test sets). In future work we plan to study how to generalise these models to other multi-modal natural language processing tasks, e.g. visual question answering.

Acknowledgments

This project has received funding from Science Foundation Ireland in the ADAPT Centre for Digital Content Technology (www.adaptcentre. ie) at Dublin City University funded under the SFI Research Centres Programme (Grant 13/RC/2106) co-funded under the European Regional Development Fund and the European Union Horizon 2020 research and innovation programme under grant agreement 645452 (QT21).

References

Dzmitry Bahdanau, Kyunghyun Cho, and Yoshua Bengio. 2015. Neural Machine Translation by Jointly Learning to Align and Translate. In *International Conference on Learning Representations, ICLR 2015*. San Diego, California.

Ondřej Bojar, Rajen Chatterjee, Christian Federmann, Barry Haddow, Matthias Huck, Chris Hokamp, Philipp Koehn, Varvara Logacheva, Christof Monz, Matteo Negri, Matt Post, Carolina Scarton, Lucia Specia, and Marco Turchi. 2015. Findings of the 2015 Workshop on Statistical Machine Translation. In *Proceedings of the Tenth Workshop on Statistical Machine Translation*. Association for Computational Linguistics, Lisbon, Portugal, pages 1–46. http://aclweb.org/anthology/W15-3001.

Iacer Calixto, Qun Liu, and Nick Campbell. 2017a. Doubly-Attentive Decoder for Multi-modal Neural Machine Translation. In *Proceedings of the 55th Conference of the Association for Computational Linguistics: Volume 1, Long Papers*. Vancouver, Canada (Paper Accepted).

Iacer Calixto, Qun Liu, and Nick Campbell. 2017b. Incorporating Global Visual Features into Attention-Based Neural Machine Translation. In *Proceedings of the 2017 Conference on Empirical Methods in Natural Language Processing*. Copenhagen, Denmark (Paper Accepted).

Kyunghyun Cho, Bart van Merrienboer, Caglar Gulcehre, Dzmitry Bahdanau, Fethi Bougares, Holger Schwenk, and Yoshua Bengio. 2014. Learning Phrase Representations using RNN Encoder–Decoder for Statistical Machine Translation. In *Proceedings of the 2014 Conference on Empirical Methods in Natural Language Processing (EMNLP)*. Doha, Qatar, pages 1724–1734. http://www.aclweb.org/anthology/D14-1179.

Michael Denkowski and Alon Lavie. 2014. Meteor Universal: Language Specific Translation Evaluation for Any Target Language. In *Proceedings of the EACL 2014 Workshop on Statistical Machine Translation*. The Association for Computer Linguistics, Gothenburg, Sweden.

Desmond Elliott, Stella Frank, Khalil Sima'an, and Lucia Specia. 2016. Multi30K: Multilingual English-German Image Descriptions. In *Proceedings of the 5th Workshop on Vision and Language, VL@ACL 2016*. Berlin, Germany. http://aclweb.org/anthology/W/W16-3210.pdf.

Yarin Gal and Zoubin Ghahramani. 2016. A Theoretically Grounded Application of Dropout in Recurrent Neural Networks. In *Advances in Neural Information Processing Systems, NIPS*. Barcelona, Spain, pages 1019–1027. http://papers.nips.cc/paper/6241-a-theoretically-grounded-application-of-dropout-in-recurrent-neural-networks.pdf.

A. Glenberg and D. Robertson. 2000. Symbol grounding and meaning: A comparison of high-dimensional and embodied theories of meaning. *Journal of Memory and Language* http://psych.wisc.edu/glenberg/.

Kaiming He, Xiangyu Zhang, Shaoqing Ren, and Jian Sun. 2015. Deep Residual Learning for Image Recognition. *arXiv preprint arXiv:1512.03385* .

Po-Yao Huang, Frederick Liu, Sz-Rung Shiang, Jean Oh, and Chris Dyer. 2016. Attention-based Multimodal Neural Machine Translation. In *Proceedings of the First Conference on Machine Translation*. Berlin, Germany, pages 639–645. http://www.aclweb.org/anthology/W/W16/W16-2360.

Philipp Koehn, Hieu Hoang, Alexandra Birch, Chris Callison-Burch, Marcello Federico, Nicola Bertoldi, Brooke Cowan, Wade Shen, Christine Moran, Richard Zens, Chris Dyer, Ondřej Bojar, Alexandra Constantin, and Evan Herbst. 2007. Moses: Open Source Toolkit for Statistical Machine Translation. In *Proceedings of the 45th Annual Meeting of the ACL on Interactive Poster and Demonstration Sessions*. Association for Computational Linguistics, Prague, Czech Republic, ACL '07, pages 177–180. http://dl.acm.org/citation.cfm?id=1557769.1557821.

Kishore Papineni, Salim Roukos, Todd Ward, and Wei-Jing Zhu. 2002. BLEU: A Method for Automatic Evaluation of Machine Translation. In *Proceedings of the 40th Annual Meeting on Association for Computational Linguistics*. Philadelphia, Pennsylvania, ACL '02, pages 311–318. https://doi.org/10.3115/1073083.1073135.

Rico Sennrich, Barry Haddow, and Alexandra Birch. 2016. Neural Machine Translation of Rare Words with Subword Units. In *Proceedings of the 54th Annual Meeting of the Association for Computational Linguistics (Volume 1: Long Papers)*. Berlin, Germany, pages 1715–1725. http://www.aclweb.org/anthology/P16-1162.

K. Simonyan and A. Zisserman. 2014. Very Deep Convolutional Networks for Large-Scale Image Recognition. *CoRR abs/1409.1556*.

Matthew Snover, Bonnie Dorr, Richard Schwartz, Linnea Micciulla, and John Makhoul. 2006. A study of translation edit rate with targeted human annotation. In *Proceedings of Association for Machine Translation in the Americas, AMTA*. Cambridge, MA, USA, pages 223–231.

Nitish Srivastava, Geoffrey Hinton, Alex Krizhevsky, Ilya Sutskever, and Ruslan Salakhutdinov. 2014. Dropout: A simple way to prevent neural networks from overfitting. *Journal of Machine Learning Research* 15:1929–1958. http://jmlr.org/papers/v15/srivastava14a.html.

The AFRL-OSU WMT17 Multimodal Translation System: An Image Processing Approach

John Duselis, Michael Hutt,
Jeremy Gwinnup
Air Force Research Laboratory
{john.duselis,michael.hutt.ctr,
jeremy.gwinnup.1}@us.af.mil

James W. Davis
Joshua Sandvick
Ohio State University
{davis.1719,sandvick.6}@osu.edu

Abstract

This paper introduces the AFRL-OSU Multimodal Machine Translation Task 1 system for submission to the Conference on Machine Translation 2017 (WMT17). This is an atypical MT system in that the image is the catalyst for the MT results, and not the textual content.

1 Introduction

Contemporary scientific meetings have examined the potential benefits of fusing image information with machine translation. For instance, the leading international conference in this area, the Conference on Machine Translation (WMT), is approaching its second year of competition on Multimodal Machine Translation (MMT). First year results in WMT16's Multimodal Task 1 were varied in approaches, informative in their findings, and indicated potential opprtunities for multimodal system improvement. (Specia et al., 2016).

In the WMT16 submissions, the seemingly predominant focal point across the systems was the fact that textual information was the driver for the translation. The image features tended towards being ancilliary inputs or outputs (Libovický et al., 2016; Guasch and Costa-Jussà, 2016; Caglayan et al., 2016) or decision-type functions (Shah et al., 2016) and not the main antagonist for translation (Specia et al., 2016; Elliott et al., 2015). This is sensible as it is an MT competition. However, approaching it from another direction, namely, having the image as the driver for the translation presents a different point of view worth investigating.

This work is sponsored by the Air Force Research Laboratory under AFRL/711 Human Performance Wing Chief Scientist Funding.

The following sections will outline the seemingly novel approach to MMT and give particulars of this unconstrained system.

2 AFRL-OSU System

This section will outline the architecture of the system. This is a first approximation into the process but is expected to undergo further development based on insights from this competition.

2.1 General Overview

Referencing Fig. 1, a generic example taken from (Specia et al., 2016) shows a method where the source caption and image are the drivers for the multimodal translation. In some of WMT16's submissions, the decomposition of the image is incorporated as an additional feature into the MMT system, while others used the features as a function to help pick the best translation.

AFRL-OSU's system is pictorially represented in Figure 2. Currently, there is much work in image captioning systems (Socher et al., 2014; Ghahramani et al., 2014; Mao et al., 2014; Kiros et al., 2014; Vinyals et al., 2015), and WMT17 has even set out a task in its competition for it. Our emphasis is not to try to produce a multilingual image captioning system, rather to use one to accomplish MT as the maturity of the caption engine research progresses.

This system architecture assumes an image caption engine can be trained in a target language to give meaningful output in the form of a set of the most probable n target language candidate captions. A learned mapping function of the encoded source language caption to the corresponding encoded target language candidate captions is thusly employed. Finally, a distance function is applied to retrieve the "nearest" candidate caption to be the translation of the source caption.

Proceedings of the Conference on Machine Translation (WMT), Volume 2: Shared Task Papers, pages 445–449
Copenhagen, Denmark, September 7–11, 2017. ©2017 Association for Computational Linguistics

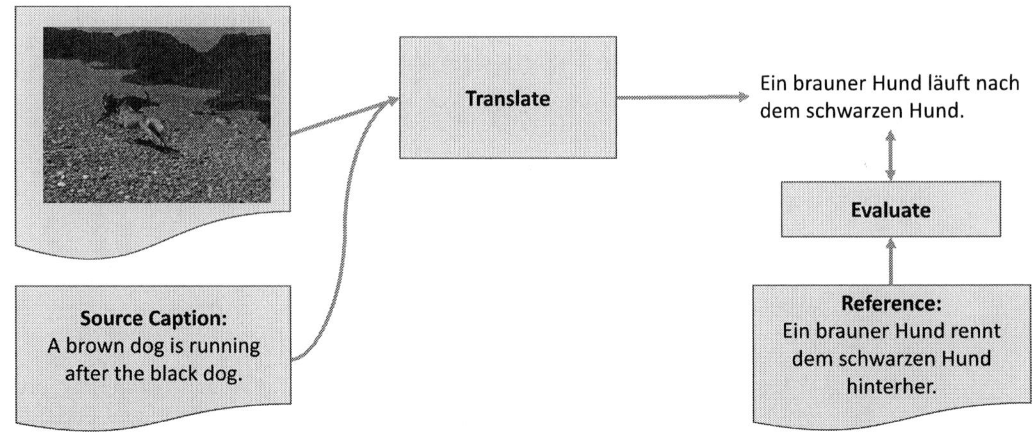

Figure 1: A Text-based Model for Multimodal Machine Translation adapted from (Specia et al., 2016)

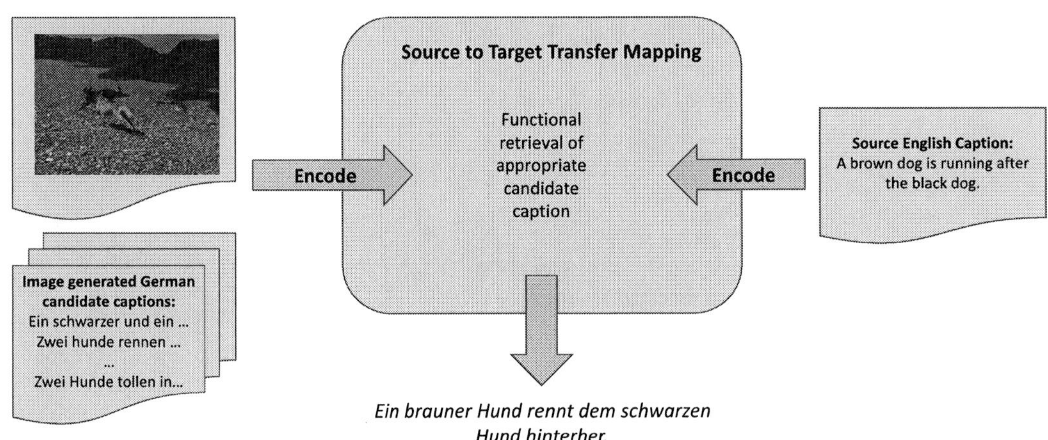

Figure 2: An Image-based Model for Multimodal Machine Translation.

2.2 Theoretical Overview

Details of the system architecture are illustrated in Figure 3. Given an image i (top left), using an image captioning engine trained in the target language t, we produce n candidate captions: $C_{i_j}^t$ for $j = 1, ..., n$.

After obtaining the candidate sentences, we transform them into a fixed vector length encoding with

$$v_{i_j}^t = G^t(C_{i_j}^t) \qquad (1)$$

where $G^t(\cdot)$ is the target encoder.

Similarly (from the top right of Figure 3), the source language caption C_i^s is encoded using

$$v_i^s = G^s(C_i^s) \qquad (2)$$

where $G^s(\cdot)$ is the source encoder.

At this point, both the target captions and the source caption are encoded in separate monolingual, monomodal subspaces. In order to execute the retrieval process, we develop a transfer mapping of the source language encodings to the space of target language encodings. We learn this source-to-target mapping using training pairs of source language encodings and target language encodings provided by traditional MT of the source language examples (Sennrich et al., 2016). Hence the mapping attempts to learn MT translation from the encoding representations themselves. The architecture employed is a multi-layer neural network.

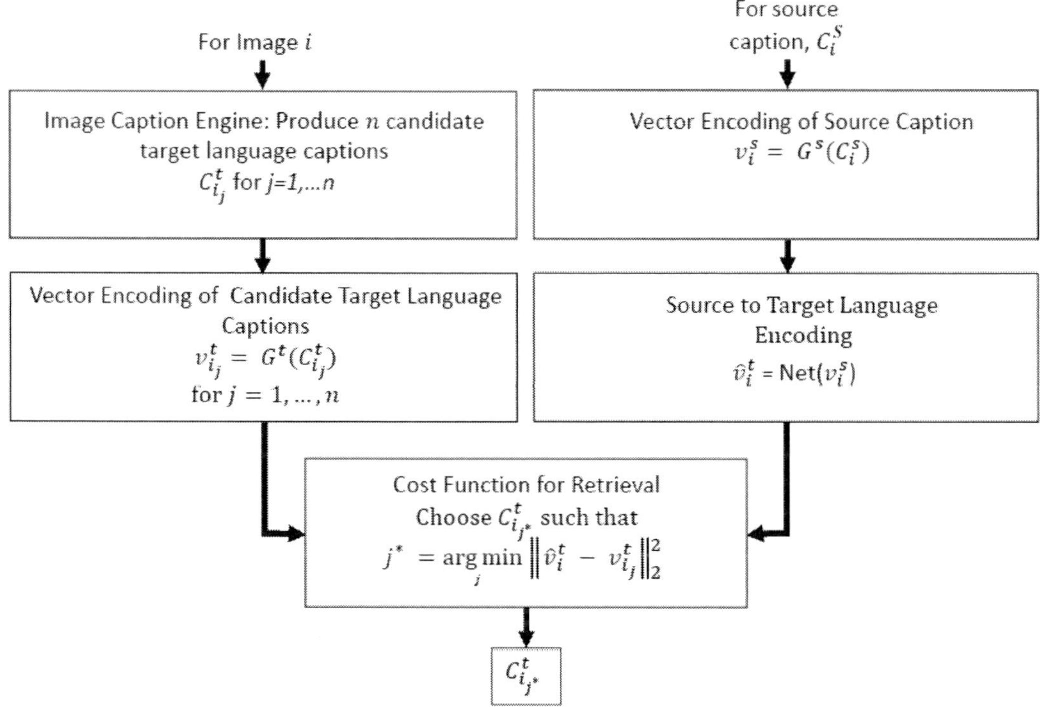

Figure 3: Architectural Diagram of the Processing Chain

2.3 Implementation

The actual AFRL-OSU unconstrained implementation went through many iterations of tool sets before settling. The captioning engine selected for this competition was Google's Show and Tell system (Vinyals et al., 2015). It was trained on the WMT16 training and validation splits using the MultiFlickr30K images and German (Elliott et al., 2016) and ImageClef 2006-2008 multilingual datasets (Rorissa et al., 2006). For testing, 1000 captions ($C_{i_j}^t$ for $j = 1, ..., 1000$) per image were produced. Any caption with sentence length less than five words was not considered, but was not replaced. Captions were put into all lowercase without punctuation.

The monolingual word encodings, G^t and G^s, used to vector encode the source language caption and target language captions employed the word encodings compiled and published by Facebook (Bojanowski et al., 2016). Because Facebook's data was chosen over any word encodings produced internally, vector length was fixed at 300. This dataset was produced by Facebook by crawling and cleaning up data from Wikipedia pages using their fastText software and encoding algorithm

outlined in (Bojanowski et al., 2016). Sentence encodings used in the AFRL-OSU system were derived from averaging of in-vocabulary constituent word encodings.

To transform source encoded data into the target language encoded subspace, a multi-layer neural network was constructed. The WMT16 training/validation splits were used for the training English source captions (5 captions per image with a total of 29000 images). These English captions were encoded into 300x1 vectors, each L2-normalized. The training target outputs were generated using Edinburgh's WMT16 Neural MT System (Sennrich et al., 2016) to translate captions from English to German in the same 300x1 vector format, and again L2-normalized. The neural network was configured with 1 hidden layer (500 nodes) and a mean squared error loss-function. To test the approach 10% of the training data was kept for evaluation. During training, 25% of the remaining training data was withheld for validation with a maximum of 10000 epochs. The resulting network provides a source-to-target mapping of the source caption encoding

$$\hat{v}_i^t = Net(v_i^s) \tag{3}$$

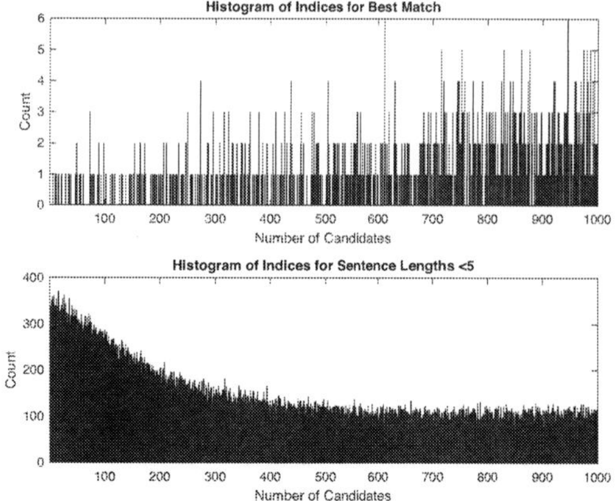

Figure 4: Histogram analysis. Top: Histogram of indices for the best match in the candidates. Bottom: Histogram of indices for candidate sentences with invalid (<5) length.

We lastly used the squared Euclidean Distance between the source transformed English caption encoding $\hat{v}_i^t$ to the collection of candidate target caption encodings to select the best candidate sentence index j^*

$$j^* = \arg\min_j ||\hat{v}_i^t - v_{i_j}^t||_2^2 \qquad (4)$$

The "best" match (to the source language caption) produced from the captioning engine is the sentence $C_{i_{j^*}}^t$. From the test data (with ground truth source-to-target labels), we received a top-1 of 77% and top-5 of 87%.

3   Results

The final submission consisted of generating 1000 captions per image with the top score being selected. The minimum of 5 words per sentence discounted 150963 candidate captions.

The top caption satisfying Eq.4 as the minimal value was scored against the output from the Edinburgh WMT16 Neural MT system and had a METEOR (Denkowski and Lavie, 2014) score of 19.8 (Sennrich et al., 2016). Figure 4 provides some trends for locations of zero vectors and top scoring vectors.

4   Conclusion

Assuming sufficient baseline results from an image-centric MMT system evaluated in this competition, there exist several opportunities for un-

derstanding the implications of such a system and also to improve its capabilities.

The captioning engine used is employed as a black box and assumed meaningful output for processing. Knowing the inner workings of the caption engine should allow tuning to produce more meaningful results. The authors also look forward to the results of this Multimodal Competition's Task 2 to obtain a better captioning engine (either improvements on the current system, or a different method altogether).

The monolingual word encodings attained from the Facebook models were constrained to 300 elemental vector length. Exploration into not only the size, but also construction of the data is warranted.

The cost function used, squared Euclidean Distance, is a first attempt. Looking at a variety of functions may harvest better results.

The authors only submitted the top ranked caption for scoring in this competition. However, 33 candidate submissions received a 0.0 sentence level METEOR score. Therefore, approaching a selection from the Top m captions that would maximize the METEOR is worth investigating.

This paper outlined the AFRL-OSU WMT17 Multimodal Translation system where the image is the focal point for MT. The authors hope that it spurs some alternative thinking and research in the area of multimodal MT.

Acknowlegements

The authors wish to thank Rebecca Young for her involvement in the human evaluation portion of the WMT17 Multimodal Translation task. The authors also wish to thank Rico Sennrich for making models and data available from the Edinburgh WMT16 Neural MT system, saving valuable time and effort during development.

References

2016. *Proceedings of the First Conference on Machine Translation, WMT 2016, colocated with ACL 2016, August 11-12, Berlin, Germany.* The Association for Computer Linguistics. http://aclweb.org/anthology/W/W16/.

Piotr Bojanowski, Edouard Grave, Armand Joulin, and Tomas Mikolov. 2016. Enriching word vectors with subword information. *arXiv preprint arXiv:1607.04606* .

Ozan Caglayan, Walid Aransa, Yaxing Wang, Marc Masana, Mercedes García-Martínez, Fethi Bougares, Loïc Barrault, and Joost van de Weijer. 2016. Does multimodality help human and machine for translation and image captioning? *CoRR* abs/1605.09186. http://arxiv.org/abs/1605.09186.

Michael Denkowski and Alon Lavie. 2014. Meteor universal: Language specific translation evaluation for any target language. In *Proceedings of the EACL 2014 Workshop on Statistical Machine Translation*.

D. Elliott, S. Frank, K. Sima'an, and L. Specia. 2016. Multi30k: Multilingual english-german image descriptions pages 70–74.

Desmond Elliott, Stella Frank, and Eva Hasler. 2015. Multi-language image description with neural sequence models. *CoRR* abs/1510.04709. http://arxiv.org/abs/1510.04709.

Zoubin Ghahramani, Max Welling, Corinna Cortes, Neil D. Lawrence, and Kilian Q. Weinberger, editors. 2014. *Advances in Neural Information Processing Systems 27: Annual Conference on Neural Information Processing Systems 2014, December 8-13 2014, Montreal, Quebec, Canada.* http://papers.nips.cc/book/advances-in-neural-information-processing-systems-27-2014.

Sergio Rodríguez Guasch and Marta R. Costa-Jussà. 2016. WMT 2016 multimodal translation system description based on bidirectional recurrent neural networks with double-embeddings. In (DBL, 2016), pages 655–659. http://aclweb.org/anthology/W/W16/W16-2362.pdf.

Ryan Kiros, Ruslan Salakhutdinov, and Richard S. Zemel. 2014. Unifying visual-semantic embeddings with multimodal neural language models. *CoRR* abs/1411.2539. http://arxiv.org/abs/1411.2539.

Jindřich Libovický, Jindrich Helcl, Marek Tlustý, Pavel Pecina, and Ondrej Bojar. 2016. CUNI system for WMT16 automatic post-editing and multimodal translation tasks. *CoRR* abs/1606.07481. http://arxiv.org/abs/1606.07481.

Junhua Mao, Wei Xu, Yi Yang, Jiang Wang, and Alan L Yuille. 2014. Explain images with multimodal recurrent neural networks. *NIPS Deep Learning Workshop* .

Abebe Rorissa, Paul Clough, William Hersh, Abebe Rorissa, and Miguel Ruiz. 2006. Imageclef and imageclefmed: Toward standard test collections for image storage and retrieval research. *Proceedings of the American Society for Information Science and Technology* 43(1):1–6. https://doi.org/10.1002/meet.14504301130.

Rico Sennrich, Barry Haddow, and Alexandra Birch. 2016. Edinburgh neural machine translation systems for WMT 16. *CoRR* abs/1606.02891. http://arxiv.org/abs/1606.02891.

Kashif Shah, Josiah Wang, and Lucia Specia. 2016. Shef-multimodal: Grounding machine translation on images. In (DBL, 2016), pages 660–665. http://aclweb.org/anthology/W/W16/W16-2363.pdf.

Richard Socher, Andrej Karpathy, Quoc V. Le, Christopher D. Manning, and Andrew Y. Ng. 2014. Grounded compositional semantics for finding and describing images with sentences. *TACL* 2:207–218.

Lucia Specia, Stella Frank, Khalil Sima'an, and Desmond Elliott. 2016. A shared task on multimodal machine translation and crosslingual image description. In *Proceedings of the First Conference on Machine Translation*. Association for Computational Linguistics, Berlin, Germany, pages 543–553. http://www.aclweb.org/anthology/W/W16/W16-2346.

Oriol Vinyals, Alexander Toshev, Samy Bengio, and Dumitru Erhan. 2015. Show and tell: A neural image caption generator. In *2015 IEEE Conference on Computer Vision and Pattern Recognition (CVPR)*.

CUNI System for the WMT17 Multimodal Traslation Task

Jindřich Helcl and **Jindřich Libovický**
Charles University, Faculty of Mathematics and Physics
Institute of Formal and Applied Linguistics
Malostranské náměstí 25, 118 00 Prague, Czech Republic
{helcl, libovicky}@ufal.mff.cuni.cz

Abstract

In this paper, we describe our submissions to the WMT17 Multimodal Translation Task. For Task 1 (multimodal translation), our best scoring system is a purely textual neural translation of the source image caption to the target language. The main feature of the system is the use of additional data that was acquired by selecting similar sentences from parallel corpora and by data synthesis with back-translation. For Task 2 (cross-lingual image captioning), our best submitted system generates an English caption which is then translated by the best system used in Task 1. We also present negative results, which are based on ideas that we believe have potential of making improvements, but did not prove to be useful in our particular setup.

1 Introduction

Recent advances in deep learning allowed inferring distributed vector representations of both textual and visual data. In models combining text and vision modalities, this representation can be used as a shared data type. Unlike the classical natural language processing tasks where everything happens within one language or across languages, multimodality tackles how the language entities relate to the extra-lingual reality. One of these tasks is multimodal translation whose goal is using cross-lingual information in automatic image captioning.

In this system-description paper, we describe our submission to the WMT17 Multimodal Translation Task. In particular, we discuss the effect of mining additional training data and usability of advanced attention strategies. We report our results on both the 2016 and 2017 test sets and discuss efficiency of tested approaches.

The rest of the paper is organized as follows. Section 2 introduces the tasks we handle in this paper and the datasets that were provided to the task. Section 3 summarizes the state-of-the-art methods applied to the task. In Section 4, we describe our models and the results we have achieved. Section 5 presents the negative results and Section 6 concludes the paper.

2 Task and Dataset Description

The challenge of the WMT Multimodal Translation Task is to exploit cross-lingual information in automatic image caption generation. The state-of-the-art models in both machine translation and automatic image caption generation use similar architectures for generating the target sentence. The simplicity with which we can combine the learned representations of various inputs in a single deep learning model inevitably leads to a question whether combining the modalities can lead to some interesting results. In the shared task, this is explored in two subtasks with different roles of visual and textual modalities.

In the multimodal translation task (Task 1), the input of the model is an image and its caption in English. The system then should output a German or French translation of the caption. The system output is evaluated using the METEOR (Denkowski and Lavie, 2011) and BLEU (Papineni et al., 2002) scores computed against a single reference sentence. The question this task tries to answer is whether and how is it possible to use visual information to disambiguate the translation.

In the cross-lingual captioning task (Task 2), the input to the model at test-time is the image alone. However, additionally to the image, the model is

Proceedings of the Conference on Machine Translation (WMT), Volume 2: Shared Task Papers, pages 450–457
Copenhagen, Denmark, September 7–11, 2017. ©2017 Association for Computational Linguistics

	en	de	fr
Train. sentences		29,000	
Train. tokens	378k	361k	410k
Avg. # tokens	13.0	12.4	14.1
# tokens range	4–40	2–44	4–55
Val. sentences		1,014	
Val. tokens	13k	13k	14k
Avg. # tokens	13.1	12.7	14.2
# tokens range	4–30	3–33	5–36
OOV rate	1.28%	3.09%	1.20%

Table 1: Multi30k statistics on training and validation data – total number of tokens, average number of tokens per sentence, and the sizes of the shortest and the longest sentence.

supplied with the English (source) caption during training. The evaluation method differs from Task 1 in using five reference captions instead of a single one. In Task 2, German is the only target language. The motivation of Task 2 is to explore ways of easily creating an image captioning system in a new language once we have an existing system for another language, assuming that the information transfer is less complex across languages than between visual and textual modalities.

2.1 Data

The participants were provided with the Multi30k dataset (Elliott et al., 2016) – a multilingual extension of Flickr30k dataset (Plummer et al., 2017) – for both training and evaluation of their models.

The data consists of 31,014 images. In Flickr30k, each image is described with five independently acquired captions in English. Images in the Multi30k dataset are enriched with five crowd-sourced German captions. Additionally, a single German translation of one of the English captions was added for each image.

The dataset is split into training, validation, and test sets of 29,000, 1,014, and 1,000 instances respectively. The statistics on the training and validation part are tabulated in Table 1.

For the 2017 round of the competition (Elliott et al., 2017), an additional French translation was included for Task 1 and new test sets have been developed. Two test sets were provided for Task 1: The first one consists of 1,000 instances and is similar to the test set used in the previous round of the competition (and to the training and validation data). The second one consists of im-

ages, captions, and their translations taken from the MSCOCO image captioning dataset (Lin et al., 2014). A new single test set containing 1,071 images with five reference captions was added for Task 2.

The style and structure of the reference sentences in the Flickr- and MSCOCO-based test sets differs. Most of the sentences in the Multi30k dataset have a similar structure with a relatively simple subject, an active verb in present tense, simple object, and location information (e.g., *"Two dogs are running on a beach."*). Contrastingly, the captions in the MSCOCO dataset are less formal and capture the annotator's uncertainty about the image content (e.g., *"I don't know, it looks like a lemon."*).

3 Related Work

Several promising neural architectures for multimodal translation task have been introduced since the first competition in 2016.

In our last year's submission (Libovický et al., 2016), we employed a neural system that combined multiple inputs – the image, the source caption and an SMT-generated caption. We used the attention mechanism over the textual sequences and concatenated the context vectors in each decoder step.

The overall results of the WMT16 multimodal translation task did not prove the visual features to be particularly useful (Specia et al., 2016; Caglayan et al., 2016).

To our knowledge, Huang et al. (2016) were the first who showed an improvement over a textual only neural system with model utilizing distributed features explicit object recognition. Calixto et al. (2017) improved state of the art using a model initializing the decoder state with the image vector, while maintaining the rest of the neural architecture unchanged. Promising results were also shown by Delbrouck and Dupont (2017) who made a small improvement using bilinear pooling.

Elliott and Kádár (2017) brought further improvements by introducing the "imagination" component to the neural network architecture. Given the source sentence, the network is trained to output the target sentence jointly with predicting the image vector. The model uses the visual information only as a regularization and thus is able to use additional parallel data without accompanying images.

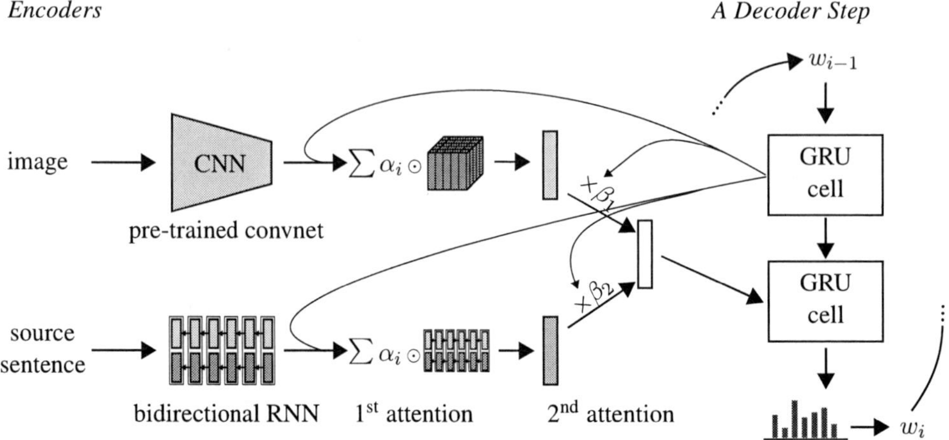

Figure 1: An overall picture of the multimodal model using hierarchical attention combination on the input. Here, α and β are normalized coefficients computed by the attention models, w_i is the i-th input to the decoder.

4 Experiments

All models are based on the encoder-decoder architecture with attention mechanism (Bahdanau et al., 2014) as implemented in Neural Monkey (Helcl and Libovický, 2017).[1] The decoder uses conditional GRUs (Firat and Cho, 2016) with 500 hidden units and word embeddings with dimension of 300. The target sentences are decoded using beam search with beam size 10, and with exponentially weighted length penalty (Wu et al., 2016) with α parameter empirically estimated as 1.5 for German and 1.0 for French. Because of the low OOV rate (see Table 1), we used vocabularies of maximum 30,000 tokens and we did not use sub-word units. The textual encoder is a bidirectional GRU network with 500 units in each direction and word embeddings with dimension of 300. We use the last convolutional layer VGG-16 network (Simonyan and Zisserman, 2014) of dimensionality $14 \times 14 \times 512$ for image processing. The model is optimized using the Adam optimizer (Kingma and Ba, 2014) with learning rate 10^{-4} with early stopping based on validation BLEU score.

4.1 Task 1: Multimodal Translation

We tested the following architectures with different datasets (see Section 4.3 for details):

- purely textual (disregarding the visual modality);

- multimodal with context vector concatenation in the decoder (Libovický et al., 2016);

- multimodal with hierarchical attention combination (Libovický and Helcl, 2017) – context vectors are computed independently for each modality and then they are combined together using another attention mechanism as depicted in Figure 1.

4.2 Task 2: Cross-lingual Captioning

We conducted two sets of experiments for this subtask. In both of them, we used an attentive image captioning model (Xu et al., 2015) for the cross-lingual captioning with the same decoder as for the first subtask.

The first idea we experimented with was using a multilingual decoder provided with the image and a language identifier. Based on the identifier, the decoder generates the caption either in English or in German. We speculated that the information transfer from the visual to the language modality is the most difficult part of the task and might be similar for both English and German.

The second approach we tried has two steps. First, we trained an English image captioning system, for which we can use larger datasets. Second, we translated the generated captions with the multimodal translation system from the first subtask.

4.3 Acquiring Additional Data

In order to improve the textual translation, we acquired additional data. We used the following

---

[1] https://github.com/ufal/neuralmonkey

technique to select in-domain sentences from both parallel and monolingual data.

We trained a neural character-level language model on the German sentences available in the training part of the Multi30k dataset. We used a GRU network with 512 hidden units and character embedding size of 128.

Using the language model, we selected 30,000 best-scoring German sentences from the SDEWAC corpus (Faaß and Eckart, 2013) which were both semantically and structurally similar to the sentences in the Multi30k dataset.

We tried to use the language model to select sentence pairs also from parallel data. By scoring the German part of several parallel corpora (EU Bookshop (Skadiņš et al., 2014), News Commentary (Tiedemann, 2012) and Common-Crawl (Smith et al., 2013)), we were only able to retrieve a few hundreds of in-domain sentences. For that reason we also included sentences with lower scores which we filtered using the following rules: sentences must have between 2 and 30 tokens, must be in the present tense, must not contain non-standard punctuation, numbers of multiple digits, acronyms, or named entities, and must have at most 15 % OOV rate w.r.t. Multi30k training vocabulary. We extracted additional 3,000 in-domain parallel sentences using these rules. Examples of the additional data are given in Table 2.

By applying the same approach on the French versions of the corpora, we were pable to extract only few additional in-domain sentences. We thus trained the English-to-French models in the constrained setup only.

Following Calixto et al. (2017), we back-translated (Sennrich et al., 2016) the German captions from the German side of the Multi30k dataset (i.e. 5+1 captions for each image), and sentences retrieved from the SDEWAC corpus. We included these back-translated sentence pairs as additional training data for the textual and multi-modal systems for Task 1. The back-translation system used the same architecture as the textual systems and was trained on the Multi30k dataset only. The additional parallel data and data from the SDEWAC corpus (denoted as additional in Table 3) were used only for the text-only systems because they were not accompanied by images.

For Task 2, we also used the MSCOCO (Lin et al., 2014) dataset which consists of 300,000 images with 5 English captions for each of them.

SDEWAC Corpus (with back-translation)	
zwei Männer unterhalten sich	· · · · · · · · · ·
	two men are talking to each other .
ein kleines Mädchen sitzt auf einer Schaukel .	· ·
	a little girl is sitting on a swing .
eine Katze braucht Unterhaltung .	· · · · · · · ·
	a cat is having a discussion .
dieser Knabe streichelt das Schlagzeug .	· · · ·
	this professional is petting the drums .

Parallel Corpora	
Menschen bei der Arbeit	*People at work*
Männer und Frauen	*Men and women*
Sicherheit bei der Arbeit	*Safety at work*
Personen in der Öffentlichkeit	
	Members of the public

Table 2: Examples of the collected additional training data.

4.4 Results

In Task 1, our best performing system was the text-only system trained with additional data. These were acquired both by the data selection method described above and by back-translation. Results of all setups for Task 1 are given in Table 3.

Surprisingly, including the data for Task 2 to the training set decreased the METEOR score on both of the 2017 test sets. This might have been caused by domain mismatch. However, in case of the additional parallel and SDEWAC data, this problem was likely outweighed by the advantage of having more training data.

In case of multimodal systems, adding approximately the same amount of data increased the performance more than in case of the text-only system. This suggests, that with sufficient amount of data (which is a rather unrealistic assumption), the multimodal system would eventually outperform the textual one.

The hierarchical attention combination brought major improvements over the concatenation approach on the 2017 test sets. On the 2016 test set, the concatenation approach yielded better results, which can be considered a somewhat strange result, given the similarity of the Flickr test sets.

The baseline system was Nematus (Sennrich et al., 2017) trained on the textual part of Multi30k only. However, due to its low score, we suspect the model was trained with suboptimal parameters because it is in principle a model identical to our constrained textual submission.

		Task 1: en → de			Task 1: en → fr	
		2016	Flickr	MSCOCO	Flickr	MSCOCO
Baseline	C	—	19.3 / 41.9	18.7 / 37.6	44.3 / 63.1	35.1 / 55.8
Textual	C	34.6 / 51.7	28.5 / 49.2	23.2 / 43.8	**50.3 / 67.0**	**43.0 / 62.5**
Textual (+ Task2)	U	36.6 / 53.0	28.5 / 45.7	24.1 / 40.7	—	—
Textual (+ additional)	U	**36.8 / 53.1**	**31.1 / 51.0**	**26.6 / 46.0**	—	—
Multimodal (concat. attn)	C	32.3 / 50.0	23.6 / 41.8	20.0 / 37.1	40.3 / 56.3	32.8 / 52.1
Multimodal (hier. attn.)	C	31.9 / 49.4	25.8 / 47.1	22.4 / 42.7	49.9 / **67.2**	42.9 / **62.5**
Multimodal (concat. attn.)	U	**36.0 / 52.1**	26.3 / 43.9	23.3 / 39.8	—	—
Multimodal (hier. attn.)	U	34.4 / 51.7	**29.5 / 50.2**	**25.7 / 45.6**	—	—
Task 1 winner (LIUM-CVC)	C	—	33.4 / 54.0	28.7 / 48.9	55.9 / 72.1	45.9 / 65.9

Table 3: Results of Task 1 in BLEU / METEOR points. 'C' denotes constrained configuration, 'U' unconstrained, '2016' is the 2016 test set, 'Flickr' and 'MSCOCO' denote the 2017 test sets. The two unconstrained textual models differ in using the additional textual data, which was not used for the training of the multimodal systems.

		Task 2
Baseline	C	**9.1 / 23.4**
Bilingual captioning	C	2.3 / 17.6
en captioning + translation	C	4.2 / 22.1
en captioning + translation	U	6.5 / 20.6
other participant	C	**9.1** / 19.8

Table 4: Results of Task 2 in BLEU / METEOR points.

	Flickr30k
Xu et al. (2015)	**19.1** / 18.5
ours: Flickr30k	15.3 / **18.7**
ours: Flickr30k + MSCOCO	17.9 / 16.6

Table 5: Results of the English image captioning systems on Flickr30k test set in BLEU / METEOR points

In Task 2, none of the submitted systems outperformed the baseline which was a captioning system (Xu et al., 2015) trained directly on the German captions in the Multi30k dataset. The results of our systems on Task 2 are shown in Table 4.

For the English captioning, we trained two models. First one was trained on the Flickr30k data only. In the second one, we included also the MSCOCO dataset. Although the captioning system trained on more data achieved better performance on the English side (Table 5), it led to extremely low performance while plugged into our multimodal translation systems (Table 4, rows labeled "en captioning + translation"). We hypothe-size this is caused by the different styles of the sentences in the training datasets.

Our hypothesis about sharing information between the languages in a single decoder was not confirmed in this setup and the experiments led to relatively poor results.

Interestingly, our systems for Task 2 scored poorly in the BLEU score and relatively well in the METEOR score. We can attribute this to the fact that unlike BLEU which puts more emphasis on precision, METEOR considers strongly also recall.

5 Negative Results

In addition to our submitted systems, we tried a number of techniques without success. We describe these techniques since we believe it might be relevant for future developments in the field, despite the current negative result.

5.1 Beam Rescoring

Similarly to Lala et al. (2017), our oracle experiments on the validation data showed that rescoring of the decoded beam of width 100 has the potential of improvement of up to 3 METEOR points. In the oracle experiment, we always chose a sentence with the highest sentence-level BLEU score. Motivated by this observation, we conducted several experiments with beam rescoring.

We trained a classifier predicting whether a given sentence is a suitable caption for a given image. The classifier had one hidden layer with 300 units and had two inputs: the last layer of the VGG-16 network processing the image, and the last state of a bidirectional GRU network processing the text. We used the same hyperparameters for the bidirectional GRU network as we did for the textual encoders in other experiments. Training data were taken from both parts of the Multi30k dataset with negative examples randomly sampled from the dataset, so the classes were represented equally. The classifier achieved validation accuracy of 87% for German and 74% for French. During the rescoring of the 100 hypotheses in the beam, we selected the one which had the highest predicted probability of being the image's caption.

In other experiments, we tried to train a regression predicting the score of a given output sentence. Unlike the previous experiment, we built the training data from scored hypotheses from output beams obtained by translating the training part of the Multi30k dataset. We tested two architectures: the first one concatenates the terminal states of bidirectional GRU networks encoding the source and hypothesis sentences and an image vector; the second performs an attentive average pooling over hidden states of the RNNs and the image CNN using the other encoders terminal states as queries and concatenates the context vectors. The regression was estimating either the sentence-level BLEU score (Chen and Cherry, 2014) or the chrF3 score (Popović, 2015).

Contrary to our expectations, all the rescoring techniques decreased the performance by 2 METEOR points.

5.2 Reinforcement Learning

Another technique we tried without any success was self-critical sequence training (Rennie et al., 2016). This modification of the REINFORCE algorithm (Williams, 1992) for sequence-to-sequence learning uses the reward of the training-time decoded sentence as the baseline. The systems were pre-trained with the word-level cross-entropy objective and we hoped to fine-tune the systems using the REINFORCE towards sentence-level BLEU score and GLEU score (Wu et al., 2016).

It appeared to be difficult to find the right moment when the optimization criterion should be switched and to find an optimal mixing factor of the cross-entropy loss and REINFORCE loss. We hypothesize that a more complex objective mixing strategy (like MIXER (Ranzato et al., 2015)) could lead to better results than simple objective weighting.

6 Conclusions

In our submission to the 2017 Multimodal Task, we tested the advanced attention combination strategies (Libovický and Helcl, 2017) in a more challenging context and achieved competitive results compared to other submissions. We explored ways of acquiring additional data for the task and tested two promising techniques that did not bring any improvement to the system performance.

Acknowledgments

This research has been funded by the Czech Science Foundation grant no. P103/12/G084, the EU grant no. H2020-ICT-2014-1-645452 (QT21), and Charles University grant no. 52315/2014 and SVV project no. 260 453.

This work has been using language resources developed and/or stored and/or distributed by the LINDAT-Clarin project of the Ministry of Education of the Czech Republic (project LM2010013).

References

Dzmitry Bahdanau, Kyunghyun Cho, and Yoshua Bengio. 2014. Neural machine translation by jointly learning to align and translate. *CoRR* abs/1409.0473. http://arxiv.org/abs/1409.0473.

Ozan Caglayan, Walid Aransa, Yaxing Wang, Marc Masana, Mercedes García-Martínez, Fethi Bougares, Loïc Barrault, and Joost van de Weijer. 2016. Does multimodality help human and machine for translation and image captioning? In *Proceedings of the First Conference on Machine Translation*. Association for Computational Linguistics, Berlin, Germany, pages 627–633. http://www.aclweb.org/anthology/W16-2358.

Iacer Calixto, Qun Liu, and Nick Campbell. 2017. Incorporating global visual features into attention-based neural machine translation. *CoRR* abs/1701.06521. http://arxiv.org/abs/1701.06521.

Boxing Chen and Colin Cherry. 2014. A systematic comparison of smoothing techniques for sentence-level bleu. In *Proceedings of the Ninth Workshop on Statistical Machine Translation*. Association for Computational Linguistics, Baltimore, Maryland, USA, pages 362–367. http://www.aclweb.org/anthology/W14-3346.

Jean-Benoit Delbrouck and Stéphane Dupont. 2017. Multimodal compact bilinear pooling for multimodal neural machine translation. *CoRR* abs/1703.08084. http://arxiv.org/abs/1703.08084.

Michael Denkowski and Alon Lavie. 2011. Meteor 1.3: Automatic metric for reliable optimization and evaluation of machine translation systems. In *Proceedings of the Sixth Workshop on Statistical Machine Translation*. Association for Computational Linguistics, Edinburgh, United Kingdom, pages 85–91. http://www.aclweb.org/anthology/W11-2107.

Desmond Elliott, Stella Frank, Loïc Barrault, Fethi Bougares, and Lucia Specia. 2017. Findings of the Second Shared Task on Multimodal Machine Translation and Multilingual Image Description. In *Proceedings of the Second Conference on Machine Translation*. Copenhagen, Denmark.

Desmond Elliott, Stella Frank, Khalil Sima'an, and Lucia Specia. 2016. Multi30k: Multilingual english-german image descriptions. *CoRR* abs/1605.00459. http://arxiv.org/abs/1605.00459.

Desmond Elliott and Ákos Kádár. 2017. Imagination improves multimodal translation. *CoRR* abs/1705.04350. http://arxiv.org/abs/1705.04350.

Gertrud Faaß and Kerstin Eckart. 2013. Sdewac– a corpus of parsable sentences from the web. In *Language processing and knowledge in the Web*, Springer, pages 61–68.

Orhan Firat and Kyunghyun Cho. 2016. Conditional gated recurrent unit with attention mechanism. https://github.com/nyu-dl/dl4mt-tutorial/blob/master/docs/cgru.pdf. Published online, version adbaeea.

Jindřich Helcl and Jindřich Libovický. 2017. Neural monkey: An open-source tool for sequence learning. *The Prague Bulletin of Mathematical Linguistics* (107):5–17. https://doi.org/10.1515/pralin-2017-0001.

Po-Yao Huang, Frederick Liu, Sz-Rung Shiang, Jean Oh, and Chris Dyer. 2016. Attention-based multimodal neural machine translation. In *Proceedings of the First Conference on Machine Translation*. Association for Computational Linguistics, Berlin, Germany, pages 639–645. http://www.aclweb.org/anthology/W/W16/W16-2360.

Diederik P. Kingma and Jimmy Ba. 2014. Adam: A method for stochastic optimization. *CoRR* abs/1412.6980. http://arxiv.org/abs/1412.6980.

Chiraag Lala, Pranava Madhyastha, Josiah Wang, and Lucia Specia. 2017. Unraveling the contribution of image captioning and neural machine translation for multimodal machine translation. *The Prague Bulletin of Mathematical Linguistics* (108):197–208. https://doi.org/doi: 10.1515/pralin-2017-0020.

Jindřich Libovický and Jindřich Helcl. 2017. Attention strategies for multi-source sequence-to-sequence learning. In *Proceedings of the 55th Annual Meeting of the Association for Computational Linguistics (Volume 2: Short Papers)*. Association for Computational Linguistics, Vancouver, Canada.

Jindřich Libovický, Jindřich Helcl, Marek Tlustý, Ondřej Bojar, and Pavel Pecina. 2016. CUNI system for WMT16 automatic post-editing and multimodal translation tasks. In *Proceedings of the First Conference on Machine Translation*. Association for Computational Linguistics, Berlin, Germany, pages 646–654. http://www.aclweb.org/anthology/W/W16/W16-2361.

Tsung-Yi Lin, Michael Maire, Serge J. Belongie, Lubomir D. Bourdev, Ross B. Girshick, James Hays, Pietro Perona, Deva Ramanan, Piotr Dollár, and C. Lawrence Zitnick. 2014. Microsoft COCO: common objects in context. *CoRR* abs/1405.0312. http://arxiv.org/abs/1405.0312.

Kishore Papineni, Salim Roukos, Todd Ward, and Wei-Jing Zhu. 2002. Bleu: a method for automatic evaluation of machine translation. In *Proceedings of 40th Annual Meeting of the Association for Computational Linguistics*. Association for Computational Linguistics, Philadelphia, Pennsylvania, USA, pages 311–318. https://doi.org/10.3115/1073083.1073135.

Bryan A. Plummer, Liwei Wang, Chris M. Cervantes, Juan C. Caicedo, Julia Hockenmaier, and Svetlana Lazebnik. 2017. Flickr30k entities: Collecting region-to-phrase correspondences for richer image-to-sentence models. *Int. J. Comput. Vision* 123(1):74–93. https://doi.org/10.1007/s11263-016-0965-7.

Maja Popović. 2015. chrf: character n-gram f-score for automatic mt evaluation. In *Proceedings of the Tenth Workshop on Statistical Machine Translation*. Association for Computational Linguistics, Lisbon, Portugal, pages 392–395. http://aclweb.org/anthology/W15-3049.

Marc'Aurelio Ranzato, Sumit Chopra, Michael Auli, and Wojciech Zaremba. 2015. Sequence level training with recurrent neural networks. *CoRR* abs/1511.06732. http://arxiv.org/abs/1511.06732.

Steven J. Rennie, Etienne Marcheret, Youssef Mroueh, Jarret Ross, and Vaibhava Goel. 2016. Self-critical sequence training for image captioning. *CoRR* abs/1612.00563. http://arxiv.org/abs/1612.00563.

Rico Sennrich, Orhan Firat, Kyunghyun Cho, Alexandra Birch, Barry Haddow, Julian Hitschler, Marcin Junczys-Dowmunt, Samuel Läubli, Antonio Valerio Miceli Barone, Jozef Mokry, and Maria Nadejde. 2017. Nematus: a toolkit for neural machine translation. In *Proceedings of the Software Demonstrations of the 15th Conference of the European Chapter of the Association for Computational Linguistics*. Association for Computational Linguistics, Valencia, Spain, pages 65–68. http://aclweb.org/anthology/E17-3017.

Rico Sennrich, Barry Haddow, and Alexandra Birch. 2016. Improving neural machine translation models with monolingual data. In *Proceedings of the 54th Annual Meeting of the Association for Computational Linguistics (Volume 1: Long Papers)*. Association for Computational Linguistics, Berlin, Germany, pages 86–96. http://www.aclweb.org/anthology/P16-1009.

Karen Simonyan and Andrew Zisserman. 2014. Very deep convolutional networks for large-scale image recognition. *CoRR* abs/1409.1556. http://arxiv.org/abs/1409.1556.

Raivis Skadiņš, Jörg Tiedemann, Roberts Rozis, and Daiga Deksne. 2014. Billions of parallel words for free: Building and using the eu bookshop corpus. In *Proceedings of the 9th International Conference on Language Resources and Evaluation (LREC-2014)*. European Language Resources Association (ELRA), Reykjavik, Iceland.

Jason R. Smith, Herve Saint-Amand, Magdalena Plamada, Philipp Koehn, Chris Callison-Burch, and Adam Lopez. 2013. Dirt cheap web-scale parallel text from the common crawl. In *Proceedings of the 51st Annual Meeting of the Association for Computational Linguistics (Volume 1: Long Papers)*. Association for Computational Linguistics, Sofia, Bulgaria, pages 1374–1383. http://www.aclweb.org/anthology/P13-1135.

Lucia Specia, Stella Frank, Khalil Sima'an, and Desmond Elliott. 2016. A shared task on multimodal machine translation and crosslingual image description. In *Proceedings of the First Conference on Machine Translation*. Association for Computational Linguistics, Berlin, Germany, pages 543–553. http://www.aclweb.org/anthology/W16-2346.

Jörg Tiedemann. 2012. Parallel data, tools and interfaces in opus. In Nicoletta Calzolari (Conference Chair), Khalid Choukri, Thierry Declerck, Mehmet Ugur Dogan, Bente Maegaard, Joseph Mariani, Jan Odijk, and Stelios Piperidis, editors, *Proceedings of the Eight International Conference on Language Resources and Evaluation (LREC'12)*. European Language Resources Association (ELRA), Istanbul, Turkey.

Ronald J Williams. 1992. Simple statistical gradient-following algorithms for connectionist reinforcement learning. *Machine learning* 8(3-4):229–256.

Yonghui Wu, Mike Schuster, Zhifeng Chen, Quoc V. Le, Mohammad Norouzi, Wolfgang Macherey, Maxim Krikun, Yuan Cao, Qin Gao, Klaus Macherey, Jeff Klingner, Apurva Shah, Melvin Johnson, Xiaobing Liu, Lukasz Kaiser, Stephan Gouws, Yoshikiyo Kato, Taku Kudo, Hideto Kazawa, Keith Stevens, George Kurian, Nishant Patil, Wei Wang, Cliff Young, Jason Smith, Jason Riesa, Alex Rudnick, Oriol Vinyals, Greg Corrado, Macduff Hughes, and Jeffrey Dean. 2016. Google's neural machine translation system: Bridging the gap between human and machine translation. *CoRR* abs/1609.08144. http://arxiv.org/abs/1609.08144.

Kelvin Xu, Jimmy Ba, Ryan Kiros, Kyunghyun Cho, Aaron Courville, Ruslan Salakhudinov, Rich Zemel, and Yoshua Bengio. 2015. Show, attend and tell: Neural image caption generation with visual attention. In David Blei and Francis Bach, editors, *Proceedings of the 32nd International Conference on Machine Learning (ICML-15)*. JMLR Workshop and Conference Proceedings, Lille, France, pages 2048–2057. http://jmlr.org/proceedings/papers/v37/xuc15.pdf.

Generating Image Descriptions using Multilingual Data

Alan Jaffe
School of Computer Science
Carnegie Mellon University
Pittsburgh, PA
`apjaffe@andrew.cmu.edu`

Abstract

In this paper we explore several neural network architectures for the WMT 2017 multimodal translation sub-task on multilingual image caption generation. The goal of the task is to generate image captions in German, using a training corpus of images with captions in both English and German. We explore several models which attempt to generate captions for both languages, ignoring the English output during evaluation. We compare the results to a baseline implementation which uses only the German captions for training and show significant improvement.

1 Introduction

Neural models have shown great success on a variety of tasks, including machine translation (Sutskever et al., 2014), image caption generation (Xu et al., 2015), and language modeling (Bengio et al., 2003). Recently, huge datasets necessary for training these models have become more widely available, but there are still many limitations. In some cases, the dataset which is available may not match the domain of the task.

In this paper, we attempt to generate image captions in German, using a training corpus of images with captions in both English and German. For each image, we have 5 independently generated captions in each language. Since the training corpus is relatively small (less than 30,000 images), we want to make use of the English language data to improve the German captions. (See figure 1).

It is important to note that since these captions were generated independently in each language rather than translated, they often differ from each other quite a bit. Not only do they often choose to describe different features of an image, but also they sometimes describe contradictory features of the image (one caption describing a man sleeping on a couch while a different caption describes a woman sleeping on a couch). This inconsistency and the relatively small amount of training data makes it very difficult to train a reliable translation system between the languages based on this corpus.

In this paper, we will start by discussing related work in image caption generation. Then we will explain the baseline German image caption generation model, the soft attention model from Xu et al. (2015). Several methods of incorporating the English data to improve the performance will be described. Finally, the experimental setup will be specified and the results will be evaluated.

2 Related Work

The task of multilingual image caption generation has been previously explored by Elliott et al. (2015). Elliott et al. (2015) used an LSTM to generate captions, using features from both a source-language multimodal model and a target-language multimodal model. Other previous work on multilingual images such as Hitschler and Riezler (2016) has focused on image caption translation, where captions are available at test time in a single language, and we wish to use the image as a guide while translating into a different language. The WMT 2016 multimodal machine translation task (Specia et al., 2016) explored precisely this task. Using existing machine translation techniques to translate the given caption provided a very strong baseline. Supplementing these translation with information from the image provided only marginal improvements. For instance Huang et al. (2016) re-ranked the translation output using image features and failed to achieve a higher METEOR score than the baseline.

Proceedings of the Conference on Machine Translation (WMT), Volume 2: Shared Task Papers, pages 458–464
Copenhagen, Denmark, September 7–11, 2017. ©2017 Association for Computational Linguistics

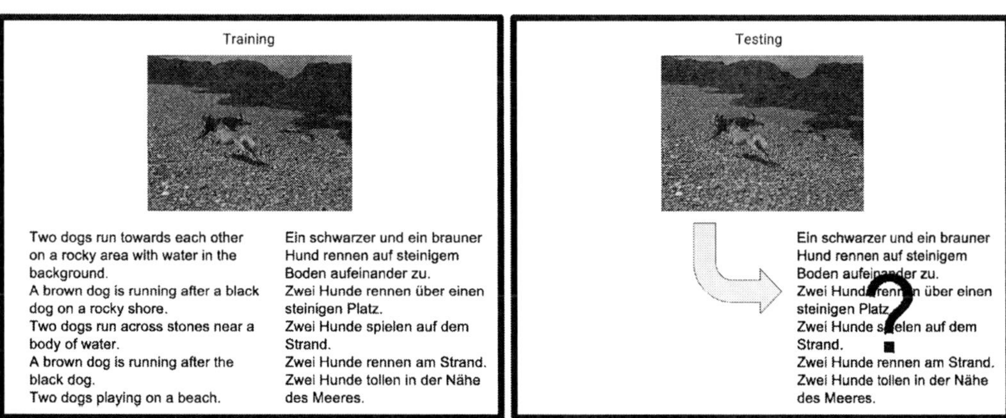

Figure 1: Training data and test data

Similarly, systems developed for the WMT 2016 crosslingual image description multimodal task had access to one or more reference English descriptions of the image (in addition to the image itself) when attempting to generate a German caption, allowing them to use attention-based models that took advantage of both pieces of information. Again though, the image seemed to provide little benefit, and in fact the highest scoring system ignored it altogether.

Generally, the long short-term memory (LSTM) model (Hochreiter and Schmidhuber, 1997) seems to be quite effective for caption generation and other natural language processing tasks. Dropout has also been shown to reduce overfitting (Srivastava et al., 2014).

Supplementing the basic LSTM model with attention model has been shown to be effective for related tasks as well, such as machine translation (Bahdanau et al., 2014). Multiple methods are possible for determining how the attention is allocated at each step, such as a simple dot-product, linear transformation, or multilayer perceptron. Several of these alternatives were explored by Luong et al. (2015).

Beyond multilingual caption generation, the over-arching task of image caption generation has also been considered before. Vinyals et al. (2015) used a convolutional neural network to encode an image, followed by an LSTM decoder to produce an output sequence. Xu et al. (2015) extended that model by adding an attentional component, using a multilayer perceptron to determine the weight of each part of the image given to the LSTM at each step.

With less than 30,000 images, it is difficult to train a convolutional neural network to identify image features. Caglayan et al. (2016) found that the ResNet (He et al., 2015) trained on ImageNet classification task was quite effective (specifically using layer 'res4fx' which is found at the end of Block-4, after ReLU). Note that this differs from Xu et al. (2015), which used pre-trained features from the Oxford VGGnet (Simonyan and Zisserman, 2014).

3 Image Caption Generation Models

3.1 Baseline

We developed several models, each of which generate both English and German captions. The models were trained on both the English and the German data, but at test time we evaluate the performance only for generating German captions.

Our baseline is implemented as an attentional neural network following the model of Xu et al. (2015). Each image is encoded as 196 vectors, each of which corresponds to a particular section of the image. Each of these vectors consists of 1024 real numbers, derived from layer 'res4fx' of ResNet. (Note that this modifies the original work by Xu et al. (2015), which used Oxford VGGnet with only 512 real numbers for each location in the image.) Xu et al. (2015) considered both a hard and a soft attentional model, but since these performed comparably, we have only re-implemented their soft attentional model.

We generate a caption as a series of words (encoded as 1-hot vectors), terminated by the end of sentence symbol </s>. At each timestep, an attention mechanism implemented as a multilayer

459

perceptron (MLP) predicts how important each part of the image is, based on the previous hidden state h_{t-1}. Softmax is applied over the attention outputs to compute a weighted average of the image vectors. The result is a 1024-dimensional context vector z_t that represents the important parts of the entire image at timestep t.

We use an LSTM as the decoder, which has decoupled input and forget gates and does not use peephole connections. We initialize the LSTM to 0, unlike Xu et al. (2015) which initializes the LSTM using two additional MLP's. Given some previous state (h_{t-1}, c_{t-1}) and input x_t, we compute $(h_t, c_t) = f(h_{t-1}, c_{t-1}, x_t)$ where $x_t = concat(embed_{t-1}, z_t)$. $embed_{t-1}$ is the word embedding of the previous word outputted (or the special token $< s >$ at the start of the sentence), and z_t is the context vector derived from attention over the image. The resulting output h_t is then transformed to $softmax(W_{yh}h_t + b_y)$ to compute the probability of each word in the vocabulary. Each timestep $(h_t, c_t) = f(h_{t-1}, c_{t-1}, x_t)$ is computed as follows (Neubig et al., 2017):

$$i_t = \sigma(W_{ix}x_t + W_{ih}h_{t-1} + b_i) \qquad (1)$$
$$f_t = \sigma(W_{fx}x_t + W_{fh}h_{t-1} + b_f + 1) \qquad (2)$$
$$o_t = \sigma(W_{ox}x_t + W_{oh}h_{t-1} + b_o) \qquad (3)$$
$$u_t = \tanh(W_{ux}x_t + W_{uh}h_{t-1} + b_u) \qquad (4)$$
$$c_t = c_{t-1} \circ f_t + u_t \circ i_t \qquad (5)$$
$$h_t = \tanh(c_t) \circ o_t \qquad (6)$$

Equation 1 is the input gate, equation 2 is the forget gate, equation 3 is the output gate, and equation 4 computes the update.

Since we re-implemented this baseline and made some changes in the process as detailed above (most notably by omitting the hard attentional model), we wanted to verify that this did not affect performance. The original paper generated English captions only, so we trained a version of our baseline model to generate English captions. Using dropout of 0.02, an English vocabulary size of 12138, and a minibatch size of 32, this achieved a BLEU score of 21.48 (lowercased, ignoring punctation).[1] That result lines up well with the BLEU score of 19.1 reported by Xu et al. (2015) on the Flickr30k dataset, so we are confident that our reimplementation has not weakened

____
[1] Dropout of 0.2 was also tested, with slightly worse results (BLEU = 20.66).

the baseline.

3.2 Shared Decoder

The first model tested was the shared decoder model. This is a multitask architecture, with one loss for each language. The idea of this model was to consider English and German as two separate vocabularies, thus each with their own set of word embeddings and word output weights W_{yh}, b_y. Other than that, the remaining parameters were shared, including the LSTM decoder and the attentional MLP. The hope was that by simply using the same parameters for a related task, we would allow data to be shared between the two languages and reduce overfitting.

3.3 Encoder-decoder Pipeline (ENCDEC)

The next model tested was the encoder-decoder pipeline (figure 2). Again, this was a relatively straightforward extension to the baseline. After the baseline model finished producing a German caption, it had some final state (h_t, c_t). We simply resumed decoding to produce an English caption starting from that final state with an independent decoder f_1, separate vocabulary, and this time without any direct access to the image. Each timestep is computed as $(h_t, c_t) = f_1(h_{t-1}, c_{t-1}, embed_{t-1})$. This should force the model to keep information about the image in the hidden state throughout the decoding process, hopefully improving the model output.

This is the model that was used as the submission to the WMT multimodal task.

3.4 Attentional Pipeline with Averaged Embeddings (ATTAVG)

Attention has been shown to improve upon simple encoder-decoder models, so we wanted to test adding an additional attentional component. Both the baseline and the previous models mentioned already include attention over the *image*, but here we add attention over the German caption output as well. Once again, the German part of this model is just the baseline. Additionally, for each German word that was actually produced, we want to consider all of the alternatives. Thus at each timestep, we average together the embeddings of every word in the German vocabulary, weighted by the probability of producing each word. The result is one vector s_w (with the same dimension as the word embedding size) for each word w in the German caption.

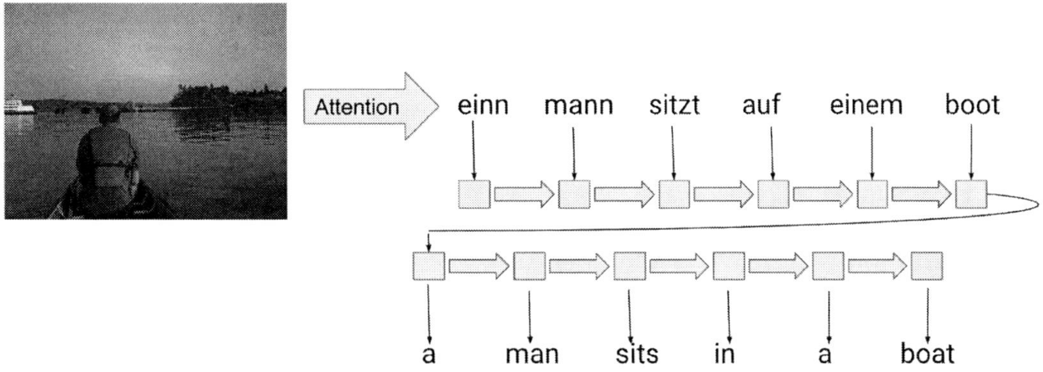

Figure 2: Encoder-decoder Pipeline. The LSTM state after producing the German caption (with attention to the image) is passed along to a new decoder. The new decoder produces an English caption using only the final hidden LSTM state, without referencing the image directly.

Then, we generate the English caption using a separate LSTM with attention over the averaged German word embeddings (and without any access to the underlying image). That is, at each timestep, an attention model f_{att} implemented as a multilayer perceptron (MLP) predicts how important each averaged word embedding s_w is, based on the previous hidden state h_{t-1}. We compute the softmax of these attention outputs and use this to compute a weighted average of the s_w embeddings. The result is a 256-dimensional context vector z_t that represents the important parts of the German sentence at timestep t. The next timestep is computed as $(h_t, c_t) = f_2(h_{t-1}, c_{t-1}, x_t)$ where $x_t = concat(embed_{t-1}, z_t)$. The process is shown in figure 3.

Unfortunately, the implementation of averaged embeddings requires more memory than the other implementations, forcing us to use a smaller word embedding size, smaller hidden layer, and smaller vocabulary. To address this issue, we consider a variant using random embeddings.

3.5 Attentional Pipeline with Random Embeddings (ATTRND)

This model is a slight variant on the attentional pipeline with averaged embeddings. At each timestep, instead of averaging together the embeddings of every word, we sample one random word from the distribution of predicted probabilities. The embedding of that word is multiplied by its probability, giving us a value that represents the contribution of that word to the weighted average.

This again yields one vector for each word in the German caption. And again we generate the English caption using an LSTM with attention over the sampled German word embeddings (and without any access to the underlying image), as shown in figure 3.

3.6 Dual Attention (DUALATT)

Finally, we tried one model with the opposite structure from the rest (figure 4). We first generate the *English* caption using the baseline method, and then train an LSTM with attention over both the English caption and the image (using two separate MLPs).

That is, after we've generated an English caption using the baseline model, we consider it as a pseudo-reference. When generating the German sentence, we take attention over the image vectors as usual to get z_t, and we take attention over the word embeddings for the actual English caption generated to get $\tilde{z}_t$, both conditioned on the hidden state h_{t-1}. That allows us to compute the next timestep as $(h_t, c_t) = f_2(h_{t-1}, c_{t-1}, x_t)$ where $x_t = concat(embed_{t-1}, z_t, \tilde{z}_t)$.

4 Experimental Setup

All models were implemented using DyNet (Neubig et al., 2017), specifically using the `VanillaLSTM` class. Models were trained using the Adam optimizer (Kingma and Ba, 2014). Multi30k, an expanded of the Flickr 30k training data, was provided for the WMT multimodal task 2 constrained setting (Elliott et al., 2016) and

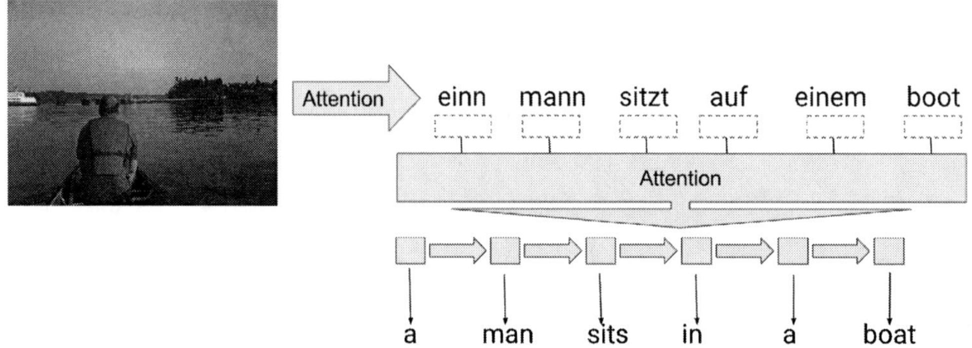

Figure 3: Attention Pipeline. At each timestep as the German caption is being generated, we produce an embedding (box with dashed outline). Depending on whether we are using averaged embeddings or random embeddings, this is either (1) the weighted average of all words in the vocabulary, or (2) the contribution of one randomly selected word to that weighted average. An LSTM with attention produces an English caption using these embeddings.

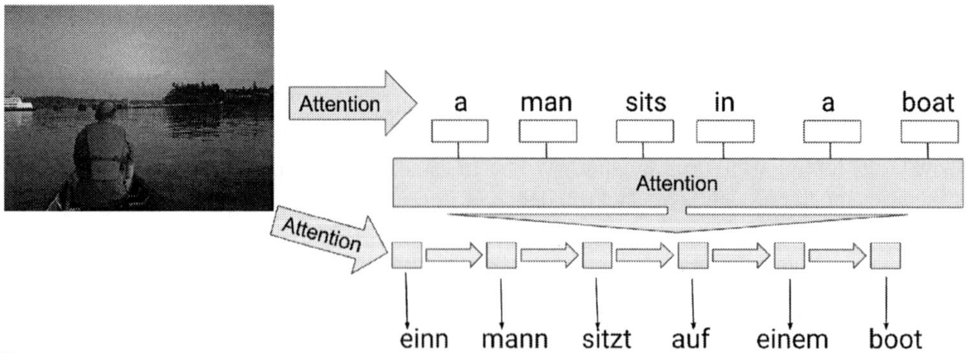

Figure 4: Dual Attention. After generating an English caption, we retrieve the embeddings for the words generated (white box with solid outline). An LSTM with attention over both the English embeddings and the image produces a German caption.

	Dropout	Vocabulary size (German/English)	Minibatch	BLEU-4	METEOR
Baseline 1	0.02	17855/12138	32	10.35	20.73
Baseline 2	0.2	9996/8368	8	10.20	18.97
Shared decoder*	0.2	17855/12138	24	11.51	20.87
ENCDEC*	0.2	9996/8368	32	11.53	21.90
ATTRND*	0.2	9996/8368	32	11.84	20.53
ATTAVG	0.2	6729/6310	8	9.18	19.67
DUALATT	0.2	17855/12138	24	10.51	19.68

Table 1: Model evaluation results. * indicates statistically significant improvement relative to baseline 1 ($p < 0.05$) with paired bootstrap resampling, based on BLEU-4 score on the 2016 test set. Multiple combinations of vocabulary size, minibatch size, and dropout were tested for each model, but only the best combination (by BLEU score on the validation set) is reported here.

used as the dataset. This dataset consists of 29000 images for training, 1014 images for validation, 1000 images for test 2016, and 1000 images for test 2017. Each image had 5 independently generated English and German captions. Since the English and German captions were generated independently, the pairing between English and German captions within each set of 5 was randomized on each epoch, for a total of 25 pairs per image. No external data was used, making this a constrained submission.

Each of the models used LSTM hidden size 512, embedding size 512, and hidden dimension 256 for the Attention MLP. The one exception was AT-TAVG which due to memory limits used LSTM hidden size 256, embedding size 256, and hidden dimension 256 for the attention MLP. Minibatching was used, with each batch formed by grouping together similar length captions to improve efficiency. Minibatch sizes, vocabulary sizes, and dropout settings are noted in table 1. The order of the batches was randomized on each epoch. Models were trained until the perplexity on the validation set no longer improved.

5 Results

The WMT 2016 multimodal task test set was used for evaluation. Results were scored using BLEU (Papineni et al., 2002) and METEOR (Denkowski and Lavie, 2014), with all sentences lower-cased and punctuation removed. Scores on the 2016 test set are shown in table 1.

The system submitted to the WMT multimodal task was ENCDEC. On the 2017 test set, it achieved a BLEU score of 9.1 (matching the official baseline and exceeding all other systems submitted). It also achieved a Meteor score of 19.8 (worse than the official baseline of 23.4) and a

TER score of 63.3 (better than the official baseline of 91.4 and all other systems submitted). The fact that each of these three scoring methods shows a different result relative to the baseline is somewhat concerning.

In general, the evaluation results did not show very good correlation between BLEU and ME-TEOR. We tested output samples derived from 52 experiments conducted with varying configurations during the course of the study. We found that the correlation between BLEU and METEOR was approximately 0.18. Strikingly, the top-ranked output according to METEOR scored more than 3 BLEU points lower than the baseline. Our informal human evaluation of the outputs tended to agree more with the BLEU evaluations than the METEOR evaluations.

6 Conclusion

We tested five alternative methods for supplementing a German caption dataset with English captions to improve performance, and in three cases achieved statistically significant improvements. This indicates that multilingual image captioning data is a valuable resource, even when learning only a single language. The best performing model measured by BLEU was the attentional pipeline with random embeddings, which improved on the baseline by 1.5 BLEU points. The best performing model measured by ME-TEOR was the encoder-decoder pipeline, which improved on the baseline by 1.2 METEOR points.

References

Dzmitry Bahdanau, Kyunghyun Cho, and Yoshua Bengio. 2014. Neural machine translation by jointly learning to align and translate. *CoRR* abs/1409.0473. http://arxiv.org/abs/1409.0473.

Yoshua Bengio, Réjean Ducharme, Pascal Vincent, and Christian Jauvin. 2003. A neural probabilistic language model. *Journal of machine learning research* 3(Feb):1137–1155.

Ozan Caglayan, Walid Aransa, Yaxing Wang, Marc Masana, Mercedes García-Martínez, Fethi Bougares, Loïc Barrault, and Joost van de Weijer. 2016. Does multimodality help human and machine for translation and image captioning? In *Proceedings of the First Conference on Machine Translation*. Association for Computational Linguistics, Berlin, Germany, pages 627–633. http://www.aclweb.org/anthology/W/W16/W16-2358.

Michael Denkowski and Alon Lavie. 2014. Meteor universal: Language specific translation evaluation for any target language. In *Proceedings of the EACL 2014 Workshop on Statistical Machine Translation*.

D. Elliott, S. Frank, K. Sima'an, and L. Specia. 2016. Multi30k: Multilingual english-german image descriptions pages 70–74.

Desmond Elliott, Stella Frank, and Eva Hasler. 2015. Multi-language image description with neural sequence models. *CoRR, abs/1510.04709* .

Kaiming He, Xiangyu Zhang, Shaoqing Ren, and Jian Sun. 2015. Deep residual learning for image recognition. *CoRR* abs/1512.03385. http://arxiv.org/abs/1512.03385.

Julian Hitschler and Stefan Riezler. 2016. Multimodal pivots for image caption translation. *CoRR* abs/1601.03916. http://arxiv.org/abs/1601.03916.

Sepp Hochreiter and Jürgen Schmidhuber. 1997. Long short-term memory. *Neural computation* 9(8):1735–1780.

Po-Yao Huang, Frederick Liu, Sz-Rung Shiang, Jean Oh, and Chris Dyer. 2016. Attention-based multimodal neural machine translation. In *Proceedings of the First Conference on Machine Translation, Berlin, Germany*.

Diederik P. Kingma and Jimmy Ba. 2014. Adam: A method for stochastic optimization. *CoRR* abs/1412.6980. http://arxiv.org/abs/1412.6980.

Minh-Thang Luong, Hieu Pham, and Christopher D. Manning. 2015. Effective approaches to attention-based neural machine translation. *CoRR* abs/1508.04025. http://arxiv.org/abs/1508.04025.

Graham Neubig, Chris Dyer, Yoav Goldberg, Austin Matthews, Waleed Ammar, Antonios Anastasopoulos, Miguel Ballesteros, David Chiang, Daniel Clothiaux, Trevor Cohn, Kevin Duh, Manaal Faruqui, Cynthia Gan, Dan Garrette, Yangfeng Ji, Lingpeng Kong, Adhiguna Kuncoro, Gaurav Kumar, Chaitanya Malaviya, Paul Michel, Yusuke Oda, Matthew Richardson, Naomi Saphra, Swabha Swayamdipta, and Pengcheng Yin. 2017. Dynet: The dynamic neural network toolkit. *arXiv preprint arXiv:1701.03980* .

Kishore Papineni, Salim Roukos, Todd Ward, and Wei-Jing Zhu. 2002. Bleu: A method for automatic evaluation of machine translation. In *Proceedings of the 40th Annual Meeting on Association for Computational Linguistics*. Association for Computational Linguistics, Stroudsburg, PA, USA, ACL '02, pages 311–318. https://doi.org/10.3115/1073083.1073135.

Karen Simonyan and Andrew Zisserman. 2014. Very deep convolutional networks for large-scale image recognition. *arXiv preprint arXiv:1409.1556* .

Lucia Specia, Stella Frank, Khalil Sima'an, and Desmond Elliott. 2016. A shared task on multimodal machine translation and crosslingual image description. In *WMT*. pages 543–553.

Nitish Srivastava, Geoffrey E Hinton, Alex Krizhevsky, Ilya Sutskever, and Ruslan Salakhutdinov. 2014. Dropout: a simple way to prevent neural networks from overfitting. *Journal of Machine Learning Research* 15(1):1929–1958.

Ilya Sutskever, Oriol Vinyals, and Quoc V. Le. 2014. Sequence to sequence learning with neural networks. *CoRR* abs/1409.3215. http://arxiv.org/abs/1409.3215.

Oriol Vinyals, Alexander Toshev, Samy Bengio, and Dumitru Erhan. 2015. Show and tell: A neural image caption generator. In *The IEEE Conference on Computer Vision and Pattern Recognition (CVPR)*.

Kelvin Xu, Jimmy Ba, Ryan Kiros, Kyunghyun Cho, Aaron C. Courville, Ruslan Salakhutdinov, Richard S. Zemel, and Yoshua Bengio. 2015. Show, attend and tell: Neural image caption generation with visual attention. *CoRR* abs/1502.03044. http://arxiv.org/abs/1502.03044.

OSU Multimodal Machine Translation System Report

Mingbo Ma, Dapeng Li, Kai Zhao[†] and Liang Huang
Department of EECS
Oregon State University
Corvallis, OR 97331, USA
{mam, lidap, zhaok, liang.huang}@oregonstate.edu

Abstract

This paper describes Oregon State University's submissions to the shared WMT'17 task "multimodal translation task I". In this task, all the sentence pairs are image captions in different languages. The key difference between this task and conventional machine translation is that we have corresponding images as additional information for each sentence pair. In this paper, we introduce a simple but effective system which takes an image shared between different languages, feeding it into the both encoding and decoding side. We report our system's performance for English-French and English-German with Flickr30K (in-domain) and MSCOCO (out-of-domain) datasets. Our system achieves the best performance in TER for English-German for MSCOCO dataset.

1 Introduction

Natural language generation (NLG) is one of the most important tasks in natural language processing (NLP). It can be applied to a lot of interesting applications such like machine translation, image captioning, question answering. In recent years, Recurrent Neural Networks (RNNs) based approaches have shown promising performance in generating more fluent and meaningful sentences compared with conventional models such as rule-based model (Mirkovic et al., 2011), corpus-based n-gram models (Wen et al., 2015) and trainable generators (Stent et al., 2004).

---

† Current address: Google Inc., 111 8th Avenue, New York, New York, USA.

More recently, attention-based encoder-decoder models (Bahdanau et al., 2014) have been proposed to provide the decoder more accurate alignments to generate more relevant words. The remarkable ability of attention mechanisms quickly update the state-of-the-art performance on variety of NLG tasks, such as machine translation (Luong et al., 2015), image captioning (Xu et al., 2015; Yang et al., 2016), and text summarization (Rush et al., 2015; Nallapati et al., 2016).

However, for multimodal translation (Elliott et al., 2015), where we translate a caption from one language into another given a corresponding image, we need to design a new model since the decoder needs to consider both language and images at the same time.

This paper describes our participation in the WMT 2017 multimodal task 1. Our model feeds the image information to both the encoder and decoder, to ground their hidden representation within the same context of image during training. In this way, during testing time, the decoder would generate more relevant words given the context of both source sentence and image.

2 Model Description

For the neural based machine translation model, the encoder needs to map sequence of word embeddings from the source side into another representation of the entire sequence using recurrent networks. Then, in the second stage, decoder generates one word at a time with considering global (sentence representation) and local information (weighted context) from source side. For simplicity, our proposed model is based on the attention-based encoder-decoder framework in (Luong et al., 2015), ref-

465

Proceedings of the Conference on Machine Translation (WMT), Volume 2: Shared Task Papers, pages 465–469
Copenhagen, Denmark, September 7–11, 2017. ©2017 Association for Computational Linguistics

ered as "Global attention".

On the other hand, for the early work of neural-basic caption generation models (Vinyals et al., 2015), the convolutional neural networks (CNN) generate the image features which feed into the decoder directly for generating the description.

The first stage of the above two tasks both map the temporal and spatial information into a fixed dimensional vector which makes it feasible to utilize both information at the same time.

Fig. 1 shows the basic idea of our proposed model (OSU1). The red character $\mathbf{I}$ represents the image feature that is generated from CNN. In our case, we directly use the image features that are provided by WMT, and these features are generated by residual networks (He et al., 2016).

The encoder (blue boxes) in Fig. 1 takes the image feature as initialization for generating each hidden representation. This process is very similar to neural-basic caption generation (Vinyals et al., 2015) which grounds each word's hidden representation to the context given by the image. On the decoder side (green boxes in Fig. 1), we not only let each decoded word align to source words by global attention but also feed the image feature as initialization to the decoder.

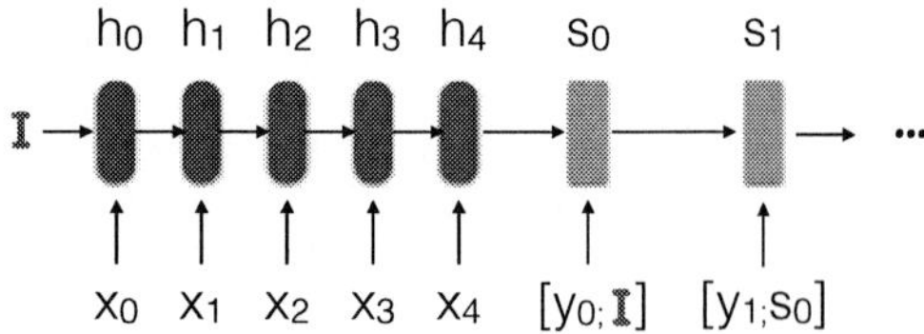

Figure 1: The image information is feed to both encoder and decoder for initialization. I (in red) represents the image feature that are generated by CNN.

3 Experiments

3.1 Datasets

In our experiments, we use two datasets Flickr30K (Elliott et al., 2016) and MSCOCO (Lin et al., 2014) which are provided by the WMT organization. For both datasets, there are triples that contains English as source sentence, its German and French human translations and corresponding image. The system is only trained on

Flickr30K datasets but are also tested on MSCOCO besides Flickr30K. MSCOCO datasets are considered out-of-domain (OOD) testing while Flickr30K dataset are considered in-domain testing. The datasets' statics is shown in Table 1

Datasets	Train	Dev	Test	OOD ?
Flickr30K	29,000	1,014	1,000	No
MSCOCO	-	-	461	Yes

Table 1: Summary of datasets statistics.

3.2 Training details

For preprocessing, we convert all of the sentences to lower case, normalize the punctuation, and do the tokenization. For simplicity, our vocabulary keeps all the words that show in training set. For image representation, we use ResNet (He et al., 2016) generated image features which are provided by the WMT organization. In our experiments, we only use average pooled features.

Our implementation is adapted from on Pytorch-based OpenNMT (Klein et al., 2017). We use two layered bi-LSTM (Sutskever et al., 2014) on the source side as encoder. Our batch size is 64, with SGD optimization and a learning rate at 1. For English to German, the dropout rate is 0.6, and for English to French, the dropout rate is 0.4. These two parameters are selected by observing the performance on development set. Our word embeddings are randomly initialized with 500 dimensions. The source side vocabulary is 10,214 and the target side vocabulary is 18,726 for German and 11,222 for French.

3.3 Beam search with length reward

During test time, beam search is widely used to improve the output text quality by giving the decoder more options to generate the next possible word. However, different from traditional beam search in phrase-based MT where all hypotheses know the number of steps to finish the generation, while in neural-based generation, there is no information about what is the most ideal number of steps to finish the decoding. The above issue also leads to another problem that the beam search in neural-based MT prefers shorter sequences due to probability-based scores for evaluating different candidates. In this paper, we use Optimal Beam Search (Huang et al., 2017) (OBS) during decoding time. OBS uses bounded length reward mechanism which allows a modified version of our beam search algorithm to remain optimal.

Figure 2 and Figure 3 show the BLEU score and length ratio with different rewards for different beam size. We choose beam size equals to 5 and reward equals to 0.1 during decoding.

3.4 Results

WMT organization provides three different evaluating metrics: BLEU (Papineni et al., 2002), METEOR (Lavie and Denkowski, 2009) and TER (Snover et al., 2006).

Table 2 to Table 5 summarize the performance with their corresponding rank among all other systems. We only show a few top performing systems in the tables to make a comparison. OSU1 is our proposed model and OSU2 is our baseline system without any image information. For MSCOCO dataset, the translation from English to German (Table 3), which is the hardest tasks compared with others since it is from English to German on OOD dataset, we achieve best TER score across all other systems.

System	Rank	TER	METEOR	BLEU
UvA-TiCC	1	**47.5**	53.5	**33.3**
NICT	2	48.1	**53.9**	31.9
LIUMCVC	3 & 4	48.2	53.8	33.2
CUNI	5	50.7	51	31.1
OSU2†	6	50.7	50.6	31
OSU1†	8	51.6	48.9	29.7

Table 2: Experiments on Flickr30K dataset for translation from English to German. 16 systems in total. $\dagger$ represents our system.

System	Rank	TER	METEOR	BLEU
OSU1†	1	**52.3**	46.5	27.4
UvA-TiCC	2	52.4	48.1	28
LIUMCVC	3	52.5	**48.9**	**28.7**
OSU2†	8	55.9	45.7	26.1

Table 3: Experiments on MSCOCO dataset for translation from English to German. 15 systems in total. $\dagger$ represents our system.

As describe in section 2, OSU1 is the model with image information for both encoder and

System	Rank	TER	METEOR	BLEU
LIUMCVC	1	**28.4**	**72.1**	**55.9**
NICT	2	28.4	72	55.3
DCU	3	30	70.1	54.1
OSU2†	5	32.7	68.3	51.9
OSU1†	6	33.6	67.2	51

Table 4: Experiments on Flickr30K dataset for translation from English to French. 11 systems in total. $\dagger$ represents our system.

System	Rank	TER	METEOR	BLEU
LIUMCVC	1	**34.2**	**65.9**	**45.9**
NICT	2	34.7	65.6	45.1
DCU	3	35.2	64.1	44.5
OSU2†	4	36.7	63.8	44.1
OSU1†	6	37.8	61.6	41.2

Table 5: Experiments on MSCOCO dataset for translation from English to French. 11 systems in total.

decoder, and OSU2 is only the neural machine translation baseline without any image information. From the above results table we found that image information would hurt the performance in some cases. In order to have more detailed analysis, we show some test examples for the translation from English to German on MSCOCO dataset.

Fig 4 shows two examples that NMT baseline model performances better than OSU1 model. In the first example, OSU1 generates several unseen objects from given image, such like knife. The image feature might not represent the image accurately. For the second example, OSU1 model ignores the object "box" in the image.

Fig 5 shows two examples that image feature helps the OSU1 to generate better results. In the first example, image feature successfully detects the object "drink" while the baseline completely neglects this. In the second example, the image feature even help the model figure out the action of the cat is "slooping".

4 Conclusion

We describe our system submission to the shared WMT'17 task "multimodal translation task I". The results for English-German and English-French on Flickr30K and MSCOCO datasets are reported in this paper. Our proposed model is simple but effective and we achieve the best performance in TER for

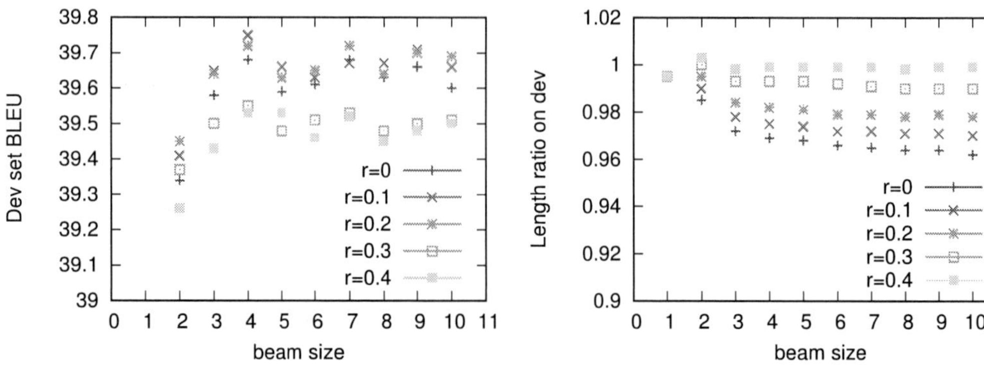

Figure 2: BLEU vs. beam size

Figure 3: length ratio vs. beam size

input	a finger pointing at a hotdog with cheese , sauerkraut and ketchup .
OSU1	ein finger zeigt auf einen hot dog mit einem messer , wischmobs und napa .
OSU2	ein finger zeigt auf einen hotdog mit hammer und italien .
Reference	ein finger zeigt auf einen hotdog mit käse , sauerkraut und ketchup .

input	a man reaching down for something in a box
OSU1	ein mann greift nach unten , um etwas zu irgendeinem .
OSU2	ein mann greift nach etwas in einer kiste .
Reference	ein mann bückt sich nach etwas in einer schachtel .

Figure 4: Two testing examples that image information confuses the NMT model.

input	there are two foods and one drink set on the clear table .
OSU1	da sind zwei speisen und ein getränk am klaren tisch .
OSU2	zwei erwachsene und ein erwachsener befinden sich auf dem rechteckigen tisch .
Reference	auf dem transparenten tisch stehen zwei speisen und ein getränk .

input	a camera set up in front of a sleeping cat .
OSU1	eine kameracrew vor einer schlafenden katze .
OSU2	eine kamera vor einer blonden katze .
Reference	eine kamera , die vor einer schlafenden katze aufgebaut ist

Figure 5: Two testing examples that image information helps the NMT model.

English-German for MSCOCO dataset.

5 Acknowledgment

This work is supported in part by NSF IIS-1656051, DARPA FA8750-13-2-0041 (DEFT), DARPA N66001-17-2-4030 (XAI), a Google Faculty Research Award, and an HP Gift.

References

Dzmitry Bahdanau, Kyunghyun Cho, and Yoshua Bengio. 2014. Neural machine translation by jointly learning to align and translate. *CoRR* .

D. Elliott, S. Frank, K. Sima'an, and L. Specia. 2016. Multi30k: Multilingual english-german image descriptions. *Proceedings of the 5th Workshop on Vision and Language* pages 70–74.

Desmond Elliott, Stella Frank, and Eva Hasler. 2015. Multi-language image description with neural sequence models. *CoRR* .

Kaiming He, Xiangyu Zhang, Shaoqing Ren, and Jian Sun. 2016. Deep residual learning for image recognition. *Conference on Computer Vision and Pattern Recognition CVPR* .

Liang Huang, Kai Zhao, and Mingbo Ma. 2017. Optimal beam search for neural text generation (modulo beam size). In *EMNLP 2017* .

G. Klein, Y. Kim, Y. Deng, J. Senellart, and A. M. Rush. 2017. Opennmt: Open-source toolkit for neural machine translation. *ArXiv e-prints* .

Alon Lavie and Michael J. Denkowski. 2009. The meteor metric for automatic evaluation of machine translation. *Machine Translation* .

Tsung-Yi Lin, Michael Maire, Serge J. Belongie, Lubomir D. Bourdev, Ross B. Girshick, James Hays, Pietro Perona, Deva Ramanan, Piotr Dollár, and C. Lawrence Zitnick. 2014. Microsoft COCO: common objects in context .

Minh-Thang Luong, Hieu Pham, and Christopher D. Manning. 2015. Effective approaches to attention-based neural machine translation. *CoRR* .

Danilo Mirkovic, Lawrence Cavedon, Matthew Purver, Florin Ratiu, Tobias Scheideck, Fuliang Weng, Qi Zhang, and Kui Xu. 2011. Dialogue management using scripts and combined confidence scores. *US Patent* pages 7,904,297.

Ramesh Nallapati, Bowen Zhou, and Mingbo Ma. 2016. Classify or select: Neural architectures for extractive document summarization. *CoRR* .

Kishore Papineni, Salim Roukos, Todd Ward, and Wei-Jing Zhu. 2002. Bleu: A method for automatic evaluation of machine translation. *Proceedings of the 40th Annual Meeting on Association for Computational Linguistics* .

Alexander M. Rush, Sumit Chopra, and Jason Weston. 2015. A neural attention model for abstractive sentence summarization .

Matthew Snover, Bonnie Dorr, Richard Schwartz, Linnea Micciulla, and John Makhoul. 2006. A study of translation edit rate with targeted human annotation. *In Proceedings of Association for Machine Translation in the Americas* .

Amanda Stent, Rashmi Prasad, and Marilyn Walker. 2004. Trainable sentence planning for complex information presentation in spoken dialog systems. *Proceedings of the 42Nd Annual Meeting on Association for Computational Linguistics* .

Ilya Sutskever, Oriol Vinyals, and Quoc V. Le. 2014. Sequence to sequence learning with neural networks. *Proceedings of the 27th International Conference on Neural Information Processing Systems* .

Oriol Vinyals, Alexander Toshev, Samy Bengio, and Dumitru Erhan. 2015. Show and tell: A neural image caption generator. *IEEE Conference on Computer Vision and Pattern Recognition* pages 3156–3164.

Tsung-Hsien Wen, Milica Gasic, Dongho Kim, Nikola Mrksic, Pei-hao Su, David Vandyke, and Steve J. Young. 2015. Stochastic language generation in dialogue using recurrent neural networks with convolutional sentence reranking. *CoRR* .

Kelvin Xu, Jimmy Ba, Ryan Kiros, Kyunghyun Cho, Aaron Courville, Ruslan Salakhudinov, Rich Zemel, and Yoshua Bengio. 2015. Show, attend and tell: Neural image caption generation with visual attention. *Proceedings of the 32nd International Conference on Machine Learning (ICML-15)* .

Zhilin Yang, Ye Yuan, Yuexin Wu, William W. Cohen, and Ruslan Salakhutdinov. 2016. Review networks for caption generation. *Advances in Neural Information Processing Systems* .

Sheffield MultiMT: Using Object Posterior Predictions for Multimodal Machine Translation

Pranava Madhyastha*, Josiah Wang* and **Lucia Specia**
Department of Computer Science
University of Sheffield, UK
{p.madhyastha, j.k.wang, l.specia}@sheffield.ac.uk

Abstract

This paper describes the University of Sheffield's submission to the WMT17 Multimodal Machine Translation shared task. We participated in Task 1 to develop an MT system to translate an image description from English to German and French, given its corresponding image. Our proposed systems are based on the state-of-the-art Neural Machine Translation approach. We investigate the effect of replacing the commonly-used image embeddings with an estimated posterior probability prediction for 1,000 object categories in the images.

1 Introduction

This paper describes the University of Sheffield's submission to the second edition of the WMT17 Multimodal Machine Translation shared task. We participate in Task 1, where the challenge is to develop a Machine Translation (MT) system to automatically translate image descriptions to a target language, given an image description in a source language and its corresponding image. We submitted systems for translating from English to both German and French.

Our submission is based on the state-of-the-art attention-based Neural Machine Translation (NMT) system, which has shown better performance than conventional phrase-based statistical MT (SMT) systems in the past years. Multimodal NMT systems have been introduced (Elliott et al., 2015; Caglayan et al., 2016; Calixto et al., 2016; Huang et al., 2016) to incorporate visual information into NMT approaches, most of which condition the NMT on an image representation (typi-

cally a vector extracted from a Convolutional Neural Network (CNN) layer). However, it has not been clear thus far whether such image features actually help in the translation task and more important, if so it is not clear which aspects of the image can play a role and how.

Recent approaches to Multimodal NMT have used low level image features, including dense fully connected vectors and spatial convolutional representations from an image classification network (Elliott et al., 2015; Huang et al., 2016). They also incorporate attention mechanisms (Calixto et al., 2016). However, the effect of image features or the efficacy of the representational contribution is still an open research question.

For our submission, we propose replacing image representations used in current Multimodal NMT systems with a class-based probabilistic distribution that is estimated directly using a state-of-the-art image classification network. The core hypothesis is that such representations offer higher level semantic information and could be more beneficial to Multimodal NMT systems.

In Section 2 we discuss the motivations behind our proposed system. In Section 3 we describe our approach, which uses CNN-based image features as input (Section 3.1) to an attention based neural machine translation system (Section 3.2), resulting in a Multimodal NMT system (Section 3.3). Experimental settings are reported in Section 4, and results discussed in Section 5. A brief overview of related work are provided in Section 6.

2 Motivation

Recent work (Wu et al., 2016; You et al., 2016) exploits explicit, higher-level semantic representation of images for the tasks of image captioning and visual question answering. Instead of feeding

---

*P. Madhyastha and J. Wang contributed equally to this work.

Proceedings of the Conference on Machine Translation (WMT), Volume 2: Shared Task Papers, pages 470–476
Copenhagen, Denmark, September 7–11, 2017. ©2017 Association for Computational Linguistics

a lower-level image representation directly to the model, such work explicitly explores predicting the occurrence of various concepts (objects, also referred to as attributes) in the image, and feeding such predictions to the language generation component. Our hypothesis is that such an approach, when applied to Multimodal NMT, should provide comparable, if not better results compared to systems that use image representations directly. This approach also offers the advantage of being more interpretable compared to end-to-end systems that use image representations directly. Finally, since the image classification network is trained directly to produce probabilistic class distributions, the predictions are more stable and encoded in simpler representations when compared with the fully connected, lower-level representations. This also presents an opportunity to fine tune the class distributions for the task using domain-specific data. In other words, we can tune the image network to produce better predictions on the classes that appear in the dataset of interest.

Motivated by these insights, we empirically evaluate the performance of a Multimodal NMT system with image features based on predicted class distributions. In most cases we are able to outperform the baseline system under similar settings. In the following section we describe our system in detail.

3 System description

We first describe the image features used in our system, more specifically, the probability prediction of an object category occurring in the image (Section 3.1). We then present the NMT system used (Section 3.2), and how the image features are combined to produce a Multimodal NMT system (Section 3.3) for the shared task. Figure 1 illustrates the proposed system.

3.1 Visual features

Visual features were extracted from the 152-layer version of ResNet (He et al., 2015), a Deep Convolutional Neural Network (CNN) pre-trained on 1,000 object categories (synsets) of the classification task of the ImageNet Large Scale Visual Recognition Challenge (ILSVRC) (Russakovsky et al., 2015). We extracted the final layer after applying the softmax function. This layer is a 1,000-dimensional vector providing class posterior probability estimates at image level for the 1,000 object

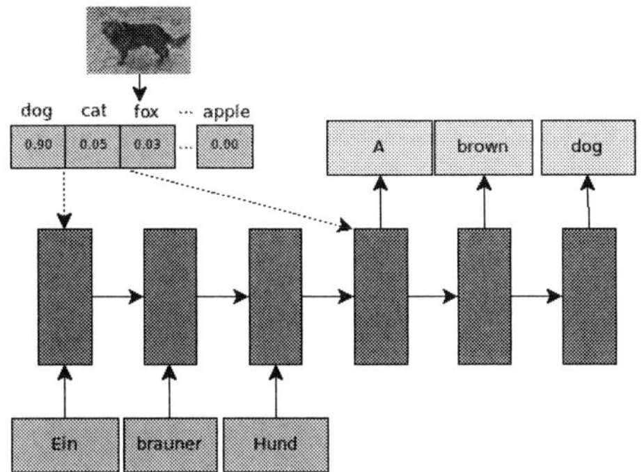

Figure 1: An illustration of our Multimodal NMT system. Departing from usual methods, we replace the lower-level image CNN representation with a vector representing the output of a 1,000-way visual classifier, where each element in the vector represents the estimated posterior probability of an object category occurring in the image. We experiment with conditioning the image representation on either the encoder or the decoder (dashed lines), and also at each source word (not shown in the Figure).

categories, each corresponding to a distinct WordNet synset.

While ResNet has been reported to perform extremely well in classification tasks (3.57% top-5 error rate in the ILSVRC2015 challenge[1], where a prediction is considered correct if the gold standard category is within a system's top 5 guesses), it is worth noting that the model is built for and tuned to the 1,000 categories of ILSVRC, some of which include very fine-grained classifications like various dog species. Thus, many of these categories may not be relevant to the shared task data which is based on the Flickr30K dataset (Young et al., 2014). Conversely, many objects depicted in Flickr30K may also not be covered in the ILSVRC dataset.

3.2 Neural Machine Translation

We use a standard LSTM-based bidirectional encoder-decoder architecture with global attention (Luong et al., 2015). All our NMT models have the following architecture: the input and output vocabulary are limited to words that appear at least twice in the training data and the remaining words are replaced by the $< UNK >$ token. The hidden layer dimensionality is set to 256 and the

---

[1] http://image-net.org/challenges/LSVRC/2015/results

471

word dimensionality is set to 128, for both the encoder and decoder, as this configuration was found to lead to faster training times without sacrificing translation performance. At decoding time, we perform greedy decoding by outputting the most probable word at each time step.

3.3 Multimodal Neural Machine Translation

To add visual features, we extend the above mentioned architecture in the following ways:

1. Image features initialising the Encoder (**InitEnc**): As shown in Figure 1, we use the predicted class distribution to initialise only the encoder (i.e. images as the first token). This can be seen as conditioning the encoder on the predicted class distribution.

2. Image features initialising the Decoder (**InitDec**): As we see in Figure 1, here we initialize the decoder's first hidden state with the predicted class distribution.

3. Image features conditioning each input token (**Proj**): In this projected representation approach, we first perform an affine transformation with a weight matrix W, where $W \in \mathcal{R}^{c \times d}$ (c and d are dimensionality of the class distribution and dimensionality of the word vectors, respectively). This is followed by a non-linearity function to squash the resulting output. We add this representation to each source word representation. The weight matrix W is learned. This can be seen as composing each source token with the visual feature at each time step.

4 Experimental settings

We use our own implementation of a multimodal NMT approach and explore a number of variants of this model in order to understand the effects of using the classification layer instead of a lower level CNN layer as input to the NMT system.

4.1 Data

The shared task is based on the Multi30K (Elliott et al., 2016) dataset. Each image contains one English description taken from Flickr30K and professional translations into German and French. In this year's edition of the shared task, the source language is English (EN) and the target languages are German (DE) and French (FR). The dataset contains 29,000 training and 1,014 development instances: an image, a description in source language, and a description for each target language. There are two test sets:

1. An in-domain test set (**Flickr**) with 1,000 images.

2. An out-of-domain test set (**MSCOCO**) with 461 images whose captions were selected to contain ambiguous verbs.

4.2 Visual features

The primary visual feature explored in this paper is the class posterior probability estimates of ResNet-152 for 1,000 object categories (**Softmax**). As a comparison, we also extract the penultimate layer of ResNet-152 (**Pool5**).

The visual features are combined with the NMT model using the three configurations described in Section 3.3 (**InitEnc, InitDec, Proj**). We also compare our systems to a text-only baseline (Section 3.2).

4.3 NMT model

We implemented our NMT system (Section 3.2) in PyTorch. We use a single layer bidirectional LSTM based encoder-decoder model. We used ReLU as the projection non-linearity and used dropout with probability of 0.2. We used the *Adadelta* optimizer (Zeiler, 2012) with the default learning rate (0.01). The batch size was set to 20. We trained it for 50 epochs and selected the model that performs best on the validation set using *BLEU* as the metric.

We normalised punctuations, lowercased and tokenised the input text using the script provided in Moses (Koehn et al., 2007). Our experiments were performed with the vocabulary size of 6,000 English words, 6,500 French words and 8,000 German words after removing words that appeared only once in the training set (these words were replaced with $< UNK >$, as described in Section 3.2). At decoding time, we post-processed the output translations by replacing $< UNK >$ with an empty string.

5 Results and discussion

We present our results on the Flickr test dataset in Table 1, for both EN–DE and EN–FR. We observe that for the **Softmax** feature, **InitDec** consistently outperformed **InitEnc** and **Proj**. It also performed better than the text-only baseline for both

Flickr	Feature	Model	Meteor	BLEU
	-	Baseline	43.7	24.4
EN-DE	Pool5	Proj	–	–
		InitEnc	43.0	23.5
		InitDec	44.3	24.6
	Softmax	Proj	43.4	24.2
		InitEnc	42.4	23.3
		InitDec	44.5	25.0
	-	Baseline	62.2	44.2
EN-FR	Pool5	Proj	–	–
		InitEnc	61.1	43.5
		InitDec	61.0	43.4
	Softmax	Proj	61.5	43.6
		InitEnc	61.0	43.3
		InitDec	62.8	45.0

Table 1: Results on the Flickr test data, for both English–German (EN–DE) and English–French (EN–FR). **Proj** was not evaluated for **Pool5** as its performance is very poor on the development set.

MSCOCO	Feature	Model	Meteor	BLEU
	–	Baseline	39.6	20.7
EN-DE	Pool5	Proj	–	–
		InitEnc	39.1	20.4
		InitDec	39.5	20.4
	Softmax	Proj	40.0	21.0
		InitEnc	37.5	18.8
		InitDec	40.7	21.4
	-	Baseline	57.4	37.2
EN-FR	Pool5	Proj	–	–
		InitEnc	56.7	36.5
		InitDec	56.7	36.9
	Softmax	Proj	57.0	36.8
		InitEnc	55.5	35.5
		InitDec	57.3	37.2

Table 2: Results on the MSCOCO test data, for both English–German (EN–DE) and English–French (EN–FR). Again, **Proj** was not evaluated for **Pool5** as its performance was very poor on the development set.

languages. In the case of **Pool5**, **InitDec** seemed to perform slightly better than **InitEnc** for German, but both yielded similar scores for French. We also observed that by using the **Pool5** feature in the **Proj** configuration, the NMT system failed to learn any useful information with extremely low *BLEU* scores on the development set, even with an increased number of epochs. Thus we do not evaluate these on the test sets.

Table 2 displays the empirical results on the MSCOCO test dataset. Similar trends are observed here for **Softmax**: **InitDec** outperformed **Proj** and **InitEnc**. For this test set, **InitDec** outperformed the baseline for EN–DE and performed comparably to the baseline for EN–FR. Interestingly, the variant with **Pool5** as a feature did not seem to perform as well, producing slightly lower scores than the baseline on this test set. Further investigation is needed to determine the reason for this phenomenon.

Overall, we observed better results for **Softmax** compared to **Pool5** with the settings used in our submission. However, more experiments need to be performed to confirm the usefulness of the posterior probabilities for the task.

Figure 2 shows example output translations from English to German and French for the test sets, for our best performing variant **InitDec** conditioned on **Softmax** class posterior predictions. We compare the output against a text-only baseline. In the first example from the Flickr test set,

InitDec produced an exact match against the reference for German, and an equally correct translation for French (differing only in the translation for 'bank'). In the second image from the MSCOCO test set, the German translation is much closer to the reference than the baseline. In the case of the French translation, the difference between the baseline and **InitDec** is much smaller, reflecting the quantitative results.

We conjecture that further hyperparameter search (increasing LSTM layers, dimensionality of the embeddings and hidden layers, etc.) and increasing the vocabulary size or using BPE could potentially improve the performance of our system on the task.

6 Related work

There has been interest in recent years in the task of generating image descriptions (also known as image captioning). Bernardi et al. (2016) provide a detailed discussion on various image description generation approaches that have been developed.

Currently, the two largest image description datasets are Flickr30K (Young et al., 2014) and MS COCO (Lin et al., 2014). These datasets are constructed in English and are aimed at advancing research on the generation of image descriptions in English. Recent attempts have been made to incorporate multilinguality into both these large-scale datasets, with the datasets being extended to

EN	A duck on the bank of a river
DE (**Baseline**)	eine ente an der kste eines flusses .
DE (**InitDec**)	eine ente am ufer eines flusses
DE (Reference)	eine ente am ufer eines flusses
FR (**Baseline**)	un canard sur l' eau , dans une rivière
FR (**InitDec**)	un canard sur la rive d' une rivière
FR (Reference)	un canard sur la berge d' une rivière

EN	A tennis player is moving to the side and is gripping his racquet with both hands.
DE (**Baseline**)	ein tennisspieler fhrt zur seite und greift nach seinem schlger .
DE (**InitDec**)	ein tennisspieler bewegt sich zur seite , whrend sein schlger mit beiden hnden .
DE (Reference)	ein tennisspieler bewegt sich zur seite und hlt den schlger mit beiden hnden .
FR (**Baseline**)	un joueur de tennis se déplaçant de côte et sa raquette avec les deux mains .
FR (**InitDec**)	un joueur de tennis se déplaçant côté et se met sa raquette avec les deux mains .
FR (Reference)	un joueur de tennis se déplace sur le cté et tient sa raquette avec ses deux mains .

Figure 2: Example output translations from English to German (DE) and French (FR), for the Flickr test set (top) and the MSCOCO test set (bottom). We show the results of **InitDec** using **Softmax** as the visual feature.

other languages such as German and Japanese (Elliott et al., 2016; Hitschler et al., 2016; Miyazaki and Shimizu, 2016; Yoshikawa et al., 2017).

The first known attempt at using NMT for machine translation of image descriptions is by Elliott et al. (2015), who conditioned an NMT system with a CNN image embedding (the penultimate layer of VGG-16 (Simonyan and Zisserman, 2014)) at the beginning of either the encoder or the decoder. The WMT16 shared task on Multimodal Machine Translation (Specia et al., 2016) has further encouraged research in this area. At the time, phrase-based SMT systems (Shah et al., 2016; Libovický et al., 2016; Hitschler et al., 2016) performed better than NMT systems (Calixto et al., 2016; Huang et al., 2016; Caglayan et al., 2016). Participants used either the penultimate fully connected layer or a convolutional layer of a CNN as image representation, with the exception of Shah et al. (2016) who used the classification output of VGG-16 as features to a phrase-based SMT system. In all cases, image information were found to provide only marginal improvements.

7   Conclusions and future work

We presented our approach that uses predicted class distribution as image features for the task of multimodal machine translation. We described three configurations for incorporating the visual representation and observed that the three methods perform differently. For our submission with the settings described in the paper, using ResNet-152's class posterior probability distribution seems to result in better scores than using the same network's pool5 features. Future experiments will aim at dissecting the type of information the image features are adding to the NMT and understand deeply the contribution of predicted class based representations.

Acknowledgments

This work was supported by the MultiMT project (EU H2020 ERC Starting Grant No. 678017).

References

Raffaella Bernardi, Ruket Cakici, Desmond Elliott, Aykut Erdem, Erkut Erdem, Nazli Ikizler-Cinbis, Frank Keller, Adrian Muscat, and Barbara Plank. 2016. Automatic description generation from images: A survey of models, datasets, and evaluation measures. *Journal of Artificial Intelligence Research* 55:409–442.

Ozan Caglayan, Walid Aransa, Yaxing Wang, Marc Masana, Mercedes García-Martínez, Fethi Bougares, Loïc Barrault, and Joost van de Weijer. 2016. Does multimodality help human and machine for translation and image captioning? In *Proceedings of the First Conference on Machine Translation*. Association for Computational Linguistics, Berlin, Germany, pages 627–633.

Iacer Calixto, Desmond Elliott, and Stella Frank. 2016. DCU-UvA Multimodal MT system report. In *Proceedings of the First Conference on Machine Translation*. Association for Computational Linguistics, Berlin, Germany, pages 634–638.

D. Elliott, S. Frank, K. Sima'an, and L. Specia. 2016. Multi30k: Multilingual English-German image descriptions. In *5th Workshop on Vision and Language*. pages 70–74.

Desmond Elliott, Stella Frank, and Eva Hasler. 2015. Multi-language image description with neural sequence models. *CoRR* abs/1510.04709.

Kaiming He, Xiangyu Zhang, Shaoqing Ren, and Jian Sun. 2015. Deep residual learning for image recognition. *CoRR* abs/1512.03385. http://arxiv.org/abs/1512.03385.

Julian Hitschler, Shigehiko Schamoni, and Stefan Riezler. 2016. Multimodal pivots for image caption translation. In *Proceedings of the 54th Annual Meeting of the Association for Computational Linguistics (Volume 1: Long Papers)*. Association for Computational Linguistics, Berlin, Germany, pages 2399–2409.

Po-Yao Huang, Frederick Liu, Sz-Rung Shiang, Jean Oh, and Chris Dyer. 2016. Attention-based multimodal neural machine translation. In *First Conference on Machine Translation*. pages 639–645.

Philipp Koehn, Hieu Hoang, Alexandra Birch, Chris Callison-Burch, Marcello Federico, Nicola Bertoldi, Brooke Cowan, Wade Shen, Christine Moran, Richard Zens, Chris Dyer, Ondřej Bojar, Alexandra Constantin, and Evan Herbst. 2007. Moses: Open source toolkit for statistical machine translation. In *ACL System Demonstration Session*. pages 177–180.

Jindřich Libovický, Jindřich Helcl, Marek Tlustý, Ondřej Bojar, and Pavel Pecina. 2016. Cuni system for wmt16 automatic post-editing and multimodal translation tasks. In *First Conference on Machine Translation*. pages 646–654.

Tsung-Yi Lin, Michael Maire, Serge Belongie, James Hays, Pietro Perona, Deva Ramanan, Piotr Dollár, and C Lawrence Zitnick. 2014. Microsoft coco: Common objects in context. In *European Conference on Computer Vision*. Springer, pages 740–755.

Minh-Thang Luong, Hieu Pham, and Christopher D Manning. 2015. Effective approaches to attention-based neural machine translation. *arXiv preprint arXiv:1508.04025* .

Takashi Miyazaki and Nobuyuki Shimizu. 2016. Cross-lingual image caption generation. In *Proceedings of the 54th Annual Meeting of the Association for Computational Linguistics (Volume 1: Long Papers)*. Association for Computational Linguistics, Berlin, Germany, pages 1780–1790.

Olga Russakovsky, Jia Deng, Hao Su, Jonathan Krause, Sanjeev Satheesh, Sean Ma, Zhiheng Huang, Andrej Karpathy, Aditya Khosla, Michael Bernstein, Alexander C. Berg, and Li Fei-Fei. 2015. ImageNet Large Scale Visual Recognition Challenge. *International Journal of Computer Vision (IJCV)* 115(3):211–252. https://doi.org/10.1007/s11263-015-0816-y.

Kashif Shah, Josiah Wang, and Lucia Specia. 2016. SHEF-Multimodal: Grounding machine translation on images. In *First Conference on Machine Translation*. pages 660–665.

Karen Simonyan and Andrew Zisserman. 2014. Very deep convolutional networks for large-scale image recognition. *CoRR* abs/1409.1556.

Lucia Specia, Stella Frank, Khalil Sima'an, and Desmond Elliott. 2016. A shared task on multimodal machine translation and crosslingual image description. In *First Conference on Machine Translation*. pages 543–553.

Qi Wu, Chunhua Shen, Lingqiao Liu, Anthony Dick, and Anton van den Hengel. 2016. What Value Do Explicit High Level Concepts Have in Vision to Language Problems? In *The IEEE Conference on Computer Vision and Pattern Recognition (CVPR)*.

Yuya Yoshikawa, Yutaro Shigeto, and Akikazu Takeuchi. 2017. STAIR captions: Constructing a large-scale japanese image caption dataset. In *Proceedings of the 55th Annual Meeting of the Association for Computational Linguistics (Volume 2: Short Papers)*. Association for Computational Linguistics, Vancouver, Canada.

Quanzeng You, Hailin Jin, Zhaowen Wang, Chen Fang, and Jiebo Luo. 2016. Image Captioning With Semantic Attention. In *The IEEE Conference on Computer Vision and Pattern Recognition (CVPR)*.

Peter Young, Alice Lai, Micah Hodosh, and Julia Hockenmaier. 2014. From image descriptions to visual denotations: New similarity metrics for semantic inference over event descriptions 2:67–78.

Matthew D Zeiler. 2012. Adadelta: an adaptive learning rate method. *arXiv preprint arXiv:1212.5701* .

NICT-NAIST System for WMT17 Multimodal Translation Task

Jingyi Zhang[1,2], Masao Utiyama[1], Eiichro Sumita[1]
Graham Neubig[2], Satoshi Nakamura[2]
[1]National Institute of Information and Communications Technology,
3-5Hikaridai, Keihanna Science City, Kyoto 619-0289, Japan
[2]Graduate School of Information Science, Nara Institute of Science and Technology,
Takayama, Ikoma, Nara 630-0192, Japan
`jingyizhang/mutiyama/eiichiro.sumita@nict.go.jp`
`neubig/s-nakamura@is.naist.jp`

Abstract

This paper describes the NICT-NAIST system for the WMT 2017 shared multimodal machine translation task for both language pairs, English-to-German and English-to-French. We built a hierarchical phrase-based (Hiero) translation system and trained an attentional encoder-decoder neural machine translation (NMT) model to rerank the n-best output of the Hiero system, which obtained significant gains over both the Hiero system and NMT decoding alone. We also present a multimodal NMT model that integrates the target language descriptions of images that are similar to the image described by the source sentence as additional inputs of the neural networks to help the translation of the source sentence. We give detailed analysis for the results of the multimodal NMT model. Our system obtained the first place for the English-to-French task according to human evaluation.

1 Introduction

We participated in the WMT 2017 shared multimodal machine translation task 1, which translates a source language description of an image into a target language description. We built systems for both English-to-German and English-to-French language pairs.

Our baseline systems only use text information. We compared three text-only approaches: a hierarchical phrase-based (Hiero) translation system (Chiang, 2005), an attentional encoder-decoder neural machine translation (NMT) system (Bahdanau et al., 2015), and a system using the NMT model to rerank the n-best output of the Hiero system.

We also explored ways to improve the NMT model with image information. Compared to previous multimodal NMT (MNMT) models that integrate visual features directly (Caglayan et al., 2016; Calixto et al., 2016; Huang et al., 2016; Calixto et al., 2017), we first exploit image retrieval methods to obtain images that are similar to the image described by the source sentence, and then integrate the target language descriptions of these similar images into the NMT model to help the translation of the source sentence. This makes it possible to exploit a large corpus with only images and target language descriptions through an image retrieval step. This is similar to Hitschler et al. (2016)'s multimodal pivots method, which uses target descriptions of similar images for reranking MT outputs, while we use these target descriptions as additional inputs for the NMT model.

2 Text-only MT

We compared three text-only approaches for this translation task.

2.1 Hierarchical Phrase-based SMT

The hierarchical phrase-based model (Chiang, 2005) extracts hierarchical phrase-based translation rules from parallel sentence pairs with word alignments. The word alignments can be learned by IBM models. Each translation rule contains several feature scores. The decoder of hierarchical phrase-based model implements a bottom-up CKY+ algorithm. The weights for different features can be tuned on the development set.

2.2 Attentional NMT

The attentional encoder-decoder networks (Bahdanau et al., 2015) include three parts: an encoder that uses a bi-directional recurrent neural network to learn representations for words in the source

Proceedings of the Conference on Machine Translation (WMT), Volume 2: Shared Task Papers, pages 477–482
Copenhagen, Denmark, September 7–11, 2017. ©2017 Association for Computational Linguistics

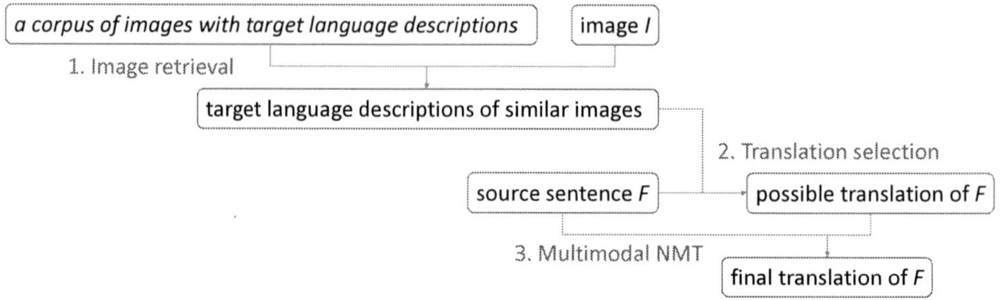

Figure 1: A overview of our multimodal method.

sentence, a decoder that generates the target sentence from left to right and an alignment model that learns which parts of the source sentence to focus on when the decoder generates each target word.

2.3 SMT reranked by NMT

The hierarchical phrase-based SMT model generates a n-best list for each source sentence. We use the attentional NMT model to assign a score to each output in the n-best list. This new NMT score together with the original SMT features is used to rerank the n-best list. The weight of the new NMT score is tuned together with other feature weights on the n-best lists of the development set.

3 Our Multimodal Approach

We propose a method to integrate the visual information into the NMT model.

Originally, the encoder of the NMT model only encodes the information of source sentence F. Our method integrates the visual information of image I into the encoder. Figure 1 is a overview of our multimodal method, which contains three steps.

Image retrieval Given image I, we search the 100 most similar images $\mathcal{I}$ from the training set and get the target language descriptions of these similar images as possible descriptions of I. When calculating image similarity, we used the Euclidean distance between averaged pooled feature vectors provided by the organizers.

Translation selection We select the most probable target word e for each source word f in sentence F as follows:

$$score\,(e, f, I) = score\,(e, f) + \lambda \cdot score\,(e, I)\,.$$
$$(1)$$

Here $score\,(e, f)$ measures the probability of f being translated into e as follows:

$$score\,(e, f) = \frac{align\,(e, f)}{\sum_{e' \in V} align\,(e', f)},\qquad (2)$$

where $align\,(e, f)$ is how many times f and e are aligned in the word-aligned training set.[1] $score\,(e, I)$ measures how related e and I are as follows:[2]

$$score\,(e, I) = idf\,(e) \cdot \sum_{I' \in \mathcal{I}} \frac{is\_in\,(e, I')}{dis\,(I, I')},\quad (3)$$

where $idf\,(e)$ is the inverse document frequency of e to punish high-frequency words, $dis\,(I, I')$ is the Euclidean distance between I and I', $is\_in\,(e, I')$ is 1/0 when e is/isn't contained in the description of I'. λ is the weight that can be tuned on the development set.

Multimodal NMT The original NMT model projects each source word f into a vector. We add an additional embedding matrix to project the selected target word e for f into a new vector. Then we concatenate both vectors and use them as the input for the bi-directional recurrent neural network of the NMT encoder.

4 Experiments

4.1 Text-only systems

We use training, development and test sets provided by the organizers (Elliott et al., 2016; Elliott

---

[1]When counting the alignment $align\,(e, f)$, we only use the intersection of the bi-directional GIZA++ alignments, so the alignments are more reliable.

[2]For e that does not occur in $\mathcal{I}$, $score\,(e, I)$ is 0.

	Description	Distance
Query 1	**a group of men are loading cotton onto a truck**	
Results	a baby camel going towards a woman , while a man takes a picture .	35.43
	person sitting in a chair selling goods outside of a building .	36.04
Query 2	**a man sleeping in a green room on a couch .**	
Results	a baby and three cats are resting on a bed .	29.85
	a man in a white t-shirt and beige shorts lies asleep on a black sofa .	29.86
Query 3	**a boy wearing headphones sits on a woman 's shoulders .**	
Results	a young blond girl in pink shirt and pigtails is sitting atop a man 's shoulders in a crowd .	28.88
	a man dressed in blue is juggling in front of an audience .	29.10
Query 4	**two men setting up a blue ice fishing hut on an iced over lake**	
Results	a man is drilling through the frozen ice of a pond .	23.49
	an inline skater in red pants and blue shirt skates between green cones .	30.05
Query 5	**a balding man wearing a red life jacket is sitting in a small boat .**	
Results	man with shawl praying by a large lake and small boat .	31.53
	four people standing on a raft sailing away on the water .	31.54

Table 1: Image retrieval examples (two most similar images for each query image). Description is the English descriptions for query and result images. Distance is the Euclidean distance between image vectors.

	Flickr		COCO	
Method	en-de	en-fr	en-de	en-fr
Hiero	27.86	50.38	24.57	41.88
NMT	30.52	50.46	24.27	41.26
Reranking	31.98	55.25	28.05	45.17

Table 2: Results of text-only approaches (BLEU).

	en-de	en-fr
$\lambda = 0$	52.17	65.60
$\lambda = 0.2$	52.93	66.31

Table 3: 1-gram BLEU score of selected target words on the development set.

et al., 2017). We lowercase, normalise punctuation and tokenise all sentences. The Hiero translation system was based on Moses (Koehn et al., 2007). We used GIZA++ (Och and Ney, 2003) and *grow-diag-final-and* heuristic (Koehn et al., 2003) to obtain symmetric word alignments. For decoding, we used standard features: direct/inverse phrase translation probability, direct/inverse lexical translation probability and a 5-gram language model, which was trained on the target side of the training corpus by IRSTLM Toolkit[3] with improved Kneser-Ney smoothing.

Attentional encoder-decoder networks were trained with Lamtram[4]. Word embedding size and hidden layer size are both 512. Training data was reshuffled between epochs. Validation was done after each epoch. We used the Adam optimization algorithm (Kingma and Ba, 2014). Because the training set is only 29K sentence pairs, we used dropout (0.5) and a small learning rate (0.0001) to reduce overfitting, which yielded improvements of $3 - 4$ BLEU on the development set. For training the NMT model, we replace words that occur less than twice in the training set as UNK. When de-

coding, we find the most probable source word for each UNK and replace the UNK using a lexicon extracted from the word-aligned training set.

We used the NMT model to rerank the unique $10,000$-best output of the Hiero system. The NMT score was used as an additional feature for the Hiero system. Feature weights were tuned by MERT (Och, 2003).

Table 2 shows results of the Hiero system, the NMT system and using the NMT model to rerank the Hiero outputs. The reranking system had the best performance on both language pairs. It is straightforward that using the NMT feature to rerank the Hiero outputs can achieve improvements over the pure Hiero system. The reason why the reranking method outperformed the NMT system should be that the training corpus is relatively small and the NMT system did not outperform the Hiero system largely. Therefore, the reranking method that takes advantages of both the Hiero and NMT systems worked the best on this task.

4.2 Multimodal systems

For the multimodal method, we found when $\lambda = 0.2$, the selected target words for the development

---

[3] http://hlt.fbk.eu/en/irstlm
[4] https://github.com/neubig/lamtram

Method	Flickr		COCO	
	en-de	en-fr	en-de	en-fr
NMT	30.52	50.46	24.27	41.26
MNMT	29.56	49.83	23.60	40.77

Table 4: Comparison of the NMT model and the MNMT model (BLEU).

		BLEU	Meteor	TER
en-de	Our system	31.9	53.9	48.1
	Best system	33.4	54.0	48.5
en-fr	Our system	55.3	72.0	28.4
	Best system	55.9	72.1	28.4

Table 5: Official evaluation results on the 2017 Flickr test sets.

		BLEU	Meteor	TER
en-de	Our system	28.1	48.5	52.9
	Best system	28.7	48.9	52.5
en-fr	Our system	45.1	65.6	34.7
	Best system	45.9	65.9	34.2

Table 6: Official evaluation results on the 2017 COCO test sets.

set had the highest 1-gram BLEU score[5] for both language pairs as shown in Table 3, which shows that visual features did help to select more accurate translations than using only translation probabilities in the translation selection step.

However, on both language pairs, our multimodal NMT model did not improve, but decreased the test set BLEU score compared to the baseline NMT model as shown in Table 4. And using the multimodal NMT as an additional feature for reranking the Hiero system did not further improve the Hiero system that had integrated the text-only NMT model. Table 5 and 6 show the official evaluation results of our system and the best system for the multimodal task (with METEOR as the primary metric). Our system is very competitive, especially with METEOR, even though only text features helped in our system, which shows with finely tuned parameters, the text-only approach that uses the NMT model to rerank the output of the Hiero system can give a strong result for this task. In addition, our system obtained the first place for the English-to-French task according to human evaluation (Elliott et al., 2017).

To further analyze the results of our multimodal method, we give some output examples for each step in Figure 1.

Table 1 gives some image retrieval results. As we can see, in the descriptions of the retrieved images, there is a lot of noise that is not useful for helping the translation of the source sentence, which is why we used 100 images with the high-

est similarities and the translation selection step to select useful information for our multimodal NMT model. Note that we used the target language (German or French) descriptions of similar images in our method, but Table 1 shows the source language (English) descriptions for easy understanding. In addition, for this image retrieval step, a large image corpus can be helpful to find more similar images and only target descriptions are needed for this image corpus.

Table 7 shows some examples for our multimodal method. For the first two examples, the visual information helped to improve the translations. In Example 1, "running" is translated into "rennt" by the NMT model incorrectly. The translation selection step selected the correct translation "läuft" for "running" and helped the MNMT model translate it correctly. In Example 2, "home" should be translated into "hauses", but it is missing in the NMT translation. The translation selection step selected "haus" as the translation for "home", which then appeared in the translation of the MNMT model.

However, for the last two examples in Table 7, the additional target descriptions decreased the translation quality. In Example 3, "looking" was correctly translated into "blickt" by the NMT model. But "schaut" was selected as the translation of "looking" at the translation selection step, which led the MNMT model translated it incorrectly. In Example 4, "flying" was correctly translated into "fliegenden" by the NMT model. But "fliegt" was selected as the translation of "flying" by the translation selection step, which led to "flying" being missing in the MNMT translation. Here, "fliegenden" and "fliegt" are different forms of the German word "fliegen", which are very difficult to distinguish using visual information. Using only the original form for these selected target words can be helpful to solve this problem.

As shown in Table 7, the target descriptions used as additional inputs for the multimodal NMT

---

[5]Because the selected target words are not reordered, so we only calculate 1-gram BLEU score.

Example 1	
Src	an adult australian shepherd follows behind a **running** australian shepherd puppy .
Ref	ein ausgewachsener australian shepherd folgt einem welpen , der vor ihm **läuft** .
NMT	ein erwachsener australischer fängt hinter einem **rennt** australischer .
TS	ein erwachsener australischer schäferhund folgt hinter ein **läuft** australischer schferhund welpe .
MNMT	ein erwachsener australischer schäferhund folgt einem **läuft** australischer hund .
Example 2	
Src	woman and child outside the front door of their scenic **home** .
Ref	eine frau und ein kind vor der tür ihres idyllischen **hauses** .
NMT	eine frau und ein kind vor der tür des malerische .
TS	frau und kind freien der vor tür von ihren malerische **haus** .
MNMT	eine frau und ein kind vor der tür eines malerische **haus** .
Example 3	
Src	a little girl is **looking** through a telescope at the beach .
Ref	ein kleines mädchen **blickt** durch ein teleskop auf den strand .
NMT	ein kleines mädchen **blickt** durch ein teleskop am strand .
TS	einem kleines mädchen ist **schaut** durch einem teleskop auf der strand .
MNMT	ein kleines mädchen **schaut** durch ein teleskop am strand .
Example 4	
Src	a dog turns on the grass to persue a **flying** ball .
Ref	ein hund dreht sich auf dem gras um einem **fliegenden** ball nachzulaufen .
NMT	ein hund dreht sich auf dem gras , um einen **fliegenden** ball zu persue .
TS	ein hund dreht auf der gras zu persue ein **fliegt** ball .
MNMT	ein hund dreht sich auf dem gras , um den ball zu persue .

Table 7: Translation examples. NMT: the translation by the NMT model; TS: the selected words for each source word in the translation selection step; MNMT: the translation by the MNMT model.

model helped the translation for some cases, but also introduced new noise, which hurt the translation performance in some other cases. In future work, we will work on how to use these target description information more effectively.

5 Conclusion

We described our system for the WMT17 multimodal translation task, including text-only approaches and a multimodal method that first searches for some possible target language descriptions of the image and then integrates these target descriptions into the NMT model to help the translation of the source sentence. Results show the text-only approach that uses a NMT model to rerank the output of a Hiero system gave a strong result for this task and the MNMT model did not further improve the text-only system, but the target descriptions did contain some useful information that can help the translations. In future work, we will work on how to make use of these related target descriptions more effectively. In addition, a larger corpus of images with only target language descriptions can be useful for our method to obtain more accurate target descriptions.

References

Dzmitry Bahdanau, Kyunghyun Cho, and Yoshua Bengio. 2015. Neural machine translation by jointly learning to align and translate. In *International Conference on Learning Representations*.

Ozan Caglayan, Walid Aransa, Yaxing Wang, Marc Masana, Mercedes García-Martínez, Fethi Bougares, Loïc Barrault, and Joost van de Weijer. 2016. Does multimodality help human and machine for translation and image captioning? In *Proceedings of the First Conference on Machine Translation*. Association for Computational Linguistics, Berlin, Germany, pages 627–633. http://www.aclweb.org/anthology/W16-2358.

Iacer Calixto, Desmond Elliott, and Stella Frank. 2016. Dcu uva multimodal mt system report. In *Proceedings of the First Conference on Machine Translation*. Association for Computational Linguistics, Berlin, Germany, pages 634–638. http://www.aclweb.org/anthology/W16-2359.

Iacer Calixto, Daniel Stein, Evgeny Matusov, Pintu Lohar, Sheila Castilho, and Andy Way. 2017. Using images to improve machine translating e commerce product listings. In *Proceedings of the 15th Conference of the European Chapter of the Association for Computational Linguistics: Volume 2, Short Papers*. Association for Computational Linguistics, Valencia, Spain, pages 637–643. http://www.aclweb.org/anthology/E17-2101.

David Chiang. 2005. A hierarchical phrase-based model for statistical machine translation. In *Proceedings of the 43rd Annual Meeting of the Association for Computational Linguistics (ACL'05)*. Association for Computational Linguistics, Ann Arbor, Michigan, pages 263–270. https://doi.org/10.3115/1219840.1219873.

D. Elliott, S. Frank, K. Sima'an, and L. Specia. 2016. Multi30k: Multilingual english-german image descriptions pages 70–74.

Desmond Elliott, Stella Frank, Loïc Barrault, Fethi Bougares, and Lucia Specia. 2017. Findings of the Second Shared Task on Multimodal Machine Translation and Multilingual Image Description. In *Proceedings of the Second Conference on Machine Translation*. Copenhagen, Denmark.

Julian Hitschler, Shigehiko Schamoni, and Stefan Riezler. 2016. Multimodal pivots for image caption translation. In *Proceedings of the 54th Annual Meeting of the Association for Computational Linguistics (Volume 1: Long Papers)*. Association for Computational Linguistics, Berlin, Germany, pages 2399–2409. http://www.aclweb.org/anthology/P16-1227.

Po-Yao Huang, Frederick Liu, Sz-Rung Shiang, Jean Oh, and Chris Dyer. 2016. Attention-based multimodal neural machine translation. In *Proceedings of the First Conference on Machine Translation*. Association for Computational Linguistics, Berlin, Germany, pages 639–645. http://www.aclweb.org/anthology/W16-2360.

Diederik Kingma and Jimmy Ba. 2014. Adam: A method for stochastic optimization. *arXiv preprint arXiv:1412.6980* .

Philipp Koehn, Hieu Hoang, Alexandra Birch, Chris Callison-Burch, Marcello Federico, Nicola Bertoldi, Brooke Cowan, Wade Shen, Christine Moran, Richard Zens, Chris Dyer, Ondrej Bojar, Alexandra Constantin, and Evan Herbst. 2007. Moses: Open source toolkit for statistical machine translation. In *Proceedings of the 45th Annual Meeting of the Association for Computational Linguistics Companion Volume Proceedings of the Demo and Poster Sessions*. pages 177–180. http://www.aclweb.org/anthology/P07-2045.

Philipp Koehn, Franz Josef Och, and Daniel Marcu. 2003. Statistical phrase-based translation. In *Proceedings of the 2003 Conference of the North American Chapter of the Association for Computational Linguistics on Human Language Technology-Volume 1*. pages 48–54.

Franz Josef Och. 2003. Minimum error rate training in statistical machine translation. In *Proceedings of the 41st Annual Meeting of the Association for Computational Linguistics*. pages 160–167. https://doi.org/10.3115/1075096.1075117.

Franz Josef Och and Hermann Ney. 2003. A systematic comparison of various statistical alignment models. *Computational linguistics* 29(1):19–51.

Automatic Threshold Detection for Data Selection in Machine Translation

Mirela-Stefania Duma and Wolfgang Menzel
University of Hamburg
Natural Language Systems Division
{mduma, menzel}@informatik.uni-hamburg.de

Abstract

We present in this paper the participation of the University of Hamburg in the Biomedical Translation Task of the Second Conference on Machine Translation (WMT 2017). Our contribution lies in adopting a new direction for performing data selection for Machine Translation via Paragraph Vector and a Feed Forward Neural Network Classifier. Continuous distributed vector representations of the sentences are used as features for the binary classifier. Most approaches in data selection rely on scoring and ranking general domain sentences with respect to their similarity to the in-domain and setting a range of thresholds for selecting a percentage of them for training various MT systems. The novelty of our method consists in developing an automatic threshold detection paradigm for data selection which provides an efficient and simple way for selecting the most similar sentences to the in-domain. Encouraging results are obtained using this approach for seven language pairs and four data sets.

1 Introduction

Data selection for Machine Translation (MT) represents a standard domain adaptation technique with the aim of tackling the problem of selecting from various general domain data the sentences that are most similar to sentences from the in-domain. Irrespective of having available vast amounts or small amounts of in-domain data, one of the advantages of data selection consists in providing more in-domain data selected from large amounts of general domain data. Two difficult tasks arise when performing data selection: what method to use for scoring the sentences from the general domain according to their similarity to the in-domain and how many of the scored sentences to keep for later use in training MT systems.

Standard state-of-the-art methods resolve the first difficulty by means of information retrieval, perplexity or edit distance methods. However, the second difficulty remains a challenge. There are no standard start-threshold and increment-threshold defined in the community. Axelrod et al. (2011), for example, uses the top N = {35k, 70k, 150k} sentence pairs from the scored general domain data, while Biçici and Yuret (2011) increasingly select N $\in$ {100, 200, 500, 1000, 2000, 3000, 5000, 10000} instances for each test sentence for training and Kirchhoff and Bilmes (2014) select subsets of 10%, 20%, 30% and 40% of the data.

We present a time and resource efficient method of performing data selection using Paragraph Vector (Le and Mikolov, 2014) for representing the sentences and a Feed Forward Neural Network Classifier for determining which general domain sentences should be considered similar to the in-domain. The paragraph vectors and the binary classifiers are trained using standard parameters and have a great advantage of dropping the need to experiment with different sentence selection thresholds. Therefore, we call our method automatic threshold detection for data selection (ATD).

The method has been applied in the Biomedical translation task of the Second Conference on Machine Translation (WMT) 2017 (Yepes et al., 2017). The in-domain corpora were made available by the competition and the general domain corpora we have chosen to select data from are the Wikipedia corpora (Wolk and Marasek, 2014) and the Commoncrawl corpora[1]. Experiments

---

[1] http://commoncrawl.org/

Proceedings of the Conference on Machine Translation (WMT), Volume 2: Shared Task Papers, pages 483–488
Copenhagen, Denmark, September 7–11, 2017. ©2017 Association for Computational Linguistics

were performed on the language pairs English-French, English-Spanish, English-Portuguese and English-German (both directions for all language pairs except for English-German as the competition did not require German-English translations). Good results have been obtained for all language pairs.

The paper is structured as follows: related work is presented in Section 2, then the data, tools and data selection method are described in Section 3. Section 4 contains the experimental results and the last section presents conclusions and suggestions for future work.

2 Related work

Given a large pool of general domain data and a small amount of in-domain data, selecting the sentences from the general domain that are most similar to the in-domain is referred in literature as data selection. The work-flow of performing data selection includes developing a metric or function that scores general domain sentences according to their relevance to the in-domain and experimenting with various ratios of top ranked sentences in order to obtain the best result in terms of one or more MT evaluation metrics.

The approaches most commonly adopted in the literature are based on information retrieval (Hildebrand et al. (2005); Tamchyna et al. (2012)), on perplexity (Moore and Lewis (2010); Axelrod et al. (2011)), or on edit distance similarity (Wang et al., 2013).

Recently, a new direction has gained interest by making use of Word or Paragraph Vectors (embeddings). Chen and Huang (2016) use word embeddings along with in-domain selected sentences as positive samples and randomly selected sentences from the general domain as negative samples in training convolutional networks that yield good results. Also, Duma and Menzel (2016) developed a new scoring method using Paragraph Vectors with positive results.

In this paper, we apply Paragraph Vectors for training FFNN classifiers that categorize the general domain sentences as being in-domain or out-of-domain. One of the most challenging tasks in data selection consists in finding the optimal threshold (how many of the scored sentences to select). It is a time-consuming process in which several experiments need to be performed, usually aiming to obtain the best BLEU score. Moreover,

there is no general consensus in the community regarding the increment ratio. We contribute to the state-of-the-art with a method that overcomes this challenge by means of a binary classifier: the problem of data selection is simplified by reducing the task of scoring and experimenting with different thresholds to a binary decision (keep/ discard a general domain sentence).

3 Experiments

This section describes the corpora and tools used, as well as the automatic threshold detection method we propose.

3.1 Data and tools

All SMT models were developed using the Moses phrase-based MT toolkit (Koehn et al., 2007) and the Experiment Management System (Koehn, 2010). The preprocessing of the data consisted in tokenization, cleaning (6-80), lowercasing and normalizing punctuation. The tuning and the test sets were provided by WMT 2016 (Bojar et al., 2016) and WMT 2017.

The SRILM toolkit (Stolcke, 2002) and Kneser-Ney discounting (Kneser and Ney, 1995) were used to estimate 5-gram language models (LM). All the trained SMT systems use a strong LM built by interpolating a LM for the in-domain and a LM for the general domain with weights that are tuned to minimize the perplexity on the tuning set (Schwenk and Koehn, 2008).

For word alignment we used GIZA++ (Och and Ney, 2003) with the default *grow-diag-final-and* alignment symmetrization method. Tuning of the SMT systems was performed with MERT (Och, 2003).

Commoncrawl and Wikipedia were used as general domains for all language pairs except for EN↔PT where no Commoncrawl data was provided by WMT. As for the in-domain corpora, EMEA (Tiedemann, 2012) was used for all language pairs and Muchmore, ECDC, Pattr and Pubmed (all from UFAL Medical Corpus[2]) for those language pairs where data was available. We also made use of the training data provided by the previous Biomedical task from 2016. The corpora corresponding to the general domain was concatenated into a single data source and the same procedure was applied for the in-domain corpora. The

---

[2]http://ufal.mff.cuni.cz/ufal_medical_corpus

size of the corpora is presented in the following table (since the bilingual corpora remain the
same for both cases of translating *Language1* to
Language2 and vice-versa, we mention only one
direction in the table):

Track / Corpora	EN-DE	EN-FR	EN-ES	EN-PT
Commoncrawl	2.4M	3.2M	1.8M	-
Wikipedia	2.4M	818K	1.8M	1.6M
EMEA	1.1M	1.09M	1.09M	1.08M
Muchmore	29K	-	-	-
ECDC	2547	2665	2357	-
Pattr	1.8M	-	-	-
Scielo-gma 2016	-	18K	175K	613K
Pubmed	-	-	285K	74K

Table 1: Corpora used for ATD

3.2 Automatic Threshold Detection for Data Selection

The data selection method we used for the WMT
Biomedical task is described in this section with a
special focus on Paragraph Vector and the FFNN
classifier employed in developing the automatic
threshold detection.

Paragraph Vector

Sentences were represented using Paragraph Vectors (Le and Mikolov, 2014) which give a continuous distributed vector representation of the input. Paragraph Vector is an extension of word
embeddings (Mikolov et al., 2013) to phrases or
sentences. Given a sentence, Paragraph Vector
learns its representation by mapping context words
and a paragraph identifier to the word to be predicted. The paragraph token acts like a memory of
the topic of the sentence (Le and Mikolov, 2014).
While the word vectors are shared between all
paragraphs, the paragraph vector is shared among
all the contexts generated from the same sentence.

We used the *gensim* toolkit[3] (Řehůřek and Sojka, 2010) that implements Doc2Vec (Paragraph
Vectors). We present results using a Doc2Vec
model trained with PV-DBOW[4] applying the default parameters of size 200 for the vectors and
window of 10 (the maximum distance between the
predicted word and context words used for prediction within a document).

---

[3]https://radimrehurek.com/gensim/models/doc2vec.html
[4]Distributed Bag of Words

Feed-forward Neural Network Classifier

The Feed-Forward Neural Network uses a supervised learning algorithm that receives as input
the Paragraph Vectors for the labeled sentences.
The feed-forward neural network classifier was
trained using the python library *sknn*[5]. We report here results obtained using a fully connected
Tanh layer of 200 units with dropout $p=0.5$ and a
Softmax output layer. The optimal dropout value
was selected in accordance with the findings from
Srivastava et al. (2014).

We experimented with both the source and the
target language, in order to determine the best use
of classified data given our settings.

For each of the language pairs we trained classifiers on $\approx$200K sentences with an equal number of
positive and negative samples. The positive samples were randomly selected from the in-domain
data and the negative samples were randomly selected from the general domain data.

4 Experimental results

We report in this section the BLEU (Papineni
et al., 2002) scores obtained by our submissions,
as well as the classifiers accuracy. For each language pair and for each test set provided by the
Biomedical task, we submitted three runs as follows:

- the selected sentences with the classifier
  trained on the source language data (run 1)

- the selected sentences with the classifier
  trained on the target language data (run 2)

- the union (without duplicates) of the selected
  sentences proposed by the two classifiers
  (run 3)

Intrinsic evaluation of the proposed data selection technique was performed by computing the
classifier accuracy. Following the recommendations from (Kohavi, 1995), we employ the stratified cross-validation method with ten folds. The
accuracy values were computed using scikit-learn
(Pedregosa et al., 2011). The following table
presents the FFNN classifier mean accuracy and
standard deviation for each of the language pairs.
The low values of standard deviation for all classifiers indicate the consistency of our proposed
method.

---

[5]http://scikit-neuralnetwork.readthedocs.io/en/latest/

Language pair	FFNN$_{source}$	FFNN$_{target}$
EN-DE	0.9715 ± 0.00085	0.9716 ± 0.00082
EN-ES	0.9403 ± 0.00221	0.9408 ± 0.00315
EN-FR	0.9585 ± 0.00364	0.9626 ± 0.00245
EN-PT	0.9596 ± 0.00197	0.9644 ± 0.00213

Table 2: Classifier accuracy (%): mean and standard deviation

This year four datasets were used in the evaluation: Scielo, EDP, Cochrane and NHS belonging to scientific publications or health information texts. The format of the datasets differed as Scielo and the EDP datasets follow the BioC format and Cochrane and NHS follow the format of the UFAL Corpus (sgm). Table 3 depicts the size of the datasets.

Language pair	Scielo	EDP	Cochrane	NHS
EN-DE	-	-	467	1044
EN-ES	1120	-	467	1044
ES-EN	1135	-	-	-
EN-FR	-	784	467	1044
FR-EN	-	662	-	-
EN-PT	1897	-	-	-
PT-EN	1825	-	-	-

Table 3: Size of the test sets

The results of our submissions are presented with respect to different datasets. Table 5 depicts all the BLEU scores of our submissions. For the Scielo dataset, our team was the only one that submitted runs. The organisers provided baselines for all language pairs and our best run improves with almost 9 BLEU points over the baseline for EN-PT and EN-ES, and almost 7 BLEU point over the baseline for PT-EN and ES-EN. There were small differences between the results of the three runs which suggests that either method could be used for gaining positive results.

For the EDP dataset (FR-EN and EN-FR) there were eight submissions and our best run for EN-FR had a gain of around 10 BLEU points over the baseline, as for FR-EN a gain of around 6 BLEU points. Considering our runs, there is 1 BLEU point difference between run 2 and run 3 for FR-EN and 0.5 difference between run 3 and run 2 for EN-FR. This indicates that the union method provides the best results.

On the Cochrane and NHS datasets our team was the only one that submitted for EN-ES obtaining high BLEU scores (48.99, 48.45 and 48.70 for Cochrane and 40.97, 41.20 and 41.22 for NHS). The differences between the runs are again very small. For EN-FR there were two teams participating. In our runs the union method gave better results for both datasets. For EN-DE there were six teams participating and the differences between our runs are again small.

In the general ranking among all participating teams, our team ranked first for EN-FR for the Cochrane and NHS datasets, second on FR-EN and third on EN-FR for the EDP datasets, last place on EN-DE for the Cochrane and NHS datasets, and was the only team submitting for Scielo (PT-EN, EN-PT, ES-EN, EN-ES) as well as for Cochrane and NHS (EN-ES).

Lavie (2010) points out that BLEU scores above 30 reflect understandable translations, while scores over 50 are considered good and fluent translations. Within 36 submitted runs by our team, 24 runs have BLEU scores between ≈32 and ≈49 (for six language pairs). Therefore, we conclude that the method presented obtains generally good translation results on a variety of language pairs.

Another important result consists in the fact that small amounts of general domain data were selected using ATD ranging from 3.1% up to 9.35%. This represents a promising direction for applying this method on much larger general domain corpora where selecting small amounts of data matters even more. The union of the selected sentences with the classifiers trained on the source and target languages ranges from 5.6% up to 12.1%.

The following table presents the amount of general data selected using ATD for the three runs along with the percentage of general domain data that it represents:

Language pair	# selected src. sent.	# selected trg. sent.	Union
EN-DE	148K (3.1%)	188K (4.0%)	263K (5.6%)
EN-ES	327K (9.35%)	257K (7.36%)	425K (12.1%)
EN-FR	223K (5.6%)	225K (5.7%)	345K (8.7%)
EN-PT	78K (4.7%)	89K (5.3%)	123K (7.4%)

Table 4: Number of selected sentences and percentage of General domain

The average duration for training the Doc2Vec models was ≈ 2.5 hours and the average duration for ten fold cross-validation was ≈ 12 minutes[6], which represents an advantage in terms of time consumption since afterwards only one MT system needs to be trained.

[6]on a 2 Ten Core Intel Xeon processor/ 128 GB of RAM machine

Language pair	EN-DE			EN-ES			ES-EN	EN-FR			FR-EN	EN-PT	PT-EN
Test set	Cochrane	NHS	Scielo	Cochrane	NHS	Scielo	EDP	Cochrane	NHS	EDP	Scielo	Scielo
run 1	22.03	18.71	36.08	**48.99**	40.97	37.14	22.43	32.46	31.79	22.64	39.14	43.84
run 2	22.37	**19.80**	35.93	48.45	41.20	37.47	22.25	32.59	31.89	22.37	**39.38**	**43.93**
run 3	**22.63**	19.66	**36.23**	48.70	**41.22**	**37.49**	**22.79**	**33.16**	**33.36**	**23.41**	39.21	43.88

Table 5: WMT results in terms of BLEU

5 Conclusions and Future Work

We presented the University of Hamburg participation to the WMT Biomedical task. The main contribution of our work consists in developing an automatic threshold detection method for data selection which yields good results for seven language pairs and four data sets. It requires little time for obtaining the general domain sentences that are considered most similar to the in-domain.

For six of the seven language pairs, the BLEU scores that our method obtained are in the range between 32 and 49. Generally, the best results among our three runs is obtained using the union approach, but with small differences among the other runs suggesting that there is no clear preference for one of the approaches.

Since we evaluated our approach only with respect to the WMT task, we intend to further apply it to other in-domains and language pairs, as well as, to compare it directly with standard state-of-the-art methods.

References

Amittai Axelrod, Xiaodong He, and Jianfeng Gao. 2011. Domain adaptation via pseudo in-domain data selection. In *Proceedings of the Conference on Empirical Methods in Natural Language Processing*. Association for Computational Linguistics, Stroudsburg, PA, USA, EMNLP '11, pages 355–362. http://dl.acm.org/citation.cfm?id=2145432.2145474.

Ergun Biçici and Deniz Yuret. 2011. Instance selection for machine translation using feature decay algorithms. In *Proceedings of the Sixth Workshop on Statistical Machine Translation*. Association for Computational Linguistics, Stroudsburg, PA, USA, WMT '11, pages 272–283. http://dl.acm.org/citation.cfm?id=2132960.2132996.

Ondřej Bojar, Rajen Chatterjee, Christian Federmann, Yvette Graham, Barry Haddow, Matthias Huck, Antonio Jimeno Yepes, Philipp Koehn, Varvara Logacheva, Christof Monz, Matteo Negri, Aurelie Neveol, Mariana Neves, Martin Popel, Matt Post, Raphael Rubino, Carolina Scarton, Lucia Specia, Marco Turchi, Karin Verspoor, and Marcos Zampieri. 2016. Findings of the 2016 conference on machine translation. In *Proceedings of the First Conference on Machine Translation*. Association for Computational Linguistics, Berlin, Germany, pages 131–198. http://www.aclweb.org/anthology/W/W16/W16-2301.

Boxing Chen and Fei Huang. 2016. Semi-supervised convolutional networks for translation adaptation with tiny amount of in-domain data. In *Proceedings of the 20th SIGNLL Conference on Computational Natural Language Learning, CoNLL 2016, Berlin, Germany, August 11-12, 2016*. pages 314–323. http://aclweb.org/anthology/K/K16/K16-1031.pdf.

Mirela-Stefania Duma and Wolfgang Menzel. 2016. Data selection for IT texts using paragraph vector. In *Proceedings of the First Conference on Machine Translation, WMT 2016, colocated with ACL 2016, August 11-12, Berlin, Germany*. pages 428–434. http://aclweb.org/anthology/W/W16/W16-2331.pdf.

Almut Silja Hildebrand, Matthias Eck, Stephan Vogel, and Alex Waibel. 2005. Adaptation of the translation model for statistical machine translation based on information retrieval. In *Proceedings of EAMT*. pages 133–142.

Katrin Kirchhoff and Jeff A. Bilmes. 2014. Submodularity for data selection in machine translation. In *Proceedings of the 2014 Conference on Empirical Methods in Natural Language Processing, EMNLP 2014, October 25-29, 2014, Doha, Qatar, A meeting of SIGDAT, a Special Interest Group of the ACL*. pages 131–141. http://aclweb.org/anthology/D/D14/D14-1014.pdf.

Reinhard Kneser and Hermann Ney. 1995. Improved backing-off for n-gram language modeling. In *Proceedings ICASSP*. pages 181–184.

Philipp Koehn. 2010. An experimental management system. *Prague Bull. Math. Linguistics* 94.87–96. http://dblp.uni-trier.de/db/journals/pbml/pbml94.html.

Philipp Koehn, Hieu Hoang, Alexandra Birch, Chris Callison-Burch, Marcello Federico, Nicola Bertoldi, Brooke Cowan, Wade Shen, Christine Moran, Richard Zens, Chris Dyer, Ondřej Bojar, Alexandra Constantin, and Evan Herbst. 2007. Moses: Open source toolkit for statistical machine translation. In *Proceedings of the 45th Annual Meeting of the ACL on Interactive Poster and Demonstration Sessions*. Association for Computational Linguistics, Stroudsburg, PA, USA, ACL '07, pages 177–180.

Ron Kohavi. 1995. A study of cross-validation and bootstrap for accuracy estimation and model selection. In *Proceedings of the 14th International Joint Conference on Artificial Intelligence - Volume 2*. Morgan Kaufmann Publishers Inc., San Francisco, CA, USA, IJCAI'95, pages 1137–1143. http://dl.acm.org/citation.cfm?id=1643031.1643047.

Alon Lavie. 2010. Evaluating the output of machine translation systems. In *AMTA*. Denver, Colorado, USA.

Quoc V. Le and Tomas Mikolov. 2014. Distributed representations of sentences and documents. In *Proceedings of the 31th International Conference on Machine Learning, ICML 2014, Beijing, China, 21-26 June 2014*. pages 1188–1196.

Tomas Mikolov, Ilya Sutskever, Kai Chen, Gregory S. Corrado, and Jeffrey Dean. 2013. Distributed representations of words and phrases and their compositionality. In *Advances in Neural Information Processing Systems 26: 27th Annual Conference on Neural Information Processing Systems 2013. Proceedings of a meeting held December 5-8, 2013, Lake Tahoe, Nevada, United States.*. pages 3111–3119.

Robert C. Moore and William Lewis. 2010. Intelligent selection of language model training data. In *Proceedings of the ACL 2010 Conference Short Papers*. Association for Computational Linguistics, Stroudsburg, PA, USA, ACLShort '10, pages 220–224. http://dl.acm.org/citation.cfm?id=1858842.1858883.

Franz Josef Och. 2003. Minimum error rate training in statistical machine translation. In *Proceedings of the 41st Annual Meeting on Association for Computational Linguistics - Volume 1*. Association for Computational Linguistics, Stroudsburg, PA, USA, ACL '03, pages 160–167. https://doi.org/10.3115/1075096.1075117.

Franz Josef Och and Hermann Ney. 2003. A systematic comparison of various statistical alignment models. *Computational Linguistics* 29(1):19–51.

Kishore Papineni, Salim Roukos, Todd Ward, and Wei-Jing Zhu. 2002. Bleu: A method for automatic evaluation of machine translation. In *Proceedings of the 40th Annual Meeting on Association for Computational Linguistics*. Association for Computational Linguistics, Stroudsburg, PA, USA, ACL '02, pages 311–318. https://doi.org/10.3115/1073083.1073135.

F. Pedregosa, G. Varoquaux, A. Gramfort, V. Michel, B. Thirion, O. Grisel, M. Blondel, P. Prettenhofer, R. Weiss, V. Dubourg, J. Vanderplas, A. Passos, D. Cournapeau, M. Brucher, M. Perrot, and E. Duchesnay. 2011. Scikit-learn: Machine learning in Python. *Journal of Machine Learning Research* 12:2825–2830.

Radim Řehůřek and Petr Sojka. 2010. Software Framework for Topic Modelling with Large Corpora. In *Proceedings of the LREC 2010 Workshop on New Challenges for NLP Frameworks*. ELRA, Valletta, Malta, pages 45–50. http://is.muni.cz/publication/884893/en.

Holger Schwenk and Philipp Koehn. 2008. Large and diverse language models for statistical machine translation. In *In Proceedings of The Third International Joint Conference on Natural Language Processing (IJCNP*.

Nitish Srivastava, Geoffrey Hinton, Alex Krizhevsky, Ilya Sutskever, and Ruslan Salakhutdinov. 2014. Dropout: A simple way to prevent neural networks from overfitting. *J. Mach. Learn. Res.* 15(1):1929–1958. http://dl.acm.org/citation.cfm?id=2627435.2670313.

Andreas Stolcke. 2002. Srilm-an extensible language modeling toolkit. In *Interspeech*. volume 2002.

Aleš Tamchyna, Petra Galuščáková, Amir Kamran, Miloš Stanojević, and Ondřej Bojar. 2012. Selecting data for english-to-czech machine translation. In *Proceedings of the Seventh Workshop on Statistical Machine Translation*. Association for Computational Linguistics, Stroudsburg, PA, USA, WMT '12, pages 374–381. http://dl.acm.org/citation.cfm?id=2393015.2393068.

Jörg Tiedemann. 2012. Parallel data, tools and interfaces in opus. In Nicoletta Calzolari (Conference Chair), Khalid Choukri, Thierry Declerck, Mehmet Ugur Dogan, Bente Maegaard, Joseph Mariani, Asuncion Moreno, Jan Odijk, and Stelios Piperidis, editors, *Proceedings of the Eight International Conference on Language Resources and Evaluation (LREC'12)*. European Language Resources Association (ELRA), Istanbul, Turkey.

Longyue Wang, Derek F. Wong, Lidia S. Chao, Junwen Xing, Yi Lu, and Isabel Trancoso. 2013. Edit distance: A new data selection criterion for domain adaptation in SMT. In *Recent Advances in Natural Language Processing, RANLP 2013, 9-11 September, 2013, Hissar, Bulgaria*. pages 727–732. http://aclweb.org/anthology/R/R13/R13-1094.pdf.

Krzysztof Wolk and Krzysztof Marasek. 2014. Building subject-aligned comparable corpora and mining it for truly parallel sentence pairs. In *Procedia Technology, 18*. Elsevier, pages 126 – 132.

Antonio Jimeno Yepes, Aurélie Névéol, Mariana Neves, Karin Verspoor, Ondřej Bojar, Arthur Boyer, Cristian Grozea, Barry Haddow, Madeleine Kittner, Yvonne Lichtblau, Pavel Pecina, Roland Roller, Amy Siu, Philippe Thomas, and Saskia Trescher. 2017. Findings of the WMT 2017 Biomedical Translation Shared Task. In *Proceedings of the Second Conference on Machine Translation (WMT17) at the Conference on Empirical Methods on Natural Language Processing (EMNLP)*. Copenhagen, Denmark.

Results of the WMT17 Metrics Shared Task

Ondřej Bojar
Charles University
MFF ÚFAL
bojar@ufal.mff.cuni.cz

Yvette Graham
Dublin City University
ADAPT
graham.yvette@gmail.com

Amir Kamran
University of Amsterdam
ILLC
a.kamran@uva.nl

Abstract

This paper presents the results of the WMT17 Metrics Shared Task. We asked participants of this task to score the outputs of the MT systems involved in the WMT17 news translation task and Neural MT training task. We collected scores of 14 metrics from 8 research groups. In addition to that, we computed scores of 7 standard metrics (BLEU, SentBLEU, NIST, WER, PER, TER and CDER) as baselines. The collected scores were evaluated in terms of system-level correlation (how well each metric's scores correlate with WMT17 official manual ranking of systems) and in terms of segment level correlation (how often a metric agrees with humans in judging the quality of a particular sentence).

This year, we build upon two types of manual judgements: direct assessment (DA) and HUME manual semantic judgements.

1 Introduction

Evaluating the quality of machine translation (MT) is critical for developers of MT systems to monitor progress as well as for MT users to select among available MT engines for their language pair of interest. Manual evaluation is however costly and difficult to reproduce. Automatic MT evaluation can resolve these issues, if it matches manual evaluation. The Metrics Shared Task[1] of WMT annually evaluates the performance of automatic machine translation metrics in their ability to provide a substitute for human assessment of translation quality.

In contrast to *MT quality estimation*, the metrics task provides participating metrics with reference translations with which MT outputs are compared. The metrics task itself then needs manual judgements of translation quality in order to check the extent to which the automatic metrics can approximate the judgement. For situations where the reference translation is not available, please consult the results of Quality Estimation Task (Bojar et al., 2017a).

We keep the two main types of metric evaluation unchanged from the previous years. In *system-level* evaluation, each metric provides a quality score for the whole translated test set (usually a set of documents, in fact). In *segment-level* evaluation, a score has to be assigned to every individual sentence.

The underlying texts and MT systems come from two other WMT tasks, namely News Translation Task (Bojar et al., 2017a, denoted as Findings 2017 in the following) and Neural MT training task (Bojar et al., 2017b), and from the EU project HimL, aiming at translation of health-related documents. The texts were drawn mainly from the news domain and, to a limited extent, from the medical domain and involve translations to/from Chinese (zh), Czech (cs), Finnish (fi), German (de), Latvian (lv), Russian (ru), and Turkish (tr), each paired with English, and additionally English into Romanian and Polish, making a total of 16 language pairs.

Two sources of golden truth of translation quality judgement are used this year:

- In *Direct Assessment* (DA) (Graham et al., 2015), humans assess the quality of a given MT output translation by comparison with a reference translation (but not the source). DA is the new standard used in WMT news translation task evaluation, requiring only monolingual evaluators. The added benefit for the metrics task is that the manual and automatic

---

[1] http://www.statmt.org/wmt17/metrics-task.html, starting with Koehn and Monz (2006) up to Bojar et al. (2016b)

Proceedings of the Conference on Machine Translation (WMT), Volume 2: Shared Task Papers, pages 489–513
Copenhagen, Denmark, September 7–11, 2017. ©2017 Association for Computational Linguistics

evaluations are now a little closer: both humans and metrics compare the MT output with the reference.

- The *HUME* score (Birch et al., 2016) is a segment-level score aggregated over manual judgements of translation quality of semantic units of the source sentence.

In contrast to previous years, the official method of evaluation changes, moving from "relative ranking" (RR, evaluating up to five system outputs on an annotation screen relative to each other) to DA and employing the Pearson correlation r in most cases. Due to difficulties in obtaining sufficient number of judgements for segment-level evaluation of some language pairs, we re-interpret DA judgements for these language pairs as relative comparisons and use Kendall's τ as a substitute, see below for details and references.

Section 2 describes our datasets, i.e. the sets of underlying sentences, system outputs, human judgements of translation quality and also participating metrics. Sections 3.1 and 3.2 then provide the results of system and segment-level metric evaluation, respectively. We discuss the results in Section 4.

2 Data

This year, we provided the task participants with two types of test sets along with reference translations and outputs of MT systems. Participants were free to choose which language pairs they wanted to participate and whether they reported system-level, segment-level scores or both.

2.1 Test Sets

We use the following test sets, i.e. sets of source sentences and reference translations:

newstest2017 is the main test set. It is the test set used in WMT17 News translation task (see Findings 2017), with approximately 3,000 sentences for each translation direction (except Chinese and Latvian which only have 2,001 sentences). The set includes a single reference translation for each direction, except English→Finnish with two reference translations.

himltest2017 is a subset of HUME Test Set Round 2 as released by the EU project HimL. More details about the original dataset are available in Deliverable D5.4 of the project.[2] Out selection contains approximately 300 sentences for each of the four language pairs (from English into Czech, German, Polish and Romanian) coming from both WMT16 news translation task as well as from HimL test sets 2015,[3] which are sentences from health-related texts by Cochrane and NHS 24. The reference translations are the standard WMT16 references for the news domain and post-edits of phrase-based MT for the Cochrane and NHS 24 sentences. No document structure has been preserved in this dataset.

2.2 Translation Systems

The results of the metrics task are likely affected by the actual set of MT systems participating in a given translation direction. For instance, if all of the systems perform similarly, it will be more difficult, even for the humans, to distinguish between the quality of translations. If the task includes a wide range of systems of varying quality, however, or systems quite different in nature, this could in some way make the task easier for metrics, with metrics that are more sensitive to certain aspects of MT output performing better.

This year, we relied on the following underlying MT systems:

News Task Systems are all machine translation systems participating in the WMT17 News translation task (see Findings 2017). The best among these systems were neural MT systems (both token- and character-based) but a good number of standard phrase-based systems and also some transfer-based and rule-based systems participated. The exact set of systems and system types depends on the language pair.

NMT Training Task systems are all instances of Neural Monkey (Helcl and Libovický, 2017) implementing the Bahdanau et al. (2014) sequence-to-sequence model with attention. Participants of the NMT training task trained a fixed NMT model using fixed training data (a subset of the news translation task training data) and these submitted models were

---

[2]`http://www.himl.eu/files/D5.4_Second_Evaluation_Report.pdf`
[3]`http://www.himl.eu/test-sets`

then run by training task organizers on new-stest2017, see Bojar et al. (2017b) for more details. All training task systems can be thus seen as regular submissions to the news translation task, with additional constraints in place. While one would expect these systems to produce outputs more similar to each other than the remaining news task systems, this is not the case, see Table 3 in Findings 2017. Based on the manual evaluation, training task systems however perform similarly, occupying the lower half of the ranking.

HUME Test Set Round 2 Systems are the MT systems translating himltest2017. For each language pair, three different MT systems are provided. The translations were run by the EU project HimL and the systems cover major MT system types for each language pair (phrase-based, neural and also syntax-based or combined systems). More details are provided in Table 3 of Deliverable 5.4 of the HimL project.[4]

To match the format of the newstest where all MT systems translate all sentences, we selected such subsets of sentences from HUME Test Set Round 2. The availability of MT systems for Romanian sentences was more varied than for other languages and we thus decided to split Romanian into two test sets, himltest2017a and himltest2017b, the first fully translated by three systems and the second fully translated only by two systems.

Important note: Due to the construction of himltest2017 for Polish, the outputs of one of the MT system were to a large part included in the HUME track last year and thus leaked to the training data we provided to metrics task participants this year. The affected test set file is `himltest2017a.Year1.en-pl` with 324 sentences out of 340 included in the training data. The file `himltest2017a.PBMT.en-pl` also contains 16 known sentences, probably due to identical translation. The performance of trained metrics for en-pl evaluation have the potential to be inflated therefore.

Hybrid Systems are created automatically with the aim of providing a larger set of systems against which to evaluate metrics, as in Graham and Liu (2016). Hybrid systems were created separately for newstest2017 and himltest2017 by randomly alternating sentences from the outputs of pairs of systems of the given dataset. In short, we create 10K hybrid MT systems for each language pair.

Excluding the hybrid systems, we ended up with 166 system outputs across 16 language pairs and 3 test sets.

2.3 Manual MT Quality Judgments

There are two distinct "golden truths" employed to evaluate metrics this year: Direct Assessment (DA) and HUME, a semantic-based manual metric.

The details of both of the methods are provided in this section, separately for system-level evaluation (Section 2.3.1) and segment-level evaluation (Section 2.3.2).

The DA manual judgements were provided by MT researchers taking part in WMT tasks and crowd-sourced workers on Amazon's Mechanical Turk.[5] Only judgements from workers who passed DA's quality control mechanism were included in the final datasets used to compute system and segment-level scores employed as a gold standard in the metrics task.

2.3.1 System-level Manual Quality Judgments

In system-level evaluation, the goal is to assess the quality of translation of an MT system for the whole test set. Our manual scoring methods DA and HUME nevertheless proceed sentence by sentence, aggregating the final score in some way.

Direct Assessment (DA) This year the translation task employed monolingual direct assessment (DA) of translation adequacy (Graham et al., 2013; Graham et al., 2014; Graham et al., 2016). Since sufficient levels of agreement in human assessment of translation quality are difficult to achieve, the DA setup simplifies the task of translation assessment (conventionally a bilingual task) into a simpler monolingual assessment. Furthermore, DA avoids bias that has been problematic in previous evaluations introduced by assessment of several alternate translations on one screen, where

---

[4]http://www.himl.eu/files/D5.4_Second_Evaluation_Report.pdf

[5]https://www.mturk.com

scores for translations were unfairly penalized if often compared to high quality translations (Bojar et al., 2011). DA therefore employs assessment of individual translations in isolation from other outputs.

Translation adequacy is structured as a monolingual assessment of similarity of meaning where the target language reference translation and the MT output are displayed to the human assessor. Assessors rate a given translation by how adequately it expresses the meaning of the reference translation on an analogue scale corresponding to an underlying 0-100 rating scale.[6]

Large numbers of DA human assessments of translations for all 14 language pairs included in the news translation task were collected from researchers and on Amazon's Mechanical Turk, via sets of 100-translation hits to ensure sufficient repeat items per worker, before application of strict quality control measures to filter out assessments from poorly performing crowd-sourced workers.

In order to iron out differences in scoring strategies attributed to distinct workers, human assessment scores for translations were standardized according to an individual worker's overall mean and standard deviation score. Mean standardized scores for translation task participating systems were computed by firstly taking the average of scores for individual translations in the test set (since some were assessed more than once), before combining all scores for translations attributed to a given MT system into its overall adequacy score. The gold standard for system-level DA evaluation is thus what is denoted "Ave z" in Findings 2017 (Bojar et al., 2017a).

Finally, although it is common to apply a sentence length restriction in WMT human evaluation, the simplified DA setup does not require restriction of the evaluation in this respect and no sentence length restriction was applied in DA WMT17.

HUME is a human evaluation measure that decomposes over the UCCA semantic units (Birch et al., 2016). UCCA (Abend and Rappoport, 2013) is an appealing candidate for semantic analysis, due to its cross-linguistic applicability, support for rapid annotation, and coverage of many fundamental semantic phenomena, such as verbal, nom-

inal and adjectival argument structures and their inter-relations. HUME operates by aggregating human assessments of the translation quality of individual semantic units in the source sentence. HUME thus avoids the semantic annotation of machine-generated text, which can often be garbled or semantically unclear. This also allows the re-use of the source semantic annotation for measuring the quality of different translations of the same source sentence, and avoids reliance on possibly suboptimal reference translations. HUME shows good inter annotator agreement, and reasonable correlation with Direct Assessment (Birch et al., 2016).

Since some translations in the HUME Test Set round 2 were annotated with HUME by more than one annotator, individual HUME scores for the same translation were combined into a single score for evaluation of metrics by taking the average of all HUME scores attributed to that translation. These segment-level HUME scores were then combined into an average score for each system.

2.3.2 Segment-level Manual Quality Judgments

Segment-level metrics have been evaluated against DA and HUME annotations for the newstest2017 and himl test sets, respectively. This year, since insufficient repeat judgements were collected for most of out-of-English language pairs to run a standard segment-level DA evaluation of metrics for the news task data, DA judgements for those language pairs were converted to relative ranking judgements to produce results similar to previous WMT metrics tasks.

Segment-level DA Adequacy assessments were collected for translations sampled from the output of systems participating in WMT17 translation task for 14 language pairs of the news translation task and 4 language pairs of the himl test set. Since the actual MT system is not important for segment-level assessment, we sampled 560 translations per language pair at random avoiding selection of identical ones.

Segment-level DA adequacy scores were collected as in system-level DA, described in Section 2.3.1, again with strict quality control and score standardization applied. To achieve accurate segment-level scores for translations, 15 distinct DA assessments were collected and com-

---

[6]The only numbering displayed on the rating scale are extreme points 0 and 100%, and three ticks indicate the levels of 25, 50 and 75%.

	DA>1	Ave	DA pairs	DARR
en-cs	2,960	6.9	67,404	32,810
en-de	2,053	3.1	8,140	3,227
en-fi	2,071	2.9	6,952	3,270
en-lv	1,616	3.4	8,047	3,456
en-tr	460	2.1	597	247

Table 1: Number of judgements for the five out-of-English language pairs employing DA converted to DARR data (DA produced by volunteer researchers in the news task manual evaluation); "DA>1" is the number of source input sentences in the manual evaluation where at least two translations of that same input sentence both received at least one DA judgement; "Ave" is the average number of translations with at least one DA judgement available for the same source input sentence; "DA pairs" is the number of all possible pairs of translations of the same source input resulting from "DA>1"; and "DARR" if the number of DA pairs with an absolute difference in DA scores greater than the 25 percentage point margin.

bined into a single mean adequacy score for each individual translation. Although in general agreement in human assessment of MT has been difficult to achieve, segment-level DA scores employing a minimum of 15 repeat assessments have been shown to be almost completely repeatable (Graham et al., 2015) and therefore provide a reliable gold standard for evaluating segment-level metrics.

HUME HUME annotations were taken from the HUME Test Set round 2 as described already in Section 2.3.1. Again, where an individual translation received more than one annotation its final segment-level score was arrived at by taking the average of all scores attributed to it.

DARR For five out-of-English language pairs (en-cs, en-de, en-fi, en-lv and en-tr) belonging to the news task, insufficient DA judgements were collected to provide reliable segment-level DA scores. When we have at least two DA scores for translations of the same source input, it is possible to convert those DA scores into a relative ranking judgement, if the difference in DA scores allows us to conclude that one translation is better than the other. In the following, we will denote these re-interpreted DA judgements as "DARR", to dis-

tinguish it clearly from the "RR" golden truth used in the past years.

Since the analogue rating scale employed by DA is marked at the 0-25-50-75-100 points, the difference in DA scores we employ to distinguish translations that are better/worse than one another is 25 points. In addition, DA judgements for these language pairs were only collected from known-reliable volunteers, and therefore avoid any inconsistency that could arise from reliance on individual DA judgements collected via crowd-sourcing, for example.

From the complete set of human assessments collected from researchers for the News task for these five language pairs, all possible pairs of DA judgements attributed to distinct translations of the same source were converted into DARR better/worse judgements. Distinct translations of the same source input whose DA scores fell within 25 percentage points (which could have been deemed equal quality) were omitted from the evaluation of segment-level metrics. Conversion of scores in this way produced a large set of DARR judgements for four of the five language pairs, shown in Table 1 due to combinatorial advantage of extracting DARR judgements from all possible pairs of translations of the same source input. Only Turkish thus remains poorly covered.

Kendall's Tau-like Formulation for DARR We measure the quality of metrics' segment-level scores against the DARR golden truth using a Kendall's Tau-like formulation, which is an adaptation of the conventional Kendall's Tau coefficient. Since we do not have a total order ranking of all translations we use to evaluate metrics, it is not possible to apply conventional Kendall's Tau given the current DARR human evaluation setup (Graham et al., 2015). Vazquez-Alvarez and Huckvale (2002) also note that a genuine pairwise comparison is likely to lead to more stable results for segment-level metric evaluation.

Our Kendall's Tau-like formulation, τ, is as follows:

$$\tau = \frac{|Concordant| - |Discordant|}{|Concordant| + |Discordant|} \quad (1)$$

where $Concordant$ is the set of all human comparisons for which a given metric suggests the same order and $Discordant$ is the set of all human comparisons for which a given metric disagrees. The formula is not specific with respect to ties, i.e.

cases where the annotation says that the two outputs are equally good.

The way in which ties (both in human and metric judgement) were incorporated in computing Kendall τ has changed across the years of WMT metrics tasks. Here we adopt the version from WMT14 and WMT15. For a detailed discussion on other options, see Macháček and Bojar (2014).

The method is formally described using the following matrix:

		Metric		
		<	=	>
Human	<	1	0	-1
	=	X	X	X
	>	-1	0	1

Given such a matrix $C_{h,m}$ where $h, m \in \{<, =, >\}^7$ and a metric, we compute the Kendall's τ for the metric the following way:

$$\tau = \frac{\sum_{\substack{h,m \in \{<,=,>\} \\ C_{h,m} \neq X}} C_{h,m} |S_{h,m}|}{\sum_{\substack{h,m \in \{<,=,>\} \\ C_{h,m} \neq X}} |S_{h,m}|} \quad (2)$$

We insert each extracted human pairwise comparison into exactly one of the nine sets $S_{h,m}$ according to human and metric ranks. For example the set $S_{<,>}$ contains all comparisons where the left-hand system was ranked better than right-hand system by humans and it was ranked the other way round by the metric in question.

To compute the numerator of our Kendall's τ formulation, we take the coefficients from the matrix $C_{h,m}$, use them to multiply the sizes of the corresponding sets $S_{h,m}$ and then sum them up. We do not include sets for which the value of $C_{h,m}$ is X. To compute the denominator, we simply sum the sizes of all the sets $S_{h,m}$ except those where $C_{h,m} = X$.

To summarize, the WMT17 matrix specifies to:

- exclude all human ties (this is already implied by the construction of DARR from DA judgements),

- count metric's ties only for the denominator (thus giving no credit for giving a tie),

---

⁷Here the relation $<$ always means "is better than" even for metrics where the better system receives a higher score.

- all cases of disagreement between human and metric judgements are counted as *Discordant*,

- all cases of agreement between human and metric judgements are counted as *Concordant*.

We employ bootstrap resampling to estimate confidence intervals for our Kendall's Tau formulation, and metrics with non-overlapping 95% confidence intervals are identified as having statistically significant difference in performance.

2.4 Participants of the Metrics Shared Task

Table 2 lists the participants of the WMT17 Shared Metrics Task, along with their metrics. We have collected 14 metrics from a total of 8 research groups.

The following subsections provide a brief summary of all the metrics that participated. The list is concluded by our baseline metrics in Section 2.4.10.

In this year's task, we asked participants whose metrics are publicly available to provide links to where the code can be accessed. Table 3 provides links for metrics that participated in WMT17 that are publicly available for download.

2.4.1 AUTODA, AUTODA.TECTO

AUTODA (Mareček et al., 2017) is a sentence-level metric trainable on any direct assessment scores. The metric is based on a simple linear regressor combining several features extracted from the automatically aligned an parsed translation-reference pair. The language-universal AUTODA uses seven features based on word-aligned parse trees in Universal Dependencies style (Nivre et al., 2016). All the features are some kind of similarity measures between two aligned nodes, e.g. lemma similarity, tag similarity, or morphosyntactic features similarity. The eighth feature used is the CHRF3 score (Popović, 2015). For the newstest2017 data, AUTODA was trained on Direct Assessment scores from newstest2015, which were available only for English. Nevertheless the same model was used for all the language pairs. For himltest2017, the metrics were trained on the provided HUMEseg2016.

The AUTODA.TECTO metric is similar to AUTODA but uses tectogrammatical trees (Hajič, 2004) instead of the Universal Dependencies. This

Metric	Seg-level	Sys-level	Hybrids	Participant
AUTODA	•	⊘	⊘	Charles University (Mareček et al., 2017)
AUTODA.TECTO	•	⊘	⊘	Charles University (Mareček et al., 2017)
BEER	•	⊘	⊘	ILLC – University of Amsterdam (Stanojević and Sima'an, 2015)
BLEND	•	⊘	⊘	ICTCAS-DCU (Ma et al., 2017)
BLEU2VEC_SEP	•	•	—	University of Tartu (Tättar and Fishel, 2017)
CHARACTER	—	•	•	RWTH Aachen University (Wang et al., 2016)
CHRF	•	⊘	⊘	(Popović, 2015)
CHRF+	•	⊘	⊘	(Popović, 2017)
CHRF++	•	⊘	⊘	(Popović, 2017)
MEANT_2.0	•	⊘	⊘	NRC (Lo, 2017)
MEANT_2.0-NOSRL	•	⊘	⊘	NRC (Lo, 2017)
NGRAM2VEC	•	•	—	University of Tartu (Tättar and Fishel, 2017)
TREEAGGREG	•	⊘	⊘	Charles University (Mareček et al., 2017)
UHH_TSKM	•	⊘	⊘	(Duma and Menzel, 2017)

Table 2: Participants of WMT17 Metrics Shared Task. "•" denotes that the metric took part in (some of the language pairs) of the segment- and/or system-level evaluation and whether hybrid systems were also scored. "⊘" indicates that the system-level and hybrids are implied, simply taking arithmetic average of segment-level scores.

AUTODA incl. TECTO	`http://github.com/ufal/auto-hume`
BEER	`http://github.com/stanojevic/beer`
BLEND	`http://github.com/qingsongma/blend`
BLEU2VEC_SEP	`http://github.com/TartuNLP/bleu2vec`
CHARACTER	`http://github.com/rwth-i6/CharacTER`
CHRF, incl. + and ++	`http://github.com/m-popovic/chrF`
MEANT_2.0 incl. NOSRL	`http://chikiu-jackie-lo.org/home/index.php/meant`
NGRAM2VEC	`http://github.com/TartuNLP/bleu2vec`
TREEAGGREG	`http://github.com/ufal/auto-hume/tree/rudolf`
Baselines:	`http://github.com/moses-smt/mosesdecoder`
BLEU, NIST	`scripts/generic/mteval-v13a.pl`
CDER, PER, TER, WER	`mert/evaluator`
SENTBLEU	`mert/sentence-bleu`

Table 3: Metrics available for public download that participated in WMT17. The baseline metrics scripts are all available with Moses, relative paths are listed.

very rich annotation allowed to use also the deep-syntactic features. It uses 18 features based on aligned tectogrammatical nodes similarity and two additional measures: CHRF3 and BLEU. The AUTODA.TECTO metric was applied only to the Czech outputs and it was trained on HUME-seg2016 en-cs data.

The AUTODA metrics are labelled as ensemble metrics because they include the scores of CHRF3 and BLEU.

2.4.2 BEER

BEER (Stanojević and Sima'an, 2015) is a trained evaluation metric with a linear model that combines features sub-word feature indicators (character n-grams) and global word order features (skip bigrams) to get language agnostic and fast to compute evaluation metric. BEER has participated in previous years of the evaluation task. The metric is identical to the 2016 run, including the training, so no 2016 data were used to train BEER in 2017.

2.4.3 BLEND

BLEND (Ma et al., 2017) is a novel combined metric that takes good advantage of merits of existing metrics. Contrary to another combined metric DPMFcomb (Yu et al., 2015), BLEND employs SVM regression for training, with DA scores as the gold standard in order to adapt to the new development of human evaluation. Experiments on WMT16 to-English language pairs show that, with a vast reduction in required training data,

BLEND still achieves improved performance over DPMFcomb when incorporated the same metrics. BLEND also finds a trade-off between its performance and efficiency by exploring the contribution of incorporated metrics. Besides, BLEND is flexible to be applied to any language pairs if incorporated metrics support the specific language pair.

BLEND is an ensemble metric, building upon scores provided by 25 lexical based metrics and 4 other metrics for to-English language pairs. Since some lexical based metrics are simply different variants of the same metric, there are only 9 kinds of lexical based metrics, namely BLEU, NIST, GTM, METEOR, ROUGE, Ol, WER, TER and PER. 4 other metrics include CharacTer, BEER, DPMF and ENTF.

BLEND for en-ru incorporates 20 lexical based metrics (the same 9 kinds of metrics mentioned above), and 2 other metrics, namely CharacTer and BEER.

2.4.4 BLEU2VEC_SEP, NGRAM2VEC

The metrics BLEU2VEC_SEP and NGRAM2VEC (Tättar and Fishel, 2017) are token-level metrics, which are trained on raw monolingual corpora. They are a direct modification of the original BLEU metric (Papineni et al., 2002) with fuzzy matches added to strict matches. The fuzzy match score is implemented via token and n-gram embedding similarities and applied to same-length n-grams in the hypothesis and reference(s).

2.4.5 CHARACTER

CHARACTER (Wang et al., 2016), identical to the 2016 setup, is a character-level metric inspired by the commonly applied translation edit rate (TER). It is defined as the minimum number of character edits required to adjust a hypothesis, until it completely matches the reference, normalized by the length of the hypothesis sentence. CHARACTER calculates the character-level edit distance while performing the shift edit on word level. Unlike the strict matching criterion in TER, a hypothesis word is considered to match a reference word and could be shifted, if the edit distance between them is below a threshold value. The Levenshtein distance between the reference and the shifted hypothesis sequence is computed on the character level. In addition, the lengths of hypothesis sequences instead of reference sequences are used for normalizing the edit distance, which effec-

tively counters the issue that shorter translations normally achieve lower TER.

Similarly to other character-level metrics, CHARACTER is applied to non-tokenized outputs and references, which also holds for this year's submission.

2.4.6 CHRF, CHRF+, and CHRF++

CHRF (Popović, 2015) is an evaluation metric which compares character n-grams in the hypothesis with those in the reference. Previous experiments have shown that the optimal set-up is to use maximal character n-gram length of 6 with uniform n-gram weights, arithmetic n-gram averaging and beta parameter set to 2. It has participated in previous two years of the evaluation task. This year's CHRF is identical to the CHRF2 from the 2016 metric task.

CHRF+ and CHRF++ (Popović, 2017) are extended CHRF metrics which, in addition to character n-grams, also compare word unigrams (CHRF+) and bigrams (CHRF++).

2.4.7 MEANT_2.0, MEANT_2.0-NOSRL

MEANT_2.0 is a non-trained evaluation metric that uses distributional word vector model to evaluate lexical semantic similarity and shallow semantic parses to evaluate structural semantic similarity between the reference and the MT output. It is a new version of MEANT (Lo et al., 2015) with improved evaluation of semantic role fillers phrasal similarity using idf-weighted n-gram similarity. Another improvement in MEANT_2.0 is its no-srl variant, MEANT_2.0-NOSRL. It provides accurate semantic evaluation of machine translation in any output language, even if no shallow semantic parser is available in that language. It considers the whole sentences as one long phrase for computing the phrasal similarity and the evaluation score.

2.4.8 TREEAGGREG

TREEAGGREG (Mareček et al., 2017) is an n-gram based metric computed over aligned syntactic structures instead of the linear representation of the translated sentences. Sentences are segmented into phrases based on their dependency parse trees, evaluating each of these phrases independently using CHRF3 metric (Popović, 2015). The resulting scores are then aggregated into a final sentence-level score using a simple weighted average.

TREEAGGREG is labelled as an ensemble metric, because it builds upon CHRF. It is however not trained at all, it only follows the dependency structure of the reference and candidate translation.

2.4.9 UHH_TSKM

UHH_TSKM (Duma and Menzel, 2017) is a nontrained metric utilizing kernel functions, i.e. methods for efficient calculation of overlap of substructures between the candidate and the reference translations. The metric uses both sequence kernels, applied on the tokenized input data, together with tree kernels, that exploit the syntactic structure of the sentences. Optionally, the match can also be performed for the candidate and a pseudo-reference (i.e. a translation by another MT system) or for the source sentence and the candidate back-translated into the source language.

2.4.10 Baseline Metrics

As mentioned by Bojar et al. (2016a), metrics task occasionally suffers from "loss of knowledge" when successful metrics participate only in one year.

We attempt to avoid this by regularly evaluating also a range of "baseline metrics":

- **Mteval.** The metrics BLEU (Papineni et al., 2002) and NIST (Doddington, 2002) were computed using the script `mteval-v13a.pl`[8] that is used in the OpenMT Evaluation Campaign and includes its own tokenization. We run `mteval` with the flag `--international-tokenization` since it performs slightly better (Macháček and Bojar, 2013).

- **Moses Scorer.** The metrics TER (Snover et al., 2006), WER, PER and CDER (Leusch et al., 2006) were produced by the Moses scorer, which is used in Moses model optimization. To tokenize the sentences, we used the standard tokenizer script as available in Moses toolkit. Since Moses scorer is versioned on Github, we strongly encourage authors of high-performing metrics to add them to Moses scorer, as this will ensure that their metric can be included in future tasks.

As for segment-level baselines, we employ the following modified version of BLEU:

- **SentBLEU.** The metric SENTBLEU is computed using the script sentence-bleu, a part of the Moses toolkit. It is a smoothed version of BLEU that correlates better with human judgements for segment-level. Standard Moses tokenizer is used for tokenization.

Chinese word segmentation is unfortunately not supported by the tokenization scripts mentioned above. For scoring Chinese with baseline metrics, we thus pre-processed MT outputs and reference translations with the script tokenizeChinese.py[9] by Shujian Huang, which separates Chinese characters from each other and also from non-Chinese parts.

For computing system-level and segment-level scores, the same scripts were employed as in last year's metrics task. New scripts have been added for generation of hybrid systems from the given hybrid descriptions.

3 Results

We discuss system-level results for news task systems (including NMT training task systems) in Section 3.1. The segment-level results are in Section 3.2.

3.1 System-Level Results

As in previous years, we employ the absolute value of Pearson correlation (r) as the main evaluation measure for system-level metrics. The Pearson correlation is as follows:

$$r = \frac{\sum_{i=1}^{n}(H_i - \overline{H})(M_i - \overline{M})}{\sqrt{\sum_{i=1}^{n}(H_i - \overline{H})^2}\sqrt{\sum_{i=1}^{n}(M_i - \overline{M})^2}} \tag{3}$$

where H_i are human assessment scores of all systems in a given translation direction, M_i are corresponding scores as predicted by a given metric. $\overline{H}$ and M are their means respectively.

Since some metrics, such as BLEU, for example, aim to achieve a strong positive correlation with human assessment, while error metrics, such as TER aim for a strong negative correlation, after computation of r for metrics, we compare metrics via the absolute value of a given metric's correlation with human assessment.

---

[8]`http://www.itl.nist.gov/iad/mig/tools/`

[9]`http://hdl.handle.net/11346/WMT17-TVXH`

	cs-en	de-en	fi-en	lv-en	ru-en	tr-en	zh-en
n	4	11	6	9	9	10	16
Correlation	$|r|$	$|r|$	$|r|$	$|r|$	$|r|$	$|r|$	$|r|$
AutoDA	**0.438**	0.959	0.925	0.973	0.907	0.916	0.734
BEER	0.972	**0.960**	**0.955**	**0.978**	0.936	0.972	**0.902**
Blend	0.968	**0.976**	**0.958**	**0.979**	**0.964**	**0.984**	**0.894**
BLEU	0.971	0.923	0.903	**0.979**	0.912	**0.976**	0.864
BLEU2VEC_SEP	**0.989**	**0.936**	**0.888**	0.966	0.907	**0.961**	**0.886**
CDER	0.989	0.930	**0.927**	**0.985**	0.922	**0.973**	**0.904**
CharacTER	0.972	**0.974**	**0.946**	0.932	**0.958**	0.949	**0.799**
CHRF	0.939	**0.968**	**0.938**	0.968	0.952	0.944	0.859
CHRF++	0.940	**0.965**	0.927	**0.973**	0.945	0.960	0.880
MEANT_2.0	0.926	0.950	**0.941**	**0.970**	**0.962**	0.932	0.838
MEANT_2.0-NOSRL	0.902	0.936	0.933	0.963	**0.960**	0.896	0.800
NGRAM2VEC	0.984	0.935	0.890	0.963	0.907	0.955	**0.880**
NIST	**1.000**	0.931	0.931	0.960	0.912	0.971	0.849
PER	0.968	**0.951**	**0.896**	0.962	0.911	0.932	**0.877**
TER	0.989	0.906	**0.952**	0.971	0.912	0.954	0.847
TreeAggreg	0.983	0.920	**0.977**	**0.986**	0.918	**0.987**	0.861
UHH_TSKM	**0.996**	0.937	0.921	**0.990**	0.914	**0.987**	**0.902**
WER	0.987	0.896	**0.948**	0.969	0.907	0.925	**0.839**
newstest2017							

Table 4: Absolute Pearson correlation of to-English system-level metrics with DA human assessment; correlations of metrics not significantly outperformed by any other for that language pair are highlighted in bold; ensemble metrics are highlighted in gray.

	en-cs	en-de	en-fi	en-lv	en-ru	en-tr	en-zh
n	14	16	12	17	9	8	11
Correlation	$|r|$	$|r|$	$|r|$	$|r|$	$|r|$	$|r|$	$|r|$
AutoDA	**0.975**	0.603	0.879	0.729	0.850	0.601	**0.976**
AutoDA-TECTO	**0.969**	–	–	–	–	–	–
BEER	**0.970**	0.842	0.976	**0.930**	0.944	**0.980**	0.914
Blend	–	–	–	–	**0.953**	–	–
BLEU	0.956	0.804	0.920	0.866	0.898	0.924	**0.981**
BLEU2VEC_SEP	**0.963**	0.810	0.942	0.859	0.903	0.911	–
CDER	**0.968**	0.813	**0.965**	**0.930**	0.924	0.957	**0.983**
CharacTER	**0.981**	**0.938**	**0.972**	0.897	**0.939**	**0.975**	0.933
CHRF	**0.976**	0.863	**0.981**	**0.955**	0.950	**0.991**	**0.976**
CHRF+	**0.976**	0.855	**0.980**	**0.956**	0.948	**0.988**	–
CHRF++	**0.974**	0.852	**0.979**	**0.956**	0.945	0.986	**0.976**
MEANT_2.0	–	0.858	–	–	–	–	**0.956**
MEANT_2.0-NOSRL	**0.976**	0.770	**0.972**	**0.959**	**0.957**	**0.991**	0.943
NGRAM2VEC	–	–	0.940	0.862	–	–	–
NIST	0.962	0.769	0.957	**0.935**	0.920	**0.986**	**0.976**
PER	**0.954**	0.687	0.949	0.851	0.887	**0.963**	0.934
TER	**0.955**	0.796	0.961	**0.909**	**0.933**	0.967	**0.970**
TreeAggreg	0.947	0.773	0.965	0.927	0.921	**0.983**	0.938
WER	**0.954**	0.802	0.960	**0.906**	**0.934**	0.956	**0.954**
newstest2017							

Table 5: Absolute Pearson correlation of out-of-English system-level metrics with DA human assessment; correlations of metrics not significantly outperformed by any other for that language pair are highlighted in bold; ensemble metrics are highlighted in gray.

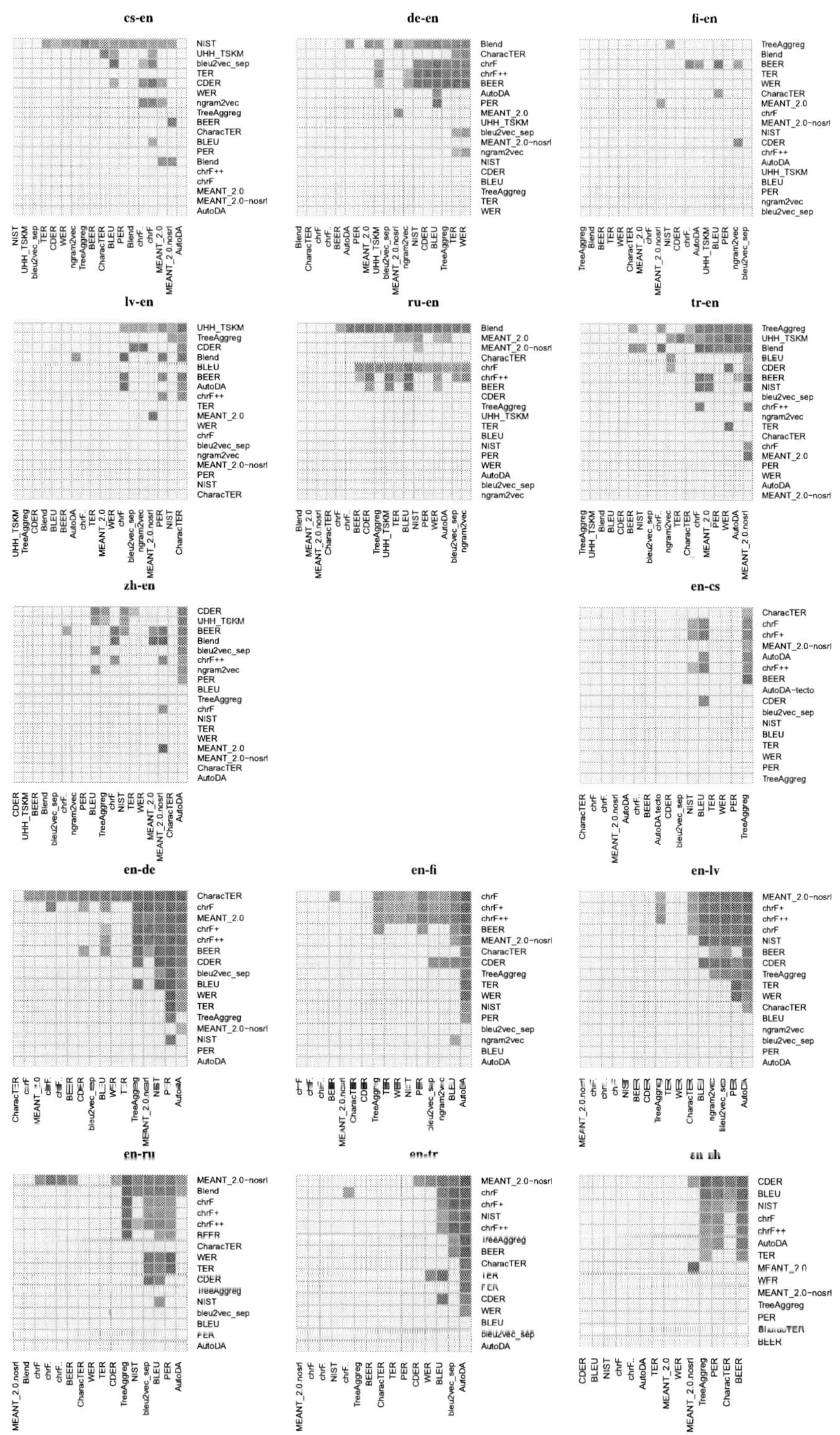

Figure 1: System-level metric significance test results for DA human assessment in newstest2017; green cells denote a statistically significant increase in correlation with human assessment for the metric in a given row over the metric in a given column according to Williams test.

	cs-en	de-en	fi-en	lv-en	ru-en	tr-en	zh-en
n	10K	10K	10K	10K	10K	10K	10K
Correlation	$|r|$	$|r|$	$|r|$	$|r|$	$|r|$	$|r|$	$|r|$
AutoDA	0.4395	0.9505	0.9220	0.9698	0.9015	0.9138	0.7341
BEER	0.9662	0.9524	0.9532	0.9740	0.9299	0.9692	**0.8970**
Blend	0.9633	**0.9685**	0.9562	0.9761	**0.9569**	0.9809	0.8897
BLEU	0.9644	0.9136	0.9061	0.9741	0.9070	0.9688	0.8523
CDER	0.9833	0.9219	0.9247	0.9814	0.9160	0.9702	**0.8975**
CharacTER	0.9628	0.9648	0.9438	0.9271	0.9484	0.9459	0.7398
CHRF	0.9330	0.9602	0.9352	0.9647	0.9456	0.9408	0.8551
CHRF++	0.9348	0.9572	0.9242	0.9696	0.9381	0.9568	0.8756
MEANT_2.0	0.9209	0.9418	0.9390	0.9668	0.9546	0.9307	0.8357
MEANT_2.0-NOSRL	0.8962	0.9275	0.9305	0.9599	0.9523	0.8951	0.7992
NIST	**0.9937**	0.9173	0.9284	0.9566	0.9035	0.9693	0.8309
PER	0.9673	0.9198	0.8917	0.9578	0.9040	0.8982	0.8659
TER	0.9830	0.8991	0.9503	0.9672	0.9051	0.9510	0.8366
TreeAggreg	0.9769	0.9133	**0.9752**	0.9828	0.9115	**0.9834**	0.8535
UHH_TSKM	0.9896	0.9294	0.9183	**0.9857**	0.9077	0.9821	0.8955
WER	0.9814	0.8894	0.9458	0.9649	0.9004	0.9222	0.8281
newstest2017 Hybrids							

Table 6: Absolute Pearson correlation of to-English system-level metrics with DA human assessment for 10K hybrid super-sampled systems; ensemble metrics are highlighted in gray.

	en-cs	en-de	en-fi	en-lv	en-ru	en-tr	en-zh
n	10K	10K	10K	10K	10K	10K	10K
Correlation	$|r|$	$|r|$	$|r|$	$|r|$	$|r|$	$|r|$	$|r|$
AutoDA	0.9670	0.6021	0.8789	0.7307	0.8501	0.5857	0.9676
AutoDA-TECTO	0.8572	—	—	—	—	—	—
BEER	0.9634	0.8285	0.9748	0.9233	0.9417	0.9684	0.9062
Blend	—	—	—	—	0.9499	—	—
BLEU	0.9447	0.7925	0.9190	0.8385	0.8929	0.9157	0.9686
CDER	0.9582	0.8030	0.9620	0.9111	0.9215	0.9484	**0.9748**
CharacTER	**0.9725**	**0.8931**	0.9698	0.8921	0.9292	0.9609	0.9140
CHRF	0.9683	0.8446	**0.9788**	0.9445	0.9474	**0.9801**	0.9686
CHRF+	0.9679	0.8375	0.9779	0.9455	0.9453	0.9779	—
CHRF++	0.9658	0.8354	0.9774	0.9441	0.9423	0.9752	0.9683
MEANT_2.0	—	0.8437	—	—	—	—	0.9444
MEANT_2.0-NOSRL	0.9682	0.7530	0.9704	**0.9470**	**0.9550**	0.9796	0.9310
NIST	0.9544	0.7607	0.9567	0.9140	0.9167	0.9760	0.9681
PER	0.9599	0.6803	0.9388	0.8169	0.8758	0.9546	0.8928
TER	0.9507	0.7899	0.9593	0.8881	0.9299	0.9582	0.9646
TreeAggreg	0.9419	0.7648	0.9630	0.9149	0.9188	0.9712	0.9331
WER	0.9489	0.7967	0.9589	0.8841	0.9310	0.9466	0.9507
newstest2017 Hybrids							

Table 7: Absolute Pearson correlation of out-of-English system-level metrics with DA human assessment for 10K hybrid super-sampled systems; ensemble metrics are highlighted in gray.

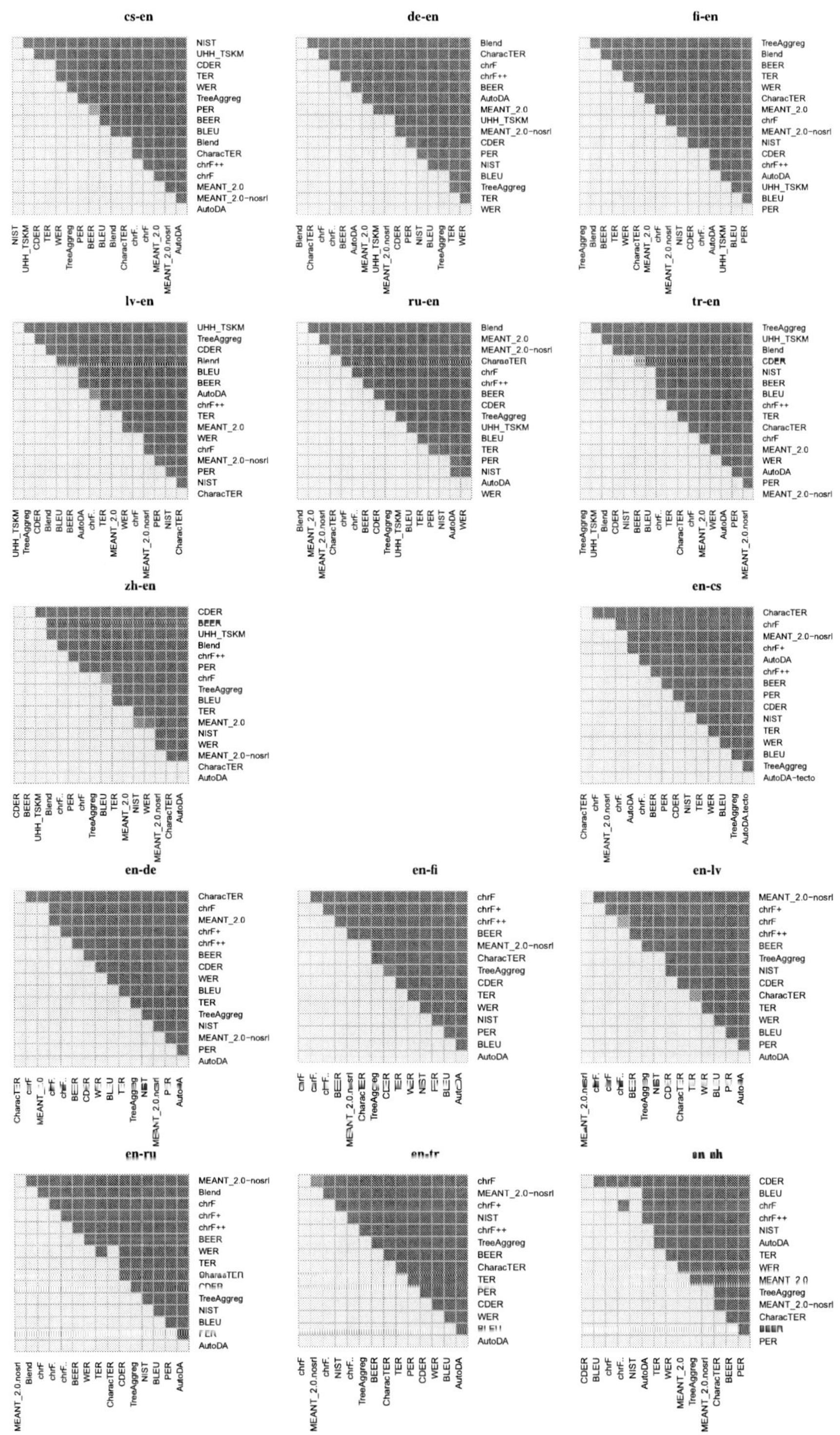

Figure 2: System-level metric significance test results for 10K hybrid systems (DA human evaluation) from newstest2017; green cells denote a statistically significant increase in correlation with human assessment for the metric in a given row over the metric in a given column according to Williams test.

3.1.1 System-Level Results for News Task

Table 4 provides the system-level correlations of metrics evaluating translation of newstest2017 into English while Table 5 provides the same for out-of-English language pairs. DA is the golden truth. The underlying texts are part of the WMT17 News Translation test set (newstest2017) and the underlying MT systems are all MT systems participating in the WMT17 news translation task. The en-cs translation direction also includes the translation systems participating in the NMT training task.

As recommended by Graham and Baldwin (2014), we employ Williams significance test (Williams, 1959) to identify differences in correlation that are statistically significant. Williams test is a test of significance of a difference in dependent correlations and therefore suitable for evaluation of metrics. Correlations not significantly outperformed by any other metric for the given language pair are highlighted in bold in Tables 4 and 5.

Since pairwise comparisons of metrics may be also of interest, e.g. to learn which metrics significantly outperform the most widely employed metric BLEU, we include significance test results for every competing pair of metrics including our baseline metrics in Figure 1.

For instance, we see that for en-cs (outputs of 14 MT systems), even the best-performing metric CHARACTER was not significantly better than any other metric except TREEAGGREG. CHRF+ and CHRF++ were significantly better than BLEU and TREEAGGREG, as were several other metrics.

The sample of systems we employ to evaluate metrics is often small, as few as four MT systems for cs-en, for example. This can lead to inconclusive results, as identification of significant differences in correlations of metrics is unlikely at such a small sample size. In addition, the Williams test takes into account the correlation between each pair of metrics and the correlation between the metric scores themselves increases the likelihood of a significant difference being identified. For cs-en, this led to one counter-intuitive result: AUTODA achieved a substantially lower correlation with human assessment compared to other metrics (0.438 compared to ~0.9 in Table 4) and yet it was not significantly outperformed by any other metric. The lack of significance here is due to the small sample size and lack of correlation of met-

ric AUTODA metric scores with the scores of the other competing metrics, reducing the likelihood of identifying a significant difference. In short, AUTODA differed too much from others, underperforming, but the four underlying MT systems are too few for the statistical significance. Other metrics are more similar to each other and the differences are sufficient for confidence as to which metric performs better. The small sample size also explains the cs-en NIST correlation of 1.0.

The situation is also interesting for de-en, with BLEND significantly outperforming numerous metrics but the second CHARACTER not being better than any other metric, and this is in part again due to the varying correlations between the metric scores themselves, as the statistical power of Williams test increases with stronger metric scores correlations between each other.

We also include significance test results for large hybrid-super-samples of systems (Graham and Liu, 2016). 10K hybrid systems were created per language pair, with corresponding DA human assessment scores by sampling pairs of systems from WMT17 translation task and NMT training task, creating hybrid systems by randomly selecting each candidate translation from one of the two selected systems. Similar to last year, not all metrics participating in the system-level evaluation submitted metric scores for the large set of hybrid systems. Fortunately, taking a simple average of segment-level scores is the proper aggregation method for most metrics this year, so wherever possible, we provided scores for hybrids ourselves.

Correlations of metric scores with human assessment of the large set of hybrid systems are shown in Tables 6 and 7, where again metrics not significantly outperformed by any other are highlighted in bold. Figure 2 also includes significance test results for hybrid super-sampled correlations for all pairs of competing metrics for a given language pair.

3.1.2 System-Level Results for HUME

In addition to the WMT17 news task, we also assess the performance of metrics on the system-level for himltest datasets. Tables 8 and 9 show correlation with human assessment of system-level metrics with HUME scores on himltest2017 "a" and "b", respectively. Since there are only two or three systems in each dataset, the sample size is too small to test for statistical significance. In fact,

	en-cs	en-de	en-pl	en-ro
n	3	3	3	3
Correlation	$|r|$	$|r|$	$|r|$	$|r|$
AutoDA	0.932	0.593	0.161	0.594
AutoDA-tecto	0.917	–	–	–
BEER	0.833	0.460	0.342	0.188
BLEU	0.815	0.537	0.675	0.064
CDER	0.751	0.461	0.211	0.285
CharacTER	0.958	0.735	0.241	0.961
chrF	0.855	0.631	0.131	0.119
chrF+	0.840	0.616	0.006	0.168
chrF++	0.836	0.573	0.119	0.172
MEANT_2.0	–	0.851	–	–
MEANT_2.0-nosrl	0.812	0.805	0.555	0.331
NIST	0.730	0.484	0.427	0.283
PER	0.704	0.738	0.853	0.239
TER	0.778	0.127	0.838	0.253
TreeAggreg	0.753	0.799	0.670	0.018
WER	0.784	0.011	0.839	0.151

himltest2017a

Table 8: Absolute Pearson correlation of system-level metrics with HUME human assessment; ensemble metrics are highlighted in gray.

	en-ro
n	2
Correlation	$|r|$
BEER	1.000
BLEU	1.000
CDER	1.000
CharacTER	1.000
chrF	1.000
chrF+	1.000
chrF++	1.000
MEANT_2.0-nosrl	1.000
NIST	1.000
PER	1.000
TER	1.000
TreeAggreg	1.000
WER	1.000

himltest2017b

Table 9: Absolute Pearson correlation of system-level metrics with HUME human assessment; ensemble metrics are highlighted in gray.

results in Table 9 are not very informative because two systems will always lie on a line, producing perfect absolute Pearson correlations. We include results nonetheless for demonstration purposes.

To obtain more meaningful results, we compute correlations for 10K hybrid systems for himltest2017a. Table 10 shows metric correlation with human assessment for the large set of 10K hybrid systems for himltest2017a and Figure 3 shows significance test results. Since a minimum of three systems is required for hybrid super-sampling and only two systems were included in himltest2017b, no hybrid results are reported for that test set.

3.2 Segment-Level Results

3.2.1 Segment-Level Results for News Task

In WMT17, since manual evaluation in the news task now takes the form of Direct Assessment of translations, this forms the basis of our segment-level metrics task results for the newstest2017 data set. Note however, that the sampling of the sentences is different, as described in Section 2.3.2. We follow the methodology outlined in Graham et al. (2015) and combine a minimum of 15 individual DA scores for a given translation by taking its average score. We then compute the absolute Pearson correlation between segment-level metric scores and segment-level DA scores where a

	en-cs	en-de	en-pl	en-ro
n	10K	10K	10K	10K
Correlation	$|r|$	$|r|$	$|r|$	$|r|$
AutoDA	**0.8700**	0.2266	0.1781	0.3494
AutoDA-tecto	0.8451	–	–	–
BEER	0.7803	0.0976	0.1859	0.0808
BLEU	0.7732	0.1546	0.4385	0.0020
CDER	0.7124	0.0911	0.2383	0.2025
CharacTER	**0.8683**	0.3900	0.0527	**0.5881**
chrF	0.8006	0.2712	0.0043	0.0405
chrF+	0.7887	0.2564	0.0960	0.0763
chrF++	0.7869	0.2131	0.1912	0.0794
MEANT2.0	–	0.5484	–	–
MEANT2.0-nosrl	0.7697	0.4630	0.4447	0.1831
NIST	0.6987	0.0559	0.3276	0.1989
PER	0.6672	0.3897	0.2342	0.0366
TER	0.7252	0.2197	0.5812	0.1686
TreeAggreg	0.7044	**0.7337**	0.4915	0.0524
WER	0.7287	0.3268	**0.5896**	0.0971

himltest2017a Hybrids

Table 10: Absolute Pearson correlation of system-level metrics with HUME human assessment for 10K hybrid super-sampled systems; ensemble metrics are highlighted in gray.

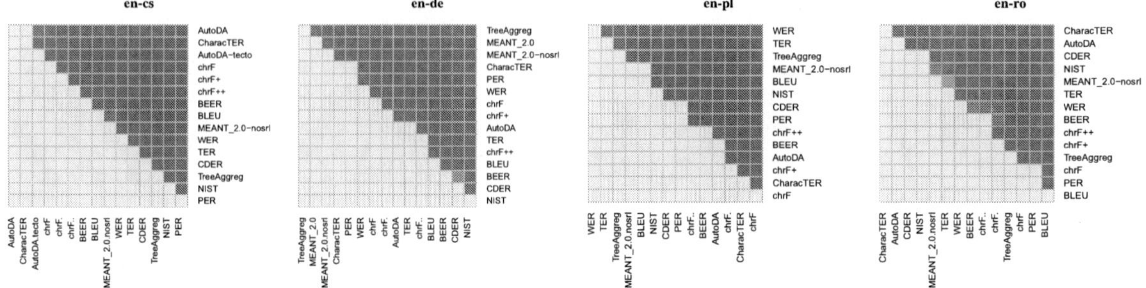

Figure 3: System-level metric significance test results for 10K hybrid systems (HUME human evaluation) from himltest2017a; green cells denote a statistically significant increase in correlation with human assessment for the metric in a given row over the metric in a given column according to Williams test.

stronger correlation indicates higher performance.

As described in Section 2.3.2, for some language pairs, insufficient human assessments were completed to provide accurate segment-level DA scores for segment-level evaluation. For those five language pairs, en-cs, en-de, en-fi, en-lv and en-tr, we therefore convert pairs of DA to DARR better/worse preferences and employ a Kendall's Tau formulation as in previous WMT metric evaluations.

Results of the segment-level human evaluation for translations sampled from the news task are shown in Tables 11 and 12, where metric correlations not significantly outperformed by any other metric are highlighted in bold. Head-to-head significance test results for differences in metric performance are included in Figure 4.

3.2.2 Segment-Level Results for HUME

For the himltest2017 datasets, we employ segment-level HUME scores also using absolute Pearson correlation.

Results of segment-level metrics task evaluated with HUME on the himltest datasets are shown in Tables 13 and 14 where metrics not significantly outperformed by any other in a given language pair are again highlighted in bold. Head-to-head significance test results for all metrics are shown in Figures 5 and 6.

4 Discussion

The major switch from RR to DA that happened this year in the main news task evaluation did not affect metrics task in any negative way, also because we trialed DA in metrics evaluation already last year.

We discuss various particular observations in the rest of this section.

4.1 Obtaining Human Judgements

The sentence sampling for segment-level evaluation is different from the sampling used to obtain system-level scores. We were aware of the difficulties in finding assessors for some language pairs on the crowdsourcing platforms, as mentioned e.g. by Birch et al. (2016), and we relied on researchers. We were indeed able to cover all the required target languages but for many of them, insufficient numbers of assessments were collected. Fortunately, DA allows to resort to a relative-ranking re-interpretation, DARR, and use a variation of Kendall's τ as in the previous years. This method proved effective and only English-Turkish segment-level evaluation suffers from having all metrics indistinguishable.

4.2 Hybrid Super-sampling vs. Document-level Evaluation

As in the previous year, hybrid super-sampling proved very effective and allowed to obtain conclusive results of system-level evaluation even for language pairs where as few as 4 MT systems participated.

We should however note that this style of aggregated evaluation may not be a substitute for truly document-level evaluation. Hybrid systems are constructed by randomly mixing sentence and they therefore may possibly break cross-sentence links in MT outputs (if such links are at all preserved by current MT systems). There is a good chance that document-level links are well represented in individual sentences of the reference, as these were created taking the whole document into

	cs-en	de-en	fi-en	lv-en	ru-en	tr-en	zh-en
Human Evaluation	DA	DA	DA	DA	DA	DA	DA
n	560	560	560	560	560	560	560
Correlation	$|r|$	$|r|$	$|r|$	$|r|$	$|r|$	$|r|$	$|r|$
AUTODA	0.499	**0.543**	0.673	0.533	0.584	0.625	0.583
BEER	0.511	0.530	0.681	0.515	0.577	0.600	0.582
BLEND	**0.594**	**0.571**	**0.733**	**0.577**	**0.622**	**0.671**	**0.661**
BLEU2VEC_SEP	0.439	0.429	0.590	0.386	0.489	0.529	0.526
CHRF	0.514	0.531	0.671	0.525	**0.599**	0.607	0.591
CHRF++	0.523	0.534	0.678	0.520	0.588	0.614	0.593
MEANT_2.0	**0.578**	**0.565**	0.687	**0.586**	**0.607**	0.596	**0.639**
MEANT_2.0-NOSRL	**0.566**	**0.564**	0.682	0.573	0.591	0.582	0.630
NGRAM2VEC	0.436	0.435	0.582	0.383	0.490	0.538	0.520
SENTBLEU	0.435	0.432	0.571	0.393	0.484	0.538	0.512
TREEAGGREG	0.486	0.526	0.638	0.446	0.555	0.571	0.535
UHH_TSKM	0.507	0.479	0.600	0.394	0.465	0.478	0.477

newstest2017

Table 11: Segment-level metric results for to-English language pairs: absolute correlation of segment-level metric scores with DA scores; correlations of metrics not significantly outperformed by any other for that language pair are highlighted in bold; ensemble metrics are highlighted in gray.

	en-cs	en-de	en-fi	en-lv	en-ru	en-tr	en-zh
Human Evaluation	DARR	DARR	DARR	DARR	DA	DARR	DA
n	32,810	3,227	3,270	3,456	560	247	560
Correlation	τ	τ	τ	τ	$|r|$	τ	$|r|$
AUTODA	0.041	0.099	0.204	0.130	0.511	**0.409**	0.609
AUTODA-TECTO	0.336	—	—	—	—	—	—
BEER	**0.398**	**0.336**	**0.557**	**0.420**	0.569	**0.490**	0.622
BLEND	—	—	—	—	0.578	—	—
BLEU2VEC_SEP	0.305	**0.313**	0.503	0.315	0.472	**0.425**	
CHRF	0.376	**0.336**	0.503	**0.420**	0.605	**0.466**	0.608
CHRF+	0.377	**0.325**	0.514	**0.421**	0.609	**0.474**	—
CHRF++	0.368	**0.328**	0.484	**0.417**	0.604	**0.466**	0.602
MEANT_2.0	—	**0.350**	—	—	—	—	**0.727**
MEANT_2.0-NOSRL	**0.395**	**0.324**	**0.565**	**0.425**	**0.636**	**0.482**	0.705
NGRAM2VEC	—	—	0.486	0.317	—	—	—
SENTBLEU	0.274	0.269	0.446	0.259	0.468	**0.377**	0.642
TREEAGGREG	0.361	**0.305**	0.509	**0.383**	0.535	**0.441**	0.566

newstest2017

Table 12: Segment-level metric results for out-of-English language pairs: absolute correlation of segment-level metric scores with human assessment variants, where τ are computed similar to Kendall's τ and over relative ranking (RR) human assessments (converted from DA scores); $|r|$ are absolute Pearson correlation coefficients of metric scores with DA scores; correlations of metrics not significantly outperformed by any other are highlighted in bold; ensemble metrics are highlighted in gray.

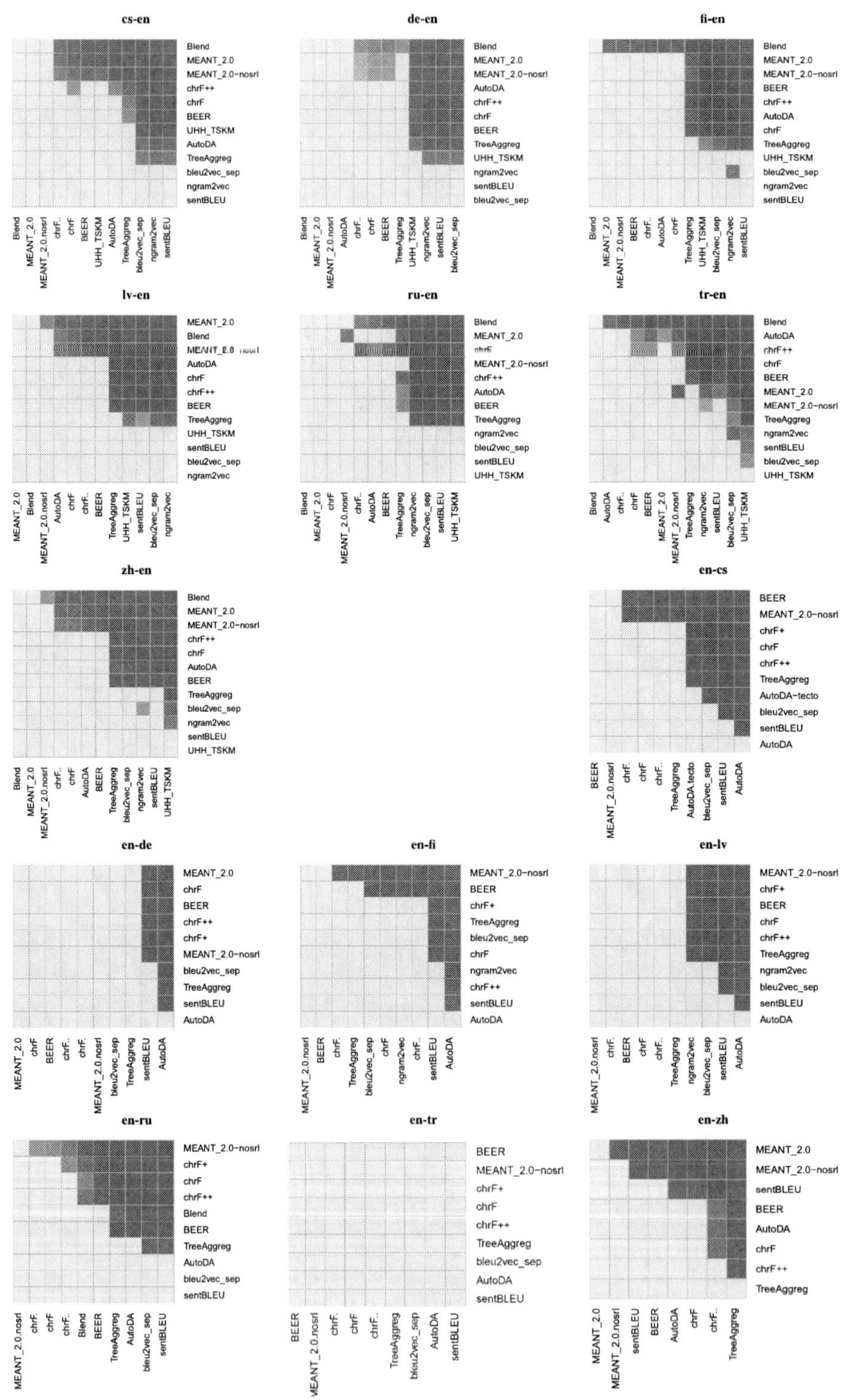

Figure 4: Direct Assessment (DA) and DARR segment-level metric significance test results for all language pairs (newstest2017): Green cells denote a significant win for the metric in a given row over the metric in a given column according to Williams test for DA (all to-English language pairs; en-ru; en-zh) and bootstrap resampling for DARR (en-cs; en-de; en-fi; en-ro; en-tr).

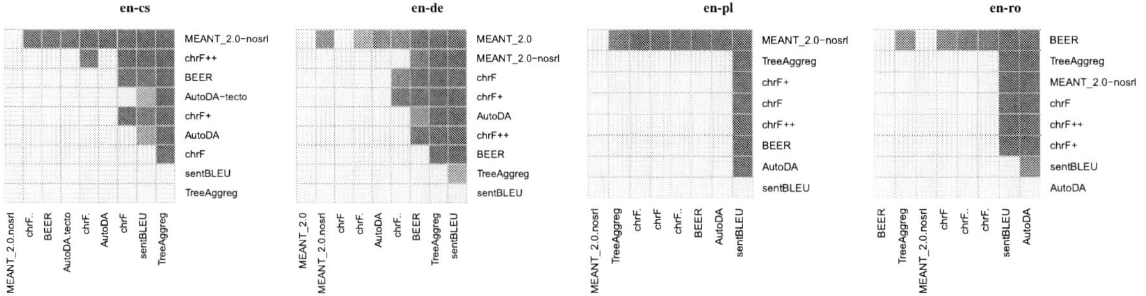

Figure 5: HUME segment-level metric significance test results (himltest2017a): Green cells denote a significant win for the metric in a given row over the metric in a given column according to Williams test for difference in dependent correlation.

	en-cs	en-de	en-pl	en-ro
n	879	891	1,020	354
Correlation	$\|r\|$	$\|r\|$	$\|r\|$	$\|r\|$
AUTODA	0.391	0.445	0.442	0.127
AUTODA-TECTO	0.400	–	–	–
BEER	0.400	0.428	0.442	**0.508**
CHRF	0.383	**0.454**	0.445	0.477
CHRF+	0.395	0.451	0.445	0.474
CHRF++	0.400	0.445	0.444	0.477
MEANT_2.0	–	**0.479**	–	–
MEANT_2.0-NOSRL	**0.473**	0.463	**0.489**	**0.479**
SENTBLEU	0.347	0.338	0.329	0.261
TREEAGGREG	0.323	0.374	0.450	0.481
himltest2017a				

Table 13: Absolute Pearson correlation of segment-level metric scores with HUME scores for himltest2017a; ensemble metrics are highlighted in gray.

	en-ro
n	350
Correlation	$\|r\|$
BEER	0.293
CHRF	0.305
CHRF+	0.314
CHRF++	0.310
MEANT_2.0-NOSRL	**0.370**
SENTBLEU	0.254
TREEAGGREG	0.244
himltest2017b	

Table 14: Absolute Pearson correlation of segment-level metric scores with HUME scores for himltest2017b; ensemble metrics are highlighted in gray.

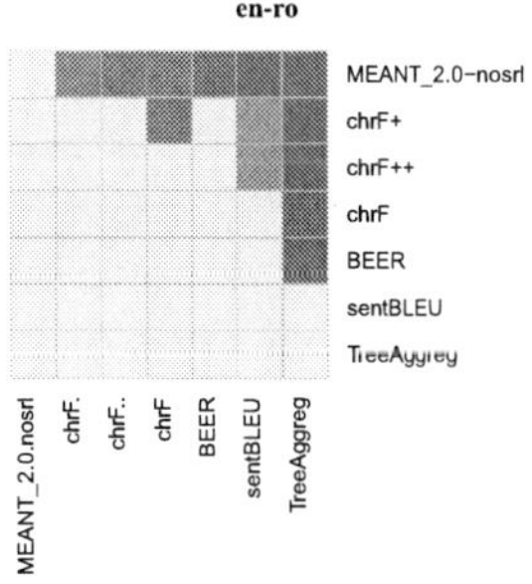

Figure 6: HUME segment-level metric significance test results (himltest2017b): Green cells denote a significant win for the metric in a given row over the metric in a given column according to Williams test for difference in dependent correlation.

account, but this would have to be empirically validated.

4.3 Overall Metric Performance

As mentioned above, the observed performance of metrics very much depends on the underlying texts and participating MT systems. We can nevertheless confirm the trend since 2014, with character-level metrics performing on average better: BEER, CHRF (and its variants) and CHARACTER.

In order to get an idea of the stability of metrics at achieving a high correlation with human assessment across all language pairs, Figure 7 shows box plots of correlations achieved by metrics.[10]

[10] We only include metrics that participated in all language pairs in each box plot, to provide a fair indication of metric performance, otherwise metrics not participating in difficult language pairs could (unfairly) appear to perform better when they did not participate in that language.

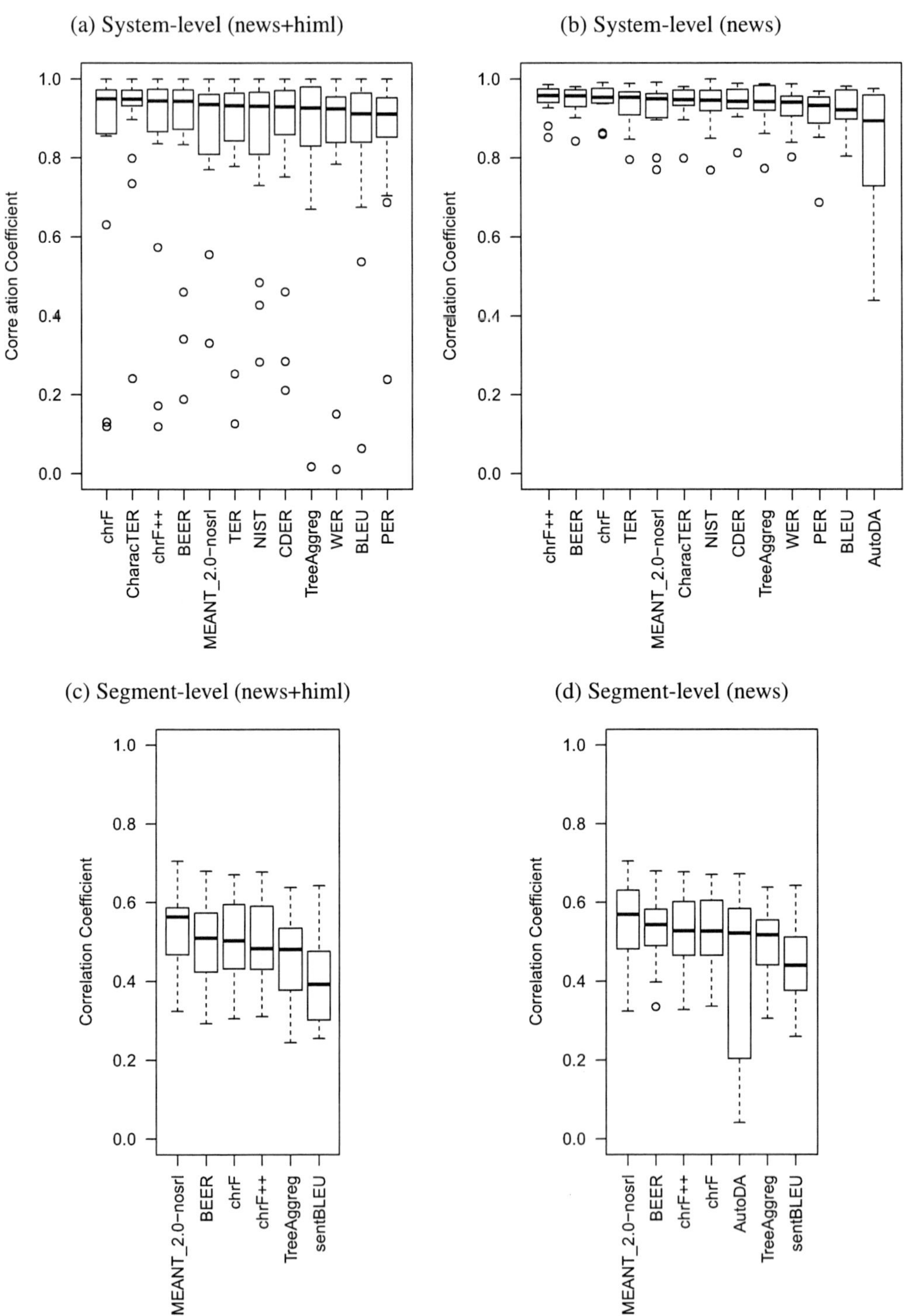

Figure 7: Plots of correlations achieved by metrics in (a) all language pairs and test sets on the system level; (b) all language pairs for newstest2017 on the system level; (c) all language pairs and test sets on the segment level; (d) all language pairs for newstest2017 on the segment-level; all correlations are for non-hybrid correlations only.

The figures confirm the observation from the past years that system-level metrics can achieve correlations above 0.9 while segment-level evaluation is only around 0.5 or slightly above. The variance in the achieved correlations across language pairs and test sets is generally acceptable, with only AUTODA getting very varied results. Comparing the plots (a) and (b) in Figure 7, we see that himl datasets allowed only for less stable results, possibly due to the smaller number of translations comprising test sets for himl. For system-level newstest, plot Figure 7(b), the variance of the majority of metrics is very low, indicating that their scores are reliable across language pairs.

The generally well-performing and stable metrics are CHRF or CHRF++, CHARACTER and BEER. MEANT_2.0-NOSRL is new this year and also performed very well, esp. in segment-level evaluation, although it is currently not yet quite as stable as others on the system-level. Traditional metrics like NIST or TER also reach relatively good results, clearly surpassing BLEU when applied in the common way with only 1 reference and not 4 as recommended by the original authors.

All of the "winners" in this years campaign are publicly available, which is very good for a wider adoption. If participants could put the additional effort of adding their code to Moses scorer, this would guarantee their long-term inclusion in the metrics task.

4.4 Data Overlap for Polish HUME

As mentioned in Section 2.2, HUME evaluation of translation into Polish suffered from a large overlap of training and evaluation data. Fortunately, only AUTODA was actually affected by this, other trained metrics such as BEER, BLEND or NGRAM2VEC either did not evaluate himltest2017 or were not retrained this year.

4.5 HUME Results

The dataset used to evaluate metrics against HUME, himltest2017, is rather small. It contains only ~300 sentences (and actually only 118 sentences for Romanian, himltest2017a) with three MT system outputs per sentence. The discriminative power of the experiment is correspondingly low.

The segment-level scores in Figures 5 and 6 however still indicate that MEANT_2.0 (in SRL and noSRL variant) performed well, significantly outperforming all others except for Romanian on

himltest2017a but still outperforming it on himltest2017b. This result nicely corresponds with the design of the manual scores of HUME, aggregated over key semantic elements of the sentence.

4.6 Metric Efficiency

This year we asked participants to submit information about the speed of their metrics in order to analyze a possible relationship between metric efficiency and performance in terms of correlation with human assessment. Many participants submitted time durations for metrics to process system outputs for the system-level news task test set. Figures 8(a) and 8(b) show scatter-plots of average correlation coefficient achieved by a given metric versus self-reported times to process a single translation (on average).[11]

Based on these plots, we can conclude that the generally good metrics are not prohibitively slow, only MEANT_2.0 being more expensive, needing up to a second per sentence. The plots show all metrics for which times were submitted, regardless the number of language pairs they took part in.

5   Conclusion

This paper summarizes the results of WMT17 shared task in machine translation evaluation, the Metrics Shared Task. Participating metrics were evaluated in terms of their correlation with human judgements at the level of the whole test set (system-level evaluation), as well as at the level of individual sentences (segment-level evaluation). For the former, best metrics reach over 0.95 Pearson correlation on average across several language pairs. For the latter, correlations between 0.4 and 0.6 Pearson's ρ or Kendall's τ are to be expected.

We confirm the main results from the previous year that character-level metrics, or metrics incorporating such a feature, generally perform better. Last year's conclusion that trained metrics generally perform better than non-trained ones is not that clear this year, good performance is observed for both trained metrics like BLEND, BEER (not retrained for this year) as well as non-trained metrics like CHRF, CHARACTER and also a new addition this year, MEANT_2.0.

____
[11]Some metric participants only submitted times for a subset of language pairs. In such cases, average correlations included in plots are only based on the correlations for which times were submitted.

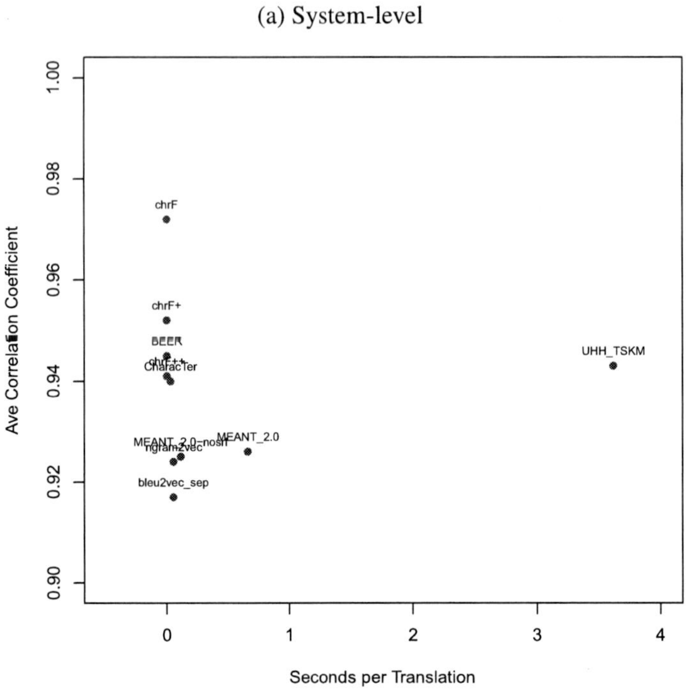

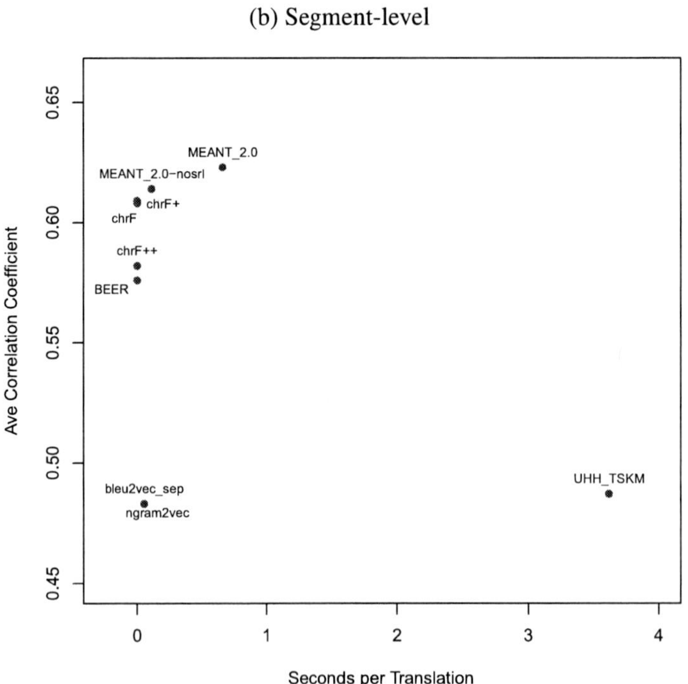

Figure 8: Scatter-plots of self-reported metric speed per translation (computed on the system-level news task datasets) versus average correlation with human assessment for (a) system-level performance and (b) segment-level performance.

Acknowledgments

We wouldn't be able to put this experiment together without tight collaboration with Christian Federmann who ran the core of WMT Shared Translation Task evaluation and also operated Appraise for us.

This study was supported in parts by the grants H2020-ICT-2014-1-645442 (QT21), H2020-ICT-2014-1-644402 (HimL), the Dutch organization for scientific research STW grant nr. 12271, ADAPT Centre for Digital Content Technology (www.adaptcentre.ie) at Dublin City University funded under the SFI Research Centres Programme (Grant 13/RC/2106) co-funded under the European Regional Development Fund, and Charles University Research Programme "Progres" Q18+Q48.

References

Omri Abend and Ari Rappoport. 2013. Universal Conceptual Cognitive Annotation (UCCA). In *Proceedings of the 51st Annual Meeting of the Association for Computational Linguistics (Volume 1: Long Papers)*, pages 228–238, Sofia, Bulgaria, August. Association for Computational Linguistics.

Dzmitry Bahdanau, Kyunghyun Cho, and Yoshua Bengio. 2014. Neural machine translation by jointly learning to align and translate. *CoRR*, abs/1409.0473.

Alexandra Birch, Omri Abend, Ondřej Bojar, and Barry Haddow. 2016. HUME: Human UCCA-Based Evaluation of Machine Translation. In *Proceedings of the 2016 Conference on Empirical Methods in Natural Language Processing*, pages 1264–1274, Austin, Texas, November. Association for Computational Linguistics.

Ondřej Bojar, Miloš Ercegovčević, Martin Popel, and Omar Zaidan. 2011. A Grain of Salt for the WMT Manual Evaluation. In *Proceedings of the Sixth Workshop on Statistical Machine Translation*, pages 1–11, Edinburgh, Scotland, July. Association for Computational Linguistics.

Ondřej Bojar, Christian Federmann, Barry Haddow, Philipp Koehn, Matt Post, and Lucia Specia. 2016a. Ten Years of WMT Evaluation Campaigns: Lessons Learnt. In *Proceedings of the LREC 2016 Workshop Translation Evaluation From Fragmented Tools and Data Sets to an Integrated Ecosystem*, pages 27–34, Portorose, Slovenia, 5.

Ondřej Bojar, Yvette Graham, , and Amir Kamran Miloš Stanojević. 2016b. Results of the WMT16 Metrics Shared Task . In *Proceedings of the First Conference on Machine Translation,*

Berlin, Germany, August. Association for Computational Linguistics.

Ondřej Bojar, Rajen Chatterjee, Christian Federmann, Yvette Graham, Barry Haddow, Matthias Huck, Philipp Koehn, Varvara Logacheva, Christof Monz, Matteo Negri, Matt Post, Raphael Rubino, Lucia Specia, and Marco Turchi. 2017a. Findings of the 2017 conference on machine translation (wmt17). In *Proceedings of the Second Conference on Machine Translation, Volume 2: Shared Tasks Papers*, Copenhagen, Denmark, September. Association for Computational Linguistics.

Ondřej Bojar, Jindřich Helcl, Tom Kocmi, Jindřich Libovický, and Tomáš Musil. 2017b. Results of the wmt17 neural mt training task. In *Proceedings of the Second Conference on Machine Translation, Volume 2: Shared Tasks Papers*, Copenhagen, Denmark, September. Association for Computational Linguistics.

George Doddington. 2002. Automatic Evaluation of Machine Translation Quality Using N-gram Co-occurrence Statistics. In *Proceedings of the Second International Conference on Human Language Technology Research*, HLT '02, pages 138–145, San Francisco, CA, USA. Morgan Kaufmann Publishers Inc.

Melania Duma and Wolfgang Menzel. 2017. Uhh submission to the wmt17 metrics shared task. In *Proceedings of the Second Conference on Machine Translation, Volume 2: Shared Tasks Papers*, Copenhagen, Denmark, September. Association for Computational Linguistics.

Yvette Graham and Timothy Baldwin. 2014. Testing for Significance of Increased Correlation with Human Judgment. In *Proceedings of the 2014 Conference on Empirical Methods in Natural Language Processing (EMNLP)*, pages 172–176, Doha, Qatar, October. Association for Computational Linguistics.

Yvette Graham and Qun Liu. 2016. Achieving Accurate Conclusions In Evaluation of Automatic Machine Translation Metrics. In *Proceedings of the 15th Annual Conference of the North American Chapter of the Association for Computational Linguistics: Human Language Technologies*, San Diego, CA. Association for Computational Linguistics.

Yvette Graham, Timothy Baldwin, Alistair Moffat, and Justin Zobel. 2013. Continuous Measurement Scales in Human Evaluation of Machine Translation. In *Proceedings of the 7th Linguistic Annotation Workshop & Interoperability with Discourse*, pages 33–41, Sofia, Bulgaria. Association for Computational Linguistics.

Yvette Graham, Timothy Baldwin, Alistair Moffat, and Justin Zobel. 2014. Is Machine Translation Getting Better over Time? In *Proceedings of the 14th Conference of the European Chapter of the Association for Computational Linguistics*, pages 443–451,

Gothenburg, Sweden, April. Association for Computational Linguistics.

Yvette Graham, Nitika Mathur, and Timothy Baldwin. 2015. Accurate Evaluation of Segment-level Machine Translation Metrics. In *Proceedings of the 2015 Conference of the North American Chapter of the Association for Computational Linguistics Human Language Technologies*, Denver, Colorado.

Yvette Graham, Timothy Baldwin, Alistair Moffat, and Justin Zobel. 2016. Can machine translation systems be evaluated by the crowd alone. *Natural Language Engineering*, FirstView:1–28, 1.

Jan Hajič. 2004. Complex Corpus Annotation: The Prague Dependency Treebank. In *Insight into Slovak and Czech Corpus Linguistics*, Bratislava, Slovakia. Jazykovedný ústav Ľ. Štúra, SAV.

Jindřich Helcl and Jindřich Libovický. 2017. Neural Monkey: An open-source tool for sequence learning. *The Prague Bulletin of Mathematical Linguistics*, 107:5–17.

Philipp Koehn and Christof Monz. 2006. Manual and Automatic Evaluation of Machine Translation Between European Languages. In *Proceedings of the Workshop on Statistical Machine Translation*, StatMT '06, pages 102–121, Stroudsburg, PA, USA. Association for Computational Linguistics.

Gregor Leusch, Nicola Ueffing, and Hermann Ney. 2006. CDER: Efficient MT Evaluation Using Block Movements. In *In Proceedings of EACL*, pages 241–248.

Chi-kiu Lo, Philipp Dowling, and Dekai Wu. 2015. Improving evaluation and optimization of MT systems against MEANT. In *Proceedings of the Tenth Workshop on Statistical Machine Translation*, Lisboa, Portugal, September. Association for Computational Linguistics.

Chi-kiu Lo. 2017. Meant 2.0: Accurate semantic mt evaluation for any output language. In *Proceedings of the Second Conference on Machine Translation, Volume 2: Shared Tasks Papers*, Copenhagen, Denmark, September. Association for Computational Linguistics.

Qingsong Ma, Yvette Graham, Shugen Wang, and Qun Liu. 2017. Blend: a novel combined mt metric based on direct assessment casict-dcu submission to wmt17 metrics task. In *Proceedings of the Second Conference on Machine Translation, Volume 2: Shared Tasks Papers*, Copenhagen, Denmark, September. Association for Computational Linguistics.

Matouš Macháček and Ondřej Bojar. 2014. Results of the WMT14 metrics shared task. In *Proceedings of the Ninth Workshop on Statistical Machine Translation*, pages 293–301, Baltimore, MD, USA. Association for Computational Linguistics.

Matouš Macháček and Ondřej Bojar. 2013. Results of the WMT13 Metrics Shared Task. In *Proceedings of the Eighth Workshop on Statistical Machine Translation*, pages 45–51, Sofia, Bulgaria, August. Association for Computational Linguistics.

David Mareček, Ondřej Bojar, Ondřej Hübsch, Rudolf Rosa, and Dusan Varis. 2017. Cuni experiments for wmt17 metrics task. In *Proceedings of the Second Conference on Machine Translation, Volume 2: Shared Tasks Papers*, Copenhagen, Denmark, September. Association for Computational Linguistics.

Joakim Nivre, Marie Catherine de Marneffe, Filip Ginter, Yoav Goldberg, Jan Haji, Christopher Manning, Ryan McDonald, Slav Petrov, Sampo Pyysalo, Natalia Silveira, Reut Tsarfaty, and Daniel Zeman. 2016. Universal dependencies v1: A multilingual treebank collection. In *Proceedings of the 10th International Conference on Language Resources and Evaluation (LREC 2016)*, pages 1659–1666, Paris, France. European Language Resources Association.

Kishore Papineni, Salim Roukos, Todd Ward, and Wei-Jing Zhu. 2002. BLEU: A Method for Automatic Evaluation of Machine Translation. In *Proceedings of the 40th Annual Meeting on Association for Computational Linguistics*, ACL '02, pages 311–318.

Maja Popović. 2015. chrF: character n-gram F-score for automatic MT evaluation. In *Proceedings of the Tenth Workshop on Statistical Machine Translation*, Lisboa, Portugal, September. Association for Computational Linguistics.

Maja Popović. 2017. chrf++: words helping character n-grams. In *Proceedings of the Second Conference on Machine Translation, Volume 2: Shared Tasks Papers*, Copenhagen, Denmark, September. Association for Computational Linguistics.

Matthew Snover, Bonnie Dorr, Richard Schwartz, Linnea Micciulla, and John Makhoul. 2006. A study of translation edit rate with targeted human annotation. In *In Proceedings of Association for Machine Translation in the Americas*, pages 223–231.

Miloš Stanojević and Khalil Sima'an. 2015. BEER 1.1: ILLC UvA submission to metrics and tuning task. In *Proceedings of the Tenth Workshop on Statistical Machine Translation*, Lisboa, Portugal, September. Association for Computational Linguistics.

Andre Tättar and Mark Fishel. 2017. bleu2vec: the painfully familiar metric on continuous vector space steroids. In *Proceedings of the Second Conference on Machine Translation, Volume 2: Shared Tasks Papers*, Copenhagen, Denmark, September. Association for Computational Linguistics.

Yolanda Vazquez-Alvarez and Mark Huckvale. 2002. The reliability of the ITU-t p.85 standard for the evaluation of text-to-speech systems. In *Proc. of ICSLP - INTERSPEECH*.

Weiyue Wang, Jan-Thorsten Peter, Hendrik Rosendahl, and Hermann Ney. 2016. CharacTer: Translation Edit Rate on Character Level. In *Proceedings of the First Conference on Machine Translation*, Berlin, Germany, August. Association for Computational Linguistics.

Evan James Williams. 1959. *Regression analysis*, volume 14. Wiley New York.

Hui Yu, Qingsong Ma, Xiaofeng Wu, and Qun Liu. 2015. CASICT-DCU Participation in WMT2015 Metrics Task. In *Proceedings of the Tenth Workshop on Statistical Machine Translation*, Lisboa, Portugal, September. Association for Computational Linguistics.

A Shared Task on Bandit Learning for Machine Translation

Artem Sokolov[*,◇] and **Julia Kreutzer**[◇] and **Kellen Sunderland**[*] and **Pavel Danchenko**[*]
and **Witold Szymaniak**[*] and **Hagen Fürstenau**[*] and **Stefan Riezler**[◇]
[*]Amazon Development Center Germany, Berlin and [◇]Heidelberg University, Germany

Abstract

We introduce and describe the results of a novel shared task on bandit learning for machine translation. The task was organized jointly by Amazon and Heidelberg University for the first time at the Second Conference on Machine Translation (WMT 2017). The goal of the task is to encourage research on learning machine translation from weak user feedback instead of human references or post-edits. On each of a sequence of rounds, a machine translation system is required to propose a translation for an input, and receives a real-valued estimate of the quality of the proposed translation for learning. This paper describes the shared task's learning and evaluation setup, using services hosted on Amazon Web Services (AWS), the data and evaluation metrics, and the results of various machine translation architectures and learning protocols.

1 Introduction

Bandit Learning for machine translation (MT) is a framework to train and improve MT systems by learning from weak or partial feedback: Instead of a gold-standard human-generated translation, the learner only receives feedback to a single proposed translation (hence the term 'partial'), in form of a translation quality judgement (a real number which can be as weak as a binary acceptance/rejection decision).

In the shared task, user feedback was simulated by a service hosted on Amazon Web Services (AWS). Participants can submit translations and receive feedback on translation quality. This is used to adapt an out-of-domain MT model, pre-trained on mostly news texts, to a new do-

main (e-commerce), for the translation direction of German (DE) to English (EN). While in our setup feedback was simulated by evaluating a reward function on the predicted translation against a gold standard reference, the reference translation itself was never revealed to the learner, neither at training nor at test time. This learning scenario has been investigated under the names of *learning from bandit feedback*[1] or *reinforcement learning* (RL)[2], and has important real world applications such as online advertising (Chapelle et al., 2014). In the advertising application, the problem is to select the best advertisement for a user visiting a publisher page. A key element is to estimate the click-through rate (CTR), i.e., the probability that an ad will be clicked by a user so that the advertiser has to pay. This probability is modeled by features representing user, page, and ad, and is estimated by trading off exploration (a new ad needs to be displayed in order to learn its click-through rate) and exploitation (displaying the ad with the current best estimate is better in the short term) in displaying ads to users.

In analogy to the online advertising scenario, one could imagine a scenario of personalization in machine translation where translations have to be adapted to the user's specific purpose and domain. Similar to online advertising, where it is unrealistic to expect more detailed feedback than a user click on a displayed ad, the feedback in adaptive machine translation should be weaker than a reference translation or a post-edit created by

---

[1]The name is inherited from a model where in each round a gambler pulls an arm of a different slot machine ('one-armed bandit'), with the goal of maximizing his reward relative to the maximal possible reward, without apriori knowledge of the optimal slot machine. See Bubeck and Cesa-Bianchi (2012) for an overview.

[2]See Sutton and Barto (1998) and Szepesvári (2009) for an overview of algorithms for reinforcement learning and their relation to bandit learning.

Proceedings of the Conference on Machine Translation (WMT), Volume 2: Shared Task Papers, pages 514–524
Copenhagen, Denmark, September 7–11, 2017. ©2017 Association for Computational Linguistics

a professional translator. Instead, the goal is to elicit binary or real-valued judgments of translation quality from laymen users (for example, Graham et al. (2016) show that consistent assessments of real-valued translation quality can be provided by crowdsourcing), or to infer feedback signals from user interactions with the translated content on a web page (for example, by interpreting a copy-paste action of the MT output as positive quality signal, and a correction as a negative quality signal). The goal of this shared task is to evaluate existing algorithms for learning MT systems from weak feedback (Sokolov et al., 2015, 2016a; Kreutzer et al., 2017) on real-world data and compare them to new algorithms, with a focus on performing online learning efficiently and effectively from bandit feedback, i.e. the best algorithms are those that perform fast online learning and, simultaneously, achieve high translation quality.

In the following, we present a description of the protocol and infrastructure of our online learning task, and of the data for pretraining, online training, and evaluation (Section 2). We introduce the online and batch evaluation metrics used in the shared task (Section 3), and describe static baseline systems (Section 4) and submitted online learning systems (Section 5). We present and discuss the results of the task (Section 6-7), showing that NMT systems with batch domain adaptation provide very good baselines, however, online learning based on SMT or NMT can catch up over time by adapting to the provided feedback.

2 Task Description

Our shared task setup follows an online learning protocol, where on each iteration, the learner receives a source sentence, proposes a translation, and is rewarded in form of a task sentence-level metric evaluation of the proposed translation with respect to a hidden reference. The learner does not know what the correct translation (reference) looks like, nor what would have happened if it had proposed a different translation. Thus, we implemented two constraints to guarantee this scenario of online learning from weak feedback. First, sentences had to be translated one by one, i.e. the next source sentence could only be received after the translation to the previous sentence was sent off. Second, feedback could be obtained only for a single translation of any given source sentence.

In our shared task, the participant systems inter-

Algorithm 1 WMT Online Bandit Learning

1: Input: MT model
2: **for** $k = 0, \ldots, K$ **do**
3:      Request source sentence s_k from service
4:      Propose a translation t_k
5:      Obtain feedback $\Delta(t_k)$ from service
6:      Improve MT model with $\langle s_k, t_k, \Delta(t_k)\rangle$

---

act online with an AWS-hosted service as shown in Algorithm 1. The service provides a source sentence to the learner (line 3), and provides feedback (line 5) to the translation predicted by the learner (line 4). The learner updates its parameters using the feedback (line 6) and continues to the next example. We did not impose any restriction on how the learner could use the feedback to improve future translations.

Infrastructure. We provided three AWS-hosted environments, that correspond to the three phases of the shared task:

1. Mock service, to test the client API (optional): hosted a tiny in-domain dataset (48 sentences).
2. Development service to tune algorithms and hyperparameters (optional): ran on a larger in-domain dataset (40,000 sentences). Several passes were allowed and two evaluation metrics were communicated to the participants via the leaderboard.
3. Training service (mandatory): served sources from a large in-domain dataset (1,297,974 sentences). Participants had to consume a fixed number of samples during the allocated online learning period to be eligible for final evaluation.

We built the shared task around the following AWS services:

- API Gateway (authentication, rate limiting, client API SDK);
- Lambda (computation);
- DynamoDB (data storage);
- CloudWatch (logging and monitoring).

In more detail, service endpoints were implemented using API Gateway, that gave us access, on a participant level, to throttle requests rates, manage accounts, etc. API Gateway enabled easy management of our public-facing endpoints and

source	reference (PE)	PE direction	PE modification
schwarz gr.xxl / xxxl	black , size xxl / xxxl	DE-EN	fixed errors in source, expanded abbreviation
, 147 cm	147 cm	DE-EN	fixed errors in source
für starke , glänzende nägel	great for strengthen your nails and enhance shine	EN-DE	poor quality source (EN) used as reference
seemless verarbeitung	seamless processing	DE-EN	source typo corrected in reference
brenndauer : mindestens 40 stunden	40 hour minimum burn time	DE-EN	translation rewritten for readability
maschinenwaschbar bei 30 ° c	machine washable at 30 degrees .	DE-EN	literal expansion of the degree symbol
32 unzen volumen	32-ounce capacity	DE-EN	language-specific typography
material : 1050 denier nylon .	material : 1050d nylon .	EN-DE	expanded source (EN) abbreviation used as reference
für e-gitarre entworfen	designed for electric guitar	DE-EN	abbreviation expanded

Table 1: Examples for non-literal PEs in the e-commerce data: The first two columns show examples[3] of source sentences and PEs used as reference translations in the shared task. The last two columns show the direction of translation post-editing, and a description of the modifications applied by the editors.

environments, and provided integrated metrics and notifications, which we monitored closely during the shared task. Data storage was implemented using DynamoDB – a NoSQL storage database which allows dynamic scaling of our back-end to match the varied requirements of the different shared task phases. The state management (e.g., forbidding multiple requests), source sentence serving, feedback calculation, keeping track of participant's progress and result processing was implemented using Lambda – a serverless compute architecture that dispenses with setting up and monitoring a dedicated server infrastructure. CloudWatch service was used to analyze logs in order to trace down errors, general monitoring and sending alarms to the shared task API maintainers. In addition to the service development, we also developed a small SDK consisting of code samples and helper libraries in Python and Java to help participants in developing their clients, as well as a leaderboard that showed the results during the development phase.

Data. For training initial or *seed* MT systems (the input to Algorithm 1), out-of-domain parallel data was restricted to DE-EN parts of Europarl v7, NewsCommentary v12, CommonCrawl and Rapid data from the WMT 2017 News Translation (constrained) task[4]. Furthermore, monolingual EN data from the constrained task was allowed. Tuning of the out-of-domain systems had to be done on the `newstest2016-deen` set.

The in-domain parallel data for online learning was taken from the e-commerce domain: The corpus was provided by Amazon and had been sampled from a large real-world collection of post-edited (PE'ed) translations of actual product descriptions. Since post-editors were following certain rules aimed at improving customer experience on the Amazon retail website (improving readability, correction of typos, rewriting of uncommon abbreviations, removing irrelevant information, etc.), naturally the resulting PEs were not always literal, sometimes adding or deleting a considerable number of tokens and resulting in low feedback BLEU scores for submitted literal translations (see Table 1 for examples). Consequently, the participants had to solve two difficult problems – domain adaptation and learning from bandit feedback. In addition, to simulate the level of noise normally encountered in real-world MT applications, and to test noise-robustness of the bandit learning algorithms, approximately half of the parallel in-domain data was sourced from the EN-DE post-editing direction and reversed.

All data was preprocessed with `Moses` scripts (removing non-printing characters, replacing and normalizing unicode punctuation, lowercasing, pretokenizing and tokenizing). No DE-side compound splitting was used, permitting custom participant decisions. Since the learning data came from a substantially different domain than the out-of-domain parallel texts, it had a large number of out-of-vocabulary (OOV) terms, aggravated by the high frequency of long product numbers and unique vendor names. To reduce the OOV rate we additionally filtered out all parallel sentences where the source contained more than one numeral (with a whitespace in between) and normalized floating point delimiters in both languages to a period. The resulting average OOV token rate with respect to the out-of-domain parallel training data (assuming the above preprocessing) is $\simeq 2\%$ for EN and $\simeq 6\%$ for DE data side. Statistics on the length distribution of in-domain and out-of-domain data is given in Table 2.

For all services, the sequence of provided

---

[3]Examples selected by Khanh Ngyuen.

[4]`statmt.org/wmt17/translation-task.html`

# tokens	out-of-domain	in-domain
mean	23.0±14.1	6.6±4.8
median	25	8
max	150	25
# lines	5.5M	1.3M

Table 2: Data statistics for source side of in-domain and out-of-domain parallel data.

source sentences was the same for all participants, with no data intersection between the services beyond natural duplicates: About 11% of data were duplicates on both (DE and EN) sides, where about 4% of DE sentences had more than one different EN side.

Feedback. Simulation of real-valued user feedback was done by calculating the smoothed sentence-level BLEU-score (Lin and Och, 2004) (with additive n-gram count smoothing with offset 0.01, applied only if the n-gram count was zero) with respect to one human reference (preprocessed as described above).

3 Evaluation Metrics

In our shared task, participants were allowed to use their favorite MT systems as starting points to integrate online bandit learning methods. This leads to the difficulty of separating the contributions of the underlying MT architecture and the online bandit learning method. We attempted to tackle this problem by using different evaluation metrics that focus on these respective aspects:

1. **Online cumulative reward:** This metric measures the cumulative sum $C = \sum_{k=1}^{K} \Delta(t_k)$ of the per-sentence BLEU score Δ against the number of iterations. This metric has been used in reinforcement learning competitions (Dimitrakakis et al., 2014). For systems with the same design, this metric favors those that do a good job at balancing exploration and exploitation to achieve high scores over the full data sequence. Unlike in these competitions, where environments (i.e., action spaces and context features) were fixed, in our task the environment is heterogeneous due to the use of different underlying MT architectures. Thus, systems that start out with a well-performing pretrained out-of-domain model have an advantage over systems that might improve more over worse starting points. Furthermore, even systems that do not perform online learning at all can achieve high cumulative rewards.

2. **Online regret:** In order to overcome the problems of the cumulative reward metric, we can use a metric from bandit learning that measures the regret $R = \frac{1}{K} \sum_{k=1}^{K} \left(\Delta(t_k^*) - \Delta(t_k) \right)$ that is suffered by the system when predicting translation t_k instead of the optimal translation t_k^* produced by an oracle system. Plotting a running average of regret against the number of iterations allows separating the gains due to the MT architecture from the gains due to the learning algorithm: Systems that do learn will decrease regret, systems that do not learn will not. In our task, we use as oracle system a model that is trained on in-domain data.

3. **Relative reward:** A further way to separate out the learning ability of systems from the contribution of the underlying MT architecture is to apply the standard corpus-BLEU score and/or an average of the per-sentence BLEU score Δ on a held-out set at regular intervals during training. Plotting these scores against the number of iterations, or alternatively, subtracting the performance of the starting point at each evaluation, allows to discern systems that adapt to a new domain from systems that are good from the beginning and can achieve high cumulative rewards without learning. We performed this evaluation by embedding a small (relative to the whole sequence) fixed held-out set in the beginning (showing the performance of the initial out-of-domain model), and again at regular intervals including the very end of the learning sequence. In total, there were 4 insertions of 700 sentences in the development data and 12 insertions of 4,000 sentences in the final training phase, which constitutes $\simeq$2% and $\simeq$0.3% of the respective learning sequence lengths. Note that this metric measures the systems' performance while they were still exploring and learning, but the relative size of the embedded held-out set is small enough to consider the models static during such periodic evaluations.

4   Baselines

As baseline systems, we used SMT and NMT models that were trained on out-of-domain data, but did not perform online learning on in-domain data. We further present oracle systems that were trained in batch on in-domain data.

4.1   Static SMT baselines.

SMT-static. We based our SMT submissions on the SCFG decoder `cdec` (Dyer et al., 2010) with on-the-fly grammar extraction with suffix arrays (Lopez, 2007). Training was done in batch on the parallel out-of-domain data; tuning was done on `newstest2016-deen`. During the development phase we evaluated MERT (on 14 default dense features) and MIRA (on additional lexicalized sparse features: rule-id features, rule source and target bigram features, and rule shape features), and found no significant difference in results. We chose MERT with dense features as the seed system for the training phase for its speed and smaller memory footprint.

4.2   Static NMT baselines.

WMT16-static. First of all, we are interested in how well the currently best (third-party) model on the news domain would perform on the e-commerce domain. Therefore, the Nematus (Sennrich et al., 2017) model that won the News Translation Shared Task at WMT 2016 (Bojar et al., 2016b)[5] was used to translate the data from this shared task. It is an attentional, bi-directional, singe-layered encoder-decoder model on sub-word units (BPE with 89,500 merge operations) with word embeddings of dimensionality 500, GRUs of size 1024, pervasive dropout and r2l reranking (details in (Sennrich et al., 2016a)). Final predictions are made with an ensemble formed of the four last training checkpoints and beam search with width 12. It was trained on a different corpus than allowed for this shared task – the WMT 2016 news training data (Europarl v7, News Commentary v11, CommonCrawl) and additional synthetic parallel data generated by translating the monolingual news crawl corpus with a EN-DE NMT model.

BNMT-static. The UNK replacement strategy of Jean et al. (2015) and Luong et al. (2015) is expected to work reasonable well for tokens that occur in the training data and those that are copied from source to target. However, the NMT model does not learn anything about these words as such in contrast to BPE models (Sennrich et al., 2016b) where the decomposition by byte pair encoding (BPE) allows for a representation within the vocabulary. We generate a BNMT system using a BPE vocabulary from 30k merge operations on all tokens and all single characters of the training data, including the UNK token. If unknown characters occur, they are copied from source to target.

4.3   Oracle SMT and NMT systems

To simulate full-information systems (oracles) for regret calculation, we trained an SMT and an NMT system with the same architectures, on the in-domain data that other learning systems accessed only through the numerical feedback. The SMT oracle system was trained on combined in-domain and out-of-domain data, while the NMT oracle system continued training from the converged out-of-domain system on the in-domain data with the same BPE vocabulary.

5   Submitted Systems

5.1   Online bandit learners based on SMT.

Online bandit learners based on SMT were following the existing approaches to adapting an SMT model from weak user feedback (Sokolov et al., 2016b,a) by stochastically optimizing expected loss (EL) for a log-linear model. Furthermore, we present a model that implements stochastic zeroth-order (SZO) optimization for online bandit learning. Cube pruning limit (up to 600), learning rate adaptation schedules (constant vs. Adadelta (Zeiler, 2012) or Adam (Kingma and Ba, 2014)), as well as the initial learning rates (for Adam), were tuned during the development phase. The best configurations were selected for the training phase. The running average of rewards as an additive control variate (CV)[6] was found helpful for stochastic policy gradient updates (Williams, 1992) for all online learning systems.

SMT-EL-CV-ADADELTA. We used the EL minimization approach of Sokolov et al. (2016a), adding Adadelta's learning rate scheduling, and a control variate (effectively, replacing the received

---

[5]From `data.statmt.org/rsennrich/wmt16_systems/de-en/`

[6]Called a *baseline* in RL literature; here we use a term from statistics not to confuse it with baseline MT models.

feedback $\Delta(t_k)$ with $\Delta(t_k) - \frac{1}{k}\sum_{k'=1}^{k}\Delta(t_{k'}))$. Sampling and computation of expectations on the hypergraph used the Inside-Outside algorithm (Li and Eisner, 2009).

SMT-EL-CV-ADAM. This system uses the same approach as above except for using Adam to adapt the learning rates, with tuning of the initial learning rate on the development service.

SMT-SZO-CV-ADAM. As a novel contribution, we adapted the *two-point* stochastic zeroth-order approach by (Sokolov et al., 2015) that required two quality evaluation per iteration to a *one-point* feedback scenario. In a nutshell, on each step of the SZO algorithm, the model parameters w are perturbed with an additive standard Gaussian noise ϵ, and the Viterbi translation is sent to the service. Such algorithm can be shown to maximize the smoothed version of the task reward: $\mathbb{E}_{\epsilon \sim N(0,1)}[\Delta(\hat{y}(w + \epsilon))]$ (Flaxman et al., 2005). The advantages of such a black-box optimization method over model-based (e.g. EL) optimization, that requires sampling of complete structures from the model distribution, are simpler sampling of standard Gaussians, and matching of the inference criterion to the learning objective (MAP inference for both), unlike the EL optimization of *expected* reward that is still evaluated at test time using MAP inference. For SZO models we found that the Adam scheduling consistently outperforms Adadelta.

5.2 Online bandit learners based on NMT.

Kreutzer et al. (2017) recently presented an algorithm for online expected loss minimization to adapt NMT models to unknown domains with bandit feedback. Exploration (i.e. sampling from the model) and exploitation (i.e. presenting the highest scored translation) are controlled by the softmax distribution in the last layer of the network. Ideally, the model would converge towards a peaked distribution. In our online learning scenario this is not guaranteed, but we would like the model to gradually stop exploring, in order to still achieve high cumulative per-sentence reward. To achieve such a behavior, the temperature of the softmax over the outputs of the last layer of the network is annealed (Rose, 1998). More specifically, let o be the scores of the output projection layer of the decoder, then $p_\theta(\tilde{y}_t = w_i | \mathbf{x}, \hat{\mathbf{y}}_{<t}) = \frac{\exp(o_{w_i}/T)}{\sum_{v=1}^{V}\exp(o_{w_v}/T)}$ is the distribution that defines the

probability of each word w_i of the target vocabulary V to be sampled in timestep t. The annealing schedule for this temperature T is defined as $T_k = 0.99^{\max(k-k_{\text{START}},0)}$, i.e. decreases from iteration k_{START} on. The same decay is applied to the learning rate, such that $\gamma_k = \gamma_{k-1}\cdot T_k$. This schedule was proven successful during tuning with the leaderboard.

WNMT-EL. Using the implementation of Kreutzer et al. (2017), we built a word-based NMT system with NeuralMonkey (Libovický et al., 2016; Bojar et al., 2016a) and trained it with the EL algorithm. The vocabulary is limited to the 30k most frequent words in the out-of-domain training corpus. The architecture is similar to WMT16-static with GRU size 1024, embedding size 500. It was pretrained on the out-of-domain data with the standard maximum likelihood objective, Adam ($\alpha = 1 \times 10^{-4}$, $\beta_1 = 0.9$, $\beta_2 = 0.999$) and dropout (Srivastava et al., 2014) with probability 0.2. Bandit learning starts from this pretrained model and continues with stochastic gradient descent (initial learning rate $\gamma_0 = 1 \times 10^{-5}$, annealing starts at $k_{START} = 700,000$, dropout with probability 0.5, gradient norm clipping when the norm exceeds 1.0 (Pascanu et al., 2013)), where the model was updated as soon as a feedback is received. As described above, UNK replacement was applied to the output on the basis of an IBM2 lexical translation model built with `fast_align` (Dyer et al., 2013) on out-of-domain training data. If the aligned source word for a generated UNK token is not in the dictionary of the lexical translation model, the UNK token was simply replaced by the source word.

BNMT-EL. The pretrained BPE model is further trained on the bandit task data with the EL algorithm, as described for BL1, with the only difference of using Adam ($\alpha = 1 \times 10^{-5}$, $\beta_1 = 0.9$, $\beta_2 = 0.999$) instead of SGD. Again, annealing started at $k_{START} = 700,000$.

BNMT-EL-CV. BNMT-EL-CV is trained in the same manner as BNMT-EL with the addition of the same control variate technique (running average of rewards) that has been previously found to improve both variance and generalization for NMT bandit training (Kreutzer et al., 2017).

5.3 Domain adaptation and reinforcement learning based on NMT (University of Maryland).

UMD-domain-adaptation. The UMD team's systems were based on an attention-based encoder-decoder translation model. The models use the BPE technique for subword encoding, which helps addressing the rare word problem and enlarges vocabulary. A further addition is the domain adaptation approach of Axelrod et al. (2011) to select training data after receiving in-domain source-side data and selecting the most similar out-of-domain data from the WMT 2016 training set for re-training.

UMD-reinforce. Another type of models submitted by UMD uses reinforcement learning techniques to learn from feedback and improve the update of the translation model to optimize the reward, based on Bahdanau et al. (2016) and Ranzato et al. (2016).

5.4 Domain adaptation and bandit learning based on SMT (LIMSI).

LIMSI. The team from LIMSI tried to adapt a seed `Moses` system trained on out-domain data to a new, unknown domain relying on two components, each of which addresses one of the challenges raised by the shared task: i) estimate the parameters of a MT system without knowing the reference translation and in a 'one-shot' way (each source sentence can only be translated once); ii) discover the specificities of the target domain 'on-the-fly' as no information about it is available. First, a linear regression model was used to exploit weak and partial feedback the system received by learning to predict the reward a translation hypothesis will get. This model can then be used to score hypotheses of the search space and translate source sentences while taking into account the specificities of the in-domain data. Second, three variants of the UCB1 (Auer et al., 2002) algorithm (vanilla UCB1, a UCB1-sampling variant encouraging more exploration, and a UCB1 with selecting only the examples not used to train the regression model) chose which of the 'adapted' or 'seed' systems should be used to translate a given source sentence in order to maximize the cumulative reward (Wisniewski, 2017).

model		cumulative reward
'translate' by copying source		64,481.8
SMT	SMT-oracle	499,578.0
	SMT-static	229,621.7
	SMT-EL-CV-ADADELTA	214,398.8
	SMT-EL-CV-ADAM	225,535.3
	SMT-SZO-CV-ADAM	208,464.7
NMT	BNMT-oracle	780,580.4
	BNMT-static	222,066.0
	WMT16-static	139,668.1
	BNMT-EL-CV	212,703.2
	BNMT-EL	237,663.0
	WNMT-EL	115,098.0
UMD-domain-adaptation		248,333.2

Table 3: Cumulative rewards over the full training sequence. Only completely finished submission are shown.

6 Results

Table 3 shows the evaluation results under the cumulative rewards metric. Of the non-oracle systems, good results are obtained by static SMT and BNMT system, while the best performance is obtained by the UMD-domain adaptation system which is also basically a static system. This result is followed closely by the online bandit learner BNMT-EL which is based on an NMT baseline and optimizes the EL objective. It outperforms the BNMT-static baseline. Cumulative rewards could not be computed for all submitted systems since some training runs could not be fully finished.

The evolution of the online regret plotted against the log-scaled number of iterations during training is shown in Figure 1. Most of the learning happens in the first 100,000 iterations, however, online learning systems optimizing structured EL objectives or based on reinforcement learning eventually converge to the same result: BNMT-EL or UMD-reinforce2 get close to the regret of the static UMD-domain adaptation. Systems that optimize the EL objective do not start from strong out-of-domain systems with domain-adaptation, however, due to a steeper learning curve they arrive at similar results.

Figures 2, 3a and 3b show the evolution of corpus- and sentence-BLEU on the heldout set that

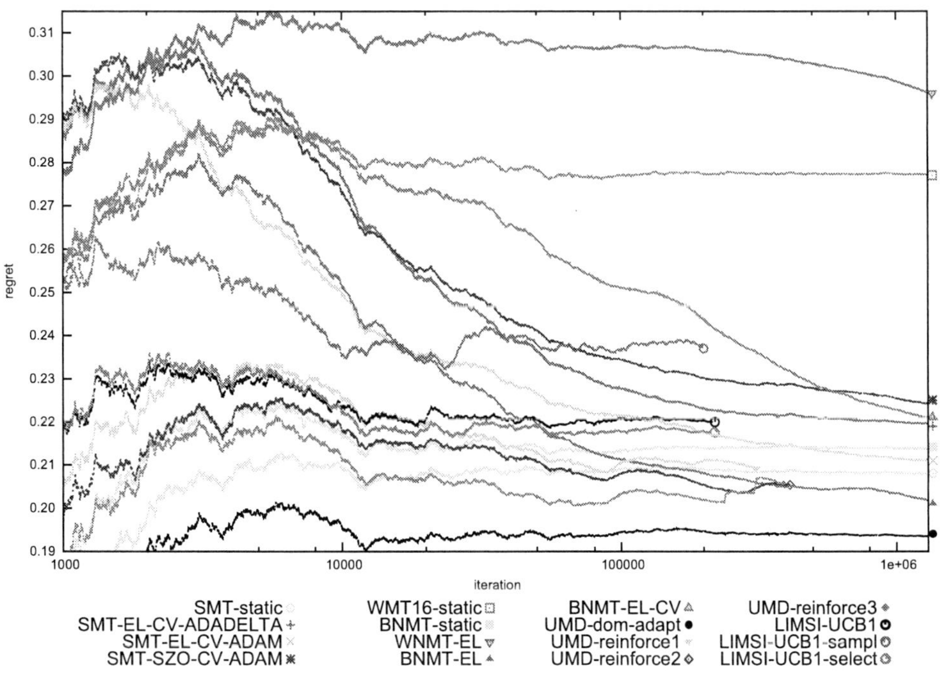

Figure 1: Evolution of regret plotted against log-scaled number of iterations during training. The steeper is the decrease of a curve, the better learning capability has the corresponding algorithm.

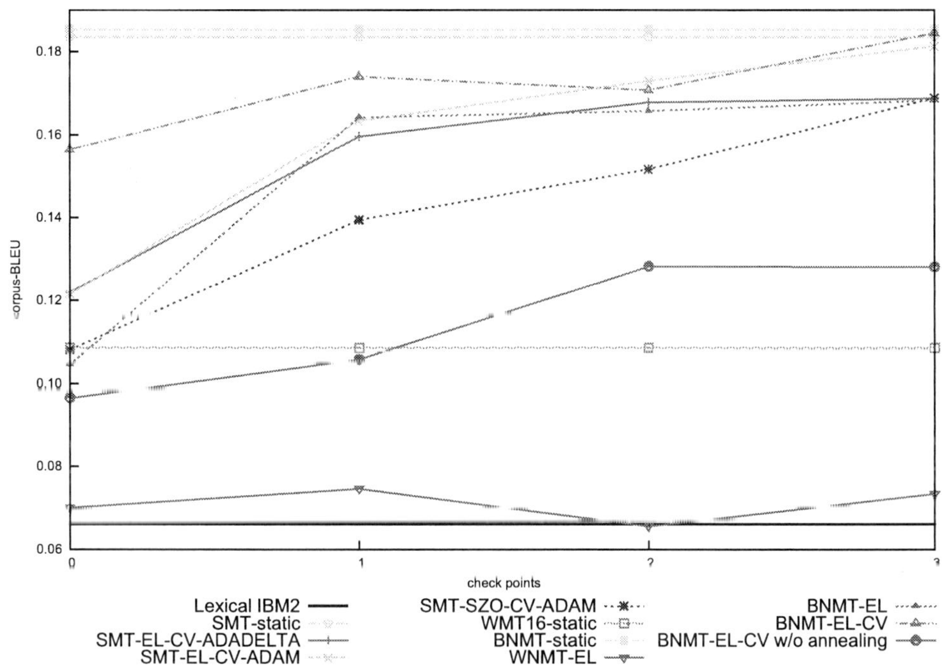

Figure 2: Evolution of corpus BLEU scores during development for configuration selected for the training phase of the competition. Each check point is comprised of the same 700 sentences spaced at a regular intervals of 12,400 sentences starting from the beginning of the development sequence.

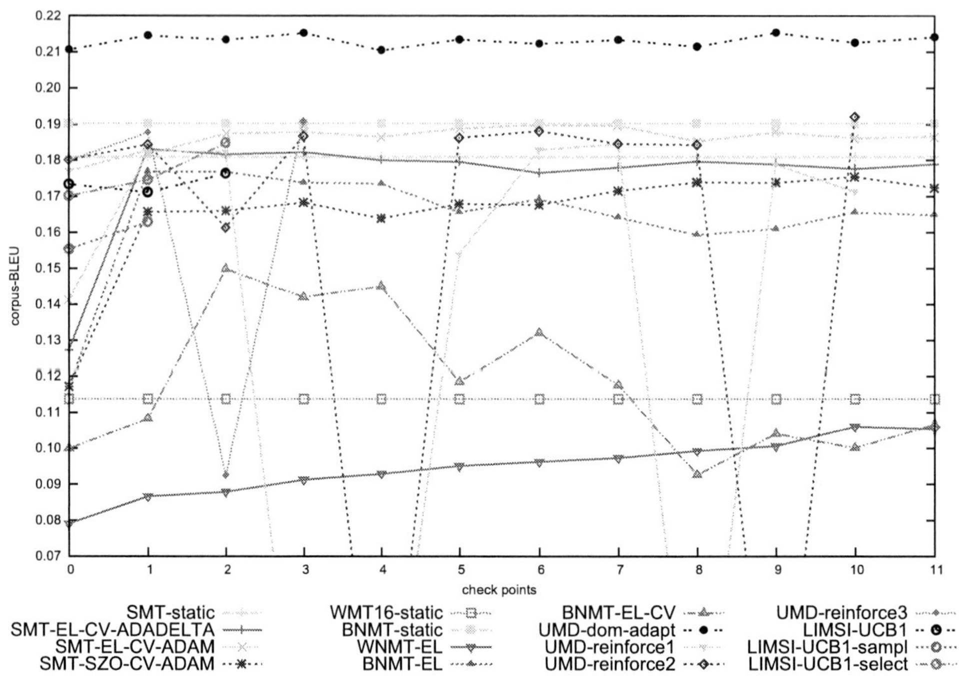

(a) corpus-BLEU

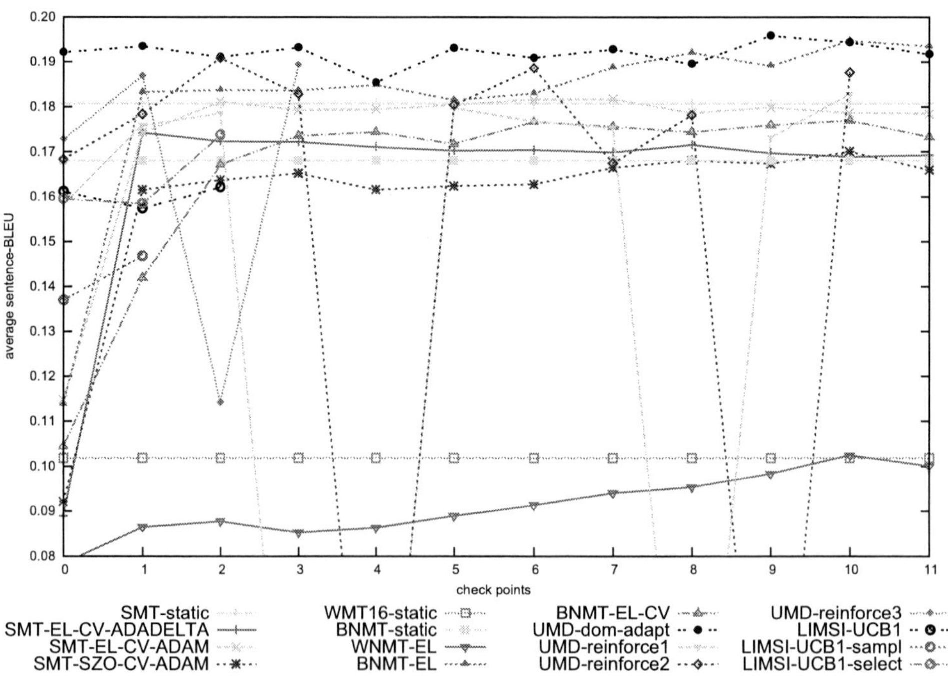

(b) sentence-BLEU

Figure 3: The evolution of corpus- and sentence-BLEU scores during training for all participant and baselines. Each check point is comprised of the same 4,000 sentences spaced at a regular intervals of 113,634 sentences starting from the beginning of the training sequence.

has been embedded in the development and the training sequences. While under corpus-BLEU, static systems always outperform online learners on the held-out embedded set, online learning systems such as BNMT-EL can catch up under corpus-BLEU during development, and under a sentence-BLEU evaluation during training. The curves for corpus- and average sentence-BLEU (Figures 3a and 3b) show a different dynamics, with the corpus-BLEU sometimes decreasing whereas the sentence-BLEU curve continues to increase. However, if the focus is online learning, the online task loss is per-sentence BLEU and so should be the evaluation metric.

7 Conclusion

We presented the learning setup and infrastructure, data and evaluation metrics, and descriptions of baselines and submitted systems for a novel shared task on bandit learning for machine translation. The task implicitly involved domain adaptation from the news domain to e-commerce data (with the additional difficulty of non-literal post-editions as references), and online learning from simulated per-sentence feedback on translation quality (creating a mismatch between the per-sentence task loss and the corpus-based evaluation metric standardly used in evaluating batch-trained machine translation systems). Despite these challenges, we found promising results for both linear and non-linear online learners that could outperform their static SMT and NMT baselines, respectively. A desideratum for a future installment of this shared task is the option to perform *offline* learning from bandit feedback (Lawrence et al., 2017), thus allowing a more lightweight infrastructure, and opening the task to (mini)batch learning techniques that are more standard in the field of machine translation.

Acknowledgments

This research was supported in part by the German research foundation (DFG), and in part by a research cooperation grant with the Amazon Development Center Germany. We would like to thank Amazon for supplying data and engineering expertise, and for covering the running costs.

References

Peter Auer, Nicolò Cesa-Bianchi, and Paul Fischer. 2002. Finite-time analysis of the multiarmed bandit problem. *Machine Learning* 47(2-3):235–256.

Amittai Axelrod, Xiaodong He, and Jianfeng Gao. 2011. Domain adaptation via pseudo in-domain data selection. In *EMNLP*. Edinburgh, Scotland.

Dzmitry Bahdanau, Philemon Brakel, Kelvin Xu, Anirudh Goyal, Ryan Lowe, Joelle Pineau, Aaron Courville, and Yoshua Bengio. 2016. An Actor-Critic Algorithm for Sequence Prediction. *eprint arXiv:1607.07086* .

Ondřej Bojar, Roman Sudarikov, Tom Kocmi, Jindřich Helcl, and Ondřej Cífka. 2016a. UFAL submissions to the IWSLT 2016 MT track. In *IWSLT*. Seattle, WA.

Ondřej Bojar, Rajen Chatterjee, Christian Federmann, Yvette Graham, Barry Haddow, Matthias Huck, Antonio Jimeno Yepes, Philipp Koehn, Varvara Logacheva, Christof Monz, Matteo Negri, Aurelie Neveol, Mariana Neves, Martin Popel, Matt Post, Raphael Rubino, Carolina Scarton, Lucia Specia, Marco Turchi, Karin Verspoor, and Marcos Zampieri. 2016b. Findings of the 2016 conference on machine translation. In *WMT*. Berlin, Germany.

Sébastian Bubeck and Nicolò Cesa-Bianchi. 2012. Regret analysis of stochastic and nonstochastic multiarmed bandit problems. *Foundations and Trends in Machine Learning* 5(1):1–122.

Olivier Chapelle, Eren Masnavoglu, and Romer Rosales. 2014. Simple and scalable response prediction for display advertising. *ACM Trans. on Intelligent Systems and Technology* 5(4).

Christos Dimitrakakis, Guangliang Li, and Nikolaos Tziortziotis. 2014. The reinforcement learning competition 2014. *AI Magazine* 35(3):61–65.

Chris Dyer, Victor Chahuneau, and Noah A. Smith. 2013. A simple, fast, and effective reparameterization of IBM model 2. In *HLT NAACL*. Atlanta, GE.

Chris Dyer, Adam Lopez, Juri Ganitkevitch, Jonathan Weese, Ferhan Ture, Phil Blunsom, Hendra Setiawan, Vladimir Eidelman, and Philip Resnik. 2010. cdec: A decoder, alignment, and learning framework for finite-state and context-free translation models. In *ACL Demo*. Uppsala, Sweden.

Abraham D. Flaxman, Adam Tauman Kalai, and H. Brendan McMahan. 2005. Online convex optimization in the bandit setting: gradient descent without a gradient. In *SODA*. Vancouver, Canada.

Yvette Graham, Timothy Baldwin, Alistair Moffat, and Justin Zobel. 2016. Can machine translation systems be evaluated by the crowd alone? *Natural Language Engineering* 23(1):3–30.

Sébastien Jean, Orhan Firat, Kyunghyun Cho, Roland Memisevic, and Yoshua Bengio. 2015. Montreal neural machine translation systems for WMT'15. In *WMT*. Lisbon, Portugal.

Diederik Kingma and Jimmy Ba. 2014. Adam: A method for stochastic optimization. *eprint arXiv:1412.6980* .

Julia Kreutzer, Artem Sokolov, and Stefan Riezler. 2017. Bandit structured prediction for neural sequence-to-sequence learning. In *ACL*. Vancouver, Canada.

Carolin Lawrence, Artem Sokolov, and Stefan Riezler. 2017. Counterfactual learning from bandit feedback under deterministic logging: A case study in statistical machine translation. In *EMNLP*. Copenhagen, Denmark.

Zhifei Li and Jason Eisner. 2009. First-and second-order expectation semirings with applications to minimum-risk training on translation forests. In *EMNLP*. Singapore.

Jindřich Libovický, Jindřich Helcl, Marek Tlustý, Pavel Pecina, and Ondřej Bojar. 2016. CUNI system for WMT16 automatic post-editing and multimodal translation tasks. In *WMT*. Berlin, Germany.

Chin-Yew Lin and Franz Josef Och. 2004. Automatic evaluation of machine translation quality using longest common subsequence and skip-bigram statistics. In *ACL*. Barcelona, Spain.

Adam Lopez. 2007. Hierarchical phrase-based translation with suffix arrays. In *EMNLP-CoNLL*. Prague, Czech Republic.

Thang Luong, Ilya Sutskever, Quoc Le, Oriol Vinyals, and Wojciech Zaremba. 2015. Addressing the rare word problem in neural machine translation. In *ACL*. Beijing, China.

Razvan Pascanu, Tomas Mikolov, and Yoshua Bengio. 2013. On the difficulty of training recurrent neural networks. In *ICML*. Atlanta, GA.

MarcAurelio Ranzato, Sumit Chopra, Michael Auli, and Wojciech Zaremba. 2016. Sequence level training with recurrent neural networks. In *ICLR*. San Juan, Puerto Rico.

Kenneth Rose. 1998. Deterministic annealing for clustering, compression, classification, regression and related optimization problems. *IEEE* 86(11).

Rico Sennrich, Orhan Firat, Kyunghyun Cho, Alexandra Birch, Barry Haddow, Julian Hitschler, Marcin Junczys-Dowmunt, Samuel Läubli, Antonio Valerio Miceli Barone, Jozef Mokry, and Maria Nadejde. 2017. Nematus: a toolkit for neural machine translation. In *EACL*. Valencia, Spain.

Rico Sennrich, Barry Haddow, and Alexandra Birch. 2016a. Edinburgh neural machine translation systems for WMT 16. In *WMT*. Berlin, Germany.

Rico Sennrich, Barry Haddow, and Alexandra Birch. 2016b. Neural machine translation of rare words with subword units. In *ACL*. Berlin, Germany.

Artem Sokolov, Julia Kreutzer, Christopher Lo, and Stefan Riezler. 2016a. Learning structured predictors from bandit feedback for interactive NLP. In *ACL*. Berlin, Germany.

Artem Sokolov, Julia Kreutzer, Christopher Lo, and Stefan Riezler. 2016b. Stochastic structured prediction under bandit feedback. In *NIPS*. Barcelona, Spain.

Artem Sokolov, Stefan Riezler, and Tanguy Urvoy. 2015. Bandit structured prediction for learning from partial feedback in statistical machine translation. In *MT Summit*. Miami, FL.

Nitish Srivastava, Geoffrey E Hinton, Alex Krizhevsky, Ilya Sutskever, and Ruslan Salakhutdinov. 2014. Dropout: a simple way to prevent neural networks from overfitting. *JMLR* 15(1):1929–1958.

Richard S. Sutton and Andrew G. Barto. 1998. *Reinforcement Learning. An Introduction.* The MIT Press.

Csaba Szepesvári. 2009. *Algorithms for Reinforcement Learning.* Morgan & Claypool.

Ronald J. Williams. 1992. Simple statistical gradient-following algorithms for connectionist reinforcement learning. *Machine Learning* 20:229–256.

Guillaume Wisniewski. 2017. LIMSI submission for WMT'17 shared task on bandit learning. In *WMT*. Copenhagen, Denmark.

Matthew D. Zeiler. 2012. ADADELTA: an adaptive learning rate method. *eprint arXiv:1212.5701* .

Results of the WMT17 Neural MT Training Task

Ondřej Bojar   Jindřich Helcl
Tom Kocmi   Jindřich Libovický   Tomáš Musil

Charles University, Faculty of Mathematics and Physics
Institute of Formal and Applied Linguistics
Malostranské náměstí 25, 118 00 Prague, Czech Republic
<surname>@ufal.mff.cuni.cz

Abstract

This paper presents the results of the WMT17 Neural MT Training Task. The objective of this task is to explore the methods of training a fixed neural architecture, aiming primarily at the best translation quality and, as a secondary goal, shorter training time. Task participants were provided with a complete neural machine translation system, fixed training data and the configuration of the network. The translation was performed in the English-to-Czech direction and the task was divided into two subtasks of different configurations—one scaled to fit on a 4GB and another on an 8GB GPU card. We received 3 submissions for the 4GB variant and 1 submission for the 8GB variant; we provided also our run for each of the sizes and two baselines. We translated the test set with the trained models and evaluated the outputs using several automatic metrics. We also report results of the human evaluation of the submitted systems.

1 Introduction

Neural machine translation (NMT) has recently replaced the "classical statistical machine translation" and became the dominant research paradigm. A large part of research on NMT is focused on architectural improvements of the neural networks or data preprocessing. However, in practice, the results of an NMT system depends not only on the architecture of the network, but also on the training techniques used to obtain the parameters.

The goal of NMT Training Task[1] is to compare

the results of various training techniques applied to a fixed network architecture. We provided task participants with the model specification, training and validation data with a fixed way of data preprocessing. We also listed a few methods as an inspiration for the participants. These methods included (but were not limited to) the following:

Curricula. The basic idea behind this technique (Bengio et al., 2009) is inspired by the fact that humans learn more easily when examples are presented in an ordering from trivial to complex ones. Neural networks could potentially also benefit from such a strategy of increasing task difficulty. This technique includes modifications of the training data in order to converge faster, or more robustly, towards possibly better local optima. Data shuffling, reordering, or back-translation (Sennrich, Haddow, and Birch, 2016a), are all techniques that can have a positive impact on the training.

Optimization algorithms. There are many optimization algorithms that can be employed to training an NMT model, such as Adadelta (Zeiler, 2012) or Adam (Kingma and Ba, 2014). Each method differs in the number of inner trainable parameters and the approach it uses them to perform gradient descent optimization. Better optimization algorithms can improve both the convergence speed and model performance.

Reinforcement learning. A significant improvement in model performance can also be achieved by using variants of the REINFORCE algorithm (Williams, 1992). MIXER (Ranzato et al., 2015), self-critical training (Rennie et al., 2016), or minimum risk training (Shen et al., 2016) all optimize the model directly to maximize the sentence-level BLEU score (Chen and Cherry, 2014) or another sequence-based metric. These

---

[1] http://www.statmt.org/wmt17/
nmt-training-task/

Proceedings of the Conference on Machine Translation (WMT), Volume 2: Shared Task Papers, pages 525–533
Copenhagen, Denmark, September 7–11, 2017. ©2017 Association for Computational Linguistics

methods deal with the exposure bias problem the traditional cross-entropy approach suffers from.

Multi-task training methods improve the model by training it to perform many tasks at once. Eriguchi, Tsuruoka, and Cho (2017) show that teaching the model how to parse helps the translation. A similar result was achieved by Elliott and Kádár (2017) who teach the network to predict the visual features of an image when translating its caption.

Knowledge distillation. The goal of knowledge distillation is to reduce the size of large trained models to smaller models while maintaining the good performance. There are two ways for employing this technique. First, train a large model and then reduce its size by removing unimportant units (Cun, Denker, and Solla, 1990; He et al., 2014; Han, Mao, and Dally, 2015). Second, train a large "teacher" model (or ensemble of models) and train a smaller "student" network on its outputs (Buciluǎ, Caruana, and Niculescu-Mizil, 2006; Hinton, Vinyals, and Dean, 2015; Kim and Rush, 2016). Both of these methods showed promising results, not only in NMT but in the deep learning field in general.

The rest of the paper is organized as follows. Section 2 describes the software and the model architectures. Details on the used dataset are given in Section 3. We summarize the submitted systems in Section 4. Section 5 presents the results of the submissions and Section 6 discusses them. We conclude in Section 7.

2   The NMT System

We used Neural Monkey (Helcl and Libovický, 2017) as the NMT system for the task. Since the software is still in development, the participants were instructed to use version 0.1.0.[2]

Neural Monkey is an open-source sequence-to-sequence learning toolkit implemented in TensorFlow[3] with simple configuration and great extensibility. Besides the basic attentive NMT pipeline (Bahdanau, Cho, and Bengio, 2014), the toolkit implements a growing collection of techniques related to sequence-to-sequence learning in general.

GPU Memory	4 GB	8 GB
embedding size	350	600
encoder state size	(2x) 350	(2x) 600
decoder state size	350	600
max sentence length	50	50
BPE merges	30,000	30,000

Table 1: Configuration for 4 and 8 GB models.

Neural Monkey conceptualizes problems of sequence-to-sequence learning as a generic encoder-decoder pipeline, with many types of individual encoders and decoders. In our task, we used the so-called sentence encoder, which maps the input sequence of tokens to a sequence of distributed representations of the tokens, and runs a bidirectional GRU (Cho et al., 2014) network over these vectors. We used the basic recurrent decoder with conditional GRU (Firat and Cho, 2016) units and attention over the encoder.

The used toolkit implements the whole training functionality, including converting token types to indices to the vocabulary, batching, and automatic validation after a specified number of training steps. It also comes with a simple configuration interface which allows the users to design their models without the requirement of writing any code.

We prepared two configurations of the models, one that fits to a GPU with 8GB of memory and a smaller one that fits into 4GB of memory. For specific details about the configuration, refer to Table 1.

3   Data

The dataset used for the NMT Training Task was a subset of the CzEng 1.6 corpus (Bojar et al., 2016). The experiments were to be executed in a constrained fashion, i.e. the participants were not allowed to augment the training corpus by additional data. However, filtering or automatically modifying the provided corpus as well as adding synthetic data (obtained using only this corpus) was permitted.

Prior to the distribution of the corpus, we removed the parts of CzEng 1.6 containing the largest amounts of noise. Specifically we removed the sections named *eu*, *navajo*, *pdfs*, *tech-docs*, and *tweets*. We also removed all sentence pairs where one of the sentences contained more

---

[2]`https://github.com/ufal/neuralmonkey/releases/tag/0.1.0`

[3]`https://www.tensorflow.org/`

than 40 tokens. The final training dataset contains 48.6 millions sentence pairs. We provided it pre-processed: tokenized and truecased by applying the casing of the lemma identified by Morphodita (Straková, Straka, and Hajič, 2014)[4] to the word form; we did not provide the lemmas to the participants. The corpus was shuffled at the level of sentences, i.e. directly suitable for training with Neural Monkey (that itself does not perform any shuffling unless the whole training data would be loaded to memory). A label file was included with the corpus indicating the original source of each sentence pair, allowing to distinguish e.g. *news* from *subtitles*.

For validation, we used the data from the WMT 2016 news test (*newstest2016*). As the test set, this year's WMT news test (*newstest2017*) was announced and used.

We provided the devset pre-processed in the same way as the training data, i.e. tokenized and truecased by applying the casing of the lemma to the word form.

The test set was not disclosed at all prior to the submission deadline.

The training corpus was analyzed to obtain the byte-pair encoding (BPE; Sennrich, Haddow, and Birch, 2016b) merge file, jointly for English and Czech. The participants were expected to use this BPE merge file in their training. (Neural Monkey, unlike other toolkits, applies BPE splitting internally, to be able to report various scores based on original tokenization and not only based on BPE tokens.) The merge file consisted of 30,000 BPE merges.

4 Training Task Participants

Including secondary and revised versions, we collected six submissions from three external participants: the Air Force Research Laboratory (AFRL), Pavel Denisov, and our students Mostafa Abdou and Vladan Glončák. Additionally, we submitted two of our systems and two baseline runs.

The following paragraphs describe the baseline systems and summarize the techniques used in the submissions for the task.

4.1 Baseline Systems

The baseline systems used the default configurations and datasets as provided to training task participants. The 4GB and 8GB baselines were trained for 60 days, each on a single Nvidia GeForce 1080 GPU.

Among other things, the baseline configuration specifies that tokens appearing only once in the training data are replaced with a special OOV token with probability 0.5.

The Adam optimizer (Kingma and Ba, 2014) with the learning rate of 10^{-4} and mini-batch size of 60 sentences are used. We used L2 regularization with weight of 10^{-8} and gradient clipping with the threshold gradient norm of 1.

The baseline model for 4 GB GPUs achieved the highest validation score after 7.5 epochs of training (47 days). The 8 GB baseline model obtained the highest score after 6.6 epochs (53 days).

4.2 AFRL

The AFRL system is described in another WMT paper by Erdmann, Young, and Gwinnup (2017). They participated in both 4GB and 8GB setups. They used knowledge distillation from an ensemble of models.

The teacher systems were enriched with factors (domain, casing, and subword position information) and trained on a cleaned dataset.

The final (student) system was trained on the news-domain data from the teacher systems dataset, output of ten teacher systems on the same dataset and data from the task training set selected to be most suitable for training a news-domain system.

The original submitted systems trained for about 5 days. We asked the participants to also submit systems trained longer that were not ready in time for the manual evaluation. The AFRL 4GB-REVISED system trained for about 11 days, and the AFRL-8GB-REVISED system trained for about 6 days.

4.3 Pavel Denisov

The system submitted by Pavel Denisov was the default 4GB system trained on 10 million longest sentences in the training dataset. The idea was to make training dataset closer to the validation dataset in the sense of sentence length. The batch size was increased from the default 60 to 90 which is possible when the 4GB model is trained on a larger GPU card. It gave promising validation BLEU score for shorter training duration (approximately 12 hours). The submitted model was trained for 4 days.

---

[4]`http://ufal.mff.cuni.cz/morphodita`

4.4 CUNI-4GB-BATCH-DECR

Our students submitted two systems, as described in the paper by Abdou, Glončák, and Bojar (2017). One of the submissions was however using a different BPE file and could not be evaluated among other systems and the other submission (CUNI-4GB-BATCH-DECR) was unfortunately left out from the manual evaluation. We therefore provide at least its automatic scores.

The submission CUNI-4GB-BATCH-DECR uses essentially the baseline configuration but it decreases the batch size from their initial value of 100 by 20 every 48 hours down to the batch size of 20. The motivation is that smaller batch sizes have been shown to converge to flatter optima, i.e. less prone to overfitting, while larger batches make a better use of the GPU. The gradual reduction could theoretically benefit from both: fast training and avoidance of local optima.

4.5 CUNI-4GB-CURRIC

The 4GB submission we provided (CUNI-4GB-CURRIC) is one instance of curriculum learning, namely learning first on short target (Czech) sentences only and gradually adding also longer sentences to the batches as the training progresses. Importantly, the batches in later stages of the training also have to include the short sentences. As a contrastive experiment, we have *only* sorted sentence pairs by the length and the training spectacularly failed.

After one epoch of curriculum learning, we continued the training on the official corpus, keeping its shuffling fixed, for 7M sentence pairs with a relatively small batch size of 20.

More details and further experiments on curriculum learning within one epoch are available in Kocmi and Bojar (2017), who document that curriculum learning can be somewhat helpful according to automatic scoring.

4.6 CUNI-8GB-DOMAIN

The CUNI-8GB-DOMAIN submission is a run forked from the BASELINE-8GB after 3.38 epochs (30.8 days) of training and trained further for 1.5 epochs (9.1 days) on a domain-adapted corpus.

The domain-adapted corpus contains 32.8M parallel lines in total and it was created by concatenating and repeating different types of extracts from the provided training corpus as listed in Table 2.

# Sents	Copies	Corpus
0.25M	4×	News section of training data
2.43M	1×	Top 5% selected by 2-grams
2.43M	1×	Top 5% selected by 4-grams
0.25M	1×	News section again
4.86M	1×	Top 10% selected by 2-grams
2.43M	1×	Top 5% selected by 4-grams
9.72M	1×	Top 20% selected by 2-grams
9.73M	1×	Top 20% selected by 4-grams

Table 2: Composition of the domain-adaptation corpus used in CUNI-8GB-DOMAIN.

Specifically, we used the annotation of the originating domain to extract all news-like sentences. This subset was rather small, only 250k sentence pairs. We therefore used the bilingual cross-entropy difference selection (Axelrod, He, and Gao, 2011) implemented in XenC (Rousseau, 2013) to select 5, 10 and 20% of the original corpus similar in terms of 2-grams and 4-grams to the news section. Presumably, the small news section made it also to these extracts and smaller extracts were probably included in larger extracts, so considering our corpus composition, the same sentences could be reused in the training corpus up to 11 times.

5 Results

The configuration file for translation was provided with the NMT system, to evaluate the model on the devset. The same configuration was used to translate the test set, with the model variables provided by the participants. Except for the chrF3 and METEOR metrics, we detokenized the output of the NMT system using the standard Moses detokenizer[5] and capitalized the first character of the sentence.

5.1 Automatic Scoring of Training Task Systems

For the results of the automatic evaluation, see Table 3.

Since the training time is an important factor in NMT, we suggested that task participants further train their systems and submit new models for automatic scoring. Two more submissions are thus

---

[5] http://github.com/moses-smt/
mosesdecoder/blob/master/scripts/
tokenizer/detokenizer.perl

	System	BLEU-dev	BLEU-test	chrF3	METEOR	BEER 2.0	CharacTER
8GB	CUNI-8GB-DOMAIN	**19.18**	**15.2**	**42.59**	**21.60**	**0.487**	**0.683**
	AFRL-8GB-REVISED	18.30	14.8	41.54	20.71	0.478	0.701
	AFRL-8GB	18.15	14.7	41.53	20.95	0.477	0.698
	BASELINE-8GB	17.47	13.8	40.75	20.44	0.472	0.704
4GB	AFRL-4GB-REVISED	**18.37**	**15.2**	**41.90**	**20.92**	**0.480**	**0.693**
	AFRL-4GB	17.58	14.2	40.97	20.64	0.474	0.702
	BASELINE-4GB	16.74	13.7	40.61	20.23	0.472	0.704
	CUNI-4GB-CURRIC	16.24	13.1	39.54	19.93	0.464	0.716
	DENISOV-4GB	15.98	12.6	40.22	20.06	0.452	0.713
	CUNI-4GB-BATCH-DECR	12.98	10.5	36.29	17.85	0.441	0.751

Table 3: Automatic scores for submissions to the WMT17 NMT Training Task.

included in the table, AFRL-4GB-REVISED and AFRL-8GB-REVISED.

BLEU scores for the development set are computed internally by Neural Monkey. For the test set, BLEU was measured on the EuroMatrix evaluation server[6] (we use the BLEU-cased variant of BLEU) as well as BEER 2.0 (Stanojević and Sima'an, 2014) and CharacTER (Wang et al., 2016) scores. We also measured chrF3 (Popović, 2015) and METEOR (Denkowski and Lavie, 2014) scores, both with the same tokenization as in the training data and our NMT system output.

5.2 Learning Curves

We asked participants to provide us with the detailed "events" file as collected by TensorFlow which logs the performance on the common validation set at a fine resolution.

For some techniques, the learning curves cannot be provided, but Figure 1 is a valuable complement to the automatic scoring above. The scores were measured internally by Neural Monkey on the devset after every 2000 batches.

Specifically, we see that the 4GB and 8GB baselines are clearly separated by about the same margin throughout the training and that CUNI-4GB-BATCH-DECR loses a little from the performance later in the training.

Interestingly, DENISOV-4GB seems to very closely follow the performance of BASELINE-8GB, i.e. a much larger setup, but it was unfortunately stopped too early so the obtained score is ultimately worse than both of the baselines. It should be however noted that the learning curves

are based on the number of training *sentences* processed, not the number of words. The longer sentences used by DENISOV-4GB have provided the model with more material to learn from, so the score could be artificially inflated.

5.3 Manual Evaluation of Training Task Systems

As announced, the official evaluation of the NMT training task is the manual scoring of the systems submitted at the deadline according to the submission instructions.

We designed training task so that it was in fact subsumed by the WMT17 News Translation Task (Bojar et al., 2017): the training data was a subset of the training data provided for English-to-Czech news task participants and the testset we used the official newstest2017 of WMT. All training task submissions can be therefore seen as regular news task submissions, with the additional constraint of a fixed MT system and further constrained training data.

With the help of WMT17 news task organizers, we included the outputs of training task submissions among the MT outputs of other MT systems for the common manual scoring.[7] Please see Bojar et al. (2017) for details on the judgment technique (direct assessment, DA) and its interpretation.

Table 4 is an extract of the official WMT17 news task results, i.e. Table 7 in Bojar et al. (2017), renaming the systems to match the naming in this paper. The horizontal lines between the systems indicate clusters according to Wilcoxon

[6]http://matrix.statmt.org

[7]Unfortunately, the submission CUNI-4GB-BATCH-DECR, despite being submitted in time, slipped through and was not included in time in the manual evaluation.

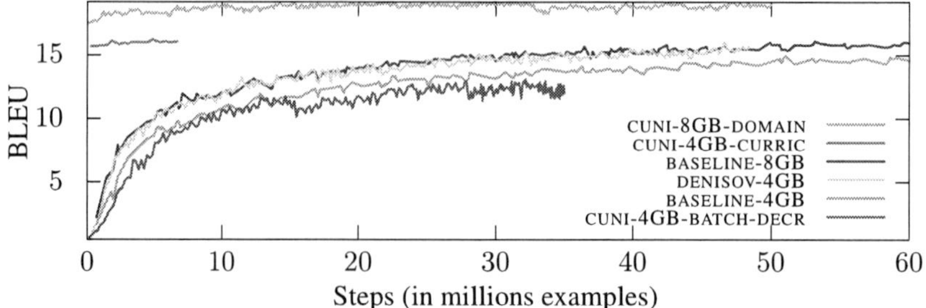

Figure 1: Learning curves for training task submissions (where available). The 8GB and 4GB baseline runs actually ran much longer, to 300M and 380M training steps, resp. CUNI-4GB-CURRIC and CUNI-8GB-DOMAIN curves are only continuations and therefore start higher.

#	Ave %	Ave z	System
~~1~~	~~42.2~~	~~-0.141~~	~~BASELINE-4GB~~
2	44.9	-0.236	CUNI-8GB-DOMAIN
3	42.2	-0.315	AFRL-4GB
	40.7	-0.373	BASELINE-8GB
	40.5	-0.376	AFRL-8GB
4	36.5	-0.486	CUNI-4GB-CURRIC
	36.6	-0.493	DENISOV-4GB

Table 4: Manual evaluation of the training task submissions. For the crossed-out BASELINE-4GB see the text.

rank-sum test at p-level $p \leq 0.05$, the column "#" is the rank of the cluster. The "Ave %" is the average DA score over all evaluated translations by the given system and it reflects the average quality as assessed by human judges against the reference translation on an absolute scale between 0 and 100. The "Ave z" first standardizes each annotator's scores and then averages them. Please see the original paper for a detailed discussion.

The manual evaluation was affected by an unfortunate omission: namely, the baseline-4GB outputs were not included in the standard batches, among other outputs, but they were scored only later, in annotation batches of their own. While the direct assessment annotation technique *in theory* evaluates translation quality on an absolute scale and such evaluations could be in principle comparable among different annotation runs, we see that this does not really work in practice. It is rather unlikely that the 4GB baseline would be significantly better than the 8GB baseline, also taking into account the big difference in BLEU. We

thus asked WMT17 news task organizers to remove baseline-4GB from their paper and we do not consider this result in our discussion below.

6 Discussion

Despite the fact that baseline-4GB was not correctly manually evaluated, the manual evaluation allows us to draw some reliable conclusions.

CUNI-8GB-DOMAIN significantly surpassed BASELINE-8GB, confirming that domain adaptation can be very helpful for NMT even with relatively simple adaptation techniques.

AFRL-8GB performed comparably to BASELINE-8GB, and based on the description of the submission, AFRL-8GB was trained for 5 days as 10 models in parallel, which could roughly correspond to the training time of the baseline. While we cannot compare AFRL-4GB and BASELINE-4GB, which would be a very interesting contrastive pair, we know that AFRL-4GB performed equally well (better, but not significantly) as AFRL-8GB. That alone is a good achievement, in line with automatic scoring.

We already knew from automatic scores that the curriculum technique tested by CUNI-4GB-CURRIC is not very effective. We cannot really compare it to BASELINE-4GB but we are not surprised by the relatively low score.

The submission DENISOV-4GB was very interesting, since it achieved the score of the 8GB baseline with just a 4GB model throughout its training, see Figure 1. We hypothesize the reason for the seemingly faster training was that while being presented longer sentences, the system is actually presented more words during training. Nevertheless, the experiment shows that the system is able to generalize to short sentences from long sentences which does not hold vice versa. Concerning the manual evaluation of DENISOV-4GB, we know that it was trained only for 4 days, so the final quality it reached was not good according to automatic scores. Manual scores in Table 4 confirm this result but it would be very interesting to see what quality would be reached if the training ran much longer.

The point of NMT training task was not to find a single winner but rather to see which techniques are more promising and important for the final performance as well as throughout the training. The short answer is domain adaptation because both CUNI-8GB-DOMAIN and AFRL used it and scored high. Further conclusions are hard to draw because the underlying data and training times differed too much.

For future similar tasks, we recommend to provide already domain-adapted training data and to attempt to keep track of further details about the training, e.g. the number of tokens processed and floating point operations needed.

7   Conclusion

We presented the results of WMT17 Neural MT Training Task, a shared task in optimizing parameters of a given NMT system when translating from English to Czech.

The best results were obtained by a standard domain adaptation technique applied before the training. Ensembling and knowledge distillation is also valuable but current results are not sufficient to assess whether the effort put into the development pays off.

Acknowledgments

This study was supported in parts by the grants SVV 260 453, GAUK 8502/2016, H2020-ICT-2014-1-645442 (QT21) and Charles University Research Programme "Progres" Q18 – Social Sciences: From Multidisciplinarity to Interdisciplinarity.

This work has been using language resources and tools stored and distributed by the LINDAT/CLARIN project of the Ministry of Education, Youth and Sports of the Czech Republic (project LM2015071).

References

Abdou, Mostafa, Vladan Glončák, and Ondřej Bojar. 2017. Variable mini-batch sizing and pre-trained embeddings. In *Proceedings of the Second Conference on Machine Translation, Volume 2: Shared Tasks Papers*, Copenhagen, Denmark. Association for Computational Linguistics.

Axelrod, Amittai, Xiaodong He, and Jianfeng Gao. 2011. Domain adaptation via pseudo in-domain data selection. In *Proceedings of the Conference on Empirical Methods in Natural Language Processing*, EMNLP '11, pages 355–362, Stroudsburg, PA, USA. Association for Computational Linguistics.

Bahdanau, Dzmitry, Kyunghyun Cho, and Yoshua Bengio. 2014. Neural Machine Translation by Jointly Learning to Align and Translate. *CoRR*, abs/1409.0473.

Bengio, Yoshua, Jérôme Louradour, Ronan Collobert, and Jason Weston. 2009. Curriculum learning. In *Proceedings of the 26th Annual International Conference on Machine Learning*, ICML '09, pages 41–48, New York, NY, USA. ACM.

Bojar, Ondřej, Ondřej Dušek, Tom Kocmi, Jindřich Libovický, Michal Novák, Martin Popel, Roman Sudarikov, and Dušan Variš. 2016. Czeng 1.6: enlarged czech-english parallel corpus with processing tools dockered. In *International Conference on Text, Speech, and Dialogue*, pages 231–238. Springer.

Bojar, Ondřej, Rajen Chatterjee, Christian Federmann, Yvette Graham, Barry Haddow, Matthias Huck, Philipp Koehn, Varvara Logacheva, Christof Monz, Matteo Negri, Matt Post, Raphael Rubino, Lucia Specia, and Marco Turchi. 2017. Findings of the 2017 conference on machine translation (wmt17). In *Proceedings of the Second Conference on Machine Translation, Volume 2: Shared Tasks Papers*, Copenhagen, Denmark. Association for Computational Linguistics.

Buciluǎ, Cristian, Rich Caruana, and Alexandru Niculescu-Mizil. 2006. Model compression. In *Proceedings of the 12th ACM SIGKDD international conference on Knowledge discovery and data mining*, pages 535–541. ACM.

Chen, Boxing and Colin Cherry. 2014. A systematic comparison of smoothing techniques for sentence-level bleu. In *Proceedings of the Ninth Workshop on Statistical Machine Translation*, pages 362–367, Baltimore, Maryland, USA. Association for Computational Linguistics.

Cho, Kyunghyun, Bart van Merrienboer, Çaglar Gülçehre, Fethi Bougares, Holger Schwenk, and Yoshua Bengio. 2014. Learning phrase representations using RNN encoder-decoder for statistical machine translation. *CoRR*, abs/1406.1078.

Cun, Yann Le, John S. Denker, and Sara A. Solla. 1990. Optimal brain damage. In *Advances in Neural Information Processing Systems*, pages 598–605. Morgan Kaufmann.

Denkowski, Michael and Alon Lavie. 2014. Meteor universal: Language specific translation evaluation for any target language. In *Proceedings of the EACL 2014 Workshop on Statistical Machine Translation*.

Elliott, Desmond and Ákos Kádár. 2017. Imagination improves multimodal translation. *CoRR*, abs/1705.04350.

Erdmann, Grant, Katherine Young, and Jeremy Gwinnup. 2017. The AFRL WMT17 neural machine translation training task submission. In *Proceedings of the Second Conference on Machine Translation (WMT17)*, Copenhagen, Denmark.

Eriguchi, Akiko, Yoshimasa Tsuruoka, and Kyunghyun Cho. 2017. Learning to parse and translate improves neural machine translation. *CoRR*, abs/1702.03525.

Firat, Orhan and Kyunghyun Cho. 2016. Conditional gated recurrent unit with attention mechanism. https://github.com/nyu-dl/dl4mt-tutorial/blob/master/docs/cgru.pdf. Published online, version adbaeea.

Han, Song, Huizi Mao, and William J Dally. 2015. Deep compression: Compressing deep neural networks with pruning, trained quantization and huffman coding. In *International Conference on Learning Representations (ICLR'16 best paper award)*.

He, Tianxing, Yuchen Fan, Yanmin Qian, Tian Tan, and Kai Yu. 2014. Reshaping deep neural network for fast decoding by node-pruning. In *Acoustics, Speech and Signal Processing (ICASSP), 2014 IEEE International Conference on*, pages 245–249. IEEE.

Helcl, Jindřich and Jindřich Libovický. 2017. Neural Monkey: An open-source tool for sequence learning. *The Prague Bulletin of Mathematical Linguistics*, (107):5–17.

Hinton, Geoffrey E., Oriol Vinyals, and Jeffrey Dean. 2015. Distilling the knowledge in a neural network. *CoRR*, abs/1503.02531.

Kim, Yoon and Alexander M. Rush. 2016. Sequence-level knowledge distillation. *CoRR*, abs/1606.07947.

Kingma, Diederik P. and Jimmy Ba. 2014. Adam: A method for stochastic optimization. *CoRR*, abs/1412.6980.

Kocmi, Tom and Ondřej Bojar. 2017. Curriculum learning and minibatch bucketing in neural machine translation. In *Recent Advances in Natural Language Processing 2017*.

Popović, Maja. 2015. chrf: character n-gram f-score for automatic mt evaluation. In *Proceedings of the Tenth Workshop on Statistical Machine Translation*, pages 392–395, Lisbon, Portugal. Association for Computational Linguistics.

Ranzato, Marc'Aurelio, Sumit Chopra, Michael Auli, and Wojciech Zaremba. 2015. Sequence level training with recurrent neural networks. *CoRR*, abs/1511.06732.

Rennie, Steven J., Etienne Marcheret, Youssef Mroueh, Jarret Ross, and Vaibhava Goel. 2016. Self-critical sequence training for image captioning. *CoRR*, abs/1612.00563.

Rousseau, Anthony. 2013. Xenc: An open-source tool for data selection in natural language processing. *The Prague Bulletin of Mathematical Linguistics*, 100:73–82.

Sennrich, Rico, Barry Haddow, and Alexandra Birch. 2016a. Improving neural machine translation models with monolingual data. In *Proceedings of the 54th Annual Meeting of the Association for Computational Linguistics (Volume 1: Long Papers)*, pages 86–96, Berlin, Germany. Association for Computational Linguistics.

Sennrich, Rico, Barry Haddow, and Alexandra Birch. 2016b. Neural machine translation of rare words with subword units. In *Proceedings of the 54th Annual Meeting of the Association for Computational Linguistics (Volume 1: Long Papers)*, pages 1715–1725, Berlin, Germany. Association for Computational Linguistics.

Shen, Shiqi, Yong Cheng, Zhongjun He, Wei He, Hua Wu, Maosong Sun, and Yang Liu. 2016. Minimum risk training for neural machine translation. In *Proceedings of the 54th Annual Meeting of the Association for Computational Linguistics (Volume 1: Long Papers)*, pages 1683–1692, Berlin, Germany. Association for Computational Linguistics.

Stanojević, Miloš and Khalil Sima'an. 2014. Fitting sentence level translation evaluation with many dense features. In *Proceedings of the 2014 Conference on Empirical Methods in Natural Language Processing (EMNLP)*, pages 202–206, Doha, Qatar. Association for Computational Linguistics.

Straková, Jana, Milan Straka, and Jan Hajič. 2014. Open-Source Tools for Morphology, Lemmatization, POS Tagging and Named Entity Recognition. In *Proceedings of 52nd Annual Meeting of the Association for Computational Linguistics: System Demonstrations*, pages 13–18, Baltimore, Maryland. Association for Computational Linguistics.

Wang, Weiyue, Jan-Thorsten Peter, Hendrik Rosendahl, and Hermann Ney. 2016. Character: Translation edit rate on character level. In *WMT*, pages 505–510.

Williams, Ronald J. 1992. Simple statistical gradient-following algorithms for connectionist reinforcement learning. *Machine learning*, 8(3-4):229–256.

Zeiler, Matthew D. 2012. Adadelta: an adaptive learning rate method. *CoRR*, abs/1212.5701.

Sentence-level quality estimation by predicting HTER as a multi-component metric

Eleftherios Avramidis

German Research Center for Artificial Intelligence (DFKI)
Language Technology Lab, Berlin, Germany
eleftherios.avramidis@dfki.de

Abstract

This submission investigates alternative machine learning models for predicting the HTER score on the sentence level. Instead of directly predicting the HTER score, we suggest a model that jointly predicts the amount of the 4 distinct post-editing operations, which are then used to calculate the HTER score. This also gives the possibility to correct invalid (e.g. negative) predicted values prior to the calculation of the HTER score. Without any feature exploration, a multi-layer perceptron with 4 outputs yields small but significant improvements over the baseline.

1 Introduction

Quality Estimation (QE) is the evaluation method that aims at employing machine learning in order to predict some measure of quality given a Machine Translation (MT) output (Blatz et al., 2004). A commonly-used subtask of QE refers to the learning of automatic metrics. These metrics produce a continuous score based on the comparison between the MT output and a reference translation. When the reference is a minimal post-edition of the MT output, the quality score produced is intuitively more objective and robust as compared to other QE subtasks, where the quality score is assigned directly by the annotators. In that case, the score is a direct reflection of the changes that need to take place in order to fix the translation. HTER (Snover et al., 2009) is the most commonly used metric as it directly represents the least required post-editing effort.

In order to predict the results of an automatic metric, QE approaches use machine learning to predict a model that associates a feature vector with the single quality score. In this case the statistical model treats the automatic metric as a black box, in the sense that no particular knowledge about the exact calculation of the quality score is explicitly included in the model.

In this submission we aim to partially break this black-box. We explore the idea of creating a QE model that does not directly predict the single HTER score, but it jointly predicts the 4 components of the metric, which are later used for computing the single score. This way, the structure of the model can be aware of the distinct factors that comprise the final quality score and also potentially learn the interactions between them. Hence, the focus of this submission will remain on machine learning and there will not be exploration in terms of features. In Section 2 we briefly introduce previous work, in Section 3 we provide details about the method, whereas the experiment results are given in Section 4. In Section 5 we describe the models submitted at the shared-task and we explain why they differ from our best models. Finally, in Section 6 we present the conclusions and some ideas for future work.

2 Previous work

The prediction of HTER first appeared as a means to estimate post-editing effort (Specia and Farzindar, 2010). Bypassing the direct calculation of HTER was shown by Kozlova et al. (2016), who had positive results by predicting BLEU instead of HTER. Predicting the HTER score with regards to post-editing operations, such as re-ordering and lexical choices, has been done by adding the relevant features in the input (Sagemo and Stymne, 2016), whereas Tezcan et al. (2016) use the word-level quality estimation labels as a feature for predicting the sentence-level score. To the best of our knowledge, all previous work used a model to directly predict a single HTER score, in con-

Proceedings of the Conference on Machine Translation (WMT), Volume 2: Shared Task Papers, pages 534–539
Copenhagen, Denmark, September 7–11, 2017. ©2017 Association for Computational Linguistics

trast to Avramidis (2014), which trained one separate model for every HTER component and used
the 4 individual predictions to calculate the final
score, albeit with no positive results. In our work
we extend that, by employing a more elegant machine learning approach that predicts four separate
labels for the HTER components but through a single model.

3 Methods

3.1 Machine Learning

The calculation of HTER is based on the count of
4 components, namely the number of insertions,
deletions, substitutions and shifts (e.g. reordering)
that are required for minimally post-editing a MT
output towards the correct translation. The final
HTER score is the total number of editing operations divided by the number of reference words.

$$\text{HTER} = \frac{\#\text{insertions} + \#\text{dels} + \#\text{subs} + \#\text{shifts}}{\#\text{reference words}} \tag{1}$$

We are here testing 4 different approaches to the
prediction of HTER:

1. **Baseline with single score**: the baseline system of the WMT17 shared task using SVM
   regression (Basak et al., 2007) to directly predict the HTER score.

2. **Combination of 4 SVM models** (4×SVM):
   this is following Avramidis (2014) so that it
   produces 4 separate SVM regression models
   that predict the amount of post-editing operations (insertions, deletions, substitutions and
   shifts respectively). Then, HTER is computed based on the 4 separate outputs (Equation 1).

3. **Single-output perceptron** (MLP): a multi-
   layer perceptron is trained to predict the
   HTER score

4. **Multi-output perceptron** (MLP4): a multi-
   layer perceptron is trained given the feature
   set in the input and the counts of the 4 post-
   editing operations as the output labels. Similar to 4×SVM, the separate predictions are
   used to compute the HTER score (Equation 1). The perceptron is depicted in Figure 1.

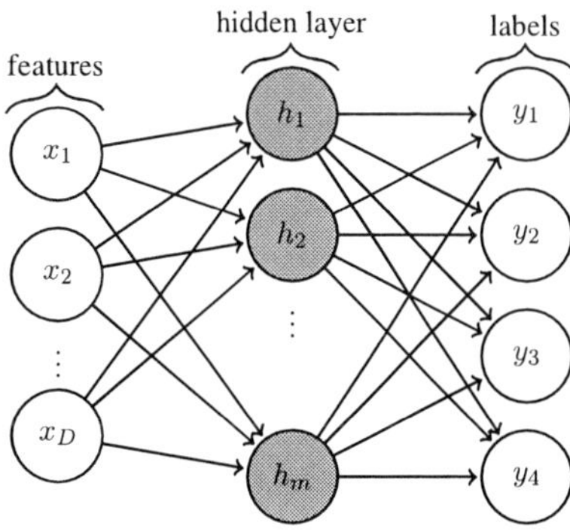

Figure 1: Network graph for the multi-layer perceptron which given the features $x_{1...D}$ can jointly
predict the amount of the post-editing operations
$y_{1...4}$

In the fist two models, SVM follows the baseline set-up of the WMT17 shared task, using SVM
regression with an RBF kernel. The hyperparameters of all three models, including the number of
the hidden units of the perceptron, are tuned via
grid search on cross-validation with 5 folds over
the training data.

3.2 Normalization of predictions

Additionally to the separate models, we are testing here some additional normalization on the predicted number of post-editing operations, before it
is used to calculate HTER:

i. **Integer rounding**: although the model was
   trained using only integers as labels, the regression model resulted into predictions including decimals. By assuming that only
   an integer amount of post-editing operations
   should be valid, we round up the post-editing
   operations to the closest integer.

ii. **Trim negative and big numbers**: MLP4
    may also predict numbers outside the valid
    integer range, e.g. providing negative num-
    bers or numbers higher than the amount of
    actual words in the sentence, particularly
    when features have not been normalized.
    Here, we trim the invalid values to the nearest
    integer within the valid range.

3.3 Optimization measure

Preliminary experiments indicated that the performance of the MLP4 may vary depending on the
optimization metric used for tuning the hyperparameters in a grid search with cross-validation. We

tested the optimization scoring the folds with R^2 and Pearson's rho (which is the official metric of the shared task) in three variations:

a) the R^2 of the predicted amount of post-editing operations against the golden amount of the post-editing operations

b) the product of 4 rhos (rho edits); each rho evaluating the predictions for one type of post-editing operation (no normalization of predictions) against the golden amount of edits for the same post-editing operation

c) the rho over the final computed HTER (rho HTER) against the golden HTER without any prior normalization of predictions

4 Experiments

Here we present the experiments of testing the various machine learning approaches on the development set. After the decisions were taken based on the development set, the models were also applied on the test-sets and the respective results are also given. The performance of the models is measured with Pearson's rho, as this is the basic metric of the WMT17 Shared Task. A test on statistical significance for comparisons is performed with bootstrap re-sampling over 1000 samples. The 4 types of post-editing operations were re-computed with TERCOM on the exact way that the workshop organizers computed the HTER scores.[1]

Similar to the baseline, features values are standardized by removing the mean and scaled to unit variance. Since the experiment is focusing on machine learning, for German-English only the baseline features are used. For English-German, we additionally performed preliminary experiments with the feature-set from Avramidis (2017) including 94 features that improved QE performance for translating into German, generated with the software Qualitative (Avramidis, 2016). The addition of these features did not result into any improvements, so we are not reporting their results during the development phase (see Section 5 for more details). The code for training quality estimation models was based on the software Quest++ (Specia et al., 2015) and Scikit-learn (Pedregosa et al., 2011) ver. 1.18.

---

[1]TERCOM ver. 0.7.25 was downloaded from `http://www.cs.umd.edu/~snover/tercom`. The scripts used for running the experiments can be found at `https://github.com/lefterav/MLP4`.

The development results concerning the presented methods are given below in this section. The model approaches are tested for both language directions, whereas the experiments on the normalization of the predictions and ML optimization are run only for German-English and these observations are applied to the models for English-German.

4.1 Best ML method

The results concerning the choice of the ML method applied on German-English are shown in Table 1.

method	dev	test
SVM	0.400	0.441
4×SVM	0.392	0.409
MLP	0.447*	0.447
MLP4	0.476*	0.475**

Table 1: Pearson rho correlation against golden labels concerning the 4 different approaches for predicting HTER for German-English. (*) indicates significant improvement ($\alpha = 0.05$) over the SVM baseline (**) significant improvement over all models

The approach of MLP4 achieves a small but significant improvement over the baseline and the 4×SVM on the development set. On the development set both MLP and MLP4 beat significantly the baseline, but MLP4 is not significantly better than MLP. Nevertheless, when applied to the test-set, the improvement achieved with MLP4 is significant as compared to all other ML methods.

method	dev	test2017	test2016
SVM	0.414	0.402	0.407
4×SVM	0.049	-0.071	0.044
MLP	0.343	0.335	0.327
MLP4	0.429*	0.412	0.412

Table 2: Performance of the 4 different approaches for predicting HTER for English-German (*) indicates a significant improvement ($\alpha = 0.1$) over the baseline

The same approaches show moderate improvements when applied to English-German with the baseline feature set (Table 2). MLP4 achieves higher correlation score than the baseline, but the difference is small and it is significant only for the development set. When compared to the other two methods, though, MLP4 achieves a significant improvement. In contrast to the direction German-English, in English-German the MLP with one output performs worse than the baseline. $4\times$SVM fails to predict HTER as its predictions achieve zero correlation. Since the individual models failed to predict the post-editing operations separately, this may be an indication that among the 4 post-editing operations in English-German there are dependencies which are stronger than the ones in German-English.

4.2 Normalization of predicted post-editing operations

The effect of the normalization of the predicted post-editing operations of MLP4, prior to the calculation of the final HTER score, is shown in Table 3.

	dev	test
original labels	0.473	0.471
trim	0.476	0.475
round	0.456	0.469
round & trim	0.456	0.467

Table 3: Performance improvements by introducing rounding and cut-off for the predicted post-editing operations (German-English)

The experiment indicates some small improvement when we trim the invalid predicted values, so we use this for all other calculations. Preliminary experiments indicated more significant improvements when the feature values have not been standardized and re-scaled prior to the training.

4.3 ML optimization

The effect of using different methods for hyperparameter optimization is show in Table 4.

	dev	test
R^2	0.440	0.454
rho HTER	0.431	0.457
rho edits	0.476	0.475

Table 4: Experimentation with different optimization measures for defining the perceptron hyperparameters (German-English model)

The product of the 4 rhos, calculated over the 4 types of post-editing operations (rho edits) has slightly better performance than the other scoring methods, nevertheless the difference is not statistically significant. Using these findings just as an indication, we perform all experiments by optimizing the hyperparameters with *rho edits*.

The optimized hyperparameters for the SVM models are shown in Table 5, whereas the ones for the MLP models are shown in Table 6. All SVMs have an RBF kernel and all MLPs are optimized with *adam* as a solver. It is noteworthy that for German-English a network topology with multiple hidden layers performed better, which is an indication that the mapping between features and labels in this language pair is much more complex than the one for German-English.

langpair	model	ϵ	C	γ
de-en	SVM	0.1	10	0.001
	$4\times$SVM (ins)	0.2	10	0.01
	$4\times$SVM (del)	0.2	10	0.01
	$4\times$SVM (shifts)	0.2	10	0.01
	$4\times$SVM (subst)	0.1	10	0.01
en-de	SVM	0.1	1	0.01
	$4\times$SVM (ins)	0.2	1	0.001
	$4\times$SVM (del)	0.1	1	0.001
	$4\times$SVM (shifts)	0.1	1	0.001
	$4\times$SVM (subst)	0.2	1	0.001

Table 5: Hyperparameters used after the optimization of the SVM models

langp.	model	act.	α	tol.	hidden units
de-en	MLP	relu	0.10	10^{-9}	1: 100
	MLP4	relu	0.10	10^{-3}	1: 300
en-de	MLP	tanh	0.01	10^{-3}	3: 150, 75, 6
	MLP4	tanh	0.10	10^{-3}	2: 300, 150

Table 6: Hyperparameters and network topology after the optimization of the MLP models

5 Submission and post-mortem analysis

Whereas previous sections described a full development phase in order to support the idea of the multi-output MLP, this section is focusing on our exact submission for the Quality Estimation Task of WMT17. Unfortunately, a development issue prior to the submission prevented our experiments from standardizing the feature values and scaling them to unit variance. Since the performance of

SVM suffers from non-scaled feature values, this led our development phase to proceed by contrasting with a much lower baseline than the one finally provided by the workshop organizers. Non-scaled features and other settings affected also the performance of MLP models, and therefore the scores on our final submissions are significantly lower than the official baseline. The issue became apparent only after the submission, so we then re-computed the all models with standardized and scaled feature values. The results presented in Section 4 are based on these corrected models.

The submitted models used both rounding and trimming of predicted integers (Section 3.2). The MLPs were optimized with an $\alpha = 0.01$, *tanh* as an activation function, and *adam* as a solver. The German-English model got optimal with 300 hidden units. The English-German was trained using the additional 52 features from Avramidis (2017) which gave good development results only with 3,000 hidden units, which is an indication of overfitting.

method	dev	test
baseline (ours)	0.32	0.34
MLP4 (submitted)	0.40	0.40
baseline (official)	0.40	0.44
MLP4 (corrected)	0.48	0.48

Table 7: Scores for the submitted models and for their corrected versions after the submission (German-English)

method	dev	test2017	test2016
baseline (ours)	0.19	0.20	0.12
MLP4 (submitted)	0.40	0.11	0.13
baseline (official)	0.41	0.40	0.40
MLP4 (corrected)	0.43	0.41	0.41

Table 8: Scores for the submitted models and for their corrected versions after the submission English-German

A comparison of the models developed before the submission and the corrected ones are shown in Tables 7 and 8. The submitted model for German-English was expected to be significantly better than the baseline, whereas the one for English-German with the additional features had strong indications of overfitting and performed indeed poorly at the final test-sets.

The corrected models perform better after scaling is added and the rounding of integers is disabled. The corrected model for English-German converges without overfitting after removing the additional features and adding one more hidden layer. These models, if submitted to the shared task, despite comparing with the baseline, they would still score lower than almost all the others submitted methods. Though, we need to note that this should still be satisfactory, as we did not perform any feature engineering, aiming at confirming our hypothesis for using multi-output models.

6 Conclusion and further work

In this submission we investigated the idea of using a multi-layer perceptron in order to jointly predict the 4 distinct post-editing operations, which are then used for calculating the HTER score. The experiments show some small but significant improvements on both the development set and the test-set for German-English, but the same approach showed improvement only on the development set when applied English-German.

Despite not having conclusive results yet, we think that the idea is promising and that further experiments could have positive impact. Concerning the current development, several issues need to be further investigated, such as possible ways to avoid the lack of robustness of the perceptron. Since this work did not focus at feature engineering, further work could profit from introducing features highly relevant to the specific types of post-editing operations, or even upscaling observations from word-level and phrase-level QE. On the machine-learning level, additional hidden layers and more work on the number of hidden units might be of benefit. Finally, evaluation specific to the types of the predicted post-editing operations could provide hints for further improvement.

Acknowledgments

This work has received funding from the European Union's Horizon 2020 research and innovation program under grant agreement N° 645452 (QT21).

References

Eleftherios Avramidis. 2014. Efforts on Machine Learning over Human-mediated Translation Edit Rate. In *Proceedings of the Ninth Workshop on Statistical Machine Translation*. Association for Computational Linguistics, Baltimore, Maryland, USA, pages 302–306. http://www.aclweb.org/anthology/W/W14/W14-3337.

Eleftherios Avramidis. 2016. Qualitative: Python Tool for MT Quality Estimation Supporting Server Mode and Hybrid MT. *The Prague Bulletin of Mathematical Linguistics (PBML)* 106:147–158. https://ufal.mff.cuni.cz/pbml/106/art-avramidis.pdf.

Eleftherios Avramidis. 2017. Comparative Quality Estimation for Machine Translation. Observations on machine learning and features. *Proceedings of the 20th Annual Conference of the European Association for Machine Translation, The Prague Bulletin of Mathematical Linguistics* (108):307–318. https://doi.org/10.1515/pralin-2017-0029.

Debasish Basak, Srimanta Pal, and Dipak Chandra Patranabis. 2007. Support vector regression. *Neural Information Processing-Letters and Reviews* 11(10):203–224.

John Blatz, Erin Fitzgerald, George Foster, Simona Gandrabur, Cyril Goutte, Alex Kulesza, Alberto Sanchis, and Nicola Ueffing. 2004. Confidence estimation for machine translation. In *Proceedings of the 20th international conference on Computational Linguistics (COLING 04)*. Association for Computational Linguistics, Stroudsburg, PA, USA. https://doi.org/10.3115/1220355.1220401.

Anna Kozlova, Mariya Shmatova, and Anton Frolov. 2016. YSDA Participation in the WMT'16 Quality Estimation Shared Task. In *Proceedings of the First Conference on Machine Translation*. Association for Computational Linguistics, Berlin, Germany, pages 793–799. http://www.aclweb.org/anthology/W/W16/W16-2385.

Fabian Pedregosa, Gael Varoquaux, Alexandre Gramfort, Vincent Michel, Bertrand Thirion, Olivier Grisel, Mathieu Blondel, Peter Prettenhofer, Ron Weiss, Vincent Dubourg, Jake Vanderplas, Alexandre Passos, David Cournapeau, Matthieu Brucher, Matthieu Perrot, and Edouard Duchesnay. 2011. Scikit-learn: Machine Learning in Python. *Journal of Machine Learning Research* 12:2825–2830.

Oscar Sagemo and Sara Stymne. 2016. The UU Submission to the Machine Translation Quality Estimation Task. In *Proceedings of the First Conference on Machine Translation*. Association for Computational Linguistics, Berlin, Germany, pages 825–830. http://www.aclweb.org/anthology/W/W16/W16-2390.

Matthew Snover, Nitin Madnani, Bonnie J Dorr, and Richard Schwartz. 2009. Fluency, Adequacy, or HTER?: Exploring Different Human Judgments with a Tunable MT Metric. In *Proceedings of the Fourth Workshop on Statistical Machine Translation*. Association for Computational Linguistics, Stroudsburg, PA, USA, StatMT '09, pages 259–268. http://www.aclweb.org/anthology/W/W09/W09-0x41.

Lucia Specia and Atefeh Farzindar. 2010. Estimating Machine Translation Post-Editing Effort with HTER. *AMTA2010 Workshop Bringing MT to the User MT Research and the Translation Industry* pages 33–41. http://mt-archive.info/JEC-2010-Specia.pdf.

Lucia Specia, Gustavo Paetzold, and Carolina Scarton. 2015. Multi-level Translation Quality Prediction with QuEst++. In *Proceedings of ACL-IJCNLP 2015 System Demonstrations*. Association for Computational Linguistics and The Asian Federation of Natural Language Processing, Beijing, China, pages 115–120. http://www.aclweb.org/anthology/P15-4020.

Arda Tezcan, Veronique Hoste, Bart Desmet, and Lieve Macken. 2016. UGENT-LT3 SCATE System for Machine Translation Quality Estimation. In *Proceedings of the First Conference on Machine Translation*. Association for Computational Linguistics, Berlin, Germany, pages 353–360. http://aclweb.org/anthology/W15-3043 http://www.aclweb.org/anthology/W/W16/W16-2393.

Predicting Translation Performance with Referential Translation Machines

Ergun Biçici

orcid.org/0000-0002-2293-2031

bicici.github.com

Abstract

Referential translation machines achieve top performance in both bilingual and monolingual settings without accessing any task or domain specific information or resource. RTMs achieve the 3rd system results for German to English sentence-level prediction of translation quality and the 2nd system results according to root mean squared error. In addition to the new features about substring distances, punctuation tokens, character n-grams, and alignment crossings, and additional learning models, we average prediction scores from different models using weights based on their training performance for improved results.

1 Introduction

Quality estimation task (QET) in WMT17 (Bojar et al., 2017) (QET17) is about prediction of the quality of machine translation output at the sentence- (Task 1), word- (Task 2), and phrase-level (Task 3) in IT and pharmaceutical domains without using reference translations. Prediction of translation performance can help in estimating the effort required for correcting the translations during post-editing by human translators if needed. RTMs are capable to model different domains and tasks while achieving top performance in both monolingual (Biçici and Way, 2015) and bilingual settings (Biçici, 2016b). We develop RTM models for all of the three subtasks of QET17, which include English to German (en-de), and German to English (de-en) translation directions. Task 1 is about predicting HTER (human-targeted translation edit rate) scores (Snover et al., 2006), Task 2 is about binary classification of word-level quality,

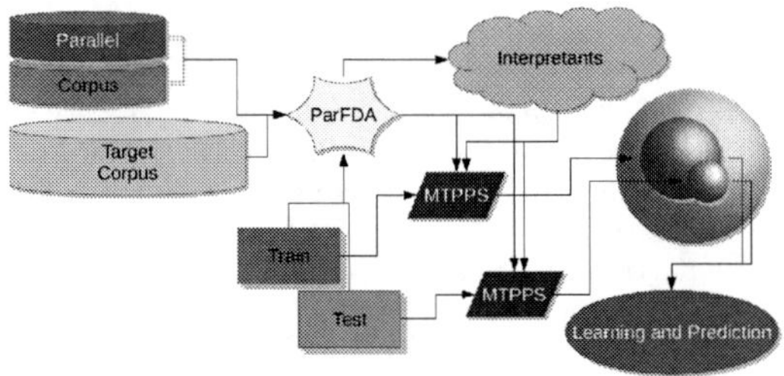

Figure 1: RTM depiction: ParFDA selects interpretants close to the training and test data using parallel corpus in bilingual settings and monolingual corpus in the target language or just the monolingual target corpus in monolingual settings; an MTPPS use interpretants and training data to generate training features and another use interpretants and test data to generate test features in the same feature space; learning and prediction takes place taking these features as input.

and Task 3 is about binary classification of phrase-level quality.

2 Referential Translation Machines

Referential translation machine (RTM) models are predict data translation between the instances in the training set and the test set. RTMs use interpretants, data close to the task instances, to derive features measuring the closeness of the test sentences to the training data, the difficulty of translating them, and to identify translation acts between any two data sets for building prediction models. RTMs are applicable in different domains and tasks and in both monolingual and bilingual settings. Figure 1 depicts RTMs and explains the model building process. RTMs use ParFDA (Biçici, 2016a) for instance selection and machine translation performance prediction system (MTPPS) (Biçici and Way, 2015) for generat-

Proceedings of the Conference on Machine Translation (WMT), Volume 2: Shared Task Papers, pages 540–544
Copenhagen, Denmark, September 7–11, 2017. ©2017 Association for Computational Linguistics

Task		Model	DeltaAvg	r_P	r_S	RMSE	MAE	RAE	MAER	MRAER	Rank
Task 1	en-de	MIX 4	8.64	0.4544	0.4768	0.1707	0.1296	0.8483	0.7594	0.7962	9
		PLS GBR	8.22	0.4302	0.4518	0.1727	0.1311	0.8586	0.7769	0.8099	10
	de-en	MIX 4	8.94	0.6004	0.5704	0.1566	0.1085	0.7034	0.7201	0.6921	4
		TREE	9.18	0.5845	0.5729	0.158	0.1186	0.7685	0.9013	0.7627	5

Table 1: Task 1 test results of the top 2 individual RTM models. RTM becomes the 2nd system according to RMSE and 3rd system in de-en and 6th system in en-de. r_P is Pearson's correlation and r_S is Spearman's correlation.

Task	Train	Test	RTM Interpretants Training	LM
Task 1, 2, 3 (en-de)	24000	2000	1.1M	17.6M
Task 1, 2, 3 (de-en)	26000	2000	1.1M	17.6M

Table 2: Number of instances used as interpretants by the RTM models.

ing features where the total number of features becomes 514, increasing depending on the order of n-grams used and we used up to 5-grams for translation features and 7-grams for language model (LM) at QET17.

We use ridge regression (RR), k-nearest neighbors (KNN), support vector regression (SVR), AdaBoost (Freund and Schapire, 1997), and extremely randomized trees (TREE) (Geurts et al., 2006) as learning models in combination with feature selection (FS) (Guyon et al., 2002) and partial least squares (PLS) (Wold et al., 1984). We use `scikit-learn` [1] for most of these models. The following parameters are optimized: λ for RR, k for KNN, γ, C, and ϵ for SVR, minimum number of samples for leaf nodes and for splitting an internal node for TREE, the number of features for FS, and the number of dimensions for PLS. For AdaBoost, we do not optimize but use exponential loss and 500 estimators like we use also with the TREE model. We use grid search for SVR. Evaluation metrics we use are Pearson's correlation (r), mean absolute error (MAE), relative absolute error (RAE), MAER (mean absolute error relative), and MRAER (mean relative absolute error relative) (Biçici and Way, 2015). DeltaAvg (Callison-Burch et al., 2012) calculates the average quality difference between the top $n - 1$ quartiles and the overall quality for the test set. Official evaluation metrics include r, MAE, and DeltaAvg.

We improved RTM models (Biçici, 2016b) with additional features:

- normalized Levenshtein distance between the

[1] http://scikit-learn.org/

source sentence and its translation and their longest common prefix, suffix, and substring (Tian et al., 2017) normalized by the minimum length of the compared sentences.

- number of tokens about punctuation in the source sentence and the translation (Kozlova et al., 2016) and the cosine between them.

- modified CHRF_3 (Popović, 2015) to compute character n-grams split by word boundary space with $n \in [3, 7]$ whereas the F_1 (Biçici, 2011) we already use compute with word n-grams up to $n = 5$.

- proportion of alignments that cross ($\curlywedge$) the link (Sagemo and Stymne, 2016) of any other alignments:

$$\sqrt{\frac{0.5 \times |a \curlywedge A|}{|A|}} \qquad (1)$$

- word alignment correspondence features (Sagemo and Stymne, 2016).

- additional learning models including KNN, AdaBoost, and gradient boosting regressor (GBR) (Tian et al., 2017; Hastie et al., 2009).

We also use prediction averaging (Biçici, 2017), where the performance on the training set is used to obtain weighted average of the top k predictions, $\hat{y}$ with evaluation metrics indexed by $j \in J$:

$$
\begin{aligned}
\hat{\boldsymbol{y}}_{\mu_k} &= \tfrac{1}{k}\sum_{i=1}^{k}\hat{\boldsymbol{y}}_i & \text{MEAN} \\
\hat{\boldsymbol{y}}_{j,w_k^j} &= \tfrac{1}{\sum_{i=1}^{k}\frac{1}{w_{j,i}}}\sum_{i=1}^{k}\tfrac{1}{w_{j,i}}\hat{\boldsymbol{y}}_i & \\
\hat{\boldsymbol{y}}_k &= \tfrac{1}{|J|}\sum_{j\in J}\hat{\boldsymbol{y}}_{j,w_k^j} & \text{MIX}
\end{aligned}
\qquad (2)
$$

MAER is used to select the predictions and weights are inverted to decrease error.

We use Global Linear Models (GLM) (Collins, 2002) with dynamic learning (GLMd) (Biçici,

	Model		splits	% error	weights
2017	word	en-de GLMd	4	0.0773	
		en-de GLMd	5	0.0668	
		de-en GLMd	4	0.0468	
		de-en GLMd	5	0.0469	
	phrase	en-de GLMd	4	0.0068	[0.5, 2]
		en-de GLMd	5	0.0059	
		de-en GLMd	4	0.0129	
		de-en GLMd	5	0.0125	
2016	word en-de	GLMd	4	0.0688	
		GLMd	5	0.0757	
	phrase en-de	GLMd	4	0.0051	
		GLMd	5	0.0051	

Table 3: RTM Task 2 training results where GLMd parallelized over 4 splits is referred as GLMd s4 and GLMd with 5 splits as GLMd s5.

	Model		F_1 BAD	F_1 OK	wF_1
Word	en-de	GLMd s4	0.318	0.8844	0.2813
		GLMd s5	0.36	0.8778	0.3158
	de-en	GLMd s4	0.3363	0.9386	0.3157
		GLMd s5	0.3381	0.9395	0.3176
Phrase	en-de	GLMd s4	0.4043	0.8079	0.3283
		GLMd s5	0.4114	0.8079	0.3323
	de-en	GLMd s4	0.2472	0.9073	0.2242
		GLMd s5	0.3598	0.8884	0.3197

Table 4: RTM Task 2 results on the test set after the challenge. wF_1 is average weighted F_1 score.

2016b) for word- and phrase-level translation performance prediction. GLMd uses weights in a range $[a, b]$ to update the learning rate dynamically according to the error rate.

3 Results

Table 2 lists the number of sentences in the training and test sets for each task and the number of instances used as interpretants in the RTM models (M for million). We tokenize and truecase all of the corpora using Moses's (Koehn et al., 2007) processing tools. [2] LMs are built using KENLM (Heafield et al., 2013).

3.1 QET 2017 Results

The results on the Task 1 test set are listed in Table 1. [3] For Task 2 and Task 3, we list the results

we obtain after the challenge for coherent presentation on the training sets in Table 3 and on the test set in Table 4. The results we obtained in the challenge are similar. Ranks for Task 1 are out of 14 submissions and 9 systems. Top RTM models that competed in Task 1 were MIX 4, which combines top 4 predictions, PLS GBR, and TREE. RTM becomes the 2nd system according to RMSE and 3rd system in de-en and 6th system in en-de.

3.2 Recomputing QET 2016 Results

QET17 also compares results on QET16 test sets. QET16 test set domain was different than the domain of QET17, overlapping on the IT domain. We use the RTM models built for QET17 to obtain results on the QET16 test sets, which is categorized as transductive transfer learning. [4] Transfer learning attempt to re-use and transfer knowledge from models developed in different domains or for different tasks such as using models developed for handwritten digit recognition for handwritten character recognition (Guyon et al., 2012). The results are in Table 5 for Task 1, which does not show improvement, and in Table 7, which show improvements with RTM models built for QET17.

3.3 Comparison with Previous Results

We compare the difficulty of tasks according to MRAER levels achieved. In Table 6, we list the RTM test results when predicting sentence-level HTER in 2013–2017. Compared with QET16, we observe improvements in MRAER and both MAE and RAE are improved when QET17 is compared with others.

4 Conclusion

Referential translation machines achieve top performance in automatic, accurate, and language independent prediction of translation performance and achieve to become the 2nd system according to RMSE when predicting the translation performance from German to English. RTMs pioneer a language independent approach for predicting translation performance and remove the need to access any task or domain specific information or resource.

---

[2] https://github.com/moses-smt/mosesdecoder/tree/master/scripts
[3] We calculate r_S using scipy.stats.

[4] www.youtube.com/watch?v=9ChVn3xVNDI; we use the RTM models for the same task in different domains.

	Model	DeltaAvg	r	MAE	RMSE	RAE	MAER	MRAER
2017	ST TREE	5.14	0.2052	0.1456	0.1875	0.9634	0.8844	0.8666
	PLS GBR	3.71	0.1875	0.1474	0.1914	0.9755	0.8706	0.8966
2016	SVR	6.38	0.3581	0.1359	0.1806	0.8992	0.7509	0.8567
	FS SVR	6.66	0.3764	0.1346	0.1781	0.8905	0.7537	0.8388

Table 5: QET16 Task 1 results are not improved with QET17 Task 1 RTM models.

Task	Translation Model		r	MAE	RAE	MAER	MRAER
QET17 Task 1 HTER	en-de	MIX 4	0.4544	0.1296	0.8483	0.7594	0.7962
	de-en	MIX 4	0.6004	0.1085	0.7034	0.7201	0.6921
QET16 Task 1 HTER	en-de	FS SVR	0.3764	0.1346	0.8905	0.7537	0.8388
QET15 Task 1 HTER	en-es	FS+PLS SVR	0.349	0.1335	0.903	0.8284	0.8353
QET14 Task 1.2 HTER	en-es	SVR	0.5499	0.134	0.8532	0.7727	0.8758
QET13 Task 1.1 HTER	en-es	PLS-SVR	0.5596	0.1326	0.8849	2.3738	1.6428

Table 6: Test performance of the top RTM results when predicting sentence-level HTER in 2013–2017.

		Model	wF_1	F_1 OK	F_1 BAD
2017	Word	GLMd s4	0.2857	0.8775	0.3256
		GLMd s5	0.3053	0.8653	0.3528
	Phrase	GLMd s4	0.3421	**0.8192**	0.4176
		GLMd s5	0.3504	**0.817**	0.4289
2016	Word	GLMd s4	0.2725	**0.8884**	0.3068
		GLMd s5	0.3081	0.8820	0.3494
	Phrase	GLMd s4	0.3070	**0.8145**	0.3770
		GLMd s5	0.3274	**0.8016**	0.4084

Table 7: QET16 Task 2 and Task 2p results show improvement.

References

Ergun Biçici. 2011. *The Regression Model of Machine Translation*. Ph.D. thesis, Koç University. Supervisor: Deniz Yuret.

Ergun Biçici. 2016a. ParFDA for instance selection for statistical machine translation. In *Proc. of the First Conference on Statistical Machine Translation (WMT16)*. Association for Computational Linguistics, Berlin, Germany. http://aclanthology.info/papers/parfda-for-instance-selection-for-statistical-machine-translation.

Ergun Biçici. 2016b. Referential translation machines for predicting translation performance. In *Proc. of the First Conference on Statistical Machine Translation (WMT16)*. Association for Computational Linguistics, Berlin, Germany. http://aclanthology.info/papers/referential-translation-machines-for-predicting-translation-performance.

Ergun Biçici. 2017. RTM at SemEval-2017 task 1: Referential translation machines for predicting semantic similarity. In *Proc. of the 11th International Workshop on Semantic Evaluation (SemEval-2017)*. Association for Computational Linguistics, Vancouver, Canada, pages 194–198. http://nlp.arizona.edu/SemEval-2017/pdf/SemEval030.pdf.

Ergun Biçici and Andy Way. 2015. Referential translation machines for predicting semantic similarity. *Language Resources and Evaluation* pages 1–27. https://doi.org/10.1007/s10579-015-9322-7.

Ondrej Bojar, Christian Buck, Rajen Chatterjee, Christian Federmann, Barry Haddow, Matthias Huck, Jimeno Antonio Yepes, Julia Kreutzer, Varvara Logacheva, Aurelie Neveol, Mariana Neves, Philipp Koehn, Christof Monz, Matteo Negri, Matt Post, Stefan Riezler, Artem Sokolov, Lucia Specia, Karin Verspoor, and Marco Turchi. 2017. Proc. of the second conference on Machine Translation. In *Proc. of the Second Conference on Machine Translation*. Association for Computational Linguistics, Copenhagen, Denmark.

Chris Callison-Burch, Philipp Koehn, Christof Monz, Matt Post, Radu Soricut, and Lucia Specia. 2012. Findings of the 2012 workshop on statistical machine translation. In *Proc. of the Seventh Workshop on Statistical Machine Translation*. Montréal, Canada, pages 10–51.

Michael Collins. 2002. Discriminative training methods for hidden markov models: theory and experiments with perceptron algorithms. In *Proc. of the ACL-02 conference on Empirical methods in natural language processing - Volume 10*. Stroudsburg, PA, USA, EMNLP '02, pages 1–8. https://doi.org/10.3115/1118693.1118694.

Yoav Freund and Robert E Schapire. 1997. A decision-theoretic generalization of on-line learning and an application to boosting. *Journal of Computer and System Sciences* 55(1):119–139. https://doi.org/10.1006/jcss.1997.1504.

Pierre Geurts, Damien Ernst, and Louis Wehenkel. 2006. Extremely randomized trees. *Machine Learning* 63(1):3–42.

Isabelle Guyon, Gideon Dror, Vincent Lemaire, Graham W. Taylor, and Daniel L. Silver, editors. 2012. *Unsupervised and Transfer Learning - Workshop held at ICML 2011, Bellevue, Washington, USA, July 2, 2011*, volume 27 of *JMLR Proceedings*. JMLR.org. http://clopinet.com/ul.

Isabelle Guyon, Jason Weston, Stephen Barnhill, and Vladimir Vapnik. 2002. Gene selection for cancer classification using support vector machines. *Machine Learning* 46(1-3):389–422. https://doi.org/10.1023/A:1012487302797.

Trevor Hastie, Robert Tibshirani, and Jerome Friedman. 2009. *The Elements of Statistical Learning: Data Mining, Inference and Prediction*. Springer-Verlag, 2nd edition.

Kenneth Heafield, Ivan Pouzyrevsky, Jonathan H. Clark, and Philipp Koehn. 2013. Scalable modified Kneser-Ney language model estimation. In *Proc. of the 51st Annual Meeting of the Association for Computational Linguistics*. Sofia, Bulgaria, pages 690–696.

Philipp Koehn, Hieu Hoang, Alexandra Birch, Chris Callison-Burch, Marcello Federico, Nicola Bertoldi, Brooke Cowan, Wade Shen, Christine Moran, Richard Zens, Chris Dyer, Ondrej Bojar, Alexandra Constantin, and Evan Herbst. 2007. Moses: Open source toolkit for statistical machine translation. In *Proc. of the 45th Annual Meeting of the Association for Computational Linguistics Companion Volume Proc. of the Demo and Poster Sessions*. Association for Computational Linguistics, pages 177–180. aclweb.org/anthology/P07-2045.

Anna Kozlova, Mariya Shmatova, and Anton Frolov. 2016. Ysda participation in the wmt'16 quality estimation shared task. In *Proceedings of the First Conference on Machine Translation*. Association for Computational Linguistics, Berlin, Germany, pages 793–799. http://www.aclweb.org/anthology/W/W16/W16-2385.

Maja Popović. 2015. chrf: character n-gram f-score for automatic mt evaluation. In *Proceedings of the Tenth Workshop on Statistical Machine Translation*. Association for Computational Linguistics, Lisbon, Portugal, pages 392–395. http://aclweb.org/anthology/W15-3049.

Oscar Sagemo and Sara Stymne. 2016. The uu submission to the machine translation quality estimation task. In *Proceedings of the First Conference on Machine Translation*. Association for Computational Linguistics, Berlin, Germany, pages 825–830. http://www.aclweb.org/anthology/W/W16/W16-2390.

Matthew Snover, Bonnie Dorr, Richard Schwartz, Linnea Micciulla, and John Makhoul. 2006. A Study of Translation Edit Rate with Targeted Human Annotation. In *Proc. of Association for Machine Translation in the Americas,*.

Junfeng Tian, Zhiheng Zhou, Man Lan, and Yuanbin Wu. 2017. Ecnu at semeval-2017 task 1: Leverage kernel-based traditional nlp features and neural networks to build a universal model for multilingual and cross-lingual semantic textual similarity. In *Proceedings of the 11th International Workshop on Semantic Evaluation (SemEval-2017)*. Association for Computational Linguistics, Vancouver, Canada, pages 182–188. http://www.aclweb.org/anthology/S17-2028.

S. Wold, A. Ruhe, H. Wold, and W. J. III Dunn. 1984. The collinearity problem in linear regression. the partial least squares (pls) approach to generalized inverses. *SIAM Journal on Scientific and Statistical Computing* 5:735–743.

Bilexical Embeddings for Quality Estimation

Frédéric Blain, Carolina Scarton and Lucia Specia
Department of Computer Science
University of Sheffield, UK
{f.blain, c.scarton, l.specia}@sheffield.ac.uk

Abstract

This paper describes the SHEF submissions for the three sub-tasks of the Quality Estimation shared task of WMT17, namely: (i) a word-level prediction system using bilexical embeddings, (ii) a phrase-level labelling approach based on the word-level predictions, (iii) a sentence-level prediction system using word embeddings and handcrafted baseline features. Results are promising for the sentence-level approach, but still very preliminary for the other two levels.

1 Introduction

Quality Estimation (QE) allows the evaluation of Machine Translation (MT) when reference translations are not available. It can be used in various ways such as in post-editing (PE) to predict whether or not an automatically generated sentence is worth publishing, editing or it should be retranslated manually. Word-level predictions can be helpful by highlighting words that cannot be relied upon or should be fixed by post-editors. More recently, QE at phrase-level has emerged as a way of using quality predictions at decoding time in phrase-based Statistical MT (SMT) systems to guide the decoder such as to keep phrases which are predicted as good, and conversely to discard those which are predicted as bad (Logacheva, 2017).

QE models are built based on a list of features along with a Machine Learning algorithm for either regression or classification. These features are usually extracted from the source and target texts or from the MT system that generated the translations. Shah et al. (2015) introduced a new set of features extracted using an unsupervised approach with the use of neural network: continuous-space language model features and word embeddings features.

In our contribution this year we investigate whether we can go beyond engineered features by learning bilexical operators over distributional representations of words in source-target text pairs. Considering the MT pipeline as a noisy black-box, our motivation is to be able to build QE models to predict if information encoded in the source sentence is preserved in the target sentence after translation.

2 Bilinear Model

Madhyastha et al. (2014) propose to use word-level embeddings to predict the strength of different types of lexical relationships between a pair of words, such as head-modifier relations between noun-adjective pairs. They designed a supervised framework for learning bilexical operators over distributional representations, based on learning bilinear forms W. We adapted their method to predict the strength of relationship between source and target words. This problem is formulated as a log-bilinear model, parametrized with W as follows:

$$\Pr(t|s; W) = \frac{\exp\left\{\phi(t)^\top W \phi(s)\right\}}{\sum_{t' \in \mathcal{T}} \exp\left\{\phi(t')^\top W \phi(s)\right\}} \quad (1)$$

where ϕ denotes the word embeddings of any given word in a vocabulary $\mathcal{V}$. The source words s and target words t are respectively taken from subspaces $\mathcal{S} \subseteq \mathcal{V}$ and $\mathcal{T} \subseteq \mathcal{V}$.

In essence, the problem can be reduced to first obtaining the corresponding word embeddings of the vocabularies of both source and target sentences using a substantially large monolingual corpus for each of the two languages, followed by using the bilinear model to estimate W. W is learned

Proceedings of the Conference on Machine Translation (WMT), Volume 2: Shared Task Papers, pages 545–550
Copenhagen, Denmark, September 7–11, 2017. ©2017 Association for Computational Linguistics

	IT		PHARMA	
	#sent	#word	#sent	#word
English	3.4M	58.3M	1.8M	78.5M
German	3.4M	57.5M	1.8M	83.6M

Table 1: Statistics of the in-domain data used to train our embeddings.

using the source-target word *alignment* by minimizing the negative log-likelihood using a ℓ_2 regularized objective as:

$$L(W) = -\sum_{s,t} \log(Pr(t|s; W)) + \lambda \|W\|_2 \quad (2)$$

where λ is the constant that controls the capacity of W with gradient descent-based optimization.

We explore this approach for both word and phrase-level QE. For training, we rely on both the word-alignments and the gold QE labels (i.e. the OK/BAD labels). The former gives us the source-target pairs, and the latter whether this pair is valid or not. Our assumption is that this approach should be able to predict whether or not a word in the target language (MT output) is correct by exploring the strength of the linguistic relation with the source word it is generated from.

3 Experimental Settings

3.1 Data and Gold labels

Each QE shared task has two datasets: English→German segments on the IT domain (with 23,000 sentences for training, 1,000 for development and 2,000 for test), and German→English segments on the Pharmaceutical domain (with 25,000 sentences for training, 1,000 for development and 2,000 for test). The same data is used for all three tasks: word, phrase and sentence-level prediction.

For the word-level task, each token of the MT is annotated with OK or BAD labels. For the phrase-level task, phrases are segmented as given by an SMT decoder and also annotated with OK or BAD labels. Finally, for the sentence-level task, the quality label is a Human-Targeted Error Rate (HTER) score (Snover et al., 2009).

3.2 Word Embeddings

Word embeddings were used in our submissions for the three tasks. We trained in-domain skip-gram embeddings on the in-domain data shown in

Table 1 using FastText[1] (Bojanowski et al., 2016) with 300 dimensions and learning rate set to 0.025. The default training settings are otherwise used. The in-domain data is the same as that used to train the SMT system that produced the translations in the QE datasets, as made available by the task organizers.

For the word and phrase-level tasks, we used our word embeddings to obtain a word vector representation of 300 dimensions for each word of both the training and development sets. For the sentence-level task, the word embeddings are averaged for each sentence, as previously applied in (Scarton et al., 2016).

3.3 Tool

To learn to predict the labels for the word-level task, we used BMAPS[2], the toolkit implementing the method in (Madhyastha et al., 2014) along with the word alignments provided by the organizers (as produced by the SMT system). BMAPS is used to learn the bilexical operators between both source and target embeddings. The tool relies on three matrices corresponding to the source and target vocabularies of the training data, and a third matrix representing the word-level lexical relation between them. This matrix is built from the word-level alignments and the gold labels to indicate which lexical items form a pair, and whether their lexical relation is OK or BAD (i.e. if two lexical items are aligned and labelled as OK, their intersection in the third matrix is set to 1, 0 otherwise).

By default, the model is trained over 100 iterations with the l_2 norm as regularizer, and using the *forward-backward splitting* algorithm (FOBOS) (Duchi and Singer, 2009) as optimization scheme ($lc = 0.1$, $tau = 0.1$).

3.4 Evaluation

We used the official task metrics to evaluate our results. For the word and phrase-level tasks, the metrics are F_1-BAD and F_1-OK which correspond to the F_1 scores on both BAD and OK labels, and F_1-multi which is the product of the two formers. For the sentence-level task, the metrics for scoring are Pearson's correlation (primary metric), Mean Average Error (MAE) and Root Mean Squared Error (RMSE), and for ranking, Spearman's rank correlation (primary metric) and DeltaAvg.

---

[1] https://github.com/facebookresearch/fastText

[2] https://github.com/f00barin/bmaps

4 Results

4.1 Word-level QE prediction (Task 2)

We investigate different context windows to build our lexical representations, ranging from a wide window considering all sentence-level context, to a much narrower approach representing each word individually:

- **Full context:** each word is associated with its left and right context to capture the exact distributional features of the specific context in which this lexical item occurs. A lexical item is thus a 900-dimensional word vector represented by the tuple $< emb_{left}, emb_{cur}, emb_{right} >$, where emb_{left} and emb_{right} are the averaged embeddings of the left/right contexts and emb_{cur} the word representation of the current word. Here our assumption is that a lexical item would represent a word within its context and at its position in the sentence, therefore if the word appears twice in the sentence, it would be represented by two different lexical items.

- **Surrounding context:** instead of considering all the left and right context of the current word, we limit ourselves to the two surrounding words. This allows for a model that is as generic as possible while still considering two distributional features corresponding to two different lexical items. Here the assumption is the same as before, the lexical item which represents a word is the same but only considering a window of one word on the left/right to compute emb_{left}/emb_{right}.

- **Unigram:** we use only the embeddings of the current word without considering any surrounding context. By doing so, we fully rely on the embeddings and the way they are trained (skipgram). In this case, the lexical item is a single word representation of 300 dimensions.

For each context we investigate two variants: with and without the use of the gold labels in order to demonstrate the capacity of our approach to learn how to discriminate the valid lexical pairs from the others.

Discussion The results of our approach for the word-level task are given in Table 2. We report the results of our official submissions to the task (†)

along with additional experiments we conducted after the task deadline. They are both compared with the official baseline of Task 2.

Our first observation is the overall low performance of our approach compared to the official baseline. However, we found very encouraging the results of our additional experiments compared to those of the systems submitted. The revised training procedure significantly improved the performance in terms of F_1-OK for all three contexts types, resulting in a boost in the F_1-multi scores.

To better understand the gap between our official and additional results, it is important to mention the technical constraints we faced performing the task with BMAPS for the official submission. In its current implementation, BMAPS relies on non-sparse matrices which in our case lead to a heavy memory print, since the source and the target matrices contain vector representations for each word in the corpus. Therefore, to be able to run BMAPS on our servers we were limited to use up to 2,000 sentences (about 9% of the training corpus) as training instances. This certainly had a significant impact on the performance of the models.

To tackle this constraint we later opted for a mini-batch training approach: we divided the training corpus into batches of 500 sentences, the training for each batch starting from the results from the training with the previous one. By doing so we are able to use all the training data. However, in BMAPS the size of the dev set (in terms of words from which the matrices are built) has to be smaller than that of the training set. Therefore, by using mini-batches we had to reduce our dev set. We selected for the dev set 250 sentences with the highest number of OK labels in order to boost performance for this class. We also refined our training parameters by switching to the nuclear norm (which is expected to converge faster when restricting the training size (Madhyastha et al., 2014)). Finally, we empirically identified the best values for the two main parameters (namely lc and tau) for different context types: for both the full and surrounding context, we used $lc = 0.1$ and $tau = 0.001$, while for the unigram approach we used $lc = 0.1$ and $tau = 0.01$.

As a second finding, one can notice the impact of considering the surrounding context when predicting each word's label. In both official and additional results, there is a substantial difference be-

	norm	training size	F_1-BAD	F_1-OK	F_1-multi
English→German (2016)					
BMAPS-full	l_2	2k	0.326	0.103	0.034
BMAPS-nolabel-full	l_2	2k	0.311	0.222	0.069
BMAPS-full	*nuclear*	23k	0.321	0.817	0.262
BMAPS-window	l_2	2k	0.328	0.207	0.068
BMAPS-nolabel-window	l_2	2k	0.315	0.170	0.053
BMAPS-window	*nuclear*	23k	0.325	0.819	0.266
BMAPS-unigram †	l_2	2k	0.316	0.501	0.158
BMAPS-nolabel-unigram †	l_2	2k	0.296	0.330	0.098
BMAPS-unigram	*nuclear*	23k	0.251	0.845	0.212
BASELINE	–	–	0.404	0.892	0.360
English→German (2017)					
BMAPS-full	*nuclear*	23k	0.336	0.812	0.273
BMAPS-window	*nuclear*	23k	0.343	0.812	0.279
BMAPS-unigram †	l_2	2k	0.325	0.484	0.157
BMAPS-nolabel-unigram †	l_2	2k	0.302	0.322	0.097
BMAPS-unigram	*nuclear*	23k	0.270	0.848	0.229
BASELINE	–	–	0.407	0.886	0.361
German→English (2017)					
BMAPS-full	*nuclear*	25k	0.231	0.447	0.103
BMAPS-window	*nuclear*	25k	0.235	0.506	0.119
BMAPS-unigram †	l_2	2k	0.210	0.419	0.088
BMAPS-nolabel-unigram †	l_2	2k	0.209	0.391	0.082
BMAPS-unigram	*nuclear*	25k	0.234	0.527	0.123
BASELINE	–	–	0.365	0.939	0.342

Table 2: Results of our word-level predictions. † denotes our official submissions to the task using the l_2 norm and single training set of 2k sentences. The other figures are obtained with mini-batch training using 500 sentences at the time. In grey are the results of the official baseline of the task.

tween the three types of context: while unigram was the best performing when limited to 2k training instances only, the exact opposite was found when using the full training set with better F_1-* scores when the context in which the word occurs is employed. Furthermore, we note a small advantage for the window context over the full context in both language pairs. We believe this means that considering the surrounding context could better help in a situation where a word would appear twice in the same sentence but should be labelled differently.

Overall, these results are encouraging and we aim to pursue further investigations towards improving this approach for the task of word-level QE.

4.2 Phrase-level QE labelling (Task 3)

While we could have chosen to predict phrase-level QE labels similarly to our word-level predictions, we opted for generating phrase-level labels from word-level labels following the labelling approaches described in Blain et al. (2016):

- **Optimistic:** if half or more of words have a label OK, the phrase has the label OK (majority labelling).

- **Pessimistic:** if 30% words or more have a label BAD, the phrase has the label BAD.

- **Super-pessimistic:** if any word in the phrase has a label BAD, the whole phrase has the label BAD.

Discussion The results of these three phrase-level labelling strategies based upon our word-level predictions are given in Table 3. We report the results of our official submissions to the task (†) along with additional experiments we conducted after the task deadline. These are compared with the official baseline for Task 3.

First, similarly to the word-level task, the performance at phrase-level improved with the additional experiments, which was expected since the labelling directly follows from the word-level predictions. Second, while we originally observed better labelling performance using the optimistic approach on test.2016 (see underlined numbers), we now observe better F_1-* scores with both pessimistic approaches for en→de. One can also observe comparable performance for en→de when the surrounding context is used: the difference in terms of F_1-* scores between the full and window context is marginal. For de→en this is different: the phrase labelling based on word predictions using the window context outperforms the phrase la-

	F_1-BAD	F_1-OK	F_1-**multi**
English→German (2016)			
BMAPS-full-opti	0.292	0.799	0.233
BMAPS-window-opti	0.284	0.798	0.227
BMAPS-unigram-opti †	0.415	0.562	0.233
BMAPS-unigram-nolabel-opti †	0.398	0.373	0.149
BMAPS-unigram-opti	0.166	0.816	0.135
BMAPS-full-pess	0.425	0.743	0.316
BMAPS-window-pess	0.426	0.742	0.316
BMAPS-unigram-pess •	0.452	0.264	0.120
BMAPS-unigram-nolabel-pess •	0.442	0.140	0.062
BMAPS-unigram-pess	0.341	0.780	0.266
BMAPS-full-superpess	0.441	0.723	0.318
BMAPS-window-superpess	0.437	0.719	0.314
BMAPS-unigram-super-pess •	0.455	0.250	0.114
BMAPS-unigram-nolabel-suppess •	0.442	0.136	0.060
BMAPS-unigram-super-pess	0.366	0.763	0.279
BASELINE	0.403	0.812	0.328
English→German (2017)			
BMAPS-full-opti	0.309	0.804	0.248
BMAPS-window-opti	0.312	0.800	0.250
BMAPS-unigram-opti †	0.409	0.553	0.226
BMAPS-unigram-nolabel-opti †	0.388	0.380	0.148
BMAPS-unigram-opti	0.184	0.823	0.152
BMAPS-full-pess	0.431	0.750	0.323
BMAPS-window-pess	0.428	0.743	0.318
BMAPS-unigram-pess	0.350	0.794	0.278
BMAPS-full-super-pess	0.438	0.733	0.321
BMAPS-window-super-pess	0.437	0.724	0.316
BMAPS-unigram-super-pess	0.368	0.781	0.287
BASELINE	0.402	0.814	0.327
German→English (2017)			
BMAPS-full-opti	0.326	0.478	0.156
BMAPS-window-opti	0.334	0.565	0.189
BMAPS-unigram-opti †	0.299	0.473	0.141
BMAPS-unigram-nolabel-opti †	0.300	0.440	0.132
BMAPS-unigram-opti	0.336	0.593	0.199
BMAPS-full-pess	0.313	0.281	0.088
BMAPS-window-pess	0.320	0.357	0.114
BMAPS-unigram-pess	0.322	0.378	0.122
BMAPS-full-super-pess	0.311	0.256	0.079
BMAPS-window-super-pess	0.317	0.332	0.106
BMAPS-unigram-super-pess	0.320	0.358	0.115
BASELINE	0.397	0.907	0.360

Table 3: Results of the phrase-level labelling strategies based upon our word-level QE predictions. † denotes our official submissions to the task and • the results of the other two labelling strategies, both using our official submissions to Task 2. The other figures are obtained with the updated word predictions from Task 2 resulting of the full batch training. In grey are the results of the official baseline of the task.

belling based on word prediction using the entire sentence as context.

4.3 Sentence-level QE prediction (Task 1)

For the sentence-level task we followed a simple approach, which had been previously applied by Scarton et al. (2016) for document-level QE. The idea was to combine word embeddings with handcrafted features.

However, whilst Scarton et al. (2016) have used

	Scoring		Ranking	
	Pearson's r	MAE	Spearman's ρ	DeltaAvg
English→German (2016)				
QUEST-EMB	0.50	0.12	0.53	9.02
BASELINE	0.40	0.13	0.44	7.42
English→German (2017)				
QUEST-EMB	0.50	0.13	0.51	8.96
BASELINE	0.40	0.14	0.43	7.45
German→English (2017)				
QUEST-EMB	0.56	0.12	0.56	8.79
BASELINE	0.44	0.13	0.45	6.81

Table 4: Results of QUEST-EMB in the sentence-level QE task. In grey are the results of the official baseline of the task.

word embeddings trained on general purpose data, our embeddings are trained over in-domain data, as previously described. Word embeddings were averaged at sentence level in order to have a single vector representing each sentence. We then concatenated source and target in-domain embeddings with the 17 sentence-level baseline features provided by the organisers. An SVM regressor was used to train our QE model with hyper-parameters optimized via grid-search. For that we used the learning module available at `QuEst++` toolkit (Specia et al., 2015).

Although the sentence-level experiment is different from the approach applied for word and phrase-level tasks, our aim was to test the usability of the in-domain word embeddings. Our results are compared with the official baseline.

Discussion The results of our sentence-level predictions are given in Table 4. Although the approach is rather simplistic, it achieves considerably good results by outperforming the baseline system and several other systems that participated in the shared task. For German→English, our system performed seventh out of 13 in the scoring task. For English→German, it performed eighth out of 13. Table 4 shows the results of our systems (called QUEST-EMB) for the different language pairs and for both scoring and ranking tasks. We also show the results of the baseline systems for comparison.

5 Conclusions

In this paper we report our submissions to the three sub-tasks of the QE campaign of WMT17. We obtained reasonably good results for the sentence-level task despite the use of a very simplistic approach. On the other hand, we significantly underperform in the two other tasks, which exploit a bilinear model. Due to limitations regarding the experimental settings of the tool used for the official submissions, it is difficult to conclude whether or not our approach is suitable for the task of QE. In follow up experiments with different training strategies, the results proved substantially better and much more promising, albeit still behind the official baseline. This is particularly encouraging considering that the approach only relies on word embeddings and word alignment information. We plan to further experiment with it and identify possible improvements in DMAP3 that could lead to better performance.

It is also worth emphasizing that the approach employed for the sentence-level task is not directly comparable to the approach used for the other tasks; they only share the embeddings trained using in-domain data. However, we can conclude that the in-domain embeddings encode useful information for all tasks.

Acknowledgments

The authors would like to thank Pranava S. Madhyastha for his support regarding the use of BMAPS. This work was supported by the QT21 project (H2020 No. 645452).

References

Frédéric Blain, Varvara Logacheva, and Lucia Specia. 2016. Phrase level segmentation and labelling of machine translation errors. In *Tenth International Conference on Language Resources and Evaluation*. Portoroz, Slovenia, pages 2240–2245.

Piotr Bojanowski, Edouard Grave, Armand Joulin, and Tomas Mikolov. 2016. Enriching word vectors with subword information. *arXiv preprint arXiv:1607.04606* .

John Duchi and Yoram Singer. 2009. Efficient online and batch learning using forward backward splitting. *Journal of Machine Learning Research* 10(Dec):2899–2934.

Varvara Logacheva. 2017. *Human Feedback in Statistical Machine Translation*. Ph.D. thesis, The University of Sheffield.

Pranava Swaroop Madhyastha, Xavier Carreras, and Ariadna Quattoni. 2014. Learning task-specific bilexical embeddings. In *Proceedings the 25th International Conference on Computational Linguistics*. Dublin, Ireland, pages 161–171. http://www.aclweb.org/anthology/C14-1017.

Carolina Scarton, Daniel Beck, Kashif Shah, Karin Sim Smith, and Lucia Specia. 2016. Word embeddings and discourse information for Quality Estimation. In *Proceedings of the First Conference on Machine Translation*. Berlin, Germany, pages 831–837.

Kashif Shah, Varvara Logacheva, Gustavo Paetzold, Frédéric Blain, Daniel Beck, Fethi Bougares, and Lucia Specia. 2015. Shef-nn: Translation quality estimation with neural networks. In *Proceedings of the Tenth Workshop on Statistical Machine Translation*. pages 342–347.

Matthew Snover, Nitin Madnani, Bonnie J. Dorr, and Richard Schwartz. 2009. Fluency, Adequacy, or HTER? Exploring Different Human Judgments with a Tunable MT Metric. In *The Fourth Workshop on Statistical Machine Translation*. Athens, Greece, pages 259–268.

Lucia Specia, Gustavo Paetzold, and Carolina Scarton. 2015. Multi-level translation quality prediction with quest++. In *Proceedings of ACL-IJCNLP 2015 System Demonstrations*. Association for Computational Linguistics and The Asian Federation of Natural Language Processing, Beijing, China, pages 115–120. http://www.aclweb.org/anthology/P15-4020.

Improving Machine Translation Quality Estimation with Neural Network Features

Zhiming Chen, Yiming Tan, Chenlin Zhang, Qingyu Xiang, Lilin Zhang,
Maoxi Li, Mingwen Wang
School of Computer Information Engineering, Jiangxi Normal University
{qqchenzhiming, tt_yymm, zhangchenlin, qingyuxian, lilinzhang, mosesli, mwwang}
@jxnu.edu.cn

Abstract

Machine translation quality estimation is a challenging task in the WMT evaluation campaign. Feature extraction plays an important role in automatic quality estimation, and in this paper, we propose neural network features, including embedding features and cross entropy features of source sentences and machine translations, to improve machine translation quality estimation. The sentence embedding features are extracted through global average pooling from word embedding and are trained by the word2vec toolkits, while the sentence cross-entropy features are calculated by the recurrent neural network language model. The experimental results on the development set of WMT17 machine translation quality estimation tasks show that the neural network features gain significant improvements over the baseline. Furthermore, when combining the neural network features and the baseline features, the system performance obtains further improvement.

1 Introduction

Quality estimation (QE) of machine translation estimates the quality of machine translation system outputs without human references using machine learning methods. It is often divided into two steps: first, it extracts various features from source sentences, translation outputs, and external language resources to describe the translation complexity, fluency and adequacy; and second, it predicts the quality of the translation outputs with the pre-trained machine learning model. Feature extraction is crucial to the performance of QE,

and traditional methods, such as QuEst (Specia et al., 2013), extract linguistically motivated features to improve the correlation between the automatic QE and human assessment. However, extracting linguistically motivated features requires part-of-speech analysis, syntactic analysis, or semantic analysis, and these linguistic analyses relate to the target language types; this consideration limits their application in other languages. To address this problem, Shah et al. (2015a, 2016) investigated continuous space language models for sentence-level QE, and Scarton et al. (2016) proposed word embedding features for document-level QE.

Inspired by their work, we propose sentence embedding features and cross-entropy features to improve the correlation between automatic QE and human assessment and to investigate how different sentence embedding dimensions of source sentences and translation outputs, as well as the size of the training corpus, affect the system performance of QE.

2 Related work

With the great success of deep learning that has been achieved in digital image processing and automatic speech recognition, deep learning has also made tremendous breakthroughs in natural language processing, e.g., the proposition of neural network language models (Bengio et al. 2003) and neural machine translation encoder decoder frameworks (Bahdanau et al. 2014). Therefore, many researchers have proposed deep learning approaches for the QE task. In the word-level QE task, Kreutzer et al. (2015) presented deep feed-forward neural networks to estimate the word confidence. Shah et al. (2015b) exploited word embedding as a feature to estimate whether the translation of the word is "good" or "bad" in machine translation outputs. Patel et al. (2016) applied a

Proceedings of the Conference on Machine Translation (WMT), Volume 2: Shared Task Papers, pages 551–555
Copenhagen, Denmark, September 7–11, 2017. ©2017 Association for Computational Linguistics

recurrent neural network language model to the word-level QE task.

In the sentence-level QE task，Shah et al. (2015a) extracted continuous space language model (Schwenk et al. 2007) probabilities of source sentences and machine translation outputs as features, and combined them with baseline features to improve the system performance of QE. In the WMT16 QE Task，Shah et al. (2016) further proposed forward sentence cross-entropy, sentence embedding features, and neural machine translation log-likelihood features based on their previous work. They extracted word embedding features and cross-entropy features by the continuous space language model.

In contrast to the work of Shah et al., we utilize a continuous bag-of-words model to extract the word embeddings, construct sentence embedding through global average pooling from word embeddings, and utilize a recurrent neural network language model to extract sentence cross-entropy features.

3 Neural Network Features

To overcome the problem that the traditional feature extraction method relies heavily on sentence linguistic analysis, in this paper, we exploit the latest deep learning method to extract the features of translation quality from source language sentences and its machine translations. The extracted features include sentence embedding features and sentence cross-entropy features.

3.1 The Embedding Features

Word representation learning has attracted the attention of many researchers in recent years. Especially after 2013, Mikolov et al. (2013a) released the open source word embedding learning tool: word2vec [1]. Word2vec, as a word embedding learning tool, has implemented two models: CBOW (Continuous Bag-of-words) and Skip-Gram model, inspired by the neural network language model proposed by Bengio (Bengio et al. 2003). The CBOW and Skip-Gram model remove the hidden layer processing of the neural network language model, which is time consuming, and add the optimization methods of Negative Sampling and Hierarchical Softmax (Mikolov et al. 2013b). This approach improves the accuracy of the model and accelerates the training of the mod-

el. The CBOW and Skip-Gram models are very similar. Their difference lies in that the CBOW model predicts the conditional probability of the current word by the context words, while the Skip-Gram model predicts the conditional probability of the context words by the current word. Because the training speed of the CBOW model is faster than that of the Skip-Gram model, we use the CBOW model to train the word embeddings of the source language and the target language.

The window size is set to 10, using the negative sampling optimization method. Additionally, the number of negative samples is set to 10. To accelerate the training, the sampling threshold of a high frequency word is set to 1e-5, and the iteration time is set to 15. We attempt various dimension of the word embedding, varied from 256 to 4096, to achieve best performance.

After obtaining the word embeddings of each word in the source sentence and the machine translation output, the sentence embeddings are computed by averaging them. This approach is applied to both the source sentences and the machine translation outputs. When the source sentence embedding (V_s) and the machine translation output embedding (V_t) are both obtained, two sentence embeddings are concatenated ($V = [V_s; V_t]$) as features for the QE task.

3.2 The Cross-Entropy Features

A language model, which occupies a significant position in natural language processing, is used for the modeling of the probability distributions of the word sequences. In section 3.1, the bag-of-words model is used to obtain the word embedding features. However, the disadvantage of the bag-of-words model is that it ignores the contextual relationships between the words.

The recurrent neural network possesses sequentiality and memorability, and it performs well in sequential data modeling. Therefore, the Recurrent Neural Network Language Model (RNNLM) (Mikolov et al. 2010) was proposed and first used in automatic speech recognition and reordering of machine translations. The experimental results indicate that the RNNLM is superior to the back-off language model. Since RNNLM accounts for the word order, we extract the source language sentences and their machine translation cross-entropies as features for the QE task.

---

[1] https://code.google.com/p/word2vec/

The RNNLM is trained by the RNNLM toolkit[2]. The number of hidden layers is set to 100, parameter "bptt" is set to 4, and the output layer class number is set to 200. The WMT17 QE development set is used to optimize the parameters of the RNNLM. The training data is shown in section 4.1. The entropy of the WMT17 QE development set that we finally trained by the RNNLM is shown in Table 1.

WMT17 QE	language	iter	entropy
en-de	en	5	7.7549
	de	3	6.5885
de-en	en	7	5.1287
	de	12	5.8929

Table 1: The entropy of each language in the WMT17 QE development set trained by the RNNLM toolkit.

4 Experimental Results

To test the performance of the neural network features for the QE task, we conduct experiments on the development set of the WMT17 sentence-level QE task.

4.1 Experiment Set

The WMT17 sentence-level QE task contains two translation directions: English to German (en-de) and German to English (de-en). Among them, the en-de corpus concerns the IT domain, while de-en concerns the pharmaceutical domain. The training set of the en-de direction consists of 23,000 sentences; the development set consists of 1,000 sentences. The training set of the de-en direction consists of 25,000 sentences; the development set consists of 1,000 sentences. A test set of 2,000 sentences is provided for each direction. HTER (Snover et al. 2006) is provided as an estimation index for the translation quality of each training set and development set. The task of the participants is to establish a QE model to predict the HTER, with the source language sentences and their machine translations.

To train the word embedding and the RNNLM, the source side and the target side of the bilingual parallel corpus for the translation task, publicly released by the WMT evaluation campaign, are used; they include Europarl v7, Common Crawl corpus, News Commentary v8 and v11; Batch1 and Batch2, localization PO files, IT-related terms from Wikipedia[3]; WMT16 and WMT17 QE task1 corpus. The statistics of the bilingual parallel corpus are shown in Table 2, the corpus are shared for the two translation directions.

The Support Vector Regression (SVR) model is utilized for the QE. To implement the model, we use the Python machine learning toolkit: scikit-learn[4], and the radial basis function is chosen for the SVR kernel function, the grid search algorithm for parameter optimization. The metrics included Pearson's correlation coefficient (Pearson r), Mean Absolute Error (MAE), Root Mean Squared Error (RMSE), Spearman's correlation coefficient (Spearman ρ) and Delta Average (DeltaAvg), which were used to evaluate the performance of the QE model. Pearson r and Spearman ρ are set as primary metrics for scoring and ranking the evaluation respectively, and higher scores mean better correlations between QE and HTER.

	English	German
Number of sentences	4.8 M	
Vocabulary size	936.0 K	1796.9 K
Number of tokens	120.8 M	115.4 M

Table 2: The statistics of the corpus size for the word embedding training and RNNLM training.

4.2 Results

We exploit SVR with different features to build the QE model. Experiments are performed on the development set of the WMT17 QE, task1. The experimental results of en-de and de-en are shown in Tables 3 and 4, respectively. The rows "Baseline" and "Word2vec" represent only used the 17 baseline features that were officially released by the evaluation campaign and only used the sentence embedding features extraction by the word2vec toolkits, while the row "Word2vec+ Baseline" represents the combination of used baseline features and sentence embedding features, and so on. The system that we finally submitted uses a combination of all of the features.

Mikolov et al. (2013c) attempt different dimensions of word embedding for the source language and the target language to achieve the best translation quality. Motivated by their work, we test the diverse dimensions of the word embedding for the source language and target language on the

---

[2] http://www.fit.vutbr.cz/~imikolov/rnnlm/
[3] http://www.statmt.org/wmt16/it-translation-task.html
[4] http://scikit-learn.org/stable/

Features set	Pearson r	MAE	RMSE	Spearman ρ	DeltaAvg
Baseline	0.414	13.564	18.660	0.466	8.622
Word2vec	0.502	13.104	17.734	0.520	9.455
Word2vec+Baseline	0.520	12.918	17.509	0.537	9.628
Word2vec+RNNLM	0.539	12.658	17.383	0.559	9.972
Word2vec+RNNLM+Baseline	**0.544**	**12.632**	**17.285**	**0.563**	**9.998**

Table 3: Results of the en-de direction on the development set of the WMT17 QE, task1.

Features set	Pearson r	MAE	RMSE	Spearman ρ	DeltaAvg
Baseline	0.401	13.702	18.163	0.404	6.845
Word2vec	0.504	13.290	17.171	0.456	7.984
Word2vec+RNNLM	0.554	12.382	16.492	0.496	8.732
Word2vec+Baseline	0.555	12.664	16.563	0.504	8.700
Word2vec+RNNLM+Baseline	**0.580**	**12.116**	**16.162**	**0.521**	**9.024**

Table 4: Results of the de-en direction on the development set of the WMT17 QE, task1.

	Features set	Pearson r	MAE	RMSE	Spearman ρ	DeltaAvg
WMT16	Baseline	0.399	0.132	0.175	0.438	7.42
	Our system	0.527[3rd]	0.122	0.163	0.552[3rd]	9.37
en-de	Baseline	0.397	0.136	0.175	0.425	7.45
	Our system	0.522[5th]	0.126	0.163	0.545[5th]	9.54
de-en	Baseline	0.441	0.128	0.175	0.45	6.81
	Our system	0.531[8th]	0.130	0.167	0.52[8th]	8.62

Table 5: The system performance on the test set of the WMT16 QE and WMT17 QE

training set. For the en-de direction, the best performance is obtained when the dimensions of the source word embedding and target word embedding are 1024 and 2048, respectively. While for de-en direction, the best performance is obtained when the dimensions of the source word embedding and target word embedding are both 2048.

Then, based on the sentence embedding features, we add the cross-entropy features extracted by the RNNLM toolkit or the baseline features. When we added the cross-entropy features, the maximum value of Pearson r increased by 9.9% on the scoring evaluation, and the maximum value of Spearman ρ increased by 7.5% on the ranking evaluation. It can be found that in the en-de direction, the result obtained by adding cross-entropy features is superior to that from adding baseline features. Finally, when we combine all of the features, the maximum value of Pearson r increases by 44.6% on the scoring task, and the maximum value of Spearman ρ increased by 29.0% on the ranking evaluation compared with the baseline.

Because the training word embedding and RNNLM require a certain size of monolingual corpus, we also investigated the effects of different corpus scales on the quality of the extracted neural network features. It was found that when the training corpus contained more than 1M sentences, the QE system performance is not reduced, and when the corpus contained less than 1M sentences, the system performance will decrease gradually as the corpus size decreases. This finding demonstrates that the training word embedding and the RNNLM are not dependent heavily on the scale of the training corpus.

Finally, Table 5 provides the results of our system and the baseline system on the test set. We take the system "Word2vec+RNNLM+Baseline" as our primary system. In WMT16 QE, the performance of our system achieves the third place. In WMT17 QE, the best result of our system achieves the fifth place. Compared with the method proposed by Shah et al (2016), we use fewer features, but achieve better result on the test set.

5 Conclusions

In this paper, we train the embedding features using the word2vec toolkit and we enrich the features with cross-entropy features extracted by RNNLM to improve the correlation between the

QE and human judgment. The experimental results show that the neural network features can significantly improve the system performance. Compared with the traditional linguistically motivated features, the extracted features of the neural network are independent of the specific language.

In the future, we will train an end-to-end pure neural network model for QE, instead of using traditional SVR methods.

Acknowledgements

This research has been funded by the Natural Science Foundation of China under Grant No.6146 2044, 6166 2031, and 6146 2045. The authors would like to extend their sincere thanks to the anonymous reviewers who provided valuable comments.

References

Dzmitry Bahdanau, KyungHyun Cho, Yoshua Bengio. 2014. Neural machine translation by jointly learning to align and translate. *arXiv preprint arXiv: 1409.0473*.

Yoshua Bengio, Réjean Ducharme, Pascal Vincent, and Christian Janvin. 2003. A neural probabilistic language model. *The Journal of Machine Learning Research*, 3(2): 1137-1155.

Julia Kreutzer, Shigehiko Schamoni and Stefan Riezler. 2015. Quality Estimation from ScraTCH (QUETCH): Deep Learning for Word-level Translation Quality Estimation. In *Proceedings of the Tenth Workshop on Statistical Machine Translation*, pages 316-322, Lisbon, Portugal.

Tomas Mikolov, Martin Karafiat, Lukas Burget, Jan Honza Cernocky, Sanjeev Khudanpur. 2010. Recurrent neural network based language model. In *Proceedings of Interspeech 2010*, pages 1045-1048, Makuhari, Chiba, Japan.

Tomas Mikolov, Kai Chen, Greg Corrado, Jeffrey Dean. 2013a. Efficient Estimation of Word Representations in Vector Space. *arXiv preprint arXiv:1301.3781*.

Tomas Mikolov, Ilya Sutskever, Kai Chen, Greg Corrado, Jeffrey Dean. 2013b. Distributed Representations of Words and Phrases and their Compositionality. *arXiv preprint arXiv:1310.4546*.

Tomas Mikolov, Quoc V. Le, Ilya Sutskever. 2013c. Exploiting Similarities among Languages for Machine Translation. *arXiv preprint arXiv:1309.4168*.

Raj Nath Patel, Sasikumar M. 2016. Translation Quality Estimation using Recurrent Neural Network. In *Proceedings of the First Conference on Machine Translation*, pages 819-824, Berlin, Germany.

Carolina Scarton, Daniel Beck, Kashif Shah, Karin Sim Smith and Lucia Specia. 2016. Word embeddings and discourse information for Machine Translation Quality Estimation. In *Proceedings of the First Conference on Machine Translation*, pages 831-837, Berlin, Germany.

Holger Schwenk. 2007. Continuous space language models. *Computer Speech & Language*, 21(3):492-518.

Kashif Shah, Raymond W. M. Ng, Fethi Bougares, Lucia Specia. 2015a. Investigating Continuous Space Language Models for Machine Translation Quality Estimation. In *Proceedings of the 2015 Conference on Empirical Methods in Natural Language Processing*, pages 1073-1078, Lisbon, Portugal.

Kashif Shah, Varvara Logacheva, Gustavo Henrique Paetzold, Frederic Blain, Daniel Beck, Fethi Bougares, Lucia Specia. 2015b. SHEF-NN: Translation Quality Estimation with Neural Networks. In *Proceedings of the Tenth Workshop on Statistical Machine Translation*, pages 342-347, Lisbon, Portugal.

Kashif Shah, Fethi Bougares, Loïc Barrault and Lucia Specia. 2016. SHEF-LIUM-NN: Sentence-level Quality Estimation with Neural Network Features. In *Proceedings of the First Conference on Machine Translation*, pages 838-842, Berlin, Germany.

Matthew Snover, Bonnie Dorr, Richard Schwartz, Linnea Micciulla, and John Makhoul. 2006. A study of translation edit rate with targeted human annotation. In *Proceedings of the 7th Conference of the Association for machine translation in the Americas*, pages 223-231, Cambridge.

Lucia Specia, Kashif Shah, Jose G. C. de Souza and Trevor Cohn. 2013. QuEst – A translation quality estimation framework. In *51st Annual Meeting of Association for Computational Linguistics: Demo Session*, pages 79-84, Sofia, Dulgaria.

UHH Submission to the WMT17 Quality Estimation Shared Task

Melania Duma and Wolfgang Menzel
University of Hamburg
Natural Language Systems Division
{duma, menzel}@informatik.uni-hamburg.de

Abstract

The field of Quality Estimation (QE) has the goal to provide automatic methods for the evaluation of Machine Translation (MT), that do not require reference translations in their computation. We present our submission to the sentence level WMT17 Quality Estimation Shared Task. It combines tree and sequence kernels for predicting the post-editing effort of the target sentence. The kernels exploit both the source and target sentences, but also a back-translation of the candidate translation. The evaluation results show that the kernel approach combined with the baseline features brings substantial improvement over the baseline system.

1 Introduction

The evaluation of Machine Translation (MT) output is a sub-field of MT research that has experienced a great amount of interest in the past years. The process of MT evaluation involves three factors: an input segment in a source language, the candidate translation (also known as target sentence) which represents the output of a MT system when translating from the source language to the target language and a reference translation in the target language. The assessment of MT quality can be divided into two categories depending on whether it requires the presence of a reference translation or not. The reference-based evaluation scores the candidate translation by comparing it to the reference translation.

On the other hand, the reference-free evaluation, also known as quality estimation (QE), predicts the quality of a candidate translation based solely on the information contained in the source and target sentences. QE can be performed at different levels of granularity: word, sentence or phrase and it involves classifying, ranking or predicting scores for the candidate translations. A sentence-level QE system is conventionally constructed based on a set of features encoding the information contained in the source and target sentences, which are used for learning a prediction model. The features employed for this task can be of different types, like surface features, language model features or linguistic features. The positive influence of syntactic features on the performance of QE systems has been extensively studied, including in Rubino et al. (2012), Avramidis (2012) or more recently in Kozlova et al. (2016). However, the process of identifying the best performing set of features, is a task that is both expensive and requires a considerable amount of engineering effort (Hardmeier, 2011). On the other hand, kernel methods do not require the explicit definition of the features, and rely on the scalar product between vectors for capturing the similarity shared by the sentence pairs.

In this paper we present our submission to the WMT17 Shared Task on sentence level Quality Estimation, that makes use of sequence and tree kernels in predicting a continuous score representing the post-editing effort for the target sentence. The novel contribution of our system is the combination of different types of kernels. Moreover, we use a back-translation of the target sentence into the source language as an additional data representation to be exploited by the kernels, together with the usual source and target sentences representations. Furthermore, we construct additional explicit features by applying the kernel functions directly on the pair of source and back-translation sentences, a method that to our knowledge has not been used before. The evaluation performed demonstrates that the combination of the kernel approach and the baseline together with the newly

Proceedings of the Conference on Machine Translation (WMT), Volume 2: Shared Task Papers, pages 556–561
Copenhagen, Denmark, September 7–11, 2017. ©2017 Association for Computational Linguistics

introduced feature vectors brings consistent improvement over the baseline system.

This paper is organized as follows. The related work is presented in Section 2, while the methods employed and the implementation are described in Section 3. The experimental setup and the evaluation results are introduced in Section 4, while the last section summarizes our findings and presents future work ideas.

2 Related work

Kernel functions have been used in a variety of NLP tasks, including Textual Similarity (e.g. (Severyn et al., 2013)), Information Extraction (e.g. (Culotta and Sorensen, 2004)), Semantic Role Labeling (e.g. (Moschitti et al., 2008)) or Textual Entailment (e.g. (Wang and Neumann, 2007)).

An approach for QE based on syntactic tree kernels is introduced in (Hardmeier, 2011), where a binary SVM classifier is trained to make predictions about the quality of the MT output. The datasets are syntactically analyzed using constituency and dependency parsers. The Subset Tree Kernel (Collins and Duffy, 2001) is used for the constituency trees, while the Partial Tree Kernel (Moschitti, 2006a) (Moschitti, 2006b) was judged as being more appropriate for the dependency trees. The evaluation shows that the combination between baseline features and the tree kernels achieves the best performance. These findings are further validated in Hardmeier et al. (2012) where a QE system is proposed based on a set of 82 explicit features combined with syntactic tree kernels.

Syntactic tree kernels for QE are also explored in Kaljahi et al. (2014), where a set of hand crafted constituency and dependency based features together with subset tree kernels applied on the constituency and dependency tree representations are used. The evaluation results demonstrate that the source constituency trees perform better than the target sentence constituency trees. This work is further extended in Kaljahi (2015), where multiple QE systems based on syntactic and semantic features are introduced.

The work presented in this paper differs from previous kernel approaches for QE by the innovative use of sequence kernels in addition to the previously utilized tree kernels. We extend on the previous kernel QE research by also making use of a back-translation of the target sentence in the computation of the kernels. While back-translations features have been previously utilized for QE (e.g.(Bechara et al., 2016)), their potential as an additional structural input representation for kernels has never been studied before. Furthermore, we exploit the potential of the scores of the kernel functions applied on the source and back-translation sentences as additional hard-coded features.

3 Methods and implementation

In this section details about the methodology and the implementation will be presented. First, tree and sequence kernels will be introduced, followed by the description of the implementation of these kernels in the context of QE. Finally, the machine learning platform used for implementing the QE systems will be presented.

3.1 Kernels for Quality Estimation

A kernel function computes the similarity between two structural representations without requiring the identification of the entire feature space (Moschitti, 2006a). To achieve this, the scalar product between vectors of substructure counts is computed in a vector space with a possibly infinite number of dimensions (Nguyen et al., 2009). Different kernel functions, depending on the type of structural input data they require, have been proposed including sequence, tree or graphs kernels. Tree kernels make use of tree representations for their computation, while sequence kernels calculate the similarity between the input sequence representations based on the number of common subsequences they share.

In the case of tree kernels, a series of algorithms have been proposed, e.g. in Collins and Duffy (2001) or Moschitti (2006a), based on the type of tree fragments (e.g. subsets, subtrees or partial trees) they take into consideration in their computation. On the other hand, sequence kernels have also been extensively studied in Bunescu and Mooney (2005) or Nguyen et al. (2009).

In this paper, we focus on the Partial Tree Kernel (Moschitti, 2006a) and the Subsequence Kernel (Bunescu and Mooney, 2005). The Partial Tree Kernel (PTK) was chosen because it is more flexible than the subtree or subset kernels in its calculation by taking partial subtrees into account. The Subsequence Kernel (SK) uses a dynamic pro-

| System | baseline features | | | | baseline+new features | | | |
| | exact | | not exact | | exact | | not exact | |
	Pearson↑	MAE↓	Pearson↑	MAE↓	Pearson↑	MAE↓	Pearson↑	MAE↓
SK src	0.408	0.145	0.416	0.143	0.413	0.144	0.422	0.143
SK src+mt	0.481	0.139	0.477	0.138	0.484	0.139	0.480	0.136
SK src+mt+mtbk	0.491	0.138	0.496	0.137	0.493	0.138	0.497	0.137
PTK src	0.449	0.137	0.452	0.138	0.459	0.137	0.463	0.137
PTK src+mt	0.495	0.133	0.499	0.133	0.50	0.133	0.505	0.132
PTK src+mt+mtbk	0.503	0.133	0.505	0.133	0.506	0.133	**0.509**	0.133
(PTK src+mt) + (SK src+mt)	0.488	0.137	0.487	0.136	0.490	0.137	0.488	0.136
(PTK src+mt+mtbk) + (SK src+mt+mtbk)	0.499	0.136	0.503	0.135	0.50	0.136	**0.504**	0.135
Baseline WMT	0.169	0.146						

Table 1: Evaluation results for the DE-EN dev set.

| System | baseline features | | | | baseline+new features | | | |
| | exact | | not exact | | exact | | not exact | |
	Pearson↑	MAE↓	Pearson↑	MAE↓	Pearson↑	MAE↓	Pearson↑	MAE↓
SK src	0.433	0.141	0.440	0.139	0.437	0.141	0.443	0.139
SK src+mt	0.478	0.138	0.483	0.137	0.480	0.138	0.484	0.139
SK src+mt+mtbk	0.466	0.142	0.478	0.140	0.467	0.142	0.479	0.140
PTK src	0.450	0.136	0.456	0.135	0.458	0.136	0.465	0.135
PTK src+mt	0.506	0.132	0.523	0.130	0.510	0.132	0.537	0.130
PTK src+mt+mtbk	0.491	0.137	0.501	0.137	0.493	0.137	0.503	0.137
(PTK src+mt) + (SK src+mt)	0.493	0.136	0.502	0.135	0.494	0.136	0.503	0.135
(PTK src+mt+mtbk) + (SK src+mt+mtbk)	0.478	0.141	0.488	0.140	0.479	0.141	0.489	0.140
Baseline WMT	0.260	0.140						

Table 2: Evaluation results for the DE-EN test set.

gramming approach to determine the number of common patterns between the two input sentences. In our experiments, the patterns taken into account were composed of the lexical items.

In order to use the tree kernel functions, the source and the target sentences were parsed using the Bohnet graph-based dependency parser (Bohnet, 2010), which was chosen because of its high accuracy. The data was first preprocessed by performing lemmatization and pos-tagging. Publicly available [1] pre-trained models were used for analyzing the source, target and back-translation sentences.

For learning using the Partial Tree Kernel, a transformation of the dependency parse tree is required, as introduced in Croce et al. (2011). We followed the lexical-centered-tree approach, where the grammatical relation and the pos-tag are encoded as the rightmost children of a dependency tree node. In the case of sequence kernels, the only preprocessing step applied was the tokenization of the input sentences. In order to investigate if prior lemmatization of the input sentences influences the results, we created two variants for each structural representation: an exact one containing the actual lexical items and a simplified non-exact one consisting of their corresponding lemmas.

Furthermore, we incorporated a back-translation of the target sentence as an additional structural input representation for both the tree kernels and the sequence kernels. The back-translation was obtained using the free online Google Machine Translation system [2]. We also exploited the full capability of the kernel functions by utilizing their explicit scores when applied on the source and back-translation sentences. We computed the scores for both the non-exact representations, and the exact ones. The scores were normalized using the formula from Croce et al. (2011)

$$score = \frac{K(T1, T2)}{\sqrt{K(T1, T1) \star K(T2, T2)}}$$

with *T1* and *T2* denoting the structural representations and *K* the type of kernel function applied.

3.2 KeLP (Kernel-based Learning Platform)

In our implementation, we applied the Partial Tree Kernel[3] and the Sequence Kernel [4] together with the epsilon-regression SVM implementations made available in the KeLP package (Filice et al., 2015b) (Filice et al., 2015a). KeLP (Kernel-based

---

[1] https://code.google.com/archive/p/mate-tools/downloads

[2] https://translate.google.com
[3] based on (Moschitti, 2006a)
[4] based on (Bunescu and Mooney, 2005)

| System | baseline features | | | | baseline+new features | | | |
| | exact | | not exact | | exact | | not exact | |
	Pearson↑	MAE↓	Pearson↑	MAE↓	Pearson↑	MAE↓	Pearson↑	MAE↓
SK src	0.446	0.137	0.434	0.140	0.450	0.137	0.436	0.140
SK src+mt	0.496	0.133	0.491	0.134	0.499	0.133	0.493	0.134
SK src+mt+mtbk	0.508	0.131	0.497	0.134	0.499	0.133	0.499	0.137
PTK src	0.467	0.134	0.469	0.134	0.476	0.134	0.477	0.133
PTK src+mt	0.516	0.130	0.524	0.129	0.480	0.134	0.530	0.129
PTK src+mt+mtbk	0.520	0.130	0.523	0.130	**0.524**	0.130	0.526	0.130
(PTK src+mt) + (SK src+mt)	0.508	0.131	0.516	0.132	0.510	0.131	0.518	0.132
(PTK src+mt+mtbk) + (SK src+mt+mtbk)	0.515	0.131	0.515	0.132	**0.516**	0.131	0.516	0.132
Baseline WMT	0.359	0.140						

Table 3: Evaluation results for the EN-DE dev set. The highlighted numbers correspond to the systems submitted to the shared task.

Learning Platform) is a Java Machine Learning library that provides the venue for implementing kernel based machine learning algorithms together with kernel functions. KeLP provides built-in support for multiple vectorial or structured data representations, which can be leveraged at the same time by combining different kernels into a single model. The package has a series of advantages, among them platform-independence, flexibility of use and its modularity that makes it easily extensible. The training of the QE prediction models was performed using the Support Vector Machine epsilon-Regression implementation with default parameters from the KeLP package. For the baseline systems a radial basis function (rbf) kernel was chosen, while for the other implemented QE systems the linear combination between the baseline features rbf kernel and the additional structural kernels was used.

4 Evaluation and results

4.1 Experimental setup

The evaluation was performed using the datasets released for the QE sentence-level shared task by the Second Conference On Machine Translation (WMT17) [5]. The data consists of tuples, containing the source segment, the target sentence and a manually post-edited version of the target sentence, together with their associated post-editing score.

The WMT17 dataset is composed of both English-German and German-English tuples. The English-German dataset, pertaining to the IT domain, consists of 23000 tuples for training, with additional 1000 instances for development. Two sets, comprised of 2000 units each, were made

available for testing. On the other hand, the German-English dataset provides 25000 tuples for training, 1000 units for development and a test set consisting of 2000 instances, with the general domain categorized as Pharmaceutical. The QE baseline systems used for evaluation are based on the sets of 17 baseline features made available by the QE sentence-level shared task. They consist of surface features (e.g the number of tokens/punctuation marks in the source sentence), language model features (e.g LM probability of the source/target sentences), but also n-gram based features (e.g percentage of unigrams in quartile 4 of frequency (higher frequency words) in a corpus of the source language).

4.2 Results

The systems were evaluated based on their predicted scores using Pearson's correlation coefficient and the Mean Average Error (MAE), with the former being chosen as the primary method of evaluation for the WMT17 sentence-level QE task. We experimented with different model combinations and the results of the evaluation are presented in the tables that follow, where we have highlighted our submissions to the sentence level shared task. To better distinguish between models, the following QE system notation scheme was utilized: [Kernel [level]], where Kernel identifies the type of kernel used: PTK or SK and level represents the input type of sentence the kernel was applied to: source (marked with src), target (marked with mt) and back-translated target (marked with mtbk). The linear combination between the different kernel functions was marked with the plus sign. The systems can be categorized according to multiple criteria. The first one considers the presence of the new kernel features, which divides the systems into *baseline features* and *baseline+new*

[5]http://www.statmt.org/wmt17/quality-estimation-task.html

System	baseline features				baseline+new features			
	exact		not exact		exact		not exact	
	Pearson↑	MAE ↓	**Pearson**↑	MAE ↓	**Pearson**↑	MAE ↓	**Pearson**↑	MAE ↓
SK src	0.448	0.131	0.443	0.132	0.456	0.131	0.451	0.132
SK src+mt	0.506	0.126	0.490	0.127	0.510	0.125	0.494	0.126
SK src+mt+mtbk	0.510	0.125	0.498	0.126	0.513	0.125	0.500	0.126
PTK src	0.461	0.129	0.439	0.130	0.474	0.128	0.452	0.129
PTK src+mt	0.508	0.124	0.500	0.124	0.515	0.124	0.508	0.123
PTK src+mt+mtbk	0.511	0.124	0.508	0.124	0.516	0.123	0.514	0.124
(PTK src+mt) + (SK src+mt)	0.517	0.125	0.508	0.125	0.520	0.126	0.511	0.125
(PTK src+mt+mtbk) + (SK src+mt+mtbk)	0.522	0.124	0.515	0.124	0.524	0.124	0.517	0.124
Baseline WMT	0.345	0.136						

Table 4: Evaluation results for the EN-DE 2016 test set

System	baseline features				baseline+new features			
	exact		not exact		exact		not exact	
	Pearson↑	MAE ↓	**Pearson**↑	MAE ↓	**Pearson**↑	MAE ↓	**Pearson**↑	MAE ↓
SK src	0.422	0.138	0.420	0.138	0.427	0.138	0.427	0.137
SK src+mt	0.482	0.132	0.470	0.133	0.485	0.132	0.473	0.133
SK src+mt+mtbk	0.494	0.131	0.482	0.132	0.495	0.131	0.483	0.132
PTK src	0.444	0.133	0.440	0.136	0.452	0.132	0.449	0.133
PTK src+mt	0.496	0.129	0.493	0.129	0.502	0.129	0.499	0.129
PTK src+mt+mtbk	0.504	0.129	0.505	0.129	0.508	0.129	0.509	0.128
(PTK src+mt) + (SK src+mt)	0.497	0.131	0.494	0.131	0.499	0.131	0.496	0.131
(PTK src+mt+mtbk) + (SK src+mt+mtbk)	0.508	0.130	0.506	0.130	0.509	0.130	0.508	0.130
Baseline WMT	0.387	0.135						

Table 5: Evaluation results for the EN-DE 2017 test set.

features systems. The second criterion is represented by the presence of the lemmatization in the pre-processing pipeline of the input sentences, which partitions the systems into *exact* and *not exact* ones.

A series of preliminary experiments was conducted which indicated that strictly structural kernel based methods could not capture all the relevant features for constructing a high performing QE system. Therefore, a combination between the baseline rbf kernel with additional structural kernels was implemented for the reported QE systems.

We can notice that all the systems, corresponding to both language pairs outperformed the baseline systems in terms of Pearson correlation. Of particular interest are the systems making use of the new kernel features, which succeeded in surpassing the corresponding systems that only used the baseline features.

The results also show that the addition of the back-translation as additional input data, proved on average beneficial for improving the correlation scores over systems that make use of only the source and target sentences as input data for the kernel functions.

In addition, we can observe that the sequence kernels based systems are highly performant in terms of Pearson's coefficient, albeit slightly worse on average than the tree kernels based implementations. This is a very important aspect, as the integration of sequence kernels into QE systems does not require additional external tools and therefore makes them well suited for low-resource language pairs, that might lack high-quality syntactic tools like parsers or taggers. Moreover, by employing a sequence kernel, the parsing of MT output is effectively bypassed. This constitutes an advantage as the parsing of target sentences often represents a challenging task due to the ungrammaticality of the MT generated output.

5 Conclusions and future work

In this paper, we presented our submission to the sentence level QE task, based on sequence and tree kernels. We have also investigated the performance of additional kernel-based features, as well as the benefit of incorporating a back-translation of the machine translation output as an additional input data representation, which to our knowledge has not been studied before. The results indicate that both ideas contribute useful additions to the baseline systems. We have also demonstrated that sequence kernels are a high performing method for predicting the quality of MT translations, that have the advantage of not requiring additional resources for their computation.

We plan to further extend the current work by using constituency trees besides dependency trees for the computation of the tree kernels. We also plan to investigate if the choice of the MT system for the back-translation, affects the evaluation results. Lastly, more combination schemes between the tree and sequence kernels will be explored together with additional datasets and language pairs.

References

Eleftherios Avramidis. 2012. Comparative Quality Estimation: Automatic sentence-level ranking of multiple Machine Translation outputs. *Proceedings of COLING 2012: Technical Papers* pages 115–132.

Hanna Bechara, Carla Parra Escartin, Constantin Orasan, and Lucia Specia. 2016. Semantic Textual Similarity in Quality Estimation. *Baltic J. Modern Computing* pages 256–268.

Bernd Bohnet. 2010. Top accuracy and fast dependency parsing is not a contradiction. *The 23rd International Conference on Computational Linguistics (COLING 2010)* .

Razvan Bunescu and Raymond Mooney. 2005. Subsequence kernels for Relation Extraction. *Advances in Neural Information Processing Systems, Vol. 18: Proceedings of the 2005 Conference (NIPS)* .

Michael Collins and Nigel Duffy. 2001. Convolution kernels for natural language. *Proceedings of NIPS 2001* pages 625–632.

Danilo Croce, Alessandro Moschitti, and Roberto Basili. 2011. Structured lexical similarity via convolution kernels on dependency trees. *Proceedings of the 2011 Conference on Empirical Methods in Natural Language Processing* pages 1034–1046.

Aron Culotta and Jeffrey Sorensen. 2004. Dependency tree kernels for Relation Extraction. *Proceedings of the 42nd Annual Meeting on Association for Computational Linguistics* .

Simone Filice, Giuseppe Castellucci, Roberto Basili, Giovanni Da San Martino, and Alessandro Moschitti. 2015a. KeLP: a Kernel-based Learning Platform in Java. *The workshop on Machine Learning Open Source Software (MLOSS): Open Ecosystems*

Simone Filice, Giuseppe Castellucci, Danilo Croce, and Roberto Basili. 2015b. KeLP: a kernel-based learning platform for Natural Language Processing. *Proceedings of ACL-IJCNLP 2015 System Demonstrations* pages 19–24.

Christian Hardmeier. 2011. Improving Machine Translation quality prediction with syntactic tree kernels. *Proceedings of the 15th Conference of the European Association for Machine Translation* pages 233–240.

Christian Hardmeier, Joakim Nivre, and Jorg Tiedemann. 2012. Tree kernels for Machine Translation Quality Estimation. *Proceedings of the 7th Workshop on Statistical Machine Translation* pages 109–113.

Rasoul Kaljahi. 2015. The role of syntax and semantics in Machine Translation and Quality Estimation of machine-translated user-generated content. *PhD Thesis* .

Rasoul Kaljahi, Jennifer Foster, Raphael Rubino, and Johann Roturier. 2014. Quality Estimation of English-French Machine Translation: A detailed study of the role of syntax. *Proceedings of COLING 2014, the 25th International Conference on Computational Linguistics: Technical Papers* pages 2052–2063.

Anna Kozlova, Mariya Shmatova, and Anton Frolov. 2016. YSDA participation in the WMT16 Quality Estimation shared task. *Proceedings of the First Conference on Machine Translation, Volume 2: Shared Task Papers* pages 793–799.

Alessandro Moschitti. 2006a. Efficient convolution kernels for dependency and constituent syntactic trees. *Proceedings of the 17th European Conference on Machine Learning* .

Alessandro Moschitti. 2006b. Making tree kernels practical for natural language learning. *Proceedings of the Eleventh International Conference of the European Association for Computational Linguistics* .

Alessandro Moschitti, Daniele Pighin, and Roberto Basili. 2008. Tree kernels for Semantic Role Labeling. *Computational Linguistics* 34(2):193–224.

Truc-Vien T. Nguyen, Alessandro Moschitti, and Giuseppe Riccardi. 2009. Convolution kernels on constituent, dependency and sequential structures for Relation Extraction. *Proceedings of the 2009 Conference on Empirical Methods in Natural Language Processing* pages 1378–1387.

Raphael Rubino, Jennifer Foster, Joachim Wagne, Johann Roturier, Rasul Samad Zadeh Kaljahi, and Fred Hollowood. 2012. DCU-Symantec submission for the WMT 2012 Quality Estimation task. *Proceedings of the Seventh Workshop on Statistical Machine Translation* pages 138–144.

Aliaksei Severyn, Massimo Nicosia, and Alessandro Moschitti. 2013. iKernels-Core: Tree kernel learning for Textual Similarity. *Second Joint Conference on Lexical and Computational Semantics (*SEM), Volume 1: Proceedings of the Main Conference and the Shared Task* pages 53–58.

Rui Wang and Gnter Neumann. 2007. Recognizing Textual Entailment using a subsequence kernel method. *AAAI* 7:937–945.

Predictor-Estimator using Multilevel Task Learning with Stack Propagation for Neural Quality Estimation

Hyun Kim[†] and **Jong-Hyeok Lee**[‡]

[†]Creative IT Engineering, [‡]Computer Science and Engineering,
Pohang University of Science and Technology (POSTECH), Republic of Korea
[†]hkim.postech@gmail.com [‡]jhlee@postech.ac.kr

Seung-Hoon Na

Computer Science and Engineering,
Chonbuk National University, Republic of Korea
nash@jbnu.ac.kr

Abstract

In this paper, we present a two-stage neural quality estimation model that uses multilevel task learning for translation quality estimation (QE) at the sentence, word, and phrase levels. Our approach is based on an end-to-end stacked neural model named *Predictor-Estimator*, which has two stages consisting of a neural word prediction model and neural QE model. To efficiently train the two-stage model, a *stack propagation* method is applied, thereby enabling us to jointly learn the word prediction model and QE model in a single learning mode. In addition, we deploy multilevel task learning with stack propagation, where the training examples available for all QE subtasks (i.e., sentence/word/phrase levels) are used to train a Predictor-Estimator for a specific subtask. All of our submissions to the QE task of WMT17 are ensembles that combine a set of neural models trained under different settings of varying dimensionalities and shuffling training examples, eventually achieving the best performances for all subtasks at the sentence, word, and phrase levels.

1 Introduction

In this paper, we describe the two-stage end-to-end neural models submitted to the Shared Task on Sentence/Word/Phrase-Level Quality Estimation (QE task) at the 2017 Conference on Machine Translation (WMT17). The task aims at estimating quality scores/categories for an unseen translation without a reference translation at various granularities (i.e., sentence/word/phrase levels) (Specia et al., 2013).

Our neural network-based models for sentence/word/phrase-level QE are based on Predictor-Estimator architecture (Kim et al., 2017; Kim and Lee, 2016), which is a two-stage end-to-end neural QE model. In this submission to WMT 2017, our Predictor-Estimator model is further advanced by extensively applying a stack propagation method (Zhang and Weiss, 2016) in order to efficiently train the two-stage model.

The Predictor-Estimator architecture (Kim et al., 2017; Kim and Lee, 2016) is the two-stage neural QE model (Figure 1) consisting of two types of stacked neural models: 1) a neural word prediction model (i.e., word predictor) trained from additional large-scale parallel corpora and 2) a neural QE model (i.e., quality estimator) trained from quality-annotated noisy parallel corpora called *QE data*. The Predictor-Estimator architecture uses word prediction as a pre-task for QE. Kim et al. (2017) showed that word prediction is helpful for improving the QE performance. In the first stage, the word predictor, which is based on a bidirectional and bilingual recurrent neural network (RNN) language model – the modification of the attention-based RNN encoder-decoder (Bahdanau et al., 2015; Cho et al., 2014) – predicts a target word conditioned with unbounded source and target contexts. QE feature vectors (QEFVs) are the approximated knowledge transferred from word prediction to QE. In the second stage, QEFVs are used as inputs to the quality estimator for estimating sentence/word/phrase-level translation quality.

Stack propagation (Zhang and Weiss, 2016) is a learning method for efficient joint learning that enables backpropagation down the stacked models. Zhang and Weiss (2016) applied stack propagation for stacked part-of-speech (POS) tagging and parsing models by alternating between stochastic updates to POS tagging or parsing objectives,

Proceedings of the Conference on Machine Translation (WMT), Volume 2: Shared Task Papers, pages 562–568
Copenhagen, Denmark, September 7–11, 2017. ©2017 Association for Computational Linguistics

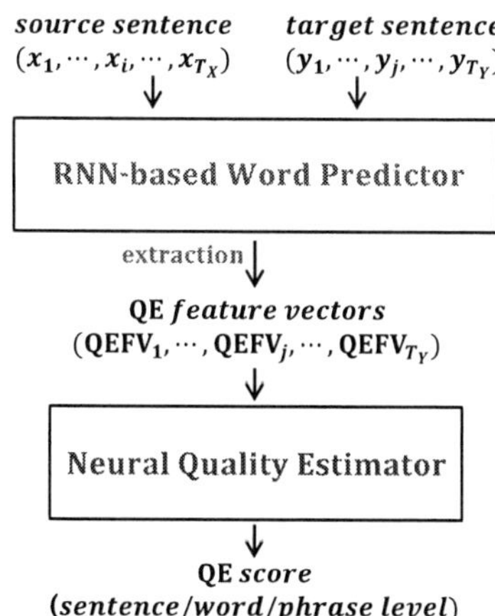

Figure 1: Two-stage Predictor-Estimator architecture (Kim et al., 2017).

where continuous hidden layer activations of the POS tagger network are used as an input to the parser network.

We applied the Predictor-Estimator architecture to the sentence/word/phrase-level QE task of WMT17. In the original Predictor-Estimator architecture proposed by Kim et al. (2017), the word predictor and quality estimator are trained individually. As a result, the backpropagation in training the quality estimator does not go down for the word predictor network. Because there exists a continuous and differentiable link between the stacked word predictor and quality estimator, we used stack propagation to jointly learn two-stage models in the Predictor-Estimator. Furthermore, we deployed multilevel task learning with stack propagation, where a task-specific Predictor-Estimator is trained by using not only the task-specific training examples but also all other training examples of QE subtasks. Finally, all of our submissions for the QE task of WMT17 were ensembles that combine a set of neural models trained under different settings of varying dimensionalities and shuffled training examples.

2 Improving Predictor-Estimator with Stack Propagation

In this section, we describe the three types of Predictor-Estimators using stack propagation: 1) the base model (*PredictorEstimator*), 2) Predictor-Estimator using stack propagation for a single-level task (*PredictorEstimator + (SingleLevel) Stackprop*),

and 3) Predictor-Estimator using multilevel task learning with stack propagation (*PredictorEstimator + MultiLevel Stackprop*).

2.1 Base Model

Our base model is the original Predictor-Estimator, where a word predictor and quality estimator are trained individually. We used the Pre&Post-QEFV/Bi-RNN model, which showed the best performance among the Predictor-Estimator models presented by Kim et al. (2017). The Pre&Post-QEFV/Bi-RNN model is a two-stage model that uses Pre&Post-QEFV extracted from the word predictor and Bi-RNN applied in the quality estimator. Pre&Post-QEFV is the summary representation in the word predictor networks and involves approximating the transferred knowledge from each target word prediction. This consists of the word prediction-based weight-inclusive indirect representation (i.e., Pre-QEFV) and direct hidden state (i.e., Post-QEFV).

2.2 Using Stack Propagation

Because the Predictor-Estimator architecture has a continuous and differentiable link between the stacked word predictor and quality estimator, allowing backpropagation from the quality estimator to the word predictor is a valuable approach. To jointly learn the two-stage models in the Predictor-Estimator, stack propagation is applied by alternating between stochastic updates to word prediction or QE objectives, thus performing backpropagation down from the quality estimator to the word predictor (Figure 2).

2.3 Using Multilevel Task Learning with Stack Propagation

We implemented multilevel task learning with stack propagation that uses the training examples available for all QE subtasks (sentence/word/phrase level) to train a task-specific Predictor-Estimator. There are mutual common parts in the Predictor-Estimator networks for sentence/word/phrase-level QE: 1) all of the word predictor networks and 2) input parts and hidden states of the quality estimator networks, except for the output parts at each level. In multilevel task learning with stack propagation, these common parts of the task-specific Predictor-Estimator networks are trained by using not only task-specific training examples but also all of the other training examples of QE subtasks.

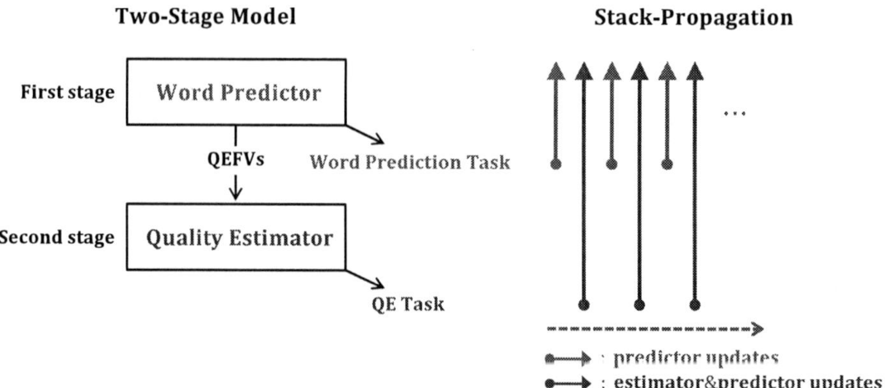

Figure 2: Applied stack propagation (Zhang and Weiss, 2016) to Predictor-Estimator architecture by alternating stochastic updates.

This approach is based on the idea that QE at all levels has a common origin because quality annotations at each level of QE data[1] are obtained by comparing the same post-edited target references with the same target translations to calculate the human-targeted translation edit rate (HTER) (Snover et al., 2006). By using multilevel task learning with stack propagation, mutually beneficial relationships can be learned between each level. We alternate not only between stochastic updates to word prediction or QE objectives but also between stochastic updates to sentence/word/phrase-level QE objectives for jointly learning mutual common parts of the Predictor-Estimator network[2].

3 Experimental Results

3.1 Experimental settings

We evaluated our models for the WMT17 QE task of sentence/word/phrase-level English-German and German-English. To train our two-stage models, we used QE data for the WMT17 QE task (Specia and Logacheva, 2017) and par-

allel corpora including the Europarl corpus, common crawl corpus, news commentary, rapid corpus of EU press releases for the WMT17 translation task[3], and src-pe (source sentences-their target post-editions) pairs for the WMT17 QE task. All Predictor-Estimator models were initialized with a word predictor and quality estimator that were pre-trained individually.

3.2 Results of the Single Predictor-Estimator Models

For a single Predictor-Estimator model, we used one type of dimensionality settings[4].

Table 1 presents the experimental results for the single Predictor-Estimator models with the English-German QE development set at the sentence, word, and phrase levels. Among the three types of models, the Predictor-Estimator using multilevel task learning with stack propagation consistently exhibited the best performance in all of our runs. Because this was the most sophisticated among our three types of models, we believe that applying more advanced approaches to Predictor-Estimator brings further improvements. The base model, which was the simplest Predictor-Estimator model, exhibited somewhat lower performance than others. The models using stack propagation for sentence/word/phrase-level QE consistently performed better than the base models without stack propagation. This result means

---

[1] QE data consist of source sentences, target translations (not references), and their target quality annotations for sentence/word/phrase levels.

[2] An original phrase-level Predictor-Estimator and original word-level Predictor-Estimator have different architectures in that the input of the former is phrase-level QEFV, which is the average of its constituent word-level QEFVs. However, in multilevel task learning with stack propagation for phrase-level QE, we use a word-level Predictor-Estimator architecture. In the word-level Predictor-Estimator for phrase-level QE, if any word in the phrase boundary is tagged as 'BAD,' the output of the phrase level has a 'BAD' tag, which exactly corresponds with the purpose of the phrase-level QE.

[3] http://www.statmt.org/wmt17/translation-task.html

[4] The vocabulary size was 70,000, the word embedding dimensionality was 500, the size of the hidden units of the word predictor was 700, and the size of the hidden units of the quality estimator was 100.

Sentence Level	Pearson's r ↑	MAE ↓	RMSE ↓	Spearman's ρ ↑	DeltaAvg ↑
PredictorEstimator	0.6436	0.1125	0.1582	0.6851	0.1190
+ (SingleLevel) Stackprop	0.6476	0.1122	0.1567	0.6957	0.1209
+ MultiLevel Stackprop	0.6785	0.1047	0.1502	0.7267	0.1234

Word Level	F_1-**mult** ↑	F_1-BAD ↑	F_1-OK ↑
PredictorEstimator	0.5104	0.5747	0.8881
+ (SingleLevel) Stackprop	0.5335	0.5906	0.9034
+ MultiLevel Stackprop	0.5374	0.6018	0.8930

Phrase Level	F_1-**mult** ↑	F_1-BAD ↑	F_1-OK ↑
PredictorEstimator	0.5262	0.6367	0.8264
+ (SingleLevel) Stackprop	0.5631	0.6674	0.8438
+ MultiLevel Stackprop	0.5664	0.6697	0.8457

Table 1: Results of the single Predictor-Estimator models on the WMT17 En-De dev set.

Sentence Level	Pearson's r ↑	MAE ↓	RMSE ↓	Spearman's ρ ↑	DeltaAvg ↑
PredictorEstimator	0.6375	0.1094	0.1480	0.6665	0.1138
+ (SingleLevel) Stackprop	0.6377	0.1092	0.1473	0.6698	0.1149
+ MultiLevel Stackprop	0.6599	0.1057	0.1450	0.6914	0.1188

Word Level	F_1-**mult** ↑	F_1-BAD ↑	F_1-OK ↑
PredictorEstimator	0.5086	0.5768	0.8818
+ (SingleLevel) Stackprop	0.5203	0.5898	0.8822
+ MultiLevel Stackprop	0.5287	0.5951	0.8883

Phrase Level	F_1-**mult** ↑	F_1-BAD ↑	F_1-OK ↑
PredictorEstimator	0.5116	0.6227	0.8216
+ (SingleLevel) Stackprop	0.5512	0.6522	0.8452
+ MultiLevel Stackprop	0.5527	0.6523	0.8473

Table 2: Results of the single Predictor-Estimator models on the WMT17 En-De test set.

that stack propagation is advantageous for efficient joint learning. The use of multilevel task learning with stack propagation for sentence-level QE significantly improved the QE performance. The use of single-level stack propagation for word/phrase-level QE also significantly improved the QE performance.

Tables 2-3 present the experimental results of the single Predictor-Estimator models for the English German and German English QE test set at the different levels.

3.3 Results of Ensembles of Multiple Instances

To develop ensemble-based submissions for the WMT17 QE task, we used two types of single models: the simplest (base model) and most sophisticated (Predictor-Estimator using multilevel task learning with stack propagation).

Martins et al. (2016) combined 15 instances of neural models to make ensembles; they used three types of neural models and trained five instances for each type by using different data shuffles.

In our experiments, we made ensembles of multiple instances trained under different set-tings of varying dimensionalities and shuffled training examples for the two selected models (i.e., the simplest and the most sophisticated single models). We averaged the predicted scores from each instance for producing the ensemble results. The ensembles for the simplest single model were made by averaging 15 predictions from each single model with five types of dimensionality settings[5] to produce three trained instances with the different shuffling training examples, called *PredictorEstimator-Ensemble*[6].

---

[5] 1) The vocabulary size was 70,000 words, the word embedding dimensionality was 500, the size of the hidden units of the word predictor was 700, and the size of the hidden units of the quality estimator was 100. 2) The vocabulary size was 70,000 words, the word embedding dimensionality was 500, the size of the hidden units of the word predictor was 700, and the size of the hidden units of the quality estimator was 150. 3) The vocabulary size was 100,000 words, the word embedding dimensionality was 700, the size of the hidden units of the word predictor was 1000, and the size of the hidden units of the quality estimator was 100. 4) The vocabulary size was 100,000 words, the word embedding dimensionality was 700, the size of the hidden units of the word predictor was 1000, and the size of the hidden units of the quality estimator was 150. 5) The vocabulary size was 100,000 words, the word embedding dimensionality was 700, the size of the hidden units of the word predictor was 1000, and the size of the hidden units of the quality estimator was 200.

[6] In the submissions for WMT17 QE task,

Sentence Level	Pearson's r ↑	MAE ↓	RMSE ↓	Spearman's ρ ↑	DeltaAvg ↑
PredictorEstimator	0.6826	0.0987	0.1428	0.6065	0.1010
+ (SingleLevel) Stackprop	0.6888	0.0977	0.1458	0.6202	0.1026
+ MultiLevel Stackprop	0.6985	0.0952	0.1461	0.6408	0.1039

Word Level	F_1-mult ↑	F_1-BAD ↑	F_1-OK ↑
PredictorEstimator	0.4864	0.5259	0.9249
+ (SingleLevel) Stackprop	0.5008	0.5361	0.9342
+ MultiLevel Stackprop	0.5051	0.5411	0.9334

Phrase Level	F_1-mult ↑	F_1-BAD ↑	F_1-OK ↑
PredictorEstimator	0.5069	0.5674	0.8934
+ (SingleLevel) Stackprop	0.5143	0.5671	0.9068
+ MultiLevel Stackprop	0.5246	0.5829	0.8999

Table 3: Results of the single Predictor Estimator models on the WMT17 De-En test set.

Sentence Level (Scoring Variant)	Pearson's r ↑	MAE ↓	RMSE ↓	Rank
PredictorEstimator-Ensemble	0.6731	0.1067	0.1412	2
PredictorEstimator-MultiLevel-Ensemble	0.6891	0.1016	0.1390	
PredictorEstimator-Combined-MultiLevel-Ensemble	0.6954	0.1019	0.1371	1
BASELINE	0.397	0.136	0.175	

Sentence Level (Ranking Variant)	Spearman's ρ ↑	DeltaAvg ↑	Rank
PredictorEstimator-Ensemble	0.7029	0.1198	2
PredictorEstimator-MultiLevel-Ensemble	0.7194	0.1221	
PredictorEstimator-Combined-MultiLevel-Ensemble	0.7253	0.1232	1
BASELINE	0.425	0.0745	

Word Level	F_1-mult ↑	F_1-BAD ↑	F_1-OK ↑	Rank
PredictorEstimator-Ensemble	0.5429	0.6069	0.8945	5
PredictorEstimator-MultiLevel-Ensemble	0.5602	0.6210	0.9021	
PredictorEstimator-Combined-MultiLevel-Ensemble	0.5679	0.6283	0.9039	1
BASELINE	0.361	0.407	0.886	

Phrase Level	F_1-mult ↑	F_1-BAD ↑	F_1-OK ↑	Rank
PredictorEstimator-Ensemble	0.5492	0.6518	0.8426	2
PredictorEstimator-MultiLevel-Ensemble	0.5808	0.6728	0.8633	
PredictorEstimator-Combined-MultiLevel-Ensemble	0.5859	0.6787	0.8633	1
BASELINE	0.327	0.402	0.814	

Table 4: Results of ensembles of multi-instance Predictor-Estimator models on the WMT17 En-De test set.

Sentence Level (Scoring Variant)	Pearson's r ↑	MAE ↓	RMSE ↓	Rank
PredictorEstimator-Ensemble	0.7146	0.0942	0.1359	2
PredictorEstimator-MultiLevel-Ensemble	0.7170	0.0907	0.1359	
PredictorEstimator-Combined-MultiLevel-Ensemble	0.7280	0.0911	0.1332	1
BASELINE	0.441	0.128	0.175	

Sentence Level (Ranking Variant)	Spearman's ρ ↑	DeltaAvg ↑	Rank
PredictorEstimator-Ensemble	0.6327	0.1044	2
PredictorEstimator-MultiLevel-Ensemble	0.6550	0.1061	
PredictorEstimator-Combined-MultiLevel-Ensemble	0.6542	0.1064	1
BASELINE	0.45	0.0681	

Word Level	F_1-mult ↑	F_1-BAD ↑	F_1-OK ↑	Rank
PredictorEstimator-Ensemble	0.5160	0.5516	0.9356	3
PredictorEstimator-MultiLevel-Ensemble	0.5271	0.5609	0.9398	
PredictorEstimator-Combined-MultiLevel-Ensemble	0.5347	0.5687	0.9402	1
BASELINE	0.342	0.365	0.939	

Phrase Level	F_1-mult ↑	F_1-BAD ↑	F_1-OK ↑	Rank
PredictorEstimator-Ensemble	0.5428	0.5990	0.9062	2
PredictorEstimator-MultiLevel-Ensemble	0.5490	0.6032	0.9101	
PredictorEstimator-Combined-MultiLevel-Ensemble	0.5611	0.6150	0.9122	1
BASELINE	0.360	0.397	0.907	

Table 5: Results of ensembles of multi-instance Predictor-Estimator models on WMT17 De-En test set.

Ensembles for the most sophisticated single model were made by averaging 15 predictions yielded from each single model with three types of dimensionality settings[7] to produce five trained instances with different shuffling training examples, called *PredictorEstimator-MultiLevel-Ensemble*. We also created an ensemble that combines both *PredictorEstimator-Ensemble* and *PredictorEstimator-MultiLevel-Ensemble*, called *PredictorEstimator-Combined-MultiLevel-Ensemble*.

Tables 4-5 present the experimental results for the ensembles of multi-instance Predictor-Estimator models with the English-German/German-English test set for sentence-/word-/phrase-level QE[8]. In all of our runs, *PredictorEstimator-Combined-MultiLevel-Ensemble* exhibited the best performance and was ranked first for all subtasks at the different levels for the WMT17 QE task.

4 Conclusion

We presented a two-stage end-to-end neural QE model that uses multilevel task learning with stack propagation for sentence/word/phrase-level QE. We used the Predictor-Estimator architecture (Kim et al., 2017; Kim and Lee, 2016) for sentence/word/phrase-level QE. We applied stack propagation (Zhang and Weiss, 2016) to the Predictor-Estimator architecture for efficient joint learning. Finally, we deployed multilevel task learning with stack propagation to use the training examples available for all QE subtasks to train a task-specific Predictor-Estimator. We developed ensembles by combining a set of neural models trained under different settings of varying dimensionalities and shuffling training examples. Our ensemble-based submissions achieved

the best performances for all subtasks at the various levels for the WMT17 QE task.

Acknowledgments

This work was partly supported by the ICT R&D Program of MSIP/IITP and ICT Consilience Creative Program of MSIP/IITP.

References

Dzmitry Bahdanau, Kyunghyun Cho, and Yoshua Bengio. 2015. Neural machine translation by jointly learning to align and translate. In *ICLR 2015*.

Kyunghyun Cho, Bart van Merrienboer, Caglar Gulcehre, Dzmitry Bahdanau, Fethi Bougares, Holger Schwenk, and Yoshua Bengio. 2014. Learning phrase representations using rnn encoder–decoder for statistical machine translation. In *Proceedings of the 2014 Conference on Empirical Methods in Natural Language Processing (EMNLP)*. Association for Computational Linguistics, Doha, Qatar, pages 1724–1734. http://www.aclweb.org/anthology/D14-1179.

Hyun Kim, Hun-Young Jung, Hongseok Kwon, Jong-Hyeok Lee, and Seung-Hoon Na. 2017. Predictor-estimator: Neural quality estimation based on target word prediction for machine translation. In *ACM Trans. Asian Low-Resour. Lang. Inf. Process (in press)*.

Hyun Kim and Jong-Hyeok Lee. 2016. A recurrent neural networks approach for estimating the quality of machine translation output. In *Proceedings of the 2016 Conference of the North American Chapter of the Association for Computational Linguistics: Human Language Technologies*. Association for Computational Linguistics, San Diego, California, pages 494–498. http://www.aclweb.org/anthology/N16-1059.

André F. T. Martins, Ramón Astudillo, Chris Hokamp, and Fabio Kepler. 2016. Unbabel's participation in the wmt16 word-level translation quality estimation shared task. In *Proceedings of the First Conference on Machine Translation*. Association for Computational Linguistics, Berlin, Germany, pages 806 811. http://www.aclweb.org/anthology/W/W16/W16-2387.

Matthew Snover, Bonnie Dorr, Richard Schwartz, Linnea Micciulla, and John Makhoul. 2006. A study of translation edit rate with targeted human annotation. In *Proceedings of association for machine translation in the Americas*. pages 223–231.

Lucia Specia and Varvara Logacheva. 2017. WMT17 quality estimation shared task training and development data. LINDAT/CLARIN digital library at the Institute of Formal and Applied Linguistics, Charles University. http://hdl.handle.net/11372/LRT-1974.

PredictorEstimator-Ensemble was denoted as *PredictorEstimator-SingleLevel-Ensemble*.

[7] 1) The vocabulary size was 70,000 words, the word embedding dimensionality was 500, the size of the hidden units of the word predictor was 700, and the size of the hidden units of the quality estimator was 100. 2) The vocabulary size was 70,000 words, the word embedding dimensionality was 500, the size of the hidden units of the word predictor was 700, and the size of the hidden units of the quality estimator was 150. 3) The vocabulary size was 70,000 words, the word embedding dimensionality was 500, the size of the hidden units of the word predictor was 700, and the size of the hidden units of the quality estimator was 200.

[8] *PredictorEstimator-Combined-MultiLevel-Ensemble* and *PredictorEstimator-Ensemble* were our two submissions for the WMT17 QE task.

Lucia Specia, Kashif Shah, Jose G.C. de Souza, and Trevor Cohn. 2013. Quest - a translation quality estimation framework. In *Proceedings of the 51st Annual Meeting of the Association for Computational Linguistics: System Demonstrations*. Association for Computational Linguistics, Sofia, Bulgaria, pages 79–84. http://www.aclweb.org/anthology/P13-4014.

Yuan Zhang and David Weiss. 2016. Stack-propagation: Improved representation learning for syntax. In *Proceedings of the 54th Annual Meeting of the Association for Computational Linguistics (Volume 1: Long Papers)*. Association for Computational Linguistics, Berlin, Germany, pages 1557–1566. http://www.aclweb.org/anthology/P16-1147.

Unbabel's Participation
in the WMT17 Translation Quality Estimation Shared Task

André F. T. Martins
Unbabel & Instituto de Telecomunicações
Lisbon, Portugal
`andre.martins@unbabel.com`

Fabio N. Kepler
Unbabel
University of Pampa, Alegrete, Brazil
`kepler@unbabel.com`

José L. Monteiro
Unbabel
Lisbon, Portugal
`jose@unbabel.com`

Abstract

This paper presents the contribution of the Unbabel team to the WMT 2017 Shared Task on Translation Quality Estimation. We participated on the word-level and sentence-level tracks. We describe our two submitted systems: (i) STACKEDQE, a "pure" QE system, trained only on the provided training sets, which is a stacked combination of a feature-rich sequential linear model with a neural network, and (ii) FULLSTACKEDQE, which also stacks the predictions of an automatic post-editing system, trained on additional data. When evaluated on the English-German and German-English datasets, FULLSTACKEDQE achieved word-level F_1^{MULT} scores of 56.6% and 52.9%, and sentence-level correlation Pearson scores of 64.1% and 62.6%, respectively. Our system ranked second in both tracks, being statistically indistinguishable from the best system in the word-level track.

1 Introduction

Quality estimation is the task of evaluating a translation system's quality without access to reference translations (Blatz et al., 2004; Specia et al., 2013). This paper describes the contribution of the Unbabel team to the Shared Task on Sentence-Level and Word-Level Quality Estimation (QE Tasks 1 and 2) at the 2017 Conference on Statistical Machine Translation (WMT 2017).

In the word-level task, the goal is to predict the word-level quality of machine translated text, by assigning a label of OK or BAD to each word in the translation. The sentence-level task attempts to predict the HTER of each sentence, along with a ranking of the sentences. Two language pairs and domains are considered: English-German (IT domain) and German-English (medical domain).

Our submission is largely based on the approach that we have recently proposed in Martins et al. (2017), which ensembles a "pure" quality estimation system with predictions derived from an automatic post-editing system. The focus was on developing a word-level system, and to use the word label predictions to predict the sentence-level HTER.

Our system architecture is described in full detail in the following sections. We first describe our "pure" QE system (§2), which consists of a neural model (NEURALQE) stacked into a linear feature-rich classifier (LINEARQE). Then, we train an APE system (using a large amount of artificial "roundtrip translations") and adapt it to predict word-level quality labels (yielding APEQE, §3). We show that the pure and the APE-based QE system are highly complementary (§4): our best system is a stacked combination of LINEARQE, NEURALQE, and APEQE. By employing a simple word-to-sentence conversion, we adapt our systems to sentence-level QE. Overall, we achieve word-level F_1^{MULT} scores of 56.6% and 52.9% and sentence-level Pearson scores of 64.1% and 62.6% for English-German and German-English, respectively.

The following external resources were used: part-of-speech tags and extra syntactic dependency information were obtained with Turbo-Tagger and TurboParser (Martins et al., 2013),[1]

---

[1]Publicly available on `http://www.cs.cmu.edu/~ark/TurboParser/`.

Proceedings of the Conference on Machine Translation (WMT), Volume 2: Shared Task Papers, pages 569–574
Copenhagen, Denmark, September 7–11, 2017. ©2017 Association for Computational Linguistics

trained on the Penn Treebank (for English) and on
the version of the German TIGER corpus used in
the SPMRL shared task (Seddah et al., 2014). For
the neural models, we used pre-trained word embeddings from Polyglot (Al-Rfou et al., 2013).

For our FULLSTACKEDQE submission, we also
use additional data to train the APE-based QE systems: for English-German, the set of 500K artificial roundtrip translations provided by Junczys-
Dowmunt and Grundkiewicz (2016), and, for
German-English, the UFAL Medical Corpus provided in the WMT17 Biomedical Translation task.

2 Pure Quality Estimation

We use the pure quality estimation system developed by the Unbabel team and described in Martins et al. (2017), which consists of an ensemble
of a linear feature-based classifier with a neural
network. We briefly describe the linear (§2.1) and
neural (§2.2) components of our system, as well as
their combination (§2.3). Further details are presented in Martins et al. (2016, 2017).

2.1 Linear Sequential Model

The linear component of our model is a discriminative feature-based sequential model (called LIN-
EARQE). The system receives as input a tuple
$\langle s, t, \mathcal{A} \rangle$, where $s = s_1 \ldots s_M$ is the source sentence, $t = t_1 \ldots t_N$ is the translated sentence, and
$\mathcal{A} \subseteq \{(m, n) \mid 1 \leq m \leq M, 1 \leq n \leq N\}$ is a
set of word alignments. It predicts as output a se-
quence $\widehat{y} = y_1 \ldots y_N$, with each $y_i \in \{\text{BAD}, \text{OK}\}$.
This is done as follows:

$$
\widehat{y} = \operatorname{argmax}_y \sum_{i=1}^{N} \boldsymbol{w}^\top \boldsymbol{\phi}_u(s, t, \mathcal{A}, y_i)
$$
$$
+ \sum_{i=1}^{N+1} \boldsymbol{w}^\top \boldsymbol{\phi}_b(s, t, \mathcal{A}, y_i, y_{i-1}). \quad (1)
$$

Above, $\boldsymbol{w}$ is a vector of weights, $\boldsymbol{\phi}_u(s, t, \mathcal{A}, y_i)$
are unigram features (depending only on a sin-
gle output label), $\boldsymbol{\phi}_b(s, t, \mathcal{A}, y_i, y_{i-1})$ are bigram
features (depending on consecutive output labels),
and y_0 and y_{N+1} are special start/stop symbols.

Table 1 shows the unigram and bigram features used in the LINEARQE system. We include
features that depend on the target word and its
aligned source word, as well as the context surrounding them.[2] We include also syntactic fea-

---

[2]Features involving the aligned source word are replaced

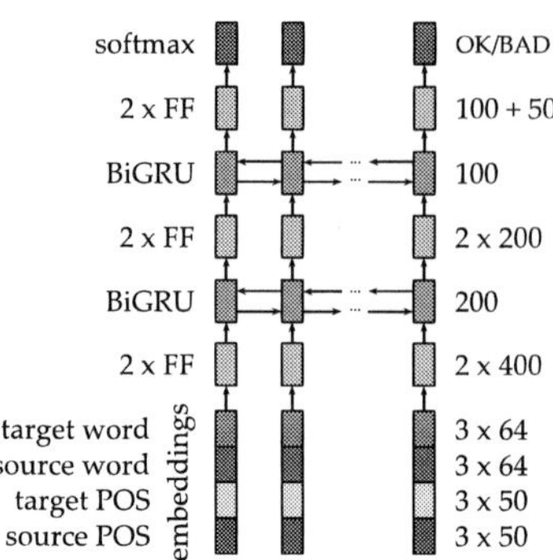

Figure 1: Architecture of our NEURALQE system.

tures to detect grammatically incorrect constructions. We use features that involve the dependency relation, the head word, and second-order
sibling and grandparent structures. Features involving part-of-speech (POS) tags and syntactic
information are obtained with TurboTagger and
TurboParser (Martins et al., 2013). The feature
weights are learned by running 50 epochs of the
max-loss MIRA algorithm (Crammer et al., 2006),
with regularization constant $C \in \{10^{-k}\}_{k=1}^{4}$ and
a Hamming cost function placing a higher penalty
on false positives than on false negatives ($c_{\text{FP}} \in
\{0.5, 0.55, \ldots, 0.95\}$, $c_{\text{FN}} = 1 - c_{\text{FP}}$), to account
for the existence of fewer BAD labels than OK la-
bels in the data. These values are tuned on the
development set.

2.2 Neural System

Next, we describe the neural component of our
pure QE system, which we call NEURALQE.

The architecture of NEURALQE is depicted in
Figure 1. We used Keras (Chollet, 2015) to implement our model. The system receives as input the source and target sentences s and t, their
word-level alignments $\mathcal{A}$, and their corresponding
POS tags obtained from TurboTagger. The input
layer follows a similar architecture as QUETCH
(Kreutzer et al., 2015), with the addition of POS
features. A vector representing each target word is
obtained by concatenating the embedding of that
word with those of the aligned word in the source.[3]
The immediate left and right contexts for source
and target words are also concatenated. We use

---

by NIL if the target word is unaligned. If there are multiple
aligned source words, they are concatenated into a single feature.

[3]For the cases in which there are multiple source words
aligned to the same target word, the embeddings are averaged.

Features	Label	Input (referenced by the ith target word)
unigram	$y_i \wedge \dots$	*BIAS *WORD, LEFTWORD, RIGHTWORD *SOURCEWORD, SOURCELEFTWORD, SOURCERIGHTWORD *LARGESTNGRAMLEFT/RIGHT, SOURCELARGESTNGRAMLEFT/RIGHT *POSTAG, SOURCEPOSTAG †WORD+LEFTWORD, WORD+RIGHTWORD †WORD+SOURCEWORD, POSTAG+SOURCEPOSTAG
simple bigram	$y_i \wedge y_{i-1} \wedge \dots$	*BIAS
rich bigrams	$y_i \wedge y_{i-1} \wedge \dots$ $y_{i+1} \wedge y_i \wedge \dots$	all above WORD+SOURCEWORD, POSTAG+SOURCEPOSTAG
syntactic	$y_i \wedge \dots$	DEPREL, WORD+DEPREL HEADWORD/POSTAG+WORD/POSTAG LEFTSIBWORD/POSTAG+WORD/POSTAG RIGHTSIBWORD/POSTAG+WORD/POSTAG GRANDWORD/POSTAG+HEADWORD/POSTAG+WORD/POSTAG

Table 1: Features used in the LINEARQE system (see Martins et al., 2016 for a detailed description). Features marked with * are included in the WMT16 baseline system. Those marked with † were proposed by Kreutzer et al. (2015).

the pre-trained 64-dimensional Polyglot word embeddings (Al-Rfou et al., 2013) for English and German, and refine them during training. In addition to this, POS tags for each source and target word are also embedded and concatenated. POS embeddings have size 50 and are initialized as described by Glorot and Bengio (2010). A dropout probability of 0.5 is applied to the resulting vector representations.

The following layers are then applied in sequence:

1. Two feed-forward layers of size 400 with rectified linear units (ReLU; Nair and Hinton (2010));

2. A layer with bidirectional gated recurrent units (BiGRU, Cho et al. (2014)) of size 200, where forward and backward vectors are concatenated, trained with layer normalization (Ba et al., 2016);

3. Two feed-forward ReLU layers of size 200;

4. A BiGRU layer of size 100 with identical configuration to the previous BiGRU;

5. Two more feed-forward ReLU layers of sizes 100 and 50, respectively.

As the output layer, a softmax transformation over the OK/BAD labels is applied. We provide ablation experiments in Martins et al. (2017) to validate this architecture choice.

We train the model with the RMSProp algorithm (Tieleman and Hinton, 2012) by minimizing the cross-entropy with a linear penalty for BAD word predictions, as in Kreutzer et al. (2015). We set the BAD weight factor to 3.0. All hyperparameters are adjusted based on the development set. Target sentences are bucketed by length and then processed in batches (without any padding or truncation).

Finally, we also trained 5 independent instances of NEURALQE with different random initializations and different data shuffles. We ensemble these systems by taking the averaged probability of each word being BAD. Tables 2–3 show the results. We observe that, for both language pairs, the neural model outperforms the linear model, and the ensemble of 5 neural systems achieves an extra boost (most noticeable in the English-German dataset).

2.3 Stacking Neural and Linear Models

We now stack the NEURALQE system (§2.2) into the LINEARQE system (§2.1) as an ensemble strategy; we call the resulting system STACKEDQE.

The individual instances of the neural systems are incorporated in the stacking architecture as different features, yielding STACKEDQE. In total, we have 5 predictions (probability values given by each NEURALQE system) for every word in the training, development and test datasets. These predictions are plugged as additional features in the

LINEARQE model. As unigram features, we used one real-valued feature for every model prediction at each position, conjoined with the label. As bigram features, we used two real-valued features for every model prediction at the two positions, conjoined with the label pair.

For the remainder of this paper, we will take STACKEDQE as our pure QE system.

3 APE-Based Quality Estimation

To develop our APE-based QE system (APEQE), we followed a similar approach as the one described in Martins et al. (2017), with a few minor differences, explained below.

Junczys-Dowmunt and Grundkiewicz (2016) applied neural translation models to the APE problem, treating different models as components in a log-linear model, allowing for multiple inputs (the source s and the translated sentence t) that were decoded to the same target language (post-edited translation p). Two systems were considered, one using s as the input ($s \rightarrow p$) and another using t as the input ($t \rightarrow p$). For English-German, we used the 500K artificial roundtrip translations provided by the shared task organizers, along with the original data from the shared task (oversampled 20 times, as in Junczys-Dowmunt and Grundkiewicz (2016)). For German-English, we only considered the $s \rightarrow p$ machine translation system, trained from a subset of the UFAL Medical Corpus provided in the WMT17 Biomedical Translation task. This subset was obtained through cross-entropy filtering. For this, we built an in-domain trigram language model from the English post-edited training data. We then calculated cross-entropy scores for the UFAL corpus according to the language model. We sorted the corpus by increasing cross-entropy and kept the first 500K sentences to be used as additional training data.

To convert the resulting APE systems into word-level quality estimators, we need to turn the automatic post-edited sentences into word quality labels. This is done in a straightforward way by using the TERCOM software tool (Snover et al., 2006)[4] with the default settings (tokenized, case insensitive, exact matching only, shifts disabled). This tool computes the HTER (the normalized edit distance) between the translated and post-edited sentence. As a by-product, it aligns the words in the two sentences, identifying substitution errors,

word deletions (i.e. words omitted by the translation system), and insertions (redundant words in the translation). This is mapped deterministically into OK and BAD labels.

Our approach for the shared task differs from Martins et al. (2017) in which we skipped the QE-tuning step when training the log-linear APE model; instead, we kept the output of the $s \rightarrow p$ and the $t \rightarrow p$ systems, converted each to word-level quality labels, and then include the two predictions as additional features in the FULL-STACKEDQE system, described below. We denote the individual systems as APEQE $s \rightarrow p$ and APEQE $t \rightarrow p$, and the combined system as FULLSTACKEDQE $s, t \rightarrow p$.

4 Full Stacked System

Finally, we consider a larger stacked system where we stack both NEURALQE and APEQE into LINEARQE. This mixes pure QE with APE-based QE systems; we call the result FULLSTACKEDQE. The procedure is analogous to that described in §2.3, with extra binary features for the APE-based word quality label predictions. For training, we used jackknifing to ensure the predictions on the training set are not biased.

4.1 Word-Level QE

The performance of the FULLSTACKEDQE system on the English-German and German-English development datasets are shown in Tables 2–3. For English-German, we compare with the system from Martins et al. (2017).

For both language pairs, we can see that the APE-based and the pure QE systems are highly complementary. For English-German, the full combination of the linear, neural, and APE-based systems improves the scores with respect to the best individual system by about 5.5 points. There is a small improvement by including also a feature from APE $t \rightarrow p$, in addition to $s \rightarrow p$. For German-English, we observe an improvement of 4.9 points.

4.2 Sentence-Level QE

We followed the same procedure of Martins et al. (2017) to convert word-level quality predictions to a sentence-level HTER prediction. For the APE system, we simply measured the HTER between the translated sentence t and the predicted corrected sentence $\hat{p}$. For a pure QE system, we ap-

---

[4] http://www.cs.umd.edu/~snover/tercom.

	F_1^{MULT} dev	F_1^{MULT} test 2016
Martins et al. (2017)	56.80	57.47
LINEARQE	47.71	48.09
NEURALQE (single)	49.58	49.95
NEURALQE (5-avg)	51.37	51.38
STACKEDQE	52.72	52.89
APEQE ($s \rightarrow p$)	51.43	52.47
APEQE ($t \rightarrow p$)	35.27	37.13
FULLSTACKEDQE ($s \rightarrow p$)	57.18	58.04
FULLSTACKEDQE ($s, t \rightarrow p$)	**57.55**	**58.36**

Table 2: Performance of the several word-level QE systems on the development and WMT16 English-German test datasets.

	F_1^{MULT} dev
LINEARQE	48.07
NEURALQE (single)	49.39
NEURALQE (avg-5)	49.58
STACKEDQE	53.22
APEQE ($s \rightarrow p$)	45.09
FULLSTACKEDQE ($s \rightarrow p$)	**58.08**

Table 3: Performance of the several word-level QE systems on the German-English development dataset.

plied the following word-to-sentence conversion technique: (i) run a QE system to obtain a sequence of OK and BAD word quality labels; (ii) use the fraction of BAD labels as an estimate for HTER. Finally, to combine the APE and pure QE systems toward sentence-level QE, we simply take the average of the two HTER predictions above.

Table 4 shows the results obtained with our pure QE system (STACKEDQE), with our APE-based system (APEQE), and with the combination of the two (FULLSTACKEDQE). We report also the performance of the system of Martins et al. (2017) for English-German, for comparison.

5 Final Results

Finally, we show in Tables 5–6 the results obtained in the test set for our two submitted systems, STACKEDQE and FULLSTACKEDQE, in word-level and sentence-level quality estimation. As expected, the inclusion of the predictions made by the APE system gave a significant boost for the word-level task (>5 F_1^{MULT} points for English-German, and >6 points for German-English) and for the sentence-level task (>5 Pearson correlation points for English-German, >4 points for German-English).

6 Conclusions

We have presented the contribution of the Unbabel team to the WMT 2017 Shared Task on Translation Quality Estimation. Our word-level system combines a pure quality estimation system, based on stacking a neural and feature-based linear model, and an APE-based quality estimation system, which uses the predictions of an automatic post-editing system to generate additional features. We applied a simple conversion strategy to obtain a sentence-level quality estimator based on the word-level one. The system is evaluated on two language pairs, English-German and German-English.

Acknowledgments

This work was partially supported by the the the EXPERT project (EU Marie Curie ITN No. 317471), and by Fundação para a Ciência e Tecnologia (FCT), through contracts UID/EEA/50008/2013 and UID/CEC/50021/2013, the LearnBig project (PTDC/EEI-SII/7092/2014), and the GoLocal project (grant CMUPERI/TIC/0046/2014).

References

Rami Al-Rfou, Bryan Perozzi, and Steven Skiena. 2013. Polyglot: Distributed word representations for multilingual nlp. *arXiv preprint arXiv:1307.1662* .

Jimmy Lei Ba, Jamie Ryan Kiros, and Geoffrey E Hinton. 2016. Layer normalization. *arXiv preprint arXiv:1607.06450* .

John Blatz, Erin Fitzgerald, George Foster, Simona Gandrabur, Cyril Goutte, Alex Kulesza, Alberto Sanchis, and Nicola Ueffing. 2004. Confidence estimation for machine translation. In *Proc. of the International Conference on Computational Linguistics*. page 315.

Kyunghyun Cho, Bart Van Merriënboer, Caglar Gulcehre, Dzmitry Bahdanau, Fethi Bougares, Holger Schwenk, and Yoshua Bengio. 2014. Learning Phrase Representations Using RNN Encoder-Decoder for Statistical Machine Translation. In *Proc. of Empirical Methods in Natural Language Processing*.

François Chollet. 2015. Keras. `https://github.com/fchollet/keras`.

Koby Crammer, Ofer Dekel, Joseph Keshet, Shai Shalev-Shwartz, and Yoram Singer. 2006. Online Passive-Aggressive Algorithms. *Journal of Machine Learning Research* 7:551–585.

		Pearson dev	Pearson test 2016	Spearman dev	Spearman test 2016
	Martins et al. (2017)	64.04	**65.56**	65.52	65.92
En-De	STACKEDQE	62.18	59.90	64.07	60.23
	APEQE	58.79	56.69	59.41	59.43
	FULLSTACKEDQE	**64.33**	65.25	**65.65**	**66.10**
	STACKEDQE	60.47	–	59.74	–
	APEQE	59.94	–	57.68	–
De-En	FULLSTACKEDQE	**67.97**	–	**62.45**	–

Table 4: Performance of our sentence-level QE systems on the English-German and German-English datasets, as measured by the official evaluation script. We show the performance of Martins et al. (2017) for comparison.

	F_1^{OK}	F_1^{BAD}	F_1^{MULT}
EN-DE STACKEDQE	88.2	58.1	51.2
EN-DE FULLSTACKEDQE	90.6	62.5	56.6
DE-EN STACKEDQE	93.6	49.7	46.6
DE-EN FULLSTACKEDQE	94.1	56.2	52.9

Table 5: Performance of the submitted word-level systems on the test set.

	Pearson	Spearman
EN-DE STACKEDQE	58.9	61.0
EN-DE FULLSTACKEDQE	64.1	65.2
DE-EN STACKEDQE	58.0	57
DE-EN FULLSTACKEDQE	62.6	61

Table 6: Performance of the submitted sentence-level systems on the test set.

Xavier Glorot and Yoshua Bengio. 2010. Understanding the difficulty of training deep feedforward neural networks. In *International Conference on Artificial Intelligence and Statistics*. pages 249–256.

Marcin Junczys-Dowmunt and Roman Grundkiewicz. 2016. Log-linear combinations of monolingual and bilingual neural machine translation models for automatic post-editing. In *Proceedings of the First Conference on Machine Translation*. pages 751–758.

Julia Kreutzer, Shigehiko Schamoni, and Stefan Riezler. 2015. Quality estimation from scratch (quetch): Deep learning for word-level translation quality estimation. In *Proceedings of the Tenth Workshop on Statistical Machine Translation*. pages 316–322.

André F. T Martins, Miguel B. Almeida, and Noah A. Smith. 2013. Turning on the turbo: Fast third-order non-projective turbo parsers. In *Proc. of the Annual Meeting of the Association for Computational Linguistics*.

André F. T. Martins, Ramón Astudillo, Chris Hokamp, and Fábio Kepler. 2016. Unbabel's participation in the wmt16 word-level translation quality estimation shared task. In *Proceedings of the First Conference on Machine Translation*.

André F. T. Martins, Marcin Junczys-Dowmunt, Fabio Kepler, Ramon Astudillo, Chris Hokamp, and Roman Grundkiewicz. 2017. Pushing the limits of translation quality estimation. *Transactions of the Association for Computational Linguistics (to appear)*.

Vinod Nair and Geoffrey E Hinton. 2010. Rectified linear units improve restricted boltzmann machines. In *Proc. of the International Conference on Machine Learning*. pages 807–814.

Djamé Seddah, Sandra Kübler, and Reut Tsarfaty. 2014. Introducing the SPMRL 2014 shared task on parsing morphologically-rich languages. In *Proceedings of the First Joint Workshop on Statistical Parsing of Morphologically Rich Languages and Syntactic Analysis of Non-Canonical Languages*. pages 103–109.

Matthew Snover, Bonnie Dorr, Richard Schwartz, Linnea Micciulla, and John Makhoul. 2006. A study of translation edit rate with targeted human annotation. In *Proc. of the 7th Conference of the Association for Machine Translation in the Americas*. pages 223–231.

Lucia Specia, Kashif Shah, Jose G.C. de Souza, and Trevor Cohn. 2013. QuEst - a translation quality estimation framework. In *Proc. of the Annual Meeting of the Association for Computational Linguistics: System Demonstrations*. pages 79–84. http://www.aclweb.org/anthology/P13-4014.

Tijmen Tieleman and Geoffrey Hinton. 2012. Rmsprop: Divide the gradient by a running average of its recent magnitude. *COURSERA: Neural Networks for Machine Learning* 4(2).

Feature-Enriched Character-Level Convolutions for Text Regression

Gustavo Henrique Paetzold and **Lucia Specia**
Department of Computer Science
University of Sheffield, UK
{g.h.paetzold,l.specia}@sheffield.ac.uk

Abstract

We present a new model for text regression that seamlessly combine engineered features and character-level information through deep parallel convolution stacks, multi-layer perceptrons and multi-task learning. We use these models to create the SHEF/CNN systems for the sentence-level Quality Estimation task of WMT 2017 and Emotion Intensity Analysis task of WASSA 2017. Our experiments reveal that combining character-level clues and engineered features offers noticeable performance improvements over using only one of these sources of information in isolation.

1 Introduction

Text regression consists in estimating a numeric label based on information available from the text. The label can represent any abstract property of said text: its appropriateness, sentiment, fluency, simplicity, quality, etc. Due to their wide applicability in both research and industry, some of these tasks have been gaining a lot of attention. These include Quality Estimation and Emotion Intensity Analysis, which are the subjects of shared tasks held at the WMT 2017 conference[1] and WASSA 2017 workshop[2] (Mohammad and Bravo-Marquez, 2017), respectively.

In Quality Estimation (QE), one attempts to estimate the quality of a machine translated text based on the information that can be extracted from the original sentence and its translation. The task has many variants, given that the quality of a translation can be estimated at word, phrase, sentence or even document level. Quality estimates can be incorporated in Machine Translation (MT) decoding or used for re-ranking of top candidates, for example, allowing for a more intelligently guided translation process (Avramidis, 2012), or they can be used to help human translators decide which automatic translations are worth post-editing, and which should be re-translated from scratch (Turchi et al., 2015). Sentence-level QE is the most popular variant, mostly due the fact that most modern statistical and neural MT systems translate one sentence at a time. In this task, the input is the original-translated sentence pair and the output is some numeric label that represents quality. The most commonly used label is HTER, which measures the human post-editing effort required to fix the translation in question (Snover et al., 2006).

As shown in (Bojar et al., 2016), the performance of QE approaches submitted to the WMT shared tasks have steadily improved in recent years. However, the nature of these approaches have not changed much: most of the top ranking systems employ well-known regression methods and extensive feature engineering. Some of the most notable examples are the RTM systems of WMT 2014 and 15, which managed to reach the top of the ranks by employing Referential Translation Machines trained with SVMs for regression (Bicici, 2016). The LORIA (Langlois, 2015) and YSDA (Kozlova et al., 2016) systems of WMT 2015 and 2016, respectively, achieved similar performance by also pairing SVMs with many resource-heavy features.

Neural Networks for sentence-level QE were introduced in WMT 2016 with the SimpleNets (Paetzold and Specia, 2016) and POSTECH (Kim and Lee, 2016) systems. While the SimpleNets system uses sequence-to-label LSTMs to predict the quality of a translation's n-grams and then

---

[1]http://www.statmt.org/wmt17
[2]http://optima.jrc.it/wassa2017

Proceedings of the Conference on Machine Translation (WMT), Volume 2: Shared Task Papers, pages 575–581
Copenhagen, Denmark, September 7–11, 2017. ©2017 Association for Computational Linguistics

combines them, the POSTECH system learns quality labels at word-level using a sequence-to-sequence model, and then combines them with a sequence-to-label model to predict quality at sentence-level. Though very interesting and distinct strategies, neither of them managed to outperform the best scoring SVM-based approach of WMT 2016.

In the task of Emotion Intensity Analysis (EIA), Neural Networks have not yet been successfully employed. Unlike typical Sentiment Analysis tasks, which are set up as either binary or multi-class classification problems that require one to determine the opinion or sentiment in a given text, EIA aims at quantifying a certain emotion in a text, such as fear, anger, joy, sadness, etc. In the Emotion Intensity shared task of SemEval 2016 (Kiritchenko et al., 2016), which is the first of its kind, none of the five systems submitted employ neural regressors. We were also unable to find any other contributions outside the SemEval 2016 task that explore neural approaches to EIA.

Given the volume of opportunities available when it comes to neural solutions for text regression, we introduce a new neural approach for the task. We innovate by using deep convolutional networks and multi-task learning to combine character-level information from the texts at hand with engineered features. Using this approach, we create the SHEF/CNN systems for the sentence-level QE task of WMT 2017 and the Emotion Intensity Analysis task of WASSA 2017. In what follows, we describe our approach in detail.

2 Overview of Tasks

As previously mentioned, we address two text regression tasks in this paper: the sentence-level Quality Estimation task of WMT 2017 and Emotion Intensity Analysis task of WASSA 2017. The next Sections describe each of those tasks.

2.1 Quality Estimation at WMT 2017

In the sentence-level QE task of WMT 2017 participants were asked to create systems that predict the human post-editing effort required to correct an automatically translated sentence. Training, development and test sets were provided for two language pairs: English-German and German-English. The training and development sets for both language pairs are composed of 23,000/25,000 and 1,000/1,000 instances, respectively. Each instance is composed of a source (original) and target (translated) sentence pair, as well as the target's manually post-edited version and an HTER label between 0 and 1 calculated based on the post-edit. The test set is composed of 2,000 instances without post-edits nor HTER labels. For training, development and test sets the organizers made available a set of 17 baseline features.

The task is divided in two sub-tasks: scoring and ranking. In the scoring task, systems had to estimate HTER scores and were evaluated through Pearson correlation. In the ranking task, systems had to rank the translations in the test set from highest to lowest quality, and were evaluated through Spearman correlation. The main difference between the data provided for the WMT 2017 QE tasks and the data of previous editions is that, for the first time, the tasks of all QE levels (sentence, word and phrase) contain annotations for the same set of translations. Because of that, one can very intuitively employ any variety of multi-task learning approaches.

2.2 Emotion Intensity at WASSA 2017

Systems submitted to the Emotion Intensity Analysis task of WASSA 2017 were asked to estimate the intensity of various emotions felt by authors while writing tweets. Training, development and test sets were made available containing four emotions: anger, fear, joy and sadness. The size of the datasets is illustrated in Table 1.

Emotion	Train	Dev	Test
Anger	857	84	760
Fear	1,147	110	995
Joy	823	79	714
Sadness	786	74	673

Table 1: Dataset sizes for the Emotion Intensity Analysis task of WASSA 2017

Each instance is composed of a tweet and an intensity label between 0 and 1 of the emotion in question. Labels were collected through crowd-sourcing. Systems were evaluated through Pearson correlation.

3 Model Architecture

Figure 1 illustrates the neural model architecture of the SHEF/CNN systems for the QE task of

WMT 2017. As it can be noticed, the model takes as input a one-hot character-level representation of the source and target, as well as a set of engineered features. As output, our model produces the numeric labels desired.

The model is divided in three main sections: a pair of deep convolution layer stacks for the source (original) and target (translated) sentences, a multi-layer perceptron for the engineered features, and a final multi-layer perceptron to combine all this information. The model used for the EIA task of WASSA 2017 is identical, except that it only has one set of convolution stacks for the tweet being analysed.

3.1 Extracting Character-Level Clues

In order to exploit the information at character-level from the text, we use a convolution architecture similar to the one introduced by (Kim et al., 2016), who successfully employ character-level information for language modelling. First we transform the one-hot character-level representation of the sentence into a sequence of character embeddings. We then feed them to a series of parallel one-dimensional convolutions of different window sizes. Each of these convolutions captures the information of character n-grams of a given length: a convolution of window size one addresses unigrams, one with size two addresses bigrams, and so on. Finally, the resulting values produced by the convolution filters are passed on to a one-dimensional max-pooling layer.

In order to capture information at different abstraction levels, we stack various convolution and max-pooling layers for each window size, thus creating a deep architecture. This deep architecture differs from the one used by (Kim et al., 2016) in the sense that they apply only one stack of convolution/max-pooling layers for each window size. The values produced by the last max-pooling layer of each window size are then flattened so that they can be easily concatenated.

The intuition behind using such an architecture lies in the assumption that sequences of characters hold important clues with respect to the text's properties, such as quality and emotion. In QE, these clues could be sequences containing morphological errors in words from the source or target sentences, or sequences in-between tokens of the target that suggest an ungrammatical segment, for example. In EIA, these clues can be emotionally charged emojis, curse words, exclamation marks, etc.

3.2 Incorporating Engineered Features

We complement character-level information with engineered features, given that the most effective QE and EIA methods in previous work heavily exploit them (Kim and Lee, 2016; Kozlova et al., 2016; Refaee and Rieser, 2016; Wang et al., 2016). To do so, we apply a simple multi-layer perceptron (MLP) over a set of input engineered features. This allows to capture abstract relations between the features provided. The output of the outermost layer is then concatenated with the flattened character-level information provided by the remainder of the network.

Finally, we pass the concatenated features and character-level information to another MLP in order for our model to be able to capture any relations between them. At the very edge of our model, we include output nodes for as many tasks as we wish to train our model over.

4 SHEF/CNN Model for QE

As illustrated in Figure 1, the sentence-level QE model employs one convolution stack for each of the source and target sides of the translation pair. We configure the model as follows:

- **Embedding size:** We train character embeddings with 50 dimensions.

- **Window range:** We use 4 parallel stacks of convolutions with window sizes from 1 to 4.

- **Convolution depth:** Each stack contains 4 pairs of convolution/max-pooling layers with 50 convolution filters each and a pool length of 4.

- **Feature MLP depth:** We stack 2 dense layers with 50 hidden units over engineered features.

- **Final MLP depth:** The MLP that combines convolutions and features is composed of 2 stacked dense layers with 50 hidden units each.

- **Engineered feature set:** We use the 17 baseline features provided by the task organizers.

This architecture was selected through experimentation. The output nodes of our multi-task QE setup predict three values:

- HTER from the sentence-level dataset;

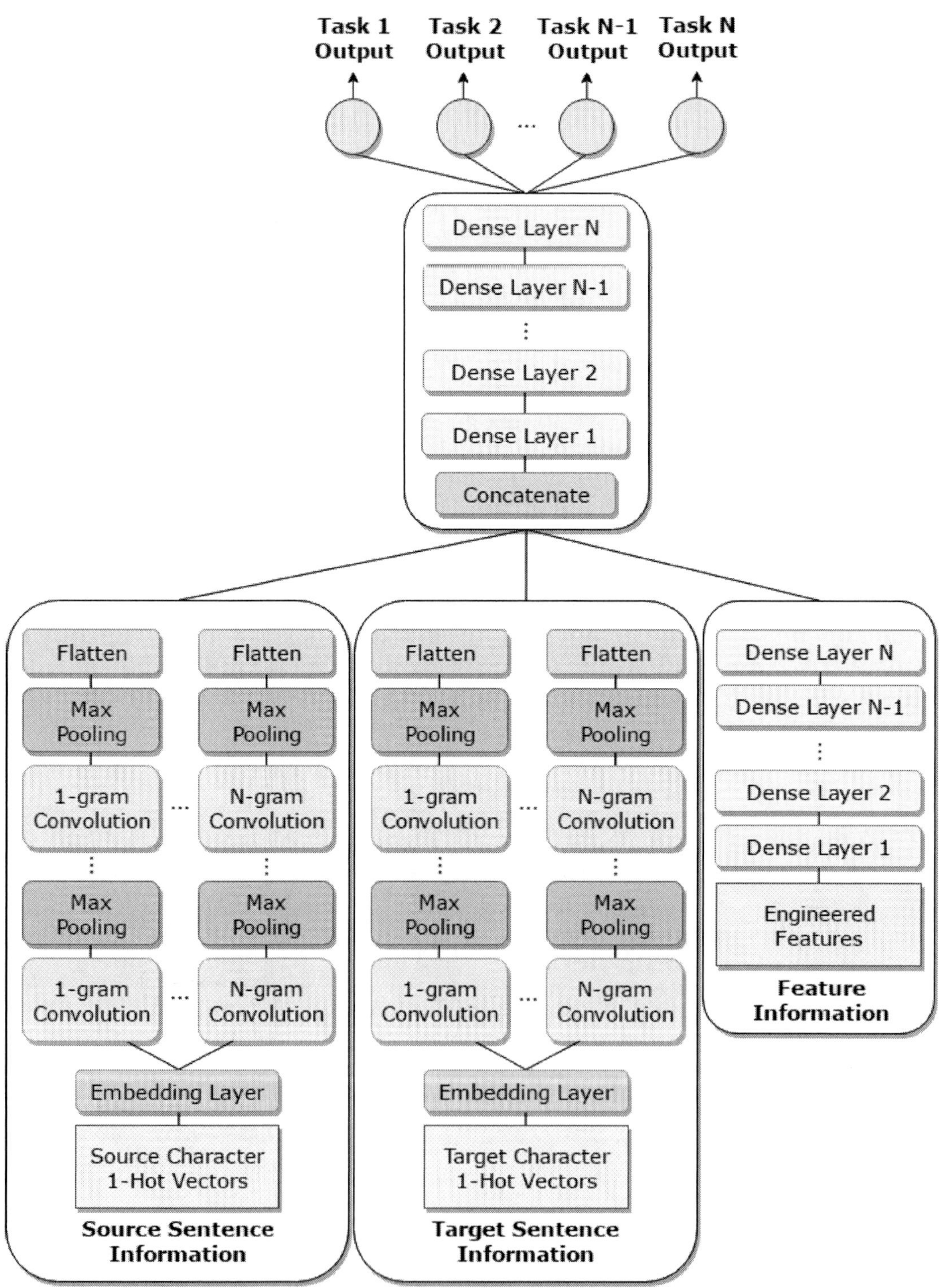

Figure 1: Architecture of the SHEF/CNN+BASE systems

- The number of BAD labels from the word-level dataset; and

- The number of BAD labels from the phrase-level dataset.

Note that the data from the word and phrase-level datasets are used as a mere complement to HTER prediction. It is important to mention that we also tried predicting the full label sequences for word and phrase-level, but the results obtained were not as promising. We train our model until convergence with Stochastic Gradient Descent and Mean Squared Error over all outputs jointly.

5   SHEF/CNN Model for EIA

The model used for the EIA task of WASSA 2017 applies only one convolution stack over the tweet being analysed, given that the task is not characterized by a sentence pair. The window range, convolution depth, as well as feature and final MLP depths are identical to the model used for the WMT 2017 task. We train one model for each emotion targeted in the shared task: anger, fear, joy and sadness.

Since the organizers did not provide a set of baseline features, we produced our own features using the Stanford Sentiment Treebank (Socher et al., 2013), which is composed of 239,232 text segments annotated with respect to their positivity probability i.e. how likely they are to convey a positive emotion. The positivity values range from 0.0 (absolutely negative) to 1.0 (absolutely positive). Using this data, we extract nine features from each tweet:

- Minimum, maximum and average positivity of single words in the tweet;

- Minimum, maximum and average positivity of bigrams in the tweet; and

- Minimum, maximum and average positivity of trigrams in the tweet.

Our multi-task learning setup is composed of two output layers that predict:

- The tweets' emotion intensity; and

- The tweets' positivity value.

We first train our models over the sentiment positivity values from the Stanford Sentiment

Treebank until convergence, then train them over the emotion intensity training sets of WASSA 2017 until convergence. The training algorithm and metric used are Stochastic Gradient Descent and Mean Squared Error, respectively.

6   WMT 2017 Results

We evaluate the performance of four variants of the SHEF/CNN model:

- **SHEF/CNN-F:** Uses only the MLP over the engineered features trained over HTER.

- **SHEF/CNN-C:** Uses only the character-level convolution stacks trained over HTER.

- **SHEF/CNN-C+F:** Uses both engineered features and character-level information trained over HTER.

- **SHEF/CNN-C+F+M:** Uses the same architecture of SHEF/CNN-C+F, but the model is trained through multi-task learning over the values listed in Section 4.

Table 2 illustrates the Pearson, Root Mean Squared Error (RMSE) and Mean Absolute Error (MAE) scores for the scoring task, and Spearman correlation scores for the ranking task of each language pair. Boldface values represent the best scores obtained across SHEF/CNN models. We also include the results from the official baseline and from the top performing team (POSTECH).

The results reveal that, although we outperform the task baseline for English-German, the SHEF/CNN models do not offer competitive performance to state-of-the-art QE systems that rely on resource-heavy strategies. Nonetheless, some valuable observations can be drawn from the results. Combining engineered features with character-level clues yields a more reliable model than simply using either of them alone, which suggests that character-level clues can be a valuable source of complementary information to engineered features. Our multi-task learning setup did not improve on the results of our model. We hypothesize that the secondary output labels could not offer a significant volume of complementary information to the model.

7   WASSA 2017 Results

Table 3 illustrates the Pearson and Spearman correlation scores for each emotion. We compare the

	English-German				German-English			
	p	MAE	RMSE	r	p	MAE	RMSE	r
POSTECH/MultiLevel	0.714	0.096	0.134	0.710	0.728	0.091	0.133	0.470
POSTECH/SingleLevel	0.686	0.101	0.139	0.690	0.715	0.094	0.136	0.440
Baseline	0.397	0.136	0.175	0.425	0.441	0.128	0.175	0.450
SHEF/CNN-F	0.384	0.176	0.137	0.412	0.092	0.208	0.145	0.034
SHEF/CNN-C	0.374	0.181	0.146	0.393	0.379	0.184	0.148	**0.408**
SHEF/CNN-C+F	**0.416**	**0.174**	**0.135**	0.441	**0.390**	**0.179**	**0.136**	0.382
SHEF/CNN-C+F+M	0.402	0.178	**0.135**	**0.448**	0.350	0.202	0.162	0.380

Table 2: Results for the sentence-level QE task of WMT 2017

	Fear		Joy		Anger		Sadness	
	p	r	p	r	p	r	p	r
Prayas	0.732	0.729	0.732	0.710	0.762	0.743	0.765	0.761
Emkay	0.690	0.690	0.705	0.692	0.726	0.703	0.767	0.764
venkatesh-1729	0.728	0.728	0.678	0.654	0.705	0.684	0.749	0.744
Baseline	0.652	0.635	0.654	0.662	0.639	0.615	0.648	0.651
SHEF/CNN-F	0.166	0.153	0.271	0.313	0.222	0.212	0.241	0.240
SHEF/CNN-C	0.217	0.221	0.328	0.302	0.120	0.142	0.259	0.253
SHEF/CNN-C+F	**0.293**	**0.284**	**0.517**	**0.510**	0.279	0.260	**0.323**	**0.326**
SHEF/CNN-C+F+M	0.109	0.096	0.407	0.392	**0.311**	**0.276**	0.233	0.228

Table 3: Results for the EIA task of WASSA 2017

performance of all SHEF/CNN variants described in the previous sections and also include the official task baseline and the three top performing approaches in the EIA task: the Prayas, Emkay and venkatesh-1729 systems.

The SHEF/CNN models are outperformed by a noticeable margin by strategies that heavily employ engineered features and external resources, such as large databases of emotion intensity labels. Nonetheless, our results reveal the same phenomenon highlighted in our experiments with QE: for all emotions, combining engineered features with character-level information yields better performance scores than using only one of these information sources. This serves as further evidence that character-level convolutions can be effectively used as a complement to engineered features.

Our multi-task learning approach only managed to obtain performance improvements for anger. We believe this is due to fact that the positivity values present in the Stanford Sentiment Treebank, which is used in our multi-task setup, accurately quantify only the degree with which the reviewer is pleased, and hence happy, or displeased, and hence angry. Because the other emotions in the WASSA 2017 task do not commonly permeate the act of writing a product review, the multi-task

setup was not able to help the model trained for them.

8 Conclusions

We introduced a text regression model that uses deep convolution neural networks and multi-layer perceptrons to combine the character-level information present in texts with the information from engineered features.

We tested several variants of our model in two text regression shared tasks: the sentence-level Quality Estimation task of WMT 2017 and the Emotion Intensity Analysis task of WASSA 2017. We found that, although our model is not able to outperform classic resource-heavy strategies, combining character-level data with engineered features results in noticeable performance gains for both tasks. We also found that, although multi-task learning can in principle help our model, the setup must be carefully crafted, otherwise it compromises its performance.

We plan to further test with other tasks the hypothesis that character-level convolutions constitute an intuitive way of complementing the performance of typical feature-based text regression models. We will also test more elaborate convolution architectures, such as using stacked LSTMs.

Acknowledgments

This work was supported by the QT21 project (H2020 No. 645452).

References

Eleftherios Avramidis. 2012. Comparative quality estimation: Automatic sentence-level ranking of multiple machine translation outputs. In *Proceedings of 24th COLING*. The COLING 2012 Organizing Committee, pages 115–132.

Ergun Bicici. 2016. Referential translation machines for predicting translation performance. In *Proceedings of the First Conference on Machine Translation*. Association for Computational Linguistics, Berlin, Germany, pages 777–781.

Ondřej Bojar, Rajen Chatterjee, Christian Federmann, Yvette Graham, Barry Haddow, Matthias Huck, Antonio Jimeno Yepes, Philipp Koehn, Varvara Logacheva, Christof Monz, Matteo Negri, Aurelie Neveol, Mariana Neves, Martin Popel, Matt Post, Raphael Rubino, Carolina Scarton, Lucia Specia, Marco Turchi, Karin Verspoor, and Marcos Zampieri. 2016. Findings of the 2016 conference on machine translation. In *Proceedings of the 1st WMT*. Association for Computational Linguistics, Berlin, Germany, pages 131–198.

Hyun Kim and Jong-Hyeok Lee. 2016. Recurrent neural network based translation quality estimation. In *Proceedings of the First Conference on Machine Translation*. Association for Computational Linguistics, Berlin, Germany, pages 787–792.

Yoon Kim, Yacine Jernite, David Sontag, and Alexander M. Rush. 2016. Character-aware neural language models. In *Proceedings of the 13th AAAI*. AAAI Press, AAAI'16, pages 2741–2749.

Svetlana Kiritchenko, Saif Mohammad, and Mohammad Salameh. 2016. Semeval-2016 task 7: Determining sentiment intensity of english and arabic phrases. In *Proceedings of the 10th SemEval*. Association for Computational Linguistics, San Diego, California, pages 42–51.

Anna Kozlova, Mariya Shmatova, and Anton Frolov. 2016. Ysda participation in the wmt'16 quality estimation shared task. In *Proceedings of the First Conference on Machine Translation*. Association for Computational Linguistics, Berlin, Germany, pages 793–799.

David Langlois. 2015. Loria system for the wmt15 quality estimation shared task. In *Proceedings of the 10th WMT*. Association for Computational Linguistics, Lisbon, Portugal, pages 323–329.

Saif M. Mohammad and Felipe Bravo-Marquez. 2017. Emotion intensities in tweets. In *Proceedings of the 6th *Sem*. Vancouver, Canada.

Gustavo Paetzold and Lucia Specia. 2016. Simplenets: Quality estimation with resource-light neural networks. In *Proceedings of the First Conference on Machine Translation*. Association for Computational Linguistics, Berlin, Germany, pages 812–818.

Eshrag Refaee and Verena Rieser. 2016. ilabedinburgh at semeval-2016 task 7: A hybrid approach for determining sentiment intensity of arabic twitter phrases. In *Proceedings of the 10th SemEval*. Association for Computational Linguistics, San Diego, California, pages 474–480.

Matthew Snover, Bonnie Dorr, Richard Schwartz, Linnea Micciulla, and John Makhoul. 2006. A study of translation edit rate with targeted human annotation. In *In Proceedings of the 2006 AMTA*. pages 223–231.

Richard Socher, Alex Perelygin, Jean Wu, Jason Chuang, Christopher D. Manning, Andrew Ng, and Christopher Potts. 2013. Recursive deep models for semantic compositionality over a sentiment treebank. In *Proceedings of the 2013 EMNLP*. Association for Computational Linguistics, Seattle, Washington, USA, pages 1631–1642.

Marco Turchi, Matteo Negri, and Marcello Federico. 2015. MT quality estimation for computer-assisted translation: Does it really help? In *Proceedings of the 53rd Annual Meeting of the Association for Computational Linguistics and the 7th International Joint Conference on Natural Language Processing (Volume 2: Short Papers)*. Association for Computational Linguistics, Beijing, China, pages 530–535.

Feixiang Wang, Zhihua Zhang, and Man Lan. 2016. Ecnu at semeval-2016 task 7: An enhanced supervised learning method for lexicon sentiment intensity ranking. In *Proceedings of the 10th SemEval*. Association for Computational Linguistics, San Diego, California, pages 491–496.

UHH Submission to the WMT17 Metrics Shared Task

Melania Duma and Wolfgang Menzel
University of Hamburg
Natural Language Systems Division
{duma, menzel}@informatik.uni-hamburg.de

Abstract

In this paper the UHH submission to the WMT17 Metrics Shared Task is presented, which is based on sequence and tree kernel functions applied to the reference and candidate translations. In addition we also explore the effect of applying the kernel functions on the source sentence and a back-translation of the MT output, but also on the pair composed of the candidate translation and a pseudo-reference of the source segment. The newly proposed metric was evaluated using the data from WMT16, with the results demonstrating a high correlation with human judgments.

1 Introduction

The evaluation of Machine Translation (MT) represents a very important domain of research, as providing meaningful, automatic and accurate methods for determining the quality of machine-translated output is a key component in the development cycle of a MT system. However, the task is inherently difficult due to the expressiveness of natural language, which often allows conveying a message in more than one equivalent ways. When translating from a source language into a target one, the input data for evaluation conventionally consists of a set of tuples, with each tuple composed of:

- a source segment, representing the sentence to be translated in the source language

- a candidate translation (also known as a target segment), obtained by translating the source segment into the target language using an MT system

- a reference translation, representing a correct human-generated translation of the source segment

As a research field, MT evaluation can be divided into two categories: reference-free evaluation and reference-based one. The reference-free evaluation, also known as Quality Estimation, aims at providing automatic methods, for assessing the quality of candidate translations, which do not require reference translations. In the case of a reference-based evaluation, the target segment is compared with the reference translation resulting in a score that measures the similarity between the two sentences. Different approaches for computing the comparison have been implemented, with the most frequently used one being BLEU (Papineni et al., 2002), which measures the quality of the candidate translation by counting the number of n-grams it has in common with the reference translations. Nonetheless, multiple disadvantages of BLEU have already been pointed out, as in Callison-Burch et al. (2006), where it is shown that an increase of the BLEU score does not necessary correlate with a better performing system. This has motivated further research into additional MT evaluation methods that rely on more than lexical matching by additionally including the syntactic and semantic structure of the sentences (e.g. (Popović and Ney, 2009), (Gautam and Bhattacharyya, 2014)).

We propose a new method for the evaluation of MT output, based on tree and sequence kernel functions, applied on the pair of reference and candidate translations. In addition, we study the impact of applying the kernels on the tuple consisting of the source segment and a back-translation, together with the pair comprised of the candidate translation and a pseudo-reference. A pseudo-reference is the result of translating the source

Proceedings of the Conference on Machine Translation (WMT), Volume 2: Shared Task Papers, pages 582–588
Copenhagen, Denmark, September 7–11, 2017. ©2017 Association for Computational Linguistics

segment into the target language, while a back-translation is obtained by translating the target segment into the source language. The evaluation results show that the new metric strongly correlates with human judgments, outperforming the state-of-the-art methods.

2 Related work

MT evaluation methods can be categorized according to the level of analysis that they address into lexical ones (e.g BLEU (Papineni et al., 2002), TER (Snover et al., 2006)), syntactic ones (e.g. (Popović and Ney, 2007), (Giménez and Màrquez, 2007)) or semantic ones (e.g. (Castillo and Estrella, 2012)), with hybrid combinations integrating more than one representational layer at a time.

A syntactic evaluation method based on tree kernels is proposed in Liu and Gildea (2005). It uses the subtree kernel introduced in Collins and Duffy (2002) to calculate the similarity between the reference and the candidate translations. Besides this, a syntactic metric based on counting the number of fixed-depth subtrees shared by the two translations is also introduced, with both metrics being applied on the constituency trees of the input data. Additionally, a dependency tree based metric is presented, which computes the number of common headword chains, where a headword chain is defined as the concatenation of words that form a path in the dependency tree.

Another MT evaluation method that makes use of tree kernels is introduced in Guzmán et al. (2014). It also uses the subtree kernel introduced in Collins and Duffy (2001), but in this case it calculates the similarity between the discourse trees of the candidate and reference translation. The evaluation combined the newly proposed metric with already existing ones and the results showed that the addition is beneficial for improving the correlation scores.

The role of back-translations has also been investigated before, like in the case of Rapp (2009) where the quality of a candidate translation is assessed by measuring the similarity, in terms of a modified version of BLEU, between its back-translation and the initial source segment. In the case of pseudo-references, they have been used as an additional source of data for tuning the parameters of MT systems, like in the case of Ammar et al. (2013). An evaluation method based on pseudo-references is presented in Albrecht and Hwa (2007) and then further extended in Albrecht and Hwa (2008), where a metric is trained to correlate with human judgments based on features extracted with the help of three pseudo-references. The features are in the form of 18 kinds of reference-based scores together with an additional set of 25 monolingual fluency scores. The results showed that the new metric correlates well with human assessments and generalizes well across different language pairs.

The novelty of the MT Evaluation metric introduced in this paper is twofold. First of all, the method makes use of the Partial Tree Kernel (PTK), a more general type of kernel function, which to the authors' knowledge has not been applied in the context of MT metrics-based evaluation before. Secondly, the proposed method also explores what impact do sequence kernels (SK) have on the quality of a kernel evaluation metric, by studying its potential individually, but also in combination with the Partial Tree Kernel. Furthermore, we extend on the previous work of pseudo-references and back-translations by studying their impact in the context of using them as input data for kernel functions.

3 Methods and implementation

A kernel function makes use of structural representations of the input data in order to calculate the number of substructures they share, without explicitly stating the feature spaces corresponding to the two representations (Moschitti, 2006a). The types of representations taken into account can be, among others, vectorial, sequential or tree-based. The tree kernels developed so far distinguish themselves from one another by the types of tree fragments (e.g. subsets, subtrees or partial trees) and the type of syntactic trees (constituency or dependency) they employ in their computation, which influences their suitability for certain tasks (see Moschitti (2006a)). Contrastively, sequence kernels (e.g (Duncscu and Mooney, 2005), (Nguyen et al., 2009)) make use of subsequences in the computation of the kernel.

The new method for the evaluation of Machine Translation proposed in this paper, denoted as TSKM, makes use of both tree and sequence kernels, which are applied on the pair of candidate and reference translations. The tree kernel used is represented by the Partial Tree Kernel (PTK)

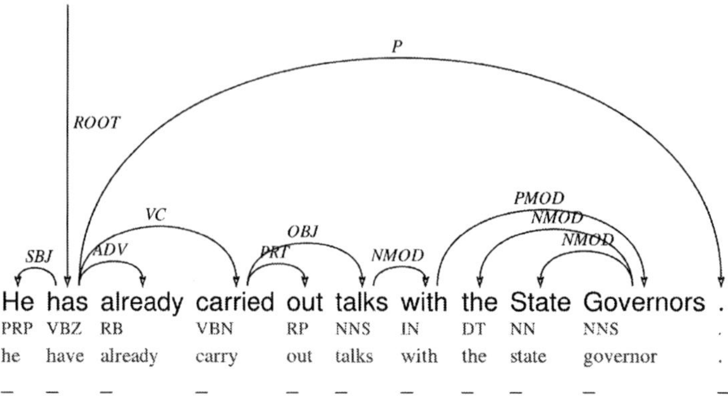

Figure 1: Example of a dependency tree.

(Moschitti, 2006a). It uses partial tree fragments, which are a generalization over subtrees and subset trees, so that a node and its partial descendants can constitute a valid fragment. An example of a dependency tree is presented in Figure 1 [1] and some possible partial trees for it are *(has(carried(out)))* or *(carried(out talks))*. For the sequence kernel (SK), the kernel introduced in Bunescu and Mooney (2005) is utilized, which computes the number of common patterns shared by the two input sentences.

Formally, TSKM can be defined as:

$$TSKM_{basic} = TSKM(r, c) = \frac{PTK(r,c)+SK(r,c)}{2} \tag{1}$$

with r and c denoting the reference and the candidate translations and *PTK* and *SK* referring to the scores of the Partial Tree Kernel and the Sequence Kernel.

Furthermore, we experimented with using an additional pseudo-reference and a back-translation in the computation of the metric in order to explore how the different combination schemes influence the performance of TSKM. One possible kind of combination can be represented as:

$$TSKM_{comb} = \frac{TSKM_{basic}+TSKM_{pseudo}+TSKM_{back}}{3} \tag{2}$$

$$TSKM_{pseudo} = TSKM(c, s_t) = \frac{PTK(c,s_t)+SK(c,s_t)}{2} \tag{3}$$

$$TSKM_{back} = TSKM(s, c_t) = \frac{PTK(s,c_t)+SK(s,c_t)}{2} \tag{4}$$

with s_t and c_t representing the pseudo-reference and the back-translation respectively and s marking the source segment. Our rationale for utilizing the pseudo-reference was motivated by two factors. In the first place, we wanted to determine whether an additional reference, even if only an approximate one, helps to better predict the quality of the candidate translation. Furthermore, we also wanted to investigate the possibility to apply our new evaluation method, in the scenario without official reference translation. Producing reference translations is a time-consuming and expensive task, therefore an evaluation method that performs well even without reference translations being available would be highly desirable.

In the case of back-translations, we wanted to investigate if the quality of a candidate translation can be approximated using the quality of its back-translation. This would prove extremely beneficial, especially in the case of low-resource language pairs, where no high quality analysis tools (e.g lemmatizers, pos-taggers or parsers) for the target language are available, a situation that would prevent TSKM from being applied. In our experiments, both the pseudo-references together with the back-translations were obtained using the free online Google Translator Toolkit [2].

To apply the tree and sequence kernels for the task of Machine Translation evaluation, a preprocessing of the input data is necessary. In the case of PTK, the input data was first tokenized and pos-tagged, followed by a parsing step using the Bohnet graph-based dependency parser (Bohnet, 2010) and the publicly available syntactic analy-

---

[1] The visualization was obtained using Arborator https://arborator.ilpga.fr/q.cgi (Gerdes, 2013)

[2] https://translate.google.com/toolkit

TSKM	not exact					exact				
	cs-en	fi-en	ru-en	tr-en	Average	cs-en	fi-en	ru-en	tr-en	Average
$SK(r,c)$	.997	.939	.958	.973	.967	.995	.850	.957	.924	.932
$SK(c,s_t)$	.993	.426	.948	.948	.829	.995	.391	.949	.895	.808
$SK(r,c)+SK(c,s_t)$	.998	.507	.955	.961	.855	.998	.454	.955	.908	.829
$PTK(r,c)$	.991	.932	.962	.957	.961	.992	.890	.959	.953	.949
$PTK(c,s_t)$	.997	.427	.961	.958	.836	.998	.403	.960	.938	.825
$PTK(r,c)+PTK(c,s_t)$	.997	.531	.969	.960	.864	.997	.492	.967	.946	.851
$SK(r,c)+ PTK(r,c)$	.990	.944	.961	.970	.965	.990	.876	.960	.944	.943
$SK(r,c)+SK(c,s_t)+ PTK(r,c)+PTK(c,s_t)$	.999	.515	.961	.964	.860	.999	.466	.960	.930	.839
mosesBLEU	-	-	-	-	-	.990	.752	.950	.765	.864
mosesWER	-	-	-	-	-	.982	.770	.958	.680	.848
mosesPER	-	-	-	-	-	.981	.770	.974	.947	.918
mosesCDER	-	-	-	-	-	.995	.846	.968	.836	.911
mtevalBLEU	-	-	-	-	-	.992	.858	.962	.899	.928
mtevalNIST	-	-	-	-	-	.988	.924	.966	.952	.958

Table 1: Evaluation results in terms of Pearson correlation for the different TSKM variants. The highlighted TSKM variant indicates the submission to the WMT17 Metrics Task.

sis models [3]. The dependency parse trees obtained were converted to tree representations which can be used by the PTK. The lexical-centered-tree approach presented in Croce et al. (2011) was utilized, which required storing both the grammatical relation and the pos-tag information as the rightmost children of a dependency tree node. The score of the kernel functions were normalized using the formula from Croce et al. (2011):

$$score = \frac{K(T1, T2)}{\sqrt{K(T1, T1) \star K(T2, T2)}} \quad (5)$$

with $T1$ and $T2$ standing for the input data tuple and K indicating the type of kernel function. Regarding SK, only a tokenization of the data was required, as the SK function was applied on substructures composed of the lexical items.

For the computation of the kernel functions we used the Partial Tree Kernel[4] and the Sequence Kernel [5] implementations, found in the KeLP (Kernel-based Learning Platform) (Filice et al., 2015b) (Filice et al., 2015a) library. KeLP is an open source Java platform encompassing kernel based Machine Learning algorithms together with multiple types of kernel functions. The implemented kernels support either vector based input representations or structural ones in the form of trees, sequences or graphs.

4 Evaluation and results

4.1 Experimental setup

The evaluation of TSKM was performed using data pertaining to the News domain from the First Conference On Machine Translation (WMT16) [6]. For the results obtained in the WMT17 Metrics Task, please refer to the official results paper. The following language pairs were used in the evaluation: English-German, Czech-English, German-English, Finnish-English, Russian-English and Turkish-English. The MT outputs evaluated correspond to systems submitted to the WMT16 News Translation Task (Bojar et al., 2016), having different types ranging from statistical phrase-based to neural or syntax-based ones. The test sets consist of approximately 3000 tuples, incorporating the source segment together with the reference and candidate translations. We evaluated TSKM in terms of Pearson correlation with human judgments. During the manual evaluation phase of WTM16, human judgments were collected by ranking five candidate translations, with ties being allowed. In order to compute a single TSKM score for an MT system, all the individual sentence scores were combined by averaging them.

Different variants of TSKM were taken into account for evaluation. To investigate how the lexical variation affects the performance of the metric, we also implemented versions of the metric where lemmas are used instead of the exact lexical items.

[3]https://code.google.com/archive/p/mate-tools/downloads

[4]based on (Moschitti, 2006a)

[5]based on (Bunescu and Mooney, 2005)

[6]http://www.statmt.org/wmt16/metrics-task/

TSKM	not exact		exact	
	de-en	en-de	de-en	en-de
SK(r,c)	.921	.643	.919	.715
SK(c,s_t)	.957	.713	.955	.752
SK(r,c)+SK(c,s_t)	.944	.705	.942	.758
SK(r,c)+SK(s,c_t)	.950	.568	.931	.640
PTK(r,c)	.941	.701	.944	.756
PTK(c,s_t)	.966	.761	.968	.789
PTK(r,c)+PTK(c,s_t)	.957	.750	.960	.792
PTK(r,c)+PTK(s,c_t)	.921	.687	.953	.735
SK(r,c)+ PTK(r,c)	.928	.667	.928	.733
SK(r,c)+SK(c,s_t)+ SK(s,c_t)	.970	.693	.964	.753
PTK(r,c)+PTK(c,s_t)+ PTK(s,c_t)	.979	.770	.973	.810
SK(r,c)+SK(c,s_t)+PTK(r,c)+PTK(c,s_t)	.948	.722	.948	.772
SK(r,c)+SK(s,c_t)+PTK(r,c)+PTK(s,c_t)	.954	.622	.931	.684
SK(r,c)+SK(c,s_t)+SK(s,c_t)+ PTK(r,c)+PTK(c,s_t)+PTK(s,c_t)	.974	.724	.969	.777
mosesBLEU	-	-	.880	.784
mosesWER	-	-	.926	.771
mosesPER	-	-	.843	.681
mosesCDER	-	-	.927	.779
mtevalBLEU	-	-	.905	.752
mtevalNIST	-	-	.887	.625

Table 2: Evaluation results in terms of Pearson correlation for the en-de and de-en language pairs

4.2 Results

The results of the evaluation are presented in Tables 1 and 2, which contain the correlation scores for the different TSKM variants taken into account. For comparison purposes, the scores for some state-of-the-art MT evaluation methods are also presented: BLEU (Papineni et al., 2002), NIST (Doddington, 2002), PER (Tillmann et al., 1997), CDER (Leusch et al., 2006) and WER. The results were obtained using the evaluation scripts made available by the WMT16 conference [7]. The following metric notation was adopted for each of the TSKM variants evaluated: *Kernel*[*level*], where *Kernel* identifies the type of kernel utilized (SK or PTK) and *level* refers to the input data tuple used in the calculation. The possible tuple types are:

- (r,c) - the pair of reference and candidate translations

- (c,s_t) - the pair of candidate translations and translated source

- (s,c_t) - the pair of source segment and back-translated candidate

In Table 1, the results of TSKM when applied to the Czech-English, Finnish-English, Russian-English and Turkish-English language pairs are

[7]http://www.statmt.org/wmt16/results.html

TSKM	exact	
	tr-en	ru-en
SPTK(r,c)	.976	.970
SPTK(c,s_t)	.960	.964
CSPTK(r,c)	.972	.968
CSPTK(c,s_t)	.968	.960

Table 3: Evaluation results in terms of Pearson correlation for SPTK and CSPTK.

presented. We first experimented with applying TSKM on the (r,c) and the (c,s_t) input data pairs. The best performing TSKM variant, SK(r,c)+ PTK(r,c), represents the combination between PTK and SK applied on the reference and candidate translations. Its average correlation score over all language pairs outperforms the state-of-the-art metrics. We can observe that the addition of the pair consisting of the candidate translation and the pseudo-reference generated mixed results. In the case of Finnish-English there was an obvious downgrade in performance, possibly due to the complex morphology of Finnish. Another observation to be pointed out is that the 'not exact' TSKM variants are stronger correlated with the human judgments than their 'exact' counterparts.

In addition to the metric variants presented in Table 1, we further extended the evaluation to the English-German and German-English language pairs by including the source and back-translation tuple in the evaluation, with the results being presented in Table 2. In this case, the best performing method for both language pairs, PTK(r,c)+PTK(c,s_t)+ PTK(s,c_t), makes use of all the three possible input data tuples, succeeding to outperform the state-of-the-art metrics. Yet another aspect worth to point out is that, in the case of English-German, the 'exact' metric variants are the ones that display better correlations. This would suggest that when choosing between 'not exact' or 'exact' variants for TSKM, the direction of the translation (e.g. in/out of English) should be taken into account. Moreover, we can observe that there is a drastic decrease of correlation in the case of English-German translations, which can possibly be explained by the highly inflectional nature of the German language.

Additional preliminary evaluation experiments, presented in Table 3, were performed after the submission to the Shared Task. Generalizations of the Partial Tree Kernel were used, namely the Smoothed Partial Tree Kernel (SPTK) (Croce et al., 2011) and the Compositional Smoothed Partial Tree Kernel (CSPTK) (Annesi et al., 2013) (Annesi et al., 2014). The SPTK uses a term similarity function to semantically match tree nodes. The term similarity function can be obtained through either word vector spaces or distributional analysis. On the other hand, the CSPTK represents a generalization of SPTK, which uses Distributional Compositional Semantics to determine the degree of similarity between tree fragments. The implementations for these kernels together with an example wordspace for English are also available in the KeLP package. The results show that by relaxing the matching constraints to allow for lexical variation these kernels outperform PTK when used by TSKM.

5   Conclusions and future work

In this paper, we introduced TSKM, our submission to the WMT17 Metrics Task, which is based on tree and sequence kernels. The metric was evaluated using multiple language pairs, with the evaluation results being very encouraging. We also experimented with applying the kernel functions on additional tuple input data, that involve back-translations and pseudo-references. In the case of the pseudo-reference the results indicate that its addition to TSKM can be beneficial, especially in the case of the PTK. However, the most important aspect to notice is that, with the exception of Finnish-English, the pseudo-reference based methods achieved correlation scores that are very similar to the official reference based ones, which suggests that TSKM could be applied even in the context of artificially generated reference translations. The addition of the back-translations of the target sentences to TSKM generated encouraging results, which prompts us to extend the evaluation to include further language pairs.

Based on the evaluation results, we can also observe that the SK metric variants succeeded in attaining correlation scores that are relatively similar to the PTK variants. This suggests that the SK metric variant can be successfully used in the case when no syntactic analysis tools are available for the target language.

Future work will be concentrated on using the constituency trees as a structural input representations for PTK in addition to the dependency trees. The evaluation will also be extended to determine how well does TSKM generalize across domains. We also plan to analyze in more detail the decrease in correlation scores when using the pseudo-reference in the case of Finnish-English, by using different MT systems to generate additional pseudo-references in order to determine if the type of MT system influences the correlation with human judgments. Another future work idea is to extend the evaluation for SPTK and CSPTK, by including them in different TSKM combinations and evaluating on additional language pairs.

References

Joshua Albrecht and Rebecca Hwa. 2007. Regression for sentence-level MT evaluation with pseudo references. In *Annual Meeting-Association for Computational Linguistics*. volume 45, page 296.

Joshua Albrecht and Rebecca Hwa. 2008. The role of pseudo references in MT evaluation. In *Proceedings of the Third Workshop on Statistical Machine Translation*. Association for Computational Linguistics, pages 187–190.

Waleed Ammar, Victor Chahuneau, Michael Denkowski, Greg Hanneman, Wang Ling, Austin Matthews, Kenton Murray, Nicola Segall, Yulia Tsvetkov, Alon Lavie, and Chris Dyer. 2013. The CMU Machine Translation systems at WMT 2013: Syntax, synthetic translation options, and pseudo-references. In *8th Workshop on Statistical Machine Translation*. page 70.

Paolo Annesi, Danilo Croce, and Roberto Basili. 2013. Towards compositional tree kernels. In *Joint Symposium on Semantic Processing.*. page 15.

Paolo Annesi, Danilo Croce, and Roberto Basili. 2014. Semantic compositionality in tree kernels. In *Proceedings of the 23rd ACM International Conference on Conference on Information and Knowledge Management*. ACM, pages 1029–1038.

Bernd Bohnet. 2010. Top accuracy and fast dependency parsing is not a contradiction. *The 23rd International Conference on Computational Linguistics (COLING 2010)* .

Ondrej Bojar, Rajen Chatterjee, Christian Federmann, Yvette Graham, Barry Haddow, Matthias Huck, Antonio Jimeno Yepes, Philipp Koehn, Varvara Logacheva, Christof Monz, Matteo Negri, Aurelie Neveol, Mariana Neves, Martin Popel, Matt Post, Raphael Rubino, Carolina Scarton, Lucia Specia, Marco Turchi, Karin Verspoor, and Marcos Zampieri. 2016. Findings of the 2016 Conference on Machine Translation. *Proceedings of the First Conference on Machine Translation, Volume 2: Shared Task Papers* pages 131–198.

Razvan Bunescu and Raymond Mooney. 2005. Subsequence kernels for Relation Extraction. *Advances in Neural Information Processing Systems, Vol. 18: Proceedings of the 2005 Conference (NIPS)* .

Chris Callison-Burch, Miles Osborne, and Philipp Koehn. 2006. Re-evaluating the role of BLEU in Machine Translation research. In *In EACL*. pages 249–256.

Julio Castillo and Paula Estrella. 2012. Semantic Textual Similarity for MT evaluation. In *Proceedings of the Seventh Workshop on Statistical Machine Translation*. Association for Computational Linguistics, pages 52–58.

Michael Collins and Nigel Duffy. 2001. Convolution kernels for natural language. *Proceedings of NIPS 2001* pages 625–632.

Michael Collins and Nigel Duffy. 2002. New ranking algorithms for parsing and tagging: Kernels over discrete structures, and the voted perceptron. In *Proceedings of the 40th annual meeting on association for computational linguistics*. Association for Computational Linguistics, pages 263–270.

Danilo Croce, Alessandro Moschitti, and Roberto Basili. 2011. Structured lexical similarity via convolution kernels on dependency trees. *Proceedings of the 2011 Conference on Empirical Methods in Natural Language Processing* pages 1034–1046.

George Doddington. 2002. Automatic evaluation of Machine Translation quality using n-gram co-occurrence statistics. In *Proceedings of the Second International Conference on Human Language Technology Research*. Morgan Kaufmann Publishers Inc., pages 138–145.

Simone Filice, Giuseppe Castellucci, Roberto Basili, Giovanni Da San Martino, and Alessandro Moschitti. 2015a. KeLP: a Kernel-based Learning Platform in Java. *The workshop on Machine Learning Open Source Software (MLOSS): Open Ecosystems* .

Simone Filice, Giuseppe Castellucci, Danilo Croce, and Roberto Basili. 2015b. KeLP: a kernel-based learning platform for Natural Language Processing. *Proceedings of ACL-IJCNLP 2015 System Demonstrations* pages 19–24.

Shubham Gautam and Pushpak Bhattacharyya. 2014. Layered: Metric for Machine Translation evaluation. *ACL 2014* page 387.

Kim Gerdes. 2013. Collaborative dependency annotation. In *DepLing*. pages 88–97.

Jesús Giménez and Lluís Màrquez. 2007. Linguistic features for automatic evaluation of heterogenous MT systems. In *Proceedings of the Second Workshop on Statistical Machine Translation*. Association for Computational Linguistics, pages 256–264.

Francisco Guzmán, Shafiq R Joty, Lluís Màrquez, and Preslav Nakov. 2014. Using discourse structure improves Machine Translation evaluation. In *ACL (1)*. pages 687–698.

Gregor Leusch, Nicola Ueffing, and Hermann Ney. 2006. Efficient MT evaluation using block movements. In *Proceedings of EACL-2006 (11th Conference of the European Chapter of the Association for Computational Linguistics)*. pages 241–248.

Ding Liu and Daniel Gildea. 2005. Syntactic features for evaluation of machine translation. In *Proceedings of the ACL Workshop on Intrinsic and Extrinsic Evaluation Measures for Machine Translation and/or Summarization*. pages 25–32.

Alessandro Moschitti. 2006a. Efficient convolution kernels for dependency and constituent syntactic trees. *Proceedings of the 17th European Conference on Machine Learning* .

Truc-Vien T. Nguyen, Alessandro Moschitti, and Giuseppe Riccardi. 2009. Convolution kernels on constituent, dependency and sequential structures for Relation Extraction. *Proceedings of the 2009 Conference on Empirical Methods in Natural Language Processing* pages 1378–1387.

Kishore Papineni, Salim Roukos, Todd Ward, and Wei-Jing Zhu. 2002. Bleu: a method for automatic evaluation of Machine Translation. In *Proceedings of 40th Annual Meeting of the Association for Computational Linguistics*. Association for Computational Linguistics, Philadelphia, Pennsylvania, USA, pages 311–318. https://doi.org/10.3115/1073083.1073135.

Maja Popović and Hermann Ney. 2007. Word Error Rates: Decomposition over POS classes and applications for error analysis. In *Proceedings of the Second Workshop on Statistical Machine Translation*. Association for Computational Linguistics, pages 48–55.

Maja Popović and Hermann Ney. 2009. Syntax-oriented evaluation measures for Machine Translation output. In *Proceedings of the Fourth Workshop on Statistical Machine Translation*. Association for Computational Linguistics, pages 29–32.

Reinhard Rapp. 2009. The back-translation score: Automatic MT evaluation at the sentence level without reference translations. In *Proceedings of the ACL-IJCNLP 2009 Conference Short Papers*. Association for Computational Linguistics, pages 133–136.

M Snover, BJ Dorr, R Schwartz, L Micciulla, and J Makhoul. 2006. A study of translation edit rate with targeted human annotation. 2006. In *Proc. AMTA*.

Christoph Tillmann, Stephan Vogel, Hermann Ney, Arkaitz Zubiaga, and Hassan Sawaf. 1997. Accelerated DP based search for statistical translation. In *Eurospeech*.

MEANT 2.0: Accurate semantic MT evaluation for any output language

Chi-kiu Lo
NRC-CNRC
Multilingual Text Processing
National Research Council Canada
1200 Montreal Road, Ottawa, ON K1A 0R6, Canada
`chikiu.lo@nrc-cnrc.gc.ca`

Abstract

We describe a new version of MEANT, which participated in the metrics task of the Second Conference on Machine Translation (WMT 2017). MEANT 2.0 uses idf-weighted distributional ngram accuracy to determine the phrasal similarity of semantic role fillers and yields better correlations with human judgments of translation quality than earlier versions. The improved phrasal similarity enables a subversion of MEANT to accurately evaluate translation adequacy for any output language, even languages without an automatic semantic parser. Our results show that MEANT, which is a non-ensemble and untrained metric, consistently performs as well as the top participants in previous years - including ensemble and trained ones - across different output languages. We also present the timing statistics for MEANT for better estimation of the evaluation cost. MEANT 2.0 is open source and publicly available.[1]

1 Introduction

We introduce a new version of MEANT, which participated in evaluating MT systems for all language pairs in the metrics task of the Second Conference on Machine Translation (WMT 2017). MEANT 2.0 is a non-ensemble and untrained metric that only requires a monolingual corpus in the output language to build the word embeddings and an automatic shallow semantic parser to obtain the predicate-argument structure to evaluate MT systems for a language pair. We have also build a degraded subversion, MEANT 2.0 - nosrl, to evaluate MT systems for any output language by re-

moving the dependency on semantic parsers for semantic role labeling (SRL) the reference and the machine translations. The correlation of MEANT with human judgments has been improved by using both inverse document frequency (idf) and distributional ngram accuracy within the phrasal similarity calculation: the former to weight the importance of each word for better adequacy, the latter to to account for word reordering for greater fluency. Our results show that MEANT consistently performs as well as the top participants in previous years across different output languages, including ensemble and trained participants. We also present the timing statistics that show the relatively low cost of running MEANT. This highly portable and open source semantic MT evaluation metric is a more accurate alternative to BLEU in evaluating translation quality for low-resource languages.

2 The family of MEANT

MEANT and its variants (Lo et al., 2015, 2014; Lo and Wu, 2011a) evaluate translation adequacy by measuring the similarity of the semantic frames and their role fillers between the human reference and machine translations. Figure 1 illustrates the concept of MEANT - the semantic roles and their fillers of the reference translation match more with those of the MT2 than with those of the MT1, therefore MT2 is a more adequate translation than MT1.

MEANT consistently outperforms the commonly used automatic MT evaluation metrics, BLEU (Papineni et al., 2002), NIST (Doddington, 2002), METEOR (Denkowski and Lavie, 2014), TER (Snover et al., 2006), CDER (Leusch et al., 2006) and WER in correlation with human adequacy judgment. It is relatively easy to port to other languages. In the full version of MEANT, it required only a monolingual corpus (for eval-

---

[1] http://chikiu-jackie-lo.org/home/index.php/meant

Proceedings of the Conference on Machine Translation (WMT), Volume 2: Shared Task Papers, pages 589–597
Copenhagen, Denmark, September 7–11, 2017. ©2017 Association for Computational Linguistics

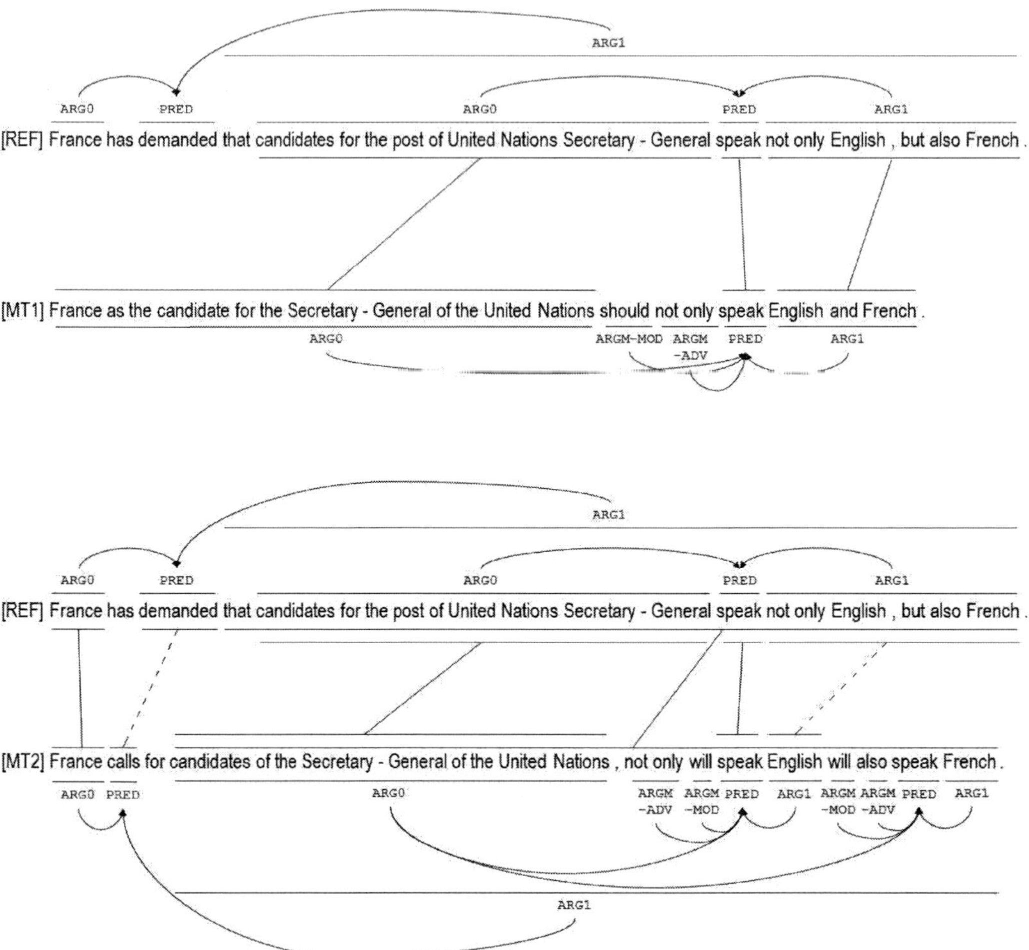

Figure 1: Example that illustrates the concept of MEANT. The solid role alignments mean the translation is mostly correct while the dotted role alignments mean the translation is partly correct. The semantic roles and fillers of the reference match more with those of MT2 than those of MT1, therefore MT2 is a more adequate translation than MT1.

uating lexical semantic similarity) and an automatic semantic parser (for evaluating frame semantic similarity) of the output language. In section 3, we describe a new subversion of MEANT that can be computed even when a semantic parser for the output language is unavailable.

MEANT is the weighted f-scores over corresponding semantic frames and role fillers in the reference and the machine translations. MEANT is generally computed as follows:

1. Apply a shallow semantic parser to both the reference and machine translations.

2. Apply the maximum weighted bipartite matching algorithm to align the semantic frames between the reference and machine translations according to the lexical similarities of the predicates.

3. For each pair of the aligned frames, apply the maximum weighted bipartite matching algorithm to align the arguments between the reference and MT output according to the lexical similarity of role fillers.

4. Compute the weighted f-score over the matching role labels of these aligned predicates and role fillers according to the following definitions:

$$q_{i,j}^0 \equiv \text{ARG } j \text{ of aligned frame } i \text{ in MT}$$

$$q_{i,j}^1 \equiv \text{ARG } j \text{ of aligned frame } i \text{ in REF}$$

$$w_i^0 \equiv \frac{\text{\#tokens filled in aligned frame } i \text{ of MT}}{\text{total \#tokens in MT}}$$

$$w_i^1 \equiv \frac{\text{\#tokens filled in aligned frame } i \text{ of REF}}{\text{total \#tokens in REF}}$$

$$w_{\text{nf}}^0 \equiv \frac{\text{\#tokens that are not fillers of any role inMT}}{\text{total \#tokens in MT}}$$

$$w_{\text{nf}}^1 \equiv \frac{\text{\#tokens that are not fillers of any role in REF}}{\text{total \#tokens in REF}}$$

$$w_{\{\text{pred}|j\}} \equiv \text{weight of similarity of predicates or ARG } j$$

$$\mathbf{e}_{\text{sent}} \equiv \text{the whole sentence string of MT}$$

$$\mathbf{f}_{\text{sent}} \equiv \text{the whole sentence string of REF}$$

$$\mathbf{e}_{i,\{\text{pred}|j\}} \equiv \text{role fillers of pred or ARG } j \text{ of the aligned frame } i \text{ of MT}$$

$$\mathbf{f}_{i,\{\text{pred}|j\}} \equiv \text{role fillers of pred or ARG } j \text{ of the aligned frame } i \text{ of REF}$$

$$s(e,f) = \text{lexical similarity of token } e \text{ and } f$$

$$\text{prec}_{\mathbf{e},\mathbf{f}} = \frac{\sum_{e \in \mathbf{e}} \max_{f \in \mathbf{f}} s(e,f)}{|\mathbf{e}|} \tag{1}$$

$$\text{rec}_{\mathbf{e},\mathbf{f}} = \frac{\sum_{f \in \mathbf{f}} \max_{e \in \mathbf{e}} s(e,f)}{|\mathbf{f}|} \tag{2}$$

$$s_{\text{sent}} = \frac{2 \cdot \text{prec}_{\mathbf{e}_{\text{sent}},\mathbf{f}_{\text{sent}}} \cdot \text{rec}_{\mathbf{e}_{\text{sent}},\mathbf{f}_{\text{sent}}}}{\text{prec}_{\mathbf{e}_{\text{sent}},\mathbf{f}_{\text{sent}}} + \text{rec}_{\mathbf{e}_{\text{sent}},\mathbf{f}_{\text{sent}}}} \tag{3}$$

$$s_{i,\text{pred}} = \frac{2 \cdot \text{prec}_{\mathbf{e}_{i,\text{pred}},\mathbf{f}_{i,\text{pred}}} \cdot \text{rec}_{\mathbf{e}_{i,\text{pred}},\mathbf{f}_{i,\text{pred}}}}{\text{prec}_{\mathbf{e}_{i,\text{pred}},\mathbf{f}_{i,\text{pred}}} + \text{rec}_{\mathbf{e}_{i,\text{pred}},\mathbf{f}_{i,\text{pred}}}} \tag{4}$$

$$s_{i,j} = \frac{2 \cdot \text{prec}_{\mathbf{e}_{i,j},\mathbf{f}_{i,j}} \cdot \text{rec}_{\mathbf{e}_{i,j},\mathbf{f}_{i,j}}}{\text{prec}_{\mathbf{e}_{i,j},\mathbf{f}_{i,j}} + \text{rec}_{\mathbf{e}_{i,j},\mathbf{f}_{i,j}}} \tag{5}$$

$$\text{precision} = \frac{\sum_i w_i^0 \frac{w_{\text{pred}} s_{i,\text{pred}} + \sum_j w_j s_{i,j}}{w_{\text{pred}} + \sum_j w_j |q_{i,j}^0|} + w_{\text{nf}}^0 s_{\text{sent}}}{\sum_i w_i^0 + w_{\text{nf}}^0} \tag{6}$$

$$\text{recall} = \frac{\sum_i w_i^1 \frac{w_{\text{pred}} s_{i,\text{pred}} + \sum_j w_j s_{i,j}}{w_{\text{pred}} + \sum_j w_j |q_{i,j}^1|} + w_{\text{nf}}^1 s_{\text{sent}}}{\sum_i w_i^1 + w_{\text{nf}}^1} \tag{7}$$

$$\text{MEANT} = \frac{\text{precision} \cdot \text{recall}}{\alpha \cdot \text{precision} + (1-\alpha) \cdot \text{recall}} \tag{8}$$

where $s(e,f)$ is the lexical similarity computed using word embeddings (Mikolov et al., 2013). By aggregating the lexical similarities, we can obtain the phrasal similarities. s_{sent} is the phrasal similarity of the whole sentence between the reference and the MT output. $s_{i,pred}$ is the phrasal similarities of the predicates between the reference translations and the MT output and $s_{i,j}$ is that of the role fillers of the arguments of role type j.

w_{pred} is the weight of the lexical similarities of the aligned predicates in step 2. w_j is the weight of the phrasal similarities of the role fillers of the arguments of role type j of the aligned frames between the reference translations and the MT output in step 3 if their role types are matching. There is a total of 12 weights for the set of semantic role labels in MEANT (Lo and Wu, 2011b) estimated by heuristics (Lo and Wu, 2012).

Finally, the weight α for the precision and recall is introduced for different usages of MEANT. α should be set to 1 so that MEANT is pure recall when it is used for MT evaluation and α should be set to 0.5 so that MEANT is the balance of precision and recall, when it is used for MT system optimization.

HMEANT (Lo and Wu, 2011a) is the variant of MEANT for human evaluation, where the semantic roles in the reference and in the MT output are annotated by humans. XMEANT (Lo et al., 2014) is the cross-lingual variant of MEANT, which estimates translation quality of the MT output against the source sentence using automatic semantic parsers for the input and output languages and alignment probabilities to determine the cross-lingual lexical semantic similarity.

3 Improvements in MEANT 2.0

We improve the performance of MEANT on evaluating translation adequacy by weighing the importance of each word by inverse document frequency when computing phrasal similarity, so that a higher score will be given to phrases with more matches for content words than for function words. We also modify the phrasal similarity calculation so that instead of aggregating lexical similarities for the bag of words in the phrase, it aggregates ngram lexical similarities. Thus, the word order of the semantic role fillers for the whole sentence is taken into account. Our development experiments showed that the optimal value of n is 2.

We also generalize the concept of weighted precision and recall when computing phrasal similarities for the semantic role fillers. Lastly, we simplify the computation of the frame semantic similarities by introducing a weight β to linearly combine the phrasal similarity of the whole sentence and the frame semantic similarity of the reference and the MT output into MEANT. Our development experiments show that the optimal value of β is 0.1. In summary, equations (1) to (8) are replaced by equations (9) to (16) as follow:

$$\text{prec}_{\mathbf{e},\mathbf{f}} \equiv \text{idf-weighted max-aligned distributional ngram precision} \tag{9}$$

$$\text{rec}_{\mathbf{e},\mathbf{f}} \equiv \text{idf-weighted max-aligned distributional ngram recall} \tag{10}$$

$$s_{i,\text{pred}} = \frac{\text{prec}_{\mathbf{e}_{i,\text{pred}},\mathbf{f}_{i,\text{pred}}} \cdot \text{rec}_{\mathbf{e}_{i,\text{pred}},\mathbf{f}_{i,\text{pred}}}}{\alpha \cdot \text{prec}_{\mathbf{e}_{i,\text{pred}},\mathbf{f}_{i,\text{pred}}} + (1-\alpha) \cdot \text{rec}_{\mathbf{e}_{i,\text{pred}},\mathbf{f}_{i,\text{pred}}}} \tag{11}$$

$$s_{i,j} = \frac{\text{prec}_{\mathbf{e}_{i,j},\mathbf{f}_{i,j}} \cdot \text{rec}_{\mathbf{e}_{i,j},\mathbf{f}_{i,j}}}{\alpha \cdot \text{prec}_{\mathbf{e}_{i,j},\mathbf{f}_{i,j}} + (1-\alpha) \cdot \text{rec}_{\mathbf{e}_{i,j},\mathbf{f}_{i,j}}} \tag{12}$$

$$s_{\text{sent}} = \frac{\text{prec}_{\mathbf{e}_{\text{sent}},\mathbf{f}_{\text{sent}}} \cdot \text{rec}_{\mathbf{e}_{\text{sent}},\mathbf{f}_{\text{sent}}}}{\alpha \cdot \text{prec}_{\mathbf{e}_{\text{sent}},\mathbf{f}_{\text{sent}}} + (1-\alpha) \cdot \text{rec}_{\mathbf{e}_{\text{sent}},\mathbf{f}_{\text{sent}}}} \tag{13}$$

$$\text{precision} = \frac{\sum_i w_i^0 \frac{w_{\text{pred}} s_{i,\text{pred}} + \sum_j w_j s_{i,j}}{w_{\text{pred}} + \sum_j w_j |q_{i,j}^0|}}{\sum_i w_i^0} \tag{14}$$

$$\text{recall} = \frac{\sum_i w_i^1 \frac{w_{\text{pred}} s_{i,\text{pred}} + \sum_j w_j s_{i,j}}{w_{\text{pred}} + \sum_j w_j |q_{i,j}^1|}}{\sum_i w_i^1} \tag{15}$$

lang.	# sent.	# tokens	# resulted vocab.
cs	67M	1,088M	1,963k
de	184M	3,444M	4,018k
en	331M	6,585M	2,368k
fi	14M	215M	1,405k
fr	38M	1,047M	950k
hi	1M	37M	82k
lv	11M	194M	586k
pl	39M	318M	885k
ro	2M	57M	233k
ru	52M	983M	1,708k
tr	2M	34M	279k
zh	61M	2,227M	911k

Table 1: Statistics of resources used to train the word embeddings and the resulted vocabulary size of the model.

$$\mathrm{MEANT} = \beta \frac{\text{precision} \cdot \text{recall}}{\alpha \cdot \text{precision} + (1 - \alpha) \cdot \text{recall}} + (1 - \beta)s_{\text{sent}} \quad (16)$$

As a result, for languages without an automatic semantic parser or sentences without a valid predicate-argument structure recognized by an automatic semantic parser, the MEANT score is the phrasal similarity of the whole sentence.

4 Setup

We use the monolingual corpora provided for the WMT translation task (Bojar et al., 2014, 2015, 2016a) to build the word embeddings for evaluating lexical similarities using `word2vec` (Mikolov et al., 2013). Table 1 summarizes the resources used to train the word embeddings and the resulting vocabulary size of the distributional lexical semantic similarity model.

We use `mateplus` (Roth and Woodsend, 2014) for German and English semantic role labeling and `mate-tools` (Björkelund et al., 2009) for Chinese semantic role labeling. Instead of the 12 semantic role types used in (Lo and Wu, 2011b), we merge the semantic role labels of Chinese, English and German into 8 role types (who, did, what, whom, when, where, why, how) for more robust performance.

For languages except Chinese, tokenization step simply involves separating punctuations at the end of the words in both the reference and the MT output. Chinese does not have clear word boundaries. Each individual Chinese character usually carries multiple meanings and relies on surrounding characters to disambiguate it. Naive Chinese character segmentation would affect the accuracy of the vector representation and the distributional lexical semantic similarity model. Thus, we use `ICTCLAS`

(Zhang et al., 2003) to segment the Chinese monolingual corpus into words before building the word embeddings.

5 Experiments and results

We use the WMT 2014-2016 metrics task evaluation set (Machacek and Bojar, 2014; Stanojević et al., 2015; Bojar et al., 2016b) for our development experiments. The official human judgments of translation quality were collected using relative ranking. The annotators were given the original input and the reference and were asked to order up to 5 different MT outputs according to the translation quality.

Two other kinds of human judgments of translation quality were collected in the WMT 2016 metrics task. The direct assessment evaluation protocol gave the annotators the reference and one MT output only and asked them to evaluate the translation adequacy of the MT output on an absolute scale. The HUME metric (Birch et al., 2016) is very similar to HMEANT, which evaluates translation adequacy via semantic units in the input sentence annotated by humans following the UCCA (Abend and Rappoport, 2013) guidelines. However, HUME also takes nominal and adjectival argument structures into account (instead of only predicate argument structure as in HMEANT).

Due to space limitations, we only report the results of MEANT 2.0, MEANT 2.0 - nosrl, BLEU and the best correlation in each of the individual language pairs. Since we use exactly the same protocol for each of the test sets, our reported results are directly comparable with those reported in Machacek and Bojar (2014); Stanojević et al. (2015); Bojar et al. (2016b). We summarize the observations in the following sections.

5.1 Correlation with human at system-level

5.1.1 On relative ranking judgment

Table 2 shows the Pearson's correlation with the WMT 2014-2016 official human relative ranking scores at system-level. As expected, MEANT 2.0 performs significantly better than MEANT 2.0 - nosrl in most of the language pairs. Overall, both MEANT 2.0 and the nosrl variant are very competitive with other metrics for all test sets.

For the WMT14 test set, MEANT 2.0 is the best metric among all participants in that year in the de-en and en-de direction. On average over from-English directions, MEANT 2.0

| | input language | cs | de | fr | hi | ru | | en | en | en | en | | en |
	output language	en	en	en	en	en	ave.	cs	fr	hi	ru	ave.	de
WMT14	MEANT 2.0	.990	**.960**	.979	.791	.843	.913	–	–	–	–	–	**.482**
RRsys	MEANT 2.0 - nosrl	.983	.957	.979	.761	.830	.902	.978	.941	.986	.938	**.961**	.236
	individual best	**.993**	.943	**.981**	**.976**	**.870**	**.944**	**.988**	**.960**	**.990**	**.941**	.959	.357
	BLEU	.909	.832	.952	.956	.789	.888	.976	.937	.973	.915	.950	.216

| | input language | cs | de | fi | fr | ru | | en | en | en | en | en | |
	output language	en	en	en	en	en	ave.	cs	de	fi	fr	ru	ave.
WMT15	MEANT 2.0	.974	.965	.946	.994	.970	.970	–	.764	–	–	–	–
RRsys	MEANT 2.0 - nosrl	.972	.956	.939	.995	.969	.966	**.984**	.676	.833	.961	.937	.878
	individual best	**.993**	**.981**	**.977**	**.997**	**.981**	**.978**	.977	**.879**	**.878**	**.964**	**.970**	**.916**
	BLEU	.957	.865	.929	.975	.851	.915	.936	.573	.602	.948	.841	.780

| | input language | cs | de | fi | ro | ru | tr | en | en | en | en | en | en |
	output language	en	en	en	en	en	en	cs	de	fi	ro	ru	tr
WMT16	MEANT 2.0	.989	.947	.953	.940	**.990**	.980	–	.540	–	–	–	–
RRsys	MEANT 2.0 - nosrl	.985	.928	.969	.917	.984	.978	.967	.541	.902	.868	.925	.933
	individual best	**.997**	**.985**	**.974**	**.970**	**.990**	**.981**	**.975**	**.915**	**.974**	**.959**	**.954**	**.956**
	BLEU	.992	.905	.858	.899	.962	.899	.968	.752	.868	.897	.835	.745

Table 2: Pearson's correlation of the metric scores with the WMT 2014-2016 official human relative ranking scores at system-level. For consistency with the task overview paper, en-de results are not included into out-of-English system average in WMT 2014 results (Machacek and Bojar, 2014); system average are not reported in WMT 2016 results (Bojar et al., 2016b).

| | input language | cs | de | fi | ro | ru | tr | en |
	output language	en	en	en	en	en	en	ru
WMT16	MEANT 2.0	.990	.950	.966	.946	.959	**.990**	–
DAsys	MEANT 2.0 - nosrl	.988	.942	.979	.930	.958	.987	.946
	individual best	**.995**	**.985**	**.980**	**.957**	**.976**	.982	**.966**
	BLEU	.989	.808	.864	.940	.837	.895	.838

Table 3: Pearson's correlation of metric scores with the WMT 2016 direct assessment of translation adequacy at system-level.

– `nosrl` is the best metric among all the participants in that year. On average over into-English directions, `MEANT 2.0` ties with the 4th-place participant in that year while `MEANT 2.0 - nosrl` is in 7th place. Both variants of MEANT lose only to ensemble and trained metrics in that year.

For the WMT15 test set, `MEANT 2.0 - nosrl` is the best metric among all the participants in that year in the en-cs direction. On average over into-English directions, `MEANT 2.0` is in 6th place while the `nosrl` variant is in 9th place. Both variants of MEANT lose only to ensemble and trained metrics in that year.

For the WMT16 test set, `MEANT 2.0` ties for 1st place with the best metric in the ru-en direction in that year. Both variants of MEANT perform as well as the leading metrics in all other directions, except en-de.

5.1.2 On direct assessment judgment

Table 3 shows the Pearson's correlation with the WMT 2016 direct assessment of translation adequacy at system-level.

Both `MEANT 2.0` and `MEANT 2.0 - nosrl` beat all the other metrics that year in the tr-en direction and perform very competitively when compared to the leading pack in other directions. `MEANT 2.0` performs better than the `nosrl` variant in all directions, except fi-en.

5.2 Correlation with human judgment at segment-level

5.2.1 On relative ranking judgment

Table 4 shows the Kendall's correlation with the WMT 2014-2016 official human relative ranking judgments at segment-level. Similar to the correlation at the system-level, `MEANT 2.0` performs significantly better than `MEANT 2.0 - nosrl` for most language pairs.

For the WMT14 test set, `MEANT 2.0` beats all the participants in the en-de direction while the `nosrl` variant beats all the participants in all other from-English directions (and their average) in that year. On the average of all the to-English directions, `MEANT 2.0` and the `nosrl` variant are in 2nd and 3rd place respectively and only lose to an ensemble and trained metric in that year.

	input language	cs	de	fr	hi	ru		en	en	en	en	en	
	output language	en	en	en	en	en	ave.	cs	de	fr	hi	ru	ave.
WMT14 RRseg	MEANT 2.0	.325	.353	.421	.421	.348	.374	–	**.279**	–	–	–	–
	MEANT 2.0 - nosrl	.312	.354	.426	.410	.341	.367	**.355**	.254	**.314**	**.294**	**.472**	**.338**
	individual best	**.328**	**.380**	**.433**	**.438**	**.355**	**.386**	.344	.268	.293	.286	.440	.319
	sentBLEU	.213	.271	.378	.300	.263	.285	.290	.191	.256	.227	.381	.269
	input language	cs	de	fi	fr	ru		en	en	en	en	en	
	output language	en	en	en	en	en	ave.	cs	de	fi	fr	ru	ave.
WMT15 RRseg	MEANT 2.0	.463	.465	.424	.402	.400	.431	–	.398	–	–	–	–
	MEANT 2.0 - nosrl	.463	.454	.421	**.406**	.401	.429	**.472**	.386	.344	.365	**.442**	**.402**
	individual best	**.495**	**.482**	**.445**	.398	**.418**	**.447**	.446	**.399**	**.380**	**.366**	.439	.400
	sentBLEU	.391	.360	.308	.358	.329	.349	.290	.191	.256	.227	.381	.269
	input language	cs	de	fi	ro	ru	tr	en	en	en	en	en	en
	output language	en	en	en	en	en	en	cs	de	fi	ro	ru	tr
WMT16 RRseg	MEANT 2.0	.355	**.453**	.414	.345	.401	.373	–	**.360**	–	–	–	–
	MEANT 2.0 - nosrl	.347	.438	.411	.338	.400	.364	**.436**	**.360**	.329	.271	**.428**	.325
	individual best	**.388**	.420	**.481**	**.383**	**.420**	**.424**	.422	.334	**.364**	**.307**	.405	**.337**
	sentBLEU	.284	.265	.368	.272	.330	.245	.359	.236	.306	.233	.328	.222

Table 4: Kendall's correlation of metric scores with the WMT 2014-2016 official human relative ranking judgments at segment-level. For consistency with the task overview paper, system averages are not reported in WMT 2016 results (Bojar et al., 2016b).

	input language	cs	de	fi	ro	ru	tr	en
	output language	en	en	en	en	en	en	ru
WMT16 DAseg	MEANT 2.0	.674	.510	.539	.607	.535	.588	–
	MEANT 2.0 - nosrl	.672	.484	.522	.587	.540	.577	.664
	individual best	**.713**	**.601**	**.598**	**.661**	**.618**	**.663**	**.666**
	sentBLEU	.557	.448	.484	.499	.502	.532	.550

Table 5: Pearson's correlation of metric scores with the WMT 2016 direct assessment of absolute translation adequacy at segment-level.

For the WMT15 test set, both MEANT 2.0 and MEANT 2.0 - nosrl beat all the participating metrics in that year in the fr-en direction. MEANT 2.0 - nosrl also has the highest correlation with human in the en-cs and en-ru directions and the overall average of the from-English directions. Again, on the average of all the to-English directions, MEANT 2.0 and the nosrl variant are in 2nd and 3rd place respectively and only lose to an ensemble and trained metric.

For the WMT16 test set, both MEANT 2.0 and MEANT 2.0 - nosrl beat all other participants in that year in the de-en, en-de directions while MEANT 2.0 - nosrl is also the champion in the en-cs and the en-ru directions. Both variants perform very competitively when compared to the leading metrics in all other directions.

5.2.2 On direct assessment judgment

Table 5 shows the Pearson's correlation of MEANT with the WMT 2016 direct assessment of absolute translation adequacy at segment-level. Both variants of MEANT perform very competitively when compared to the leading pack in other directions. MEANT 2.0 performs better than the

	input language	en	en	en	en
	output language	cs	de	pl	ro
HUME	MEANT 2.0	–	**.522**	–	–
	MEANT 2.0 - nosrl	.508	**.522**	.619	**.479**
	individual best	**.544**	.480	**.639**	.435
	sentBLEU	.349	.377	.550	.328

Table 6: Pearson's correlation of metric scores with the WMT 2016 HUME human assessment at segment-level.

nosrl variant in all directions, except ru-en.

5.2.3 On HUME evaluation

Table 6 shows the Pearson's correlation of MEANT with the HUME human assessment on the himltest test set at segment-level.

Both MEANT 2.0 and MEANT 2.0 - nosrl beat all other participating metrics in that year in the en-de direction. MEANT 2.0 - nosrl also has the highest correlation with HUME among all the participants in that year in the en-pl direction.

5.3 Evaluation speed

Table 7 shows the average time (in seconds) for each step of a typical WMT system evaluation

lang.	# pairs	tok.	load	srl	score
cs	2.8k	3	158	–	56
de	2.6k	2	333	1010	41
en	2.8k	2	195	1120	46
fi	2.3k	2	114	–	24
fr	3.0k	4	77	–	61
hi	2.5k	4	7	–	35
lv	2.0k	2	47	–	13
pl	0.3k	1	72	–	4
ro	2.0k	1	19	–	10
ru	2.9k	5	142	–	27
tr	3.0k	4	23	–	17
zh	2.0k	501	75	1175	16

Table 7: Average time in seconds for each step of evaluating a typical WMT system using MEANT: tokenizing both the reference and the MT output; loading the distributional lexical semantic similarity model; semantic role labeling the reference and the MT output; and scoring the MT output.

on different output languages using MEANT. The time taken for punctuation tokenization is almost negligible. This is because in common practice for MT system development, the validation and evaluation set are reused frequently, so the processing of the reference translation is typically pre-computed. Furthermore, the MT system is trained to output tokenized translations, so it is not necessary to run the tokenization step on the MT output. Therefore, the tokenization step does not affect the time cost of MEANT in practical applications (even in the case of Chinese, where word segmentation takes significantly longer).

The loading time of the word embedding model is proportional to the vocabulary size of the model reported in table 1; it takes less than a second to load 10k vocabularies into memory.

Automatic semantic role labeling (SRL) is the most time consuming step in running MEANT. The time reported in table 7 includes parsing both the reference and the MT output. However, as pointed out above, common practice for MT system development is to frequently reuse the validation and evaluation sets. Thus, semantic role labeling of the reference translation could be pre-computed to reduce the time taken for the SRL step in the development cycle.

Finally, the time used in computing the MEANT score is proportional to the size of the evaluation set and the word embedding model. The scoring step processes around 50 to 100 sentences each second.

6   Conclusion

We present a new version of MEANT that participated in evaluating MT systems for all language pairs in the metrics task of the Second Conference on Machine Translation (WMT 2017). The correlation of MEANT with human judgment has been improved by better addressing translation adequacy via weighing the importance of each word in the phrasal similarity computation by inverse document frequency, and better addressing translation fluency via using distributional ngram accuracy to account for word reordering in the computation. Our results show that MEANT consistently performs well across different output languages in the previous year's test set at both system-level and segment-level.

MEANT 2.0 - nosrl is a non-ensemble and untrained metric that requires only a monolingual corpus in the output language for building the word embeddings to evaluate MT systems for a new language pair. Although there is an overhead time cost in semantic role labeling sentence pairs in MEANT 2.0 and loading the word embedding model in both MEANT 2.0 and its nosrl subversion, the time cost can be reduced almost by half in real applications. This highly portable and open source semantic MT evaluation metric is a more accurate alternative to BLEU in evaluating translation quality for low-resource languages.

Acknowledgement

The author would like to thank Markus Saers, Karteek Addanki and Meriem Beloucif for providing code review before the software release and Roland Kuhn for editing the paper.

References

Omri Abend and Ari Rappoport. 2013.   UCCA: A Semantics-based Grammatical Annotation Scheme. In *Proceedings of the 10th International Conference on Computational Semantics (IWCS 2013) – Long Papers*. Association for Computational Linguistics, Potsdam, Germany, pages 1–12. http://www.aclweb.org/anthology/W13-0101.

Alexandra Birch, Omri Abend, Ondřej Bojar, and Barry Haddow. 2016.   HUME: Human UCCA-Based Evaluation of Machine Translation. In *Proceedings of the 2016 Conference on Empirical Methods in Natural Language Processing*. Association for Computational Linguistics, Austin, Texas, pages 1264–1274.   https://aclweb.org/anthology/D16-1134.

Anders Björkelund, Love Hafdell, and Pierre Nugues. 2009. Multilingual semantic role labeling. In *Proceedings of the Thirteenth Conference on Computational Natural Language Learning (CoNLL 2009): Shared Task*. Association for Computational Linguistics, Boulder, Colorado, pages 43–48. http://www.aclweb.org/anthology/W09-1206.

Ondrej Bojar, Christian Buck, Christian Federmann, Barry Haddow, Philipp Koehn, Johannes Leveling, Christof Monz, Pavel Pecina, Matt Post, Herve Saint-Amand, Radu Soricut, Lucia Specia, and Aleš Tamchyna. 2014. Findings of the 2014 Workshop on Statistical Machine Translation. In *Proceedings of the Ninth Workshop on Statistical Machine Translation*. Association for Computational Linguistics, Baltimore, Maryland, USA, pages 12–58. http://www.aclweb.org/anthology/W14-3302.

Ondřej Bojar, Rajen Chatterjee, Christian Federmann, Yvette Graham, Barry Haddow, Matthias Huck, Antonio Jimeno Yepes, Philipp Koehn, Varvara Logacheva, Christof Monz, Matteo Negri, Aurelie Neveol, Mariana Neves, Martin Popel, Matt Post, Raphael Rubino, Carolina Scarton, Lucia Specia, Marco Turchi, Karin Verspoor, and Marcos Zampieri. 2016a. Findings of the 2016 Conference on Machine Translation. In *Proceedings of the First Conference on Machine Translation*. Association for Computational Linguistics, Berlin, Germany, pages 131–198. http://www.aclweb.org/anthology/W16-2301.

Ondřej Bojar, Rajen Chatterjee, Christian Federmann, Barry Haddow, Matthias Huck, Chris Hokamp, Philipp Koehn, Varvara Logacheva, Christof Monz, Matteo Negri, Matt Post, Carolina Scarton, Lucia Specia, and Marco Turchi. 2015. Findings of the 2015 Workshop on Statistical Machine Translation. In *Proceedings of the Tenth Workshop on Statistical Machine Translation*. Association for Computational Linguistics, Lisbon, Portugal, pages 1–46. http://aclweb.org/anthology/W15-3001.

Ondřej Bojar, Yvette Graham, Amir Kamran, and Miloš Stanojević. 2016b. Results of the WMT16 Metrics Shared Task. In *Proceedings of the First Conference on Machine Translation*. Association for Computational Linguistics, Berlin, Germany, pages 199–231. http://www.aclweb.org/anthology/W16-2302.

Michael Denkowski and Alon Lavie. 2014. METEOR universal: Language specific translation evaluation for any target language. In *9th Workshop on Statistical Machine Translation (WMT 2014)*.

George Doddington. 2002. Automatic evaluation of machine translation quality using n-gram co-occurrence statistics. In *The second international conference on Human Language Technology Research (HLT '02)*. San Diego, California.

Gregor Leusch, Nicola Ueffing, and Hermann Ney. 2006. CDer: Efficient MT evaluation using block movements. In *11th Conference of the European Chapter of the Association for Computational Linguistics (EACL-2006)*.

Chi-kiu Lo, Meriem Beloucif, Markus Saers, and Dekai Wu. 2014. XMEANT: Better semantic MT evaluation without reference translations. In *Proceedings of the 52nd Annual Meeting of the Association for Computational Linguistics (Volume 2: Short Papers)*. Association for Computational Linguistics, pages 765–771. https://doi.org/10.3115/v1/P14-2124.

Chi-kiu Lo, Philipp Dowling, and Dekai Wu. 2015. Improving evaluation and optimization of MT systems against MEANT. In *Proceedings of the Tenth Workshop on Statistical Machine Translation*. Association for Computational Linguistics, Lisbon, Portugal, pages 434–441. http://aclweb.org/anthology/W15-3056.

Chi-kiu Lo and Dekai Wu. 2011a. MEANT: An inexpensive, high-accuracy, semi-automatic metric for evaluating translation utility based on semantic roles. In *Proceedings of the 49th Annual Meeting of the Association for Computational Linguistics: Human Language Technologies*. Association for Computational Linguistics, pages 220–229. http://aclweb.org/anthology/P11-1023.

Chi-Kiu Lo and Dekai Wu. 2011b. SMT Versus AI Redux: How Semantic Fames Evaluate MT More Accurately. In *Proceedings of the Twenty-Second International Joint Conference on Artificial Intelligence - Volume Volume Three*. AAAI Press, IJCAI'11, pages 1838–1845. https://doi.org/10.5591/978-1-57735-516-8/IJCAI11-308.

Chi-kiu Lo and Dekai Wu. 2012. Unsupervised vs. supervised weight estimation for semantic MT evaluation metrics. In *Proceedings of the Sixth Workshop on Syntax, Semantics and Structure in Statistical Translation*. Association for Computational Linguistics, Jeju, Republic of Korea, pages 49–56. http://www.aclweb.org/anthology/W12-4206.

Matous Machacek and Ondrej Bojar. 2014. Results of the WMT14 Metrics Shared Task. In *Proceedings of the Ninth Workshop on Statistical Machine Translation*. Association for Computational Linguistics, Baltimore, Maryland, USA, pages 293–301. http://www.aclweb.org/anthology/W14-3336.

Tomas Mikolov, Ilya Sutskever, Kai Chen, Greg Corrado, and Jeffrey Dean. 2013. Distributed representations of words and phrases and their compositionality. In *Proceedings of the 26th International Conference on Neural Information Processing Systems*. Curran Associates Inc., USA, NIPS'13, pages 3111–3119. http://dl.acm.org/citation.cfm?id=2999792.2999959.

Kishore Papineni, Salim Roukos, Todd Ward, and Wei-Jing Zhu. 2002. BLEU: a method for automatic evaluation of machine translation. In *40th Annual Meeting of the Association for Computational Linguistics (ACL-02)*. Philadelphia, Pennsylvania, pages 311–318. https://doi.org/10.3115/1073083.1073135.

Michael Roth and Kristian Woodsend. 2014. Composition of word representations improves semantic role labelling. In *Proceedings of the 2014 Conference on Empirical Methods in Natural Language Processing (EMNLP)*. Association for Computational Linguistics, Doha, Qatar, pages 407–413. http://www.aclweb.org/anthology/D14-1045.

Matthew Snover, Bonnie Dorr, Richard Schwartz, Linnea Micciulla, and John Makhoul. 2006. A study of translation edit rate with targeted human annotation. In *7th Biennial Conference Association for Machine Translation in the Americas (AMTA 2006)*. Cambridge, Massachusetts, pages 223–231.

Miloš Stanojević, Amir Kamran, Philipp Koehn, and Ondřej Bojar. 2015. Results of the WMT15 Metrics Shared Task. In *Proceedings of the Tenth Workshop on Statistical Machine Translation*. Association for Computational Linguistics, Lisbon, Portugal, pages 256–273. http://aclweb.org/anthology/W15-3031.

Hua-Ping Zhang, Hong-Kui Yu, De-Yi Xiong, and Qun Liu. 2003. HHMM-based Chinese Lexical Analyzer ICTCLAS. In *Proceedings of the Second SIGHAN Workshop on Chinese Language Processing*. Association for Computational Linguistics, Sapporo, Japan, pages 184–187.

Blend: a Novel Combined MT Metric Based on Direct Assessment

— CASICT-DCU submission to WMT17 Metrics Task

Qingsong Ma[1] Yvette Graham[2] Shugen Wang[1] Qun Liu[2,1]
[1]Key Laboratory of Intelligent Information Processing,
Institute of Computing Technology, University of Chinese Academy of Sciences
[2] ADAPT Centre, School of Computing, Dublin City University
maqingsong@ict.ac.cn, graham.yvette@gmail.com
wangshugen@ict.ac.cn, qun.liu@dcu.ie

Abstract

Existing metrics to evaluate the quality of Machine Translation hypotheses take different perspectives into account. DPM-Fcomb, a metric combining the merits of a range of metrics, achieved the best performance for evaluation of to-English language pairs in the previous two years of WMT Metrics Shared Tasks. This year, we submit a novel combined metric, Blend, to WMT17 Metrics task. Compared to DPMFcomb, Blend includes the following adaptations: i) We use DA human evaluation to guide the training process with a vast reduction in required training data, while still achieving improved performance when evaluated on WMT16 to-English language pairs; ii) We carry out experiments to explore the contribution of metrics incorporated in Blend, in order to find a trade-off between performance and efficiency.

1 Introduction

Automatic machine translation evaluation (AMTE) has received much attention in recent years, with the aim of providing quick and stable measurements of the performance of machine translation (MT) systems. Various metrics for AMTE have been proposed and most operate via computation of the similarity between the MT hypothesis and the reference translation. However, different metrics focus on different perspectives in terms of measuring similarity. For lexical based metrics, BLEU (Papineni et al., 2002) and NIST (Doddington, 2002) count n-gram co-occurrence,

Meteor (Denkowski and Lavie, 2014) and GTM (Melamed et al., 2003) catch different kinds of matches, ROUGE (Lin and Och, 2004) captures common subsequences, WER (Nießen et al., 2000), PER (Tillmann et al., 1997) and TER (Snover et al., 2009) compute the post-editing distance between the hypothesis and the reference translation. Syntactic based metrics mainly use shallow syntactic structures (Chan and Ng, 2008; Zhu et al., 2010), dependency tree structures or constituent tree structures (Owczarzak et al., 2007; Liu and Gildea, 2005). Semantic measures (Lo et al., 2012) and discourse similarity based metrics (Guzmán et al., 2014) have also been proposed.

Different metrics evaluate similarity between hypotheses and reference translations from various perspectives, each of which has pros and cons. One straightforward and effective method to take advantage of the merits of existing metrics is to combine quality scores assigned by these metrics, like DPMFcomb (Yu et al., 2015a).

In WMT15 and WMT16 Metrics tasks, DPM-Fcomb was the best metric on average for to-English language pairs (Stanojević et al., 2015; Bojar et al., 2016). DPMFcomb incorporates lexical, syntactic and semantic based metrics, using ranking SVM[1] to train parameters of each metric score and achieves a high correlation with human evaluation. Human evaluations in terms of relative ranking (RR) accumulated in WMT Metrics tasks are adopted to generate training data and to guide the training process. Human relative ranking is carried out by ranking the quality of 5 MT hypotheses of the same source segment from 1 to 5 via comparison with the reference translation.

---

[1]http://www.cs.cornell.edu/People/tj/svm_light/svm_rank.html

Proceedings of the Conference on Machine Translation (WMT), Volume 2: Shared Task Papers, pages 598–603
Copenhagen, Denmark, September 7–11, 2017. ©2017 Association for Computational Linguistics

	cs-en	de-en	fi-en	ro-en	ru-en	tr-en	en-ru
WMT15	500	500	500	–	500	–	500
WMT16	560	560	560	560	560	560	560

Table 1: The number of sampled DA data for each language pair in WMT15 and WMT16.

Therefore, human RR only provides relative differences in quality of a given 5 hypotheses rather than the overall absolute quality of hypotheses. Besides, the low inter-annotator agreement level in RR (Callison-Burch et al., 2007) has been a long-lasting issue in MT human evaluation. The ability and the reliability of RR raise our concern whether the capability of the model trained with RR as the golden standard may be limited.

Fortunately, a new emerged evaluation approach, direct assessment (DA) (Graham et al., 2013), has been proven more reliable for evaluation of metrics and was recently adopted as the official human evaluation in WMT17. DA produces absolute quality scores of hypotheses, by measuring to what extend the hypothesis adequately expresses the meaning of the reference translation, through a 1-100 continuous rating scale that facilitates reliable quality control of crowd-sourcing. Large numbers of repeat human assessments per translation are standardized and then combined into a mean score as the final quality score of the MT hypothesis.

The recent development in human evaluation of MT motivates us to propose a new combined metric, named as Blend [2], by adopting DA, as opposed to RR, to guide the training process indicating that a more reliable gold standard can lead to more reliable results even with less training data. Furthermore, we explore the contribution of metrics incorporated in Blend, aiming at finding a trade-off between performance and efficiency of Blend.

What follows is a brief review of DPMFcomb, before a description of Blend formulation is provided in Section 2, followed by experiments and results in Section 3, before the conclusions in section 4.

2 Metrics

2.1 Review of DPMFcomb

DPMFcomb utilizes human relative ranking data to train a combined metric that produces quality scores for MT hypotheses. In the training pro-

cess, metrics are incorporated as features in the form of metric scores attributed to the same hypotheses, with relative ranks as the gold standard to guide SVM-rank to learn parameters for features. When testing, the predicted ranking scores produced by DPMFcomb reflect the quality of hypotheses. DPMFcomb allows the combination of the advantages of a set of arbitrary metrics resulting in a metric with a high correlation with human assessment. DPMFcomb includes default metrics provided by Asiya MT evaluation toolkit (Giménez and Màrquez, 2010), as well as three other metrics, namely ENTF (Yu et al., 2015c), REDp (Yu et al., 2014) and DPMF (Yu et al., 2015b). Over the past two years of WMT metrics tasks, DPMFcomb has achieved the best performance for evaluation of MT of to-English language pairs.

2.2 Blend: A Novel Combined Metric based on DA

Although RR reflects the quality of hypotheses to some extent, it has two obvious defects. Firstly, RR provides relative ranks of the given competing MT hypotheses, which only reflects relative differences in quality rather than the absolute quality of hypotheses. On the other hand, RR suffers from low inter-annotator agreement levels. As a result, the capability of the model trained with RR as the golden standard could be limited. However, DA with carefully design of criteria (Graham et al., 2013) produces highly reliable overall quality scores for each hypothesis (Graham et al., 2015). In addition, since DA has replaced RR as the official human evaluation in the news domain in WMT17, more DA data would become available in the coming years. These motivate our new combined metric, specially designed based on DA, rather than RR, named as Blend, which means it is a metric that can blend advantages of arbitrary metrics in a combined metric that has a high correlation with human assessment.

Our metric follows the basic formulation of DPMFcomb. However, since DA is an absolute quality judgment, which is different from RR, the

---

[2]Blend is available: https://github.com/qingsongma/blend

	cs-en	de-en	fi-en	ro-en	ru-en	tr-en	avg
Blend.all	**.991**	**.954**	.969	.879	**.942**	.972	**.951**
MPEDA	.988	.923	**.971**	**.905**	.923	**.975**	.948
BEER	.985	.871	.964	.828	.894	**.975**	.920

Table 2: System-level Pearson correlation of metric scores and DA human scores with 10K hybrid systems for to-English language pairs on WMT16, where "avg" denotes the average Pearson correlation of all language pairs.

	cs-en	de-en	fi-en	ro-en	ru-en	tr-en	avg
Blend.all	.710	**.615**	**.602**	.636	**.622**	.658	**.641**
DPMFcomb	**.713**	.598	.584	.627	.615	**.663**	.633
METRICS-F	.696	.601	.557	**.662**	.618	.649	.631

Table 3: Segment-level Pearson correlation of metric scores and DA human scores for to-English language pairs on WMT16, where "avg" denotes the average Pearson correlation of all language pairs.

training data and the method of Blend are different from that of DPMFcomb. We employ SVM regression from libsvm (Chang and Lin, 2011) [3] for training, with training data consisting of features in terms of incorporated metric scores for hypotheses and the gold standard in terms of DA human scores.

3 Experiments

We carry out experiments to compare the performance of DPMFcomb and Blend. We also explore the contribution of incorporated metrics in Blend to find a trade-off between performance and efficiency.

3.1 Setups

Our experiments are tested on WMT16 to-English and English-Russian (en-ru) language pairs. We use DA data sampled from WMT15 and WMT16 (Table 1) for Blend. Since there is only a limited amount of DA data available at present, we employ all other to-English DA data as training data (4800 sentences) when testing on each to-English language pair (560 sentences) in WMT16. For en-ru, we use en-ru DA data in WMT15 (500 sentences) to train and test on en-ru DA data in WMT16 (560 sentences).

Features in both the training data and the test data are scaled to be in [-1,1]. We use epsilon-SVR with RBF kernel, and the epsilon is set to 0.1.

[3] http://www.csie.ntu.edu.tw/ cjlin/libsvm/

3.2 Blend vs DPMFcomb

In WMT16, DPMFcomb incorporates 57 metrics and was trained with SVM-rank on 445K training segments extracted from WMT12-WMT14 to-English language pairs according to human judgments in terms of RR. For comparison, Blend incorporates the same 57 metrics but is trained with SVM regression on only 4,800 training data extracted from sampled DA data in WMT15-WMT16 for each to-English language pair. We name it Blend.all.

We present the system and segment-level Pearson correlation results in Table 2 and Table 3, respectively. Table 2 shows Blend.all has higher average system-level Pearson correlation (.951) with DA human scores compared to the two high performing metrics MPEDA (.948) and BEER (.920) on WMT16 for to-English language pairs.

Table 3 shows segment-level Pearson correlations of Blend.all and two other high-performing metrics DPMFcomb and EMTRICS-F on WMT16 for to-English language pairs. From Table 3 we can see Blend.all achieves the best performance in 3 out of 6 to-English languages pairs and state-of-the-art performance on average. It is worth noting that even though the training data of Blend.all is far less than that of DPMFcomb, Blend.all has higher average Pearson correlation (.641), trained on DA scores, than that of DPMFcomb (.633), trained on RR scores.

In all, the above results show Blend trained with DA data outperforms DPMFcomb trained with RR data on WMT16 for to-English language pairs.

	cs-en	de-en	fi-en	ro-en	ru-en	tr-en	avg
Blend.all	**.710**	**.615**	**.602**	**.636**	**.622**	.658	**.641**
Blend.lex	.704	.589	.583	.625	.620	**.674**	.632
Blend.syn	.656	.528	.494	.560	.533	.610	.564
Blend.sem	.610	.533	.492	.507	.501	.554	.533

Table 4: Segment-level Pearson correlation of Blend incorporating different level of linguistic metrics for to-English language pairs on WMT16, where "avg" denotes the average Pearson correlation of all language pairs.

	cs-en	de-en	fi-en	ro-en	ru-en	tr-en	avg
Blend.lex	.704	.589	.583	.625	.620	.674	.632
Blend.lex+CharacTer	.707	.596	.575	.628	.620	**.680**	.634
Blend.lex+BEER	**.709**	.589	.580	.627	.622	.673	.634
Blend.lex+DPMF	.706	.592	**.590**	.632	.626	.670	.636
Blend.lex+ENTF	.703	.595	.588	.629	.629	.676	.637
Blend.lex+4	**.709**	**.601**	.584	**.636**	**.633**	.675	**.640**

Table 5: Segment-level Pearson correlation of Blend.lex incorporating 4 other metrics for to-English language pairs on WMT16, where "avg" denotes the average Pearson correlation of all language pairs.

3.3 Trade-off between Performance and Efficiency

It is convenient for Blend to combine arbitrary metrics in order to achieve a high correlation with human assessment. However, it would be useful to know if any metric does not contribute greatly to Blend in terms of performance, while at the same time leads to low efficiency. To explore this, we separate out the default metrics for to-English language pairs provided by Asiya toolkit into three categories, namely, lexical, syntactic, and semantic based metrics. Blend.lex is the variant that incorporates only default lexical based metrics in Asiya toolkit, while Blend.syn, and Blend.sem, incorporate only syntactic and semantic metrics, respectively. Blend.lex includes 25 metrics, but with only 9 kinds of metrics, since some of them are simply different variants of the same metric. Blend.syn includes 17 metrics and Blend.sem 13 metrics but in reality each only corresponds to 3 distinct metrics, similar to Blend.lex.

The experimental results on WMT16 are shown in Table 4. It is not all that surprising that Blend.all incorporated with all default Asiya metrics achieves the best performance in 5 out of 6 language pairs and on average. However, it may be worth noting that the average Pearson correlation of Blend.lex is only 0.009 less than that of Blend.all, while the performance of Blend.syn and Blend.sem are quite far worse than that of Blend.all, and even that of Blend.lex. Since syntactic and semantic based metrics are usually complex, and the performance of Blend.lex is comparable with that of Blend.all, Blend can operate effectively with only incorporating the default lexical based metrics from Asiya toolkit.

We further add 4 other metrics to Blend.lex., CharacTer(Wang et al., 2016), a novel character-based metric; BEER(Stanojević and Sima'an, 2015), a metric combining different kinds of features; DPMF and ENTF, which proved to be effective. All of these 4 metrics are convenient to use. Table 5 shows *Blend.lex+4* (.640) achieves better performance than that of Blend.lex (.632), and is very close to that of Blend.all (.641) as shown in Table 3.

Hence, we submit *Blend.lex+4* to WMT17 Metrics task for to-English language pairs, since it provides a good trade-off between performance and efficiency for Blend.

3.4 Experiments on from-English language pairs

Blend can be effective to evaluate the quality of from-English MT hypotheses if incorporated metrics support from-English language pairs. We carry out experiments on WMT16 for en-ru language pair as shown in Table 6.[4] Blend.default

---

[4]For from-English language pairs, there is only en-ru DA data available at present.

	en-ru
Blend.default	.613
Blend.default+2	**.675**
BEER	.666

Table 6: Segment-level Pearson correlation for en-ru in WMT16.

is trained on only 500 sentences and incorporates default lexical based metrics from Asiya toolkit for en-ru, including 20 metrics, but with 9 kinds of metrics only. Compared with Blend.default, Blend.default+2 incorporates two more metrics, CharacTer and BEER, but achieves great improvement with segment-level Pearson correlation from .613 to .675. The incorporated metric BEER is the best performing metric (.666) on WMT16 for en-ru, which is trained with large amounts of data. Beer contributes to Blend apparently, meanwhile Blend can further improve the performance of BEER, indicating the effectiveness of the combined metric Blend. We submit Blend.default+2 to WMT17 Metrics task for en-ru.

4 Conclusions

The performance of DPMFcomb proves the effectiveness of the idea of combining metrics. However, DPMFcomb cannot extend itself to the new development of human evaluation. Therefore, we propose a novel metric Blend to employ DA data. Blend is also a combined metric that can take good advantage of the merits of existing metrics, and performs better than DPMFcomb, even with far less training data. Blend is easy to be trained and flexible to be applied to any language pairs. In this paper we present experiments on WMT16 Metrics task, which shows Blend achieves state-of-the-art performance on average for to-English language pairs and for en-ru. Furthermore, we carry out experiments with different settings and find a good trade-off for Blend in terms of performance and efficiency.

Acknowledgments

This research is supported by Chinas NSFC grant 61379086 and the European Union Horizon 2020 Programme (H2020) under grant agreement no. 645452 (QT21). The ADAPT Centre for Digital Content Technology is funded under the SFI Research Centres Programme (Grant 13/RC/2106) and is co-funded under the European Regional Development Fund.

References

Ondřej Bojar, Yvette Graham, Amir Kamran, and Miloš Stanojević. 2016. Results of the wmt16 metrics shared task. In *Proceedings of the First Conference on Machine Translation*. Association for Computational Linguistics, Berlin, Germany, pages 199–231. http://www.aclweb.org/anthology/W16-2302.

Chris Callison-Burch, Cameron Fordyce, Philipp Koehn, Christof Monz, and Josh Schroeder. 2007. (meta-) evaluation of machine translation. In *Proceedings of the Second Workshop on Statistical Machine Translation*. Association for Computational Linguistics, pages 136–158.

Yee Seng Chan and Hwee Tou Ng. 2008. Maxsim: A maximum similarity metric for machine translation evaluation. In *ACL*. pages 55–62.

Chih-Chung Chang and Chih-Jen Lin. 2011. LIBSVM: A library for support vector machines. *ACM Transactions on Intelligent Systems and Technology* 2:27:1–27:27. Software available at http://www.csie.ntu.edu.tw/~cjlin/libsvm.

Michael Denkowski and Alon Lavie. 2014. Meteor universal: Language specific translation evaluation for any target language. In *In Proceedings of the Ninth Workshop on Statistical Machine Translation*. Citeseer.

George Doddington. 2002. Automatic evaluation of machine translation quality using n-gram co-occurrence statistics. In *Proceedings of the second international conference on Human Language Technology Research*. Morgan Kaufmann Publishers Inc., pages 138–145.

Jesús Giménez and Lluís Màrquez. 2010. Asiya: An open toolkit for automatic machine translation (meta-) evaluation. *Prague Bull. Math. Linguistics* 94:77–86.

Yvette Graham, Timothy Baldwin, and Nitika Mathur. 2015. Accurate evaluation of segment-level machine translation metrics. In *HLT-NAACL*. pages 1183–1191.

Yvette Graham, Timothy Baldwin, Alistair Moffat, and Justin Zobel. 2013. Continuous measurement scales in human evaluation of machine translation. In *Proceedings of the 7th Linguistic Annotation Workshop & Interoperability with Discourse*. pages 33–41.

Francisco Guzmán, Shafiq R Joty, Lluís Màrquez, and Preslav Nakov. 2014. Using discourse structure improves machine translation evaluation. In *ACL (1)*. pages 687–698.

Chin-Yew Lin and Franz Josef Och. 2004. Automatic evaluation of machine translation quality using longest common subsequence and skip-bigram statistics. In *Proceedings of the 42nd Annual Meeting on Association for Computational Linguistics*. Association for Computational Linguistics, page 605.

Ding Liu and Daniel Gildea. 2005. Syntactic features for evaluation of machine translation. In *Proceedings of the ACL Workshop on Intrinsic and Extrinsic Evaluation Measures for Machine Translation and/or Summarization*. pages 25–32.

Chi-kiu Lo, Anand Karthik Tumuluru, and Dekai Wu. 2012. Fully automatic semantic mt evaluation. In *Proceedings of the Seventh Workshop on Statistical Machine Translation*. Association for Computational Linguistics, pages 243–252.

I Dan Melamed, Ryan Green, and Joseph P Turian. 2003. Precision and recall of machine translation. In *Proceedings of the 2003 Conference of the North American Chapter of the Association for Computational Linguistics on Human Language Technology: companion volume of the Proceedings of HLT-NAACL 2003–short papers-Volume 2*. Association for Computational Linguistics, pages 61–63.

Sonja Nießen, Franz Josef Och, Gregor Leusch, Hermann Ney, et al. 2000. An evaluation tool for machine translation: Fast evaluation for mt research. In *LREC*.

Karolina Owczarzak, Josef van Genabith, and Andy Way. 2007. Evaluating machine translation with lfg dependencies. *Machine Translation* 21(2):95–119.

Kishore Papineni, Salim Roukos, Todd Ward, and Wei-Jing Zhu. 2002. Bleu: a method for automatic evaluation of machine translation. In *Proceedings of the 40th annual meeting on association for computational linguistics*. Association for Computational Linguistics, pages 311–318.

Matthew Snover, Nitin Madnani, Bonnie Dorr, and Richard Schwartz. 2009. Fluency, adequacy, or HTER? Exploring different human judgments with a tunable MT metric. In *Proceedings of the Fourth Workshop on Statistical Machine Translation*. Association for Computational Linguistics, Athens, Greece, pages 259–268.

Miloš Stanojević, Amir Kamran, Philipp Koehn, and Ondřej Bojar. 2015. Results of the wmt15 metrics shared task. In *Proceedings of the Tenth Workshop on Statistical Machine Translation*. Association for Computational Linguistics, Lisbon, Portugal, pages 256–273. http://aclweb.org/anthology/W15-3031.

Miloš Stanojević and Khalil Sima'an. 2015. Beer 1.1: Illc uva submission to metrics and tuning task. In *Proceedings of the Tenth Workshop on Statistical Machine Translation*. Association for Computational Linguistics, Lisbon, Portugal, pages 396–401. http://aclweb.org/anthology/W15-3050.

Christoph Tillmann, Stephan Vogel, Hermann Ney, Arkaitz Zubiaga, and Hassan Sawaf. 1997. Accelerated dp based search for statistical translation. In *Eurospeech*.

Weiyue Wang, Jan-Thorsten Peter, Hendrik Rosendahl, and Hermann Ney. 2016. Character: Translation edit rate on character level. In *ACL 2016 First Conference on Machine Translation, Berlin, Germany*.

Hui Yu, Qingsong Ma, Xiaofeng Wu, and Qun Liu. 2015a. Casict-dcu participation in wmt2015 metrics task. In *Proceedings of the Tenth Workshop on Statistical Machine Translation*. Association for Computational Linguistics, pages 417–421.

Hui Yu, Xiaofeng Wu, Wenbin Jiang, Qun Liu, and Shouxun Lin. 2015b. An automatic machine translation evaluation metric based on dependency parsing model. *arXiv preprint arXiv:1508.01996* .

Hui Yu, Xiaofeng Wu, Wenbin Jiang, Qun Liu, and Shouxun Lin. 2015c. Improve the evaluation of translation fluency by using entropy of matched sub-segments. *arXiv preprint arXiv:1508.02225* .

Hui Yu, Xiaofeng Wu, Jun Xie, Wenbin Jiang, Qun Liu, and Shouxun Lin. 2014. Red: A reference dependency based mt evaluation metric. In *COLING*. volume 14, pages 2042–2051.

Junguo Zhu, Muyun Yang, Bo Wang, Sheng Li, and Tiejun Zhao. 2010. All in strings: a powerful string-based automatic mt evaluation metric with multiple granularities. In *Proceedings of the 23rd International Conference on Computational Linguistics: Posters*. Association for Computational Linguistics, pages 1533–1540.

CUNI Experiments for WMT17 Metrics Task

David Mareček   **Ondřej Bojar**
Ondřej Hübsch   **Rudolf Rosa**   **Dušan Variš**

Charles University, Faculty of Mathematics and Physics
Institute of Formal and Applied Linguistics
Malostranské náměstí 25, 118 00 Prague, Czech Republic
surname@ufal.mff.cuni.cz, except hubschondrej@gmail.com

Abstract

In this paper, we propose three different methods for automatic evaluation of the machine translation (MT) quality. Two of the metrics are trainable on direct-assessment scores and two of them use dependency structures. The trainable metric AutoDA, which uses deep-syntactic features, achieved better correlation with humans compared e.g. to the chrF3 metric.

1 Introduction

With the ongoing research of the machine translation (MT) systems in the past the need for accurate automatic evaluation of the translation quality became unquestionable. Even though the human judgment of the MT system outputs still holds as the most reliable form of evaluation, the high cost of human evaluation together with the amount of time required for such evaluation makes human judgment unsuitable for large scale experiments where we need to evaluate many different system configurations in a relatively short timespan. An additional important limitation of human evaluation is that it cannot be exactly repeated. This led to development of various methods for automatic MT evaluation in the past with the aim to eliminate the need for the expensive human assessment of the developed MT systems.

In this paper we suggest three novel methods for automatic MT evaluation together with their direct comparison:

1. AutoDA: A linear regression model using semantic features trained on WMT Direct Assessment scores (Bojar et al., 2016) or HUMEseg scores (Birch et al., 2016).

2. TreeAggreg: N-gram based metric computed over aligned syntactic structures instead of the linear representation of the translated sentences.

3. NMTScorer: A neural sequence classifier which assigns correct/incorrect flags to the evaluated sentence segments.

Table 1 shows the main properties of the proposed methods. Some of them were mainly developed for Czech as the target language and were later modified to be applied to other languages. The differences in the data preprocessing and their impact on the resulting evaluator are also described in this paper.

2 AutoDA: Automatic Direct Assessment

AutoDA is a sentence-level metric trainable on any direct assessment scores. The metric is based on a simple linear regression combining several features extracted from the automatically aligned translation-reference pair. There may be also other established metrics within the features.

The training data with golden direct-assessment scores available are shown in Table 2.

We describe two variants. The first one works only on Czech and uses many semantic features based of rich Czech tectogrammatical annotation (Böhmová et al., 2003). The second one uses much fewer features, however, it is language universal and needs only a dependency parsing model available.

2.1 AutoDA Using Czech Tectogrammatics

This metric automatically parses the Czech translation candidate and the reference translation and uses various semantic features to compute the final score.

2.1.1 Word Alignment

AutoDA relies on automatic alignment between the translation candidate and the reference trans-

Proceedings of the Conference on Machine Translation (WMT), Volume 2: Shared Task Papers, pages 604–611
Copenhagen, Denmark, September 7–11, 2017. ©2017 Association for Computational Linguistics

Method	Resource Type	Trainable	Metric Type
AutoDA	Monolingual/Bilingual*	Yes	Segment-level Linear Regression
TreeAggreg	Monolingual	No	Tree Segment-level ChrF**
NMTScorer	Bilingual	Yes	Segment-level Classification

Table 1: Overview of the examined methods. Currently, AutoDA uses only monolingual resources even though extracting additional features from the bilingual data (*) is possible. TreeAggreg can use any string-level metric for score computation instead of ChrF (**).

Dataset	Source	Target	# Sentences
WMT16 DAseg	TR/FI/CS/RO/RU/DE	EN	560
	EN	RU	
WMT15 DAseg	DE/RU/FI/CS	EN	500
	EN	RU	
WMT16 HUMEseg	EN	CS/DE/PL/RO	∼350

Table 2: Overview of the available data for training AutoDA.

lation. The easiest way of obtaining word alignments is to run GIZA++ (Och and Ney, 2000) on the set of sentence pairs. GIZA++ was designed to align documents in two languages and it can obviously also align documents in a single language, although it does not benefit in any way from the fact that many words are identical in the aligned sentences. GIZA++ works well if the input corpus is sufficiently large, to allow for extraction of reliable word co-occurrence statistics. While the test sets alone are too small, we have a corpus of paraphrases for Czech (Bojar et al., 2013). We thus run GIZA++ on all possible paraphrase combinations together with the reference-translation pairs we need to align and then extract alignments only for the sentences of interest.

2.1.2 Tectogrammatical Parsing

We use Treex[1] framework (Popel and Zabokrtský, 2010) to do the tagging, parsing and tectogrammatical annotation. Tectogrammatical annotation of sentence is a dependency tree, in which only content words are represented by nodes. The main label of the node is a tectogrammatical lemma — mostly the same as the morphological lemma, sometimes combined with a function word in case it changes its meaning. Other function words and grammatical features of the words are expressed by other attributes of the tectogrammatical node. An example of a pair of tectogrammatical trees is provided in Figure 1. The main attributes are:

- **tectogrammatical lemma (t-lemma)**: the lexical value of the node,

- **functor**: the semantic value of the syntactic dependency relation. Functors express the functions of individual modifications in the sentence, e.g. ACT (Actor), PAT (Patient), ADDR (Addressee), LOC (Location), MANN (Manner),

- **sempos**: semantic part of speech: n (noun), adj (adjective), v (verb), or adv (adverbial),

- **formeme**: morphosyntactic form of the node. The formeme includes for example prepositions and cases of the nouns, e.g. *n:jako+1* for nominative case with preposition *jako*.

- **grammatemes**: tectogrammatical counterparts of morphological categories, such as number, gender, person, negation, modality, aspect, etc.

2.1.3 Scores for Matching Attributes Ratios

Given the word- (or node-) alignment links between tectogrammatical annotations of the translation and reference sentences, we can count the percentage of links where individual attributes agree, e.g. the number of pairs of tectogrammatical nodes that have the same tectogrammatical lemma. These scores capture only a portion of what the tectogrammatical annotations offer, for instance, we they do not consider the structure of the trees at all. For the time being, we take these scores as individual features and use them in a combined model.

[1] http://ufal.mff.cuni.cz/treex

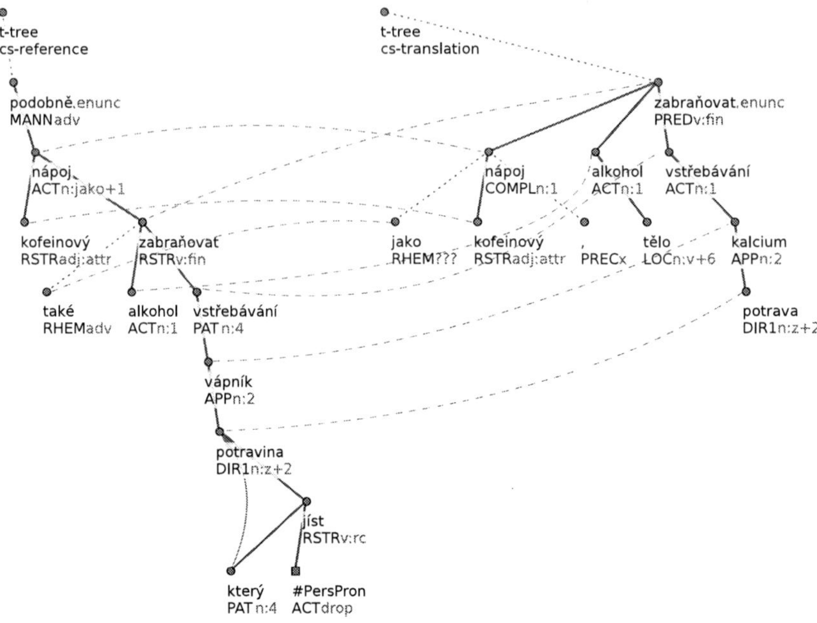

Figure 1: Example of aligned tectogrammatical trees of the reference *"Podobně jako kofeinový nápoj také alkohol zabraňuje vstřebávání vápníku z potravin, které jíme."* and the candidate translation *"Jako kofeinový nápoj, alkohol v těle zabraňuje vstřebávání kalcia z potravy."*

2.1.4 Linear Regression Training

We collect 83 various features based on matching tectogrammatical attributes computed on all nodes or a subsets defined by particular semantic part-of-speech tags. To this set of features, we add two BLEU scores (Papineni et al., 2002) computed on forms and on lemmas and two chrF3 scores (Popovic, 2015) computed on trigrams and sixgrams, so we have 87 features in total.

We train a linear regression model to obtain a weighted mix of features that fits best the WMT16 HUMEseg scores. Since the amount of annotated data available is low, we use the jackknife strategy:

- We split the annotated data into ten parts.

- For each tenth, we train the regression on all the rest data and apply it to this tenth.

By this procedure, we obtain automatically assigned scores for all sentences in the data. The correlation coefficients are shown in Table 3, along with the individual features.

In addition to the regression using all 87 features, we also did a feature selection, in which we manually chose only 23 features with a positive impact on the overall correlation score. For instance, we found that the BLEU scores can be

metric	en-cs
aligned-tnode-tlemma-exact-match	0.449
aligned-tnode-formeme-match	0.429
aligned-tnode-functor-match	0.391
aligned-tnode-sempos-match	0.416
lexrf-form-exact-match	0.372
lexrf-lemma-exact-match	0.436
BLEU on forms	0.361
BLEU on lemmas	0.395
chrF3	0.540
AutoDA (87 features)	0.625
AutoDA (selected 23 features)	**0.659**

Table 3: Selected Czech deep-syntactic features and their correlation against WMT16 HUMEseg dataset. Comparison with BLEU, chrF3, and our trainable AutoDA (using chrF3 as well).

easily omitted without worsening the correlation. Conversely, the chrF scores are very valuable and omiting them would lower the correlation significantly.

We see that chrF3 alone performs reasonably well (Pearson of 0.54), If we combine it with a selected subset our features, we are able to achieve the correlation of up to 0.659.

2.2 Language Universal AutoDA

We have seen that deep-syntactic features help to train an automatic metric with higher correlation for Czech. Even though we have no similar tools for other languages so far, we try to extract similar features for them as well. The source code is available online. [2]

2.2.1 Universal Parsing

We use Universal Dependencies (UD) by Nivre et al. (2016b), a collection of treebanks in a common annotation style, where all our testing languages are present – version 1.3 covers 40 languages (Nivre et al., 2016a). For syntactic analysis, we use UDPipe by Straka et al. (2016), a tokenizer, tagger, and parser in one tool, which is trained on UD. The UD tagset consists of 17 POS tags; the big advantage is that the tagset is the same for all the languages and therefore we can easily extract e.g. content words, prepositional phrases, etc.

2.2.2 Monolingual Alignment

Unlike from Czech, we did not known about the existing corpus of paraphrases available across other languages,[3] so we used a simple monolingual aligner based on word similarities and relative positions in the sentence. Our implementation is inspired by the heuristic Monolingual Greedy Aligner written by Martin Popel (Rosa et al., 2012), which is available in the Treex framework.[4]

First, we compute scores for all possible alignment connections between tokens of the reference and translated sentence:

$$score(i, j) = w_1 \mathrm{JaroWinkler}(W_i^t, W_j^r)$$
$$+ w_2 I(T_i^t = T_j^r)$$
$$+ w_3(1 - |(i/len(t) - j/len(r)|), \tag{1}$$

where $\mathrm{JaroWinkler}(W_i^t, W_j^r)$ defines similarity between the given words (Winkler, 1990), $I(T_i^t = T_j^r)$ is a binary indicator testing the identity of POS tags, and $(1 - |(i/len(t) - j/len(r)|)$ tells us how close are the two words according to their relative positions in the sentences. The weights were set manually to $w_1 = 8$, $w_2 = 3$, and $w_3 = 3$; they were not tuned for this specific task. When we have the scores, we can simply produce unidirectional alignments (i.e. find the best token in the translation for each token in the reference and vice versa) and then symmetrize them to create intersection (one-to-one) or union (many-to-many) alignments. We finally use union symmetrization, since it achieved slightly better correlation with humans.

2.2.3 Extracting Features

We distinguish content words from function ones by the POS tag. The tags for nouns (NOUN, PROPN), verbs (VERB), adjectives (ADJ), and adverbs (ADV) correspond more or less to content words. Then there are pronouns (PRON), symbols (SYM), and other (X), which may be sometimes content words as well, but we do not count them. The rest of POS tags represent function words.

Now, using the alignment links and the content words, we can compute numbers of matching content word forms and matching content word lemmas. The universal annotations contains also morphological features of words: case, number, tense, etc. Therefore, we also create equivalents of tectogrammatical formemes or grammatemes. Our features can thus check for instance the percentage of aligned words with matching morphological number or tense.

2.2.4 Regression and Results

We compute all the scores proposed in the previous section on the four languages and test the correlation on WMT16 HUMEseg dataset (Birch et al., 2016). German UD annotation does not contain lemmas and morphological features, so some scores for German could not be computed.

Similarly as in Section 2.1.4, we trained a linear regression on all the features together with *chrF3* score. The results computed by 10-fold cross-validation on WMT16 HUMEseg dataset and comparison with chrF and NIST[5] scores is shown in Table 4.

3 Tree Aggregated Evaluation

TreeAggreg is a simple sentence-level metric, remotely inspired by HUME. Rather than being a full standalone metric, it can be regarded as

---

[2] https://github.com/ufal/auto-hume

[3] Multilingual corpus of paraphrases has been released by Chris Callison-Burch's group and is available here: http://paraphrase.org/#/download

[4] https://github.com/ufal/treex/

[5] Unlike in previous experiment, we compare the results using NIST rather than BLEU since it is better suited for segment-level evaluation.

metric	en-cs	en-de	en-pl	en-ro
NIST	0.436	0.481	0.418	0.611
NIST cased	0.421	0.481	0.410	0.611
chrF1	0.505	0.497	0.428	0.608
chrF3	0.540	0.511	0.419	0.638
NIST on content lemmas	0.416	–	0.361	0.542
matching lemmas	0.431	–	0.393	0.565
matching forms	0.372	0.478	0.405	0.576
matching content lemmas	0.359	–	0.408	0.536
matching content forms	0.321	0.470	0.427	0.552
matching formemes	0.347	0.170	0.357	0.420
matching tense	-0.094	–	-0.118	0.079
matching number	0.286	–	0.205	0.404
AutoDA (linear regression)	**0.604**	**0.525**	**0.453**	**0.656**

Table 4: Pearson correlations of different sentence-level metrics on WMT16 HUMEseg dataset. Standard NIST and chrF metrics are compared with our individual features matching. AutoDA combines all the features together with the chrF3 score and the NIST score computed on content lemmas only. Other NIST scores are not included in AutoDA, since they do not bring any improvement.

a *metric template*, for in principle, any string-based MT metric can be plugged into it; we used chrF3 (Popovic, 2015) in our work.

In TreeAggreg, we are trying to improve an existing string-based metric by applying it in a syntax-tree-based context. This is motivated by our belief that dependency trees are a good means of capturing sentence structure, which may be relevant for MT evaluation metrics, as the MT output should presumably transfer the information present in the source sentence into a similar syntactic structure as the reference translation uses. However, in string-based MT metrics, the syntactic structure of a sentence is typically ignored.

In our rather light-weight attempt to employ syntactic analysis in MT evaluation, we segment the sentences into phrases based on their dependency parse trees, and evaluate these phrases independently with the string-based MT metric. The resulting scores are then aggregated into a final sentence-level score using a simple weighted average.

Our source codes are available online.[6]

3.1 Method

To be able to apply TreeAggreg to measuring the correspondence of a translation t to the reference r, we first need to apply a set of NLP tools in a pre-processing pipeline:

1. align reference and translation

2. parse reference

3. parse translation

We use the monolingual aligner presented in Section 2.2.2, using the unidirectional alignment from reference to translation; i.e. for each reference word we get exactly one translation word aligned to it (not necessarily unique). We use the UDPipe tool to provide the dependency parse trees (see Section 2.2.1).

Next, both the reference and the translation are split into the following types of segments:

1. the whole sentence (s_r, s_t)

2. the sentence root (r_r, r_t)

3. for each immediate dependent (d_r^i, d_t^i) of the root, the continuous span defined by its subtree (p_r^i, p_t^i)

Whole sentence This is simply the base string-based MT metric applied in the standard way.

Sentence root The sentence root is selected according to the parse trees; usually this is the main verb in the sentence.

Subtree spans As we expect the dependency analysis of the reference to be much more accurate than that of the translation, we only use the reference parse tree to identify the root dependents'

[6] https://github.com/ufal/auto-hume/tree/rudolf

spans, and the word alignment to identify the corresponding spans in the translation:

- p_r^i contains all words from s_r that are transitively dependent on d_r^i, the ith dependent of r_r; p_r^i includes d_r^i but excludes r_r

- p_t^i contains the first and last word from s_t which are aligned to any of the words in p_r^i, and all of the words between them

The string-level metric $m(r, t)$ is then computed on each corresponding pair of the reference and translation segments. A weighted average of the segment-level scores is computed, where longer segments are given higher weight: the weight is the sum of the numbers of words in the reference segment and in the translation segment. Additionally, for the (s_r, s_t) segment pair, which is still the most important component of the metric, we use a double weight. Thus, the final score m is computed as follows:

$$m_s = m(s_r, s_t) \cdot (|s_r| + |s_t|) \cdot 2$$
$$m_r = m(r_r, r_t) \cdot 2$$
$$m_p^i = m(p_r^i, p_t^i) \cdot (|p_r^i| + |p_t^i|)$$
$$m = \frac{m_s + m_r + \sum_{i \in Dep(r_r)} m_p^i}{2|s_r| + 2|s_t| + 2 + \sum_{i \in Dep(r_r)} |p_r^i| + |p_t^i|}$$

$Dep(r_r)$ are all immediate dependents of r_r.

3.2 Development

When developing the TreeAggreg metric, we tried multiple configurations, evaluating each of them on the WMT16 HUMEseg dataset for correlation with human judgments, and then selected the one that performed best, which we have just described.

For example, we also experimented with more fine-grained segmentations, such as taking each node together only with its immediate dependents as a span. However, such setups performed poorer, probably because they depend more heavily on the high structural similarity of the translation to the reference. Still, it seems reasonable to assume that at least the arguments of the root node should usually correspond well between the reference and the candidate translation.

We also tried to put more weight to certain words that we expected to be more important, such as d_r^i (immediate dependents of the root r_r) However, this always led to a deterioration in the correlation of the metric to human judgments. Thus, an

Lang.	chrF3	TreeAggreg	Difference
en-cs	0.5403	**0.5473**	+0.0070
en-de	**0.5111**	0.5078	−0.0033
en-pl	0.4186	**0.4266**	+0.0080
en-ro	**0.6314**	0.6226	−0.0088
Average	0.5254	**0.5261**	+0.0007

Table 5: Evaluation of TreeAggreg (our metric) and chrF3 (baseline) with Pearson's correlation to human judgments.

important property of our metric seems to be that each reference word is taken into account exactly twice.[7]

3.3 Evaluation

To evaluate our metric, we measured Pearson's correlation of chrF3-based TreeAggreg scores with sentence-level human judgments on the WMT16 HUMEseg dataset. For comparison, we also measure the correlation of a baseline metric, which is the vanilla sentence-level chrF3.

As shown in Table 5, our metric performs comparably to the chrF3 baseline, leading to a slight improvement for two language pairs, and a slight deterioration for the other two.

Thus, our approach of employing sentence syntactic structure into a string-based MT metric seems to affect the metric only minimally. Moreover, the TreeAggreg metric was developed and evaluated on the same data and therefore the comparison in Table 5 is not quite fair, however, the number of configurations tested was very little.

4 Neural MT Scorer

Neural MT Scorer is a model that predicts a probability for a given source/target translation pair using a simplified architecture that is based on existing NMT models with attention. The predicted number should reflect how much the meaning of source and target matches. We used that model for a different task (scoring phrase table entries in PBMT) where it performed well. Note that as of now, Neural MT Scorer indeed does not make any use of the reference translation, so it is effectively a quality estimation method.

The training data for the model are bilingual corpus (set of sentences that should be classified

---

[7]The same holds for words in the translation only if the p_t^i spans do not overlap, are contiguous, include both the first and the last word in the sentence, and do not include r_r.

as entirely correct) as well as a set of sentences that should be classified as incorrect (we obtain these by performing some random operations on the bilingual corpus). We do not train it on data specific for the metrics task (i.e. the model is only trained to recognize correct and incorrect translations, but small differences among different translations of the same sentence might not be recognized), therefore there is a room for potential improvement.

We do not use any smoother labeling than 0/1 (correct/incorrect), since even a single word omission may cause completely different meaning of the sentence. At inference time, the output is a float number between 0 and 1.

4.1 Architecture

We use two LSTM encoders, one for source and one for target side. The vector representations of the source words are fed into the source LSTM encoder to obtain one representation p_s of the entire sentence. Also, the intermediate outputs of the source LSTM encoder are used in an attentional layer when processing the target sentence in the target LSTM encoder. The final cell states p_s and p_t are used to measure the bilingual similarity by $\sigma(p_s^T p_t)$. The entire architecture is very similar to (Bahdanau et al., 2014), except that we use the attention mechanism while encoding the target side. Note that there is also no softmax layer over the word dictionary – we know the entire source and target sentences and so we do not need to predict the next word; we just need one score between 0 and 1. This should allow for faster training of the model; however, we need to provide labeled training data. We currently generate wrong sentences using these basic operations:

- change a few words to completely random ones from the source/target dictionary

- take a translation of a completely different sentence

- utilize WordNet to change the polarity of a sentence

- remove/add some random words at a random place

4.2 Evaluation

We evaluated the model on the WMT16 HUMEseg dataset, but currently it performs poorly. It

Languages	NMT Scorer
en-cs	0.4099
en-de	0.3462
en-pl	0.3261
en-ro	0.4792
Average	0.3903

Table 6: Evaluation of NMT Scorer with Pearson correlation to human judgments.

should be possible to improve it significantly by optimizing the training process for the metrics task (for example by adding another layer that uses the final representations p_s and p_t to predict human scores and finetune the entire model on some manually evaluated datasets). The Pearson correlation coefficients to human judgements are shown in Table 6.

5 Conclusion

We presented three metrics. AutoDA is a trainable metric combining syntactic features matching and chrF and naturally significantly outperforms chrF on all four tested languages.

In TreeAggreg, we tried to enrich a string-based MT metric with light-weight information about the syntactic structure of the sentences, but the results seem rather disappointing.

NMTScorer in which we used two LSTM encoders for source sentence and candidate translation and predicted sentence similarity also did not prove to work well.

Acknowledgments

This work has been in part supported by the European Union's Horizon 2020 research and innovation programme under grant agreements No 644402 (HimL) and 645452 (QT21), by the LINDAT/CLARIN project of the Ministry of Education, Youth and Sports of the Czech Republic (projects LM2015071 and OP VVV VI CZ.02.1.01/0.0/0.0/16_013/0001781), by the grant No. DG16P02B048 of the Ministry of Culture of the Czech Republic and by the SVV 260 453 grant.

References

Dzmitry Bahdanau, Kyunghyun Cho, and Yoshua Bengio. 2014. Neural machine translation by jointly learning to align and translate. *CoRR* abs/1409.0473. http://arxiv.org/abs/1409.0473.

Alexandra Birch, Omri Abend, Ondrej Bojar, and Barry Haddow. 2016. HUME: Human UCCA-based evaluation of machine translation. *arXiv preprint arXiv:1607.00030* .

Alena Böhmová, Jan Hajič, Eva Hajičová, and Barbora Hladká. 2003. The Prague dependency treebank. In *Treebanks*, Springer, pages 103–127.

Ondřej Bojar, Matouš Macháček, Aleš Tamchyna, and Daniel Zeman. 2013. Scratching the Surface of Possible Translations. In *Proc. of TSD 2013*. Západočeská univerzita v Plzni, Springer Verlag, Berlin / Heidelberg, Lecture Notes in Artificial Intelligence.

Ondřej Bojar, Rajen Chatterjee, Christian Federmann, Yvette Graham, Barry Haddow, Matthias Huck, Antonio Jimeno Yepes, Philipp Koehn, Varvara Logacheva, Christof Monz, Matteo Negri, Aurelie Neveol, Mariana Neves, Martin Popel, Matt Post, Raphael Rubino, Carolina Scarton, Lucia Specia, Marco Turchi, Karin Verspoor, and Marcos Zampieri. 2016. Findings of the 2016 conference on machine translation. In *Proceedings of the First Conference on Machine Translation*. Association for Computational Linguistics, Berlin, Germany, pages 131–198. http://www.aclweb.org/anthology/W/W16/W16-2301.

Joakim Nivre, Ž. Agić, L. Ahrenberg, M. J. Aranzabe, M. Asahara, A. Atutxa, M. Ballesteros, J. Bauer, K. Bengoetxea, Y. Berzak, R. A. Bhat, C. Bosco, G. Bouma, S. Bowman, G. Cebirolu Eryiit, Giuseppe G. A. Celano, Ç. Çöltekin, M. Connor, Marie-Catherine de Marneffe, A. Diaz de Ilarraza, K. Dobrovoljc, T. Dozat, K. Droganova, T. Erjavec, R. Farkas, J. Foster, D. Galbraith, S. Garza, F.and Goenaga I. Ginter, K. Gojenola, M. Gokirmak, Y. Goldberg, X. Gómez Guinovart, B. Gonzáles Saavedra, N. Grūzītis, B. Guillaume, J. Hajič, D. Haug, B. Hladká, R. Ion, E. Irimia, A. Johannsen, H. Kaşkara, H. Kanayama, J. Kanerva, B. Katz, J. Kenney, S. Krek, V. Laippala, L. Lam, A. Lenci, N. Ljubešić, O. Lyashevskaya, T. Lynn, A. Makazhanov, C. Manning, C. Mărănduc, D. Mareček, H. Martínez Alonso, J. Mašek, Y. Matsumoto, R. McDonald, A. Missilä, V. Mititelu, Y. Miyao, S. Montemagni, K. S. Mori, S. Mori, K. Muischnek, N. Mustafina, K. Müürisep, V. Nikolaev, H. Nurmi, P. Osenova, L. Øvrelid, E. Pascual, M. Passarotti, C. Perez, S. Petrov, J. Piitulainen, B. Plank, M. Popel, L. Pretkalnia, P. Prokopidis, T. Puolakainen, S. Pyysalo, L. Ramasamy, L. Rituma, R. Rosa, S. Saleh, B. Saulīte, S. Schuster, W. Seeker, M. Seraji, L. Shakurova, M. Shen, N. Silveira, M. Simi, R. Simionescu, K. Simkó, K. Simov, A. Smith, C. Spadine, A. Suhr, U. Sulubacak, Z. Szántó, T. Tanaka, R. Tsarfaty, F. Tyers, S. Uematsu, L. Uria, G. van Noord, V. Varga, V. Vincze, Jing Xian Wang, J. N. Washington, Z. Žabokrtský, Daniel Zeman, and Hanzhi Zhu. 2016a. Universal dependencies 1.3. LINDAT/CLARIN digital library at the Institute of Formal and Applied Linguistics, Charles University. http://hdl.handle.net/11234/1-1699.

Joakim Nivre, Marie-Catherine de Marneffe, Filip Ginter, Yoav Goldberg, Jan Hajič, Christopher Manning, Ryan McDonald, Slav Petrov, Sampo Pyysalo, Natalia Silveira, Reut Tsarfaty, and Daniel Zeman. 2016b. Universal Dependencies v1: A Multilingual Treebank Collection. In *Proceedings of the 10th International Conference on Language Resources and Evaluation (LREC 2016)*. European Language Resources Association, Portorož, Slovenia.

Franz Josef Och and Hermann Ney. 2000. A Comparison of Alignment Models for Statistical Machine Translation. In *Proceedings of the 17th conference on Computational linguistics*. Association for Computational Linguistics, pages 1086–1090.

Kishore Papineni, Salim Roukos, Todd Ward, and Wei-Jing Zhu. 2002. Bleu: A method for automatic evaluation of machine translation. In *Proceedings of the 40th Annual Meeting on Association for Computational Linguistics*. Association for Computational Linguistics, Stroudsburg, PA, USA, ACL '02, pages 311–318. https://doi.org/10.3115/1073083.1073135.

Martin Popel and Zdeněk Žabokrtský. 2010. TectoMT: Modular NLP framework. In Hrafn Loftsson, Eirikur Rögnvaldsson, and Sigrun Helgadottir, editors, *Lecture Notes in Artificial Intelligence, Proceedings of the 7th International Conference on Advances in Natural Language Processing (IceTAL 2010)*. Iceland Centre for Language Technology (ICLT), Springer, Berlin / Heidelberg, volume 6233 of *Lecture Notes in Computer Science*, pages 293–304.

Maja Popovic. 2015. chrF: character n-gram F-score for automatic MT evaluation. In *Proceedings of the 10th Workshop on Statistical Machine Translation (WMT-15)*. pages 392–395.

Rudolf Rosa, Ondřej Dušek, David Mareček, and Martin Popel. 2012. Using parallel features in parsing of machine-translated sentences for correction of grammatical errors. In *Proceedings of Sixth Workshop on Syntax, Semantics and Structure in Statistical Translation (SSST-6), ACL*. ACL, Jeju, Korea, pages 39–48.

Milan Straka, Jan Hajič, and Straková. 2016. UDPipe: trainable pipeline for processing CoNLL-U files performing tokenization, morphological analysis, pos tagging and parsing. In *Proceedings of the Tenth International Conference on Language Resources and Evaluation (LREC'16)*. European Language Resources Association (ELRA), Paris, France.

William E. Winkler. 1990. String comparator metrics and enhanced decision rules in the fellegi-sunter model of record linkage. In *Proceedings of the Section on Survey Research Methods (American Statistical Association)*. pages 354–359.

CHRF^{++}: words helping character n-grams

Maja Popović
Humboldt University of Berlin, Germany
`maja.popovic@hu-berlin.de`

Abstract

Character n-gram F-score (CHRF) is shown to correlate very well with human relative rankings of different machine translation outputs, especially for morphologically rich target languages. However, its relation with direct human assessments is not yet clear. In this work, Pearson's correlation coefficients for direct assessments are investigated for two currently available target languages, English and Russian. First, different β parameters (in range from 1 to 3) are re-investigated with direct assessment, and it is confirmed that $\beta = 2$ is the optimal option. Then separate character and word n-grams are investigated, and the main finding is that, apart from character n-grams, word 1-grams and 2-grams also correlate rather well with direct assessments. Further experiments show that adding word unigrams and bigrams to the standard CHRF score improves the correlations with direct assessments, though it is still not clear which option is better, unigrams only (CHRF+) or unigrams and bigrams (CHRF++). This should be investigated in future work on more target languages.

1 Introduction

Recent investigations (Popović, 2015; Stanojević et al., 2015; Popović, 2016; Bojar et al., 2016) have shown that the character n-gram F-score (CHRF) represents a very promising evaluation metric for machine translation, especially for morphologically rich target languages – it is fast, it does not require any additional tools or information, it is language independent and tokenisation independent, and it correlates very well with hu-

man relative rankings (RR) (Callison-Burch et al., 2008). In order to produce these rankings, human annotators have to decide which sentence translation is better/worse than another without giving any note about the absolute quality of any of the evaluated translations. This type of human judgment has been the offical evaluation metric and gold standard for all automatic metrics at WMT shared tasks from 2008 until 2016.

Another type of human judgment, direct human assessment (DA) (Bojar et al., 2016), has become additional official evaluation metric for WMT-16, and the only one for WMT-17. These assessments consist of absolute quality scores for each translated sentence. Contrary to RR, the relation between CHRF and DA has still not been investigated systematically. Preliminary experiments in previous work (Popović, 2016) shown that, concerning DA, the main advantage of character-based F-score CHRF in comparison to word-based F-score WORDF is better correlation for good translations for which WORDF often assigns too low scores.

In this work, we systematically investigate relations between DA and both character and word n-grams, as well as their combinations. The scores are calculated for all available translation outputs from the WMT-15 and WMT-16 shared tasks (Bojar et al., 2016) which contain two target languages, English (translated from Czech, German, Finnish, Romanian, Russian and Turkish) and Russian (translated from English), and then compared with DAs on segment level using Pearsons's correlation coefficient.

2 n-gram based F-scores

The general formula for an n-gram based F-score is:

$$ngrF\beta = (1 + \beta^2)\frac{ngrP \cdot ngrR}{\beta^2 \cdot ngrP + ngrR} \quad (1)$$

Proceedings of the Conference on Machine Translation (WMT), Volume 2: Shared Task Papers, pages 612–618
Copenhagen, Denmark, September 7–11, 2017. ©2017 Association for Computational Linguistics

where $ngrP$ and $ngrR$ stand for n-gram precision and recall arithmetically averaged over all n-grams from $n = 1$ to N:

- $ngrP$
  n-gram precision: percentage of n-grams in the hypothesis which have a counterpart in the reference;

- $ngrR$
  n-gram recall: percentage of n-grams in the reference which are also present in the hypothesis.

and β is a parameter which assigns β times more weight to recall than to precision.

WORDF is then calculated on word n-grams and CHRF is calculated on character n-grams. As for maximum n-gram length N, previous work reported that there is no need to go beyond N=4 for WORDF (Popović, 2011) and N=6 for CHRF (Popović, 2015).

CHRF++ score is obtained when the word n-grams are added to the character n-grams and averaged together. The best maximum n-gram lengths for such combinations are again N=6 for character n-grams and N=2 or N=1 for word n-grams, which will be discussed in Section 4.3.

3 Motivation for adding word n-grams to CHRF

A preliminary experiment on a small set of texts reported in previous work (Popović, 2016) with different target languages and different types of DA[1] shown that for poorly rated sentences, the standard deviations of CHRF and WORDF scores are similar – both metrics assign relatively similar (low) scores. On the other hand, for the sentences with higher human rates, the deviations for CHRF are (much) lower. In addition, the higher the human rating is, the greater is the difference between the WORDF and CHRF deviations. These results indicate that CHRF is better than WORDF mainly for segments/systems of higher translation quality – the CHRF scores for good translations are more concentrated in the higher range, whereas the WORDF scores are often too low.

In order to further investigate these premises, scatter plots in Figure 1 are produced for CHRF and WORDF with DA for the Russian→English and English→Russian WMT-16 data.

---

[1]none of them equal to the variant used in WMT

Figure 1 confirms the findings from previous work, since a number of WORDF values is indeed pessimistic – high DA but low WORDF, whereas CHRF values are more concentrated, i.e. correlate better with DA values. However, these plots raised another question – are CHRF scores maybe too optimistic (i.e. segments with high CHRF score and low DA score)? Certainly not to such extent as WORDF scores are pessimistic, but still, could some combination of character and word n-grams improve the correlations of CHRF?

4 Pearson correlations with direct assessments

In order to explore combining CHRF with word n-grams, the following experiments are carried out in terms of calculating Pearson's correlation coefficient between DA and different n-gram F-scores:

1. As a first step, β parameter is re-investigated for DA, both for CHRF and WORDF in order to check if $\beta = 2$ is a good option for DA, too;

2. Individual character and word n-grams are investigated in order to see if some are better than others and to which extent;

3. Finally, various combinations of character and word n-grams were explored and the results are reported for the most promising ones.

4.1 β parameter revisited

Previous work (Popović, 2016) reported that the best β parameter both for CHRF and for WORDF is 2 in terms of Kendall's τ segment level correlation with human relative rankings (RR). However, this parameter has not been tested for direct human assessments (DA) – therefore we tested several β in terms of Pearson correlations with DA. It is confirmed that putting more weight on precision is not good, and the results for $\beta = 1,2,3$ are reported in Table 1. Both for CHRF and WORDF, the correlations for $\beta = 2,3$ are comparable, and better than for $\beta = 1$. Since there is almost no difference between 2 and 3, and putting too much weight to recall could jeopardise some other applications such as system tuning or system combination (for example, (Sánchez-Cartagena and Toral, 2016) decided to use CHRF1 because CHRF3 lead to generation of too long sentences), we decided to choose $\beta = 2$ which will be used for all further experiments.

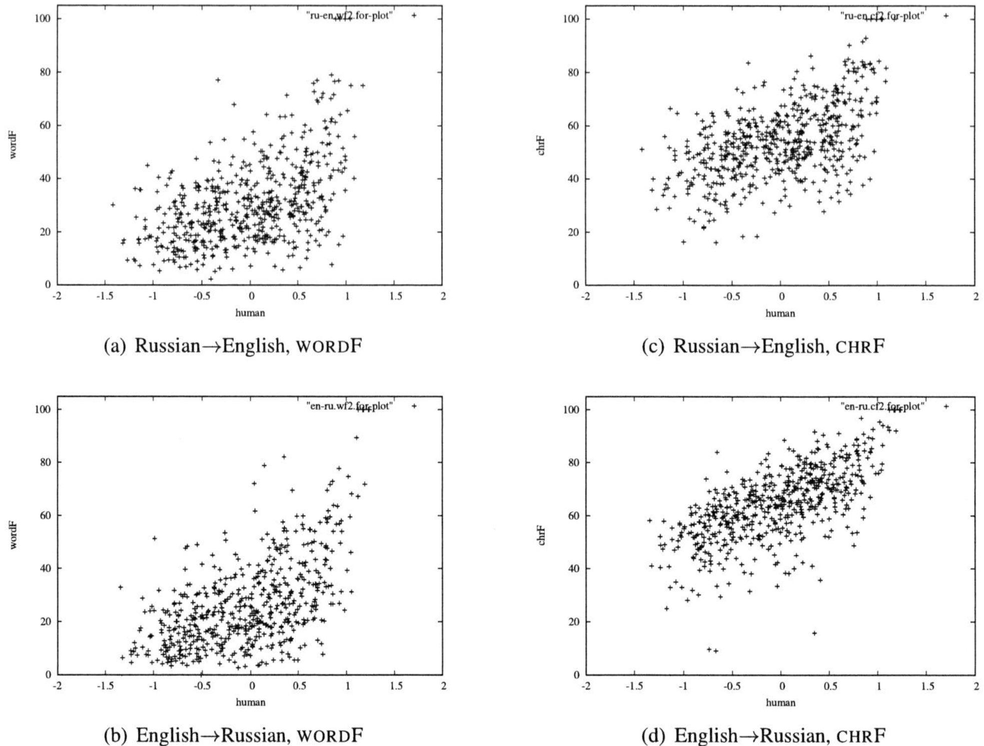

(a) Russian→English, WORDF

(c) Russian→English, CHRF

(b) English→Russian, WORDF

(d) English→Russian, CHRF

Figure 1: Scatter plots for (a)(b) WORDF and (c)(d) CHRF with DA for (a)(c) Russian→English and (b)(d) English→Russian WMT-16 texts confirm that WORDF values are overly pessimistic – a number of WORDF points lies in the lower right quadrant, i.e. a number of segments with high DA values has a low WORDF value. On the other hand, CHRF points are more concentrated, especially for morphologically rich Russian. However, are some of them too optimistic? (i.e. segments with high CHRF scores and low DA scores)

4.2 Individual character and word n-grams

Individual n-grams were also investigated in previous work, however (i) only character n-grams and (ii) only compared with RR, not with DA. In this work, we carried out systematic investigation on both character and word n-grams' correlations with DA, and the results are reported in Table 2. It should be noted that, to the best of our knowledge, word n-grams with order less than 4 have not been investigated yet in the given context of correlations with RR or DA. Implicitly, the ME-TEOR metric (Banerjee and Lavie, 2005) is based on word unigrams with additional information and generally correlates better with human rankings than the BLEU metric (Papineni et al., 2002) based on uni-, bi-, 3- and 4-gram precision.

The results show that, similarly to the correlations with RR, the best character n-grams are of the middle lengths i.e. 3 and 4. The main finding is, though, that the best word n-grams are the short ones, namely unigrams and bigrams.

Following these results for individual n-grams, several different experiments have been carried out, involving different character n-gram weights, combining character and word n-grams with different weights, etc., however no consistent improvements have been noticed in comparison to the standard uniform n-gram weights, not even by removing or setting low weight for character unigrams. The only noticeable improvement was observed when word 4-grams and 3-grams were removed.

4.3 The emergence of CHRF++

Findings reported in the previous section raised the following questions: (i) are word 3-grams and 4-grams the "culprits" for overly pessimistic behaviour of WORDF described in Section 3? (ii) Could the "good guys", i.e. word unigrams and

2016/2015	cs-en	de-en	fi-en	ro-en	ru-en	tr-en	en-ru	*mean*
CHRF1	.644/.542	.452/.600	.454/.565	.570	.522/.601	.551	.642/.606	.562
CHRF2	.658/**.552**	.469/**.605**	**.457/.573**	.581	.534/.613	**.556**	**.661/.624**	**.574**
CHRF3	**.660/.552**	**.472**/.604	.455/.572	**.582**	**.535/.614**	.555	**.661**/.622	**.574**
WORDF1	.587/.503	.453/.540	.428/.525	.504	.498/.549	.531	.572/.527	.519
WORDF2	.598/.512	.462/.543	.437/.535	.518	.504/.559	.536	.580/.533	.526
WORDF3	.600/.514	.464/.543	.439/.537	.522	.504/.561	.536	.582/.534	.528

Table 1: Pearson's correlation coefficients of CHRF and WORDF with direct human assessments (DA) for different β parameters. Bold represents the best character level value and underline represents the best word level value. The best β values are 2 and 3.

2016/2015	cs-en	de-en	fi-en	ro-en	ru-en	tr-en	en-ru	*mean*
chr1-gram	.544/.448	.355/.407	.313/.417	.443	.358/.527	.337	.531/.489	.431
chr2-gram	.644/.537	.441/.556	.420/.547	.554	.504/.599	.513	.652/.631	.550
chr3-gram	**.662**/.539	**.472**/.604	.459/**.582**	.579	.533/**.613**	.559	**.683/.661**	**.579**
chr4-gram	.657/**.542**	**.472/.614**	**.460**/.581	**.582**	**.538**/.602	**.562**	.682/.655	**.579**
chr5-gram	.644/.540	.467/.611	.456/.559	.576	.532/.588	.559	.676/.640	.571
chr6-gram	.627/.539	.463/.599	.447/.539	.568	.521/.578	.553	.662/.623	.560
word1-gram	.631/.509	.481/.529	.434/.566	.504	.505/.606	.510	.601/.564	.537
word2-gram	.611/.528	.473/.546	.441/.513	.529	.513/.551	.539	.575/.549	.531
word3-gram	.546/.461	.426/.513	.387/.470	.498	.469/.519	.475	.536/.472	.481
word4-gram	.479/.382	.385/.458	.337/.369	.427	.404/.468	.380	.478/.397	.414

Table 2: Pearson's correlation coefficients of CHRF and WORDF with direct human assessments (DA) for individual character and word n-grams. Bold represents the best character level value and underline represents the best word level value.

bigrams diminish potentially too optimistical behaviour of CHRF?

In order to get the answers, the Pearson correlations are calculated for CHRF combined with four WORDFs with different maximum n-gram lengths, i.e. N=1,2,3,4 and the results are presented in Table 3. In addition, correlations are presented also for CHRF and two variants of WORDF (usual N=4 and the best N=2).

First, it can be seen that removing word 3-grams and 4-grams improves the correlation for WORDF which becomes closer to CHRF (and even better for one of the two German→English texts). Furthermore, it can be seen that adding word unigrams and bigrams to CHRF improves the correlations of CHRF in the best way. Therefore this is the variant which is chosen to be the CHRF++. Next best option (CHRF+) is to add only word unigrams i.e. words, and this one is the best one for translation into Russian. Possible reasons are morphological richness of Russian as well as rather free word order, however the test set in this experiment is too small to draw any conclusions. Both CHRF++ and CHRF+ should be further tested on more texts and on more morphologically rich languages.

Scatter plots presented in Figure 2 visualise the improvement of correlations by CHRF++: WORDF with N=4 (a) is, as already shown, too pessimistic. Lowering the maximum n-gram length to 2 (b) moves a number of pessimistic points upwards, thus improving the correlation. When added to slightly overly optimistic CHRF (c), the points for both metrics are moved more towards the middle (d).

5 Conclusions

The results presented in this work show that adding short word n-grams, i.e. unigrams and bigrams to the character n-gram F-score CHRF improves the correlation with direct human assessments (DA). Since the amount of available texts with DA is still small, it is still not possible to conclude which variant is better: adding only unigrams (CHRF+) or unigrams and bigrams (CHRF++). This is especially hard to conclude for translation into morphologically rich languages, since only Russian was available until now. In order to explore both CHRF+ and CHRF++ more systematically, both are submitted to the WMT-17 metrics task for translations from English. For

translation into English, only CHRF++ is submitted since it outperformed the other variant for English. For Chinese, only the raw CHRF has been submitted since the concept "Chinese words" is generally not clear. Further work should include more data and more distinct target languages.

The tool for calculating CHRF++ (as well as CHRF+ and CHRF since it is possible to change maximum n-gram lengths) is publicly available at `https://github.com/m-popovic/chrF`. It is a Python script which requires (multiple) reference translation(s) and a translation hypothesis (output) in the raw text format. It is language independent and does need tokenisation or any similar preprocessing of the text. The default β is set to 2, but it is possible to change. It provides both segment level scores as well as document level scores in two variants: micro- and macro-averaged.

Acknowledgments

This work has been supported by the TraMOOC project funded from the European Unions Horizon 2020 research and innovation programme under grant agreement No 644333.

References

Satanjeev Banerjee and Alon Lavie. 2005. METEOR: An Automatic Metric for MT Evaluation with Improved Correlation with Human Judgements. In *Proceedings of the ACL-05 Workshop on Intrinsic and Extrinsic Evaluation Measures for MT and/or Summarization*. Ann Arbor, MI, pages 65–72.

Ondřej Bojar, Yvette Graham, Amir Kamran, and Miloš Stanojević. 2016. Results of the WMT16 Metrics Shared Task. In *Proceedings of the First Conference on Machine Translation (WMT-16)*. Berlin, Germany, pages 199–231.

Chris Callison-Burch, Cameron Fordyce, Philipp Koehn, Christof Monz, and Josh Schroeder. 2008. Further Meta-Evaluation of Machine Translation. In *Proceedings of the 3rd ACL 08 Workshop on Statistical Machine Translation (WMT-08)*. Columbus, Ohio, pages 70–106.

Kishore Papineni, Salim Roukos, Todd Ward, and Wie-Jing Zhu. 2002. BLEU: a method for automatic evaluation of machine translation. In *Proceedings of the 40th Annual Meeting of the Association for Computational Linguistics (ACL-02)*. Philadelphia, PA, pages 311–318.

Maja Popović. 2011. Morphemes and POS tags for n-gram based evaluation metrics. In *Proceedings of*

2016/2015	cs-en	de-en	fi-en	ro-en	ru-en	tr-en	en-ru	*mean*
WORDF (4-gram)	.598/.512	.462/.543	.437/.535	.518	.504/.559	.536	.580/.533	.526
WORD2-F	.642/.537	.490/.557	.455/.563	.535	.526/.592	.553	.603/.575	.552
CHRF (6-gram)	.658/.552	.469/.605	.457/.573	**.581**	.534/613	.556	.661/.624	.574
c6w4F	.656/.555	.483/.598	.470/.580	.572	.538/.608	.573	.665/.630	.577
c6w3F	.663/.559	.486/.603	**.471**/.584	.578	.542/.615	**.574**	.672/.641	.582
c6w2F (CHRF++)	**.668/.561**	**.487/.606**	.470/**.585**	.580	**.544**/.619	.570	.679/.650	**.585**
c6w1F (CHRF+)	.665/.558	.480/**.606**	.464/**.585**	.579	.540/**.620**	.562	**.685/.654**	.583

Table 3: Pearson's correlation coefficients with direct human assessments (DA) of CHRF enhanced with word n-grams together with CHRF and two variants of WORDF: N=4 and N=2. Bold represents the best overall value.

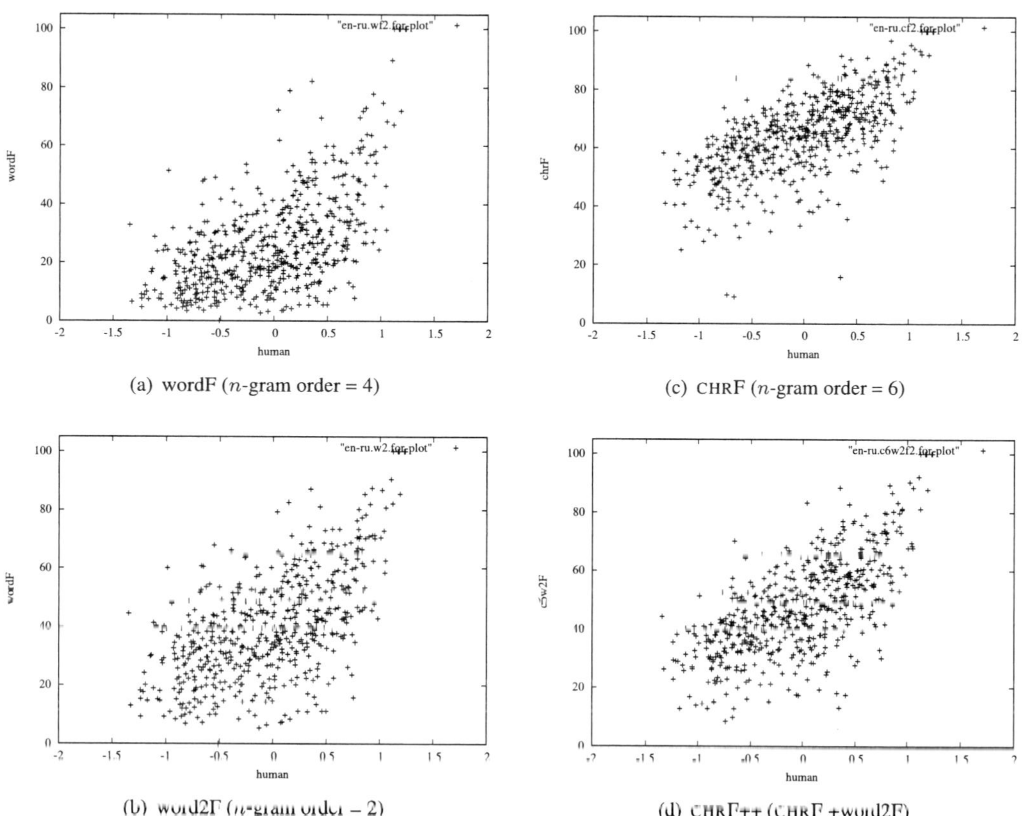

(a) wordF (n-gram order = 4)

(c) CHRF (n-gram order = 6)

(b) word2F (n-gram order = 2)

(d) CHRF++ (CHRF +word2F)

Figure 2: Scatter plots for (a) WORDF with N=4, (b) WORDF with N=2, (c) CHRF and (d) CHRF++ (CHRF enhanced with word bigrams) with DA for English→Russian WMT-16 text. Removing word 3-grams and 4-grams decreases the number of "pessimistic" WORDF points in the lower right quadrant. Combining CHRF with word unigrams and bigrams further decreases the frequency of such points and also lowers overall CHRF scores pushing the points more towards the middle.

the Sixth Workshop on Statistical Machine Translation (WMT-11). Edinburgh, Scotland, pages 104–107.

Maja Popović. 2015. chrF: character n-gram F-score for automatic MT evaluation. In *Proceedings of the 10th Workshop on Statistical Machine Translation (WMT-15)*. Lisbon, Portugal, pages 392–395.

Maja Popović. 2016. chrF deconstructed: beta parameters and n-gram weights. In *Proceedings of the First Conference on Machine Translation (WMT-16)*. Berlin, Germany, pages 499–504.

Víctor M. Sánchez-Cartagena and Antonio Toral. 2016. Abu-matran at wmt 2016 translation task: Deep learning, morphological segmentation and tuning on character sequences. In *Proceedings of the First Conference on Machine Translation (WMT-16)*. Berlin, Germany, pages 362–370.

Miloš Stanojević, Amir Kamran, Philipp Koehn, and Ondřej Bojar. 2015. Results of the WMT15 Metrics Shared Task. In *Proceedings of the 10th Workshop on Statistical Machine Translation (WMT-15)*. Lisbon, Portugal, pages 256–273.

BLEU2VEC: the Painfully Familiar Metric on Continuous Vector Space Steroids

Andre Tättar and **Mark Fishel**
Institute of Computer Science
University of Tartu, Estonia
{andre.tattar, fishel}@ut.ee

Abstract

In this participation in the WMT'2017 metrics shared task we implement a fuzzy match score for n-gram precisions in the BLEU metric. To do this we learn n-gram embeddings; we describe two ways of extending the WORD2VEC approach to do so. Evaluation results show that the introduced score beats the original BLEU metric on system and segment level.

1 The Painfully Familiar Metric

The BLEU metric (Papineni et al., 2002) has deeply rooted in the machine translation community and is used in virtually every paper on machine translation methods. Despite the well-known criticism (Callison-Burch et al., 2006) and a decade of collective efforts to come up with a better translation quality metric (from Callison Burch et al., 2007 to Bojar et al., 2016) it still appeals with its ease of implementation, language independence and competitive agreement rate with human judgments, with the only viable alternative on all three accounts being the recently introduced CHRF (Popovic, 2015).

The original version of BLEU is harsh on single sentences. One of the factors of the score is a geometric mean of n-gram precisions between the translation hypothesis and reference(s) and as a result sentences without 4-gram matches get a score of 0, even if there are good unigram, bigram and possibly trigram matches. There have been several attempts to "soften" this approach by using arithmetic mean instead (NIST, Doddington, 2002), allowing for partial matches using

lemmatization and synonyms (METEOR, Banerjee and Lavie, 2005) and directly implementing fuzzy matches between n-grams (LEBLEU, Virpioja and Grönroos, 2015).

Our work is most closely related to LEBLEU, where BLEU is augmented with fuzzy matches based on the character-level Levenshtein distance. Here we use independently learned word and n-gram embeddings instead.

2 The Continuous Vector Space Steroids

Together with neural networks came the necessity to map sparse discrete values (like natural language words) into dense continuous vector representations. This is done explicitly e.g. with WORD2VEC (Mikolov et al., 2013), as well as learned as part of the whole learning process in neural networks-based language models (Mikolov et al., 2010) and translation approaches (Bahdanau et al., 2015). The approach of learning embeddings has since been extended for example to items in a relational database (Barkan and Koenigstein, 2016), sentences and documents (Le and Mikolov, 2014) and even users (Amir et al., 2017).

The core part of this work consists of n-gram embeddings, the aim of which is to find similarities between short phrases like "research paper" and "scientific article", or "do not like" and "hate". We propose two solutions, both reducing the problem to the original WORD2VEC; the first one only handles n-grams of the same length while the second one is more general. These are described in the following sections.

2.1 Separate N-gram Embeddings

Our first approach is learning separate embedding models for unigrams, bigrams and trigrams. While

Proceedings of the Conference on Machine Translation (WMT), Volume 2: Shared Task Papers, pages 619–622
Copenhagen, Denmark, September 7–11, 2017. ©2017 Association for Computational Linguistics

unigram embeddings are handled by the baseline WORD2VEC method, in this approach we group the n-gram tokens into a single entry, ignoring the overlapping parts, for example:

Uni-grams: this is a test .
Bi-grams: this_is is_a a_test test_.
Tri-grams: this_is_a is_a_test a_test_.

and then compute embeddings for the new tokens with the baseline approach.

Since the number of different n-grams is much higher than single tokens, we filter out bi-grams that occur less than 30 times and tri-grams that occur less than 50 times.

2.2 Joint N-gram Embeddings

Our first method can only learn similarities between n-grams of the same lengths. While it is enough for this submission's metric, it also runs the danger of learning overlapping n-grams, as these are generated next to each other. We therefore define a more general solution.

By modifying the process of extracting input-output training pairs from text sentences we can achieve direct inclusion of both the words and the n-grams, with each of them being treated a separate lexical entry. See Figure 1 for an example of skip-gram training:

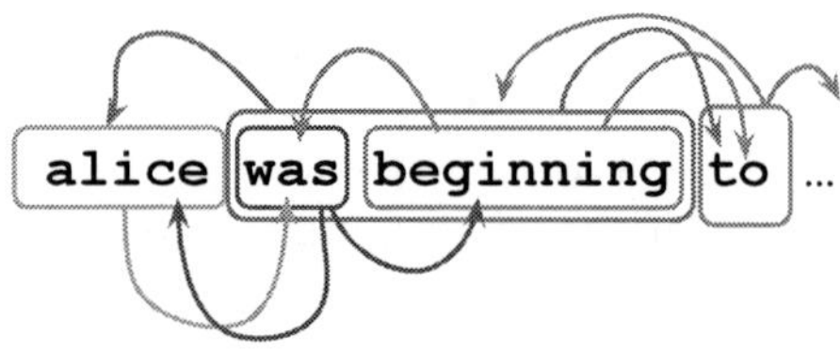

Figure 1: Example of skip-gram training for words and n-grams. Boxes show the input entries and arrows point to output entries; context window width of 1 is used for a simpler figure's sake. We follow (Yu and Dredze, 2015) and predict single words on the output side while feeding words and n-grams on the input side.

In addition to frequency filtering we also sample the n-grams randomly, sometimes including or excluding them from training. To increase the chances of more rare n-grams being included we define the sampling probability based on smoothed reverse frequency:

$$p = \exp(-\beta \log(f)) = \frac{1}{f^\beta},$$

where f is the n-gram absolute frequency, p is the sampling probability and β is a small weight. For example with $\beta = \frac{1}{8}$ the sampling likelihood of an tri-gram with minimum frequency (50) is 0.613, while a high frequency like 10000 will have the probability of 0.316. Using this dynamic probability is equivalent to down-sampling the more frequent n-grams, leaving more exposure to the entries with lower frequency.

Finally, by sampling only n-grams that do not overlap we reduce the problem to the original word-level WORD2VEC by randomly re-deciding which n-grams to join into a single lexical entry at each epoch. This also means that n-grams are present as both the input and output entries.

In the next section we apply the learned n-gram embeddings to compute a soft-constraint translation metric score.

3 BLEU2VEC

The original BLEU metric defines a hard constraint: a word or n-gram from the hypothesis is considered either precise or not. Our modification is defined as follows:

- a hypothesis translation word or n-gram present in the reference translation is considered precise (weight 1)

- all other words and n-grams in the hypothesis are aligned to same-length n-grams in the reference by greedily selecting the most similar pair first. Similarity is computed via the cosine of the embeddings, and is used as the pair's weight

- overlaps are not allowed: once a pair is aligned it is removed from the search space for the next n-grams

The rationale behind this simple modification is that partially correct words will be hopefully considered similar by the embedding model, while completely wrong words will only find alignments with lower similarity.

4 Evaluation

In order to evaluate the metric we trained word and n-gram embeddings using the monolingual

Metric	fi-en	de-en	cs-en	ru-en	Average
BLEU	0.929	0.865	0.958	0.851	0.901
BLEU2VEC_SEP	0.953	0.867	0.970	0.857	0.912
BLEU2VEC_JOINT	0.946	0.863	0.969	0.846	0.906

Table 1: System-level correlation between human judgments from WMT'2015 and the original BLEU metric as well as our two modifications. BLEU2VEC_SEP stands for separate n-gram embedding learning and BLEU2VEC_JOINT stands for the joint learning model.

Metric	fi-en	de-en	cs-en	ru-en	Average
SENT-BLEU	0.308	0.360	0.391	0.329	0.347
BLEU2VEC_SEP	0.327	0.366	0.422	0.320	0.359
BLEU2VEC_JOINT	0.326	0.363	0.417	0.318	0.356

Table 2: Segment-level correlation between human judgments and the SENT-BLEU metric as well as our two modifications.

data from the WMT'2017 news translation shared task: we took a random 50 million sentences from the News Crawl corpora for each language (except Chinese, where we used a portion of Common Crawl).

While this year's human judgments are still being annotated at the time of final submission, we present correlation results based on WMT 2015 data for English in Table 1 for system-level correlations and Table 2 for segment-level correlations.

Results show that both our metrics perform better than the baseline on system-level evaluation. In all cases the joint n-gram embedding learning model performs slightly worse than the separate learning approach.

The same effect can be seen on segment-level evaluations, whereas for Russian-English translations the correlation of both our metrics is worse than SENT-BLEU.

5 Discussion and Conclusions

We defined BLEU2VEC, a modification of the BLEU score that uses word and n-gram embedding similarities for fuzzy matches. Compared to our expectations the metric is underwhelming, but still has higher system-level and segment-level correlations than the original BLEU metric in most evaluated cases.

The main disadvantage of the metric is that the embedding models need to be trained for it to work. On one hand, only raw text is needed for the training. On another hand, this means that the results depend on the size of the training material, as well as the text domain overlap and other similar-

ities/dissimilarities between the training data and the evaluated translations. Evaluating how much this affects the metric remains to be done in future work.

Our future plans include evaluating the metric on other languages; one can expect a bigger difference in metric performance for morphologically complex languages, since our metric aims at reducing the sparsity effect of the original BLEU metric. Other ways of representing words with embeddings have to be experimented with, especially the ones where word and character-level representations are mixed, like Charagram (Wieting et al., 2016). It is also interesting to see, whether this metric can be used for hill-climbing and system development.

The code of our implementation is available on GitHub[1].

References

Silvio Amir, Glen Coppersmith, Paula Carvalho, Mário J. Silva, and Byron C. Wallace. 2017. Quantifying mental health from social media with neural user embeddings. *CoRR* abs/1705.00335. http://arxiv.org/abs/1705.00335.

Dzmitry Bahdanau, Kyunghyun Cho, and Yoshua Bengio. 2015. Neural Machine Translation by Jointly Learning to Align and Translate. *Proceedings of the International Conference on Learning Representations (ICLR)* .

Satanjeev Banerjee and Alon Lavie. 2005. METEOR: An automatic metric for mt evaluation with improved correlation with human judgments. In *Pro-*

---

[1]https://github.com/TartuNLP/bleu2vec

ceedings of the ACL workshop on intrinsic and extrinsic evaluation measures for machine translation and/or summarization. volume 29, pages 65–72.

Oren Barkan and Noam Koenigstein. 2016. Item2vec: Neural item embedding for collaborative filtering. *CoRR* abs/1603.04259. http://arxiv.org/abs/1603.04259.

Ondřej Bojar, Yvette Graham, Amir Kamran, and Miloš Stanojević. 2016. Results of the wmt16 metrics shared task. In *Proceedings of the First Conference on Machine Translation*. Berlin, Germany, pages 199–231.

Chris Callison-Burch, Cameron Fordyce, Philipp Koehn, Christof Monz, and Josh Schroeder. 2007. (Meta-)evaluation of Machine Translation. In *Proceedings of the Second Workshop on Statistical Machine Translation*. Prague, Czech Republic, pages 136–158.

Chris Callison-Burch, Miles Osborne, and Philipp Koehn. 2006. Re-evaluation the role of bleu in machine translation research. In *EACL*. volume 6, pages 249–256.

George Doddington. 2002. Automatic evaluation of machine translation quality using n-gram co-occurrence statistics. In *Proceedings of the second international conference on Human Language Technology Research*. pages 138–145.

Quoc Le and Tomas Mikolov. 2014. Distributed representations of sentences and documents. In *Proceedings of the 31st International Conference on Machine Learning (ICML-14)*. pages 1188–1196.

Tomas Mikolov, Kai Chen, Greg Corrado, and Jeffrey Dean. 2013. Efficient estimation of word representations in vector space. *CoRR* abs/1301.3781. http://arxiv.org/abs/1301.3781.

Tomas Mikolov, Martin Karafiát, Lukas Burget, Jan Cernocký, and Sanjeev Khudanpur. 2010. Recurrent neural network based language model. In *Interspeech*. volume 2, page 3.

Kishore Papineni, Salim Roukos, Todd Ward, and Wei-Jing Zhu. 2002. Bleu: a method for automatic evaluation of machine translation. In *Proceedings of the 40th annual meeting on association for computational linguistics*. pages 311–318.

Maja Popovic. 2015. chrf: character n-gram f-score for automatic mt evaluation. In *Proceedings of the 10th Workshop on Statistical Machine Translation (WMT-15)*. pages 392–395.

Sami Virpioja and Stig-Arne Grönroos. 2015. Lebleu: N-gram-based translation evaluation score for morphologically complex languages. In *Proceedings of the Tenth Workshop on Statistical Machine Translation*. Lisbon, Portugal, pages 411–416.

John Wieting, Mohit Bansal, Kevin Gimpel, and Karen Livescu. 2016. Charagram: Embedding words and sentences via character n-grams. In *Proceedings of the 2016 Conference on Empirical Methods in Natural Language Processing*. Austin, Texas, pages 1504–1515.

Mo Yu and Mark Dredze. 2015. Learning composition models for phrase embeddings. *Transactions of the Association for Computational Linguistics* 3:227–242.

LIG-CRIStAL System for the WMT17 Automatic Post-Editing Task

Alexandre Bérard   Olivier Pietquin

Univ. Lille, CNRS, Centrale Lille, Inria, UMR 9189 CRIStAL

`alexandre.berard@ed.univ-lille1.fr`
`olivier.pietquin@univ-lille1.fr`

Laurent Besacier

LIG, Univ. Grenoble Alpes, CNRS

`laurent.besacier@univ-grenoble-alpes.fr`

Abstract

This paper presents the LIG-CRIStAL submission to the shared Automatic Post-Editing task of WMT 2017. We propose two neural post-editing models: a mono-source model with a task-specific attention mechanism, which performs particularly well in a low-resource scenario; and a chained architecture which makes use of the source sentence to provide extra context. This latter architecture manages to slightly improve our results when more training data is available. We present and discuss our results on two datasets (*en-de* and *de-en*) that are made available for the task.

1 Introduction

It has become quite common for human translators to use machine translation (MT) as a first step, and then to manually post-edit the translation hypothesis. This can result in a significant gain of time, compared to translating from scratch (Green et al., 2013). Such translation workflows can result in the production of new training data, that may be re-injected into the system in order to improve it. Common ways to do so are retraining, incremental training, translation memories, or automatic post-editing (Chatterjee et al., 2015).

In Automatic Post-Editing (APE), the MT system is usually considered as a blackbox: a separate APE system takes as input the outputs of this MT system, and tries to improve them. Statistical Post-Editing (SPE) was first proposed by Simard et al. (2007). It consists in training a Statistical Machine Translation (SMT) system (Koehn et al., 2007), to translate from translation hypotheses to a human post-edited version of those. Béchara et al. (2011) then proposed a way to integrate both the transla-

tion hypothesis and the original (source language) sentence. More recent contributions in the same vein are (Chatterjee et al., 2016; Pal et al., 2016).

When too little training data is available, one may resort to using synthetic corpora: with simulated PE (Potet et al., 2012), or round-trip translation (Junczys-Dowmunt and Grundkiewicz, 2016).

Recently, with the success of Neural Machine Translation (NMT) models (Sutskever et al., 2014; Bahdanau et al., 2015), new kinds of APE methods have been proposed that use encoder-decoder approaches (Junczys-Dowmunt and Grundkiewicz, 2016, 2017; Libovický et al., 2016; Pal et al., 2017; Hokamp, 2017), in which a Recurrent Neural Network (RNN) encodes the source sequence into a fixed size representation (encoder), and another RNN uses this representation to output a new sequence. These encoder-decoder models are generally enhanced with an attention mechanism, which learns to look at the entire sequence of encoder states (Bahdanau et al., 2015; Luong et al., 2016).

We present novel neural architectures for automatic post-editing. Our models learn to generate sequences of edit operations, and use a task-specific attention mechanism which gives information about the word being post-edited.

1.1 Predicting Edit Operations

We think that post-editing should be closer to spelling correction than machine translation. Our work is based on Libovický et al. (2016), who train a model to predict edit operations instead of words. We predict 4 types of operations: `KEEP`, `DEL`, `INS(word)`, and `EOS` (the end of sentence marker). This results in a vocabulary with three symbols plus as many symbols as there are possible insertions.

A benefit of this approach is that, even with little

Proceedings of the Conference on Machine Translation (WMT), Volume 2: Shared Task Papers, pages 623–629
Copenhagen, Denmark, September 7–11, 2017. ©2017 Association for Computational Linguistics

training data, it is very straightforward to learn to output the translation hypothesis as is (MT baseline). We want to avoid a scenario where the APE system is weaker than the original MT system and only degrades its output. However, this approach also has shortcomings, that we shall see in the remainder of this work.

Example If the MT sequence is `"The cats is grey"`, and the output sequence of edit ops is `"KEEP DEL INS(cat) KEEP KEEP INS(.)"`, this corresponds to doing the following sequence of operations: keep `"The"`, delete `"cats"`, insert `"cat"`, keep `"is"`, keep `"grey"`, insert `"."` The final result is the post-edited sequence `"The cat is grey ."`

We preprocess the data to extract such edit sequences by following the shortest edit path (similar to a Levenshtein distance, without substitutions, or with a substitution cost of $+\infty$).

1.2 Forced Attention

State-of-the-art NMT systems (Bahdanau et al., 2015) learn a global attention model, which helps the decoder look at the relevant part of the input sequence each time it generates a new word. It is defined as follows:

$$attn_{global}(\mathrm{h}, s_t) = \sum_{i=1}^{A} a_i^t h_i \qquad (1)$$

$$a_i^t = softmax(e_i^t) \qquad (2)$$

$$e_i^t = v^T tanh(W_1 h_i + W_2 s_t + b_2) \qquad (3)$$

where s_t is the current state of the decoder, h_i is the ith state of the encoder (corresponding to the ith input word). A is the length of the input sequence. W_1, W_2 and b_2 are learned parameters of the model. This attention vector is used to generate the next output symbol w_t and to compute the next state of the decoder s_{t+1}.

However, we don't predict words, but edit operations, which means that we can do stronger assumptions as to how the output symbols align with the input. Instead of a soft attention mechanism, which can look at the entire input and uses the current decoder state s_t to compute soft weights a_i; we use a hard attention mechanism which directly aligns t with i. The attention vector is then $attn_{forced}(h, s_t) = h_i$.

The $t \rightarrow i$ alignment is pretty straightforward: i is the number of KEEP and DEL symbols in the decoder's past output $(w_1, \ldots, w_{t-1})$ plus one.

Task	Train	Dev	Test 2016	Extra
en-de	23k (12k + 11k)	1000	2000	500k 4M
de-en	24k	1000	none	none

Table 1: Size of each available corpus (number of SRC, MT, PE sentence tuples).

Following the example presented earlier, if the decoder's past output is `"KEEP DEL INS(cat)"`, the next token to generate is naturally aligned with the third input word ($i = 3$), i.e., we've kept `"The"` and replaced `"cats"` with `"cat"`. Now, we want to decide whether we keep the third input word `"is"`, delete it, or insert a new word before it.

If the output sequence is too short, i.e., the end of sentence marker EOS is generated before the pointer i reaches the end of the input sequence, we automatically pad with KEEP tokens. This means that to delete a word, there must always be a corresponding DEL symbol. This ensures that, even when unsure about the length of the output sequence, the decoder remains conservative with respect to the sequence to post-edit.

1.3 Chaining Encoders

The model we proposed does not make any use of the source side SRC. Making use of this information is not very straightforward in our framework. Indeed, we may consider using a multi-encoder architecture (Zoph and Knight, 2016; Junczys-Dowmunt and Grundkiewicz, 2017), but it does not make much sense to align an edit operation with the source sequence, and such a model struggles to learn a meaningful alignment.

We propose a chained architecture, which combines two encoder-decoder models (see fig. 1). A first model SRC $\rightarrow$ MT, with a global attention mechanism, tries to mimic the translation process that produced MT from SRC. The attention vectors of this first model summarize the part of the SRC sequence that led to the generation of each MT token. A second model MT $\rightarrow$ OP learns to post-edit and uses a forced attention over the MT sequence, as well as the attention vectors over SRC computed by the first system. Both models are trained jointly, by optimizing a sum of both losses.

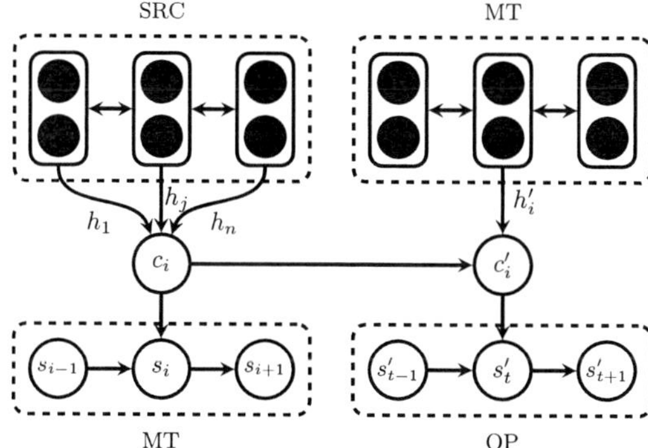

Figure 1: There are two bidirectional encoders that read the SRC and MT sequences. We maximize two training objectives: a translation objective (SRC $\rightarrow$ MT) and a post-editing objective (MT $\rightarrow$ OP). The OP decoder does a forced alignment with the MT encoder ($t \rightarrow i$), and uses the corresponding global attention context c_i over SRC: $c'_i = tanh(H_1 c_i + H_2 h'_i + b')$. The MT decoder and MT encoder share the same embeddings.

2 Experiments

This year's APE task consists in two sub-tasks: a task on English to German post-editing in the IT domain (*en-de*), and a task on German to English post-editing in the medical domain (*de-en*). Table 1 gives the size of each of the corpora available. The goal of both tasks is to minimize the HTER (Snover et al., 2006) between our automatic post-editing output, and the human post-editing output.

The *en-de 23k* training set is a concatenation of last year's *12k* dataset, and a newly released *11k* dataset. A synthetic corpus was built and used by the winner of last year's edition (Junczys Dowmunt and Grundkiewicz, 2016), and is available this year as additional data (*500k* and *4M* corpora).

For the *en-de* task, we limit our use of external data to the 500k corpus. For the *de-en* task, we built our own synthetic corpus, using a technique similar to (Junczys-Dowmunt and Grundkiewicz, 2016).

2.1 Synthetic Data

Desiderata We used similar data selection techniques as Junczys-Dowmunt and Grundkiewicz (2016), applied to the *de-en* task. However, we are very reticent about using as much parallel data as the authors did. We think that access to such amounts of parallel data is rarely possible, and the round-trip translation method they used too cumbersome and unrealistic. To show a fair comparison, this paper should show APE scores when translating from scratch with an MT system trained with all this parallel data.

To mitigate this, we decided to limit our use of external data to monolingual English (*commoncrawl*). So, the only parallel data we use is the *de-en* APE corpus.

PE side Similarly to Junczys-Dowmunt and Grundkiewicz (2016) we first performed a coarse filtering of well-formed sentences of commoncrawl. After this filtering step, we obtained about 500M lines. Then, we estimated a trigram language model on the PE side of the APE corpus, and sorted the 500M lines according to their logscore divided by sentence length. We then kept the first 10M lines. This results in sentences that are mostly in the medical domain.

MT and SRC sides Using this English corpus, and assuming its relative closeness to the PE side of the APE corpus, we now need to generate SRC and MT sequences. This is where our approach differs from the original paper.

Instead of training two SMT systems PE $\rightarrow$ SRC and SRC $\rightarrow$ MT on huge amounts of parallel data, and doing a round-trip translation of the monolingual data, we train two small PE $\rightarrow$ SRC and PE $\rightarrow$ MT Neural Machine Translation systems on the APE data only.

An obvious advantage of this method is that we do not need external parallel data. The NMT systems are also fairly quick to train, and evaluation is very fast. Translating 10M lines with SMT can take a very long time, while NMT can translate dozens of sentences at once on a GPU.

However, there are strong disadvantages: for one, our SRC and MT sequences have a much poorer vocabulary as those obtained with roundtrip translation (because we only get words that belong to the APE corpus). Yet, we hope that the richer target (PE) may help our models learn a better language model.

TER filtering Similarly to Junczys-Dowmunt and Grundkiewicz (2016), we also filter the triples to be close to the real PE distribution in terms of TER statistics. We build a corpus of the *500k* closest tuples. For each tuple in the real PE corpus,

Token	Count	Percentage
KEEP	326581	66.9%
DEL	76725	15.7%
"	5170	1.1%
,	3249	0.7%
die	2461	0.5%
der	1912	0.4%
zu	1877	0.4%
werden	1246	0.3%
KEEP	18367	90.4%
DEL	801	3.9%
"	199	1.0%
>	130	0.6%
,	93	0.5%
zu	63	0.3%
werden	37	0.2%
wird	30	0.1%

Table 2: Top 8 edit ops in the target side of the training set for *en-de* (top), and most generated edit ops by our primary (500k + 23k) system on dev set (bottom).

we select a random subset of *1000* tuples from the synthetic corpus and pick the tuple whose euclidean distance with the real PE tuple is the lowest. This tuple cannot be selected again. We loop over the real PE corpus until we obtain a filtered corpus of desirable size (*500k*).

2.2 Experimental settings

We trained mono-source forced models, as well as chained models for both APE tasks. We also trained mono-source models with a global attention mechanism, similar to (Libovický et al., 2016) as a measure of comparison to our forced models.

For *en-de*, we trained two sets of models (with the same configuration) on the 12k train set (to compare with 2016 competitors), and on the new (23k) train set.

The encoders are bidirectional LSTMs of size 128. The embeddings have a size of 128. The first state of the decoder is initialized with the last state of the forward encoder (after a non-linear transformation with dropout). Teacher forcing is used during training (instead of feeding the previous generated output to the decoder, we feed the ground truth). Like Bahdanau et al. (2015), there is a maxout layer before the final projection.

We train our models with pure SGD with a batch size of 32, and an initial learning rate of 1.0.

We decay the learning rate by 0.8 every epoch for the models trained with real PE data, and by 0.5 every half epoch for the models that use additional synthetic data. The models are evaluated periodically on a *dev* set, and we save checkpoints for the best TER scores.

We manually stop training when TER scores on the dev set stop decreasing, and use the best checkpoint for evaluation on the test set (after about 50k steps for the small training sets, and 120k steps for the larger ones).

Unlike Junczys-Dowmunt and Grundkiewicz (2016), we do not use subword units, as we found them not to be beneficial when predicting edit operations. For the larger datasets, our vocabularies are limited to the 30,000 most frequent symbols.

Our implementation uses TensorFlow (Abadi et al., 2015), and runs on a single GPU.[1]

2.3 Results & Discussion

As shown in table 3, our *forced* (contrastive 1) system gets good results on the *en-de* task, in limited data conditions (*12k* or *23k*). It improves over the MT and SPE baselines, and over the global attention baseline (Libovický et al., 2016). The chained model, which also uses the source sentence, is able to harness larger volumes of data, to obtain yet better results (primary model). However, it lags behind large word-based models trained on larger amounts of data (Junczys-Dowmunt and Grundkiewicz, 2016, 2017; Hokamp, 2017).[2]

Figure 2 compares alignments performed by our attention models. We see that the global attention model struggles to learn a meaningful alignment on a small dataset (12k). When more training data is available (23k), it comes closer to our forced alignment.

We see that our good results on *en-de* do not transfer well to *de-en* (see table 4). The BLEU scores are already very high (about 16 points above those of the *en-de* data, and 10 points above the best APE outputs for *en-de*). This is probably due to the translation direction being reversed (because of its rich morphology, German is a much harder target that English). The results obtained with a vanilla SMT system (SPE) seem to confirm this difficulty.

---

[1] Our source code, and the configurations used in the experiments are available here: https://github.com/eske/seq2seq/tree/APE

[2] More results are published on the web page of the task: http://statmt.org/wmt17/ape-task.html

Model	PE attention	Data	dev	test 2016	test 2017		Steps
				TER		BLEU	
Baseline		none	24.81	24.76	24.48	62.49	
SPE		12k		24.64	24.69	62.97	
Best 2016 (AMU)		4M + 500k + 12k	21.46	21.52			
Best 2017 (FBK)		23k + ?			**19.60**	70.07	
Mono-source	global	12k	24.15	24.26			29000
	forced (contr. 1)		23.20	23.32	23.51	64.52	16600
Chained	forced (contr. 2)		23.40	23.30	23.66	64.46	23600
	forced (primary)	500k + 12k	22.77	**22.94**	**23.22**	65.12	119200
Mono-source	global	23k	23.60	23.55			47200
	forced (contr. 1)		23.07	22.89	23.08	65.57	38800
Chained	forced (contr. 2)		22.61	22.76	23.15	64.94	50400
	forced (primary)	500k + 23k	22.03	**22.49**	**22.81**	65.91	121200

Table 3: Results on the *en-de* task. The SPE results are those provided by the organizers of the task (SMT system). The AMU system is the winner of the 2016 APE task (Junczys-Dowmunt and Grundkiewicz, 2016). FBK is the winner of this year's edition. We evaluate our models on *dev* every 200 training steps, and take the model with the lowest TER. The *steps* column gives the corresponding training time (SGD updates). 500k + 12k is a concatenation of the 500k synthetic corpus with the 12k corpus oversampled 20 times. 500k + 23k is a concatenation of 500k with 23k oversampled 10 times.

The only reason why our *de-en* systems are able to not deteriorate the baseline, is that they only learned to do nothing, by producing arbitrarily long sequences of KEEP symbols. Furthermore, we see that the best results are obtained very early in training, before the models start to overfit and deteriorate the translation hypotheses on the dev set (see *steps* column).

The difference between our scores on the *de-en* dataset is not statistically significant, therefore we cannot draw conclusions as to which model is the best. Furthermore, it turns out that our models output almost only KEEP symbols, resulting in sequences almost identical to the MT input, which explains why the scores are so close to those of the baseline (see table 5).

Adding substitutions is not particularly useful as it leads to even more data sparsity: it doubles the vocabulary size, and results in less DEL symbols, and less training feedback for each individual insertion.

Future work One major problem when learning to predict edit ops instead of words, is the class imbalance. There are much more KEEP symbols in the training data as any other symbol (see tables 2 and 5). This results in models that are very good at predicting KEEP tokens (*do-nothing* scenario), but very cautious when producing other symbols. This

also results in bad generalization as most symbols appear only a couple of times in the training data.

We are investigating ways to get a broader training signal when predicting KEEP symbols. This can be achieved either by weight sharing, or by multi-task training (Luong et al., 2016).

Another direction that we may investigate, is how we obtain sequences of edit operations (from PE data in another form). Our edit operations are extracted artificially by taking the shortest edit path between MT and PE. Yet, this does not necessarily correspond to a plausible sequence of operations done by a human. One way to obtain more realistic sequences of operations, would be to collect finer-grained data from human post-editors: key strokes, mouse movements and clicks could be used to reconstruct the 'true' sequence of edit operations.

Finally, we chose to work at the word level, when a human translator often works at the character level. If a word misses a letter, he won't delete the entire word and write it back. However, working with characters poses new challenges: longer sequences means longer training time, and more memory usage. Also, it is easier to learn semantics with words (a *character embedding* does less sense). Yet, using characters means more training data, and less sparse data, which could be very useful in a post-editing scenario.

Model	PE attention	Data	train-dev	dev	test 2017		Steps
				TER		BLEU	
Baseline	none		16.11	15.58	15.55	79.54	
SPE		24k			15.74	79.28	
Best 2017 (FBK)		24k + ?			**15.29**	79.82	
Mono-source	global		16.06	15.55			5200
	forced (contr. 1)	24k	16.05	15.57	15.62	79.48	3400
Chained	forced (contr. 2)		16.02	15.63	15.68	79.35	7000
	forced (primary)	500k + 24k	15.98	15.67	15.53	79.46	27200

Table 4: Results on the *de-en* task. Because the test set was not available before submission, we used a small part (1000 tuples) of the training set as a *train-dev* set. This set was used for selecting the best models, while the provided dev set was used for final evaluation of our models. The *500k + 24k* corpus is a concatenation of our synthetic corpus with the 24k corpus oversampled 10 times.

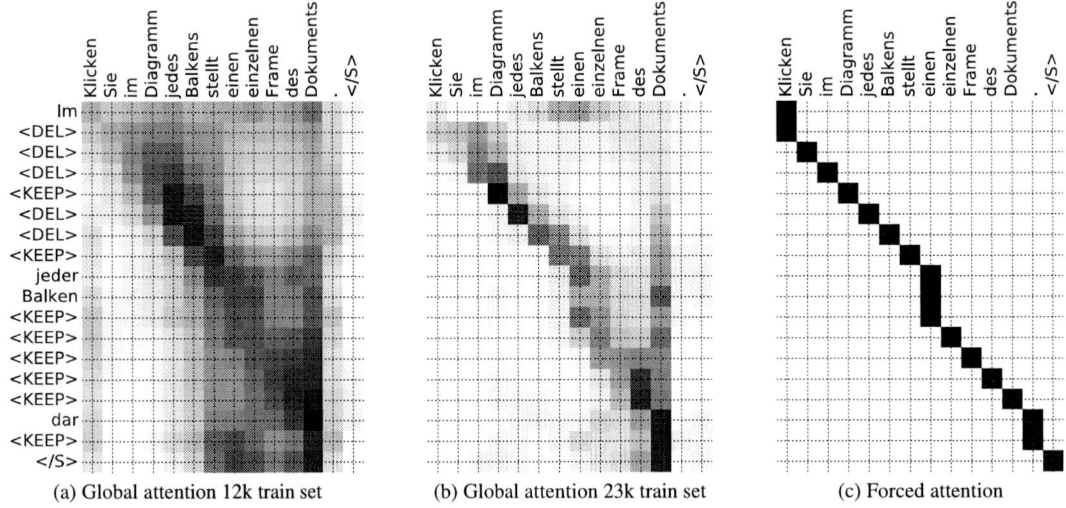

(a) Global attention 12k train set   (b) Global attention 23k train set   (c) Forced attention

Figure 2: Alignments of predicted edit operations (OP) with translation hypothesis (MT), on *en-de* dev set, obtained with different attention models.

Token	Count	Percentage
KEEP	382891	78.19%
DEL	51977	10.61%
the	2249	0.46%
,	1691	0.35%
of	1620	0.33%
to	1022	0.21%
a	952	0.19%
in	919	0.19%

Token	Count	Percentage
KEEP	17861	99.62%
DEL	52	0.29%
UNK	4	0.02%
:	3	0.02%
the	2	0.01%
Have	2	0.01%
A	1	0.01%
>	1	0.01%

Table 5: Top 8 edit ops in the target side of the training set for *de-en* (left), and most generated edit ops by our primary system on train-dev (right).

References

Martín Abadi, Ashish Agarwal, Paul Barham, Eugene Brevdo, Zhifeng Chen, Craig Citro, Greg S. Corrado, Andy Davis, Jeffrey Dean, Matthieu Devin, Sanjay Ghemawat, Ian Goodfellow, Andrew Harp, Geoffrey Irving, Michael Isard, Yangqing Jia, Rafal Jozefowicz, Łukasz Kaiser, Manjunath Kudlur, Josh Levenberg, Dan Mané, Rajat Monga, Sherry Moore, Derek Murray, Chris Olah, Mike Schuster, Jonathon Shlens, Benoit Steiner, Ilya Sutskever, Kunal Talwar, Paul Tucker, Vincent Vanhoucke, Vijay Vasudevan, Fernanda Viégas, Oriol Vinyals, Pete Warden, Martin Wattenberg, Martin Wicke, Yuan Yu, and Xiaoqiang Zheng. 2015. TensorFlow: Large-Scale Machine Learning on Heterogeneous Systems. Software available from tensorflow.org.

Dzmitry Bahdanau, Kyunghyun Cho, and Yoshua Bengio. 2015. Neural Machine Translation by Jointly Learning to Align and Translate. In *ICLR 2015*. San Diego, California, USA, pages 3104–3112.

Hanna Béchara, Yanjun Ma, and Josef van Genabith. 2011. Statistical Post-Editing for a Statistical MT System. In *MT Summit XIII*. Xiamen, China, pages 308–315.

Rajen Chatterjee, José G. C. de Souza, Matteo Negri, and Marco Turchi. 2016. The FBK Participation in the WMT 2016 Automatic Post-Editing Shared Task. In *Proceedings of the First Conference on Machine Translation (WMT 2016)*. Association for Computational Linguistics, Berlin, Germany, pages 745–750.

Rajen Chatterjee, Marion Weller, Matteo Negri, and Marco Turchi. 2015. Exploring the Planet of the APEs: a Comparative Study of State-of-the-art Methods for MT Automatic Post-Editing. In *Association for Computational Linguistics*. pages 156–161.

Spence Green, Jeffrey Heer, and Christopher D Manning. 2013. The Efficacy of Human Post-Editing for Language Translation. In *Proceedings of the SIGCHI conference on Human Factors in Computing Systems*. ACM, pages 439–448.

Chris Hokamp. 2017. Ensembling Factored Neural Machine Translation Models for Automatic Post-Editing and Quality Estimation. *arXiv preprint arXiv:1706.05083* .

Marcin Junczys-Dowmunt and Roman Grundkiewicz. 2016. Log linear Combinations of Monolingual and Bilingual Neural Machine Translation Models for Automatic Post-Editing. In *Proceedings of the First Conference on Machine Translation (WMT 2016)*. Association for Computational Linguistics, Berlin, Germany, pages 751–758.

Marcin Junczys-Dowmunt and Roman Grundkiewicz. 2017. An Exploration of Neural Sequence-to-Sequence Architectures for Automatic Post-Editing. *arXiv preprint arXiv:1706.04138* .

Philipp Koehn, Hieu Hoang, Alexandra Birch, Chris Callison-Burch, Marcello Federico, Nicola Bertoldi, Brooke Cowan, Wade Shen, Christine Moran, Richard Zens, et al. 2007. Moses: Open Source Toolkit for Statistical Machine Translation. In *Proceedings of the 45th annual meeting of the ACL on interactive poster and demonstration sessions*. Association for Computational Linguistics, pages 177–180.

Jindřich Libovický, Jindřich Helcl, Marek Tlustý, Ondřej Bojar, and Pavel Pecina. 2016. CUNI System for WMT16 Automatic Post-Editing and Multimodal Translation Tasks. In *Proceedings of the First Conference on Machine Translation (WMT 2016)*. Association for Computational Linguistics, Berlin, Germany, pages 646–654.

Minh-Thang Luong, Quoc V Le, Ilya Sutskever, Oriol Vinyals, and Łukasz Kaiser. 2016. Multi-task Sequence to Sequence Learning. In *ICLR 2016*. San Juan, Puerto Rico.

Santanu Pal, Sudip Kumar Naskar, Mihaela Vela, and Josef van Genabith. 2017. Neural Automatic Post-Editing Using Prior Alignment and Reranking. In *EACL 2017*. volume 2, pages 349–355.

Santanu Pal, Marcos Zampieri, and Josef van Genabith. 2016. USAAR: An Operation Sequential Model for Automatic Statistical Post-Editing. In *Proceedings of the First Conference on Machine Translation (WMT 2016)*. Association for Computational Linguistics, Berlin, Germany, pages 759–763.

Marion Potet, Laurent Besacier, Hervé Blanchon, and Marwen Azouzi. 2012. Towards a Better Understanding of Statistical Post-Edition Usefulness. In *IWSLT 2012*. Hong Kong, pages 284–291.

Michel Simard, Cyril Goutte, and Pierre Isabelle. 2007. Statistical Phrase-based Post-editing. In *NAACL-HLT 2007*. Rochester, New-York, USA, pages 508–515.

Matthew Snover, Bonnie Dorr, Richard Schwartz, Linnea Micciulla, and John Makhoul. 2006. A Study of Translation Edit Rate with Targeted Human Annotation. In *Proceedings of Association for Machine Translation in the Americas*. volume 200.

Ilya Sutskever, Oriol Vinyals, and Quoc V Le. 2014. Sequence to Sequence Learning with Neural Networks. In *Advances in Neural Information Processing Systems (NIPS 2014)*. Montral, Canada, pages 3104–3112.

Barret Zoph and Kevin Knight. 2016. Multi-Source Neural Translation. In *NAACL-HLT 2016*. Denver, Colorado, USA.

Multi-source Neural Automatic Post-Editing:
FBK's participation in the WMT 2017 APE shared task

Rajen Chatterjee[1,2]**, Amin Farajian**[1,2]**, Matteo Negri**[2]**, Marco Turchi**[2]**,**
Ankit Srivastava[3]**, Santanu Pal**[4]
[1]University of Trento
[2]Fondazione Bruno Kessler
[3] German Research Center for Artificial Intelligence
[4]Saarland University

Abstract

Previous phrase-based approaches to Automatic Post-editing (APE) have shown that the dependency of MT errors from the source sentence can be exploited by jointly learning from source and target information. By integrating this notion in a neural approach to the problem, we present the multi-source neural machine translation (NMT) system submitted by FBK to the WMT 2017 APE shared task. Our system implements multi-source NMT in a weighted ensemble of 8 models. The n-best hypotheses produced by this ensemble are further re-ranked using features based on the edit distance between the original MT output and each APE hypothesis, as well as other statistical models (n-gram language model and operation sequence model). This solution resulted in the best system submission for this round of the APE shared task for both *en-de* and *de-en* language directions. For the former language direction, our primary submission improves over the MT baseline up to -4.9 TER and +7.6 BLEU points. For the latter, where the higher quality of the original MT output reduces the room for improvement, the gains are lower but still significant (-0.25 TER and +0.3 BLEU).

1 Introduction

Automatic post-editing (APE) aims to correct systematic machine translation (MT) errors, thereby reducing translators workload and eventually increasing translation productivity. The task, well motivated in (Bojar et al., 2015) and (Bojar et al., 2016), becomes necessary when working in a "black-box" condition where the MT engine used

to translate is not directly accessible for retraining or for more radical internal modifications. As pointed out in (Bojar et al., 2015), from the application point of view an APE system can help to: *i)* improve MT output by exploiting information unavailable to the decoder, or by performing deeper text analysis that is too expensive at the decoding stage; *ii)* provide professional translators with improved MT output quality to reduce (human) post-editing effort and *iii)* adapt the output of a general-purpose MT system to the lexicon/style requested in a specific application domain.

Different APE paradigms based on statistical methods (Simard et al., 2007; Dugast et al., 2007; Isabelle et al., 2007; Lagarda et al., 2009; Potet et al., 2012; Rosa et al., 2013; Lagarda et al., 2015; Chatterjee et al., 2017) have been proposed in the past showing the effectiveness of APE systems. In the previous round of the APE shared task (WMT16), neural (Junczys-Dowmunt and Grundkiewicz, 2016), hybrid (Chatterjee et al., 2016), and phrase-based (Pal et al., 2016b) solutions were all able to significantly improve MT output quality in domain-specific settings, with neural system being the best in 2016. Some of the previous approaches, both phrase-based (Béchara et al., 2011; Chatterjee et al., 2015b) and neural (Libovický et al., 2016) also suggested the importance of jointly learning both from the source sentences and from the corresponding translations in order to take advantage of the strict dependency between translation errors and the original source sentences.

Learning from these lessons, this year the FBK participation in the APE task is based on a multi-source neural sequence-to-sequence architecture. We extend the existing NMT implementation in the Nematus toolkit (Sennrich et al., 2016a) to facilitate multi-source training and decoding. This year we participated in both translation directions

Proceedings of the Conference on Machine Translation (WMT), Volume 2: Shared Task Papers, pages 630–638
Copenhagen, Denmark, September 7–11, 2017. ©2017 Association for Computational Linguistics

(*en-de* and *de-en*) with similar system architectures consisting of an ensemble of 8 neural models followed by a re-ranker. On both tasks, our primary submissions achieved the best results, with significant improvements over the baseline (-4.9 TER and +7.6 BLEU for *en-de* and -0.25 TER and +0.3 BLEU for *de-en*).

2 Neural Machine Translation

As normally done in APE, we cast the problem as a "monolingual translation" task in which a system is trained on (*src, mt, pe*) triplets to "translate" (*i.e.* correct) rough MT output (*mt*) into fluent and adequate translations by learning from human post-edits (*pe*). Following the recent success of neural approaches (to MT in general and APE in particular), we develop our neural APE systems around the sequence-to-sequence encoder-decoder architecture proposed in (Bahdanau et al., 2014) and further developed by Sennrich et al. (2016a) in the Nematus toolkit (Sennrich et al., 2017).

Neural machine translation aims to optimize the parameters of the model to maximize the log-likelihood of the training data. The ultimate goal is to estimate a conditional probability model $p_\Theta(y|x)$, where Θ is the parameter set of the model (the weights and biases of the network), y is a target sentence and x is a source sentence. Thus, the objective function is:

$$argmax_\Theta \frac{1}{N} \sum_{n=1}^{N} log(p_\Theta(y_n|x_n)); \qquad (1)$$

where N is the total number of sentence pairs in the training corpus. The conditional probability is computed as:

$$p_\Theta(y|x) = \prod_{t=1}^{T_y} p_\Theta(y_t|y_{<t}, x) \qquad (2)$$

where T_y is the number of words in the target sentence. Given all the previous target words $y_{<t}$ and the source x, the probability of target word y_t, is modelled by the decoder network as follows:

$$p_\Theta(y_t|y_{<t}, x) = g(\dot{y}_{t-1}, s_t, c_t) \qquad (3)$$

where $\dot{y}_{t-1}$ is the word embedding of the previous target word, s_t is the hidden state of the decoder, and c_t the source context vector (encoding of the source sentence x) at time t. The decoder state s_t is computed by a gated recurrent unit (GRU) (Cho

et al., 2014) in two steps. First, the previous hidden state and the previous target word embedding are used to compute an intermediate hidden state by a GRU unit:

$$s'_t = f'(s_{t-1}, \dot{y}_{t-1}) \qquad (4)$$

Then, the intermediate hidden state and the source context vector are passed to another GRU to compute the final hidden state of the decoder. In short:

$$s_t = f(s'_t, c_t) \qquad (5)$$

The source context vector is a weighted sum of all the hidden states of a bi-directional encoder (Bahdanau et al., 2014).[1]

$$c_t = \sum_{j=1}^{T_x} a_{tj} h_j \qquad (6)$$

where a_{tj} is the attention weight given to the j-th encoder hidden state at decoding time t, and T_x is the number of words in the source sentence. The attention weight represents the importance of the j-th hidden state of the encoder in generating the target word of time t. It is drawn from a probability distribution over all the hidden states of the encoder, which is computed by applying a $softmax$ operator over all the scores of the hidden units of the encoder:

$$a_{tj} = \frac{exp(e_{tj})}{\sum_{k=1}^{T_x} exp(e_{tk})} \qquad (7)$$

where e_{tj} and e_{tk} are the score of the j-th and k-th hidden units of the encoder at time step t, which is a function of the intermediate hidden state of the decoder (as mentioned in Equation 4) and the hidden state of the encoder, as shown below:

$$e_{tj} = a(s'_t, h_j) \qquad (8)$$

The hidden state h_j of the j-th source word is a concatenation of the hidden states of the forward and backward encoders:

$$h_j = [\overrightarrow{h_j}; \overleftarrow{h_j}] \qquad (9)$$

where $\overrightarrow{h_j}$ and $\overleftarrow{h_j}$ are respectively the hidden state of the forward and backward encoders. These hidden states are computed by the GRU unit that takes

---

[1] In rest of the paper, by encoder we mean bi-directional encoder

previous/next hidden state and the word embedding of the j-th source word ($\dot{x}_j$).

$$\overrightarrow{h}_j = f(\dot{x}_j, \overrightarrow{h}_{j-1}) \tag{10}$$

$$\overleftarrow{h}_j = f(\dot{x}_j, \overleftarrow{h}_{j+1}) \tag{11}$$

3 Multi-source implementation

The strict connection between MT errors and the input source sentences suggests to develop APE systems that leverage information both from the source (*src*) and it's corresponding translation (*mt*) instead of looking at the machine-translated sentence in isolation. Exploiting source information as an additional input can in fact help the system to disambiguate corrections applied at each time step. For example, the German phrase "mein Haus" (EN: my house) looks correct but if the source phrase was "my home" then the correct translation would be "mein Zuhaus". In this case, an APE system ignoring the source would have left the sub-optimal MT output untouched.

Jointly learning from both source and translation has been previously proved to be effective in (Béchara et al., 2011; Chatterjee et al., 2015b). Such works, however, exploit the idea of a "joint representation" of the input mainly in the statistical phrase-based APE framework while, within the neural paradigm, recent prior work mostly focuses on single-source systems (Pal et al., 2016a; Junczys-Dowmunt and Grundkiewicz, 2016; Pal et al., 2017). The only exception, to the best of our knowledge, is the approach of Libovický et al. (2016), who developed a multi-source neural APE system. According to the authors, however, the resulting network seems to be inadequate to learn how to perform the minimum edits required to correct the MT segment. Rather, it learns to paraphrase the input, which results in a high chance of performing unnecessary corrections that would be penalized by reference-based evaluations against human post-edits. Therefore, to mitigate this problem, they represented the target as a minimum-length sequence of edit operation needed to turn the machine-translated sentence into the reference post-edit.

Our multi-source APE implementation, which is built on top of the network architecture discussed in §2, is similar to (Libovický et al., 2016) but extends it with a context dropout, and considers the target as a sequence of words rather than minimum-length sequence. We extend the architecture to have two encoders, one for *src* and another for *mt*. Each encoder has its own attention layer that is used to compute the weighted context (Equation 6). The *src* and the *mt* weighted contexts (c_t^{src} and c_t^{mt} respectively) are then passed to a merger layer to obtain the final context ($c_{t-merge}$). The merger layer concatenates both contexts and applies a linear transformation, thus the final context captures information from both the inputs:

$$c_{t-merge} = [c_t^{src}; c_t^{mt}] * W_{ct} + b_{ct} \tag{12}$$

where, W_{ct}, b_{ct} are respectively the weight and the bias of the merger layer. The final context ($c_{t-merge}$) is used by the decoder to compute target word probabilities (similar to Equation 3)

$$p_\Theta(y_t|y_{<t}, x) = g(\dot{y}_{t-1}, s_t, c_{t-merge}) \tag{13}$$

Context Dropout: Dropout was proposed by Hinton et al. (2012) as a regularization technique for deep networks to avoid over-fitting. The key idea is to randomly drop some units (along with its incoming and outgoing connections) from the neural network to prevent co-adaption on the training data. It has been shown to be very effective on a wide range of supervised learning tasks in vision, speech recognition, document classification and computational biology (Srivastava et al., 2014). When applying dropout with a recurrent neural network, Gal and Ghahramani (2016) showed that using same dropout mask at each timestep is better than ad hoc techniques where different dropout are sampled at each time step. This strategy is also retained in the Nematus toolkit with the exception of using dropout at the token level instead of type level. Since our multi-source architecture is implemented on top of this toolkit, we also follow the same dropout strategy. We use context dropout at different layers of the network:

- To compute the attention score in Equation 8 we apply a shared dropout to the hidden state of both encoders;

- To compute the final hidden state of the decoder in equation 5, we apply a dropout to the merged context of the encoders ($c_{t-merge}$).

We have observed that the use of context dropout helps the model to avoid overfitting and allows more stable performance on the validation set when the model converges.

4 Experiments and Development Results

In this section we summarize how our systems have been trained, tuned and combined to produce the FBK submissions to the WMT 2017 APE shared task.

4.1 Data

EN-DE: We use $\sim$4M artificially-created training data from (Junczys-Dowmunt and Grundkiewicz, 2016) to train generic models that are later fine-tuned with $\sim$500K artificial[2] and 23K (replicated 20 times) real post-edited training data collected from previous year and this year shared task (Bojar et al., 2016).[3] The development set released in the previous year shared task is used to evaluate and compare different models' performance. All the data is segmented using the byte pair encoding technique to obtain sub-word units following (Sennrich et al., 2016b) in order to avoid the problem of out-of-vocabulary words.

DE-EN: We create artificial post-editing training data by a round-trip translation using the subset of parallel data released in the medical task at WMT'14 (Bojar et al., 2014). The parallel data is used to build a phrase-based MT system (PBMT) for both *en-de* and *de-en* language directions. The monolingual English data (considered as *pe*) is first translated into German (considered as *source*) using the *en-de* PBMT system, and then back-translated into English (considered as *mt*) using the *de-en* PBMT system. The parallel and monolingual data each consists of $\sim$2M segments. To train the APE systems we concatenate the round-trip translated data, the parallel data where we consider the reference as the MT output itself, and the shared task training data (25K triplets) replicated 160 times to avoid possible biases towards the artificial data. All the data is segmented in sub-word units (similar to the *en-de* direction), and the systems are evaluated on the development set released for this years' shared task.

4.2 Evaluation Metric

We run case-sensitive evaluation with TER, which is based on edit distance, and BLEU (Papineni et al., 2002), which is based on modified n-gram precision. In addition to the standard evaluation

metrics, we also measure the precision of our APE system using sentence level TER score as defined in (Chatterjee et al., 2015a):

$$\text{Precision} = \frac{\text{Number of Improved Sentences}}{\text{Number of Modified Sentences}}$$

where "Number of Improved Sentences" is the count of APE outputs that have lower TER than the corresponding MT output, and "Number of Modified Sentences" is the count of APE outputs that have TER scores different from the TER of the corresponding MT output.

4.3 Hyper parameters

The hyper parameters of all the systems in both language directions are the same. The vocabulary is created by selecting 50K most frequent subwords. Word embedding and GRU hidden state size is set to 1024. Network parameters are optimized with Adagrad (Duchi et al., 2011) with a learning rate of 0.01 following the work by Farajian et al. (2016), which empirically showed that Adagrad has a faster convergence rate and better performance than Adadelta (Zeiler, 2012). Source and target dropout is set to 10%, whereas, encoder and decoder hidden states, weighted source context, and embedding dropout is set to 20% (Sennrich et al., 2016a). After each epoch, the training data is shuffled and the batches are created after sorting 2000 samples in order to speed-up the training. The batch size is set to 100 samples, with a maximum sentence length of 50 sub-words.

4.4 Models

For both language directions, we trained four types of networks to capture different information that can be leveraged together via ensemble techniques. The results of the single best model for *en-de* and *de-en* from each network type are respectively reported in Tables 1 and 2. The performance trends among different networks are similar for both language directions. However, the variation are less visible in the case of *de-en* given the fact that the room of improvement is much lower due to higher MT quality (15.58 TER and 79.46 BLEU scores). Therefore, we base our discussion for each model below on the results achieved on the development data for the *en-de* direction, where the performance variations among different networks are much more visible.

---

[2]https://github.com/amunmt/amunmt/wiki/AmuNMT-for-Automatic-Post-Editing
[3]http://www.statmt.org/wmt17/ape-task.html

SRC_PE This system is similar to a NMT system used for bilingual translation from a source language to a target language. The parallel corpus consist of source text and post-edits of MT segments. We notice that the performance of this system is below the MT Baseline indicating that learning only from the source text is not enough to improve the translation quality. Most likely, this system generates (alternative, potentially correct) translations that diverge from the MT output and are thus penalized by automatic evaluation metrics that use human post-edits as references. This can be confirmed from the fact that when we used the reference test set for evaluation,[4] the APE system outperformed the MT Baseline by +4.2 BLEU points (47.97 vs 43.79 BLEU scores).

MT_PE This is a single-source neural APE system similar to the previous one. However, in this case the objective is "monolingual" translation as opposed to bilingual in the previous case. Both source and target languages are the same, and the goal is to translate rough MT segments into their corrected version. The results in Table 1 show that learning from machine-translated text is better than learning from the corresponding source sentences (-3.2 TER and +6.0 BLEU points over the MT Baseline). Though quite large, the performance gain does not indicate if all the MT segments are improved. To better understand this aspect, we use the precision metric (as defined in Section 4.2). A precision of 72% for this system indicates that the majority of the MT segments that are modified results in a better translation quality. The remaining 28% of deteriorated sentences gives evidence of the "over-correction" problem discussed in last years' APE task overview (Bojar et al., 2016).

MT+SRC_PE One limitation of the "monolingual translation" approach is that the APE system is only trained on data in the target language, disregarding information about the source language: mappings learned from (*mt, pe*) pairs lose the connection between the translated words (or phrases) and the corresponding source terms (*src*). This implies that information lost or distorted in the translation process is out of the reach of the APE component, and the resulting errors are impossible to recover. To overcome this limitation and to leverage both source and MT output, we introduced the

[4] http://hdl.handle.net/11234/1-2334

Systems	TER	BLEU	Prec. (%)
MT_Baseline	24.81	62.92	-
SRC_PE	26.66	61.91	49.07
MT_PE	21.57	69.09	72.01
MT+SRC_PE	19.77	70.72	78.22
MT+SRC_PE_TSL	20.07	70.52	78.77
Ens8	19.26	71.63	78.50
Ens8+Re-rank-A	**19.22**†	**71.89**†	**78.84**
Ens8+Re-rank-AB	19.35	70.94	78.07

Table 1: Performance of the APE systems on dev. 2016 (*en-de*) ("†" indicates statistically significant differences wrt. MT_Baseline with p<0.05).

Systems	TER	BLEU	Precision (%)
MT_Baseline	15.58	79.46	-
SRC_PE	28.50	58.17	20.22
MT_PE	15.97	78.43	36.29
MT+SRC_PE	15.61	78.59	44.67
MT+SRC_PE_TSL	15.89	78.48	42.58
Ens8	15.14	79.41	54.18
Ens8+Re-rank-A	**15.04**†	**80.00**†	**68.86**

Table 2: Performance of the APE systems on dev. 2017 (*de-en*) ("†" indicates statistically significant differences wrt. MT_Baseline with p<0.05).

multi-source neural sequence-to-sequence model described in §3. Our multi-source neural APE model clearly outperforms the strong monolingual single-source model (-1.8 TER and +1.6 BLEU). The improvement is also visible in terms of precision (+8.2%), which indicates that the source segment might be useful to disambiguate if the MT word should be corrected or kept untouched, thus helping to mitigate the over-correction problem.

MT+SRC_PE_TSL The low TER score of the MT baseline (24.8 and 15.5 respectively for *en-de* and *de-en*) indicates that the majority of the MT words are correct. In order to induce a conservative approach (in other words, to induce the APE system to preserve the correct MT words) we use a task-specific loss (TSL) function that takes into consideration the attention score of the MT words before computing the target word probabilities. The attention scores can act as a reward to the target words that are present in the MT segment. To this aim, first we add the attention scores from the *mt* encoder (Equation 8) to the respective target words in the softmax layer. Then, we apply softmax to obtain the target word probabilities. More formally:

$$p_\Theta(y_t|y_{<t}, X^{src}, X^{mt}) = \frac{e^{y_t}_{dec} + \sum e^{y_t}_{enc}}{\sum_{y'}(e^{y'}_{dec} + \sum e^{y'}_{enc})}$$

(14)

where, e^y_{dec} and e^y_{enc} are respectively the scores of the target word computed by the decoder layer and the attention layer of the *mt* encoder ($e^y_{enc} = 0$ if $y \notin MT$). Since a target word can occur multiple times in the MT segment, we sum the scores of all occurrences. In case a target word is not present in the MT segment the score is 0.

Ensemble (Ens8) In order to leverage all the network architectures discussed above, we ensemble the two best models for each of them. Since the networks are very diverse in terms of information learned from the input representation we observed that weighing all the models equally does not improve over the single system. Therefore, we generate 50-best hypothesis from the ensemble system and then tune the model weights with Batch-MIRA (Cherry and Foster, 2012) on the development set to maximize the BLEU score. We observe that, after 3 cycles of decoding and tuning, the performance converges. The weighted ensemble of 8 models further improves the translation quality (-0.8 TER and +1.1 BLEU) over the best single multi-source model (MT+SRC_PE).

Re-ranking Following the improvements obtained by re-ranking n-best hypotheses as shown in (Pal et al., 2017), we use a re-ranker in our submissions with two different sets of features:

Edit Distance (Re-rank-A) The first set consists of shallow features that can be easily extracted on-the-fly. It captures different types of edit operations performed by an APE system over the MT output. These features include number of insertions, deletions, substitutions, shifts, and length ratio between the MT segment and each APE hypothesis, computed using TER. In addition, we compute precision and recall of the APE hypotheses in order to avoid over-correction by rewarding the hypotheses that are closer to the MT segment. Precision is the percentage of words generated by the APE system that are present in the MT segment, and recall is the percentage of words in the MT segment that are generated

by the APE system. The feature weights are optimized with Batch-MIRA on the development set to maximize the BLEU score. Re-ranking with these features gave further improvements over the ensemble system. Since this is the best configuration (as seen from Table 1 and 2), we evaluate this system on the 2016 APE test set. The results of this evaluation are reported in Table 3. We observe that this system achieves significant improvement over the MT baseline (-5.4 TER and 8.7 BLEU points) also on the 2016 test set.

Systems	TER	BLEU
MT_Baseline	24.76	62.11
APE_Baseline	24.64	63.47
Ens8+Re-rank-A	**19.32†**	**70.88†**

Table 3: Performance of the APE systems on the 2016 test set (*en-de*) ("†" indicates statistically significant differences wrt. MT_Baseline with p<0.05).

Statistical (Re-rank-AB) This re-ranker is similar to the one used in (Pal et al., 2017). The feature set consists of the log probability given by the neural models itself, the statistical n-gram language model probability as well as the perplexity normalized by sentence length, and features from operation sequence model. In addition to this, we also integrate all the features used by the previous re-ranker, following the same procedure to optimize their weights. The result of this system is reported in Table 1 (Ens8+Re-rank-AB). We observe that this re-ranker does not yield performance improvements, probably due to over-fitting. We leave further investigations on this aspect for future work.

5 Results on Test Data

The shared task evaluation has been carried out on 2,000 unseen samples consisting of *src* and *mt* pairs from the same domain of the training data. Our primary submission is Ens8+Re-rank-A (in Table 1 and 2) that is a weighted ensemble of 8 neural APE models (2 best models from SRC_PE, MT_PE, MT+SRC_PE, and MT+SRC_PE_TSL). As a contrastive submission, we wanted to evaluate the performance of a simpler system with a higher throughput. Therefore, we select a single best multi-source model (MT+SRC_PE) with a re-ranker that is based only on edit-distance features (labelled as Contrastive-A in Table 4). For *en-de* we also submitted (Ens8+Re-rank-AB) another contrastive system that is based on ensemble system plus the whole set of re-ranking features (labelled as Contrastive-B in Table 4). According to the shared task results, as reported in Table 4, our primary and contrastive submissions achieve significant improvement over the MT baseline for both language directions. It is interesting to note that our contrastive-A submission, which is a much simpler version of the full-fledged system, performs almost similar to our primary submission for *de-en* and slightly worse (+0.7 TER points) for *en-de*.

Systems	en-de		de-en	
	TER	**BLEU**	**TER**	**BLEU**
MT Baseline	24.48	62.49	15.55	79.54
APE Baseline	24.69	62.97	15.74	79.28
Primary	**19.6**	**70.07**	**15.29**	**79.82**
Contrastive-A	20.3	69.11	15.31	79.64
Contrastive-B	21.55	67.28	-	-

Table 4: Official results on 2017 test set.

6 Conclusion

Based on the lessons learned from previous work on APE, which suggest that the dependency of MT errors from the source sentence can be exploited by jointly learning from source and target information, we developed a multi-source NMT system. Our implementation extends the existing NMT toolkit (Nematus) to train multi-source APE systems that learn from source and MT text together in order to increase robustness and precision. We trained several networks with different input representation (single-source/multi-source) to finally built an ensemble of 8 neural models. The n-best hypotheses generated by this ensemble were further re-ranked using features based on the edit distance between the original MT output and each APE hypothesis, as well as other statistical models (n-gram language model and operation sequence model). On the *en-de* and *de-en* test data released for the WMT 2017 APE shared task, our primary submissions achieved significant improvements over the task baselines, which we outperformed by a large margin (+7.6 and +0.3 BLEU points on *en-de* and *de-en*) ranking first on both language directions.

Acknowledgments

This work has been partially supported by the EC-funded H2020 project QT21 (grant agreement no. 645452).

References

Dzmitry Bahdanau, Kyunghyun Cho, and Yoshua Bengio. 2014. Neural machine translation by jointly learning to align and translate. *arXiv preprint arXiv:1409.0473* .

Hanna Béchara, Yanjun Ma, and Josef van Genabith. 2011. Statistical Post-Editing for a Statistical MT System. In *Proceedings of the 13th Machine Translation Summit*. Xiamen, China, pages 308–315.

Ondrej Bojar, Christian Buck, Christian Federmann, Barry Haddow, Philipp Koehn, Johannes Leveling, Christof Monz, Pavel Pecina, Matt Post, Herve Saint-Amand, Radu Soricut, Lucia Specia, and Aleš Tamchyna. 2014. Findings of the 2014 workshop on statistical machine translation. In *Proceedings of the Ninth Workshop on Statistical Machine Translation*. Association for Computational Linguistics, Baltimore, Maryland, USA, pages 12–58.

Ondřej Bojar, Rajen Chatterjee, Christian Federmann, Yvette Graham, Barry Haddow, Matthias Huck, Antonio Jimeno Yepes, Philipp Koehn, Varvara Logacheva, Christof Monz, Matteo Negri, Aurelie Neveol, Mariana Neves, Martin Popel, Matt Post, Raphael Rubino, Carolina Scarton, Lucia Specia, Marco Turchi, Karin Verspoor, and Marcos Zampieri. 2016. Findings of the 2016 conference on machine translation. In *Proceedings of the First Conference on Machine Translation*. Association for Computational Linguistics, Berlin, Germany, pages 131–198.

Ondřej Bojar, Rajen Chatterjee, Christian Federmann, Barry Haddow, Matthias Huck, Chris Hokamp, Philipp Koehn, Varvara Logacheva, Christof Monz, Matteo Negri, Matt Post, Carolina Scarton, Lucia Specia, and Marco Turchi. 2015. Findings of the 2015 workshop on statistical machine translation. In *Proceedings of the Tenth Workshop on Statistical Machine Translation*. Association for Computational Linguistics, Lisbon, Portugal, pages 1–46.

Rajen Chatterjee, José G. C. de Souza, Matteo Negri, and Marco Turchi. 2016. The fbk participation in the wmt 2016 automatic post-editing shared task. In *Proceedings of the First Conference on Machine Translation*. Association for Computational Linguistics, Berlin, Germany, pages 745–750.

Rajen Chatterjee, Gebremedhen Gebremelak, Matteo Negri, and Marco Turchi. 2017. Online automatic post-editing for mt in a multi-domain translation environment. In *Proceedings of the 15th Conference of the European Chapter of the Association for Computational Linguistics: Volume 1, Long Papers*. Association for Computational Linguistics, Valencia, Spain, pages 525–535.

Rajen Chatterjee, Marco Turchi, and Matteo Negri. 2015a. The fbk participation in the wmt15 automatic post-editing shared task. In *Proceedings of the Tenth Workshop on Statistical Machine Translation*. pages 210–215.

Rajen Chatterjee, Marion Weller, Matteo Negri, and Marco Turchi. 2015b. Exploring the Planet of the APEs: a Comparative Study of State-of-the-art Methods for MT Automatic Post-Editing. In *Proceedings of the 53rd Annual Meeting of the Association for Computational Linguistics)*. Beijing, China.

Colin Cherry and George Foster. 2012. Batch tuning strategies for statistical machine translation. In *Proceedings of the 2012 Conference of the North American Chapter of the Association for Computational Linguistics: Human Language Technologies*. Association for Computational Linguistics, Stroudsburg, PA, USA, NAACL HLT '12, pages 427–436.

Kyunghyun Cho, Bart Van Merriënboer, Caglar Gulcehre, Dzmitry Bahdanau, Fethi Bougares, Holger Schwenk, and Yoshua Bengio. 2014. Learning phrase representations using rnn encoder-decoder for statistical machine translation. *arXiv preprint arXiv:1406.1078* .

John Duchi, Elad Hazan, and Yoram Singer. 2011. Adaptive Subgradient Methods for Online Learning and Stochastic Optimization. *Journal of Machine Learning Research* .

Loïc Dugast, Jean Senellart, and Philipp Koehn. 2007. Statistical post-editing on systran's rule-based translation system. In *Proceedings of the Second Workshop on Statistical Machine Translation*. Association for Computational Linguistics, pages 220–223.

M Amin Farajian, Rajen Chatterjee, Costanza Contorti, Shahab Jalalvand, Vevake Balaraman, Mattia A Di Gangi, Duygu Ataman, Marco Turchi, Matteo Negri, and Marcello Federico. 2016. Fbks neural machine translation systems for iwslt 2016. In *Proceedings of the ninth International Workshop on Spoken Language Translation, USA*.

Yarin Gal and Zoubin Ghahramani. 2016. A theoretically grounded application of dropout in recurrent neural networks. In *Advances in Neural Information Processing Systems*. pages 1019 1027.

Geoffrey E Hinton, Nitish Srivastava, Alex Krizhevsky, Ilya Sutskever, and Ruslan R Salakhutdinov. 2012. Improving neural networks by preventing co-adaptation of feature detectors. *arXiv preprint arXiv:1207.0580* .

Pierre Isabelle, Cyril Goutte, and Michel Simard. 2007. Domain adaptation of mt systems through automatic post-editing .

Marcin Junczys-Dowmunt and Roman Grundkiewicz. 2016. Log-linear combinations of monolingual and bilingual neural machine translation models for automatic post-editing. In *Proceedings of the First Conference on Machine Translation*. Association for Computational Linguistics, Berlin, Germany, pages 751–758.

A-L Lagarda, Vicente Alabau, Francisco Casacuberta, Roberto Silva, and Enrique Diaz-de Liano. 2009. Statistical post-editing of a rule-based machine translation system. In *Proceedings of Human Language Technologies: The 2009 Annual Conference of the North American Chapter of the Association for Computational Linguistics, Companion Volume: Short Papers*. Association for Computational Linguistics, pages 217–220.

Antonio L Lagarda, Daniel Ortiz-Martínez, Vicent Alabau, and Francisco Casacuberta. 2015. Translating without in-domain corpus: Machine translation post-editing with online learning techniques. *Computer Speech & Language* 32(1):109–134.

Jindřich Libovický, Jindřich Helcl, Marek Tlustý, Ondřej Bojar, and Pavel Pecina. 2016. Cuni system for wmt16 automatic post-editing and multimodal translation tasks. In *Proceedings of the First Conference on Machine Translation*. Association for Computational Linguistics, Berlin, Germany, pages 646–654.

Santanu Pal, Sudip Kumar Naskar, Mihaela Vela, Qun Liu, and Josef van Genabith. 2017. Neural automatic post-editing using prior alignment and reranking. In *Proceedings of the 15th Conference of the European Chapter of the Association for Computational Linguistics: Volume 2, Short Papers*. Association for Computational Linguistics, Valencia, Spain, pages 349–355.

Santanu Pal, Sudip Kumar Naskar, Mihaela Vela, and Josef van Genabith. 2016a. A neural network based approach to automatic post-editing. In *Proceedings of the 54th Annual Meeting of the Association for Computational Linguistics (Volume 2: Short Papers)*. Association for Computational Linguistics, Berlin, Germany, pages 281–286.

Santanu Pal, Marcos Zampieri, and Josef van Genabith. 2016b. USAAR: An Operation Sequential Model for Automatic Statistical Post-Editing. In *Proceedings of the 11th Workshop on Statistical Machine Translation (WMT)*.

Kishore Papineni, Salim Roukos, Todd Ward, and Wei-Jing Zhu. 2002. Bleu: a method for automatic evaluation of machine translation. In *Proceedings of the 40th annual meeting on association for computational linguistics*. pages 311–318.

Marion Potet, Laurent Besacier, Hervé Blanchon, and Marwen Azouzi. 2012. Towards a better understanding of statistical post-edition usefulness. In *IWSLT*. pages 284–291.

Rudolf Rosa, David Marecek, and Ales Tamchyna. 2013. Deepfix: Statistical post-editing of statistical machine translation using deep syntactic analysis. In *ACL (Student Research Workshop)*. pages 172–179.

Rico Sennrich, Orhan Firat, Kyunghyun Cho, Alexandra Birch, Barry Haddow, Julian Hitschler, Marcin Junczys-Dowmunt, Samuel Läubli, Antonio Valerio Miceli Barone, Jozef Mokry, and Maria Nadejde. 2017. Nematus: a toolkit for neural machine translation. In *Proceedings of the Software Demonstrations of the 15th Conference of the European Chapter of the Association for Computational Linguistics*. Association for Computational Linguistics, Valencia, Spain, pages 65–68.

Rico Sennrich, Barry Haddow, and Alexandra Birch. 2016a. Edinburgh Neural Machine Translation Systems for WMT 16. In *Proceedings of the First Conference on Machine Translation*. Association for Computational Linguistics, Berlin, Germany, pages 371–376.

Rico Sennrich, Barry Haddow, and Alexandra Birch. 2016b. Neural machine translation of rare words with subword units. In *Proceedings of the 54th Annual Meeting of the Association for Computational Linguistics (Volume 1: Long Papers)*. Association for Computational Linguistics, Berlin, Germany, pages 1715–1725.

Michel Simard, Cyril Goutte, and Pierre Isabelle. 2007. Statistical phrase-based post-editing. In *Human Language Technology Conference of the North American Chapter of the Association of Computational Linguistics, Proceedings, April 22-27, 2007, Rochester, New York, USA*. pages 508–515.

Nitish Srivastava, Geoffrey E Hinton, Alex Krizhevsky, Ilya Sutskever, and Ruslan Salakhutdinov. 2014. Dropout: a simple way to prevent neural networks from overfitting. *Journal of Machine Learning Research* 15(1):1929–1958.

Matthew D Zeiler. 2012. ADADELTA: an adaptive learning rate method. *arXiv preprint arXiv:1212.5701* .

The AMU-UEdin Submission to the WMT 2017 Shared Task on Automatic Post-Editing

Marcin Junczys-Dowmunt
Information Systems Laboratory
Adam Mickiewicz University in Poznań
junczys@amu.edu.pl

Roman Grundkiewicz
School of Informatics
University of Edinburgh
rgrundki@exseed.ed.ac.uk

Abstract

This work describes the AMU-UEdin submission to the WMT 2017 shared task on Automatic Post-Editing. We explore multiple neural architectures adapted for the task of automatic post-editing of machine translation output. We focus on neural end-to-end models that combine both inputs mt and src in a single neural architecture, modeling $\{mt, src\} \rightarrow pe$ directly. Apart from that, we investigate the influence of hard-attention models which seem to be well-suited for monolingual tasks, as well as combinations of both ideas.

1 Introduction

During the WMT 2016 APE two systems relied on neural models, the CUNI system (Libovický et al., 2016) and the shared task winner, the system submitted by the Adam Mickiewicz University (AMU) team (Junczys-Dowmunt and Grundkiewicz, 2016). This submission explored the application of neural translation models to the APE problem and achieved good results by treating different models as components in a log-linear model, allowing for multiple inputs (the source src and the translated sentence mt) that were decoded to the same target language (post-edited translation pe). Two systems were considered, one using src as the input ($src \rightarrow pe$) and another using mt as the input ($mt \rightarrow pe$). A simple string-matching penalty integrated within the log-linear model was used to control for higher faithfulness with regard to the raw MT output. The penalty fires if the APE system proposes a word in its output that has not been seen in mt. The influence of the components on the final result was tuned with Minimum Error Rate Training (Och, 2003) with regard to the task metric TER.

With neural encoder-decoder models, and multi-source models in particular, the combination of mt and src can be now achieved in more natural ways than for previously popular phrase-based statistical machine translation (PB-SMT) systems. Despite this, results for multi-source or double-source models in APE scenarios are incomplete or unsatisfying in terms of performance.

In this work, we explore a number of single-source and double-source neural architectures which we believe to be better fits to the APE task than vanilla encoder-decoder models with soft attention. We focus on neural end-to-end models that combine both inputs mt and src in a single neural architecture, modeling $\{mt, src\} \rightarrow pe$ directly. Apart from that, we investigate the influence of hard-attention models which seem to be well-suited for monolingual tasks. Finally, we create combinations of both architectures.

Following (Junczys-Dowmunt and Grundkiewicz, 2016), we also attempt to generate more artificial data for the task. Instead of relying on filtering towards specific error rates, we generate text with fitting error rates from the start which allows us to retain more data.

2 Encoder-Decoder Models with APE-specific Attention Models

2.1 Standard Attentional Encoder-Decoder

The attentional encoder-decoder model in Marian[1] is a re-implementation of the NMT model in Nematus (Sennrich et al., 2017). The model differs from the standard model introduced by Bahdanau et al. (2014) by several aspects, the most important being the conditional GRU with attention. The summary provided in this section is based on the description in Sennrich et al. (2017). More details on the specific architectures in this shared

---

[1] https://github.com/marian-nmt/marian

Proceedings of the Conference on Machine Translation (WMT), Volume 2: Shared Task Papers, pages 639–646
Copenhagen, Denmark, September 7–11, 2017. ©2017 Association for Computational Linguistics

task submission are given in Junczys-Dowmunt and Grundkiewicz (2017).

Given the raw MT output sequence $(x_1, \ldots, x_{T_x})$ of length T_x and its manually post-edited equivalent $(y_1, \ldots, y_{T_y})$ of length T_y, we construct the encoder-decoder model using the following formulations.

Encoder context A single forward encoder state $\overrightarrow{\mathbf{h}}_i$ is calculated as:

$$\overrightarrow{\mathbf{h}}_i = \text{GRU}(\overrightarrow{\mathbf{h}}_{i-1}, \mathbf{F}[x_i])$$

where $\mathbf{F}$ is the encoder embeddings matrix. The GRU RNN cell (Cho et al., 2014) is defined as:

$$\text{GRU}(\mathbf{s}, \mathbf{x}) = (1 - \mathbf{z}) \odot \underline{\mathbf{s}} + \mathbf{z} \odot \mathbf{s}, \quad (1)$$
$$\underline{\mathbf{s}} = \tanh\left(\mathbf{W}\mathbf{x} + \mathbf{r} \odot \mathbf{U}\mathbf{s}\right),$$
$$\mathbf{r} = \sigma\left(\mathbf{W}_r\mathbf{x} + \mathbf{U}_r\mathbf{s}\right),$$
$$\mathbf{z} = \sigma\left(\mathbf{W}_z\mathbf{x} + \mathbf{U}_z\mathbf{s}\right),$$

where $\mathbf{x}$ is the cell input, s is the previous recurrent state, $\mathbf{W}, \mathbf{U}, \mathbf{W}_r, \mathbf{U}_r, \mathbf{W}_z, \mathbf{U}_z$ are trained model parameters[2]; σ is the logistic sigmoid activation function. The backward encoder state is calculated analogously over a reversed input sequence with its own set of trained parameters.

Let $\mathbf{h}_i$ be the annotation of the source symbol at position i, obtained by concatenating the forward and backward encoder RNN hidden states, $\mathbf{h}_i = [\overrightarrow{\mathbf{h}}_i; \overleftarrow{\mathbf{h}}_i]$, the set of encoder states $\mathbf{C} = \{\mathbf{h}_1, \ldots, \mathbf{h}_{T_x}\}$ then forms the encoder context.

Decoder initialization The decoder is initialized with start state s_0, computed as the average over all encoder states:

$$\mathbf{s}_0 = \tanh\left(\mathbf{W}_{init} \frac{\sum_{i=1}^{T_x} \mathbf{h}_i}{T_x}\right)$$

Conditional GRU with attention We follow the Nematus implementation of the conditional GRU with attention, cGRU$_{\text{att}}$:

$$\mathbf{s}_j = \text{cGRU}_{\text{att}}\left(\mathbf{s}_{j-1}, \mathbf{E}[y_{j-1}], \mathbf{C}\right) \quad (2)$$

where $\mathbf{s}_j$ is the newly computed hidden state, $\mathbf{s}_{j-1}$ is the previous hidden state, C the source context and $\mathbf{E}[y_{j-1}]$ is the embedding of the previously decoded symbol y_{i-1}.

The conditional GRU cell with attention, cGRU$_{\text{att}}$, has a complex internal structure, consisting of three parts: two GRU layers and an intermediate attention mechanism ATT.

---

[2]Biases have been omitted.

Layer GRU$_1$ generates an intermediate representation $\mathbf{s}'_j$ from the previous hidden state $\mathbf{s}_{j-1}$ and the embedding of the previous decoded symbol $\mathbf{E}[y_{j-1}]$:

$$\mathbf{s}'_j = \text{GRU}_1\left(\mathbf{s}_{j-1}, \mathbf{E}[y_{j-1}]\right).$$

The attention mechanism, ATT, inputs the entire context set C along with intermediate hidden state $\mathbf{s}'_j$ in order to compute the context vector $\mathbf{c}_j$ as follows:

$$\mathbf{c}_j = \text{ATT}\left(\mathbf{C}, \mathbf{s}'_j\right) = \sum_i^{T_x} \alpha_{ij} \mathbf{h}_i,$$
$$\alpha_{ij} = \frac{\exp(e_{ij})}{\sum_{k=1}^{T_x} \exp(e_{kj})},$$
$$e_{ij} = \mathbf{v}_a^{\mathsf{T}} \tanh\left(\mathbf{U}_a \mathbf{s}'_j + \mathbf{W}_a \mathbf{h}_i\right),$$

where α_{ij} is the normalized alignment weight between source symbol at position i and target symbol at position j and $\mathbf{v}_a, \mathbf{U}_a, \mathbf{W}_a$ are trained model parameters.

Layer GRU$_2$ generates $\mathbf{s}_j$, the hidden state of the cGRU$_{\text{att}}$, from the intermediate representation $\mathbf{s}'_j$ and context vector $\mathbf{c}_j$:

$$\mathbf{s}_j = \text{GRU}_2\left(\mathbf{s}'_j, \mathbf{c}_j\right).$$

Deep output Finally, given $\mathbf{s}_j$, y_{j-1}, and $\mathbf{c}_j$, the output probability $p(y_j|\mathbf{s}_j, y_{j-1}, \mathbf{c}_j)$ is computed by a softmax activation as follows:

$$p(y_j|\mathbf{s}_j, y_{j-1}, \mathbf{c}_j) = \text{softmax}\left(\mathbf{t}_j \mathbf{W}_o\right)$$
$$\mathbf{t}_j = \tanh\left(\mathbf{s}_j \mathbf{W}_{t_1} + \mathbf{E}[y_{j-1}] \mathbf{W}_{t_2} + \mathbf{c}_j \mathbf{W}_{t_3}\right)$$

$\mathbf{W}_{t_1}, \mathbf{W}_{t_2}, \mathbf{W}_{t_3}, \mathbf{W}_o$ are the trained model parameters.

This rather standard encoder-decoder model with attention is our baseline and denoted as ENCDEC-ATT.

The following models reuse most parts of the architecture described above wherever possible, most differences occur in the decoder RNN cell and the attention mechanism. The encoders are identical, so are the deep output layers.

2.2 Hard Monotonic Attention

Aharoni and Goldberg (2016) introduce a simple model for monolingual morphological reinflection with hard monotonic attention. This model looks at one encoder state at a time, starting with the left-most encoder state and progressing to the right until all encoder states have been processed.

The target word vocabulary V_y is extended with a special step symbol ($V_y' = V_y \cup \{\langle \text{STEP} \rangle\}$) and whenever $\langle \text{STEP} \rangle$ is predicted as the output symbol, the hard attention is moved to the next encoder state. Formally, the hard attention mechanism is represented as a precomputed monotonic sequence $(a_1, \ldots, a_{T_y})$ which can be inferred from the target sequence $(y_1, \ldots, y_{T_y})$ (containing original target symbols and T_x step symbols) as follows:

$$a_1 = 1$$
$$a_j = \begin{cases} a_{j-1} + 1 & \text{if } y_{j-1} = \langle \text{STEP} \rangle \\ a_{j-1} & \text{otherwise.} \end{cases}$$

For a given context $\mathbf{C} = \{\mathbf{h}_1, \ldots, \mathbf{h}_{T_x}\}$, the attended context vector at time step j is simply h_{a_j}.

Following the description by Aharoni and Goldberg (2016) for their LSTM-based model, we now adapt the previously described encoder-decoder model to incorporate hard attention. The encoder as well as the output layer of the previous model remain unchanged. Given the sequence of attention indices $(a_1, \ldots, a_{T_y})$, the conditional GRU cell (Eq. 2) used for hidden state updates of the decoder is replaced with a simple GRU cell (Eq. 1) (thus removing the soft-attention mechanism):

$$\mathbf{s}_j = \text{GRU}\left(\mathbf{s}_{j-1}, \left[\mathbf{E}[y_{j-1}]; \mathbf{h}_{a_j}\right]\right) \qquad (3)$$

where the cell input is now a concatenation of the embedding of the previous target symbol $E[y_{j-1}]$ and the currently attended encoder state $\mathbf{h}_{a_j}$. This model is labeled ENCDEC-HARD.

We find this architecture compelling for monolingual tasks that might require higher faithfulness with regard to the input. With hard monotonic attention, the translation algorithm can enforce certain constraints:

1. The end-of-sentence symbol can only be generated if the hard attention mechanism has reached the end of the input sequence, enforcing full coverage;

2. The $\langle \text{STEP} \rangle$ symbol cannot be generated once the end-of-sentence position in the source has been reached. It is however still possible to generate content tokens.

Obviously, this model requires a target sequence with correctly inserted $\langle \text{STEP} \rangle$ symbols. For the described APE task, using the Longest Common Subsequence algorithm (Hirschberg, 1977), we first generate a sequence of match, delete and insert operations which transform the raw MT output $(x_1, \cdots x_{T_x})$ into the corrected post-edited sequence $(y_1, \cdots y_{T_y})^3$. Next, we map these operations to the final sequence of steps and target tokens according to the following rules:

- For each matched pair of tokens x, y we produce symbols: $\langle \text{STEP} \rangle$ y;

- For each inserted target token y, we produce the same token y;

- For each deleted source token x we produce $\langle \text{STEP} \rangle$;

- Since at initialization of the model $a_1 = 1$, i.e. the first encoder state is already attended to, we discard the first symbol in the new sequence if it is a $\langle \text{STEP} \rangle$ symbol.

2.3 Hard and Soft Attention

While the hard attention model can be used to enforce faithfulness to the original input, we would also like the model to be able to look at information anywhere in the source sequence which is a property of the soft attention model.

By re-introducing the conditional GRU cell with soft attention into the ENCDEC-HARD model while also inputting the hard-attended encoder state h_{a_j}, we can try to take advantage of both attention mechanisms. Combining Eq. 2 and Eq. 3, we get:

$$\mathbf{s}_j = \text{cGRU}_{\text{att}}\left(\mathbf{s}_{j-1}, \left[\mathbf{E}[y_{j-1}]; \mathbf{h}_{a_j}\right], \mathbf{C}\right). \qquad (4)$$

The rest of the model is unchanged; the translation process is the same as before and we use the same target step/token sequence for training. This model is called ENCDEC-HARD-ATT.

2.4 Soft Double-Attention

Neural multi-source models (Zoph and Knight, 2016) seem to be natural fit for the APE task, as raw MT output and original source language input are available. Although application to the APE problem have been reported (Libovický and Helcl, 2017), state-of-the-art results seem to be missing.

In this section we give details about our double-source model implementation. We rename the existing encoder C to $\mathbf{C}^{mt}$ to signal that the first encoder consumes the raw MT output and introduce

---

^{3}Similar to GNU wdiff.

a structurally identical second encoder $C^{src} = \{\mathbf{h}_1^{src}, \ldots, \mathbf{h}_{T_{src}}^{src}\}$ over the source language. To compute the decoder start state s_0 for the multi-encoder model we concatenate the averaged encoder contexts before mapping them into the decoder state space:

$$\mathbf{s}_0 = \tanh\left(\mathbf{W}_{init}\left[\frac{\sum_{i=1}^{T_{mt}} \mathbf{h}_i^{mt}}{T_{mt}}; \frac{\sum_{i=1}^{T_{src}} \mathbf{h}_i^{src}}{T_{src}}\right]\right).$$

In the decoder, we replace the conditional GRU with attention, with a doubly-attentive cGRU cell (Calixto et al., 2017) over contexts $\mathbf{C}^{mt}$ and $\mathbf{C}^{src}$:

$$\mathbf{s}_j = \text{cGRU}_{2\text{-att}}\left(\mathbf{s}_{j-1}, \mathbf{E}[y_{j-1}], \mathbf{C}^{mt}, \mathbf{C}^{src}\right) \quad (5)$$

The procedure is similar to the original cGRU, differing only in that in order to compute the context vector $\mathbf{c}_j$, we first calculate contexts vectors $\mathbf{c}_j^{mt}$ and $\mathbf{c}_j^{src}$ for each context and then concatenate the results:

$$\mathbf{s}_j' = \text{GRU}_1\left(\mathbf{s}_{j-1}, \mathbf{E}[y_{j-1}]\right),$$

$$\mathbf{c}_j^{mt} = \text{ATT}\left(\mathbf{C}^{mt}, \mathbf{s}_j'\right) = \sum_i \alpha_{ij} \mathbf{h}_i^{mt},$$

$$\mathbf{c}_j^{src} = \text{ATT}\left(\mathbf{C}^{src}, \mathbf{s}_j'\right) = \sum_i \alpha_{ij} \mathbf{h}_i^{src},$$

$$\mathbf{c}_j = \left[\mathbf{c}_j^{mt}; \mathbf{c}_j^{src}\right],$$

$$\mathbf{s}_j = \text{GRU}_2\left(\mathbf{s}_j', \mathbf{c}_j\right).$$

This could be easily extended to an arbitrary number of encoders with different architectures. During training this model is fed with a tri-parallel corpus, during translation both input sequences are processed simultaneously to produce the corrected output. This model is denoted as ENCDEC-DOUBLE-ATT.

2.5 Hard Attention with Soft Double-Attention

Analogously to the procedure described in section 2.3, we can extend the doubly-attentive cGRU to take the hard-attended encoder context as additional input:

$$\mathbf{s}_j = \text{cGRU}_{2\text{-att}}\left(\mathbf{s}_{j-1}, \left[\mathbf{E}[y_{j-1}]; \mathbf{h}_{a_j}^{mt}\right], \mathbf{C}^{mt}, \mathbf{C}^{src}\right)$$

In this formulation, only the first encoder context $\mathbf{C}^{mt}$ is attended to by the hard monotonic attention mechanism. The target training data consists of the step/token sequences used for all previous hard-attention models. We call this model ENCDEC-HARD+DOUBLE-ATT.

Data set	Sentences	TER
training set 2016	12,000	26.22
training set 2017	11,000	–
development set 2016	1,000	24.81
test set 2016	2,000	–
artificial-large 2016	4,335,715	36.63
artificial-small 2016	531,839	25.28
artificial 2017	15,158,354	27.45

Table 1: Statistics for artificial data sets in comparison to official training and development data, adapted from Junczys-Dowmunt and Grundkiewicz (2016).

3 Artifical Data

We also attempt to generate more artificial data for the task. Instead of relying on filtering towards specific error rates, we generate text with fitting error rates from the start which allows us to retain more data. To obtain the monolingual source data we follow the steps described by (Junczys-Dowmunt and Grundkiewicz, 2016). Next we train a English-to-German MT system using data from the WMT2016 shared task on IT translation. This system is used to translate it's own training data into German. Although input sentence have been seen, the translations are far from perfect. Next we create an MT system to translate from correct German to imperfect German MT output. This system can now be applied to create raw German MT output from correct German text.

In order to achieve matching TER statistics we use a simple implementation of the Nelder-Mead algorithm for parameter tuning. For unknown reasons, MERT or kb-Mira would not create output with the desired error-rates.

Using this system we create a new large set of pseudo-PE data, translating domain-selected monolingual data from German into German pseudo-MT output. The English input is created with an German-to-English phrase-based MT system. We translate about 15 million sentences in this manner, creating new artificial APE triplets.

4 Experiments and Results

4.1 Training, Development, and Test Data

We perform all our experiments with the official WMT16 (Bojar et al., 2016) automatic post-

Model	dev 2016		test 2016		test 2017	
	TER↓	BLEU↑	**TER**↓	BLEU↑	**TER**↓	BLEU↑
WMT17-baseline 1	–	–	–	–	24.48	62.49
WMT17-baseline 2	–	–	–	–	24.69	62.97
Constrastive	19.74	70.61	19.30	70.34	19.83	69.38
Primary	–	–	19.21	70.51	19.77	69.50

Table 2: Submitted system results

editing data and the respective development and test sets. The training data consists of a small set of 23,000 post-editing triplets (src, mt, pe), where src is the original English text, mt is the raw MT output generated by an English-to-German system, and pe is the human post-edited MT output. The MT system used to produce the raw MT output is unknown, so is the original training data. The task consist of automatically correcting the MT output so that it resembles human post-edited data. The main task metric is TER (Snover et al., 2006) – the lower the better – with BLEU (Papineni et al., 2002) as a secondary metric.

Table 1 summarizes the data sets used in this work. To produce our final training data set we oversample the original training data 20 times and add all three artificial data sets (they may overlap). This results in a total of slightly more than 21M training triplets. We keep the development set as a validation set for early stopping and report results on the WMT16 test set. The data is already tokenized, additionally we truecase all files and apply segmentation into BPE subword units. We reuse the subword units distributed with the artificial data set. For the hard-attention models, we create new target training and development files following the procedure from section 2.2.

4.2 Training parameters

All models are trained on the same training data. Models with single input encoders take only the raw MT output (mt) as input, double-encoder models use raw MT output (mt) and the original source (pe). The training procedures and model settings are the same whenever possible:

- All embedding vectors consist of 512 units, the RNN states use 1024 units. We choose a vocabulary size of 40,000 for all inputs and outputs. When hard attention models are trained the maximum sentence length is 100

to accommodate the additional step symbols, otherwise 50.

- To avoid overfitting, we use pervasive dropout (Gal, 2015) over GRU steps and input embeddings, with dropout probabilities 0.2, and over source and target words with probabilities 0.2.

- We use Adam (Kingma and Ba, 2014) as our optimizer, with a mini-batch size of 64. All models are trained with Asynchronous SGD (Adam) on three to four GPUs.

- We train all models until convergence (early-stopping with a patience of 10 based on dev-set cross-entropy cost), saving model checkpoints every 10,000 mini-batches.

- The best eight model checkpoints w.r.t. dev-set cross-entropy of each training run are averaged element-wise (Junczys-Dowmunt et al., 2016) resulting in new single models with generally improved performance.

- For the multi-source models we repeat the mentioned procedure four times with different randomly initialized weights and random seeds to later form model ensembles.

Training time for one model on four NVIDIA GTX 1080 GPUs or NVIDIA TITAN X (Pascal) GPUs is between two and three days, depending on model complexity.

4.3 Submitted System

We chose an ensemble of four ENCDEC-HARD+DOUBLE-ATT systems (four distinct training runs with different random weights initializations) as our final system. In Table 2, this system is marked as CONSTRASTIVE. We also noticed that providing the system output once more as system input to the same system results in a small im-

Model	dev 2016		test 2016	
	TER↓	BLEU↑	**TER**↓	BLEU↑
WMT16-baseline 1 (Bojar et al., 2016)	25.14	62.92	24.76	62.11
WMT16-baseline 2 (Bojar et al., 2016)	–	–	24.64	63.47
Junczys-Dowmunt and Grundkiewicz (2016)	21.46	68.94	21.52	67.65
Pal et al. (2017) SYMMETRIC	–	–	21.07	67.87
Pal et al. (2017) RERANKING	–	–	20.70	**69.90**

Table 3: Results from the literature for the WMT 2016 APE development and test set

Model	dev 2016		test 2016	
	TER↓	BLEU↑	**TER**↓	BLEU↑
ENCDEC-ATT	22.01	68.11	22.27	66.90
ENCDEC-HARD	22.72	66.82	22.72	65.86
ENCDEC-HARD+ATT	22.11	67.82	22.10	67.15
ENCDEC-DOUBLE-ATT	20.79	69.28	20.69	68.56
ENCDEC-DOUBLE-ATT × 4	20.10	**70.24**	**19.92**	69.40
ENCDEC-HARD+DOUBLE-ATT	20.83	69.02	20.87	68.14
ENCDEC-HARD+DOUBLE-ATT × 4	**20.08**	70.05	20.34	68.96

Table 4: Post-submission results, the main task metric is TER (the lower the better)

provement. This one-time looped system is our primary submission PRIMARY.

5 Post-submission analysis

This section is based on the work in Junczys-Dowmunt and Grundkiewicz (2017). After the submission we performed a number of in-depth experiments to verify our intuitions about the selected models for a better controlled data setting. We restricted all training, development data to data available during the WMT 2016 shared task on APE and test on test set 2016. We also only used artificial data made available by Junczys-Dowmunt and Grundkiewicz (2016), dicarding the newly created data in this work. To produce our final training data set we oversample the original training data 20 times and add the artificial data sets. This results in a total of slightly more than 5M training triplets. For the hard-attention models, we create new target training and development files following the LCS-based procedure outlined in section 2.2.

Table 3 contains a selection of most relevant results for the WMT16 APE shared task – during the task and afterwards. WMT 2016-baseline 1 is the raw uncorrected mt output, baseline 2 is the results of a vanilla phrase-based Moses system (Koehn et al., 2007) trained only on the official 12,000 sentences. Junczys-Dowmunt and Grundkiewicz (2016) is the best system at the shared task. Pal et al. (2017) SYMMETRIC is the currently best reported result on the WMT16 APE test set for a single neural model (single source), whereas Pal et al. (2017) RERANKING – the overall best reported result on the test set – is a system combination of Pal et al. (2017) SYMMETRIC with phrase-based models via n-best list re-ranking.

In Table 4 we present the results for the models discussed in this work. The double-attention models outperform the best WMT16 system and the currently reported best single-model Pal et al. (2017) SYMMETRIC. The ensembles also beat the system combination Pal et al. (2017) RERANK-ING in terms of TER (not in terms of BLEU though). The simpler double-attention model with no hard-attention ENCDEC-DOUBLE-ATT reaches slightly better results on the test set than its counterpart with added hard attention ENCDEC-HARD+DOUBLE-ATT, but the situation would have been less clear if only the dev set were used to choose the best model.

Acknowledgments

This research was funded by the Amazon Academic Research Awards program.

References

Roee Aharoni and Yoav Goldberg. 2016. Sequence to sequence transduction with hard monotonic attention. *arXiv preprint arXiv:1611.01487* .

Dzmitry Bahdanau, Kyunghyun Cho, and Yoshua Bengio. 2014. Neural machine translation by jointly learning to align and translate. *CoRR* abs/1409.0473. http://arxiv.org/abs/1409.0473.

Ondřej Bojar, Rajen Chatterjee, Christian Federmann, Yvette Graham, Barry Haddow, Matthias Huck, Antonio Jimeno Yepes, Philipp Koehn, Varvara Logacheva, Christof Monz, Matteo Negri, Aurelie Neveol, Mariana Neves, Martin Popel, Matt Post, Raphael Rubino, Carolina Scarton, Lucia Specia, Marco Turchi, Karin Verspoor, and Marcos Zampieri. 2016. Findings of the 2016 conference on machine translation. In *Proceedings of the First Conference on Machine Translation*. Association for Computational Linguistics, Berlin, Germany, pages 131–198. http://www.aclweb.org/anthology/W/W16/W16-2301.

Iacer Calixto, Qun Liu, and Nick Campbell. 2017. Doubly-attentive decoder for multi-modal neural machine translation. *CoRR* abs/1702.01287. http://arxiv.org/abs/1702.01287.

Kyunghyun Cho, Bart Van Merriënboer, Caglar Gulcehre, Dzmitry Bahdanau, Fethi Bougares, Holger Schwenk, and Yoshua Bengio. 2014. Learning Phrase Representations Using RNN Encoder-Decoder for Statistical Machine Translation. In *Proc. of Empirical Methods in Natural Language Processing*.

Yarin Gal. 2015. A Theoretically Grounded Application of Dropout in Recurrent Neural Networks. *ArXiv e-prints* .

Daniel S. Hirschberg. 1977. Algorithms for the longest common subsequence problem. *J. ACM* 24(4):664–675. https://doi.org/10.1145/322033.322044.

Marcin Junczys-Dowmunt, Tomasz Dwojak, and Hieu Hoang. 2016. Is neural machine translation ready for deployment? A case study on 30 translation directions. *arXiv preprint arXiv:1610.01108* http://arxiv.org/abs/1610.01108.

Marcin Junczys-Dowmunt and Roman Grundkiewicz. 2016. Log-linear combinations of monolingual and bilingual neural machine translation models for automatic post-editing. In *Proceedings of the First Conference on Machine Translation*. pages 751–758.

Marcin Junczys-Dowmunt and Roman Grundkiewicz. 2017. An exploration of neural sequence-to-sequence architectures for automatic post-editing. *CoRR* abs/1706.04138. https://arxiv.org/abs/1706.04138.

Diederik P. Kingma and Jimmy Ba. 2014. Adam: A method for stochastic optimization. *arXiv preprint arXiv:1412.6980* http://arxiv.org/abs/1412.6980.

Philipp Koehn, Hieu Hoang, Alexandra Birch, Chris Callison-Burch, Marcello Federico, Nicola Bertoldi, Brooke Cowan, Wade Shen, Christine Moran, Richard Zens, et al. 2007. Moses: Open source toolkit for statistical machine translation. In *Proceedings of the 45th Annual Meeting of the Association for Computational Linguistics*. Association for Computational Linguistics, pages 177–180.

Jindrich Libovický and Jindrich Helcl. 2017. Attention strategies for multi-source sequence-to-sequence learning. *CoRR* abs/1704.06567. http://arxiv.org/abs/1704.06567.

Jindřich Libovický, Jindřich Helcl, Marek Tlustý, Ondřej Bojar, and Pavel Pecina. 2016. CUNI system for WMT16 automatic post-editing and multimodal translation tasks. In *Proceedings of the First Conference on Machine Translation*. Association for Computational Linguistics, Berlin, Germany, pages 646–654. http://www.aclweb.org/anthology/W/W16/W16-2361.

Franz Josef Och. 2003. Minimum error rate training in statistical machine translation. In *Proc. of the Annual Meeting on Association for Computational Linguistics*. pages 160–167.

Santanu Pal, Sudip Kumar Naskar, Mihaela Vela, Qun Liu, and Josef van Genabith. 2017. Neural automatic post-editing using prior alignment and reranking. In *Proceedings of the European Chapter of the Association for Computational Linguistics*. pages 349–355.

Kishore Papineni, Salim Roukos, Todd Ward, and Wei-Jing Zhu. 2002. BLEU: A method for automatic evaluation of machine translation. In *Proceedings of the 40th Annual Meeting on Association for Computational Linguistics*. Association for Computational Linguistics, Stroudsburg, PA, USA, ACL '02, pages 311–318. https://doi.org/10.3115/1073083.1073135.

Rico Sennrich, Orhan Firat, Kyunghyun Cho, Alexandra Birch, Barry Haddow, Julian Hitschler, Marcin Junczys-Dowmunt, Samuel Läubli, Antonio Valerio Miceli Barone, Jozef Mokry, and Maria Nadejde. 2017. Nematus: a toolkit for neural machine translation. In *Proceedings of the Software Demonstrations of the 15th Conference of the European Chapter of the Association for Computational Linguistics*. Association for Computational Linguistics, Valencia, Spain, pages 65–68. http://aclweb.org/anthology/E17-3017.

Matthew Snover, Bonnie Dorr, Richard Schwartz, Linnea Micciulla, and John Makhoul. 2006. A Study of Translation Edit Rate with Targeted Human Annotation. In *Proceedings of Association for Machine Translation in the Americas,*.

Barret Zoph and Kevin Knight. 2016. Multisource neural translation. *CoRR* abs/1601.00710. http://arxiv.org/abs/1601.00710.

Ensembling Factored Neural Machine Translation Models for Automatic Post-Editing and Quality Estimation

Chris Hokamp
ADAPT Centre
Dublin City University
`chokamp@computing.dcu.ie`

Abstract

This work presents a novel approach to Automatic Post-Editing (APE) and Word-Level Quality Estimation (QE) using ensembles of specialized Neural Machine Translation (NMT) systems. Word-level features that have proven effective for QE are included as input factors, expanding the representation of the original source and the machine translation hypothesis, which are used to generate an automatically post-edited hypothesis. We train a suite of NMT models that use different input representations, but share the same output space. These models are then ensembled together, and tuned for both the APE and the QE task. We thus attempt to connect the state-of-the-art approaches to APE and QE within a single framework. Our models achieve state-of-the-art results in both tasks, with the only difference in the tuning step which learns weights for each component of the ensemble.

1 Introduction

Translation destined for human consumption often must pass through multiple editing stages. In one common scenario, human translators correct machine translation (MT) output, correcting errors and omissions until a perfect translation has been produced. Several studies has shown that this process, referred to as "post-editing", is faster than translation from scratch (Specia, 2011), or interactive machine translation (Green et al., 2013).

A relatively recent line of research has tried to build models which correct errors in MT automatically (Simard et al., 2007; Bojar et al., 2015; Junczys-Dowmunt and Grundkiewicz, 2016). Automatic Post-Editing (APE) typically views the system that produced the original translation as a black box, which cannot be modified or inspected. An APE system has access to the same data that a human translator would see: a source sentence and a translation hypothesis. The job of the system is to output a corrected hypothesis, attempting to fix errors made by the original translation system. This can be viewed as a sequence-to-sequence task (Sutskever et al., 2014), and is also similar to multi-source machine translation (Zoph and Knight, 2016; Firat et al., 2016). However, APE intuitively tries to make the minimum number of edits required to transform the hypothesis into a satisfactory translation, because we would like our system to mimic human translators in attempting to minimize the time spent correcting each MT output. This additional constraint on APE models differentiates the task from multi-source MT.

The Word Level QE task is ostensibly a simpler version of APE, where a system must only decide whether or not each word in an MT hypothesis belongs in the post-edited version – it is not necessary to propose a fix for errors. Most recent work has considered word-level QE to be a sequence labeling task, and employed the standard tools of structured prediction to solve it, i.e. structured predictors such as CRFs or structured SVMs, which take advantage of sparse representations and very large feature sets, as well as dependencies between labels in the output sequence (Logacheva et al., 2016; Martins et al., 2016). However, Martins et al. (2017) recently proposed a new method of word-level QE using APE, which simply uses an APE system to produce a "pseudo-post-edit" given a source sentence and an MT hypothesis. Their approach, which we call **APE-QE**, is the basis of the work presented here. In APE-QE, the original MT hypothesis is then aligned with the pseudo-post-edit from the APE system using word level edit-

Proceedings of the Conference on Machine Translation (WMT), Volume 2: Shared Task Papers, pages 647–654
Copenhagen, Denmark, September 7–11, 2017. ©2017 Association for Computational Linguistics

distance, and words which correspond to *Insert* or *Delete* operations are labeled as incorrect. Note that this also corresponds exactly to the way QE datasets are currently created, with the only difference being that human post-edits are typically used to create gold-standard data (Bojar et al., 2015).

A key similarity between the QE and APE tasks is that both use information from two sequences: (1) the original source input, and (2) an MT hypothesis. Martins et al. (2017), showed that APE systems with no knowledge about the QE task already provide a very strong baseline for QE. Because the essential training data for the APE and QE tasks is identical, consisting of parallel triples of (SRC, MT, PE), it is also natural to consider these tasks as two subtasks that make use of a single underlying model.

In this work, we explicitly design ensembles of NMT models for both word-level QE, and APE. This approach builds upon the approach presented in Martins et al. (2017), by incorporating features which have proven effective for Word Level QE as "factors" in the input to Neural Machine Translation (NMT) systems. We achieve state-of-the-art results in both Automatic Post-Editing and Word-Level Quality Estimation, matching the performance of much more complex QE systems, and significantly outperforming the current state-of-the-art in APE.

The main contributions of this work are:

- Novel Input Representations for Neural APE models

- New tuned ensembles for APE-QE

- An open-source decoder supporting ensembles of models with different inputs[1]

The following sections discuss our approach to creating hybrid models for APE-QE, which should be able to solve both tasks with minimal modification.

2   Related Work

Two important lines of research have recently made breakthroughs in QE and APE.

2.1   Automatic Post-Editing

APE and QE training datasets consist of (SRC, MT, PE) triples, where the post-edited reference is created by a human translator in the workflow described above. However, publicly available APE datasets are relatively small in comparison to parallel datasets used to train machine translation systems. Junczys-Dowmunt and Grundkiewicz (2016) introduce a method for generating a large synthetic training dataset from a parallel corpus of (SRC, REF) by first translating the reference to the source language, and then translating this "pseudo-source" back into the target language, resulting in a "pseudo-hypothesis" which is likely to be more similar to the reference than a direct translation from source to target. The release of this synthetic training data was a major contribution towards improving APE.

Junczys-Dowmunt and Grundkiewicz (2016) also present a framework for ensembling SRC $\rightarrow$ PE and SRC $\rightarrow$ PE NMT models together, and tuning for APE performance. Our work extends this idea with several new input representations, which are inspired by the goal of solving both QE and APE with the same model.

2.2   Quality Estimation

Martins et al. (2016) introduced a stacked architecture, using a very large feature set within a structured prediction framework to achieve a large jump in the state of the art for Word-Level QE. Some features are actually the outputs of standalone feedforward and recurrent neural network models, which are then stacked into the final system. Although their approach creates a very good final model, the training and feature extraction steps are quite complicated. An additional disadvantage of this approach is that it requires "jackknifing" the training data for the standalone models that provide features to the stacked model, in order to avoid overfitting in the stacked ensemble. This requires training k versions of each model type, where k is the number of jackknife splits.

Our approach is most similar to Martins et al. (2017), the major differences are: we do not use any internal features from the original MT system, and we do not need to "jackknife" in order to create a stacked ensemble. Using only NMT with attention, we are able to surpass the state-of-the-art in APE and match it in QE.

---

[1] code avaiable at https://github.com/chrishokamp/constrained_decoding

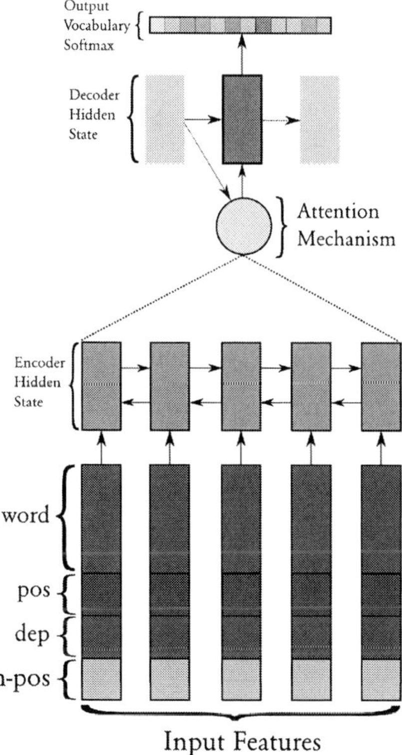

Figure 1: Schematic of the architecture of our factored NMT systems

2.3 Factored Inputs

Alexandrescu and Kirchoff (2006) introduced linguistic factors for neural language models. The core idea is to learn embeddings for linguistic features such as part-of-speech (POS) tags and dependency labels, augmenting the word embeddings of the input with additional features. Recent work has shown that NMT performance can also be improved by concatenating embeddings for additional word-level "factors" to source-word input embeddings (Sennrich and Haddow, 2016). The input representation e_j for each source input x_j with factors F thus becomes Eq. 1:

$$e_j = \prod_{k=1}^{|F|} \mathbf{E}_k x_{jk} \qquad (1)$$

where $||$ indicates vector concatenation, $\mathbf{E}_k$ is the embedding matrix of factor k, and x_{jk} is a one hot vector for the k-th input factor.

3 Models

In this section we describe the five model types used for APE-QE, as well as the ensembles of these models which turn out to be the best-performing overall. We design several features to be included as inputs to APE. The operating hypothesis is that that features which haven proven useful for Quality Estimation should also have a positive impact upon APE performance.

Our baseline models are the same models used in Junczys-Dowmunt (2016)[2]. The authors provide trained $SRC \rightarrow PE$ and $MT \rightarrow PE$ models, which correspond to the last four checkpoints from fine-tuning the models on the *500K* training data concatenated with the task internal APE data upsampled 20 times. These models are referred to as **SRC** and **MT**.

3.1 Word Alignments

Previous work has shown that alignment information between source and target is a critical component of current state-of-the-art word level QE systems (Kreutzer et al., 2015; Martins et al., 2016). The sequential inputs for structured prediction, as well as the feedforward and recurrent models in existing work obtain the source-side features for each target word using the word-alignments provided by the WMT task organizers. However, this information is not likely to be available in many real-world usecases for Quality Estimation, and the use of this information also means that the MT system used to produce the hypotheses is not actually a "black box", which is part of the definition of the QE task. Clearly, access to the word-alignment information of an SMT system provides a lot of in sight into the underlying model.

Because our models rely upon synthetic training data, and because we wish to view the MT system as a true black-box, we instead use the **SRC** NMT system to obtain these alignments. The attention model for NMT produces a normalized vector of weights at each timestep, where the weights can be viewed as the "alignment probabilities" for each source word (Bahdanau et al., 2014). In order to obtain the input representation shown in table 3, we use the source word with the highest weight from the attention model as an additional factor in the input to another MT-aligned $\rightarrow$ PE system.

---

[2]These models have been made available by the authors at `https://amunmt.github.io/examples/postedit/`

649

WMT 2016 Dev

Model Input	BLEU	TER ↓	F1-Mult	Accuracy
WMT 16 Best	68.94	.215	.493	–
Martins et al (2017)	–	–	**.568**	–
SRC	55.47	.315	.506	.803
MT	66.66	.232	.328	.834
MT-aligned	68.32	.215	.437	.852
SRC+MT	69.17	.211	.477	.857
SRC+MT-factor	69.75	.209	.484	.859
Avg-All Baseline	71.02	.199	.476	.862
Avg-All APE-Tune	**71.22**	**.197**	.510	**.866**
Avg-All QE-Tune	66.92	.228	.554	.857
4-SRC+Avg-All QE-Tune	67.16	.225	.567	.860

WMT 2016 Test

Model Input	BLEU	TER ↓	F1-Mult	Accuracy
WMT Baseline	62.11	.248	.324	–
WMT 16 Best	67.65	.215	.493	–
Martins et al (2017)	67.62	.211	**.575**	–
SRC	55.58	.304	.519	.809
MT	65.85	.234	.347	.837
MT-aligned	67.69	.216	.447	.854
SRC+MT	68.03	.212	.477	.857
SRC+MT-factor	68.28	.211	.473	.857
Avg-All Baseline	**70.05**	.198	.492	.865
Avg-All APE-Tuned	70.04	**.196**	.516	**.868**
Avg-All QE-Tuned	66.93	.219	.573	.864
4-SRC+Avg-All QE-Tune	66.94	.219	**.575**	.865

Table 1: Results for all models and ensembles on WMT 16 development and test datasets

The **MT-aligned** → PE system thus depends upon the **SRC** → PE system to produce the additional alignment factor.

3.2 Inputting Both Source and Target

Following Crego et al. (2016), we train a model which takes the concatenated source and MT as input. The two sequences are separated by a special *BREAK* token. We refer to this system as **SRC+MT**.

3.3 Part-of-Speech and Dependency Labels

Sennrich and Haddow (2016) showed that information such as POS tags, NER labels, and syntactic roles can be included in the input to NMT models, generally improving performance. Inspired by this idea, we select some of the top performing features from Martins et al. (Martins et al., 2016), and include them as input factors to the **SRC+MT-factor** model. The base representation is the concatenated SRC+MT (again with a special *BREAK* token). For each word in the English source and the German hypothesis, we obtain the part-of-speech tag, the dependency relation, and the part-of-speech of the head word, and include these as input factors. For both English and German, we use spaCy[3] to extract these features for all training, development, and test data. The resulting model is illustrated in figure 1.

3.4 Extending Factors to Subword Encoding

Our NMT models use subword encoding (Sennrich et al., 2016), but the additional factors are computed at the word level. Therefore, the factors must also be segmented to match the BPE segmentation. We use the {BILOU}- prefixes common in sequence-labeling tasks such as NER to extend

[3]https://spacy.io/

factor vocabularies and map each word-level factor to the subword segmentation of the source or target text.

Table 3 shows the input representations for each of the model types using an example from the WMT 2016 test data.

3.5 Ensembling NMT Models

We average the parameters of the four best checkpoints of each model type, and create an ensemble of the resulting five models, called **Avg-All Baseline**. We then tune this ensemble for TER (APE) and F1-Mult (QE), using MERT (Och, 2003). The tuned models are called **Avg-All APE-Tuned** and **Avg-All QE-Tuned**, respectively. After observing that source-only models have the best single-model QE performance (see section 5), we created a final F1-Mult tuned ensemble, consisting of the four individual **SRC** models, and the averaged models from each other type (an ensemble of eight models total), called **4-SRC+Avg-All QE-Tune**.

3.6 Tuning

Table 2 shows the final weights for each ensemble type after tuning. In line with the two-model ensemble presented in Martins et al. (2017), tuning models for F1-Mult results in much more weight being allocated to the SRC model, while TER tuning favors models with access to the MT hypothesis.

	APE (TER)	QE (F1-Mult)
SRC	.162	.228
MT	.003	-.183
MT-aligned	.203	.229
SRC+MT	.222	.231
SRC+MT-factor	.410	.129

Table 2: Final weights for each model type after 10 iterations of MERT for tuning objectives TER and F1-Mult.

4 Experiments

All of our models are trained using Nematus (Sennrich et al., 2017). At inference time we use our own decoder, which supports weighted log-linear ensembles of Nematus models[4]. Following Junczys-Dowmunt and Grundkiewicz (2016), we

first train each model type on the large (4M) synthetic training data, then fine tune using the 500K dataset, concatenated with the task-internal training data upsampled 20x. Finally, for **SRC+MT** and **SRC+MT-factor** we continued fine-tuning each model for a small number of iterations using the min-risk training implementation available in Nematus (Shen et al., 2016). Table 4 shows the best dev result after each stage of training.

For both APE and QE, we use only the task-specific training data provided for the WMT 2017 APE task, including the extra synthetic training data[5]. However, note that the SpaCy models used to extract features for the factored models are trained with external data – we only use the off-the-shelf models provided by the SpaCy developers.

To convert the output sequence from an APE system into OK, BAD labels for QE, we use the APE hypothesis as a "pseudo-reference", which is then aligned with the original MT hypothesis using TER (Snover et al., 2006).

5 Results

Table 1 shows the results of our experiments using the WMT 16 development and test sets. For each system, we measure performance on BLEU and TER, which are the metrics used in APE task, and also on F1-Mult, which is the primary metric used for the Word Level QE task. Overall tagging accuracy is included as a secondary metric for QE.

All systems with input factors significantly improve APE performance over the baselines. For QE, the trends are less clear, but point to a key difference between optimizing for TER vs. F1_product: F1_product optimization probably lowers the threshold for "changing" a word, as opposed to copying it from the MT hypothesis. This hypothesis is supported by the observation that the source-only APE system outperforms all other single models on the QE metrics. Because the source-only systems cannot resort to copying words from the input, they are forced to make the best guess about the final output, and words which are more likely to be wrong are less likely to be present in the output. If input factors were used with a source-only APE system, the performance on word-level QE could likely be further improved. However, this hypothesis needs more

---

[4]https://github.com/chrishokamp/
constrained_decoding

[5]http://www.statmt.org/wmt17/ape-task.
html

SRC	auto vector masks apply predefined patterns as vector masks to bitmap and vector objects .
MT	automatische Vektor- masken vordefinierten Mustern wie Vektor- masken , Bitmaps und Vektor- objekte anwenden .
MT-aligned	automatische|auto Vektor-|vector masken|masks vordefinierten|apply Mustern|patterns wie|as Vektor-|vector masken|masks ,|to Bitmaps|to und|and Vektor-|vector objekte|objects anwenden|apply .|.
SRC+MT	auto vector masks apply predefined patterns as vector masks to bitmap and vector objects . BREAK automatische Vektor- masken vordefinierten Mustern wie Vektor- masken , Bitmaps und Vektor- objekte anwenden .
SRC+MT Factored	Auto|JJ|amod|NNS vector|NN|compound|NNS masks|NNS|nsubj|VBP apply|VBP|ROOT|VBP predefined|VBN|amod|NNS patterns|NNS|dobj|VBP as|IN|prep|NNS vector|NN|compound|NNS masks|NNS|pobj|IN to|TO|aux|VB bitmap|VB|relcl|NNS and|CC|cc|VB vector|NN|compound|NNS objects|NNS|conj|VB .|.|punct|VBP BREAK|BREAK|BREAK|BREAK Automatische|ADJA|nk|NN Vektor-|B-NN|B-sb|B-VVINF masken|I-NN|I-sb|I-VVINF vordefinierten|ADJA|nk|NN Mustern|NN|pd|NN wie|KOKOM|cd|NN Vektor-|B-NN|B-cj|B-KOKOM masken|I-NN|I-cj|I-KOKOM ,|\$,|punct|NN Bitmaps|NN|cj|NN und|KON|cd|NN Vektor-|B-NN|B-cj|B-KON objekte|I-NN|I-cj|I-KON anwenden|VVINF|ROOT|VVINF .|\$.|punct|VVINF
PE (Reference)	Automatische Vektormasken wenden vordefinierte Mustern als Vektormasken auf Bitmap- und Vektorobjekte an .
Gold Tags	OK OK BAD OK BAD OK BAD BAD OK OK BAD OK

Table 3: Examples of the input for the five model types used in the APE and QE ensembles. The pipe symbol '|' separates each factor. '-' followed by whitespace indicates segmentation according to the subword encoding.

Model	General	Fine-tune	Min-Risk
MT-aligned	60.31	67.54	–
SRC+MT	59.52	68.68	69.44
SRC+MT-factor	57.59	68.26	69.76

Table 4: Best BLEU score on dev set after each of the training stages. *General* is training with 4M instances, *Fine-tune* is training with 500K + upsampled in-domain data, *Min-Risk* uses the same dataset as *Fine-tune*, but uses a minimum-risk loss with BLEU score as the target metric.

analysis and experimentation to confirm.

6 Conclusion

This work has presented APE-QE, unifying models for APE and word-level QE by leveraging the flexibility of NMT to take advantage of informative features from QE. Models with different input representations are ensembled together and tuned for either APE or QE, achieving state of the art performance in both tasks. The complementary nature of these tasks points to future avenues of exploration, such as joint training using both QE labels and reference translations, as well as the incorporation of other features as input factors.

Acknowledgments

This project has received funding from Science Foundation Ireland in the ADAPT Centre for Digital Content Technology (www.adaptcentre.ie) at Dublin City University funded under the SFI Research Centres Programme (Grant 13/RC/2106) co-funded under the European Regional Development Fund and the European Union Horizon 2020 research and innovation programme under grant agreement 645452 (QT21). Marcin Junczys-Dowmunt provided essential guidance on the tuning implementation for APE and QE ensembles.

References

Andrei Alexandrescu and Katrin Kirchhoff. 2006. Factored neural language models. In *Proceedings of the Human Language Technology Conference of the NAACL, Companion Volume: Short Papers*. Association for Computational Linguistics, Stroudsburg, PA, USA, NAACL-Short '06, pages 1–4. http://dl.acm.org/citation.cfm?id=1614049.1614050.

Dzmitry Bahdanau, Kyunghyun Cho, and Yoshua Bengio. 2014. Neural machine translation by jointly learning to align and translate. *arXiv preprint arXiv:1409.0473* .

Ondřej Bojar, Rajen Chatterjee, Christian Federmann, Barry Haddow, Matthias Huck, Chris Hokamp, Philipp Koehn, Varvara Logacheva, Christof Monz, Matteo Negri, Matt Post, Carolina Scarton, Lucia Specia, and Marco Turchi. 2015. Findings of the 2015 workshop on statistical machine translation. In *Proceedings of the Tenth Workshop on Statistical Machine Translation*. Association for Computational Linguistics, Lisbon, Portugal, pages 1–46. http://aclweb.org/anthology/W15-3001.

Josep Crego, Jungi Kim, Guillaume Klein, Anabel Rebollo, Kathy Yang, Jean Senellart, Egor Akhanov, Patrice Brunelle, Aurelien Coquard, Yongchao Deng, et al. 2016. Systran's pure neural machine translation systems. *arXiv preprint arXiv:1610.05540* .

Orhan Firat, Kyunghyun Cho, and Yoshua Bengio. 2016. Multi-way, multilingual neural machine translation with a shared attention mechanism. In Kevin Knight, Ani Nenkova, and Owen Rambow, editors, *HLT-NAACL*. The Association for Computational Linguistics, pages 866–875.

Spence Green, Jeffrey Heer, and Christopher D. Manning. 2013. The efficacy of human post-editing for language translation. In *Proceedings of the SIGCHI Conference on Human Factors in Computing Systems*. ACM, New York, NY, USA, CHI '13, pages 439–448. https://doi.org/10.1145/2470654.2470718.

Marcin Junczys-Dowmunt and Roman Grundkiewicz. 2016. Log-linear combinations of monolingual and bilingual neural machine translation models for automatic post-editing. In *Proceedings of the First Conference on Machine Translation*. Association for Computational Linguistics, Berlin, Germany, pages 751–758. http://www.aclweb.org/anthology/W16-2378.

Julia Kreutzer, Shigehiko Schamoni, and Stefan Riezler. 2015. Quality estimation from scratch (quetch): Deep learning for word-level translation quality estimation. In *Proceedings of the Tenth Workshop on Statistical Machine Translation*. Association for Computational Linguistics, Lisbon, Portugal, pages 316–322. http://aclweb.org/anthology/W15-3037.

Varvara Logacheva, Chris Hokamp, and Lucia Specia. 2016. MARMOT: A toolkit for translation quality estimation at the word level. In *Proceedings of the Tenth International Conference on Language Resources and Evaluation LREC 2016, Portorož, Slovenia, May 23-28, 2016* http://www.lrec-conf.org/proceedings/lrec2016/summaries/1054.html.

André F. T. Martins, Ramón Astudillo, Chris Hokamp, and Fabio Kepler. 2016. Unbabel's participation in the wmt16 word-level translation quality estimation shared task. In *Proceedings of the First Conference on Machine Translation*. Association for Computational Linguistics, Berlin, Germany, pages 806–811. http://www.aclweb.org/anthology/W16/W16-2387.

André FT Martins, Marcin Junczys-Dowmunt, Fabio N Kepler, Ramón Astudillo, and Chris Hokamp. 2017. Pushing the limits of translation quality estimation .

Franz Josef Och. 2003. Minimum error rate training in statistical machine translation. In *Proc. of the Annual Meeting on Association for Computational Linguistics*. pages 160–167.

Rico Sennrich, Orhan Firat, Kyunghyun Cho, Alexandra Birch, Barry Haddow, Julian Hitschler, Marcin Junczys-Dowmunt, Samuel Läubli, Antonio Valerio Miceli Barone, Jozef Mokry, and Maria Nadejde. 2017. Nematus: a toolkit for neural machine translation. In *Proceedings of the Software Demonstrations of the 15th Conference of the European Chapter of the Association for Computational Linguistics*. Association for Computational Linguistics, Valencia, Spain, pages 65–68. http://aclweb.org/anthology/E17-3017.

Rico Sennrich and Barry Haddow. 2016. Linguistic input features improve neural machine translation. In *Proceedings of the First Conference on Machine Translation, WMT 2016, colocated with ACL 2016, August 11-12, Berlin, Germany*. The Association for Computer Linguistics, pages 83–91. http://aclweb.org/anthology/W/W16/W16-2209.pdf.

Rico Sennrich, Barry Haddow, and Alexandra Birch. 2016. Neural machine translation of rare words with subword units. In *Proceedings of the 54th Annual Meeting of the Association for Computational Linguistics, ACL 2016, August 7-12, 2016, Berlin, Germany, Volume 1: Long Papers*. http://aclweb.org/anthology/P/P16/P16-1162.pdf.

Shiqi Shen, Yong Cheng, Zhongjun He, Wei He, Hua Wu, Maosong Sun, and Yang Liu. 2016. Minimum risk training for neural machine translation. In *Proceedings of the 54th Annual Meeting of the Association for Computational Linguistics, ACL 2016, August 7-12, 2016, Berlin, Germany, Volume 1: Long Papers*.

Michel Simard, Nicola Ueffing, Pierre Isabelle, and Roland Kuhn. 2007. Rule-based translation with statistical phrase-based post-editing. In *Proceedings of the Second Workshop on Statistical Machine Translation*. pages 203–206.

Matthew Snover, Bonnie Dorr, Richard Schwartz, Linnea Micciulla, and John Makhoul. 2006. A study of translation edit rate with targeted human annotation. In *In Proceedings of Association for Machine Translation In the Americas*. pages 223–231.

Lucia Specia. 2011. Exploiting objective annotations for measuring translation post-editing effort. In *Proceedings of the 15th Conference of the European Association for Machine Translation*. pages 73–80.

Ilya Sutskever, Oriol Vinyals, and Quoc V. Le. 2014. Sequence to sequence learning with neural networks. In *Proceedings of the 27th International Conference on Neural Information Processing Systems*. MIT Press, Cambridge, MA, USA, NIPS'14, pages 3104–3112. http://dl.acm.org/citation.cfm?id=2969033.2969173.

Barret Zoph and Kevin Knight. 2016. Multi-source neural translation. In Kevin Knight, Ani Nenkova, and Owen Rambow, editors, *NAACL HLT 2016,*

*The 2016 Conference of the North American Chap-
ter of the Association for Computational Linguistics: Human Language Technologies, San Diego
California, USA, June 12-17, 2016.* The Association for Computational Linguistics, pages 30–34.
http://aclweb.org/anthology/N/N16/N16-1004.pdf.

Neural Post-Editing Based on Quality Estimation

Yiming Tan, Zhiming Chen, Liu Huang, Lilin Zhang,
Maoxi Li, Mingwen Wang
School of Computer Information Engineering, Jiangxi Normal University
{tt_yymm, qqchenzhiming, ufhuangliu, lilinzhang, mosesli, mwwang}
@jxnu.edu.cn

Abstract

Automatic post-editing (APE) is a challenging task on WMT evaluation campaign. We find that only a small number of edit operations are required for most machine translation outputs, through analysis of the training set of WMT17 APE en-de task. Based on this statistics analysis, two neural post-editing (NPE) models are trained depended on the edit numbers: single edit and minor edits. The improved quality estimation (QE) approach is exploited to rank models, and select the best translation as the post-edited output from the n-best list translation hypotheses generated by the best APE model and the raw translation system. Experimental results on the datasets of WMT16 APE test set show that the proposed approach significantly outperformed the baseline. Our approach can bring considerable relief from the overcorrection problem in APE.

1 Introduction

Automatic post editing (APE) aims to learn how to correct machine translation errors by use of the human post-editing feedback. The traditional statistical post-editing builds monolingual statistical phrased-based machine translation system to translate the wrong raw outputs into good translations (Simard et al., 2007; Bechara et al., 2011; Chatterjee et al., 2015). In recent years, with the great success of deep learning achieved in machine translation, many works have applied neural machine translation (NMT) to the APE task.

Pal et al. proposed to exploit the bidirectional source RNN encoder-decoder model to establish a monolingual machine translation system for APE (Pal et al., 2016). Compared with the traditional statistical post-editing approaches, their approach gained more improvement. In the light of the context information of the translation, Pecina et al. proposed to respectively establish independent encoders for source sentences and raw machine translations (Pecina et al., 2016). Their approach is similar to the multi-source NMT (Zoph et al., 2016); the difference lies in the input information are source sentences and raw machine translation outputs. Grundkiewicz et al. proposed to combine the outputs of monolingual NMT and bilingual NMT to improve the performance of APE task (Grundkiewicz et al., 2016).

This paper presents a new approach for APE which was submitted by the JXNU team to WMT17 APE shared task. In order to effectively reduce the overcorrection problem, we propose to build two specific neural post-editing (NPE) models in term of the edit numbers, and select the best model by machine translation quality estimation (QE). The experiment results indicate that the proposed approach gains great improvement over the baseline officially released by the evaluation campaign.

2 Data analysis

Overcorrection problem refers to edit the machine translation output more times than it really needed, among these edit operations, some are not necessary or even wrong. Overcorrection may cause the resulting outputs of APE have lower translation quality than the raw translation outputs. To estimate the number of edit operations needed on the test set, we count the number of edit operations, including deletion, insert, substitution, and shift of word chunk, for the raw machine translation outputs on the training set of WMT16 and WMT17 APE shared task by the open source

Proceedings of the Conference on Machine Translation (WMT), Volume 2: Shared Task Papers, pages 655–660
Copenhagen, Denmark, September 7–11, 2017. ©2017 Association for Computational Linguistics

TER script[1]. The combination training set has 23,000 triples that are source sentence, raw machine translation output, and its human reference translation.

The distribution of the number of edit operations needed for raw machine translation outputs on the training set of WMT16 and WMT17 APE shared task are showed as Figure 1. The statistics indicate that the average number of edit operations for the raw machine translation outputs is 4. And the machine translation outputs need more than 1 edit operation account for 20.47%, while 58.03% of machine translation outputs need to be edited 4 times or less.

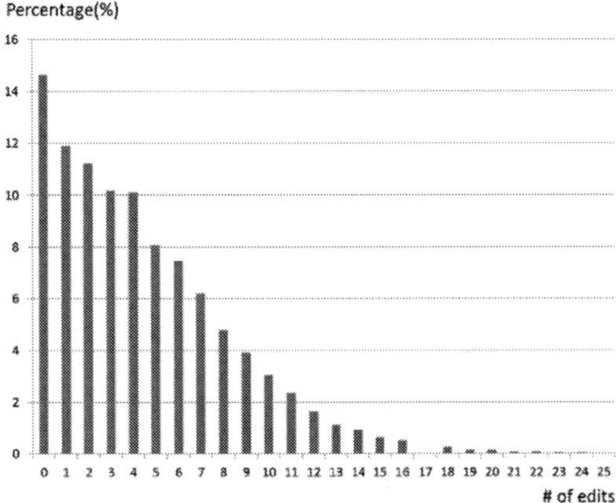

Figure 1: Distribution of the number of edit operations needed for machine translation outputs in the training set of WMT16 and WMT17 APE shared task.

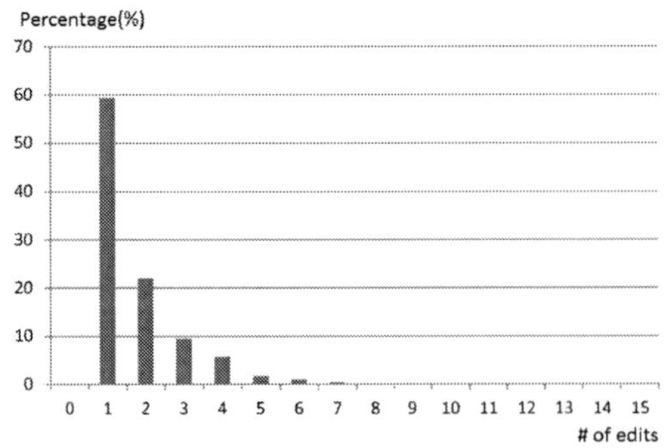

Figure 2: Distribution of the number of only one type edit operations needed for machine translation outputs.

Because the raw machine translation outputs can be converted to good translation by deletion, insert, substitution, and shift of word chunk operations, we also extract the machine translation outputs that only one type of edit operation are needed to convert them into good translation, the distribution of the number of edit operations on the subset is shown as Figure 2, it shows that more than 80% of raw machine translation outputs needed 2 or less one type edit operations.

3 Model

From the distribution of the number of edit operations in the training set, there are a lot of raw machine translation outputs needed a small amount of edit operations, less than 4 times; and there also exist a lot of raw machine translation outputs needed only one type edit operations. Thus, we speculate that this phenomenon is also available for the test set. In order to reduce the overcorrection in the test set, we train two NPE models aiming at these two conditions.

Follow by Grundkiewicz et al. (2016) work, a NPE model is build and trained with the training set officially released by the evaluation campaign, called $NPE_{BASELINE}$.

We extract a triplet corpus with raw machine translation outputs needed 4 or less edit operations from the training dataset, and train a NPE system, called NPE_{MINOR}. In the meantime, in order to strengthen the ability of editing the raw machine translation outputs by one single type edit operations, we use a triplet corpus contained machine translations with 2 or less one single edit operations from the training dataset, and train a NPE system, called NPE_{SINGLE}.

In order to combine $NPE_{BASELINE}$, NPE_{MINOR} and NPE_{SINGLE}, we merge outputs of these three systems which are regarded as an n-best list translation hypothesis, and introduce the sentence-level QE approach (Specia et al., 2013) to score and rank the n-best list translation hypothesis.

QE approach aim is to estimate the qualities of translation without human references on the basis of features abstracted from the source sentences and machine translation outputs which reflect translation complexity, fluency and adequacy.

Adopted the sentence-level QE approach to score and rank translation outputs in the n-best lists, we find that the QE approach can be proved to be very effective when it comes to one source sentence with great difference in qualities of translation, however, it's not very effective when one source sentence with small difference in qualities of translation.

---

[1]http://www.cs.umd.edu/~snover/tercom/

In order to reduce the impact of misjudgment, a hierarchical classification method is used to select the best translation output among the merged *n*-best list. First, the translation hypotheses are score by the QE method and the scores are converted into the five-point scale. Thus, if the qualities of translation hypotheses are classified into different level, they can be ranked according to the quality level; if they are in the same level, a statistical language model, SRILM (Stolckeet al., 2002), is introduced to score and rank the translation hypotheses to get the best one.

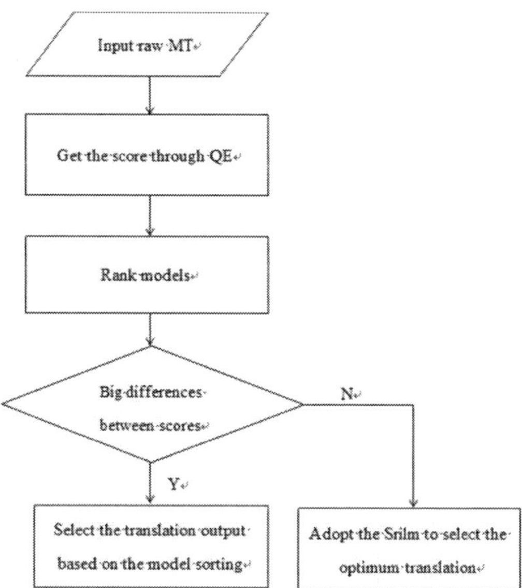

Figure 3: The flow chart of how to select the best translation by the QE approach

4 Experiments

In order to test the performance of the proposed approach, we conduct experiment on the test set of the WMT16 APE Task. The task focuses on the information technology domain, in which English source sentences have been translated into German (en-de) by an unknown MT system. The goal of the APE shared task is to examine automatic methods for correcting errors.

4.1 Experiments setting

Experimental data consist of corpus of WMT16 and WMT17 APE shared task released by the evaluation campaign, and publicly released artificial post-editing data (Grundkiewicz et al., 2016), including source language sentences, raw machine translation outputs and human references. Table 1 shows more details about this corpus.

Due to the provided training triplets for en-de direction is too small to train neural models, Grundkiewicz et al. created artificial training triplets through applying cross-entropy filtering and round-trip translation to extend the provided training triplets and publicly released the extended one (Grundkiewicz et al., 2016). Therefore, we integrate these two corpora into a training set for training NPE systems.

Data set	Sentences	length	TER
WMT16 training set	12,000	17.89	26.22
WMT17 training set	11,000	17.69	24.41
WMT16 development set	1,000	19.75	24.81
WMT16 test set	2,000	17.41	24.76
Artificial data 500K	531,839	20.92	25.28
Artificial data 4M	4,335,715	15.86	36.63

Table 1: Statistics of the provided data sets: number of sentences, average sentence lengths and TER score.

The sentences in the corpus have been tokenized and truecased when preprocessing. To deal with the limited ability of neural translation models to handle out-of-vocabulary words, tokens are splited into subword units (Sennrich et al., 2015b) to improve the systems' performance.

We apply Nematus[2] to train the bidirectional RNN encoder-decoder model with attention mechanism. The size of minibatches is set 80, vocabulary size is set 40000, maximum sentence length is set 50, the dimension of word embeddings is set 500, the size of hidden layers is set 1024, and the optimization algorithm proposed by Adadelta (Zeiler, 2012) is used. Compared with Nematus's approach, AmuNMT[3] based on C++/CUDA (Grundkiewicz et al., 2016) decode at a faster speed on CPU. Thus, we apply AmuNMT's approach to decode to-be-edited machine translations with a beam size of 12 and length normalization when decoding.

4.2 Experiments result

4.2.1 NPE$_{BASELINE}$ system

The APE corpus with size of 4M is used to train the NPE$_{BASELINE}$ system, while the combined corpus of APE corpus with size of 500k and the

---

[2]http://github.com/rsennrich/nematus
[3]http://github.com/emjotde/amunmt

WMT16 and WMT17 training set are used to optimize the parameters of the system.

4.2.2 NPE$_{\text{MINOR}}$ & NPE$_{\text{SINGLE}}$ systems

Filtered the above training set by the following rules respectively: machine translations needed 4 or less edits and machine translations needed 2 or less single edit operations, two sub training sets, contained 278.9 K and 160.6 K training triples, are obtained. At the same time, the development set of the WMT16 APE shared task are filtered by the rules, and two sub development sets, contained 1199 and 810 triples, are obtained.

System	TER	BLEU
Raw MT output	12.66	76.13
NPE$_{\text{BASELINE}}$	12.20	78.53
NPE$_{\text{MINOR}}$	**10.24**	**81.80**

Table 2: System performance of the NPE$_{\text{MINOR}}$ and the NPE$_{\text{BASELINE}}$ systems in the sub development set.

System	TER	BLEU
Raw MT output	8.25	82.31
NPE$_{\text{BASELINE}}$	8.04	84.48
NPE$_{\text{MINOR}}$	6.20	88.07
NPE$_{\text{SINGLE}}$	**5.58**	**89.02**

Table 3: System performance of NPE systems in the sub development set.

We respectively train and tune the NPE$_{\text{BASELINE}}$ model with the sub training set and sub development set, two NPE systems, called NPE$_{\text{MINOR}}$ and NPE$_{\text{SINGLE}}$, are gained. The system performance on the two sub development sets are shown in Table 2 and Table 3.

4.2.3 Joint system

To gain better system performance, the outputs of NPE systems and raw machine translations were combined into an n-best list of translation hypotheses. The improved machine translation QE was exploited to select the best outputs among the n-best list.

As shown in Table 4, the system performance of combining the outputs of NPE$_{\text{BASELINE}}$ and NPE$_{\text{MINOR}}$ systems and raw machine translations gained 0.7 TER score and 1.76 BLEU score improvement over that of the NPE$_{\text{BASELINE}}$ system in the test set of WMT16 APE shared task. The system performance was further improved by 0.75 TER score and 0.61 BLEU score when combined the NPE$_{\text{SINGLE}}$ outputs. The result shows the effectiveness of the proposed approach.

System	TER	BLEU
Baseline1(Raw MToutput)	24.76	62.11
Baseline2(Moses PBAPE)	24.64	63.47
NPE$_{\text{BASELINE}}$	**23.78**	**64.97**
NPE$_{\text{BASELINE}}$ + NPE$_{\text{MINOR}}$	23.08	66.73
NPE$_{\text{BASELINE}}$ + NPE$_{\text{MINOR}}$ + NPE$_{\text{SINGLE}}$	**22.33**	**67.34**

Table 4: Results of NPE systems in the WMT16 test set

4.3 Analysis

In order to look into the reasons for system performance improvement, we extract 500 triples from the test set of WMT16 APE shared task, in which the NPE$_{\text{BASELINE}}$ system performed worse than the raw machine translations. The machine translations in the 500 triples are all over-corrected by the NPE$_{\text{BASELINE}}$ system, however, the total amount of sentences occurring overcorrection reduce to 372 in the outputs of the jointed models. And it was found that 58.8% of machine translation sentences only need 4 or less edits, this illustrates that the jointed model contributes greatly to reducing overcorrection.

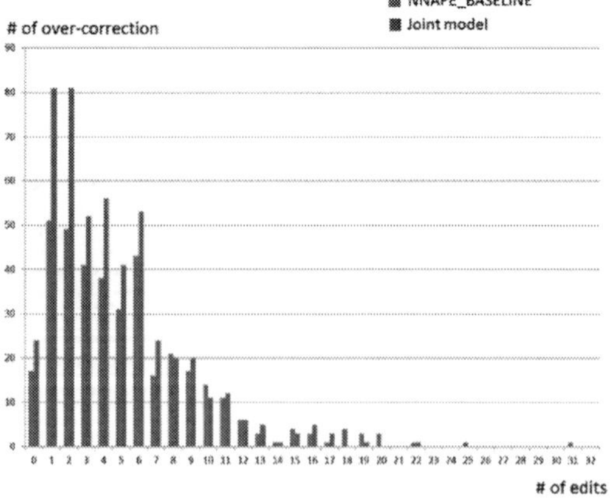

Figure 4: Distribution of the number of edits needed in overcorrection sentences from outputs of NPE$_{\text{BASELINE}}$ and jointed systems.

To show their differences on the number of edits more clearly, Figure 4 describes the distribution of the number of edits from outputs of NPE$_{\text{BASELINE}}$ system and jointed systems. The Figure 4 reveals that the frequency of overcorrection of the joint system is lower than the NPE$_{BASELINE}$ system when corrected machine translation needed a small amount of edits (<=4).

5 Conclusion

Our submission to the WMT17 APE shared task en-de translation direction gains significantly improvements over the baselines, scoring 23.30 on TER and 65.66 on BLEU in the official results. This indicates that it is necessary to build a NPE system for machine translations needed a smaller amount of edits. Future work should include the investigation of the proposed approach application to the de-en translation direction of the WMT APE shared task.

Acknowledgements

This research has been funded by the Natural Science Foundation of China under Grant No.6166 2031, 6146 2044, and 61462045. The authors would like to extend their sincere thanks to the anonymous reviewers who provided valuable comments.

References

Dzmitry Bahdanau, Kyunghyun Cho, and Yoshua Bengio. 2015. Neural machine translation by jointly learning to align and translate. In *Proceedings of the International Conference on Learning Representations*, San Diego, CA.

Hanna Béchara, Yanjun Ma and Josef van Genabith. 2011. Statistical post-editing for a statistical MT system. In *MT Summit*, pages 308-315, Xiamen, China.

Ondřej Bojar, Rajen Chatterjee, Christian Federmann, Barry Haddow, Matthias Huck, Chris Hokamp, Philipp Koehn, Varvara Logacheva, Christof Monz, MatteoNegri, Matt Post, Carolina Scarton, Lucia Specia, and Marco Turchi. 2015. Findings of the 2015 Workshop on Statistical Machine Translation. In *Proceedings of the Tenth Workshop on Statistical Machine Translation*, pages 1–46, Lisbon, Portugal.

Rajen Chatterjee, Marco Turchi, and Matteo Negri. 2015a. The FBK participation in the WMT15 automatic post-editing shared task. In *Proceedings of the Tenth Workshop on Statistical Machine Translation*, pages 210–215, Lisbon, Portugal.

Rajen Chatterjee, Marion Weller, Matteo Negri, and Marco Turchi. 2015b. Exploring the planet of the APEs: a comparative study of state-of-the-art methods for MT automatic post-editing. In *Proceedings of the 53rd Annual Meeting of the Association for Computational Linguistics and the 7th International Joint Conference on Natural Language Processing*, pages156–161, Beijing, China.

Marcin Junczys-Dowmunt and Roman Grundkiewicz. 2016. Log linear combinations of monolingual and bilingual neural machine translation models for automatic post-editing. In *Proceedings of the First Conference on Machine Translation*, pages 751–758, Berlin, Germany, August.

Kevin Knight and Ishwar Chander. 1994. Automated post-editing of documents. In *Proceedings of the 12th National Conference on Artificial Intelligence*, pages 779-784, Seattle, WA, USA.

Philipp Koehn, Hieu Hoang, Alexandra Birch, Chris Callison-Burch, Marcello Federico, Nicola Bertoldi, Brooke Cowan, Wade Shen, Christine Moran, Richard Zens, et al. 2007. Moses: Open source toolkit for statistical machine translation. In *Proceedings of the 45th Annual Meeting of the Association for Computational Linguistics*, pages 177–180.

Santanu Pal, Sudip Kumar Naskar, Mihaela Vela, and Josefvan Genabith. 2016. A neural network based approach to automatic post-editing. In *Proceedings of the 54th Annual Meeting of the Association for Computational Linguistics*, pages 281–286, August.

Kishore Papineni, Salim Roukos, Todd Ward, and Wei Jing Zhu. 2002. BLEU: A method for automatic evaluation of machine translation. In *Proceedings of the 40th Annual Meeting on Association for Computational Linguistics, ACL'02*, pages 311–318, Stroudsburg, PA, USA.

Kashif Shah, Raymond W. M. Ng, Fethi Bougares and Lucia Specia. 2015. Investigating Continuous Space Language Models for Machine Translation Quality Estimation. *Proceedings of the 2015 Conference on Empirical Methods in Natural Language Processing*, pages 1073-1078, Lisbon, Portugal.

Lucia Specia, Kashif Shah, Jose G.C. de Souza and Trevor Cohn. 2013. QuEst - A translation quality estimation framework. *51st Annual Meeting of the Association for Computational Linguistics: System Demonstrations*, pages 79-84, Sofia, Bulgaria.

Michel Simard, Cyril Goutte, and Pierre Isabelle. 2007. Statistical phrase-based post-editing. In *Proceedings of the Conference of the North American Chapter of the Association for Computational Linguistics*, pages 508–515, Rochester, New York.

Matthew Snover, Bonnie Dorr, Richard Schwartz, John Makhoul, Linnea Micciulla and Ralph Makhoul. 2006. A Study of Translation Edit Rate with Targeted Human Annotation. *Proceedings of*

Association for Machine Translation in the Americas, pages 223-231, Cambridge.

Rico Sennrich, Barry Haddow, and Alexandra Birch. 2015a. Improving neural machine translation models with monolingual data. *arXiv preprint arXiv*: 1511.06709.

Rico Sennrich, Barry Haddow, and Alexandra Birch. 2015b. Neural machine translation of rare words with subword units. *arXiv preprint arXiv*: 1508.07909.

Andreas Stolcke. 2002. SRILM - an extensible language modeling toolkit. In *Proceedings of International Conference on Spoken Language Processing, volume 2*, pages 901-904

CUNI System for WMT17 Automatic Post-Editing Task

Dušan Variš and Ondřej Bojar
Charles University, Faculty of Mathematics and Physics,
Institute of Formal and Applied Linguistics,
Malostranské náměstí 25, 118 00 Prague, Czech Republic
{varis,bojar}@ufal.mff.cuni.cz

Abstract

Following upon the last year's CUNI system for automatic post-editing of machine translation output, we focus on exploiting the potential of sequence-to-sequence neural models for this task. In this system description paper, we compare several encoder-decoder architectures on a smaller-scale models and present the system we submitted to WMT 2017 Automatic Post-Editing shared task based on this preliminary comparison. We also show how simple inclusion of synthetic data can improve the overall performance as measured by an automatic evaluation metric. Lastly, we list few example outputs generated by our post-editing system.

1 Introduction

Even with the recent substantial improvements of the machine translation (MT) quality mainly thanks to the increasingly popular neural models (neural MT, NMT), many errors still remain in the output require further post-editing. This can be done manually, or as the automatic post-editing (APE) task expects, automatically.

When phrase-based machine translation (PBMT) was the indisputable state of the art, some automatic post-editing (APE) systems were based on the PBMT techniques (Simard et al., 2007). With source-sentence information (Béchara et al., 2011), post-editing results were quite promising. It is therefore not surprising that with the rise of the neural machine translation, neural APE systems based on the findings in NMT research were built (Pal et al., 2016) and even won last year's WMT16 Shared Task (Junczys-Dowmunt and Grundkiewicz, 2016).

In this paper, we present a baseline comparison of several recent neural sequence-to-sequence architectures, motivations behind our primary submission for the WMT17 Shared Task and further improvements of this submission with regard to model size and additional synthetic data.

2 Experiments

In automatic post-editing, we are expected to take the output of an MT system that usually contains various errors (morphological, lexical etc.) and to generate a corrected version of the output. Most of the time, there is also additional information available, e.g. the original sentence in the source language and sometimes also some internal scores or features from the primary MT system.

2.1 Examined Setups

If we look at the recent developments in the field of NMT, we can see that there are many different novel approaches that often bring significant improvements to the overall performance of the NMT system. It is natural to ask how these findings can be applied to APE task and how much they can contribute to the APE system performance. We experimented in two areas: (1) how to feed simultaneously the source sentence and the MT output (multi-source input), and (2) whether to use subword units or individual characters.

2.1.1 Multi-Source Input

All our experiments use both the source sentence and the MT output to be corrected. As far as encoding the input is concerned, we examined two basic approaches. We tried using a single encoder that received the concatenation of the source sentence and the corresponding MT output as suggested by Niehues et al. (2016). The resulting input sequence becomes longer and it may thus be more difficult to encode, but it was reported that

Proceedings of the Conference on Machine Translation (WMT), Volume 2: Shared Task Papers, pages 661–666
Copenhagen, Denmark, September 7–11, 2017. ©2017 Association for Computational Linguistics

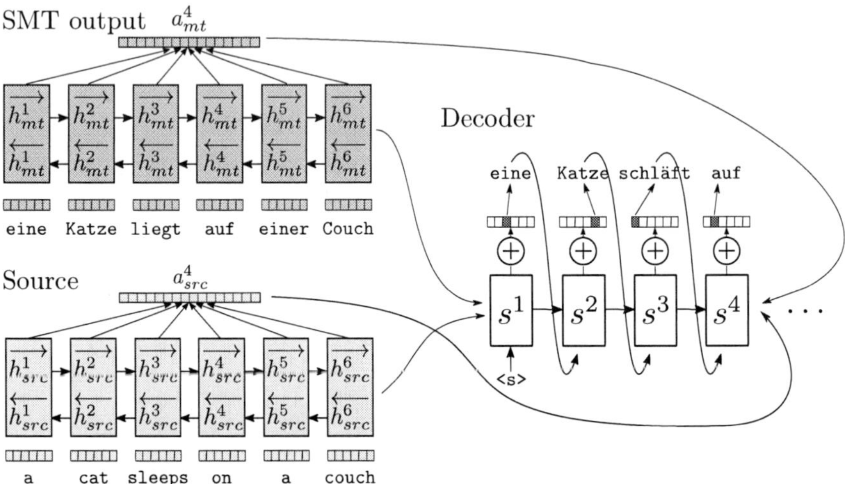

Figure 1: Illustration of a multiple-encoder sequence-to-sequence architecture as illustrated in Libovický et al. (2016).

(through the attention mechanism) the decoder is able to attend to relevant parts of the concatenated sentences when generating output.

As an alternative option, we also tried using two separate encoders, one for the source sentence and one for the MT output (Libovický et al., 2016) as shown in Figure 1. In this case, both encoders encode their corresponding input sequences separately and the concatenation of their final states is passed to the decoder. The attention is computed over the hidden states of both encoders as if they were produced by a single encoder. Libovický and Helcl (2017) present other options for combining the attention of multiple encoders, but the investigation of these methods is not covered in this paper.

2.1.2 Subword Units or Characters

All data-driven approaches to MT suffer in quality when translating rare words (including words not seen during training at all) and NMT is no exception. In out neural approach to APE, we would still like our APE system to address errors in rare words (e.g. by fixing their endings). A popular approach of reducing the vocabulary size in NMT is called byte-pair encoding (BPE, Sennrich et al., 2015) which creates a vocabulary of most frequent words, subword units and individual characters. This way, even rare words can be successfully handled by modifying their parts.

Another option is to use a fully character-level encoder-decoder architecture. However, this ap-proach in its basic form results in much longer sequences that are generally much harder to learn for the underlying recurrent neural network (RNN, Pascanu et al., 2012). Another downside is the increased training and inference time for each sentence. Recently, Lee et al. (2016) presented an encoder architecture that uses RNN over the output of several hundreds convolutional filters that are applied on the character-level embeddings, combining the benefits of both convolutional and recurrent approaches.

2.2 Baseline Comparison

Based on the approaches described in the previous section, we decided to compare the following system variations:

- a single encoder (concatenated input, "concat") vs. two separate encoders ("two-enc"),

- BPE2BPE vs. CHAR2CHAR architecture.

Each system variation was trained using a single Nvidia Tesla K20 5GB GPU. We set embedding size and both encoder and decoder RNN size to 300 for all the systems. We used BPE vocabulary of size 50k for the BPE2BPE systems and character vocabulary of size 500 for the CHAR2CHAR systems. We did not use dropout during training. For the CHAR2CHAR setups (i.e. RNN over convolutional encoder by Lee et al., 2016), we reduced the number of convolutional filters proportionally to the size of the used GPU, used segment size 5 and highway network of depth 1.

System	BLEU
BPE2BPE two-enc	42.36
BPE2BPE concat	42.13
CHAR2CHAR two-enc	49.82
CHAR2CHAR concat	49.94

Table 1: Automatic evaluation of the proposed architectures we trained. The model size was downscaled to 5GB due to the limited computation resources.

The experiments were carried out in Neural Monkey[1] (Helcl and Libovický, 2017), a framework for sequence-to-sequence modeling. Most of the required neural network components together with necessary preprocessing and postprocessing were already implemented in the framework. We added the RNN over convolutional encoder in this work.

We used 12k sentences WMT16 APE training dataset for training and we computed BLEU (Papineni et al., 2002) on WMT16 APE development dataset to compare the baselines. The evaluation was performed during training. We thus did not use beam search and simply greedily chose the most probable output at each decoding step to get the validation output.

The best results for each architecture are shown in Table 1. We can see that the character-level post-editing models outperform the subword-level models. However, the training was done using only a small dataset which may possibly indicate that the character level architecture is able to better exploit the training data. Nevertheless, we chose the character-level system for our remaining experiments.

3 CUNI System for WMT17 APE Task

After the baseline comparison of the smaller sequence-to-sequence models, we moved towards training of the primary submission for the WMT17 post-editing task.

3.1 Common Settings

We decided to use the two-encoder character-level architecture. Even though the single encoder character-level architecture with concatenated inputs performed slightly better during the baseline evaluation, we believe that the multi-encoder ar-

chitecture offers higher potential for further improvement.[2]

The model was trained using GeForce GTX 1080 with 8GB memory with the following parameters:

- shared character-level vocabulary size: 500

- encoder RNN size: 256

- input embedding size: 300

- segment size: 5

- highway network depth: 2

- convolutional filters (size, number of filters): (1,150), (2,200), (3,250), (4,250), (5,300), (6,300), (7,350), (8,350)

- decoder RNN size: 512

- output embedding size: 300

During the inference, we used beam-search of beam size 20 and length normalization to penalize shorter sentences. Beam search parameters were chosen based on the Lee et al. (2016).

First, we used only 23k sentences from WMT17 training dataset to train the system. We used this model as a baseline which we tried to further improve.

3.2 Synthetic Data

Since the basic training dataset provided for the task was rather small we also tried to include the training dataset from the previous WMT16 post-editing task and furthermore, we added the synthetic data (smaller dataset, ~500k sentences) as provided by last year's submission of Junczys-Dowmunt and Grundkiewicz (2016). To balance the ratio of genuine and synthetic sentences in the final dataset, we duplicated the WMT16 and WMT17 sentence pairs several times to match the size of the synthetic dataset. We then took all the data and shuffled them randomly to create a dataset consisting of ~1M training sentences. We used WMT16 APE dev set to evaluate the model during the training.

---

[1] https://github.com/ufal/neuralmonkey

[2] This still needs to be confirmed though by the future research.

Source	You can also perform many types of transformations by dragging the bounding box for a selection .
OrigMT	Sie können auch zahlreiche Transformationsarten durchführen , indem Sie den Begrenzungsrahmen für eine Auswahl .
Synth	Sie können auch zahlreiche Transformationsarten durchführen , indem Sie den Begrenzungsrahmen für eine Auswahl **ziehen** .
Ref	Sie können auch zahlreiche Transformationsarten durchführen , indem Sie den Begrenzungsrahmen für eine Auswahl ziehen .
Source	3D comments added to other views are listed as components of that view in the Model Tree .
OrigMT	3D hinzugefügten Kommentare zu anderen Ansichten als Komponenten anzuzeigen , die in der Modellhierarchie aufgeführt sind .
Synth	3D-Kommentare zu anderen Ansichten **werden** als Komponenten **angezeigt** , die in der Modellhierarchie aufgeführt sind .
Ref	Anderen Ansichten hinzugefügte 3D-Kommentare werden in der Modellhierarchie als Komponenten dieser Ansicht aufgeführt .
Source	Choose an option from the Key Algorithm menu .
OrigMT	Wählen Sie eine Option aus dem Menü " Algorithm . "
Synth	Wählen Sie eine Option aus dem Menü " Algorithmu . "
Ref	Wählen Sie eine Option aus dem Menü " Schlüsselalgorithmus . "
Source	Shift-drag to constrain the movement of the object horizontally , vertically , or diagonally .
OrigMT	Halten Sie beim Ziehen des Zeigers über die Bewegung des Objekts horizontal , vertikal oder diagonal einzuschränken .
Synth	Halten Sie beim Ziehen die Bewegung des Objekts die Bewegung des Objekts horizontal , vertikal oder diagonal eingeschränkt .
Ref	Halten Sie beim Ziehen des Objekts die Umschalttaste gedrückt , um nur horizontale , vertikale oder diagonale Bewegungen zuzulassen .

Figure 2: Sample outputs from the original MT and our submitted model "Synth". In the first two examples, our model helped to produce correctly the main verb (in **bold**). In the third example, it introduced a spelling error (underlined). The last example shows that the model can also severely damage the sentence, introducing repetitions common in NMT output. The original output for the last sentence was not perfect either, it does not mention the shift key at all (and our model does not fix it).

3.3 Predicting Edit Operations

Finally, inspired by Libovický et al. (2016), we also trained a separate model that generates a sequence of post-editing operations ("editops") instead of directly generating the target sequence of characters. Aside from generating characters present in the training data, the model learns to use special tokens "<keep>" and "<delete>", or to normally produce characters present in the training data, to indicate the modifications needed for the MT output. We used the same network parameters and data (including the synthetic dataset) for the model with and without BPE.

3.4 Evaluation

We evaluated these three models using the WMT16 APE test set[3], computing the BLEU score on the produced outputs: baseline CHAR2CHAR setup (Baseline), the model trained with synthetic data (Synth) and the model which produces edit operations instead of complete sentences (Synth+editops). Table 2 shows the results of the evaluation.

We can see that even when we choose the best architecture based on the relative comparison and increase the model capacity ("Baseline"), it is still not enough to even get close to the original MT output quality ("Original MT"). Introducing additional synthetic data ("Synth") fixed this and actually outperformed the original MT, reaching

System	BLEU
Original MT	62.09 ($\pm$1.04)
Baseline	50.86 ($\pm$3.96)
Synth	**66.04 ($\pm$1.16)**
Synth+editops	62.08 ($\pm$1.05)

Table 2: Automatic evaluation of the final 8GB APE setups. The score of the original MT output is shown for comparison. The $\pm$ values are empirical confidence intervals reflecting the variance in the test set (Koehn, 2004).

BLEU of 66.04. We chose this system as our primary submission for the WMT16 APE task.

We were a little surprised that there was no improvement when using model that learned to generate post-editing operations ("Synth+editops"). When we manually examined the generated output, we found out that the system took the safer path of keeping most of the machine translation output because it probably resulted in fewer errors than trying to change it. This could be probably avoided by discouraging the model from keeping the whole MT output unchanged and we plan investigating this approach in the future.

Even though we did not perform a thorough manual evaluation, we present some examples of our submitted system ("Synth") outputs to give the reader some insight to the model performance in Figure 2. Our post-editing helped with the main verb, but in other cases, it also damaged the sentence structure or introduced spelling errors.

---

[3]http://www.statmt.org/wmt16/ape-task.html

4 Conclusion

In this paper, we compared several sequence-to-sequence architectures that were previously proposed for the NMT task and evaluated their performance in automatic post-editing of English-to-German MT output. Our setup relies on the original source sentence and uses either subword units (BPE) or individual characters.

With additional synthetic data, we were able to improve over the original MT output in terms of BLEU, but a quick manual inspection reveals that errors can be easily also introduced and BLEU (or other automatic metric) is not likely to give a reliable picture of the post-editing performance.

Acknowledgments

This work has been in part supported by the EU grants no. H2020-ICT-2014-1-644402 (Health in my Language) and H2020-ICT-2014-1-645452 (QT21), as well as by the LINDAT/CLARIN project of the Ministry of Education, Youth and Sports of the Czech Republic (project LM2015071) and Charles University SVV project no. 260 453.

Computational resources were also supplied by the Ministry of Education, Youth and Sports of the Czech Republic under the Projects CESNET (Project No. LM2015042), CERIT-Scientific Cloud (Project No. LM2015085) provided within the program Projects of Large Research, Development and Innovations Infrastructures.

References

Hanna Béchara, Yanjun Ma, and Josef van Genabith. 2011. Statistical Post-Editing for a Statistical MT System. In *Proceedings of the 13th Machine Translation Summit*. pages 308–315.

Jindřich Helcl and Jindřich Libovický. 2017. Neural monkey: An open-source tool for sequence learning. *The Prague Bulletin of Mathematical Linguistics* (107).5–17. https://doi.org/10.1515/pralin-2017-0001.

Marcin Junczys-Dowmunt and Roman Grundkiewicz. 2016. Log-linear combinations of monolingual and bilingual neural machine translation models for automatic post-editing. In *Proceedings of the First Conference on Machine Translation, WMT 2016, colocated with ACL 2016, August 11-12, Berlin, Germany*. The Association for Computer Linguistics, pages 751–758. http://aclweb.org/anthology/W/W16/W16-2378.pdf.

Philipp Koehn. 2004. Statistical Significance Tests for Machine Translation Evaluation. In *Proceedings of EMNLP 2004*. Barcelona, Spain.

Jason Lee, Kyunghyun Cho, and Thomas Hofmann. 2016. Fully character-level neural machine translation without explicit segmentation. *CoRR* abs/1610.03017. http://arxiv.org/abs/1610.03017.

Jindřich Libovický and Jindřich Helcl. 2017. Attention strategies for multi-source sequence-to-sequence learning. In *Proceedings of the 55th Annual Meeting of the Association for Computational Linguistics (Volume 2: Short Papers)*. Association for Computational Linguistics, Vancouver, Canada.

Jindřich Libovický, Jindřich Helcl, Marek Tlustý, Ondřej Bojar, and Pavel Pecina. 2016. Cuni system for wmt16 automatic post-editing and multimodal translation tasks. In *Proceedings of the First Conference on Machine Translation*. Association for Computational Linguistics, Berlin, Germany, pages 646–654. http://www.aclweb.org/anthology/W16-2361.

Jan Niehues, Eunah Cho, Thanh-Le Ha, and Alex Waibel. 2016. Pre-translation for neural machine translation. In Nicoletta Calzolari, Yuji Matsumoto, and Rashmi Prasad, editors, *COLING 2016, 26th International Conference on Computational Linguistics, Proceedings of the Conference: Technical Papers, December 11-16, 2016, Osaka, Japan*. ACL, pages 1828–1836. http://aclweb.org/anthology/C/C16/C16-1172.pdf.

Santanu Pal, Sudip Kumar Naskar, Mihaela Vela, and Josef van Genabith. 2016. A neural network based approach to automatic post-editing. In *Proceedings of the 54th Annual Meeting of the Association for Computational Linguistics, ACL 2016, August 7-12, 2016, Berlin, Germany, Volume 2: Short Papers*. The Association for Computer Linguistics. http://aclweb.org/anthology/P/P16/P16-2046.pdf.

Kishore Papineni, Salim Roukos, Todd Ward, and Wei-Jing Zhu. 2002. Bleu: A method for automatic evaluation of machine translation. In *Proceedings of the 40th Annual Meeting on Association for Computational Linguistics*. Association for Computational Linguistics, Stroudsburg, PA, USA, ACL '02, pages 311–318. https://doi.org/10.3115/1073083.1073135.

Razvan Pascanu, Tomas Mikolov, and Yoshua Bengio. 2012. Understanding the exploding gradient problem. *CoRR* abs/1211.5063. http://arxiv.org/abs/1211.5063.

Rico Sennrich, Barry Haddow, and Alexandra Birch. 2015. Neural machine translation of rare words with subword units. *CoRR* abs/1508.07909. http://arxiv.org/abs/1508.07909.

Michel Simard, Cyril Goutte, and Pierre Isabelle. 2007. Statistical phrase-based post-editing. In

Human Language Technologies 2007: The Conference of the North American Chapter of the Association for Computational Linguistics; Proceedings of the Main Conference. Association for Computational Linguistics, Rochester, New York, pages 508–515. http://www.aclweb.org/anthology/N/N07/N07-1064.

The UMD Neural Machine Translation Systems
at WMT17 Bandit Learning Task

Amr Sharaf and **Shi Feng** and **Khanh Nguyen** and **Kianté Brantley** and **Hal Daumé III**
Department of Computer Science
University of Maryland, College Park
{amr,shifeng,kxnguyen,kdbrant,hal}@cs.umd.edu

Abstract

We describe the University of Maryland machine translation systems submitted to the WMT17 German-English Bandit Learning Task. The task is to adapt a translation system to a new domain, using only *bandit feedback*: the system receives a German sentence to translate, produces an English sentence, and only gets a scalar score as feedback. Targeting these two challenges (adaptation and bandit learning), we built a standard neural machine translation system and extended it in two ways: (1) robust reinforcement learning techniques to learn effectively from the bandit feedback, and (2) domain adaptation using data selection from a large corpus of parallel data.

1 Introduction

We describe the University of Maryland systems for bandit machine translation. For the shared translation task of the EMNLP 2017's second conference on machine translation (WMT17), we focused on the task of bandit machine translation. This shared task was set up, consistent with (Kreutzer et al., 2017), simultaneously as a bandit learning problem *and* a domain adaptation problem. This raises the natural question: can we combine these potentially complementary information sources?

To investigate this question, we started from a standard neural machine translation (NMT) setup §2[1], and then we:

1. applied domain adaptation techniques by data selection (Moore and Lewis, 2010) to the out-of-domain data, with the goals of filtering out harmful data and fine-tuning the training process to focus only on relevant sentences (§4).

2. trained robust reinforcement learning algorithms that can effectively learn from bandit feedback (§3); this allows our model to "test" proposed generalizations and adapt from the provided feedback signals.

Tackling the problem of learning with bandit feedback is important because neural machine translation systems, like other natural language processing technology, currently learn almost exclusively from labeled data for a specific domain. While this approach is useful, it cannot scale to a broad variety of language and domains, as linguistic systems often cannot generalize well beyond their training data. Machine translation systems need to be able to learn to improve their performance from naturalistic interaction with users in addition to labeled data.

Bandit feedback (Robbins, 1985) offers systems the opportunity to "test" proposed generalizations and receive feedback on their performance; particularly interesting are *contextual* bandit systems, which make predictions based on a given input context (Auer et al., 2002; Langford and Zhang, 2008; Beygelzimer et al., 2010; Dudik et al., 2011). For example, a neural translation system trained on parliament proceedings often performs quite poorly at translating anything else. However, a translation system that is deployed to facilitate conversations between users might receive either explicit feedback (e.g. thumbs up/down) on its translations, or even implicit feedback, for example, the conversation partner asking for clarifications. There has recently been a flurry of work specifically addressing the bandit structured prediction problem (Chang et al., 2015; Sokolov et al., 2016a,b), of which machine translation is a special case.

---

[1] Our implementation is based on OpenNMT (Klein et al., 2017), an open-source toolkit for neural MT.

Proceedings of the Conference on Machine Translation (WMT), Volume 2: Shared Task Papers, pages 667–673
Copenhagen, Denmark, September 7–11, 2017. ©2017 Association for Computational Linguistics

Because this task is—at it's core—a domain adaptation problem (for which a bandit learning signal is available to "help"), we also explored the use of standard domain adaptation techniques. We make a strong assumption that a sizable amount of *monolingual, source language* data is available *before* bandit feedback begins.[2] We believe that in many realistic settings, one can at least get some amount of unlabeled data to begin with (we consider $40k$ sentences). Using this monolingual data, we use data selection on a large corpus of parallel out-of-domain data (Europarl, NewsCommentary, CommonCrawl, Rapid) to seed an initial translation model.

Overall, the results support the following conclusions (§5), based on the limited setting of one new domain and one language pair:

1. data selection for domain adaptation alone improves translation quality by about 1.5 BLEU points.

2. on *top* of the domain adaptation, reinforcement learning (which requires exploration) leads to an *initial* degradation of about 3 BLEU points, which is recovered (on development data) after approximately $40k$ sentences of bandit feedback.[3]

One limitation of our current setup is that we used bandit feedback on development data to train a "critic" function for our reinforcement learning implementation, which, in the worst case, means that our results over-estimate performance on the first $120k$ examples (more details in §5.3).

2 Neural MT architecture

We closely follow Luong et al. (2015) for the structure of our neural machine translation (NMT) systems. Our NMT model consists of an encoder and a decoder, each of which is a recurrent neural network (RNN). We use a bi-directionaral RNN as the encoder and a uni-directional RNN as the decoder. The model directly estimates the posterior distribution $P_\theta(\boldsymbol{y} \mid \boldsymbol{x})$ of translating a source sentence $\boldsymbol{x} = (x_1, \cdots, x_n)$ to a target sentence

$\boldsymbol{y} = (y_1, \cdots, y_m)$:

$$P_\theta(\boldsymbol{y} \mid \boldsymbol{x}) = \prod_{t=1}^{m} P_\theta(y_t \mid \boldsymbol{y}_{<t}, \boldsymbol{x}) \quad (1)$$

where $\boldsymbol{y}_{<t}$ are all tokens in the target sentence prior to y_t.

Each local distribution $P_\theta(y \mid \boldsymbol{y}_{<t}, \boldsymbol{x})$ is modeled as a multinomial distribution over the target language vocabulary. We represent this as a linear transformation followed by a softmax function on the decoder's output vector $\tilde{\boldsymbol{h}}_t^{dec}$:

$$P_\theta(y \mid \boldsymbol{y}_{<t}, \boldsymbol{x}) = \text{softmax}(\boldsymbol{W}_s \, \tilde{\boldsymbol{h}}_t^{dec}; \tau) \quad (2)$$

$$\tilde{\boldsymbol{h}}_t^{dec} = \tanh(\boldsymbol{W}_o[\boldsymbol{h}_t^{dec}; \boldsymbol{c}_t]) \quad (3)$$

$$\boldsymbol{c}_t = \text{attend}(\boldsymbol{h}_{1:n}^{enc}, \boldsymbol{h}_t^{dec}) \quad (4)$$

where $[.;.]$ is the concatenation of two vectors, $\text{attend}(.,.)$ is an attention mechanism,[4] τ is the temperature hyperparameter of the softmax function, $\boldsymbol{h}^{enc}$ and $\boldsymbol{h}^{dec}$ are the hidden vectors generated by the encoder and the decoder, respectively.

During training, the encoder first encodes $\boldsymbol{x}$ to a continuous vector $\boldsymbol{\Phi}(\boldsymbol{x})$, which is used as the initial hidden vector for the decoder. The decoder performs RNN updates to produce a sequence of hidden vectors:

$$\begin{aligned} \boldsymbol{h}_0^{dec} &= \boldsymbol{\Phi}(\boldsymbol{x}) \\ \boldsymbol{h}_t^{dec} &= f_\theta \left(\boldsymbol{h}_{t-1}^{dec}, \left[\tilde{\boldsymbol{h}}_{t-1}^{dec}; \boldsymbol{e}(y_t) \right] \right) \end{aligned} \quad (5)$$

where $\boldsymbol{e}(.)$ is a word embedding lookup operation, f_θ is an LSTM cell.[5]

At prediction time, the ground-truth token y_t in Eq. 5 is replaced by the model's own prediction $\hat{y}_t$:

$$\hat{y}_t = \arg\max_y P_\theta(y \mid \hat{\boldsymbol{y}}_{<t}, \boldsymbol{x}) \quad (6)$$

In a supervised learning framework, an NMT model is typically trained under the maximum log-likelihood objective:

$$\mathcal{L}_{sup}(\theta) = \mathbb{E}_{(\boldsymbol{x},\boldsymbol{y}) \sim D_{\text{tr}}} [\log P_\theta (\boldsymbol{y} \mid \boldsymbol{x})] \quad (7)$$

where D_{tr} is the training set.

However, this learning framework is not applicable to our problem since reference translations are not available.

---

[2] This raises a natural question: in the cases where this assumption is unreasonable, could we do adaptation online?

[3] Unfortunately, due to our implementation bug, our evaluation of the test server is incomplete for the reinforcement learning setting; see §5.3 for a discussion.

[4] We use the "concat" mechanism in (Luong et al., 2015).

[5] Feeding $\tilde{\boldsymbol{h}}_t^{dec}$ to the next step is "input feeding."

3 Reinforcement Learning

The translation process of an NMT model can be viewed as a Markov decision process operating on a continuous state space. The states are the hidden vectors h_t^{dec} generated by the decoder. The action space is the target language's vocabulary.

3.1 Markov decision process formulation

To generate a translation from a source sentence x, an NMT model commences at an initial state h_0^{dec}, which is a representation of x computed by the encoder. At time step $t > 0$, the model decides the next action to take by defining a stochastic policy $P_\theta(y_t \mid y_{<t}, x)$, which is directly parametrized by the parameters θ of the model. This policy takes the previous state h_{t-1}^{dec} as input and produces a probability distribution over all actions (words in the target vocabulary). The next action $\hat{y}_t$ is chosen either by taking $\arg\max$ or sampling from this policy. The encoder computes the current state h_t^{dec} by applying an RNN update on the previous state h_{t-1}^{dec} and the next action taken $\hat{y}_t$ (Eq. 5).

The objective of bandit NMT is to find a policy that maximizes the expected quality of translations sampled from the model's policy:

$$\mathcal{L}_{pg}(\theta) = \mathbb{E}_{\substack{x \sim D_{tr} \\ \hat{y} \sim P_\theta(y|x)}} \left[R(\hat{y}, x) \right] \qquad (8)$$

where R is a reward function that returns a score in $[0, 1]$ reflecting the quality of the input translation.

We optimize this objective function by policy gradient methods. The gradient of the objective in Eq. 8 with respect to θ is: [6]

$$\nabla_\theta \mathcal{L}_{pg}(\theta) = \mathbb{E}_{\hat{y} \sim P(\cdot)} \left[R(\hat{y}) \nabla_\theta \log P_\theta(\hat{y}) \right] \quad (9)$$

$$= \sum_{t=1}^{m} \mathbb{E}_{\hat{y}_t \sim P(\cdot|\hat{y}_{<t})} \left[R(\hat{y}) \nabla_\theta \log P_\theta(\hat{y}_t \mid \hat{y}_{<t}) \right]$$

3.2 Advantage Actor-Critic

Algorithm 1 The A2C algorithm for NMT.

---
1. **for** $k = 0 \cdots K$ **do**
2:    receive a source sentence x
3:    sample a translation, $\hat{y} \sim P_\theta(y \mid x)$
4:    receive reward $R(\hat{y}, x)$
5:    update the NMT model using the gradient in Eq. 9
6:    update the critic model using the gradient in Eq. 12
7: **end for**

We follow the approach of the advantage actor-critic (A2C) algorithm (Mnih et al., 2016), which

combines the REINFORCE algorithm (Williams, 1992) with actor-critic. The algorithm approximates the gradient in Eq. 9 by a single-point sample and normalize the rewards by V values to reduce variance:

$$\nabla_\theta \mathcal{L}_{pg}(\theta) \approx \sum_{t=1}^{m} \nabla_\theta \log P_\theta(\hat{y}_t \mid \hat{y}_{<t}, x) \bar{R}_t(\hat{y}_{<t}, x)$$

$$\text{with } \bar{R}_t(\hat{y}_{<t}, x) \equiv R(\hat{y}, x) - V(\hat{y}_{<t}, x)$$

$$(10)$$

where $\hat{y}_t \sim P(\cdot \mid \hat{y}_{<t}, x)$ and $V(\hat{y}_{<t}, x) = \mathbb{E}[R(\hat{y}, x) \mid \hat{y}_{<t}, x]$ is a baseline that estimates the expected future reward given x and $\hat{y}_{<t}$.

We train a critic model V_ω to estimate the V values. This model is an attention-based encoder-decoder model that encodes a source sentence x and decodes a predicted translation $\hat{y}$. At time step t, it computes $V_\omega(\hat{y}_{<t}, x) = W_o \tilde{h}_t^{dec}$ where $\tilde{h}_t^{dec}$ is the hidden state of the RNN decoder, and W_o is a matrix that transforms a vector into a scalar. [7]

The critic model is trained to minimize the MSE between its estimates and the true values:

$$\mathcal{L}_{crt}(\omega) = \mathbb{E}_{x \sim D_{tr}} \left[\sum_{t=1}^{m} \| R(\hat{y}, x) - V_\omega(\hat{y}_{<t}, x) \|^2 \right]$$

$$(11)$$

Given a fixed x, the gradient with respect to ω of this objective is:

$$\nabla_\omega \mathcal{L}_{crt}(\omega) = \sum_{t=1}^{m} [R(\hat{y}) - V_\omega(\hat{y}_{<t})] \nabla_\omega V_\omega(\hat{y}_{<t})$$

$$(12)$$

Algorithm 1 describes our algorithm. For each x, we draw a single sample $\hat{y}$ from the NMT model, which is used for both estimating the gradient of the NMT model (Eq. 10) and the gradient of the critic model (Eq. 12). We update the NMT model and the critic model simultaneously.

4 Domain Adaptation

We performed domain adaptation by choosing the best out-of-domain parallel data for training using Moore and Lewis (2010) cross-entropy based data selection technique.

Cross-Entropy Difference

The Moore and Lewis method uses the cross-entropy difference $H_I(s) - H_O(s)$ for scoring a

---

[6] For notation brevity, we omit x from this equation. The expectations are also taken over all given x.

[7] We abuse the notation $\tilde{h}^{dec}$ to denote the decoder output. But since the translation model and the critic model do not share parameters, their decoder outputs are distinct.

given sentence s, based on an in-domain language model LM_I and an out-of-domain language model LM_O (Moore and Lewis, 2010). We trained LM_O using the German-English Europarl, NewsCommentary, CommonCrawl and Rapid (i.e. out-of-domain) data sets and LM_I using the e-commerce domain data provided by Amazon. After training both language models, we follow Moore and Lewis method by applying the cross-entropy difference to score each sentence in the out-of-domain data. The cross-entropy is mathematically defined as:

$$H(W) = -\frac{1}{n} \sum_{i=1}^{n} \log P_{LM}(w_i|w_1, \cdots, w_{i-1})$$

where P_{LM} is the probability of a LM for the word sequence W and $w_1, \cdots, w_{i-1}$ represents the history of the word w_i.

Sentences with the lowest cross-entropy difference scores are the most relevant because they are the more similar to the in-domain data and less similar to the average of the out-of-domain data. Using this criteria, the top n out-of-domain sentences are used to create the training set D_{tr}. In this work we consider various n sizes, selecting the n that provides the best performance on the validation set.

5   Experiments

This section describes the experiments we conducted in attempt to assess the challenges posed by bandit machine translation and our exploration of efficient algorithms to improve machine translation systems using bandit feedback.

As explained in previous sections, this task requires performing domain adaptation for machine translation through bandit feedback. With this in mind, we experimented with two types of models: simple domain adaptation without using the feedbacks, and reinforcement learning models that leverage the feedbacks. In the following sections, we explain how we train the regular NMT model, how we select training data for domain adaptation, and how we use reinforcement learning to leverage the bandit feedbacks.

We trained our systems using the out-of-domain parallel data restricted by the shared task. The entire out-of-domain dataset contains 4.5 millions parallel German-English sentences from Europarl, NewsCommentary, CommonCrawl and

Word embedding size	500
Hidden vector size	500
Number of LSTM layers	2
Batch size	64
Epochs	13
Optimizer	SGD
Initial learning rate	1
Dropout	0.3
BPE size	20000
Vocab size	$\sim$25k (*)

Table 1: NMT model's training hyperparameters. (*) with BPE we no longer need to prune the vocabulary, and the exact size depends on the training data.

Rapid data for the News Translation (constrained) task. Our NMT model is based on OpenNMT's (Klein et al., 2017) PyTorch implementation of attention-based encoder-decoder model. We extended their implementation and added our implementation of the A2C algorithm. Details of the model configuration and training hyperparameters are listed in Table 1.

5.1   Subword Unit for Neural Machine Translation

Neural machine translation (NMT) relies on first mapping each word into the vector space, and traditionally we have a word vector corresponding to each word in a fixed vocabulary. Due to the data scarcity, it's hard for the system to learn high quality representations for rare words. To address this problem, with the goal of open vocabulary NMT, Sennrich et al. (2015) proposed to learn subword units and perform translation on a subword level. We incorporated this approach in our system as a preprocessing step. We generate the so-called byte-pair encoding (BPE), which is a mapping from words to subword units, on the whole training set (WMT15), for both the source and target languages. The same mapping is used for all the training sets in our system. After the translation, we do an extra post-processing step to convert the target language subword units back to words. With BPE, the vocabulary size is reduced dramatically and we no longer need to prune the vocabularies. We find this approach to be very helpful and use it for all our systems.

5.2 Domain Adaptation

As explained in Section 4, we use the data selection method of (Moore and Lewis, 2010) for domain adaptation. We use the kenlm toolkit (Heafield, 2011) to build all the language models used for the data selection. We train 4-gram language models. For computing the cross-entropy similarity scores, we use the XenC (Rousseau, 2013) open source data selection tool. We use the mono-lingual data selection mode of XenC on the in-domain and out-of-domain source sentences.

We have two parameters in this data selection process: the size of in-domain dataset that is used for training the in-domain language model, and the size of the out-of-domain training data that we select. We experimented with different configurations and the results on the development server are listed in Table 2. For obtaining the in-domain data, we pre-fetch the source sentences from development and training servers. For the training server, we do not have enough keys to test all combinations, so we picked several configurations and for each sentence, we select randomly a system to translate it. In addition, we also compare with and without beam search. The purpose for this is to provide another comparable baseline for the later reinforcement learning model, for which beam search cannot be used. Thus, the domain adaptation system that we submit to the training server is the uniformly random combination of 6 systems, and their individual average BLEU scores are listed in Table 3.

It can be seen from these results that most configurations of data selection improve the overall BLEU score. The model without data selection achieves 18.70 BLEU on the development server, while the best data selection configurations achieves 20.16, while on the training server the scores are 18.65 without data selection and 20.13 with. It can also be seen from Table 3 that beam search does help with improving the BLEU score.

5.3 Reinforcement Learning Results

While translating with the domain adaptation models to the development server, we collect 320,000 triples of (source sentence, translation, feedback) from 8 submitted systems. We use these triples to pre-train the critic in the A2C algorithm. We use the same pre-trained critic for all A2C-trained systems. The critic for each model is then

| | in-domain size | | |
o.o.d.%	40k	200k	800k
10%	18.50	18.57	18.85
20%	19.56	19.41	19.23
30%	19.54	**20.16**	19.11
40%	**19.58**	19.37	19.36
60%	18.88	18.81	**19.59**
85%	19.12	18.69	18.26
(*) 100%	18.70	18.70	18.70

Table 2: average BLEU scores of domain adaptation systems on the development server with different combinations of in-domain size (x-axis) and the percentage of out-of-domain data selected (y-axis). (*) we show the BLEU score of using all the out-of-domain data, do data selection performed for this row.

i.d. size	o.o.d. %	beam=1	beam=5
0	100%	18.07	18.65 (+0.58)
40k	40%	18.77	19.51 (+0.74)
200k	30%	**19.67**	**20.13 (+0.46)**

Table 3: Average BLEU scores of domain adaptation systems on the training server with different combinations of in-domain size, out-of-domain percentage, beam size, and the corresponding BLEU scores.

updated jointly with the actor respectively. We use Adam (Kingma and Ba, 2014) with learning rate of 10^{-4} to update the both the translation model and the critic model. We do not use dropout (Srivastava et al., 2014) during training with A2C as it makes learning less stable.

We note that there are some drawbacks when using the A2C algorithm when it comes to generating translations. Normally we generate translations by greedy decoding, which means at each time step we pick the word with the highest probability from the distribution produced by the model. But with A2C, we need to sample from the distribution of words to ensure exploration. As a direct consequence, it is not clear how to apply beam search for A2C (and for policy gradient methods in general). To control the trade-off between exploration and exploitation, we use the temperature hyperparameter τ in the softmax function. In our experiments τ is set to $\frac{2}{3}$, which produces a more

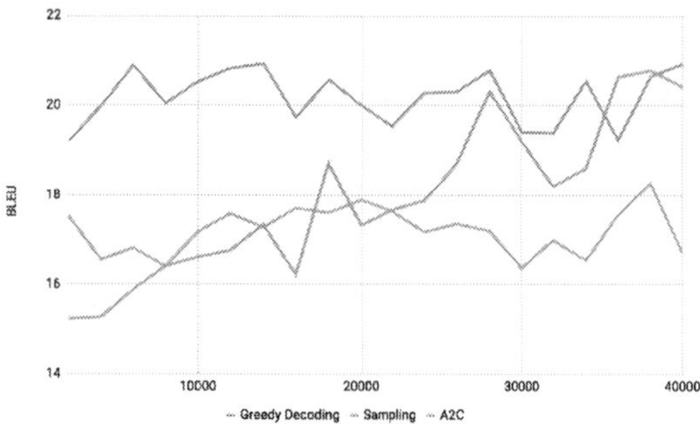

Figure 1: Comparing sampling, greedy decoding, and the A2C algorithm on the development data. Lines show average BLEU scores of every 2000 consecutive sentences.

peaky distribution and makes the model explore less.

It is best to have batching during bandit training for stability. Due to the limitation of the submission servers, that is, we only get the single reward feedback each time, we had to devise a method for batching for the feedback from the server. We cache the rewards until we reach the batch size, then do a batch update. However, due to some bugs in the implementation of this method, some sentences are not submitted in the correct order. And at some test points on the training server the scores are near or equal to zero.

In Figure 1 we present some results from the development server. We use a data selection model (200k in-domain data, 30% out-of-domain training data) as the baseline translation model, upon which we use the A2C algorithm to improve further. From this model, we generate translations with both sampling and greedy decoding to see how much the exploration required by the A2C algorithm hurts the performance. Figure 1 shows the average BLEU score of every 2000 sentences from the development server. A2C loses at the beginning because of exploration, and catches up as it sees more examples. Using sampling instead of greedy decoding, but exploration eventually improves the model.

6 Conclusion

We present the University of Maryland neural machine translation systems for the WMT17 bandit MT shared task. We employ two approaches: out-of-domain data selection and reinforcement learning. Experiments show that the best performance is achieved with a model pre-trained with only one-third of the available out-of-domain data. When applying reinforcement learning to further improve this model with bandit feedback, the model performance degrades initially due to exploration but gradually improves over time. Future work is to determine if reinforcement learning is more effective on a larger bandit learning dataset.

Acknowledgements

The authors thank the anonymous reviewers for many helpful comments. We would like to thank the task organizers: Pavel Danchenko, Hagen Fuerstenau, Julia Kreutzer, Stefan Riezler, Artem Sokolov, Kellen Sunderland, and Witold Szymaniak for organizing the task and for their help throughout the process.

This work was supported by NSF grants IIS-1320538 and IIS-1618193, as well as an Amazon Research Award and LTS grant DO-0032. Any opinions, findings, conclusions, or recommendations expressed here are those of the authors and do not necessarily reflect the view of the sponsor(s).

References

Peter Auer, Nicolo Cesa-Bianchi, Yoav Freund, and Robert E Schapire. 2002. The nonstochastic multi-armed bandit problem. *SIAM journal on computing* 32(1):48–77.

Alina Beygelzimer, Lihong Li, Robert E Schapire, John Langford, and Lev Reyzin. 2010. An optimal high probability algorithm for the contextual bandit problem. Technical report.

Kai-Wei Chang, He He, Hal Daumé III, and John Langford. 2015. Learning to search for dependencies. *arXiv preprint arXiv:1503.05615* .

Miroslav Dudik, Daniel Hsu, Satyen Kale, Nikos Karampatziakis, John Langford, Lev Reyzin, and Tong Zhang. 2011. Efficient optimal learning for contextual bandits. *arXiv preprint arXiv:1106.2369* .

Kenneth Heafield. 2011. Kenlm: Faster and smaller language model queries. In *Proceedings of the Sixth Workshop on Statistical Machine Translation*. Association for Computational Linguistics, pages 187–197.

Diederik P. Kingma and Jimmy Ba. 2014. Adam: A method for stochastic optimization. *CoRR* abs/1412.6980. http://arxiv.org/abs/1412.6980.

Guillaume Klein, Yoon Kim, Yuntian Deng, Jean Senellart, and Alexander M Rush. 2017. Opennmt: Open-source toolkit for neural machine translation. *arXiv preprint arXiv:1701.02810* .

Julia Kreutzer, Artem Sokolov, and Stefan Riezler. 2017. Bandit structured prediction for neural sequence-to-sequence learning. In *Association of Computational Linguistics*.

John Langford and Tong Zhang. 2008. The epoch-greedy algorithm for multi-armed bandits with side information. In *Advances in neural information processing systems*. pages 817–824.

Minh-Thang Luong, Hieu Pham, and Christopher D. Manning. 2015. Effective approaches to attention-based neural machine translation. In *Empirical Methods in Natural Language Processing (EMNLP)*. Association for Computational Linguistics, Lisbon, Portugal, pages 1412–1421. http://aclweb.org/anthology/D15-1166.

Volodymyr Mnih, Adria Puigdomenech Badia, Mehdi Mirza, Alex Graves, Timothy P Lillicrap, Tim Harley, David Silver, and Koray Kavukcuoglu. 2016. Asynchronous methods for deep reinforcement learning. In *International Conference on Machine Learning*.

Robert C Moore and William Lewis. 2010. Intelligent selection of language model training data. In *Proceedings of the ACL 2010 conference short papers*. Association for Computational Linguistics, pages 220–224.

Herbert Robbins. 1985. Some aspects of the sequential design of experiments. In *Herbert Robbins Selected Papers*, Springer, pages 169–177.

Anthony Rousseau. 2013. Xenc: An open-source tool for data selection in natural language processing. *The Prague Bulletin of Mathematical Linguistics* (100):73–82.

Rico Sennrich, Barry Haddow, and Alexandra Birch. 2015. Neural machine translation of rare words with subword units. *arXiv preprint arXiv:1508.07909* .

Artem Sokolov, Julia Kreutzer, Christopher Lo, and Stefan Riezler. 2016a. Learning structured predictors from bandit feedback for interactive nlp. ACL.

Artem Sokolov, Julia Kreutzer, Stefan Riezler, and Christopher Lo. 2016b. Stochastic structured prediction under bandit feedback. In *Advances in Neural Information Processing Systems*. pages 1489–1497.

Nitish Srivastava, Geoffrey Hinton, Alex Krizhevsky, Ilya Sutskever, and Ruslan Salakhutdinov. 2014. Dropout: A simple way to prevent neural networks from overfitting. *The Journal of Machine Learning Research* 15(1):1929–1958.

Ronald J Williams. 1992. Simple statistical gradient-following algorithms for connectionist reinforcement learning. *Machine learning* 8(3-4):229–256.

LIMSI Submission for WMT'17 Shared Task on Bandit Learning

Guillaume Wisniewski

LIMSI, CNRS, Univ. Paris-Sud, Université Paris-Saclay, 91 405 Orsay, France

`guillaume.wisniewski@limsi.fr`

Abstract

This paper describes LIMSI participation to the WMT'17 shared task on Bandit Learning. The method we propose to adapt a seed system trained on out-domain data to a new, unknown domain relies on two components. First, we use a linear regression model to exploit the weak and partial feedback the system receives by learning to predict the reward a translation hypothesis will get. This model can then be used to score hypotheses in the search space and translate source sentences while taking into account the specificities of the in-domain data. Second, we use the UCB1 algorithm to choose which of the 'adapted' or 'seed' system must be used to translate a given source sentence in order to maximize the cumulative reward.

Results on the development and train sets show that the proposed method does not succeed in improving the seed system. We explore several hypotheses to explain this negative result.

1   Introduction

The first Bandit Learning for Machine Translation shared task (Sokolov et al., 2017) aims at adapting a 'seed' MT system trained on out-domain corpora to a new domain considering only a 'weak' signal, namely a translation quality judgment rather than a reference translation or a post-edition. Such a situation arises when the user is not a skilled translator but can nevertheless decide whether a translation is useful or not. The signal is qualified as 'weak' as only the score of the translation produced by a system can be known, the same sentence can not be translated twice and no reference is ever revealed.

Adapting a MT system from a weak signal raises three main challenges. First, the parameters of the MT system must be estimated without knowing the reference translation which rules out most of the usual optimization methods for MT such as MERT, MIRA or the computation of likelihood at the heart of NMT systems (Neubig and Watanabe, 2016). Second, the system must be trained in a 'one-shot' way as each source sentence can only be translated once and will result in a single reward. Third, no information about the target domain is available and its specificities must be discovered 'on-the-fly'.

To address these challenges, we propose an adaptation method that relies on two components. First, we use a linear regression model to exploit the weak and partial feedback the system receives by learning to predict the reward a translation hypothesis will get. This model can then be used to score hypotheses of the search space and translate source sentences while taking into account the specificities of the in-domain data. Second, we use the UCB1 algorithm to choose which of the 'adapted' or 'seed' system must be used to translate a given source sentence in order to maximize the cumulative reward.

The rest of this article is organized as follows: we will first describe the shared task and the different challenges it raises (§2). Then we will describe the proposed method (§3–4) and discuss their results in §5.

2   Task Description

Bandit learning for MT follows an online learning protocol: at the i-th iteration, a new source sentence x_i is received; the learner translates it and gets a reward $r_i \in [0, 1]$ (a smoothed sentence-level BLEU score in this shared task). The higher the reward, the better the translation but no infor-

Proceedings of the Conference on Machine Translation (WMT), Volume 2: Shared Task Papers, pages 674–679
Copenhagen, Denmark, September 7–11, 2017. ©2017 Association for Computational Linguistics

mation about the actual reference is available. The goal of the task is to maximize the cumulative reward over T rounds: $\sum_{i=1}^{T} r_i$.

Maximizing the cumulative reward faces an exploration/exploitation dilemma: if all the sentences are translated using the seed system (i.e. a system trained on out-domain data), the specificities of the domain will never be taken into account and only 'average' translations will be predicted (assuming the seed system is 'good enough'). However, training a new MT system from scratch is also not a good strategy as, at the beginning the system will predict many bad translations which i) will have a negative impact on the cumulative reward ii) might hinder training as the system will only see bad hypotheses (i.e. only a small part of the search space of a MT system will be explored). Moreover, as no information about the target domain is available, the seed system may be, in fact, very good for some input sentences and the best strategy will simply be not to do any adaptation.

3 System Overview

We will now describes the two components of our system: the first one (§3.1) will allow us to exploit the weak and partial feedback we receive and the second one (§3.2) will allow to discover the MT system that translates in-domain data the best.

3.1 Optimizing a MT System from Weak Feedback

Estimating the parameters of a MT system from the rewards can not be done with the usual MT optimization methods: as the reference is not known, it is impossible to score a n-best list as required by methods optimizing a classification criterion such as MERT or MIRA (Neubig and Watanabe, 2016). Moreover, as only one translation hypothesis is scored, methods optimizing a ranking criterion, such as PRO, can also not be used.

Instead we propose to simply learn a linear regression to predict the reward a translation hypothesis will get based on a joint feature representation $\phi(h_i, x_i)$ of the hypothesis and the source sentence. Using a linear model allows us to easily integrate it into the decoder to score translation hypotheses: given a weight vector w, translating a source sentence x consists in looking, in the search space, for the hypothesis that maximizes the predicted reward, which amounts to finding the longest path in a weighted directed acyclic

graph (Wisniewski et al., 2010; Wisniewski and Yvon, 2013).

More precisely the weights of the MT system are chosen by optimizing the regularized mean squared error (MSE):

$$\min_{w} \sum_{i} (r_i - w \cdot \phi(h_i, x_i))^2 + \lambda_2 \cdot ||w||_2^2 + \lambda_1 \cdot ||w||_1 \tag{1}$$

where λ_1 and λ_2 are hyper-parameters controlling the strength of the regularization. Solving Equation (1) with a stochastic gradient descent allows us to update the weight vector each time a new reward is received and to integrate learning in the bandit protocol. Features and optimization methods are detailed in Section 4.2.

It is important to note that in the context of Bandit MT, examples are not independently distributed: the score of the i-th observation depends on the current value of the weight vector that, in turn, depends on all the examples that have been previously observed. This is a second aspect of the exploration/exploitation dilemma described in Section 2 as we have to trade off exploration of the search space (to ensure that we correctly predict the reward of any 'kind' of hypotheses and eventually discover better translations) while focusing on the part of the search space that contains, according to our current knowledge (i.e. value of the weight vector), the best hypotheses.

In the following, we will denote ADAPTED the MT system that uses the predicted reward to translate a source sentence.

3.2 Trading off Exploration and Exploitation

Our system relies on the observation that each new source sentence can be translated by different systems: either the SEED system, the parameters of which have been estimated on an out-domain data set or the ADAPTED system the parameters of which are continuously updated from the rewards. The bandit learning task aims at deciding, for a given input sentence, which system must be used to translate it in order to maximizes the cumulative reward.

The quality of a translation predicted by a given system i can be modeled by a $[0, 1]$-valued random variable X_i distributed with an unknown distribution and possessing an unknown expected value μ_i. Would μ_i be known, the best strategy would be to always translate sentences with the system that has the highest μ_i. The challenge here is that

μ_i is unknown and can change over time.

This framework corresponds to the multi-armed bandit scenario (Bubeck and Cesa-Bianchi, 2012). Many algorithms have been proposed to find the best *policy*.[1] In this shared task, we considered the UCB1 algorithm (Auer et al., 2002), that consists in choosing the system that maximizes $\bar{x}_j + \sqrt{2\log\frac{t}{n_j}}$, where n_j represents the number of times system j was chosen so far, t the number of rounds and $\bar{x}_j$ the empirical mean reward of the j-th system. After each decision, a reward is observed and used to i) update the estimated empirical mean reward of the system that has just been chosen and ii) update the weight vector of the ADAPTED system by doing one SGD step. Intuitively, this strategy selects a decision that has either a 'good' expected reward or has not been played for long. Importantly it never permanently rules out a system no matter how poorly it performs.

It can be proven (Auer et al., 2002) that the UCB1 expected cumulative regret after T rounds is at most $\mathcal{O}\left(\sqrt{K \cdot T \cdot \log T}\right)$ where K is the number of decisions that can be made. This means that the difference between the cumulative reward achieved by the UCB1 strategy and the cumulative reward that would have been achieved by always making the best decision is upper-bounded, i.e. the UCB1 will allow us to discover which was the best decision to make without making too many bad decisions.

In the following, we denote UCB1 the strategy that consists in using the UCB1 algorithm to choose between the SEED and ADAPTED translation systems.

3.3 Variants

After analyzing our results on the development set (see §5), we decide to consider two more strategies:

- UCB1-SELECT that considers the same systems as the UCB1 strategy but only the translation hypothesis associated to a reward r in $[0.1, 1[$ are considered to estimate the weights of the ADAPTED system (other observations are discarded);

- UCB1-SAMPLING in which two more MT systems are considered (in addition to the

ADAPTED and SEED systems): the first one, SAMPLE-SEED samples translations from the search space according to their score predicted by the SEED system (the higher its predicted score, the higher the probability to select this hypothesis); the other one, SAMPLE-UNIFORM samples translation hypotheses uniformly from the search space.

The latter strategy allows us to increase the diversity of translation hypotheses seen when estimating the weights of the ADAPTED system. The former is motivated by our observations that many good translation hypotheses have very low rewards because the references used to compute them are not a direct translation that can be produced by the MT system (i.e. the references are unreachable) or that many source sentence do not actually need to be translated (i.e. the source and the reference are the same). Table 1 shows such examples. We assume that these observations hinder the estimation of the model used to predict the rewards has its gold value is completely unrelated to the features describing the hypothesis.

source	einfach genial und absolut cool !
hyp.	simply brilliant and totally cool !
score	0.008633400213704501
source	schwarz gr.xxl / xxxl
hyp.	black gr.xxl / xxxl
score	0.0360645288
source	00603.117 , bt .
hyp.	00603.117 , bt .
score	1.0

Table 1: Example of a 'good' translation with very bad rewards and of a perfect translation.

4 Experimental Details

4.1 The SEED System

We consider as our SEED system a phrase-based system trained using the standard Moses pipeline (Koehn et al., 2007): all corpora are cleaned[2] and tokenized; compounds are split on the German side using our re-implementation of (Koehn and Knight, 2003). Parallel data are

---

[1] A policy is a randomized algorithm which makes a decision in each round based on the history of decisions and observed rewards so far

[2] Moses scripts are applied in the following order to clean corpora: removing non-printing characters, replacing and normalizing Unicode punctuation, lowercasing, pre-tokenizing.

aligned using FASTALIGN (Dyer et al., 2013) and 5-gram language models is estimated using KENLM (Heafield et al., 2013).

The language model is estimated on the monolingual corpus resulting from the concatenation of the EUROPARL (v7), NEWSCOMMENTARY (v12) and NEWSDISCUSS (2015–2016) corpora. At the end, our monolingual corpus contain 193,292,548 sentences. The translation model is estimated from the `CommonCrawl`, `NewsCo`, `Europarl` and `Rapid` corpora, resulting in a parallel corpus made of 5,919,142 sentences.

Weights of the MT systems are estimated with MERT on `newstest-2016`.

4.2 Training the Regression Model

We use Wowpal Wabbit (Agarwal et al., 2014) to efficiently train a regressor to predict the rewards by optimizing the Mean Squared Error with a stochastic gradient descent. We consider 32 features: the 15 features of a baseline Moses system[3] as well the score of the SEED system. We also consider the logarithm of these features.

To account for the different feature ranges and the mix of continuous and discrete features, we enhance the standard SGD by adding the following three additional factors affecting the weight updates when optimizing the MSE objective function:

- normalized updates to adjust for the scale of each feature (Ross et al., 2013);

- adaptive, individual learning rate for each feature (Duchi et al., 2011);

- Importance aware update (Karampatziakis and Langford, 2011).

The value of the hyper-parameters λ_1 and λ_2 are chosen by maximizing prediction performance on the 5,000 first examples on the development set.

5 Results

Performance of the proposed methods have been evaluated on the two corpora provided by the shared task organizers: a development set containing about 40,000 sentences and an official training set containing 1,300,000 sentences, which will be use to rank the participants. Unfortunately, given

---

[3] 1 language model score, 4 translation model scores, 6 scores describing lexical reordering, one distortion score, as well as word, phrase and unknown word penalty

Strategy	Cumulative BLEU
SEED	6970.21399
UCB1	6533.67157
UCB1-SAMPLING	6059.92188
UCB1-SELECT	6596.03351

Table 2: Results on the Development data set

its size, we were not able to translate all the training set.

The quality of the systems is evaluated both by the cumulative reward (see §2) and by computing the BLEU score on a specific corpus at different 'checkpoints'.

Table 2 shows the cumulative reward achieved by our systems on the development set. It appears that all the methods we proposed are outperformed by the seed system. Looking at the number of times each system was used by the different strategies (Table 3), shows that, most of the time, the seed system is selected, which confirms that it achieves the best translation performance. Results of the off-line evaluation, reported in Figure 1 and on the training set confirm these observations.

Several hypotheses can be formulated to explain these negative results:

- trying to adapt an MT system by changing only the scores of a few models and without additional resources or knowledge of the target domain may not offer enough flexibility;

- the estimation error of regressor may be too large to discriminate the best translation hypothesis of the search space. In practice the mean squared error on the training data is around 0.06.

- Our exploration strategy is not efficient enough, and the learners never learns to score 'good' hypotheses. Indeed, as shown in Figure 2, most of the hypotheses seen during training are of very low quality or correspond to very short sentences that can be translated trivially. In both cases, extracting useful information is difficult.

Analyzing these hypotheses in more depth is difficult without access to the references and results on the training set.

Strategy	Out-Domain	In-Domain	Sample Moses	Sample Uniform
SEED	100%	—	—	—
UCB1	90.77%	9.23%	—	—
UCB1-SAMPLING	78.04%	7.67%	7.36%	6.94%
UCB1-SELECT	90.15%	9.85%	—	—

Table 3: Number of times each translation system is chosen by the UCB1 strategy on the development set. 'Out-Domain' refers to the seed system, In-Domain to the system trained on the rewards and the last two systems to systems sampling randomly hypotheses from the search space.

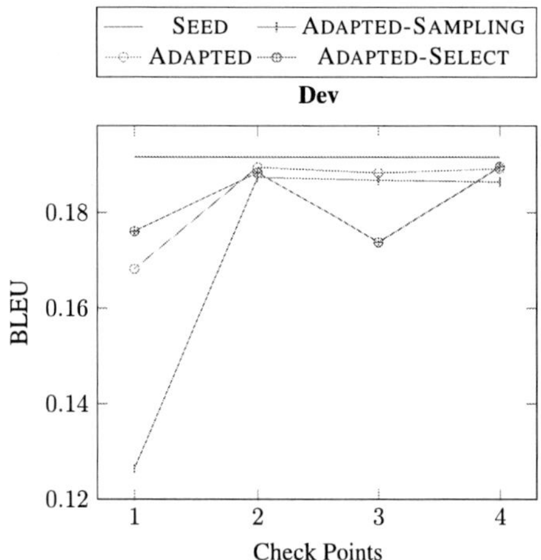

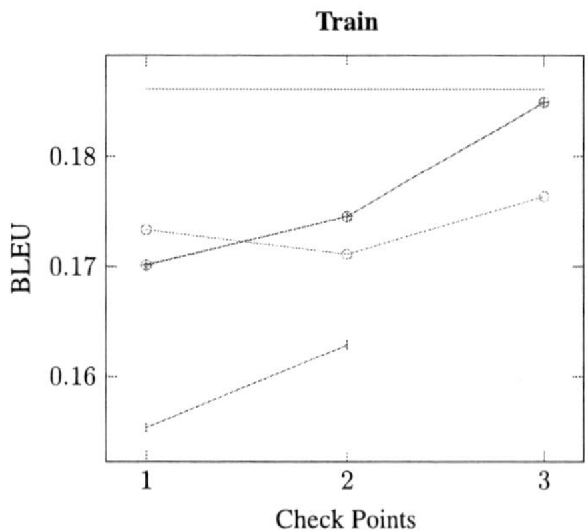

Figure 1: Evolution of the BLEU score at the different 'check-points' of the development and training datasets.

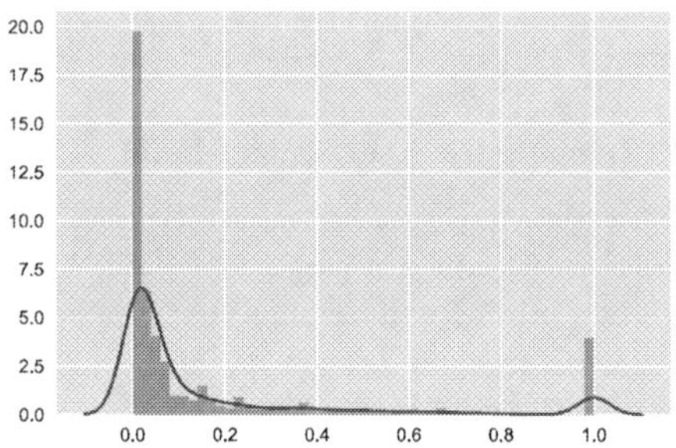

Figure 2: Distributions of the rewards the SEED system got on the development dataset.

Acknowledgments

This work has been partially funded by the *Agence Nationale de la Recherche* (ParSiTi project, ANR-16-CE33-0021). Warm thanks to François Yvon for his feedback on this work.

References

Alekh Agarwal, Olivier Chapelle, Miroslav Dudík, and John Langford. 2014. A reliable effective terascale linear learning system. *J. Mach. Learn. Res.*, 15(1):1111–1133.

Peter Auer, Nicolò Cesa-Bianchi, and Paul Fischer. 2002. Finite-time analysis of the multiarmed bandit problem. *Machine Learning*, 47(2-3):235–256.

Sébastien Bubeck and Nicolò Cesa-Bianchi. 2012. Regret analysis of stochastic and nonstochastic multi-armed bandit problems. *Foundations and Trends in Machine Learning*, 5(1):1–122.

John Duchi, Elad Hazan, and Yoram Singer. 2011. Adaptive subgradient methods for online learning and stochastic optimization. *J. Mach. Learn. Res.*, 12:2121–2159.

Chris Dyer, Victor Chahuneau, and Noah A. Smith. 2013. A simple, fast, and effective reparameterization of ibm model 2. In *Proceedings of the 2013*

Conference of the North American Chapter of the *Association for Computational Linguistics: Human Language Technologies*, pages 644–648, Atlanta, Georgia. Association for Computational Linguistics.

Kenneth Heafield, Ivan Pouzyrevsky, Jonathan H. Clark, and Philipp Koehn. 2013. Scalable modified Kneser-Ney language model estimation. In *Proceedings of the 51st Annual Meeting of the Association for Computational Linguistics*, pages 690–696, Sofia, Bulgaria.

Nikos Karampatziakis and John Langford. 2011. Online importance weight aware updates. In *UAI 2011, Proceedings of the Twenty-Seventh Conference on Uncertainty in Artificial Intelligence, Barcelona, Spain, July 14-17, 2011*, pages 392–399. AUAI Press.

Philipp Koehn, Hieu Hoang, Alexandra Birch, Chris Callison-Burch, Marcello Federico, Nicola Bertoldi, Brooke Cowan, Wade Shen, Christine Moran, Richard Zens, Chris Dyer, Ondrej Bojar, Alexandra Constantin, and Evan Herbst. 2007. Moses: Open source toolkit for statistical machine translation. In *Proceedings of the 45th Annual Meeting of the Association for Computational Linguistics Companion Volume Proceedings of the Demo and Poster Sessions*, pages 177–180, Prague, Czech Republic. Association for Computational Linguistics.

Philipp Koehn and Kevin Knight. 2003. Empirical methods for compound splitting. In *Proceedings of the Tenth Conference on European Chapter of the Association for Computational Linguistics - Volume 1*, EACL '03, pages 187–193, Stroudsburg, PA, USA. Association for Computational Linguistics.

Graham Neubig and Taro Watanabe. 2016. Optimization for statistical machine translation: A survey. *Computational Linguistics*, 42(1):1–54.

Stéphane Ross, Paul Mineiro, and John Langford. 2013. Normalized online learning. In *Proceedings of the Twenty-Ninth Conference on Uncertainty in Artificial Intelligence, UAI 2013, Bellevue, WA, USA, August 11-15, 2013*. AUAI Press

Artem Sokolov, Julia Kreutzer, Kellen Sunderland, Pavel Danchenko, Witold Szymaniak, Hagen Fürstenau, and Stefan Riezler. 2017. A shared task on bandit learning for machine translation. In *Proceedings of the Second Conference on Machine Translation (WMT)*.

Guillaume Wisniewski, Alexandre Allauzen, and François Yvon. 2010. Assessing phrase-based translation models with oracle decoding. In *Proceedings of the 2010 Conference on Empirical Methods in Natural Language Processing*, pages 933–943, Cambridge, MA. Association for Computational Linguistics.

Guillaume Wisniewski and Franois Yvon. 2013. Fast large-margin learning for statistical machine translation. In *International Conference on Intelligent Text Processing and Computational Linguistics (CI-CLing 2013)*, page 12p.

Variable Mini-Batch Sizing and Pre-Trained Embeddings

Mostafa Abdou and **Vladan Glončák** and **Ondřej Bojar**
Charles University, Faculty of Mathematics and Physics,
Institute of Formal and Applied Linguistics
`mostafahany56@gmail.com`, `{gloncak,bojar}@ufal.mff.cuni.cz`

Abstract

This paper describes our submission to the WMT 2017 Neural MT Training Task. We modified the provided NMT system in order to allow for interrupting and continuing the training of models. This allowed mid-training batch size decrementation and incrementation at variable rates. In addition to the models with variable batch size, we tried different setups with pre-trained word2vec embeddings. Aside from batch size incrementation, all our experiments performed below the baseline.

1 Introduction

We participated in the WMT 2017 NMT Training Task, experimenting with pre-trained word embeddings and mini-batch sizing. The underlying NMT system (Neural Monkey, Helcl and Libovický, 2017) was provided by the task organizers (Bojar et al., 2017), including the training data for English to Czech translation. The goal of the task was to find training criteria and training data layout which leads to the best translation quality. The provided NMT system is based on an attentional encoder-decoder (Bahdanau, Cho, and Bengio, 2014) and utilizes BPE for vocabulary size reduction to allow handling open vocabulary (Sennrich, Haddow, and Birch, 2016).

We modified the provided NMT system in order to allow for interruption and continuation of the training process by saving and reloading variable files. This did not result in any noticeable change in the learning. Furthermore, it allowed for mid-training mini-batch size decrementation and incrementation at variable rates.

As our main experiment, we tried to employ pre-trained word embeddings to initialize embeddings in the model on the source side (monolin-gually trained embeddings) and on both source and target sides (bilingually trained embeddings).

Section 1.1 describes our baseline system. Section 2 examines the pre-trained embeddings and Section 3 the effect of batch size modifications. Further work and conclusion (Sections 4 and 5) close the paper.

1.1 The Baseline System

Our baseline model was trained using the provided NMT system and the provided data, including the given word splits of BPE (Sennrich, Haddow, and Birch, 2016). Of the two available configurations, we selected the 4GB one for most experiments to fit the limits of GPU cards available at MetaCentrum.[1] This configuration uses a maximum sentence length of 50, word embeddings of size 300, hidden layers of size 350, and clips the gradient norm to 1.0. We used a mini-batch size of 60 for this model.

Due to resource limitations at MetaCentrum, the training had to be interrupted after a week of training. We modified Neural Monkey to enable training continuation by saving and loading the model and we always submitted the continued training as a new job. When tested with restarts every few hours, we saw no effect on the training. In total, our baseline ran for two weeks (one restart), reaching BLEU of 15.24.

2 Pre-trained Word Embeddings

One of the goals of NMT Training Task is to reduce the training time. The baseline model needed two weeks and it was still not fully converged. Due to the nature of back-propagation, variables closer to the expected output (i.e. the decoder) are trained faster while it takes a much higher number of iterations to propagate corrections to early parts

---

[1] `https://metavo.metacentrum.cz/`

Proceedings of the Conference on Machine Translation (WMT), Volume 2: Shared Task Papers, pages 680–686
Copenhagen, Denmark, September 7–11, 2017. ©2017 Association for Computational Linguistics

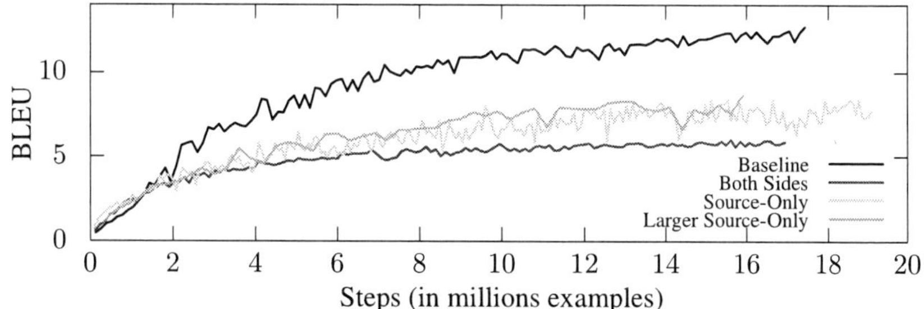

Figure 1: Results of pre-trained embeddings initialized models as compared to baseline model.

	Baseline	Source-Only	Both Sides	Larger Source-Only
Config for	4GB	4GB	4GB	8GB
Mini-batch size	60	60	60	150
Aux. symbols init.	$\mathcal{N}(0, 0.01^2)$	$U(0, 1)$	$\mathcal{N}(0, 0.01^2)$	$\mathcal{N}(0, 0.01^2)$
Pre-trained embeddings	none	source	source and target	source
Embeddings model	–	CBOW	Skip-gram	CBOW
Pre-trained with	–	gensim	bivec	gensim

Table 1: The different setups of models initialized with pre-trained embeddings.

of the network. The very first step in NMT is to encode input tokens into their high-dimensional vector embeddings. At the same time, word embeddings have been thoroughly studied on their own (Mikolov et al., 2013b) and efficient implementations are available to train embeddings outside of the context of NMT.

One reason for using such pre-trained embeddings could lie in increased training data size (using larger monolingual data), another reason could be the faster training: if the NMT system starts with good word embeddings (for either language but perhaps more importantly for the source side), a lower number of training updates might be necessary to specialize the embeddings for the translation task. We were not allowed to use additional training data for the task, so we motivate our work with the hope for a faster convergence.

2.1 Obtaining Embeddings

We trained monolingual word2vec CBOW embeddings (continuous bag of words model, Mikolov et al., 2013a) of size 300 on the English side of the corpus after BPE was applied to it, i.e. on the very same units that the encoder in Neural Monkey will be then processing. The training was done using Gensim[2] (Řehůřek and Sojka, 2010).

We started with CBOW embeddings because they are significantly faster to train. However, as

they did not lead to an improvement, we decided to switch to the Skip-gram model which is slower to train but works better for smaller amounts of training data, according to T. Mikolov.[3]

Bilingual Skip-gram word embeddings were trained on the parallel corpus after applying BPE on both sides. The embeddings were trained using the bivec tool[4] based on the work of Luong, Pham, and Manning (2015).

In all setups, the pre-trained word embeddings were used only to initialize the embedding matrix of the encoder (monolingual embeddings) or both encoder and decoder (bilingual embeddings). These initial parameters were trained with the rest of the model.

The embeddings of the four symbols which are added to the vocabulary for start, end, padding, and unknown tokens were initialized randomly with uniform and normal distributions.

2.2 Experiments with Embeddings

The tested setups are summarized in Table 1 and the learning curves are plotted in Figure 1. The line "Config for" indicates which of the provided model sizes was used (the 4GB and 8GB setups differ in embeddings and RNN sizes, otherwise, the network and training are the same).

---

[2]https://radimrehurek.com/gensim/

[3]https://groups.google.com/d/
msg/word2vec-toolkit/NLvYXU99cAM/
E5ld8LcDxlAJ

[4]https://github.com/lmthang/bivec

Embeddings from	Monolingual Training		NMT Training	
	CBOW (no BPE)	**CBOW (BPE)**	**Baseline**	**Source-Only**
Vocabulary	Full	Common subset (265 words)		
WordSim-353 (ρ)	0.320	0.610	0.571	**0.621**	0.527
MEN (ρ)	0.300	0.610	**0.621**	0.583	0.591
SimLex-999 (ρ)	0.064	0.173	0.171	**0.519**	0.267

Table 2: Pairwise cosine distances between embeddings correlated with standard human judgments for the common subset of the vocabularies. Best result in each row in bold.

We used uniform distribution from 0 to 1 in the first experiment with embeddings and returned to the baseline normal distribution in subsequent experiments.

The best results we were able to obtain are from a third experiment "Larger Source-Only" with batch size increased to 150 but also with differences in other model parameters. (We ran this setup on a K80 card at Amazon EC2.) This run is therefore not comparable with any of the remaining runs, but we nevertheless submitted it as our secondary submission for the WMT 2017 training task (i.e. not to be evaluated manually).

2.3 Discussion

Due to lack of resources, we were not able to run pairs of directly comparable setups. As Figure 1 however suggests, all our experiments with pre-trained embeddings performed well below the baseline of the 4GB model. This holds even for the larger model size.

2.3.1 Analysis of Embeddings

In search for understanding the failure of pre-trained embeddings,[5] we tried to analyze the embeddings we are feeding and getting from our system.

Recent work by Hill et al. (2017) has demonstrated that embeddings created by monolingual models tend to model non-specific relatedness of words (e.g. *teacher* being related to *student*) while those created from NMT models are more oriented towards conceptual similarity (*teacher* $\approx$ *professor*) and lexical-syntactic information (the Mikolov-style arithmetic with embedding vectors for morphosyntactic relations like pluralization but not for "semantic" relations like *France-Paris*). It is therefore conceivable, that embeddings pre-trained with the monolingual methods are not suitable for NMT.

We performed a series of tests to diagnose four sets of embeddings: the baseline for the comparison are embeddings trained monolingually with the CBOW model without BPE processing. BPE may have affected the quality of embeddings, so we also evaluate CBOW trained on the training corpus after applying BPE. These embeddings were used to initialize the Source-Only setup. Finally two sets of embeddings are obtained from Neural Monkey after the NMT training: from the Baseline run (random initialization) and Source-Only (i.e. the CBOW model used in initialization and modified through NMT training).

The tests check the capability of the respective embeddings to predict similar words, as manually annotated in three different datasets: WordSim-353, MEN and Simlex-999. WordSim-353 and MEN contain a set of 353 and 3000 word pairs, respectively, rated by human subjects according to their relatedness (any relation between the two words). Simlex-999, on the other hand, is made up of 999 word pairs which were explicitly rated according to their similarity. Similarity is a special case of relatedness where the words are related by synonymy, hyponymy, or hypernymy (i.e. an "is a" relation). For example, *car* is related to but not similar to *road*, however it is similar to *automobile* or to *vehicle*. Spearman's rank correlation (ρ) is then computed between the ratings of each word pair (v, w) from the given dataset and the cosine distance of their word embeddings, $\cos(\text{emb}(v), \text{emb}(w))$ over the entire set of word pairs. The results of the tests are shown in Table 2.

The tests were performed for the intersecting subset of all four vocabularies, i.e. the words not broken by BPE and known to all three datasets. (265 words). For the CBOW embeddings which were trained without BPE being applied, the scores of the full vocabulary (which has a much higher coverage of the testing dataset pairs) is also included.

As expected from Hill et al. (2017) results, on SimLex-999 the Baseline embeddings com-

---

[5]This negative result actually contradicts another set of experiments using the Google News dataset embeddings currently carried out at our department.

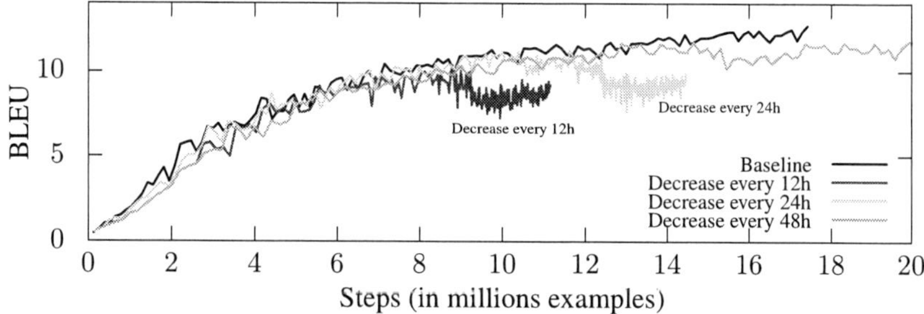

Figure 2: Results of mini-batch decrementation compared to baseline model.

	Baseline	Decrease every 12h	Decrease every 24h	Decrease every 48h*
Starting mini-batch Size	60	100	100	150
Lowest mini-batch Size	60	5	5	20
Decreased every	—	12 hours	24 hours	48 hours

Table 3: The different setups with mini-batch size decrementation. The run reducing every 48h was our primary submission (*).

ing from NMT perform markedly better (0.519) than other embeddings. The embeddings extracted from the Source-Only model which was initialized with the CBOW embeddings score somewhere in the middle (0.267), which indicates that the NMT model is learning word similarity and it moves towards similarity from the general relatedness.

To a little extent, this is apparent even in the values of the embedding vectors of the individual words: we measured the cosine distance between the embedding attributed to a word by the Baseline NMT training and the embedding attributed to it by "CBOW (BPE)". The average cosine distance across all words in the common subset of vocabularies was 1.003. After the training from "CBOW (BPE)" to "Source-only", the model has moved closer to the Baseline, having an average cosine distance of 0.995 (cosine of "Baseline" vs. "Source-only" averaged over all words in the common subset). In other words, the training tried to "unlearn" something from the pre-trained CBOW (BPE).

For MEN, the general relatedness test set, CBOW (BPE) embeddings perform best (0.621) but Baseline NMT is also capable of learning these relations quite well (0.583). The Source-Only setup again moves somewhat to the middle in the performance.

The poor performance of the CBOW embeddings on the full vocabulary (cf. columns 1 and 2 in Table 2) can be attributed to a lack of sufficient coverage of less frequent words in the training cor-

pus. When "CBOW (no BPE)" is tested on the common subset of vocabulary, it performs much better. Our explanation is that words not broken by BPE are likely to be frequent words. If the corpus was not big enough to provide enough context for all the words which were tested against the human judgment datasets, suitable embeddings would only be learned for the more frequent ones (including those that were not broken by BPE). Indeed, 263 words out of the set of 265 are among the 10000 most frequent words in the full vocabulary (of size 350881).

3 Mini-Batch Sizing

The effect of mini-batch sizing is primarily computational. Theoretically speaking, mini-batch size should affect training time, benefiting from GPU parallelization, and not so much the final test performance. It is common practice to choose the largest mini-batch size possible, due to its computational efficiency. Balles, Romero, and Hennig (2016) have suggested that dynamic adaptation of mini-batch size can lead to faster convergence. What we experiment with in this set of experiments is a much naiver concept based on incrementation and decrementation heuristics.

3.1 Decrementation

The idea of reducing mini-batch size during training is to help prevent over-fitting to the training data. Smaller mini-batch sizes results in a nosier

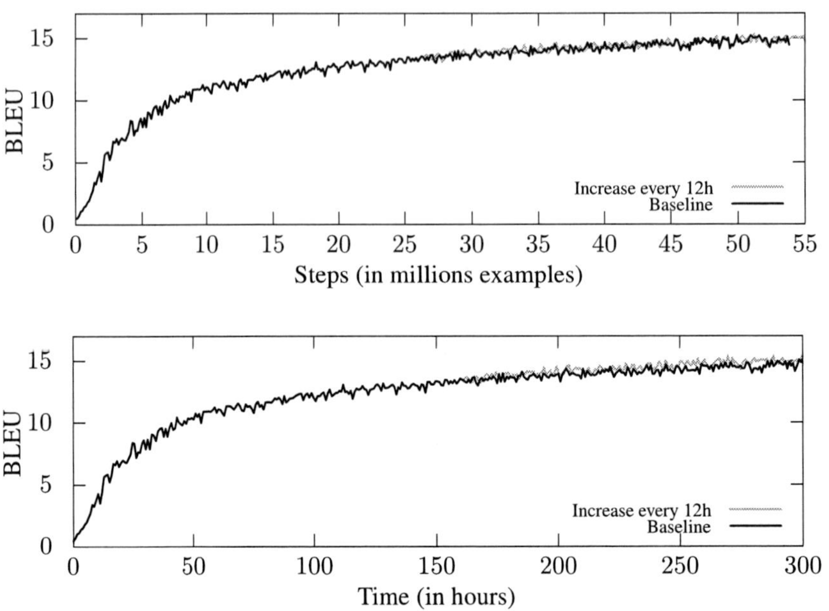

Figure 3: Results of the setup with increasing mini-batch size.

approximation of the gradient of the entire training set. Previous work by Keskar et al. (2016) has shown that models trained with smaller mini-batch size consistently converge to flat minima which results in an improved ability to generalize (as opposed to larger mini-batch size which tends to converge to sharp minima of the training function). By starting with a large mini-batch size, we aim to benefit from larger steps early in the training process (which means the optimization algorithm will proceed faster) and then to reduce the risk of over-fitting in a sharp minimum by gradually decrementing mini-batch size.

In the first experiment, our primary submission, we begin with the mini-batch size of 100 and decrease it by 20 every 48 hours down to mini-batch size of 20. This was chosen heuristically.

In another two experiments, the mini-batch size was decremented every 12 hours and every 24 hours starting from 100 and reaching down to the size of 5. For these, the mini-batch size was reduced by 20 at each interval till it reached 20, then it was halved twice and fixed at 5. A summary of the different mini-batch size decrementation settings tried can be seen in Table 3.

The performance of the setups when reducing mini-batch is displayed in Figure 2. We see that the more often we reduce the size, the sooner the model starts losing its performance.

The plots are the performance on a held-out dataset (as provided by the task organizers), so what we are be seeing is actually over-fitting, the opposite of what we wanted to achieve and what one would expect from better generalization.

3.2 Incrementation

Due to time and resource restrictions, we managed to complete the set of experiments with batch size increasing only after the deadline for the training task submissions. Interestingly, it is the only experiment which managed to outperform our baseline.

The model was trained for a week with mini-batch size 65 and then for another week with mini-batch size increased to 100. Although both the baseline and this run are yet to converge, the increased mini-batch size resulted in a very small gain in terms of learning speed (measured in time), as seen in the lower part of Figure 3. In terms of training steps, there is no observable difference.

4 Further Work

4.1 Mini-Batch Size

In one of our experiments, have demonstrated that variable mini-batch sizing could be possibly beneficial. We suggest using different, smoother, incrementation and decrementation functions or trying some method online mini-batch size adaptation, e.g. based on the dissimilarity of the current section of the corpus with the rest. This could be particularly useful in the common technique of model fine-tuning when adapting to new domains.

Contrary to our expectations, reducing mini-batch size during training leads to a loss on both the heldout dataset and the training dataset. It is therefore not a simple overfitting but rather genuine loss in ability to learn. We assume that the larger mini-batch size plays an important role in model regularization and reducing it makes the model susceptible to keep falling into very local optima. Our not yet published experiments however suggest that if we used the smaller mini-batch from the beginning, the model would not perform badly, which is worth further investigation.

4.2 Pre-Trained Embeddings

The word2vec embeddings were not suitable for the model. Scaling the whole embedding vector space so that the euclidean distances are very small but the cosine dissimilarities are preserved could make it easier for the translation model to adjust the embeddings but so far we did not manage to obtain any positive results in this respect.

We can also speculate that since NMT models produce embeddings which are best suited to the translation task, initializing word embeddings using embeddings from previously trained models could be a promising method of speeding up training.

5 Conclusion

In our submission to the WMT17 Training Task, we tried two approaches: varying the mini-batch size on the fly and initializing the models with pre-trained word2vec embeddings. None of these techniques resulted in any improvement, except for a setup with mini-batch incrementation where at least the training speed in wallclock time increased (thanks to better use of GPU).

When analyzing the failure of the embeddings, we confirmed the observation by Hill et al. (2017) than NMT learns direct word similarity while monolingual embeddings (CBOW) learn general word relatedness.

Acknowledgments

We would like to thank Jindřich Helcl and Jindřich Libovický for their advice and their previous work that we were able to use.

This work has been supported by the EU grant no. H2020-ICT-2014-1-645452 (QT21), as well as by the Ministry of Education, Youth and Sports of the Czech Republic SVV project no. 260 453.

Computational resources were in part supplied by the Ministry of Education, Youth and Sports of the Czech Republic under the Projects CESNET (Project No. LM2015042), CERIT-Scientific Cloud (Project No. LM2015085) provided within the program Projects of Large Research, Development and Innovations Infrastructures. We are also grateful for Amazon EC2 vouchers we obtained at MT Marathon 2016.

References

Bahdanau, Dzmitry, Kyunghyun Cho, and Yoshua Bengio. (2014). Neural Machine Translation by Jointly Learning to Align and Translate. *CoRR.* `arXiv: 1409.0473v7`.

Balles, Lukas, Javier Romero, and Philipp Hennig. (2016). Coupling adaptive batch sizes with learning rates. *Computing Research Repository.* `arXiv: 1508.07909v1`.

Bojar, Ondřej, Jindřich Helcl, Tom Kocmi, Jindřich Libovický, and Tomáš Musil. (2017). Results of the WMT17 Neural MT Training Task. In *Proceedings of the Second Conference on Machine Translation (WMT17)*, Copenhagen, Denmark.

Helcl, Jindřich and Jindřich Libovický. (2017). Neural Monkey: An open-source tool for sequence learning. *The Prague Bulletin of Mathematical Linguistics.* `doi:10.1515/pralin-2017-0001`.

Hill, Felix, Kyunghyun Cho, Sébastien Jean, and Yoshua Bengio. (2017). The representational geometry of word meanings acquired by neural machine translation models. *Machine Translation.* `doi: 10.1007/s10590-017-9194-2`.

Keskar, Nitish Shirish, Dheevatsa Mudigere, Jorge Nocedal, Mikhail Smelyanskiy, and Ping Tak Peter Tang. (2016). On large-batch training for deep learning: Generalization gap and sharp minima. `arXiv:1609.04836v2`.

Luong, Minh-Thang, Hieu Pham, and Christopher D. Manning. (2015). Bilingual word representations with monolingual quality in mind. In *North American Association for Computational Linguistics (NAACL) Workshop on Vector Space Modeling for NLP*, Denver, United States.

Mikolov, Tomáš, Kai Chen, Greg Corrado, and Jeffrey Dean. (2013)a. Efficient Estimation of Word Representations in Vector Space. *Computing Research Repository*. `arXiv:1301.3781v3`.

Mikolov, Tomáš, Ilya Sutskever, Kai Chen, and Greg Corrado. (2013)b. Distributed Representations of Words and Phrases and their Compositionality. `arXiv:1310.4546v1`.

Řehůřek, Radim and Petr Sojka. (2010). Software Framework for Topic Modelling with Large Corpora. In *Proceedings of the LREC 2010 Workshop on New Challenges for NLP Frameworks*, pages 45–50, Valletta, Malta. ELRA.

Sennrich, Rico, Barry Haddow, and Alexandra Birch. (2016). Neural machine translation of rare words with subword units. In *Proceedings of the 54th Annual Meeting of the Association for Computational Linguistics (Volume 1: Long Papers)*, pages 1715–1725, Berlin, Germany. Association for Computational Linguistics.

The AFRL WMT17 Neural Machine Translation Training Task Submission

Grant Erdmann, Katherine Young, Jeremy Gwinnup
Air Force Research Laboratory
grant.erdmann@us.af.mil, katherinemccreightyoung@gmail.com, jeremy.gwinnup.1@us.af.mil

Abstract

The WMT17 Neural Machine Translation Training Task aims to test various methods of training neural machine translation systems. We describe the AFRL submission, including preprocessing and its knowledge distillation framework. Teacher systems are given factors for domain, case, and subword location. Student systems are given multiple teachers' output and a subselected set of the training data designed to match the target domain. Numerical results indicate that the student systems surpass the teachers in translation quality and that this benefit comes directly from the inclusion of the teachers' output.

1 Introduction

This paper describes our development of systems for the WMT17 Neural Machine Translation (NMT) Training Task (WMT, 2017). This task tests methods of adjusting the NMT training process, with a fixed size and format for the final English-to-Czech system. A large (approx. 50 million line) general-domain (mostly subtitles) bilingual corpus is provided as a training set. A domain is provided for each line of this corpus. News text, the application domain, composes about 0.5% of the corpus (see Table 1, column "Given"). A subword expansion to be used is explicitly provided as well. We preprocess the training data to standardize some punctuation and character encoding differences. We filter the data to remove some lines of foreign languages and little information, approximately 5% of the training data.

We follow a teacher-student (aka knowledge distillation) paradigm for this task (Ba and Caruana, 2014). We train ten replicate systems larger than the final system, based on all the training data

available. These systems are aware of different factors (domain, case, subword location) for each subword, allowing them to use this information to learn finer details of translation. They also produce different outputs, based on randomness in training. We translate the entire news-domain training corpus with all replicate systems. These outputs are added to the most applicable training data as another set of references, and the final NMT systems are trained from this decimated and augmented training set.

We choose to resist making many changes to the given systems, in order to provide useful *a posteriori* comparisons. To this end, we use:

- only neuralmonkey, or branches thereof, for NMT

- the given data only

- alterations to given 4GB and 8GB configurations only.

for all intermediate systems.

2 Preprocessing of Training Data

2.1 Normalization

We use several simple steps of text normalization to produce a more standardized training set. Some lines had been doubly-tokenized, and we correct these (e.g., "& quot ;" becomes """). Punctuation and spacing indicators are made uniform (e.g., "Tha \x09D s" becomes "That ' s"). Several characters were denoted by non-standard Unicode codepoints, and these are normalized. For instance, both of the codepoint sequences \x03BF and \x043E look similar to and were used for "o" in the English text.

2.2 Factor definition

We add several factors to the training set for the teacher systems.

Proceedings of the Conference on Machine Translation (WMT), Volume 2: Shared Task Papers, pages 687–691
Copenhagen, Denmark, September 7–11, 2017. ©2017 Association for Computational Linguistics

We add a sentence-level factor of domain, with the following given categories: fiction, subtitles, paraweb, medical, and news.

We add a word-level factor for case (e.g., for the line "Why did Dr . Henry Philip McCoy use BASIC ?") with the values:

1. no case (".", "?")

2. lowercase ("did", "use")

3. all uppercase, more than one character ("BASIC")

4. mixed-case: any uppercase noninitial letter ("McCoy")

5. capitalized, at the beginning of a line or after punctuation ("Why", "Henry")

6. capitalized abbreviation: preceding period and not last word ("Dr")

7. other ("Philip")

A word's case factor comes from the first matching condition in the above list.

Lowercasing is performed after this step, on both the source and target sides, for the teachers' training data. Information as to how the source word is mixed-case is lost for the teacher systems (e.g., "mPa" and "MPa" are equivalent).

Byte-pair-encoded (Gage, 1994) source text is given a subword-level factor for position in subword (non-subword, subword start, subword interior, subword end).

These factors are embedded into spaces with dimension equal to that of the square of the number of factors (e.g., 25 dimensions for the five factors in domain). While theoretically unimportant at convergence, this increase in dimension might encourage the training optimization to spend more effort in understanding factors.

2.3 Cleanup

Byte-pair-encoded source text is filtered for use as training data, based on two conditions. An English line must be at least 75% alphanumeric or spaces. An English line must be at most 25% "@" (two "@" being the subword continuation marker, so this is a measure of rare subwords). The filtering is based on the lowercased parallel corpus used by the teacher, but the filtered lines are also excluded from the students' cased training data.

This rough filter removes many of the non-English lines of the source text. The English lines that are filtered out appear to have little usable content. Table 1 shows how severely the different domains were filtered and their relative representation in the cleaned-up data used for training the teacher systems. The effect of filtering can be seen by comparing the "Given" and "Teacher" columns.

Approximately 5% of the initial data is filtered out by this process. Both the normalization and cleanup processes have little quantitative effect in final system quality, as seen by comparing "Given" to "Teacher" in §5. However, the processes require few resources, and we expect they have minor time and quality benefits.

3   Factored teacher systems

The teacher systems are based on the given 8 GB model configuration and trained using neuralmonkey's bandit-neuralmonkey branch[1], which seems to have good support for factors. The teacher systems are provided the lowercased general-domain training dataset, along with its domain, case, and subword location factors. Vectors for the factor embeddings are merely concatenated to the subword vectors. Convergence is declared when none of the ten teacher systems improve its validation set score for two days of training. This occurred after approximately seven passes through the training dataset. At that time, each teacher's model with the best validation score was used to translate the news-domain from the training data. The performance of the teacher systems on the validation set newstest2016 is provided in Table 2.

4   Student systems

Training data for the student systems consist of three parts. First, we include the news-domain data from the "Teacher" set. Second, we add the output of all ten teacher systems from translating this news-domain training data.

The third component is the bilingual training data from other domains, selected to be most suitable for training a news-domain system. To make this corpus, we first limit the data to lines where both languages (after the BPE process) are less than 50 words, which is a limit in the model specification. We next remove duplicate lines in the data, since some long lines similar to news data are repeated many times, and we do not want them

---

[1] github.com/juliakreutzer/bandit-neuralmonkey

Table 1: Breakdown of training corpora by domain, with numbers of lines in millions. "Given" is all data provided for the task. "Teacher" is cleaned data used to train teachers. "Subselector" is length-filtered and deduplicated data from which we subselect, along with news-domain data from "Teacher". "Selected" is output of subselector, along with news-domain data. "Student" is subselected data, along with news-domain data, both from "Teacher" and as translated by the ten teacher systems.

Domain	Given		Teacher		Subselector		Selected		Student	
	Lines	%	Lines	%	Lines	%	Lines	%	Lines	%
fiction	5.9	12.2	5.8	12.5	5.4	16.2	1.6	22.7	1.6	16.7
subtitles	38.6	79.5	37.1	80.1	26.6	80.1	4.6	67.3	4.6	49.5
paraweb	2.3	4.7	1.8	3.9	0.5	1.6	0.3	3.9	0.3	2.9
medical	1.5	3.1	1.4	3.0	0.4	1.3	0.2	2.4	0.2	1.8
news	0.2	0.5	0.2	0.5	0.2	0.7	0.2	3.6	0.2	2.7
teacher news	0.0	0.0	0.0	0.0	0.0	0.0	0.0	0.0	2.5	26.5
Total	48.6		46.4		33.3		6.8		9.3	

represented disproportionately. The distribution of the remaining lines is given by the "Subselector" columns (non-news rows) of Table 1.

Next, we break the corpus (approximately 33 million lines) into 44 parts (approximately 750,000 lines each) and apply our subselection algorithm (Gwinnup et al., 2016). We use 4-grams and below in the subselection coverage metric, and monolingual coverage scores are summed to get the bilingual coverage score that determines whether to include a line. We find a total of 6.6 million news-like lines from the non-news domains to use in training the student system, distributed as given by the "Selected" column of Table 1. It is noteworthy that the "fiction" domain was the most useful non-news domain, with its percentage of the training data increasing dramatically from "Given" to "Selected".

The final training data distribution for the student system is given in Table 1, in the "Student" columns. Our submitted student models had both the 4 GB and 8 GB configurations provided by the task organizers. Our 4 GB model made 8 passes through the student training set, and our 8 GB model made 4 passes. The performance on the validation set newstest2016 is provided in Table 2. Two replicates of each configuration were trained, and the systems with the highest validation set scores were submitted.

5 Analysis

From Table 2 we see that the student systems perform even better on the validation set than the teacher systems. The 4 GB systems perform about half a BLEU point better, and the 8 GB systems

Table 2: Validation set BLEU scores of intermediate, factored 8GB teacher systems and final student systems. Scores are computed internally by neuralmonkey. Starred systems are submission systems.

System	Replicate	Score
Teacher	0	17.19
Teacher	1	16.98
Teacher	2	16.96
Teacher	3	17.07
Teacher	4	17.10
Teacher	5	17.01
Teacher	6	17.09
Teacher	7	16.82
Teacher	8	16.80
Teacher	9	17.14
Student 4GB	0	17.47
⋆Student 4GB	1	17.58
∗Student 8GB	0	18.15
Student 8GB	1	18.05

perform about one BLEU point better. To determine which stage in processing yielded the most benefit, 4 GB systems matching the submission criteria are built using all five of the training sets seen in Table 1. Graphical training histories are shown in Figure 1, summarized in Table 3. We see clearly that using the "Student" training data set both trains the fastest and leads to the highest-scoring systems, beating others by about a BLEU point on the validation set. The systems trained on other datasets lead to scores within about half a BLEU point of each other, with the smallest dataset (i.e., "Selected") training fastest and the largest datasets (i.e., "Given" and "Teacher") training the most slowly.

We believe that the success of the "Student" training data is caused by using training data with reachable and realistically conflicting translations. The conflicting translations provide "translator noise" and might prevent a system from over-training or finding a strictly local optimum.

To test this theory, we build systems with exactly the same size training set as "Student", but with different composition. For these, the teacher output is replaced with:

- DupNews: ten identical copies of the news data from the given bilingual corpus (for a total of eleven copies).

- DupTeach: ten identical copies of the output from the best teacher system (i.e., from replicate Teacher-0).

As shown in Table 3, both of these adjustments begin training somewhat faster than "Selected" but are negligibly different after one week of training, at which point training is halted. This behavior supports our hypothesis that realistically conflicting translations improve the final system.

6 Discussion

We have given our method for creating the systems we submitted to the WMT17 Neural Machine Translation Training Task. After cleaning the data, we used factors to teach larger, teacher NMT systems. We trained our student submission systems using in-domain output from the teacher systems, rounded out with the most in-domain data from the general training data. The output from multiple teacher systems was used to encourage the student systems to include language ambiguity in their training. Numerical results show that we

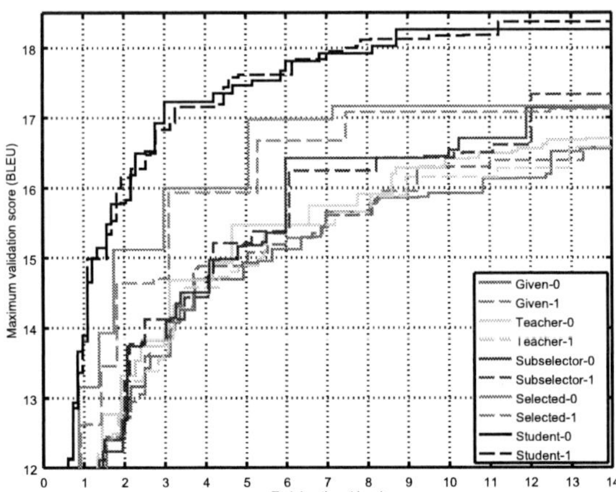

Figure 1: Scores of 4GB systems on validation set throughout training, with differing training data. Two replicates were trained per dataset. Scores are computed internally by neuralmonkey.

Table 3: Validation set BLEU scores of 4GB systems trained using different data. Scores are computed internally by neuralmonkey. "Dup-News" and "DupTeach" training was halted after one week, since negligible improvement over "Selected" was found.

System-Replicate	4-day	7-day	14-day
Given-0	14.69	15.66	16.56
Given-1	14.88	15.44	16.57
Teacher-0	14.69	15.75	16.70
Teacher-1	14.58	15.48	16.58
Subselector-0	14.50	16.43	17.14
Subselector-1	14.44	16.25	17.33
Selected-0	16.00	16.98	17.17
Selected-1	15.94	16.67	17.13
Student-0	17.23	17.92	18.26
Student-1	17.15	17.95	18.37
DupNews-0	16.83	16.83	
DupNews-1	16.68	16.68	
DupTeach-0	16.66	16.99	
DupTeach-1	16.66	16.94	

can distill knowledge of multiple well-informed
teacher systems into smaller student systems.

References

Jimmy Ba and Rich Caruana. 2014. Do deep nets really
need to be deep? *Advances in Neural Information
Processing Systems* pages 2654–2662.

Philip Gage. 1994. A new algorithm for data compression. *C Users Journal* 12:23–38.

Jeremy Gwinnup, Tim Anderson, Grant Erdmann,
Katherine Young, Michaeel Kazi, Elizabeth
Salesky, and Brian Thompson. 2016. The AFRL-
MITLL WMT16 news-translation task systems.
In *Proceedings of the First Conference on Ma-
chine Translation*. Association for Computational
Linguistics, Berlin, Germany, pages 296–302.
http://www.aclweb.org/anthology/W16-2313.

WMT. 2017. Findings of the 2017 Conference on Statistical Machine Translation. In *Proc. of the Second Conference on Statistical Machine Translation
(WMT '17)*. Copenhagen, Denmark.

Opinions, interpretations, conclusions and recommendations are those of the authors and are not necessarily endorsed by the United States Government. Cleared for public
release on 22 May 2017. Originator reference number RH-
17-117141. Case number 88ABW-2017-2505.

Author Index